Pat Stratton, LCSW

Lisa Tolliver, M.S. LPsy A

DISORDERS OF PERSONALITY

SECOND EDITION

DISORDERS OF PERSONALITY
DSM-IV™ and Beyond

THEODORE MILLON
with Roger D. Davis

and Contributing Associates

Carrie M. Millon
Andrew Wenger
Maria H. Van Zuilen
Marketa Fuchs
Renée B. Millon

A Wiley-Interscience Publication

John Wiley & Sons, Inc.

New York • Chichester • Brisbane • Toronto • Singapore

Copyright © 1996 by John Wiley & Sons, Inc.

Library of Congress Cataloging-in-Publication Data:

Millon, Theodore.
    Disorders of personality : DSM-IV and beyond / Theodore Millon
  with Roger D. Davis ; and contributing associates, Marketa Fuchs . . .
  [et al.] — 2nd ed.
        p.   cm. — (A Wiley-Interscience publication)
    Includes bibliographical references and indexes.
    ISBN 0-471-01186-X (cloth : alk. paper)
    1. Personality disorders.   2. Personality disorders—
  Classification.   3. Diagnostic and statistical manual of mental
  disorders.   I. Davis, Roger D.   II. Title.   III. Series.
    [DNLM: 1. Personality Disorders.   WM 190 M656d 1996]
  RC554.M54   1995
  616.85′82—dc20   95-9045

ISBN: 0-471-01186-X

Printed in the United States of America

10   9   8   7   6   5   4   3

To the Memory of

Gardner Murphy, Kurt Goldstein, and Ernst Kris
Who Built the Foundations

and to

Mel Sabshin, Herb Reich, and Niels Strandbygaard
Who Paved the Way

Preface

As with its instructive and well-received first edition (21 printings), this book may be seen as a companion volume to the most recent *Diagnostic and Statistical Manual of Mental Disorders (DSM-IV)*, published by the American Psychiatric Association in 1994. Although this latest edition of the DSM is more comprehensive descriptively than its several predecessors, it was not designed to provide fully detailed clinical or theoretical presentations of the disorders it encompasses. The lack of such materials has been especially troublesome to those seeking substantial information on the many historical, modern, and contemporary conceptions of the personality disorders. These syndromes have now "come of age," having been transformed from a class of disorders possessing only incidental relevance to the diagnostic enterprise into one that is central to the comprehensive multiaxial format. Although clinicians and researchers will find considerable literature on most psychopathologic syndromes in standard texts and journals, such information has only begun to accumulate among the majority of the personality disorders. Now that these syndromes have advanced to the status of major clinical entities, the need to develop a comprehensive professional reference and student text to fill the void is all the more acute. It is in the sense of filling this void that this revised text, comprising some 800 pages as compared to the DSM-IV's Axis II section of 44 pages, may be seen as a useful, and perhaps needed, companion volume to both the DSM-IV and the even briefer personality section of the ICD-10, the official manual of the World Health Organization.

Personalities are like Impressionistic paintings. At a distance, each person is "all of a piece"; up close, each is a bewildering complexity of moods, cognitions, and motives. The thesis or rationale for this text stems from a similar, but more ancient injunction to physicians: "Ask not what disease the patient has, but rather who the patient is who has the disease." Disorders of personality are not medical entities; nor should they be seen as human perversities either. Viewed from an ecological and evolutionary perspective, we conceive them as problematic styles of human adaptation. They represent intriguing and often unique individuals whose constitutional make-up and early life experiences have not only misdirected their development, but have also constructed an unsatisfying sense of self, a problematic way of expressing thoughts and feelings, as well as a troublesome manner of behaving and relating to others. Each of the "classical" personality types, as well as their subvarieties, demonstrate for us the many complex structures and styles in which we become the persons we are.

Beyond the fact that each of the personality disorders is a clinical syndrome in its own right, the DSM multiaxial schema lends these disorders a unique role. Rather than seen merely as a supplement to the more traditional diagnostic entities of Axis I, personality serves as a distinctive context, a constraining and shaping pattern of persistent influences that gives meaning and character to whatever clinical disorders may also be present in the individual, be it of a physical nature, such as cancer or heart disease, or a psychic one, such as schizophrenia. To illustrate within our own field, a unipolar depression will be experienced and reacted to differently in an individual with an avoidant personality than in one with a narcissistic personality. Not only will dissimilar circumstances provoke the divergent vulnerabilities that characterize each of these personalities, but they will also evoke contrasting ways of perceiving and coping with these circumstances. For these and other reasons, we believe that clinicians should be oriented to the "context of personality" when they deal with all medical diseases and, of course, all forms of psychiatric disorders.

It is no overstatement to describe the growth of the field of personality disorders as exponential since the first edition of this book was published a decade and a half ago. The speed of both theoretical and empirical developments continues at an accelerated pace, fostered greatly by the inaugural publication of the *Journal of Personality Disorders* in 1987, and the formal organization of the *International Society for the Study of Personality Disorders* in 1988. Owing to the senior author's close participation and continued involvement in both ventures, each of which serve as a primary vehicle to advance the status and cross-cultural importance of personologic studies, this text's authors have had a front row seat as the quickening pace of this evolving field has progressed. Despite the ever-expanding nature of pertinent concepts and findings, there is little in this avalanche of information and trends to which we have not been privy.

As one of the first appointees in 1974 to the American Psychiatric Association's Task Force on Nomenclature and Statistics, the committee responsible for developing the DSM-III, the senior author was most fortunate to participate in the group's deliberations from the very start. Especially gratifying were the opportunities to persuade colleagues of the utility of an innovative multiaxial format and, substantively, to provide the initial drafts and diagnostic criteria for each of the personality disorders. Similarly, the senior author was again pleased to be called on to serve as a full member of the DSM-IV, Axis II Work Group. Those who are acquainted with this author's prior writings will recognize his influence on the DSM-III (e.g., the concept of an Avoidant Personality) and, more recently, on the DSM-IV, (e.g., the concept of a Negativistic Personality Disorder).

As in prior publications, it was my intent to write a sequentially unified book, one that would demonstrate how the many varieties of personality pathology could be logically derived from a few basic concepts and principles. Most authors in psychiatry and psychology split their texts down the middle, so to speak, providing little or no continuity between the theoretical notions they presented in the early chapters of their books and the syndromes that comprised later ones. More recently, several writers have sought to bridge this gap and to develop a degree of consistency in their treatment of the subject.

Unfortunately, most have shaped their materials in line with narrow theoretical models, for example, neurobiologic, statistical, or psychoanalytic; inevitably, these works compressed the rich diversity of clinical data into Procrustean beds, discarding what did not suit their author's predilections, and imposing a false sense of harmony and order on the remainder. In the hope of gaining the best of both worlds—that is, of being

logically and sequentially consistent—we have borrowed liberally from several schools of thought, adapting and refashioning what appear to be divergent views to fit a coherent *integrative* model, one grounded fundamentally on theoretical principles. The historical and conceptual background of this integrative model is elaborated in Chapters 1 through 3; Chapters 4 and 5 provide the logic and techniques for personality assessment and therapy; the application of these concepts to both the diagnosis of personality pathology and their treatment is elaborated in Chapters 6 to 20.

Given the many advances in conceptual and empirical research these past two decades, the time has come for developing fresh and far-reaching theoretical models that interweave not only psychological and biological factors, but also coordinate them to knowledge gained in adjacent fields of scientific endeavor. Toward that end, we have sought to devise a new classification schema, one constructed from its inception by coalescing several principles drawn from evolutionary theory and biosocial development. Chapters 2 and 3, in addition to reviewing historically diverse conceptions of classification and deduction, provide the theoretical rationale and logic for an "evolutionary approach" to the motivation and learning of pathological styles of behavior. Not only does the schema serve to connect personality pathology to other realms of scientific theory and research, it also demonstrates the developmental continuity of pathological functioning throughout life and the interconnections that exist among ostensibly unrelated syndromes, still considered discrete entities according to the official DSM system. To make this developmental continuity explicit, an organizational sequence is arranged in the text in which more severe stages of disorder are seen to arise as seriously problematic extensions of the more basic personality patterns (e.g., schizotypal viewed as a more severe variant of basic schizoid and avoidant patterns).

Followers of my work will be pleased that my earlier views have not changed appreciably. Previous contributions have not only been retained in great measure, but have found a significant place in the framework and substance of both DSM-III and DSM-IV. Nevertheless, modern ideas and research generated in the 15 years since the first edition has lead me to reformulate certain aspects of my previous conceptions. Issues relating to matters of taxonomy and diagnosis have become dominant themes in our profession, and imaginative theoretical proposals have come to the fore, each seeking to introduce novel models for focusing and cohering the personality disorders. As noted previously, we have progressed in our work from what was first labeled a "biosocial framework" to one now termed an "evolutionary model." Despite their seeming divergence, these two conceptual schemas are both consonant and consistent. The former derives its constructs largely from learning theory and undergirds developmental ontogenesis, whereas the latter includes constructs derived from evolutionary theory that are applicable both to phylogenesis and human adaptive styles. In this reformulation, elaborated for the reader in Chapters 2 and 3, we believe that a major step has been taken to coordinate concepts of human motivation and behavior with those more typically found in other spheres of scientific inquiry, such as cosmogony and population biology. To readers who gravitate to such admittedly more speculative, but potentially more fruitful, ventures, I suggest they read my recent book, *Toward a New Personology: An Evolutionary Model*, also published by Wiley-Interscience.

As is evident by its size and weight, this revised edition is a substantially enlarged text, more than twice the length of the first, a consequence that owes much to the impressive advancements in the field these past two decades. As before, the book brings together the sparse, widely scattered and highly doctrinaire clinical literature on personality disorders. Seeking in a single sourcebook to both coordinate and evaluate what has been written on the subject, as well as to maximize scholarly and practical utility, it contains contrasting historical and modern viewpoints, and provides extensive coverage of the work of contemporary thinkers. Chapter 2 brings this information together in a historical review that progresses from the distant past to innovative proposals in our present time. More detailed presentations and extensive excerpts relevant to the disorders themselves are found in the clinical chapters, one devoted to each of the personalities comprising Axis II of DSM-III, DSM-III-R, and DSM-IV.

We believe that a substantial expansion of the Clinical Picture section in each personality disorder chapter will prove of considerable utility to all practitioners. Whereas the first edition limited its purview to only four realms of patient data, the current text encompasses eight, enabling mental health professionals of rather diverse persuasions (e.g., cognitive, interpersonal, self-theory, object relations) to recognize those features and traits

with which they are most acquainted and comfortable. These eight domains also set the groundwork for selecting among matching and distinct modalities of therapy (e.g., behavioral, pharmacologic, psychoanalytic, as well as those noted in the previous sentence).

In addition to providing comprehensive reviews of each of the newer personality prototypes, for example: avoidant, narcissistic, borderline, schizotypal, depressive, sadistic, and masochistic, also of special use to clinicians, particularly in this day of managed care, are detailed discussions of frequent Comorbid Axis I and Axis II diagnoses. These are presented to alert practitioners to differences in vulnerabilities among the personalities to each of the major Axis I syndromes, such as depression and anxiety. Equally useful in each chapter are sections elucidating each personality's most plausible biogenic and psychogenic origins and course.

Other areas of expansion and restructuring in this edition should also be noted. Most evident to the reader will be the addition of two major chapters, one pertaining to personality assessment, the other to personality therapy. We have undertaken the task of providing not only a rationale for what should be assessed in the personality disorders, but also an up-to-date review of the newly constructed and recently refurbished instruments available to contemporary clinicians and researchers. Of potential interest to experienced assessment psychologists are brief sections in each clinical chapter that record indices from well-known instruments, such as the Rorschach, the TAT, and the MMPI. These venerable tools may be seen as complementing the diagnostic efficacy of the MCMI, an inventory designed specifically to aid in personality disorder appraisals. Similarly, we have also expanded the logic of a strategic model for the "integrative treatment" of the personality disorders, as well as providing the reader with a focused review of the many tactical modalities that may be usefully employed to that end. Both assessment and therapy chapters lay the foundation for substantially enlarged discussions in later clinical chapters.

The overall sequence of the clinical Chapters (6–20) has been realigned to represent the text's reformulated theoretical model. Personality disorders that are characterized by their marked "pleasure-deficiency" (e.g., schizoid, avoidant, depressive) begin the sequence. The second grouping is comprised of personalities that are "interpersonally-imbalanced," that is, strongly inclined to be oriented either to *others* (e.g., dependent, histrionic), or to *self* (e.g., narcissistic, antisocial). The third classification features disorders that are primarily "intrapsychically-conflicted" (e.g., sadistic, obsessive-compulsive, negativistic, masochistic). And finally, the most severe of the personality pathologies also are assembled together, they comprise patients whose primary personality difficulty stems from their being "structurally-defective" (e.g., schizotypal, borderline, paranoid).

The most innovative section in each clinical chapter, and perhaps in the book as a whole, concerns personality disorder subcategories, ranging from normal styles, to childhood syndromes, to adult subtypes. It is the author's belief that our field should progress "beyond" our present conceptions of these disorders, conceptions that owe in part to the assumption that each is a clinically homogeneous category composed of distinctive and uniformly covariant diagnostic attributes. We believe this assumption is a misleading one, a point of view that not only narrows one's thinking, but also distorts clinical reality, especially for students with modest levels of clinical experience. Although there is a considerable measure of pedagogic utility in formulating modal or textbook prototypes, clinical experience teaches us that great diversity exists within all personality categories; some exhibit its features in essentially normal ways; others are young children who demonstrate the most problematic extremes; still others exhibit various mixtures and combinations of the adult genre. Hence, in addition to the 15 basic personality "prototypes" that constitute the prime focus of each clinical chapter, a further breakdown has been made, resulting thereby in over 60 additional adult subtypes, as well as several normal variants and childhood syndromes. The introduction of these subdivisions may also help resolve the pernicious categorical-dimensional debate and, perhaps more importantly, sensitize the serious reader to the many and diverse "species" that comprise each personality disorder.

It is a pleasure to record the contributions of those who have been most directly involved in this text; there are many to whom I owe much. Several of those who have improved or expedited this work have been listed on the title page. Foremost is my wife Renée who, as before, has contributed her distinctive editorial talents to make the text more lucid and readable, but also more humane and sensitive. It is a joy of no lesser significance to add to this editorial team my daughter Carrie, a Ph.D. psychologist who is rapidly becoming a full partner in several of my endeavors. Also on the list are Marketa Fuchs and Maria (Rose) Van Zuilen, two graduate students who were given responsibility

for writing first drafts of several sections on therapy. And not to be overlooked is Andrew Wenger, who served masterfully as my eyes and fingers while I reflected on inchoate ideas, and then faithfully transcribed my initial draft dictations on the word processor. It is not merely a charitable act that prompts me to record the contributions of these valued associates.

Roger Davis is a special case on the title page, one who well deserves to be listed as the text's co-author. Not only has he written substantial drafts and major sections of several of the new chapters (e.g., Personality Assessment, Personality Therapy), but he has become, while still a University Fellow and Ph.D. candidate, a true professional colleague in the best sense of the word. Never succumbing to the temptation of oversimplification, but always clear and concise in expressing his thoughts, Roger has been endowed with a first-rate mind, perhaps unmatched among my 250 graduate students over the past 40 years in academia. I have bequeathed the task of updating this book to him, should it call for future revisions.

Over the years of writing this and earlier works, I have accumulated numerous intellectual debts to other colleagues and students. None of my theoretical writings have sprung from my mind unaided, nor was the execution of my research endeavors the product of my labors alone. As I have noted in earlier acknowledgments, there are a few who have been foremost in furnishing the stimulus of intellectual discourse and collegial encouragement so necessary to spur an author through his otherwise isolated scholarly labors. Heading this list are Addi Geist Agar, Cathy Green-Goldstein, and Bob Meagher, along with scores of other colleagues to whom I am deeply obliged for their unstinting support at crucial times, namely Flo Grabel, Rose Wilansky, Audrey Melamed, Naomi Grossman, Sally Perlis, Jean Jones, Mary-Lou McGinnis, Leila Foster, JoAnn Lederman, Michael Antone, Robert Tringone, George Everly, and Joseph Zubin.

To these associates must be added my co-founding Editor-In-Chief of the *Journal of Personality Disorders,* Allen Frances; his contributions to the Journal and his diplomatic talents as the DSM-IV Task Force Chairperson will continue to foster advances in the field for many-a-decade. The two six-year stints I spent with colleagues on the DSM-III Task Force (1974–1980) and the DSM-IV, Axis II Work Group (1988–1994) were richly rewarding challenges and opportunities that I shall never forget. Among those who made the DSM-III period intellectually exciting were the innovative and polemical talents of Don Klein, Jean Endicott, Nancy Andreasen, and Bob Spitzer. Several colleagues on the DSM-IV Work Group, where I learned to constrain my more contentious inclinations, are among the most productive thinkers and researchers in the field today, notably Larry Siever, Kathy Phillips, Tracie Shea, Tom Widiger, Bob Hirschfield, Bruce Pfohl, Roger Blashfield, and, most especially, the Work Group's sagacious, fiercely fair-minded, and clinically astute Chairperson, John Gunderson. Along with other valued colleagues at Harvard Medical School/McLean Hospital, such as Elsa Ronningstam and Mary Zanarini, leaders of the Psychosocial and Personality Treatment Group, he has made my visits to Cambridge and Belmont extremely fruitful. Similarly, Ed Murray, Paul Blaney, and Bob McMahon, three colleagues at the University of Miami, have been among my most valued associates. Among my psychoanalytic compatriots, I must single out Otto Kernberg and Michael Stone from whose creative writings and erudite discussions I have profited greatly. Added to these men are a host of distinguished nonanalysts whom I also count as esteemed thinkers and friends, namely Lorna Benjamin, Aaron (Tim) Beck, and Gerry Klerman: their warmth and personal instruction pervade the pages of this book.

For the past decade, I have been the recipient of numerous opportunities to share my ideas with colleagues around the world; many have been extremely generous in their welcome and I would like to record my appreciation for their kindness. Particular affection is due those who promulgated the central role of the personality disorders in Denmark: notable here are Erik Simonsen, Gunilla Øberg, Morten Birket-Smith, Bent Rosenbaum, Fini Schulsinger and, most especially, Niels Strandbygaard, of whom I will say more shortly. In the Netherlands I have been impressed by numerous clinicians of diverse, but exceptional talent, namely Jan Derksen, Wim van den Brink, Franz Luteyn, Herman Groen, Theo Bouman, and Robert Abraham. Among my most esteemed colleagues, few demonstrate the psychometric skills and inventiveness of Hedwig Sloore of the University of Brussels. At the Karolinska Institute in Stockholm, I have been both persuaded and charmed by the broad perspectives of Robert Weinryb and Marie Äsberg. The fine research and theoretical skills of Svenn Torgersen, Per and Sonya Vaglum, Bjørn Østberg, and Alv Dahl of the University of Oslo have been most illuminating. Among associates in Japan, where communication among colleagues is

but a modest problem, I shall like to record the colleagueship of Masaaki Kato of Tokyo Medical College and Kazuhisa Nakao of the University of Osaka. Closer to home in Canada I have very much appreciated the friendship and highly productive contributions of W. John Livesley of the University of British Columbia, and those of Joel Paris and Chris Perry at McGill University.

Of no minor interest to me personally are a group of "Millon Inventory Trainers," knowledgeable and talented instructors who furnish informative workshops to clinical psychologists and other mental health professionals throughout the United States; among those who have not otherwise been noted in these pages, I am happy to record the contributions of Joseph McCann, Paul Retzlaff, Steve Strack, Darwin Dorr, Frank Dyer, Bob Craig, and Jim Choca. The recently organized *Institute for Advanced Studies in Personology and Psychopathology* has inaugurated a national and international Study Group Program led by my able associate Luis Escovar. Collaboration with the Leaders of these Groups over the next several years will be an activity to which I look forward with great enthusiasm. Last, members of the staff of both National Computer Systems, and The Psychological Corporation deserve no small measure of thanks for their competence and indulgence these past several years; deserving special note are Jeffrey Sugerman, Carol Watson, and Scott Allison of NCS, and Larry Weiss and Aurelio Profitera of PsyCorp.

A few words are in order concerning the revolution in health care delivery in which all of us, consumers and providers alike, are involved these days. The beneficial potentials and problematic pitfalls of this radical change are many. They need not be elaborated here; most readers of this text, professionals and professionals-in-training, are well-acquainted with the upheaval that is underway. I do wish to comment, however, on one, rather pernicious consequence of "managed care," namely the belief that the diagnosis of personality disorders is no longer relevant to our profession, owing to the "fact" that insurance companies are loathe to underwrite the costs of extended treatment. Our response to this noxious attitude it two-fold. *First,* personality disorders *can* be treated effectively and efficiently; brief focused therapy can be carried out successfully and swiftly *if* one understands the character of these disorders accurately. Long term treatment is not inevitable; the problem is that we spend too much time wandering hither and yon searching to find what our patients' difficulties may be. With new, brief, and personality-oriented assessment tools, plus the availability of a few solid reference works on the subject (e.g., Beck/Freeman, Benjamin) we should be able to identify the key clinical features which, if directly resolved, should advance the health status of the patient both favorably and rapidly. *Second,* knowledge of the patient's personality disorder can be of inestimable value in helping resolve his or her Axis I clinical syndrome. The treatment focus in these conditions in not that of reworking an Axis II personality disorder, but rather in utilizing the "context of personality" for identifying the patient's core vulnerabilities quickly, vulnerabilities that lead to clinical syndromes such as depression, anxiety, marital tensions, and the like. Knowledge of personality and its disorders is now *more* critical than ever before inasmuch as such knowledge enables the clinician to promptly address the "context" that gives meaning to the patient's syndrome or problem. Such information is all the more important now owing to the fact that clinicians have only a few sessions to accurately appraise and treat their "managed care" patients.

As in the first edition, I have retained my dedication to three early mentors, Gardner Murphy, Kurt Goldstein, and Ernst Kris; without their direct tuition, inspiration, and warm friendship during my student years, the foundations for this book would never have been built. In this revised edition, I have added to these early mentors three peerless colleagues who have aided me immeasurably in building on these early foundations, enabling me to move forward in all of my more mature scholarly efforts. Mel Sabshin, Medical Director of the American Psychiatric Association, has been a much honored and much treasured personal associate of mine for more than a quarter-of-a-century. It was Mel's foresight and tenacity that opened the pathway to the trail-blazing advances of the DSM-III—a little known fact that typifies his courage and integrity. Herb Reich is another generous and cherished friend, no less an editor of singular talent. Not content to merely acquire worthy manuscripts, he takes on a genuinely collaborative role in overseeing the work of his many authors, ferreting out trivial facts and digressions, as well as inelegant and obscure prose, pressing always for clarity and logical consistency, but invariably with wit, grace, and gentility. Finally, my early entree into the European community, where my writings are perhaps as well known as they are in the States, owes much to the intellectual curiosity and creative energies of a great Dane, Niels Strandbygaard. Not only did Niels translate my work for much of Scandinavia, but he was instrumental in organizing the First Congress of the *International Society for the Study of Personality Disorders;* no less significant on a personal basis was his role in leading the First European *Millon Study Group.* My hat is off to each of these three companions "who paved the way."

THEODORE MILLON, PH.D., D.SC.

Coral Gables, Florida
June 1995

Contents

PART I

CONCEPTUAL AND CLINICAL FOUNDATIONS

CHAPTER 1

Personality Disorders:
Issues, Principles, and Classification

Personality disorders have historically been in a tangential position among diagnostic syndromes, never having achieved a significant measure of recognition in the literature of either abnormal psychology or clinical psychiatry. Prior to the *Diagnostic and Statistical Manual of Mental Disorders* (DSM-III; APA, 1980) they were categorized in the official nomenclature with a melange of other, miscellaneous, and essentially secondary syndromes. Today, personality disorders occupy a place of diagnostic prominence, having been accorded a contextual role in the multiaxial schema. Personality pathologies comprise one of two required "mental disorder" axes. Henceforth, clinicians must assess not only the patient's current symptom picture via Axis I, but, in addition, those pervasive features recorded on Axis II that characterize the patient's enduring personality pattern. In effect, the revised multiaxial format requires that symptom states no longer be assessed as clinical entities isolated from the broader context of the patient's lifelong style of relating, coping, behaving, thinking, and feeling—that is, his or her personality.

Beyond the pragmatics of adhering to official DSM nosological requirements, there are substantive reasons for attending to the personality disorders. Lifelong personality traits serve as a substrate and as a context for understanding more florid and distinct forms of psychopathology. Since the early 1960s, our society has been increasingly committed to the early identification and prevention of mental disorders. This emphasis has led clinicians to attend to both premorbid behavioral signs and the less severe variants of emotional disturbance. Ordinary anxieties, minor personal conflicts, and social inadequacies are now seen as the forerunners of more serious problems. A significant impetus to this movement in the 1960s was the emergence of community mental health centers whose attentions are directed to the needs of the less seriously disturbed. As a result of these developments, the scope of clinical psychopathology was broadened far beyond its historical province of "state hospital" psychiatry. As a field, it now encompassed the full spectrum of mild to severe mental disorders. With personality as a contextual foundation, diagnosticians can now more ably grasp the dynamics and more clearly trace the sequences through which both subtle and dramatic clinical symptoms unfold.

Once an area of academic interest has been identified, academic activity within that area increases exponentially. As always, there are periods of creative expansion during which many diverse hypotheses are advanced, and periods of consolidation during which critical activity increases and those ideas that are to become organizing principles for future thinking are sifted into the foreground. Recent years have witnessed a creative expansion of ideas in the area of personality disorders, with the proposal of new models in any of several data domains. Interpersonal (e.g., Lorna Benjamin, Donald Kiesler, Jerry Wiggins), neurobiological (e.g., C. Robert Cloninger, Larry Siever), statistical (e.g., Lee Anna Clark, Paul Costa, Douglas Jackson, W. John Livesley, Thomas Widiger), cognitive (e.g., Aaron Beck, Albert Ellis), and psychoanalytic (e.g., John Gunderson, Otto Kernberg, Michael Stone) adherents have been especially vigorous. As a result of this inevitable stage of scientific growth, the centrifugal forces of specialization currently dominate thinking in the field. Personality disorders are awash in a conceptual pluralism that, while enriching, nevertheless stands in remarkable contrast to the intrinsically integrative epistemology of the personality construct itself. The totality of personality is today increasingly conceptualized through the lens of particular perspectives. The implicit assumption is that cohesive and highly focused systems of thought are best for understanding personologic phenomena, and therefore should serve as the foundation for a taxonomy of personality disorders.

Chapter 1 introduces this emergence of a new discipline by analyzing the constructs of personality and personality disorders. As a point of departure, we emphasize the role of prior assumptions in constraining scientific thought and research. Functionally, prior assumptions are to future scientific thought what object representations are to the phenomenology of the individual. Just as object-relations theorists are interested in uncovering latent assumptions that channel the continuous stream of personal experience into predetermined phenomenological sets, our own underlying conceptual assumptions must be illuminated if we are to determine how they constrain our thinking and research. Although all representations are simplifications of reality, and therefore false in the strictest sense, different models have different strengths and weakness depending on the assumptions one takes to model building. As such, the focus of this chapter is on paradigms and definitions, not on issues of content. The questions asked concern personality disorders in an abstract sense. What is personality? How does our definition of personality inform our definition of personality disorder? Do assumptions underlying the concept of personality support the use of the term "disorder"? Assuming that personality disorder can be defined, on what basis should we determine the classification into disordered and nondisordered groups? How useful can we expect classification schemas to be when the things classified are personalities?

ISSUES OF DEFINITION

What is personality? The question is simple to pose, but difficult to answer, even though, as an idea, personality must be many thousands of years old. Historically, the word personality derives from the Greek term *persona,* originally representing the theatrical mask used by dramatic players. Its meaning has changed through history. As a mask assumed by an actor, it suggested a pretense of appearance, that is, the possession of traits other than those that actually characterized the individual behind the mask. In time, the term persona lost its connotation of pretense and illusion, and began to represent, not the mask, but the real person, his or her apparent, explicit, and manifest features. The third and final meaning that the term personality has acquired

delves beneath surface impressions and turns the spotlight on the inner, less revealed, and hidden psychological qualities of the individual. Thus through history, the meaning of the term has shifted from external illusion to surface reality, and finally to opaque or veiled inner traits. It is this third meaning that comes closest to contemporary use. Personality is seen today as a complex pattern of deeply embedded psychological characteristics that are largely nonconscious and not easily altered, expressing themselves automatically in almost every facet of functioning. Intrinsic and pervasive, these traits emerge from a complicated matrix of biological dispositions and experiential learnings, and ultimately comprise the individual's distinctive pattern of perceiving, feeling, thinking, coping, and behaving.

THE NOMOTHETIC PERSPECTIVE: UNIVERSAL TRUTH IN PERSONALITY

In modern times, personality may be prototypally approached from either of two great historical traditions, both of which go back at least to the time of the early Greeks. The first of these, the nomothetic or construct-centered (Allport, 1937) approach, is concerned with personality in an abstract sense, not with any one individual. The emphasis is on discovering how certain constructs tend to relate or cohere with others, and why. Most often this means focusing on constructs subsidiary to personality as an integrated phenomenon, such as needs, motives, mechanisms, traits, schemas, and defenses. Questions grounded in this approach include "What is the relationship of locus of control to depression?" and "How does the continuum of self-schema complexity relate to stress vulnerability?" Nowhere is mention made of any individual person.

Strongly nomothetically-oriented psychologists often believe that once the fundamental units of personality are isolated, it will be possible to express each particular personality in terms of these units, with little or no relevant information about the person left over. Experimental error or residual variance is seen as reflecting an ignorance of important independent variables that, when accounted for, render what is yet to be explained vanishingly small.

In this perspective, personality is described in terms of the deviation of individual scores from the group mean. The combination of various levels of individual difference variables constitutes individuality, for which the subject's personality profile or codetype then becomes an intervening variable. Nowhere is this assumption more obvious than in taxonomies constructed using factor analytic methods. Here, numerous scales representing a selection of personality traits are factor analyzed for "latent" patterns of covariation, and the larger factors are taken as fundamental dimensions of personality. The variance not accounted for by the factor model is typically rejected as error variance, that is, as being due to measurement error. The derived factors are then accorded causal primacy in the specification of other more circumscribed traits of personality, and ultimately become the axes of a nomothetic hyperspace in which any particular personality may be plotted. In this particular version of the nomological approach, parsimony is emphasized; thousands of traits may be telescoped into a handful of dimensions. However, such a position also requires important auxiliary assumptions, such as the adequacy and appropriateness of both the methodology and the means of sampling the content domain.

The advantage of the nomothetic perspective is that it serves the needs of science by looking at personality in the abstract, by not being grounded to any one person. Toward this end, the nomothetic perspective is indispensable if personality is ever to be considered a genuinely scientific enterprise, not merely a descriptive one. Because science thrives on generalizability, personality cannot afford to be limited to the discovery and explication of laws of behavior that are specific to one person, or to a very small group of persons. If science is defined as the discovery and explanation of invariances across instances, the instances cannot be singular. Instead, science must show the applicability of its theories in realms of manifest phenomena not heretofore seen, approachable, or understood. To locate such universal propositions about behavior, personality psychologists look for regularities or covariations that hold across many different people, rather than merely within one person. Allport (1937, p. 4) compared the nomothetic approach to "finding a single thread running from individual nature to individual nature, visible only through the magical spectacles of a special, theoretic attitude."

The Idiographic Perspective: Particular Truths about Particular Persons

Whereas the nomothetically oriented perspective emphasizes commonalities between people or regularities consistent across a class of objects, the idiographic perspective emphasizes the individuality, complexity, and uniqueness of each person. Obviously, people have different personalities. The idiographic perspective reminds us that personality is not only that which makes each individual what he or she is, it is also that which makes each person different from others. Were everyone the same, were there no variation between persons, then personality as a construct would be unnecessary. In fact, it would be undiscoverable.

Perhaps the most important point of this perspective is the idea that individuality is the result of a unique history of transactions between biological (e.g., temperament and genetic constitution) and contextual factors (e.g., the mother's womb, the family environment, social roles to which the child is exposed, culture, and socioeconomic status), a history that has never existed before and will never be repeated. Because each personality is such a singular product, it cannot be understood through either the application of universal laws or through dimensions of individual differences. Instead, understanding personality requires a developmental approach potentially as descriptively rich as the person's own history, so rich in fact that ultimately it might only be called biographical. According to Henry Murray (1938, p. 604), originator of the term "personology," "the history of personality *is* the personality." Whereas the nomological approach asks about the "what" of personality, the idiographic perspective asks about the "how" and the "why." The question is: How has the person become the unique creature he or she is? Accordingly, the focus in this perspective shifts from the description of each individual personality as a positive phenomenon, that is, classification of the person as an antisocial or the dimensionalization of the person as a codetype in some nomothetic space, to the view that personality is a richly contextualized and intrinsically transactuated phenomenon that emerges from a nearly infinite ground of possibilities. Here, science requires not only a cross-sectional description of the person, for this is only the beginning point, but also an explanation concerning why that person evolved into who he or she is rather than anything else, an elucidation of the specific developmental constraints by which the particular individual as a distinct entity was culled from an infinite universe of possibilities. Because of the antithesis of this perspective to universal laws, it is not impossible that these constraints might include such softer concepts as free will and chance.

In its extreme form, the idiographic approach militates against all taxonomy as an illusion that maintains the pretense of science, but is not in itself scientific. Where taxonomies must be used, they are only provisional explanatory systems to be modified as needed when additional evidence becomes available. Thus, in this book, we have established a series of *prototypes* that are essentially nomothetic in character in that they comprise hypothetical or abstract constructs derived from theoretically posited universals (evolutionary polarities); however, in addition, we have also provided a wide range of personality *subtypes* representing trait constellations that approach more specific and idiographic levels of description. Absolute individuality is too complex and varied to be organized into classes or placed along dimensions of individual differences. If these are used at all, they must be used self-consciously as contrivances to facilitate the investigation of individuality and not as end points. Given the interpenetrant and multidetermined nature of any personality construct, we must resist the ever-present linguistic compulsion to separate constructs from their behavioral field and treat them as if their manifestations in personality were achieved through some causality of their own. Constructs (e.g. personality prototypes) are to be used heuristically, as guidelines to be replaced and reformulated as necessary; it is only the unique manifestation or instantiation of the construct or trait in the individual that is of immediate clinical interest. For this reason, the idiographic perspective is not so much concerned with construct validity as it is with content and descriptive validity. Idiographic psychologists don't care much about the question "What are the fundamental units of personality?" Constructs are only points of departure. What is important is achieving a relatively complete and descriptively rich characterization of the individual as he or she exists, and why. Any construct from personality, or even literature, is free game if it is relevant and effective in communicating something about the patient.

For clinicians, the implication of such extreme individualism is that even officially sanctioned taxonomies of personality and personality disorders are limited in their explanatory power and clinical utility. How many clinicians, when faced with a patient whose personality and its relationship to psychopathology must be understood, would confine themselves to the constructs and attributes of the DSM-IV (American Psychiatric Association, 1994)? Probably none. Not only is the DSM-IV *not* an exhaustive listing of personality constructs that might be relevant to any particular individual, it does not even begin to scratch the surface. From this perspective, a DSM-IV diagnosis alone, unsupplemented by information from additional descriptive domains, constitutes an insufficient basis by which to explain the dynamics of the individual. Nomothetic propositions and diagnostic labels are mere superficialities to be overcome as understanding is gained. They are necessary, but not sufficient and, in fact, if left on their own as cross-sectional rather than developmentally oriented entities, they may even be regarded as pseudoscientific. As Sartre wrote, "Once you label me, you defeat me," an existential take on how reified diagnostic schemas so exaggerate within-group homogeneity at the expense of individuality (Cantor & Genero, 1986) that, functionally, it is a form of defeat through reductionism.

For nosologists, the inexact fit between patient and diagnosis is a nagging and noisome reminder of individuality. Fortunately, this incessant nagging has influenced and fueled the development of modern psychiatric taxonomies. Ideally, a diagnosis alone should be both necessary and sufficient to begin treatment—all you need to know. Were ideals realities, individuals would fit their diagnostic categories perfectly with pristinely prototypal presentations. Yet such a thing seldom occurs. A famous developmental theorist, Heinz Werner, argued that development always proceeds from the global to the more differentiated. The monotypic categories of earlier DSMs may be seen as the global beginnings of a march toward specification and the accommodation of the DSM taxonomy to individuality. In the initial phases of its development, a diagnostic taxonomy should consist generally of entities of broad bandwidth, but little specificity. Inevitably, some diagnostic categories will begin to be viewed as invalid and discarded wholesale. As theoretical knowledge and empirical studies accrue, however, manifestations of most diagnostic entities become better delineated—broad diagnostic taxons begin to be broken down into multiple, narrow taxons of greater specificity and descriptive value, as we have begun to do in later chapters when describing the several *subtypes* of each broader-based personality disorder category. As the process continues, an interesting structural change occurs in the taxonomy: It begins to take on a hierarchical structure that allows it to accommodate to the contextualism in the world at large. Its coverage increases as big taxons are broken down into little taxons. The Anxiety Disorders, for example, now include Panic Disorder, Agoraphobia, and Posttraumatic Stress Disorder, among others. No one argues that what these disorders have in common is anxiety—but now it has become apparent that a diagnosis of anxiety alone is insufficient to understand the client and inform intervention efforts.

The same kind of hierarchical evolution is already occurring on Axis II. Whenever kinds of schizoids or antisocials or borderlines are discussed, a hierarchical conception is implicit. In this volume, following the nomothetic tradition, subvarieties of the Axis II constructs have been abstracted from historical works to provide further refinement, sharper distinctions, and greater descriptive power within these diagnostic entities throughout the clinical chapters of this text. In the idiographic tradition, Millon (1986b, Table 1.1) has articulated each of the Axis II prototypes as integrative personality patterns that are expressed in a variety of functional and structural clinical domains. Among assessment instruments, which are much more easily constructed and altered than official nosologies, the evidence of contextualism is even more clear. Despite its metatheoretical weaknesses, one strength of the lexical approach is its assertion that personality traits are hierarchically organized. Personality descriptors are broad, but somewhat inaccurate, near the top of the hierarchy, becoming increasingly narrow, but more precise, as one moves down into regions of lower traits and

ultimately into behavioral acts. The Neuroticism, Extroversion, Openness to Experience-Personality Inventory (NEO-PI) for example, includes facet scales of each of its five broadband factors. The Minnesota Multiphasic Personality Inventory (MMPI)-2 Content Scales have been broken up into experimental Content Component scales (Butcher, Graham, Williams, & Ben-Porath, 1990). Moreover, content subscales have recently been designed for the personality disorder scales of the Millon Clinical Multiaxial Inventory-III (Millon, Davis, & Fuchs, in press), the Millon Adolescent Clinical Inventory (Millon & Davis, in press), and the Millon Index of Personality Styles (Millon & Davis, in press). As a result of a cluster analysis of 158 patients' profiles on their Dimensional Assessment of Personality Problems-Basic Questionnaire, Livesley, Schroeder, Jackson, and Lang (1994) argued for three types of narcissism, noting that if these "types" are placed together into one category, they are effectively represented under a single label with little justice done to their uniqueness. The hierarchical issue will be revisited in Chapter 4, as will the value of demonstrating the clinical utility of positing subtypes of each disorder in Chapters 6 to 20.

AN INTEGRATIVE PERSPECTIVE

Both the nomothetic and idiographic perspectives on personality are unsatisfying in their extreme forms. The nomothetic approach fails to recognize the singularity of each person, and so loses sight of the very point of departure, the desire to understand the individual, that formed the reason for the whole venture. The idiographic approach fails to recognize that each individual must be compared and contrasted with others. Each person is conceived ultimately as the embodiment of a unique transactional history between contextual and constitutional factors that has never existed before and that will never be repeated. Although every biography is unique and highly relevant, biography alone lacks the vision and generalizability we expect from science. Individuals cannot be made so individual that they become ineffable. Constructs cannot exist without individuals to be compared; individuals cannot be understood except through constructs.

The divergence between these two broad perspectives parallels that between the role of personality as a pure science and the role personality plays in an applied clinical science. As previously

TABLE 1.1   Some Principles for Conceptualizing Personality and Its Disorders

Principle 1.	Personality disorders are not diseases.
Principle 2.	Personality disorders are internally differentiated functional and structural systems, not internally homogenous entities.
Principle 3.	Personality disorders are dynamic systems, not static, lifeless entities.
Principle 4.	Personality consists of multiple units at multiple data levels.
Principle 5.	Personality exists on a continuum. No sharp division exists between normality and pathology.
Principle 6.	Personality pathogenesis is not linear, but sequentially interactive and multiply distributed through the entire system.
Principle 7.	Personality criteria by which to assess pathology should be logically coordinated with the systems model itself.
Principle 8.	Personality disorders may be assessed, but not definitively diagnosed.
Principle 9.	Personality disorders require strategically planned and combinatorial modes of tactical intervention.

noted, the onus of individuality has become a primary motivating force in the revision of modern taxonomies. Pure personality psychologists tend to be construct-focused, interested in creating and validating a network of nomological relationships. Clinical scientists, however, are always faced with understanding a single person.

The integrative perspective seeks a synthesis of these two broad traditions. Ideally, both aspects of our science would be completely integrated, so that we not only would possess exhaustive knowledge of every personality construct and its relationships with other constructs across every domain of personality, but also would have exhaustive knowledge of the universe of transactional mechanisms through which individual personalities are transformed during their development. Any attempt must recognize, first, that some point of departure is necessary for understanding the individual and, second, that universal and particular truth cannot be completely reconciled, that ultimately the individual is a singular phenomenon only partially accessible to science and its methods. In more complex systems, nature simply does not afford the degree of structure and lawfulness that we would have it possess. Every scientific theory must be judged according to the degree to which it is simultaneously both a complete and a parsimonious explanation of behavior. A ratio is at work. Models that are either one or the other are far easier to invent than those that to a large measure satisfy both criteria simultaneously. Unfortunately, such models also tend to be either very consistent but narrow, derived from one perspective or domain of personality, or of wide scope, but cumbrous and difficult to apply with precision, as for example with psychodynamic formulations.

In addition to the steps taken to specify comparable clinical domains for refining appraisals of personalities, as well as steps to differentiate each personality prototype into its several subtypes, the authors believe that the concept of a *system* offers an optimal level of scope and precision for purposes of bridging nomothetic and idiographic perspectives. By definition, a system is an integrative construct consisting of both structural and functional elements. Part and whole are bound together by self-regulating processes. The appropriate unit of analysis in systems is neither trait nor taxon, but constraint. A constraint is simply something that acts to diminish the number of states or configurations other parts of the system can assume. Some constraints are more severe than others, in that they exclude more possibilities than others.

Assume, for example, that a recently married couple has only one car. Having one car instead of two is an unfortunate circumstance that requires both husband and wife to plan their lives carefully in order to accomplish their mutual goals. If other constraints arise, one person's immediate goals may not get met. The husband cannot get his hair trimmed at two o'clock if his wife has an important job interview across town at exactly the same time. However, if the couple has two cars, one of which is low on gas, the tank can easily be filled. Being low on gas is not much of a constraint.

If personality as a science is to inform the individual case, it must strive toward formulations in which the diverse nomothetic constructions may be integrated as an organic whole. The structure of the field should mirror its subject matter. Although we must all be eclectics to some degree, if we believe that nature itself is unintegrated and pluralistic, then we must be content to let Axis II consist of only a collection of diagnostic attributes or characteristics organized by content domain (e.g., cognitive styles, defense mechanisms, interpersonal behaviors), without any organization of these into broader and less arbitrary units. Were we dogmatic pluralists, the kind of validity that we would be concerned with in a symptom- or attribute-oriented (as opposed to a syndrome-oriented) taxonomy would be mainly content validity: whether the cognitive domain contains everything it should contain and nothing superfluous, whether the domain of regulatory (defense) mechanisms contains everything it should and nothing superfluous, and so on. In fact, if we really believe that personalities can "hold themselves together," given almost any mixture of parts, there is no need for higher-order syndromes at all. Then, of course, we must also be prepared to believe that there are no higher-order principles inherent in nature by which covariations found between these attributes "make sense."

Few, however, would argue that this is the case. On the contrary, the essence of personality lies in its implicit holism. Not every defense mechanism goes equally well with every interpersonal style. Although needs, motives, mechanisms, traits, schemas, and defenses are part of personality, they are never the whole story. As a construct, personality seeks to capture the entire matrix of the person, to distill from the swirl of the behavioral stream some set of underlying, logical, organizing principles that precisely capture individual functioning. Personality asks us to look at manifest behaviors not one at a time as if each were simply the next on the list or next in a sequence, relevant to, yet isolated from the larger whole, but rather to examine behaviors in connection with one another as a means by which to infer some underlying theme or unity of purpose to which each aspect of the whole is somehow accountable. As a construct, personality begs us dive beneath the surface, to make inferences, and to integrate manifest diversities based on latent logical principles. As scientists, we are called on not merely to record behavior in this or that domain, but to explain it.

What are these nomological principles? In the authors' view, they are based in evolutionary tasks that are applicable to every living organism as a biopsychosocial system: Existence (Pleasure-Pain), Adaptation (Active-Passive), Replication (Self-Other), and Abstraction (Thinking-Feeling). Each task is coupled with a polarity or bipolarity that lends the system content. Chapters 2 and 3 provide a detailed discussion of the attributes and development of this evolutionary model. At the conclusion of the Contemporary Proposals section of each clinical chapter of this text (Ch. 6–20), a diagram is presented showing how that particular personality style is conceptualized in terms of the polarity framework.

At this point in our discussion, however, we are interested in the formal properties of systems, rather than their content, and the implications of a systems metaphor for personality and personality disorders. Several ideas implicit in the idea of a system not only are relevant to personality as a construct, but also serve as a welcome nostrum for certain paradigmatic misconceptions that continue to plague the personality disorders, despite the fact that Axis II has now moved into its second decade of life. Fortunately, personality may be discussed in systems concepts without any reference to content, and without reference to any one individual. The idea of a system is a more structurally robust unit of analysis than is a trait or category, though these latter units may be convenient for purposes of clinical communication. The implications and benefits of systems concepts for the personality disorders are abstracted as a set of principles and summarized in Table 1.1. All are intrinsically interconnected logically; their enumeration for pedagogic purposes in this chapter should not imply that these principles are intended to be logically discrete. They are set forth as principles simply because of the limitations of human memory. Principles tend to be remembered; paragraphs forgotten. As the reader will undoubtedly note, there is substantial thematic overlap as these principles are discussed.

Principle 1 Personality Disorders Are Not Diseases

The systems conception of personality, implicitly made central in the DSM-III through the multiaxial model, breaks the long-entrenched habit of conceiving syndromes of psychopathology as one or another variant of a disease, that is, as some "foreign" entity or lesion that intrudes insidiously within the person to undermine his or her so-called normal functions. The archaic notion that all mental disorders represent external intrusions or internal disease processes is an offshoot of prescientific ideas such as demons or spirits that ostensibly "possess" or cast spells on the person. The role of infectious agents and anatomical lesions in physical medicine has reawakened this archaic view. Although we no longer see demons, many still see personality disorders as involving some alien or malevolent force that invades and unsettles the patient's otherwise healthy status. This view is an appealing simplification to the layperson, who can attribute his or her irrationalities to some intrusive or upsetting agent. It also has its appeal to the less sophisticated clinician, for it enables him or her to believe that the insidious intruder can be identified, hunted down, and destroyed.

Such naive notions carry little weight among modern-day medical and behavioral scientists. As a result of our increasing awareness of the complex nature of both health and disease, we now recognize, for example, that most physical disorders result from a dynamic and changing interplay between individuals' capacities to cope and the environment within which they live. It is the patients' overall constitutional makeup—their vitality, stamina, and immunological system—that serves as a substrate inclining them to resist or to succumb to potentially troublesome environmental forces. To illustrate: Infectious viruses and bacteria proliferate within the environment; it is the person's defenses that determine whether or not these microbes will take hold, spread, and, ultimately, be experienced as illness. Individuals with robust immune activity counteract the usual range of infectious microbes with ease, whereas those with weakened immunosuppressive capacities are vulnerable, fail to handle these "intrusions," and quickly succumb. Similarly, structural disorders such as coronary artery disease are not merely a consequence of food consumed or life stress but reflect instead each individual's metabolic capacity to break down lipoprotein intake;

it is the body's ability to process nutritional excess that is the major determinant of whether arterial disease does or does not occur. Those with balanced enzymatic functions will readily transform and dispose of excess lipids, whereas those with less adequate equipment will cumulate arterial plaques that gradually develop into disease. Psychopathology should be conceived as reflecting the same interactive pattern. Here, however, it is not the immunological defenses or enzymatic capacities but the patient's personality pattern— that is, coping skills and adaptive flexibilities— that determines whether or not the person masters or succumbs to his or her psychosocial environment. Just as physical ill health is likely to be less a matter of some alien virus than it is a dysfunction in the body's capacity to deal with infectious agents, so too is psychological ill health likely to be less a product of some intrusive psychic strain than it is a dysfunction in the personality's capacity to cope with life's difficulties. Viewed this way, the structure and characteristics of personality become the foundation for the individual's capacity to function in a mentally healthy or ill way.

Principle 2   Personality Disorders Are Internally Differentiated Functional and Structural Systems, Not Internally Homogenous Entities

Implicit in the idea of a system is the notion of internal differentiation and cooperation between constituent parts. For a system to do its work, it must contain various structural elements, each of which is physically differentiated toward some functional purpose essential to the operation of the whole. Much as an organism may be studied from the viewpoints of both physiology and anatomy, a system may be said to possess both structural and functional properties. If a system contained no internal parts, it could not exist as a system at all. Moreover, if each of these parts did not subserve some systemic function, the system would be nothing more than a collection of noninteracting pieces, much like a machine that was never assembled. Structures without functions remain inanimate, whereas functions without structures to subserve them are but disembodied ghosts, if that.

Just as evolution has endowed each organism with certain functional and structural properties in phylogenetic time, in ontogenetic time the structural characteristics of each personality begin to take on a more permanent mold. The structural attributes of the personality system represent deeply embedded and relatively enduring templates of imprinted memories, attitudes, needs, fears, conflicts, schemas, and so on, that guide the experience and transform the nature of ongoing life events. Because they subserve functional domains of personality only insofar as their structural properties permit, these psychic structures have an orienting and preemptive effect whereby the character of action and the impact of subsequent experiences are altered in line with preformed inclinations and expectancies. Once psychic structures are in place, they are difficult to transform or uproot. By selectively lowering thresholds for transactions that are consonant with either constitutional proclivities or early learnings, present events and future anticipations are experienced as variations of the past. Schemas, for example, provide a structural means of organizing the world into a set of categories, thereby helping to achieve cognitive economy, and a sense of existential competency, among other things. Once formed, however, the schematic prototype preempts consideration of each member of a set as an entity with qualities unique in its own right. For purposes of definition, structural domains may be conceived as "substrates and action dispositions of a quasi-permanent nature." Possessing a network of interconnecting pathways, these structures contain the internalized residues of the past in the form of memories and affects that are associated intrapsychically with conceptions of self and others.

Principle 3   Personality Disorders Are Dynamic Systems, Not Static, Lifeless Entities

Perhaps the most annoying misconception about personality disorders, perpetuated in part by the medical disease model, and in part by linguistic habits embedded in our language, is that personality disorders are things, much like any other physical object, rather than heuristic constructs. In the parlance of philosophy, this is called reification, the transformation of a thought intended to guide further investigation into a thing.

To be truly lifelike, structures must be coupled with functions that animate the system and allow it to make transactions both internally and between itself and outside world. If a system is to perpetuate itself, it must maintain its integrity against both external and internal threats and stressors. Doing so requires modalities of action that continually make adjustments of fit within the system and between the system and the environment. Functional characteristics may be said to represent dynamic processes that transpire within the intrapsychic world and between the individual's self and psychosocial contexts. For definitional purposes, we might say that functional domains represent "expressive modes of regulatory action," that is, behaviors, social conduct, cognitive processes, and unconscious mechanisms that manage, adjust, transform, coordinate, balance, discharge, and control the give and take of inner and outer life. Accordingly, functional characteristics are especially important with regard to the self-regulation of systems.

Because the precise physical constitution of the various structural elements of personality remains largely unknown, and because their functional roles are highly intermeshed and intrinsically intercontextualized, leading to ambiguous boundaries, the structural elements and functional processes of the personality system are best referred to pedagogically as structural and functional domains. This descriptive convenience simply recognizes that certain part-oriented aspects of personality have a more enduring and ingrained quality, whereas others are by definition transactional in character.

Principle 4 Personality Consists of Multiple Units at Multiple Data Levels

Concepts are not reality. They are not inevitable and true representations of the objective world. The conceptual language of a theory is an optional tool utilized to organize observable experience in a logical manner. Theorists often engage in intense debates as to which concepts are best, and readers often invest much time and energy in trying to decide who is correct. Unfortunately, pure empiricism fails to take cognizance of fundamental and complex philosophical issues. To make sense of or give direction to observations, it is necessary first to choose the kinds of data that will be conceptualized. Only when we know which data have been selected for this purpose by the various theories will we be able to compare them in terms of their success in giving meaning and coherence to the observations they share.

A major source of confusion for students stems from the fact that psychopathologists have traditionally observed different types of data. The complex components of personality lend themselves to being conceived in almost an infinite number of ways. Which observations should be grouped or

combined to form conceptual abstractions is a matter of theoretical orientation. Observational units may range from past events to current situations, from specific acts to dimensional traits, or from unconscious motives to biological temperaments. No single focus of observation is sufficient to encompass all the complex and multidimensional components that make up personality pathology.

Psychopathologists have no choice but to approach their subject from different vantage points, selecting only those elements they believe will enable them to best answer the questions they pose. Nature does not lend itself to our need to conceptualize a tidy and well-ordered universe (Millon, 1967). The complexity of the natural world makes difficult not only the identification of lawful relationships among events, but also their classification. In our desire to uncover the essential order of nature, we necessarily select only a few of the infinite number of elements that could be chosen. In this selection process, we narrow our choices largely in terms of the traditions of our science, with the hope that this will focus our attention and facilitate our search for answers.

Personality psychology, however, is a science rich in diverse perspectives which suggest competing ways that data might prove fruitful. Psychopathologists who view patients at a *behavioral* level are likely to conceive personality as a collection of specific and largely unrelated responses to particular stimulus events. Those who view personality from a *phenomenological* perspective are inclined to attend to signs of personal discomfort as subjectively experienced and consciously reported. Approached with a *biophysical* orientation, these same events are likely to be conceived as intricate sequences of neural or chemical activity. Those of a *psychoanalytic* persuasion will be disposed to organize personality as complex unconscious processes that reflect instinctual drives and the residues of childhood anxieties and conflicts. As a consequence of these diverse perspectives, the raw data of personality may be conceived by some as conditioned habits, by others as cognitive expectancies, or neurochemical dysfunctions, or reaction formations, and so on.

While all these levels of data are necessary for a complete perspective on personality, none in itself is sufficient or best. Alternative levels of data are merely different. Once a particular level is chosen, it leads to conceptualizations and conclusions that do not readily translate into the vocabulary of others. For this reason, theories must be differentiated in terms of the kinds of data they elect to conceptualize. Although this material is elaborated in greater detail elsewhere (Millon, 1967, 1973), it will be useful to briefly describe the major levels of data that distinguish contemporary theories:

Biophysical Data. Those who follow in the tradition of medical psychiatry are oriented to biophysical data. Most adhere to the medical "disease" model, as illustrated by the search for the origins of disease in infections, obstructions, imbalances, or other disruptions of normal physiological functioning. As regards psychopathology, biophysically oriented theorists are likely to believe that structural defects or chemical deficiencies will ultimately be found to account for symptoms such as bizarre behaviors, labile emotions, and disorganized thinking. The major difference they see between psychological and physical disease is that the former, reflecting disruptions in the nervous system, will manifest itself in the realms of behavior, emotions, and thought, whereas the latter, arising from defects in other organ systems, will be manifest in physical symptoms.

Intrapsychic Data. Those within the psychodynamic tradition of psychiatry focus their attention on intrapsychic data. They emphasize the impact of early experience and view adult disorders to be a consequence of the unrelenting and insidious operation of past events. Personality pathology reflects the inappropriate persistence of unconscious defensive maneuvers that were devised initially to protect against the upsurge or recurrence of early difficulties. The obscure and objectively elusive data of the unconscious are uncovered and used for intrapsychic concepts.

Phenomenological Data. Theorists whose views reflect humanistic and existential traditions attend primarily to the data of conscious, phenomenological experience. From this perspective, each individual must be studied only on his or her own terms—from that individual's unique perception of the world. No matter how transformed or unconsciously distorted this perception may be, it is the person's idiosyncratic way of seeing and experiencing events that gives meaning to his or her behavior. Concepts must be formulated, therefore, not in terms of objective reality or unconscious processes, but in accord with how things are directly felt and known by the patient.

Behavioral Data. Those working in the traditions of academic and experimental psychology direct their observations to overt behavioral data. To them, concepts and propositions are anchored to tangible and measurable properties in the empirical world. Subjective introspection and unconscious dynamics are viewed as unscientific and are replaced by references to empirically observable events and actions. Environmental influences are given prominence and are conceived as stimulus properties that reinforce and control behavior pathology.

Sociocultural Data. Finally, there are theorists whose data derive mainly from sociological and anthropological perspectives. No longer is the focus on the individual, the overt behavior, neurochemical processes, self-concept, or unconscious mechanisms; rather, larger units of sociocultural phenomena such as families, groups, or ethnic and minority status are the primary data. Concepts are devised to represent these social forces and are employed largely to provide a context for understanding pathological behaviors.

Principle 5   Personality Exists on a Continuum; No Sharp Division Is Possible between Normality and Pathology

Numerous attempts have been made to develop definitive criteria for distinguishing psychological normality from abnormality. Some of these criteria focus on features that characterize the so-called normal, or ideal, state of mental health, as illustrated in the writings of Shoben (1957), Jahoda (1958), and Offer and Sabshin (1974, 1991); others have sought to specify criteria for concepts such as abnormality or psychopathology, exemplified in the work of Scott (1958), Buss (1966), and Strack and Lorr (1994).

Obviously, all such distinctions between normality and pathology are in part social constructions or cultural artifacts. Although persons may be segregated into groups according to overt and reproducible criteria, lending such classifications the respectability and occasionally even the substance of science, the desire to segregate and the act of segregating such persons are uniquely social phenomena. Hence, all definitions of pathology, ailment, malady, sickness, illness, disorder, or derangement are ultimately value laden and circular (Feinstein, 1977). Disorders are what doctors treat, and what doctors treat is defined implicitly by social standards that for the most part are assumed and thus exist at a nonconscious level.

Because of its social heritage, positive aspects of normality are best exemplified by participation in those behaviors and customs that are prototypal for the individual's reference group. Conversely, pathology or abnormality is exemplified by behaviors that are uncommon, irrelevant, or hostile to that reference group. However uncomfortable one may be with the knowledge that abnormality is largely a social construction, the origins of this construction may at least be acknowledged and dealt with heuristically, without reification. Accordingly, normality and pathology must be viewed as relative concepts; they represent arbitrary points on a continuum or gradient—no sharp line divides normal from pathological behavior. Among diverse and ostensibly content- and culture-free criteria used to signify normality are a capacity to function autonomously and competently, a tendency to adjust to one's social milieu effectively and efficiently, a subjective sense of contentment and satisfaction, and the ability to self-actualize or to fulfill one's potentials. Psychopathology would be noted either by deficits among the preceding or by the presence of characteristics that actively undermine these capacities. Then again, perhaps these criteria are too Westernized to be universal. Whereas the unfolding and rich differentiation of some immanent plan of organismic potentials would seem to be generic to all development, its ultimate expression is specified by social and cultural forces. In some Asian cultures, for example, where the individual is expected to subordinate individual ambitions to group consensus, the capacity to function autonomously might be praiseworthy, but an intense desire to do so is not.

Developmentally, personality pathology results from the same forces that are involved in the development of normal functioning. Important differences in the character, timing, and intensity of these influences lead some individuals to acquire pathological constraints and others to develop more adaptive traits. When an individual displays an ability to cope with the environment in a flexible manner, and when his or her typical perceptions and behaviors foster increments in personal satisfaction, then the person is deemed by the larger reference group to possess a normal or healthy personality. Conversely, when average or everyday responsibilities are responded to inflexibly or defectively, or when the individual's perceptions and behaviors result in increments in personal discomfort or curtail opportunities to learn and to grow, then we may speak as a linguistic contrivance of a pathological or maladaptive pattern.

Despite the foregoing, it should be noted that the traits which compose a number of personality styles are likely in certain historical periods or cultures, such as contemporary Western societies, to promote healthy functioning (e.g., Histrionic, Compulsive, Narcissistic traits). Similarly, in our society, there are personality styles and traits that are highly conducive to pathological functioning (e.g., Avoidant, Dependent, Masochistic). There are other personality patterns (e.g., Schizotypal, Borderline, Paranoid) which have a *very* small probability of falling at the normal end of the continuum in almost all cultures.

Principle 6   Personality Pathogenesis Is Not Linear, but Sequentially Interactive and Multiply Distributed throughout the Entire System

By definition, systems are characterized by interdependencies among their constituent elements. Consequently, operations of the system cannot be described simply as A causes B causes C causes D, and so on. Instead, each domain or part of the system directly or indirectly constrains and is constrained by every other through a reciprocal causality. Changes in system functioning are changes in the entire "causal field" of personality variables.

A systems conception of personality has important implications for psychotherapy and psychotherapy research. On the optimistic side, the interdependency of system components means that almost any point in the system can be targeted for change and will produce results, whether cognitive, behavioral, psychodynamic, or pharmacological. Reciprocal causality allows these effects to be distributed, potentially changing the entire person.

On the pessimistic side, systems tend toward homeostasis. Interventions aimed at one domain of functioning alone produce effects that dissipate as they are distributed. Regulatory mechanisms of defense, for example, provide the organism with an active means of coping with incongruities between habitual modes of self-conception and new information that is potentially damaging to the self-concept. Only information that is confirmatory, or at least not disconfirmatory, of established and cherished ideas passes through the defensive filter for conscious recognition and deliberation. The same can be said for cognitive schemas, which accomplish the same end passively simply by neglecting to process schematically incongruent information. To the credit of short-term psychotherapists, they have recognized that real change cannot be produced unless these homeostatic mechanisms are suspended, producing anxiety.

Principle 7 Criteria by Which to Assess Personality Pathology Should Be Logically Coordinated with the Systems Model Itself

Despite knowledge that normality and abnormality exist on a continuum, there is often a difference between practice and theory. In the real world of clinical work, practitioners are called on to make decisions that lead to a clinical bifurcation: To treat or not to treat? What criteria should be implemented to assist in making this judgment? As always, the best judgements are those that are somehow articulated with the overarching paradigm in which those decisions must be made. Personality may be viewed as a closed system, as an open system actively in transaction with its environment, and as an open system that evolves across time. Each of these three levels of conception is really just a way of slicing the pie when trying to understand persons. The person can be looked at on his or her own terms, against the background of his or her environment, or as an evolved entity with a long and unique history. These modes parallel three essential and interdependent criteria for personality pathology that may be abstracted to judge the severity of personality pathology: (a) tenuous stability under stress, (b) adaptive inflexibility, and (c) a tendency to foster vicious or self-defeating circles (Millon, 1969). Like the normality-pathology continuum, each of these may be characteristic of each individual to various degrees:

Tenuous Stability. The first feature that tends to characterize clinical personality patterns is a fragility or lack of resilience under conditions of subjective stress. Like all working systems, normal personalities exhibit functional-structural integration among their various aspects. Normal personalities, for example, engage behaviors that minimize the incompatibility between organismic needs and environmental press, a negative feedback process for maintaining the integrity of their psychic systems. So-called pathological personalities, however, practice strategies that inadvertently produce positive feedback, amplifying their adaptive difficulties. Ultimately, because of the ease with which the already troubled are vulnerable to events that reactivate the past, as well as their inflexibility and paucity of effective coping mechanisms, they may become extremely susceptible to new difficulties and disruptions. Faced with recurrent failures, anxious lest old and unresolved conflicts reemerge, and unable to recruit new adaptive strategies, these persons are likely to revert to pathological ways of coping, to less adequate control over their emotions, and, ultimately, to increasingly subjective and distorted perceptions of reality. The ultimate disintegration of personality is represented in psychotic decompensation.

Adaptive Inflexibility. Rather than being merely passive receptacles ready for environmental input, personality systems are open systems with the opportunity to actively transact with their physical, familial, social, and cultural environments. For personalities that function in the normal range, this means role flexibility, knowing when to take the initiative and modify one's environment, and knowing when to adapt to what the environment offers. Normal persons exhibit flexibility in their interactions, such that their initiatives or reactions are proportional and appropriate to what the situation requires.

If person and environment are conceptualized as structural features of a larger dynamic system, then the evolution of the system through successive states may be said to be subject to constraints that issue from both. When environmental constraints dominate, the behavior of individuals tends to converge, regardless of their prepotent dispositions: Almost everyone stops when stoplights are red. Such situations are highly scripted, in that almost everyone knows what to do and behaves the same way. In contrast, when environmental constraints are few or poorly defined, there is opportunity for flexibility, novelty, and the expression of individual differences in behavior.

What happens, however, when the person-environment interaction is pervasively constrained by personologic factors? In this case, the variability of the individual's behavior is no longer appropriate and proportional to what the environment requires. We might say that the interaction is driven by the person. The alternative strategies the individual employs for relating to others, for achieving goals, and for coping with stress are, prototypally, few in number and practiced rigidly; that is, they are imposed on conditions for which they are ill suited. Not only may the individual be unable to adapt effectively to the circumstances of his or her life, he or she may also arrange the environment to avoid objectively neutral events that are perceived as stressful. As a consequence, the individual's opportunities for testing and acquiring new, more adaptive strategies are reduced, with the result that life experiences become even more narrowly circumscribed.

Vicious Circles. As noted, individuals and their environments are always in active transaction. Sometimes environmental constraints dominate. Sometimes personologic constraints dominate—all of us manipulate our environments to suit our needs. The last characteristic that distinguishes pathological from normal patterns is a consequence of their rigidity and inflexibility—a tendency to foster vicious circles. The many constraints personality-disordered individuals bring to their social milieu inevitably result in feedback processes that perpetuate and intensify preexisting difficulties. Protective constriction, cognitive distortion, overgeneralization—all are processes by which individuals restrict their opportunities for new learning, misconstrue essentially benign events, and provoke reactions from others that reactivate earlier problems. In effect, then, pathological personality patterns are themselves pathogenic; that is, they generate and perpetuate extant dilemmas, provoke new predicaments, and set into motion self-defeating sequences with others, which cause their already established difficulties not only to persist, but to be aggravated further.

Principle 8   Personality Disorders May Be Assessed, but Not Definitively Diagnosed

This rather strong statement is inconsistent with the disease model, but consistent with the multiaxial model and systems conceptions. If personality disorders are not diseases (so that the word "disorder" is itself unjustified), then this conclusion is straightforward, inevitable, and obvious. With the advent of the multiaxial system of DSM-III, personality was given a contextual role with respect to the classical psychopathologies of Axis I. What mode of conception would best free personality from the distortions of the medical model while simultaneously maintaining fidelity to the construct, thereby illuminating its contextual role and clinical utility?

Through a systems model, the value-laden normality-abnormality ascription can be translated into terminology that maintains standards of scientific respectability and continually reminds clinical scientists of the artificiality of any such distinction. In short, talk of normal and abnormal functioning must be replaced by a discussion of systemic constraints. Unlike the terms disorder and pathology, which pull for discrete, binary, categorical conceptions that implicitly embed clinical activity in the disease model, the idea of the "constraint" embeds clinical activity in a systems perspective; it thereby simultaneously reports the existence of substantial limitations on current personality functioning, and makes salient the idea of new possibilities for the person should these constraints be relaxed.

Not only is the systems perspective more realistic (in the sense of having greater fidelity to the personality construct) than the medical model, it is also much more optimistic. In contrast, the mindset that currently dominates the clinical milieu is doubly pessimistic for those "diagnosed" with clinical personality features: To be disordered or diseased is bad enough. What is worse, however, is to be diseased in way that is deeply ingrained and pervasive across time and situations. Imagine the hopelessness and helplessness such clients would feel if told they "had" a personality disorder. Imagine the hopelessness and helplessness their therapists feel believing it! Paradigms, by definition, inform everything that we do. A systems model provides not only realism, but also welcome relief and hope for clinicians everywhere. To be sure, the techniques for doing therapy are, like the systems model itself, more complex and integrative than what might be called linear or "main-effects" psychotherapy, which proceeds from the perspective of a single domain (as when cognitive therapy, or psychodynamic therapy, or behavior therapy, are practiced alone), but they are also likely to be more efficacious.

Also relevant and important are the dimensional connotations of the constraint concept. Unlike the binary disorder, which must be either present or absent, on or off, constraints are explicitly stronger or weaker. The idea of constraint pulls for a continuum. When these constraints are more or less invariant across time and pervasive across situations, they may be thought of as personality traits. Some persons, however, exhibit more consistency than others, so that consistency itself may be thought of as traitlike in nature. If individuals see themselves as generally inconsistent, their self-reports do not predict their behaviors (Bem & Allen, 1974). Accordingly, the constraint notion adds the idea that personality may be crystallized to various degrees in various domains across different persons. There are individual differences in the degree to which a particular trait construct can be used to inform the characterization of a particular individual, that is, individual differences in the degree to which a particular trait construct is applicable *at all* where some individuals are concerned. Empirical research supports this notion. When persons judge themselves to be relatively consistent on some trait, its correlation with ratings made by friends and parents is approximately twice as high as on average, .60 versus about .27 (e.g., Kenrick & Stringfield, 1980). Individual differences not only in overall consistency, but also differences in the consistency of particular traits across persons argue strongly for limitations of the nomothetic approach and the importance of addressing individuality in personality assessment.

What does this mean for personality assessment? Because individuals do not fit neatly into taxonomies for ontological rather than epistemological reasons (i.e., because individuality overflows the taxonomy), the taxonomy can only be considered a point of departure in characterizing the individual. Ultimately, this amounts to more than saying than that no one individual represents the incarnation of a given personality prototype. Because representations are inherently simplifications of reality rather than reality itself, any set of representations, no matter how elaborate, is ultimately false where the individual is concerned. Even a well-written biography is an intervening variable. The greater the bandwidth of the descriptive units of a taxonomy, the sooner their heuristic value expires (an important fact in driving the evolving hierarchical structures of modern taxonomies of mental disorders). In fact, the only way assessing clinicians can know that they have done their job well is if the limitations of the taxonomy are discovered. If individuality is to be unearthed, a taxonomy must be driven until it is falsified. The ultimate primacy of the person works toward ends opposite those of classification in the sense of the medical model, and are an important reason why personality disorders are not disorders or diseases, and therefore cannot be diagnosed. Such "diagnostic" terms are best used self-consciously as a linguistic convenience, or not at all. In light of this argument, one must question of the wisdom of merely reporting personality disorders on Axis II as part of a multiaxial diagnosis. A short paragraph communicates the complexity and irreducibility of personality, while a few short labels do not.

Principle 9   Personality Disorders Require Strategically Planned and Combinatorial Modes of Tactical Intervention

The homeostatic characteristics of personality are manifested in personality traits that are enduring across time and pervasive across situations. Unfortunately, the worldview of single-domain interventions (cognitive therapy alone, behavioral therapy alone, psychodynamic therapy alone) is congruent with linear, mechanistic modes of conception, but not with a systemic, reciprocal ones. The methodology for treating personality disorders must not be set at odds with the integrative nature of the construct. The interdependency and synergistic tenacity of personality argues for interventions that are not only multidomained but also coordinated across time in a logical fashion. In the same way that personality is more than the sum of its parts, a logical basis allows "potentiating pairings" and "catalytic sequences" to function as more than the sum of each intervention applied separately or alone. As such, they form the reparative equivalents of "adaptive inflexibility" and "vicious circles," two cardinal characteristics of personality disorders. Because personality disorders are by nature interwoven and multifaceted, interventions that are congruent with the nature of the "disorder" must be interwoven and multifaceted as well.

PERSONALITY: CONTRAST WITH RELATED CONSTRUCTS

What are the boundaries and principal features of the concept of personality, and how shall it be distinguished from other closely related concepts whose meanings overlap and often are used synonymously with it? Gordon Allport (1937) raised the following concerns in his early text, *Personality: A Psychological Interpretation:*

The term "personality" is a perilous one for [the psychologist] to use unless he is aware of its many meanings. Since it is remarkably elastic, its use in any context seldom is challenged. Books and periodicals carry it in their titles for no apparent reason other than its cadence, its general attractiveness, and everlasting interest. Both writer and reader lose their way in its ineffectual vagueness, and matters are made much worse by the depreciation of the word in the hands of journalists, beauty doctors, and peddlers of gold bricks labeled "self improvement."

"Personality" is one of the most abstract words in our language, and like any abstract word suffering from excessive use, its connotative significance is very broad, its denotative significance negligible. Scarcely any word is more versatile. (p. 12)

Allport sought to clarify the origins of the term and to revitalize this frayed concept. A review of his efforts, along with a similar enterprise by Roback (1927), will prove illuminating to students of the history of personality. The task here, however, is more modest, that of seeking to distinguish among seemingly synonymous concepts and thereby focus the reader more sharply on those features that are most relevant to personality pathology.

Two words, character and temperament, have often been employed in the literature interchangeably with personality. Each term has a distinguished history, portions of which are elaborated in Chapter 2. Both should be differentiated from the concept of personality, however. In brief, character has come to mean those personal qualities that represent the individual's adherence to the values and customs of society; temperament, in contrast, has come to signify those biologically based dispositions that underlie the energy level and color the moods of the individual. Let us review their origins briefly.

Personality versus Character

Derived from the Greek word for "engraving," the term character was used initially to signify distinctive features that served as the "mark" of the person. Two distinct meanings of the term evolved over time, producing a confusion that has rendered its utility for descriptive purposes somewhat less than it might otherwise have been. Most similar to the current meaning of personality is the European use of the term character, frequently associated with psychoanalytic writings on characterology. In employing the labels "character structure" and "character disorders," analytic theorists refer to those pervasive features of behavior and thinking that are deeply etched and relatively unchanging throughout life. Although this formulation corresponds closely to the concept of personality described earlier, character is conceived by analytic writers as somewhat more restricted in scope, as conveyed in this quote from Fenichel (1945):

Character, as the habitual mode of bringing into harmony the tasks presented by internal demands and by the external world, is necessarily a function of the constant, organized, and integrating part of the personality which is the ego. (p. 467)

As previously noted, the analytic concept of character limits its range to only the integrating part of the personality (i.e., the ego), thereby excluding functions carried out by those parts of the personality referred to as id and superego. The second

meaning of the term character, however, has proved the more problematic. When we speak of a person's character in contemporary language (e.g., Cloninger, Svrakic, & Przybeck, 1993), we are likely to be applying a *moral standard* in judging behavior. In this sense, character has taken on (to use psychoanalytic terminology) features associated with the superego—how and to what extent the individual has incorporated the precepts and social customs of his or her cultural group.

Personality versus Temperament

In turning to the term temperament, the focus shifts to the third of the tripartite division of personality formulated by the psychoanalysts, that of the id. The word temperament came into the English language in the Middle Ages to represent formulations such as the four humors, and it meant, as it does today, the raw biological materials from which personality emerges. It reflects the constitutional soil, if you will, the biochemistry, endocrinology, and neurological structure that underlie the tendency to respond to stimulation in particular areas. Temperament would be represented in the literature of personality pathology by the individual's prevailing mood, its type, periodicity, and intensity. In the same ways as the term character has come to be limited largely to the moral or social valuation dimensions of personality, so too has the term temperament come to be restricted to the individual's constitutional disposition to activity and emotionality.

Personality: Relationship to Axis I Disorders

Personality disorders are related to Axis I disorders in several ways. One has already been proposed, that which considers personality as the equivalent of the immune system. As noted in Chapter 9, this relates to the predisposition or vulnerability model; additionally, there is the complication model, the spectrum model, and the pathoplasty model, as schematized in Figure 1.1. According to the vulnerability model, personality disorders work to dispose the individual to the development of an Axis I disorder. When coping responses are limited or impoverished, the probability of developing an Axis I disorder such as anxiety or depression is greatly increased. Of course, personality disorder patients often evoke

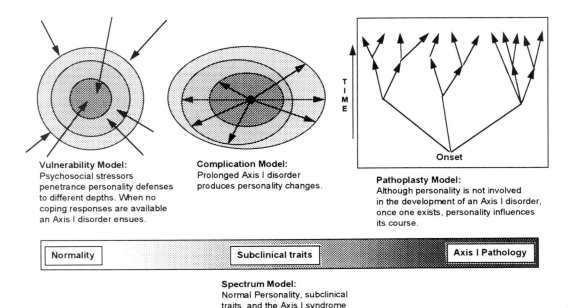

Vulnerability Model:
Psychosocial stressors penetrance personality defenses to different depths. When no coping responses are available an Axis I disorder ensues.

Complication Model:
Prolonged Axis I disorder produces personality changes.

Pathoplasty Model:
Although personality is not involved in the development of an Axis I disorder, once one exists, personality influences its course.

Spectrum Model:
Normal Personality, subclinical traits, and the Axis I syndrome exist on a continuum.

Figure 1.1   Relationships between Axis I and Axis II.

the very stressors under which these disorders will be developed. Interpersonally, for example, they may become involved in vicious circles that perpetuate stressful conditions keeping their "immune systems" chronically weakened, and disposed to the development of more severe clinical conditions.

In the complication model, the causality of the vulnerability model is reversed, so that Axis I conditions, however initiated, create a predisposition to personality change. Individuals experiencing their first schizophrenic episode may on receiving medication realize the significance of the disorder for their life course and become greatly depressed. The knowledge of their condition changes the individual's self-concept and self-efficacy expectations, a form of personality change. Patients who experience a severe and long-lasting depression may internalize pessimism and hopelessness, creating personality change at the trait level.

In contrast to the vulnerability and complication models, which conceptualize Axis I and Axis II conditions as relatively distinct, personality disorders and Axis I conditions may be seen as developing from the same constitutional soil and therefore as existing on a continuum, as in the spectrum model. Here, biologically based subclinical traits so preempt the development of other more adaptive

characteristics that they effectively become the organizing principle for the entire personality. In the appropriate circumstances, a genetic predisposition toward an Axis I condition may be amplified into a full-blown disorder. Kraepelin and Kretschmer were both of this persuasion, as is Akiskal (1981) today.

In contrast to the preceding models, which see Axis I and Axis II conditions as either directly causally related or derived from the same "third variable" of constitution, the pathoplasty model holds that personality influences the course of an Axis I disorder, but does not in itself dispose toward the development of the disorder. Consequently, if the form of particular Axis I conditions is related to personality, it is only because the course of the disorder tends to be canalized by certain personality features. The onset of an Axis I disorder itself is independent of personality style.

All these models are possible and likely to be true for different individuals. In fact, it is not impossible that all are applicable within a single individual to some degree. Assume that a dependent personality begins to experience panic attacks when a close relationship ends, desperately seeks therapy, and goes on to develop a more confident and independent style. Although her personality provided an enduring vulnerability to panic attack, the attacks themselves functioned as the direct impetus for change. For some individuals, then, Axis I and Axis II disorders transact to influence personality development. Compensation for perceived inferiorities may be assumed to be an analogous but less severe phenomenon, in which an individual who possesses some ego-dystonic characteristic becomes highly motivated to turn weakness into strength. Moreover, it is likely that personality disorders not only contribute to vulnerability, but also influence the course of illness. There is no reason to believe that either onset (pathoplasty model) or course (vulnerability model) must be conceptualized as independent of personality style.

CLASSIFICATION ISSUES

Classification has been a particularly contentious issue throughout the history of psychopathology. That tradition endures in the area of personality disorders. Both clinically and scientifically, a taxonomy serves certain functional ends. Clinically, it provides a means of organizing pathological phenomena, the signs and symptoms or manifestations of mental disorder; it formalizes certain clinical commonalities and relieves the clinician of the burden of conceptualizing each patient *sui generis,* as an entity so idiographically unique it has never been seen before, nor ever will again. Stone (1993, p. 37) likens the classification problem to the situation faced by librarians: "A 'perfect' system is impossible." Although the fit between diagnosis and individual is always inexact, if psychopathology is to be practiced at all, there cannot be as many groups or dimensions as there are individuals. Even if the formal categories that constitute a taxonomy are but convenient fictions of dubious reality serving only to draw ostensibly similar presentations together under a single rubric, it is better to have an imperfect grouping system than to be defeated by a multiplicity of observations unassimilable to any larger framework.

Scientifically, an explicit and operationally defined taxonomy provides a potent organizing force for research activities. Although many considerations must be weighed in constructing a taxonomy, the validity of a classification system is bounded by its reliability. Where researchers cannot agree on the meaning of their terms (e.g., how to operationalize the content of the constructs "histrionic" or "projection"), the generalizability of their conclusions is compromised. Ultimately, when reliability dips too low, scientific statements effectively

have no more objectivity than personal opinion. One might as well write an essay entitled "What Borderline Means to Me . . ." In the best of all possible worlds, the objectivity afforded by operationalizing diagnostic criteria serves to open the construct system up to possibilities of revision as theory is informed by empirical findings. Each diagnostic entity may be viewed as a small theory that unites presentation, etiology, and intervention for those so diagnosed. As empirical findings accrue, some taxons prove to be of limited validity or utility and are overthrown entirely; others are elaborated into entities of successively more logical coherency and longitudinal consistency.

How can we best conceptualize and organize the clinical data that comprise personality disorders? Not only are these data complex, they can be approached from a variety of frames of reference. As described previously, they can be conceived and grouped behaviorally as complex response patterns to environmental stimuli. Biophysically, they can be approached and analyzed as sequences of complex neural and chemical activity. Intrapsychically, they can be inferred and categorized as networks of entrenched unconscious processes that bind anxiety and conflict. Quite evidently, the complexity and intricacy of personologic phenomena make it difficult not only to establish clear-cut relationships among phenomena but to find simple ways in which these phenomena can be classified or grouped. Should we artificially narrow our perspective to one data level to obtain at least a coherency of view? Or should we trudge ahead with formulations that bridge domains but threaten to crumble by virtue of their complexity and potentially low internal consistency?

CAN PERSONALITY DISORDERS BE CLASSIFIED?

There is a clear logic to classifying syndromes in medical disorders. Bodily changes wrought by infectious diseases and structural deteriorations repeatedly display themselves in a reasonably uniform pattern of signs and symptoms that make sense in terms of how anatomic structures and physiological processes are altered and dysfunction. Moreover, these biological changes provide a foundation not only for identifying the etiology and pathogenesis of these disorders but also for anticipating their course and prognosis. Logic and fact together enable us to construct a rationale to explain why most medical syndromes express themselves in the signs and symptoms they do, as well as the sequences through which they unfold.

Can the same be said for personologic classifications? Is there a logic, perhaps evidence, for believing that certain forms of clinical expression (e.g., behaviors, cognitions, affects, defense mechanisms) cluster together as do medical syndromes—in other words, that they not only covary frequently, but "make sense" as a coherently organized and reasonably distinctive group of characteristics? Are there theoretical and empirical justifications for believing that the varied features of personality display a configurational unity and expressive consistency over time? Will the careful study of individuals reveal congruency among attributes such as overt behavior, intrapsychic functioning, and biophysical disposition? Is this coherence and stability of psychological functioning a valid phenomenon and not merely imposed on observed data by virtue of clinical expectation or theoretical bias?

There are reasons to believe that the answer to each of the preceding questions is yes. Stated briefly and simply, the observations of covariant patterns of signs and symptoms and traits may be traced to the fact that each person's relatively enduring biophysical disposition gives a consistent coloration to his experience, and the range of experience to which people are exposed throughout their lives is both limited and repetitive (Millon, 1969, 1981). Because of the limiting and shaping character of these biogenic and psychogenic factors, it should not be surprising that individuals develop clusters of prepotent and deeply ingrained behaviors, cognitions, and affects clearly distinguishing them from others of dissimilar backgrounds. Moreover, once a number of the components of a particular clinical pattern are identified, knowledgeable observers are able to trace the presence of other, unobserved, but frequently correlated features composing that pattern.

If we accept the assumption that most people do display a pattern of internally consistent characteristics, we are led next to the question of whether groups of patients evidence commonality in the patterns they display. The notion of clinical categories rests on the assumption that there exist a limited number of such shared covariances; for example, regular groups of diagnostic signs and symptoms that can confidently be used to distinguish certain classes of patients (the fact that patients can profitably be classified into categories does not negate the fact that patients so classified

display considerable differences as well—differences we routinely observe with medical diseases).

Another question that must be addressed about the nature of personological classification concerns the covariation of clinical attributes. Why does possession of characteristic A increase the probability, appreciably beyond chance, of also possessing characteristics B, C, and so on? Less abstractly, why do particular behaviors, attitudes, mechanisms, and so on covary in repetitive and recognizable ways, instead of exhibiting themselves in a more or less haphazard fashion? And even more concretely, why should, say, behavioral defensiveness, interpersonal provocativeness, cognitive suspicion, affective irascibility, and excessive use of the projection mechanism co-occur in the same individual, instead of being uncorrelated and randomly distributed among different individuals?

First, temperament and early experience simultaneously affect the development and nature of several emerging psychological structures and functions; a wide range of behaviors, attitudes, affects, and mechanisms can be traced to the same origins, leading thereby to their frequently observed covariance. Second, once an individual possesses these initial characteristics, they set in motion a series of derivative life experiences that shape the acquisition of new psychological attributes causally related to the characteristics that preceded them in the sequential chain. Common origins and successive linkages increase the probability that certain psychological characteristics will frequently be found to pair with specific others, resulting thereby in repetitively observed symptom or trait clusters.

LATENT VERSUS MANIFEST TAXONOMY: THE NATURE-NUMBER ISSUE

At a minimum, persons within a taxon should be more alike clinically than those selected across taxons. Unfortunately, although similarity-dissimilarity is the organizing principle on which taxonomies are constructed, similarity itself is a fuzzy notion. In what way are patients who receive the same diagnosis alike? At the coarsest level, two kinds of similarity—manifest and latent—may be distinguished. Such a distinction is necessary for two reasons. First, surface similarities (and all intervening variables, including personality tests, qualify as "surface" data) often belie latent diversity. All seas are more or less "flat" on top, whereas at bottom they may have vastly different topographies. Patients whose pathologies are similar at a manifest level present in similar ways. In an exclusively empirical nosology, these patients would be classified together on the basis of similarities in their surface characteristics. For example, they may be classified according to a cluster analysis of their personality profiles. In contrast, the latent level is concerned with genotypic similarity, with the way things are presumed to actually exist according to theoretical or etiologic inferences. Patients are classified together regardless of (what appears to be) diversity of presentation.

How do these kinds of similarity interact to bear on the validity of a taxonomy of personality disorders? Figure 1.2 presents diagnostic matches and mismatches concerning the two kinds of similarity. As can be seen, this figure resembles others that present the logic of diagnostic efficiency statistics—true positives, false negatives, and so on (e.g., Baldessarini, Finklestein, & Arieti, 1983). Whereas diagnostic efficiency tables compare the apparent or obtained diagnosis with some so-called criterion standard, illustrating the diagnostic dilemma associated with imperfect predictors in the ignorance of the true diagnostic disposition, Figure 1.2 represents the "nosological dilemma." Here, multiple taxons must be established for multiple subjects, the "true" taxonic membership of each being unknown. Starting in the first quadrant, two presentations that appear similar, may indeed be similar. In this case, etiologically similar pathways have produced manifestly similar results. Second, two presentations that appear similar, may in fact require different diagnoses. Because of a "convergent causality," diverse etiologic pathways have produced manifestly similar results that are difficult to tease apart. Third, two presentations that appear different, many in fact be different. Diverse outcomes

legitimately depict distinctive etiologies. Fourth, two presentations that appear different, may in fact be similar. Here, the transaction of the same pathology with individual differences has produced two diverse presentations.

The scenario depicted in Figure 1.2 is hypothetical; we have been speaking as if the degree of similarity at both manifest and latent levels were known, otherwise no comparison could be made. In fact, neither is ever known with certainty. At a manifest level, the distinction between intervening variables and hypothetical constructs ensures that there are a variety of psychometric issues at work that render any measurement of psychological variables fuzzy and fraught with error. Regarding the latent level, the underlying patterning of mechanisms and processes—true taxonicity—is by definition inferred rather than observed. This is the Catch-22 of taxonomic development. Given the inherently imprecise measurement of a set of indicators whose completeness, and perhaps even relevance, to the latent state of affairs is unknown, how can the "true" variables and their patterning be systematically inferred? How are ideas about the latent state of affairs to be subjected to a strong risk of falsification comparable to that in the more developed sciences such as chemistry and physics? Personologic theory provides one means of guiding these explorations. Other answers to this question are outside the scope of this text. Interested readers are directed to numerous papers by Meehl (e.g., 1978, 1986, 1992) for interesting and persuasive answers.

As seen in Figure 1.2, an exclusively empirical approach to the personality disorders is beset with difficulties. In quadrant four, patients who have essentially the same condition, albeit one whose appearance is mediated by a variety of factors, will be categorized separately and treated differently. Moreover, because the state of the art for different sets of patients is likely to be in different stages of progression, some patients will receive highly specific and effective interventions, whereas others will be treated symptomatically. In quadrant two, the combination of latent heterogeneity-manifest similarity means that one prototype will be established due to indicator covariance where multiple taxons are in fact required. The DSM category of schizophrenia is likely an example of one of these categories. No method of subtyping this disorder has proven clinically satisfying or valid. In a review of research in the field, R.W. Heinrichs (1993, p. 230) noted, "The likelihood that researchers are studying different illnesses without being able to

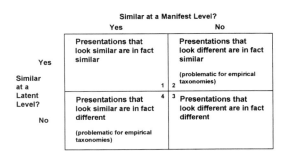

Figure 1.2 Taxonomy and the latent-manifest distinction.

specify these differences must be recognized as the superordinate problem. It is not a subproblem that can be ignored. It is the major obstacle to scientific progress." Among the personality disorders, historically the borderline has also been notoriously heterogenous. The double-barreled "bet" of pure empiricism—that things which look alike always are alike, and that things which look different always are different—cannot easily be sustained.

To support inferences that get beneath surface similarities, the major divisions of a classification system cannot merely be specified arbitrarily, but instead should be set out according to some logical undergirding principle or principles. In ancient biological taxonomies, such as that of Linnaeus, animals that looked alike were classified together. Modern empirical taxonomic methods (e.g., Sneath & Sokal, 1963) essentially represent a continuation of pre-Darwinian methods, extreme rigorization in the organization of surface similarities. These authors, identified with the phrase "numerical taxonomy," advocate entering all attributes into the taxonomic analysis, regardless of theoretical ideas that might narrow the scope of available indicators to more relevant and rational choices. To believe in the validity of this procedure, one must be prepared to believe that reality can be revealed by numerical methods alone. Although indiscriminate multivariate data crunching may occasionally yield some small insight, modern philosophers of science recognize that surface characteristics alone form an insufficient, if not false, basis for a taxonomy. Modern biological classifications, for example, have as their foundation the principles of evolution and speciation. When logically based, a taxonomy takes on a generative character that Hempel (1961) termed "systematic import." By appealing to nature's deeper order, the taxonomy suggests hypotheses that can be used in its specification and further elaboration.

APPROACHES TO CLASSIFICATION OF PERSONALITY DISORDERS

Two broad polarities influence the ultimate structure and evolution of a taxonomy of personality disorders. The first is concerned with conceptual openness versus conceptual specificity. The second is concerned with whether the ultimate aim is to achieve logical coherence and understanding within a single taxon, or whether it is to erect an entire taxonomic system *ex nihilo*.

Theoretical versus Empirical Approaches: Issue of Conceptual Openness versus Conceptual Specificity

How should the nature of personologic phenomena be investigated? Should we remain close to the assumptions of common sense, carefully refining our measures until we can advance with sure-footed precision? Or should we seek conceptual innovations that will partition the personologic realm in ways that are believed to be more theoretically and clinically auspicious?

The first option requires that we anchor personological phenomena directly in the empirical world of observables. In the extreme, each attribute would be tied to only one observable indicator as its operational definition (Bridgman, 1927). The virtue of operational definitions lies in their precision; their vice lies in their scope. Ultimate empirical precision can only be achieved if each defining feature of a taxon is anchored to a single observable in the real world; that is, a different datum for every difference observed between personality syndromes. This goal is simply not feasible, nor desirable: The subject domain of personology is inherently more weakly organized than that of the so-called hard sciences. As one moves from physics and chemistry into biological and psychological arenas, unidirectional causal pathways give way to feedback and feedforward processes, which in turn give rise to emergent levels of description that are more inferential than the physical substrates underlying them. Intrapsychic formulations, for example, are inferential by nature. Owing to their abstract and hypothetical character, their tendency to float above a data plane to which they can only in part be anchored, and the fact that they are naturally fuzzy at the edges (Meehl, 1978), these operationally indeterminate intervening variables are referred to as open concepts (Pap, 1953). The polar distinction between operational definitions and open concepts forms a epistemological duality best represented by those who prefer to employ data derived from empirical-practical contexts, at one end, versus those who prefer to draw their ideas from more causal-theoretical sources, at the other (Millon, 1987a).

The advantage of operationism lies in its promise to reduce diagnostic confusion by tethering personality syndromes and the attributes of which they are composed tightly to real world referents, thereby rendering them clinically unambiguous. Here, clinical diagnosis is directly translated into diagnostic procedures so rigorously defined that they could conceivably be applied by a clerk instead of a clinician. This direct one-to-one mapping of attributes to measurement procedures amounts to a kind of psychometric repression that ignores the biases consequent to any one procedure or method and the incumbent necessity of gathering information across multiple instruments and data sources (Campbell & Fiske, 1959). Precision is exalted at the expense of validity.

In contrast, open concepts acknowledge the desirability of multiple measurement procedures and encourage their user to move freely in more abstract and inferential realms. Each construct may be embedded in a theoretical matrix of propositions from which its meaning is contextually derived through a ramified nomological network of relations with other open concepts, with only indirect and incomplete reference to explicit observables. Some concepts are more open than others. Some are so circuitous in their references that they become tautological. Others are so inferential in character that they are completely decoupled from observables, resulting in untestable propositions that may be used to explain almost anything. Clarity gets muddled in statements like "in the borderline the mechanisms of the ego disintegrate when libidinous energies overwhelm superego introjections." In such formulations, the highly inferential character of the theory overwhelms the testability of its empirical linkages, resulting in a loss of precision so profound that there is a complete inability to sustain the operational definitions that allow theory to be tested and subjected to the dangers of falsification.

Monotaxonomic Approaches versus Polytaxonic Approaches

In what is here called the "monotaxonic approach," a smaller piece of the larger pie becomes the object of taxonomic interest. As its name suggests, this approach is concerned only with a single entity of content, whatever its taxonic representation, be it category, dimension, prototype, or circumplical segment. Whatever the unit of analysis, its core feature is that it does not attempt to bring order to the entire personality milieu in one fell swoop through a some set of undergirding principles or totalistic methodology, but rather limits itself to some more circumscribed area. Opposite this is the "polytaxonic approach," which seeks to impose some structural edifice on the entire personologic domain, effectively creating an entire taxonomic schema

out of a vacuum. Whether derived deductively from theory or from multivariate statistical methods, the emphasis here is on the explication of so-called "latent entities," fundamental units or principles that are sufficient to account for observed variation in the subject domain. Whatever the unit of analysis, the core feature of the polytaxonic approach is its intention to parse the entire personologic domain at once, reducing a large number of variables or observations to a smaller number of theoretical principles or multivariate dimensions.

Crossing these two polarities—the first concerning a disposition to take perspective on observations in order to generate a coherent theoretical account versus a disposition to remain close to preexisting constructs and refine already extant observations, the second concerning a disposition to parse a portion of the personologic totality versus a disposition to be concerned with the totality itself—leads to a four-category metataxonomy of approaches to the classification of personality disorders (see Figure 1.3). The derived categories are best viewed as prototypes. Just as there is a natural heterogeneity among clinical features of personality, such that not all patients exhibit identical features, there is also a heterogeneity among approaches to the personologic domain. Many, but not all, approaches or methodologies will easily be placed within this framework.

The Monotaxonic Empirical Approach

Prototypally, this approach tends to focus on a single diagnostic category. As with all empirical approaches to taxonomy, the direction of argument is prototypally from already existing intervening variables to reality. Accordingly, knowledge is gained through exploring the structure of the measures or instruments that already exist, not through the generation of new concepts by some process of theoretical refinement. Typically, single or multiple measures are decomposed psychometrically

	All of Personality	Single Content Area
Theory (Openness)	Explanatory Polytaxonic	Explanatory Monotaxonic
Descriptive (Specificity)	Descriptive Polytaxonic	Descriptive Monotaxonic

Figure 1.3 Approaches to taxonomy for the personality disorders.

into their constituent elements, often through factor analysis or inspection of a cluster analytic dendrogram, a graphical representation of the extent of interrelationship among empirically derived clusters of items or scales.

Like all empirical methods, the validity of this approach demands a perfect correspondence between intervening variables and constructs, that is between manifest and latent structures. Accordingly, it is at its weakest when it employs only a single scale or procedure: Method biases and content deficiencies intrinsic to any particular scale tend to distort the necessary correspondence and compromise the validity of the argument that results are definitive of "what actually exists." Thus, most studies of this kind employ multiple measures, as a means of extending the aggregation principle to a scale level: Just as the randomly distributed errors of many single items cancel each other out when summated and thereby lead only to an accumulation of signal in a large representative sample of items, biases intrinsic to any one scale presumably fail to accumulate when many scales are examined at once. Assuming a representative sample of intervening variables with all errors randomly distributed, the extracted factors or components are assumed to represent facets of the construct as it in fact exists in reality. The direction of the argument is from intervening variable to the nature of the personality construct of interest. When this argument cannot be sustained, the entire edifice crumbles.

The inherently decompositional methodology of this "top-down empiricism" sometimes gets this approach associated with a reductionism that multiplies the number of essential personologic features without bound. Consider the history of trait psychology. If there were only a small number of traits, it would be easy to believe that these were necessary and sufficient to describe the domain of personality. As the number of traits grows, however, the question concerning exactly which traits are fundamental begins to loom larger. Ultimately, as the growing number of traits exceeds the capacity of human cognition to grasp their interactions and relationships, the reality of any one individual trait comes into question. A more parsimonious and structurally incisive way of representing the universe of descriptors becomes sorely needed. Apparently, our need to believe in the ultimate truth of a classification system can sustain shorter lists of categories or dimensions better than longer lists. With a shorter list, there is the feeling that the boundaries of a domain are firm. As the length

of the list increases, the model becomes increasingly unwieldy.

The Polytaxonic Empirical Approach

Methodologically, like its previously discussed cousin, the descriptive polytaxonic empirical approach is driven by the mathematical induction or distillation of intervening variables. Taxonomically, however, it is concerned with deriving an entire set of categories or dimensions for the personality domain. As with all empirical approaches to taxonomy, the polytaxonic approach depends crucially on an isomorphism between reality and instrumentation. What is learned is learned by gathering many diverse measures and subjecting these to some multivariate analysis that reveals their dimensions or clusters. Typically, no in-depth process of theoretical reflection and refinement is engaged beyond deciding what constitutes the limits of the domain to be sampled. Whereas the monotaxonic approach may be thought of as working from the top down, moving in the direction of greater specificity as broader units are distilled into smaller ones, this approach works from the bottom up, moving in the direction of greater commonality, combining more narrow measures into ones of greater and greater bandwidth.

The five-factor model is perhaps the epitome of the descriptive polytaxonic empirical approach. The emphasis on already extant intervening variables is evidenced in the lexical hypothesis, which assumes that "most of the socially relevant and interpersonally salient personality characteristics have become encoded in the natural language" (John, 1990, p. 67). More esoteric or inferential dimensions of personality not accessible to nonpsychologists, such as mechanisms of defense or styles of information processing, are not included in the analysis (even though a representative sampling of the content domain of personality would seem to demand they be). The factor analytic method lends the empiricist a way of dealing with the intercorrelations, so confusing when a large matrix must be understood, through the method of factor rotation, the explicit purpose of which is to render the factors more interpretable. Although rotations that yield intercorrelated factors are possible, an orthogonal rotation is by far the most popular, suppressing ambiguous intercorrelations out of existence, thus creating a model of laudable scope, if somewhat illusory precision. Whereas the "discreteness" of categorical models is inherent in the concept of a category itself, here discreteness is cloaked as the angle between dimensions, and dimensions that are maximally discrete or orthogonal are preferred. Because this kind of discreteness is methodologically imposed, it must be considered as repugnant as that associated with categories, a fact played down by those who believe personality consists exclusively of dimensions that can be revealed by factor analytic methods.

Because of its ability to rotate factors and produce completely independent dimensions, factor analysis offers a means of ordering a chaotic universe consisting of thousands of traits into a more manageable hierarchy. Recall that the top-down or monotaxonic approach tends to multiply the number of units of analysis without bound. Factor analysis restores a shorter list (George Miller's 7 plus or minus 2) more amenable to the limits of human cognition. However, the question of completeness still dogs this approach, first, in terms of how many factors should be extracted from the data, and second, in terms of the boundaries of the content domain to which the methodology should be applied. Obviously, the validity of the five-factor model rests on the validity of the lexical hypothesis. To examine this hypothesis in relation to the lexical hypothesis, we might ask whether nonpsychologists are equally sensitive to characteristics across domains, regardless of the level of inference at which each domain exists, for example, defense mechanisms (highly inferential) versus interpersonal traits (relatively less inferential). There is no reason to believe that those domain attributes to which common persons are not sensitive have become encoded in the language. Although factor analysis has currently been applied only within particular domains, an alternative and more persuasive approach would be to sample descriptors from across a variety of domains and subject these—represented in approximately equal numbers to indicate that no domain is more prototypally important causally than any other (Principle 3, Table 1.1)—to the methodology.

The Monotaxonic Theoretical Orientation

Two kinds of theory must be distinguished. Again, the distinction is one concerning the scope of inquiry, whether a single or a few diagnostic categories are addressed, here referred to as a monotaxonic orientation, or whether the entire domain of personality pathology is parsed in its entirety, here referred to as a polytaxonic orientation. The "within-category" theoretical orientation is probably what comes to mind when most people think about theory or theory testing. Because of its

limited scope, it is primarily concerned with the essential elements that eventuate in and sustain a particular kind of personality pattern; it is particularly impressive in its longitudinal incarnation, wherein models of personality pathology may be explicated through diagrams and flowcharts that detail the developmental history of a disorder, complete with the inputs of various factors which predispose or immunize against the disorder along the way. Alternately, it may develop as a stage model, with pathology representing the regression to earlier stages of development, as in the oral character, the anal character, and so on.

Although advocates of the monotaxonic theoretical explanatory approach assert gains in conceptual precision, these are only achieved at the expense of scope. Monotaxonic theories for bridging clinical domains are far fewer, perhaps because any attempt to do so seeks the assimilation of elements that to some extent intrinsically resist integration—otherwise they could not be thought of as existing as domains at all. An integrative model, for example, holds that personality styles are expressed across multiple domains. Each domain is involved in creating the full picture of the disorder; no domain is necessarily more causally potent in creating pathology than any other. Because theorists tend to be of a particular persuasion or school, however, they tend to ignore alternative approaches or to reduce other content domains to that of their own expertise. Thus the tendency to parse particular personality patterns in terms of a single area clinical domain, whether behavioral, phenomenological, intrapsychic, or biophysical. The classical view of narcissism, for example, contends that it is the result of developmental arrests or injuries, with consequent reactivations, compensations, or regressions to earlier periods of psychic trauma. An important elaborator of the narcissism construct is Kohut (1971). He believed that in the narcissistic personality, narcissism does not fade away by becoming transformed into object-libido, as contended by classical theorists, but instead unfolds into its own set of mature narcissistic processes and structures. Pathology occurs as a consequence of failures to integrate one of the two major spheres of self-maturation, the "grandiose self" and the "idealized parent imago." If disillusioned, rejected, or forced to experience cold and unempathic care at the earliest stages of self-development, serious pathology, including psychotic and borderline states, will result. Trauma or disappointment at a later phase will have somewhat different repercussions depending on whether the difficulty centered on the development of the grandiose self or on the parental imago.

Other internally consistent developmental accounts of narcissism could be given from behavioral or cognitive perspectives. Because these formulations are so "domain-bound," it is difficult to see how such developmental models could ever give rise to the kind of taxonomies of scope needed for the DSMs. Thus, although this kind of theoretical approach may illuminate the developmental origins of personality pathology from a particular perspective, it works best when it is not held to account for why certain patterns of personality disorder exist in the first place—it cannot answer the question, "Why these diagnostic categories rather than others?" Instead, it must be given the pathology to begin with, for it cannot generate categories of personality pathology on its own.

The Polytaxonic Theoretical Orientation

The monotaxonic theoretical orientation seeks to explain the origins of personality pathology but must be given its raw material, the disorder of interest, first, and work backward from there. Can a complete science of personology rest on such a foundation? Is it enough merely to accept some authoritative dispensation that a particular disorder exists, without wondering why this particular constellation of disorders exists at all? Whereas the periodic table is the unique province of chemistry, the problematic behaviors that are to be carved up into diagnostic categories are implicitly given to psychopathologists by parties whose standards are extrinsic to psychopathology as a science. In contrast, the polytaxonic theorist asks that the units of personality pathology account for themselves, by persistently asking, "Why these categories rather than others?"

Philosophers of science agree that the system of kinds undergirding any domain of inquiry must itself be answerable to the question forming the very point of departure for the scientific enterprise: Why does nature take this particular form rather than some other? Such questions explicitly seek answers beyond the manifest diversity of what is immediately observable. According to this perspective, one cannot merely accept any list of kinds or dimensions as given, even if arrived at by committee consensus. Instead, a taxonomic scheme must be justified, and to be justified scientifically, it must be justified theoretically, through a search for underlying principles that can be logically coordinated to yield the observed pathologies.

Is such a classification possible? The stakes are nothing less than whether personology is to become an autonomous field possessing its own intrinsic taxonomy, or remain a pseudoscience servicing the larger society, with diagnostic entities established according to what extrinsic cultural conventions deem problematic. Perhaps we live in a more enlightened age, but was it not so long ago that Sullivan proposed the "homosexual personality"? Or that the "masochistic personality" came under fire as being prejudicial against women? If particular characteristics or attributes are not to be spuriously elevated to a taxonic level, some set of logical principles will be required to assist in making this distinction. Although the DSM was deliberately and appropriately formulated to be atheoretical (but see Faust & Miner, 1986) in order not to alienate special interest groups among psychological consumers, ultimately we will require some way of culling the wheat from the chaff that depends on the generativity of scientific theory rather than decision by committee.

The explanatory polythetic or deductive approach generates a true taxonomy to replace the primitive aggregation of taxons that preceded it, thus forming a true diagnostic schema. This generative power is what Hempel (1965) meant by the "systematic import" of a scientific classification. According to Meehl (1978), theoretical systems comprise related assertions, shared terms, and coordinated propositions that provide fertile grounds for deducing and deriving new empirical and clinical observations. What is elaborated and refined in theory is understanding, an ability to see relations more clearly, to conceptualize categories more accurately, and to create greater overall coherence in a subject; that is, to integrate its elements in a more logical, consistent, and intelligible fashion. Pretheoretic taxonomic boundaries that were set according to clinical intuition and empirical research can now be affirmed or refined by critically examining the disorders in relation to fundamental undergirding principles or polarities. Entirely new diagnostic categories may be generated, as was the case with the Avoidant personality, derived from Millon's theoretical system (1969). The polarities of this schema lent the model a holistic, cohesive structure that facilitated the comparison and contrast of groups along basic axes of content, not only sharpening the meanings of the taxonomic constructs so derived, but also protecting them from the construct drift incumbent to single-domain formulations and the vicissitudes of diagnostic faddishness.

CATEGORIES, DIMENSIONS, AND PROTOTYPES

In addition to questions concerning the content of personality and how a taxonomy may be established and investigated are questions concerning the basic units in which personality data should be organized. What units of analysis are best for the assessment of personalities functioning in the clinical range? Though a number of formulations are possible, including the radex and class-quantitative approaches (Degerman, 1972), the answer to this question has traditionally turned on whether one believes that the individual should be embedded in the diagnostic system, or whether the diagnostic system should be embedded in the individual—the perennial controversy between categories and dimensions. Both have advantages and disadvantages.

CATEGORICAL MODELS

Among the advantages of categorical typologies is their ease of use by clinicians who must make relatively rapid diagnoses with large numbers of patients whom they see briefly. Although clinical attention in these cases is drawn to only the most salient features of the patient, a broad range of traits that have not been directly observed is often strongly suggested. In fact, the capacity to suggest characteristics beyond those immediately manifest adds special value to an established system of types. For example, let us assume that an individual is suspected of being histrionic following the observation of seductive and dramatic behaviors, and labile and shallow emotions. After observing behaviors associated with only these two traits, what clinician would not want to inquire whether the person is stimulus seeking, needful of attention, interpersonally capricious, emotionally labile, and so on? In effect, assignment to a particular type or category often proves useful by alerting the clinician to a range of unobserved but frequently correlated behaviors. The ability of categories to extend the scope of associated characteristics contrasts with the tendency of dimensional schemas to fractionate the intrinsic unity of personality into separate and uncoordinated traits. As such, typologies restore and recompose the unity of personality by integrating seemingly diverse elements into a single syndrome. Moreover, the availability of well-established syndromes provides a standard reference for clinicians who would otherwise be faced with repeated analyses and de novo personality constructions that could not be generalized from one patient to the next.

Widiger and Sanderson (1994), ardent proponents of dimensional classification, noted a number of disadvantages of the categorical model. Categories assume the existence of discrete boundaries both between separate personality styles and between normality and abnormality, a feature felicitous to the medical model, but not so for personality functioning, which exists on a continuum. Consequently, diagnostic thresholds, far from being coordinated with the definition of personality disorder in a generic sense, are essentially arbitrary, with the result that small changes in diagnostic criteria may radically influence prevalence estimates. Moreover, by being oriented to the presence or absence of a disorder, even groups rigorously diagnosed by structured interviews may be biased by a substantial subsample that possesses subclinical traits for another disorder. To state the problem more generally, assume a researcher is interested in an Axis I condition: If the Axis I disorder and an Axis II personality diagnosis are strongly comorbid, is it better for research purposes to include only those with the Axis I condition to obtain a pure representation of this disorder, or to include individuals also diagnosed with the Axis II condition on the grounds that this sample is in fact more representative?

DIMENSIONAL MODELS

Dimensional models possess a number of virtues. Most important is that they combine several clinical features or personality traits into a single profile, which can be grasped and interpreted by experienced clinicians almost *in toto.* Because of their comprehensiveness, little information of potential significance is lost; nor is any single trait given special attention, as when only one distinctive characteristic is brought to the foreground in a typology. Further, a trait profile permits the assessment of unusual or atypical cases; in typologies, odd, infrequent, or mixed conditions are often excluded because they do not fit the prescribed categories. Given the diversity and idiosyncratic character of many clinical personalities, a dimensional system encourages the representation of individuality, rather than forcing patients into categories for which they are ill suited. A final advantage of a dimensional format is that the strength of traits is gauged quantitatively—each characteristic extends into the normal range; as a consequence, normality and abnormality are merely arranged as points on a continuum rather than as distinct and separable phenomena. In contrast to categories, dimensional schemas recognize the tenuous nature of the normal-abnormal distinction. Indeed, continuity is the cardinal feature of dimensional systems as they are usually articulated.

The arguments of those who favor the adoption of dimensional models center mainly around one theme—that the categorical model, because it entails discrete boundaries between the various disorders and between normality and abnormality, is simply inappropriate for the personality disorders; however, the kind of discreteness that dimensional systems often bring to personality assessment—discreteness between dimensions—tends to be largely overshadowed by the continuity characteristic of each dimension itself. Many dimensional systems, for example, have been created methodologically through factor analytic techniques explicitly designed to extract independent or orthogonal factors (e.g., the five-factor model). In other words, an individual's standing on any one dimension is in no way related to his or her standing on any other dimension.

One can ask, however, as dimensional proponents have of the categorical model, does the world really work this way? The answer to this question is to be found in the systems concept of personality. The cardinal feature of systems is their functional-structural interdependence. What exists in one domain of the system constrains what can comfortably coexist elsewhere. A child born with a reactive, choleric temperament, for example, might develop any number of future personality characteristics but would probably not grow up to become a sanguine diplomat, delicately weighing this and that to the satisfaction of all sides with great premeditation. Thus, whereas a system is a system precisely because of interrelationship between essential variables, a taxonomy of orthogonal dimensions is orthogonal precisely because it presumes independence among essential variables, an absence of interrelationships. Although the world does not exist in categories, neither can it be supposed to exist in "rows and columns" (Loevinger, 1994).

Other complications and limitations have been noted in the literature, and these should be recorded also. Some traits possess inherently positive connotations, and so are anchored in normality; other traits possess inherently negative connotations, and so are anchored exclusively in the undesirable or clinical realm. An example here would be emotional stability versus emotional vulnerability. Other trait dimensions may be conceived that are psychologically curvilinear, such that both extremes have negative implications; an example of this would be an activity dimension such as listlessness versus restlessness.

Additionally, although trait dimensions have a number of desirable properties, there is little agreement among their proponents concerning either the nature or number of traits necessary to represent personality adequately. For example, Menninger (1963) contends that a single dimension will suffice; Eysenck (1960) asserts that 3 are needed, whereas Cattell (1965) claims to have identified as many as 33 and believes there to be many more. Theorists may, in fact, "invent" dimensions in accord with their expectations rather than "discovering" them as if they were intrinsic to nature, merely awaiting scientific detection. Apparently, the number of traits required to assess personality is not determined by the ability of our research to disclose some inherent truth but rather by our predilections for conceiving and organizing our observations. Describing personality with more than a few such trait dimensions produces schemas so complex and intricate that they require geometric or algebraic representation. Although there is nothing intrinsically wrong with such quantitative formats, they pose considerable difficulty both in comprehension and in communication among professionals. Most mental health workers are hesitant about working with complex multivariate statistics, and the consequent feeling that one is lost in one's own professional discipline is not likely to make such schemas attractive, no less practical for everyday use.

Apart from matters of convenience and comfort, dimensional profiles are often grouped into categories before the information they contain can be communicated. Indeed, it is not clear that dimensional models can free themselves from ultimately embracing the categorylike entities their proponents so much eschew. Paradoxically, as more and more external variables are correlated with a particular profile, the profile itself begins to take on aspects of an integrative hypothesis, effectively acquiring a constructlike nature. Thus, clinicians and researchers begin to focus, for example, on 4-9 and 1-2 profiles, and these *groups* become an area of interest and investigation. The tendency to simplify dimensional profiles suggests that even if a dimensional format were universally adopted, researchers might well end up studying populations of profiles rather than persons.

PROTOTYPAL MODELS

Prototypes are a relatively recent diagnostic innovation, first implicitly adopted in the DSM-III. The prototype is neither category nor dimension, but a synthesis of both. For several reasons, prototypal models may become the preferred schema for representing personality disorders and clinical syndromes. First, most contemporary typologies neither imply, nor were constructed, as all-or-none categories. Most advocates of the dimensional approach to clinical practice overlook the fact that the word "category" has been used very loosely in the DSM. Second, the prototype construct recognizes the explicit heterogeneity of personality-disordered patients. Pure prototypal cases are extremely rare; most patients meet criteria for multiple disorders and may have subclinical features of other personality styles as well. Indeed, the problems imputed to categorical models largely evaporate if categories are regarded as prototypes. Prototypal constructs do not assume discrete boundaries (Cantor & Genero, 1986) and have the advantage that they are already implicit in the diagnostic system. Horowitz, Post, French, Wallis, and Siegelman (1981) describe the construct succinctly:

A prototype consists of the most common features or properties of members of a category and thus describes a theoretical ideal or standard against which real people can be evaluated. All of the prototype's properties are assumed to characterize at least some members of the category, but no one property is necessary or sufficient for membership in the category. Therefore, it is possible that no actual person would match the theoretical prototype perfectly. Instead different people would approximate it to different degrees. The more closely a person approximates the ideal, the more closely the person typifies the concept. (p. 575)

Explicit in this description is the use of diagnostic criteria as a heuristic method, not as a reified model. The surplus causal meaning associated with latent taxons need not be postulated. Such an approach would seem thoroughly consonant with the atheoretical orientation of the DSM, which, if taken to its logical conclusion, should be atheoretical not only with regard to the various schools of psychopathology but *structurally* as well. Because certain literatures, methodologies, and structural models appear to cohere tenaciously—for example, empiricism, the lexical approach, factor analysis, and dimensional models—this point cannot be underestimated.

How might prototypes actually be used in clinical contexts? As Horowitz et al. (1981) noted, the resemblance of an individual to the prototype is necessarily a qualitative as well as a quantitative affair. Although categories and dimensions inevitably sacrifice one or the other kind of information, the prototype conserves both. By its heuristic nature, the prototype asks both how and how much the individual resembles the prototype. Because patients will likely resemble more than one of these theoretical ideals, the clinician is encouraged to use prototypes constructively in order to look beyond the one-disorder, one-cause, one-therapy perspective implicit in the current diagnostic system (i.e., to get the flavor of the patient's pathology in its dynamic totality and to integrate any interventions with this conception). To be used successfully, however, the prototype requires (a) a willingness on the part of the professional to move flexibly between categorical and dimensional paradigms as utility requires, regarding each as what it essentially is—a clinical point of departure and nothing more; and (b) valid criteria sets.

This text extends the concept and use of prototypes in two new directions, one essentially *theoretical,* the other *clinical.*

1. We have taken the liberty of employing the concept of prototype as representing a *theoretically derived construct,* whose essential qualities are posited on the basis of concepts or dimensions that have been articulated as the central elements of a theoretical schema. For example, Freud and his disciples have frequently used the concepts of *ego, superego,* and *id* to serve as the fundamental elements to characterize various personality patterns. According to their theoretical model, antisocial personalities are seen as individuals whose superego is deficient and whose id is intense; similarly, compulsive personalities are conceptualized as persons with a dominant superego and a constrained id. In a similar prototypal derivation from the five-factor model, Costa and Widiger (1993) speak of the passive-aggressive (negativistic) personality as stemming from low *agreeableness,* low *conscientiousness,* high *neuroticism,* and high *extroversion.* In Cloninger's (1987) tridimensional model, the antisocial personality prototype is seen to derive from high *novelty seeking,* low *harm avoidance,* and low *reward dependence.* In Millon's (1990) formulations, bipolarities related to an evolutionary model are employed to derive personality prototypes. For example, the depressive personality is conceived as stemming from high *life-preservation* (pain avoidance), high *ecologic-accommodation* (passivity), and low *individuation* (deficient self-focus). In line with the preceding, we believe that the *prototype* concept should be considered to be a theoretically derived "ideal" type (Cantor & Genero, 1986; Rosch, 1978; Schwartz, Wiggins, & Norko, 1989).

2. There is a logic to the syndromal concept in medical disorders. Bodily images wrought by infectious diseases and structural deteriorations repeatedly display themselves in reasonably uniform patterns of signs and symptoms that make sense in terms of how anatomic structures and physiological processes are altered and dysfunctional. The key word noted in the preceding sentence, for our purposes, is "reasonably uniform." Thus, not all persons who have coronary artery disease (CAD) have the same blockages in their arteries; some have them in the left descending main, some in the circumflex, and so on. However, all have CAD. Similarly, not all persons with metastatic carcinoma are identical in their pathology; the disease of some is relatively localized, others are widespread, some are slow growing, others faster, yet all importantly evidence the same basic disease process.

Can the same be said for personality prototypes? Is there a logic for believing that certain behaviors, cognitions, and moods cluster together as do medical syndromes? Do they not only co-vary frequently, but make sense as a coherently organized and reasonably distinctive group of clinical characteristics evidencing configurational unity and expressive consistency? And last, are there not *variations* in these reasonably uniform patterns of clinical characteristics? It is our contention that the answer to each of the preceding questions is yes.

Although each personality *prototype* displays a cluster of cohesive characteristics, it is also clear that these personalities vary in the manifestation of their clinical features. We have termed these variations *prototypal variants.* Phrased differently, the fact that patients can profitably be classified into personality prototypes does not negate the fact that patients, so categorized, display considerable clinical differences as well, a fact observed quite routinely, as noted previously, with medical diseases.

Each theoretically generated prototype can serve usefully as a conceptually relevant anchoring point, a logically rational and cohesive framework of descriptors around which *clinically realistic variants* take form. Few pure or ideal prototypes are seen in reality. However, numerous variants are encountered in clinical work that give evidence of the core features of each prototype. These variants or subtypes differ to some degree and in certain of their particulars (e.g., not all tables are rectangular or have four legs, though the construct "table" is well understood as distinct from a chair or a lamp). In a like manner, the prototype "histrionic personality" comprises consensually agreed on descriptive clinical features, whatever the theoretical schema is from which it was derived, be it Freud (1932), the five-factor model (1993), Cloninger (1987), Millon (1990), and so on.

The widely publicized categorical versus dimensional debate may, in part, be resolved by identifying the numerous prototypal variants that exist for each personality disorder. It should be noted that only a small subset of the basic dimensions that may be theoretically (e.g., Cloninger's neurobiological thesis, 1987) or empirically (e.g., Costa & Widiger's five-factor schema, 1993) proposed are found to combine in clinically relevant ways. Every possible dimensional combination does *not* emerge as a clinically observed personality variant; nor are many of the combinations that are mathematically possible found to be theoretically coherent or clinically plausible. It is only those variants which cohere "realistically" that clinicians see in their practices. And it is these clinically observed personality *variants* that will be described in the following chapters.

As implied in the preceding paragraph, theoretically derived prototypes are just the beginning of an adequate clinical study. These "pure ideal types" must be differentiated to illustrate the many ways in which they are manifested in the world of clinical reality. In this text, we have illustrated these clinical divergences in a wide range of populations, from normal types, to childhood syndromes, to adult subtypes. For the most part, these variants evince relatively minor clinical deviations from their theoretically-generated prototypes.

It is our belief that the prototypal approach permits us to specify an ideal or pure type whose essential elements can be understood as having been logically derived from a set of theoretically posited core factors, dimensions, structures, or polarities. Which set of theoretical constructs should be employed remains an issue for future research and scholarly thought. Only further work will tell whether a five-factor model, based on a lexical approach to descriptors, Cloninger's dimensional schema, derived from ostensive neurobiological substrates (Cloninger, Svrakic, & Przybeck, 1993), Freud's (1931/1950) intrapsychic model, grounded in conflicts among the mind's fundamental structures, or Millon's (1990) biosocial model, framed in terms of evolutionary principles and polarities, or some other, perhaps interpersonal model, will prove most fruitful and enduring.

EMPIRICAL ISSUES

The previous section dealt with conceptual issues concerning the organization of personality data. Questions raised by these issues are resolved largely by logic, utility, and preference. In contrast, the two issues addressed in this section, and the questions they raise, are approached empirically. Answers must be sought through objective and quantitative research. The first of these issues concerns whether clinical syndromes are in fact discrete entities; that is, whether each is a separate unit composed of distinct constituent symptoms or whether syndromes overlap and interrelate by virtue of important shared symptoms. Referred to as syndromal continuity versus discontinuity, the problem is similar in certain respects to the conceptual issue of types versus dimensions. The second empirical issue is whether personality characteristics do, in fact, display consistency from one time and situation to another, or whether they are transient and situationally specific. We would have great difficulty in justifying the concept of personality if little or no behavioral stability was observed over time and circumstance.

Syndromal Continuity versus Discontinuity

The notion of syndromal discontinuity is an outgrowth of the belief that all psychopathologies are qualitatively distinct disease entities. Syndromal continuity reflects the view that all psychological abnormalities are quantitative deviations from the average on a distribution of traits. Discontinuity implies that some unusual process has intruded on the individual's functioning, and now sets this person apart from others who vary normally from each other in accord with natural individual differences. The discontinuity thesis is strongly supported if it can be demonstrated empirically that a clear boundary exists between the features of one syndrome and those of others. Kendall (1975) has discussed this issue in terms of the bimodality thesis:

If the putative boundary lies between one syndrome and another this means demonstrating, on an unselected population, that patients with features of both conditions are less common than those with symptoms appropriate only to one or the other. And in the related case where the presumed boundary lies between a syndrome and normality, it means demonstrating that patients with partial or half-fledged symptoms are less common than those who have all or none. Either way the mixed forms, the greys, must be shown to be less common than the pure forms, the blacks and the whites. The mere existence of patients with mixed symptoms is not evidence that the boundary is not a genuine one, any more than the existence of a few hermaphrodites invalidates the distinction between male and female, but such differences must be relatively infrequent. In graphical terms, this means that the distribution curve of the total population must be bimodal rather than unimodal. (p. 65)

Empirical research does little to support the view that syndromes can be clearly separated, nor is there evidence that distribution curves tend to be bimodal. Numerous borderline cases are usually found between supposedly discrete categories. Some investigators have uncovered an occasional bimodality, but these findings appear to reflect methodological artifacts. Strauss (1973), for example, has noted several complications with studies that report bimodal findings, including sampling problems, procedural distortions, poor interjudge reliabilities, rater preconceptions, and so on.

Both factor and cluster analytic techniques have been employed to demonstrate the existence of discrete syndromes or dimensions. Findings obtained with factorial techniques have been seriously questioned, however. For example, factors may be mere artifacts of redundant variables or preselected patient populations. Others have questioned whether the characteristics included in most factor studies represent meaningful clinical features found in patients (Armstrong & Solberg, 1968; Maxwell, 1971). Although cluster analysis is the most advanced technique for identifying patient similarities, the groupings it derives do not represent commonalities inherent in patients; rather, they reflect statistical characteristics that impose group clusters on data even when there is little to support them as discrete clinical syndromes (Bartko, Strauss, & Carpenter, 1971; Fleiss & Zubin, 1969). Particularly disturbing is that different cluster computer programs frequently produce dissimilar patient groupings, a finding that strongly suggests that the statistical method, rather than the raw data themselves, plays the major role in producing the emergent patterns or categories. As noted by Meehl (1978), cluster analysis has yet to produce a single consensually accepted diagnostic category.

Where then do we stand on the issue of syndromal continuity or discontinuity?

The view that mental disorders are composed of distinct entities may reflect our level of scientific development more than a characteristic intrinsic to psychopathological phenomena. Hempel (1961) noted that all sciences, in their early stages, tend to order their variables into separate or discrete classes. As progress occurs, advanced methods of analysis become available to enable scientists to deal with the interplay of elements comprising their field and, thereby, specify how formerly unconnected characteristics overlap and interrelate. As science progresses, syndromes should begin to be conceived less as discrete and independent, and more as converging and reciprocal, exhibiting both interconnected and distinct features—displaying greater continuity, both theoretically and empirically.

On the other hand, although categories are evidence of a more primitive science, they are not, to use Meehl's (1978) phrase, "two-way pathognomic" of a primitive science; the mere presence of categories in itself does not establish a science as being primitive, no more than their absence establishes a science as being advanced. The taxonicity or dimensionality of a given content domain remains an empirical question. Meehl has written lucidly on a methodology he calls taxonometrics, by which the hypothesized latent taxonicity of a domain can be subjected to the threat of falsification. Trull, Widiger, and Guthrie (1990) applied

this methodology to the borderline personality disorder. They concluded a dimensional model was most consistent with their results but also noted a peak at the end of the MAXCOV curve, a result "which is perhaps inconsistent with both dimensional and categorical models" (Widiger & Sanderson, 1995). Unfortunately, because the borderline construct has been historically almost as labile as those so diagnosed, the borderline is a poor candidate if one wishes to generalize to the entire schema of Axis II categories. Taxonicity, or lack thereof, must be established for each disorder independently of others.

Recent expositions on the categories versus dimensions controversy indicate that implicit assumptions underlying this debate have become increasingly clear. As described by Blashfield and McElroy (1995) for example, categorical and dimensional models may be discussed in either a structural or measurement context, and the confounding of these contexts has confounded the debate. When embedded in a measurement context, categorical refers to a nominal level (e.g., male vs. female), whereas dimensional refers to either an interval (e.g., intelligence quotient) or ratio level of measurement (e.g., temperature). In this context, it is asserted that the use of diagnostic categories results in a loss of information by dichotomizing what is in fact a continuum of personality functioning that spans both normality and pathology. When discussed structurally, however, in terms of the concordance between the observed distributional properties of the data and those properties ontologically required by the model, a dimensional schema assumes that individuals are approximately equally distributed throughout the dimensional space, whereas "the categorical model is a dimensional model with the additional assumption that patient data form descriptive clusters when plotted in a space defined by the dimensions" (Blashfield & McElroy, 1995). Because the categorical model makes additional assumptions about the structure of reality, it effectively disallows more than does the dimensional model, which in fact is the more basic of the two. We should not be surprised, then, if the scope of applicability of the categorical model is proportionally decreased. Some Axis II pathologies, perhaps those which have been proposed to exist on a spectrum with some Axis I disorder, may show evidence of latent taxonicity. Others will be more amenable to dimensional modeling. In any case, the trend in personality disorders is definitely toward specifying the structural properties of various models and testing these empirically.

Personality Consistency versus Situational Specificity

Personality is a heuristic construct; as such, it is intended as a point of departure, not as an arrival. Like all heuristic constructs, personality begins to fray at the edges (but does not completely unravel) when submitted to empirical evidence. The assumption that the way an individual behaves typically at one time or in one situation will be closely related to the way he or she behaves at others has in the past been seriously questioned. That personality traits endure or persist over time has been spoken of as stability; that behaviors displayed in one situation will be exhibited in others has been referred to as consistency. Stability and cross-situational consistency are fundamental to the concept of personality. If individuals fail to exhibit reasonably stable and consistent behaviors, then the very notion of personality itself may be in jeopardy. Although both seem intuitively self-evident, there are those who have vigorously argued that research fails to support both assumptions (Mischel, 1969). If true, then the very concept of personality could not be sustained. Mischel, in an early critique favoring the situationist position, presented a wide array of evidence indicating that behaviors over time and situation rarely achieve correlations beyond the .30 level, the so-called "personality coefficient." In contrast, he referred to a substantial body of data that show that behaviors are affected significantly by situational variations. Mischel also pointed out that the data of studies finding purported consistency were, in fact, spurious, a consequence of anticipated and rater-imposed regularities.

Consistency and stability have become pseudoissues in recent years. Mischel (1979), has asserted that the controversy never existed because it has always been known that people behave in a stable manner in certain situations and variably in others. In his first rethinking of this matter, he phrased his position as follows: "No one suggests that the organism approaches every new situation with an empty head, nor is it questioned by anyone that different individuals differ markedly in how they deal with most stimulus conditions" (1973b, p. 255). What Mischel has come around to is referred to in the literature as the interactionist position. Ekehammer (1974), in a review of interactionism, has concluded that the situationist-personologist issue should be reformulated as follows: Which personality and situational factors interact to produce consistent behaviors and which to produce variable behaviors? Behavior, from this viewpoint, results from reciprocal transactions between personality and situational characteristics.

Empirical research shows that individuals differ in the degree to which their behaviors exhibit consistency (Endler & Magnusson, 1976; Epstein, 1979). Moreover, each individual displays consistency only in certain characteristics; each of us possesses particular traits that are relatively resistant to situational influence and others that can be readily modified. Stated differently, the several characteristics composing our personality do not display equal degrees of consistency and stability. Furthermore, the traits that exhibit consistency in one person may not exhibit consistency in others (Kenrick & Stringfield, 1980). In general, consistency is found only in traits that are central to the individual's style of functioning. For some, what is of significance is being compliant and agreeable, never differing or having conflict; for another, it may be crucial to keep one's distance from people so as to avoid rejection or the feeling of being humiliated; and for a third, the influential characteristic may be that of asserting one's will and dominating others. Thus, each individual possesses a small and distinct group of primary traits that persist and endure, and exhibit a high degree of consistency across situations. These enduring (stable) and pervasive (consistent) characteristics are what we mean when we speak of personality. Going one step further, personality pathology comprises those stable and consistent traits that persist inflexibly, are exhibited inappropriately, and foster vicious circles that perpetuate and intensify already present difficulties.

CHAPTER 2

Personality Theories:
Historical, Modern, and Contemporary

Current classifications of personality are the result of a long and continuing history. Despite the desultory nature of our path to knowledge, there appear to be certain themes and concepts to which clinicians and theorists return time and again; these are noted as the discussion proceeds in this chapter. Commonalities notwithstanding, the classification schemas to be summarized here represent different notions concerning which data are important to observe and how they should be organized to best represent personality. Thus, to Kretschmer (1925), body morphology was a significant variable in conceptualizing pathological types; for Cattell (1957, 1965), statistically derived trait dimensions were given preeminence; for Horney (1950), it was the interpersonal orientation developed to resolve unconscious conflicts that received emphasis. What should be especially heartening is that theorists and classifiers have been convinced that the complexities and intricacies of personality can, in fact, be studied systematically and will, it is hoped, yield to our efforts at scientific comprehension. Each classification schema is not only a model for arranging thinking about personality but poses significant questions and provides interesting, if not necessarily valid, answers to them. Moreover, these abstract formulations furnish frameworks to organize clinical concepts and to appraise the everyday utility of observations.

It is not the intent of this chapter to enable the reader to master the details of personality classification. The purpose is simply that of outlining the diverse theories into which personality pathology has been cast through history. Much is to be gained by reading original or primary sources, but the aim of this synopsis is to distill the essentials of what theorists have written and to present them as an orientation to the personality syndromes described in later chapters.

We will divide our presentation into three time periods: the first, referred to as "Historical Antecedents," encompasses theorists whose major works were promulgated from ancient times to World War I; the second, termed "Modern Formulations," represents the contributions of those whose key publications were prominent from World War I to World War II; and the third, noted as "Contemporary Proposals," includes thinkers whose significant writings are to be found from mid-century to the present.

HISTORICAL ANTECEDENTS

The history of formal personality characterization can be traced to the early Greeks. A survey of these notions can be found in the detailed reviews published by Roback (1927) and Allport (1937). These fine secondary sources make it unnecessary to record here any but the most central concepts of these early characterologists. Also worthy of brief mention are those who may be considered the forerunners of contemporary systems of classification.

LITERARY DESCRIPTIONS

Allport has referred to "character writing" as a minor literary style originating in Athens, probably invented by Aristotle and brought to its finest and most brilliant form through the pen of Theophrastus. Presented as "verbal" portraits, these depictions of character are brief sketches that capture certain common types so aptly as to be identified and appreciated by readers in all walks of life. In these crisp delineations, a dominant trait is brought to the forefront and accentuated and embellished to highlight the major flaws or foibles of the individual. In essence, they are stylized simplifications that often border on the precious or burlesque. Among literature's most incisive and brilliant portrayals are the character depictions found in the works of Butler, Carlyle, Chaucer, Donne, Eliot, La Bruyère, La Rochefoucauld, Montesquieu, Pascal, Proust, Stendhal, and Tolstoy.

Whether the work is penetrating or poignant, novelists are free to write about their subjects without the constraints of psychological or scientific caution. Lively and spirited characterizations most assuredly capture one's interest, but many mislead us regarding the true nature of causes and correlates. Allport noted the facile wordplay of literary characterology and its frequent insubstantial nature in the following:

One of his characters may have "menial blood in his veins," another "a weak chin." A hand may possess "a wonderfully cruel greed" and a blond head "radiate fickleness." Such undisciplined metaphors give cadence and inspire a kind of bland credulity, but for science they are mere idle phrases. (1937, p. 62)

For all its graphic and compelling qualities, literary characterology is a limited and often misleading form of personality description. In the hands of an astute observer, sensitive to the subtleties and contradictions of behavior, such portrayals provide a pithy analysis of both the humor and anguish of personal functioning. However, the unique and picturesque quality of the presentations draws attention to the fascinating, and away from the mundane behaviors that typify everyday human conduct. Artistic accentuations may serve the purpose of dramatic rendition but falsify the true nature of psychic operations. Intriguing though such portrayals may be, they often depict types that are either unidimensional or rarely seen in clinical observation, and are, hence, of minimal diagnostic utility. Perhaps less delightful and amusing, the characteristics required for purposes of clinical classification must be both more systematic and more commonplace.

HUMORAL DOCTRINES

The first explanatory system to specify personality dimensions is likely to have been the doctrine of bodily humors posited by early Greeks some 25 centuries ago. Interestingly, history appears to have come full circle. The humoral doctrine sought to explain personality with reference to alleged body fluids, whereas much of contemporary psychiatry seeks answers with biochemical and endocrinological hypotheses. In the fourth century B.C., Hippocrates concluded that all disease

stemmed from an excess of or imbalance among four bodily humors: yellow bile, black bile, blood, and phlegm. Humors were the embodiment of earth, water, fire, and air—the declared basic components of the universe according to the philosopher Empedocles. Hippocrates identified four basic temperaments, the choleric, melancholic, sanguine, and phlegmatic; these corresponded, respectively, to excesses in yellow bile, black bile, blood, and phlegm. Modified by Galen centuries later, the choleric temperament was associated with a tendency toward irascibility, the sanguine temperament prompted the individual toward optimism, the melancholic temperament was characterized by an inclination toward sadness, and the phlegmatic temperament was conceived as an apathetic disposition. Although the doctrine of humors has been abandoned, giving way to scientific studies on topics such as neurohormone chemistry, its terminology and connotations still persist in such contemporary expressions as being sanguine or *good humored.*

PHYSIOGNOMIC/PHRENOLOGIC CONCEPTIONS

The ancients speculated also that body structure was associated with the character of personality. Whereas the humoral doctrine may be seen as the forerunner of contemporary psychiatric neurobiology, phrenology and physiognomy may be conceived as forerunners of modern psychiatric morphology. Physiognomy, first recorded in the writings of Aristotle, seeks to identify personality characteristics by outward appearances, particularly facial configurations and expressions. People have sought to appraise others throughout history by observing their countenance, the play in their face, and the cast of their eyes, as well as their postural attitudes and the style of their movements. It was not until the late 18th century, however, that the first systematic effort was made to analyze external morphology and its relation to psychological functions.

Despite its discredited side, phrenology, as practiced by Franz Josef Gall, was an honest and serious attempt to construct a science of personology. Although Gall referred to his studies of "brain physiology" as "organology" and "cranioscopy," the term *phrenology,* coined by a younger associate, came to be its popular designation. The rationale that Gall presented for measuring contour variations of the skull was not at all illogical given the limited knowledge of 18th-century anatomy. In fact, his work signified an important advance over the naive and subjective studies of physiognomy of his time in that he sought to employ objective and quantitative methods to deduce the inner structure of the brain. Seeking to decipher personality characteristics by their ostensible correlations with the nervous system, he was among the first to claim that a direct relationship existed between mind and body. Contending that the brain was the central organ of thought and emotion, Gall concluded, quite reasonably, that both the intensity and character of thoughts and emotions would correlate with variations in the size and shape of the brain or its encasement, the cranium. Thus, Gall asserted that just as it is logical to assume that persons with large bicep muscles are stronger than those with thin or small ones, so too would it be logical to assume that persons possessing large cranial projections would display corresponding psychological characteristics to a greater extent than those who evidence smaller protuberances. That these assertions proved invalid should not be surprising when we recognize, as we do today, the exceedingly complex structure of neuroanatomy and its tangential status as a substrate for personality functions. Despite the now transparent weaknesses of Gall's system, he was the first to attempt a reasoned thesis for the view that personality characteristics may correlate with body structure.

CHARACTER PROPOSITIONS

T. Ribot

A late 19th-century French psychologist, Ribot (1890), attempted to formulate character types in a manner analogous to botanical classifications. By varying the intensity level of two traits, those of sensitivity and activity, Ribot sought to construct several major types. Among the personalities proposed were: (a) the "humble character," noted by excess sensibility and limited energy; (b) the "contemplative character," marked by keen sensibility and passive behavior; and (c) the "emotional type," combining extreme impressionability and an active disposition. Among other major categories were the "apathetic" and the "calculative" characters.

F. Queyrat

A similar method of permutation was applied by another French theorist, F. Queyrat (1896), in his formulation of nine normal character types; this was achieved by intensity combinations of three

dispositions: emotionality, activity, and meditation. Where only one disposition was preeminent, the character took the form of a pure emotional, active, or meditative type. A second group of normal characters were noted by the simultaneous predominance of two dispositions, yielding an active-emotional, or "passionate," type; an active-meditative, or "voluntary," character; and a meditative-emotional, or "sentimental," personality. In the third set of characters, Queyrat identified those in which the three dispositions were balanced: Here were noted the "equilibrated," the "amorphous," and the "apathetic" characters. When one or more of the three tendencies functioned irregularly or erratically, Queyrat designated them as semimorbid characters, specifically the "unstable," the "irresolute," and the "contradictory" types.

G. Heymans and E. Wiersma

Writing a decade or so later were a number of theorists from other European nations. Most notable among them were the Dutch psychologists Heymans and Wiersma (1906–1909). On the basis of a series of highly sophisticated empirical studies, they identified three fundamental criteria for evaluating character: activity level, emotionality, and susceptibility to external versus internal stimulation. These criteria anticipated identical threefold schemas (each based, however, on highly dissimilar theoretical models) developed by McDougall (1908/1932), Meumann (1910), Freud (1915/1925b), and Millon (1969). By combining these criteria, Heymans and Wiersma deduced the presence of eight character types:

1. The "amorphous" character, reflecting the interplay of passive, nonemotional, and external susceptibility.
2. The "apathetic" character, developing from a passive, nonemotional, and internal orientation.
3. The "nervous" character, a product of a passive, emotional, and external responsiveness.
4. The "sentimental" character, who is passive, emotional, and internally impressed.
5. The "sanguine" character, noted as active, nonemotional, and externally receptive.
6. The "phlegmatic" character, typified by active, nonemotional, and internal tendencies.
7. The "choleric" character, reflecting an active, emotional, and external susceptibility.
8. The "impassioned" character, representing an active, emotional, and internal sensitivity.

As noted, the criteria developed by Heymans and Wiersma correspond extremely well with clinical dimensions derived by later theorists, specifically the polarities of activity-passivity, pleasure-pain emotionality, and an internal, or self, responsivity versus an external, or other, responsivity.

A. Lazursky

Brief note should be made of the work of the Russian psychologist Lazursky, whose book *An Outline of a Science of Characters* was first published in 1906. Lazursky had been greatly influenced by the experimental approach of Pavlov and his colleagues. Foreshadowing personality dimensions that were given special significance in later decades, Lazursky concluded, following a series of "systematic" studies, that the seeming diversity among characters can be grouped into three higher-order types: (a) those who relate to society negatively, appear detached from everyday affairs, and are only minimally adapted to the demands of their environment; (b) those who are molded by their environment and are dependent on external circumstances to guide their behavior and actions; and (c) those who are masters of their fate, controlling their environment and capable of functioning independently of the will of others.

TEMPERAMENT HYPOTHESES

Attempts were made in the early 20th century to identify the constituents of temperament and determine the ways in which they blend into distinctive patterns. The ideas proposed by four theorists are briefly described to illustrate this line of thinking.

E. Hirt

Among the first of these was the psychiatrist Hirt, director of a German asylum and author of *Die Temperamente,* published in 1902. Extrapolating from work with institutionalized cases, Hirt divided temperament in accord with the classical four humors, but, in addition, he attempted to find their parallels among psychiatric populations. To Hirt, those who possessed an accentuated phlegmatic temperament were inclined to exhibit a morbid apathy such as seen in cases of dementia praecox; these patients were not only inactive but lacked insight, seemed detached from the world, and were too indifferent to complain about their plight. Patients endowed with a sanguine temperament to an extreme degree were characterized by superficial excitability, enthusiasm, and unreliability, and were therefore typically diagnosed as hysterical types; to Hirt, vanity, a craving for attention, and the seeking of enjoyment served as their primary stimuli for action. The choleric temperament was found among several subcategories of patients, including suspicious characters who were forever anticipating treachery and ill will, and grumbling types who were invariably critical of others, claiming their personal superiority to all if only they were given a chance. Those of a melancholic disposition were divided into two categories: Those of an active inclination were filled with an irritable pessimism and bitterness, and those more passively inclined were found among speculative and brooding types.

W. McDougall

Best known in the United States was William McDougall, who proposed the "consolidation of sentiments" in his *Introduction to Social Psychology,* first published in 1908. In a manner not dissimilar from Heymans and Wiersma, McDougall derived eight "tempers" based on different combinations of three fundamental dimensions: the intensity (strength and urgency), the persistency (inward versus outward expression), and the affectivity (emotional susceptibility) of behavioral impulses. Those of high intensity were viewed as active individuals, whereas those disposed to low intensity were seen as passive. High persistency directed the person to the external world, whereas those with low persistency were oriented toward internal matters. By affectivity McDougall meant susceptibility to pleasure and pain such that those characterized by high affectivity were particularly susceptible to these influences, whereas those of low affectivity were not. Combining these three dimensions led McDougall to form the following eight tempers:

1. The "steadfast" temper, noted by high intensity, high persistency, and low affectivity.
2. The "fickle" temper, characterized by low intensity, high persistency, and high affectivity.
3. The "unstable" temper, defined by high intensity, low persistency, and high affectivity.
4. The "despondent" temper, distinguished by high intensity, low persistency, and low affectivity.

5. The "anxious" temper, designated by low intensity, high persistency, and high affectivity.
6. The "hopeful" temper, identified by high intensity, high persistency, and high affectivity.
7. The "placid" temper, depicted by low intensity, high persistency, and low affectivity.
8. The "sluggish" temper, specified by low intensity, low persistency, and low affectivity.

Of interest is the similarity between McDougall's temperament typology and the characterology of Heymans and Wiersma, especially with regard to parallels between their basic dimensions of intensity and the polarity of activity-passivity, between persistency and the internal versus external orientation, and between affectivity and the emotions of pain and pleasure. As noted earlier, frameworks based on essentially the same three dimensions were formulated by other theorists, such as the two discussed next.

E. Meumann

A major effort to construct a theory of temperament was proposed by the distinguished German psychologist Meumann in his 1910 text *Intelligenz und Wille*. Meumann specified eight fundamental qualities of feeling. Central among them were the polarity of pleasure versus displeasure and the two excitative modes of expression, the active and the passive. A number of other features were considered by Meumann to be of lesser significance, such as the ease of excitability and the intensity of affect. By combining the pleasure-displeasure and active-passive dimensions, Meumann sought to account for the four classical humors: The active mode and the pleasurable quality blended to produce the sanguine temperament; an active mode merged with displeasurable feelings to form the choleric temperament; the combination of a passive mode with a pleasurable feeling accounted for the phlegmatic temperament; and the passive and displeasure amalgam created the melancholic temperament.

J. Kollarits

Another schema was formulated by the Hungarian psychiatrist Kollarits in his *Charakter und Nervositat,* published in 1912. Here again, the dimensions of pleasantness versus unpleasantness and of excited (active) versus calm (passive) were brought to the foreground as a basis for deriving major character types. For example, Kollarits spoke of the pleasantly toned "calm euphoric," whom he contrasted with both the "calm depressive," who is unpleasantly toned, and the "indifferent," who lacks the capacity to experience both pleasant and unpleasant affects. In a manner similar to Meumann, Kollarits related these dimensions to the four humors. In his schema, the sanguine temperament reflected an interaction of the calm and unpleasant modes, the choleric was an excited and unpleasant blending, and the phlegmatic corresponded essentially to the indifferent type.

MODERN FORMULATIONS

Attempts to classify nosological systems are doubly problematic; not only must we identify the essential quality that each classifier intends as the core of the schema, but we must also find a framework by which these diverse systems themselves can be grouped. Unfortunately, no principle exists to unify or organize the various classifications that have been proposed throughout history. One useful distinction that may be made differentiates those that focus on normal as opposed to abnormal personalities. In accord with this distinction, this discussion separates theorists of character and temperament, who concern themselves with nonpathological traits and types, from psychiatric theorists, who are likely to attend to pathological symptoms and syndromes.

The majority of theorists presented in this section are of European origin, as were most scientific contributors in the early decades of this century. As psychological interest and talent crossed the Atlantic, and as psychoanalysis gained its preeminent status in the 1930s, 1940s, and 1950s, acquaintance with the theorists discussed here faded rapidly. The loss of their contributions is regrettable because many of them proposed concepts that had to be rediscovered in contemporary work. Present thinking might have progressed more rapidly had their ideas been in more common use.

DESCRIPTIVE PSYCHIATRY

Just prior to the turn of the century, the professions of psychology and psychiatry began one of their first, albeit tentative, mergers. Psychologists and psychiatrists undertook to study in each other's laboratories, to read each other's treatises, and to explore the overlap between normal and abnormal characteristics of behavior. The following paragraphs note a number of contributions made by psychiatrists who broadened their primary focus on psychopathological "diseases" so as to include the "morbid" personalities, that is, the "deviant" character types described by psychologists.

Emil Kraepelin

The prime psychiatric nosologist at the turn of the century, Emil Kraepelin did not systematize his thinking on personality disorders until the eighth edition of his major text, in 1913. Until then, Kraepelin paid but scant attention to personality disturbances, concentrating his organizing efforts on the two major syndromes of dementia praecox and maniacal depressive insanity. In his efforts to trace the early course of these syndromes, Kraepelin uncovered two premorbid types: the "cyclothymic disposition," exhibited in four variants, each inclined to maniacal-depressive insanity; and the "autistic temperament," notably disposed to dementia praecox. In addition, Kraepelin wrote on a number of so-called morbid personalities, those whom he judged as tending toward criminality and other dissolute activities. The four varieties of the cyclothymic disposition were labeled the "hypomanic," the "depressive," the "irascible," and the "emotionally unstable." Kraepelin stated the following with regard to the hypomanic type:

They acquire, as a rule, but scant education, with gaps and unevenness, as they show no perseverance in their studies, are disinclined to make an effort, and seek all sorts of ways to escape from the constraints of a systematic mental culture. The emotional tone of these patients is persistently elated, carefree, self-confident. Toward others they are overbearing, arbitrary, impatient, insolent, defiant. They mix into everything, overstep their prerogatives, make unauthorized arrangements, as they prove themselves everywhere useless. (p. 221)

Turning to the depressive personality, Kraepelin noted the following:

There exists in these patients from youth a special sensitiveness to the cares, troubles, and disappointments of life. They take all things hard and feel the little unpleasantnesses in every occurrence. They lack self-confidence, decision, and seek the advice of others on the slightest occasions. Owing to the timidity these patients never come to a quick decision. (p. 221)

Those categorized as displaying the irascible makeup are ostensibly endowed simultaneously with both hypomanic and depressive inclinations. To Kraepelin:

They are easily offended, hot-headed, and on trivial occasions become enraged and give way to boundless outbursts of energy. Ordinarily the patients are, perhaps, serene, self-assertive, ill-controlled; periods, however, intervene in which they are cross and sullen. (p. 222)

The emotionally unstable variant presumably also possesses both hypomanic and depressive dispositions but manifests them in an alternating or, as Kraepelin viewed it, true cyclothymic pattern. He described these patients as follows:

It is seen in those persons who constantly swing back and forth between the two opposite poles of emotion, now shouting with joy to heaven, now grieved to death. Today lively, sparkling, radiant, full of the joy of life, enterprise, they meet us after a while depressed, listless, dejected, only to show again several months later the former liveliness and elasticity. (p. 222)

Kraepelin's *autistic* temperament serves as the constitutional soil for the development of dementia praecox. The most fundamental trait of this type is a narrowing or reduction of external interests and an increasing preoccupation with inner ruminations. Of particular note was Kraepelin's (1919) observation that children of this temperament frequently "exhibited a quiet, shy, retiring disposition, made no friendships, and lived only for themselves" (p. 109). They were disinclined to be open and become involved with others, were seclusive, and had difficulty adapting to new situations. They showed little interest in what went on about them, often refrained from participating in games and other pleasures, seemed resistant to influence (but in a passive rather than active way), and were inclined to withdraw increasingly in a world of their own fantasies.

Among the "morbid personalities," Kraepelin included a wide range of types disposed to criminal activities; he described in considerable detail the so-called shiftless, impulsive types, liars and swindlers, troublemakers, and other disreputable characters.

Psychiatric typologies prior to World War I were also formulated by other clinical theorists, notably Bleuler and Weygandt. Their lists are bypassed since they overlap substantially with the conceptions of Kraepelin. Attention is turned next to those personality systems that gained recognition after World War I and have retained to the present some following in either Europe or the United States. As noted earlier, there is no simple principle or intrinsic logic to suggest the order in which various personality classifications might best be presented. They could be separated into those which focus on "normal" versus "abnormal" subjects, as sketchily done in the previous section. This format breaks down too readily among modern classifiers, who frequently include both normal and abnormal types within their purview. Instead, and by no means resolving all complications, the sequence followed here presents, in rough order, theorists who draw on biological dispositions (constitutional/temperament exponents) as the basis for their personality classification, followed by theorists who give primacy to experiential learning (psychoanalytic theorists). But first a few words about the prime personality psychopathologist to carry forth the inventive and informative ideas of Kraepelin.

Kurt Schneider

The best known European classification of disordered personalities was proposed by Kurt Schneider (1950), first published in 1923 and revised through several editions. Schneider differed from many of his contemporaries, most notably Kretschmer, in that he did not view personality pathology to be a precursor to other mental disorders but conceived it as a separate group of entities that covaried with them. Although he has justly been viewed as the inheritor of Kraepelin's descriptive psychiatry, Schneider was at heart a disciple of Jaspers and his phenomenological perspective. Whereas Kraepelin sought to objectify the mental disorders, Schneider's intent was to more clearly elucidate the patient's inner experiences.

In the last edition of his text on psychopathological personalities, Schneider described the following 10 variants often seen in psychiatric work.

"Hyperthymic" personalities reflect a mix of high activity, optimism, and shallowness; they tend to be uncritical, cocksure, impulsive, and undependable. Many seem unable to concentrate, and those who achieve occasional insights fail to retain them as lasting impressions. Those in the second category, the "depressive" personalities, have a skeptical view of life, tend to take things

seriously, and display little capacity for enjoyment. They are often excessively critical and deprecatory of others; at the same time, they are full of self-reproach and exhibit hypochondriacal anxieties. "Insecure" personalities are grouped by Schneider into two subvarieties, the "sensitives" and the "anankasts" (compulsives). These individuals ruminate excessively over everyday experience but have little capacity for expressing or discharging the feelings these thoughts stir up. Chronically unsure of themselves, they are apt to see life as a series of unfortunate events. They tend to behave in a strict and disciplined manner, holding closely to what is judged as socially correct. "Fanatic" personalities are expansive individuals inclined to be inhibited, combative, and aggressive in promoting their views; they are often querulous and litigious. Among the "attention-seeking" personalities are those with heightened emotional responses, who delight in novelty and give evidence of excess enthusiasms, vivid imaginations, and a striving to be in the limelight; they are showy and capricious, many are boastful and are inclined to lie and distort. "Labile" personalities do not evidence a simple chronic emotionality but are characterized by abrupt and volatile mood changes, impulsive urges, sudden dislikes, and a "shiftless" immaturity. The "explosive" personality is characterized by being impulsively violent, disposed to be fractious, and likely to become combative without warning and without provocation. "Affectionless" personalities lack compassion and are often considered callous and cold; they appear distant or indifferent to friends and strangers alike. Historically, these patients correspond to those identified in the literature as exhibiting "moral insanity." The so-called weak-willed personalities are not only docile and unassuming but are easily subjected to seduction by others and readily exploited "to no good end"; they are inevitably fated to trouble and disillusionment. The last of Schneider's types, the "asthenic" personality, subjects him- or herself to intense hypochondriacal scrutiny and is so preoccupied with bodily functions that external events fade into the background and appear strange or unreal.

CONSTITUTIONAL/TEMPERAMENT NOTIONS

Perhaps the most perceptive observer of human character, Shakespeare, wrote the following in *Julius Caesar* (Act I, Scene 2):

Let me have men about me that are fat;
Sleek-headed men and such as sleep o'nights;
Yon Cassius has a lean and hungry look;
He thinks too much; such men are dangerous.

Since times of antiquity, observant persons have noted that bodily form was in some way related to characteristics of behavior. This section briefly discusses the views of a few theorists who have furnished a rationale for this relationship.

Ernst Kretschmer

Ernst Kretschmer is the prime modern constitutionalist, suggesting a series of inventive propositions that he sought to support empirically (1926). In his early research, Kretschmer categorized individuals in accord with their physical build and attempted to relate morphological differences to schizophrenia and manic-depressive psychosis. As his work progressed, he extended the presumed relationship of physique, not only to severe pathology but also to premorbid personality and to "normal" temperament. Kretschmer proposed that people could be grouped into four basic physical types: the "pyknic," viewed as compactly built, with a large thorax and abdomen, soft and poorly muscled limbs, and a tendency toward obesity; the "athletic," noted for extensive muscular development and a broad skeletal endowment; the "asthenic," seen as fragile, possessing thin muscularity and a frail bone structure; and the "dysplastic," a mixture of the other three variants that formed an awkwardly constructed bodily structure. Kretschmer's early findings led him to claim a clear-cut relationship between manic-depressive disease and the pyknic build, and a similarly strong correlation between schizophrenia and the asthenic type.

Kretschmer considered psychotic disorders to be accentuations of essentially normal personality types, a position not commonly held by the majority of his psychiatric colleagues. Thus, the schizophrenic, the schizoid, and the schizothymic possessed different quantities of the same disposition or temperament; a distinctly pathological level existed among schizophrenics, a moderate degree among schizoids, and a minimal amount among relatively well-adjusted schizothymics. Similarly, cycloids were viewed as moderately affected variants of those with manic-depressive psychosis, and cyclothymic personalities were normal types possessing minor portions of the disposition. As far as the relationship between bodily structure and temperament are concerned,

Kretschmer contended that normal asthenic individuals were inclined toward introversion, timidity, and a lack of personal warmth, that is, lesser intensities of the more withdrawn and unresponsive schizophrenics to whom they were akin. Normal pyknics were conceived as gregarious, friendly, and interpersonally dependent, that is, less extreme variants of the moody and socially excitable manic-depressive.

To complicate matters somewhat, Kretschmer expanded his notions into what he termed the four fundamental reaction types. The first of these, the "asthenic" reaction, was noted by depressive lethargy, a tendency toward sadness and weariness, and an inability to gather sufficient energy to be anxious about life's events. The second, the "primitive" reaction, was to be found in individuals who discharged the impact of their experiences immediately, who lacked a capacity to retain and integrate experience—a pattern Kretschmer found most clearly among those he termed the "explosive," "shiftless," "delinquent," "instinct-driven," and "immature" personality types. The third set, the "expansive" reactions, included patients who were highly vulnerable to distressing events, overly sensitive to the thoughts of others, and unable to deal with social frustrations; their supersensitivity and irritability disposed them toward suspicious and aggressively paranoid behaviors. The fourth reaction pattern was labeled the "sensitive type," and was distinguished by inclinations to dam up emotions, a high level of intrapsychic activity, and poor powers of expression—all of which resulted in a brooding, anxious, restricted, and unconfident behavioral style. In addition, Kretschmer identified a number of intermediary types, notably the "placating," the "submissive," and the "histrionic."

William Sheldon

William H. Sheldon is the best-known American constitutional theorist (1940, 1954; Sheldon & Stevens, 1942). A disciple of Kretschmer, Sheldon also formulated a series of hypotheses concerning the relationship between body physique, temperament, and psychopathology. He identified three basic dimensions in his morphological schema: first is "endomorphy," noted by a predominance of body roundness and softness; second is "mesomorphy," characterized by muscular and connective tissue dominance; and third is "ectomorphy," identified by a linearity and fragility of structure.

In his temperament typology, Sheldon specified three clusters: "viscerotonia," "somatotonia," and "cerebrotonia." The viscerotonic component, which parallels endomorphy, is characterized by gregariousness, an easy expression of feeling and emotion, a love of comfort and relaxation, an avoidance of pain, and a dependence on social approval. Somatotonia, the counterpart to mesomorphy, is noted by assertiveness, physical energy, low anxiety, courage, social callousness, indifference to pain, and a need for action and power when troubled. Cerebrotonia, corresponding to ectomorphy, is defined by a tendency toward restraint, self-consciousness, introversion, social awkwardness, and a desire for solitude when troubled.

Correlating measures of morphology and temperament to psychiatric syndromes led Sheldon to construct what he termed the three primary components of psychopathology. The first, labeled the "affective," was found in its extreme from among manic-depressive patients; Sheldon proposed that a high relationship exists between this component, the endomorphic physique, and the viscerotonic temperament. The affective component is characterized by a low threshold for behavioral reaction and emotional expression, and results from a weakened or feeble inhibitory capacity; with minimal prompting these individuals display either marked elation or intense dejection, depending on the nature of events in their immediate environment. The "paranoid" component corresponds in its most intense form to the traditional diagnostic category of the same name and to both mesomorphy and somatotonia. It reflects a "fighting against something," a driving antagonism and resentment that is projected against the environment; the power delusions of persecution that characterize paranoids are seen as extremes of this dimension. If physically capable, the patient will be overtly aggressive and arrogant; if weak or otherwise deterred from manifesting hostility, the patient will use circuitous methods of attack or become preoccupied ideationally with feelings of persecution. The third component, labeled by Sheldon as "heboid," is typified by marked withdrawal and regression, features characteristic of the traditional diagnosis of hebephrenic schizophrenia. It is found in ectomorphic individuals since these individuals lack both energy and viscerotonic affect. These patients learn to withdraw from social participation and actively avoid the disastrous consequences of attempting, with their feeble energies, to cope and compete with others.

The theorists that follow are similar to the preceding constitutionalists; they differ in that their focus is not on explicit structural or morphological features but on implicit endocrinological or neuroanatomical variations. It should be noted that temperament is a psychological, and not a physiological, concept; it attempts to represent psychologically relevant physiological processes inferred from observed differences in behavioral activity, persistence, intensity, variability, and, especially, susceptibility to emotional stimulation.

J. Sjobring

The major Scandinavian theorist of personality is J. Sjobring (1914, 1973). Influenced primarily by Dutch psychologist Heymans and, to a lesser extent, Janet and Kraepelin, Sjobring formulated his first ideas about temperament in 1913. Writing over a 45-year span, he termed the various temperaments as basic "physiological constructs" that underlie interindividual or personality variations. The four main constructs were labeled: "capacity," denoting the genetic substrate for intellectual development; "validity," indicating the degree of energy available for nervous system functioning; "stability," meaning the maximum potential achievable given the person's nervous substrate; and "solidity," signifying the extent to which this potential must be replenished by experience to maintain its maximum level. Sjobring conceived each of these four factors as independent of the others and distributed in accord with the normal curve. Although personality combinations of these constructs were recognized, clinical interest centered on features that characterized those who were high (super) and those who were low (sub) on each of the four factors. Among the eight "pure" types are the "subcapable," referring to those who are seen as inadaptable, crude, coarse, and blunt. They contrast with the "supercapable," who are appraised as sensitive, subtle, talented, and adaptable. "Subvalid" personalities are conceived as cautious, reserved, precise, industrious, and scrupulous; "supervalid" types are characterized as venturesome, active, persevering, alert, and confident. Those judged to be primarily "substable" types are identified as warm, hearty, clumsy, naive, and sociable; whereas "superstables" are described as cool, clever, abstract, sophisticated, and elegant. The "subsolid" person is assessed as quick, agile, histrionic, unpredictable, subjective, and impulsive; finally, the "supersolid" individual is noted as slow, steady, earnest, dependable, circumspect, and dependable.

E. Kahn

An early classification of temperaments for personality pathology was also constructed by E. Kahn, in 1931. Interweaving the concepts of impulse, temperament, and character, Kahn constructed several innovative types. In line with earlier theorists, Kahn identified a number of basic dimensions, notably the polarities of activity versus passivity, self-orientation versus non-self-orientation, negative versus positive outlook, and so on. On the bases of their interaction, Kahn deduced the presence of four basic temperaments: the "hyperthymic," noted by excitability, rapidity, and explosiveness; the "athymic," characterized by dull or weak affect; the "dysphoric," identified by an anxious timidity and peevishness; and the "poikilothymic," distinguished by a high degree of emotional lability. Unusual among temperament theorists was Kahn's proposal that biological bases may exist to orient the person either toward the self and individual needs or toward others and the external environment.

M. Tramer

Another early system of temperament classification was constructed by M. Tramer in 1931. Twelve types were derived from his schema. The "hyperthyme" was noted by a ready emotionality and a sanguine disposition; in its extreme form, Tramer categorized the troublemakers, the shiftless, and the unreliable. The "depressive" personality was characterized by a phlegmatic and sluggishly reacting temperament; among them were found the morose and ill-tempered depressives. The "labile" types and the "impulsive" characters were distinguished by their inflammable moods, which died down quickly after discharge; among them were the cyclothymics and those disposed to immature acting out. Tramer also identified a "hypothymic" personality, those who exhibited little or no affect, often found among the more withdrawn and schizoid types. "Explosive" personalities gave evidence of a passionate temperament that tended to short-circuit reactions; these individuals were disposed, according to Tramer, to conversion reactions and alcoholism. The seventh type, the "suspicious," or hypersensitive, temperament was seen clinically among paranoids. The "suggestible," or weak-willed, types encompassed addicts, the thin-skinned, and the "morally inferior." Following the lead of Kahn, Tramer included types that represent two aspects governing the self; the sense of

self may be either strong or weak, and the relation to the environment may be active or passive. Among the passive types with a weak sense of self were found those who give evidence of "martyrdom" and masochistic tendencies; among the active types could be found the "reformers" and adventurers. The eleventh subtype, the "attention seekers," were noted by their exhibitionism and boastfulness, and were often inclined toward hysterical disorders. Finally, Tramer noted the "poorly integrated," insecure types who lacked confidence, had difficulty in discharging tensions, and were disposed to obsessive compulsive conditions.

PSYCHOANALYTIC THEORISTS

The best-known and perhaps most fully conceptualized of personality disorders are those formulated by psychoanalytic theorists. Their work was crucial to the development of an understanding of the causal agents and progressions that typify the background of these disorders.

Owing to their central role in providing a framework for understanding the personality disorders, a few words should be said concerning the basic hypotheses that guide the psychoanalytic perspective.

Psychoanalytic theorists have stressed the importance of early childhood experiences because it is these experiences that dispose the individual to lifelong patterns of pathological adaptation. In what has been termed the psychogenetic hypothesis, early events establish deeply ingrained defensive systems that may lead the individual to react to new situations as if they were duplicates of what occurred in childhood. These anticipatory defensive styles persist throughout life and result in progressive maladaptations or personality disorders. Subsequent patterns of behavior are not a function of random influences but arise from clear-cut antecedent causes. For the most part, these causes remain out of awareness, kept unconscious owing to their potentially troublesome character, notably the memories and impulses they contain and the primitive nature with which defenses and emotions are expressed. Central to the analytic viewpoint is the concept of psychic conflict. In this notion, behavior is seen to result from competing desires and their prohibitions which, through compromise and defensive maneuver, express themselves overtly. Further, all forms of behavior, emotion, or cognition will likely serve multiple needs and goals.

We turn first to the originators of the psycho-analytic perspective on what we now call "personality disorders," eschewing their preferred earlier designation of "character types" for the present.

Sigmund Freud and Karl Abraham

It was Sigmund Freud (1908/1925, 1932/1950), Karl Abraham (1921/1927, 1925/1927), and Wilhelm Reich (1933) who laid the foundation of the psychoanalytic character typology. These categories were conceived initially as a product of frustrations or indulgences of instinctual or libidinous drives, especially in conjunction with specific psychosexual stages of maturation. Because the essentials of this typology may be traced to Freud, it may be of value to note alternative formulations he proposed at different times as potential schemas for personality, based on conceptions other than psychosexual theory.

Freud wrote in 1915 what many consider to be his most seminal papers, those on metapsychology and, in particular, the section entitled "Instincts and Their Vicissitudes." Speculations that foreshadowed several concepts developed more fully later were presented in this paper. Particularly notable is a framework that Freud proposed as central to the understanding of personality functioning; unfortunately, this framework was never fully developed as a system for personality dynamics, as Freud appears to have intended. His conception was formulated as follows:

> . . . *Our mental life as a whole is governed by three polarities, namely, the following antitheses:*
> *Subject (ego)-Object (external world),*
> *Pleasure-Pain,*
> *Active-Passive.*
> *The three polarities within the mind are connected with one another in various highly significant ways. (pp. 76–77)*
> *We may sum up by saying that the essential feature in the vicissitudes undergone by instincts is their subjection to the influences of the three great polarities that govern mental life. Of these three polarities we might describe that of activity-passivity as the biological, that of the ego-external world as the real, and finally that of pleasure-pain as the economic respectively. (1915/1925b, p. 83)*

These same three dimensions were well known prior to Freud's writings in 1915; recall earlier references to the ideas of Heymans and Wiersma, McDougall, Meumann, and Kollarits, each of whom identified the pain-pleasure, active-passive, and subject-object distinction as central. Despite the prominence Freud gave these three polarities by identifying them as the elements that govern all of mental life, he failed to capitalize on them as a framework for formulating character types. Some 50 years later, Millon (1969) utilized these same polarities in constructing a series of eight basic personality patterns.

At another time in his exploration of personality dimensions, Freud speculated that character classification might best be based on his threefold structural distinction of id, ego, and superego. Thus, in 1932 he sought to devise character types in accord with which intrapsychic structure was dominant. First, he proposed an "erotic" type whose life is governed by the instinctual demands of the id; second, in what he termed the "narcissistic" type, are found persons so dominated by the ego that neither other persons nor the demands of id or superego can affect them; third, he suggested a "compulsive" type whose life is regulated by the strictness of the superego such that all other functions are dominated; and last, Freud identified a series of mixed types in which combinations of two of the three intrapsychic structures outweigh the third. Freud's compulsive character type has been well represented in the literature, but only in the past 10 years have his proposals for a narcissistic personality disorder gained attention.

Freud's 1908 paper set the seeds for psychoanalytic character types. Freud's primary interest at that time was not in tracing the formation of character structure but rather in discovering the derivatives of instincts as they evolve during particular psychosexual stages. Although Freud noted that developmental conflicts give rise to broadly generalized defensive tendencies, these were noted only incidentally, written largely as minor digressions from the main point of his early papers. Unlike Karl Abraham, he did not focus on character structure derivatives but attempted to identify the psychosexual roots of specific and narrowly circumscribed symptoms, such as compulsions or conversions. It was Abraham who was most responsible for framing the conceptions of libidinal character development, the features of which will be presented in later paragraphs, following an outline of the work of Reich.

Wilhelm Reich

It was not until the writings of Wilhelm Reich in 1933 that the concept of character appeared in its current psychoanalytic formulation. Reich asserted that the neurotic solution of psychosexual conflicts was accomplished by a pervasive restructuring of the individual's defensive style, a set of changes that ultimately crystallizes into what he spoke of as a "total formation" of character. In contrast to his forerunners, Reich claimed that the emergence of specific pathological symptoms was of secondary importance when compared with the total character structuring that evolved as a consequence of these experiences. As Reich put it: "Our problem is not the content or the nature of this or that character trait" (1949, p. 46). To him, the particular defensive modes acquired in dealing with early experience become stable, even ossified, or as he put it, "a character armor." As the consolidation process hardens, the response to earlier conflicts becomes "transformed into chronic attitudes, into chronic automatic modes of reaction" (p. 46).

Reich's contribution broadened the impact of early instinctual vicissitudes from that of specific symptom formations to that of character or personality types. However, it remained a limited notion in that it failed to specify nondefensive ways in which character traits or structures might develop. Character formations, according to Reich, had an exclusively defensive function, comprising an inflexible armor against threats from the external and internal world. Although the habits of character were employed in dealing with current realities and were no longer limited to early conflicts, these functions remained exclusively defensive and protective; thus, Reich did not recognize that character traits may emerge from sources other than early conflicts. It is in this last regard that contemporary modifications to psychoanalytic characterology have been introduced; we will address some of these more recent developments in a later section on contemporary proposals. It may be useful at this point to briefly summarize the major character types formulated by Freud, Abraham, and Reich. Organizing this literature is best done with reference to the common practice of differentiating types by the psychosexual stages in which problematic development occurs.

Oral Characters

The oral period is usually differentiated into two phases: the oral-sucking phase, in which food is accepted indiscriminately, followed by the oral-biting phase, in which food is accepted selectively, occasionally rejected, and aggressively chewed. An overly indulgent sucking stage leads to what is frequently referred to as the *oral-dependent* type. Characteristic of these individuals is an imperturbable optimism and naive self-assurance; such

persons are inclined to be happy-go-lucky and emotionally immature in that serious matters do not seem to affect them. An ungratified sucking period is associated with excessive dependency and gullibility; for example, deprived children may learn to "swallow" anything to ensure that they get something; here, external supplies are all important, but the children yearn for them passively.

Frustrations experienced at the *oral-biting* stage typically lead to the development of aggressive oral tendencies such as sarcasm and verbal hostility in adulthood. Sometimes referred to as the *oral-sadistic* character, this person is in many ways characterologically the opposite of the oral-sucking or dependent character. The basic pattern is one of pessimistic distrust, an inclination to blame the world for unpleasant matters, and a tendency to be cantankerous and petulant.

Anal Characters

Difficulties associated with the anal period likewise lead to distinctive modes of adult personality. During this time, children can both control their sphincter muscles and comprehend the expectancies of their parents; for the first time in their lives, children have the power to actively and knowingly thwart their parents' demands, and they now have the option of either pleasing or spoiling their desires. Depending on the outcome, children will adopt attitudes toward authority that will have far-reaching effects. So-called anal characters are quite different from each other depending on whether their conflict resolutions are during the anal-expulsive or the anal-retentive period. Characteristics emerging from the *anal-expulsive* period are primarily those of suspiciousness and megalomania, a tendency toward extreme conceit and ambitiousness, and a pattern of self-assertion, disorderliness, and negativism. Difficulties that emerge in the late anal, or *anal-retentive,* phase are usually associated with frugality, obstinacy, and orderliness. There is a predominance of parsimony and pedantry, a hairsplitting meticulousness, and a rigid devotion to societal rules and regulations. As Fenichel (1945) put it, these individuals are in constant conflict between "I want to be naughty" and "I must be good." Although writers such as Fenichel have proposed what may be called a *urethral* character, there is little consensus that a distinct pattern exists. The most outstanding personality features attributed here are those of ambition and competitiveness, both of which are presumed to be reactions against feelings of shame and inadequacy.

Phallic Characters

The next major psychosexual phase in which a distinct set of character types are associated is the so-called phallic stage. This period of psychosexual development is one that Reich (1933) conceived as troubled by narcissistic sexuality. Although libidinal impulses normally are directed toward the opposite sex, they may become excessively self-oriented. Either intense frustration or overindulgence during this period of need for genital contact may produce conflict and defensive armoring. As a result, according to Reich, there will be a striving for leadership, a need to stand out in a group, and poor reactions to even minor defeats. The traits of this *phallic narcissistic* character were depicted by Reich as vain, brash, arrogant, self-confident, vigorous, cold, reserved, and defensively aggressive. If these persons succeed in gaining the attentions of others, they often become delightful and spontaneous high achievers; conversely, if they are not greatly appreciated or sought after, they are inclined to downgrade themselves or to become exhibitionistic and provocative.

In early analytic theory, the genital stage was viewed as the pinnacle of maturity, the attainment of a fully socialized and adjusted adult. However, Reich, in disagreement with other analysts, saw two pathological complications associated with this final period: the *hysterical* and the *masochistic* characters. Among the hysterical characters are people fixated at the genital level, who have little inclination to sublimate their impulses and are preoccupied with sexual excitations and discharge. They are noted by a characteristic fearfulness and skittishness, a pseudoseductiveness, interpersonal superficiality and flightiness, and an inability to sustain endeavors. In what he refers to as the masochistic character, Reich describes a pattern that results from the repression of exhibitionistic tendencies during the genital stage. The masochist is characterized by self-criticism, a querulous disposition, and a habit of tormenting both self and others. The masochist is in a terrible bind, however. Love and affection are sought but result in pain; by making themselves unlovable, masochists avoid pain but, as a consequence, prevent themselves from achieving the love they desire.

The next sections turn to the proposals of Carl Gustav Jung and Alfred Adler, early disciples of Freud known best as the first dissidents. Both present essentially normal character typologies free of clinical symptomatology. Parallels do exist between their types and various personality syndromes, but their intent was to provide a theoretical foundation for normal lifestyles.

Carl Gustav Jung

Jung is among the more seminal thinkers in psychopathology. Most practitioners and laypeople are acquainted with his distinction between extroversion and introversion; few, however, are aware of their subdivisions and characteristics. To refresh the reader's memory, *extroversion* represents the flowing of energy toward the outer world, whereas *introversion* is a flow inward (Jung, 1921). Extroverts explain events from the viewpoint of the environment, seeing things as coming from without. The introvert's approach is essentially subjective, drawing from the environment whatever is perceived as necessary to satisfy inner inclinations. Interacting with introversion and extroversion are four psychological modes of adaptation or functioning: thinking, feeling, sensation, and intuition. "Thinking" refers to logical and directed thought such that situations are approached in a cool, detached, and rational fashion. "Feeling" is a subjective and value-laden process to be distinguished from emotion in that the former is a more rational and less impulsive activity. "Sensation" refers to perceptions geared to the present moment that are experienced immediately by the senses and by bodily excitations. "Intuition," in contrast, relates to a future orientation that anticipates situational possibilities. Thinking and feeling are conceived as rational functions, whereas sensation and intuition are viewed as irrational. Jung created a four-by-two matrix of eight basic types by combining his extroversion-introversion dimension with each of the four psychological functions. The "extroverted thinking" type is inclined to base actions only on intellectual appraisals and to reconstruct events in line with these appraisals. Intellectual formulas serve as ruling life principles to which people are expected to subordinate themselves. As a consequence, such persons are often considered martinets or quibblers who force their views on others. In the "extroverted feeling" type is found a predominance of traditional standards, a willingness to adjust to external expectations, and an avoidance of criticism and reflection. Personal judgments are suppressed and efforts are made to be consistent and loyal, and to adhere to the standards of others. The "extroverted sensation" type pursues enjoyment as the true reality. There is little inclination to reflect on matters and no desire to examine either the past or the future. What is not experienced spontaneously is seen as suspect. Thoughts and feelings are reduced to their immediate, so-called objective qualities. Such individuals are inclined to become crude pleasure seekers, "degenerates," or "unscrupulous effetes." In the "extroverted intuitive" type, there are expectations concerning the potential of things, a search for the new and for the possibilities in people. Stability is experienced as monotonous and suffocating; new situations are seized on with intensity, only to be abandoned as soon as their potentials are anticipated.

Turning to the introverted types, there is a shift from the environment toward inner processes, a centering in the self as opposed to external objects or persons. The "introverted thinking" type does not draw from objective data, as does the extroverted thinker, but from subjective reflections. Such thinkers often are inarticulate because they construct images that have little correspondence to objective events. Often taciturn, this type only rarely makes the effort to gain the approval of others. The "introverted feeling" type also tends to be silent and inaccessible, and frequently hides behind a mask of childishness and melancholy. Although appearing reserved at times, these persons feel intensely but tend to express it in a personal manner such as in art or poetry. The "introverted sensation" type is characterized by peculiarities that stem from highly subjective reactions to objective events. There is often no logical relationship between reality and subjective response; as a consequence, these persons tend to be seen as unpredictable and arbitrary in their behaviors. Persons of this type often become involved in the spiritual interests that are not accessible to objective understanding. Finally the "introverted intuitive" type draws from the deepest layer of the unconscious and is inclined to mystical dreaming and artistic forms of expression. Often an enigma to others, these persons may appear aloof and unrelated to conventional reality.

Jung's typology has but limited utility to the understanding of patients since it reflects his theoretical speculations about the essence of personality structure and not the problems of everyday clinical practice. Difficulties in extrapolating Jung's types to clinical reality are found also in the classification formulated by Freud's other early disciple, and later dissident, Alfred Adler.

Alfred Adler

As the reader may recall, the cardinal concept in Adler's (1964) theoretical system is that of *over-compensation,* an inborn tendency to counteract deficiencies or inadequacies through reparative striving. Compensation for feelings of inferiority takes the form of what Adler referred to as fictive goals, that is, unrealistic aspirations by which the individual could redress shortcomings. Compensating strategies, which Adler termed "neurotic safeguards," help the individual keep fictive goals intact by various protective maneuvers. The individual's "style of life" represents distinctive patterns of striving that derive from shortcomings and the adaptive compensations employed to cope with them. Adler formulated his lifestyle typology on the basis of two polarities, active-passive and constructive-destructive. The "active-passive" dimension reflects whether the individual has learned to be a giver and initiator as opposed to being a receiver or getter. The "constructive-destructive" polarity refers essentially to levels of social interest. High levels of social interest reflect the constructive orientation, and low levels signify a destructive orientation. Combining the two polar extremes led Adler to propose four basic lifestyles: active-constructive, passive-constructive, active-destructive, and passive-destructive (Adler, 1964; Ansbacher & Ansbacher, 1956).

It is the "active-constructive" lifestyle that Adler considers the healthy or ideal individual. He described these persons as feeling at home in life and sensing their existence to be worthwhile; such individuals are disposed to face advantages and disadvantages with equal firmness, to be concerned with serving humanity, and to overcome difficulties with creative efforts. The "passive-destructive" style is characterized by oppositional tendencies. These individuals are seen as accusatory; they are inclined to fix blame, expect to get things from others, lean on them, and act in a passive-aggressive and despairing fashion—or what Adler described as a neurotic style of life. The "passive-constructive" lifestyle is noted by attention seeking, behaving in a charming manner, and seeking to gain recognition simply by being oneself rather than for what one has achieved. The final group, the "active-destructive" style, is one in which attention getting takes the form of becoming a nuisance, of behaving in a rebellious, vicious, tyrannical, and often delinquent manner with others.

Both Jung and Adler reoriented characterology toward the social aspects of personal functioning. What ultimately became the interpersonal orientation took its clearest form in the personality descriptions of Karen Horney, Erich Fromm, and Harry Stack Sullivan. We will discuss Sullivan in the section Contemporary Proposals because many contemporary thinkers trace their origins to the foundations laid down by him.

Karen Horney

Karen Horney's descriptive eloquence is perhaps without peer; nevertheless, difficulties arise in attempting to summarize what she refers to as the major "solutions" to life's basic conflicts. Although her primary publications were written over a short period, she utilized different terms to represent similar conceptions (1937, 1939, 1942, 1945, 1950). An attempt is made here to synthesize these diverse formulations, albeit briefly.

Faced with the insecurities and inevitable frustrations of life, Horney identified three broad modes of relating that will emerge: "moving toward" people, "moving against" people, or "moving away" from them. In her 1945 book, Horney formulated three character types to reflect each of these three solutions: Moving toward is found in a "compliant" type; moving against, in an "aggressive" type, and moving away, in a "detached" type. In 1950, Horney reconceptualized her typology in line with the manner in which individuals solve intrapsychic conflicts. Corresponding roughly to the prior trichotomies, they were termed the "self-effacement" solution, the "expansive" solution, and the solution of "neurotic resignation." Although these sets of three do not match perfectly, they do correspond to the essential themes of Horney's characterology, which are briefly summarized next.

In the *moving-toward,* compliant, and self-effacing orientation are individuals with a marked need for affection and approval, a willingness to deny personal aspirations and self-assertion, and an assumption that love solves all problems. Self-esteem is determined by what others think, personal desires are subordinated, and there are tendencies toward self-accusation, helplessness, passivity, and self-belittlement. In the extreme form, a morbid dependency emerges; at a more advanced and complicated level, there is a masochistic wallowing in guilt and self-degradation.

In the *moving-against,* aggressive type with expansive solutions, individuals glorify themselves, and there is a rigid denial of weakness and inadequacy. Life is seen as a struggle for survival; there is a need to control or exploit others, to excel, to outsmart, and to belittle those who have power. Three subdivisions of this solution were described by Horney. The first, the "narcissistic" solution, suggests that individuals believe that they are, in fact, their idealized selves; and to the extent that others reinforce this belief, they are able to maintain their sense of eliteness and superiority. The second subdivision is referred to as "perfectionism"; persons in this type believe that they are, in fact, what social standards expect them to be, and they are heavily invested in repressing all indications that they may fail to live up to these standards. The third subdivision, most similar to the aggressive type that Horney described in her earlier work, is referred to as "vindictive sadism," in which individuals arrogate to themselves all powers and rights, and seek to deny them to others. In the extreme form, there is an effort to be omnipotent, invulnerable, and inviolable. Satisfaction is gained by subjecting others to pain or indignity, and there is a perverse joy in sadistically deprecating them; through these actions vindictive types feel that they restore their pride and glory.

The third of the triad of broad modes of relating is the *moving-away,* detached type. Employing the solution of neurotic resignation, these persons have as their primary goal the active avoidance of others, fearing that relationships will evoke feelings and desires that will lead ultimately only to conflict and frustration. They restrict their life, become detached onlookers, and achieve peace by curtailing needs and wishes. In extreme form, this type becomes severely alienated, moves to the periphery of life, and becomes an automaton who drifts in a dream, unconnected to others.

Erich Fromm

Erich Fromm (1947) was one of the early theorists to reinterpret Freud's psychopathological theories along social lines. Although constructing his model in accord with themes first formulated by Freud, Fromm questioned the relevance of libidinous forces as the prime elements in character development. Primary emphasis was given to the interpersonal transactions at each stage between parent and child. For example, the compulsive pattern was seen to result not from frustrations experienced at the anal stage but from the behavioral models exhibited by a rigid and meticulous parent who imposed cleanliness and orderliness as standards for the child during toilet training.

Fromm distinguished five character orientations that develop from such interpersonal learning experiences; four are identified as nonproductive orientations and are of primary interest. The first is termed the "receptive orientation" and is characterized by a deep need for external support from parents, friends, and authorities. All things that are good or necessary are found outside one's self. A search takes place for a "magic helper," and anxiety is experienced when external sources of support and nurturance are threatened. Similar to the classical analytic oral-sucking character, these individuals find consolation in eating and drinking, and in dependency on others; they behave in an optimistic, receptive, and friendly manner, except when anticipating loss or rebuff.

The second orientation is entitled the "exploitative" character; these persons seek to extract what they wish from others by either force or cunning. Pessimistic, suspicious, and angry, these individuals feel they are not capable of producing on their own and, hence, must usurp or steal what they can, claiming that what they take from others is of greater value than what they can produce themselves. This type is similar to the analytic oral-biting character and to Horney's aggressive style.

The third orientation, labeled the "hoarding" character by Fromm, is closest to the psychoanalytic anal-retentive type. Security for these personalities is achieved by saving and keeping, by surrounding oneself with a protective wall and drawing in as much as possible, while letting out virtually nothing. There is a rigid and compulsive orderliness, a miserliness in the sharing of both possessions and thoughts, and an inability to express love, as well as an unreceptiveness to both feelings and new ideas.

In the fourth orientation, "marketing," Fromm has made an original contribution to characterology, that is, one not developed by earlier writers. Such individuals mold themselves to fit whatever others expect or require of them; they have little that is stable and genuine in their makeup since they are ever-ready to adapt and "sell" themselves to fulfill the desires that others wish of them. There is a superficiality, a lack of depth and genuineness in one's relationships, a manipulation of oneself to appeal to the fashions of the moment.

The fifth of Fromm's orientations, the "productive" character, is seen as the healthy and creative personality, who fully develops his or her powers, is capable of thinking independently while respecting the views of others, and is responsive to the experience of love and the sensuous pleasures, without being either indulgent or self-centered.

CONTEMPORARY PROPOSALS

Over 80 years ago, Karl Jaspers (1913/1948) wrote the following:

While the work of the psychiatrist is entirely with individual cases, he nevertheless requires to be also a psychopathologist, to look for general concepts and rules, in order to solve the problems presented by the individual case. . . . He wishes to know and understand, characterize and analyze, not the individual person but the general case. . . . He requires ideas which can be conceptualized, which can be communicated, which can be fitted into an orderly scheme and which can be systematized. (p. 87)

What Jaspers recommended then is equally true today; an effort must be made to construct a consistent framework that will create order and give coherence to the broad spectrum of mental disorders. A review of the theorists described earlier in this chapter indicates that many have pursued this goal, but few, if any, have succeeded in formulating as comprehensive and integrated a framework as is necessary to encompass even the personality disorders. Given the intrinsic difficulty of the task, one must ask whether there are good reasons to continue the pursuit of systematizing our knowledge of psychopathology in a theoretically anchored fashion? The following paragraphs briefly answer this question before describing the classification model for this section.

Several benefits derive from systematizing knowledge in a theoretically anchored fashion. For example, given the countless ways in which the complex of clinical behaviors can be observed and analyzed, a system of explanatory propositions becomes an extremely useful guide and focus. Thus, rather than shifting from one aspect of behavior to another, according to momentary impressions of importance, the clinician is led to pursue only those aspects that are likely to prove fruitful and clinically relevant. Another major value of a theoretical system is that it enables researchers to generate hypotheses about relationships that have not been observed before. Thus, in the same manner as in nuclear physics (where theory may *predict* the presence of particles that have yet to be experimentally observed), psychopathology theory may accurately deduce the presence of clinical entities even though they may never have been previously conceived as syndromal types. In this way, theoretical frameworks may enlarge the scope of knowledge by directing observers to potentially significant clinical relationships and constellations. More commonplace, yet significant, is that a theory may enable the clinician to tie new and old observations into an orderly and coherent pattern.

Although general psychopathology theories can prove extremely useful, the personality pathologies they subsume should be as diverse in scope as possible. One of the problems noted in the review of earlier formulations is the limited number of syndromes subsumed within most classifications. For example, though extremely rich in its clinical details, the analytic *psychosexual theory* generates no more than five or six personality characters; factor analytic theorist Eysenck, to be discussed briefly, specifies only three types; Sheldon also notes only three basic categories, as does Horney in her three solutions, and so on. None provide distinctions sufficient in number to correspond to the diversity seen in clinical work. Of equal importance, they do not match in reasonable detail the list of personality disorders described in the DSM classification schema. Thus, in evaluating the utility and accuracy of a theory of personality pathology, the clinician must ask whether it generates a typology that both encompasses and corresponds to all the established and formally recognized personality syndromes. Only in this manner can the prime goal of a clinical science be achieved, that of establishing agreement between theory, empirical data, and clinical observation.

Psychodynamic Frameworks

Despite the decline in the status and centrality of psychoanalysis over the past 20 or 30 years, adherents of this school of thought have continued to be highly productive and insightful. Many of the most innovative and illuminating papers and books on the personality disorders originate in psychoanalytic foundations. Of special significance have been contributions by ego-analytic theorists and the British object-relations school, as well as proposals from a number of contemporary thinkers of special note, each of whom has helped illuminate and organize our understanding of these disorders. We will turn to these clinical scholars in the following sections.

Major Ego-Analytic Theorists

O. Fenichel (1945), perhaps the most impressive of psychoanalytic scholars, classified character traits into "sublimation" and "reactive" types, depending on whether normally maturing instinctual energies were compatible with the ego, and thereby fashioned into conflict-free or neutral patterns (sublimation), or whether they were dammed up by the aims of the ego and countermanded by conflict-resolving defensive measures (reactive). In making this distinction, Fenichel was the first to recognize that instinctual energy can develop into character forms free of conflict resolution. Although Fenichel considered the sublimation character traits to be as deeply ingrained as the reactive types, he viewed them to be nonpathological and, hence, paid little attention to the diverse forms into which they might take shape. In this regard, he failed to recognize the possibility that pathological personality traits could arise from conflict-free sources, simply as a result of deficient or other inappropriate experiences that set the seeds for maladaptive learnings. Fenichel limited his attention to reactive characters and differentiated them into the "avoidance" and "oppositional" types, each representing a major form of defensive control. Fenichel died without being fully satisfied with the classification schema he had just begun to sort out; his well-delineated, yet somewhat disjointed, format is not detailed here, but the reader might benefit by studying his original text (1945).

Heinz Hartmann (1939/1958), David Rapaport (1958), and Erik Erikson (1950) also recognized that the origins of character may be found in instinctual energies that are independent of conflicts and their resolutions. To both Hartmann and Rapaport, the ego and id instincts derived from a common matrix of biological potentials, differentiating into separable energies for adaptive functioning. Termed "autonomous apparatuses," these ego potentials were seen as "preadapted to handle average expectable environments."

Erikson extended the preceding notion of autonomous apparatuses by stating that character development emerges out of three interwoven roots: instinctual energies, the maturational capacities of the ego, and the external standards that society provides at each developmental stage. It would appear logical for Hartmann, Rapaport, and Erikson to have taken the next step and propose character types that develop from conflict-free ego energies, that is, nonreactive traits that prove to be pathological because they are inadequate or ill-suited to the expectancies of the social environment. Since none of them attempted such a characterology, the schema of psychoanalytic character types remained largely the same as had been formulated by Freud, Abraham, and Reich some 50 years earlier.

British Object-Relations Theorists

Several major thinkers from Great Britain began to formulate new directions for psychoanalytic theory in the 1940s and 1950s. Perhaps the most inventive of these theorists was Melanie Klein (1948), one of the originators of child psychoanalysis. It was her view that fantasy was a major primitive ability; furthermore, that these fantasies exhibit a regular developmental sequence that reflects the infant's relationship with its mother. The key element of Klein's object-relations theory is that the mind is composed of preformed internal representations of the infant's external relationships (i.e., its "objects"). This contrasted with Freud's view that the mind possesses instinctual urges that are object-seeking, but are not preformed in their character; in this formulation, objects become part of the mind only secondarily. Klein believed that the mind possessed "prewired" fantasies, implying unlearned knowledge that gave shape to and prepared the child for subsequent experiences.

Similar conceptions to those of Klein may be found in the early writings of Jung and, subsequently, in a number of her followers, such as Fairbairn, Winnicott, and Guntrip. For example, Jung attributed the existence of instinctive object-relationships to racially derived archetypes that are then projected on the external world. Fairbairn, in this vein, proposed "infantile endopsychic objects"—universal pristine images in the unconscious of children. Fairbairn asserted that these objects may fail to mature unless children obtain satisfying experiences with their real-world counterparts. Deprivation of these instinctively sought-for relationships would result in a loss of social capacities or in the aversion to social contacts, each of which may become a forerunner of later personality disorders.

Otto Kernberg

Although numerous analytic theorists have contributed in recent years to the study of character, the work of Otto Kernberg deserves special note (1967, 1975, 1980, 1984, 1989,1992). Taking steps to develop a new characterology, Kernberg constructed a useful framework for organizing established types in terms of their level of severity. Breaking away from a rigid adherence to the psychosexual model, Kernberg proposed another dimension as primary, that of structural organization. Coordinating character types in accord with severity and structural organization led Kernberg to speak of "higher, intermediate, and lower levels" of character pathology; both intermediate and lower levels are referred to as "borderline" personality organizations. To illustrate his ordering of types, Kernberg assigns most hysterical, obsessive-compulsive, and depressive personalities to the higher level. At the intermediate level of organization, Kernberg locates the "infantile" and most narcissistic personalities. Last, clear-cut antisocial personalities are classified as distinctly of a lower borderline organization.

Despite having been strongly influenced by the major ego and object-relations theorists, and despite the innovative nature of his proposals, Kernberg has remained anchored to the view that all pathological character types are inevitably reactive in their formation rather than potentially conflict-free in their origins. Nevertheless, many of Kernberg's innovative and insightful proposals regarding the personality disorders will be detailed in later chapters.

Heinz Kohut

It was Kohut (1971, 1977) who developed an influential variant of analytic theory that furnished a special role for the self-construct as the major organizer of psychological development. To him, self-psychology was the proper next step following the earlier orientations of id-psychology and ego-psychology. Kohut's primary focus was on the development of self from its infantile state of fragility and fragmentation to that of a stable and cohesive adult structure. Disagreeing with classical analytic views concerning the role of conflicts as central to pathology, Kohut asserted that most disorders stemmed from deficits in the structure of the self. Owing to failures in empathic mothering, aspects of the self remain fragile and enfeebled, resulting in a variety of "narcisisstically injured" personality disorders. Paying special attention to the importance of empathic responsiveness as a foundation for effective psychotherapy, Kohut has added a new group of populations treatable by psychoanalytic methods. Unfortunately, Kohut was unable to continue his important contributions and hence, may remain a less-than-significant figure in the development of psychoanalytic characterology.

John Gunderson

Although trained originally in the psychoanalytic approach, John Gunderson (1977, 1979, 1988) has progressively broadened his perspective to include a wide range of theoretical schools of thought; nevertheless, his work on the analytically based borderline personality remains the central focus of his efforts. In recent books and papers, Gunderson and his colleagues have been major advocates of the notion that the borderline personality should be seen as a discrete disorder, not merely a level of psychodynamic organization or a level of pathology, as other notable analytic theorists such as Kernberg contend.

Gunderson has formulated a conceptual framework that organizes the DSM disorders in terms of a continuum from normality to psychosis. Those at the least pathological level, what Gunderson terms "trait disorders," would include obsessive-compulsives, histrionics, avoidants, and dependents. The middle range, or what Gunderson terms the "self-disorders," encompasses the schizoid, antisocial, and borderline. Those at the most severe level in this personality grouping are noted as "spectrum disorders," owing to their close relationship with several of the major Axis I psychotic syndromes. Included in the spectrum group are the schizotypal, paranoid, and depressive personality disorders.

In his early work with Margaret Singer (1975), Gunderson reviewed a wide range of psychological test data and developmental histories, as well as engaged in the direct observation of borderline patients. Offering perhaps the clearest explication of the borderline construct in its day, Gunderson proposed a series of "criteria" for diagnosing borderline cases, notably minimal work achievement, impulsiveness, superficial social skills but disturbed intimate relationships, manipulative suicide gestures, and brief psychotic episodes. This work broadened the usage of the borderline construct beyond those oriented to psychoanalytic thought, providing the wider community of mental health clinicians the fruits of his careful methodological and statistical analysis. As in the parallel work of Michael Stone, to be presented next, Gunderson has demonstrated the wisdom of marshaling a solid database in support of his hypotheses.

Gunderson's progression shows his continued adherence to traditional analytic concepts while, at the same time, extending his view to encompass newer models and approaches to the subject. Thus, his recent work includes the development of several structured interviews for the personality disorders, as well as attempts to synthesize dynamic, trait, biological, and sociological theoretical models, a view adopted recently by other multidimensionally oriented investigators (e.g., Paris, 1994).

Michael Stone

Another recent contributor to the understanding of personality disorders, also noted by his highly informed contributions in explicating the borderline construct, is Michael Stone (1980, 1986, 1990a, 1993). As with Gunderson, Stone's views, though broad-ranging and open-minded, remain deeply anchored to psychodynamic foundations. Not only has Stone articulated insightful proposals concerning the history and nature of the borderline but, in contrast to most analytically oriented thinkers, his scholarly work has been enriched by a series of carefully designed long-term investigations (1990a). Most authors of note have espoused a singular approach to the subject, but Stone and Gunderson have become innovative and comprehensive personality disorder scholars as well; moreover, their analyses are clinically incisive and illuminating, as well as integrative of biogenic, psychogenic, and sociogenic propositions.

This clinically relevant and integrative mindset is well illustrated in a major study undertaken by Stone in concert with his colleagues at the New York State Psychiatric Institute (Stone, 1990a). They sought to investigate the history and course of some 502 patients hospitalized over a 14-year period. Analyses were undertaken at the culmination of the study and provided a detailed database on rehospitalization, work history, social activities, marital and child-rearing status, and subsequent therapy. As is typical of Stone, the presentation of these otherwise dry data was gracefully written and provided numerous illuminating case vignettes. Most impressive was the unique character of this study, both in the size of the population investigated, and in the details it brought to light concerning the divergent course of these patients' histories.

COGNITIVE SCHEMAS

Few fields have gained as much ground in the past two decades as that of cognitive sciences. Along with the increasing significance of the personality disorders and rapid growth among neurosciences, there has literally been an explosion of both theoretical and empirical work centered on the role of cognitive processes in both the understanding and treatment of psychopathological conditions.

Cognitivists stress that individuals react to the world in terms of their unique perception of it. No matter how unconsciously distorted these perceptions may be, it is the person's way of construing events that determines behavior. Concepts and therapies must be formulated, therefore, not in terms of objective realities or unconscious processes, but in accord with how events are interpreted by the individual. Any datum which represents the person's portrayal of his or her experience is grist for the cognitivist's mill.

According to Murray (1988), the cognitive approach reflects the Kantian tradition in which the individual actively imposes meaning on life experiences, developing a schemata, or belief system, for organizing his or her physical and social world. As both Kelly (1955) and Beck (1963) have described it, significant cognitive structures are formed that categorize and organize these schemas into more complex hierarchies. Dysfunctional feelings and behaviors reflect the operation of consistently biased schemas and result in repetitive perceptual and interpersonal errors. It is notable that the cognitive approach is based on the impact of attributional biases rather than motivational or unconscious ones. Hence, therapeutic change requires the reorientation of faulty assumptions, misperceptions, and erroneous expectancies.

Aaron T. Beck

Beck has been the most prominent and insightful contributor to the methodology known as "cognitive therapy," especially as it has applied to a wide range of Axis I disorders (Beck, 1963, 1967, 1976). More recently, he and his associates (Beck & Freeman, 1990b) have addressed the subject of personality, articulating "cognitive schemas" that shape the experiences and behaviors of numerous personality disorders.

In a manner similar to Millon (1990), Beck formulates a model anchored to evolution. He speculates on how the prototypes of personality may be derived from our phylogenetic heritage. What may be conceived as genetically determined strategies are seen to have facilitated survival and reproduction through natural selection. Derivatives of these evolutionary strategies may be identified, according to Beck, in exaggerated form among the Axis I clinical syndromes, and in less dramatic expression among the personality disorders.

The cognitive dimensions of these strategies are embedded in relatively stable structures labeled "schemas," which then select and organize incoming experiences, translating them into habitual emotional and behavioral strategies. By assigning meanings to events, cognitive schemas start a chain reaction culminating in overt patterns of behavior that come to characterize what we call personality traits. Dysfunctional and distorting schemas give rise to maladaptive strategies that, in turn, make the individual susceptible to repetitive and pervasive life difficulties. For example, the dependent personality is hypersensitive to the possibility of a loss of love and help, and quickly interprets signs of such loss as signifying its reality. These highly personalized cognitive schemas displace and perhaps inhibit other schemas that may be more adaptive or more appropriate for a given situation. As a result, they introduce a persistent and systematic bias into the individual's processing machinery.

Beck recognizes the presence of both overdeveloped and underdeveloped cognitive assumptions. Thus, individuals with a dependent personality will quickly activate their overdeveloped, widely generalized, and erroneous cognitive expectancies of personal loss. Conversely, other personalities will have comparatively underdeveloped cognitive schemas. For example, antisocial personalities are likely to have an underdeveloped disposition to find reasons to be responsible or to feel guilt for their behavioral deficiencies. Whereas obsessive-compulsives are disposed to judge themselves responsible and guilt-ridden, they show a marked underdevelopment in the inclination to interpret events spontaneously, creatively, and playfully.

Although Beck is fully acquainted with the role of both self-schemas and interpersonal schemas, his primary emphasis lies in the realm of the former, specifying in great detail distorting cognitive schemas for each of the personality disorders, and doing so in a manner that provides a basis for planning cognitive therapy.

Albert Ellis

No less significant to the cause of the cognitive approach to pathology is the work of Albert Ellis

(1962, 1987). As the originator of what he terms *rational-emotive* psychotherapy, Ellis has argued vigorously for the view that psychological disturbances are largely a result of thinking illogically or irrationally. Moreover, he contends that mental unhappiness, ineffectuality, and other disturbances can be eliminated when people learn how to maximize their rational thinking. To Ellis, the task of the therapist is to show patients that their difficulties result largely from distorted perceptions and erroneous beliefs. All effective therapy teaches or induces patients to reperceive or rethink their life events and thereby change their unrealistic thoughts. Ellis does not articulate a series of categories of personality disorder, preferring to address cognitive misinterpretations as the basis of psychic difficulties. He does state clearly that personality difficulties reflect an individual's unrealistic and self-defeating assumptions about him- or herself and others.

Ronald Forgus and Bernard Schulman

Prior to the recent work by Beck, Freeman, et al. (1990b), a book by Forgus and Schulman (1979) outlined an analysis of several major personality disorders in terms of cognitive processes. Like Ellis and Beck, they assumed that mistaken beliefs lie at the heart of maladaptive behaviors and feelings. The key organizational framework for these distorted belief systems was referred to as the *core rubric,* which comprised self-perceptions, worldviews, and behavioral instructions. The resulting lifestyle (a construct first enunciated by Alfred Adler) validates and perpetuates the basic beliefs that makeup the core rubric. Each personality has a distinctive cognitive structure, but there are similarities among individuals in the nature of these cognitive structures. Forgus and Schulman outline the core rubrics for five personality disorders. Thus, paranoid personalities believe that they are disliked by others, that life is a competitive struggle against external enemies, and therefore they can excuse themselves for their failures by attributing blame to others. For the antisocial personality, the core rubric encompasses the belief that they are entitled to what they want, that life is a "dog eats dog jungle," and therefore they would be guided by the behavioral dictum that they must "eat others before they are eaten" as well as defy the efforts of others to control them. Similarly, obsessive-compulsive personalities believe that they will be held liable and responsible for things that may go wrong, that life is unpredictable, and

that they must stand guard to protect against anything that might go wrong.

INTERPERSONAL CIRCUMPLEXES

The interpersonal perspective on personality and personality disorders has become a major direction of thought in recent years. Despite variations among theorists in the specific constructs and rationales employed, there is agreement that personality can best be understood in terms of recurrent interpersonal tendencies that shape and perpetuate styles of behavior, thought, and feeling. Those of the interpersonal point of view usually suggest that a circumplical structural model can serve best as a framework for organizing their fundamental dimensions. All share the view that there are maladaptive causal sequences between interpersonal perceptions, behavioral enactments, and psychosocial reactions. These interpersonal sequences are rigid and extreme, being activated regardless of their ultimate inappropriateness across numerous social situations. As instrumental styles of coping, these behaviors prove self-defeating in that they are adaptively inflexible and tend to perpetuate and foster difficulties rather than resolve them. As McLemore and Brokaw (1987) have noted, the avoidant personality, for example, enacts a consistently fearful and self-effacing stance toward an environment that resists exhibiting the very experiences of acceptance and intimacy so desperately desired. Such avoidant behaviors usually elicit rejection or allow others to be ignoring, and hence reinforce the person's avoidant tendencies.

We will begin this contemporary historical review with reference to the work of Sullivan.

Harry Stack Sullivan

Although central to the development of the interpersonal orientation in psychiatry, the personality typology presented by Harry Stack Sullivan (1947) is not notably interpersonal in character. Nevertheless, the framework he proposed in his general writings set the basis for seeing the interpersonal basis of clinical difficulties. In an attempt to identify syndromes seen in everyday clinical practice, Sullivan briefly outlined a set of 10 personality varieties.

The first type, labeled "nonintegrative" personalities, is characterized by fleeting involvements with people, a failure to profit from experience, and a disregard for the consequences of one's behavior. These individuals constantly disappoint others by their superficiality and wandering inclinations, but this does not dispose them to experience discontent or to wonder why others react as they do. The second of Sullivan's syndromes, termed the "self-absorbed," or fantastic personality, is characterized by autistic and wish-fulfilling thinking. Conflicted as to whether the world is essentially good or bad, these persons see relationships as either marvelous or despicable; they engage in a series of intimacies that inevitably terminate in profound disillusionment, only to be sought after and repeated again. The "incorrigible" personality is identified by hostility toward others and a pattern of unfriendly, morose, and forbidding behaviors. Authority is viewed as especially hostile and there is a tendency to complain bitterly about those in superior positions. The fourth syndrome is the "negativistic" personality, individuals who cope with their considerable insecurity by refusing to subscribe to the views of others, by passively or subtly resisting social norms, or by a cynical form of conciliation. The fifth type, conceived by Sullivan as a supernegativistic variety, is the "stammerer"; stammering is perceived as a symptom disorder by most theorists, and Sullivan offers little reason for conceiving it as a personality type. "Ambition-ridden" personalities are noted by their exploitation of others, their competitiveness, and their unscrupulous manipulations. Those with the seventh syndrome, "asocial" personalities, are typically detached and lonely, unable to establish and maintain warm and gratifying personal relationships. They seem unable to appreciate the possibility that others may value them; though some asocials are sensitive, others seem obtuse and drift through life without intimate relationships. The "inadequate" personality is distinguished by a need for guidance from a strong person who will take responsibility for everyday decisions; these persons appear to have learned that a clinging helplessness is an adequate adaptation to life. The ninth syndrome is labeled by Sullivan the "homosexual" personality; its distinguishing feature is that love appears to extend only to persons of the same sex. Here, again, Sullivan has identified a specific symptom with the totality of personality. The final syndrome is labeled the "chronically adolescent" personality. These individuals are perennially seeking to achieve ideals but rarely are able to fulfill their aspirations in either love-objects or mature vocations; some will ultimately resolve their frustrations, whereas some will become cynical, others will turn lustful, or celibate, and so on.

Timothy Leary

Drawing inspiration from the work of Horney, Fromm, and Sullivan, Timothy Leary (1957), along with associates at the Kaiser Permanente Foundation, constructed an interpersonal typology based on two dimensions: dominance-submission and hate-love. Utilizing gradations and permutations, Leary separated 16 behavioral segments, which he then grouped into eight distinct interpersonal types. Each is identified by two variants, a mild and an extreme form; two labels are used here to designate each of the eight types, the first to signify the mild or more adaptive variant; the second, the more extreme or pathological variant.

The "rebellious-distrustful" personality, the first of Leary's types, is characterized by an attitude of resentment and by feelings of deprivation. These persons handle anxiety and frustration by actively distancing themselves from others and by displays of bitterness, cynicism, and passively resistant behaviors. Although not wishing to be distant, desiring both closeness and tenderness as alternatives, experience has taught them that it is best not to trust others, to be skeptical of the so-called goodwill of others, and to be alert to and rebel against signs of phoniness and deceit on their part.

In the "self-effacing-masochistic" personality, there is a modesty and an unpretentious reserve, a tendency to avoid appearing capable and confident; in extreme form, efforts are made to evoke deprecation and humiliation from others, with consequent feelings of depression and uncertainty.

The behavior of the "docile-dependent" personality is primarily submissive and is characterized by overt displays of both friendliness and affiliation. Its central feature is that of soliciting help by behaving weakly and incompetently, and by voicing unusual trust and admiration of others; in the extreme form we might observe an ingratiating and clinging dependency, and a constant beseeching for help, advice, and direction.

The fourth pattern, the "cooperative-overconventional" personality, identifies those who strive to be liked and accepted by others, and who display an extraverted friendliness and sociability. There is a willingness to compromise to maintain harmony; in more extreme form this personality displays an effusiveness, a shallow optimism, an immature naïveté, a histrionic or dramatic expressiveness, and a hyperdistractibility.

The "responsible-hypernormal" personality is noted by efforts to maintain the appearance of personal integrity, self-sacrifice, and concern for others. Variants of this type strive excessively to achieve an inner ideal of proper and conventional behavior, and to avoid appearances of emotionality and weakness; they are orderly and perfectionistic, and are intolerant of impulsive feelings such as anger in either themselves or others. In extreme form, this personality may experience life as a "hollow man," isolated by pretensions of propriety and correctness from both the external realities of life and from one's own inner feelings.

The "managerial-autocratic" personality is characterized by an air of strength and confidence, and by communicating an attitude of leadership that often evokes obedience and respect from others. In the maladaptive form, we might observe domineering and dictatorial attempts to control others, power-ridden manipulations of their lives, an inability to relax, and an insistence that others behave efficiently and competently.

In the "competitive-narcissistic" personality is seen a proud, independent, self-enhancing style in which others are either exploited, put down, or benignly invited to be submissive. These personalities are most secure when they are in control, independent of others, feel triumphant, or are assured of a competitive advantage or superior status. In pathological form, there is a blind selfishness, a frantic effort to impress, and a boastfulness and exhibitionism that becomes flagrant and irrational.

The eighth and final of Leary's types is the "aggressive-sadistic" personality, individuals noted by their cold sternness and punitiveness, who gain security and pleasure in mocking others, acting hard-boiled, and in provoking fear through intimidating displays of power; although intentionally provocative, these persons may feel a measure of guilt over the consequences of their behaviors.

Lorna S. Benjamin

As is characteristic of most innovative thinkers, Benjamin (1974, 1993a) recognizes the interplay of cognitive, affective, and interpersonal dimensions in her effort to articulate the fundamental qualities of each of the personality disorders. Thus, her model encompasses many of the elements of the work of Leary, and of Beck, no less those of a psychodynamic orientation. Her special venue, however, is centered in the interpersonal sphere (although her schematic includes intrapsychic features as well). Perhaps the most detailed and verstatile model of interpersonal interaction, Benjamin brings into clear relief one of the major strengths of the interpersonal approach, namely that it can accommodate behavioral, self, and intrapsychic dimensions to personality analysis.

Benjamin terms her approach the Structural Analysis of Social Behavior (SASB), an orientation and methodology that permits an operational description, not only of the major interpersonal patterns, but also of their impact on one's concept of self. Her model of interpersonal interactions is built on three orthogonal dimensions: focus on others, focus on self, and introjective focus. Each of these dimensions can be organized in a circumplical framework. This schema enables one to test and understand, on a symptom-by-symptom basis, how the DSM personality disorders can be analyzed in terms of specific social learning experiences and the social context in which they are activated.

Personality is seen by Benjamin to be a consequence of early interactions with parents and later social learning experiences with significant others. Central to her thesis is that adult interpersonal patterns reflect (a) the development of instrumental interpersonal competence; (b) learning the consequences of neediness and illness; (c) the emergence of a self-concept and social identity; and (d) learning the interpersonal consequences of expressing affect. Translating the preceding into specific personality consequences of expressing anger, for example, Benjamin speculates as follows: In the borderline personality, anger is exhibited when the caregiver/lover is seen as neglectful and abandoning. The borderline wonders whether the significant other is caring and giving enough. Activated by panic, borderlines will recklessly and erratically force the caregiver to provide the desperately needed nurturance. By contrast, the angry histrionic will also mount tantrums, but to manipulatively evoke praise and admiration. The angry antisocial will act cold, maintain control by distancing, and have no remorse for the damage these actions create. Narcissists, by contrast, will become angry if their needs are not automatically fulfilled, reacting with arrogance and withdrawal to elicit their desired attentions. To Benjamin, therefore, different precipitants of anger, and different forms of its expression, can be logically understood from differences in a personality's interpersonal history.

In contrast to many present-day theorists, Benjamin seeks to provide testable hypotheses, not only of the features or traits of each disorder, but of their social pathogenesis. She argues further that the dynamic interplay of the dimensions she articulates will give coherence to the overall personality configuration. Moreover, she believes that treatment interventions should be a natural outgrowth of her interpersonal analysis, hence coordinating both diagnosis and therapy, a necessary element for scientific and clinical progress.

Donald J. Kiesler

Employing what has been termed "interpersonal communication theory," Kiesler (1983, 1986) has centered attention on the transactions that occur between individuals and others throughout their life experiences. As he has formulated it, people transmit an "evoking message" to others through various verbal and nonverbal channels; the message is intended to create a particular encoder-decoder relationship. Kiesler conceptualizes the emotional and personality difficulties of individuals as stemming from problematic countercommunications they unknowingly elicit from others.

In his highly detailed and precise analysis of the interpersonal circle formulated in 1982, Kiesler arranges his personality taxonomy in terms of two major dimensions: affiliation (love-hate) and control (dominance-submission). According to his developmental perspective, a child will settle on a distinctive interpersonal style, role, and self-definition early in life, which then leads the child repeatedly to engage others in terms of how intimate and how controlling he or she wishes to relate them. These relatively constant interpersonal patterns and self-presentations are repeatedly validated in subsequent interactions by the responses the child "pulls" from others.

The classification Kiesler formulated contains some 350 bipolar interpersonal items, 3 to 9 of which define some 64 subclasses that may in turn be grouped into 16 major segments. Kiesler offers a series of translations that relate the DSM personality disorders to their profiles in his interpersonal circle. For example, the histrionic personality fits the frenetically gregarious octant, the dependent personality parallels the unassured-submissive octant, and the passive-aggressive matches the antagonistic-aloof octant.

Kiesler recognizes that not all personality traits or dimensions apply to all people; each of us displays consistency only in those behaviors crucial to our interpersonal style. Accurate personality representations require, therefore, that we designate those styles of behavior that are most important or salient for an individual. It is notable that these central interpersonal styles are likely to be more resistant to situational influences than more peripheral behaviors. As with Benjamin, Kiesler has utilized his model as a basis for conceptualizing optimal approaches to interpersonal psychotherapy.

Jerry S. Wiggins

This author (Wiggins, 1973, 1982; Wiggins & Pincus, 1989) is another creative theorist whose model is based on the interpersonal circumplex. According to his view, interpersonal dimensions of personality that are arranged in a circle have identifiable and useful properties. Adjacent dimensions should be more highly correlated than nonadjacent ones, and the degree of correlation between any two segments should be directly proportional to their distance from each other on the circle.

As with Kiesler, Wiggins organizes 16 segments of interpersonal functioning built around two axes: affiliation (warm-agreeable vs. cold-quarrelsome) and dominance (ambitious-dominant vs. lazy-submissive); as Wiggins sees it, each of the interpersonal segments represents a blend of affiliation and dominance. Although the patterns of correspondence between his interpersonal model and the DSM-IV personality disorders have their shortcomings, a sufficient level of correspondence may be derived for several disorders. If we use numbers of the clock for reference, Wiggins locates the compulsive personality at 12:00, the histrionic at 3:00, the dependent at 4:30, the passive-aggressive at 6:00, and so on.

Specifically, Wiggins sees the compulsive personality as an exaggeration of the ambitious-dominant interpersonal segment, involving excessive formality and preoccupation with rules and trivial details. The narcissistic personality is judged to be an exaggeration of the arrogant-calculating segment and involves exhibitionism and a lack of empathy for others. The paranoid personality is considered an exaggeration of the cold-quarrelsome segment, involving hypersensitivity, readiness to counterattack, and restricted affectivity.

As with other circumplex models in which only two or three dimensions are employed to characterize the many variations of personality disorder, these models fall short of completeness in their formal derivations. Their richness derives as much from their authors' descriptive talents as from their formal theoretical structure.

STATISTICAL CONSTRUCTIONS

Factor and cluster analyses are statistical methods that calculate intercorrelations among a large group of variables such as traits, behaviors, and symptoms. Patterns or groupings among these correlations are referred to as first-order, or primary: The elements making up these factors or clusters are interpreted to provide them with relevant psychological meaning. Second or higher-order groupings may be derived from the original components by combining them into larger units; it is usually these second-order groupings that possess the scope necessary to encompass the breadth of a concept such as personality.

As with the neurobiological temperament theorists, to be described shortly, models that employ statistical analyses seek to identify the basic dimensions or factors of personality through a variety of numerical methods. Once these elements have been identified, the task facing theorists is to regroup them into higher order combinations that correspond to various overt personality styles or patterns. The sequence is first analytic, and then synthetic.

Fundamental questions have arisen with regard to the specification of the basic dimensions, traits, or factors. How many are there? Are they consistent with one another? Do they conflict? Although ostensibly derived on objective numerical grounds, is there no subjectivity in how the basic elements were initially selected and subsequently recombined? This is not the place to elaborate these issues, but they raise significant questions, nevertheless. For example, impressive descriptions of personality derived by numerical approaches can provide only surface characterizations. Lacking is an understanding of *how* these elements relate dynamically. Moreover, there is no basis for tracing or understanding each disorder's developmental origins, nor its etiologic course. Interesting though they may be, ostensively objective and quantitative gauges of trait dimensions are insufficient to achieve a complete characterization of personality pathology (Davis & Millon, 1993). Finally, it would be difficult to justify a preference among alternate statistical schemas on descriptive grounds alone; extrastatistical information is needed, not only to understand the character of these disorders, but to specify why one's schema is preferable to the others.

Most theorists of a statistical bent share a common heritage in Great Britain. Almost all have been trained in English universities, carrying on a mathematical tradition laid down in the early part of the century by Spearman and Burt. The thinkers represented in the following sections are the most persuasive proponents of a psychometric/quantitative approach to the study of personality.

Raymond Cattell

One of the earliest and most productive of those utilizing a factorial approach in constructing personality dimensions is Raymond Cattell (1957, 1965). His research has led him to identify 16 primary factors, or source traits, which he then arranged in the following sets of bipolar dimensions: "schizothymia" (reserved, detached, aloof) versus "cyclothymia" (outgoing, warm, sociable); "dull" (low intelligence, concrete thinking) versus "bright" (intelligent, abstract thinking); "low ego strength" (easily upset, emotionally unstable) versus "high ego strength" (mature, calm, stable); "submissiveness" (obedient, conforming) versus "dominance" (assertive, independent); "desurgency" (serious, glum, sober) versus "surgency" (enthusiastic, happy-go-lucky); "low superego strength" (expedient, casual, undependable) versus "high superego strength" (conscientious, rule-bound, persistent); "threctia" (timid, restrained, fearful) versus "parmia" (adventurous, thick-skinned, uninhibited); "harria" (tough, self-reliant, realistic) versus "prensia" (sensitive, overprotected, tenderminded); "alaxia" (trusting, easy to get on with) versus "protension" (suspicious, jealous, opinionated); "praxemia" (practical, careful, conventional) versus "autia" (imaginative, unconcerned, unconventional); "naïveté" (forthright, guileless, natural) versus "shrewdness" (calculating, sophisticated, polished); "confident" (self-assured, placid, unshakable) versus "guilt-prone" (apprehensive, troubled, insecure); "conservatism" (traditional, uncritical) versus "radicalism" (experimental, liberal); "group adherence" (joiner, follower, imitator) versus "self-sufficiency" (resourceful, independent-minded); "weak-willed" (aimless, careless, impulsive) versus "self-disciplined" (controlled, compulsive, socially precise); and "low ergic tension" (relaxed, tranquil, phlegmatic) versus "high ergic tension" (tense, overwrought, driven).

Cattell's second-order factor dimensions may be described as follows: creativity versus conventionality, independence versus dependence, tough versus sensitive, neurotic versus stable, leadership versus followership, high anxiety versus low anxiety, and introversion versus extroversion, Cattell gives primacy to the latter two second-order factors in constructing four personality types. The first type, "high anxiety-introversion," is noted as being tense, excitable, suspicious, insecure, jealous, unstable, silent, timid, and shy. The second type, "low anxiety-introversion," tends to be phlegmatic, unshakable,` trustful, adaptable, mature, calm, self-sufficient, cold, timid, unconcerned, and resourceful. In the third personality type, the "high anxiety-extroversion" group, is found someone who is tense, excitable, insecure, suspicious, jealous, and unstable but, at the same time, sociable, enthusiastic, talkative, practical, and dependent. The last of the types, "low anxiety-extroversion," is identified by being phlegmatic, confident, unshakable, adaptable, mature, calm, warm, sociable, enthusiastic, practical, and conventional. As noted in the first chapter, problems arise when efforts are made to synthesize trait dimensions into a diverse set of coherent clinical types. This problem is evident in Cattell's typology since the traits that cluster factorially in his work neither consolidate into clinically relevant syndromes nor generate enough variety to comprise a comprehensive classification.

Several other factor analysts at work today are worthy of note.

Hans Eysenck

Eysenck (1952, 1960; Eysenck & Eysenck, 1969) has contributed to many areas of learning and behavioral research. On the basis of his studies he has selected three dimensions of personality that are fundamental to psychopathology: "neuroticism," "introversion-extroversion," and "psychoticism." Stimulated by the ideas of Jung, Kretschmer, and Pavlov, Eysenck has built an explanatory schema in terms of autonomic nervous system reactivity and ease of conditionability. Those who are highly reactive autonomically are prone to neurotic disorders, whereas those who readily form conditioned responses are inclined to introverted behavior. People at the high end of both conditionability and autonomic reactivity are disposed to develop fears and compulsions, whereas those who are subject to minimal conditioning are likely to become extroverted and potentially antisocial. As in the case of Cattell, Eysenck's formulations provide us with a rather skimpy range of clinically diverse personality types.

H. J. Walton

Mention should be made of the recent work of the Scottish psychiatrist H. J. Walton and his associates

(Walton, Foulds, Littman, & Presley, 1970; Walton & Presley, 1973a, 1973b). Although Walton has employed clustering procedures in his studies, this research has led him to conclude that a dimensional format is likely to be a more accurate means of representing personality than categorical schemas. Walton differentiates personality disorders into three levels of severity: mild, moderate, and gross. Mild personalities are individuals who are dissatisfied with the quality of their lives or relationships; they characteristically seek assistance on their own initiative rather than being brought to the attention of clinicians because of difficulties with others. Mild personality pathologies are termed "character disorders," and Walton specifies three varieties: the "withdrawn" type, noted by being socially isolated and emotionally inhibited; the "dependent" type, characterized by compliance, helplessness, and a seeking of support; and the "overassertive" type, identified by an overbearing or officious style, often associated with feelings of guilt. Moderately severe personalities are those whose maladjustments are associated with other mental disturbances, such as psychosomatic ailments or neurotic symptoms; in addition, their behaviors are sufficiently unusual or eccentric to be evident to others. Among moderately severe types, referred to by Walton as "personality disorders," five varieties may be found: (a) the "schizoid" type, noted by being reserved, aloof, and lonely, often appearing queer and incapable of intimacy; (b) the "hysterical" type, characterized by histrionic dress and behavior, sociability, and vivaciousness, and a tendency toward the theatrical, shallow, and insincere; (c) the "paranoid" type, seen as basically mistrustful, hypersensitive, upset by imagined criticism, and envious and suspicious of others; (d) the "cyclothymic" type, giving evidence of mood phases, with spells of spontaneous, outgoing activity turning into dejection and loss of drive; and (e) the "obsessional" type, noted by being orderly, neat, punctual, and pedantic, and by tightly controlled emotions. The third level of severity, the gross personality disorders, refers to persons whose deviance is so marked that they are unable to fit into their social group and often come into conflict with its laws and customs. Among these are two major types: the "aggressive sociopath," who is unable to inhibit aggressive impulses, is affectionless and harmful to society, and cannot form close relationships or loyalty to others; and the "passive sociopath," who is inept, inclined to poor judgment, lacking in drive and stamina, aimless, and having poor work records and few ties to others.

Peter Tyrer

As noted previously, statistical methodologies have been especially prominent among British clinical psychometricians. Along with their forerunners, Cattell and Eysenck, as well as their contemporaries, Walton and Livesley, the group headed by Peter Tyrer (1988) have sought to specify a wide range of personality traits that they see as varying quantitatively from normal to disordered. Developing a factorially derived list of 24 separable traits, Tyrer calculated their intensity or severity with patients who were clinically diagnosed as having a personality disorder. In a series of studies, Tyrer sought to identify which traits clustered together to characterize various groupings or subtypes of personality. Four major clinical clusters were developed, termed "sociopathic," "passive-dependent," "inhibited," and "anankastic" (obsessive-compulsive). In the sociopathic, for example, prominent factors included impulsiveness, aggression, and irresponsibility. In the passive-dependent, primary factors noted were vulnerability, anxiousness, and lability. In the inhibited group, the factors listed were conscientiousness, anxiousness, rigidity, and shyness. In the withdrawn group, the primary features were sensitivity, anxiousness, lability, and shyness.

Following an earlier model proposed by Leonhard (1968), Tyrer and his associates employ their Personality Assessment Schedule (Tyrer, 1988) also to specify what they term "accentuated personality styles or traits"; this level of severity addresses the presence of factors that lie somewhere between normality and disorder. By employing this concept, Tyrer reinforces his belief that personality characterizations are best conceived on a continuum and that differences in personality accentuation or disorder reflect combinations of traits or factors that differ from person to person, even though they may be categorized under the same designation.

W. John Livesley

Perhaps the most sophisticated of investigators employing the factorial structure of personality and pathology are W. John Livesley and his associates (1986, 1987, 1989, 1992). Drawing initially on descriptive characterizations found in a wide range of personality-oriented texts and articles, Livesley generated a set of 100 separate traits for the personality disorders in DSM-III and DSM-III-R. Utilizing both self-report scales and psychiatrically rated trait/behavioral items, he has sought to evaluate the degree to which each trait item was prototypical of the disorder. Decomposing the correlation matrix on the basis of a principal components analysis of the 100 self-report and clinician-rated traits, he initially found that 15 interpretable factors could reliably be identified to account for a large proportion of the data's variance. Solutions with more components yielded factors with only one, usually unreliable trait-item. Conversely, solutions with fewer factors became highly complex in that many trait-items loaded on several factors, hence reducing their independence.

Specifically, the following initial components were identified and labeled: Identity Disturbance, Rejection, Restricted Expression, Compulsive Behaviors, Perceptual-Cognitive Distortion, Insecure Attachment, Interpersonal Disesteem, Diffidence, Intimacy Avoidance, Narcissism, Passive Oppositionality, Stimulus-Seeking, Social Apprehension, and Conduct Problems.

According to Livesley, these components provide a readily interpretable and clinically meaningful structure that is consistent with a number of the DSM personality disorders. As he sees it, the obsessive-compulsive and narcissistic personality disorders are clearly represented by a single component. Others are represented by combinations of several components. For example, dependent personality disorder is represented by two components, insecure attachment and diffidence, whereas antisocial personality disorder is best represented by conduct problems and interpersonal disesteem.

In contrast with many of his statistically oriented colleagues, Livesley does not evince a naive empiricism. Although he sees factor analysis to be an appropriate tool for data reduction, he records several limitations, most notably the necessity to make numerous subjective decisions (e.g., in selecting criteria and items, choosing a method of factor rotation, refining imprecise diagnostic definitions, arranging appropriate patient populations, labeling statistically derived trait/factors).

P. T. Costa, R. R. McCrae, and T. Widiger

The most vigorous and persuasive exponents of the dimensional approach to the study of personality and its disorders are those who follow the five-factor model (FFM), most notably Widiger, Costa, and McCrae (Costa & McCrae, 1985, Costa & Widiger, 1993).

As early as 60 years ago, McDougall (1932), a leading theorist of personality and social psychology, suggested that personality may be best analyzed as expressions of five distinguishable but separable factors. Approaching the subject of personality from a different point of view, Thurstone (1934) analyzed 60 descriptive adjectives characterizing personality, and found that they could be reduced to five independent factors. Cattell (1947, 1965) followed up on Thurstone's work and concluded that five *higher order* factor solutions could be developed to represent the 16-plus basic factors that he had investigated. Drawing next on the work of Fiske (1949), Tupes and Christal (1961), Norman (1963), Goldberg (1990, 1992), as well as others, recent five-factor investigators contend that they have identified the core trait dimensions that characterize personality and its disorders.

The five-factor model derives its data primarily from studies of folk lexicals, that is, the codification of descriptive words found in the language of laypersons. Although disagreements exist regarding the labels to be used to represent the five factors, there is sufficient commonality from one context and culture to another to view the following as highly reliable: Factor 1, Neuroticism, reflecting chronic levels of emotional instability and susceptibility to psychological distress; Factor 2, Extroversion, signifying a disposition to interpersonal interactions, activity, and stimulus seeking, as well as a capacity for joy; Factor 3, Openness to Experience, seen typically in an appreciation for new experiences, a willingness to entertain novel ideas, as well as curiousness and imaginativeness; Factor 4, Agreeableness, representing those who are disposed to be good natured, trusting, helpful, and altruistic; and Factor 5, Conscientiousness, signifying a high degree of organization, reliability, persistence, ambitiousness, and control.

Although there have been serious criticisms of this model, both in its assumptions and empirical support (Davis & Millon, 1993), it can provide an interesting schema of factorial traits that may serve to characterize the DSM personality disorders. For example, histrionic and schizoid disorders appear to fall on opposite extremes of the extroversion factor. Agreeableness may be seen among dependents and compulsives, whereas deficits in agreeableness are likely to be found among antisocials and paranoids. Low scores on conscientiousness appear to be consistently associated with antisocial and passive-aggressive (negativistic) personality disorders. And neuroticism seems especially notable among borderline personalities.

Despite the extensive support garnered by Costa et al., favoring the view that FFM is *the* dimensional model to subserve the personality disorders, all such schemas must be seen as essentially cross-sectional in nature; they fail to provide an understanding of their developmental background. Moreover, they fail to come to grips with numerous combinations and subtle variations that other theoretical schemas provide. Nevertheless, the FFM has proven to be extremely robust across numerous factor solutions, are found in a number of cultures and languages, appear stable across observers, and correlate well with a variety of nonfactorially based clinical measures.

NEUROBIOLOGICAL TEMPERAMENTS

To get a clearer description of a complex system such as personality, many theorists attempt to dissect the phenomenon under analysis into its fundamental or underlying components and then synthesize them on the basis of how the components interrelate. Thus, if we examine the Interpersonal Circumplexes section described previously, we can see that the processes of human relationships have been broken down into certain fundamental polarities; these are then combined (e.g., Leary) to give a more complete picture of each of several personality types. Similarly, in the section on Statistical Constructions, theorists seek to break down the essential constituents or factors that underlie personality styles and disorders, segmenting personality into traits such as neuroticism, extroversion, agreeableness, and so on. These are then recombined in various ways to account for the complexities of a personality disorder. Once again in this section, the majority of the theorists discussed attempt to identify the basic temperaments of personality and then to explicate the character of each disorder in terms of which components combine with which other components (e.g., Siever & Cloninger). Not all of those oriented to the understanding of personality disorders pursue this combinatorial or analytic-synthetic style. What is common among the theorists in this section is the belief that biological/constitutional mechanisms and dispositions are central to the understanding personality disorders.

A. Thomas and S. Chess

Although they have not derived clinical personality types from their work, mention should be made of the studies conducted by two groups of collaborators, one associated with the New York Medical School (Thomas & Chess, 1977; Thomas, Chess, & Birch, 1963, 1968) and the other with the Menninger Foundation (Escalona, 1968; Escalona & Heider, 1959; Escalona & Leitch, 1953; Murphy et al., 1962; Murphy & Moriarty, 1976). Their research has been especially useful in identifying temperament characteristics in the young child.

Several hundred infants were observed from birth through the early years of adolescence. Rating scales were employed to quantify behavior dimensions such as activity level, rhythmicity, inclinations toward approach or withdrawal, adaptability, intensity of reaction, quality of mood, and so on. It was found that the majority of children displayed a recognizable and distinctive way of behaving from the first few months of life. Some were predictably regular in their schedule, whereas others followed chaotic sequences. Some reached out for everything presented; others avoided anything new. Although any of a number of different dimensions could be used to differentiate children, two dimensions subsumed several characteristics considered significant, if not crucial, to later development. The first of these was labeled the child's "activity pattern." Active children displayed a decisiveness and vigor in their behavior; they related continuously to their environment and insisted that events take place in accord with their desires. In contrast, passive children displayed a receptive orientation; they seemed to be content to wait and see what would be done to meet their needs, accepting matters until their wishes were ultimately fulfilled. The second set of central temperament constellations was organized around what the researchers termed "adaptability." One group of children was characterized by a regularity, a positive approach to new stimuli, and a high degree of flexibility in response to changing conditions. Another group displayed irregularity in their biological functions, exhibited withdrawal reactions to new stimuli, showed minimal flexibility in response to change, and expressed intense and often negative moods.

Arnold Buss and Robert Plomin

The temperament theory of personality development proposed by Buss and Plomin (1975, 1984) is grounded firmly on an empirical research base. They have suggested three fundamental temperaments; activity, emotionality, and sociability. "Activity" refers to total energy output such that active persons are typically busy, in a hurry, constantly

moving, and seemingly tireless, whereas passive or lethargic persons display opposite inclinations. "Emotionality" is conceived as equivalent to intensity of reaction; thus, the emotional person is easily aroused, has an excess of affect, and displays strong tempers, violent mood swings, and a high degree of expressiveness. The third temperament, that of "sociability," consists of a need to be with others. Those at the "gregarious" extreme of the sociability dimension find that interaction with others is very gratifying, far more rewarding than nonsocial experiences; they contrast with those at the opposite extreme of the dimension, which Buss and Plomin refer to as "detached." Although all possible permutations of two or three temperaments might be expected theoretically, Buss and Plomin stated that this is not supported in either the research or clinical literature. Low activity or passivity combined with high emotionality appears to underlie agitated depressions. Those high in emotionality and sociability would be inclined to seek the company of others but would perhaps be inhibited by strong anxieties over potential rejection and ridicule. The combination of high sociability and high activity is seen as relating to the classical extrovert pattern, whereas those low in both temperaments are conceived as similar to the introvert.

Donald Klein

This theorist differs from most temperament/neurobiological thinkers in that he (Klein, 1967, 1972; Klein, Gittleman, Quitken, & Rifkind, 1980) is not impressed by efforts to explain the overt forms of psychiatric and personality disorders as mere outcroppings of a set of interacting underlying variables. To Klein, piecing together the manifest expression of a personality disorder with reference to ostensive deeper temperaments or neurohormonal processes is not the way to explicate the character of these disorders. Klein notes that each of these theoretical formulations is but one of several competing explanatory schemas, will often contradict other synthetic viewpoints, and that there are no methods available for determining which, if any, is correct.

The method that Klein prefers analyzes the overt pathology in terms of its response to medication. Rather than search for underlying temperaments or personality factors that can be combined into relatively discrete syndromes, Klein seeks to determine which specific psychiatric symptoms are optimally predictive of a criterion variable, such as prognosis or medication response. Thus, in the absence of firm etiologic knowledge, or objectively based syndromes, Klein would opt for the identification of features that are reactive to treatment success.

Using this preceding framework, Klein deduces a variety of different personality types. One group is termed the "hysteroid-dysphoric," which he describes as emotionally labile, shallow, seductive, demanding, and love intoxicated. A second type is termed the "emotionally unstable," noted by tension, empty unhappiness, withdrawal, irritability, sudden impulsiveness, and a shortsighted hedonism. Also described is what Klein refers to as the "phobic-anxious" type, characterized as socially backward, inept, and fearful, with notable anticipatory anxiety and low self-esteem.

Larry Siever

In many regards, Siever's proposals concerning the temperamental underpinning of personality dispositions and disorders can be traced back through history to the humoral thesis of Hippocrates. However, as is evident from reading his papers (Siever & Davis, 1991; Siever, Klar, & Coccaro, 1985), the specificity and clarity of Siever's reasoning shows how advanced this old temperament notion has become. Although not intended to accommodate all of the particulars and complexities of the many varieties of personality disorders in the current classification system, it integrates the clinical characteristics of several of these disorders and their possible psychobiological and developmental roots.

Siever develops a dimensional model that has major Axis I syndromes at one extreme and milder personality inclinations at the other end. He proposes four major predispositions: "cognitive/perceptual organization," "impulsivity/aggression," "affective instability," and "anxiety/inhibition." For example, schizophrenic disorders are seen as disturbances of a cognitive/perceptual nature, exhibiting themselves in thought disorders, psychotic symptoms, and social isolation; the schizotypal disorder would serve as the prototype among the personality types. Disorders of impulsivity/aggression are hypothesized as resulting in poor impulse control, particularly as seen in aggressive actions. In the more distinct Axis I forms, Siever suggests its presence in explosive disorders, pathological gambling, or kleptomania. When this dimension is more pervasive and chronic, as in Axis II, the predisposition may be seen in persistent self-destructive

behaviors, such as in Axis II borderline and antisocial personality disorders. Problems of affective instability are most clearly observed in the intensity and dysregulation of mood disorders. Where this inclination is more sustained over time, it may interfere with the development of stable relationships and self-image, as may be seen manifested in borderline or histrionic personality disorders. Lastly, the anxiety/inhibition dimension appears to be related to the Axis I anxiety disorders (e.g., social phobia, compulsive rituals); when present at a low threshold over extended periods of development, we may observe a resulting avoidant, compulsive, or dependent Axis II personality disorder.

Siever hypothesizes biological correlates undergirding each of these dimensions, although this evidence is largely circumstantial and speculative. The rich possibilities in Siever's four-dimensional schema can readily be extended to cover numerous personality disorders beyond those in his current framework (e.g., in addition to affective dysregulation, one can hypothesize affective *deficits,* which might provide a grounding for the schizoid personality disorder). Thus, as proposed by Millon, the schizoid personality would not be seen as a milder variant of either the schizotypal personality, nor of the more extreme Axis I schizophrenic, the latter two resulting from cognitive/perceptual disorganization, but rather (despite the similarity in their names), reflect a deficiency in their affective temperament.

C. Robert Cloninger

In a rather elegant model that seeks to draw on genetic and neurobiological substrates, Cloninger proposes a complex theory based on the interrelationship of several trait dispositions. Central to his formula are a series of heritable characteristics or dimensions, notably: novelty seeking, harm avoidance, and reward dependence. Each of these is associated with different neurobiological systems, respectively dopaminergic, serotonergic, and noradrenergic. The interaction of these heritable traits shapes the development of personality by influencing learning experiences, processing information, mood reactions, and general adaptation. Depending on the combinations of these three core dimensions, individuals will be inclined to develop particular patterns of behavior and personality styles.

More specifically, "novelty seeking" is hypothesized to dispose the individual toward exhilaration or excitement in response to novel stimuli, which leads to the pursuit of potential rewards as well as an active avoidance of both monotony and punishment. Second, "harm avoidance" reflects a disposition to respond strongly to aversive stimuli, leading the individual to inhibit behaviors to avoid punishment, novelty, and frustrations. Third, "reward dependence" is hypothesized as a tendency to respond to signals of reward (e.g., verbal signals of social approval), and to resist extinction of behaviors previously associated with rewards or relief from punishment. Extending the theme of novelty seeking, for example, individuals with this disposition, but average of the other two dimensions, would be characterized as impulsive, exploratory, excitable, quick tempered, and extravagant, likely to seek out new interests, but inclined to neglect details and to become quickly distracted or bored. Anchored fundamentally to the dopamine neuromodulator, individuals who might be low in this neurobiological substrate (e.g., underaverage in novelty seeking) are likely to be characterized as slow to engage in new interests, be preoccupied with narrow details, and inclined to be reflective, rigid, stoic, slow-tempered, orderly, and persistent.

Drawing on various combinations of these three fundamental dispositions or temperaments, Cloninger describes a series of second-order personality trait patterns, as well as third-order clusters of personality types or disorders. For example, the histrionic personality is seen as exhibiting high novelty seeking, low harm avoidance, and high reward dependence; these derive from second-order trait patterns of being impulsive, emotionally vulnerable, and narcissistic.

Cloninger, Svrakic, and Przybeck (1993) have extended the original model to include a fourth dimension, labeled persistence, and three dimensions of character, as they put it, that mature in adulthood and influence personal and social effectiveness as well as the acquisition of self-concepts. Each aspect of self-concept corresponds to the three character dimensions.

The process of deriving prototypal personality disorders through a sequence of analyses of fundamental neurobiological dispositions and their secondary behavioral characteristics is a potentially rich and fruitful schema for tying together the complex network of influences that give rise to these disorders. The recent expansion of the original neurobiological temperament model appears to weaken the strength of the original model by encompassing highly culturally bound and philosophically tenuous constructs. Although the original neurobiological grounding of Cloninger's schema had its critics,

it nevertheless sought to interrelate neurobiological processes and psychological disorders, albeit in a highly speculative manner. Despite these and other questions, the enterprise could serve as a heuristic model for future work in this area.

Hagop Akiskal

Although Akiskal's (1981, 1984, 1990) contributions focus primarily on the depressive disorders spectrum, his proposals are of significance in that he seeks to articulate subtle variations within that problematic group of pathologies. His basic premise is that personality variants of depression represent milder expressions of basic, neurobiologically determined mood disorders. To him, personality traits and affective episodes are derived from the same underlying neurotransmitter dysfunctions. The core group of the affective spectrum is termed "subaffective dysthymics"; these individuals manifest a series of personality traits akin to those described by Schneider as possessing a depressive temperament.

Akiskal has extended his notions to encompass individuals with cyclothymic personality traits as well (e.g., tempestuous relationships, emotional instability, irritable periods). In a recent expansion of his affective spectrum concept, Akiskal has proposed a series of intermediary variables, termed "temperamental disorders," which serve to link a number of etiologic risk factors to the clinical expression of an affective disorder. As Akiskal conceives it, these temperamental dispositions are subclinically active at all times and can be easily triggered by environmental challenges. Among the temperaments that Akiskal lists as inclining individuals into the affective spectrum are the following: cyclothymic, noted by abrupt shifts from one phase to another, and seen most prominently in what Akiskal terms the "irritable cyclothymic patient"; hyperthymic, characterized by exuberance, overconfidence, boastfulness, as well as meddlesomeness, and lack of judgment; depressive, typified by a persistent gloominess, brooding, lethargy, and self-reproach. Also included in the subaffective spectrum are a subgroup of borderline personalities with concurrent affective or mood disorders. What differentiates them from other subaffective dysthymics is their "chronic tempestuous course," a developmental sequence that derives from a mixture of affective distress and impulsiveness, as well as the interpersonal consequences of these emotions and behaviors.

INTEGRATIVE MODELS

There are those who would view the preceding approaches and theories as being too doctrinaire in their assumptions and focus. In fact, the majority of theorists do recognize the interplay of several different sources of data and a variety of diverse influences. Even though we have categorized them for pedagogic purposes, the majority of theorists described previously are quite comprehensive and broad-ranging in their approach to the field. Some have made an effort to integrate the diversity of data relevant to understanding personality disorders (e.g., Cloninger).

Despite these pioneering efforts at partial integration, no theorist discussed thus far starts out with an integrative model as he or she seeks to locate the place and character of personality disorders. The following presentation represents two approaches that begin with an integrative worldview. It states that "nature is one," that all facets, both cross-sectionally and longitudinally, are unified by common principles, and compose an interwoven network of characteristics that have been segmented for either scientific or pedagogic purposes. Thus, chemistry is not merely an emergent property of physical phenomena; biological systems are not reducible to chemical and physical but are, in effect, one and the same thing, facets of nature expressed in different forms and processes. These formal and traditional subjects view nature from different vantage points, and analyze nature employing different methodologies.

It is argued in the second of the following sections that common principles underlie all scientific data levels. Moreover, these principles are anchored to the progression of evolution. The essential elements of evolution are seen to operate in all aspects of scientific endeavor, from cosmogony, at one end, to human interactions, at the other. Pathological human functioning is seen as disruptions or imbalances in these evolutionary principles. From this viewpoint, personality disorders are not fully understood by addressing cognitive preconceptions, or unconscious repetition compulsions, or neurochemical dysfunctions. Rather they are most fundamentally seen as expressions of evolutionary processes that have gone awry. Cognitions, unconscious structures, interpersonal styles, and neurohormonal dynamics are viewed, in this formulation, as overt forms of expression or as underlying mechanisms that merely reflect and correlate with fundamental evolutionary processes. Each of them is important

in that it identifies domains in which evolution's pathology manifests itself, and hence becomes a useful vehicle for specifying and understanding that pathology. However, these manifestations and correlates are not the pathology itself, but expressions and mechanisms of it in the cognitive, behavioral, affective, and biological realms.

Theodore Millon: Biosocial-Learning Theory

This section turns to a contemporary, yet recently supplanted formulation for deducing and coordinating personality syndromes. The full scope of this schema was published by the senior author in a text some 25 years ago (Millon, 1969) and was elaborated in later writings (Millon, 1977, 1981, 1986a, 1986b). Identified as a *biosocial-learning* theory (and subsequently as an evolutionary model, to be described in the next section), Millon sought to generate the established and recognized personality categories through formal deduction and to show their covariation with other mental disorders.

A major theme of the biosocial-learning theory, which served to designate its title, was that personality and psychopathology develop as a result of the interplay of organismic and environmental forces; such interactions start at the time of conception and continue throughout life. Individuals with similar biological potentials emerge with different personalities and clinical syndromes depending on the experiences to which they were exposed. According to the theory, biological factors can shape, facilitate, or limit the nature of an individual's experiences and learning in a number of ways. For example, the same objective environment will be perceived as different by individuals who possess different biological sensibilities; people register different stimuli at varying intensities in accord with their unique pattern of alertness, sensory acuity, and temperamental disposition. From this fact, significant differences in experience itself are shaped at the outset by the biological equipment of the person.

The theory asserted further that the interaction between biological and psychological factors was not unidirectional such that biological determinants always precede and influence the course of learning and experience; the order of effects can be reversed, especially in the early stages of development. Moreover, biological maturation was judged to be largely dependent on favorable environmental experience. The development of the biological substrate itself could be disrupted, even completely arrested, by depriving the maturing organism of stimulation at sensitive periods of rapid neurological growth.

Beyond the crucial role of these early experiences, the theory argued further that there is a circularity of interaction in which biological dispositions in young children evoke counterreactions from others that accentuate their disposition. Children play an active role, therefore, in creating their own environmental conditions, which, in turn, serve as a basis for reinforcing their biological tendencies.

Each person possesses a biologically based pattern of sensitivities and behavioral dispositions that shapes the nature of his or her experiences and may contribute directly to the creation of environmental difficulties. Two facets of this interactive biological social learning system were noted because of their special pertinence to the development of pathology, a theme that will be developed further in Chapter 3.

First, the biological dispositions of the maturing individual are important because they strengthen the probability that certain kinds of behavior will be learned. Second, it is clear that early temperamental dispositions evoke counterreactions from others that accentuate these initial tendencies; that is, a child's biological endowment shapes not only his behavior but that of his parents as well. The reciprocal interplay of temperamental dispositions and parental reactions has only now begun to be explored. It may be one of the most fruitful spheres of research concerning the etiology of psychopathology.

In reviewing the many theories presented in this chapter, the reader cannot help but be impressed by both the number and diversity of concepts and types. In fact, one might well be inclined to ask, first, where the catalog of possibilities will end and, second, whether these different frameworks overlap sufficiently to enable the identification of common trends or themes.

In response to the second question, we find that theorists, going back to the turn of the century, began to propose a threefold group of dimensions that were used time and again as the raw materials for personality construction. Thus Freud's "three polarities that govern all of mental life" were "discovered" by theorists both earlier and later than he in France, Germany, Russia, and other European nations, as well as in the United States. The dimensions of active-passive, subject-object, and pleasure-pain were identified either in part or in all their components by Heymans and Wiersma (1906–1909), McDougall (1908/1932), Meumann

(1910), Kollarits (1912), Kahn (1928), Fiske and Maddi (1961), and others. For example, the subject-object distinction parallels Jung's introversive-extroversive dichotomy; active-passive is the same polarity utilized by Adler and is traceable directly to a major distinction drawn by Aristotle. A review of the basic ingredients selected for building personality typologies since the turn of the century uncovers an unusual consensus. It is these very concepts that were "discovered" once more by Millon (1969).

When the theory refers to the *active-passive* dimension it means that the vast range of behaviors engaged in by a person may be fundamentally grouped in terms of whether the individual takes the initiative in shaping surrounding events or whether behavior is largely reactive to those events. The distinction of *pleasure-pain* recognizes that motivations are ultimately aimed in one of two directions, toward events that are attractive or positively reinforcing versus away from those that are aversive or negatively reinforcing. Similarly, the distinction of subject-object, or *self-other,* recognizes that among all objects and things in our environment there are two that stand out above all others in their power to affect us: our own selves and others.

Using this threefold framework as a foundation, Millon (1969) derived personality coping patterns that ultimately corresponded closely in detail to each of the official personality disorders in the DSM-III. These coping patterns were viewed as complex forms of instrumental behavior, that is, ways of achieving positive reinforcements and avoiding negative reinforcements. These strategies reflect what kinds of reinforcements individuals learned to seek *or* to avoid (pleasure-pain), where individuals looked to obtain them (self-others), and how they learned to behave to elicit or to escape them (active-passive). Eight basic coping patterns and three severe variants were derived by combining the *nature* (positive or pleasure vs. negative or pain), the *source* (self vs. others), and the *instrumental behaviors* (active vs. passive) engaged in to achieve various reinforcements. Describing pathological strategies of behavior in reinforcement terms merely casts them in a somewhat different language than that utilized in the past.

A major theoretically derived distinction was that people could be differentiated in terms of whether their primary source of reinforcement was within themselves or within others. This distinction corresponded to what were termed the dependent and independent patterns. *Dependent* personalities have learned that those feelings associated with pleasure or the avoidance of pain—feeling good, secure, confident, and so on—are best provided by others. Behaviorally, these personalities display a strong need for external support and attention; should they be deprived of affection and nurturance, they will experience marked discomfort, if not sadness and anxiety. *Independent* personality patterns, in contrast, were characterized by a reliance on the self. These individuals learned that they obtain maximum pleasure and minimum pain if they depend on themselves rather than others. In both dependent and independent patterns, individuals demonstrate a distinct preference as to whether to turn to others or to themselves to gain security and comfort. Such clear-cut commitments are not made by all personalities. Some, those whom Millon spoke of as *ambivalent,* remain unsure as to which way to turn; they are in conflict regarding whether to depend on themselves for reinforcement or on others. Some of these patients vacillated between turning to others, in an agreeable conformity one time, and turning to themselves, in efforts at independence, the next. Other ambivalent personalities displayed overt dependence and compliance; beneath these outwardly conforming behaviors, however, were strong desires to assert independent and often hostile feelings and impulses. Finally, certain patients were characterized by their diminished ability to experience both pain and pleasure; they have neither a normal need for pleasure nor a normal need to avoid punishment. Another group of patients are also distinguished by a diminished ability to feel pleasurable reinforcers, but they are notably sensitive to pain; life is experienced as possessing few gratifications but much anguish. Both groups share a *deficit capacity* to sense pleasurable reinforcers, although one is hyperreactive to pain. Millon described both of these as *detached* patterns; unable to experience rewards from themselves or from others, they drift increasingly into socially isolated and self-alienated behaviors.

Another theory-derived distinction reflected persons who instrumentally elicit the reinforcements they seek in essentially one of two ways: actively or passively. Descriptively, those who are typically *active* tend to be characterized by their alertness, vigilance, persistence, decisiveness, and ambitiousness in goal-directed behaviors. They plan strategies, scan alternatives, manipulate events, and circumvent obstacles, all to the end of eliciting pleasures and rewards, or avoiding the distress of punishment, rejection, and anxiety.

Although their goals may differ from time to time, they initiate events and are enterprising and energetically intent on controlling the circumstances of their environment. By contrast, *passive* personalities engage in few overtly manipulative strategies to gain their ends. They often display a seeming inertness, a lack of ambition and persistence, an acquiescence, and a resigned attitude in which they initiate little to shape events and wait for the circumstances of their environment to take their course.

Using these three pairs of polarities as a basis, Millon (1969) derived a biosocial-learning taxonomy that combined in a four-by-two matrix the dependent, independent, ambivalent, and detached styles with the activity-passivity dimension. This produced eight basic types, to which three severe disorders were added, for a total of 11 theory-derived personality patterns. Despite their ultimate correspondence to the official DSM-III personality disorders, these coping patterns were considered to be conceptual and prototypal, and not reified diagnostic entities. In the following paragraphs, the eight basic pathological patterns are described first, followed by the three more severe variants:

1. The *passive-dependent* pattern (Millon Submissive personality; DSM-III Dependent disorder) was characterized by a search for relationships in which one can lean on others for affection, security, and leadership. This personality's lack of both initiative and autonomy was considered to be a consequence largely of parental overprotection. As a function of these early experiences, these individuals simply learned the comforts of assuming a passive role in interpersonal relations, accepting whatever kindness and support they found, and willingly submitting to the wishes of others in order to maintain their affection.

2. The *active-dependent* pattern (Millon Gregarious personality; DSM-III Histrionic disorder) shows an insatiable and indiscriminate search for stimulation and affection. This personality's sociable and capricious behaviors give the appearance of considerable independence of others, but beneath this guise lies a fear of autonomy and an intense need for signs of social approval and attention. Affection must be replenished constantly and must be obtained from every source of interpersonal contact.

3. The *passive-independent* pattern (Millon Narcissistic personality; DSM-III Narcissistic disorder) is noted by an egotistic self-involvement. As a function of early experience, these persons have learned to overvalue their self-worth; their confidence in their superiority may, however, be based on false premises. Nevertheless, they assume that others will recognize their specialness, maintain an air of arrogant self-assurance, and, without much thought or even conscious intent, benignly exploit others to their own advantage.

4. The *active-independent* pattern (Millon Aggressive personality; DSM-III Antisocial disorder) reflects a learned mistrust of others and a desire for autonomy and retribution for what are felt as past injustices. There is an indiscriminate striving for power and a disposition to be rejecting of others; these actions are seen as justified because people are unreliable and duplicitous. Autonomy and hostility are claimed to be the only means to head off deceit and betrayal.

5. The *passive-ambivalent* pattern (Millon Conforming personality; DSM-III Compulsive disorder) is based on a conflict between hostility toward others and a fear of social disapproval. These persons resolve their ambivalence not only by suppressing resentment but by overconforming and overcomplying, at least on the surface. Lurking behind this front of propriety and restraint, however, are anger and intense oppositional feelings that, on occasion, break through their controls.

6. The *active-ambivalent* pattern (Millon Negativistic personality; DSM-III Passive-aggressive disorder) represents an inability to resolve conflicts similar to those of the passive-ambivalent; however, this ambivalence remains close to consciousness and intrudes into everyday life. These individuals get themselves into endless wrangles and disappointments as they vacillate between deference and conformity, at one time, and aggressive negativism, the next. Their behavior displays an erratic pattern of explosive anger or stubbornness intermingled with moments of guilt and shame.

7. The *passive-detached* pattern (Millon Asocial personality; DSM-III Schizoid disorder) is characterized by social impassivity. Affectionate needs and emotional feelings are minimal, and the individual functions as a passive observer detached from the rewards and affections, as well as from the demands, of human relationships.

8. The *active-detached* pattern (Millon Avoidant personality; DSM-III Avoidant disorder) represents a fear and mistrust of others. These individuals maintain a constant vigil lest their impulses and longing for affection result in a repetition of the pain and anguish they have experienced with others previously. Only by active withdrawal can they protect themselves. Despite

desires to relate, they have learned that it is best to deny these feelings and keep an interpersonal distance.

Three additional personality patterns are identified at the moderately severe or borderline level of pathology. These are differentiated from the first eight by several criteria, notably deficits in social competence and periodic (but reversible) psychotic episodes. Less integrated and effective in coping than their milder personality counterparts, they appear especially vulnerable to the strains of everyday life. Their major features and similarities to DSM-III personality disorders are briefly summarized.

9. The *Cycloid personality* corresponds to the DSM-III "Borderline personality disorder" and represents a moderately dysfunctional dependent or ambivalent orientation. These personalities experience intense endogenous moods, with recurring periods of dejection and apathy interspersed with spells of anger, anxiety, or euphoria. Many reveal recurring self-mutilating and suicidal thoughts, appear preoccupied with securing affection, and display a cognitive-affective ambivalence evident in simultaneous feelings of rage, love, and guilt toward others.

10. The *Paranoid personality* is described in a similar fashion in both Millon and the DSM-III. Here are seen a vigilant mistrust of others and an edgy defensiveness against anticipated criticism and deception. There is an abrasive irritability and a tendency to precipitate exasperation and anger in others. Expressed often is a fear of losing independence, leading this personality to vigorously resist external influence and control.

11. The DSM-III Schizotypal disorder and Millon's *Schizoid* personality both display a constellation of behaviors that reflect a poorly integrated or dysfunctional detached personality pattern. These persons prefer isolation with minimal personal attachments and obligations. Behavioral eccentricities are notable, and the individual is often perceived by others as strange or different. Depending on whether the pattern is passive or active, there will be either an anxious wariness and hypersensitivity, or an emotional flattening and deficiency of affect.

Theodore Millon: Evolutionary Model

In 1990, Millon reconceptualized his model of personality and its disorders. The fundamental shift reflected a reevaluation of the deeper or latent features that undergird human functioning. For the past 20 to 25 centuries, people have attempted to decode the underlying characteristics of personality functioning by reviewing the diverse forms in which behaviors, thoughts, and feelings are expressed. Drawing inspiration from Godel's incompleteness theorem (1931) that no self-contained system can prove its own propositions, Millon made the decision to turn the spotlight away from psychology proper to expressions of nature that fall outside the field of psychology itself. Just as in Godel's theorem, Millon concluded that the deeper laws of human functioning may be best explicated by examining universal principles derived from other, nonpsychological manifestations of nature (e.g., physics, chemistry, and especially biology). Within these other spheres, it was felt that one might uncover more than just the biophysical underpinnings of psychological functioning, or the unconscious forms in which experience takes shape, or the phenomenological world of cognitive experience, or the behavioral observations of the preceding.

What Millon deduced from these reevaluations was that the principles and processes of *evolution* are essentially universal, expressed in a variety of different forms, as seen in diverse subjects such as physics, chemistry, biology, and psychology. In his 1990 book, Millon attempted to illustrate the universals he judged were fundamental to all spheres of evolution's progression, including those of human experience. What was most gratifying in this exploratory search was the close correspondence between the 1969 biosocial-learning theory and the key elements of the evolutionary model. In addition, the ontogenetic theory of neuropsychological stages presented in the 1969 book also paralleled closely the new theoretical conception of evolutionary phylogenesis (see Chapter 3).

To summarize the preceding, we believe it was necessary to go beyond traditional conceptual boundaries in psychology to find a fresh and fundamental grounding for organizing and understanding both personality and its disorders. More specifically, we chose to explore carefully reasoned, as well as "intuitive" hypotheses that drew their principles, if not their substance, from more established adjacent sciences, such as evolutionary biology. Not only did such steps bear new conceptual fruits, but they provided a foundation that both undergirded and guided our explorations.

Much of personology, no less psychology as a whole, appears to have been adrift, divorced from broader spheres of scientific knowledge, isolated from firmly grounded, if not universal principles, leading psychologists and psychiatrists to continue building the patchwork quilt of concepts and data domains that has characterized the field. Preoccupied with but a small part of the larger puzzle of scientific endeavors, or fearing accusations of reductionism, most failed to draw on the rich possibilities to be found in adjacent realms of scholarly pursuit. With few exceptions, cohering concepts that would connect the subject of personality to those of its sister sciences have not been developed.

And what better sphere is there within the psychological sciences to undertake such syntheses than with the subject matter of personology? Persons are the only organically integrated system in the psychological domain, evolved through the millennia and inherently created from birth as natural entities, rather than culture-bound and experience-derived gestalts. The intrinsic cohesion of persons is not merely a rhetorical construction, but an authentic substantive unity. Personologic features may often be dissonant, and may be partitioned conceptually for pragmatic or scientific purposes, but they are segments of an inseparable biopsychosocial entity, as well as a natural outgrowth of evolution's progression.

What makes evolutionary principles as relevant as we propose? Owing to the mathematical and deductive insights of our colleagues in physics, we have a deeper and clearer sense of the early evolution and structural relations among matter and energy. So too has knowledge progressed in our studies of physical chemistry, microbiology, evolutionary theory, population biology, ecology, and ethology. How odd it is (is it not?) that we have only now again begun to investigate—as we did at the turn of the past century—the interface between the basic building blocks of physical nature and the nature of life as we experience and live it personally? How much more is known today, yet how hesitant are people to undertake a serious rapprochement.

Each evolved species displays commonalities in its adaptive or survival style. Within each species, however, there are differences in style and differences in the success with which its various members adapt to the diverse and changing environments they face. In these simplest of terms, *personality* would be conceived as representing the more-or-less *distinctive style of adaptive functioning* that an organism of a particular species exhibits as it relates to its typical range of environments. *Disorders of personality,* so formulated, would represent particular *styles of maladaptive functioning* that can be traced to deficiencies, imbalances, or conflicts in a species' capacity to relate to the environments it faces.

To provide a conceptual background from these sciences, and to furnish a rough model concerning the styles of personality, normal and abnormal, four spheres in which evolutionary and ecological principles can be applied were labeled as "Existence," "Adaptation," "Replication," and "Abstraction." The first relates to the serendipitous transformation of random or less organized states into those possessing distinct structures of greater organization; the second refers to homeostatic processes employed to sustain survival in open ecosystems; the third pertains to reproductive styles that maximize the diversification and selection of ecologically effective attributes; and the fourth concerns the emergence of competencies that foster anticipatory planning and reasoned decision making. We will restrict this brief discussion to the first three principles to illustrate normal and abnormal processes. The various components of the fourth have been discussed elsewhere (Millon, 1990, 1994a) and will be elaborated in Chapter 3.

Aims of Existence

The following pages summarize the rationale and characteristics of the first of the four segments of the polarity model to be described. In each section, we will draw on the model as a basis for establishing criteria for both "normality" and "abnormality," grounding these interpretations in modern evolutionary and ecological theory.

Life Enhancement and Life Preservation: Pleasure-Pain Polarity. Two intertwined strategies are required, one to achieve existence, the other to preserve it. The aim of the first is the enhancement of life, that is, creating or strengthening ecologically survivable organisms; the aim of the second is the preservation of life, that is, avoiding events that might terminate it.

Existence reflects a to-be or not-to-be issue. In the inorganic world, "to be" is essentially a matter of possessing qualities that distinguish a phenomenon from its surrounding field, that is, not being in a state of entropy. Among organic beings, to be is a matter of possessing the properties of life as well as being located in ecosystems that facilitate the enhancement and preservation of that life. In the phenomenological or experiential world of sentient organisms, events that extend life and preserve it

correspond largely to metaphorical terms such as pleasure and pain, that is, recognizing and pursuing positive sensations and emotions, on the one hand, and recognizing and eschewing negative sensations and emotions, on the other. An interweaving and shifting balance between the two extremes that comprise the pain-pleasure bipolarity typifies normality. Both of the following criteria should be met in varying degrees as life circumstances require. In essence, a synchronous and coordinated personal style would have developed to answer the question of whether the person should focus on experiencing only the pleasures of life versus concentrating his or her efforts on avoiding its pains.

Life Enhancement: Seeking Rewarding Experiences. At one end of the "existence polarity" are attitudes and behaviors designed to foster and enrich life, to generate joy, pleasure, contentment, fulfillment, and thereby strengthen the capacity of the individual to remain vital and competent physically and psychically. This polarity asserts that existence/survival calls for more than life preservation alone; beyond pain avoidance is pleasure enhancement.

A note or two should be recorded on the pathological consequences of a failure to attend to a polarity. These are seen most clearly in the personality disorders labeled schizoid and avoidant. In the former, there is a marked hedonic deficiency, stemming either from an inherent deficit in affective substrates or the failure of stimulative experience to develop either or both attachment behaviors or affective capacity (Millon 1981). Among those designated avoidant personalities, constitutional sensitivities or abusive life experiences have led to an intense attentional sensitivity to psychic pain and a consequent distrust in either the genuineness or durability of the pleasures, such that these individuals can no longer permit themselves to experience them. Both of these personalities tend to be withdrawn and isolated, joyless and grim, neither seeking nor sharing in the rewards of life.

Life Preservation: Avoiding Danger and Threat. One might assume that a criterion based on the avoidance of psychic or physical pain would be sufficiently self-evident not to require specification. As is well known, debates have arisen in the literature as to whether mental health/normality reflects the absence of mental disorder, being merely the reverse side of the mental illness or abnormality coin. That there is a relationship between health and disease cannot be questioned; the two are intimately connected, conceptually and physically. On the other hand, to define health solely as the absence of disorder will not suffice. As a single criterion among several, however, features of behavior and experience that signify both the lack of (e.g., anxiety, depression) and an aversion to (e.g., threats to safety and security) pain in its many and diverse forms provide a necessary foundation on which other, more positively constructed criteria may rest. Substantively, positive normality must comprise elements beyond mere nonnormality or abnormality. And despite the complexities and inconsistencies of personality, from a definitional point of view normality does preclude nonnormality.

It may be of interest to record some of the psychic pathologies of personality that can be traced to aberrations in meeting this second polarity. For example, among those termed avoidant personalities (Millon 1969, 1981), we see an excessive preoccupation with threats to one's psychic security, an expectation of and hyperalertness to the signs of potential rejection that lead these persons to disengage from everyday relationships and pleasures. At the other extreme of the polarity, we see a risk-taking attitude, a proclivity to chance hazards and to endanger one's life and liberty, a behavioral pattern characteristic of those we label antisocial personalities. Here there is little of the caution and prudence expected in the normal polarity range of avoiding danger and threat; rather, we observe its opposite, a rash willingness to put one's safety in jeopardy, to play with fire and throw caution to the wind.

Modes of Adaptation

For an organism to maintain its unique structure, differentiated from the larger ecosystem of which it is a part, to be sustained as a discrete entity among other phenomena that compose its environmental field, requires good fortune and the presence of effective modes of functioning.

Ecological Accommodation and Ecological Modification: The Passive-Active Polarity.   This evolutionary principle relates to what we have termed the modes of adaptation; it is also framed as a two-part polarity. The first may best be characterized as the mode of ecological accommodation, signifying inclinations to passively "fit in," to locate and remain securely anchored in a niche, subject to the vagaries and unpredictabilities of the environment, all acceded to with one crucial proviso: that the elements making up the surroundings will furnish

both the nourishment and the protection needed to sustain existence. Though based on a somewhat simplistic bifurcation among adaptive strategies, this passive and accommodating mode is one of the two fundamental methods that living organisms have evolved as a means of survival. It represents the core process employed in the evolution of what has come to be designated as the plant kingdom, a stationary, rooted, yet essentially pliant and dependent survival mode. By contrast, the second of the two major modes of adaptation is seen in the lifestyle of the animal kingdom. Here we observe a primary inclination toward ecological modification, a tendency to change or rearrange the elements constituting the larger milieu, to intrude on otherwise quiescent settings, a versatility in shifting from one niche to another as unpredictability arises, a mobile and interventional mode that actively stirs, maneuvers, yields, and, at the human level, substantially transforms the environment to meet its own survival aims. The active-passive polarity means that the vast range of behaviors engaged in by humans may fundamentally be grouped in terms of whether initiative is taken in altering and shaping life's events or whether behaviors are reactive to and accommodate those events.

"Normal" or optimal functioning, at least among humans, appears to call for a flexible balance that interweaves both polar extremes. In the first evolutionary stage, that relating to existence, behaviors encouraging both life enhancement (pleasure) and life preservation (pain avoidance) are likely to be more successful in achieving survival than actions limited to one or the other alone. Similarly, regarding adaptation, modes of functioning that exhibit both ecological accommodation and ecological modification are likely to be more successful than either by itself.

As with the polarity pair representing the aims of existence, a balance should be achieved between the two elements comprising modes of adaptation, those related to ecological accommodation and ecological modification, or what I have termed in the biosocial-learning model as the passive-active polarity. Normality calls for a synchronous and coordinated personal style that weaves a balanced answer to the question of whether one should accept what the fates have brought forth or take the initiative in altering the circumstances of one's life.

Ecological Accommodation: Abiding Hospitable Realities.   On first reflection, it would seem to be less than optimal to submit meekly to what life

presents, to adjust obligingly to one's destiny. As described earlier, however, the evolution of plants is essentially grounded (no pun intended) in environmental accommodation, in an adaptive acquiescence to the ecosystem. Crucial to this adaptive course, however, is the capacity of these surroundings to provide the nourishment and protection requisite to the thriving of a species.

To the extent that the events of life have been and continue to be caring and giving, is it not perhaps wisest, from an evolutionary perspective, to accept this good fortune and "let matters be"? This accommodating or passive life philosophy has worked extremely well in sustaining and fostering those complex organisms that make up the plant kingdom. Hence passivity, the yielding to environmental forces, may be in itself not only unproblematic but, where events and circumstances provide the pleasures of life and protect against their pains, positively adaptive and constructive.

An example of the inability to leave things as they are is seen in what the DSM terms the histrionic personality disorder. The persistent and unrelenting manipulation of events by persons with this disorder is designed to maximize the receipt of attention and favors as well as to avoid social disinterest and disapproval. They show an insatiable if not indiscriminate search for stimulation and approval. Their clever and often artful social behaviors may give the appearance of an inner confidence and self-assurance; but beneath this guise lies a fear that a failure on their part to ensure the receipt of attention will, in short order, result in indifference or rejection, and hence their desperate need for reassurance and repeated signs of approval. Tribute and affection must constantly be replenished and are sought from every interpersonal source. As they are quickly bored and sated, they keep stirring up things, becoming enthusiastic about one activity and then another. There is a restless stimulus-seeking quality in which they cannot leave well enough alone.

At the other end of the polarity are personality disorders that exhibit an excess of passivity, failing thereby to give direction to their own lives. Several Axis II disorders demonstrate this passive style, although their passivity derives from and is expressed in appreciably different ways. Dependents typically are average on the pleasure/pain polarity. Passivity for them stems from deficits in self-confidence and competence, leading to deficits in initiative and autonomous skills as well as a tendency to wait passively while others assume leadership and guide them. Passivity among obsessive-compulsive personalities stems from their fear of acting independently, owing to intrapsychic resolutions they have made to quell hidden thoughts and emotions generated by their intense self-other ambivalence. Dreading the possibility of making mistakes or engaging in disapproved behaviors, they became indecisive, immobilized, restrained, and passive. High on pain and low on both pleasure and self, self-defeating personalities operate on the assumption that they dare not expect nor deserve to have life go their way; giving up any efforts to achieve a life that accords with their true desires, they passively submit to others' wishes, acquiescently accepting their fate. Finally, narcissists, especially high on self and low on others, benignly assume that "good things" will come their way with little or no effort on their part; this passive exploitation of others is a consequence of the unexplored confidence that underlies their self-centered presumptions.

Ecological Modification: Mastering One's Environment. The active end of the bipolarity signifies the taking of initiative in altering and shaping life's events. As stated previously, such persons are best characterized by their alertness, vigilance, liveliness, vigor, and forcefulness, their stimulus-seeking energy and drive. Others exhibiting this tendency to master their environment become problematic owing to the fact that it is not balanced or oriented in psychologically healthful ways. This may be seen in the antisocial personality who is impulsive, precipitate, excitable, rash, and hasty, seeking to elicit pleasures and rewards in a less than culturally acceptable manner. Although specific expressions and goals vary and change from time to time, actively aroused individuals will intrude on passing events and energetically and busily modify the circumstances of their environment.

Strategies of Replication

If an organism merely duplicates itself prior to death, then its replica is "doomed" to repeat the same fate it suffered. However, if new potentials for extending existence can be fashioned by chance or routine events, then the possibility of achieving a different and conceivably superior outcome may be increased. And it is this co-occurrence of random and recombinant processes that leads to the prolongation of a species' existence. This third hallmark of evolution's procession also undergirds another of nature's fundamental polarities, that between self and other.

Reproductive Individuation and Reproductive Nurturance: The Self-Other Polarity. Recombinant replication, with its consequential benefits of selective diversification, requires the partnership of two parents, each contributing its genetic resources in a distinctive and species-characteristic manner. Similarly, the attention and care given the offspring of a species' matings is also distinctive. Worthy of note is the difference between the mating parents in the degree to which they protect and nourish their joint offspring. Although the investment of energy devoted to upbringing is balanced and complementary, rarely is it identical or even comparable in either devotion or determination. This disparity in reproductive investment strategies, especially evident among animal species (insects, reptiles, birds, mammals), underlies the evolution of the male and female genders, the foundation for the third cardinal polarity we propose to account for evolution's procession.

Of special interest is the extreme diversity among *and* within species in the number of offspring spawned and the consequent nurturing and protective investment the parents make in the survival of their progeny. Designated the *r*-strategy and *K*-strategy in population biology, the former represents a pattern of propagating a vast number of offspring but exhibiting minimal attention to their survival; the latter is typified by the production of few progeny followed by considerable effort to assure their survival.

Not only do species differ in where they fall on the *r*- to *K*-strategy continuum, but *within* most animal species an important distinction may be drawn between male and female genders. This latter differentiation undergirds what has been termed the self-versus other-oriented polarity. Humans can be both self-actualizing and other-encouraging, although most persons are likely to lean toward one or the other side. A balance that coordinates the two provides a satisfactory answer to the question of whether one should be devoted to the support and welfare of others or fashion one's life in accord with one's own needs and desires.

Reproductive Individuation: Actualizing Self. The converse of reproductive nurturance is not reproductive propagation but rather the lack of reproductive nurturance. Thus, to fail to love others constructively does not assure the actualization of one's potentials. Both may and should exist in normal/healthy individuals.

Carl Jung's (1961) concept of individuation shares important features with that of actualization in that any deterrent to becoming the individual one may have become would be detrimental to life. Any imposed "collective standard is a serious check to individuality," injurious to the vitality of the person, a form of "artificial stunting." Where do we see failures in the achievement of self-actualization, a giving up of self to gain the approbation of others? One personality disorder may be drawn upon to illustrate forms of self-denial.

Those with dependent personalities have learned that those feelings associated with pleasure or the avoidance of pain—feeling good, secure, confident, and so on—are provided almost exclusively in their relationship with others. Behaviorally, these persons learn early that they themselves do not readily achieve rewarding experiences; the experiences are secured better by leaning on others. They learn not only to turn to others as their source of nurturance and security but to wait passively for others to take the initiative in providing safety and sustenance. Clinically, most are characterized as searching for relationships in which others will reliably furnish affection, protection, and leadership. Lacking both initiative and autonomy, they assume a dependent role in interpersonal relations, accepting what kindness and support they may find and willingly submitting to the wishes of others in order to maintain nurturance and security.

Reproductive Nurturance: Constructively Loving Others. As described earlier, recombinant replication achieved by sexual mating entails a balanced though asymmetric parental investment in both the genesis and nurturance of offspring.

Before we turn to some of the indexes and views of the self-other polarity, let us be mindful that these conceptually derived extremes do not evince themselves in sharp and distinct gender differences. Such proclivities are matters of degree, not absolutes, owing not only to the consequences of recombinant "shuffling" and gene "crossing over" but to the influential effects of cultural values and social learning. Consequently, most "normal" individuals exhibit intermediate characteristics on this as well as on the other two polarity sets.

The pathological consequences of a failure to embrace the polarity criterion of "others" are seen most clearly in the personality disorders termed antisocial and narcissistic. Both personalities exhibit an imbalance in their replication strategy; in this case, however, there is a primary reliance on self rather than others. They have learned that reproductive success as well as maximum pleasure and minimum pain is achieved by turning exclusively to themselves. The tendency to focus on self follows two major lines of development.

In the narcissistic personality, development reflects the acquisition of a self-image of superior worth, learned largely in response to admiring and doting parents. Providing self-rewards is highly gratifying if one values oneself or possesses either a real or inflated sense of self-worth. Displaying manifest confidence, arrogance, and an exploitative egocentricity in social contexts, this self-orientation has been termed the passive-independent style in the theory, as the individual already has all that is important—him- or herself. The person then blithely assumes that others will recognize his or her specialness.

Those whom the theory characterizes as exhibiting the active-independent orientation resemble the outlook, temperament, and socially unacceptable behaviors of the DSM Antisocial personality disorder. They act to counter the expectation of pain at the hand of others by actively engaging in duplicitous or illegal behaviors in which they seek to exploit others for self-gain. Skeptical regarding the motives of others, they desire autonomy and wish revenge for what are felt as past injustices. Many are irresponsible and impulsive, actions they see as justified because they judge others to be unreliable and disloyal. Insensitivity and ruthlessness with others are the primary means they have learned to head off abuse and victimization.

Processes of Abstraction

The fourth level of analysis pertains to the capacity to symbolize one's world, both internal and external. We will postpone discussing the integrative elements involved in this evolutionary stage until Chapter 3, when we elaborate the features of neuropsychological development.

In the following chapters, we will develop many of the themes generated by the evolutionary theory, especially as they serve deductively to generate each of the DSM and ICD personality disorders. These deductions will lead to the formation of the *Personality Prototypes* that comprise clinical Chapters 6 through 20 of this book. Specifically, we will argue that *deficiencies, imbalances, conflicts,* and *structural defects* that arise in these polarities are

the most fruitful basis for deriving personality prototypes. Also to be described in these chapters are several *Subtypes* of the core prototype. Subtypes are variations in the manner in which the theoretically derived prototypes are reshaped and manifested by virtue of the special circumstances of personal upbringing and culture.

Although it is our belief that the evolutionary principles elaborated in the preceding paragraphs represent the most fundamental elements of nature's progressions, including those that manifest themselves in human functioning, we also believe that these conceptions do not invalidate other theoretical models. As we see it, there is no inherent inconsistency between our formulations and those of other theorists (neurobiological, behavioral, etc.). In fact, they should parallel one another; however, we believe that all other models should be superimposed or mapped onto the evolutionary framework. This view may be seen by some as arrogant and presumptuous in that it asserts that other models are composed essentially of biological mechanisms (neurohormonal substrates) or psychological expressions (interpersonal behavior) of more latent and fundamental evolutionary processes; we ask the reader to forego conclusions until completing the text.

We will conclude this chapter with reference to official manuals, initiating the presentation with the DSM-III, owing to its significance as a major breakthrough in our thinking about these disorders.

OFFICIAL DESCRIPTIVE MANUALS

The Task Force assigned to develop the DSM-III acknowledged that the personality disorders represented syndromes that were "fuzzy at the edges" (Task Force, 1976). On the one hand, these disorders shade imperceptibly into "normal problems of everyday life"; and, on the other, they have few clear and distinguishing symptoms to serve as identifying markers. Nevertheless, the Task Force recognized that personality disorders possess features that are not shared with other syndromes, qualities noted more by the pervasiveness and duration of their expression than by their symptomatological distinctiveness. It was recognized, further, that personality "traits" had to be differentiated from personality "disorders." Although the behaviors that signify traits often underlie and may be difficult to discriminate from those constituting disorders, they can be distinguished on two grounds: Disorders are associated with subjective feelings of distress and/or significantly impaired social functioning.

This text is arranged in accord with DSM-III, DSM-III-R, and DSM-IV categories for several reasons other than the fact that they have been the standard and official schemas. Despite the many compromises their products represent, the end results achieved are a reasonable reflection of the state of the art as judged by a well-respected and highly competent committee of practicing clinicians and academic researchers. Moreover, the syndromes included in the final drafts had been extensively pretested with large and representative samples of mental health professionals. Earlier drafts were revised in light of these studies, and several categories were proposed anew while others were dropped.

A major goal of the DSM-III committee was to include as many clinically useful personality syndromes as justified. Despite objections from certain quarters, a decision was made to incorporate categories that had not been fully validated by systematic research but nevertheless had much to commend them in terms of their everyday clinical applicability. Failure to include these tentative, but clinically useful, categories would have deprived the profession of an opportunity to encourage the systematic research necessary to determine whether these syndromes hold up under careful clinical and research scrutiny.

The spelling out of formal *diagnostic criteria* was notably beneficial to the practitioner in that it served to highlight the specific inclusion and exclusion components of a diagnostic decision. It is this very precision in articulating specific and uniform rules of definition, originally and significantly termed "operational criteria," that made the DSM-III so serviceable and potentially fruitful also as a research tool. Not only did the criteria delineate the components that would enable homogeneous group assignments, but its application as a standard national (and, it is hoped, international) gauge would ensure at least a modicum of reliability and comparability among studies undertaken at diverse research settings.

It is reasonable to assume that greater reliability and research comparability flow from the use of standard diagnostic criteria, but it should be recorded that increased reliability is no assurance of increased validity and that the criteria offered *no more than a promise* at that time.

At best, then, the diagnostic criteria of the DSM-III represented a significant *conceptual* step

toward a future goal when clinical characteristics of appropriate specificity and breadth would provide both reliable and valid indexes for identifying the major syndromal prototypes. Although this chapter has neither the space nor is the setting within which to elaborate the theme, it should be said that the categorical syndromes of the DSM-III were conceptual prototypes and not tangible entities.

The formal adoption of the *multiaxial schema* in the DSM-III signified a reformulation of the task of psychodiagnoses that approached the magnitude described by Kuhn (1962) as a paradigm shift. It represented a distinct turn from the traditional medical disease model where the clinician's job was to disentangle and clear away "distracting" symptoms and signs so as to pinpoint the underlying or "true" psychophysiological state. By contrast, the multiaxial assessment model not only recognized that distracting features such as course, etiology, social functioning, and personality traits were aspects worthy of attention, but recorded each of them on its own representative axis as part of an integrative complex of elements that, only in their entirety, were the pathological state.

Henceforth, the official classification directed the clinician to address, not just the specific symptoms and signs which defined the disease entity, but an entire panorama of contextual dimensions, notably the person's overall style of psychological functioning, the qualities of his or her current situational environment, and his or her strengths and potentials for constructive and healthy coping.

It was not a failure to acknowledge axes beyond the five listed in the DSM-III that accounted for their absence. For example, "cause" and "severity" were debated extensively in Task Force discussions. In both cases, it was concluded that they lacked universal applicability and, hence, should be coded selectively in syndromal categories where they would provide useful information. Unfortunately, the number of coded digits available for purposes such as these proved to be appreciably less than originally anticipated. Hence, severity, though originally scheduled for use in several diagnostic classes, failed to survive in any category. The fate of course as an informational code was only slightly less sullied; it survived as a recorded datum in a few syndromal categories, notably as the fifth digit code in both schizophrenic and substance abuse groups.

Considerable attention was given also to two other potentially quite useful informational axes: "etiology" and "treatment response." Although insufficient time was available for an empirical field trial or even a systematic review, the notion of devising an etiologic axis that would permit clinicians to formulate their thoughts on both the origins and development of a disorder was an appealing one to several Task Force members.

The most important fact concerning the DSM-III personality disorders was their partition from the main body of clinical syndromes and their placement in a separate axis. Clinicians in the past were often faced with the task of deciding whether a patient was best diagnosed as possessing a personality or a symptom syndrome; that choice is no longer necessary. Henceforth, clinicians may record not only the current clinical picture, but also those characteristics that typify the individual's behavior over extended periods, both prior to and concurrent with the present complaint. The new multiaxial format enabled practitioners to place the clinical syndromes of Axis I within the context of the individual's lifelong and pervasive style of functioning, recorded as Axis II.

Although an early aspiration of the committee was the differentiation of personality types along the dimension of severity, criteria for such distinctions were never developed. Rather than drawing severity discriminations, as proposed by both Kernberg (1967, 1970) and Millon (1969), associates of the Task Force grouped the personality syndromes into three symptomatological clusters. The first includes the paranoid, schizoid, and schizotypal disorders, unified as a group in that their behaviors appear odd and eccentric. The second cluster subsumes the histrionic, narcissistic, antisocial, and borderline disorders, grouped together on the basis of their tendency to behave dramatically, emotionally, or erratically. The third cluster groups the avoidant, dependent, compulsive, and passive-aggressive personalities on the grounds that these types often appear anxious or fearful. A memo distributed by the author for discussion at the DSM-III Task Force meeting of June 1978 addressed these recommended clusters as follows:

I never quite understood the importance of those dimensions that led us to cluster personality disorders in the manner described. Any number of different dimensions could have been selected to group the eleven personality disorders in any of an almost infinite arrangement of sets or combinations. Why the specific one suggested in the text was selected out of these is not clear to me. Does it have some prognostic significance, some etiological import, logic in terms of a deductive theoretical

model? If I were to develop a cluster or factorial framework for the personality disorders I am sure I would come up with a different schema than the one suggested. The characteristics specified are clear enough, but of what value is it to know that three are "eccentric," that four are "emotional," and that four appear "anxious"?

My own preference was either to drop the grouping entirely and list them alphabetically or to group them in terms of their known prevalence or potential severity. The likely severity of pathology, such as the probability to which these syndromes succumb to severe versus mild disorders, struck me as a useful distinction if we were to make any one at all among these disorders. If we looked through our DSM-III list we might have noted that disorders such as paranoid, schizotypal and borderline, and possibly schizoid and avoidant, were likely to exhibit a greater propensity to severe pathology than the others. Conversely, types such as the histrionic, narcissistic, antisocial, dependent and compulsive, and perhaps passive-aggressive, tend to stabilize at the mild-to-moderate level of severity.

If the DSM-III had followed the preceding suggestion, we would have had a logical distinction of some clinical import among the categories. It would be at least in line with earlier plans to note the dimension of severity with each personality disorder.

The DSM-III-R introduced a series of modest criterion changes (e.g., histrionic, avoidant, and schizoid disorders) as well as adding to the Appendix two highly controversial personality syndromes, the Self-Defeating (Nee Masochistic), and the Sadistic; as will be noted, these latter two disorders were dropped in the DSM-IV. Other changes of note involved the reformulation of all criteria sets into a uniform polythetic format. This resulted in an increased base rate and comorbidity among the various disorders, as well as evoking concern regarding the disruption of ongoing studies.

DSM-IV was introduced with the thought that a firmer empirical base could be established to justify the characterizations and diagnostic criteria of the disorders it subsumed. Insofar as the personality disorders were concerned, discussions occurred regarding several major issues. At the most general level, questions were raised regarding the logic of the cluster system (eccentric, dramatic, and anxious) that served as a framework for organizing these disorders. Although evidence supporting this tripartite division was equivocal, and its conceptual grounding subject to numerous criticisms, it continued as a general schema for DSM-IV.

Proposals were made for the introduction of a dimensional system to supplant or supplement the categorical model used in the DSM. Several alternative schemas were evaluated but none achieved sufficient consensus. Specific modifications regarding the DSM-III-R criteria were introduced on the basis of the Axis II committee's review of numerous published and unpublished studies concerning the sensitivity, specificity, positive predictive power, and negative predictive power rates for the criteria sets. Also considered was the contribution of these criteria to the overlap or comorbidity among the personality disorders. Several criterion items were deleted as a consequence of these empirical studies.

Major reviews were carried out and field trials conducted to examine the characteristics of the antisocial personality disorder and resulted in the elimination of several specific behavioral indicators and the introduction of trait characterizations. On the basis of extensive literature reviews this past decade, there was an increased awareness of the importance of impulse regulation as a major component of the borderline personality disorder. An additional criterion was introduced to the borderline criteria list to reflect the frequency with which they evince transient, stress-related dissociative symptoms or paranoid ideation.

A notable modification occurred with the decision to place the passive-aggressive personality disorder in the DSM-IV Appendix. Discontent concerning the narrow characterization in prior manuals, its formulation in situation-specific terms, as well as its reflecting no more than a single symptom led the committee to recast their conception of the disorder as a "negativistic personality disorder." More broadly conceived than heretofore, the changes introduced were of sufficient magnitude to justify placement in the Appendix, where its new definition and criteria could be evaluated in future work.

Joining the new passive-aggressive/negativistic formulation in the Appendix was the new Depressive personality disorder. This latter decision followed considerable debate concerning distinctions between it and similar formulations in Axis I (e.g., dysthymia).

Finally, and as noted previously, the self-defeating and sadistic personalities were dropped from the manual owing, in our judgment, more to political considerations than to substantive clinical

ones. Hence, our decision in this text to include both as major forms of personality disturbance.

CLASSIFYING PERSONALITY SEVERITY

In presenting the syndromes of personality disorder in the following chapters, this text sequences them in terms of our judgment of their level of severity. Before doing so, a question must be asked: How shall severity levels be gauged; that is, what criteria should be employed to determine whether one personality disorder is typically more severe than another?

Two theoretically derived classification systems have given special attention prior to the DSM proposals concerning criteria that would differentiate personality disorders along the dimension of severity, those of Kernberg (1967, 1970) and of Millon (1969). Direct comparison is not feasible since the character types presented by Kernberg did not correspond to the DSM-III personality disorders. Nevertheless, it will be useful to put aside DSM-III comparability and consider the conceptual distinctions that differentiated Kernberg's views from those of Millon.

As noted earlier, Kernberg groups personality disorders into higher, intermediate, and lower levels of character pathology. Millon also categorized his types into several subsets, including those of mild, moderate, and marked severity. The major distinction between Kernberg and Millon was not found in the clinical signs they included to gauge severity but rather in the ones they chose to emphasize. For Kernberg, primary attention was given to the *internal* structural characteristics of the personality, whereas for Millon the *external* social system and interpersonal dynamics were given a status equal that of internal organization.

Kernberg focused on "nonspecific manifestations of ego weakness," as illustrated in shifts toward primary process thinking, defensive operations characterized as "splitting," increasingly primitive idealizations, and early forms of projection and omnipotence. Though differences do exist, Millon and Kernberg identified the following similar features: loss of impulse control that disturbed psychological cohesion, rigid versus diffused ego functions, adaptive inflexibility, ambivalent or conflict-ridden defenses, blurrings of self and nonself, and so on. Millon went beyond these, however, by stressing a systems perspective that interprets the internal structure as being functional or dysfunctional depending on its efficacy and stability within the context of interpersonal, familial, and other social dynamics. Thus, he spoke additionally of such severity criteria as deficits in social competence, checkered personal relationships, digressions from early aspirations, and repetitive interpersonal quandaries and disappointments. From this view, severity was conceived as a person-field interaction that includes not only intrapsychic dynamics but interpersonal dynamics as well. Although Kernberg (1975) recognized the importance of internalized object relations, Millon assigned them a major role by stressing both internalized past and contemporary real social relationships. In this way, the boundaries of both structure and dynamics were expanded such that internal structural features were placed within a context or system of external social dynamics.

A positive consequence of broadening the criteria of severity was that personality pathology no longer needed to be traced exclusively to intrapsychic origins in conflict and defense. By enlarging our vista so as to include interpersonal efficacy within a social context, the reference base for conceptualizing disordered personality has been expanded. A shift from the view that all pathogenic sources derive from internal conflicts was consistent with Fenichel's notion of sublimation character types and reinforced the ego analysts' assertion of conflict-free spheres of development and learning. No longer restricted by the limiting intrapsychic outlook, personality disorders could now be conceived as any behavior pattern that was consistently inappropriate, maladaptive, or deficient in the social and familial system within which the individual operated. And, in accord with this broader systems perspective, several personality syndromes described in Millon (1969) and formulated for the DSM-III were recognized as having developed "conflict free"—They could be products of inadequate or misguided learning; others were conceived more traditionally as primarily "reactive"—they were consequences of conflict resolutions. For example, some dependent personalities unfold in large measure as a result of simple parental overprotection and insufficiently learned autonomous behaviors, and not from instinctual conflicts and regressive adaptations.

The logic for broadening the criteria of severity to include the interplay of both individual and social systems seems especially appropriate when considering personality syndromes. Not only do personality traits express themselves primarily within group and familial environments, but the patient's style of communication, interpersonal competency, and social skill will, in great measure, elicit reactions that feed back to shape the future course of whatever impairments the person may already have. Thus, the behavior and attitudes that individuals exhibit with others will evoke reciprocal reactions that influence whether their problems will improve, stabilize, or intensify. Internal organization or structure is significant, but the character or style of relating interpersonally may have as much to do with whether the sequence of social dynamics will prove rewarding or destructive. It is not only the structural ego capacity, therefore, but also the particular features of social and familial behavior that will dispose the patient to relate to others in an increasingly adaptive or maladaptive manner.

Utilizing a systems perspective that includes the interplay of both internal and external dynamics has led us to group the 14 personality disorders listed in the DSM-III, DSM-III-R, and DSM-IV into several broad categories for the present text.

The first group has been termed "pleasure-deficient" styles; it includes what we have labeled the detached types, which now subsumes the schizoid, avoidant, and depressive personalities in the DSM-IV. These three deficient styles are judged at a mid- to moderate-level of severity because of their characteristic isolation or estrangement from external support systems. As a consequence, they are likely to have few subliminatory channels and fewer still interpersonal sources of nurturance and stability, the lack of which will dispose them to increasing social isolation, autistic preoccupation, or depressive regressions.

The second grouping includes the dependent, histrionic, narcissistic, and antisocial personality disorders, usually mild in severity level. These four personality patterns are conceptualized as being "interpersonally-imbalanced" styles according to the theoretical model; they are *either* primarily oriented to relationships with others, or primarily toward the fulfillment of their self-needs. We speak of this imbalanced grouping as *either* dependent or independent in its style of interpersonal functioning. The intrapsychic structures of these personalities enable them to conceive themselves and to deal with others in a relatively coherent, "nonsplit," or nonconflictful manner that is consistent and focused rather than diffused or divided. Moreover, because the needs and traits that underlie their personality style dispose them either to seek out others consistently, or to orient their actions in their own favor consistently, they are able to find a stable niche in their interpersonal environment, while maintaining psychic cohesion.

The third group includes what we are terming "intrapsychically-conflicted" styles, namely, the sadistic (aggressive), obsessive-compulsive, negativistic (passive-aggressive), and masochistic (self-defeating) personality disorders. These four conflicted types may reflect a somewhat more severe level of functioning than the second group for several reasons. Each possesses a split within both its interpersonal relations and intrapsychic structures; in other words, they are unable to maintain a coherent or consistent direction by which to orient both their personal relationships and their defensive operations. They are in conflict, split between assuming either an independent or dependent stance for one pair (obsessive-compulsive, negativistic/passive-aggressive) or, for the second, experience a marked discordance or reversal between their pain and pleasure polarities (sadistic/aggressive and masochistic/self-defeating). As a consequence, all four disorders regularly undo or reverse their interpersonal behaviors and frequently feel intrapsychically divided.

The fourth set, reflecting moderately severe levels of personality functioning, is termed "structurally-defective"; it includes the DSM-IV schizotypal, borderline, and paranoid disorders. All three personalities are seen as socially incompetent, difficult to relate to, and often isolated, hostile, or confused; hence, they are not likely to elicit the interpersonal support that might bolster their flagging defenses and orient them to a more effective and satisfying lifestyle. Moreover, a clear breakdown in the cohesion of personality organization is seen in both schizotypal and borderline disorders. The converse is evident in the paranoid, where there is an overly rigid and narrow focus to the personality structure. In the former pair, there has been a dissolution or diffusion of ego capacities; in the latter, the paranoid pattern, there is an inelasticity and constriction of personality, giving rise to a fragility and inadaptability of functions.

A final group of personality disorders, those of marked severity which we have termed "decompensated structures," will close the book's clinical presentations. Here, we will address patients who give evidence of a relatively permanent state of psychic disintegration in which all psychological functions have been seriously compromised.

But before proceeding to the many personality disorders to be detailed in this text, let us first discuss the general principles and processes involved in their development. For that we turn next to Chapter 3.

CHAPTER 3

Personality Development: Origins, Sequences, and Outcomes

Tracing the developmental background of psycho-pathology is one of the most difficult but rewarding phases in the study of medical and psychological science. This study of causation has been termed *etiology* by some, and *developmental pathogenesis* by others. It attempts to establish the relative importance of a number of determinants of pathology and seeks to demonstrate how overtly unrelated determinants interconnect to produce a clinical picture. Methods such as laboratory tests, case histories, clinical observation, and experimental research are combined in an effort to unravel this intricate developmental sequence.

We will first consider briefly the logic, terminology, and problems associated with the study of developmental causes, and will argue that alternative approaches to etiology are reconcilable, necessary, and fruitful.

LOGIC AND TERMINOLOGY OF DEVELOPMENTAL CAUSAL ANALYSIS

Certain events typically precede others in time, and it is often assumed that the second set of events must be an inevitable consequence of the first. Associations of this kind are spoken of as *causal,* that is, earlier events are viewed as the "cause" of later events. It should be noted, however, that causality, as it might be used in the sentence "A is the cause of B," implies nothing more than a description of an empirically observed association between A and B in which A has always preceded B in time.

Philosophers point out that there is no *logical* reason to assume that time sequence relationships which have been demonstrated in the past will, perforce, continue in the future. Naturally, the longer and more consistent an association has been in the past, the stronger will be our confidence in predicting its continuance in the future. But this belief

rests on verified empirical observations rather than logical processes of deduction. If we keep this restricted meaning of causality clearly in mind, we can proceed to use the term.

Most people have been conditioned to think of causality in a simple format in which a single event, known as the cause, results in a single effect. Scientists have learned, however, that particular end results usually arise from the interaction of a large number of causes. Furthermore, it is not uncommon for a single cause to play a part in a variety of end results. Each of these individual end results may set off an independent chain of events that will progress through different intricate sequences.

The study of developmental etiology is complicated further by the fact that a particular end result, such as a physical disease, may be produced by any one of a number of different and, on occasion, even mutually exclusive causal sequences (e.g., one can get a cold from a chill or a virus). It should be obvious from the foregoing that causation in psychopathology is not a simple matter of a single cause leading to a single effect. Disentangling the varied and intricate pathways to pathology is a difficult task indeed.

In philosophy, causes are frequently divided into three classes: necessary, sufficient, and contributory.

A *necessary* cause is an event that *must* precede another event for it to occur. For example, certain theorists believe that individuals who do not possess a particular genetic defect will not become schizophrenic; they believe further that this inherent defect must be supplemented, however, by certain types of detrimental experiences before the schizophrenic pattern will emerge. In this theory, the genetic defect is viewed as a necessary but not a sufficient cause of the pathology.

A *sufficient* condition is one that is adequate *in itself* to cause pathology; no other factor need be associated with it. However, a sufficient condition is neither a necessary nor an exclusive cause of a particular disorder. For example, a neurosyphilitic infection may be sufficient in itself to produce certain forms of psychopathology, but many other causes can result in these disorders as well.

Contributory causes are factors that increase the probability that a disorder will occur, but are neither necessary nor sufficient to do so. These conditions, such as economic deprivation or racial conflict, add to a welter of other factors that, when taken together, shape the course of pathology. Contributory causes usually influence the form in which the pathology is expressed, and play relatively limited roles as primary determinants.

In psychopathology, causes are divided traditionally into predisposing and precipitating factors.

Predisposing factors are contributory conditions that usually are neither necessary nor sufficient to bring about the disorder but that serve as a foundation for its development. They exert an influence over a relatively long time span and set the stage for the emergence of the pathology. Factors such as heredity, socioeconomic status, family atmosphere, and habits learned in response to early traumatic experiences are illustrations of these predispositions.

No hard-and-fast line can be drawn between predisposing and precipitating causes, but a useful distinction may be made between them. Precipitating factors refer to clearly demarcated events that occur shortly before the onset of the manifest pathology. These factors either bring to the surface or hasten the emergence of a pathological disposition; that is, they evoke or trigger the expression of established, but hidden, dispositional factors. The death of a loved one, a severe physical ailment, the breakup of an engagement and so on, illustrate these precipitants.

A few words of a more-or-less philosophic nature are in order concerning the concept of etiology itself; as in other matters that call for an incisive explication of psychopathological constructs, the reader is directed to the writings of Meehl (1972, 1977). In these essays, it is made abundantly clear that the concept of etiology itself is a "fuzzy notion" that not only requires the careful separation of constituent empirical elements, but calls for differentiating its diverse conceptual meanings, ranging from "strong" influences that are both causally necessary and/or sufficient, through progressively weaker levels of specificity, in which causal factors exert consistent, though quantitatively marginal differences to those that are merely coincidental or situationally circumstantial.

The premise that early experience plays a central role in shaping personality attributes is shared by numerous theorists. To say the preceding, however, is not to agree as to which specific factors during these developing years are critical in generating particular attributes, nor is it to agree that known formative influences are either necessary or sufficient. Analytic theorists almost invariably direct their etiologic attentions to the realm of early childhood experience. Unfortunately, they differ vigorously among themselves (e.g., Kernberg, Kohut, Mahler/Masterson, Erikson) as to which aspects of nascent life are crucial to development.

To be more concrete, there is reason to ask whether etiologic analysis is even possible in psychopathology in light of the complex and variable character of developmental influences. Can this most fundamental of scientific activities be achieved with an interactive and sequential chain of "causes" comprising inherently inexact data of a highly probabilistic nature in which even the slightest variation in context or antecedent condition, often of a minor or random character, produces highly divergent outcomes? Because this "looseness" in the causal network of variables is unavoidable, are there any grounds for believing that such endeavors could prove more than illusory? Further, will the careful study of individuals reveal repetitive patterns of symptomatic congruence, no less consistency among the origins of such diverse clinical attributes as overt behavior, intrapsychic functioning, and biophysical disposition? And will etiologic commonalities and syndromal coherence prove to be valid phenomena, that is, not merely imposed on observed data by virtue of clinical expectation or theoretical bias (Millon, 1986a, 1986b, 1987a)?

Among other concerns is that the "hard data," the unequivocal evidence from well-designed and well-executed research, are sorely lacking. Consistent findings on causal factors for specific clinical entities would be extremely useful were such knowledge only in hand. Unfortunately, our etiologic database is both scanty and unreliable. As noted, it is likely to remain so owing to the obscure, complex, and interactive nature of influences that shape psychopathological phenomena. The yearning among theorists of all viewpoints for a neat package of etiologic attributes simply cannot be reconciled with the complex philosophical issues, methodological quandaries, and difficult-to-disentangle subtle and random influences that shape mental disorders. In the main, almost all etiologic theses today are, at best, perceptive conjectures that ultimately rest on tenuous empirical grounds, reflecting the views of divergent "schools of thought" positing their favorite hypotheses. These speculative notions should be conceived as questions that deserve empirical evaluation, rather than be promulgated as the gospel of confirmed fact.

Inferences drawn in the consulting room concerning past experiences, especially those of early childhood, are of limited, if not dubious, value by virtue of having only the patient as the primary, if not the sole, source of information. Events and relationships of the first years of life are notably unreliable, owing to the lack of clarity of retrospective memories. As will be detailed in later chapters, the presymbolic world of infants and young toddlers comprises fleeting and inarticulate impressions that remain embedded in perceptually amorphous and inchoate forms that cannot be reproduced as the growing child's cognitions take on a more discriminative and symbolic character. What is "recalled," then, draws on a highly ambiguous palette of diffuse images and affects, a source whose recaptured content is readily subject both to direct and subtle promptings from contemporary sources, such as a theoretically oriented therapist. In Grunbaum's (1984) meticulous examination of the logical and empirical underpinnings of psychoanalytic theory, the philosopher concludes that its prime investigatory method, the case history, and, in particular, data generated "on the couch" through so-called free associations, are especially fallible. Commenting on the influences of the therapist in directing the flow and content of the patient's verbal production, Grunbaum writes (1984):

The clinical use of free association features epistemic biases of selection and manipulative contamination as follows: (1) the analyst selects thematically from the patient's productions, partly by interrupting the associations—either explicitly or in a myriad more subtle ways at points of his or her own theoretically inspired choosing; and (2) when the Freudian doctor harbors the suspicion that the associations are faltering because of evasive censorship, he uses verbal and also subtle nonverbal promptings to induce the continuation of the associations until they yield theoretically appropriate results. (pp. 210–211)

A third of a century ago, the analyst Marmor (1962), commenting on the ease and inevitability

with which therapeutic colleagues of contending analytic orientations would "discover" data congenial to their theoretical predilections, wrote:

Depending upon the point of view of the analyst, the patients of each school seem to bring out precisely the kind of phenomenological data which confirm the theories and interpretations of their analysis. Thus, each theory tends to be self-validating. Freudians elicit material about the Oedipus complex and castration anxiety, Adlerians about masculine strivings and feelings of inferiority, Horneyans about idealized images, Sullivanians about disturbed interpersonal relationships, etc. (p. 289)

Arguments pointing to thematic or logical continuities between the character of early experience and later behaviors, no matter how intuitively rational or consonant with established principles they may be, do not provide unequivocal evidence for their causal connections; different, and equally convincing, developmental hypotheses can be and are posited. Each contemporary explication of the origins of most personality disorders is persuasive, yet remains but one among several plausible possibilities. Most theorists favor one cause, a singular experiential event or process—be it the splitting of good and bad introjects, or fears engendered during the individuation-separation phase—that is the sine qua non, for example, of borderline personality development. Unfortunately, causal attributions appear no more advanced today than they were in former times. As Marmor (1986) has commented more recently:

One of the major fallacies of classical psychoanalytic theory is that Freud, in keeping with the thinking of his time, kept looking for a single cause for neurosis (akin to the tubercle bacillus), such as an infantile sexual trauma or castration anxiety. Causality in the genesis of neurosis is now understood to be multifactorial and to have biological and sociological roots as well as psychological ones. Even the tubercle bacillus is no longer assumed to be the sole sufficient cause of tuberculosis without also considering the contributory role of the host's immune system as well as sociological factors such as poverty, malnutrition, and overcrowding. Recognizing the complex systemic context in which psychopathology originates eliminates the tendency toward psychological reduction. (p. 249)

Rather sadly, our current literature abounds with brilliantly rationalized yet "competing" unifactorial conceptions.

Among other troublesome aspects of contemporary proposals are the diverse syndromal consequences attributed to essentially identical causes. Although it is not unreasonable to trace different outcomes to similar antecedents, there is an unusual inclination among theorists to assign the same "early conflict" or "traumatic relationship" to all varieties of psychological ailment. For example, an almost universal experiential ordeal that ostensibly undergirds such varied syndromes as narcissistic and borderline personalities, as well as a host of schizophrenic and psychosomatic conditions, is the splitting or repressing of introjected aggressive impulses engendered by parental hostility, an intrapsychic mechanism requisite to countering the dangers these impulses pose to dependency security, should they achieve consciousness or behavioral expression.

Not only is it unlikely that singular origins would be as ubiquitous as clinicians often posit them, but even if they were, their ultimate psychological impact would differ substantially depending on the configuration of other concurrent or later influences to which individuals were exposed. "Identical" causal factors cannot be assumed to possess the same import, nor can their consequences be traced without reference to the larger context of each individual's life experiences. One need not be a Gestaltist to recognize that the substantive impact of an ostensive process or event, however formidable it may seem in theory—be it explicit parental spitefulness or implicit parental abandonment—will differ markedly as a function of its developmental covariants.

To go one step further, there is good reason, as well as evidence, to believe that the significance of early troubled relationships may inhere less in their singularity or the depth of their impact than in the fact that they are precursors of what is likely to become a recurrent pattern of subsequent parental encounters. It may be sheer recapitulation and consequent cumulative learning that ultimately fashions and deeply embeds the entrenched pattern of distinctive personality attributes we observe. Although early encounters and resolutions may serve as powerful forerunners and substantive templates, the presence of persistent and pervasive clinical symptoms may not take firm root in early childhood, but may stem from conscious replication and reinforcement. Fisher and Greenberg (1977), though highly supportive of the scientific credibility of Freudian theories, conclude with this thesis following their examination of the etiologic origins of the anal character:

Several investigators have identified significant positive relationships between the anality of individuals and the intensity of anal attitudes present in their mothers. This obviously suggests that anal traits derive from associating with a parent who treats you in certain ways or provides you with models of how the world is to be interpreted. One should add that since a mother's anal traits are probably a permanent part of her personality repertoire, it would be reasonable to assume they would continue to affect her offspring not only during the toilet-training period but also throughout her contacts with him. . . . The only thing we can state with even moderate assurance is that a mother with anal character traits will tend to raise an offspring with analogous traits. (pp. 164–165)

Despite the foregoing, I share the commonly held view that, unit for unit, the earlier the experience, the likely greater its impact and durability. For example, the presymbolic and random nature of learning in the first few years often precludes subsequent duplication, and hence "protects" what has been learned. But, I believe it is also true that singular etiologic experiences, such as "split introjects" and "separation-individuation" struggles, are often only the earliest manifestation of a recurrent pattern of parent-child relationships. Early learnings fail to change, therefore, not because they have jelled permanently, but because the same slender band of experiences that helped form them initially, continue and persist as influences for years.

FOCUS AND LEVEL OF PATHOGENIC ANALYSIS

The things scientists look for as causes of pathology depend largely on their habits of thinking and their theoretical frames of reference. Two aspects of causal analysis may be differentiated for our purposes: the *unit of time* a scientist prefers to focus on, and the *conceptual level* the scientist habitually uses.

TIME UNIT

Some scientists focus on contemporaneous events, that is, factors in the present environment that influence the individual's behavior. Others are developmentally oriented and attempt to trace the historical sequence of past experiences that have resulted in present behavior.

Contemporaneous Analysis

This analysis takes as its subject only that which is significant for the moment in the life of the individual; this approach may be pictured as a cross-sectional analysis of current events and processes. Etiologists of this persuasion are *not* concerned with the chain of historical events that has led to the present, but with the state of the individual and his or her environment as it *currently exists.*

Adherents of this view claim that a full depiction of an individual's current state can supply all the data necessary for a causal analysis of his behavior. To them, a historical analysis is both unwieldy and unnecessary. For example, let us assume that a patient presently displays a marked hostility to his wife and children. Is it necessary, they ask, to trace the sequence of past events that gave rise to his hostility? Would this not lead to a tortuous and irrelevant search for "first causes?" This search might trace his hostility to an earlier need to compensate for feelings of inadequacy that stemmed from parental rejection, which, in turn, resulted from their preference for a younger sibling. Should his hostility toward his present family be ascribed to his childhood relationship with his brother? The historical analysis may be correct, but is it relevant to the patient's current behavior? The job of disentangling this sequence of causes to its earliest roots not only presents its own difficulties but may lead us to matters far afield from our original interests. Would it not be more expedient to account for his hostility by examining the stresses in his current environment and their impact on his present personality makeup?

Developmental Analysis

Pathogenecists who prefer a *developmental analysis* of causality contend that a cross-sectional study cannot produce sufficient data to account for present behavior. Furthermore, they believe that contemporary events must be reinterpreted in light of the individual's past history. To them, present experiences can be understood only in terms of their similarity to experiences in the past; likewise, present behaviors take on significance as only as extensions of past behaviors.

Developmental theorists assume not only that past conditions exercise an influence on the present, but that the residues of the past, in large measure, continue to operate in the present. Thus, the patient's present responses are being made to past rather than present events. For example, in the previous illustration, they would contend that the patient is reacting to his present family as if its members were duplicates of his childhood family; the feelings and behaviors he expresses now are *not* a function of what his wife and children are doing, but what his brother and parents did. Without knowing what these past experiences were, it would be impossible to understand the causes of his present behavior.

These theorists note further that behaviors which are indistinguishable in a contemporaneous analysis may be clearly differentiated in a developmental analysis. For example, pacifism in one individual may represent imitative behaviors learned through contact with thoughtful and gentle parents; in another individual, pacifism may have its roots in a fear of hostility based on painful experiences with harsh and brutal parents. According to the developmental viewpoint, similar current behaviors often take on very different meanings when analyzed longitudinally.

Contemporary and developmental approaches are neither mutually exclusive nor irreconcilable; they are complementary points of focus. One examines the interplay of current factors on behavior, and the other traces the historical antecedents which preceded that behavior. The philosophical and practical justifications of one approach versus the other may be argued endlessly, but they are merely two sides of the same coin. Both are necessary.

CONCEPTUAL LEVEL

As indicated in earlier chapters, a multiplicity of diverse viewpoints prevails in personality theory; this extends equally to developmental causal analysis. Depending on the frames of reference or the kinds of concepts a scientist has become accustomed to deal with, he or she will explore and organize the causal events of pathology from one of a number of different levels. Biophysical theorists direct their attention to neurological structures and physiochemical processes, expecting to find the key to causality among these phenomena. In a like manner, behavior theorists search for maladaptive reinforcement and conditioning experiences, and ascribe causation in those terms. Conceptual levels are complementary; none, in itself, is sufficient to answer the different kinds of questions that psychopathologists ask because these questions are posed at the start in different conceptual languages.

Some useful conceptual distinctions can be made in the study of developmental pathogenesis. First, clear-cut biological or psychological sources can occasionally be pinpointed as the primary precipitant of a disorder. For example, a paralysis of an arm due to a gunshot wound of the brachial nerve can meaningfully be differentiated from an emotionally based paralysis of the arm, even though we know that every psychic process is at the same time a process of the nervous system, and vice versa. Second, biological and psychological scientists delimit their research to those variables they are best equipped to pursue. As a result, the present literature on pathogenesis has been divided rather than coordinated. But first a few words on their synthesis.

On the Interactive Nature of Developmental Pathogenesis

Despite the title of this book, personality disorders are not disorders at all in the medical sense. Rather, personality disorders are reified constructs employed to represent varied styles or patterns in which the personality system functions *maladaptively* in relation to its environment. This relational aspect is an important one because it is an interactional conception of personality disorder: Normal persons exhibit flexibility in their interactions with their environment. Their responses or behaviors are appropriate to the given situation and over time. If person and environment are conceptualized as a dynamic system, then the evolution of the system through successive states must be subject to constraints that lie both in the person and in the environment. When environmental constraints dominate, the behavior of individuals tends to converge, regardless of their prepotent dispositions: Almost everyone stops when stoplights are red. When environmental constraints are few or poorly defined, there is opportunity for flexibility, novelty, and the expression of individual differences in behavior.

However, if the person-environment interaction is pervasively constrained by personologic factors, the variability of an individual's behavior is no longer appropriate and proportional to what the environment requires. The interaction is driven by the person. When the alternative strategies employed to achieve goals, to relate to others, and to cope with stress are few in number and rigidly practiced (*adaptive inflexibility*), when habitual perceptions, needs, and behaviors perpetuate and intensify preexisting difficulties (*vicious circles*), and when the person tends to lack resilience under conditions of stress (*tenuous stability*), we speak of a clinically significant personality pattern. Borrowing terminology from the medical model, we may even say that a personality "disorder" exists, if we keep in mind that the disorder is an interactional aberration that admits of degrees, shading gently from normality to clinicality, and has at a latent level no single underlying cause or disease pathogen, but instead must be as multidetermined as the personality system itself is multifaceted.

For pedagogical purposes, the multifaceted personality system can be heuristically decomposed into various clinical domains. Although these facilitate clinical investigation and experimental research, no such division exists in reality. Personality development represents the complex interplay of elements within and across each of these domains. Not only is there an interaction between person and environment; in addition, there are interactions and complex feedback loops operating within the person as well at levels of organization both biological and psychological. It is the essentially probabilistic character of these interactions, representing the person's own unique history, that binds the individual together as an organic whole with its own unique coloration we call personality. Our guiding metaphor, then, is organismic and dynamic, rather than mechanistic and reductionistic.

This very organismic-dynamic metaphor leads to a curious paradox between what is desired of an exposition of personality development and what is possible. Because all scientific theories are to some extent simplifications of reality, the map rather than the territory, all theories involve trade-offs between scope and precision. Most modern developmental theories are organismic and contextual in character. By embracing a multidomain organismic-contextual model, we aspire to *completely* explain personality disorder development as a totality. However, we must simultaneously accept the impossibility of any such explanation given the probabilistic character of the interactions espoused by the model we have assumed. Despite our aspirations, a certain amount of "ontological" imprecision is built into the guiding metaphor. The term ontological is aptly used, since its posits the existence or reality of experimental error—the interaction of personality variables is very often synergistic or nonlinear rather than additive.

Certain conceptual gimmicks could be used to recover this imprecision or to present an illusion of precision. We might give an exposition of personality disorder development from a "one-domain" perspective, whether cognitive, psychodynamic, or behavioral. Such explanations might increase the precision of their derived theses, but this feat would be accomplished only by denying essential aspects of the whole person. Such reductionism with respect to content is incommensurate with the guiding metaphor, that of the *total* organism. Thus, whereas any one of these personologic domains could be abstracted from the whole to give an exposition of personality disorder development from a particular and narrow perspective, this would not do justice to a "pathology" that pervades the entire matrix of the person.

Accordingly, interaction and continuity are the major themes of this chapter. The discussion stresses that numerous biogenic and psychogenic determinants covary to shape personality disorders, the relative weights of each varying as a function of time and circumstance. Further, this interaction of influences persists over time. The course of later characteristics is related intrinsically to earlier events; individual history itself is a constraint on future development. Personality disorder development must be viewed, therefore, as a process in which organismic and environmental forces display not only a mutuality and circularity of influence, but also an orderly and sequential continuity throughout the life of the individual.

For pedagogical purposes, it is necessary to separate biogenic from psychogenic factors as influences in personality disorder development; as noted, this bifurcation does not exist in reality. Biological and experiential determinants combine in an inextricable interplay throughout life. Thus, constitutional dispositions not only shape the character of experience but also are themselves modified through constant transactions with the environment. This sequence of biogenic-psychogenic interaction creates a never-ending spiral; each step in the interplay builds on prior interactions and creates, in turn, new potentials and constraints for future reactivity and experience. There are no unidirectional effects in development; it is a multideterminant transaction in which unique biogenic potentials and distinctive psychogenic influences mold each other in reciprocal and successively more intricate ways. The circular feedback and the

serially unfolding character of the developmental process defy simplification, and must constantly be kept in mind when analyzing the background of personality disorders.

PATHOGENIC BIOLOGICAL FACTORS

That characteristics of anatomic morphology, endocrine physiology, and brain chemistry would not be instrumental in shaping the development of personality is inconceivable. Biological scientists know that the central nervous system cannot be viewed as a simple and faithful follower of what is fed into it from the environment; not only does it maintain a rhythmic activity of its own, it also plays an active role in regulating sensitivity and controlling the amplitude of what is picked up by peripheral organs. Unlike a machine, which passively responds to external stimulation, the brain has a directing function that determines substantially what, when, and how events will be experienced. Each individual's nervous system selects, transforms, and registers objective events in accord with its distinctive biological characteristics.

Unusual sensitivities in this delicate orienting system can lead to marked distortions in perception and behavior. Any disturbance that produces a breakdown in the smooth integration of functions, or a failure to retrieve previously stored information, is likely to create chaos and pathology. Normal psychological functioning depends on the integrity of certain key areas of biological structure, and any impairment of this substrate will result in disturbed thought, emotion, and behavior. It must be carefully noted, however, that although biogenic dysfunctions or defects may produce the basic break from normality, psychological and social determinants almost invariably shape the *form* of its expression. Acceptance of the role of biogenic influences, therefore, does *not* negate the role of social experience and learning (Eysenck, 1967; Meehl, 1962, 1990; Millon, 1981, 1990).

Although the exact mechanisms by which biological functions undergird personality disorders will remain obscure for some time, the belief that biogenic factors are intimately involved is not new. Scientists have been gathering data for decades, applying a wide variety of research methods across a broad spectrum of biophysical functions. The number of techniques used and the variety of variables studied are legion. These variables often are different avenues for exploring the same basic hypotheses. For example, researchers focusing on biochemical dysfunctions often assume that these dysfunctions result from genetic error. However, the methods they employ and the data they produce are quite different from those of researchers who approach the role of heredity through research comparing monozygotic with dizygotic twins. With this in mind, this chapter proceeds to subdivide the subject of development into several arbitrary (but traditional) compartments, beginning first with heredity.

HEREDITY

The role of heredity is usually inferred from evidence based on correlations among traits in members of the same family. Most psychopathologists admit that heredity must play a role in personality disorder development, but they insist that genetic dispositions are modified substantially by the operation of environmental factors. This view states that heredity operates not as a fixed constant but as a disposition that takes different forms depending on the circumstances of an individual's upbringing. Hereditary theorists may take a more inflexible position, referring to a body of data that implicate genetic factors in a wide range of psychopathologies. Although they are likely to agree that variations in these disorders may be produced by environmental conditions, they are equally likely to assert that these are merely superficial influences that cannot prevent the individual from succumbing to his or her hereditary inclination. The overall evidence seems to suggest that genetic factors serve as predispositions to certain traits, but with few exceptions, similarly affected individuals display important differences in their symptoms and developmental histories. Moreover, genetically disposed disorders can be aided by psychological therapies, and similar symptomatologies often arise without such genetic dispositions.

A number of theorists have suggested that the milder pathologies, such as personality disorders, represent undeveloped or minimally expressed defective genes; for example, the schizoid personality may possess a schizophrenic genotype, but in this case the defective gene is weakened by the operation of beneficial modifying genes or favorable environmental experiences (Meehl, 1990). An alternate explanation might be formulated in terms of polygenic action; polygenes have minute, quantitatively similar, and cumulative effects. Thus, a continuum of increasing pathological severity can be accounted for by the cumulative effects of a large number of minor genes acting on the same trait.

The idea that psychopathological syndromes comprise well-circumscribed disease entities is an attractive assumption for those who seek a Mendelian or single-gene model of inheritance. Recent thinking forces us to question the validity of this approach to nosology and to the relevance of Mendelian genetic action. Defects in the infinitely complex central nervous system can arise from innumerable genetic anomalies (Plomin, 1990). Moreover, even convinced geneticists make reference to the notion of phenocopies, a concept signifying that characteristics usually traceable to genetic action can be simulated by environmental factors; thus, overtly identical forms of pathology may arise from either genetic or environmental sources. Because similar appearances do not necessarily signify similar etiologies, the clinical picture of a disorder may give no clue to its origins. To complicate matters further, different genes vary in their responsiveness to environmental influences; some produce uniform effects under all environmental conditions, whereas others can be entirely suppressed in certain environments (Plomin, DeFries, & McClearn, 1990). Moreover, it appears that genes have their effects at particular times of maturation and that their interaction with environmental conditions is minimal both before and after these periods.

Despite these ambiguities and complications, there can be little question that genetic factors do play some dispositional role in shaping the morphological and biochemical substrate of certain traits. However, these factors are by no means necessary to the development of personality pathology, nor are they likely to be sufficient in themselves to elicit pathological behaviors. They may serve, however, as a physiological base that makes the person susceptible to dysfunction under stress or inclined to learn behaviors that prove socially troublesome.

BIOPHYSICAL INDIVIDUALITY

The general role that neurological lesions and physiochemical imbalances play in producing pathology can be grasped with only a minimal understanding of the structural organization and functional character of the brain. However, it is important to avoid naive misconceptions. Among these is the belief that psychological functions can be localized in neurohormonal depots or precise regions of the brain. Psychological processes such as thought, behavior, and emotion derive from complex and circular feedback properties of brain activity. Unless the awesomely intricate connections within the brain that subserve these psychological functions are recognized, the result will be simplistic propositions that clinical or personality traits can arise as a consequence of specific chemical imbalances or focal lesions (Purves & Lichtman, 1985). Psychological concepts such as emotion, behavior, and thought represent diverse and complex processes that are grouped together by theorists and researchers as a means of simplifying their observations. These conceptual labels must not be confused with tangible events and properties within the brain. Certain regions are more involved in particular psychological functions than others, but it is clear that higher processes are a product of brain area interactions. For example, the frontal lobes of the cortex orchestrate a dynamic pattern of impulses by selectively enhancing the sensitivity of receptors, comparing impulses arising in other brain spheres and guiding them along myriad arrangements and sequences. In this regnant function, it facilitates or inhibits a wide range of psychological functions.

With the exception of a few well-circumscribed lesions that are directly associated with specific organic syndromes, the data relating neurological damage to psychopathology are equivocal. We are only beginning to cross the threshold of knowledge about normal brain functions. When we have a firm grasp of these normal processes, we may have an adequate base for specifying how disruptions impair psychological processes.

The problem of correlating psychopathology with neurological structures is complicated immensely by individual differences in the organization of the brain. There is more variability in internal morphology than there is in external morphology. The location of and interconnections among brain regions differ markedly from person to person. These naturally occurring individual differences are important in another regard. Variations among individuals in the constitutional density, range, and branching of comparable brain regions will have a direct bearing on emerging psychological functions. Possessing more or less of the neurological substrate for a particular function, such as pleasure or pain, can markedly influence the character of experience and the course of learning and development. Quite evidently, the role of neuroanatomical structures in psychopathology is not limited to problems of tissue defect or damage. Natural interindividual differences in structural anatomy and organization can result in a wide continuum of relevant psychological effects.

Anatomic differences are only part of the story. The highly popular current search for biochemical dysfunctions in psychopathology is equally handicapped by the high degree of natural variability in physiochemical processes among humans. Roger Williams (1973), the eminent biochemist, has made us aware that each individual possesses a distinctive physiochemical pattern that is wholly unlike others and bears no relationship to a hypothetical norm. Such patterns of biological individuality comprise crucial factors that must be built into the equation before we can properly appraise the role of biogenic influences in the development of personality pathology.

TEMPERAMENT DISPOSITIONS

Each child enters the world with a distinctive pattern of dispositions and sensitivities. Nurses know that infants differ from the moment they are born, and perceptive parents notice distinct differences in their successive offspring. Some infants suck vigorously; others seem indifferent and hold the nipple feebly. Some infants have a regular cycle of hunger, elimination, and sleep, whereas others vary unpredictably (Michelsson, Rinne, & Paajanen, 1990). Some twist fitfully in their sleep, whereas others lie peacefully awake in hectic surroundings. Some are robust and energetic; others seem tense and cranky.

The question that must be posed, however, is not whether children differ temperamentally but whether a particular sequence of subsequent life experiences will result as a consequence of these differences; childhood temperament would be of little significance if it did not constrain subsequent patterns of functioning. In this regard, the clinician must ask whether the child's characteristics evoke distinctive reactions from his or her parents and whether these reactions have a beneficial or a detrimental effect on the child's development (Kagan, Reznick, & Snidman, 1989; Maccoby & Martin, 1983). Rather than limit attention to the traditional question of what effect the environment has on the child, the focus might be changed to ask what effect the child has on the environment and what the consequences of these are on the child's development.

Patterns of behavior observed in the first few months of life are apparently more biogenic rather than psychogenic in origin. Some researchers speak of these patterns as "primary" because they are displayed before postnatal experience can fully account for them. Investigators have found that infants show a consistent pattern of autonomic system reactivity; others have reported stable differences on such biological measures as sensory threshold, quality and intensity of emotional tone, and electroencephalographic waves. Because the pertinence of psychophysiological differences to later personality is unknown, investigators have turned attention to the relationship between observable behavior and later development.

The studies of a number of research groups (Escalona, 1968; Escalona & Heider, 1959; Escalona & Leitch, 1953; Murphy & Moriarty, 1976; Murphy et al., 1962; Thomas & Chess, 1977; Thomas et al., 1963, 1968) have been especially fruitful in this regard. Their work has contributed not only to an understanding of personality development in general but also to the development of personality pathology in particular. Several behavioral dimensions were found to differentiate the temperament patterns of infants. Children differ in the regularity of their biological functions; including autonomic reactivity, gauged by initial responses to new situations; sensory alertness to stimuli and in adaptability to change; characteristic moods; and in intensities of response, distractibility, and persistence (Goldsmith & Goldsmith, 1981). Although early patterns were modified only slightly from infancy to childhood, this continuity could not be attributed entirely to the persistence of innate endowments. Subsequent experiences served to reinforce the characteristics that were displayed in early life (Kagan, 1989). This occurred in great measure because the infant's initial behaviors transformed the environment in ways that intensified and accentuated initial behaviors.

Theorists have often viewed disorders to be the result of experiences that individuals have no part in producing themselves (Jones & Raag, 1989; Zanolli, Saudargas, & Twardosz, 1990). This is a simplification of a complex interaction (Sroufe & Waters, 1976). Each infant possesses a biologically based pattern of sensitivities and dispositions that shapes the nature of his or her experiences. The interaction of biological dispositions and environmental experience is not a readily disentangled web but an intricate feedback system of crisscrossing influences. Several components of this process are elaborated because of their pertinence to development.

Adaptive Learning

The temperament dispositions of the maturing child are important because they strengthen the probability that certain traits will become prepotent (Bates, 1980, 1987; Thomas, Chess, & Korn, 1982). For example, highly active and responsive children relate to and rapidly acquire knowledge about events and persons in their environment. Their zest and energy may lead them to experience personal gratification quickly or, conversely, their lively and exploratory behavior may result in painful frustrations if they run repetitively into insuperable barriers. Unable to fulfill their activity needs, they may strike out in erratic and maladaptive ways. Moreover, temperament also influences the expression of psychological variables such as attachment (Belsky & Rovine, 1987).

Organismic action in passive children is shaped also by their biological constitution. Ill-disposed to deal with their environment assertively and disinclined to discharge their tensions physically, they may learn to avoid conflicts and step aside when difficulties arise. They may be less likely to develop guilt feelings about misbehavior than active youngsters, who more frequently get into trouble and receive punishment, and who are therefore inclined to develop aggressive feelings toward others. Passive youngsters may also deprive themselves of rewarding experiences, feel "left out of things," and depend on others to protect them from events they feel ill-equipped to handle on their own.

Interpersonal Reciprocity

Previously, we spoke of personality as a system. However, a systems notion need not be confined to operations that take place within the organism. Interpersonal theorists often speak of dyads and triads as systems of reciprocal influence. Childhood temperament evokes counterreactions from others that confirm and accentuate initial temperamental dispositions (Papousek & Papousek, 1975). Biological moods and activity levels shape not only the child's own behaviors but also those of the child's parents. If the infant's disposition is cheerful and adaptable and care is easy, the mother will quickly display a positive reciprocal attitude (Osofsky & Danzger, 1974). Conversely, if the child is tense, or if his or her care is difficult and time consuming, the mother may react with dismay, fatigue, or hostility. Through this distinctive behavioral disposition, then, the child elicits parental reactions that reinforce the initial pattern. Innate dispositions can be reversed, of course, by strong environmental pressures. A cheerful outlook can be crushed by parental contempt and ridicule. Conversely, shy and reticent children may become more self-confident in a thoroughly encouraging family atmosphere (Smith & Pederson, 1988).

There is an unfortunate tendency of clinicians and theorists to speak of parental responses to their children as if they were identical (e.g., uniformly abusive; uniformly loving). In fact, what is most likely is that parents will differ in their attitudes and behaviors toward the child, often rather strikingly so. When parental consistency occurs, it may be relatively easy to trace the connection between early experiences and later behavior styles. However, when these crucial parental relationships differ appreciably, the equation of influence becomes much more complex, especially if one also considers the effects of one or more siblings, perhaps some older and others younger.

Depending on the character and mix of influences, the child may learn any number of behavioral and attitudinal styles. Some youngsters may develop conflicting or "split" images of self; others may find a way to "synthesize" these contrasting patterns; still others may shift or vacillate from circumstance to circumstance, depending on their similarity to their parents' divergent behaviors (e.g., learning to behave in a caring and affectionate manner with women, owing to the actions of a consistently nurturing and valuing mother; with men, however, this *same* person will inevitably behave in a competitive and hostile manner, owing to the father's rejecting and derogating attitudes).

Although the idea that biophysical aspects constrain future development is easily understood, it must also be remembered that *not* all features of an individual's constitution are activated at the moment of birth. Individuals mature at different rates. Potentials may unfold only gradually as maturation progresses. Thus, some biologically rooted influences may not emerge until the youngster is well into adolescence, and it is not inconceivable that these late-blooming patterns may supplant those displayed earlier.

A crucial determinant of whether a particular temperament will lead to personality pathology appears to be parental acceptance of the child's individuality. Parents who accept their child's temperament, and then modify their practices accordingly, can deter what might otherwise become pathological. On the other hand, if parents experience daily feelings of failure, frustration, anger, and guilt, regardless of the child's disposition, they are likely to contribute to a progressive worsening of the child's adjustment. These comments point once more to the fact that biogenic and psychogenic factors interact in complex ways.

PATHOGENIC EXPERIENTIAL HISTORY

In the previous section, we stressed that biological functions play an active role in regulating what, when, and how events will be experienced; the nervous and endocrine systems do not accept passively what is fed into it. This active process means that unusual biological sensitivities or defects may result in perceptual distortions, thought disorders, and pathological behaviors.

Although behavior pathology may be triggered by biogenic abnormalities, the mere specification of a biogenic cause is not sufficient for an adequate etiologic analysis. Even in cases where clear-cut biogenic factors can be identified, it is necessary to trace the developmental sequence of experiences that transform these defects into a manifest form of psychopathology; the need for this more extensive developmental analysis is evident by the fact that some individuals with biological defects function effectively, whereas other, similarly afflicted individuals succumb to maladaptation and psychopathology (Davidson, 1986). The biological defect, in itself, cannot account for such divergences in development. Pathological behaviors that are precipitated initially by biological abnormalities are not simple or direct products of these defects; rather, they emerge through a complex sequence of interactions that include environmental experience and learning.

A major theme of this chapter is that psychopathology develops as a result of an intimate interplay of intraorganismic and environmental forces; such interactions start at the time of conception and continue throughout life. Individuals with similar biological potentials emerge with different personality patterns depending on the environmental conditions to which they were exposed. These patterns unfold and change as new biological maturations interweave within the context of new environmental encounters. In time, these patterns stabilize into a distinctive hierarchy of behaviors that remain relatively consistent through the ever-changing stream of experience.

To state that biological factors and environmental experiences interact is a truism; we must be more specific and ask how, exactly, these interactions take place.

Before we begin, let us discount questions about the proportionate contribution of biological factors as contrasted to environmental learning. The search to answer such questions is not only impossible from a methodological point of view, but is logically misleading. We could not, given our present state of technical skill, begin to tease out the relative contribution of these two sources of variance. Furthermore, a search such as this would be based on a misconception of the nature of interaction. The character and the degree of contribution of either biogenic or psychogenic factors are inextricably linked to the character and degree of the contribution of the other. For example, biological influences are not uniform from one situation to the next but vary as a function of the environmental conditions within which they arise. The position we take then is that both factors contribute to all behavior patterns and that their respective contributions are determined by reciprocal and changing combinations of interdependence.

Let us return now to the question of how, exactly, biogenic and psychogenic factors interact in the development of personality and psychopathology.

In the previous section, we examined a number of ways in which biological factors shape, facilitate, or limit the nature of the individual's experiences and learning. For example, the same objective environment will be perceived as different by individuals who possess different biological sensibilities; people register different stimuli at varying intensities in accord with their unique pattern of alertness and sensory acuity. From this fact, we should see that experience itself is shaped at the outset by the biological equipment of the person. Furthermore, the constitutional structure of an individual will strengthen the probability that he or she will learn certain forms of behavior. Not only will body build, strength, energy, neurological makeup, and autonomic system reactivity influence the stimuli the person will seek or be exposed to, but they will determine, in large measure, which types of behaviors he or she will find are successful in dealing with these encounters.

We must recognize further, that the interaction between biological and psychological factors is not unidirectional such that biological determinants always precede and influence the course of learning and experience; the order of effects can be reversed, especially in the early stages of development. From recent research, we learn that biological maturation is largely dependent on favorable environmental experience; the development of the biological substrate itself, therefore, can be disrupted, even completely arrested, by depriving the maturing organism of stimulation at sensitive periods of rapid neurological growth. The profound effect of these experiences on biological capacities will be a central theme in this chapter; we will contend that the sheer quantity as well as the quality of these early experiences is a crucial aspect in the development of several pathological patterns of personality.

Beyond the crucial role of these early experiences, we will argue further that there is a circularity of interaction in which initial biological dispositions in young children evoke counterreactions from others accentuating their disposition. The notion that the child plays an active role in creating environmental conditions that, in turn, reinforce his or her biological tendencies is illustrated well in this observation from Cameron and Magaret (1951):

. . . the apathy that characterizes an unreactive infant may deprive him of many of the reactions from others which are essential to his biosocial maturation. His unresponsiveness may discourage his parents and other adults from fondling him, talking to him or providing him with new and challenging toys, so that the poverty of his social environment sustains his passivity and social isolation. If such a child develops behavior pathology he is likely to show an exaggeration or distortion of his own characteristic reactions in the form of retardation, chronic fatigue or desocialization. (p. 97)

This thesis suggests, then, that the normally distributed continuum of biological dispositions that exists among young children is widened gradually because initial dispositions give rise to experiences that feed back and accentuate these dispositions. Thus, biological tendencies are not only perpetuated but intensified as a consequence of their interaction with experience.

The argument that biogenic and psychogenic factors are intimately connected does not mean that psychogenic events cannot produce psychopathology of their own accord. Geneticists refer to the concept of phenocopies, which are characteristics arising entirely from the action of environmental events that simulate those produced by genes. In a like fashion, psychogenic experiences may lead to pathological behaviors that are indistinguishable from those generated by the interplay of biological and psychological forces. Severe personal trauma, social upheaval, or other more insidious pressures can reverse an individual's normal pattern and prompt a pathological reaction. Thus, not only are there exceptions to the general rule that biological dispositions and experiences interact to shape the course of adjustment, but a promising beginning may be upset by unusual or unfortunate circumstances.

Although in some cases later experience can reverse early behavior patterns, we cannot understand these cases fully without reference to the historical background of events that precede them. We assert that there is an intrinsic continuity throughout life of personality functioning; thus, the present chapter has been organized to follow the sequence of natural development. Furthermore, not only do we contend that childhood events are more significant to personality formation than later events but we also believe that later behaviors are related in a determinant way to early experience. Despite an occasional and dramatic disjunctiveness in development, there is an orderly and sequential continuity, engendered by mechanisms of self-perpetuation and social reinforcement, that links the past to the present. The format for this chapter demonstrates this theme of developmental continuity.

EFFECT OF STIMULATION ON MATURATION

Certain forms of pathological behavior appear immutable, resistant to change under all forms of therapy. Psychoanalytic techniques may uncover deeply hidden infantile strivings, environmental management may remove aggravating precipitants, and programs of extinction and conditioning may zero in on specific symptoms, but all to no avail. The behavior is so deeply and pervasively ingrained that it is judged to be not only unalterable but an intrinsic part of the individual's biological makeup.

Such deeply rooted traits need not signify the presence of an innate disposition, nor need they stem from the effects of a biological trauma or disease. Embedded patterns of behavior may arise entirely as a product of psychological experience that shapes the development of biological structures so profoundly as to transform it into something substantially different from what it might otherwise have been.

Under what circumstances can psychological experience exert so profound an effect? An answer that enjoys a great degree of acceptance among psychopathologists is experience during infancy and early childhood. The major impetus for this view can be traced to the seminal writings of Freud at the turn of this century. The observations of a number of eminent European ethnologists on the effects of early stimulation on adult behavior in animals added substantial naturalistic evidence to support this position (Rakic, 1985, 1988). Experimental work during this period has shown more precisely that environmental stimulation is crucial to the maturation of several psychological functions.

The thesis that early experience has a paramount effect on personality formation is taken for granted by many theorists and researchers; this consensus is not reason enough, however, to accept it without further elaboration. We must ask why early experience is crucial and, more specifically, how this experience shapes the biological substrate of personality.

Several answers advanced in response to these questions will be elucidated throughout the chapter. For the moment we will concentrate on one: the dependence of maturation on early environmental stimulation. The thesis may be stated simply: Certain biological capacities will fail to develop fully as a result of impoverished stimulation; conversely, these same capacities may be overdeveloped as a consequence of enriched stimulation (Lipton & Kater, 1989).

PLASTICITY OF THE MATURING BIOLOGICAL SUBSTRATE

Maturation refers to the intricate sequence of ontogenetic development in which initial diffuse and inchoate structures of the body progressively unfold into specific functional units. Early stages of structural differentiation precede and overlap with more advanced stages in which lower level units interweave and connect into a complex and integrated network of functions displayed only in the adult organism. It was once believed that the course of maturation—from diffusion to differentiation to integration—arose exclusively from inexorable forces laid down in the genes. Maturation was thought to evolve according to a preset timetable that operated autonomously of environmental conditions. This view no longer is tenable. Maturation follows an orderly progression, but the developmental sequence and level of the organism's ultimate biological equipment are substantially dependent on a variety of stimuli and nutritional supplies from the environment. Thus, maturation progresses not in a fixed course leading to a predetermined level, but is subject to numerous variations that reflect the character of the organism's environment.

Early experiences are more crucial to development than later experiences in part because the peak period of maturation occurs from the prenatal stage through the first years of postnatal life. Granting that experience can influence the course of maturation, it is reasonable to conclude that the organism is subject to more alteration in the early, or more plastic years, than when it has fully matured. An example in the sphere of body structure may illustrate this point well. Inadequate nutrition in childhood may result in stunted bone development, leading to a permanently shortened stature; no amount of nutrition in adult life can compensate to increase the individual's height. However, had adequate nutrition been given during the formative or maturing years, the child might have grown to his or her full potential. Similarly, in the nervous system, prenatal deficiencies in nutrition will retard or arrest the differentiation of gross tissue into separable neural cells; early postnatal deficiencies will deter or preclude the proliferation of neural collaterals and their integration. However, deficiencies arising later in life will have little or no effect on the development of these neural structures.

CONCEPT OF STIMULUS NUTRIMENT

We must look at the concept of nutrition more broadly than we commonly view it if we are to understand its role in the development of biological maturation. Nutrition should be conceived as including not only obvious supplies such as those found in food, but also sources such as those found in what Rapaport (1958) had termed "stimulus nutriment." This notion of nutrition suggests that the simple impingement of environmental stimuli on the maturing organism has a direct bearing on the chemical composition, ultimate size, and patterns of neural branching within the brain (Lipton & Kater, 1989; Purves & Lichtman, 1985). Stated simply, the sheer amount of stimulation to which the child is exposed has a determinant effect on the maturation of his or her neural capacities. (We are bypassing, for the moment, any reference to the effects of the timing and quality of the stimulative source, which also have a bearing on development.)

The notion that degree of stimulation can produce changes in neural development is not new. Spurzheim, in 1815, proposed that the organs of the brain increase by exercise. Ramon y Cajal suggested in 1895 that since neural cells cannot multiply after birth, cerebral exercise will result in the expansion of neural collaterals and in the growth of more extended intercortical connections. For more than 50 years, experimental biologists have reported that the development and maintenance of neural connections are dependent on periodic stimulus activation. As early as 1915, Bok showed that nerve fibers grow out along the path of repeated stimuli; he termed this phenomenon *stimulogenous fibrillation.* Similar observations in the 1930s led Kappers to formulate the concept of neurobiotaxis. Valid criticisms have been leveled at certain features of these concepts, but there appears to be considerable support from recent research that neurochemical processes, essential to the growth and branching of neural structures, are activated by stimulation; extremes of stimulus impoverishment or enrichment appear to prompt an under- or overdevelopment of neural connections and patterns.

The belief that the maturing organism must receive periodic stimulus nutriments for proper development has led some theorists to suggest that the organism actively seeks an optimum level of stimulation. Thus, just as the infant cries out in search of food when deprived, or wails in response to pain, so too the child may display behaviors that provide sensory stimulation requisite to maturation. Murphy (1947) and Butler and Rice (1963), for example, have proposed that the maturing organism possesses a series of "adient drives or stimulus hungers." They note that although infants are restricted largely to stimulation supplied by environmental agents, they often engage in what appear to be random exercises, that, in effect, furnish them with the stimulation they require. Thus, in the first months of life, infants can be seen to track auditory and visual stimuli; as they mature further, they grasp incidental objects, and then mouth, rotate, and fondle them. Furthermore, we observe that the young of all species engage in more exploratory and frolicsome behavior than adults. These seemingly "functionless" play activities may not be functionless at all; they may be essential to growth, an instrumental means of self-stimulation that is indispensable to the maturation and maintenance of biological capacities (Ainsworth, Bleher, Waters & Wall, 1978; Bowlby, 1969, 1982; Bretherton, 1985; Volkmar & Provence, 1990).

Implicit in the preceding is the view that the organism's partly matured capacities enable it to provide for itself sources of stimulation necessary for further maturation; according to this thesis, each stage of maturational development establishes a foundation of capacities that are prerequisites for, and conducive to, the development. For example, children with deficient sensory capacities such as vision may be unable to maneuver within their environment and consequently may be delayed in the development of motor capacities such as walking and running. Similarly, children with a marked hearing loss may develop inarticulate speech because they are unable to discriminate sounds.

Consequences of Early Stimulus Impoverishment

It should be evident from the foregoing, that unless certain chemicals and cells are activated by environmental stimulation, the biological substrate for a variety of psychological functions may be impaired irrevocably. Furthermore, deficiencies in functions that normally mature in early life may set the stage for a progressive retardation of functions that mature later.

What evidence is there that serious consequences may arise from an inadequate supply of early stimulation? Beach and Jaynes (1954), Killackey (1990), Melzack (1965), Newton and Levine (1968), Rakic (1985, 1988), Scott (1968), and Thompson and Schaefer (1961) provide extensive reviews of relevant experimental findings; we shall refer here only briefly to some of the principal conclusions derived from this growing body of work.

Numerous investigators have shown that an impoverished environment in early life results in permanent adaptational difficulties. For example, experimental animals reared in isolation tend to be markedly deficient in such traits as emotionality, activity level, social behavior, curiosity, and learning ability. As adult organisms, they possess a reduced capacity to manipulate their environments, to discriminate or abstract essentials, to devise strategies, and to cope with stress.

Comparable results have been found among humans. Children reared under unusually severe conditions of restriction, such as in orphanages, evidence deficits in social awareness and reactivity, are impulsive, deficient in solving intellectual problems, susceptible to sensorimotor dysfunctions, and display a generally low resistance to stress and disease. These consequences have double-barreled effects. Not only are these children hampered by their specific deficiency, but each of these deficiencies yields progressive and long-range consequences in that it precludes or retards the devel-

opment of more complex capacities. Thus, early deficits may precipitate a whole series of stunted or distorted adaptive capacities (Ainsworth et al., 1978; Bowlby, 1960; Bretherton, 1985; Volkmar & Provence, 1990).

Consequences of Early Stimulus Enrichment

Intense levels of early stimulation also have effects. Several investigators have demonstrated among animals that an enriched environment in early life results in measurable changes in brain chemistry and brain weight. Others have found that early stimulation accelerates the maturation of the pituitary adrenal system, whereas equivalent stimulation at later stages is ineffective. On the behavioral level, enriched environments appear to enhance problem-solving abilities and increase the capacity of the organism to withstand stress. Comparable data among humans is either lacking or equivocal. Nevertheless, several theorists have proposed that enriching experiences can foster the development of higher intellectual abilities and adaptive coping behaviors.

There has been little systematic exploration of the potentially detrimental effects of environmental enrichment because researchers and clinicians alike are inclined to assume that the opposite side of the coin, that of impoverishment, is more conducive to pathological consequences. This assumption probably is correct, but it should not lead us to overlook the possibility that excessive stimulation can lead to an overdevelopment of certain biological capacities that may prove disruptive to effective psychological functioning. Thus, just as excessive food nutrition leads to obesity and physical ill health, so too may stimulus enrichment produce unhealthy psychological growth. For example, the enhancement or strengthening of certain neural patterns, such as those associated with emotional reactivity, may dispose the organism to overreact to social situations. The predominance of any biological response tendency may throw off key what would otherwise have been a normal or more balanced pattern of psychological functioning. Thus, the enrichment of biological capacities does not produce beneficial consequences only; whether enhanced functions prove advantageous or disadvantageous to the individual depends on which of the many and diverse capacities have been enriched, and whether the resultant pattern is balanced or unbalanced.

NEUROPSYCHOLOGICAL DEVELOPMENT

The previous section focused only on the determinant effects of *volume* of early stimulation. Our attention now will turn from the issue of "how much" to that of "when"; here we will explore the view that the specific time of stimulation has a direct relationship to its effect. The question can be raised: Are the effects of extremes in stimulation greater at certain periods of early maturation than others? Interest will be directed and limited to the *interaction* of volume and timing, not to the content or quality of the stimulative source. Questions about the effects of different kinds of stimuli will be discussed in the next section; for the present, we shall deal only with the interplay between "how much" and "when," not with "what." In reality, of course, these three elements are not separable. We distinguish among them, however, not only for pedagogical purposes; we believe that each of these variables can produce different and specifiable effects on the development of personality; they should be distinguished, therefore, for theoretical clarification and research execution as well.

Two kinds of relationships may be observed between the effect of a stimulus and the time of its occurrence; we may term these *recurrent periods* and *sensitive developmental periods.*

The first relates to recurrent tissue needs, best illustrated in periodic deficit conditions known as hunger and thirst. At various times each day, the depletion of certain nutritional substances leads to increased levels of neurological activation and the selective focusing of sensory receptors. As a consequence, stimuli to which attention is not ordinarily given become dominant and have a marked impact on the organism. For example, while driving along a road, we tend to notice signs pertaining to food if we are hungry; after a good meal, however, these signs pass by in a blur. The role of these recurrent periods will be elaborated when we discuss, in a later section, the operation of what is known as "motivation" in learning.

The second, and less obvious, relationship between timing and stimulus impact will be our principal focus in this section. It refers to the observation that certain types of stimuli have an especially pronounced effect on the organism at particular and well-circumscribed periods of maturation. At these periods or stages, the organism is unusually responsive to and substantially influenced by the action of these stimuli.

CONCEPT OF SENSITIVE DEVELOPMENTAL PERIODS

The contention that stimuli produce different effects at different ages can scarcely be questioned (e.g., the shapely legs of an attractive girl catch the eye of most young and middle-aged men but rarely draw the attention of preadolescent boys and senile men). The concept of sensitive or critical periods of development states more than this, however. It argues, first, that there are limited time periods during which particular stimuli are necessary for the full maturation of an organism, and second, that if these stimuli are experienced either before or after the sensitive period, they will have minimal or no effects. Thus, if critical periods pass without proper stimulus nourishment, the organism will suffer certain forms of maldevelopment that are irremediable; they cannot be compensated for by the presentation of the "right" stimuli at a later date.

The rationale for the sensitive period concept was presented initially in the field of experimental embryology. One of the early researchers, Child (1941), found that rapidly growing tissues of an embryo are especially sensitive to environmental stimulation; the morphological structure of proliferating cells was determined, in large part, by the character of the stimulus environment within which it was embedded. At later stages, where growth had slowed down, these same cells were resistant to environmental influences. These embryological findings suggested that the effects of environmental stimuli on morphological structure are most pronounced *when tissue growth is rapid* (Killackey, 1990; Rakic, 1985–1989).

It is unclear which mechanisms operate to account for the special interaction between stimulation and periods of rapid neural growth. First, there is evidence that stimulation itself promotes a proliferation of neural collaterals, and that this effect is most pronounced when growth potential is greatest. Second, early stimulation may result in a selective growth process in which certain collaterals establish particular interneuronal connections to the exclusion of others. Third, we may hypothesize that once these connections are embedded biologically, the first stimuli that traverse them preempt the circuit and thereby decrease the chance that subsequent stimuli will have comparable effects. Whatever the sequence and mechanisms may be, the effects of stimulation are maximal at periods of rapid tissue growth; at this point in our knowledge, we only can speculate on the apparatus involved.

The notion that brief early experiences may produce a permanent modification of functions has been theorized by scientists in fields other than embryology. Lorenz, the eminent European ethologist, discovered critical periods during which primary social bonds are permanently established in birds. In human research, McGraw (1943) demonstrated the existence of peak periods for learning specific motor skills, and illustrated the resistance of these skills to subsequent extinction. Murphy (1947) reports a number of studies to support the concept of canalization, a notion signifying an irreversible initial learning process.

Numerous theorists have proposed, either by intention or inadvertently, developmental schemas based on a concept of sensitive periods. Among these are Heinz Werner (1940), Jean Piaget (1952) and, of course, both Sigmund Freud (1908) and Erik Erikson (1950). None, however, have presented their notions in terms of evolutionary-neuropsychological growth stages, although G. Stanley Hall (1916) sought to formulate a developmental theory of "recapitulation" anchored to Darwin's model. Although such compound terminology may seem formidable, it is intended to communicate first the fact that personological developmental constraints derive from the history of human adaptation, and second that the ultimate instantiation of these constraints lies in universal evolutionary principles, whether they be expressed in personality traits, cognitive schemas, or sociocultural customs (Wilson, 1978).

EVOLUTIONARY PHASES

Broadly speaking, an individual human organism must pass through four "stages" and must fulfill a parallel set of four "tasks" to perform adequately in life. The first three pairs of these stages and tasks, and in part the fourth as well, are shared by lower species and may be thought of as recapitulating four phases of *evolution* (Millon, 1990). Each stage and task corresponds to one of the four evolutionary phases: existence, adaptation, replication, and abstraction. Polarities, that is, contrasting functional directions, representing the first three of these phases (pleasure-pain, passive-active, other-self) have been used to construct a theoretically anchored classification of personality styles and disorders, such as described in this text. Such bipolar or dimensional schemes are almost universally present throughout the world's literature, as well as in psychology at large (Millon, 1990). The earliest may be traced to ancient Eastern religions, most notably the Chinese *I Ching* texts and the Hebrew *Cabala*.

In the life of the individual organism, each evolutionary phase is recapitulated and expressed ontogenetically; that is, each individual organism moves through developmental stages that have functional goals related to their respective phases of evolution. Within each stage, every individual acquires personologic dispositions representing a balance or predilection toward one of the two polarity inclinations; which inclination emerges as dominant over time results from the inextricable and reciprocal interplay of intraorganismic and extraorganismic factors. Thus, during early infancy, the primary organismic function is to "continue to exist." Here, evolution has supplied mechanisms that orient the infant toward life-enhancing environments (pleasure) and away from life-threatening ones (pain).

The expression of traits or dispositions acquired in early stages of development may have their expression transformed as later faculties or dispositions develop (Millon, 1969). Temperament is perhaps a classic example. An individual with an active temperament may develop, contingent on contextual factors, into an avoidant or an antisocial personality. The transformation of earlier temperamental characteristics takes the form of what we will call "personologic bifurcations." Thus, if the individual is inclined toward a passive orientation and later learns to be self-directed, a narcissistic style ensues. But if the individual possesses an active orientation and later learns to be self-directed, an antisocial style ensues. Thus, early developing dispositions may undergo vicissitudes, whereby their meaning in the context of the whole organism is subsequently re-formed into more complex personality trait configurations.

As previously noted, the authors believe that the development of personality disorders should be organized in terms of fundamental personologic axes embedded in evolutionary theory. These are discussed in the following sections.

Phase 1   Existence

The first phase, existence, concerns the survival of integrative phenomena, whether a nuclear particle, virus, or human being, against the forces of entropic decompensation. Evolutionary mechanisms associated with this stage relate to the processes of *life-enhancement* and *life-preservation*. The former are concerned with orienting individuals toward improving the quality of life; the latter with orienting individuals away from actions or environments that decrease the quality of life, or even jeopardize existence itself. These two superordinate processes may be called *existential aims*. At the highest level of abstraction, such mechanisms form, phenomenologically or metaphorically, a pleasure-pain polarity. Most humans exhibit both processes, those oriented toward enhancing pleasure and avoiding pain. Some individuals, however, appear to be conflicted in regard to existential aims (e.g., the sadistic), whereas others possess deficits in such aims (e.g., the schizoid). In terms of evolutionary-neuropsychological stages (Millon, 1969, 1981, 1990), orientations on the pleasure-pain polarity are set during a "sensory-attachment" developmental stage, the purpose of which is to further mature and selectively refine and focus the largely innate ability to discriminate between pain and pleasure signals.

Phase 2 Adaptation

Everything that exists, exists in an environment. To come into existence as a surviving particle or living creature is but an initial phase. Once an integrated structure exists, it must maintain its existence through exchanges of energy and information with its environment. This second evolutionary phase relates to what is termed the modes of adaptation; it also is framed as a two-part polarity: a passive orientation, that is, to be *ecologically accommodating* in one's environmental niche, versus an active orientation, that is, to be *ecologically modifying* and to intervene in or to alter one's surrounds. These *modes of adaptation* differ from the first phase of evolution, in that they relate to how that which has come to exist, endures. In terms of neuropsychological development, this polarity is ontogenetically expressed as the "sensorimotor-autonomy stage," during which the child typically progresses from an earlier, relatively passive style of accommodation to a relatively active style of modifying his or her physical and social environment.

The accommodating-modifying polarity necessarily derives from an expansion of the systems concept. Whereas in the existence phase the system is seen as being mainly intraorganismic in character, the adaptation phase expands the systems concept to its logical progression, from person to person-in-context. Some individuals, those of an active orientation, operate as genuine agencies, tending to modify their environments according to their desires. For these individuals, an active-organism model is appropriate. Other persons, however, seek to accommodate to whatever is offered or, rather than work to change what exists, seek out new, more hospitable venues when current ones become problematic. For these individuals, a passive-organism model is appropriate.

Phase 3 Replication

Although organisms may be well adapted to their environments, the existence of any life-form is time limited. To circumvent this limitation, organisms exhibit patterns of the third polarity, *replicatory strategies*, by which they leave progeny. These strategies relate to what biologists have referred to as an *r*- or *self*-propagating strategy, at one polar extreme, and a *K*- or *other*-nurturing strategy at the second extreme. Psychologically, the former is disposed toward individually oriented actions that are perceived by others as egotistic, insensitive, inconsiderate, and uncaring; whereas the latter is disposed toward nurturant-oriented actions that are seen as affiliative, intimate, protective, and solicitous (Gilligan, 1981; Rushton, 1985; Wilson, 1978). Like pleasure-pain, the self-other polarity is not unidimensional. Whereas most humans exhibit a reasonable balance between the two polar extremes, some personality disorders are quite conflicted on this polarity, as are the compulsive and negativistic personalities. In terms of neuropsychological growth stages, an individual's orientation toward self and others evolves largely during the "pubertal-gender identity" stage.

As with the passive-active polarity, the self-other bipolarity necessarily derives from an expansion of the systems concept. Whereas the adaptation phase exists contemporaneously within an environment, replication is seen as evolving longitudinally over time. As before, the goal of the organism is its survival or continuance. When expressed across time, however, survival means reproducing, and strategies for doing so.

Phase 4 Abstraction

The reflective capacity to transcend the immediate and concrete, to interrelate and synthesize diversity, to represent events and processes symbolically, to weigh, reason, and anticipate, each signifies a quantum leap in evolution's potential for change and adaptation (Millon, 1990). Emancipated from the real and present, unanticipated possibilities and novel constructions may routinely be created by various styles of abstract processing. It is these capacities that are represented in the neuropsychological stage of "intracortical-integration."

The capacity to sort and to recompose, to coordinate and to arrange the symbolic representations of experience into new configurations is, in certain ways, analogous to the random processes of recombinant replication, though they are more focused and intentional. To extend this rhetorical liberty, genetic replication represents the recombinant mechanism underlying the adaptive progression of phylogeny, whereas abstraction represents the recombinant mechanism underlying the cognitive progression of ontogeny. The uses of replication are limited, constrained by the finite potentials inherent in parental genes. In contrast, experiences, internalized and recombined through cognitive processes, are infinite. Over one lifetime, innumerable events of a random, logical, or irrational character transpire, construed and reformulated time and again, some of which proving more, and others less adaptive than their originating circumstances may have called forth. Whereas the actions of most subhuman species derive from successfully evolved genetic programs, activating behaviors of a relatively fixed nature suitable for a modest range of environmental settings, the capabilities of both implicit and intentional abstraction give rise to adaptive competencies that are suited to radically divergent ecological circumstances that themselves may be the result of far-reaching acts of symbolic and technological creativity.

The abstract mind may mirror outer realities, but reconstructs them in the process, reflectively transforming them into subjective modes of phenomenological reality, rendering external events subject to individualistic designs. Every act of apprehension is transformed by processes of abstract symbolism. Not only are internal and external images emancipated from direct sensory and imaginal realities, allowing them to become entities, but contemporaneous time also loses its immediacy and impact, becoming as much a construction as a substance. Cognitive abstractions bring the past effectively into the present, and their power of anticipation brings the future into the present, as well. With past and future embedded in the here and now, humans can encompass, at once, not only the totality of our cosmos, but its origins and nature, its evolution, and how they have come to pass. Most impressive of all are the many visions

humans have of life's indeterminate future, where no reality as yet exists.

Comment. Because any classification system is a simplification of nature, the most important aspect of a taxonomy is where the boundaries are drawn. The authors believe their evolutionary system's conception, linked to fundamental stages of development, provides the most secure foundation for dissecting the personologic sphere. Accordingly, and in contrast to earlier formulations (e.g., Freud, Piaget, Erikson), it seems more reasonable to us to construct a developmental model based on the evolutionary phases and their related neuropsychological stages and tasks rather than on ones oriented to psychosexual or cognitive processes and periods. As noted, part-function models such as the latter two fail to encompass the entire person, are unconnected to the deeper laws of evolutionary progression and, hence, cannot form either a comprehensive or a firm grounding for a modern developmental theory.

A qualification should be noted before describing the developmental stages derived from the model. First, individuals differ with regard to the degree to which they are constrained at each level of organization. Biologically speaking, children of the same chronological age, for example, often are not comparable in the level and character of their biological capacities. Not only does each infant start life with distinctive neurological, physiochemical, and sensory equipment, each also progresses at his or her own maturational rate toward some ultimate but unknown level of potential. The same is true for constraints of a sociocultural nature.

Second, although we differentiate four seemingly distinct stages of development in the following section, it is important to state at the outset that all four stages and their related primary processes begin in utero and continue throughout life—they proceed simultaneously and overlap throughout the developmental process. For example, the elements that give shape to "gender identity" are underway during the sensory-attachment phase, although at a modest level; and the elements that give rise to attachment behaviors continue and extend well into puberty. Stages are differentiated only to bring attention to peak periods of development when certain processes and tasks are prominent and central. The concept of sensitive periods implies that developmental stages are not exclusionary; rather, they merely demarcate a period in life when certain developmental potentialities are salient in their maturation and in their receptivity to relevant life experiences.

The characteristics and consequences of the four "overlapping" stages of neuropsychological development are discussed next, as are their roots in the evolutionary phase theory.

NEUROPSYCHOLOGICAL STAGES

The four stages of development to be described here parallel the four evolutionary phases discussed previously. Moreover, each evolutionary phase is related to a different stage of ontogenetic development (Millon, 1969). For example, life enhancement–life preservation corresponds to the sensory-attachment stage of development in that the latter represents a period when the young child learns to discriminate between those experiences that are enhancing and those that are threatening.

STAGE 1   SENSORY-ATTACHMENT

The Life-Enhancement (Pleasure)– Life-Preservation (Pain) Polarity

The first year of life is dominated by sensory processes, functions basic to subsequent development in that they enable the infant to construct some order out of the initial diffusion experienced in the stimulus world, especially that based on distinguishing pleasurable from painful "objects." This period has also been termed that of attachment because infants cannot survive on their own (Fox, Kimmerly, & Schafer, 1991) but must "fasten" themselves to others who will protect, nurture, and stimulate them (provide them with experiences of pleasure rather than those of pain).

Such themes are readily understood through an evolutionary theory of personality development. Whereas evolution has endowed adult humans with the cognitive ability to project future threats and difficulties as well as potential rewards, human infants are comparably impoverished, being as yet without the benefit of these abstract capacities. Evolution has therefore "provided" mechanisms or substrates that orient the child toward life-enhancing activities or venues (pleasure), and away from potentially life-threatening ones (pain). Existence during this highly vulnerable stage is quite literally a to-be or not-to-be matter.

As noted previously, life-enhancing actions or sensations can be subsumed under the rubric of "pleasure," whereas life-threatening actions or sensations can be subsumed under the metaphorical term "pain." Such a pleasure-pain polarity simply recognizes that although the behavioral repertoire of the young child—the operational means, so to speak—may be manifestly diverse (e.g., smiles, coos, stranger anxiety, primitive reflexes), the end, or *existential aim,* is universal and has as its bare minimum the maintenance of life itself. In the normal organism, both pleasure and pain are coordinated toward ontogenetic continuity. However, whether as a result of genetic factors, early experiences, or their interaction, some pathological patterns display aberrations in their orientation toward pleasure or pain. Deficits in the strength of both painful and pleasurable drives, for example, either constitutionally given or experientially derived, are involved in the schizoid pattern, whereas a reversed or conflicted pleasure-pain orientation inclines toward the masochistic or sadistic disorders.

Development of Sensory Capacities

The early neonatal period is characterized by undifferentiation. The organism behaves in a diffuse and unintegrated way, and perceptions are unfocused and gross. Accordingly, the orientation of the infant is toward sensations that are proportionately broad and undifferentiated, although increasingly the distinction between pleasure and pain becomes central to subsequent refinements. Freud recognized that the mouth region is a richly endowed receptor system through which neonates establish their first significant relationship to the world, but it is clear that this oral unit is merely the focal point of a more diverse system of sensory capacities for making significant distinctions. Through oral and other tactile contacts, the infant establishes a sense, or "feel," of the environment that evokes pleasurable or painful responses.

According to neuropsychological and evolutionary theories, it would be expected that the amount and quality of tactile stimulation to which the neonate is exposed will contribute significantly to the infant's development as precocities or retardations, depending on the level of stimulation. Moreover, it is likely that the quality and patterning of this stimulation may lead the infant to experience inchoate feelings tentatively drawn against the background of pleasure-pain. These form the phenomenological prototypes of such later-evolving emotions such as fear, joy, sadness, anger.

Development of Attachment Behaviors

The neonate cannot differentiate between objects and persons; both are experienced simply as stimuli. How does this initial indiscriminateness become progressively refined into specific attachments? For all essential purposes, the infant is helpless and dependent on others to avoid pain and supply his or her pleasurable needs. Separated from the womb, the neonate has lost the physical attachment to the mother's body and the protection and nurturance it provided; the infant must turn toward other regions or sources of attachment to survive and obtain nourishment and stimulation for further development (Bowlby, 1969/1982; Gewirtz, 1963; Hinde, 1982; Lamb, Thompson, & Gardner, 1985; Ribble, 1943; Spitz, 1965). Attachment behaviors may be viewed, albeit figuratively, as an attempt to reestablish the unity lost at birth that enhanced and protected life. In fact, recent investigations show that although initial attachments are transformed across stages of development, they remain important across the life span (e.g., Sroufe & Fleeson, 1986). Whether the infant's world is conceptualized as a buzz or a blank slate, the child must begin to differentiate venues or objects that further his or her existential aims, supplying nourishment, preservation, and stimulation, from those that diminish, frustrate, or threaten them. These initial relationships, or "internal representational models" (e.g., Crittenden, 1990), apparently "prepared" by evolution, become the context through which other relationships develop.

Consequences of Impoverishment

A wealth of clinical evidence is available showing that humans deprived of adequate maternal care in infancy display a variety of pathological behaviors. We cannot, of course, design studies to disentangle precisely which of the complex of variables that compromise maternal care account for these irreparable consequences; the lives of babies cannot be manipulated to meet our scientific needs.

However, extensive reviews of the consequences in animals of early stimulus impoverishment show that sensory neural fibers atrophy and cannot be regenerated by subsequent stimulation (Beach &

Jaynes, 1954; Riesen, 1961). Inadequate stimulation in any major receptor function usually results in decrements in the capacity to utilize these sensory processes in later life. The profound effects of social isolation have been studied thoroughly and show that deprived monkeys are incapable at maturity of relating to peers, of participating effectively in sexual activity, and of assuming adequate roles as mothers. Abstracting to those substrates and pathways that undergird pleasure-pain, we might expect that such underelaboration, if pervasive, might at the least render emotional discriminations of a more refined or narrow character impossible, or worse, result in the wholesale impoverishment of all affective reactions, as seen in the schizoid pattern.

The potential effects of moderate levels of early sensory impoverishment have been little researched. The reader should note, however, that the degree of sensory impoverishment varies along a gradient or continuum; it is not an all-or-none effect. Children who receive less than an optimum degree of sensory stimulation will be likely to grow up less "sensory oriented" and less "socially attached" than those who have experienced more (Bowlby, 1952, 1969, 1973; Goldfarb, 1955; Yarrow, 1961). Such variations are especially relevant to the study of personality disorders, which lie on a continuum with normal functioning.

Consequences of Enrichment

Data on the consequences of too much, or enriched, early sensory stimulation are few and far between; researchers have been concerned with the effects of deficit, rather than excess, stimulation.

A not unreasonable hypothesis, however, is that excess stimulation during the sensory-attachment stage would result in overdevelopments among associated neural structures (Rosenzweig et al., 1962); these may lead to oversensitivities that might, in turn, result in potentially maladaptive dominance of sensory functions or pleasurable substrates. Along this same line, Freud hypothesized that excess indulgence at the oral stage was conducive to fixations at that period. Eschewing both oral and fixation notions, the authors propose that excess sensory development in childhood will require a high level of maintenance in adulthood, as seen in persistent sensory-seeking or pleasure-seeking behaviors. These individuals might be characterized by their repetitive search for excitement and stimulation, their boredom with routine, and their involvement in incidental and momentarily gratifying adventures. Exactly what neural or chemical mechanisms undergird such a stimulus-seeking pattern is a matter for speculation. Whatever the mechanisms may be, it appears plausible both neurologically and clinically that overenriched early stimulation can result in pathological stimulus-seeking behavior, a pattern dominated by relatively capricious and cognitively unelaborated, pleasurable pursuits.

Excess stimulation, especially if anchored exclusively to a parental figure, might result in an overattachment to him or her. This is demonstrated most clearly in symbiotic children, where an abnormal clinging to the mother and a persistent resistance to stimulation from other sources often result in overwhelming feelings of isolation and panic, as when they are sent to nursery school or "replaced" by a newborn sibling.

STAGE 2   SENSORIMOTOR-AUTONOMY

The Ecologically Accommodating (Passive)–Ecologically Modifying (Active) Polarity

Not until the end of the first year has the infant matured sufficiently to engage in actions independent of parental support. Holding the drinking cup, the first few steps, or a word or two, all signify a growing capacity to act autonomously. As the child develops the functions that characterize this stage, he or she begins to comprehend the attitudes and feelings communicated by stimulative sources. No longer is rough parental handling merely excess stimulation, undistinguished from the playful tossing of an affectionate father; the child now discerns the difference between harshness and good-natured roughhousing.

In the sensorimotor-autonomy stage, the focus shifts from existence in itself to existence within an environment. From an evolutionary perspective, the child in this stage is learning a *mode of adaptation,* an *active* tendency to modify his or her ecological niche, versus a *passive* tendency to accommodate to whatever the environment has provided. The former reflects a disposition toward taking the initiative in shaping the course of life events; the latter a disposition to be quiescent, placid, unassertive, to react rather than act, to wait for things to happen, and to accept what is given. In the prior sensory-attachment stage, the infant was in his or her native mode, so to speak, largely passive, mostly dependent upon parental figures to meet existential needs. Although the child may have engaged in behaviors (e.g., crying) that seemed active by virtue of the arousal they evoked in others, these signals were intended to recruit others in the service of fundamental needs. Here it was parental figures, rather than the child itself, who either modified the ecological milieu or sought out a more hospitable one. With the development of autonomous capacities, the young child finds that he or she is embedded in an environment which can either be explored and later modified, or feared and accommodated to. The child must "decide" whether to "break out" of dependence on parental figures or to perpetuate this dependent pattern into later years. Whatever alternative is pursued, it is, of course, a matter of degree rather than a yes-no decision. Undoubtedly important in children's orientation toward the environment are their attachments. Those children who possess a "secure base" will explore their environments without becoming fearful that their attachment figure cannot be recovered (Ainsworth, 1967). On the other hand, those without such a base tend to remain close to their caretakers, assuming the more passive mode, which is likely to ultimately restrict their range of coping resources through decreased or retarded sociocognitive competence (Millon, 1969).

Development of Sensorimotor Capacities

The unorganized movements of the neonate progressively give way to focused muscular activity. As the neural substrate for muscular control unfolds, the aimless motor behavior of infants is supplanted by focused movements. These newly emergent functions coordinate with sensory capacities to enable children to explore, manipulate, play, sit, crawl, babble, throw, walk, catch, talk, and otherwise intervene in their ecological milieu as desired. The maturing fusion between the substrates of sensory and motor functions is strengthened by children's exploratory behavior. Manipulative play and the formation of babbling sounds are methods of self-stimulation that facilitate the growth of action-oriented interneuronal connections; the child is building a neural foundation for more complicated and refined skills such as running, handling utensils, controlling sphincter muscles, and articulating precise speech. Children's intrinsic tendency to "entertain" themselves represents a necessary step in establishing capacities that are more substantial than maturation alone would have furnished. Stimulative experiences, either self-provided or provided by relations with others, are requisites for the development of normal, activity-oriented sensorimotor skills. Unless retarded by environmental restrictions, biological handicaps, or insecure attachments, toddlers' growing sensorimotor capacities prepare them to take an active rather than passive role in coping with their environment.

Development of Autonomous Behaviors

Perhaps the most significant aspect of sensorimotor development is that it enables children to begin to take an active stance in doing things for themselves, to influence their environment, to free themselves from domination, and to outgrow the dependencies of their first years. Children become aware of their increasing competence and seek new ventures. Needless to say, conflicts and restrictions arise as they assert themselves (Erikson, 1959; White, 1960). These are seen clearly during toilet training, when youngsters often resist submitting to the demands of their parents. A delicate exchange of power and cunning often ensues. Opportunities arise for the child to actively extract promises or deny wishes; in response, parents may mete out punishments, submit meekly, or shift inconsistently. Important precedents for attitudes toward authority, power, and autonomy are generated during this period of parent-child interaction.

Consequences of Impoverishment

A lack of stimulation of sensorimotor capacities can lead to retardations in functions necessary to the development of autonomy and initiative, leading children to remain within a passive adaptational mode. This is seen most clearly in children of overprotective parents—spoon-fed, excused from chores, restrained from exploration, curtailed in friendships, and protected from danger—all these practices illustrate controls that restrict growing children's opportunities to exercise their sensorimotor skills and develop the means for autonomous behavior. A self-perpetuating cycle often unfolds. These children may fear abandoning their over-learned dependency on their parents since they are ill-equipped to meet other children on the latter's terms. They may become timid and submissive when forced to venture out into the world, likely to avoid the give and take of competition with their peers, and they may seek out older children who will protect them and upon whom they can lean. Here the passive mode that began as dependence on parental figures is continued in the larger social context (Millon, 1969).

Consequences of Enrichment

The consequences of excessive enrichment during the sensorimotor-autonomy stage are found most often in children of excessively lax, permissive, or overindulgent parents. Given free rein with minimal restraint, stimulated to explore and manipulate things to their suiting without guidance or control, these children will often become irresponsibly undisciplined in their behaviors. Their active style compels these children to view the entire ecological milieu as a playground or medium to be modified according to their whims. Carried into the wider social context, these behaviors run up against the desires of other children and the restrictions of less permissive adults. Unless the youngsters are extremely adept, they will find that their actively self-centered and free-wheeling tactics fail miserably. For the few who succeed, however, a pattern of egocentrism, unbridled self-expression, and social arrogance may become dominant. The majority of these youngsters fail to gain acceptance by peers and never quite acquire the flexibility to shift between active and passive styles according to contextual demands. Such children are conspicuous in their lack of the normal give-and-take skills that form the basis of genuine social relationships.

Equally important as a form of enrichment is the intensity of attachments. Children acquire representations about the world, themselves, and others through their interactions with attachment figures (Bowlby, 1969/1982; 1973). Constant concern about a child's welfare may cause it to view itself as an object of frailty, resulting later in a passive style wherein the older child or adult constantly makes bids for others to take the initiative in transforming the environment.

STAGE 3   PUBERTAL-GENDER IDENTITY

The Progeny Nurturance (Other)– Individual Propagation (Self) Polarity

Somewhere between the 11th and 15th years, a rather sweeping series of hormonal changes unsettle the psychic state that was so carefully constructed in preceding years. These changes reflect the onset of puberty and the instantiation of sexual and gender-related characteristics that are preparatory for the emergence of the r- and K-strategies—strong sexual impulses and adultlike features of anatomy, voice, and bearing. Erratic moods, changing self-images, reinterpretations of one's view of others, new urges, hopeful expectancies, and a growing physical and social awkwardness, all upset the relative equanimity of an earlier age. Disruptive as it may be, this turbulent stage of growth bifurcates and focuses many of the remaining elements of the youngster's biological potential. Not only is it a preparatory phase for the forthcoming independence from parental direction, but it is when the psychological equivalent of the r- and K-strategies, self (male) and other (female) orientations, begin to diverge and then coalesce into distinct gender roles.

With the unsettling influences of adolescence, both physiological and social, and the emergence of the individual as a being of genuine reproductive potential, the r- and K-strategies begin to take on an implicitly criterial role in the selection of the behaviors of the moment, as well as future goals, from a universe of implicit alternatives. These strategies are psychologically expressed, at the highest level of abstraction, in an orientation toward self and an orientation toward others. Here the male can be prototypally described as more dominant, imperial, and acquisitive, and the female more communal, nurturant, and deferent.

These representations—self and other and their coordination—are essential to the genesis of the personality system. Both attachment theory and the evolutionary model presented here recognize the importance of self and other constructs. From an attachment perspective, these constructs represent inchoate interpersonal relationships, the intricacies of which are made possible by cognitive developments. No longer is the world an unorganized swirl of events; increasingly, it is organized around relationships and expectations. Although relationships are organic wholes (Sroufe & Fleeson, 1986), within these wholes the individual's orientation (i.e., expectations about future states of the relationship and outcomes desired from the relationship) is toward self and other, and the individual may possess positive or negative models of each (Bartholomew & Horowitz, 1991).

Development of Pubertal Maturation

Pubescence is characterized by the rapidity of body growth, genital maturity, and sexual awareness. A series of transformations take place that are qualitatively different from those developed earlier in childhood. They create an element of discontinuity from prior experiences, confronting the youngster, not only with an internal "revolution" of a physiological nature, but also with a series of psychological tasks that are prompted by emergent sexual feelings. Perhaps more applicable to this stage of life than those which Freud considered paramount in infancy, the emergence of pubertal sexuality is central to the psychic development of the adolescent. Much effort is invested both consciously and unconsciously to incorporate these new bodily impulses into one's sense of self and one's relationship to others. Youngsters must establish a gender identity that incorporates physiological changes and the powerful libidinal feelings with which they are associated. The increase in pubertal libidinal drives requires a reorganization of the child's sense of adolescent identity. When developed in a satisfactory manner, the adolescent is enabled to search out relevant extrafamilial love objects.

Development of Gender Identity

Developing a gender identity is not so much acquiring a means for satisfying libidinal impulses as it is a process of refining the youngster's previously diffused and undifferentiated sense of self. This is achieved most effectively by reflecting the admiration of a beloved other. The feedback received in real and fantasized love relationships assists the teenager to revise and define his or her gender-identity. It serves also to clarify and further develop a new self-concept that encompasses relationships with peer companions of both genders, rather than parents or siblings.

Not uncommonly, the definition of one's own gender identity brings forth a rejection of the opposite sex. "They" are treated with derision and contempt. A turning toward the same-sex peer group is of value in defining one's identity, a process that is deeply embedded by a self-conscious selection and alliance of same-sex peers. Pubertal boys avoid girls, belittle them and strongly reject female sentimentality. Girls turn for affection and support toward their same-sex peers, sharing secrets, intimacies, and erotically tinged fantasies and romances. All these efforts add a psychosocial dimension and gender definition to increasingly powerful pubertal processes.

Consequences of Impoverishment

The goal of the adolescent is in part to achieve a libidinous extrafamilial object, an aim ultimately resulting in a richer and more mature emotional life. As noted, with the onset of puberty, parental identification declines and is replaced by identifications with valued peers, both real friendships and romanticized heroes. The lack of such identifications and role models during adolescence may culminate in imaginary infatuations, unreal and ineffectual substitutes for the desirable qualities that usually emerge from everyday personal relationships.

Without direct tuition from their elders, teenagers will be left to their own devices to master the complexities of a varied world, to control intense aggressive and sexual urges that well up within, to channel their fantasies and to pursue their goals. They may become victims of their own growth, unable to discipline impulses or fashion acceptable means for expressing their desires. Scattered and unguided, they cannot get hold of a sense of personal identity, a consistent direction and purpose to their existence. Such teenagers become an "other-directed" individuals who vacillate at every turn, overly responsive to fleeting stimuli, and who shift from one erratic course to another. Ultimately, without an inner core or anchor to guide their future, they may flounder or stagnate. Deficient gender identifications and inadequate sexual initiations may interfere in significant ways with the development of their emotional maturity.

Borderline personality disorders often characterize this pattern of gender diffusion. Their aimlessness and disaffiliation from the mainstream of traditional American life may be traced, in part, to the failure of experience to provide a coherent set of gender role-models and values around which they can focus their lives and orient themselves toward a meaningful future.

Consequences of Enrichment

In contrast to the problems that arise from a deficiency of gender-role models, we frequently observe excessive dependency on peer group sexual habits and values. Some adolescents who have been ill disposed to the values of problematic peer groups may find themselves isolated and avoided, if not ridiculed and ostracized. To protect themselves against this discomforting possibility, these teenagers may submerge their identity to fit the roles given them by others. They may adopt gender models that have been explicitly or implicitly established by group customs. They act, dress, use language, and enact their gender roles in terms of peer-group standards.

Not untypically, peer groups provide a formal structure to guide the youngster, with uniforms,

rituals, and even specified heroes as imitative models. Such identities, gender and otherwise, are provided by belonging to neighborhood gangs or "hippie" subcultures. Many high-school students conform unquestioningly to the sexual standards of their peers in order to be accepted, to be enmeshed in the good feeling of group solidarity, and to boost their sense of identity through identification. In effect, these youngsters have jettisoned parental norms for peer group norms, and it is these latter norms that foreclose independent thought and feeling. What is seen in these identifications is an increase in narcissism, a posture of arrogance and rebellion, as well as defiance against conventional societal norms.

As the diffusion of earlier bisexual trends gives way to a distinct heterosexual orientation, sexuality becomes the most prominent feature of these "enriched" youngsters. Many become sensitive, almost exclusively, to erotic stimuli, in contrast to the more global and varied aspects of normal heterosexual relationships. Such adolescents often "back off," stating that they are worried that they might be getting "too involved." Hence, pubertal maturation in these youngsters may not only intensify their libidinal drives, but may also increase in equal measure their aggressive/hostile drives. As a consequence of these developments and transformations, these youngsters may now have developed behaviors that accentuate the stereotypical roles of masculinity and femininity.

STAGE 4 INTRACORTICAL-INTEGRATION

The Intellective Reasoning (Thinking)–Affective Resonance (Feeling) Polarity

The intracortical-integration stage coordinates with the fourth phase of the evolutionary progression, the thinking-feeling polarity. The peak period of neurological maturation for these psychological functions generally occurs between the ages of 4 and 18. The amount and kind of intrapsychic and contextual stimulation at these times of rapid growth will have a strong bearing on the degree to which these functions mature. Thinking and feeling are broad and multifaceted constructs with diverse manifestations. Whereas the focus in the first three stages of development was on the child's existential aims, modes of adaptation, and gender identification, here the focus shifts to the individual as a being-in-time.

Initially, the child must acquire abstract capacities to transcend the purely concrete reality of the present moment and project the self-as-object into myriad futures contingent on the child's own style of action or accommodation. Such capacities are both cognitive and emotional, and may have wide-ranging consequences for the personality system if they fail to cohere as integrated structures, as in the more severe personality disorders (e.g., borderline and schizotypal).

What capacities unfold during this stage, and what consequences can be attributed to differences in the quality and intensity of relevant experience?

Development of Intracortical Capacities

Progressively more complex arrangements of neural cells become possible as children advance in maturation. Although these higher-order connections begin in early infancy, they do not form into structures capable of rational foresight and adult-level planning until the youngsters have fully developed their more basic sensorimotor skills and pubertal maturations. With these capacities as a base, they are able to differentiate and arrange the objects of the physical world. As verbal skills unfold, they learn to symbolize concrete objects; soon they are able to manipulate and coordinate these symbols as well as, if not better than, the tangible events themselves. Free of the need to make direct reference to the concrete world, they are able to recall past events and anticipate future ones. As increasingly complex cortical connections are established, higher conceptual abstractions are formulated, enabling the children to transfer, associate, and coordinate these symbols into ideas of finer differentiation, greater intricacy, and broader integration. These internal representations of reality, the product of symbolic thought, the construction of events past, present, and future, take over as the primary elements of the representational world. Especially significant at this period is a fusion between the capacities to think and to feel.

Development of Integrative Processes

When the inner world of symbols is mastered, giving objective reality an order and integration, youngsters are able to create some consistency and continuity in their lives. No longer are they buffeted from one mood or action to another by the swirl of changing events; they now have an internal anchor, a nucleus of cognitions that serves as a base and imposes a sense of sameness and continuity on an otherwise fluid environment. As they grow in their capacity to organize and integrate their world,

one configuration becomes increasingly differentiated and begins to predominate. Accrued from experiences with others and their reactions to the child, an image or representation of self-as-object has taken shape. This highest order of abstraction, the sense of individual identity as distinct from others becomes the dominant source of stimuli that guides the youngster's thoughts and feelings. External events no longer have the power they once exerted; the youngster now has an ever-present and stable sphere of internal representations, transformed by rational and emotional reflections, which govern his or her course of action and from which behaviors are initiated.

Consequences of Impoverishment

The task of integrating a consistent self-other differentiation, as well as consolidating the divergencies of thought and feeling, is not easy in a world of changing events and pluralistic values. From what sources can a genuine balance between reason and emotion be developed?

The institutions that interweave to form the complex fabric of society are implicitly designed to shape the assumptive world of its younger members. Family, school, and church transmit implicit values and explicit rules that guide children in behaving and thinking in a manner consonant with those of others. Youngsters not only are subject to cultural pressures but require them to give direction to their proliferating capacities and impulses. Without them, potentials may become overly diffuse and scattered; conversely, too much guidance may narrow children's potentials and restrict their adaptiveness. In either case, the sense of self and other, as well as the relationship of thought and emotion, are no longer expressed in personally elaborated and multifaceted forms. Instead, they are manifested narrowly or rigidly, with the result that the individual lacks the flexibility required to successfully navigate life's social contexts on his or her own. Once basic patterns of thought and feeling are shaped during this period, it is difficult to orient them along new pathways.

What are the effects of inadequate or erratic stimulation during the peak years of intracortical integration? As noted in discussions of Stage 3, youngsters may be left to their own devices to master the complexities of a varied world, to control intense urges, to channel fantasies, and to pursue the goals to which they aspire. They may become victims of their own growth, unable to orient their impulses or fashion acceptable means for expressing their desires. Scattered and unguided, they may be unable to construct a sense of internal cohesion, nor a consistent direction and purpose to their existence. As noted, such youngsters may vacillate at every turn, overly responsive to fleeting stimuli, shifting from one erratic course to another. Without an inner core or anchor to guide their future, they may flounder or stagnate.

Evidently, the impoverishment of integrative stimuli will have a profound effect. Fortunately, with proper guidance, the "immaturity and irresponsibility" of many adolescents may be salvaged in later years. But for others, the inability to settle down into a consolidated path may become a problem of increasingly severe proportions.

Consequences of Enrichment

The negative consequences of overenrichment at the fourth stage usually occur when parents are controlling and perfectionistic. Overly trained, overly disciplined, and overly integrated youngsters are given little opportunity to shape their own destiny. Whether by coercion or enticement, children who, too early, are led to control their emergent feelings, to focus their thoughts along narrowly defined paths and to follow the prescriptions of parental demands, have been subverted into adopting the identities of others. Whatever individuality they may have acquired is drowned in a model of adult orderliness, propriety, and virtue. Such oversocialized and rigid youngsters lack the spontaneity, flexibility, and creativeness we expect of the young; they have been trained to be old men and women before their time, too narrow in perspective to respond to excitement, variety, and the challenge of new events. Overenrichment at this stage has fixed them on a restrictive course and has deprived them of the rewards of being themselves.

It may be useful to represent the first three of the theory's polarities in terms of their initial potentials and their ultimate levels of expression. Figure 3.1 portrays the gradual ontological development of these polarities in two persons.

Let us first look at Person 1. Across the top row are the names of the three evolutionary polarities: pleasure-pain, active-passive, and self-other. The furthest left column of Figure 3.1 records the range these polarities may achieve, zero at the bottom, 100 at the top. Looking to the right, we find the first elongated rectangle under the *pleasure* polarity of the pleasure-pain pairing. It is composed of a dashed-line vertical rectangle; this rectangle represents the *constitutional* potential in Person 1 for

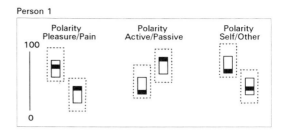

Person 1

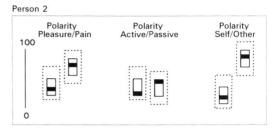

Person 2

┈┈ Constitutionally disposed potential.

☐ Actual range of potential achieved through life experiences.

▬ Current dispositional state, as influenced by the inducements and constraints of present life circumstances.

Figure 3.1 Polarity dispositions: Constitutional, achieved, and current.

experiencing pleasure. As can be seen, this potential extends from levels 50 to 100. What these numbers translate into is a high inherent capacity of Person 1 to experience life as reasonably gratifying to exceptionally gratifying. However, this *constitutionally* disposed range (within the dotted lines) is merely the upper and lower boundary of this inherent potential in Person 1. Within this extended rectangle is a smaller rectangle, one noted by straight lines on all four sides. It indicates the *actual* bandwidth for experiencing pleasure (life enhancement) that derives from the early life events to which Person 1 has been exposed. The experiences of life narrow the range of constitutional potentials to a smaller bandwidth than might have possibly been, that is, these experiences produce a *dispositional reality* below the upper and above the lower constitutional potentials of the individual. As we can see with Person 1, this actual range (straight-line rectangle) leans slightly toward the lower end of the constitutional potential, indicating that the person's life experiences have been of a less than favorable sort. In sum, the dotted and straight line rectangles indicate that this person is still well disposed and favorably exposed to experience life in positive/pleasure-enhancing manner.

There is a third solid rectangle within the second straight-line rectangle. Its placement within the second rectangle indicates that person's current or immediate dispositional state, shaped largely by present life circumstances. In Person 1, we see that this rectangle leans slightly toward the upper end of the second rectangle, that is, the actual dispositional range. What this final rectangle tells us, in sum, is that pleasure is a high constitutional disposition, that the actual potential achieved by virtue of life's experiences have also been moderately positive, and that current life circumstances appear to bring positive inclinations out further.

It would be useful, by contrast, to examine the *pain* component polarity of Person 1. Here we see that Person 1's inclinations were quite weak constitutionally (*neither* fearful, anxious, aversive); this is gauged by the relatively low position of the dotted rectangle. Within this constitutional rectangle lies the second or straight-line rectangle, which signifies the actual range of potential achieved by virtue of life experiences. As can be seen, this rectangle falls at a mid-point within the constitutional range. However, the solid horizontal rectangle, representing current life circumstances, is located at the high end of the actual rectangle, suggesting that current life circumstances make this individual feel as unhappy, depressed, and anxious as he is capable of, which is not very much.

Combining the pain and pleasure components for Person 1, we appear to be dealing with an individual who is not only potentially inclined to view the world in a sanguine and optimistic manner, but whose life circumstances have led that inherent disposition to continue in its inclined direction. Moreover, although current circumstances are distressing to him, he is inherently not capable of experiencing much of these discomforting emotions and, hence, remains basically optimistic in his outlook.

If we shift to the second bipolarity, that relating to active/passive inclinations, what we see in Person 1 is a constitutional tendency more disposed to passivity than to activity. Further, early life events have reinforced this disparity (the straight-line rectangle within the dotted-line rectangle), and current life circumstances bring out the passive/accommodating inclination to its fullest extent. A similar analysis may be made in the self/other bipolarity. Here, constitutional potentials are strongly in the self direction, early life events create dispositions at the lower end of

this inborn potential, and current life circumstances further reduce achieved inclinations.

If we turn to Person 2, we see that the pleasure-pain polarity contrasts with that of Person 1, that is, the constitutional inclination to preserve life or avoid pain stands at a higher level than does the life-enhancing/pleasure inclination. The relative positions achieved on the active-passive bipolarity are rather similar between these two persons; however, the dissimilarity between them continues on the bipolarity of self-other. There are times when the potentials for one or another of the bipolarity pairs are close to identical, as in the active-passive polarity of Person 2. Moreover, in this case, extended life circumstances appear to have brought the range of actual achieved dispositions even closer, that is, an initial minor inequality between active and passive was further reduced; however, current life circumstances are having a pronounced effect, such that the equalized potentials now diverge appreciably, given present inducements or constraints (as seen in the placement of the smaller black rectangles).

To summarize briefly, Figure 3.1 tells us that people start off life with a genetic/constitutional disposition that falls somewhere between the highest and lowest boundaries in which that disposition can be expressed among persons. The dotted-line rectangle, the outer bandwidth for each person, indicates the constitutional *potential* possible for that individual. The second, or straight-line rectangle indicates the *actual* degree to which this potential is achieved by virtue of lifelong experiences. The third, or solid rectangle, represents the effects of present life circumstances that further constrain the range within which the actual disposition is likely to be manifested currently.

Comment.   It would be an error to leave this discussion of evolutionary-neuropsychological development with the impression that personality growth is merely a function of stimulation at sensitive maturational periods. Impoverishment and enrichment have their profound effects, but the quality or kind of stimulation the youngster experiences is often of greater importance. The impact of parental harshness or inconsistency, of sibling rivalry or social failure, is more than a matter of stimulus volume and timing. Different dimensions of experience take precedence as the meaning conveyed by the source of stimulation becomes clear to the growing child. We will discuss this facet of psychogenesis shortly, as well as the central tasks that must be undertaken at each of the four sequential stages of development.

Normal psychological processes depend on a substrate of orderly neuronal connections. The development of this intricate neural substrate unfolds within the organism in accord with genetically determined mechanisms, but there remain substantial numbers of fibers whose direction of growth is modifiable. To summarize the previous section, it might be said that the basic architecture of the nervous system is laid down in a relatively fixed manner, but refinements in this linkage system do not develop without the aid of additional experiences. Environmental experience not only activates neural collaterals but alters these structures so as to preempt them for similar subsequent experiences. Thus, early experiences not only construct new neural pathways but, in addition, selectively prepare them to be receptive to later stimuli that are qualitatively similar.

This second consequence of experience, representing the selective lowering of thresholds for the transmission of similar subsequent stimuli, is described in the conceptual language of psychology as learning. It reflects the observation that behaviors that have been subject to prior experience are reactivated with increasing ease. With this second consequence of stimulation, we begin to conceive the nervous system as more than a network of abstract pathways; it is now viewed as possessing the residues of specific classes of environmental stimuli. These environmentally anchored neural connections interweave to form patterns of perception and behavior that relate to discriminable events in the external world. By including qualitatively discriminable features of the stimulus world within our purview, we shift our attention to observational units that transcend neural mechanisms located strictly within the anatomic limits of the body. It is necessary to represent these complex external-internal relationships in a conceptual language that is broader in scope than that of neurology.

We noted further that there are sensitive periods in the maturation of the nervous system when the effects of stimulation are especially pronounced; these occur at points of rapid neural growth. Stimulus impoverishment at these critical stages leads to an underdevelopment among neural connections; deficit neural development will have long-range deleterious effects because early growth serves as a prerequisite to the development of subsequent capacities; comparable complications may arise as a function of stimulus enrichment.

What conceptual level and units of observation will best enable us to describe and analyze the effects of the *quality* or content of experience?

As noted earlier, the qualitative aspect of stimulation alters the threshold of neural transmission for similar subsequent stimuli. This change in the probability of neural transmission is descriptively similar to the psychological process known as learning; learning often is defined as an increment in the probability that previously experienced stimulus situations will be perceived rapidly, and that responses previously associated with them will be elicited.

Both neurological and learning concepts can be utilized to describe changes in response probabilities arising from prior stimulus exposure. But, because learning concepts are formulated in terms of behavior-environment interactions, it would appear reasonable, when discussing the specific properties of qualitatively discriminable stimulus events, to utilize the conceptual language of learning. Moreover, the principles derived from learning theory and research describe subtle features of psychological behavior that cannot begin to be handled intelligently in neurological terms. With the principles and conceptual language of learning, we can formulate precisely our ideas about the effects of qualitatively discriminable stimulus events, that is, differences not only in the magnitude but in the variety and content of the stimulus world as we experience it.

Let us keep in mind that learning concepts and neurological concepts do not represent intrinsically different processes; we are using the former because they have been more finely differentiated and, therefore, are more fruitful tools for formulating notions about qualitatively different stimulus-behavior interactions.

STAGE-RELATED DEVELOPMENTAL TASKS

As noted in prior sections, experience is likely to have a more profound effect at certain stages in the developmental sequence than at others. This statement reiterates a conviction stated earlier that pronounced environmental influences occur at periods of rapid neurological growth. A further reason for the stage-specific significance of experience is the observation that children are exposed to a succession of culturally related social tasks that they are expected to fulfill at different points in the developmental sequence. These stage-specific tasks are timed to coincide with periods of rapid neurological growth (e.g., the training of bladder control is begun when the child possesses the requisite neural equipment for such control; similarly, children are taught to read when intracortical development has advanced sufficiently to enable a measure of consistent success). In short, a reciprocity appears between periods of rapid neurological growth and exposure to related experiences and tasks. To use Erikson's (1950) terms, the child's newly emerging neurological potentials are challenged by a series of "crises" with the environment. Children are especially vulnerable at these critical stages because experience both shapes their neurological patterns and results in learning a series of fundamental attitudes about themselves and others.

What experiences typically arise at the four neuropsychological stages described earlier, and what are the central attitudes learned during these periods?

In seeking answers to these questions, this discussion turns briefly to the fertile ideas of Freud and Erikson. During the sensory-attachment stage, when pleasure and pain discriminations are central, the critical attitude learned deals with one's *trust of others*. The sensorimotor-autonomy stage, when the progression from passive to active modes of adaptation occurs, is noted by learning attitudes concerning *adaptive confidence*. During the pubertal-gender identity stage, when the separation between self and other is sharpened, we see the development of reasonably distinct *sexual roles*. The intracortical-integrative stage, when the coordination between intellectual and affective

processes develops, may best be characterized by the acquisition of a balance between *cognition and emotion*. A brief elaboration of these is in order (Table 3.1).

TASK 1   DEVELOPING TRUST OF OTHERS (PAIN-PLEASURE POLARITY)

Trust may be described as a feeling that one can rely on the affections and support of others. There are few periods of life when an individual is so wholly dependent on the goodwill and care of others as during the relatively helpless state of infancy. Nothing is more crucial to the infant's well-being than the nurturance and protection afforded by caretakers. Through the quality and consistency of this support, deeply ingrained feelings of trust are etched within the child. From the evolutionary model presented earlier, trust and mistrust represent facets of the pleasure and pain constructs, generalized to adaptational venues within the physical environment, such as the nursery, as well as to the environment of prototypal social objects. Within the infant's world, of course, trust and mistrust lack their phenomenological and moral dimensions, resembling more global and undifferentiated feelings of soothing calm (pleasure) or tense apprehension (pain) than consciously abstracted states.

Such perceptual indiscriminateness of associations is highly significant. Thus, feelings and expectancies arising from specific experiences become highly generalized and come to characterize the child's image of the entire environment. Because children are unable to make fine

TABLE 3.1 Four Components of the Evolutionary Model

Evolutionary Phase	Survival Functions	Neuropsychological Stage	Developmental Task
Existence	Life enhancement (pleasure) Life preservation (pain)	Sensory-attachment	Developing trust of others
Adaptation	Ecological modification (active) Ecological accommodation (passive)	Sensorimotor-autonomy	Acquiring adaptive confidence
Replication	Progeny nurturance (other) Individual propagation (self)	Pubertal-gender identity	Assimilating sexual roles
Abstraction	Intellective-reasoning (thinking) Affective resonance (feeling)	Intracortical integration	Balancing reason and emotion

discriminations, their early attachments become pervasive and widespread. Nurtured well and given comfort and affection, they will acquire a far-reaching trust of others; they learn that discomfort will be moderated and that others will assist them and provide for their needs. Deprived of warmth and security or handled severely and painfully, they will learn to mistrust their environment, to anticipate further stress, and view others as harsh and undependable. Rather than developing an optimistic and confident attitude toward the future, they will be disposed to withdraw and avoid people for fear that these persons will recreate the discomfort and anguish that were experienced in the past.

TASK 2   ACQUIRING ADAPTIVE CONFIDENCE (ACTIVE-PASSIVE POLARITY)

Children become progressively less dependent on their caretakers during the sensorimotor-autonomy stage. By the second and third years, they are ambulatory and possess the power of speech and control over many elements in their environment. They have acquired the manipulative skills to venture forth and test their competence to handle events on their own (White, 1960). In terms of the evolutionary model, this stage concerns the active-passive polarity. Here children struggle to break out of the inherently dependent and passive mode of infancy. Rather than remain a passive receptacle for environmental forces, clay to be molded, they acquire competencies that enlarge their vistas and allow them to become legitimate actors in their environments.

However, subtle, as well as obvious, parental attitudes shape children's confidence in their ability to exercise these growing competencies. These attitudes markedly influence behavior since it is not only what the children can do that determines their actions but how they feel about what they can do. The rewards and punishments to which they are exposed and the degree of encouragement and affection surrounding their first performances will contribute to their confidence in themselves. Severe discipline for transgressions, humiliating comments in response to efforts at self-achievement, embarrassment over social awkwardness, deprecations associated with poor school performance, and shame among one's peers as a result of physical inadequacies, all weigh heavily to diminish self-esteem. Faced with rebuffs and ridicule, children learn to doubt their competence and adequacy. Whether they actually possess the skills to handle events is no longer the issue; they simply lack the confidence to try, to venture out, or to compete. Believing their efforts will be ineffectual and futile, these children often adopt a passive, wait-and-see attitude toward their environment and their future.

TASK 3   ASSIMILATING SEXUAL ROLES (SELF-OTHER POLARITY)

The many crushes and infatuations experienced during the pubertal period serve as a genuine source of development. Gender roles emerge in significant ways by interacting with others, especially as enacted in peer group relationships. Adhering to the models of peer behaviors helps the youngster find and evaluate how certain gender roles fit. The high school clique, the neighborhood gang, the athletic team, all aid the teenager in discovering his or her gender identity, providing both useful role models and instant social feedback. The bull session among boys and the endless phone conversations between girls serve significant goals by providing evaluative feedback as youngsters search to define themselves. It is particularly during the time of rapid body changes when genital impulses stimulate sexual fantasies that the adolescent learns to rely on peers as important guides and sounding boards.

Security is found in peer relationships in that youngsters share a code as to what constitutes appropriate gender behaviors. No less important is the mutuality they experience in struggling through the same pubertal issues. The importance of the influence of the peer group is perhaps nowhere more significant than in the realm of sexual behaviors. For the most part, the adolescent finds security in accepting the peer-gender norms as preliminary guides regarding how to regulate impulses, feelings, and sexual inclinations.

TASK 4   BALANCING REASON AND EMOTION (THINKING-FEELING POLARITY)

The emergence of this final developmental stage—with its capacities for thinking, feeling, evaluating, and planning—leads youngsters to formulate a clear image of themselves as a certain "kind of adult," an identity discernible from others, capable of having independent judgments and of fashioning their own course of action. Healthy children must acquire a coherent system of internalized values that will guide them through a changing and varied environment. They must find their own anchor and compass by which to coordinate both their feelings and ideas about life. Equipped by successful efforts toward autonomy, they will have confidence that they possess a direction in life that is valued by others and that can safely withstand the buffeting of changing events. In terms of the evolutionary model, such children are capable of integrating their feelings and thoughts, setting their own agendas, and becoming masters of their own fate.

Conversely, if deprived of rewarded achievements and unable to construct a picture of a valued identity, they will lack the means to meet life's tasks rationally and be unable to handle discouraging emotional forces that may arise. In such cases, their identity may come to be defined through the goals and needs of others rather than through self. Without an integrated and consistent integration of thought and feeling, the growing adolescent or adult will flounder from one tentative course to another and be beset with amorphous and vague feelings of discontent and uselessness.

SOURCES OF PATHOGENIC LEARNING

Attitudes and behaviors may be learned as a consequence of instruction or indoctrination on the part of parents, but most of what is learned accrues from a haphazard series of casual and incidental events to which the child is exposed. Not only is the administration of rewards and punishments meted out most often in a spontaneous and erratic fashion, but the everyday and ordinary activities of parents provide the child with unintended models to imitate.

These conditions *do not* activate protective or defensive behaviors as do emotionally disruptive events; they merely reinforce styles of behavior that prove deleterious when generalized to settings other than those in which they were acquired. The roots of behavior—how people think, talk, fear, love, solve problems and relate to others, aversions, irritabilities, attitudes, anxieties and styles of interpersonal communication—are all adopted and duplicated by children as they observe the everyday reactions of their parents and older siblings. Children mirror these complex

behaviors without understanding their significance and without parental intentions of transmitting them. The old saying, "practice what you preach," conveys the essence of this thesis. Thus, as noted in the quote, a parent who castigates the child harshly for failing to be kind may create an intrinsically ambivalent learning experience; the contrast between parental manner and the verbalized injunction teaches the child simultaneously to think kindly but to behave harshly.

The particulars and the coloration of many pathological patterns have their beginnings in the offhand behaviors and attitudes to which the child is incidentally exposed. It is important, therefore, in reviewing this chapter, that the reader keep in mind that children acquire less from intentional parental training methods than from casual and adventitious experience. People simply do not learn in neatly arranged alley mazes with all confounding effects nicely controlled; the sequence is complicated not only by manifold "extraneous variables" to which learning becomes attached, but is subject to highly irregular "schedules of reinforcement."

A few words must be stated again on a matter that should be self-evident but is often overlooked or simplified in presenting pathogenic influences. It relates to our prior notation that most children acquire their ideas and models from *two parents,* as well as one or more siblings. As a consequence, children are exposed to and frequently learn different and contrasting sets of perceptions, feelings, attitudes, behaviors, and so on, as well as a mixed set of assumptions about themselves and others. In a manner similar to *genetic recombination,* where the child's heredity-based dispositions reflect the contribution of both parents, so too the child's experiences and learnings reflect the input and interweaving from both parents. To illustrate, one parent may have been cruel and rejecting, whereas the other may have been kindly and supportive. How this mix will ultimately take psychological form, and which set of these differential experiences will predominate, will be a function of numerous other factors. The point to note, however, is that we should expect that children will be differentially affected by each parent, and that pathogenesis will reflect a complex interaction of these combined experiences. In reading the following, as well as what has already been presented, the reader should be mindful that few experiences are singular in their impact, but are modulated by the interplay of multiple forces, especially the commingling and consolidation of two sets of parental influences.

We might pause briefly, before going further, and note what is meant by the term "pathogenic." Three types of events may be described to illustrate the concept:

1. First, there are events that provoke undue anxiety within the individual because they make demands beyond the child's capacity, or because they otherwise undermine his or her feelings of security and comfort. Persistence of these emotionally disruptive events elicit coping reactions that, ultimately, may lead to the *learning* of *generalized defensive strategies.* These strategies may be successful in diminishing certain feelings of discomfort, but they may prove detrimental in the long run to healthy functioning in that they may be applied to circumstances for which they are ill-suited.

2. The second class of pathogenic events are emotionally neutral conditions that lead to the *learning of maladaptive behaviors.* These conditions do not activate protective or defensive behaviors as do emotionally disruptive events; they merely teach or reinforce styles of behavior that prove deleterious when generalized inappropriately to settings other than those in which they were acquired. The roots of these difficulties, therefore, do not lie in stress, anxiety, or unconscious mechanisms of defense, but rather in the simple conditioning or imitation of maladaptive behavior patterns.

3. The third source of psychopathology arises from an *insufficiency* of experiences requisite to the learning *of adaptive behavior.* Thus, general stimulus impoverishment, or minimal social experience, may produce deficits in the acquisition of adaptive behaviors. The sheer lack of skills and competence for mastering the environment is a form of pathological *underlearning* that may be as severe as those disorders generated either by stressful experiences or by defective or maladaptive learning.

The research and theoretical literature on pathogenic sources do not lend themselves to the preceding threefold schema; another format must be used to present this body of work. Nevertheless, it will be helpful for the reader to keep these distinctions in mind while studying the ensuing pages.

A few preliminary comments are advisable before detailing the pathogenic sources of learning.

The belief that early interpersonal experiences within the family play a decisive role in the development of psychopathology is well accepted among professionals, but reliable and unequivocal data supporting this conviction are difficult to find. The deficits in these data are not due to a shortage of research efforts; rather, they reflect numerous methodological and theoretical difficulties that stymie progress. For example, and as discussed in prior pages, most of these data depend on retrospective accounts of early experience; these data are notoriously unreliable. Patients interviewed during their illness are prone to give a warped and selective accounting of their relationships with others; information obtained from relatives often is distorted by feelings of guilt or by a desire to uncover some simple event to which the disorder can be attributed. In general, then, attempts to reconstruct the complex sequence of events of yesteryear that may have contributed to pathological learning are fraught with almost insurmountable methodological difficulties.

To these procedural complications may be added problems of conceptual semantics and data organization; these complications make comparisons among studies difficult, and deter the systematic accumulation of a consistent body of research data, For example, what one investigator calls a "cold and distant" parent, another may refer to as "hostile or indifferent"; an "indulgent" mother in one study may be referred to as a "worrier" in another or "overprotective" in a third. Furthermore, descriptive terms such as "cold," "overprotective," and so on represent gross categories of experience; variations, timing sequences, and other subtleties of interpersonal interaction are lost or blurred when experiences are grouped together into these global categories. The precise element of these experiences that effectively accounts for maladaptive learning remains unclear because of the gross or nonspecific categories into which these experiences are grouped. We must know exactly what aspect of parental "coldness" or "overprotectiveness" is pathogenic. Such specifications may be detailed more precisely in future research. Until such time, however, we must be content with the global nature of these categories of psychogenesis.

In the following sections, we will differentiate the sources of pathological learning into two broad categories. The first comprises experiences that exert an influence throughout the child's entire developmental sequence; these shall be referred to as *enduring and pervasive experiences.* The second category will include adverse conditions of relatively brief duration that occur at any point in the life span but that exert a profound influence on development; they shall be noted as *traumatic experiences*.

ENDURING AND PERVASIVE EXPERIENCES

An atmosphere, a way of handling the daily and routine activities of life, or a style and tone of interpersonal relatedness—all come to characterize the family setting within which the child develops. Events, feelings, and ways of communicating are repeated day in and day out. In contrast to the occasional and scattered events of the outside environment, the circumstances of daily family life have an enduring and cumulative effect on the entire fabric of the child's learning. Within this setting, the child establishes a basic feeling of security, imitates the ways in which people relate interpersonally, acquires an impression of how others perceive and feel about him or her, develops a sense of self-worth, and learns how to cope with feelings and the stresses of life. The influence of the family environment is preeminent during all of the crucial growth periods in that it alone among all sources exerts a persistent effect on the child.

In what ways can these enduring experiences be differentiated? Because the ebb and flow of everyday life consists of many inextricably interwoven elements, any subdivision that can be made must reflect some measure of arbitrariness. To avoid the errors of etiologic simplification, the reader should keep in mind that the features separated into each of the five categories described in the following sections represent only single facets of an ongoing and complex constellation of events.

The five categories are:

1. Parental feelings and attitudes
2. Methods of behavior control
3. Family styles of communication
4. Content of teachings
5. Family structure.

PARENTAL FEELINGS AND ATTITUDES

The most overriding, yet the most difficult to appraise, aspect of learned experience is the extent to which the child develops a feeling of acceptance or rejection by his or her parents. With the exception of cases of blatant abuse or overt deprecation, investigators have extreme difficulty in specifying, no less measuring, the signs of parental neglect, disaffiliation, and disaffection. Despite the methodological difficulties that researchers encounter, the child who is the recipient of rejecting cues has no doubt about being unappreciated, scorned, or deceived.

Children who are exposed throughout their early years to parents who view them as unwanted and troublesome can only establish a deep and pervasive feeling of isolation in a hostile world. Deprived of the supports and security of home, these children may be ill disposed to venture forth with confidence to face struggles in the outer world. Rejected by their parents, they may anticipate equal devaluation by others (Emde, 1989). As a defense against further pain, they may learn the strategy of avoiding others; they may utilize apathy and indifference as a protective cloak to minimize the impact of the negative reinforcements they now expect from others. Different strategies may evolve, of course, depending on other features associated with rejection; children may imitate parental scorn and ridicule, and learn to handle their disturbed feelings by acting in a hostile and vindictive fashion (Cicchetti & Carlson, 1989; Mueller & Silverman, 1989). When children are rejected by parents, they are likely to anticipate equal devaluation by others (Dodge, Murphy, & Buchsbaum, 1984; Dornbusch, Ritter, & Leiderman et al., 1987; Steinberg, Elmen, & Mounts, 1989).

Rejection is not the only parental attitude that may result in insidious damage to the child's personality; attitudes represented by terms such as seduction, exploitation, and deception contribute their share of damage as well. But it is usually the sense of being unwanted and unloved that proves to have the most pervasive and shattering effect (Cicchetti & Beeghly, 1987). Children can tolerate substantial punishment and buffeting from their environment if they sense a basic feeling of love and support from their parents; without this support, their resistance, even to minor stress, is tenuous (Billings & Moos, 1982; Lewinsohn, 1974).

More important than heretofore considered is that parental feelings and attitudes need not be the same, nor uniformly conveyed by both parents. Differences in parental relationships are the norm for most children. One parent may be attentive and overprotective while the other is hostile or indifferent. In a sense, the recombinant process of hereditary transmission, in which children receive half their chromosomes from each of two parents, is duplicated at the experiential level, as well. Dissimilar aspects of human thought, feeling, and behavior are conveyed by each parent through implicit modeling or direct tuition. Children incorporate these two variant models, either keeping them as separate modes of experience or fusing them in a combinatorial synthesis.

Hence, it is not uncommon for children to acquire attitudes and feelings about themselves that are divided or split, partly reflecting the relationship with their mother, and partly with their father, no less also with older siblings or relatives. As we read the typical background of one or another of several personality disorders, we may find individuals who have experienced two or more of the characteristic histories described. Exposed to a "single" parent who was consistent and whose attitudes and feelings were not subverted or countermanded by other adult models, the child may develop into a "pure" textbook type. For the most part, however, youngsters reflect the impact of a variety of adult models, hence resulting in a mixed personality configuration (e.g., somewhat narcissistic and somewhat compulsive; partly dependent and partly avoidant). In later sections pertaining to "adult subtypes," we will see personality mixtures that reflect different, and sometimes conflictual combinations of parental feelings and attitudes to which the youngster was exposed.

Methods of Behavior Control

What training procedures are used to regulate the child's behavior and to control what he learns? As noted earlier, incidental methods used by parents may have a more profound effect than what the parent intended, that is, the child acquires a model of interpersonal behavior by example and imitation as well as by verbal precept. What are some of the pathogenic methods of control? Five will be noted.

Punitive Methods

Parents disposed to intimidate and ridicule their offspring, using punitive and repressive measures to control their behavior and thought, may set the stage for a variety of maladaptive patterns (El Sheikh, Cummings, & Goetsch, 1989; Loeber & Stouthamer-Loeber, 1986).

If these children submit to pressure and succeed in fulfilling parental expectations (i.e., learn instrumentally to avoid the negative reinforcement of punishment), they are apt to become overly obedient and circumspect. Quite typically, these individuals learn not only to keep in check their

impulses and contrary thoughts but, by vicarious observation and imitation, to adopt the parental behavior model, and begin to be punitive of deviant behavior on the part of others. Thus, an otherwise timid and hypertense 16-year-old boy, whose every spark of youthful zest had been squelched by harshly punitive parents, was observed to be "extremely mean" and punitive when given the responsibility of teaching a Sunday school class for 7-year-olds.

Should these youngsters fail to satisfy excessive parental demands, and be subject to continued harassment and punishment, they may develop a pervasive anticipatory anxiety about personal relationships, leading to feelings of hopelessness and discouragement, and resulting in such instrumental strategies as social avoidance and withdrawal. Others, faced with similar experiences, may learn to imitate parental harshness and develop hostile and aggressively rebellious behaviors. Which of these reactions or strategies evolves will depend on the larger configuration of factors involved (Ferster, 1973; Lazarus, 1968; Lewinsohn, 1974; Patterson, 1982).

Contingent Reward Methods

Some parents rarely are punitive but expect certain behaviors to be performed *prior to* giving encouragement or doling out rewards. In other words, positive reinforcements are contingent on approved performance. Youngsters reared under these conditions tend to be socially pleasant and, by imitative learning, tend to be rewarding to others. But, quite often, we observe that they seem to have acquired an insatiable and indiscriminate need for social approval. For example, a 15-year-old girl experienced brief periods of marked depression if people failed to comment favorably on her dress or appearance. In early childhood, she had learned that parental approval and affection were elicited only when she was "dressed up and looked pretty"; to her, failure on the part of others to note her attractiveness signified rejection and disapproval. It would appear then that contingent reward methods condition children to develop an excessive need for approval; they manifest not only a healthy social affability but also a dependency on social reinforcement.

Inconsistent Methods

Parental methods of control often are irregular, contradictory, and capricious (Maccoby & Martin, 1983; Patterson, 1982). Some degree of variability is inevitable in the course of every child's life, but there are parents who display an extreme inconsistency in their standards and expectations, and an extreme unpredictability in their application of rewards and punishments. Youngsters exposed to such a chaotic and capricious environment cannot learn consistently and cannot devise nonconflictive strategies for adaptive behavior; whatever behavior they display may be countermanded by an unpredictable parental reaction.

To avoid the suspense and anxiety of unpredictable reactions, the child may protectively become immobile and noncommittal. Others, imitatively adopting what they have been exposed to, may come to be characterized by their own ambivalence and their own tendency to vacillate from one action or feeling to another. We know that irregular reinforcements build difficult-to-extinguish behavior patterns; thus, the immobility or ambivalence of these youngsters may persist long after their environment has become uniform and predictable.

Protective Methods

Some parents so narrowly restrict the experiences to which their children are exposed that these youngsters fail to learn even the basic rudiments of autonomous behaviors (Baumrind, 1967). Overprotective mothers, worried that their children are too frail or are unable to care for themselves or make sensible judgments on their own, not only succeed in forestalling the growth of normal competencies but, indirectly, give children a feeling that they are inferior and frail. These children, observing their actual inadequacies, have verification that they are weak, inept, and dependent on others (Millon, 1981; Parker, 1983). Thus, not only are these youngsters trained to be deficient in adaptive and self-reliant behaviors but they also learn to view themselves as inferior, and become progressively fearful of leaving the protective "womb."

Indulgent Methods

Overly permissive, lax, or undisciplined parents allow children full rein to explore and assert their every whim. These parents fail to control their children and, by their own lack of discipline, provide a model to be imitated that further strengthens the child's irresponsibility. Unconstrained by parental control, and not guided by selective rewards, these youngsters grow up displaying the inconsiderate and often tyrannical characteristics of undisciplined children. Having had their way for so long, they tend to be exploitive, demanding,

uncooperative, and antisocially aggressive. Unless rebuffed by external disciplinary forces, these youngsters may persist in their habits and become irresponsible members of society (Millon, 1969).

FAMILY STYLES OF COMMUNICATION

The capacity of humans to symbolize experience enables them to communicate with one another in ways more intricate and complex than are found in lower species. Free of the simple mechanisms of instinctive behavior, and capable of transcending the tangibles of the objective world, humans can draw from events of the distant past and project to those of the distant future. The symbolic units and syntax of language provide people with a powerful instrumentality for thought and communication.

Each family constructs its own style of communication, its own pattern of listening and attending, and its own way of fashioning thoughts and conveying them to others. The styles of interpersonal communication to which children are exposed serve as a model for attending, organizing and reacting to the expressions, thoughts and feelings of others. Unless this framework for learning interpersonal communication is rational and reciprocal, they will be ill-equipped to function in an effective way with others. Thus, the very symbolic capacities that enable people to transcend their environment so successfully may lead to serious misdirections and confusions; this powerful instrument for facilitating communication with others may serve instead to undermine social relationships. Although illogical ideas, irrational reactions, and irrelevant and bizarre verbalizations often arise as a consequence of extreme stress, their roots can be traced as frequently to the simple exposure to defective styles of family communication (Campbell, 1973; Mash & Johnston, 1982; Morrison, 1980; Tizard & Hodges, 1978).

The effects of amorphous, fragmented, or confusing patterns of family communication have been explored by numerous investigators (Bateson et al., 1956; Singer & Wynne, 1965). Not only are messages attended to in certain families in a vague, erratic, or incidental fashion, with a consequent disjunctiveness and loss of focus, but when they are attended to, they frequently convey equivocal or contradictory meanings. The transmission of ambivalent or opposing meanings and feelings produces what Bateson refers to as a *double-bind*. For example, a seriously disturbed 10-year-old boy was repeatedly implored in a distinctly hostile tone by his equally ill mother as follows: "Come here to your mother; mommy loves you and wants to hug and squeeze you, hug and squeeze you." The intrinsically contradictory nature of these double-bind messages precludes satisfactory reactions; the recipient cannot respond without running into conflict with one aspect of the message (he is "damned if he does, and damned if he doesn't"). Exposed to such contradictions in communication, the youngster's foundation in reality becomes increasingly precarious (Reid, Patterson, & Loeber, 1982; Reiss, 1981). To avoid confusion, such children learn to distort and deny these conflicting signals; but in this defensive maneuver they succumb even further to irrational thought. Unable to interpret the intentions and feelings of others and encumbered with a progressively maladaptive pattern of self-distortions, they fall prey to a vicious circle of increasing interpersonal estrangement.

CONTENT OF TEACHINGS

Parents transmit a wide range of values and attitudes to their children either through direct tuition or unintentional commentary (Dorr, 1985; Emde, 1979). The family serves as the primary socialization system for inculcating beliefs and behaviors. Through these teachings the child learns to think about, be concerned with, and react to certain events and people in prescribed ways.

What kinds of teachings lend themselves to the learning of pathological attitudes and behaviors? Just a few will be mentioned.

Anxiety

The most insidious and destructive of these teachings is training in anxiety. Parents who fret over their own health, who investigate every potential ailment in their children's functioning and who are preoccupied with failures or the dismal turn of events teach and furnish models for anxiety proneness in their children (Coolidge & Brodie, 1974; Parker, 1983; Waldron, Shrier, Stone, & Tobin, 1975). Few incidents escape the pernicious effects of a chronically anxious and apprehensive household. Fantasies of body disease, vocational failure, loss of prized objects, and rejection by loved ones illustrate the range of items that can intrude on and color otherwise neutral events when there is a tendency toward this general disposition.

Guilt and Shame

Feelings of guilt and shame are generated in the teachings of many homes. A failure to live up to parental expectations, a feeling of having caused parents to make undue sacrifices and of having transgressed rules and embarrassed the family by virtue of some shortcoming or misbehavior illustrate events that question the individual's self-worth and produce marked feelings of shame and guilt. Furthermore, the sacrificing and guilt-laden atmosphere of these parental homes provides a model for behavioral imitation. Youngsters who are admonished and reproached repeatedly for minor digressions often develop a deep and pervasive self-image of failure. If those children admit their misdeeds, and adopt their parents' injunctions as their own, they will come to view themselves as unworthy, shameful, and guilty. To protect against feelings of marked self-condemnation, such children may learn to restrict their activities, to deny themselves the normal joys and indulgences of life, and to control their impulses far beyond that required to eschew shame and guilt; In time, even the simplest of pleasures may come to be avoided.

Other Destructive Attitudes

These attitudes can be taught directly through narrow or biased parental outlooks; feelings of inferiority and social inadequacy are among the most frequent. Particularly damaging are teachings associated with sexual urges. Unrealistic standards that condemn common behaviors such as masturbation and petting create unnecessary fears and strong guilt feelings; sexual miseducation may have long-range deleterious effects, especially during periods of courtship and marriage.

FAMILY STRUCTURE

The formal composition of the family often sets the stage for learning pathogenic attitudes and relationships. A number of these structural features will be noted.

Deficient Models

The lack of significant adult figures within the family may deprive children of the opportunity to acquire, through imitation, many of the complex patterns of behavior required in adult life (Emery, 1982; Ferri, 1976; Millon, 1987). Parents who provide undesirable models for imitation, at the very least, are supplying some guidelines for the intricate give-and-take of human relationships.

The most serious deficit usually is the unavailability of a parental model of the same sex (Hetherington, Cox, & Cox, 1982). The frequent absence of fathers in underprivileged homes, or the vocational preoccupations of fathers in well-to-do homes, often produce sons who lack a mature sense of masculine identity; they seem ill-equipped with goals and behaviors by which they can orient their adult lives.

Family Discord

Children subject to persistent parental bickering and nagging not only are exposed to destructive models for imitative learning but are faced with upsetting influences that may eventuate in pathological behaviors (Crockenberg, 1985; Cummings, Pelligrini, Notarius, & Cummings, 1989; Rutter & Giller, 1983). When strife and marked controversy prevail, they shatter the stability of life so necessary for the acquisition of a consistent pattern of behaving and thinking. There is an ever-present apprehension that one parent may be lost through divorce; dissension often leads to the undermining of one parent by the other; an air of mistrust frequently pervades the home, creating suspicions and anxieties: a nasty and cruel competition for the loyalty and affections of children may ensue. Children often become scapegoats in these settings, subject to displaced parental hostilities (Hetherington, 1972). Constantly dragged into the arena of parental strife, the child not only loses a sense of security and stability but may be subjected to capricious hostility and to a set of conflicting and destructive behavior models.

Sibling Rivalry

Sibling relationships often are overlooked as a major element in shaping the pattern of peer and other intimate competitions (Circirelli, 1982; Dunn & Kendrick, 1981; Wagner, Schubert, & Schubert, 1979). The presence of two or more children within a family requires that parents divide their attention and approval. When disproportionate affection is allotted to one child, or when a newborn child supplants an older child as the "apple of daddy's eye," seeds of discontent and rivalry flourish. Intense hostility often is generated; because hostility fails to eliminate the intruder and gains, not the sought-for attention, but parental disapproval, the aggrieved child often reverts to regressive or infantile maneuvers, (e.g., baby talk or bed-wetting). If these methods succeed in winning back parental love, the youngster will have been reinforced through instrumental learning to continue these childish techniques. More often than not, however, efforts to alter parental preferences fail miserably, and the child may continue to experience deep resentments and a sense of marked insecurity. In the future, such persons often display a distrust of affections, fearing that those who express them will prove to be as fickle as their parents. Not unlikely also is the possibility that the intense hostility they felt toward their siblings will linger and generalize into envious and aggressive feelings toward other competitors.

Ordinal Position

It seems plausible that the order of a child's birth within the family would be related to the kinds of problems the child faces, and the kinds of strategies he or she is likely to adopt. For example, the *oldest child,* once the center of parental attention, experiences a series of displacements as new sibs are born; this may engender a pervasive expectation that "good things don't last." However, to counteract this damaging experience, the youngster may be encouraged to acquire the skills of autonomy and leadership, may be more prone to identify with adult models and may learn, thereby, to cope with the complications of life more effectively than less mature siblings. The *youngest child,* although petted, indulged, and allotted the special affections and privileges due the family "baby," may fail to acquire the competencies required for autonomous behaviors. He or she may be prone to dependency and prefer to withdraw from competition; the higher incidence of mental disorder among the last-born in families lends support to these interpretations (Dohrenwald & Dohrenwald, 1966; Gregory, 1958). *Only children* appear to be especially resilient to severe emotional difficulty. This may reflect their special status as sole recipient of parental attention, approval, and affection. In this singular and unhampered state, children may learn to view themselves as especially gifted; with this confidence in self-worth as a base, they may venture into the larger society secure in the conviction that they will be as well-received there as in the parental home. Despite this sound beginning, they are ill-equipped to cope with the give-and-take of peer relationships because they have not experienced the sharing and competition of sibling relationships.

Numerous other features of the family environment, some relating to structural elements (e.g., sex of sibs and presence of "problem" sibs) and some to roles assumed by family members (e.g., domineering or seductive mothers or inadequate or effeminate fathers), can be specified, and their likely effects on learning speculated about. A listing of such events and relationships, however, would be too exhaustive for our purposes. A number of these elements will be raised in later chapters when we present characteristic experiential histories.

TRAUMATIC EXPERIENCES

It is a common belief, attributable in large measure to popularizations of psychology in our literature and news media, that most forms of psychopathology can be traced to a single, very severe experience, the hidden residues of which account for the manifest disorder. Freud's early writings gave impetus and support to this notion, but he reversed himself in his later work when he was made aware that patient reports of early trauma often were imaginative fabrications of their past. Current thinking in the field suggests that most pathological behaviors accrue gradually through repetitive learning experiences.

Despite the primacy that enduring and pervasive experiences play in shaping most pathological patterns, there are occasions when a particularly painful event can shatter the individual's equanimity and leave a deeply embedded attitude that is not readily extinguished. An untimely frightening experience, be it abusive or not, or an especially embarrassing and humiliating social event, illustrate conditions that can result in a persistent attitude.

The impact of these events may be particularly severe with young children because they usually are ill prepared for them and lack the perspective of prior experience that might serve as a context for moderating their effects (Field, 1985; Garmezy, 1986; Weissman & Paykel, 1974). If a traumatic event is the first exposure for a youngster to a particular class of experiences, the attitude he or she learns in reaction to that event may intrude and color all subsequent events of that kind. Thus, an adolescent whose first sexual venture resulted in devastating feelings of guilt, inadequacy, or humiliation may harbor such feelings long after the event has passed.

Traumatic events persevere in their learned effects for essentially two reasons. First, a high level of neural activation ensues in response to most situations of marked distress or anxiety. This means that many diverse neural associations become connected to the event; the greater the level of neural involvement, the more deeply and pervasively will be the learned reaction, and the greater the difficulty will be in extinguishing what was learned. Second, during heightened stress, there often is a decrement in the ability to make accurate discriminations within the environment; as a consequence,

traumatized individuals generalize their emotional reaction to a variety of objects and persons who are only incidentally associated with the traumatic source. For example, a youngster injured in an auto accident may develop a fear reaction not only to cars but to all red couch covers (the color of the seat of the car in which he was riding), to men in white jackets (the color of the medical intern's uniform who attended to him after the accident) and so on. Because of the seemingly illogical nature of these fears (the difficulty of tracing their connection to the accident), they are not readily amenable to rational analysis and unlearning.

Despite the severity and persistence of the effects of certain traumatic events, they tend to be stimulus-specific, that is, limited to stimulus conditions that are highly similar to those in which they were first learned. In certain cases, however, these experiences may give rise to a chain of reactions and events that establish pervasive pathological trends. Thus, in the next section we will see that the conditions of early experience, whatever their nature, may persist long after the event that prompted them has passed.

Comment. We have taken the liberty in this section of bringing together many of the diverse notions and findings that theorists have used to identify the principal psychogenic sources of personality pathology; only briefly have we commented on the adequacy of these data, or the methods employed in obtaining them. Our presentation would be amiss if we failed to appraise, albeit briefly, the soundness of the evidence.

The view that the particular setting and events of early experience play a decisive part in determining personality is assumed by psychologists of all theoretical persuasions. But where, in fact, are the "hard data," the unequivocal evidence derived from well-designed and well-executed research? Such data, unfortunately, are sorely lacking. Most of the research in the field can be faulted on methodological grounds, biased populations, poor assessment techniques, unreliable diagnostic categories and, most significantly, failures to include appropriate control groups by which comparative evaluations can be made. Without controls, for example, it is impossible to determine whether the specific parental attitude, training procedure, or traumatic event under investigation can be assigned the significance attributed to it.

There are disconcerting findings that show us that there may be no substantial difference in deleterious childhood experiences between normal men and psychiatric patients. It is known, furthermore, that many adults who have been reared in seemingly devastating childhood environments not only survive but thrive, whereas adults raised under idealistic conditions often deteriorate into severe pathological patterns. The combination of factors, and the sequence of events involved in producing pathology, is awesomely complex and difficult to unravel. Unless future lines of research are based on sound premises and executed with the utmost of methodological care, investigators will continue to go around in circles, confirming only what their naive prejudices incline them to find.

The importance of well-reasoned and well-designed studies is nowhere more evident than in the investigation of psychogenic sources of personality pathology; few studies of the past have met the basic criteria of good research. We have minimized reference to specific studies in this section lest we lead the student to believe that there are data from well-designed research to support the notions presented. The student should view these notions as propositions that will be confirmed or disconfirmed as a result of *future* research.

CONTINUITY OF EARLY LEARNINGS

We have contended in the preceding sections that childhood experiences are crucially involved in shaping lifelong patterns of behavior. To support this view, we elaborated several conditions of early upbringing and their consequences, noting first the impact of the sheer quantity of stimulation on maturation and second, the effect of particular kinds of experiences on the learning of complex behaviors and attitudes. Although few theorists of psychopathology would deny the paramount role we have attributed to early experience, they may differ among themselves as to not only "why" these experiences are important but "how" exactly they come to play their significant role in later behavior.

Comment. A few words should be said about why early experience should be more important than later experiences. Throughout evolutionary history, early life has been a preparation for later life. Until recently, and except at times of massive environmental upheavals, all species have lived in the same basic ecological niches throughout their history. Under these conditions, the experiences of early life provide an opportunity for the young organism to acquire sensitivities and behaviors that enable it to function more adequately in its environment. It learns to become acquainted with the elements of its habitat, differentiating those components that are gratifying from those that are endangering. It learns to imitate the behavior of its parents, acquiring thereby methods and competencies that would otherwise take appreciably longer to learn, if ever learned at all.

The importance of early learning cannot be overstated for creatures that continue to live in the same environments as their ancestors. Until recently, this continuity has been true for humans, as well. Thus, if a boy's father was a farmer, the young son quickly learned how to function in an environment where farming was a primary and important occupation. And if a girl's mother tended to the children and the home, the young daughter observed and imitated her parent's behaviors and attitudes. In these earlier times, the ambience of the children's neighborhood, its values, beliefs, and customs were likely to have been the very same beliefs, values, and customs of their ancestors; similarly, these attitudes corresponded with those shared by the larger community in adulthood and, in time, with that likely to be experienced by progeny, as well.

Infancy and childhood prepares children well for life in adulthood, perhaps too well. Problems have arisen in the past century since radical environmental and cultural shifts have taken place, upsetting the continuity between past and present family and societal values and customs. This sharp break between what may have been learned in childhood and what one may have to face in adulthood accounts in part for many of the personality difficulties we observe today. In infancy and toddlerhood each child learns a series of thoughts, feelings, and behaviors that are retained and carried into later childhood and adulthood. This continuity served the youngster well in the past because the patterns of adulthood life were well ingrained in childhood. In recent decades, however, childhood learnings are often inapplicable and inappropriate when applied to the family, neighbors, and societies of adulthood. Children who learned to fear humiliating and disparaging parents will carry what they have learned into new relationships that may be radically different than those of childhood. Their aversive behaviors may no longer be appropriate nor applicable, yet they will likely persist and generate new difficulties owing to this continuity of past learnings into the present.

It is this persistence of early learned behaviors into adulthood, what psychoanalysts speak of as transference, and behaviorists refer to as generalization, that underlies many of the problems we consider to be personality disorders. And now that we are in a society in which few constants persevere, where values and customs are in conflict, and where the styles of human interaction today are likely to change tomorrow, we see the emergence of a new unstructured and highly fluid personality style, the borderline disorder. In these adults, we find a reflection of the contradictory and changing customs and beliefs of contemporary society. This newest pattern of childhood adaptation leaves the person unable to find the "center" of him- or herself. Such persons have learned *not* to demonstrate consistency and continuity in their behaviors, thoughts and feelings, no less in their way of relating to others. More will be said about these unstable and contradictory cultural patterns in a later section. Similarly, we will discuss the impact of experiential discontinuities as a key factor in creating the borderline personality in a later chapter.

Is the impact of early experience, as we have asserted in previous sections, a consequence of the young child's susceptibilities during "sensitive" maturational stages? Are early experiences more significant than later experiences because the developing child is more plastic and impressionable than the fully matured adult? Can other explanations be offered to account for the special status in shaping behavior assigned to early experience?

A review of the literature will uncover several alternate explanations that contend children are not intrinsically different from adults in their responsiveness to experience. Despite these occasional differences in opinion, most theorists believe that early experiences do contribute a disproportionately larger share to learned behavior than later experiences.

Among the alternate interpretations offered for this phenomenon are the following. Influences common to children and adults arise more often in childhood: There is nothing distinctive about childhood other than the *frequency* with which certain experiences occur; were these events equally frequent in adulthood, there would be no reason to assume that they would affect adults less than they do children. Others state that the difference may be due to the fact that children experience the impact of events more intensely than adults because they have fewer skills to handle challenges and threats. A somewhat similar hypothesis suggests that the importance of childhood experience lies in

its *primacy*—the first event of a set of similar effects will have a more marked impact than later ones. According to this view, an event experienced initially in adulthood will have the same effect on an adult as it does on a child; these theorists note, however, that it is more likely that the first of a series of similar experiences will occur in childhood.

There is little question that the special status of early experience can be ascribed in part to the simple facts of frequency and primacy; events that come first or more often will have a bearing on what comes later and thereby justify our assigning them special impact value. The question remains, however, as to whether frequency and primacy, in themselves, are sufficient to account for the unusual significance attributed to childhood experiences.

Acceptance of the role played by these two factors does not preclude additional hypotheses that assign unusual vulnerabilities or sensitivities to young children. There is no fundamental conflict between these views; each factor, primacy, frequency, and biological sensitivity may operate conjointly and with undiminished singular effects. A later discussion will attempt to show how these varied influences weave together to give early experience its special role.

We will concentrate in this section on the notion of continuity in behavior, because we believe that the significance of early experience lies not so much in the intensity of its impact but in its durability and persistence. Experiences in early life are not only ingrained more pervasively and forcefully, but their effects tend to persist and are more difficult to modify than later experiences. For example, early events occur at a presymbolic level and cannot easily be recalled and unlearned; they are reinforced frequently as a function of the child's restricted opportunities to learn alternatives; they tend to be repeated and perpetuated by the child's own behavior. For many reasons, then, a continuity in behavior—a consistent style of feeling, thinking, and relating to the world—once embedded in early life, perseveres into adulthood.

Part of the continuity we observe between childhood and adulthood may be ascribed to the stability of biological constitutional factors, factors described earlier in this chapter. But numerous psychological processes contribute as well to this longitudinal consistency (Chess & Thomas, 1984; Kagan, Reznick, & Snidman, 1989; Plomin & Dunn, 1986; Robins & Rutter, 1990). Because these processes enable us to see more clearly how pathology develops, we cannot afford to take them for granted or merely enumerate them without elaboration.

Broadly speaking, the processes that coalesce to bring about continuity may be grouped into three categories: resistance to extinction, social reinforcement, and self-perpetuation.

RESISTANCE TO EXTINCTION

Acquired behaviors and attitudes usually are not fixed or permanent. What has been learned can be modified or eliminated under appropriate conditions, a process referred to as *extinction*. Extinction usually entails exposure to experiences that are similar to the conditions of original learning but that provide opportunities for new learning to occur. Essentially, old habits of behavior change when new learning interferes with, and replaces, what previously had been learned; this progressive weakening of old learnings may be speeded up by special environmental conditions, the details of which are not relevant to our discussion.

What happens if the conditions of original learning cannot be duplicated easily? According to contiguity learning theory, failure to provide opportunities for interfering with old habits means that they will remain unmodified and persist over time; in other words, learnings associated with events that are difficult to reproduce are resistant to extinction.

The question we next must ask is: Are the events of early life experienced in such a manner as to make them difficult to reproduce and, therefore, resistant to extinction? An examination of the conditions of childhood suggests that the answer is yes! The reasons for asserting so have been formulated with extraordinary clarity by David McClelland (1951); we will draw on several of his ideas in the following sections.

Presymbolic Learning

Biologically speaking, the young child is a primitive organism. The child's nervous system is incomplete, he or she perceives the world from momentary and changing vantage points and is unable to discriminate and identify many of the elements of experience. What the child sees and learns about the environment through infantile perceptual and cognitive systems will never again be experienced in the same manner in later life.

The presymbolic world of fleeting and inarticulate impressions recedes gradually as the child acquires the ability to identify, discriminate and symbolize experience. By the time youngsters are four or five, they view the world in preformed categories and they group and symbolize objects and events in a stable way that is quite different from that of infancy.

Once these perceptions have taken on discriminative symbolic forms, children can no longer duplicate the perceptually amorphous, presymbolic and diffusely inchoate experiences of their earlier years. Unable to reproduce these early experiences in subsequent life, children will not be able to extinguish what they learned in response to them; no longer perceiving events as initially sensed, they cannot supplant the early reactions with new ones. These early learnings will persist, therefore, as feelings, attitudes, and expectancies that crop up pervasively in a vague and diffuse way.

Random Learning

Young children lack not only the ability to form a precise image of their environment but the equipment to discern logical relationships among its elements. Their world of objects, people, and events is connected in an unclear and random fashion; they learn to associate objects and events that have no intrinsic relationship; clusters of concurrent but only incidentally connected stimuli are fused erroneously. Thus, when a small boy experiences fear in response to his father's harsh voice, he may learn to fear not only that voice but the setting, the atmosphere, the pictures, the furniture, and the odors, a whole bevy of incidental objects that by chance were present at that time. Unable to discriminate the precise source in his environment that "caused" his fear, he connects his discomfort randomly to all associated stimuli; now each of them become a precipitant for these feelings.

Random associations of early life cannot be duplicated as the child develops the capacity for logical thinking and perception. By the time children are four or five, they can discriminate cause-and-effect relationships with considerably accuracy. Early random associations do not "make sense" to them; when they react to a precipitant derived from early learning, they are unable to identify what they are reacting to in the environment. They cannot locate the source of their difficulty because they now think more logically than before. To advise the young boy that he is reacting to a picture or piece of furniture simply will be rejected; he cannot fathom the true features that evoke his feelings since these sources are so foreign to his new, more rational mode of thought. His difficulty in extinguishing the past is compounded because it is difficult not only for him to reexperience the world as it once may have been but he will be misled in his search for these experiences if he applies his more developed reasoning powers.

Generalized Learning

Young children's discriminations of their environment are crude and gross. As they begin to differentiate the elements of their world, they group and label them into broad and unrefined categories. All men become "daddy"; all four-legged animals are called "doggie"; all foods are "yumyum." A child who learns to fear a particular dog, for example, will learn to fear not only that dog but all strange, mobile four-legged creatures. To the child's primitive perception, all of these animals are one of a kind.

Generalization is inevitable in early learning. It reflects more than the failure of young children to have had sufficient experiences to acquire greater precision; their indiscriminateness represents an intrinsic inability to discriminate events because of their undeveloped cortical capacities.

As the undifferentiated mass of early experiences becomes more finely discriminated, learning gets to be more focused, specific, and precise; a 10-year-old will learn to fear bulldogs as a result of an unfortunate run-in with one but will not necessarily generalize this fear to collies or poodles because the youngster knows and can discern differences among these animals.

Generalized learning is difficult to extinguish. Young children's learned reactions are attached to a broader class of objects than called for by their specific experiences. To extinguish these broadly generalized reactions in later life, when discriminative capacities are much more precise, will require exposure to many and diverse experiences. This may be a difficult point to grasp, and an illustration may be useful to clarify it.

Let us assume that a 2-year-old girl was frightened by a cocker spaniel. Given her gross discriminative capacity at this age, this single experience may have conditioned her to fear dogs, cats, and other small animals. Let us assume further, that in later life she is exposed repeatedly to a friendly cocker spaniel. As a consequence of this experience, we find that the child has extinguished her fear, but only of cocker spaniels, not of dogs in general, or of cats or other small animals. Her later experience, seen through the discriminative eye of an older child, was that *spaniels* are friendly but not dogs in general. The extinction experience applied then to only one part of the original widely generalized complex of fears she had acquired. Her original learning experience incorporated a much broader range of stimuli than her later experience, even though the objective stimulus conditions were essentially the same. Because of the child's more precise discriminative capacity, she now must have her fear extinguished in a variety of situations to compensate for the single but widely generalized early experience.

These three interlocking conditions—presymbolic, random, and generalized learning—account in large measure for the unusual difficulty of reexperiencing the events of early life, and the consequent difficulty of unlearning the feelings, behaviors, and attitudes generated by these events.

SOCIAL REINFORCEMENT

Of the many factors that contribute to the persistence of early behavior patterns, none plays a more significant role than social and interpersonal relationships. These relationships can be viewed fruitfully from the perspective usually taken by sociologists and social psychologists. To these scientists, the varied cultural and institutional forces of a society promote continuity by maintaining a stable and organized class of experiences to which most individuals of a particular group are repeatedly exposed. Reference to these broader social determinants of continuity will be made occasionally in later chapters. For the present, our focus will be on the more direct and private side of interpersonal experience.

As pointed out in an earlier section, ingrained personality patterns develop as a consequence of enduring experiences generated in intimate and subtle relationships with members of one's immediate family. We described a number of events that lead to the acquisition of particular types of behaviors and attitudes. Here our attention will be not on the content of what is learned but on those aspects of relationships that strengthen what has been learned and that lead to their perpetuation. Three such influences will be described: repetitive experiences, reciprocal reinforcement, and social stereotyping.

Repetitive Experiences

The typical daily activities in which young children participate are restricted and repetitive; there is not much variety in these routine experiences. Day in and day out, they eat the same kind of food, play with the same toys, remain essentially in the same physical environment, and relate to the same people. This constricted environment, this repeated exposure to a narrow range of family attitudes and training methods, not only builds in deeply etched habits and expectations but prevents children from having new experiences that are so essential to change. The helplessness of infants, and the dependency of children, keep them restricted to a crabbed and tight little world with few alternatives for learning new attitudes and responses. Early behaviors fail to change, therefore, not because they may have jelled permanently but because the same slender band of experiences that helped form them initially may continue and persist in influence for many years.

Reciprocal Reinforcement

The notion that parents' responses to a child's early behaviors may accentuate those behaviors was raised earlier in the chapter; we noted that a circular interplay often arises that intensifies the child's initial biological reactivity pattern. Thus, unusually passive, sensitive, or cranky infants frequently elicit feelings on the part of their mothers that perpetuate their original tendencies.

This model of circular or reciprocal influences may be applied not only to the perpetuation of biological dispositions but to behavior tendencies that are acquired by learning. Whatever the initial roots may have been—constitutional or learned—certain forms of behaviors provoke or pull from others, reactions that result in a repetition of these behaviors (Leary, 1957). For example, a suspicious, chip-on-the-shoulder and defiant child eventually will force others, no matter how tolerant they may have been initially, to counter with perplexity, exasperation, and anger; the child undermines every inclination on the part of others to be nurturant, friendly, and cooperative. An ever-widening gulf of suspicion and defiance may develop as parents of such children withdraw, become punitive, or "throw up their hands in disgust"; controls or affections that might have narrowed the gulf of suspicion and hostility break down. Each participant, in feedback fashion, contributes his or her share; the original level of hostile behavior is aggravated and intensified. Whether the "cause" was the child or the parent, the process has gotten out of hand, and will continue its vicious and inexorable course until some benign influence interferes, or until it deteriorates into pathological form (Gottman & Katz, 1989).

Social Stereotypes

The dominant features of a child's early behavior form a distinct impression on others. Once this early impression is established, people expect the child to continue behaving in a distinctive manner; in time, they develop a fixed and simplified image of "what kind of person the child is." The term "stereotype," borrowed from social psychology, represents this tendency to simplify and categorize the attributes of others.

Once people have stereotyped a child, they no longer view the youngster passively and objectively because they now are sensitized to those distinctive features they have learned to expect. Stereotypes take on a life of their own; they operate as a screen through which children's behaviors are selectively perceived so as to fit the characteristics attributed to them. Children who are cast in such a mold will experience a consistency in other people's reactions that fails to recognize the varieties and complexities of individual behavior. No matter what these children do, they find their behavior is interpreted in the same fixed and rigid manner. Exposed time and time again to the same reactions and attitudes of others, these children may give up efforts to change. For example, if a defiant young boy displays the slightest degree of resentment to unfair treatment, he will be jumped on as hopelessly recalcitrant; should he do nothing objectionable, questions will be raised as to the sincerity of his motives. Faced with repeated negative appraisals and unable to break the stereotype into which he has been cast, the youngster will relapse after every effort to change, and continue to behave as he did originally, and as others expect.

SELF-PERPETUATION

Significant experiences of early life may never recur again, but their effects remain and leave their mark. Physiologically, we may say they have etched a neurochemical change; psychologically, they are registered as memories, a permanent trace and an embedded internal stimulus. In contrast to the fleeting stimuli of the external world, these memory traces become part and parcel of every stimulus complex that activates behavior. Once registered, the effects of the past are indelible, incessant, and inescapable. They now are intrinsic elements of the individual's makeup; they latch on and intrude into the current events of life, coloring, transforming, and distorting the passing scene.

Although the residuals of subsequent experiences may override them, becoming more dominant internal stimuli, earlier memory traces remain in one form or another. In every thought and action, the individual cannot help but carry these remnants into the present. Every current behavior is a perpetuation, then, of the past, a continuation and intrusion of these inner stimulus traces.

The residuals of the past do more than passively contribute their share to the present. By temporal precedence, if nothing else, they guide, shape, or distort the character of current events. Not only are they ever present, then, but they operate insidiously to transform new stimulus experiences in line with past. We will elaborate four of these processes of perpetuation in this section: protective constriction, perceptual and cognitive distortion, behavior generalization, and repetition compulsion.

Protective Constriction

Painful memories of the past are kept out of consciousness, a process referred to as repression. Similarly, current experiences that may reactivate these repressed memories are judiciously avoided. The individual develops a network of conscious and unconscious protective maneuvers to decrease the likelihood that either of these distressing experiences will occur.

As a consequence of these protective efforts, however, the person narrows or constricts his or her world. Repression reduces anxiety by enabling the individual to keep the inner sources of discomfort from awareness, but it also thwarts the person from "unlearning" these feelings or learning new and potentially more constructive ways of coping with them. Likewise, by defensively reducing activities to situations that will not reactivate intolerable memories, the individual automatically precludes the possibility of learning to be less anxious than in the past, and diminishes the chances for learning new reactions to formerly stressful situations. For example, a highly intelligent and physically attractive 15-year-old girl had progressively withdrawn from school and social activities; for several years there had been marked disharmony at home, culminating in a well-publicized scandal involving her parents. Although her teachers and peers viewed her personally in a favorable light and made efforts to show their continued acceptance, her embarrassment and fear of social ridicule led her into increasing isolation and fantasies that she would be humiliated wherever she went. As a result of her

own protective actions, then, the young girl preserved unaltered her memories of the past; in addition, they persisted and forced her along paths that prevented their resolution. Moreover, the more vigilant her protective maneuvers and the more constrictive her boundaries, the more limited would be her competencies for effective functioning and the more she would be deprived of the positive rewards of life.

Perceptual and Cognitive Distortion

Certain processes not only preserve the past but transform the present in line with the past. Cameron (1947) described this process, which he referred to as *reaction-sensitivity,* with insight and clarity. To him, once people acquire a system of threat expectancies, they respond with increasing alertness to similar threatening elements in their life situation. For example, persons who develop bodily anxieties often become hypochondiracal, that is, hyperalert to physiological processes that most people experience but ignore.

Kelly's notion of *personal constructs* (1955) may be seen as an extension of the concept of reaction-sensitivity. To him, people acquire anticipatory cognitive attitudes as a consequence not only of threatening but of all forms of past experience; these constructs guide, screen, code, and evaluate the stream of new experiences to which the individual is exposed. Thus, a person who has learned to believe "everyone hates me" will tend to interpret the incidental and entirely innocuous comments of others in line with this premise.

The role of habits of language as factors shaping one's perceptions are of particular interest. As Whorf (1956) and others have shown, the words we use transform our experiences in line with the meaning of these words. For example, a child who has been exposed to parents who respond to every minor mishap as "a shattering experience" will tend to use these terms himself in the future; as a consequence, he will begin to feel that every setback he experiences is shattering because he has labeled it as such.

The importance of expectancies, reaction-sensitivities, and language habits lies in the fact that they lead to the distortion of objective realities. Disturbed individuals may transform what most people would have perceived as a beneficent event into one that is humiliating, threatening, and punishing. Instead of interpreting events as they objectively exist, these individuals selectively distort them to "fit" their expectancies and habits of thought. These expectancies may channel their attention and magnify their awareness of irrelevant and insignificant features of their environment intruding constantly to obscure and to warp an accurate perception of reality. The following quote from Beck illustrates this process well (1963):

A depressed patient reported the following sequence of events which occurred within a period of half an hour before he left the house: His wife was upset because the children were slow in getting dressed. He thought, "I'm a poor father because the children are not better disciplined." He then noticed a faucet was leaky and thought this showed he was also a poor husband. While driving to work, he thought, "I must be a poor driver or other cars would not be passing me." As he arrived at work he noticed some other personnel had already arrived. He thought, "I can't be very dedicated or I would have come earlier." When he noticed folders and papers piled up on his desk, he concluded, "I'm a poor organizer because I have so much work to do."

Often inexact labeling *seems to contribute to this kind of distortion. The affective reaction is proportional to the descriptive labeling of the event rather than to the actual intensity of a traumatic situation.*

A man reported during his therapy hour that he was very upset because he had been "clobbered" by his superior. On further reflection, he realized that he had magnified the incident and that a more adequate description was that his superior "corrected an error he had made." After reevaluating the event, he felt better. He also realized that whenever he was corrected or criticized by a person in authority he was prone to describe this as being "clobbered."

Selective abstraction *refers to the process of focusing on a detail taken out of context, ignoring other more salient features of the situation and conceptualizing the whole experience on the basis of this element.*

A patient, in reviewing her secretarial work with her employer, was praised about a number of aspects of her work. The employer at one point asked her to discontinue making extra carbon copies of his letters. Her immediate thought was, "He is dissatisfied with my work." This idea became paramount despite all the positive statements he had made. (p. 327)

This distortion process has an insidiously cumulative and spiraling effect. By misconstruing reality in such ways as to make it corroborate their expectancies, individuals, in effect, intensify their misery. Thus, ordinary, even rewarding events, may be perceived as threatening. As a result of this distortion, patients subjectively experience neutral events "as if" they were, in fact, threatening. In this process, they create and accumulate painful experiences for themselves where none exists in reality.

One sometimes sees in patients a progressive worsening of their behavior, although the objective conditions of their life have improved. Once the pathological process of distortion has begun, these patients misinterpret experiences in terms of their outlook; they now are caught in a downward spiral in which everything, no matter how objectively "good" it might be, is perceived as distressing, disheartening, or threatening. Their initial distortions have led to a succession of subjectively experienced stresses; this progressive cumulation of stress drives patients further and further away from an objective appraisal of reality; all efforts to counter and reverse the pathological trend are utterly useless at this point. The process of perceptual and cognitive distortion has built up its own momentum, resulting not only in its perpetuation but in its intensification.

Behavior Generalization

We have just described a number of factors that lead individuals to perceive new experiences in a subjective and frequently warped fashion; perceptual and cognitive distortions may be viewed as the defective side of a normal process in which new stimulus conditions are seen as similar to those experienced in the past. This process, though usually described in simpler types of conditions, commonly is referred to as *stimulus generalization*. In the present section, we will turn our attention to another closely related form of generalization, the tendency of people to react to new stimuli in a manner similar to the way in which they reacted in the past; we may speak of this process as *behavior generalization*.

Stimulus generalization and behavior generalization often are two sides of the same coin; thus, if an individual distorts an objective event so as to perceive it as identical to a past event, it would be reasonable to expect that the person's response to it would be similar to that made previously. For example, let us assume that a child learned to cower and withdraw from a harshly punitive mother. Should the child come into contact with a somewhat firm teacher, possessing physical features similar to those of the mother, the child may distort his perception of the teacher, making her a duplicate of the mother, and then react to her as he had learned to react to his mother.

This tendency to perceive and to react to present events as if they were duplicates of the past has been labeled by intrapsychic theorists as the process of *transference*. This concept signifies the observation that patients in treatment often magnify minor objective similarities between their parents and the therapist, and then transfer to the therapist responses learned within the family setting.

The transference of past behaviors to novel situations is necessary to efficient functioning; we cannot approach each and every new circumstance of life without some prior notion of how to perceive and react to it. From the viewpoint of efficiency, then, generalization enables us to apply what we have learned—to react in the same way to comparable situations. A problem arises, however, when we transfer responses incorrectly because we have failed to discriminate between dissimilar situations (e.g., reacting to novel circumstances in the present as if they were duplicates of the past).

The tendency to generalize inappropriate behaviors has especially far-reaching consequences because it often elicits reactions from others that not only perpetuate these behaviors but aggravate the conditions giving rise to them. Thus, Bateson and Ruesch (1951) have noted that communications between people convey more than a statement; they carry with them some anticipation of what the response will be. Leary (1957), along similar lines, suggests that interpersonal behaviors often are designed unconsciously to pull a reaction from others. For example, a phrase such as "I think I'm doing poorly" is not merely a message denoting a person's feelings but a social statement that normally elicits a reciprocal reaction such as "Of course not! You did beautifully."

How does the generalization of interpersonal behavior perpetuate conditions that give rise to these behaviors? An example may be useful. A young man whose past experiences led him to anticipate punitive reactions from his parents may be hyperalert to signs of rejection from others. As a consequence of his suspiciousness, he may distort innocuous comments, seeing them as indications of hostility. In preparing himself to ward off and counter the hostility he expects, he freezes his posture, stares coldly and rigidly, and passes a few aggressive comments himself. These actions communicate a message that quickly is sensed by others as unfriendly and antagonistic. Before long, others express open feelings of disaffection, begin to withdraw and display real, rather than imagined, hostility. The person's generalized suspicious behavior has evoked the expected punitive responses. He now has experienced an objective form of rejection similar to what he received in childhood; this leads him to be more suspicious and arrogant, beginning the vicious circle all over again.

By intruding old behaviors into new situations, individuals will provoke, with unfailing regularity, reactions from others that reinforce their old responses. Almost all forms of generalized behavior set up reciprocal reactions that intensify these behaviors; docile, ingratiating, or fearful interpersonal actions, for example, draw domineering and manipulative responses; confident and self-assured attitudes elicit admiration and submissiveness. In short, not only is generalization a form of perpetuation itself but it creates conditions that promote perpetuation.

Repetition Compulsion

Maladaptive behaviors persist not only as a consequence of generalized learned habits. Intrapsychic sources also "drive" the individual to recreate situations of the past that were frustrating or unresolved. Freud spoke of this process as repetition compulsions; by this, he meant the unconscious tendency to reconstruct situations in the present that parallel failures or disappointments of the past, and to persist in the attempt to undo these disappointments even though these attempts repeatedly have proven unrewarding.

A contradiction may appear, on first reading, between protective constriction, noted earlier, and repetition compulsion. The inconsistency can be resolved if we think of protective constriction as a process of avoiding conditions that have no hope of resolution. Repetition compulsions, in contrast, may be viewed as a process of reinstating conditions that provided partial gratification in the past, and that give promise of ultimate fulfillment. In this process, individuals arrange situations so as to utilize maneuvers that were *periodically* successful. They employ these partially reinforced behaviors again and again in the hope of finally achieving a full measure of the ends they sought.

The derivatives of these partially fulfilled drives constitute a reservoir of strivings that persist and seek gratification. Thus, the individual repeats past patterns not only through generalization but through active efforts to recreate and overcome what was not achieved fully. For example, a highly charged sibling rivalry between two sisters generated intense hostile and destructive feelings on the part of the older sister, a 21-year-old college student seen at her university's counseling service. These feelings were vented in a variety of malicious maneuvers, some of which were successful some of the time, but never fully gratified; that is, the drive to undo, humiliate and even destroy the younger sister remained only a partially fulfilled striving. In new interpersonal situations, the older sister recreated the sibling relationship; time and time again she made friends, only to repeat the malicious maneuvers of deprecation and humiliation she had employed with her sister in the past. These relationships only partially fulfilled her needs, however, because the real object of her hatred was her sister, and the goal she really sought, that of total destruction of her competitor, never was achieved. She repeated compulsively, in one relationship after another, the same destructive behavior patterns she had learned in the past; although she never gratified her unconscious objectives fully, she obtained sufficient symbolic rewards in these peer relationships to perpetuate her behavior.

In contrast to protective constriction, then, a process limited to conditions in which failure and pain are inevitable, repetition compulsions apply to those conditions where rewards are periodically achieved and where the motivation to obtain greater fulfillment persists. Nevertheless, intolerable duplicates of the past are recreated.

SOCIOCULTURAL INFLUENCES

We would be remiss in our presentation if we failed to recognize that personality pathology may be shaped by the institutions, traditions, and values that compose the cultural context of societal living; these cultural forces serve as a common framework of formative influences that set limits and establish guidelines for members of a social group. However, we must be careful to view "society" and "culture" not as entities but as convenient abstractions that characterize the pattern of relationships and responsibilities shared among group members.

The continuity and stability of cultural groups depend largely on the success with which their young are imbued with common beliefs and customs. To retain what has been wrought through history, each group must devise ways of molding its children to "fit in," that is, to accept and

perpetuate the system of prohibitions and sanctions that earlier group members have developed to meet the persistent tasks of life. All infants undergo a process of socialization by which they learn to progressively surrender their impulsive and naive behaviors, and to regulate or supplant them with the rules and practices of their group. Despite the coerciveness of this process and the loss of personal freedom that it entails, children learn, albeit gradually, that there are many rewards for cooperative and sharing behaviors. Societal rules enable them to survive, to predict the behaviors of others, to obtain warmth and security, and to learn acceptable strategies for achieving the rich and diverse rewards of life. It is important to recognize, then, that the traditions of a culture provide its members with a shared way of living by which basic needs are fulfilled for the greater majority with minimal conflict and maximal return.

In previous sections, we noted that for many children cultural training and inculcation are far from ideal; methods by which parents transmit societal rules and regulations often are highly charged and erratic, entailing affection, persuasion, seduction, coercion, deception, and threat. Feelings of stress, anxiety, and resentment may be generated within the young, leaving pathological residues that are perpetuated and serve to distort their future relationships; several of these pathogenic experiences have been dealt with earlier.

Attention in this sociocultural section will focus, not on the more private experiences of particular children in particular families, but on those more public experiences that are shared in common among members of a societal group. In a sense, we shall be speaking of forces that characterize "society as the patient," a phrase that Lawrence K. Frank suggested close to 60 years ago. He wrote (1936):

Instead of thinking in terms of a multiplicity of so-called social problems, each demanding special attention and a different remedy, we can view all of them as different symptoms of the same disease. That would be a real gain even if we cannot entirely agree upon the exact nature of the disease. If, for example, we could regard crime, mental disorders, family disorganization, juvenile delinquency, prostitution and sex offenses, and much that now passes as the result of pathological processes (e.g., gastric ulcer) as evidence, not of individual wickedness, incompetence, perversity or pathology, but as human reactions to cultural disintegration, a forward step would be taken. (p. 42)

The notion that many pathological patterns observed today can best be ascribed to the perverse, chaotic, or frayed conditions of our cultural life has been voiced by many commentators of the social scene; these conditions have been characterized in phrases such as "the age of anxiety," "growing up absurd," and "the lonely crowd." It is not within the scope of this book to elaborate the themes implied in these slogans; a brief description of three conditions of contemporary life will suffice to provide the reader with some idea of what these writers are saying. First, we will note the operation of forces that compel individuals to surpass the standards to which they were exposed in early life; second, we will point up the effects of changing, ambiguous, and contradictory social values; and third, we will describe the consequences of the disintegration of social beliefs and goals.

ACHIEVEMENT STRIVING AND COMPETITION

Few characterizations of American life are more apt than those that portray our society as upwardly mobile. Stated differently, our culture has maximized the opportunity of its members to progress, to succeed, and to achieve material rewards once considered the province only of the aristocracy and well-to-do. With certain notable and distressing exceptions, the young of our society have been free to rise, by dint of their wits and their talents, above the socioeconomic status of their parents. Implicit in this well-publicized option to succeed, however, is the expectancy that each person will pursue opportunities and will be measured by the extent to which he or she fulfills them. Thus, our society not only promotes ambition but expects each of its members to meet the challenge successfully. Each aspiring individual is confronted, then, with a precarious choice; along with the promising rewards of success are the devastating consequences of failure, as may be seen in the developmental background of certain *narcissistic* personality disorders.

The upwardly mobile opportunities shared by most members of our society can only bring forth intense competition. The struggle for achievement is geared, therefore, not only to transcend one's past but to surpass the attainments of others. No better illustration can be seen of the consequences of competitive failure and inadequacy than in the constant testing and grading that children experience throughout their school years; this early form of teaching competitiveness persists and pervades every fabric of societal life. It is evident in athletics, in the desire to be accepted by prestigious colleges, in the search for "pretty" dates, in the effort to get a job with a "title," in the quest for high income, in the purchase of a status car, in affiliation with the "right" country club, and so on.

The competitive success struggle is insatiable and fruitless since few can reach the "top," and there are no spheres of life in which invidious comparisons cannot be made. Thus, a depressed 47-year-old man, who had risen from a poor immigrant family background to a respected and financially rewarding career as a lawyer, became despondent and considered himself a failure following his unsuccessful bid for the elective office of county judge.

Guilt for having let others down, self-devaluation for one's limitations and self-recrimination for failures, all of these pathogenic feelings well up within many members of our society. We have been well trained to compete and to seek public achievements without examining their aims, their inevitable frustrations, and their limited rewards.

UNSTABLE AND CONTRADICTORY SOCIAL STANDARDS

Achievement strivings refer to the need to surpass one's past attainments; competition describes the struggle among individuals to surpass each other in these achievements. What happens, however, if the standards by which people gauge their achievements keep changing or are ambiguous? What happens if people cannot find dependable and unequivocal standards to guide their aspirations?

It has been the historical function of cultural traditions to give meaning and order to social life, to define the tasks and responsibilities of existence and to guide group members with a system of shared beliefs, values, and goals. These traditions, transmitted from parents to children, provide the young with a blueprint for organizing their thoughts, behaviors, and aspirations.

One of the problems we face today is the pace of social change, and the increasingly contradictory standards to which members of our society are expected to subscribe. Under the cumulative impact of rapid industrialization, immigration, urbanization, mobility, technology, and mass communication, there has been a steady erosion of traditional values and standards. Instead of a simple and coherent body of customs and beliefs, we find ourselves confronted with constantly shifting and increasingly questioned standards whose durability is uncertain and precarious. No longer can we find the certainties and absolutes that guided earlier generations. The complexity and diversity of everyday experience play havoc with simple archaic beliefs and render them useless as instruments to deal with contemporary realities. Lacking a coherent view of life, we find ourselves groping and bewildered, swinging from one set of standards to another, unable to find stability and order in the flux of changing events. There have been few times in the history of humankind when so many have faced the tasks of life without the aid of accepted and durable traditions. As will be elaborated in our discussion of the *borderline* personality disorder's experiential background, the previously described factors are likely to be central influences in giving shape to their internal psychic dissonance.

This profusion of divergent standards is compounded by intrinsic contradictions among the beliefs to which people are exposed; we are sermonized to "turn the other cheek," but exhorted to "compete and win" as well. The strain of making choices among conflicting values and loyalties besets us at every turn. Competing claims on our time and divergent demands to behave one way here and another there keep us in constant turmoil and prevent us from finding a stable anchor or from settling on a fixed course.

For example, an anxious and dejected 36-year-old mother of three could not resolve the problem of whether to follow her former career as a lawyer, which she had interrupted at the time of her first child's birth, or whether to remain a housewife; when first seen, she was torn between the desire to accept a position as legal counsel for a public agency engaged in humanitarian social programs, and feelings of guilt that by so doing she would fail to fulfill her responsibilities to her husband and children. With no system of consistent values, we drift erratically from one action to another; countervailing pressures only lead us into uncertainty, confusion, conflict, and hypocrisy.

DISINTEGRATION OF REGULATORY BELIEFS AND GOALS

There are large segments of our society that find themselves out of the mainstream of American life; isolated by the circumstance of social prejudice or economic deprivation, they struggle less with the problem of achieving in a changing society than with managing the bare necessities of survival. To them, the question is not which of the changing social values they should pursue, but whether any social values are worthy of pursuit.

Youngsters exposed to poverty and destitution, attending inadequate schools, living in poor housing set within decaying communities, raised in chaotic and broken homes, deprived of parental models of success and attainment and immersed in a pervasive atmosphere of hopelessness, futility, and apathy, cannot help but question the validity of the "good society." In these settings, children quickly learn that there are few worthy standards to which they can aspire successfully. Whatever efforts they make to raise themselves from these bleak surroundings run hard against the painful restrictions of poverty, the sense of a meaningless and empty existence, and an indifferent, if not hostile, world.

As will be discussed in our presentation of the so-called *antisocial* personality disorder, many young black people today reject outright the idea of finding a niche in American society; they question whether a country that has preached equality but has degraded their parents and deprived them of their rights and opportunities, is worth saving at all. Why make a pretense of accepting patently "false" values or seeking the unattainable goals of the larger society, when reality undermines every hope, and social existence is so evidently and pervasively painful and harsh?

Deteriorating and alienated communities feed on themselves; not only do they perpetuate their decay by destroying the initiative and promise of their young but they attract the outcast and unstable who drift into their midst. Caught in this web of disintegration, the young and the downwardly mobile join those who already have retreated from the values of the larger society. Delinquency, prostitution, broken homes, crime, violence, and addiction increasingly characterize these communities, and the vicious circle of decay and disintegration not only persists but is intensified.

We must keep in mind, however, that harsh cultural and social conditions rarely "cause" personality pathology; rather, they serve as a context within which the more direct and immediate experiences of interpersonal life take place. They color and degrade personal relationships, and establish maladaptive and pathogenic models for imitation.

CONCLUDING COMMENTS

The obstacles confronting investigators engaged either in the design, the execution, or the interpretation of studies of personality disorders are formidable. Numerous questions have been raised regarding both the methodological adequacy of earlier research and the likelihood that these studies will prove more fruitful in the future. Let us briefly note again some of these problems.

Because it is impossible to design an experiment in which relevant variables can systematically be controlled or manipulated, it will be impossible to establish unequivocal cause-effect relationships among these variables and personality pathology. Investigators cannot arrange, no less subvert and abuse, an individual or a social group for purposes of scientific study; research in this field must, therefore, continue to be of a naturalistic and correlational nature. The problem that arises with naturalistic studies is the difficulty of inferring causality; correlations do not give us a secure base for determining which factors were cause and which were effect. For example, correlations between socioeconomic class and personality disorders may signify both that deteriorated social conditions produce mental disorders *and* that mental disorders result in deteriorated social conditions.

Despite efforts on the part of the DSM-IV committees to make progress in establishing a scientific base for research in this field, we are likely to continue to be plagued by unreliable and nonuniform diagnostic criteria. We know that the basis for assigning one or another diagnostic label varies tremendously.

Throughout the chapter are comments indicating the appalling lack of definitive research to support assertions regarding the role of pathogenic factors in personality pathology. That pathogenic factors of both a psychosocial and biological nature are significantly involved seems axiomatic to most theorists, but science progresses not by supposition and belief but by hard facts gained through well-designed and well-executed research. This paucity of evidence does not signify neglect on the part of researchers; rather, it indicates the awesome difficulties involved in unraveling the intricate interplay of influences productive of personality pathology. Despite these apologetics, there is reason for caution in accepting the contentions of pathogenic theorists.

We have no choice but to continue to pursue the suggestive leads provided us by both plausible speculation and exploratory research; difficulties notwithstanding, we must caution against inclinations to revert to past simplifications, or to abandon efforts out of dismay or cynicism. Our increasing knowledge of the multideterminant and circular character of pathogenesis, as well as the inextricable developmental sequences through which it proceeds, should prevent us from falling prey to simplifications that led early theorists to attribute personality pathology to single factors. Innumerable pathogenic roots are possible; the causal elements are so intermeshed that we must plan our research strategies to disentangle, not isolated determinants, but their convergencies, their interactions, and their continuities.

CHAPTER 4

Personality Assessment: Domains, Validity, and Instruments

As noted in previous chapters, rather than developing independently and being left to stand as an unconnected body of structures and functions, a truly mature, integrated clinical science must embody and coordinate (a) explicit *theories*—explanatory and heuristic conceptual schemas that are consistent with established knowledge in both their own and related sciences, from which reasonably accurate propositions concerning pathological conditions can be both deduced and understood, enabling thereby the development of (b) a formal *nosology*—a taxonomic classification of disorders derived logically from the theory and arranged to provide a cohesive organization within which its major categories can be grouped and differentiated, permitting thereby the development of (c) coordinated *instruments*—tools that are empirically grounded and sufficiently sensitive quantitatively to allow the theory's propositions and hypotheses to be adequately investigated and evaluated, and the constructs composing its nosology to be dimensionalized and measured, specifying therefrom target areas for (d) planned *interventions*—strategies and techniques of therapy, designed in accord with the theory and oriented to modify problematic clinical characteristics in a manner consonant with professional standards and social responsibilities. It is the third of these elements that comprises the body of this chapter.

The current state of clinical psychopathology resembles that of medicine a century ago. Not only do the complexly interwoven causal networks underlying the personality disorders have yet to be untangled, there is no explicit consensus among informed researchers concerning the content areas in which personality disorders are expressed. Bereft of a solid and officially recognized theoretical foundation, personality disorders cannot automatically be anchored to a list of definitive indicators that might be systematically inquired for diagnostic purposes. Even among more theoretically minded researchers, there is disagreement concerning the nature of the fundamental dimensions of personality, with the result that different disorders may be derived from different models. Benjamin (1993), Cloninger (1987), and Millon (1990), for example, elaborate polytaxonic theories of personality. Nevertheless, although each theory is logically coherent, it makes different assumptions about the nature of personality, carving the domain in a different way. The resulting taxonomies contain interesting, and possibly illuminating, points of correspondence, but are no means identical.

To note that there are different theories, however, is only the beginning. There are a variety of different implicit definitions of theory as well as differing opinions as to how theory should be translated into methodology and how it should be applied in the treatment of each individual case. At one polar extreme lie the descriptive-polytaxonic models of the inductivists, whose theoretical grounding consists of no more than the argument that their methodology of vogue, factor analysis, is both necessary and sufficient to reveal nature's intrinsic structure. Theory here is simply a theory about a methodology, not about any dimension of content that issues from the methodology. Nevertheless, the phrase "five-factor theory" is occasionally seen. Following a "theory-strong" orientation is Millon (1990), a thorough-going polytaxonic deductivist, for whom the personality disorders are derived by linking stages of evolution to personologic polarities. Meehl (e.g., 1986, 1992), although not a prominent researcher in this area, might also be included in this company, as only

Meehl makes much of the importance of subjecting theories to the strong threat of falsification in the tradition of Karl Popper.

An abundance of models stands to enrich our thinking over the long term, but if the clinician is a scientific realist, believing that validity ultimately rests in some one conceptual system or taxonomy that maps nature's intrinsic structure, such controversy must be distressing at the current time. Despite the enthusiasm of the five-factor proponents, no convergence or finality on some single conceptual system for personality disorders has yet been established, with the result that no strong and consensually agreed-on link between theory, nosology, assessment, and intervention currently exists. Furthermore, there are no "external" or "paradigm-free" criteria by which to judge the merits of competing conceptual systems. From a standpoint external to any one particular model of the personality disorders, then, descriptive validity is the maximum that an assessment might be certain to achieve at the current time. The four domains of clinical science remain loosely articulated and rather disjoint.

And yet, clinical work must go on. First, we discuss questions that might motivate a personality disorder assessment. Second, the issue of content validity is considered in terms of the eight functional (e.g., expressive acts) and structural (e.g., self-image) domains through which personality is expressed. Concerns associated with psychometric methodology are presented next, followed by two major models of validation, that labeled "idiographic validity," which seeks to appraise assessment accuracy within the *single subject,* as contrasted with "nomothetic *or* construct validity," which seeks to verify the accuracy of a concept or generalizable measure by employing a broad sample-based gauge or test. Subsequent sections deal with current instruments in use by clinicians such as self-report inventories, interviews, and checklists oriented specifically to the DSM Axis II personality constructs. The chapter closes with speculations concerning the future course of assessment for the personality disorders.

ISSUES AND QUESTIONS CONCERNING ASSESSMENT

What is assessment? What are the goals of an assessment? Every new patient presents a large number of unknowns. Some unknowns, however, are so salient and relevant they warrant a standardized procedure in which certain questions are explicitly formulated by one party and explicitly answered by another. This procedure is called assessment.

WHEN SHOULD PERSONALITY CHARACTERISTICS BE ASSESSED?

Why would a patient's personality be assessed? A personality disorder need not exist for a personality assessment to be useful. In the course of clinical work, a thorough personality assessment is always good advice as a head start on therapy, whether the client is an inpatient or outpatient, or simply a normal who enters therapy desiring to become a more fully functioning and self-actualized person. The question "Why this particular pattern of traits or behaviors rather than some other?" may be less urgent, but it is no less useful as a point of departure for therapy for individuals who have no personality disorder and no diagnosed or subclinical Axis I condition. Even among normal persons, there are areas of ridigity or dysfunction relative to their intraindividual norm.

Some patients, however, present in the throes of crisis or the depths of a depressive episode. Personality profiles obtained during treatment for an Axis I condition are often different from those obtained following recovery. Reich, Noyes, Coryell, and Gorman (1986), for example, obtained personality measures on 56 patients suffering from panic disorder and agoraphobia. Data on the same measures were obtained 6 weeks later. The 40 patients who had improved (defined in advance as a decline of 5 or more points on the Hamilton Anxiety Rating Scale) showed a significantly increased emotional strength and extroversion, and significantly decreased interpersonal dependence. From an integrative perspective, these results are not unexpected. Each person exists as a single integrated organism. The cognitive theory of depression, for example, holds that depressed subjects are negatively biased toward the self, world, and future (Beck & Freeman, 1993). Because their schemas are chronically activated, depressed subjects may endorse items indicating more severe pathology than is in fact warranted, leading to elevated profiles, increased comorbidity, and presumably, more severe personality pathology. Individuals who feel overwhelmed by their problems and helpless to solve them may exaggerate their pathologies as a help-seeking maneuver, effectively endorsing any test item having content that might get the attention of test interpreters.

In addition, it is likely that different Axis I conditions systematically affect the Axis II profiles in qualitatively different ways. If so, then obtaining a more "true" representation of the patient's characteristics is not merely a matter of adjusting the whole profile upward or downward. Although the diagnostic efficiency of its corrections has yet to be fully explored, the Millon Clinical Multiaxial Inventory (MCMI) includes base rate score modifications for the effects of anxious and depressive states on several personality disorders scales: the depressive, masochistic (self-defeating), borderline, avoidant, and schizotypal. Clinicians need to consider the possibility of pathology by presentation interactions for inventories and batteries when it is determined that personality should be assessed.

IS A PERSONALITY DISORDER DIAGNOSIS WARRANTED?

Asking whether a personality disorder diagnosis is warranted is quite different from asking, "Does the patient 'have' a personality disorder?" The former frames the problem as a functional issue, the latter as a medical or record-keeping one, for which a "present or absent" judgment will be sufficient. Such a distinction may appear subtle, but it has profound implications that inevitably color the entire clinical process. Undoubtedly, the temptation to reify personality disorders, especially in casual conversation, is almost irresistible. Unless carefully checked, it leads to metatheoretical and epistemological misconceptions. Personality disorders are disorders of the entire matrix of the person, of the entire patterning of personality variables at levels as easily observed as behavioral acts and as highly inferential as defense regulatory mechanisms. Personality disorders cannot be medicalized and transformed into disease entities that are readily isolated and expunged through some approved and effective course of treatment. In this sense, the choice of the word "disorders" for the Axis II abnormalities is unfortunate, because it lards Axis II with suppositions that are more consonant with Axis I. No person is currently alive, has ever been born, nor will ever be born, who "has" a personality disorder. As noted in Chapter 1, such syntactical shortcuts may be

useful for convenience in clinical communication, but the nature of the construct disallows their possessing any truth value. Diagnosis, then, is not, as in the medical model, a determination of the presence or absence of a disease process and the specification of its unique manifestations in the particular patient. Instead, it is only concerned with whether the individual represents a "case," and how the individual's personality is tied up in the meaning of past and current problems. In other words, diagnosis must be regarded as a pragmatic, rather than an ontological, issue.

The exact threshold at which a client with personality problems functionally becomes a case has not yet been satisfactorily operationalized, much less standardized across disorders, for a variety of reasons. Just as individuals are embedded in larger social milieus, the idea of caseness is embedded in an implicit network of social assumptions. Undoubtedly, this situation plays an important role in limiting the reliability of Axis II diagnoses and in distorting base rate estimates within and across diagnostic settings. There is, for example, little validity in saying there are more avoidants than negativistics if the negativistics diagnosed with current criteria are far more dysfunctional, and therefore likely to be far fewer in number, than the avoidants. This problem will no doubt loom large in discussions regarding the DSM-V. In Chapter 1, we suggested that personality could be usefully conceptualized as a system and that the criteria for personality dysfunction are most usefully derived when coordinated with the systems model itself. Ideally, some content-free or personality-generic criteria would exist that operationalize personality functioning contextually.

The same critique might be applied to almost all existing personality assessment instruments. Because these are overwhelmingly content oriented, there is the further problem of separating scale elevations that indicate inflexibility or maladaptive behavior from those that are elevated but for whatever reason are not creating psychosocial difficulties. Unfortunately, the degree to which a given trait is problematic is not a direct function of the quantity of the trait expressed as a scale elevation but instead is a function of (a) its interaction with other characteristics of the organism in which the trait is embedded, and (b) the interaction between the organism and the context in which the organism is embedded. Thus not one, but two interactions modulate the implications of the quantity of a trait for flexibility and pervasiveness.

How Should the Patient's Personality Be Diagnosed?

After "when" and "whether" comes "what": What constellation of Axis II constructs best captures the essence of the patient's personality style? If it is decided that the patient in fact warrants a personality disorder diagnosis, then this question is important for at least two reasons. First, it must be answered in formulating a multiaxial diagnosis for the clinical report. Second, the purpose of the multiaxial model is not merely to assign diagnoses; some answer is necessary so that the relationship between the patient's Axis I and Axis II difficulties can be considered and the logic of the case decoded.

With the evolution of competing conceptions to the Axis II prototypes, the what question has become more complex. Clinicians who open-mindedly consider dimensions other than those officially sanctioned risk becoming entangled in a conceptual pluralism that renders the assessment process either heavily biased in favor of one personologic domain at the expense of others, or almost cryptic and nonrepeatable by other clinicians. Assume for the moment that data from the Wisconsin Personality Disorders Inventory, grounded in Benjamin's interpersonal model, and the Tridimensional Personality Questionnaire, grounded in Cloninger's neurobiological model, are available and lead to certain hypotheses about the client that both converge and diverge in some respects. What should be done? No formal rules exist for integrating disparate data from multiple personologic domains into a single integrated picture. Two solutions appear possible. First, one set of findings might simply be rejected as irrelevant. Because those that remain originate from a single personologic domain, they at least have the virtue of internal consistency. However, they do not have the virtue of scope. Second, both sets of findings might be retained and integrated, albeit only through a nonspecifiable process of clinical intuition, resulting in a conceptually fuzzier, but possibly more complete description of personality. Both solutions are scientifically unpalatable, but are acceptable given the state of the science at this time. The preference of individual clinicians may in fact depend more on their own personality styles (tolerance for ambiguity vs. desire for consistency), than on any objective criteria. The idea of evolving simultaneously a set of instruments, each (a) coordinated with the others and (b) oriented toward a specific structural or functional domain in which personality is expressed, in order to (c) maximize convergent validity while optimizing incremental validity, has yet to work its way into personality disorders' literature in a self-conscious manner. Ideally, personality structures and functions would be assessed in their totality, and the instruments to do so would be conjointly designed.

Evaluating the Relationship between Axis I and Axis II

With the multiaxial model, first adopted in the DSM-III, personality disorders (Axis II) and the psychosocial environment (Axis IV) have been assigned contextual roles. The multiaxial model has been deliberately constructed such that the Axis I symptoms seek their reason for being in the context of the patient's larger personality style and its interaction with the current social milieu. The transaction between Axes II and IV produces Axis I. What is being assessed, then, are not diseases, but contexts that transform the meaning of diseases, of the existing Axis I symptomatology. An anxiety disorder in a dependent individual is different from an anxiety disorder in a negativistic individual. Were this not true, were there an independence between clinical syndrome and personality style, there would be no reason for the multiaxial model to exist at all. The logic of the case would reducible to the logic of the disorder. In this sense, the most important question an integrative assessment must answer is: Why this set of symptoms rather than some other? Answering this question means that the assessment must achieve idiographic validity. Here is yet another reason why personality disorders cannot be approached as diseases or even as reified entities. In the logic of the multiaxial model, personality disorders are functionally inherently more allied with ground than figure. Whereas they are circumscribed as diagnostic syndromes as a linguistic necessity, they are not diseases or "things" at all, but contexts in which the more diseaselike entities that we think of as belonging on Axis I derive a significance unique to each individual case.

Selecting Therapeutic Options

After "when," "whether," and "what" comes "how." If the assessment is relatively complete and at least has descriptive validity, then various avenues for approaching the patient's problems will be relatively clear. After all, the ultimate purpose of assessment is to constrain the number of hypotheses the clinician must entertain with respect to patient intervention. Prior to the assessment, the patient could easily be anyone, with nearly an infinite number of possibilities for a personality style, for presenting problems, and interrelationships between the two. If there has been a good assessment, what is known works to constrain what should be done. Assuming treatment is indicated, the Axis II pattern bears on how it should proceed. Axis II would be of little use if every Axis I disorder could be treated in the same way regardless of the patient's personality style. In Chapter 5, we note that personality disorders specifically require an integrative mode of therapy, achieved through what are called "potentiating pairings" and "catalytic sequences." The essence of this idea is simply that the intervention cannot be less tenacious than the problem it is intended to remedy. If many hypotheses exist that are sufficient to account for the patient's current state and its integration with his or her personality, the clinician cannot possibly know which treatments to combine in order to achieve synergistic efficacy.

APPRAISING THERAPEUTIC PROGRESS

Any evaluation of treatment efficacy requires a follow-up assessment. Should treatment continue? How severe are the residuals of the presenting problem? Where should treatment go from here? Does the further increment in functioning believed achievable justify the expenditure of resources needed to achieve that increment? The economic forces currently operating in our managed care health system seem bent on achieving cost reduction, even when this means only symptomatic relief of uncertain duration. For this reason, follow-up and perhaps even "in-progress" assessments are likely only to become more important in the future, at least where the Axis I disorders are concerned. In contrast, third-party payers are not inclined to reimburse for personality disorder therapy, even though personality pathology entails an adaptive inflexibility and the perpetuation of preexisting difficulties that, almost by definition, create a vulnerability to Axis I problems as enduring and pervasive as personality itself. Personality disorder therapy, then, if it is to occur at all, occurs in the context of treatment for an Axis I condition. Unlike traditional long-term therapy, brief therapy, at least for the personality disorders, means not a cure, but merely engaging the constructive forces of personality long enough to open up possibilities that are likely to be achieved only *after* termination.

Ideally, the operational definition of personality pathology, defined in a contextual or generic sense, would be so precise that the efficacy of therapy would be gauged specifically with reference to personality functioning, rather than to the particular disorders. As previously noted, this is not the case. A widely tested, content-free, and consensually accepted operationalization of personality pathology does not yet exist. Nor is there a specialized suite of conjointly constructed instruments intended specifically to assess personality in its totality. At the current time, the best that can be achieved is to administer the same diagnostic inventory at two or more points in time, examining profile congruence and overall elevation for evidence of progress, broadly conceived.

CONTENT VALIDITY OF THE ASSESSMENT

"The problem with personality assessment is that there is little agreement as to what one is assessing, much less how to assess it; from this it follows that there is little agreement concerning the domain it covers" (Rorer, 1990, p. 693). In a situation where so many fundamental issues remain undecided, it is probably best to aim for content validity. Measure everything that needs to be measured in order to get as complete a picture of the client as possible. Idiographic validity will be impossible to achieve if essential information has been neglected.

The question we must ask, then, is "In what domains should personality disorders be ascribed and therefore assessed?" Although personality may be considered as being exclusively psychodynamic or exclusively biological, the authors regard such positions as overly narrow and restrictive. The integrative perspective encouraged here views personality as a multidetermined and multireferential construct that may be profitably studied and assessed across a variety of content areas. The term "multireferential" is an important one for assessment purposes. Earlier, we noted that one way of dealing with conceptual and theoretical pluralism is simply to assess personality in accord with a single model, effectively eliminating the eclecticism of divergent perspectives through a dismissive dogmatism. A truly comprehensive assessment, however, one that is logically consonant with the integrative nature of personality as a construct, requires that personality be assessed systematically across multiple personologic spheres if the assessment is to be content valid. Constraints on system functioning may exist in any of these areas. Assessment instruments that do not address these domains must be regarded as incomplete with respect to content, whether accidentally, pragmatically, or ideologically.

On what basis will we distinguish the major domains of personality from more narrow areas of study? Several criteria were used to select and develop the clinical domains listed herein: (a) that they be varied in the features they embody; they must not be limited just to behaviors or cognitions, but instead encompass a full range of clinically relevant characteristics; (b) that they parallel, if not correspond, to many of our profession's therapeutic modalities (e.g., self-oriented phenomenological techniques for altering dysfunctional cognitions; group treatment procedures (for modifying interpersonal conduct); and (c) that they not only be coordinated to the official DSM schema of personality disorder prototypes, but also that each disorder possess a distinctive feature within each clinical domain. As portrayed in Table 4.1, these diagnostic features are distinguished in accord with the data levels they represent—behavioral, phenomenological, intrapsychic, and biophysical. This differentiation reflects the four historic approaches that characterize the study of psychopathology. More narrow clinical domains can be systematically organized in a manner similar to distinctions drawn in the biological realm, that is, by dividing them

TABLE 4.1 Functional and Structural Domains of Personality

Functional Domains	Structural Domains
Behavioral Level	
Expressive acts	
Interpersonal conduct	
Phenomenological Level	
Cognitive style	Object representations
	Self-image
Intrapsychic Level	
Regulatory mechanisms	Morphologic organization
Biophysical Level	
	Mood/temperament

into structural and functional attributes. The science of anatomy investigates embedded and essentially permanent structures that serve, for example, as substrates for mood and memory. Its functional counterpart, physiology, is concerned with processes that regulate internal dynamics and external transactions. Together, structures and functions bind the organism together as a coherent entity. Dividing the characteristics of the psychological world into structural and functional realms is, of course, by no means a novel notion. Psychoanalytic theory has dealt since its inception with topographic constructs such as conscious, preconscious, and unconscious, and later with structural concepts such as id, ego, and superego. Likewise, a host of quasi-stationary functional processes, such as the so-called ego apparatuses, have been posited and studied (Gill, 1963; Rapaport, 1959).

Each of the clinical chapters in this text lists functional and structural attributes for its particular personality disorder. These attributes have been constructed to be both comprehensive (exhaustive of the major domains of personality) and comparable (existing at approximately equal levels of abstraction) across domains. Incorporating all the personalities of the DSM-III-R and DSM-IV yields an 8×14 domain by disorder matrix (Figure 4.1). Each cell of the matrix contains the diagnostic attribute or criterion that in the authors' judgment best captures the expression of that personality style within that domain. Vertically considered, the matrix facilitates ready comparison and contrast of the disorders across content areas. Horizontally, it suggests that criteria must be appraised conjointly across a variety of content areas in order to arrive a comprehensive picture of each ideal type. The first gets at discriminate validity; the second at convergent validity.

In contrast, the criteria of the DSM-IV are both noncomprehensive (no real scheme through which to coordinate and anchor personality attributes has been developed) and noncomparable (the criteria run the gamut from very broad to very narrow). Further, these problems exist both within and between disorders, so that different disorders evince different content distortions. Consider, for example, the obsessive-compulsive personality disorder. Criterion 5 is relatively narrow and behavioral: "Is unable to discard worn-out or worthless objects even when they have no sentimental value." In contrast, criterion 8 requires more inference: "Shows rigidity and stubbornness." In fact, the inability to discard

Domain / Disorder	Expressive Acts	Interpersonal Conduct	Cognitive Style	Self-Image	Object Representations	Regulatory Mechanisms	Morphologic Organization	Mood/ Temperament
Schizoid	Impassive	Unengaged	Impoverished	Complacent	Meager	Intellectualization	Undifferentiated	Apathetic
Avoidant	Fretful	Aversive	Distracted	Alienated	Vexatious	Fantasy	Fragile	Anguished
Depressive	Disconsolate	Defenseless	Pessimistic	Worthless	Forsaken	Asceticism	Depleted	Melancholic
Dependent	Incompetent	Submissive	Naive	Inept	Immature	Introjection	Inchoate	Pacific
Histrionic	Dramatic	Attention-Seeking	Flighty	Gregarious	Shallow	Dissociation	Disjointed	Fickle
Narcissistic	Haughty	Exploitive	Expansive	Admirable	Contrived	Rationalization	Spurious	Insouciant
Antisocial	Impulsive	Irresponsible	Deviant	Autonomous	Debased	Acting-Out	Unruly	Callous
Sadistic	Precipitate	Abrasive	Dogmatic	Combative	Pernicious	Isolation	Eruptive	Hostile
Compulsive	Disciplined	Respectful	Constricted	Conscientious	Concealed	Reaction Formation	Compartmentalized	Solemn
Negativistic	Resentful	Contrary	Skeptical	Discontented	Vacillating	Displacement	Divergent	Irritable
Masochistic	Abstinent	Deferential	Diffident	Undeserving	Discredited	Exaggeration	Inverted	Dysphoric
Schizotypal	Eccentric	Secretive	Autistic	Estranged	Chaotic	Undoing	Fragmented	Distraught or Insentient
Borderline	Spasmodic	Paradoxical	Capricious	Uncertain	Incompatible	Regression	Split	Labile
Paranoid	Defensive	Provocative	Suspicious	Inviolable	Unalterable	Projection	Inelastic	Irascible

Figure 4.1 Expression of personality disorders across the domains of clinical science.

worthless objects could well be considered simply a behavioral manifestation of the trait of rigidity. Failure to coordinate criteria across domains may also lead to redundancies. Consider, for example, the dependent personality disorder. Criterion 1 states, "Has difficulty making everyday decisions without an excessive amount of advice and reassurance from others." Criterion 2, however, says almost the same: "Needs others to assume responsibility for most major areas of his or her life." In fact, five of the eight dependent personality criteria seem oriented toward the interpersonal conduct domain, two seem oriented toward the self-image domain, and only one is concerned with cognitive style, leaving the domains of regulatory mechanisms, object representations, morphologic organization, mood/temperament, and expressive acts completely unaddressed.

Failure to multioperationalize the personality disorders through comprehensive and comparable attributes certainly means that the content validity of the criteria sets has been compromised, quite probably contributing to diagnostic invalidity and diagnostic inefficiency. Because the DSM is usually taken as the "gold standard" by which other measures of personality disorder are judged, the degree of distortion is an open question at this point—there is no gold standard for the gold standard. One scenario reads as follows: Clinical wisdom states correctly that, in principle, multiple data sources and construct gauges should be sought as a means of obtaining diagnostic confirmation. Because the DSM criteria sets are noncomprehensive and noncomparable, there are substantive reasons for bringing extra-DSM notions and instruments not intended explicitly to instantiate DSM criteria to bear on each assessment case. To the extent that DSM criteria are successfully operationalized in two instruments A and B, distortions latent in the criteria are built into both, providing users with information that, while ostensibly confirmatory if the instruments agree, is in fact of unknown incremental validity. The agreement is, after all, achieved through two highly redundant gauges of the same flawed criteria sets. Although the diagnosis is reliably DSM, then, the use of noncomparable and noncomprehensive items in both instruments makes its validity uncertain. Once again, we see that reliability is not validity, even for a DSM diagnosis. Instruments embracing the same constructs but constructed independent of the DSM considerations, that is, instruments whose findings would be truly independent and thus bear most strongly on the validity of a given diagnosis,

are few and far between. Every extant instrument is to some extent contaminated by the problem. The degree to which a worst-case scenario represents clinical reality is unknown. In all likelihood, matters are not this severe, but it is wise to be aware of the possibilities. What *is* certain is that the role of clinical judgment in making diagnostic decisions has by no means been usurped by the current constellation of instrumentalities and criteria sets.

In conducting a domain-oriented assessment, clinicians should beware of regarding each domain as concretized, independent entity, and thereby falling into a naive and reducing operationism. Each domain is an legitimate, but highly contextualized, part of a single integrated whole (see Figure 4.2). All domains are necessary if the functional-structural integrity of the organism is to be maintained. Nevertheless, individuals differ with respect to the domains they enact most frequently. Real patients vary not only in the degree to which they approximate each personality prototype, but also in the extent to which constraints in each domain shape their overall behavior. Conceptualizing personality as a system, we might say that the constraints on the states the system may assume inhere in different parts of the system for different individuals, even where those individuals share a diagnosis. Only those aspects of the system that are sufficiently crystallized possess the enduring and pervasive character we associate with personality. In this sense, the goal of an assessment is to illuminate constraints that perpetuate the system's narrow, rigid functioning, and consequent adaptive inflexibility. Thus identified, the purpose of therapy should be to relax these constraints, allowing the system to assume a greater variety of states or adaptive behaviors across situations than before.

Although comprehensive and comparable diagnostic attributes are important to clinical work,

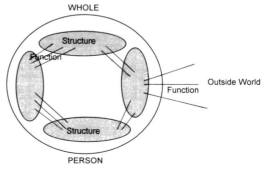

Figure 4.2 Each structural and functional domain is contextualized as part of the whole person.

they are no less important to researchers. An explicit purpose of operationalizing the personality disorders by clinical domain is to achieve content validity, the foundation of construct validity, as the first necessary step toward the construction of a taxonomy sufficiently valid to allow knowledge to accumulate. Unfortunately, this first necessary step has not yet been officially taken. Consequently, whereas the DSM criteria may be criticized for any number of reasons, including lack of internal consistency, redundancy, and comorbidity, it is not clear whether criticisms of the criteria are in fact criticisms of the constructs, because the constructs have never been adequately represented. Proposals radically revise DSM schema, then, must be regarded as premature. The intervening variables through which the validity of the constructs might be judged have never been comprehensively and comparably specified. How can the validity of a set of constructs whose epistemology requires they be anchored across multiple domains be judged through criteria that neglect some domains of content completely while weighting others disproportionately? Even radically empirically oriented researchers in the Sneath and Sokal (1961) tradition, who assert that methodology alone is sufficient to reveal the intrinsic topography of a subject domain, insist that all relevant attributes be entered into the statistical analysis.

FUNCTIONAL DOMAINS

Functional characteristics represent dynamic processes that transpire within the intrapsychic world and between the individual's self and psychosocial environment. Transactional processes take place through the medium of functional domains. For definitional purposes, we might say that functional domains represent "expressive modes of regulatory action": behaviors, social conduct, cognitive processes, and unconscious mechanisms that manage, adjust, transform, coordinate, balance, discharge, and control the give and take of inner and outer life. Four functional domains relevant to the personality disorders will be described briefly.

Expressive Acts

These attributes relate to the observables seen at the "behavioral level" of data, and are usually recorded by noting what and how the patient acts. Through inference, observations of overt behavior enable us to deduce either what the patient

unknowingly reveals about him- or herself or, conversely, what he or she wishes others to think or to know about him or her. Not only are the range and character of expressive actions wide and diverse, but they convey distinctive and worthwhile clinical information, from communicating a sense of personal incompetence to exhibiting general defensiveness to demonstrating a disciplined self-control, and so on. This domain of clinical data is likely to be especially productive in differentiating patients on the passive-active polarity of Millon's (1990) theoretical model.

For Buss and Craik (1983), acts represent the basic unit of analysis in personality. Dispositions consist of summaries of act frequencies that may be studied as hierarchically organized natural cognitive categories (e.g., Rosch & Mervis, 1975). A dispositional attribution means simply that the subject of the attribution has exhibited a higher number of acts relevant to a particular disposition in a certain time frame than what is considered to be the norm or average. The act-frequency perspective leads quite naturally to a method of scale construction. First, a large pool of acts representative of the disposition of interest are nominated by peers, family members, clinicians, or experts. Second, each act is rated for prototypicality by a panel of raters and the ratings are then averaged. Third, items are ranked by prototypicality and the top 20 or so items are retained to form a scale, which can then be given to actual samples and further refined, if desired.

Buss and Chiodo (1991) used this procedure to identify manifestations of narcissism in everyday life. Separate act pools were solicited for seven narcissistic traits or facets identified in the DSM-III-R criteria set—exhibitionistic, grandiose, self-centered, sense of entitlement, self-aggrandizing, lack of empathy, and exploitative. Refinement by prototypicality ratings ultimately yielded 140 acts, 20 for each of the seven traits related to narcissism. The prototypicality of each of the 140 acts was then assessed in relation to narcissism as a means of studying the centrality of the seven dispositions, ultimately yielding a set of 20 narcissistic acts, including "I expected others to step aside as I walked by" (grandiosity) and "I insisted that my friend drop everything to see me" (exploitativeness). When followed in this way, the act nomination approach can be used in a stepwise manner to operationalize concretely even constructs existing at high levels of inference, yielding not only summary measures of these constructs, but also subscales as measures of their component traits.

Regretfully, no instrument as yet exists that has applied this methodology to the entire schema of officially recognized personality disorders.

Interpersonal Conduct

A patient's style of relating to others also is noted essentially at the "behavioral" data level and may be captured in a number of ways, such as how his or her actions impact on others, intended or otherwise; the attitudes that underlie, prompt, and give shape to these actions; the methods by which he or she engages others to meet his or her needs; or his or her way of coping with social tensions and conflicts. Extrapolating from these observations, the clinician may construct an image of how the patient functions in relation to others, be it antagonistically, respectfully, aversively, secretively, and so on.

Whereas the interpersonal approach had its origins in the seminal contributions of Sullivan (1953), the circumplex model was developed by associates of the University of California and the Kaiser Foundation Health Plan. Freedman, Leary, Ossorio, and Coffey presented the circle in 1951, and this research was summarized and elaborated by Timothy Leary (1957), thus providing a coherent theory and taxonomy around which future contributions in the interpersonal paradigm could be researched and organized. The basic model has been refined by numerous researchers, though the efforts of Donald Kiesler (1982), Jerry Wiggins (1982), and the innovative theoretical conceptions of Lorna Benjamin (1974, 1993a), are especially notable. Tenets of interpersonal theory, encoded in the circumplex representation, make this taxonomy a promising one for the assessment of personality disorders. According to its most basic conception, each person constricts the response repertoire of others to evoke specifically those responses that confirm his or her perception of the self and world (Kiesler, 1982). Each party in the interpersonal system is co-opted by the other in an effort to elicit validation. Together, the parties must find a stable system state that is mutually confirmatory, thereby maintaining and perpetuating their respective self-concepts. These system states can be based on either reciprocity (on the vertical axis) or correspondence (on the horizontal axis). Thus dominance and submission are opposite and pulls for each other, whereas love pulls for love and hate for hate.

What is most important for assessment purposes is the existence of a coherent theoretical basis, one that permits a structural representation of the theory's propositions and the derivation of clinically testable hypotheses about actual cases. Theory, taxonomy, and assessment are embodied in the geometric representation of clinical personalities on the interpersonal circle itself. Although usually presented two dimensionally, the circumplex can also be visualized as a bivariate distribution with increasing densification toward the center, and increasing sparsity toward the edges. Healthy or flexible styles appear as balanced or circular patterns concentric with the circle. Such individuals possess a full range of styles by which to relate to others, regardless of the kinds of others with whom they find themselves involved. In other words, they are able to achieve stable system states with a maximum number of others; to confirm and be confirmed regardless of the nature of the interactants. In statistical parlance, a dyad composed of such relatively flexible individuals possesses many more degrees of freedom than one composed of characterologically rigid participants. Such a system may evolve a rich subtlety and variety of states, which, though perhaps unanticipated by the participants, nevertheless do not elicit anxiety (defined as a failure to "save face" or maintain the illusion) precisely because they are confirmatory at each successive interval of time.

Personality pathology is expressed geometrically through distortions of the healthy circular and concentric pattern. Some, for example, are highly shifted along one axis. To the extent that an individual's pattern approaches the periphery of the circle, the personality style may be assumed to be increasingly intense. To the extent that a particular segment of the circle dominates the totality, the personality style may be assumed to be increasingly narrow or rigid in its range of coping maneuvers, interpersonal behaviors, and role characteristics.

Despite the elegance of its undergirding theory, some personality disorders appear to be more related to the dimensions of the interpersonal circumplex than others (Pincus & Wiggins, 1990; Romney & Bynner, 1989; Wiggins & Pincus, 1989). In particular, schizoid, avoidant, dependent, histrionic, narcissistic, and antisocial personality disorders seem better assessed by the interpersonal circumplex than compulsive, borderline, negativistic (passive-aggressive), paranoid, and schizotypal disorders (Pincus & Wiggins, 1989). These findings are consistent with the domain-oriented conception of personality disorders previously presented, illustrating that interpersonal behavior is necessary but not sufficient as a complete model of these disorders. We must conclude then that any assessment of personality disorder anchored only in the interpersonal domain, while informative, must be regarded as incomplete. Clinicians of an interpersonal bent must balance the increased specificity gained by using an exclusively interpersonally-oriented instrument with the knowledge that the paradigm itself is acknowledged to be an incomplete representation of personality pathology. Clinicians who desire to assess their patients for compulsive, borderline, negativisitic, paranoid, and schizotypal pathology are advised to use additional inventories.

Cognitive Style

How the patient focuses and allocates attention, encodes and processes information, organizes thoughts, makes attributions, and communicates reactions and ideas to others represent data at the "phenomenological" level, and are among the most useful indexes to the clinician of the patient's distinctive way of functioning. By synthesizing these signs and symptoms, it may be possible to identify indications of what may be termed an impoverished style, or distracted thinking, or cognitive flightiness, or constricted thought, and so on.

Beck, Freeman, and associates (1990b) have made a genuine contribution in illuminating the relation of maladaptive core beliefs in this organisimic functional domain to the personality disorders. The unpublished Belief Questionnaire Beck (1990a) has been developed to assess the prominence of these cognitive constructs. The questionnaire consists of nine scales, each 14 items long, assessing the avoidant, dependent, passive-aggressive, obsessive-compulsive, antisocial, narcissistic, histrionic, schizoid, and paranoid personality disorders. Unfortunately, no scales are provided for the borderline and schizotypal disorders, although these disorders may be seen as typically clinically severe. Trull, Goodwin, Schopp, Hillenbrand, and Schuster (1993) found generally high internal consistencies, ranging from .77 to .93, and adequate test-retest reliabilities at approximately one month, ranging from .63 to .82, in a sample of normal college freshman. Unfortunately, positive intercorrelations were found even for nearly opposite disorders (e.g., schizoid-histrionic = .22).

Also relevant to this domain are instruments that assess what may be called *cognitive modes* concerning the sources employed to gather knowledge about one's life and surroundings and the manner in which this information is transformed. Four bipolarities, the constructs they reflect, and the eight scales developed to represent them were developed to compose the cognitive modes segment of the Millon Index of Personality Styles (MIPS). The first three of these cognitively oriented polarities parallel the ideas of Carl Jung (1921). The first two of these cognitive modes refer to the *information sources* to which attention and perception are drawn to provide cognitions. One scale contrasts individuals who are disposed to look outward or external to self for information, inspiration, and guidance (termed *extroversing*), versus those inclined to turn inward or internal to self (referred to as *introversing*). The second contrasts predilections for direct observational experiences of a tangible, material, and concrete nature (labeled *sensing*) with those geared more toward inferences regarding phenomena of an intangible, ambiguous, symbolic, and abstract character (named *intuiting*). The second pair of cognitive mode polarities relate to *processes of transformation,* that is, ways in which information and experiences, once apprehended and incorporated, are subsequently evaluated and reconstructed mentally. The first of these two transformation scales differentiates processes based essentially on intellect, logic, reason, and objectivity (entitled *thinking*), from those that depend on affective empathy, personal values, sentiment, and subjectivity (designated *feeling*). The second of the transformational scales is likewise divided into a bipolar pairing. At one end are reconstruction modes that transform new information so as to make it assimilate to preconceived formal, tradition-bound, well-standardized, and conventionally structured schemas (called *systematizing*); at the other polar scale are represented inclinations to avoid cognitive preconceptions, to distance from what is already known and to originate new ideas in an informal, open-minded, spontaneous, individualistic, and often imaginative manner (termed *innovating*). Whereas the MIPS is not explicitly intended for clinical personality disorders, it is nevertheless representative of the kinds of constructs that might be brought to bear to assess personality functioning in the cognitive domain. The normative data for the MIPS are, however, based on nonclinical populations (Millon, 1990). More will be said about this instrument later in a discussion of theory-based inventories.

Regulatory Mechanisms

Although "mechanisms" of self-protection, need gratification, and conflict resolution are consciously recognized at times, they represent data derived primarily at the intrapsychic level. Because defense mechanisms are internal processes, they are more difficult to discern and describe than processes anchored closer to the observable world. As such, they are not directly amenable to assessment by self-reflective appraisal in their pure form, but only as derivatives potentially many levels removed from their core conflicts and their dynamic regulation. By definition, these dynamic regulatory mechanisms co-opt and transform both internal and external realities before they can enter conscious awareness in a robust, unaltered form. When chronically enacted, they often perpetuate a sequence of events that intensifies the very problems they were intended to circumvent. Despite the methodological problems involved, the task of identifying which mechanisms are chosen (e.g., rationalization, displacement, reaction formation) and the extent to which they are employed is extremely useful in a comprehensive personality assessment. No organizing principle has yet been found by which a periodic table or taxonomy of defense mechanisms might be rationally constructed (Vaillant, 1971) and thereby put on a nonarbitrary basis. Consequently, those mechanisms ultimately selected for measurement may be conceptualized through theoretically disparate orientations and at diverse levels of abstraction, as the history of psychodynamic literature well illustrates.

Nevertheless, several researchers (e.g., Ihilevich & Gleser, 1986, 1991) are attempting to tackle the methodological problems inherent in the phenomena of this personological domain. As an example of research in this area, Perry and Cooper (1989) reported on the reliability of the Defense Mechanism Rating Scales (DMRS). The DMRS provides a framework by which to measure 30 defense (regulatory) mechanisms across four levels of functioning, from immature to mature. A psychodynamically oriented clinical interview— including recent life history discussed by the subject, life vignettes, and subject-interviewer interaction—serves as the basis for the ratings of each regulatory mechanism. To increase the objectivity of the rating process, the interviewer does *not* assist in rating the subject. Each defense mechanism is scored 0 (no examples present) to 1 (probable use of defense) to 2 (definite use of defense) during a 2-year time frame. To increase the objectivity of the scales and to enhance discriminate validity and interrater reliability, these anchor points are descriptively embellished by explanations and examples of the defense, as well as text that differentiates each defense from other near-neighbors defenses (e.g., hypochondriasis

vs. passive-aggression). Perry and Cooper (1989) report a median intraclass interrater reliability of .57 using group consensus of nonprofessional raters, half of whom were graduate students.

Similar measures of regulatory mechanisms have been constructed using projective instruments. Cooper, Perry, and Arnow (1988) discussed the reliability and validity of their 15 Rorschach defense scales, consisting of higher level denial, isolation, intellectualization, reaction formation, rationalization, Pollyannaish denial, repression, devaluation, primitive idealization, projective identification, splitting, omnipotence, projection, massive denial, and hypomanic denial. Criteria are content-oriented, not determinant or score-dependent. Intraclass correlation coefficients for individual defense scales range from .45 (rationalization) to .80 (primitive idealization).

Together, the preceding studies seem to indicate that although the measurement of defense mechanisms has improved through content objectification and specification, current procedures still leave something to be desired. In particular, because the size of the correlation coefficient that can be achieved between measures is limited by their reliabilities, it is likely that the external validity of defensive measures will remain more difficult to establish than that of self-report inventories for some time to come.

STRUCTURAL DOMAINS

In contrast to functional characteristics, structural attributes represent a deeply embedded and relatively enduring template of imprinted memories, attitudes, needs, fears, conflicts, and so on, that guide experience and transform the nature of ongoing life events. Psychic structures have an orienting and preemptive effect in that they alter the character of action and the impact of subsequent experiences in line with preformed inclinations and expectancies. By selectively lowering thresholds for transactions that are consonant with either constitutional proclivities or early learnings, future events are often experienced as variations of the past. Of course, the residuals of the past do more than passively contribute their share to the present. By temporal precedence, if nothing else, they guide, shape, or distort the character of current events and objective realities.

For purposes of definition, structural domains may be conceived as "substrates and action dispositions of a quasi-permanent nature." Possessing a network of interconnecting pathways, these structures contain the internalized residues of the past in the form of memories and affects that are associated intrapsychically with conceptions of self and others. Structures serve to close the organism to novel interpretations of the world and limit the possibilities of expression to those that have already become prepotent. Their preemptive and channeling character plays an important role in perpetuating the maladaptive behavior and vicious circles of personality pathology. Four structural domains relevant to personality will be briefly described.

Self-Image

As the inner world of symbols is mastered through development, the "swirl" of events that buffets the young child gives way to a growing sense of order and continuity. One major configuration emerges to impose a measure of sameness on an otherwise fluid environment, the perception of self-as-object, a distinct, ever-present, and identifiable "I" or "me." Self-identity stems largely from conceptions formed at this phenomenological level of analysis. It is especially significant in that it provides a stable anchor to serve as a guidepost and to give continuity to changing experience. Most persons have an implicit sense of who they are, but differ greatly in clarity, accuracy, and complexity (Millon, 1986b) of their self-introspections. Few can articulate the psychic elements that make up this image, such as stating knowingly whether they view themselves as primarily alienated, or inept, or complacent, or conscientious, and so on. Several instruments may be drawn on to aid in the identification of differences in self-image, e.g., the Ego Identity Scale (EIS), and the Rosenberg Self-Esteem Scale (RSES).

Object Representations

As noted previously, significant early experiences with others leave an inner imprint, a structural residue composed of memories, attitudes, and affects that serves as a substrate of dispositions for perceiving and reacting to life's ongoing events. Analogous to the various organ systems of which the body is composed, both the character and substance of these internalized representations of significant figures and relationships of the past can be differentiated and analyzed for clinical purposes. Variations in the nature and content of this inner world can be associated with one or another personality and lead us to employ descriptive terms to represent them, such as shallow, vexatious, undifferentiated, concealed, and irreconcilable.

Although there are numerous informal procedures for decoding the presence and character of the inner template of object representations, there are few formalized procedures designed for this purpose. A potentially useful formal tool that focuses on object relations characteristics among adolescents can be adapted for use with adults as well. This instrument (Levine, Green, & Millon, 1986) called the Separation-Individuation Test of Adolescence (SITA) comprises six scales: nurturance-symbiosis; engulfment-anxiety; separation-anxiety; need-denial; self-centeredness; and healthy-separation.

Morphologic Organization

The overall architecture that serves as a framework for an individual's psychic interior may display weakness in its structural cohesion, exhibit deficient coordination among its components, and possess few mechanisms to maintain balance and harmony, regulate internal conflicts, or mediate external pressures. The concept of morphologic organization refers to the structural strength, interior congruity, and functional efficacy of the personality system. "Organization" of the mind is a concept almost exclusively derived from inferences at the "intrapsychic level" of analysis, and are akin to and employed in conjunction with current psychoanalytic notions such as borderline and psychotic levels; this usage, however, tends to be limited, relating essentially to quantitative degrees of integrative pathology, not to qualitative variations in either integrative structure or configuration. "Stylistic" variants of this structural attribute may be employed to characterize each of the personality prototypes; their distinctive organizational attributes are represented with descriptors such an inchoate, disjoined, and compartmentalized.

A particularly promising although difficult to execute interview procedure designed to uncover the morphologic organization of a patient's intrapsychic world has been formulated by Kernberg (1984). Although he begins his interview with a relatively standardized history taking and mental status examination, his "structural interview" seeks to highlight three potential levels of personality organization. The interview progresses by focusing on symptoms, conflicts, and defensive processes employed by the patient, paying special attention to the degree of identity integration, the type of defensive operations that predominate, and the capacity for reality testing. He summarizes his structural interview as follows:

Clarification *is a nonchallenging, cognitive means of exploring the limits of the patient's awareness of certain material.* Confrontation *attempts to make the patient aware of potentially conflictual and incongruous aspects of that material.* Interpretation *tries to resolve the conflictual nature of the material by assuming underlying unconscious motives and defenses that make the previously contradictory appear logical.* Transference interpretation *applies all these preceding modalities of technique to the current interaction between the patient and the diagnostician. (p. 9)*

Mood or Temperament

Few observables are clinically more relevant from the biophysical level of data analysis than the predominant character of an individual's affect and the intensity and frequency with which he or she expresses it. The meaning of extreme emotions is easy to decode. This is not so with the more subtle moods and feelings that insidiously and repetitively pervade the patient's ongoing relationships and experiences. Not only are the expressive features of mood and drive conveyed by terms such as distraught, labile, fickle, or hostile (communicated via self-report), but they are revealed as well, albeit indirectly, in the patient's level of activity, speech quality, and physical appearance. The most useful aspect of this attribute as it relates to the theory is its utility in appraising features relevant to the pleasure-pain and active-passive polarities.

Numerous instruments have been designed to identify the dimensions of temperament. Among the more relevant are two that will be described in later sections, the Tridimensional Personality Questionnaire (Cloninger, 1987a) and the Schedule of Nonadaptive and Adaptive Personality (Clark, 1993).

VALIDITY ISSUES AND MODELS

The quality and accuracy of the individual assessment is contingent on the validity of the measures used in the assessment, and these are contingent on many factors. Included are, first, structural assumptions on which the instrument is based (i.e., whether personality is conceived in terms of categories, dimensions, or prototypes) and second, issues related to measurement sources and their degree of precision.

THE TAXONIC ISSUE REVISITED

In Chapter 1, the controversy between categories and dimensions was briefly discussed. That issue is revisited here as it is relevant to clinical work. The validity of the assessment depends on the validity of the system of types and dimensions that might be brought to bear on the individual case. Perhaps the most relevant question is this: Should the individual be embedded in the classification system (categorical) or the classification system embedded in the person (dimensional)? Phrasing the question this way translates the controversy into a question of ontological priority; recent debates in the personality disorders area have focused on the ontological status of personologic categories and personality dimensions (e.g., Livesley, Schroeder, Jackson, & Lang, 1994). Which one is "really real"? Returning to Loevinger's definition of the structural component of validity, personologic taxonomies and their operational or assessment measures should reflect only those dimensions or categories that can be genuinely shown to exist in nature. For this reason, the categorical-dimensional controversy, as it is relevant to assessment, is here discussed under the heading of validity.

Categories

From an assessment viewpoint, a categorical model is valuable in drawing attention to covarying attributes that might otherwise go unassessed. Categorical models ask us to synthesize the constellation of problematic personologic attributes our clients possess into a single substantive and integrative formulation. The intrinsic holism of categorical models is a reminder that single traits must never be allowed to stand on their own in any personality assessment. Individual traits are adaptive or maladaptive only by virtue of their place in an entire constellation of characteristics.

Unfortunately, a categorical model does lead to a sacrifice of essentially continuous information, the degree of pathology. As noted earlier, where to draw the line between functional and dysfunctional (i.e., the criteria for "caseness") is not well operationalized in the DSM-IV, in part because the

DSM cutting scores are based largely on considerations of content internal to each disorder, and not on contextual factors, where personalities actually function. No discrete boundaries between normality and pathology of personality have in fact been shown to exist. Such artificially imposed divisions are not problematic for clinicians if their heuristic character is constantly kept in mind. However, the synthetic emphasis of categories can become problematic for inexperienced clinicians, who may project clinical stereotypes onto those who seem to fall within the category, inflating their similarity to categorical exemplars at the expense of accurate description (Cantor & Genero, 1986).

Much of the effort to resolve the controversy between categorical and dimensional models has been fueled empirically using categorically oriented latent class methods and dimensionally oriented multivariate techniques, such as factor analysis and multidimensional scaling. With regard to categorically oriented methods, the results of cluster analytic procedures have proven so notoriously sensitive to methodological options that the validity of any cluster result has come into doubt. As noted by Blashfield (1986), "No way exists of solving the number of clusters problems." In and of itself, cluster analysis is widely acknowledged as an insufficient basis by which to constrain either the nature or number of categories in a taxonomy. In another approach, Meehl (1962, 1990) has argued elegantly for the existence of a schizotaxia taxon, a superordinate "open" (Pap, 1953) construct represented as a spectrum of gene penetrance and consequent pathology, encompassing soft neurological signs at one end, schizotypal personality traits at a moderately severe level, and leading finally to schizophrenia at its most severe. A set of MMPI items referred to as the Schizoidia scale selected by Meehl's techniques (Golden & Meehl, 1979) may be used to diagnose membership in the schizotaxia taxon. Widiger (1982) applied Meehl's techniques to the DSM borderline personality and failed to find evidence of taxonicity. Failure to find taxonicity is not conclusive evidence of dimensionality, however, because it is impossible to prove the null hypothesis. Comprehensive studies of the other personality disorders have not yet been attempted. Conceivably, Meehl's techniques could be applied to each of the DSM disorders to assess taxonicity, estimate base rates, and yield optimal cutting scores. Much work remains to be done in this area.

Dimensions

Dimensional models emphasize quantitative gradations among persons rather than qualitative, discrete, all-or-nothing boundaries. Where instruments contain a variety of scales at comparable levels of bandwidth, scale scores are readily summarized in a configuration, profile, or codetype. Dimensions facilitate the handling of atypical cases, which either fail to fit prescribed criteria in categorical models, or else meet so many criteria across disorders that the amount of comorbidity approaches absurdity. Moreover, the dimensional model recognizes that clinicality and normality of personality must be considered as points on a continuum rather than as phenomena with sharp, discriminable boundaries. And, unlike the categorical model (for which in the DSM-IV caseness is determined by content), the continuity of dimensions readily lends itself to functional appraisals. Clinicians who assess patients in a dimensional framework are less likely to succumb to distortions wrought by the medical model.

Dimensional models do, however, have an uglier side: Dimensions fractionate individuals. The dimensional flip side of the discreteness issue, so often put forward as a deficiency of categories, for some reason goes unnoticed where dimensions are concerned. Fundamental or basic dimensions of personality are often derived through factor analysis or multidimensional scaling techniques. Whereas these techniques represent each personality dimension as orthogonal or independent to all others in the model, thus achieving considerable descriptive parsimony for the population at hand, it is unclear how these dimensions are to be interpreted with regard to the individual assessment case. Personality is a system precisely because what exists in one domain constrains what can exist elsewhere; scores on orthogonal dimensions, however, are independent precisely because each dimension does not constrain (account for any of the variance) of the others. A model consisting of orthogonal dimensions thus runs hard against the integrative philosophy that undergirds the personality construct itself. Just as persons do not exist in categories, it must also be said that neither do they exist fractionated along some set of dimensions.

Finally, a nature-number issue, similar to that which exists for cluster analysis, also besets factor analytic models. How many dimensions exist on which patients' should be assessed? Eysenck prefers a three-factor solution, consisting of neuroticism, introversion-extroversion, and psychoticism. Tellegen (1993), however, prefers a seven-factor over a five-factor solution, the factor-based alternative preferred by Costa and McCrae (1990). Tellegen's preference is based on criteria that are essentially extraempirical or extramethodological in nature; for those who find his argument persuasive, a five-factor model must be regarded as an insufficient basis by which to assess personality disorders. However, even among those methodologists who agree that there are five factors, there is disagreement as to the nature of these factors. Costa and McCrae (1990, 1992) and Widiger (1993) argue that the essential dimensions are Neuroticism, Extroversion, Openness to Experience, Agreeableness, and Conscientiousness. Goldberg (1992), however, notes that there are two five-factor models. Apparently, both should be regarded as sufficient models of the personality domain owing to their content coverage. For clinicians, however, the point is that the question concerning the ultimate dimensions of personality disorder has not yet been settled. Nevertheless, dimensions do seem to be an excellent point of departure; they present personality in its complexity, thus facilitating descriptive validity in the individual assessment.

Prototypes

The prototype construct represents a synthesis of the categorical and dimensional models, an approach adopted with the DSM-III. As noted in Chapter 1, prototypal models assume that no necessary or sufficient criteria exist by which personality disorders can be unequivocally diagnosed. The synthetic character of the prototypal model can be seen by comparing what is saved and discarded in all three approaches. The categorical model sacrifices quantitative variation in favor of the discrete, binary judgments. The dimensional model sacrifices qualitative distinctions in favor of quantitative scores: The question is where the person should be placed on a certain so-called latent dimension. Because this question focuses exclusively on an appraisal of quantity, a strict dimensionalist should refrain from examining particular scale items to determine how an elevation was achieved, when such scales are supposed to tap unitary latent traits. Of the three models, the prototypal is the only one that conserves both qualitative and quantitative clinical information. Ideally, to use the model to its fullest, clinicians should ask both "how" and "how much" the client resembles the prototypes of the diagnostic schema. Asking

how much merely transforms the prototypes first into a set of dimensions, and then into a set of categories as diagnostic thresholds are assessed. Asking how builds qualitative information important for the intervention into the assessment. Unfortunately, because the diagnostic criteria of DSM-IV are noncomparable and noncomprehensive, the utility of this approach is limited. For example, it is very difficult on the basis of solicited information to make a DSM-IV diagnosis as to what subspecies of schizoid a particular patient might be—the criteria to discriminate subgroups simply does not yet exist. Fortunately, the subtype write-ups given in the clinical chapters of this text may be used as a descriptive supplement to the official schema.

MEASUREMENT SOURCES AND PSYCHOMETRIC PRECISION

One of the vexing problems in psychological assessment and research concerns the method and source of personologic information, along with the level of precision at which this information is gathered.

Method Variance

Instruments that gather information in similar ways tend to be more highly intercorrelated than those that gather information in different ways (Campbell & Fiske, 1959). Two self-report measures of narcissism are likely to correlate more highly than a self-report measure and a semistructured interview. Self-report instruments and interviews for personality disorders often show little agreement in terms of the patients they classify as personality disordered (e.g., Zimmerman & Coryell, 1990). In fact, Miller, Streiner, and Parkinson (1992) concluded in a methodologically sophisticated study incorporating three criterion measures, the MCMI and SIDP (in their unrevised versions) and the MMPI personality disorder scales, that "of the instruments studied here, there is no one technique that can serve as an adequate defining criterion for personality disorders." This does not necessarily mean that one instrument is right or wrong, as each could tap nearly orthogonal pieces of the same construct, getting at unique pieces of information. Additionally, correlations between scales that purport to measure the same construct may also be modest simply because the nature of the constructs differs somewhat between instruments, as for example, with the atheoretical DSM-III MMPI scales

(Morey, Waugh, & Blashfield, 1985) and those of the theoretically grounded MCMI. Finally, it is also possible for two self-report instruments to exhibit strong evidence of concurrent validity, for the pairing of one of these instruments with a structured interview to show modest concurrent validity, and for the other pairing to show much less concurrent validity, with all three possessing approximately equal validity considered separately, as evidenced by the amount of true variance taken into account! Figure 4.3 illustrates this possibility. Because the degree to which a given intervening variable is construct faithful is always unknown (the perimeter of the shaded circle can never really be determined), the frequency with which similar situations occur must likewise remain unknown. Perhaps they rarely occur and perhaps they are common. Either belief is an article of faith. These possibilities make definitive judgments about the quality of any instrument extremely difficult, and are simply further proof that clinical judgment, though undoubtedly supplemented by a variety of operational measures, will remain important in the final analysis for a long time to come.

Why should method variance exist at all? A partial answer comes from the assumption that one can only report what one knows. Simple differences in the mere availability and perspective of information may account in large part for the insufficiency of self and other ratings as complete assessments of personality. No one can know everything there is to know about oneself. On principle alone, we know that one's idea of oneself is like any other intervening variable, that it is an open concept (Pap, 1953), and that as such it is susceptible to any number of insufficiencies and distortions, such as those introduced by confirmatory biases and defense mechanisms. Conversely, others may know aspects of our personality that

we have not quite got into perspective or perhaps never even thought about. Yet no one can know us thoroughly. There are private aspects of ourselves, such as secrets and private wishes, to which others never have access. Even when both a patient and an informant are administered with the same instrument, different conclusions may be reached. Zimmerman, Pfohl, Stangl, and Corenthal (1986) found that almost 20% of a sample of 82 patients interviewed changed in terms of a present or absent judgment of personality disorder when informant data were used. Further, individuals who have had years of insight-oriented psychotherapy likely know more of what exists to be known. These individuals will likely give more veridical self-reports, as will those high on traits such as self-consciousness. What is clear, however, is that only one realm of data contributes to the convergence of external raters and self-reports, while another may contribute to divergence, and yet another may be accessible only through special instrumentation or methods, such as psychophysiological measurement or perhaps hypnosis. Given the poor correlations found between interviews and self-report, the contribution of each is apparently small relative to the others when the interviewer does not know the subject well, even when the interviewer has been provided with a standardized way of asking questions about the subject's personality.

Moreover, there is no reason why the relative value of each source of data must be consistent across personality styles. If personalities are assumed to vary in terms of the schematic complexity of their self- and other-representations, then surely the validity of the self-report modality varies from personality to personality in a similar manner. Compulsive personalities, for example, because of their desire to appear normal to others and conform to sanctioned social codes, rarely endorse obviously pathological items. Whereas an interviewer can guide the interview into particular directions, detection of the compulsive personality on self-report inventories is complicated by this characteristic of the syndrome. For compulsives, faking good, not only in the appraisals of others, but in their self-appraisals, is a core part of their disorder. Similar arguments might be advanced for other personality disorders. Because schizoids are deficient on the pleasure polarity and withdraw from the world, their self-schemas remain global or gross. Many schizoids will be incapable of offering valid self-descriptions at more narrow and differentiated levels of the trait hierarchy simply because

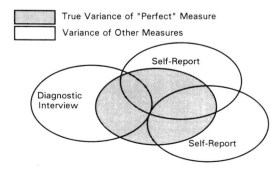

Figure 4.3   The relationship between intervening variables and hypothetical constructs.

more narrow constructs, and the questions designed to assess them, simply mean something else to schizoids than to other personalities. Thus, a valid assessment must somehow control for distortions that accrue as a result of the character of the disorders themselves.

Bandwidth versus Fidelity

The idea that indicators exist at different levels of generality quite naturally leads to the notion of a hierarchy. In general, no scientific scheme is a perfect (i.e., a complete and consistent), representation of nature. Every scientific model involves trade-offs between scope and precision. The wider ranging a scientific model, the more abstract it tends to be, and the more difficulty it encounters in informing judgments about concrete realities. Clinical sciences differ from pure sciences in that clinical sciences must make contact with pressing matters concerning individual human suffering. The inverse relation between scope and precision has been discussed as the bandwidth-fidelity problem (Cronbach & Gleser, 1965). The choice (Widiger & Frances, 1987) is between somewhat inaccurate information and limited accurate information. The problem can also be cast in the language of diagnostic efficiency statistics: As the sensitivity of an indicator increases, its specificity generally declines, leading to an increase in false positives.

All taxonic schemes attempt to address the bandwidth-fidelity dilemma. Dimensional systems often do so through the notion of a hierarchy of traits. Superordinate, or higher-order traits are assumed to assess that which is common to a set of lower-order traits. The covariance of traits or characteristics at each lower level becomes the variance for traits or characteristics at each higher level. The implication is that assessment at higher levels alone results in a substantial loss of information, since there is no way to determine which lower order constituents are responsible for the obtained score. Accordingly, the assessment loses precision. In a personality disorders assessment, the grossest level of description is conveyed in a question congruent with the disease model: "Personality disorder, present or absent?" The categorical or prototypal analogue of the trait hierarchy can be seen in the DSM in the adoption of prototypal criteria sets. Just as higher order traits underspecify personality description, requiring traits of a narrower bandwidth to flesh out the personality portrait, personality disorder diagnoses specify

diagnostic attributes that represent core features of these disorders. Had these criteria been conceived not as a hodgepodge, but as being comprehensive across personologic domains and comparable at approximately equal levels of generality, more focused and precision-oriented questions (How does the person meet diagnostic criteria, that is, what kind of narcissistic or antisocial personality?) necessary for treatment planning would have become genuinely meaningful. The idea of a hierarchy of related traits is synthesized with that of personologic domains and presented schematically in Figure 4.4.

The bandwidth-fidelity problem has long been an issue in personality assessment. The challenge is to get individuality out of a set of scales, each of which exists at a fairly abstract level. The conventional solution is to consider the scales conjointly, as a profile or configuration of scales. There are other ways of getting increased specificity out of an inventory, however. The MCMI-II adopted an item-weighting scheme, continued in part in the MCMI-III, which contains items corresponding to DSM-IV diagnostic criteria. Prototypal or core features of each disorder are weighted more than peripheral characteristics, forming a subgroup of so-called critical items that can be inspected to achieve greater specification of problematic diagnostic attributes. The NEO-PI contains "facet scales" that "partition" each factor of the Costa and McCrae (1985) version of the five-factor model. The relatively homogeneous content scales derived for the MMPI-II can be seen as an effort to get at purer sources of information than those available through the dustbowl empiricism of the mostly heterogeneous clinical scales. Recent attempts to develop inventories that assess personality disorders' traits at lower levels of the trait hierarchy are represented in the research of Livesley, Jackson, and Schroeder (1989) and Clark (1990, 1993), whose inventories consist of 15 to 20 relatively narrow factor analytically derived personality scales. Harkness (1993) identified 39 even more narrow dimensions within personality disorder criteria translated into the lay language. One could easily argue that the increasing specificity of personality inventories through the inclusion of more narrow characteristics represents an attempt to deal with the contextualism of the world at large. As noted in Chapter 1, the poor fit between diagnostic schemes and individual realities has been an important force driving the development of modern taxonomies.

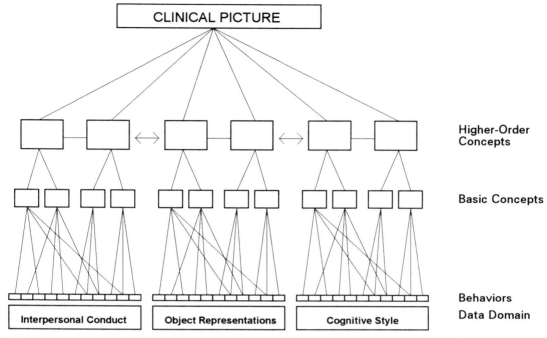

Figure 4.4   Synthesis of hierarchical and domain models of personality.

Criterion Inadequacies

In general, any given personality construct may be operationalized in a variety of ways. Narcissism, for example, might be measured with a self-reported scale, as the proportion of time spent looking in a mirror, or as the proportion of conversation spent in self-referential commentary. Each is obviously related, yet different, containing its own measurement biases. Reminiscent of the prototype construct, we might say that these measures neither singly nor collectively exhaust narcissism as an ideal, for which an almost infinite number of intervening variables are possible, limited only by the imagination and ingenuity of psychologists.

How can the validity of an instrument be assessed in the absence of an objectively defined and consensual criterion? Without an absolute reference point or objective standard, not only does no rigorous feedback loop exist that might directly quantify and therefore guarantee the validity of an instrument, no such feedback loop *can* exist. Personality constructs are by definition inferential and therefore, not anchored to any absolute criterion. This fact requires a different conception of validity than criterion validity, one which is parallel to the

nature of the psychological constructs. Where the constructs are multireferential and hierarchical, construct validity must be acknowledged as being multireferential and hierarchical as well. Just as any single behavioral act not only will, but must, fail as an unequivocal measure of the construct of interest simply because its bandwidth is too narrow to represent the construct in its totality, a single study, conducted as it is in the particularities of time, circumstance, and sample characteristics, must also be viewed as inadequate to establish the construct validity of an instrument.

How then, is the construction of personality assessment instruments possible at all? Without a construct validity coefficient and the rigorous feedback it would make possible, we have only our expectations concerning what an instrument should do to guide us, both in construction and evaluation. Two general principles apply.

First, our expectations, whether explicit or not, really are theories about relationships between constructs. Accordingly, since all we have with which to evaluate construct validity is our expectations and not some single, external, and absolute criterion, the content of the constructs to be included in the inventory and the relations between them should be specified as precisely as possible. Otherwise, we will be left, despite our time and effort, with something the quality of which can only be determined after the fact, by delineating post hoc what should have been specified from the beginning.

Second, we must distinguish between variables that are internal and external to those of our inventory, and specify these internal-external relationships as well. If our inventory is intended to assess personality disorders, we might expect, for example, that those classified as dependent personalities will also be classified as experiencing depressive episodes more often than, say, antisocials, simply because dependents are likely to feel helpless and hopeless more often than antisocials, who are more likely to take matters into their own hands and change the world around them, albeit in a destructive fashion. Together, these internal-internal and internal-external expectations form a set of constraints that our inventory must be constructed to satisfy. The larger this set of constraints, the better, for if the inventory can satisfy many such constraints at the outset, then validity has been built into the instrument from the beginning. In general, the more such constraints the test has been shown to satisfy, the better the instrument, and the greater confidence we can have that it will meet whatever challenges are put to it in the future. Each constraint is an additional point through which the pattern of findings that emerge from the instrument are triangulated with reality as it is assumed to exist in theory.

Sometimes, after the instrument has been constructed, certain variables about which we had no preformed ideas show a significant relationship. Perhaps in the beginning we believed that antisocial personalities should also report high family distress and a high incidence of alcoholism. Perhaps we also believed that dependents' personalities should report overprotective parents and an inability to end relationships, and these expectations were built into the instrument. About the relationship between dependent personality and incidence of alcoholism, however, we may have no a priori notions at all, so that, with regard to the expectations we held in the context of constructing the instrument, the magnitude of this relationship was "free to vary," simply because we did not know how much about it, how it should be evaluated, or whether it should even exist. How do we evaluate this observed, but unexpected, relationship? Having constructed our instrument to satisfy multiple

constraints in the form of theoretically driven expectations, we are no longer working with just any item pool, but with a system of scales of demonstrated validity. The more the tests satisfy these constraints, the greater our expectations of the generalizability of the entire system of instrumentation. Demonstrated validity in diverse areas of the nomological network becomes a promissory note that observed relationships between intervening variables elsewhere is not peculiar to their mode of operationalization, but is instead representative of nature's structure and, so, worthy of genuine scientific interest. In addition to their shortcomings in comprehensiveness and comparability, one of the problems of the DSM-IV criteria is that they have not been subjected to such a process of refinement, but were instead constructed through committee consensus.

CONCEPTUAL MODELS OF VALIDITY

Two broad kinds of validity may be distinguished. The first is here referred to as *idiographic validity* because it is concerned with the fidelity of the clinician's personality description to the patterning of variables as they exist within a *single* individual. Whether articulated in a rich and developmentally detailed manner or left to languish as a single Axis II diagnostic label, this description is an intervening variable for the whole individual, and it is on the basis of this description that treatment decisions with real world implications will be made. The second continues our elaboration of nomothetic or construct validity begun in the previous section. This is essentially an impersonal approach to instrument development using large samples of respondents (e.g., broad dimensions of personality traits common to many individuals). We now turn to a brief discussion of the first of these approaches, the idiographic model.

IDIOGRAPHIC VALIDITY

Apart from the validity of each scale or instrument used in the assessment, there is the issue of the validity of the individual assessment itself, an issue different from but connected to and ultimately dependent on the validity of psychological measures. Although this focus would seem less lofty, it is no less problematic, as all the issues currently swirling around the personality disorders suddenly come pouring forth. First, there is the taxonic issue: Those who believe that personality must be assessed in an exclusively dimensional format will likely regard any categorical assessment as invalid. Moreover, there are those who believe that the entire Axis II set of constructs are not working and should be replaced with those derived through an empirical methodology. Clinicians of this persuasion are likely to render DSM diagnoses only as a means of satisfying official formalities, for the most part bypassing the official schema and using their own constellation of pet dimensions as a jumping-off point en route to descriptive validity for the individual case.

The Person-Population Paradox

Whatever one decides about current controversies such as optimal content boundaries, taxonic format, and method variance, there is the problem of how to synthesize the clinical data obtained. Researchers usually deal with large samples of subjects. Arguments for the validity of their methods and the instruments they create rest on sample-based statistics. Clinicians, however, are usually faced with one patient (or perhaps a family) at a time. Paradoxically, the methodology through which assessment instruments are created is in spirit opposed to the goal that directs their use. In tapping dimensions of individual differences, only those dimensions taken as being common or fundamental to most persons are abstracted. Rich biographical specificities, the very thing that many would argue makes each individual, are left behind as residual variance, effectively aggregated out of the analysis. First, some corpus of generalities is created: Persons are aggregated over to test or specify portions of a nomological network, and then these abstractions are *generalized back* to any individual who becomes a clinical focus. Profiles, for example, are profiles of population-based dimensions, refined through clinical samples, and then considered conjointly as a means of finding the individual in the instrument. The circle completes itself as a synthesis: From (a) rich idiographic individuality (all that the person is), we abstract (b) certain nomothetic commonalities, which in turn inform the individual assessment, giving rise to a kind of (c) nomothetic individuality. The fractionated person who lies dispersed across many dimensions and

content areas is put back together again as an organic whole. The scale scores that once were each an intervening variable for a population-based hypothetical construct now become personality profiles. The personality profile in turn becomes an intervening variable for the individual's entire personality. This kind of reflexivity in the clinical process is reminiscent of Loevinger's (1957) integrated process model of validity, and argues for the process-character of the validity in the individual assessment as well.

Meehl (1978) has written that because psychologists have failed to embrace methodologies that subject their theories to the threat of falsification, multiple sufficient theories accumulate, with no real means of choosing between them. First there is a period of enthusiasm, but ultimately they simply suffer the fate of old generals, fading nobly away. Any personality assessment must seek a theory of the patient. The advantages, which are much the same as those obtaining in science at large, include all the benefits that accrue to theoretical-explanatory orientations as opposed to those that are merely descriptive: The unification of ostensibly diverse findings, an economy of presentation, and most importantly, a generative character which affords a logical means of evaluating intervention possibilities. In the absence of a strong theory of the person, the intervention and the assessment cannot be tightly coupled, leaving the relationship between the patient's personality and current problems to be explored primarily during therapy time. Without theory, our patients, like old generals, may soon tire and just fade away, or at least have their insurance run out before they are substantially benefited.

As with the creation of nomothetically oriented psychological instruments, one may begin with either a strong-theory or a strong-data bias, that is, with or without some more-or-less explicit body of preconceived notions. The multidetermined nature of personality argues that clinicians should not be too doctrinaire in their approach, appraising personality exclusively from a single perspective. Returning to ideas introduced in Chapter 1, the idea of a system serves as a powerful metaphor through which to conceptualize personality function from the idiographic tradition. In this framework, the purpose of assessment should be to elucidate constraints on system functioning. These constraints cannot be identified if the assessment is less than comprehensive. Accordingly, clinicians must be prepared to readily generate, integrate, test, and discard propositions from diverse data levels—

behavioral, phenomenological (cognitive), intrapsychic, and biophysical.

As in science itself, theories of compelling necessity and those of mere sufficiency should be distinguished. Obviously, there is the way things are, and the way we think they are. The end goal of the assessment process is *the* theory of the patient, one in which every loose end has been so tied up that the theory seems to follow a logic intrinsic to the patient's own psyche, a theory so compelling one gets the feeling that things could be not be otherwise than they have been supposed to be. Only such an eminently integrative theory allows the referral question to be addressed with confident words and concrete suggestions. As we have seen, the danger of an exclusively inductive approach is that it tends to result in models that give an adequate accounting of the data at hand; they are merely sufficient, and so, suffer from imprecision. In the absence of absolute knowledge, there are usually many different ways things might be supposed to be in accounting for a given set of observations. A comprehensive database allows competing explanations to be sifted. In an ideal clinical world, an assessment would answer not only "what" questions, but also "why" questions.

Construct (Nomothetic) Validity

The second form of validity is usually termed construct validity (Cronbach & Meehl, 1955), although *nomothetic validity* would seem to be equally appropriate. Construct validity is concerned with the scaling of psychological concepts. Individuals are sampled and aggregated over as a means of eliminating the very individuality that must be recaptured in the assessment process.

Perhaps the easiest way to understand construct validity is to contrast it with criterion validity, which is easily understood. A test may be evaluated with respect to criterion validity when some criterion exists for appraising the performance of the test, such as the ability of an IQ test to predict which members of a group of aspiring pilots will complete their training and which will not, or which graduate students will obtain their PhD degree in five years or less, and which will not. The current test score stands in place of some performance; the criterion validity of the test is the degree to which it predicts this performance. When this performance is the future, criterion validity is referred to as predictive validity. When

this performance is in the present, it is referred to as concurrent validity.

Test construction would be greatly simplified if there were some unequivocal criterion to serve as a standard by which to evaluate every psychological test. The worth of the test, its validity, could then be directly quantified with a kind of "validity coefficient" by comparing predictions made by the test to actual results. The percentage of pilots who complete their training, for example, can be known with absolute certainty. Time to complete the PhD degrees is likewise directly quantifiable. In this simplified world, making an instrument better would simply mean making the discrepancy between prediction and performance as small as possible. For the aspiring pilots, a good test would misclassify as few individuals who completed their training as possible. Such concrete feedback allows new items to be written and readily tested for incremental efficiency in prediction.

For better or worse, personality psychologists are usually interested in constructs rather than in explicit, concrete, and easily coded performances. Whereas one either flies solo or is granted the PhD, personality traits are by definition continuous and inferential variables that often far removed from observable and objective behavior. Some, including the regulatory (defense) mechanisms, have spawned vast literatures without even submitting themselves to the requirement of interrater reliability. Because any trait, defense, schema, or other construct may be manifested in so many different ways across so many different situations, behavior in any given situation becomes an insufficient basis on which to characterize the whole person. In other words, traits and behaviors exist at different levels of generality. They do not map onto one another in a one-to-one fashion.

An Integrated Process Model

The preceding short discussion of construct validity and test construction accords well with the integrated or process-oriented model of construct validity advanced by Jane Loevinger (1957). Previously, the different forms of validity were discussed or listed simply as separate kinds of validity, much as the personality disorders today are simply listed in the DSM. Her model divides the validation process into three components: substantive, structural, and external, which are "mutually exclusive, exhaustive of the possible

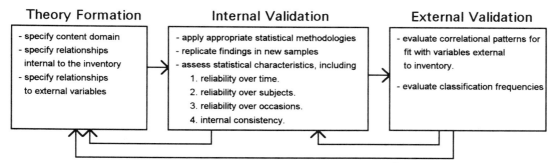

Figure 4.5   Loevinger's process-model of validity (adapted from Skinner, 1986).

lines of evidence for construct validity, and mandatory" (p. 92). Construct validity, then, is no more a static entity to be assessed as either present or absent than are the personality disorders. Both are multireferential and integrative. Skinner (1986) schematized Loevinger's model as shown in Figure 4.5.

As can be seen, Loevinger emphasizes the iterative interplay of theory and empirical research. Although Loevinger apparently wrote her monograph with the idea of formalizing a process for the validation of scales considered one at a time, her framework may also be applied to the development and validation of an entire classification system. In fact, her framework could be applied to the validation of scales in any of the descriptive monotaxonic, descriptive polytaxonic, explanatory monotaxonic, or explanatory polytaxonic approaches to personality taxonomy described in Chapter 1. However, it is with regard to the descriptive polytaxonic and explanatory polytaxonic models that Loevinger's conceptions have proven most influential in the area of personality disorders. Both Millon's explanatory polytaxonic approach (Millon, 1977, 1987) and Livesley (1986, 1987) descriptive polytaxonic approach have been heavily influenced by Loevinger's ideas. Referring back to Figure 4.4, we might say that Millon's approach is top-down or deductive, based on ostensive evolutionary polarities such as pleasure-pain, active-passive, and self-other. As such, it gives rise to relatively fewer constructs at a relatively high level of bandwidth. Further specification of these theoretical constructs is gained by elucidating their referents across significant domains of personality pathology at approximately equal levels of generality, making for criteria that are both comprehensive and comparable. The dependent type, for example, is said to use introjection as a regulatory mechanism; in addition, it is

expressively incompetent; interpersonally submissive; cognitively naive; and possessed of an inept self-image, immature object representations, an inchoate morphologic organization, and a pacific mood. In contrast, the approach of Livesley et al. is bottom-up, or inductive. As such, it begins by searching out and defining many lower-level constructs of comparatively great fidelity. Constructs of greater generality are derived through the rigor of statistical procedures, notably the mathematically inductive technique of factor analysis. In the following subsections these two approaches are compared through each of Loevinger's stages.

Theoretical-Substantive Component

The substantive component was likened by Loevinger (1957) to content validity, in that the constructs or contents with which the classification is to be concerned are here selected and defined. Theory at this stage includes whatever implicit assumptions and explicit propositions that must hold for the resulting taxonomy to be representative of the intrinsic structure of the domain of interest. As a beginning step, the content domain must be defined and delimited on some rational basis. Theory may play either a very strong or very weak role. Content selection may occur logically within the theory, as with Millon's model, where the content of the eight personologic domains are defined deductively through the theory within the framework of the clinical domains. Or, the role of theory may be limited to the assertion that whatever is relevant is already encoded or given in some external source, as with the inductive model of Livesley, Jackson, and Schroeder (1989). In the five-factor tradition, this assumption is even known by a formal name, the so-called lexical hypothesis (e.g., Goldberg, 1990).

A second proposition that must be sustained concerns whether the methodology to be used in the internal-structural and external stages is compatible with the theory, and if so, whether it is sufficient to illuminate the structure of personality, or whether the methodology itself inherently distorts the subject domain. This issue is an especially significant one for inductive approaches, where the initial role of theory is weak and the structure of the taxonomy issues more from the methodology, usually factor analysis, than the theory. Theory in these approaches tends to be limited to two propositions: (a) that the content domain has been properly defined, and (b) that the structure the methodology imparts to the content is consonant with its intrinsic topology, or at least not a serious distortion of this topology. Because the true topology is unknown, the extent of the distortion is impossible to quantify rigorously. The propositions subserving the inductive approach, then, are difficult to test in the sense of being open to falsification. The content of the taxonomy thus issues from the methodology, and its appeal rests not so much on the model's ability to resist attempts at falsification (Popper, 1973), but rather on the ability of its authors to convince their fellow researchers that a given point of departure makes assumptions that, while somewhat arbitrary, are not altogether unreasonable. Accordingly, the primary challenge with which such theories are faced is a deficiency of precision, and the paradigm in which such theories flourish or die is Kuhnian (1962), not Popperian (1973). As inductive taxonomies of the personality disorders multiply, each being a "theory" of the personologic domain (Costa & McCrae, 1990; Goldberg, 1990), it has become clear that their ultimate structure is exquisitely sensitive to initial boundary and sampling conditions.

Whereas the five-factor and psycholexical researchers have been working in the direction of normality to pathology, Livesley et al. (1989), undertook a content analysis of the clinical literature to identify personality disorders constructs, for which explicit definitions were written. Next, each construct was scaled through a rational methodology that relied on expert judgment to select highly prototypal or core features. Theory here does not derive the entire taxonomy in its totality, but is encoded in the definitions of each selected construct. In contrast, Millon's (1969, 1981, 1986a, 1990) approach to the first of Loevinger's components was to explicitly elaborate a three-polarity theoretical

model through which fundamental personality disorder prototypes could be deduced. Rather than being selected by virtue of their representation in some external literature, and then specified on the basis of expert opinion, these constructs issue from, are defined in terms of, and have their items pools written, on the basis of the generative theory. For Millon, then, content was determined by the theory, from the top down. Specification proceeded by elucidating the referents of these theory-derived dimensions in terms of organismic functional-structural domains that correspond to the traditional approaches or "data levels" of clinical science. Thus each theory-derived personality construct is operationalized in terms of the total functioning of the organism, eliminating content biases that might accrue as a result of research fads or other historical factors.

The Internal-Structural Component

"The structural component of validity refers to the extent to which structural relations between test items parallel the structural relations of other manifestations of the trait being measured" (Loevinger, 1957, p. 97). The relationships among the various components of a test or putative taxonomy should parallel those relationships believed to be intrinsic to the subject domain itself. The criterion is fidelity: The map should resemble the territory. As noted previously, to the extent that a test satisfies a constellation of structural constraints, we may have faith in its utility in areas for which the test is at yet untried. Livesley et al. (1989) and Millon (1977) again chose somewhat different approaches. After selecting their constructs through a content analysis of the clinical literature, the former authors combined scales or segregated the items of a single scale mainly on internal consistency grounds. Just as in the scientific method a good manipulation varies one and only one factor at a time, a good measure assesses one and only one construct at a time. Next, to determine the "underlying" dimensions, the resulting one hundred scales were factor analyzed with an oblique rotation. Fifteen components were extracted, which subsequently became the basis for the DAPP-BQ (Schroeder, Wormworth, & Livesley, 1993).

Millon also emphasized internal consistency in scale development. However, for Millon the choice of an inductive technique would have been incommensurate with the overarching deductive theoretical framework. The test developed to operationalize the theory, the MCMI (Millon, 1977), was assessed for structural validity by comparing the obtained pattern of correlations with those expected on the basis of theory. Thus, Millon elaborated a nonfactorial logic of validity by which essential features of the subject domain were argued to be theoretically specifiable and intrinsically intercorrelated. In this deductive schema, the theory serves a feedforward function by which expectancies for parameters of correlations internal and external to the instrument are constrained or specified in advance, rather than left to emerge from the methodology.

External Component

In the final stage of the construction of a personality scale (monotaxonic) or inventory (polytaxonic), expected patterns of covariation are evaluated with reference to variables outside or external to the inventory. Like other stages, findings here are expected to inform the ultimate structure of the inventory through changes in item assignments or item weights, and perhaps eventually through the addition of entire scales. Whereas the previous stage dealt with the structural pattern of internal relations, here the inventory is modified until it conforms to a pattern of expected external relations as well. In practice, because comprehensive external data are difficult to gather, the external stage tends to be drawn out across years of research in which important issues that must be addressed in future revisions gradually emerge. An example of an approximation to the external stage is given in the manual for the MCMI-II, in which the positive and negative predictive power, sensitivity, and specificity are derived for each scale on the basis of "expert" clinical judgment.

ASSESSMENT INSTRUMENTS

Current tools for appraising personality disorders may be divided into four broad categories. Most popular today are the recently devised *self-report inventories* and *structured clinical interviews*. Although a long established method of general assessment, the use of personality-oriented *checklists* is a more contemporary development. At the other end are the well-established instruments known as *projective techniques*. These latter tools were not specifically designed to diagnose personality disorders; however, they can provide useful insights into their intrapsychic dynamics and interpersonal implications.

SELF-REPORT INVENTORIES

The self-report modality of assessment has become the most frequently employed technique for diagnosing and assessing the characteristics of personality disorders. A number of the more popular and useful instruments are described in this chapter. They will be divided into two major subcategories. The *first* includes instruments designed specifically to identify the personality disorders themselves; they focus their efforts with scales specific to each or many of the disorders that are commonly diagnosed today. The *second* group of instruments is essentially designed to identify the underlying principles or concepts that help identify the factors, dimensions, or polarities that theorists consider the fundamental substrates for deriving personality disorders. Their scales are not personality disorder scales per se, but are conceptual scales based on theory.

Inventories Assessing Manifest Personality Disorders

The inventories described next may be anchored to theory, or may reflect factorially developed empirical procedures, or may stem from careful clinical observation. Whatever origins may have prompted their construction, each of them possesses distinct and separable scales to identify the presence and magnitude of each (or most) of the DSM Axis-II disorders.

Millon Clinical Multiaxial Inventory-III (MCMI-III)

The MCMI may best be considered an *objective psychodynamic* instrument in that it is composed and administered in a structured and standardized manner, but is interpreted by examining the interaction of scale scores, and by drawing on clinically established relationships among cognitive processes, interpersonal behaviors, and intrapsychic forces. In this regard, it is akin to the MMPI in its item format and administrative procedures, but rather like the Rorschach and TAT in its interpretive style and content.

A few words regarding the origin and sequential construction of the various forms of the MCMI may be of value in explicating the intended rigorous logic, but ultimately desultory character of the instrument's progressive development.

In early 1971, Millon was directing a research supervision group composed of psychologists- and psychiatrists-in-training during their internship and residency periods. All of them had read *Modern Psychopathology* (Millon, 1969) and found the proposal of working together to develop instruments to identify and quantify the text's personality constructs to be both worthy and challenging. Some were asked to analyze the possibilities of identifying new indexes from well-established projective techniques, such as the Rorschach and the Thematic Apperception Test (TAT); others were to investigate whether relevant scales from existing objective inventories could be composed, such as the Sixteen-Factor Personality Questionnaire (16PF) and the Minnesota Multiphasic Personality Inventory (MMPI). Another group examined the potential inherent in developing a new and original structured interview. After 4 or 5 months of weekly discussions, the group concluded that an entirely new instrument would be required to represent the full scope of the theory, especially its diverse and then-novel pathological personality patterns (this work, it should be recalled, preceded the establishment of the DSM-III Task Force by several years). It was further judged that it would be best to construct both a self-report inventory and a semistructured interview schedule. The framework and preliminary item selections of the inventory were well underway by the end of the first full year of work and were described briefly in *Research Methods in Psychopathology* (Millon & Diesenhaus, 1972). The initial forms of the clinical instrument were entitled the Millon-Illinois Self-Report Inventory (MI-SRI).

Soon thereafter, Millon became involved in the development of the DSM-III, playing a role in formulating both the constructs and criteria that were to characterize its Axis II personality disorders. Although the MI-SRI was regularly refined and strengthened on the basis of theoretical logic and research data, an effort was made during this period to coordinate both its items and scales with the forthcoming syndromes of DSM-III. So modified, its name was changed to that of the Millon Clinical Multiaxial Inventory, published in 1977 by National Computer Systems (Millon, 1977).

In the ensuing 10-year period, numerous refinements of the inventory (retrospectively labeled MCMI-I) were introduced (e.g., corrections for response-distorting tendencies such as current emotional state), as were expansions made to incorporate theoretical extensions and the newly published DSM-III-R (e.g., the addition of the self-defeating and sadistic personality

disorder scales). The MCMI-II, reflecting the preceding changes and additions, was published by Millon in 1987. Ongoing investigations, further refinements in its undergirding theory, and modifications in the anticipated DSM-IV personality disorders criteria served as the primary impetus to refashion the inventory into its latest form, the MCMI-III (Millon, Millon, & Davis, 1994), designed to reflect its theoretical foundations while providing as much consonance with the most recent edition of the official classification system as these dual goals would allow.

A principal goal in constructing each form of the MCMI was to keep the total number of items small enough to encourage use in diverse diagnostic and treatment settings, yet large enough to permit the assessment of a wide range of clinically relevant behaviors. At 175 items, these forms are well within the tolerance of most patients. Potentially objectionable items were screened out, and terminology was geared to an eighth-grade reading level. The majority of clients can complete the MCMI in 20 to 30 minutes, facilitating relatively simple and rapid administration, while minimizing client resistance and fatigue.

The current MCMI-III consists of 24 clinical scales, as well as three "modifier" scales available for interpretive analysis. The purpose of the modifier indexes (Disclosure, Desirability, and Debasement) is to identify distorting tendencies that characterize patients and their responses. The first two clinical sections constitute all the personality disorder scales, encompassing Axis II of both DSM-III-R and DSM-IV (including the appendixed self-defeating/masochistic and sadistic personality disorders of DSM-III-R and the depressive personality disorder of DSM-IV). The first of these sections (Scales 1 to 8B) appraises what are viewed as the moderately severe personality pathologies, ranging from the Schizoid to the Masochistic scales; the second section (Scales S, C, and P) represents what Millon views as the more severe or structural-defective personality pathologies, encompassing Schizotypal, Borderline, and Paranoid disorders. The following two sections cover several of the more prevalent Axis I syndromes, ranging from the more moderate to the more severe clinical syndromes. The division between personality disorder and clinical syndrome scales is intended to make MCMI interpretations congruent with the DSM's multiaxial logic. The most recent MCMI-III revision was devised to correspond as fully with the 1994 DSM-IV criteria, as it was with the underlying theoretical model that spurred the development of the original MCMI.

Each of the clinical chapters of this book includes an assessment of a personality-disordered patient, presenting the corresponding MCMI-III profile and segments of the interpretive report. Detailed reviews of the inventory may be found in several recent books as well as in numerous chapters and articles.

MMPI Personality Disorder Scales

In many ways, the MMPI is not so much a standardized test as a standardized item pool that belongs to psychology itself. Literally hundreds of personality scales have been derived from the MMPI throughout its long career. In fact, there are now more auxiliary scales than there are items on the MMPI (Graham, 1990).

Morey, Waugh, and Blashfield (1985) constructed a set of MMPI-I scales to represent the 11 DSM-III personality disorders, based on the strategy used by Wiggins (1966) in the construction of the Wiggins content scales. Item selection proceeded through two stages. In the initial phase, scales were rationally derived by four experienced clinicians who culled the item pool for items representative of DSM-III personality disorder criteria. Those items selected by two or more clinicians formed the preliminary scales; items could be assigned to more than one scale, mirroring the diagnostic overlap of DSM-III. These were then subjected to empirical refinement. Nonoverlapping scales were constructed by assigning each overlapping item to the scale with which it exhibited the highest correlation. This approach would seem to have the advantage of maximizing both convergent and discriminate validity, within the limitations on content imposed by the MMPI item pool. The final scales consist of 14 to 38 items for the overlapping scales, and 13 to 20 items for the nonoverlapping scales. As should be expected, the internal consistencies of the longer, overlapping scales are appreciably higher, ranging between .675 (compulsive scale) and .859 (avoidant scale). Those of the nonoverlapping scales range from .619 (histrionic scale) to .791 (schizotypy scale). These internal consistencies are superior to those of the clinical scales, and comparable to those of the Wiggins (1966) content scales. Specific item assignments are available in Morey, Waugh, and Blashfield (1985). Although used in a number of studies, most of which examine its correlation with other gauges of personality disorders,

studies showing support for its external validity are currently limited in number.

Personality Diagnostic Questionnaire (PDQ)-Revised

Unlike other self-report inventories, the PDQ-R is a direct translation of the DSM-III-R personality disorders criteria into a true-false self-report format. An updated version of the original PDQ, which was derived from the criteria of DSM-III, the current inventory consists of 152 questions and is completed in about one-half hour. Prospects are that a DSM-IV-related version will be forthcoming in the near future.

Hyler, Skodol, Kellman, Oldham, and Rosnick (1990) examined the validity of the PDQ-R in relation to the Personality Disorder Examination and the Structured Clinical Interview for DSM-III-R Personality Disorders (see descriptions later in this chapter). Results showed that although the PDQ-R exhibits high sensitivity, it often yields numerous false positive diagnoses. The authors conclude that it should not be used to substitute for a structured interview, but that it can be employed as a screening instrument in populations where personality disorders are relatively prevalent. Specifically, schizoid and histrionic disorders were much more frequently diagnosed by the PDQ-R than by the Structured Clinical Interview for DSM (SCID) or the Personality Disorders Examination (PDE). In a comment about the lack of an infallible criterion by which any instrument can be judged, the authors also noted only modest agreement between the interviews, and that "for about half of the personality disorders the PDQ-R agreed with either of the two interviews about as well as they agreed with each other" (Hyler et al., 1990, p. 1046). The relative brevity of the PDQ-R can be an advantage, but it may expose the instrument to appreciable unreliability.

Other Self-Report Inventories

Several other, nontheoretically guided inventories appear promising, but supporting empirical literature is rather modest currently.

A well-developed and previously discussed new instrument is the Dimensional Assessment of Personality Pathology-Basic Questionnaire (DAPP-BQ) constructed by Livesley (1987) and his associates (Livesley, Jackson, & Schroeder, 1992; Livesley & Schroeder, 1990; Schroeder, Wormworth, & Livesley, 1994). After an extensive literature review, Livesley compiled an initial list of descriptors for each DSM-III-R diagnosis.

Consensual judgments by knowledgeable clinicians were used to identify the most prototypical features of each diagnosis. A series of trait categories were then developed based on these prototypical features. Ultimately, each disorder was defined by a cluster of traits; for example, schizoid disorder was composed of clusters such as low affiliation, avoidant attachment, and restricted affective expression. In these preliminary studies, 79 traits were required to define the 11 personality diagnoses in the DSM-III-R. A series of self-report scales were developed on the basis of these trait clusters. The initially constructed 100-scale questionnaire was too long for practical use; hence, its components were factored into 18 DAPP-BQ scales, each possessing between 14 and 16 items. Several additional studies were carried out employing canonical correlation and multiple regression analyses. At present, the instrument is composed of 290 items, divided into 18 factor scales, and provides a basis for deriving the DSM personality disorders.

Coolidge and Merwin (1992) reported on the reliability and validity of the Coolidge Axis II Inventory (CATI). The CATI consists of 200 items scored from *strongly false* to *strongly true* on a four-point scale. Reminiscent of the PDQ, each item was created from DSM-III-R criteria in an effort to ensure maximal classificatory correspondence between the two. All 13 personality disorders listed in the DSM-III-R are represented in scales ranging from 45 items in length, for the antisocial, to 16 items in length, for the avoidant, sadistic, and self-defeating. A 3-item validity scale, a 21-item social desirability scale, and a 71-item adjustment index, which measures overall psychopathology, and three Axis I scales—anxiety, depression, and brain dysfunction—are also included. In a study of 609 presumably normal subjects, Coolidge and Merwin reported a median internal consistency of .76 for all 13 personality disorder scales. Unfortunately, the internal consistencies of three of these scales—the sadistic, obsessive-compulsive, and self-defeating—are slightly less than .70 and therefore of marginal quality. Concurrent validity with respective MCMI-II scales ranged from .87 (borderline) to .10 (obsessive-compulsive), with a median of .58.

The Personality Assessment Inventory (Morey, 1992) consists of 344 items on 4 validity scales, 11 clinical scales, 5 treatment scales, and 2 interpersonal scales. Only three scales, however, the Paranoia, Borderline Features, and Antisocial Features, directly assess personality pathology. Ten scales are each subdivided into subscales consisting of

either eight or six items. The Paranoia scale consists of Hypervigilance, Persecution, and Resentment; the Antisocial Features, of Antisocial Behaviors, Egocentricity, and Stimulus Seeking; and the Borderline Features, of Affective Instability, Identity Problem, Negative Relationships, and Self-Harm. Two interpersonal scales are also provided; one is oriented toward a warmly affiliative versus a cold rejecting dimension, the other toward a dominating, controlling versus meekly submissive dimension.

Inventories Assessing Latent Theoretical Mathematical Constructs

Whether anchored to mathematically "latent" entities constructed through factor analytic methods, or composed of more theoretically latent constructs specific to a particular personologic domain and ensconced in some strongly structural model, the following inventories either do not assess personality disorders directly, propose to do so only if the test user believes that the content domain or perspective through which the personality disorders are there conceived is somehow primary to all others, or provide a set of secondary scales on which personality disorders can be scored. The exception to this is the complex SNAP, which synergizes factor methods with a temperament model, while also containing DSM-translated items.

Neuroticism, Extroversion, Openness to Experience-Personality Inventory-Revised (NEO-PI-R)

The "big five" were originally based on a lexical approach, which assumes that "most of the socially relevant and interpersonally salient personality characteristics have become encoded in the natural language" (John, 1990, p. 67). It derives from a particular philosophy of science (empiricism), a particular methodology (factor analysis), a particular structural model (dimensional traits), and a particular research tradition (the so-called lexical hypothesis).

Proponents of the five-factor model argue that all of personality, abnormal and normal, can be conceptualized in terms of five broad orthogonal dimensions. Although the exact nature of these dimensions is still in dispute (see Goldberg, 1990), the NEO-PI-R is currently the most popular five-factor inventory, assessing what Costa and McCrae (1985) refer to as Neuroticism, Extroversion, Openness to Experience, Agreeableness, and Conscientiousness. The current inventory has its origins in the original 1978 NEO Inventory, which tapped three of the five factors and 18 facets. Short scales for Agreeableness and Conscientiousness were added in 1983, and the revision was published in 1985. Facet scales for A and C were added in 1990. Each of the 240 items of the NEO-PI-R is scored on a 5-point scale varying from strongly disagree to strongly agree. An observer rating form, NEO-PI-R Form R, phrased from the perspective of a third person, can be used to obtain information from relevant third-party sources, such as spouses, peers, or employers. Form R is further differentiated by gender, depending on whether the individual to be rated is male or female. Among other things, points of convergence and divergence 'between self- and other-informants may be clinically useful in assessing the functioning of dyadic relationships. Costa and McCrae (1990) report reliability and validity for self-report and observer-rated forms to be approximately comparable. All forms require a sixth-grade reading level, and can be completed in 30 to 40 minutes. Internal consistencies of the factor scales are uniformly high, ranging from .86 to .95 (Costa & McCrae, 1992). Those of the facet scales are in some cases much lower (alpha for the tender-mindedness facet of the agreeableness scale equals .56), but are largely adequate considering the length of the scales.

Costa and McCrae (1992) address the bandwidth-fidelity issue by presenting six facets for each of the five factors, yielding a total of 30 facet scales. Because the same factor score may be obtained in any number of ways, examination of the facet scales allows a level of descriptive specificity not afforded by the more global factor alone. In other words, two individuals may have the same score on a particular factor scale, for different reasons. Neuroticism is viewed as consisting of Anxiety, Angry Hostility, Depression, Self-Consciousness, Impulsiveness, and Vulnerability. Extroversion is viewed as consisting of Warmth, Gregariousness, Assertiveness, Activity, Excitement Seeking, and Positive Emotions. Openness is viewed as consisting of Fantasy, Aesthetics, Feelings, Actions, Ideas, and Values. Agreeableness is viewed as consisting of Trust, Straightforwardness, Altruism, Compliance, Modesty, and Tender-Mindedness. Conscientiousness is viewed as consisting of Competence, Order, Dutifulness, Achievement Striving, Self-Discipline, and Deliberation. Such an approach legitimately recognizes that personality cannot be sufficiently described in terms of five broad factors alone, but instead requires assessment through more narrow constructs. The final profile

presents scores both on the five factors and on the facet scales. These are grouped together by factor, yielding a mini-profile within the broad domain each factor represents. Nevertheless, for situations in which scores on the five factors are sufficient, a 60-item version, the NEO-Five-Factor Inventory (NEO-FFI), is available.

Although the facet scales go far toward contributing to the descriptive validity of the instrument, it is not clear that they contribute to its construct validity. These facets were "chosen to represent constructs frequently identified in the psychological literature that embody important distinctions within each of the five domains" (Costa & McCrae, 1992, p. 39). From a scientific, rather than descriptive perspective, the issue is one of necessity rather than sufficiency. Scientists seek a "natural" classification scheme or taxonomy, one that "inheres" in the subject domain, not one "imposed" on it. Such a taxonomy exists apart from the vicissitudes of human purpose, and so asserts its necessity, not merely its instrumentality, through its generative theory (Hempel, 1965). The system of kinds or dimensions undergirding any domain of inquiry must itself be answerable to the question that forms the very point of departure for the scientific enterprise: Why does nature take this particular form rather than some other? The facet scales do not account for themselves in this way. For those interested in this perspective, Widiger, Trull, Clarkin, Sanderson, and Costa (1994) present a translation of the DSM personality disorders into the NEO-PI-R framework.

Other conceptually interesting and worthy five-factor instruments include Block's (1961) five-factor version of the California *Q*-Sort and the six-factor Hogan Personality Inventory (1986), which splits E into Sociability and Ambition.

Schedule of Nonadaptive and Adaptive Personality (SNAP)

The SNAP is a 375-item, true-false instrument designed in the best inductive tradition. Although based on a series of factor analyses of personality disorder symptomatology and designed to uncover the internal structure of these disorders by the development of personality trait clusters, its promptings were anchored at its core to the theoretically generated temperament model formulated by Tellegen (1982, 1985). The SNAP yields personality-relevant information at a more fundamental level than that provided by a straightforward Axis II diagnosis; however, as noted in the following paragraphs, the instrument lends itself to personality disorder derivations from its 15 personality trait scales (e.g., mistrust, manipulativeness, aggression, detachment, dependency, impulsivity).

Whereas researchers working from the lexical approach (e.g., Costa & McCrae, 1985; Goldberg, 1990) define the personality domain in terms of English language descriptors, Clark (1990) chooses instead personality disorder criteria from all the DSMs, classic non-DSM personality disorder conceptions, and criteria from the personality-related Axis I conditions of dysthymia, cyclothymia, and generalized anxiety disorder. From this initial pool, 22 symptom clusters were identified through factor analysis. Next, items were written for 16 of the clusters and administered to university students. Then, a series of factor analytic studies with university, outpatient, and inpatient samples assessed and refined the resulting scales, ultimately yielding 12 trait dimensions: Mistrust, Manipulativeness, Aggression, Self-Harm, Eccentric Perceptions, Dependency, Exhibitionism, Entitlement, Detachment, Impulsivity, Propriety, and Workaholism. These have been shown to possess acceptable to high internal consistencies (median alpha = .76 to .85 for three student and patient samples) and to be stable over periods of one week to one month. Moreover, the scales are for practical purposes uncorrelated, with only one intercorrelation above .50 in college and mixed outpatient samples.

Factor analysis of the 12 primary scales yielded three factors—Negative Temperament, Positive Temperament, and Disinhibition (vs. Constraint)—which were then added as temperament dimensions (corresponding to the remaining 6 of the original 22 symptom clusters) for a total of 15 scales. Clinically, the temperament dimensions, essentially paralleling those of the General Temperament Survey and the Multidimensional Personality Questionnaire, lend the instrument a hierarchical structure that may be useful in terms of deriving developmental hypotheses about a patient's basic biophysical predisposition. If these three dimensions are seen as the "soil" of personality development, then the question "How did the patient's broad temperament characteristics come to be expressed through particular trait dimensions (as represented in the 12 primary scales) rather than others?" becomes a point of idiographic interest that can be explored in therapy.

In addition to its inductively derived trait and temperament scales, the SNAP also includes diagnostic scales oriented to the DSM-III-R Axis II criteria. Each criterion is operationalized through at least two items. Clark (1993) gives an example for the Histrionic criterion "is overly concerned with physical attractiveness," which is instantiated with these items: "I like to turn heads when I walk into a room" and "I wear clothes that draw attention."

A number of studies (e.g., Clark, Vorhies, & McEwen, 1994) examined the relationship between the SNAP scales and the five-factor model. Scores from the self-reported NEO-PI of Costa and McCrae and five-factor rating scales of Goldberg were standardized and added together to yield a composite variable for each factor. Next, a series of multiple regressions was performed using the composite FFM indexes to predict each SNAP scale. Multiple R's ranging from .40 to .70 were found, indicating that a substantial portion of the variance of the SNAP scales was accounted for by the FFM. However, three scales—Entitlement, Eccentric Perceptions, and Propriety—were not well accounted for by the FFM variables, an interesting finding since FFM proponents hold that the model is a complete representation of the personality domain, both normal and abnormal. Equivocal findings in personality psychology may always be attributed either to intervening variables or to the constructs themselves. The weak interpretation is that FFM measures, developed using normal populations, are simply not sensitive to dimensions rarely found among normals. The strong interpretation is that the FFM constructs, while obviously related, are nevertheless unable to encompass the domain of personality pathology in its totality. The intrinsic ambiguity between intervening variables and hypothetical constructs promises to keep this debate alive for a long time.

Tridimensional Personality Questionnaire (TPQ)

Guided by putative neurobiological substrates, Cloninger (1987a) has specified three behavioral dimensions (Novelty Seeking, Harm Avoidance, and Reward Dependence) that ostensibly underlie the styles of learning and adaptive interactions of personality traits and disorders. Cloninger, Przybeck, and Svrakic (1991) presented U.S. normative data for the 100-item, self-administered TPQ. Each superordinate dimension consists of 30 to 34 items, which in turn are broken up into four lower-order bipolar dimensions. The Novelty-Seeking scale (34 items) is divided into Exploratory Excitability versus Stoic Rigidity (9 items), Impulsiveness versus Reflection (8 items), Extravagance versus Reserve (7 items), and Disorderliness versus Regimentation (10 items). The Harm Avoidance scale (34 items) consists of Anticipatory Worry versus Uninhibited Optimism (10 items), Fear of Uncertainty versus Confidence (7 items), Shyness with Strangers versus Gregariousness (7 items), and Fatigability and Asthenia versus Vigor (10 items). The Reward

Dependence scale (30 items) is partitioned into Sentimentality versus Insensitiveness (5 items), Persistence versus Irresoluteness (9 items), Attachment versus Detachment (11 items), and Dependence versus Independence (5 items).

Independence of the dimensions of the TPQ has been examined in a number of confirmatory factor studies, including those of Bagby, Parker, and Joffe (1992), and Waller, Lilienfeld, Tellegen, and Lykken (1991). Both groups of researchers reported good results, with the exception of certain facets of the Reward Dependence dimension, as reported by Waller and associates, who further argued that the Harm Avoidance dimension in fact measures neuroticism or negative emotionality rather than the postulated disposition of behavioral inhibition, a point that will no doubt be the subject of future research. Given its promising preliminary findings, it would appear that the clinical utility of the TPQ is likely to be limited more by the inaccessibility of neurochemical and neuroanatomic knowledge to the larger community of mental health practitioners than by the generativity and coherence of its theoretical framework. Recent changes in the theory, namely the addition of four more dimensions beyond the original three (Cloninger, Svracic, & Przybeck, 1993), will require substantial modifications in the original instruments if it is to serve as a gauge of the conceptual model.

Wisconsin Personality Disorders Inventory (WISPI)

One of the more innovative approaches to interpersonal theory is represented in Benjamin's (1974, 1984) Structural Analysis of Social Behavior (SASB). As described in prior chapters, Benjamin's model conceptualizes interpersonal behavior in terms of two dimensions (affiliation and interdependence) within three domains (focus on other, focus on self, focus within self), which describe parentlike, childlike, and introjected behaviors, respectively. Benjamin's formulation resolves a controversy in interpersonal theory concerning the opposite of domination, which Schaefer (1965) labeled autonomy, and Leary, submission. Autonomy is taken to be the opposite of domination in the parentlike plane, whereas submission is viewed as its complement in the childlike plane. The resulting three-circumplex model thus integrates object representations and intrapsychic attitudes with interpersonal behavior.

Klein, Benjamin, Rosenfeld, Treece, Husted, and Griest (1993) reported on the use of the SASB model to guide the development of the 360-item

WISPI. In a multistage strategy similar to that recommended by Loevinger (1957), interpersonal descriptors were developed for each of the DSM-III and DSM-III-R Axis II criteria according to SASB principles. An important feature of these items is that they are phased to appear functional within the subjective worldview held by each disorder: "For example, an item that simply restates a DSM-III criterion such as: 'People say I am cold and aloof' (Schizoid criterion A1) would be less likely to be endorsed by persons with schizoid disorders than an item such as 'Because I wall myself off from others, I'm not affected by people' (WISPI item 86)" (Klein et al., 1993, p. 287). Consequently, although narcissistics, antisocials, sadistics, and paranoids might all be considered cold, phrasing the items in a way that provides not only the item content, but also a "why" behind that content, improves the discriminative validity of the inventory. Patients rate each item on a 10-point scale (1 = never or not at all true of you; 10 = always or extremely true of you).

Test-retest reliability at an interval of "within two weeks" varied from a high of .94 (dependent) to a low of .71 (schizoid), with an average of .88. Overlap between the scales appears to reflect that defined in the DSM, with the average intercorrelation being a rather high .62. Concurrent validity with the PDQ was moderate, averaging .69, but was somewhat lower with the MCMI-I, averaging .39. Correlations with the PDE and SCID-II in a small sample were also lower, averaging .19 and .28, respectively. As noted earlier, correlations across assessment modalities (e.g., interview to self-report), may be expected to be lower than those within the same modality (e.g., self-report to self-report). Research done to test the WISPI's differentiation between patient and nonpatient samples showed that patients did not differ significantly from nonpatients on the histrionic and antisocial scales in both the validation and reliability groups. Nor did the patients differ from nonpatients in the reliability sample on the schizoid scale, and in the validation sample on the narcissistic scales on which groups were examined. Similar results have been found with histrionic and narcissistic patients for the MCMI and MMPI-PD (Morey, Blashfield, Webb, & Jewell, 1982) scales, further evidence that the validity of self-report measures varies by disorder.

Millon Index of Personality Styles (MIPS)

Whereas the MCMI is designed to identify the personality disorders more or less directly, the MIPS (Millon et al., 1994), in the same manner as the NEO-PI and the Tridimensional instruments described earlier, focuses its scales on constructs that underlie these personality types, that is, the *latent elements* that combine to give rise to them. This 180-item inventory, useful for appraising personality *styles* rather than disorders, groups its scales to correspond directly to Millon's undergirding theory (Millon, 1990). For example, it possesses separate scales for *motivational aims* such as "life-enhancement (pleasure)" and "life-preserving (pain)." In a similar manner, it possesses separate scales to represent dispositions to "actively modify" one's environment versus "passively accommodating" to it. Also included are a "self-oriented" scale (individuating), and an "other-oriented" (nurturing) one. Noted in an earlier section were MIPS scales representing *cognitive modes,* as well as scales designed to represent polarities of *interpersonal behavior.*

To illustrate the process of synthesizing latent constructs into personality styles/disorder derivatives, we might note the following: The histrionic personality disorder scale of the MCMI represents in manifest form what can be derived by combining the latent construct MIPS scales "active-modifying," on the active-passive polarity, and "other-nurturing," on the self-other polarity. By focusing on these latent components, rather than their manifest derivations, the MIPS scales serves as a more direct gauge of the theory's evolutionary constructs than can be determined by the MCMI scales.

STRUCTURED INTERVIEW SCHEDULES

Structured and semistructured interviews have often been thought of as the criterion standard in psychopathology. Together with the specification of diagnostic criteria and the adoption of the prototypal model in DSM-III, the development of interview schedules marks a watershed in the history of measurement in psychopathology.

Because of their apparent scientific rigor, interviews have frequently been used to select samples against which self-report and rating scales are to be evaluated. Unfortunately, with the exception of the Bayesian superbootstraps methodology developed by Meehl (1978), there is simply no way around the criterion problem. No intervening variable measures 100% true variance; all intervening variables measure both true and error variance. When populations of clients are selected by interview to derive self-report inventories or checklists,

for example, these derived measures inherit both the advantages and shortcomings of their criterion forefathers. The specificities and eccentricities of the interview are then built into the instrument itself.

Moreover, the lengthy administration time and special personnel requirements of structured interviews do not facilitate concurrent validity studies that might assess the convergent and discriminant validity of various interviews. Those studies which have been done find that comparability between interviews is generally poor (e.g., Skodal, Oldham, Rosnick, Kellman, & Hyler, 1991). In fact, interviews may be so respected simply because they require that clinicians invest a considerable amount of time in the assessment process, thus becoming much more ego involved in the validity of the results than with a self-report inventory, where the time spent face-to-face with the patient is minimal.

A review of some of the more prominent interview schedules follows. They will be differentiated in terms of their scope. First, we will describe the features of instruments that seek to encompass a wide range of personality disorder categories or traits. The second section will focus on interviews that address a single personality disorder in depth.

Multidisorder and Multitrait Schedules

A number of interviews are based on the identification of the personality disorders directly. Others attempt to uncover a variety of traitlike features and characteristics. We will discuss these structured interviews beginning with those geared primarily to the disorders themselves and progress to those that are more domain or trait-oriented, yet designed to serve as a basis for identifying the disorders.

Structured Clinical Interview for DSM (SCID)

As we go to press, there is a high likelihood that this extensively researched instrument will undergo further revisions to accommodate to changes that have taken place in the DSM-IV. Although used in numerous investigations, the distinctive quality of the instrument lies in its close coordination with the criteria of each form of the DSM, first that of DSM-III, then DSM-III-R and, in all likelihood, the recently completed DSM-IV.

Developed originally by Spitzer and Williams (1986), this 120-item semistructured interview is usually included in a broad-based Schedule designed to assess many of the Axis 1 syndromes. Phrased to accord with the language employed in the DSM diagnostic criteria, the clinician uses a four-point measuring scale for appraising the degree to which the characteristic being examined is present. Specific probing questions are recommended to explore the extent to which the patient possesses adequate information concerning the item in question.

Beginning with an introductory set of general questions, the interview proceeds in turn to cover each of the personality disorders. Eight to 12 symptoms are used for each disorder. If it is evident that the patient cannot qualify for a specific disorder, the interviewer may skip onto the questions for the next personality category. A major advantage of the SCID is its speed of administration, at least in comparison with most other structured interviews. Personality disorder diagnoses are determined by cumulating the scores on the 4-point scale (inadequate information, negative, subthreshold, and threshold) for each criterion item. As noted, investigations at numerous psychiatric sites nationally have employed the several forms of the SCID. Despite its extensive employment as a "subthreshold lead standard," the instrument may not be quite as psychometrically acceptable as the frequency of its usage suggests. Though selected by many investigators to serve as their external criterion, owing to its content validity (DSM criteria), its conceptual scope (breadth of clinical domains encompassed), and ostensive construct validity (theoretical logic and internal consistency), the instrument has never been extensively evaluated. Other promising tools composed of interview questions may prove at least as accurate or valid.

Structured Interview for DSM Personality Disorders-Revised (SIDP-R)

The SIDP-R (Pfohl, Blum, Zimmerman, & Stangl, 1989) is a semistructured interview of approximately 160 items geared to the criteria of the DSM-III-R; a new form coordinated to the DSM-IV may soon be forthcoming. Questions are grouped into 17 topical sections, not into the DSM personality disorders. Subjects are encouraged to respond according to "what you are like when you are your usual self." Thus, no time frame for the interview is explicitly specified, although if the subject's personality has changed substantially, whichever personality that has dominated "for the greatest amount of time in the last five years" is scored as typical. Questions appear at the beginning of each section; the diagnostic criteria to which they relate appear at

the end. To improve interrater reliability, a 3-point scale is listed below each criterion to help anchor its level of severity. Thus "is overly concerned with physical attractiveness" may be rated "(0) physical appearance is not of overwhelming importance," "(1) more concerned with physical attractiveness than most people," or "(2) preoccupied with appearance." Interviewers are free to make additional inquiries when necessary.

Interviewers familiar with the instrument can administer it in 60 to 90 minutes. If an informant is available, 15 to 30 minutes of further inquiry may be necessary. Transcription of scores to the summary sheet of the interview booklet and scoring consume another 20 to 30 minutes. Together, these make for a minimum of about $1\frac{1}{2}$ hours to a maximum of $2\frac{1}{2}$ hours to complete the entire interview process. Diagnostic criteria are rated only after the end of the interview. Accordingly, the interview proceeds fluidly and without interruption, but may require that the diagnostician take copious notes to supplement his or her memory in the process.

Personality Assessment Schedule (PAS)

The PAS was developed in 1979 by Tyrer and Alexander, before the introduction of the DSM-III in 1980. Twenty-four traits are included: pessimism, worthlessness, optimism, lability, anxiousness, suspiciousness, introspection, shyness, aloofness, sensitivity, vulnerability, irritability, impulsiveness, aggression, callousness, irresponsibility, childishness, resourcelessness, dependence, submissiveness, conscientiousness, rigidity, eccentricity, and hypochondriasis. These traits are not assessed on a content basis alone, but rather are scored on a 9-point scale (0 to 8), depending on the degree to which the trait dominates the individual's life and results in dysfunction. Zero represents the complete absence of the trait; eight represents disturbance so profound that institutional care has been often been required over the course of the subject's life. Each intermediate point is anchored to a short descriptive paragraph, which facilitates reliability in scoring. The authors note that traits at the more normal end of the continuum are scored at three or less, with very few normals receiving higher ratings.

The authors recommend that both the subject and a knowledgeable informant be interviewed for ratings on all 24 traits. Where discrepancies of two or more points exist, some attempt should be made to reconcile the ratings through additional questions or independent information, where available.

Near the end of the interview, the interviewer also rates the validity of both the subject's and the informant's responses on a 9-point scale, zero representing a reliable witness or informant whose reports are consistent with information from other sources, 8 representing inconsistency and no validity. Final scores on each trait dimension are assigned according to the validity of the information. Thus on some dimensions, the subject's scores may be retained; on other dimensions, the informant's scores may be substituted. The role of method variance in the final ratings is presumably minimized by such a procedure. One study found good-to-excellent intraclass correlation coefficients across several raters in the United States and Great Britain for both informants (.66 to .94) and subjects (.51 to .91), with informants' ratings being generally less biased.

Although the PAS was not intended to directly parallel the DSM Axis II constructs, the authors do provide a means of translating the scores on the PAS trait dimensions into DSM dimensional scores, with the caveat that the narcissistic and passive-aggressive are not as well assessed as the other disorders. Each DSM construct is scored as the average of four PAS dimensions. Thus, the paranoid personality is the sum of scores on suspiciousness, sensitivity, vulnerability, and irritability, divided by four. Schizoid is the sum of scores on introspection, aloofness, eccentricity, and pessimism, divided by four. Narcissistic is the sum of childishness, vulnerability, optimism, and irritability, divided by four, and so on.

Personality Disorders Examination-Revised (PDE-R)

The PDE-R was developed over several years by Loranger, Susman, Oldham, and Russakoff (1987) as a means of surveying the phenomenology and life experiences relevant to personality disorder diagnoses. Dimensional scores are obtained on some 328 items that are grouped under six headings: Work, Self, Interpersonal Relations, Affects, Reality Testing, and Impulse Control. An open-ended question introduces each domain, and the subject may elaborate as much as he or she chooses in answering. Criteria are listed above their respective items to facilitate scoring. Each item is assigned "0" if the behavior is judged absent or clinically insignificant, "1" if present but of unknown significance, "2" if present and significant, and "?" if the subject does not respond or if the response cannot be clarified sufficiently to be scored. In addition, the interviewer is free to ask whatever questions

seem clinically relevant to explore the subject's response. An informant version is also available.

Diagnostic criteria may be scored in two ways. The first is statistical. Responses for each criterion are summed and compared with a threshold score. Loranger et al. (1987) suggest that this method probably maximizes interrater reliability. Alternately, criteria may be scored by clinical judgment, an approach that draws on the expertise of the clinician and the value of additional exploratory questions, where necessary. Research with the original PDE has shown interrater reliabilities for dimensional scores to be quite high, with most above .95 for a convenience sample of 60 inpatients. A kappa of .80 was found in diagnosing any personality disorder present or absent.

Widiger (1987, p. 51) notes that the PDE "may at times rely too heavily on the patient's opinions and self-evaluations rather than [on] more objective, behavioral data." A related problem is that the PDE presents its questions in obviously pathological forms. For example, an inquiry for the DSM compulsive criterion is "Are you so devoted to your work that you neglect your relationships with other people?" Individuals with personality disorders may not be aware of the extent to which their own behaviors are problematic, and may in fact view their behavior as quite functional.

Despite methodological concerns and limited validity data, the PDE-R's format and open-ended question structure is an attractive feature of the instrument, and has led to its translation into several languages and its use in numerous international studies on the personality disorders.

Single Disorder Interview Schedules

Whereas the preceding interview instruments attended to the full scope of personality disorders/traits, the following ones focus on one specific disorder at a time. A variety of such inventories have been devised; we will limit ourselves, however, to what we judge to be the most promising.

Diagnostic Interview for Borderlines-Revised (DIB-R)

The DIB was developed "to achieve diagnostic reliability specifically for borderline patients" (Gunderson, Kolb, & Austin, 1981, p. 896) on the basis of Gunderson and Singer's (1975) review of borderline conditions. Five content areas associated with these authors' conception of borderline conditions are assessed: Social adaptation, impulse action patterns, affects, psychosis, and interpersonal relations. On the plus side, such an explicitly domain-oriented approach favors content, and ultimately construct, validity through the coverage of attributes across the range of relevant and varied spheres in which personality is expressed. As a practical negative, however, the DIB was designed before the Borderline personality was elaborated in the DSM-III, and is intended to instantiate the authors' conception of the construct, and not that represented in the DSM. Accordingly, there is partial but imperfect overlap between the two. Nevertheless, despite its "nonofficial" status, the DIB-R represents a more precisely articulated concept of a construct that has historically proven to be almost as labile as those so diagnosed.

Due to the subtlety of judgments in the interpersonal and psychosis domains, the interviewer is free to probe for more information. Scaled scores of 0 to 2 are computed for each section, and these are then summed to yield an overall diagnostic score ranging from 0 to 10. Scores of 7 or more are considered to be indicative of a borderline personality disorder. The entire interview takes about an hour.

Numerous studies utilizing or evaluating the DIB have been published. Interrater reliability (e.g., Frances, Clarkin, Gilmore, Hurt, & Brown, 1984; Gunderson, Kolb, & Austin, 1981) and discriminant validity relative to Axis I disorders such as schizophrenia and major depression (e.g., Koenigsberg, Kernberg, & Schomer, 1983; Kolb & Gunderson, 1980) have been established. Some researchers, however, have questioned the grouping of the DIB's scored questions into the five content areas and found that some items failed to discriminate between borderline and nonborderline groups and between inpatients and outpatients; others found that the DIB lacked discriminate validity with respect to other Axis II personality disorders (Kolb & Gunderson, 1980; Soloff & Ulrich, 1981). For these reasons, the DIB was revised on the basis of conjoint interviews to "refine its format, phrasing, and scoring system" (Zanarini, Gunderson, Frankenburg, & Chauncey, 1989). Diagnostic efficiency statistics for the DIB-R have been shown to be superior to those of the DIB in a sample of 237 inpatients and outpatients (Zanarini et al., 1989).

Diagnostic Interview for Narcissism (DIN)

The DIN is a semistructured diagnostic interview by Gunderson, Ronningstam, and Bodkin (1990),

the second to focus comprehensively on a particular disorder. Prior to their effort, narcissistic personality disorder could only be diagnosed via interview as part of a schedule oriented toward all the Axis II categories. The DIN was developed from a literature review and from the authors' clinical exposure and systematic examination of narcissistic patients over a 2-year period. Characteristics were borrowed from a variety of traditions and theoretical frameworks. All probes are rated on a scale of 2, 1, or 0. Administering the interview takes about 45 minutes.

The DIN assesses narcissism in five content areas: Grandiosity, interpersonal relations, reactiveness, affects and mood states, and social and moral adaptation. The grandiosity section is oriented toward assessing the patient's unrealistic view of self (e.g., Do you have special abilities or talents?). Interpersonal probes are drawn primarily from the psychoanalytic writings of Kohut (e.g., idealization of others and lack of empathy) and Kernberg (e.g., sense of entitlement and exploitation of others).

Diagnostic Interview for Depressive Personality (DIDP)

The DIDP has proved to be prophetic in that it anticipated the inclusion of a depressive personality category in the DSM-IV (Phillips, Gunderson, Hirschfeld, & Smith, 1990). Both affective (e.g., chronic unhappiness) and cognitive (e.g., negativism) traits are given primacy. The major categories include (1) quiet, (2) tense, (3) unhappy, (4) negativistic, and (5) unassertive. Usage guidelines state that the ratings should be characteristic of "usual and enduring traits typical of and present for most of the patient's adult life." This distinction is critical, since depressive personality and major depression must not be confounded. Accordingly, patients are instructed to respond to the interviewer's questions according to what their personality is like when not experiencing a depressive episode. Those patients currently experiencing a depressive episode are instructed to respond according to what is characteristic of their premorbid personality.

CHECKLISTS

Checklists blur the boundaries between personality scales and diagnostic criteria. Since the intent of a checklist is to assist in making a typological or diagnostic decision, checklist items typically exist at a higher level of inference than those of self-report inventories, which may be very specific or act oriented. In this sense, checklist items approach diagnostic criteria. A checklist, however, differs from DSM criteria in two important ways. First, a checklist usually provides more attributes or items than the DSM. Second, unlike the DSM personality disorders' criteria sets, these attributes or items are usually subjected to some kind of psychometric refinement and thus exhibit respectable internal consistency.

Three checklists will be noted owing to their special character. The first is a *simple adjective* checklist, quite popular in studies of personality traits in general; the second has the uniqueness of addressing a number of the *clinical domains* that were presented earlier in this chapter; the third is focused on a *single disorder,* but has a well established empirical history supporting its utility.

Personality Adjective Checklist (PACL)

Using the adjective checklist format, the initial forms (both clinician rated and self-reported) of the PACL were composed of 405 items. The structure of the checklist was designed to reflect the eight basic clinical types that were initially formulated in Millon's (1969, 1981) theory of personality disorders. Although based originally on a conception of personality pathology, the PACL's adjectival items were selected to help identify personality types in the normal range. Owing to its high correlation with independent gauges of personality pathology, the instrument lends itself quite nicely for use with clinical populations as well.

Item refinements and initial validation studies were based on data from over 2,000 "normal" adults from a variety of diverse national settings. A wide range of validity data have been gathered and reported (Strack, 1987, 1993), including correlations with various other sources of personality and biographical data on current and past behavior. Each scale of the PACL appears consonant with theoretical expectations and their expected personality characterizations. Thus, the PACL Inhibited scale (which reflects a milder variant of the Millon's and DSM's Avoidant personality disorder) is positively correlated with measures of shyness, submissiveness, and social anxiety, while being negatively correlated with measures of sociability, dominance, and emotional well-being. Similarly, the PACL Forceful scale (a milder version of the theory's and DSM's Antisocial and Sadistic disorders) is positively related to gauges

of aggressiveness, arrogance, and dominance, and is negatively related to gauges of deference, submissiveness, and conscientiousness.

Owing to the common linkage in theory, there is a possibility that the results of the PACL might be erroneously confused with parallel versions of the MCMI. High scores on the PACL scales do not signify the presence of personality *disorders,* as they do on the MCMI; rather, they suggest the presence of distinctive personality traits. As Strack (1993) notes, all persons in the PACL development group were presumed to have normal personalities, hence the special utility of the instrument as a measure of normality rather than abnormality.

Millon Personality Diagnostic Checklist (MPDC)

Throughout this chapter, we have stressed the need to operationalize personality across the clinical domains in which the disorders are expressed. Eight structural and functional domains were identified to serve as a basis of analysis. The MPDC is grouped into several categories that offer a diagnostician the opportunity to systematically assess patients in five of these eight domains: expressive acts, interpersonal conduct, cognitive style, self-image, and mood/temperament. The other three domains proved to be too difficult and inferential for clinicians to utilize with any degree of reliability or comfort.

All 14 personality disorders are represented in the checklist items that make up the MPDC. For some personalities, there may be as many as 15 or more descriptive phrases that the clinician might want to check; most have 10 to 12. Thus, for the schizoid, one will find two items relating to expressive acts, three for interpersonal conduct, two for cognitive style, three for self-image, and two for mood/temperament.

Like the other Millon instruments, the MPDC was constructed employing a three-stage sequence in which a larger pool of items is whittled down on the basis of theoretical, internal-statistical, and external validity data to form the final checklist. The current form consists of 160 phrases retained on the basis of their discriminative and predictive power relative to the clinicians' judgments of their patients' Axis II personality diagnoses. Representative phrases include "displays intolerance of boredom and inactivity" (from the expressive behavior domain), "is callous and insensitive" (from the mood/temperament domain), "withdraws into reveries to fulfill needs" (from the cognitive style domain), "expects special favors without reciprocating" (from the interpersonal conduct domain), and "has a grandiose sense of self-importance" (from the self-image domain).

Clinicians complete the MPDC in two stages. First, the entire checklist is surveyed and those items judged to be characteristic of the client are marked in the first circle next to each item. Most clinicians mark between 35 and 50 items when appraising a patient they know reasonably well. Next, the marked items are reread again, and those that describe aspects of the patient's personality judged most prominent have their second circle bubbled in as well. Like other instruments in the Millon family, the MPDC uses an item-weighting scheme. Like the MCMI-II (but unlike the MCMI-III), items are weighted 3, 2, or 1. Final scoring yields a base rate score for each of the personality disorders.

Psychopathy Checklist—Revised (PCL-R)

The original PCL was published in 1980 by Hare as a representation of the psychopathy construct as conceived by Cleckley (1941). Two items were deleted in a later revision in order to better represent the higher-order oblique two-factor structure of the instrument (Hare, 1985), yielding the PCL-R. Factor 1, defined by eight items, is negatively correlated with empathy and anxiety measures and is positively correlated with ratings of narcissistic and histrionic personality disorder (Hare, 1991). A survey of these items shows that those who score high on this factor are likely to be egocentric and manipulative; lack remorse, guilt, or empathy; and exhibit a superficial charm or glibness. Factor 2 refers more to lifestyle components of the psychopathy construct, including poor behavioral control, impulsivity, and lack of long-term goals. Not surprisingly, it is this factor that correlates more highly with the concretized DSM-III-R antisocial diagnosis.

Unlike the DSM-III-R antisocial personality disorder, however, PCL-R traits are thought of as open concepts with multiple referents (Hare, 1991). Raters are provided with descriptions and behavioral exemplars, from which judgments are made about the degree to which the individual possesses each trait on a 0 (definitely does not apply) to 3 (definitely does apply) scale. These ratings are made after a review of file data and clinical interview. Interrater reliability with trained raters is high.

Ample evidence for the construct validity of the PCL-R is available. Concurrent validation evidence has been accumulated from correlations with DSM-III and DSM-III-R antisocial personality disorder criteria, the Psychopathic Deviate and Hypomania scales of the MMPI, the CPI Socialization scale, the MCMI Antisocial scale, and many indexes of criminality and recidivism (Hare, 1991). Although the PCL and PCL-R were developed with a mainly white adult male prison population, there are strong suggestions that the generalizability of the PCL-R extends to other populations as well, including blacks and young male offenders (Forth, Hart, & Hare, 1990). Moreover, the PCL and PCL-R have served as a platform from which to investigate verbal, psychophysiological, and attentional hypotheses regarding psychopaths.

PROJECTIVE TECHNIQUES

Despite numerous assaults of an empirical and methodological nature, projective techniques such as the Rorschach and TAT have not only endured, but flourished, firmly grounded in the idiographic tradition. Like interviews and self-reports, projective techniques may be described as necessary but not sufficient for a complete personality assessment.

As with all measurement procedures, projectives involve potential gains and losses. The gain is comprehensiveness: Projectives are explicitly intended to access more inferential aspects of personality that exist outside of self-awareness, including the domains of object representations, regulatory mechanisms, and morphologic organization. The loss is one of precision: To the extent that the psychological interpretation of projective material is constrained by factors outside the clinician's own awareness, the end results become as projective to him or her as the material to be interpreted. The very open-endedness that makes projectives so clinically rich in turn creates interpretational ambiguities that are inherently problematic. Self-report instruments do not suffer this shortcoming, since one cannot even embark on the creation of a scale or inventory without explicit content definition and delimitation, as explained earlier. Self-reports, of course, suffer other limitations. Patients can only report what is known, or at least what is believed to be known, and self-image is distorted both by the inaccessibility of relevant information and the introjection of other appraisals of dubious validity. Just as phenomenology is not all of mentality, self-reports cannot be regarded as the end-all of personality assessment.

Consequently, projectives play an important and complementary role in getting at those aspects of personality that are not known to self, and quite possibly not known to others. McClelland, Koestner, & Weinberger (1989), for example, argue that the low correlations found between clinical ratings of motive disposition and self-reported disposition, far from indicating poor convergent validity in the tradition of Campbell and Fiske (1959), instead reflect a distinction that in fact exists in nature between what are called self-attributed and implicit motives. By definition, implicit motives are not explicitly owned by the person. Indeed, they are acquired before the development of language. Self-attributed motives, on the other hand, reflect information stored in the self-schema; it is this information that is tapped by self-report inventories. McClelland et al. state (p. 699), "In evolutionary terms, a conscious motivational system has been built on top, so to speak, of a more primitive motivational system." The tension between drive states, as represented in McClelland's work through the language of needs, and conscious contents and beliefs, has long been of fundamental importance to the dynamics of personality.

Although there are guides to the assessment of certain aspects of personality with projective methods—the work of Perry & Cooper, (1989) in assessing regulatory or defense mechanisms using the Rorschach was described in an earlier section—as yet there exists no systematic and comprehensive method of directly assessing the DSM personality constructs using projective techniques. Certainly some indicators, such as Exner's Obsessive-Compulsive and Egocentricity Indexes, may be suggestive of DSM-like personality pathology, but their utility for making differential diagnostic decisions, as might be gauged, for example, by calculating positive predictive power relative to some structured interview or expert judgment, remains largely unstudied.

FUTURE DIRECTIONS

What future directions might be pursued to advance the assessment of personality disorders? One distinction noted in this chapter regards a content-bound versus contextually-oriented assessment of personality. Although a contextually-oriented assessment is consonant with the epistemology of the construct, no such assessment measures have been constructed by which to operationalize levels of personality health and abnormality. The development of such measures promises to free personality disorder diagnosis from both more content-oriented (which dimensions are fundamental to personality?) and structurally-oriented (categories, dimensions, or prototypes?) disputes. Perhaps the word diagnosis can be eventually dispensed with in favor simply of assessment of functioning. In Chapter 1, we argued that personality disorders criteria are best coordinated with the systems metaphor through which personality itself may be conceived. Unfortunately, there are as yet no instruments specifically designed that assess the tenuous stability, adaptive inflexibility, and vicious circles of personality pathology. No dimensional assessment that looks simply at scale elevations is sufficient to answer questions in these areas. As previously noted, although some traits are by definition maladaptive, the quantity of any given trait is twice removed, separated by two interactions, from the implications of that quantity for contextual functioning. Consequently, it is possible that a considerable amount of slippage and consequent loss of classification accuracy may occur if personality disorders are to be diagnosed on the basis of dimensional scores alone.

Along similar lines, no effort has been made in the official nosology to equate diagnostic thresholds with particular levels of psychosocial dysfunction across disorders, leading to a variety of unsavory possibilities. First, individuals meeting diagnostic criteria for some disorders may be functioning relatively adequately, whereas others who present with features currently considered subclinical may nevertheless possess considerable personality pathology. Second, to the extent that the DSM personality disorders represent dimensions that in fact extend into normality but are not equated in terms of criteria that are generic with respect to the functional consequences of personality pathology, the possibility exists that prevalence rate estimates based on current criteria sets are hopelessly confounded. As a result, diagnostic efficiency statistics, which depend in part on the relative prevalence rates between disorders, may also be muddled, with the result that research attempts to identify auxiliary indicators of high positive predictive power will be either unsuccessful, successful to different degrees across disorders, ultimately prove to be an epiphenomenon dependent on particular criteria sets, or be in some other way distorted.

Another innovation brewing in the assessment of personality disorders derives from the long advocated, and now widely recognized, conviction that normal and abnormal personality exist on a continuum (Offer & Sabshin, 1991; Strack & Lorr, 1994). Because the difference between the two is one of degree rather than kind, any method or construct relevant to the assessment of normal personality must be considered relevant to the assessment of clinical personality as well. No longer must or should clinicians confine themselves to modes of assessment traditional to clinical science. Such conceptions as personal projects (Little, 1983) and public and private self-consciousness (Fenigstein, Scheier, & Buss, 1975) are free game in the assessment process, as are any other perspectives from the mainstream, or even the fringe, of personality psychology. Even though additional perspectives promise to enrich the field, in and of themselves they do not specify how competing models are to be integrated when the object of study is a single individual. Unless checked by some integrative principle, conceptual pluralism may degenerate into clinical confusion. The domain-oriented approach discussed earlier provides, at the least, an extensible means of accommodating additional enriching concepts by classifying them into domains that parallel the profession's current therapeutic modalities, while putting the integrity of the personality directly into the foreground.

Future assessment instruments are also likely to become more methodologically sophisticated. Because of the importance of the state-trait issue and the impact of state factors on the subject's presentations, especially self-report, those involved in the construction of future instruments might consider refining their items pools first by administering these pools at a minimum of two time points. Those items that show the greatest reliability over time would presumably be most insensitive to state factors and therefore tap only more enduring trait-like characteristics. Given the generally modest correlations and poorer diagnostic correspondence between self-reports and structured interviews and checklists, another direction might be to derive both instruments from the same normative sample simultaneously, thereby optimizing their correspondence while using one as a validity check on the other. We may in the not too distant future be able to derive and refine entire systems of instrumentation.

Other innovations might be pursued by placing the official nosology on a basis that would be more dynamic and continuity oriented with respect to revisions. Jackson and Livesley (1995) compared the psychiatric DSM method of taxonomy revision to that involved in the revision of personality assessment instruments. Among other things, these authors noted that the structural component of DSM revision is particularly deficient. Although experts submit revisions and replacements for criteria that are not performing well, these candidate criteria are not subjected to any further selection or data-driven evaluation process. In effect, poor criteria are replaced by criteria whose performance is uncertain. In an effort to strengthen the structural component, a limited number of *provisional* diagnostic criteria might be proposed by each Axis II committee member for future study alongside the official criteria in the interval until the DSM-V revision. These criteria, although not officially endorsed for making diagnostic classifications, would nevertheless constitute an officially public item pool out of which those items with better empirically verified convergent and discriminant characteristics would be substituted for poorer performers during DSM-V revision meetings. In the absence of some radical shift in diagnostic standards, an official pool would eliminate philosophical bickering among committee members by reducing criterion replacement decisions to a common empirical framework. Simultaneously, taxonomic revision would be radically "democratized" because researchers not on the Axis II committee would inevitably target particular sections of the taxonomic matrix for study, depending on the availability of samples, their interest patterns, and so on. Data from these multisite studies would then be periodically compiled using meta-analytic strategies. Eventually, such a model might even be expanded so that "rolling replacements" could be made at semiannual or annual intervals, giving the process of taxonomic revision a genuinely dynamic dimension. Poorly performing items would be put back into the pool for further study or deleted entirely as artifacts of taxonomic history. Content validity and construct validity would inevitably expand as comprehensive and comparable criteria are adopted across a variety of personologic domains. In contrast, the current DSM categories and criteria appear to be frozen for a decade or more.

CHAPTER 5

Personality Therapy:
Planning, Modalities, and Integration

Today, economic forces—not theoretical developments and empirical research—increasingly drive the direction of developments in psychotherapy. Although modern times continue to see an explosion in the total number of therapies, brief therapies are in the ascendancy. These claim to accomplish in less time through patient selectivity and therapeutic structure and specificity almost as much, if not more, than the longer term, more inclusive therapies of the past. The message to psychotherapists today is "do more, with less," meaning, unfortunately, not only fewer sessions, but more patients, and therefore less time spent thinking about the dynamics of any one patient's problems. For better or worse, the emphasis on efficiency has been and continues to be a primary impetus in the development of programmatic forms of therapy. Moreover, these forms have been adapted to variables at levels of analysis congruent with what is afforded by current economic constraints. Operationalizing the content of therapy not only achieves experimental control, it diminishes the therapist's need to "think," at least at the "depth" levels characteristic of psychotherapy's psychodynamic origin, while presumably maintaining or even improving levels of efficacy. Interventions are linked more rigidly to diagnoses, and the need for case conceptualization is minimized.

The personality disorders, however, would seem to stand squarely and intrinsically in opposition to the current trend toward briefer and briefer therapies. The more focal Axis I disorders admit to more focal, and therefore, briefer, interventions, but the personality disorders, long-standing and pervasive, stand like stone monoliths unmoved in the face of economic necessity. Is it reasonable to expect 10, or even fewer, hours with a therapist to "cure" a personality disorder? Persons are not clay waiting to be passively resculpted. Furthermore, the personality system, functioning as the immune system of the psyche, actively resists the influence of outside forces. To uproot a personality disorder, the clinician must wrangle with the ballast of a lifetime, a developmental disorder of the entire matrix of the person, produced and perpetuated across years. By any reasoning, the pervasiveness and entrenched tenacity of the pathology soak up therapeutic resources, leading inevitably to pessimism and disaffection for therapists.

And yet, no clinician would deny the importance of personality to psychotherapy. In fact, "the characteristics that the patient brings to the treatment experience are the single most powerful sources of influence on the benefit to be achieved by treatment" (Beutler & Clarkin, 1990, p. 31). Beyond the more obvious and widely discussed influences, such as transference and countertransference and the problems and opportunities these offer, the presence of a personality disorder creates, by definition, a psychic vulnerability that not only disposes the individual to the development of an Axis I disorder, but also complicates the course of that disorder once it in fact exists. These, in turn create levels of stress and anxiety that keep the "immune system" chronically weakened, extending the illness and making recovery even more problematic. Treating the Axis I disorder without treating the personality disorder is like neutralizing the symptoms without treating the disease. Whether it will prove cost-effective for mental health care concerns to follow such a course cannot be known with certainty in advance. Efforts to develop therapies that can be applied with automaticity *do* offer incremental gains over psychotherapy's unstructured classical past. How long these gains will forestall the development of structured therapies specifically addressed to the personality disorders, to the disease, in a society that seems bent on producing such pathology, is likewise an empirical question. Some diseases, after all, linger in the background and handicap the quality of life, but necessitate care only in times of acute crisis.

Much, of course, depends on what it means to "remedy" a personality disorder. Those who have examined the disease concept (e.g., Feinstein, 1977) have found it troublingly tautological, imprecise, and informed more by social factors than by scientific ones. The concept cannot be defined nonarbitrarily. If the concept of disease is problematic and paradigmatically bound, then so is a remedy to the disease. In the psychodynamic perspective, human beings are seen as being inevitably and perpetually at the mercy of conflicting internal forces and external pressures. Here, successful therapy leads back from highly individualized pathologies of compromise to the generic "psychopathology of everyday life," the so-called human situation. If one comes from a "fulfillment" perspective, however, successful therapy means self-actualization, with the possibility of a conflict-free existence. Both of these worldviews obviously influence the idea of a remedy. For example, one of the most important questions in psychotherapy is when to terminate. The emphasis on process rather than product in the fulfillment perspective seems to paradigmatically proscribe therapy ever coming to an end, since growth is, presumably, always possible. In the comparatively Hobbesian world of the "conflict" perspective, however, where resources are now limited and psychological problems are dismissed as being too fuzzy and probabilistic to treat effectively, therapy itself begins to resemble the lives of those who are treated, being ethically nasty, technically brutish, and definitely short. Here, personality problems are treated in a cursory manner, and the therapeutic relationship is terminated, even while real Axis I problems and Axis II vulnerabilities remain.

Although there is still cause for optimism, it requires a return to first principles. The idea of a personality disorder is only that, an ideal or reference point to which real persons are compared. Recall again from Chapter 1 that personality disorders are not diseases at all, but reified entities useful for conceptual or heuristic purposes. Like all representations, the ideal of a personality disorder (rather than any particular personality disorder or particular individual) is a prototype realized to various degrees and in different ways in different people. Not only do individuals vary in the degree to which they approximate any given personality diagnosis, they also vary in the degree to which their pathologies approximate the ideal of a personality disorder at all, that is, the degree to which they exhibit tenuous stability under conditions of subjective stress, adaptive inflexibility across the contexts in which life finds them, and the degree to which these two factors lead them into vicious circles of self-perpetuating pathology. Real persons fulfill the generic ideal of a personality disorder only in part. One of the messages of Chapter 4 was the need for specificity in the assessment as a means to specificity in the intervention. In real individuals, the ideal assessment finds different aspects of personality impaired to various degrees. Some operate as severe constraints, others as areas of flexibility or strength. For this reason, if the focus is on the therapy of a real individual rather than the therapy of a personality disorder prototype, the situation need not be as bad as it first appears. In particular, the constraint construct provides an excellent reframe for the psychotherapist. Embedded in a systems perspective rather than in the medical model, the patient's difficulties are conceived ecologically, against a background of possibilities to be realized when the constraints are relaxed.

This chapter is divided into several sections. The first is a very broad overview of what has become our current treatment philosophy, specifically eclecticism and its variants, the identification of common factors among diverse therapies, and *integrationism*. The argument is essentially that of the three, only from the last is it possible to derive a form of therapy that is both personality oriented and theoretically logical. As an integrative construct, the idea of personality itself contains structural implications that legislate over the form of any therapy that would propose to remedy its pathologies.

The second section details several of these implications, and proposes a new model for therapeutic action that we call *personologic psychotherapy*. This model gives promise of a new level of efficacy and may, in fact, contribute to making therapy briefer. However, it has not been conceptualized in the service of economic forces. Far from representing merely rationales or justifications, it provides a means of optimizing psychotherapy by making the nature of the intervention parallel to that of the pathology. For this reason, it is not an option to be adopted or dismissed as congruent or incongruent with one's own therapeutic style. Rather, we believe that this approach is *required* for the personality disorders.

The next section of the chapter concerns the assessment of the individual for purposes of *treatment planning*. Following that, there is a review of the several *domains* of clinical functioning and structure that call for specialized techniques of intervention. The question addressed in this section is "How should therapy be done?" In the final major segment of the chapter, the question addressed is "How shall this be done in an *integrative* fashion?" The distinction here is between the tactics employed in therapy and the coordination of these tactics to optimize achieving the strategic goals of treatment.

ECLECTIC AND INTEGRATIVE THERAPY: A GROWING TREATMENT PHILOSOPHY

Heinz Werner, the developmental theorist, held that development proceeds in three stages: (a) from the relatively global, to (b) the relatively differentiated, to (c) an integrated totality. Had the development of psychotherapy followed this model, modern therapies would not only address psychological problems with unprecedented specificity and therapeutic efficacy, they would also do so from the vantage point of a single, unifying theoretical perspective.

Clinical science did not develop into such an integrative totality, for at least two reasons. First, the original clinical theory within which therapy developed, psychoanalysis, ultimately proved to be only a partial theory of human nature, beset with terminological ambiguities that have proven highly resistant to operationalization and clarification. In fact, the case has been made that evolution of psychoanalysis is an evolution away from what Freud had originally conceptualized. Thus hobbled by metatheoretical obscurities, psychoanalysis did not gave birth to a true taxonomy of psychopathology offering both precision and coverage. As noted in Chapter 1, personality disorders are multireferential constructs. Although some disorders display themselves with a greater degree of salience in some domains rather than others, a taxonomy cannot be generated that encompasses all the personality disorders on the basis of a single perspective or domain. Consequently, psychoanalysis largely failed to profit from the synergism between theory and empirical research of the kind begun by the DSM-III and now continued through DSM-IV.

Second, other "data domains" of personality (see Chapters 1 and 4), some primarily from academic psychology and others from clinical science, also gave rise to sophisticated philosophies of human nature that were just as imperious, totalistic, and exclusionary as psychoanalysis.

Behaviorism emerged and dominated for a time, only to eventually give way to cognitive psychology, which today may itself be considered a subdiscipline of cognitive science. Other perspectives oriented both to harder (e.g., the neurobiological) and softer (e.g., interpersonal) levels of organization have also emerged and flourished. Each of these spawned its own schools of intervention and theoretically derived techniques (in the neurobiological perspectives these techniques take the form of medications). For the most part, each also became submerged in the specificities of its own program, and having developed largely in isolation, transfixed by its own internal consistency, was either not attentive to or dismissive of the advances of related perspectives on the same field.

For better or worse, the "dynamics of the knowledge situation" (Pepper, 1942) are such that multiple perspectives on the same subject domain tend to call each other into question, and end up creating doubts concerning the completeness of any one perspective; the raw materials of psychodynamic, biological, behavioral, and phenomenological data levels are, after all, psychopathology and human nature (Millon, 1969). Understandably, this disputation tends to be more intense when the various perspectives all exhibit high internal consistency, for then they "close off" from each other, and no common ground can be found outside each perspective on which some rapprochement might be achieved. Internally consistent perspectives are like "infallible" authorities that vehemently disagree—eventually infallibility itself becomes suspect, for on whatever grounds reasonable people choose to test infallibility, it is a grounds required to stand apart from and yet legislate over it. If Werner's thesis can be applied to the development of disciplines as well as organisms, these conflicts probably represent an inevitable intermediate stage in the evolution of a truly integrated clinical science.

Eclecticism, dogmatism, and integrationism are all reactions to this situation. Of the two, eclecticism at least has the virtue of humility, and integrationism, those of persistence and optimism. Dogmatism, however, is more of a "compromise" that is usually intended to veil underlying self-doubt and insecurity concerning one's own convictions. Alternately, it can also derive from a fear of growth, in that growth points to the insufficiency or inadequacy of what currently exists. Epistemologically, it is found in its most obtuse form in debates concerning which treatment orientation (cognitive, behavioral, biological, intrapsychic) is "closer to the truth," or which therapeutic method is the most intrinsically efficacious. What differentiates these orientations and treatment methods has little to do with their theoretical underpinnings or their empirical support. Their differences are akin to physicists, chemists, and biologists arguing over which of their fields is a more "true" representation of nature. Such schisms have been constructed less by philosophical considerations or pragmatic goals than by the accidents of history and professional rivalries. In the following pages, we will offer discussions of eclecticism, common factors, and integrationism. Because the discussions are brief, we will sharpen the positions somewhat, thereby bringing the contrast between perspectives into higher relief.

GENERAL ECLECTICISM

Today, the compensating insecurity of dogmatism has succumbed to an eclecticism of practical necessity; the tendency is to conceptualize cases "completely," even if internal consistency is sacrificed. No one on a treatment team waits until a common vocabulary has been evolved that bridges and unifies the perspectives of the team members in a single overarching framework. Each person simply presents his or her own opinion where that perspective informs the case; this practice recognizes, if only in practice, that there is something about the totality of human nature that resists being put into a single conceptual system or taxonomy. Unlike school-oriented psychotherapies, eclecticism is viewed as being atheoretical, as encouraging research of all kinds, and as being devoted pragmatically to what actually helps people. In contrast, school-oriented forms of psychotherapy make strong prescriptions about the perspectives from which cases are conceptualized and the techniques that may be used in psychotherapy.

What is ironic about the modern position, however, is that eclecticism itself seems to have become dogmatic, a kind of psychotherapeutic liberalism. The irony lies in the contrast between the intent of eclecticism and what it is becoming. There are two preconditions for intelligent eclecticism: first, practical necessity, and second, a measure of ignorance concerning the nature of the subject at hand. In the absence of a complete and internally consistent theory of human nature, that would exhaust individuality in every case, we must all remain eclectics. To this extent, eclecticism, far from being dogmatic, simply co-opts whatever present theory seems to go the farthest given the difficulties to be resolved. As a form of psychotherapeutic pragmatism, eclecticism is motivated by self-conscious ignorance; it essentially functions as a means of coping with complexity until better and more integrative schemas come along. Eclecticism, then, is a movement, not a theoretical orientation.

In the history of psychotherapy, the adherents of particular perspectives have often worn their devotion like religious disciples. Eclecticism, however, is more like agnosticism than faith or atheism. Both faith and atheism are dogmatic: They make decisions about an issue that is undecidable on empirical evidence alone, the existence of God (if God's existence or lack thereof was empirically demonstrable, either faith would not be required or atheism would be proven). In contrast, agnostics simply say that given their empirical experience thus far, they must reserve judgment. In fact, the most honestly ignorant agnostic (the most self-consistent kind) would probably not even go so far as to say that the existence of God is empirically undecidable, for fear of making a dogma of indecision; somehow one knows and knows *absolutely* such matters to be rationally out of bounds. Just as agnostics, then, can self-consistently make no prescriptions about what how their own beliefs will develop or what the beliefs of others should be, eclecticism cannot look to the future, but only report the past. Like pragmatism, eclecticism prescribes whatever works, and whatever works is "the truth." In the case of psychotherapy, this means recording those techniques that have proven efficacious thus far with certain types of persons. When eclecticism begins to exist as a self-conscious movement and sets up first principles, including "thou shall be an eclectic," it has made the transition to dogmatism and makes no more sense than an agnostic church. Eclecticism prescribes nothing.

TECHNICAL ECLECTICISM

Technical eclecticism holds that therapeutic procedures may be divorced from their generative theories and applied independently of them, without the need of either endorsing the theory or subjecting the theory to validation (e.g., Beutler & Clarkin, 1990; Lazarus, 1968, 1981). Only the efficacy of specific techniques need be justified. At the beginning of Chapter 4, we noted that, ideally, a clinical science should integrate theory, taxonomy, instrumentation, and intervention. Technical eclecticism is a laudable effort to move forward in the face of stubborn difficulties, not the least of which is the contentious climate of hundreds of therapies and the contextualism of the disorders themselves. By promising an independence of technique and theory, the problem of a large number of theories and therapies of human nature is bypassed completely.

However, an independence of theory and technique entails a clinical science that is specifically unintegrated. What would clinical science look like if the two were in fact entirely disjoint—if techniques were truly theory-free? Most importantly, there would be no scientific basis on which to choose a particular technique, only an empirical one. Deprived of the guidance of theory, clinical science would then be completely in bondage to methodology. Where empirical evidence did not exist to guide the therapist, there would be no more reason to decide between one technique and any other, for there would be no theory, however implicit, on which to base the decision or narrow the range of options. Those clients experiencing difficulties as yet unresearched would either be assigned to the experimental or control group or simply be dismissed from the office as possessing problems outside the scope of psychology in its current form. Psychotherapy research would consist exclusively of filling in the cells of a problems-by-techniques matrix with empirical findings (which would then be compulsively "refined" by repeated meta-analyses).

Just as philosophers of science recognize that there are no theory-neutral facts, similarly, we would argue that there are no theory- and therapy-neutral techniques, either in content or in application. Undoubtedly, those therapeutic techniques that have been derived from the propositions of a particular data domain will be most efficacious for problems anchored primarily in that domain; for example, the treatment of phobias from a behavioral perspective, or the use of cognitive techniques to reframe a client's distorted perceptions. However, the odds and ends of diverse schemas and perspectives no more form a theory than do several techniques, randomly chosen, form a therapy. Such a hodgepodge will lead only to illusory syntheses and interventions that cannot long hold together. Sechrest and Smith (1994, p. 2), for example, note that the addition of relaxation training to psychodynamic therapy "does not constitute integration unless relaxation itself has been integrated into psychodynamic theory as a construct and as an aim of therapy." Again, the problem is that different

perspectives on human nature come with different sets of assumptions. By virtue of its internal consistency, each set of assumptions carves out its own universe of discourse, the terms and propositions of which are not readily translatable into those of any other. Like theoretical constructs, each technique is embedded in a particular perspective, a preformed body of nomological relationships. To lift it out of that perspective is to dissociate it from the assumptive world from where it takes its meaning. If applied in another context, the technique must either be translated, or be applied meaninglessly, without regard to the antecedent conditions that might justify its use or the consequences that might follow.

Eclectic psychotherapy, of course, might be applied to any disorder. There are, however, positive reasons for preferring a more integrative approach specifically for the personality disorders, which go beyond the insufficiencies of eclecticism. Whereas eclecticism is motivated by the necessity of action in the face of insufficient knowledge, no such state exists with regard to the personality disorders, for the structural properties of personality are explicitly integrative and are specifically included in the definition of the construct itself. In a generic sense, these structural properties set up *ideal* forms of therapy, which we call potentiated pairings and catalytic sequences. These forms of therapy will be discussed toward the end of this chapter.

IDENTIFYING COMMON FACTORS

If development does proceed from the relatively global to the relatively differentiated, then perhaps it is possible to look for commonalities among the many differentiated schools as a means of identifying the core features that drive successful psychotherapy. This is a reasonable and honest point of beginning. Like Descartes, the common-factors approach seeks to jettison the entire corpus of accumulated conceptual heterogeneities and specificities, in order to discover some one or small number of fundamental truths from which to begin again with a firm foundation.

The problem with the common-factors approach, however, is that it is insufficiently theoretical; it is a necessary, but not sufficient, basis for a scientific psychotherapy. Even if these factors could be concretely and consensually defined across either theories of psychotherapy or even across very good therapists, merely identifying common factors does not explicate the underlying mechanisms that mediate their efficacy. Most readers probably know therapists whose clinical intuition is so incisive that they almost instinctively know exactly what to say and do in therapy, yet cannot fully explain the rational basis on which their actions are narrowed from an almost infinite constellation of possibilities. For these individuals, attempts to link explanatory schemas directly to intervention, what we would think of as the very substance of a scientific psychotherapy, may be experienced as counterproductive, in that they disrupt a graceful automaticity that the rest of us are still struggling to achieve. Nevertheless, that some psychotherapists are apparently "loaded" with common factors and are so good at what they do begs the questions "How do they do it?" and "Why does it work?", which bring the insufficiency of a common-factors approach into the foreground. As noted earlier, there are no theory-neutral observations; in this sense, the common-factors approach suffers the problems of any inductive methodology. Once regularities or patterns have been observed again and again, their existence is clear, but not why they exist, what creates them, or how they work. We might say that common factors are to psychotherapy what factor analysis is to personality.

The common-factors approach is useful, however, as a gauge by which to estimate the incremental efficacy achieved by theoretically integrative efforts. Because of their distilled quality, the common factors become a kind of lowest common denominator of psychotherapies. As such, they constitute the bare minimum of what good therapy should embody, but not the maximum of what it might achieve. If a "common-factors" therapy could be manualized, a useful point of reference would be created for outcome studies. Ideally, the waiting-list control group would show some or no improvement, the common-factors therapy group would show significant gains, and the integrative-therapy group would show the greatest gains. Nevertheless, the fact that technique seems to account for only a small portion of variance in outcome (about 15% of the improvement; Lambert, 1992), argues that, beyond merely jargonizing therapy, theory has yet to make a substantial contribution to its actual conduct.

There are other equally compelling reasons why technique and theory might make only small contributions to the success of therapy. Most clinicians are quite capable of grasping abstract principles of the various theoretical orientations. Most clinicians are also intuitively sensitive to what their patients need at the moment. However, especially where the theory is rich, clinicians may not be as good as integrating these two levels, such that their interventions are explicitly guided by and consonant with their avowed theoretical persuasion. All interpersonal interactions are highly contextualized, with communications taking place at many different levels. Psychotherapy is even more complex. Truly integrative therapy, where the therapist has one mind on the patient's communications, one mind on theory, and one mind on how his or her own presentation is being received, may require a level of integration between the declarative principles of theory and the almost instinctive procedural knowledge of human relations that is difficult to achieve.

INTEGRATIONISM: SYSTEMS PRINCIPLES

Unlike eclecticism, integration insists on the primacy of an overarching gestalt that gives coherence, provides an interactive framework, and creates an organic order among otherwise discrete units or elements. Each personality is a synthesized and substantive system whose distinctive meaning derives from that old chestnut: The whole is greater than the sum of its parts. Personality problems are an inextricably linked nexus of behaviors, cognitions, intrapsychic processes, and so on. They flow through a tangle of feedback loops and serially unfolding concatenations that emerge at different times in dynamic and changing configurations. Behavioral acts, self-image cognitions, defense mechanisms, indeed, each functional and structural domain, is contextualized by and interdigitated with all others so as to form a single organism. No one domain can be segregated out and made to stand on its own. Moreover, each component of these configurations has its role and significance altered by virtue of its place in these continually evolving constellations. In parallel form, so should integrative psychotherapy be conceived as a configuration of strategies and tactics in which each intervention technique is selected not only for its efficacy in resolving particular pathological features but also for its contribution to the overall constellation of treatment procedures of which it is but one.

In our view current debates regarding whether "technical eclecticism" (Lazarus, 1981) or "integrative therapy" (Arkowitz, 1992) is the more suitable designation for our approach are both mistaken. They have things backward, so to speak, because they start the task of intervention by focusing on methodology first. Integration does not inhere in treatment techniques or theories, be they eclectic or otherwise. Natural integration is in the person, not in modalities or tactics. It stems from the dynamics and interwoven character of the patient's traits and symptoms. Our task as therapists is not to see how we can blend discordant models of therapeutic techniques, but to match the integrative pattern that characterizes each patient, and *then* to select treatment goals and tactics that mirror this pattern optimally. It is for this reason, among others, that we have chosen to employ the label "persondogic therapy" to represent our brand of integrative treatment.

Integration is an important concept in considering not only the psychotherapy of the individual case but also the role of psychotherapy in clinical science. For the treatment of a particular client to be integrated, the elements of a clinical science should be integrated as well. One of the arguments advanced earlier against a radical technical eclecticism is that it further and explicitly insulates psychotherapy from clinical science. In contrast to eclecticism, wherein techniques are justified methodologically, all integrative treatment takes place in the context of some theory of human nature. All so-called grand theories are inviting because they attempt to explain the totality of human behavior, so that a psychotherapy seems to grow naturally out of the theory. In technical eclecticism, however, theory is actively dissociated from technique. In the common-factors approach, theory is ostensibly eliminated by aggregating across various psychotherapies. Although we may have our doubts about whether the various grand theories in fact fulfill their promise, they nevertheless stand as an ideal that integrates theory, taxonomy, assessment, and intervention.

What exactly do we mean when we say that therapy must be integrated and must be grounded in a logical and coordinated theory (Arkowitz, 1992; Millon, 1988)? Unfortunately, much of what travels under the eclectic or integrative banner sounds like the talk of a "goody goody"—a desire to be nice to all sides, and to say that everybody is right. These labels have become platitudinous buzzwords, philosophies with which open-minded people certainly would wish to ally themselves. But, integrative theory and psychotherapy must signify more than that (Beutler & Clarkin, 1990; Norcross & Goldfried, 1992; Stricker & Gold, 1993).

First, it is *not* eclecticism. Perhaps it might be considered *posteclecticism,* if we may borrow a notion used to characterize modern art just a century ago. Eclecticism is not a matter of choice. We all must be eclectics, engaging in differential (Frances, Clarkin, & Perry, 1984) and multimodal (Lazarus, 1981) therapeutics, selecting the techniques that are empirically the most efficacious for the problems at hand (Beutler & Clarkin, 1990). Moreover, integration is more than the coexistence of two or three previously discordant orientations or techniques. We cannot simply piece together the odds and ends of several theoretical schemas, each internally consistent and oriented to different data domains. As stated, such a hodgepodge will lead only to illusory syntheses that cannot long hold together. Efforts such as these, meritorious as they may be in some regards, represent the work of peacemakers, not innovators and not integrationists. Integration is eclectic, of course, but more. It is a synthesized and substantive system.

The personality problems that our patients bring to us are an inextricably linked nexus of behaviors, cognitions, intrapsychic processes, and so on. As described previously, they flow through a tangle of feedback loops and serially unfolding concatenations that emerge at different times in dynamic and changing configurations. To restate matters, each component of these configurations has its role altered by virtue of its place in these evolving constellations. In a similar manner, integrative psychotherapy should be seen as a configuration of strategies and tactics in which each intervention technique is selected for its efficacy in resolving particular pathological conditions and also for its contribution to the overall pattern of treatment procedures *of which it is but one.*

Whether we work with "part functions" that focus on behaviors, or cognitions, or unconscious processes, or biological defects, and the like, *or* whether we address contextual systems that focus on the larger environment, the family, or the group, or the socioeconomic and political conditions of life, the crossover point, the place that links parts to contexts, is the person. The individual is the intersecting medium that brings them together.

But persons are more than just crossover mediums. As noted in prior pages, they are the only organically integrated system in the psychological domain, inherently created from birth as natural entities, rather than experience-derived gestalts, constructed through cognitive attribution. Moreover, it is persons who lie at the heart of the psychotherapeutic experience, the substantive beings who give meaning and coherence to symptoms and traits—be they behaviors, affects, or mechanisms—as well as those beings, those singular entities, who give life and expression to family interactions and social processes.

It is our contention that integrative therapists should take cognizance of the person from the start, for the parts and the contexts take on different meanings, and call for different interventions in terms of the person to whom they are anchored. To focus on one social structure or one psychic form of expression, without understanding its undergirding or reference base is to engage in potentially misguided, if not random, therapeutic techniques.

It may be useful to record a major shift in medical thinking that parallels what we have been saying. It highlights the fact that modern-day health providers no longer focus on symptoms—as they did a century ago—nor do they focus on intruding infectious agents—as they did a decade or two ago—but have turned their attention to the structure and mechanisms of the immune system.

The concentric circles in Figure 5.1 are designed to represent changes that have evolved in medicine over the past century; they mirror, as well, shifts that must advance more rapidly in our thinking about psychopathology and psychotherapy. In the center of the figure, we find (to use DSM terms) Axis I, the so-called clinical syndromes, (e.g., depression, anxiety). The parallel to Axis I in physical disorders characterizes where medicine was 100 and more years ago; in

the early and mid-19th century, physicians defined their patients' ailments in terms of manifest symptomatology—their sneezes and coughs and boils and fevers, labeling "diseases" with terms such as consumption and smallpox. Shifting to the outer ring of Figure 5.1, that paralleling Axis IV of the DSM, the related medical focus, uncovered approximately 100 years ago, was that illness should no longer be conceived only in terms of overt symptomatology, but with reference to minute microbes that intruded upon and disrupted the body's normal functions; in time, medicine began to assign diagnostic names that reflected ostensive etiologies—such as infectious sources (e.g., dementia paralytica was relabeled neurosyphilis).

Psychopathology has progressed in making this shift from symptom to cause all too slowly. We still focus on what can be done about "dysthymia" or "anxiety," giving our prime attention to the surface symptoms that constitute the syndromes of Axis I. Among those who consider themselves to be sophisticated about such matters, there is recognition that dysthymia and anxiety are merely a psychic response to life's early or current stressors, such as those that comprise the DSM-IV's Axis IV—marital problems, child abuse, and the like—psychic intruders, if you will, that parallel the infectious microbes of a century ago.

But medicine has progressed in the past decade or two beyond its turn-of-the-century "intrusion disease" model, an advance most striking these past 15 years owing to the tragedy of the AIDS epidemic. This progression reflects a growing awareness of the key role of the immune system, the body's intrinsic capacity to contend with the omnipresent multitude of potentially destructive infectious and carcinogenic agents that pervade our physical environment. What medicine has learned is that it is not the symptoms (the sneezes and coughs) and not the intruding infections (the viruses and bacteria) that are the key to health or illness. Rather, the ultimate determinant is the competence and the vulnerability of the immune system. So too, in psychopathology, it is not anxiety or dysthymia, nor the stressors of early childhood or contemporary life that are the key to psychic well-being. Rather, it is the mind's equivalent of the body's immune system—that structure and style of psychic processes that represents our overall capacity to perceive and to cope with our psychosocial world—in other words, the psychological construct we describe as "personality." We have begun to catch up with medicine this past decade, to turn our attentions from symptoms and stressors

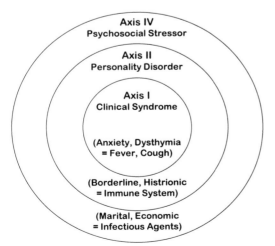

Figure 5.1   Interactive nature of the multiaxial system.

toward "persons," and the psychic structures and styles that signify their vulnerabilities and disordered character.

Simply to make a platitudinous announcement that personality disorders constitute an integrative construct, however, or that it is the natural parallel and setting for integrative therapies, is not enough. So too might it be merely sententious to speak of an "integrative theory." In building a science of psychopathology, we must seek to discover the essential principles about which a subtantive personology and corresponding integrative theory can be organized.

A THEORETICAL BASIS FOR INTEGRATIVE THERAPY

Before proceeding, however, we would like to make some comments in favor of the utility of theory. Kurt Lewin (1936) wrote some 60 years ago, "There is nothing so practical as a good theory." Theory, when properly fashioned, ultimately provides more simplicity and clarity than unintegrated and scattered information. Unrelated knowledge and techniques, especially those based on surface similarities, are a sign of a primitive science, as has been effectively argued by contemporary philosophers of science (Hempel, 1961; Quine, 1961).

All natural sciences have organizing principles that not only create order but also provide the basis for generating hypotheses and stimulating new knowledge. A good theory not only summarizes and incorporates extant knowledge, but is heuristic, that is, has "systematic import," as Hempel has phrased it, in that it originates and develops new observations and new methods. As we have seen over the past century, both learning and analytic theories have generated new therapeutic techniques of considerable power and utility, for example, the behavior methods of desensitization and skill acquisition, as well as the psychodynamic methods of free association and dream analysis.

We do not as yet have a unifying theory for all human behavior and psychotherapy. In the interim, however, we can generate fruitful microtheories that may encompass and give coherence to many of the facets that make up our subject domain. It is toward that end that an effort has been made to develop an integrative or unified microtheory of the personality disorders (Millon, 1969, 1981, 1986a, 1990), disorders that are

themselves exemplar integrative constructs in the larger domain of psychopathology.

The "theorizing" that characterized the field in the 1940s and 1950s failed to fulfill its promise, resulting in few unifying proposals. The confidence that integrative schemas in realms such as personality and psychotherapy could be fashioned by the convergence of a few basic psychological variables gave way as a feasible aspiration by the 1960s. A hesitant conservatism, either antitheoretical or proempirical in character, gained sway, illustrated in the field of personality by the growth of what was referred to as the anticonsistency and anticoherency movements (Millon, 1990). Fortunately, the integrative mind-set has been reemerging in the form of tentative proposals of an ecumenical nature that seek to bridge diverse psychological methods and processes. The dislodging of behavioral concretism, the rebirth of cognitive science, and the growth of therapeutic eclecticism illustrate this encouraging shift.

It is necessary, however, to go beyond current conceptual boundaries, more specifically to explore carefully reasoned, as well as intuitive hypotheses that draw their principles, if not their substance, from more established, adjacent sciences. Not only may such steps bear new conceptual fruits, but they may provide a foundation that can undergird and guide our own discipline's explorations. As discussed in prior chapters, much of personology, no less psychology as a whole, remains adrift, divorced from broader spheres of scientific knowledge, isolated from firmly grounded, if not universal principles, leading us to continue building the patchwork quilt of concepts and data domains that characterize the field. Preoccupied with but a small part of the larger puzzle, or fearing accusations of reductionism, many fail thereby to draw on the rich possibilities to be found in other realms of scholarly pursuit. With few exceptions, cohering concepts that would connect personology to those of its sister sciences have not been developed.

We seem preoccupied by horizontal refinements. A search for integrative schemas and cohesive constructs that link its seekers closely to relevant observations and laws developed in more advanced fields is needed. The goal—albeit perhaps a rather grandiose one—is to refashion the patchwork quilt into a well-tailored and aesthetic tapestry that interweaves the diverse forms in which nature expresses itself.

And what better sphere is there within the psychological sciences to undertake such syntheses than with the subject matter of personology? As noted in prior chapters, persons are the only integrated system in the psychological domain, evolved through the millennia as natural entities. The intrinsic cohesion of persons is not merely a rhetorical construction, but an authentic substantive unity. Whereas personologic features may often be dissonant, and may be partitioned conceptually for pragmatic or scientific purposes, they are nonetheless segments of an inseparable biopsychosocial entity.

To take this view is not to argue that different spheres of scientific inquiry should be equated, nor is it to seek a single, overarching conceptual system encompassing biology, psychology, and sociology (Millon, 1990). Arguing in favor of establishing explicit links between these domains calls neither for a reductionistic philosophy, a belief in substantive identicality, or efforts to so fashion them by formal logic. Rather, the researcher should aspire to their substantive concordance, empirical consistency, conceptual interfacing, convergent dialogues, and mutual enlightenment.

Integrative consonance is not an aspiration limited to ostensibly diverse sciences, but is a worthy goal within the domains of each science. To restate matters, relevant in this regard are efforts that seek to coordinate the often separate realms of a clinical science, namely, its theories, the classification system it formulated, the diagnostic tools it employs, and the therapeutic techniques it implements. Rather than developing independently and being left to stand as autonomous and largely unconnected functions, a truly mature clinical science should embody explanatory and heuristic conceptual schemas that are consistent with established knowledge in both its own and related sciences. From these sources, reasonably accurate propositions concerning pathological conditions can be both deduced and understood, enabling thereby the development of a formal taxonomic classification of disorders derived logically *from the theory*. In turn, this formal organization will permit the development of coordinated assessment instruments that are empirically grounded and sufficiently sensitive quantitatively to enable the theory's propositions and hypotheses to be adequately investigated and evaluated. In such a framework, the categories that make up the nosology should be readily identifiable and measurable, thus making target areas for treatment interventions apparent.

When translated into psychological terms, a theory of psychopathology should be able to generate answers to a number of key questions. For example,

how do its essential constructs interrelate and combine to form specific personality disorders? And, if it is to meet the criteria of an integrative or unifying schema, can it derive all the personality disorders with the same set of constructs (i.e., not employ one set of explanatory concepts for borderline personalities, another for schizoids, a third for compulsives, etc.)? One of the great appeals of early analytic theory was its ability to explain several "character types" from a single developmental model of psychosexual stages. Can the same be said for other, more encompassing theories? Moreover, can these theories provide a structure and serve as a guide for planning psychotherapy with the personality disorders?

PERSONOLOGIC THERAPY

A historic and still frequently voiced complaint about diagnosis, be it based or not on the official classification system, is its lack of utility for therapeutic purposes. Most therapists, whatever their orientation or mode of treatment, pay minimal attention to the possibility that diagnosis can inform the philosophy and technique they employ. It matters little what the syndrome or disorder may be, a family therapist is likely to select and employ a variant of family therapy, a cognitively oriented therapist will find that a cognitive approach will probably "work best," and so on, including integrative therapists who are beginning to become a "school" and join this unfortunate trend of asserting the "truth" that their approach is the most efficacious.

Do we think that there is some truth to the integrative faith, that is, that there is a class of disorders for whom the logic of the integrative mind-set is the optimal, if not the most efficacious therapeutic choice?

Although the approach that has come to be called integrative therapy has its applications to a variety of diverse clinical conditions (e.g., Norcross & Goldfried, 1992)—a view I wholeheartedly endorse—we will seek in this chapter to outline some reasons why personality disorders *may* be that segment of psychopathology for which integrative psychotherapy is ideally and distinctively suited—in the same sense that behavioral techniques appear most efficacious in the modification of problematic actions, cognitive methods optimal for reframing phenomenological distortions, and intrapsychic techniques especially apt in resolving unconscious processes.

The cohesion (or lack thereof) of complexly interwoven psychic structures and functions is what distinguishes the disorders of personality from other clinical syndromes; likewise, the orchestration of diverse, yet synthesized techniques of intervention is what differentiates integrative from other variants of psychotherapy. These two, parallel constructs, emerging from different traditions and conceived in different venues, reflect shared philosophical perspectives, one oriented toward the understanding of psychopathology, the other toward effecting its remediation. It is not that integrative psychotherapies are inapplicable to more focal pathologies, but rather that these therapies are *required* for the personality disorders (whereas depression may successfully be treated either cognitively or pharmacologically); it is the very interwoven nature of the components of personality disorders that makes a multifaceted and synthesized approach a necessity.

In the following pages, we will present a few ideas in sequence. First, that integrative therapies require a foundation in a coordinated theory; they must be more than a schema of eclectic techniques, a hodgepodge of diverse alternatives assembled de novo with each case. Second, although the diagnostic criteria for DSM syndromes are a decent first step, they must be comprehensive and comparable through systematic revision, so as to be genuinely useful for treatment planning. Third, a logical rationale can be formulated as to how the clinician can and should integrate diversely focused therapies when treating the personality disorders.

Before turning to these themes, we would like to comment briefly on some philosophical issues. They bear on a rationale for developing theory-based treatment techniques, that is, methods that transcend the merely empirical (e.g., electroconvulsive therapy for depressives). It is our conviction that the theoretical foundations of our science must be further advanced if we are to succeed in constructing an integrative approach to psychotherapy.

As we have stated in this and previous chapters, we believe that four features signify and characterize mature clinical sciences:

1. They embody conceptual theories from which propositional deductions can be derived.

2. These theories should lead to the development of coherent taxonomies that characterize the central features of their subject domain (in our case, that of personality and its disorders, the substantive realm within which scientific and psychotherapeutic techniques are applied).

3. These sciences possess a variety of empirically oriented instruments with which they can identify and quantify the concepts that comprise their theories (in the personality disorders, methods that uncover developmental history and furnish cross-sectional assessments).

4. In addition to theory, nosology, and diagnostic tools, mature clinically oriented sciences possess change-oriented intervention techniques that are therapeutically optimal in modifying the pathological elements of their domain.

Most current therapeutic schools share a common failure to coordinate these four components of an applied science. What differentiates them has more to do with the fact that they attend to different levels of data in the natural world. It is to the credit of those of an eclectic persuasion that they have recognized, albeit in a fuzzy way, the arbitrary if not illogical character of such contentions, as well as the need to bridge schisms that have been constructed less by philosophical considerations or pragmatic goals than by the accidents of history. There are numerous other knotty issues with which psychopathology and integrative therapy must contend (e.g., differing worldviews concerning the essential nature of psychological experience). There is no problem, as we see it, in encouraging active dialectics among these contenders—although we personally hold to an "organismic" or "synthetic" view of nature's phenomena.

Let us turn to issues more substantively relevant to the concerns of this chapter—not that we wish to obviate philosophical matters; they are often more fundamental to the problems we face than matters of ostensibly direct or palpable psychological significance.

In Chapter 1, we noted that the concept of a *system* is a useful metaphor for personality. Systems function as a whole, but are composed of parts. In Chapter 4, we partitioned personality pedagogically into *eight structural* and *functional* domains. These domains are not themselves the parts of personality, but they do serve as a means of classifying the parts or constructs of personality in accord with the *four data levels* (e.g., biophysical, phenomenological) that represent traditional approaches to clinical science. In every individual, elements from each of these domains constrain what can exist elsewhere in other domains of the system. An individual born with a phlegmatic temperament, for example, is unlikely to mature into a histrionic adult. An individual whose primary defensive mechanism is intellectualization is more likely to mature into a schizoid than an antisocial. The nature and intensity of the constraints in each of these domains limit the potential number of states that the system can assume at any moment in time; this configuration of constraints *is* individuality.

Such complex and dynamic interdependency is cause for both optimism and pessimism in the psychotherapy of personality disorders. Optimistically, the interdependency of system structures and functions means that any point in the system, any functional or structural domain, can become the object of therapeutic efforts and actually achieve results. Cognitive, behavioral, psychodynamic, and interpersonal approaches are all likely to demonstrate some level of efficacy with the personality disorders over waiting-list control groups. Even though consistently channeled through a particular therapeutic bias and directed at a particular data level, some interventions will in fact gather enough momentum to eventually change much of the entire personality. More often, however, the personality will be most changed only at that particular focus. In cases where the whole personality is largely reconfigured, it is not the intervention per se that produces the change, but a synergistic interaction between a fairly focal intervention and the personologic context in which that intervention takes place. Such changes occur, but they are more often serendipitous than planned, so that the interdependent nature of the organism compensates for an inadequacy of therapeutic scope. The capacity of a system to spread the effect of any input throughout its entire infrastructure is likely to be a principal reason why no major school of therapy (i.e., behavioral, cognitive, psychodynamic, interpersonal) has yet been able to consistently demonstrate an intrinsic superiority across all disorders.

Pessimistically speaking, however, it must be remembered that the primary function of any system is homeostasis. In Chapter 1, personality was likened to an immune system for the psyche, such that stability, constancy, or internal equilibrium, are the "goals" of personality. Obviously, these are directly contrary to the explicit goal of therapy, which is change. Usually, the dialogue between client and therapist is not so directly confrontational that it is experienced as particularly threatening. In these cases, the personality system functions for the client as a form of passive resistance, albeit one that may be experienced as a positive force (or trait) by the therapist. In fact, the schematic nature of self-image and object representations is so preemptive and confirmation-seeking that the true meaning of the therapist's comments may never reach the level of conscious processing. Alternately, even if a client's equilibrium is initially upended by a particular interpretation, his or her defensive mechanisms may kick in to ensure that the therapist's comment is somehow distorted, misunderstood, interpreted in a less threatening manner, or even ignored. The first is a passive form of resistance; the second an active form. No wonder then, that effective therapy is often considered anxiety provoking, for it is in situations where the patient really has no effective response, where the functioning of the immune system is temporarily suppressed, that the scope of his or her response repertoire is most likely to be broadened. Personality "goes with what it knows," and it is with the "unknown" where learning is most possible. Arguing essentially the same point, Kiesler (1966) states that the therapist is obliged to make the "asocial" response, one other than that which the client is specifically trying to evoke.

If personality is regarded as a system, then the question becomes: How can the characteristics that define systems be co-opted to facilitate rather than retard transactive change? A coordinated schema of treatment strategies and methods that seek to accomplish these ends is what we have labeled "personologic psychotherapy." Through various coordinated approaches that mirror the system-based structure and style of personality disorders, an effort is made to select what may be termed session-focused tactics designed to fulfill the long-term, strategic goals of treatment.

Session-Focused Tactics.   A first principle is that each session of therapy should be focused; here we are referring to what actually is planned to happen in each therapy period. The efficacy of these tactics can be understood through an analogy with physical force. Whereas 10 pounds of force is insignificant when distributed over an area of several feet, if those same 10 pounds are applied at a pinpoint, the point underneath the pin experiences a force equal to several tons per square foot. To personalize the analogy, imagine that a friend places both hands on your shoulders and pushes back with 10 pounds of force, 5 pounds for each hand. You will easily be able to resist by leaning forward a little. Now imagine that your friend comes at you with a long hypodermic needle, bearing the same 10 pounds of force. The outcome is easily visualized. Unless you take some action, the needle will soon be buried up the hilt. With diffusion applied, you can easily resist 10 pounds of force by essentially passive measures, merely using your own weight. When applied at a pinpoint, however, the same 10 pounds is enough to motivate the fight-flight system of an organism.

Focus or tactical specificity works essentially the same way in psychotherapy. If interventions are unfocused, rambling, and diffuse, the patient will merely "lean forward a little," passively resisting change by using his or her own "weight," that is, habitual characteristics already intrinsic to the system. Although creating rapport is always important, nothing happens unless the system is eventually "shook up" in some way. Therapists should not always be toiling to expose their patient's defenses, but sooner or later, something must happen that cannot be readily fielded by habitual processes—something that often will be experienced as uncomfortable or even threatening.

In fact, personality change is probably more like a "punctuated equilibrium" than a slow and continuous process. The systems model argues for periods of rapid growth during which the personality system reconfigures itself in a new gestalt, alternating with periods of relative constancy. The purpose of tactical focus or specificity, knowing what you are doing and why you are doing it, is to keep the whole of psychotherapy from being diffused. The systems model runs counter to the deterministic universe-as-machine model of the late 19th century, which features slow but incremental gains. In the systems model, diffuse interventions are experienced simply as another input to be discharged homeostatically, producing zero change. In the machine model, in which conservation laws play a prominent role, diffuse interventions produce small increments of change, with the promise that therapeutic goals will be reached given enough time and effort. In contrast, in the systems model, therapeutic goals may never be reached, unless something is done which has genuine transactive potential. This potential is optimized through what are called potentiated pairings and catalytic sequences, discussed a bit later in the chapter.

Tactical specificity is also required because of the level of analysis at which therapy usually is practiced. Most often, the in-session dialogue between patient and therapist is dominated by a discussion of specific behaviors, feelings, and events, *not* by traits or diagnostic syndromes. When the latter are discussed, they are usually discussed through more specific behaviors, feelings, and events. When traits or diagnostic syndromes become the focus of discussion, they are usually perceived by the patient as an ego-alien intrusive force or lesion that must be removed by a professional, against which the client's efforts will be futile. The statement "I have a bad personality" presents the person as a vessel filled by some noxious substance. The professional is expected to empty and refill the vessel with something more desirable; the patient relinquishes control and responsibility and simply waits passively for the therapist to perform some mystical ritual, one of the worst assumptive sets in which to begin psychotherapy. Whatever the physical substates and dynamic forces involved in creating and sustaining particular traits, terms are evoked as inferences from particular constituent behaviors. Negative trait attributions should be broken down into smaller units of analysis. Behavior can be changed; traits have a more permanent connotation.

Viewing traits in this way is beneficial to both patient and the therapist. Knowing what behaviors are descriptively linked to particular traits helps clients understand how others perceive them, and that these behaviors should not be repeated. Additionally, if patients are led to understand that their personalities are, or are derived from, their behaviors, there is hope because behavior is more easily controlled and changed than is a diagnosis, especially a personality disorder diagnosis, which is by definition pervasive, enduring, and not easily treated even with medication. In this sense, the paradigm itself is the enemy. There is, after all, a difference between what is practically impossible because it is at the limits of one's endurance or ability, and what is logically impossible. With support and courage, human beings can be coaxed into transcending their limitations, into doing what was before considered practically impossible. No one, however, can do what is logically impossible. When personality disorders are framed through the medical model, personality change *is* paradigmatically impossible. Individuals who see themselves as vessels for a diseased personality should be disabused of this notion.

For the therapist, operationalizing traits as clusters of behavioral acts or cognitive expectancies can be especially beneficial in selecting tactical modalities. First, some behaviors are linked to multiple traits, and some of these traits are more desirable than others, so that some play exists in the interpretation or spin put on any particular behavior at the trait level. This play can be exploited by the therapist to reframe patient attributions about self and others in more positive ways. The avoidant's social withdrawal can be seen as having enough pride in oneself to leave a humiliating situation. The dependent's clinging to a significant other can be seen as having the strength to devote oneself to another's care. Of course, these reframes will not be sufficient in and of themselves to produce change. They do, however, seek a bond with the patient by way of making positive attributions, and thereby raising self-esteem, while simultaneously working to disconfirm or make the client reexamine other beliefs that lower esteem and function to keep the person closed off from trying on new roles and behaviors.

Second, understanding traits as clusters of behaviors and/or cognitions is just as beneficial for the therapist as for the patient when it comes to overturning the medical model of personality pathology and replacing it with a systems model. One of the problems of personality disorder patients is that their range of attributions and perceptions is too narrow to characterize the richness that in fact exists in their social environment. As a result, they end up perpetuating old problems by interpreting even innocuous behaviors and events as noxious. Modern therapists have a similar problem, in that the range of paradigms they have to bring to their personality disorder patients is too narrow to describe the rich set of possibilities that exist for every individual. The belief that personality pathologies are medical diseases, monolithically fixed and beyond remediation, should itself be viewed as a form of paradigmatic pathology, almost sufficient in and of itself to evoke self-defeating countertransference responses to personality disorder patients, and one hopefully to be remedied by supervision or self-correction.

Long-Term Strategies. "Tactics" and "strategies" keep in balance the two conceptual ingredients of therapy, the first refers to what goes on in a particular session with a particular intervention, whereas the second refers to the overall plan or design that characterizes the entire course of therapy. Both are required. Tactical specificity without strategic objectives implies doing without knowing why in the big picture, whereas objectives without specificity implies knowing where to go, but having no way to get there. Obviously, one uses short-term modality tactics to accomplish higher level strategies or goals over the long term.

Psychotherapies seem to vary on the amounts of tactical specificity and strategic objectives they

prefer. Often, this is not merely an accident of history, but can rather be tied back to paradigmatic assumptions latent in the therapies themselves as a product of the times. Historically, the progression seems to be in the direction of both greater specificity and clearer goals. More modern approaches to psychotherapy, such as cognitive-behavioral, put into place highly detailed elements (e.g., agreed-on goals, termination criteria, and ongoing assessments) through which therapy itself becomes a self-regulating system. Ongoing assessments ensure the existence of a feedback process that is open to inspection and negotiation by both therapist and patient. The expectancy is one of action rather than talk. Talk is viewed as incapable of realizing possibilities in and of itself, but is merely a prerequisite for action, used to reframe unfortunate circumstances so that obstacles to action are removed or minimized. Action is more transactive than talk, and therapy is forward-looking and concentrates on realizing present possibilities as a means of creating or opening up new ones. The organism is changed more through action than by unraveling the problems of the past. Insight is not necessary for change.

In the next section, we consider two extremes of strategic structure and tactical specificity; first, unstructured and nonspecific, as exemplified in classic psychoanalytic therapy, and hyperstructured and hyperspecific, as exemplified in the traditional outcome study. We argue that for therapy to be effective, it should be structured and specific enough that something gets done in a planful way, but not so structured and specific that what gets done is set in stone, regardless of the needs and characteristics of the patient. The best psychotherapy should be adaptable over time.

Some Illustrations.   In classical psychoanalytic therapy, the therapist plays the part of a passive observer who requires that the patient report the contents of consciousness as an ongoing stream of associations. These associations are different from person to person, and the question the therapist asks is: "Why these particular associations rather than others?" The analyst's interpretations are relatively sparse, lest these somehow contaminate the stream and lead the analyst astray.

The worldview (Pepper, 1942) latent in the classical analytic drive model is mechanism, which flourished up until the late 19th century. Whatever else Freud was, he was embedded in the times, and the drive or "pressure cooker" model was created to be consonant with the prevailing biological determinism. Mechanism is concerned with inter-actions. In an interaction, the participants are like billiard balls. Although they may career off each other at different positions in space and head off in different directions, they nevertheless remain billiard balls. If one knows the precise position of the balls and their velocities, then all past and future configurations can be calculated with certainty. Thus time is unimportant, a medium in which the inevitabilities implied by the initial conditions are played out. The whole is equal to the sum of its parts, and nothing is ever really new. Mechanism proscribes change.

How does the practice of psychotherapy in Freud's drive model square with the mechanistic paradigm? One of the limitations of mechanism is stated in the uncertainty principle. In quantum theory, this principle states that it is impossible to determine both the position and momentum of a particle simultaneously. When generalized to other scientific domains, the essence of the principle states simply that the act of measurement itself requires some kind of interaction between the measuring device and the thing measured. This in turn changes the thing measured in some unpredictable way, making absolute and complete knowledge of all its dimensions impossible. If you have ever reached for something, only to have the clumsiness of your own hand push it out of your reach, then you have experienced a frustrating existential analogue to the uncertainty principle. In psychological assessment and therapy, this means not only that the validity of psychological tests are compromised when those tests are given too close together (the organism is changed in that a memory of the experience is created), but more importantly that the very procedure of assessment or the very act of making contact with a professional may be ameliorative of some psychological problems and symptoms.

To minimize the effects of the uncertainty principle, the dyad between patient and therapist had to be dissolved insofar as possible. Only then could the therapist learn as much as possible about the inner workings of the patient as a machine while holding his or her own input to a minimum. The therapist-patient dyad was "neutralized" as a means of gaining experimental control with a single subject. Without such control, the therapist would be transacting with the patient, aiming at a moving target. Not knowing the current configurational state of the personality system with certainty (if the present is known, past and future can be calculated), the therapist's extrapolations backward into

the patient's childhood would lose their precision and validity. If therapy were not to be self-confounding, the therapist would need to sit in a chair behind the couch, not even within the patient's view, making only occasional comments and inquiries, and waiting until fairly certain of the latent pathology to announce these. Because the past determines the future in mechanism, the emphasis was on freeing the patient from problems created in childhood, on "making the unconscious conscious."

Interestingly, the practice of classical psychoanalysis may be viewed as sending a paradoxical message to patients. Without an active therapist with which to transact, the client must become the moment force of his or her own salvation, so that if change occurs at all, it occurs through some process of self-transcendence. Yet, change is epiphenomenal in mechanism; past and future are both determined. Ironically, the kind of change required by the methodology was itself proscribed by the mechanistic paradigm in which the classical economic view was embedded. One of the goals of this chapter is to prevent double binds between theory and therapy by thinking through the relevance of implications latent in the construct of personality for the psychotherapy of personality disorders.

The distinction between interaction and transaction does in fact prescribe to the practice of psychotherapy. Because the goal of personality therapy is personality change, patient and therapist cannot be satisfied merely to interact like billiard balls and emerge from therapy unchanged. Instead, we must invent modes of therapy that maximize the transactive potential of the therapeutic dyad. Because of its lack of structure and feedback, traditional insight-oriented psychotherapy may be schematized as in Figure 5.2. The starting point is at the center, with termination somewhere at the periphery, at a point unknown to both therapist and patient (an agreed-on point of termination would provide a constraint on the projective process). Diverging arrows indicate that therapy can potentially take any direction at any time. There is no overall structure, and no feedback process whereby therapist and patient might collaboratively seek goals. As a result, therapy may wander around essentially indefinitely, without ever reaching termination. In fact, since patient and therapist have not previously determined what constitutes success, it is not inconceivable that an appropriate point of termination might be reached without either the therapist or client ever realizing it, only for new issues to be raised and the process to begin again.

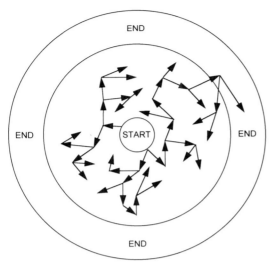

Figure 5.2   The course of traditional, unstructured, long-term psychodynamic therapy.

Opposite traditional insight-oriented psychotherapy on a continuum of structure is the traditional therapy outcome study, schematized in Figure 5.3. Here, a group of individuals with some pathology is corralled and administered a particular intervention. In the better designed studies, the exact nature of intervention is even specified in great detail, rather than being merely listed as cognitive, behavioral, and so on. The end point of therapy may be clearly defined as consisting of a fixed number of sessions, after which the dependent variables of the study are again assessed and compared.

Although this design at least has the virtue of direction and specificity, it contains one important failing—it completely lacks ecological validity. Real therapy simply isn't like this. The design implicitly assumes that the experimental and control groups are homogeneous with respect to their pathologies, that is, that patients are therapeutically interchangeable. The possibility that some combination of interventions might prove

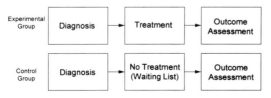

Figure 5.3   Totally structured traditional psychotherapy outcome study.

synergistic if tailored to the individual patient is neglected. For this kind of design to make a valuable contribution to psychotherapy research, the latent pathology or disease process "present" in each patient would need to so dominate, coerce, or canalize other variables into a characteristic expression during the development of the disease that its interaction with premorbid individual differences could be almost completely neglected. Only then could every client be treated in the same way.

ASSESSMENT FOR TREATMENT PLANNING

Neither unstructured, as done in the classical psychodynamic setting, nor completely structured therapy, as done in the traditional outcome design, is appropriate for the personality disorders. The unstructured approach is not incisive enough to penetrate personality in its immunological role. Therapy may drag on incessantly, without ever coming to termination, and without ever producing any real change. The totally structured approach assumes clients to be practically interchangeable, and minimizes the substantive role of individual differences in the planning and course of therapy.

If therapy and theory are to be part of a single integrated clinical science, then diagnoses should in fact prescribe certain forms of intervention, based on theory. In an atheoretical empirical classification, such as the DSM-IV, where diagnostic syndromes are inductive summaries of observations, rather than validated latent taxa, the linkage between theory and therapy will probably be weak. Recall the distinction between manifest and latent similarity observed in Chapter 1. Taxons formed on the basis of overt similarities alone, that is, by inductive methods, risk classifying together individuals who look alike, but whose pathologies are actually radically different in terms of their underlying pathological process. In turn, these latent heterogeneities frustrate outcome research, if only because the statistics that evaluate efficacy aggregate over individuals who do not form a homogeneous group, thus muddying up the design and affecting the magnitude of the statistical error term in unpredictable ways. In Chapter 1, we noted that since a manifest level is by definition all that is ever available to study, it is impossible to know with certainty the extent to which the manifest taxa of DSM-IV in fact classify ostensibly similar, but pathologically different, groups of individuals together. No outcome study classifying psychotically depressed individuals and schizophrenics as a single group would be acceptable today. Exclusionary criteria are used to make a distinction that might not otherwise be made given the salience of psychotic thinking. How often we fail to make distinctions that future DSMs will someday observe can only be known in time. We can say however that to the extent that manifest taxa, as inductive summaries, not only draw diagnostic boundaries with imprecision, but also lump together distinct pathological processes that should in fact be separated, the yield of outcome research will be disappointing.

Although the fit between the manifest and latent situation is difficult to determine for any one diagnostic syndrome (e.g., schizophrenia), much less for an entire taxonomy, a number of considerations argue that the inductive summaries of the DSM-IV are not a faithful mirror of nature's intrinsic structure. One theme that has been stressed throughout the introductory chapters of this text is that theory, taxonomy, assessment, and intervention are the four domains of an integrated clinical science. We know that interventions based on specified theoretical principles are the ideal of therapy. The fact that a movement such as technical eclecticism, which explicitly advocates the disjoining of therapy and theory, can find such a wide readership, argues that the current taxonomy has been constructed too much on the basis of clinical observation, and not enough on the basis of clinical theory. Efforts to construct taxonomies on more rigorously inductive grounds (e.g., factor analysis or cluster analysis) have not proven fruitful either.

Even in situations where the taxonicity of a diagnostic syndrome has been validated, however, the one-disease, one-therapy model leaves something to be desired. Taxonicity itself may be thought of as lying on a continuum. Where taxonicity is weak, the power of a latent pathological process to constrain or mold other variables into some characteristic expression is similarly weak, so that individual differences dominate the symptom picture. Where taxonicity is strong, however, the latent pathological process overrides individual differences, so all class members come to resemble each other in the expression of the pathology. In weak taxonic situations, the initial or premorbid conditions influence the course of the illness. In strong taxonic situations, this influence is not nearly as strong. Thus, premorbid individual differences interact with latent pathological processes to produce degrees of heterogeneity even in situations where taxonicity has been validated. Heterogeneity need not be

approached as an epistemic problem, the product of our ignorance of some underlying set of categories, which when uncovered, will lead to diagnostic classes that "carve nature at its joints" with discrete boundaries. Instead, heterogeneity should be looked at as a substantive part of our world. The prototype construct recognizes this fact, and the internal consistency of the prototype and its diagnostic threshold should mirror it.

How should the prototype construct inform the practice and structure of therapy? If no one subset of diagnostic criteria is necessary or sufficient for membership in a diagnostic class, and if the structure of the taxonomy and the planning and practice of therapy are to be linked in a meaningful way, it seems likely that no one therapy or technique can be regarded as a necessary or sufficient remediation as well. Diagnostic heterogeneity-therapeutic heterogeneity is a more intrinsically agreeable pairing than diagnostic heterogeneity-therapeutic homogeneity, which, like the traditional psychotherapy outcome study, treats every person diagnosed the same way, ignoring individual differences. The argument is one of parallelism: The palette of methods and techniques available to the therapist must be commensurate with the heterogeneity of the diagnostic class for which the methods and techniques are intended. Such an approach is schematized in Figure 5.4.

A diagnosis, then, constrains what interventions might be considered appropriate but can only determine any one intervention to the degree that individual differences are unimportant in the expression of the pathology. This means that in cases of moderate to weak taxonicity, a diagnosis is a necessary, but not sufficient basis for planning an intervention. Ideally, a diagnosis functions as a means of narrowing the universe of therapies and techniques to some small set, and within this small set, individual factors legislate over the choice between techniques or the order in which the techniques might be applied. At this level of treatment planning, an idiographic level, the therapist is working at the very limits of the heuristic power of the taxonomy.

The preceding discussion could be applied as easily to Axis I as Axis II, but the emphasis on idiographic factors should probably be greater on Axis II than Axis I, simply because of the greater level of comorbidity that is observed on Axis II.

More importantly, however, the Axis II constructs are fundamentally different from those of Axis I. As has been repeatedly stressed, the Axis I conditions may be thought of as medical diseases,

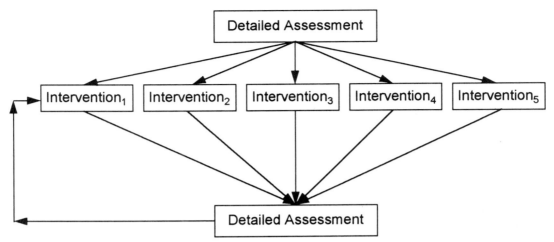

Figure 5.4   A self-regulatory model of therapy that accommodates to individuality.

but the Axis II constructs are pathologies of the entire matrix of the person. They are not diseases. Nor were the Axis II constructs intended to exhaust all of personality. Like a plane that lands somewhere short of your ultimate destination, the Axis II constructs will take you quite far, but not all the way. However you get to your destination, you are required to accommodate to the particulars of the terrain, and personality is full of particularities. Although patients rarely present as pure prototypes on any diagnostic axis, they do so much less frequently on Axis II than Axis I. As a result, the intraindividual patterning of personality variables across personologic domains does not, by definition, readily lend itself to taxonomic classification.

The diagnostic criteria of the DSM-IV have not been explicitly constructed to facilitate personologic psychotherapy. Criteria should do more than classify persons into categories, a rather minimalistic function. Instead, diagnostic criteria should encourage a substantive and integrative understanding of the patient across all those domains in which personality is expressed. The DSM-IV criteria, disproportionately weighted in some domains and nonexistent in others, cannot perform this function. At this point in time, truly personologic therapy requires that the official diagnostic criteria be supplemented by clinical judgment. Effective personologic therapy requires a detailed assessment of all those domains which can exist as constraints on system functioning. Because the DSM-IV therapist simply would not be cognizant of such abnormalities, techniques appropriate to those domains

would not be used either in combination or in series. Using DSM-IV criteria alone as a guide to the substantive characteristics of personality would effectively leave some systems constraints completely unobserved, free to operate insidiously in the background to perpetuate the pathological tenacity of the system as a whole. Consequently, a DSM-IV-based therapy is not necessarily a personologic therapy.

Responses to the preceding issues point to the inadequacy of any approach that links taxonomic criteria to intervention without theoretical guidance that encompasses the functional-structural nature of personality. Look again at Figure 5.4. The argument is merely that diagnosis should constrain therapy in manner consonant with accepted diagnostic standards, the prototypal model. The scope of the interventions that might be considered appropriate and the form of their application has been left unattended. Any set of interventions or techniques might be applied singly or in combination, without regard to the axis of the treated disorder. In the actual practice of therapy, techniques within a particular personologic data level, that is, psychodynamic techniques, behavioral techniques, and so on, are, in fact, often applied conjointly. Thus systematic desensitization might be followed by in vivo exposure, or a patient might keep a diary of his or her thoughts, while at the same time reframing those thoughts in accordance with the therapist's directions when they occur. In these formulations, however, there is no strong a priori reason why any two therapies or techniques should be combined at all. When techniques from different modalities are applied together, it is because the combination seems required by the logic of the case, not because it is required by the logic of the disorder.

ESTABLISHING STRATEGIC GOALS

Historically, treatment planning accrues as the result of transactions between the therapist's conceptions of his or her patient and the therapist's entire scholarly and experiential background. If the structure of his or her learning and experiences were different, then, within limits, so would the therapist's conception of the patient's personality be altered, a reality that is recognized across numerous literatures that discuss the concept of countertransference.

Simply to note that individual differences between patients within a diagnostic category might prove useful in optimizing the course of therapy, however, is not enough; taxonomy and intervention must be linked back to theory, as well. Does a theoretical grounding to the organization of personality types contain guidelines that can inform the psychotherapy of personality pathologies? The principles that underlie a taxonomy, such as Millon's evolutionary theory of pain-pleasure, active-passive, self-other, and thinking-feeling polarity, may provide a useful framework and point of departure for getting from conception to treatment, a means of understanding the patient and a guide to plan treatment strategy and tactics.

Balancing Polarities

In Millon's model, a theoretical basis is developed from the principles of evolution, to which four polarities are considered fundamental: the pain-pleasure, the active-passive, the self-other, and the thinking-feeling. As a general philosophy, specific treatment techniques are selected as tactics to achieve polarity-oriented balances. Depending on the pathological polarity to be modified, and the integrative treatment sequence the clinician has in mind, the goals of therapy are to overcome *pleasure deficiencies* in schizoids, avoidants, and depressives; to reestablish *interpersonally imbalanced* polarity disturbances in dependents, histrionics, narcissists, and antisocials; to undo the *intrapsychic conflicts* in sadists, compulsives, masochists, and negativists; and to reconstruct the *structural defects* in the schizotypal, borderline, and paranoid personalities. These are to be achieved by the use

of modality tactics that are optimally suited to the clinical domains in which these pathologies are expressed.

Table 5.1 provides a synopsis of what may be considered the primary goals of personologic therapy according to the polarity model. Therapeutic efforts responsive to problems in the pain-pleasure polarity would, for example, have as their essential aim life-enhancement among schizoid, avoidant, and depressive personalities (increased pleasure). Given the probability of intrinsic deficits in this area, schizoids and depressives might require the use of pharmacologic agents designed to lift their melancholic or to activate their apathetic mood/temperament. Increments in life-enhancement for avoidants, however, are likely to depend more on cognitive techniques designed to alter their alienated self-image, and behavioral methods oriented to counter their aversive interpersonal conduct. Equally important for avoidants is reducing their hypersensitivities, especially to social rejection (decreased pain); this may be achieved by coordinating the use of medications for their characteristic anguished mood/temperament with cognitive methods geared to desensitization.

Among imbalances in the passive-active polarity, efforts may be made to increase the capacity and skills for taking a less reactive and more proactive role in dealing with life affairs (decreased passive; increased active). This would be a major goal of treatment for schizoids, depressives, dependents, narcissists, masochists, and

TABLE 5.1   Goals of Polarity-Oriented Personologic Therapy

Modifying the Pain-Pleasure Polarity
+ Pleasure (Schizoid, Avoidant, Depressive)
− Pain (Avoidant, Depressive)
Pain ↔ Pleasure (Self-Defeating, Sadistic)

Balancing the Passive-Active Polarity
+ Passive − Active (Avoidant, Histrionic, Antisocial, Sadistic, Negativistic)
− Passive + Active (Schizoid, Depressive, Dependent, Narcissistic, Self-Defeating, Compulsive)

Altering the Other-Self Polarity
− Other + Self (Dependent, Histrionic)
+ Other − Self (Narcissistic, Antisocial)
Other ↔ Self (Compulsive, Negativistic)

Rebuilding the Personality Structure
+ Cognitive, Interpersonal Cohesion   Schizotypal
+ Affective, Self Cohesion   Borderline
− Cognitive, Affective-Rigidity   Paranoid

---

compulsives. Interpersonal imbalances in the self-other polarity found among narcissists and antisocials, for example, suggest that a major aim of their treatment would be a reduction in their predominant self-focus, and a corresponding augmentation of their sensitivity to the needs of others (increased other; decreased self). Among dependents and histrionics, a major objective of therapy is to stimulate greater self-interest, rather than focus on those of others. For the intrapsychic conflicts that underlie the behavior and feelings of compulsives and negativists, attention should be directed to help them recognize the nature of their ambivalences and to assist them in overcoming their inner disharmony. Similarly, the pain-pleasure discordance that undergirds the difficulties of sadists and masochists will require efforts to reverse these pathological inclinations.

Countering Perpetuating Tendencies

As noted in an earlier chapter, continuity in personality functioning may be attributed in great measure to the stability of constitutional factors and the deeply ingrained character of early experiential learning. Every behavior, attitude, and feeling that is currently exhibited is a perpetuation, a remnant of the past that persists into the present. Not only do these residuals passively shape the present by temporal precedence, if nothing else, but they insidiously distort and transform ongoing life events to make them duplicates of the past. It is this re-creative process of self-perpetuation that becomes so problematic for the personality disorders. In other words, as we have said previously, personality disorders are themselves pathogenic. They set into motion *new* life experiences that are pathology-producing.

A major goal of what we have called personologic psychotherapy is to stop these perpetuating inclinations, to prevent their continued exacerbation and intensification of the patients' established pathologic habits and attitudes. Much of what therapists must do is reverse self-pathogenesis, the intruding into the present of erroneous expectations, the perniciousness of maladaptive coping styles, the repetitive establishing of new, self-entrapping vicious circles. To achieve these counteracting effects, for example, dependents should be guided to reduce their self-deprecating attitudes, and encouraged to acquire adultlike skills. Avoidants should be taught to reverse their habitual social detachments, and be assisted in diminishing their fearful assumptions about the inevitable malice of

others. Depressives should be helped to undo their pessimistic expectations, to enhance their mood with antidepressants, and to reappraise their negative assessments of their self-worth. Similarly, the repugnant attitudes and deceptive behaviors of antisocials should be confronted and neutralized. Sadists must be shown how to control their abusive behaviors, and to learn to identify the precipitants of their precipitous acting-out. In each of the preceding, the goal of the therapist is not only to dislodge these provocative and aggravating actions, attitudes, and feelings, but to stop them from generating new difficulties.

SELECTING TACTICAL MODALITIES

Tactics are like strategies, except that they are chosen and played out on the more focal venue of the personologic domains, rather than on a polarity level. Turning to the specific domains in which clinical problems exhibit themselves, we can address dysfunctions in the realm of interpersonal conduct by employing any number of family (Gurman & Kniskern, 1981) or group (Yalom, 1985) therapeutic methods, as well as a series of recently evolved and explicitly formulated interpersonal techniques (Anchin & Kiesler, 1982). Modern intrapsychic and phenomenological methods may be especially suited to the realm of object-representations, as would the techniques of Beck (1976; Beck & Freeman, 1990b), Ellis (1970), and Meichenbaum (1977) be well chosen to modify difficulties of cognitive style and self-image.

The modalities of personologic intervention mirror the clinical domains we have discussed in prior chapters. Rather than proceed in the order that we followed previously, we will begin our presentation with a description of treatment modes that are geared primarily to the modification of the mood/temperament domain, that which we have termed biophysical modalities.

Biophysical Modality Interventions

At one time, biophysical treatment included the use of electroconvulsive and psychosurgical procedures; these were never suitable for the personality disorders and, with rare exceptions, are judged today to be technologies of the past. An early period of unjustified optimism, characterized by the belief that pharmacological wonder drugs would cure all mental illnesses and deplete the rolls of every state hospital, has passed. Nevertheless, the field continues to be subjected to a flood of new products, each of which is preceded by massive and tantalizing advertisements that promise "a new life" for the psychiatric patient. Despite this bewildering array of highly touted medications, we note that psychiatrists' offices, community clinics, and mental health hospitals are no less busy than before. Formerly agitated and assaultive patients are easier to handle, as are anxious and depressed syndromes less severe and of briefer duration, but there has been no sweeping change in the prevalence or variety of most psychopathological conditions. In short, these wonder drugs have assumed a solid scientific and commercially successful place as one of many tools in the broadly trained therapist's treatment kit.

When a psychopharmacological agent has been shown to exert an effect on an organism, questions arise as to the precise nature of its psychological consequences (e.g., whether it influences, singly or in combination, motor behavior, sensory processes, perception, affective states, memory, and cognitive processes), the specific biophysical mechanisms altered by the drug (e.g., whether it activates or inhibits certain neurohormonal transmitter substances or has different kinds of effects on cortical regions, reticular pathways, limbic divisions), and the relationship between these psychological and biophysical changes and the final clinical effect.

Answers to the first question are largely obtained through animal laboratory studies, although certain functions (e.g., higher cognitive processes) can be appraised only in human clinical trials. Answers to the second question involve the use of exceedingly complex technical procedures that specify the anatomic site of action and trace the precise character and sequence of the induced chemical changes; the task of unraveling the neurophysiological concomitants of drugs must disentangle effects throughout the awesomely intricate histological structure of the brain and the complicated network of interactions that operates among its diverse components. Attempts to answer the third question are even more difficult since the observed "final" clinical outcome reflects not only the action of interacting chemical and neurological pathways, but the individual's experiential history and the conditions prevailing in his or her current environment.

Because of the varied questions that can be posed regarding the nature of pharmacological action, and because of the complexity of the factors involved, theorists have had a relatively open

field to speculate on "why" and "how" these drugs produce their effects. These formulations may be grouped into three categories: neurohormonal defect theories, which hypothesize that drugs overcome endogenous chemical dysfunctions in synaptic transmission; neurophysiological imbalance theories, which assume that these agents reestablish equilibrium among ill-matched functional systems; and psychological reaction theories, which posit that these substances result in energy and temperament changes that alter patients' coping competencies and lead them to modify their self-image.

Speculations of drug action formulated in accord with the first viewpoint assume that pharmacological agents counteract endogenous defects in synaptic transmission. Implicit, if not explicit, in this thesis is a belief that the major forms of psychopathology stem from disturbances in one or another of the neurohormonal transmitter substances. Among the more prominent speculations of this type are those referred to as the serotonin and norepinephrine hypotheses. According to these theories, drugs reestablish normal synaptic transmission by facilitating the release of formerly bound transmitter substances, by blocking competing but faulty metabolites, or by inhibiting enzymes that have depleted crucial neurotransmitters.

It is likely that endogenous disturbances of neurohormones would result in intensely maladaptive behaviors and place afflicted individuals at a marked disadvantage in regulating events, even in benign social environments. Any drug that would compensate for these chemical aberrations would be expected to improve patients' coping competencies and enhance their prospects for normal functioning. However, the thesis that psychopathology has its roots in neurohormonal defects is far from proved, and imaginative speculations have been seriously questioned or sharply revised in light of ongoing empirical evidence. In short, there are ambiguous data to support the notion that specific endogenous chemical defects play a determinant role in the major psychopathologies, no less in the personality disorders. Thus, the thesis that pharmacological substances achieve their beneficial effects by repairing existent biochemical disturbances is equivocal, given our present state of knowledge.

One of the major complications of neurohormonal defect theories is that synaptic transmitter substances may be unevenly distributed in the brain and produce opposite effects in several of the principal regions of the nervous system. The architectural complexity of the limbic, midbrain, cortical, and reticular systems and the vast number of pathways which chemicals traverse make it evident that drug effects are varied and complicated. Moreover, pharmacological agents can release endogenous chemical substances in one neurological system and suppress those of other systems arguing for a thesis formulated in terms of neurophysiological relationships rather than singular or localized effects. Accordingly, some theorists have proposed that these drugs reestablish disturbed homeostatic balances among neurophysiological systems. Equilibrium, according to these speculations, is achieved by the drugs' selective facilitation and inhibition of neural regions that have been either out of phase with one another or weighted unequally in their regulative powers.

These formulations contend that the principal forms of personality pathology stem from endogenous imbalances among functional neural groups. For example, the normal interplay between sympathetic and parasympathetic components of the autonomic nervous system may have been impaired; the borderline's impulsiveness and affective dysregulation may be considered a formulation of this type. Along similar lines, some have proposed that pharmacological agents restore balances among visceropsychic systems (structures subserving consciousness of affect), sensoripsychic systems (consciousness of objects and reality), and corticopsychic systems (consciousness of concepts and symbols). According to this conjecture, psychopharmacological agents can best be described in terms of their ability to counteract different patterns of disequilibria among these three psychophysiological systems through selective excitatory and inhibitory effects.

The intricate relationships among intracerebral regions are gradually being unraveled through refined technical procedures, but the precise role and sequence through which pharmacological substances traverse these topologically complex systems is still far from thoroughly understood. As such, neurophysiological imbalance models, consistent though they are with the fact that chemical substances have varying effects throughout the nervous system, must be viewed as only a plausible schema, and not a verified theory.

Although the direct action of pharmacological drugs is chemical and their effects formulable in terms of altered neurophysiological relationships, there are those who believe that the crucial variable is not chemical or neurophysiological, but psychological. To them, the factors that determine the patient's response are not molecular events or processes, but the patient's prior psychological state and the environment within which he or she currently functions. According to this view, biophysical changes induced by drugs take on a meaning to the patient, and it is this meaning which determines the final clinical response.

Theorists of this persuasion pay less attention to specifying the mechanisms and pathways of biophysical change than to the impact of these changes on the patient's self-image, coping competencies, social relationships, and the like. To support their thesis, they note that barbiturates, which typically produce sedative reactions, often produce excitement and hyperactivity. Similarly, many persons exhibit a cheerful state of intoxication when given sodium amytal in a congenial social setting, but succumb to a hypnotic state when the drug is administered to them in a therapeutic environment. Of even greater significance than social factors according to this view, is the patient's awareness of the energy and temperamental changes that have taken place within as a consequence of drug action. Freyhan (1959), discussing the effect of "tranquilizers" in reducing mobility and drive, states that patients with compulsive traits, who need intensified activity to control their anxiety, may react unfavorably to their loss of initiative, resulting thereby in an upsurge rather than a decrement in anxiety. Other patients, such as avoidants who are comforted by feelings of reduced activity and energy, may view the drug's tranquilizing effect as a welcome relief. Thus, even if a drug produced a uniform biophysical effect on all patients, its psychological impact would differ from patient to patient, depending on the meaning these changes have in the larger context of the patient's needs, attitudes and coping strategies. As Sarwer-Foner remarked (1959):

If the pharmacologic effect threatens the patient by interfering with vital defenses, new waves of energy are produced, alerting and disturbing him. Here these arise precisely because of the medication he is receiving. . . .

When the changes produced affect the patient, physician, hospital, and their interrelations in a way that makes the patient feel less inferior, worthless, and dangerous, a new opportunity for a more adult level of functioning is produced. When this situation continues for a sufficiently long time, further ego reintegration can take place. The symptomatic action of the drugs leads therefore to a variable therapeutic effect. (p. 207)

In short, the "psychological reaction" model contends that the effectiveness of pharmacological agents is determined primarily by the patient's premedication self-image and coping strategy. If the drug facilitates the control of disturbing impulses or if it activates a new sense of competence and adequacy, then it may be spoken of as beneficial. Conversely, if the effect is to weaken the patient's defenses and upset his or her self-image, it may prove detrimental. The key to the effectiveness of a drug, then, is not its chemical impact, but the psychological significance of these changes.

The several theories of psychopharmacological action we have just presented focus on different facets of a broad constellation of factors that contribute to drug efficacy. Although resting on different etiologic premises, they are not nearly as divergent as they appear to be in the writings of their exponents. As we see it, they merely stress different levels and variables of the same process, each of which is an important dimension of psychopharmacological study: neurohormonal changes, alterations in neurophysiological balance, and their psychological significance.

Behavioral Modality Interventions

As we conceive the *behavioral* construct, it includes both concrete and observable actions, the prime subject for modification among *pure* behaviorists, as well as the expressive significance of these actions, and the transactive meaning of these behaviors in social interactions, the prime subject of *interpersonal* behaviorists. In a later section, we will discuss what is commonly referred to as *cognitive* behaviorists, those who are primarily concerned with how phenomenological distortions affect their perceptions and actions.

Our attention in this section will turn first to *behavioral purists*. Secondarily, we will touch on the formal procedures of "interpersonal therapy," as well as those referred to as "group therapy." Although family therapies overlap in significant ways with the interpersonal model, we consider them separately in a later section, owing to our belief that this approach to therapy is not focused on patients themselves, but is oriented to a cohesive unit composed of several individuals who relate to one another primarily *outside* of therapy.

Expressive Act Therapies

Behaviorists of a *pure* variety consider objectively observable actions and events to be the primary subject matter of psychological science; they eschew, where possible, all reference to subjective or unconscious processes that play a central role in phenomenologically and intrapsychically oriented therapies.

Pure behaviorists argue that the procedures of therapy should consist of the systematic application of experimentally derived and corroborated principles. They avoid "loosely formulated" techniques derived from unverifiable clinical observations, which they contend typify the methodology of other treatment approaches. Despite certain theoretical differences, most pure behavior therapists subscribe in common to the concepts and methods of learning research. This orientation reflects both their desire to adhere to scientific principles and their belief that personality pathology is learned behavior that is viewed to be socially maladaptive or deficient. According to this view, whatever has been learned, adaptive or maladaptive, can be "unlearned" by the therapeutic application of the same principles and conditions that led to its initial acquisition. To achieve the goals of treatment, the therapist must first specify both the maladaptive behaviors (overt symptoms) and the environmental conditions (stimuli and reinforcements) that sustain them. Once these have been identified, the therapist can arrange a program of learning procedures tailored specifically to the elimination of the maladaptive responses and to the institution of more adaptive ones.

As noted, behavior therapists share a number of beliefs. They consider overt actions and observable events to be the most fruitful data for their concepts and treatment variables. Therapy, to them, consists of the systematic application of experimentally corroborated learning principles. Personality pathology is viewed to be deficiently learned or maladaptively learned behaviors that can be unlearned or relearned in accord with the same principles by which they were first acquired.

Pure behaviorists assert that nonbehavioral therapists unwittingly apply learning principles in their treatment procedure. Nonbehavioral therapists formulate their methods in elaborate conceptual systems and engage in circuitous maneuvers, such as providing interpretations and promoting the release of repressed emotions, but the crucial element in their technique, according to these behaviorists, is the selective if inadvertent manner in which they reinforce the patient's adaptive behaviors and extinguish those that are maladaptive. They contend that the benefits of psychological treatment will be maximized if therapists knowingly apply these learning principles in a planned and systematic fashion. Accordingly, behavior therapists take great care to unburden themselves of all of the more traditional therapeutic activities considered to be peripheral to effective treatment. They make no effort to trace and unravel the developmental roots of the patient's problem, considering this historical analysis to be an unnecessary diversion from the task at hand. Similarly, they do not "waste their time" exploring unconscious conflicts or facilitating patient insights because these are considered nonproductive of therapeutic gain. In short, they divest themselves of all the superfluous and time-consuming paraphernalia associated with other treatment procedures and concentrate exclusively on those basic learning principles that have been proved to be scientific and efficacious.

Pure behaviorists contend further that other therapeutic approaches are method-oriented rather than problem-oriented. Nonbehaviorists are seen to proceed in a uniform fashion regardless of the particular character of the patient's difficulty, utilizing the same psychoanalytic or cognitive procedure with all forms and varieties of pathology. In contrast, they claim that behavioral approaches are flexible and problem-oriented. There is no fixed technique in pure behavior therapy; rather, the therapist identifies the distinguishing elements of each problem and then fashions a procedure designed specifically to effect changes only in that problem. For example, if the patient complains of a phobia, procedures are designed to eliminate just that symptom, and therapy is completed when it has been removed.

Numerous methods have been developed utilizing a variety of procedures designed to eliminate problematic behaviors and to facilitate the formation of suitable ones. For example, in what is termed *counterconditioning,* an incompatible response is introduced to block maladaptive behaviors. Such actions can be neutralized or blocked by evoking a response that is antithetical to it. Counteracting the habit of avoidant personalities to respond with fretfulness can be done by interposing and associating a relaxation response to events that were formerly provocative. Whereas desensitization seeks to eliminate a fretful response that inhibits more adaptive behaviors (e.g., overcoming feared situations among avoidants), what is known as *aversive learning* seeks only to extinguish undesirable behavioral acts, such as may be seen among sadistic or antisocial personalities (e.g., their impulsive or hostile behaviors). Thus, in aversive learning, a formerly rewarding behavior to the individual (e.g., alcohol or sexual excitement) is associated therapeutically with an unrewarding one (e.g., evoking nausea or pain). Other techniques such as *implosive methods* reverse the procedure by therapeutically introducing extremely distressful conditions both immediately and forcefully. Thus, avoidant patients may be subjected to conditions of imaginative and overwhelming threat, rather than conditions that may calm or relax them. The argument here is that by flooding the imagination of patients with the very worst of their fears in a setting in which no actual harm is forthcoming, these patients may learn that their fears are largely unfounded. In other techniques designed to alter problematic behaviors, reinforcements that previously sustained them are therapeutically withdrawn in the hope that these undesirable acts may dissipate gradually. *Reinforcement withdrawal* is most suitable for combating behaviors that *should* be inhibited, such as a sadist's aggressive behaviors and a compulsive's habit persistence. Techniques that manipulate an individual's behaviors through *selective positive reinforcement* may prove useful in strengthening more adaptive behaviors. In procedures termed *assertiveness training,* efforts are made to develop personal confidence and self-reliance among dependent personalities. Behavioral procedures specifically oriented to the clinical management of the personality disorders have been described by Turkat (1990).

The feature that most clearly distinguishes pure behavior therapies from other approaches is their commitment to an action-suppressive process. Behaviorists consider emotional ventilation and insight, the bedrocks of other schools of therapy, to be of dubious value; not only are these two procedures viewed as time-consuming digressions, but they are often thought to be counterproductive, that is, to strengthen rather than weaken maladaptive behaviors (Bandura, 1969; Davison, 1968; Kahn, 1960; Linehan, 1992). As behaviorists see it, the task of therapy is to achieve as directly as possible changes in real-life action, not greater self-understanding or affective expression.

Pure behaviorists point to a number of advantages inherent in their approach. First, they argue that the principles that guide their methods are anchored to "scientific" laboratory data and can be tested and revised, therefore, in an objective and systematic fashion. Second, because behaviorists focus their efforts on clearly delimited and carefully defined symptom problems, they assert that they will accumulate a body of quantitative data concerning the efficacy of their approach, not "in general," but with specific and identifiable syndromes. Third, if pure behavioral methods can be shown to be of equal or superior efficacy to other treatment approaches, their benefits will be twofold because they achieve their results in far fewer sessions. This advantage is especially significant for patients in lower socioeconomic groups who can ill afford the greater expense and time involved in more traditional therapies. Fourth, straightforward and pure behavioral therapy can be carried out by persons who are appreciably less sophisticated psychologically than those who can perform other types of therapy. The need for more therapists in our society is great, and the expediency and economy of employing hospital nurses and attendants, as well as parents, teachers, and other auxiliary persons, cannot be readily overlooked.

Nonbehavioral therapists do not accept the contentions of pure behaviorists. They note numerous disadvantages and objections.

First, critics assert that behaviorists ennoble themselves by falsely appropriating the prestige of "scientific" learning theories. Not only is their distinctive affinity to principles of learning questioned (other therapists adhere to learning theories as well), but the very existence of established "laws" of learning is doubted. These critics ask whether such dubious laws can be systematically applied to complex therapeutic processes when their applicability to simple situations is still a matter of dispute. Questions are also raised as to whether the sparse language of learning theories—stimuli, conditioning, response, and reinforcement—is a sufficiently sensitive conceptual instrument for dealing with the subtle and complex processes of psychological treatment. Although learning and environmental events are central to an understanding of therapeutic interactions, forcing these processes into the meager verbal formulations of behavior theories may blunt rather than sharpen the clinician's powers of observation and analysis. Third, it is noted that the actual processes of behavior therapy are far from pure applications of learning principles. Most behavior modification procedures include elements that are incidental to the theoretically formulated plan of therapy. For example, in desensitization, is therapeutic gain entirely a function of counterconditioning learning or is it at least in part attributable to the therapist's personality, enthusiasm, and powers of suggestion? The fourth, and perhaps the most vigorously argued criticism of pure behavior therapy, contends that these procedures deal only with superficial and narrowly defined symptoms; they ignore not only the underlying causes of overt symptoms, but many important although difficult to define conditions such as existential anxiety, identity crises, and personality traits. Because deeper and more pervasive difficulties are left untouched, behavior therapy is considered a technique of markedly limited utility. In short, the ostensive benefits of pure behavioral methods are considered to be either limited, temporary, or illusory.

Interpersonal Conduct Therapies

There are two major variants of treatment that focus on the interpersonal realm of behavior. The first engages one patient exclusively at a time in a dyadic patient-therapist medium, but centers its attentions primarily on the patient's relationships with others; these techniques are known as "interpersonal psychotherapy." The second set of techniques assembles an assortment of patients together in a group so that their habitual styles of behaving and relating to others can be observed and analyzed as the interactions among the participants unfold; these techniques are known as "group psychotherapy."

Interpersonal Psychotherapy. Broadening the behavioral focus in significant ways are therapists who describe themselves as *interpersonally oriented.* Although they address the behavioral conduct of the patient, it is their assertion that behaviors which relate and transact communications with others are by far the most significant. Preceded by several theorists around mid-century (e.g., Sullivan, Leary, Berne), there has been a marked upsurge in the use of formal interpersonal therapies in recent decades (Anchin & Kiesler, 1982; Benjamin, 1993a; Klerman, Weissman, Rounsaville, & Chevron, 1984).

To paraphrase Kiesler (1984), the essential problems of individuals reside in the person's recurrent transactions with significant others. These stem largely from disordered, inappropriate, or inadequate communications, and result from failing to attend and/or not correct the unsuccessful and self-defeating nature of these communications. The interpersonal approach centers its attention on the individual's closest relationships, notably current family interactions, the family of origin, past and present love affairs and friendships, as well as neighborhood and work relations. It is the patient's habitual interactive and hierarchical roles in these social systems that are the focus of interpersonal therapy. The dyadic treatment interaction, despite its uniqueness, is seen as paralleling other venues of human communication. The interpersonal therapist becomes sensitized to the intrusions of the patient's habitual styles of interaction by the manner in which he or she draws out or "pulls" the therapist's feelings and attitudes. These evocative responses provide a good indication of how the patient continues to relate to others. This transactive process mirrors in many ways what psychoanalysts refer to in their concepts of transference and countertransference. More will be said on these matters when we later discuss treatment modalities oriented to modifying the patient's "object relationships."

McLemore and Brokaw (1987) outline a number of the prescriptive assumptions of the interpersonal model. In contrast to other behaviorally oriented therapists, they assert that the deeply ingrained, long-standing, and dysfunctional interpersonal styles of the patient are psychologically more significant than are discrete "symptoms." Their judgment is that personality disorders are primarily a function of disordered relationships with other persons. More pertinently, effective treatment of a personality disorder requires that a genuine interpersonal relationship be established with the therapist, and that the individual's "self-defeating interpersonal cycles" be directly interrupted.

Once a past history assessment has been undertaken and its elements clarified, the task of the interpersonal therapist is to help patients identify the persons with whom they are currently having difficulties, what these difficulties are, and whether there are ways in which they can be resolved or made more satisfactory. Problems in patients' current environment should be stated explicitly (e.g., being intimidated on the job, arguing over trivia with their spouse, missing old friends) and shown to be derivations from past experiences and relationships.

Foremost among the early interpersonal therapists was Harry Stack Sullivan (1953, 1954). He directed his efforts not only to "parataxic distortion," a process akin to the classical transference phenomenon, but to a host of other habitual maneuvers such as selective inattention, memory dissociation and inaccurate social evaluations. The task of his therapy was to unravel this pattern of self-protective, but ultimately self-defeating interpersonal measures. At times, Sullivan, a former psychoanalyst, sought to elicit childhood memories and dream materials; however, his focus was directed primarily to present interpersonal

problems. Sullivan believed that the classical passive or blank-screen attitude should be replaced by a more natural expression of the therapist's *real* feelings and thoughts. Beyond this, he proposed that certain attitudes be simulated by the therapist so as to throw the patient "off guard," thereby provoking interpersonally illuminating responses. In short, Sullivan tried to participate actively in an interpersonal treatment relationship, exploiting his own reactions and feigning others, both designed to uncover the patient's distortions and unconscious styles of behavior. The primary instrument of Sullivan's therapy was skillful interviewing. By this, Sullivan meant subtly drawing out the patient's interpersonal distortions by careful listening and questioning, suggesting that the patient may harbor unwarranted preconceptions of self and others, and offering tentative speculations as to how these self and interpersonal attitudes may have caused problem relationships in the past and how they may be altered in the future. The interview interaction, then, rather than the passive free association technique, was considered by Sullivan to be the most fruitful means of disentangling the web of interpersonal distortions.

As noted, interpersonal approaches broaden the behavioral modality from a focus on individual symptoms to an overall pattern of behaviors that represents the patient's relationships to others. In what has been called *transactional analysis,* the progression continues toward the sociocultural end of the continuum by directing attention to the "roles" assumed by the patient. Employing patient-therapist communications as their data and drawing their models from mathematical game theorists such as von Neumann and Morgenstern (1944), or social role theorists such as Mead (1934), a number of therapists formulated the transactional analytic technique. The best known of these persons, due largely to the witty and phrase-making character of his popular works, is Eric Berne (1961). To him, therapeutic interactions provided insight into the patient's characteristic interpersonal maneuvers and mirrored the several varieties of his or her everyday social behaviors. These maneuvers were translated into caricature forms known as "pastimes" or "games," each of which highlighted an unconscious strategy of the patient to defend against "childish" relationship anxieties and to secure "immature rewards." These distorting transactional processes are also akin to the analysts' notions of transference phenomena, although Berne dramatizes these operations by tagging them with rather clever and humorous labels. As a consequence of transactional analyses, patients were expected to gain insight into the foolish "games" they "played" in their current relationships, as well as reinforce those skills and attitudes that comprise a more mature and adaptive style.

More contemporary methods of interpersonal treatment have been proposed, as noted earlier, by Kiesler (1982), Klerman et al. (1984), and Benjamin (1993a).

In perhaps the most detailed model of dyadic interactions, called the *Structural Analysis of Social Behavior* (SASB), Benjamin bridges both intrapsychic and behavioral realms of functioning. Her key medium for exploring these functions is the interview process, which Benjamin believes should contain at least six features. First, a collaboration must be established in which the therapist can affirm the patient's views and responses; the task of the interviewer is to be acutely aware of the patient's behaviors, feelings, and indirect communications throughout the interview process, identifying such communications as evinced in silences, affective expressions, resistances when revisiting difficult subjects, and so on. Second, unconscious processes should be tracked in a "free-form" flow of conversation. Thus, rather than seeking to control topical progressions, the interviewer should permit the patient to proceed with seemingly disorganized or random digressions, identifying fantasies, metaphors, and the like, as well. Third, the therapist should assume that the narrative storyline that unfolds "makes sense." The basic task here is to understand the interpersonal and intrapsychic patterns that emerge in terms of where they came from and what their purposes may be. Fourth, Benjamin refers to the achievement of "interpersonal specificity," by which she means gaining an awareness of patterns of interpersonal relevance as they relate to dimensions such as love-hate and enmeshment-differentiation. Fifth, the therapist should avoid reinforcing preexisting destructive patterns. Here, Benjamin recommends that the interviewer *not* show empathy for symptomatic behaviors, nor attend actively to the task of gathering symptomatic data. Lastly, Benjamin enjoins the therapist to correct "errors" as quickly as possible. To her, errors are interventions that do not conform to the previous five interviewing recommendations.

Thus, in Benjamin's model, the key role is that of establishing a collaboration, in which empathic processes may or may not be appropriate. In addition, she stresses the importance of facilitating the patient's recognition of his/her interpersonal patterns of behavior. Equally significant is the task of "blocking maladaptive patterns," as well as the necessity for addressing the patient's underlying fears and wishes. And finally, new learning should be facilitated; the clinician should encourage the acquisition of interpersonal behaviors that are more adaptive and more gratifying than those previously employed.

Group Psychotherapy. Developed as a comprehensive modality of treatment more than a half-century ago (e.g., Slavsen, 1943), the impact of *group psychotherapy* in molding and sustaining interpersonal behaviors has been thoroughly explored in recent decades. During a more recent period, there has been growing support for the use of trained personnel to meet an increasing number of patients who cannot afford themselves, nor be adequately covered financially by an ever-tightening managed care environment. Spurred by these practical considerations, therapists appear to be turning increasingly to more expeditious ways of treating patients for whom individual therapy is neither available nor economically feasible. The manifest need for more efficient forms of therapy may lead to a rapid growth of group treatment methods in the 1990s.

Group therapists contend that in the semirealistic group setting, patients display most clearly those attitudes and behavioral habits that intrude and complicate their real, everyday relationships with others. The interplay among group members provides numerous opportunities to observe distortions in perception and behavior that aggravate and perpetuate interpersonal difficulties. Because mutual support characterizes the atmosphere and intent of the group, these distortions can be rectified and more socially constructive alternatives acquired in their stead. Moreover, since each patient expresses deep feelings and attitudes with the knowledge that similar experiences are shared by fellow group members, the patient gradually learns self-tolerance and sympathy toward the needs of others. As a consequence, patient's develop greater self-acceptance, a capacity to view things from the perspective of others, a freedom from self-defeating interpersonal strategies, and the ability to participate more effectively in social relationships.

There are several advantages to group therapy, at least as seen by its exponents:

1. Perhaps most significant, is that the patients acquire new behaviors in a setting that is similar

to their natural interpersonal world; relating to peer group members is a more realistic experience than that of the hierarchic therapist-patient dyad. It is easier to generalize to the extratherapeutic world what one learns in peer-group settings since it is closer to reality than is the individual treatment setting.

2. Because patients must cope with a host of different personalities in their group, they acquire a range of flexible interpersonal skills; in this way, they learn to relate not only to the neutral or uniform style of a single therapist, but to a variety of disparate personality types.

3. The semirealistic atmosphere of the group provides patients with ample opportunities to try out new attitudes and behaviors; group therapy serves, then, as a proving ground, an experimental laboratory within which the formative stages of new learnings can be rehearsed and refined.

4. By observing that their feelings are shared by others, patients are not only reassured that they are not alone in their suffering, but regain thereby some of their former self-confidence and self-respect.

5. No longer ashamed of their thoughts and emotions, patients can give up the barriers they have defensively placed between self and others, enabling them to relate to others without fear and embarrassment.

6. Able to accept criticism and to forgo pathological interpersonal defenses, patients begin to see themselves as others do and develop a more realistic appraisal than heretofore of their social strengths and weaknesses.

7. Concurrent with increased accuracy of self-perception, the patients learn to observe others more objectively and gradually relinquishes previous tendencies to distort interpersonal judgments.

8. Now able to respect the feelings of others, patients can share their perspectives and begin to provide each other with assistance in resolving difficulties.

PHENOMENOLOGICAL MODALITY INTERVENTIONS

In this section, we will turn our attention, as we have previously in differentiating the clinical domains, to three spheres of personality structure and

functioning that may be usefully considered significant targets of therapeutic intervention, notably *cognitive styles,* and the content areas of *self-image* and *object-representations.* Important modalities of intervention have been developed with each of the preceding in mind, albeit somewhat tangentially. Before we begin these presentations, we would like to note three factors that phenomenologically oriented therapists exhibit in common and that set them apart from other schools of thought:

1. In contrast to behaviorists and in common with intrapsychic therapists, phenomenologists place heavy emphasis on internal processes that mediate overt actions. To them, personality pathology is best conceived in terms of enduring and pervasive traits that shape and give consistency to behavior. No matter how widely generalized and consistent certain behaviors may be, they are but "surface" derivatives of these inner mediators. It follows, therefore, that phenomenologists focus their therapeutic efforts on internal dispositions of feeling, thought, and behavior.

2. Phenomenologists differ from both behavior and intrapsychic therapists with regard to which events and processes they consider central to the pathogenesis and treatment of personality pathology. Behaviorists emphasize the role of environmental events such as stimuli and reinforcements; intrapsychic therapists consider unconscious forces to be crucial. As a consequence of these orientations, behaviorists seek to alter pathology by manipulating stimulus events and reinforcement contingencies, and intrapsychic therapists direct their efforts toward uprooting and reconstructing the elements of the unconscious. In contrast to both, phenomenologists concern themselves with the data of conscious perceptions and attitudes, believing that these cognitive processes are crucial to both the development and perpetuation of personality pathology. Therapy, then, is directed to the reorientation of consciously discordant feelings and erroneous beliefs, and not to the modification of isolated behaviors or to the disgorging of the past and its associated unconscious derivatives.

3. Because of their emphasis on conscious attitudes and perceptions, phenomenological therapists are inclined to follow an insight-expressive rather than an action-suppressive treatment process. Both phenomenological and intrapsychic therapists employ the insight-expressive approach, but the focus of their explorations differs, at least in theory. Phenomenologists attend to dissonant interpersonal assumptions and self-perceptions that

can be consciously acknowledged by an examination of their patients' everyday relationships and activities. In contrast, intrapsychic therapists view consciously acknowledged attitudes to be "superficial verbalizations" that cloak hidden beliefs and emotions; to them, the task of therapy is to bring into awareness repressed materials that resist conscious examination. Phenomenologists consider intrapsychic "depth" probing to be both unnecessary and time consuming; they believe that reorienting patients' conscious assumptions and feelings, without exploring their historical origins or dissolving their unconscious roots, will more than suffice to enable them to rectify difficulties and find a more constructive outlook of life.

Cognitive Style Therapies

These therapies seek to address how patients perceive the events of their lives, focus their attentions, process information, organize their thoughts, and communicate their reactions and ideas to others. They provide some of the most useful indexes to the clinician regarding a patient's distinctive way of functioning. By synthesizing these data, it may be possible to identify such general features as constricted thought, cognitive distractibility, impoverished thinking, and so on.

The philosophy underlying *cognitive style* procedures contrasts in emphasis with those of *self-image* or *object-relations* methods. They are not *primarily* concerned with, nor do they specifically focus on either the person's self-conception or attitudes toward others. Rather, their efforts are more general, that of counteracting the patient's erroneous or distorted ways of thinking, whatever realm may be involved.

Patients may be viewed as inept, irresponsible, or sick, and therefore unwilling or unable to choose the course they must take for their own well-being. The therapist not only assumes authority for deciding the objectives of treatment, but confronts patients with the irrationalities of their thinking; moreover, the therapist may employ intimidating tactics to indoctrinate patients with a value system that is considered universally beneficial.

The first systematic formulation of what may be called a direct approach to modifying a patient's cognitive assumptions was published by DuBois (1909) and Dejerine (1913), both of whom sought to impart "reason" to patients whose emotions had confused or distorted their capacity to think sensibly. It was their belief that mental disorders were irrational preoccupations with minor symptoms, causing these symptoms to become

"mountains, instead of molehills." To counter these foolish absorptions, they enjoined patients to disregard their troubles and reorient their thoughts in the direction of their virtues and accomplishments. The therapists inspired their patients to believe that happiness was best achieved through self-denial and a dedication to others. DuBois' philosophy of "positive thinking" and "selfless altruism" was promptly borrowed as a guiding principle among pastoral counselors, but it had little impact on clinical practitioners.

In the mid-1940s, Thorne (1944, 1948), viewing the growth of what he considered to be the narrow-minded and sentimentalistic practices of most therapists, proposed an approach that revived modern cognitive procedures. In contrast to DuBois, who sought to smooth over the strains and vexations of life, Thorne induced conflicts deliberately by confronting patients with their contradictory and self-defeating attitudes. Provoked in this manner, patients were forced to examine their destructive habits and to explore more adaptive alternatives.

Other cognitive style approaches gained favor in the 1950s and 1960s because they sought to bridge the gap between well-known principles of learning and the primary vehicle of most therapies, verbal interaction. Several semiformal systems were proposed along these lines (Breger and McGaugh, 1965; Kelly, 1955; Kanfer & Saslow, 1965; Miller, Galanter and Pribam, 1960; Philips, 1956; Rotter, 1954); we cannot expand on these interesting proposals, given limitations in space.

As noted, a number of features distinguish cognitive style approaches from other phenomenological procedures. For example, there is the practice of exposing the patient's erroneous or irrational attitudes, and imposing a particular philosophy of life in its stead. Of interest in this regard are the diametrically opposite philosophies espoused by the two historic approaches (DuBois, Thorne) discussed in prior paragraphs.

Modern *cognitive style* therapy has been most clearly formulated by Ellis (1958, 1962, 1967) and by Beck (1964, 1976, 1990), although their respective origins can be traced to the writings of earlier thinkers. In what he terms "rational-emotive" therapy, Ellis (1967) has considered the primary objective of therapy to be countering the patient's tendency to perpetuate difficulties through illogical and negative thinking. By reiterating these unrealistic and self-defeating beliefs in a self-dialogue, the patient constantly reaffirms irrationality and aggravates distress. To overcome these implicit but pervasive attitudes, the therapist confronts the patient with them and induces him or her to think about them consciously and concertedly and to "attack them" forcefully and unequivocally until they no longer influence behavior. By revealing and assailing these beliefs and by "commanding" the patient to engage in activities which run counter to them, their hold on the patient's life is broken and new directions become possible. An especially useful variant of Ellis' work, more in line with the integrative mind-set, is a book by Greenberg and Safran (1987), designed to synthesize affective, cognitive, and interpersonal perspectives and techniques.

A currently highly regarded cognitive approach has been developed by Beck and his associates (Beck et al., 1993b). Central to Beck's approach is the concept of "schema"—specific rules that govern information processing and behavior. These schemas may be classified into a variety of categories, such as personal, familial, and cultural. They are inferred directly from behavior or from interviews and history taking. To Beck, the disentangling and clarification of these schemas lie at the heart of therapeutic work with personality disorders. They persist, despite their dysfunctional consequences, largely because patients find ways to extract short-term benefits from them, thereby diverting these patients from pursuing more effective, long-term solutions. Beck recognizes that an important treatment consideration with personality disorders is recognizing that cognitive restructuring, by forcing patients to reexamine or reframe their schemas, will inevitably evoke problematic anxieties.

As does Benjamin in her interpersonal approach, Beck sets out a sequence of necessary steps in his cognitive style therapy. Not only must one first conceptualize the core schemas that undergird the patient's pathological outlook, but the therapist must keep in mind the underlying goals for reframing them. As with other sophisticated therapists, Beck emphasizes the therapist-patient relationship as central to the therapeutic endeavor. As he notes further, considerable artistry is involved in unraveling the origins of the patient's beliefs and in exploring the meaning of significant past events. Toward this goal, therapists must examine "transferencelike" reactions, but never be judgmental or perjorative in their responses. He provides a list of 18 problems in establishing a good collaboration to illustrate issues that can undo this constructive process. Potentially problematic also are procedures for confronting schemas that repetitively distort the expectancies

and assumptions of personality-disordered patients. A variety of "schematic restructuring" techniques are outlined to help build new schemas or to shore up defective ones. Beck recommends the use of role playing, imagery, and the reliving of childhood experiences as a means of schema modification and decision making. Important cognitive therapy developments, as they apply to the personality disorders, have recently been introduced by Young (1990) and by Wessler (1993), expanding the range of recommended procedures in this realm.

The variety of philosophies, goals, and therapeutic procedures that differentiate cognitive style approaches make it difficult to group and evaluate these therapies as a unit. Despite these substantive differences, however, certain merits and criticisms may be assigned in common to all these methods. Let us note some of them.

Cognitive style therapists are more active in the treatment process than most of those who follow the self-image focus. They encourage patients to alter their self-defeating perceptions and cognitions instead of allowing them to work things out for themselves. Also in contrast to self-image therapists, they tend to prejudge the patient's cognitive errors in accord with a fixed philosophy, such as "rationality"; they seem to have an "axe to grind," a set of alternative beliefs they seek to inculcate. Their plan is to reorient the patient's misguided attitudes, whatever these may be and toward whatever direction may prove more constructive. Although many subscribe to principles of learning, these cognitive therapists differ from behavioral therapists in that treatment is focused not on overt symptom behaviors, but on those internal mediating processes (perceptions and attitudes) that give rise to and perpetuate these behaviors.

Self-Image Therapies

As touched on in earlier chapters, the diffuse swirl of events buffeting the young child gives way over time to an increasing sense of order and continuity. The most significant configuration that imposes a measure of sameness on a previously more fluid environment is self-as-object, a distinct, ever-present, and identifiable "I" or "me." Self-identity, the image of who we are provides a stable anchor to serve as a guidepost that creates continuity in an ever-changing world. Although few can articulate clearly the psychic elements in this image, it serves to color favorably or unfavorably the nature of one's continuing experiences. For some, the character and valuation of this image is a problematic one, an unhappy and dismaying self-reality, such as may be seen in the *avoidant's* feeling of being alienated, or the *depressive's* image of worthlessness, or the *negativist's* sense of self-discontent. On the other hand, there are those whose self-image is one of complacence, as is seen in the *schizoid,* or that of being gregarious among *histrionics,* or admirable among *narcissists.* Thus, self-images, despite the many particulars of their character, appear to be predominantly either of a positive or a negative quality. The self-image techniques we will describe next appear to fall into the same positive and negative division noted in the prior sentence. An especially insightful and sensitive presentation focusing on issues of self-disavowal and self-confirmation has been formulated by Andrews (1991). Although his integrative therapeutic model will not be detailed in the following paragraphs, it is recommended as a highly fruitful direction for assisting patients in restructuring their sense of self.

We will turn first to those self-image therapists whose orientations are to "free" patients to develop a more positive and confident image of self-worth. Liberated in this manner, patients will learn to act in ways that are individually "right" and thereby "actualize" their inherent potentials. To promote these objectives, the therapist views events from the patient's frame of reference and conveys both a "caring" attitude and a genuine respect for the patient's worth as a human being.

The goal of self-actualization is most prominent in the *client-centered* therapeutic approach of Rogers' "self theory" (1959). This variant of self-image therapy is based on the optimistic premise that humans possess an innate drive for socially constructive behaviors; the task of therapy is to "unleash" these wholesome growth forces. The thesis that humans are driven to "actualize their potentials" may be traced to the seminal writings of Carl Jung and Otto Rank. Jung (1916, 1923) contended that people possessed a singular "life urge" that craved self-realization. Rank (1929, 1936) translated the notion of a drive for self-fulfillment into a philosophy of therapy. To Rank and his disciples—the social worker Jessie Taft (1933) and the child psychiatrist Frederick Allen (1942)—the paramount aim of therapy was to free the patient's "will," a somewhat mystical but powerful energy that leads to self-reliance and uniqueness in personality. This end could best be achieved, according to Rank, by making the patient the central figure in the therapeutic relationship. In effect, the patient became his or her own therapist and the professional helper became, not an all-knowing authority, but a catalyst to strengthen the patient's will toward growth.

Carl Rogers (1942, 1951, 1961, 1967), working independently of Rank and his associates, developed the notion of "client-centered" therapy most clearly and effectively. According to Rogers, patient "growth" is a product neither of special treatment procedures nor professional know-how; rather, it emerges from the quality and character of the therapeutic relationship. More specifically, it occurs as a consequence of certain attitudes of therapists, notably their *genuineness,* that is, their ability to be themselves in therapy and to express their feelings and thoughts without pretensions or the cloak of professional authority. Such therapists offer *unconditional positive regard,*—the capacity to feel respect for the patient as a worthy being, no matter how unappealing and destructive the patient's behaviors may be. They also provide *accurate empathic understanding,* that is, sensitivity to the patient's subjective world, and have the ability to communicate this awareness to the patient. In line with Rogers' therapeutic model, the patient assumes full responsibility for the subject and goals of therapeutic discussion; the therapist reflects rather than interprets the patient's thoughts and feelings and encourages, but does not recommend, efforts toward growth and individual expression. Experience appears to show that these techniques work best with patients who are already endowed with a positive sense of self-worth, perhaps narcissists and histrionics who are going through a particularly trying period in their lives.

More suitable for those who have experienced the anguish of a chronically troubled life, such as *avoidants, depressives, negativists, masochists,* even *borderlines,* are the philosophies and techniques of modern-day "existential therapists," who seek to enable patients to deal with their unhappiness realistically, yet in a constructive and positive manner. The existential school possesses a less sanguine view of humans' inherent fate, believing that they must struggle to find a valued meaning to life; therapy, then, attempts to strengthen the patient's capacity to choose an "authentic" existence.

Self-image therapists of this persuasion are committed to the view that people must confront and accept the inevitable dilemmas of life if they are to achieve a measure of authentic self-realization. Themes such as these were first formulated in the philosophical writings of Kierkegaard, Nietzsche, Husserl, Heidegger and, more recently, in those of Jaspers, Buber, Sartre, and Tillich. From these sources, also, may be traced the foundations of existential therapy, notably those advanced by Ludwig Binswanger (1942, 1947, 1956), Medard Boss (1957, 1963), Viktor Frankl (1955, 1965), and Rollo May (1958, 1963). Despite differences in terminology and philosophical emphasis, these existential variants are similar insofar as their approach to therapy.

Important to all existential therapists is the "being-together encounter" between patient and therapist. This encounter, characterized by mutual acceptance and self-revelation, enables patients to find an authentic meaning to their existence, despite the profound and inescapable contradictions that life presents. The focus both in *logotherapy* (Frankl) and *daseinsanalyse* (Binswanger, Boss), the two major variants of existential treatment, is to utilize the insoluble predicaments and suffering of life as a way of discovering self-meaning and purpose. By facing the "inevitable" with equanimity, patients rise above petty frustrations and discovers the fundamentals upon which the genuine self can unfold. As mentioned previously, the philosophy espoused by these existentially oriented self-image therapists may be especially suitable to personality disorders for whom life has been a series of alienations and unhappiness (e.g., *avoidants, depressives*).

The underlying assumption of "client-centered," perhaps even "rational-emotive therapy," is that people may have been too harsh with themselves, tending to blame and judge their actions more severely than is necessary. No more opposite a philosophy could be found than that espoused in Glasser's "reality therapy" (1961, 1965) or Mowrer's "integrity therapy" (1961, 1965, 1966). In effect, these men claim that patients are sick because they are irresponsible; they are *not* "over-socialized" victims of too rigid standards, but "undersocialized" victims of a failure to adhere to worthy social or moralistic standards. Anguish stems not from too much guilt and self-derogation but from an unwillingness to admit guilt and irresponsibility, such as may be found among *antisocials, sadists,* and *paranoids.* The task of therapy, according to this approach to altering self-image is to confront patients with their misbehaviors and irresponsibilities, and to make them "confess" their wrongdoings. Therapists do not accept patients' facile rationalizations or other efforts to find scapegoats for their misfortunes. Only by facing and admitting the "reality" of their deceit and guilt can patients regain self-integrity and learn to deal with the future truthfully and objectively. No longer needing to hide their sins, they can rectify past mistakes and find a more socially responsible style of life, without shame or the fear of being discovered. Therapists of this persuasion would not be suitable for dealing with a variety of personality disorders, such as avoidants, dependents, and masochists. Moreover, where their philosophy may seem appropriate, as previously noted, there may be some difficulty in getting these patients to agree that they possess attitudes that promote and perpetuate their difficulties. Nevertheless, their methods may prove to be a useful entrée into the self-image conceptions these troublesome patients possess.

Object-Representations Therapies

As described in prior chapters, and as will be elaborated further in later chapters, significant experiences from the past, especially those involving important figures of childhood, leave an inner imprint, a structural residue composed of memories, attitudes, and affects that serve as a substrate of dispositions for anticipating, perceiving, and reacting to life's ongoing events, especially those related to significant persons in their current world. The character and specifics of these internalized representations of others from the past remain as templates for interpreting and reacting to new relationships in the present. It is this inner template that shapes our perceptions of other persons that requires identification and analysis. These "object-representations" are, along with self-image, the major components and content of the mind. They bridge the division we have made between the phenomenological and intrapsychic realms in that they are essentially unconscious images, assumptions, and emotions that persistently intrude in the patient's ongoing relationships. Moreover, they can be readily reactivated into consciousness and thereby be available for phenomenological analysis and intervention.

Object-representations follow from Freud's observation that patients often expressed totally unwarranted beliefs and attitudes toward him. He noted that these seemingly irrational thoughts and assumptions reflected deeply embedded and usually hidden anticipations and feelings toward significant persons from the patient's past. This "transference" phenomenon, which illuminated important aspects of the repressed unconscious, could be facilitated if the therapist remained a totally neutral object; assumption of this passive role, "forced" the patient to attribute traits to the therapist drawn from earlier relationships with parents or other significant childhood figures.

The task of therapy was to uproot these elements of the unconscious, to free them of all conscious appraisal and understanding, as well as to release potentially constructive energies that had been tied up in the task of keeping them repressed. To do this, Freud employed numerous procedures such as of free association, dream interpretation and, most importantly, the analysis of the "transference neurosis," a process that characterizes what we are referring to as *object-relations* therapy (Greenberg & Mitchell, 1983).

All modern phenomenological and classical intrapsychic therapists recognize that patients project onto the therapist attitudes and emotions that derive from past relationships. Object-relations therapists consider these transference phenomena to represent the nucleus of the patient's infantile conflicts and pathological defenses. More than classical analytic therapists, however, they not only seek to foster the expression of transference materials and reveal their current manifestations, but center their attentions on making them conscious and to subject them to careful reworking in present life circumstances.

Should object-relations transference phenomena be actively resisted, the therapist attempts to break through these resistances by interpreting their irrational and childhood basis. Conscious insight into these object-relations distortions is designed to free the patient from their pernicious effects by breaking the hold of childhood misconceptions and anticipations. Not only do these procedures reframe the distortions of the past, but they liberate energies tied up in their repression, and thereby provide a renewed sense of self-mastery.

Although the uncovering of unconscious materials is a necessary phase in their work, object-relations therapists pay less heed to matters of the past than they do to the resolution of present difficulties. In another deviation from classical psychoanalytic doctrines, they assert that adult pathology is not simply a repetition of "nuclear" infantile neuroses. Early experiences are recognized as the basis for later difficulties, but intervening events are thought to modify their impact; problematic learnings and anticipations acquired early in life promote new difficulties that, in turn, provoke new maladaptive strategies. By adulthood, then, an extensive series of events have occurred, making present behaviors and cognitions far removed from their initial childhood origins. Consequently, and in contrast to classical analysts, they consider it digressive, if not wasteful, to become enmeshed in the details of the roots of infantile neuroses. In

their stead, efforts can more fruitfully be expended in uncovering and resolving the patient's *current phenomenological* schemas and strategies.

Although face-to-face discussion is the more typical treatment procedure, free association may be used to uncover the character of the patient's unexpressed beliefs and assumptions. Similarly, relevant childhood experiences are probed and unraveled, but not for the purpose of resolving them, as in classical analysis. Rather they are exposed to demonstrate both the foundations of current difficulties and the repetitive sequence of destructive consequences they have caused. The therapist actively interprets the patient's object-relations distortions, not only in the treatment interaction, but as they are expressed in the patient's everyday relationships with others. The focus on the current ramifications of distorted phenomenological assumptions, and the direct mode of attack on the vicious circles they engender, further distinguishes the object-relations treatment approach from both other phenomenological methods and classical analysis.

Among the merits ascribed by proponents of phenomenological modalities are the following:

1. The language of phenomenological discourse represents events in terms that are meaningful to patients rather than in the obscure vernacular of intrapsychic therapies or the overly objectivized terminology of behavioral schools. Consequently, patients understand what is "going on" in the consulting room and can readily translate into reality what they have learned. Discussions at the phenomenological level, then, facilitate both the acquisition of insight and its application to current realities.

2. Phenomenological therapies are carried out in a face-to-face interpersonal interaction that resembles normal extratherapeutic relationships to a greater degree than those of most other therapeutic schools. Consequently, what is learned in the setting of phenomenological treatment should more readily generalize to the natural life settings for which they are ultimately intended.

3. Phenomenological approaches focus on internal mediating processes that underlie behavior. Consequently, they are more efficient instruments for solving pervasive or complex difficulties than are behavior therapies that deal primarily with isolated or well-circumscribed symptoms. Similarly, phenomenological therapies can grapple with such nebulous symptom clusters as "existential dilemmas" and "identity crises" that are further obscured by the conceptual schema of intrapsychic schools and resist formulation in the overly precise language of behavior therapies.

On the other hand, there have been many criticisms leveled at phenomenological therapies, such as the following:

1. Many phenomenologists formulate their procedures in a vague and unsystematized manner, presenting a discursive melange of sporadic recommendations as to how therapy should be conducted. Upon careful analysis, these recommendations prove to possess no more substance than those of supportive reassurance, ventilation, and persuasion, although they are cloaked in pretentious semantics and specious social philosophies. Critics note that all psychotherapies employ the processes that phenomenological therapists consider essential; thus, phenomenologists make a virtue out of the commonplace.

2. Phenomenological therapies fail to deal with the historical course or the unconscious roots of personality pathology. According to intrapsychic therapists, consciously acknowledged attitudes and feelings, which characterize the data of phenomenological therapy, are but superficial verbalizations that cloak deeper motives and emotions. As they see it, unless the patient comes fully to grips with these hidden events, true insight and action will constantly be subverted, and therapeutic progress will be blunted or prove illusory.

3. Phenomenological approaches may be of minimal value with patients who otherwise are unable to face or analyze their attitudes and emotions. In short, these procedures are limited to relatively stable and moderately intelligent adults whose functional capacities are sufficiently intact to enable them to engage in calm self-exploration or symbolic verbal discourse.

INTRAPSYCHIC MODALITY INTERVENTIONS

Intrapsychic therapy had its formal beginning in the pioneering studies of Freud during the last decade of the nineteenth century. We have discussed both frequently and at length the history, rationale, and variants of intrapsychic theory in Chapter 2; more will be said concerning this model of the mind in each of the clinical chapters later in the book; hence, there is no need to review these matters at length here. However, and

despite inevitable controversies and divergencies in emphasis, often appearing more divisive upon first than later examination, intrapsychic therapists share certain beliefs and goals that are worthy of note and distinguish them from other modality orientations; two will be noted here.

First, intrapsychic therapists focus on *internal mediating* processes and structures that ostensibly underlie and give rise to overt behavior. In contrast to phenomenologists, however, their attention is directed to those mediating events that operate at the unconscious rather than the conscious level. To them, overt behaviors and phenomenological reports are merely surface expressions of dynamically orchestrated, but deeply repressed emotions and associated defensive strategies, all framed in a distinctive structural morphology. Because these unconscious processes and structures are essentially impervious to surface maneuvers, techniques of behavior modification are seen as mere palliatives, and methods of phenomenological reorientation are thought to resolve only those difficulties that are so trivial or painless as to be tolerated consciously. "True" therapy occurs only when these deeply ingrained elements of the unconscious are fully unearthed and analyzed. The task of intrapsychic therapy, then, is to circumvent or pierce resistances that shield these insidious structures and processes, bring them into consciousness, and rework them into more constructive forms.

Second, intrapsychic therapists see as their goal the *reconstruction* of the patient's personality, not the removal of a symptom or the reframing of an attitude. Disentangling the underlying structure of personality pathology, forged of many interlocking elements that build into a network of pervasive strategies and mechanisms, is the object of their therapy. To extinguish an isolated behavior or to redirect this or that belief or assumption, is too limited an aim, touching but a mere fraction of a formidable pathological system whose very foundations must be reworked. Wolberg (1967) illustrated this philosophy in the following analogy:

A leaky roof can expeditiously be repaired with tar paper and asphalt shingles. This will help not only to keep the rain out, but also ultimately to dry out and to eliminate some of the water damage to the entire house. We have a different set of conditions if we undertake to tear down the structure and to rebuild the dwelling. We will not only have a watertight roof, but we will have a better house . . . If our object is merely to keep the rain out of the house, we will do better with the short-term repair focused on the roof and not bother with the more hazardous, albeit ultimately more substantial reconstruction. (p.137)

Reconstruction, then, rather than repair is the option chosen by intrapsychic therapists. They set for themselves the laborious task of rebuilding those functions (regulatory mechanisms) and structures (morphologic organization) that comprise the substance of personality, not merely its facade.

In brief, intrapsychic therapists contend that treatment approaches designed merely to modify behavioral conduct and phenomenological complaints or distortions fail to deal with the root source of pathology and are bound therefore to be of short-lived efficacy. As they view it, therapy must reconstruct the "inner" structures and processes that underlie overt behaviors and beliefs. It does not sacrifice the goal of personality reconstruction for short-term behavioral or cognitive relief. Reworking the source of the problem rather than controlling its effects is what distinguishes intrapsychic therapy as a treatment procedure. Once the unconscious roots of the impairments are disclosed and dislodged, patients should no longer precipitate new difficulties for themselves and will be free to develop strategies that are consonant with their healthy potentials.

As noted previously, intrapsychic therapists were the founders of *transference analyses,* a broad-based approach that continues to be a major treatment technique employed to this day, whatever other therapeutic measures they find congenial to achieve their goals.

There are other tools of *intrapsychic therapy* that are quite distinctive to this treatment technique. They are designed not only to uncover the *content* of the mind, such as described previously in our section on object-representations, a realm shared with phenomenologically oriented therapists, but are features of the mind that are *exclusively* in the unconscious, namely the *dynamic* regulatory mechanisms and the *structural* morphologic organization, both of which are investigated and treated simultaneously in intrapsychic therapies. The following procedures address these aspects of structure and functioning that are distinctively intrapsychic.

Many patients seem unable to bring their memories and feelings into consciousness. To overcome this obstacle, classical analysts employ the method of *free association,* that is, having the patient relax on a couch and articulate any thoughts that cross the mind, no matter how trivial or embarrassing they may appear to be. This procedure circumvents many of the memory blocks that may preclude the recall of significant past events and the discharge of their associated emotions.

Residuals of the past may be uncovered by methods of *dream analysis,* which Freud referred to as the "royal road to the unconscious." Repressed fears and desires are filtered through the patient's defenses at night, although they take form in various symbolic disguises. By an introspective analysis of his own dreams, Freud (1900) formulated this brilliant technique for deciphering the unconscious meaning and significance of dream symbols.

Other techniques have been devised to facilitate the exposure and manipulation of unconscious processes and structures in cases that are resistant to standard analytical procedures. Only one of these will be noted here, that of *hypnotherapy.* Hypnotic induction, either through verbal means or by use of drugs (narcotherapy), may be employed to circumvent barriers to both insight and action. During the trance state, achieved at the hands of a trusted therapist, the patient may be able to ease repressive controls and thereby revive memories and emotions that resist free association and dream techniques. Similarly, posthypnotic suggestions may provide a needed impetus to behaviors for which the patient is psychologically prepared, but is unable to muster the courage to carry out. As a rule, hypnosis should be utilized as an adjunct to rather than the primary instrument of a treatment program.

No one can question the goals of intrapsychic therapy; they are highly commendable, if difficult to achieve. It is not the goals of the intrapsychic approach that are viewed critically; rather, dissent arises with regard to the theoretical rationale, technique, and feasibility of these methods. Let us note several of the objections.

First, and perhaps the most persistent criticism, is the assertion that intrapsychic data are both vague and inaccessible. Therapists are expected to manipulate metaphysical entities whose very existence is unverifiable and whose modification can never be empirically confirmed. Exerting efforts to alter these unobservable processes is considered nothing less than foolishness, and claiming success in such ventures as nothing but an article of faith. In short, dealing with matters of the unconscious is a throwback to the days when mysticism flourished, a continuation of a prescientific way of thinking from which psychotherapy must be liberated.

Second, the process of intrapsychic treatment is considered unnecessarily involved and digressive, dredging up facts and events that are entirely subsidiary, if not irrelevant to the nature of the patient's problem. Rather than focusing directly on the difficulty, as do therapists of other schools, the intrapsychic therapist pursues a host of activities that focus on the patient's past, regulatory mechanisms, morphologic structure, and underlying motivations. Such circuitous pathways to the resolution of personality pathology are seen not only as wasteful and time consuming, but as a sign of presumption and arrogance on the part of the therapist, who is asserting that the patient is troubled by something other than the problem stipulated by that patient. By therapeutic maneuvers, the therapist "forces" the patient to accept ostensible ailments that fit the therapist's theoretical presuppositions. That the discovery of these underlying problems proves to be a laborious and prolonged task of doubtful therapeutic value, in this day of tight finances and managed-care systems, is a further reason to question the utility of the intrapsychic approach.

Third, as just noted, even if intrapsychic therapies were shown to be efficacious, few patients are able to devote the time or expend the funds required to pursue a full course of treatment. Classical analytic techniques demand at least three or four sessions per week over a 2- to 5-year span. Assuming treatment was feasible on these accounts, problems would still arise because there are too few trained therapists to make this approach available to the masses. In short, intrapsychic therapies must be relegated to a secondary position among treatment techniques on wholly practical grounds, if on no other.

ASSOCIATED MODALITY INTERVENTIONS

There are modalities of treatment that do not fit readily into the four data levels we have separated for the preceding discussions. Nevertheless, they are of sufficient import to deserve notation in the following paragraphs.

Family and Couples Interventions

The patient who comes to therapy is often but one member of a pathological family unit. Not uncommonly, interactions between family members form a complex of shared personality pathologies, the patient being merely its most dramatic "symptom."

The primary patient is enmeshed in daily encounters in a system of interlocking attitudes and behaviors that not only intensify the patient's illness, but sustain the pathological family unit. Each member, through reciprocal perceptual and behavioral distortions, reinforces pathogenic reactions in others, thus contributing to a vicious circle of self-perpetuating responses. It follows logically from this premise that therapy must intervene not only with the patient, but with the total family; in short, what is needed is family therapy, not individual therapy.

Several variants in technique have been proposed to achieve the goal of disentangling these reciprocally reinforcing pathological family relations (Ackerman, 1958; Boszormenyi-Nagy & Framo, 1965; Wachtel & Wachtel, 1986). Essentially, the therapist brings several members of the family together, explores major areas of conflict, and exposes the destructive behaviors that have perpetuated their difficulties. The therapist clarifies misunderstandings, dissolves barriers to communication, and neutralizes areas of prejudice, hostility, guilt, and fear. In this manner, the clinician gradually disengages the pathogenic machinery of the family system and enables its members to explore healthier patterns of relating. By recommending new, more wholesome attitudes and behaviors and by supporting family members as they test out these patterns, the therapist may succeed in resolving not only the difficulties of the primary patient, but pathological trends that have taken root in all members.

Environmental Management

Little progress can be expected in therapy if the patient's everyday environment provides few gratifications and is filled with tension and conflict. Like the proverbial high-priced automobile that uses up gasoline faster than it can be pumped in, an unwholesome life situation may set the patient back faster than therapy can move the person forward. For these reasons, it may be necessary to control or modify disruptive home or work influences, or perhaps encourage the patient to move away from these disorganizing effects.

Beyond relief and protection, environmental manipulation may be employed to achieve positive therapeutic ends such as releasing potentials or developing social skills. These two elements, the alleviation of situational stress and the exploitation of situational opportunities for constructive change, constitute the chief goals of environmental management. The deeply rooted habits of personality disorders are not readily diverted by mere changes in environmental conditions; nevertheless, they are worth a try should opportunities for their use present themselves.

Supportive Procedures

Whereas environmental management focuses on situational context seeking to exploit the persons and activities surrounding the patient's daily life for therapeutic purposes, the procedures of supportive therapy focus directly on the patient. In contrast to other individual treatment approaches, however, supportive therapy does not seek to make fundamental changes in the patient's premorbid attitudes and strategies, but to reactivate and strengthen more adaptive patterns so that he can again function as he did prior to succumbing to a current clinical syndrome. All personality disorders can benefit by periods of supportive treatment.

Supportive procedures are employed either as the principal mode of therapy or as adjuncts to other treatment methods. In his illuminating texts on psychotherapy, Wolberg (1954, 1967) outlines the chief indications of the supportive approach, distinguishing between principal and adjunctive uses; we will paraphrase several of his recommendations as they may apply to the personality disordered.

1. Mildly disturbed personalities who have succumbed temporarily to a transient clinical syndrome. A brief period of therapeutic intervention, designed to alleviate upsetting symptoms and to shore up formerly adequate behaviors and attitudes, may suffice to bring the patient to his habitual level of equilibrium and stability.

2. Personality-disordered patients whose current outlook and actions constitute a serious threat to themselves and others. As a necessary expedient, supportive measures may serve to prevent suicidal impulses, calm intense anxieties and panic reactions or deter the acting-out of homicidal and other destructive tendencies.

3. Structurally defective personalities whose stability is perpetually in doubt, and who may be kept from more severe disorders requiring long-term therapeutic work. In these more extended supportive contacts, patients are guided to avoid and "ride through" recurring conflicts and tensions that might otherwise precipitate psychotic episodes.

4. As adjuncts to other forms of therapy, supportive measures may be fruitfully employed to strengthen the patient's coping resources during periods of marked or unanticipated anxiety or depression. During these exigencies, supportive approaches may revive patients' flagging hopes, bolster their coping strategies, and ameliorate tensions that can seriously disrupt the normal progress of treatment.

Central to the varied techniques that compose supportive therapy is the patient's acceptance of the therapist's "benevolent authority," as Wolberg put it. The therapist must maintain a sympathetic but firm attitude, exhibiting a tolerance of the patient's irrational emotions or behavioral deviance, yet inspiring strength through the force of authority and forthright honesty. As a consequence, the patient will be inclined to trust the therapist's judgments and view the clinician as an ally worthy of identification and respect. With this as a foundation, the therapist may achieve the desired ends.

INTEGRATING MODALITY TECHNIQUES

What specifically are the procedures that distinguish *integrative* personologic therapy from other models of an eclectic nature?

Modern therapies are often practiced in a linear format, which assumes that a simple additivity of effects within a clinical data level will be sufficient to deal with the problems at hand. In Chapter 4, we spoke of content-bound versus content-free assessment. In this chapter, we have outlined a series of *domain-bound modality therapies*. Unfortunately, there remains the practice of some mental health professionals of employing single modalities, exclusively cognitive therapy, exclusively behavioral therapy, exclusively pharmacological therapy, and so on, to every patient they encounter.

If personality disorders were anchored exclusively to one particular structural or functional domain (as phobias are thought of being primarily behavioral in nature), domain-bound psychotherapy would be appropriate and desirable. Personality disorders, however, are not exclusively behavioral or cognitive constructs confined to particular clinical data levels. Instead, they are multioperational and systemic. No part of the system exists in complete isolation. Instead, every part is directly or indirectly tied to every other, such that an emergent synergism lends the whole a clinical tenacity that makes personality a "real" thing to be reckoned with in any therapeutic endeavor. Therapies should possess at least as much content validity as the disorders they seek to remedy. If the scope of the therapy is insufficient relative to the scope of the disorder, the refurbished system will have considerable difficulty fulfilling its broad adaptive roles. Both unstructured intrapsychic therapy and highly structured behavioral techniques, to note the extremes, share this deficiency.

Domain-bound psychotherapy is increasingly becoming part of the past. In growing numbers, clinicians are identifying themselves, not as psychodynamic or as cognitive-behavioral, but as eclectic or integrative. As noted previously, eclecticism is insufficient to undergird personologic therapy. As a movement, not a construct, it cannot prescribe to personality the form of those therapies that will remedy its pathologies. Eclecticism is too open with regard to content and too imprecise to achieve focused goals. The intrinsically configurational nature of personality disorders, their multioperationism, and the interwoven character of personologic domains, simply are not as integrated in eclecticism as they are in personality.

Establishing a polarity-oriented and domain-focused treatment strategy is fundamental, but only an initial step. Two elements of clinical focus and logic may be distinguished. As outlined as our framework in previous sections, the first concerns the long-range *goals* of therapy that endure across numerous sessions and against which progress is measured; the second concerns the specific *tactics* by which these goals are pursued in each therapy hour. The first focus has been called *strategies,* the second that of *modalities.* The distinction is similar but not quite the same as that between theory and technique; they are less useful because the term theory is often doctrinaire and technique often domain-bound.

Ideally, strategies and tactics should be integrated, with the tactics chosen to accomplish strategic goals, and the strategies chosen on the basis of what tactics might actually achieve given other constraints, such as the number of therapy sessions and the nature of the problem. In retrospect, intrapsychic therapies are highly strategic, but tactically impoverished; pure behavioral therapies are highly tactical, but strategically narrow and inflexible. There are, in fact, many different ways that strategies might be operationalized. Just as diagnostic criteria are neither necessary nor sufficient for membership in a given class, it is likely that no technique is an inevitable consequence of a given clinical strategy. Subtle variations in technique and the ingenuity of individual therapists to invent techniques ad hoc assure that an almost infinite number of ways exist to operationalize or put into action a given clinical strategy.

In the first of the *integrative procedures* we recommend (Millon, 1988, 1990), what has been called "potentiated pairings," treatment methods are combined simultaneously to overcome problematic characteristics that might be refractory to each technique if they were administered separately. These composites pull and push for change on many different fronts, so that the therapy becomes as multioperational and as tenacious as the disorder itself. A currently popular illustration of these treatment pairings is found in what has been referred to as "cognitive-behavior" therapy.

The term "catalytic sequences" has been proposed to represent procedures whose intent is to plan the order in which coordinated treatments are executed. They comprise therapeutic arrangements and timing series to optimize the impact of changes that would be less effective if the sequential combination were otherwise arranged. In a catalytic sequence, for example, the clinician might seek first to alter a patient's stuttering by direct modification procedures that, if achieved, may facilitate the use of cognitive methods in producing self-image changes in confidence. These, in turn, may foster the utility of interpersonal techniques in effecting improvements in social relationships.

There are no discrete boundaries between potentiating pairings and catalytic sequences, just as there is no line between their respective pathological analogues (i.e., adaptive inflexibility and vicious circles). Nor should therapists be concerned about when to use one rather than another. Instead, they are intrinsically interdependent phenomena whose application is intended to foster increased flexibility and, we hope, a beneficent rather than a vicious circle. As Figure 5.5 illustrates, potentiated pairings and catalytic sequences represent but the first order of therapeutic synergism. The idea of a "potentiated sequence" or a "catalytic pairing" recognizes that these logical composites may build on each other in proportion to what the tenacity of the disorder requires.

One question we may want to ask concerns the limits to which the content of personologic therapy can be specified in advance at a tactical level, that is, the extent to which specific potentiating pairings and catalytic sequences can be identified for each of the personality disorders. Each of the clinical chapters in this text contains a chart presenting the salience of each of the clinical domains for that disorder. To the extent that each patient's presentations is prototypal, the potentiating pairings and catalytic sequences that are actually used should derive from modality tactics oriented to several of

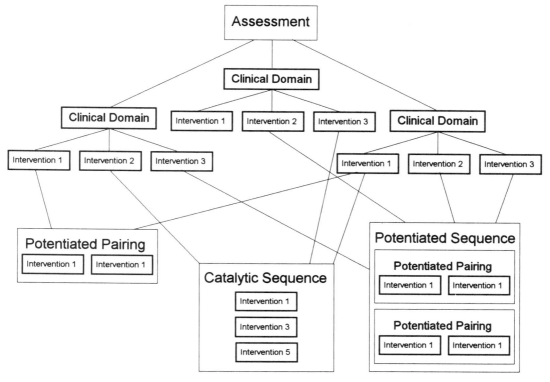

Figure 5.5   Therapy from assessment to domain to actual practice.

the more salient domains. That, however, probably represents the limits to which theory can guide practice in an abstract sense, that is, without knowing anything about the history and characteristics of the *specific* individual case to which the theory is to be applied. Just as individuality is ultimately so rich that it cannot be exhausted by any taxonomic schema, personologic therapy, ideally performed, is full of specificities that cannot readily be resolved into generalities. Potentiating pairings, catalytic sequences, and whatever other higher order composites that therapists may evolve, are conducted at an idiographic rather than at a nomothetic or disorder level. Accordingly, their precise content is specified as much by the logic of the individual case as by the logic of the disorders themselves. At an idiographic level, we must all be open-mindedly eclectic.

Perhaps we can best grasp the intergrative process of personologic therapy if we think of personality domains as analogous to the sections of an orchestra, and the pathological characteristics of a patient as a clustering of discordant instruments. To extend the analogy, therapists may be seen as conductors whose task is to bring forth a harmonious balance among all the instruments, muting some here, accentuating others there, all to the end of fulfilling their knowledge of how "the composition" can best be made consonant. The task is not that of altering just one instrument, but of altering all, in concert. Just as music requires a balanced score, composed of harmonic counterpoints, rhythmic patterns, and melodic combinations, what is needed in personologic therapy is a likewise balanced and synergistic program, a coordinated strategy of counterpoised techniques designed to optimize treatment effects in an idiographically combinatorial and sequential manner.

Obviously, a tremendous amount of knowledge, both about the nature of the patient's disorders and about diverse modes of intervention, is required to perform personologic therapy. To maximize this synergism requires that the therapist be a little like a jazz soloist. Not only should the professional be fully versed in the various musical keys, (i.e., in techniques of psychotherapy that span all personologic domains), he or she should also be prepared to respond to subtle fluctuations in the patient's thoughts, actions, and emotions, any of which could take the composition in a wide variety of directions, and integrate these with the overall plan of therapy *as it evolves*. After the instruments have been packed away and the band goes home, a retrospective account of the entire process should reveal a level of thematic continuity and logical order commensurate with that which would have existed had all relevant constraints been known in advance.

The integrative processes of personologic therapy are dictated by the nature of the construct. The content of personologic therapy, however, must be specified on some other basis. Whereas personality is, by definition, the patterning of intraindividual variables, the nature of these variables does not follow from the definition, but must be supplied by some principle or on some basis "outside" the construct. In Millon's model, for example, the content of personality is derived from evolutionary theory, a discipline that informs but exists apart from personology. In and of itself, personality is a structural-functional concept that refers to the intraorganismic patterning of variables; it does not in itself say what these variables are, nor can it, no more than it can describe the personality of an individual person.

Ideally, in a truly integrated clinical science, the theoretical basis that lends personality its content—the basis on which its taxonomy is generated and patients assessed and classified—would also provide the basis for the clinical goals and tactics of therapy. Without such a basis, anarchy ensues, for we will have no rationale by which to select from an almost infinite number of specific domain techniques that can be used, except the dogmas of past traditions. The "truth" is what works in the end, a pragmatism based on a contemporary integrationism.

Final Word: Context and System Considerations

The individual person represents but one structural level of life's systems; other levels of organization might also be considered and analyzed. Thus, individuals may be viewed as system units that exist within larger ecological milieus, such as dyads, families, communities, and ultimately, cultures. Like the personality system, these higher-level systems contain homeostatic processes that tend to sustain and reinforce their own unique patterning of internal variables. In this sense, both dyads and families may be said to possess their own distinct personalities, and to contain regulatory mechanisms whereby functional constancy is maintained within their respective levels of structural organization. Some systems theorists argue that these larger systems are solely responsible for creating and sustaining person-level pathology, and that individual pathology, in effect, simply does not exist because it is derivable from and can be "reduced" to these more encompassing systems. The authors of this book philosophically reject such forms of system reductionism, whether it is a reductionism to the part, as when personality is predicated to only a particular clinical domain, or reductionism to the whole, as when the content of personality problems, or even Axis I pathologies, are believed to be the *sole* product of and completely explainable by wider-system interactions (e.g., family relationships).

The homeostatic pull of larger ecologies may often work at cross purposes with therapeutic change. Constancy within the family system, for example, depends among other things on each individual's conformity to the conscious, as well as unconscious or implicit, expectancies of others. These expectancies may be viewed as constraints on higher-order systems, in much the same way that personologic domains may be viewed as constraints on personality functioning.

When an individual involved in personologic therapy begins to change or changes suddenly, his or her role in larger systems is likely to change as adaptability and role flexibility increase. From the perspective of the individual, this change may be welcome and constructive. From the perspective of some system in which the individual is embedded, however, individual change may seem disruptive or hostile to the larger structural organization, threatening a whole pattern of interrelationships and expectancies, thus pitting the individual in his or her changed role against implicit contextual factors that work to maintain the status quo. In the family therapy literature, the "identified patient," or IP, is the classic example. The IP, usually a problem child, is someone whose problem exists in order to conceal some other pathology latent in the family system, often a conflict of some kind between the parents. Functionally, the identified patient redirects attention away from something that, if recognized openly, would be much more dangerous to the family. When conflict begins to flare, the IP's pathology intensifies as well, bringing the family back to homeostasis, albeit one of pathology rather than health. Because some form of feedback must occur for the IP's pathology to be coordinated to parental conflict, the IP role may correctly be thought of as an active form of defense that emerges at a family systems level of organization. Undoubtedly, the family system has other emergent properties that influence the development of personality, if only by establishing and sustaining normal and pathological patterns of object representations within a family and influencing the character of these object representations across generations of family life.

The fact that the ecology of personality and personality disorders is itself organizational and systemic argues for another principle of therapy: Pull as much of the surrounding interpersonal context into the therapeutic process as possible, or risk being defeated by it. Where ecological factors are operative, therapeutic gains may be minimized and the risk of relapse increased. In the best case scenario, family members can be brought into therapy as a group or as needed, no latent pathologies will exist, and the family and other systems will cooperate in discussing characteristics of the status quo that perpetuate pathology and contingencies that might be established to promote change. In the worst-case scenario, family members will refuse to come into therapy under some thin rationale, probably because nonparticipation is one way to passively undermine a change they in fact fear. If family members are not motivated to assist in the therapeutic process, it is likely that the individual is in therapy either because the person must be, as in cases of court referral, or because family members do not want the burden of guilt that would accrue from actively refusing assistance. In fact, the goal of a cursory trial of therapy may be to "prove" that the disturbed individual cannot be reached, even by a professional, and therefore is a "hopeless" case as far as the family is concerned.

Group therapy operates on essentially the same principle. Here, however, instead of trying to co-opt a context that already exists and may be implicitly unfriendly to change, the therapist creates a new transactional context whose explicit purpose *is* change. In individual therapy, the client gains only one additional relationship to learn through, the transference relationship. In group therapy, however, the client has the opportunity to learn through the experiences of many different others, and to gain a diversity of perspectives and reactions to his or her own behavior. Whereas the observations of the therapist are observations of just one person, the consensus of a well-balanced group provides powerful and invaluable feedback, the validity of which is truly ecological. Group therapy represents the one chance the therapist has to create a higher-order system whose explicit purpose and only reason for being is to facilitate change. In cases of personality pathology of moderate severity, where the individual possesses enough structural strength to tolerate disparate opinions and still maintain self-cohesion, that opportunity should be utilized whenever possible.

PART II

PLEASURE-DEFICIENT PERSONALITIES

CHAPTER 6

Schizoid Personality Disorders: The Asocial Pattern

We begin our presentation of the major pathological patterns with personalities that are grouped together by virtue of their marked *pleasure deficiencies:* the capacity to experience that crucial component of the polarities pertaining to life enhancement and life preservation. The three personality patterns in this classification group, for one reason or another, lack the ability to experience the rewards, joys, and positive experiences of life. Included among them are the schizoid, avoidant, and depressive personality prototypes. In the first category, the *schizoid* disorder, there appears to be a significant deficit in the person's intrinsic capacity to experience the joyful and pleasurable aspects of life. Patients in the second category, the *avoidant* personality, show an excessive preoccupation and oversensitivity to the stresses of life, such that they invest all their energies in avoiding pain and misfortune; their hyperalertness to the possibility of troublesome events appears to preclude their ability to attend, to seek, and hence to experience the pleasures of life. Theirs is not an intrinsic deficit, but a preoccupation with matters of danger and distress. In the third prototypal group, the *depressive* personality, there is a sense of hopelessness and futility that inclines these individuals not to expect and therefore not to experience the rewards and joys of life. They would rather not expose themselves to the possibility of pleasure for fear that it will either not be forthcoming, or would prove ultimately to be deceptive and disappointing. Thus, for different reasons, intrinsic deficiency, preoccupation elsewhere, or despairing its possibility, we see personalities take similar but different forms of expression—schizoid, avoidant, depressive.

The present chapter focuses on the schizoid personality, individuals distinguished by their aloof, introverted, and seclusive nature. They have difficulty in establishing friendships, prefer distant or limited involvements with others, and seem uninterested in (if not aversive to) social

activities. In general, they appear to gain little satisfaction in personal relationships. Two personality syndromes, schizoid and avoidant comprise what we have differentiated as the *passive* and *active* variants of a "socially detached" pattern. Although neither of these types is entirely homogeneous, each exhibits distinctive clinical features and experiential histories. The first type, the passively detached variant, or what has been labeled the "schizoid personality" in the DSM-IV, displays emotional and cognitive deficits that hinder the development of close or warm relationships. The second variant, the actively detached, or DSM-IV "avoidant" personality, includes individuals whose experiences of interpersonal rejection and deprecation have led them to be mistrustful of and to keep distance from close relationships.

This chapter attends to schizoid personalities. Relatively normal variants of these individuals are seen in every walk of life; they appear untroubled and indifferent, and function adequately in their occupations, but are judged by their associates as rather colorless and shy, seeming to prefer to be by themselves and to be lacking in the need to communicate with or relate affectionately to others. Typically, they remain in the background of social life, work quietly and unobtrusively at their jobs, and are rarely noticed even by those with whom they have routine contact. They would fade into the passing scene, to live their lives in a tangential and undisturbed inconspicuousness, were it not that there are persons who expect or wish them to be more vibrant, alive, and involved.

Most distinctive among clinical variants is a profound defect in the ability to form social relationships and an underresponsiveness to all forms of stimulation. These individuals exhibit an intrinsic emotional blandness; an imperviousness to joy, anger, or sadness. Seemingly unmoved by emotional stimuli, the schizoid appears to possess a generalized inability to be aroused and activated;

a lack of initiative and vitality. Their interpersonal passivity then, is not by intention or for self-protective reasons, but due to a fundamental imperceptiveness to the needs and moods of others.

What appears most distinctive about these individuals is that they seem to lack the equipment for experiencing the finer shades and subtleties of emotional life. They appear especially unaware of, if not insensitive to, the feelings and thoughts of others. Some interpret their interpersonal passivity as a sign of hostility and rejection; it does not represent, however, an active disinterest but rather a fundamental *incapacity* to sense the moods and needs that are experienced by others, and that others normally expect will evoke thoughtful or empathic responses. As noted, schizoid individuals are unfeeling, not by intention or for self-protective reasons, but because they possess an intrinsic emotional blandness and interpersonal imperceptiveness. They lack spontaneity, resonance, and color, are clumsy, unresponsive, and boring in relationships, and appear to lead dull, if not bleak, and stolid lives.

Because schizoids experience few rewards in social interaction, they often turn their talents and interests toward things, objects, or abstractions. As children, for example, they are likely to have been disinclined to competitive games and frolicsome activities, preferring to concentrate their energies on hobbies such as stamp or rock collecting, computer games, electronic equipment, or academic pursuits such as mathematics or engineering. Many find considerable gratification in nonsocial and abstract activities, often developing rather intricate fantasy lives in conjunction with these. The drab and withdrawn characteristics of developing schizoids often make them easy targets for teasing and condemnation by their peers, leading frequently to an intensification of their isolation and self-absorption activities.

In the past, the label "schizoid" was applied to individuals with a mix of features that the DSM now differentiates into three separate personality syndromes: the "schizoid," the "avoidant," and the "schizotypal." The designation schizoid is limited to personalities characterized by an intrinsic defect in the capacity to form social relationships. The label avoidant represents those who possess both the capacity and desire to relate socially, but who fear humiliation and disapproval, and, hence, distance themselves from such relationships. The term schizotypal is reserved for individuals who are noted by the eccentric character of their social

communications and behaviors, and for an ostensive genetic linkage to schizophrenia. These distinctions are elaborated more fully and sharply as the discussion proceeds.

HISTORICAL ANTECEDENTS

The designation of schizoid personality could not have been made prior to Eugen Bleuler's formulation of the concept of schizophrenia, offered as an alternative to the diagnostic label of "dementia praecox" in 1911. Nevertheless, during the two decades prior to Bleuler's concept, Kahlbaum (1890), Ribot (1890), and Hoch (1910) argued the view that the dramatic symptoms seen in clinical states such as dementia praecox were often accentuations of the individual's preexisting personality traits that had been thrust into sharp relief as a consequence of some unusual event or trauma. For example, Kahlbaum introduced the term "heboid" to represent the personality pattern that was structurally connected to clinical hebephrenia, referring to it as a "deviation of psychic individuality in social relationships." Similarly, Ribot coined the term anhedonia as a "counterdesignation to analgesia" and as a syndrome indicating a lessened ability to experience pleasure, a quality seen as central to the schizoid. Particularly relevant also to the syndrome of dementia praecox was August Hoch's study (1910) of the background histories and personal characteristics of these patients. He was to conclude from this research that most had exhibited a "shut-in" personality that predated their manifest illness by several years. These "shut-in" types were described as persons who:

> do not have a natural tendency . . . to get into contact with the environment, who are reticent, seclusive, who cannot adapt themselves to situations, who are hard to influence . . . and stubborn . . . in a passive than an active way. They do not let others know what their conflicts are; they do not unburden their minds, are shy, and have a tendency to live in a world of fancies. What is, after all, the deterioration in dementia praecox if not the expression of the constitutional tendencies in their extreme form, a shutting out of the outside world, a deterioration of interests in the environment, a living in a world apart? (p. 219)

Farrar (1927) expanded Hoch's notion of "shut-in" personalities by distinguishing five subtypes:

1. The "backward" variant lacked ambition, appeared absent-minded, and was disinclined to attend to work or school responsibilities.
2. The "precocious" type was seen as bookish, serious-minded, and prudish, and was often considered as having been a model child.
3. The "neurotic" pattern was noted by frequent temper tantrums, self-centeredness, secretiveness, and persistent physical complaints.
4. The "asocial" style was best characterized by seclusiveness, an indifference to worldly affairs, and a preference for extended daydreaming.
5. The "juvenile" kind remained childlike and dependent, refusing to, or otherwise unable to, grow up.

Emil Kraepelin (1913) also wrote of a prodromal form of dementia praecox in the eighth edition of his text. He described it as follows:

Certain abnormal personalities with mild defect states . . . [are] a product of dementia praecox experienced in earliest childhood, and then brought to a standstill. (p. 237)

In addition to this prodromal variant of dementia praecox, which slows to a halt before reaching clinical proportions, Kraepelin also spoke of a healed and stable prepsychotic state. Notable in this formulation is the absence of the persistent deterioration that was so central to Kraepelin's original view that dementia praecox followed an inevitable downward course. These "milder personality defects," though akin to dementia praecox, differed from the more serious and florid psychotic form. Using modern terminology, mild schizophrenic disorders that came to a standstill prior to decompensation would be likely to be labeled as "schizoid" personalities. Kraepelin (1919), however, had his own terminology for these individuals, designating them as "autistic personalities." To him, the trait that disposed them to dementia praecox, and that characterized the prodromal and quiescent stages, was their tendency to "narrow or reduce their external interests and contacts and their preoccupation with inward ruminations" (p. 213).

MODERN FORMULATIONS

Eugen Bleuler coined the term *schizoidie* (1922, 1929) to represent a pattern of traits closely allied to Hoch's "shut-in" type and Kraepelin's "autistic" personality. The tendency to schizoidness was seen by Bleuler as present in everyone, differing among individuals only in the quantity of its potential biological penetrance. In its clinical or schizophrenic form, this tendency achieved its full level of morbid intensity, whereas in moderate form it could assume the character of only a mild schizoid personality, described by Bleuler (1924) as "people who are shut in, suspicious, incapable of discussion, people who are comfortably dull" (p. 441). The fundamental symptoms that Bleuler spelled out as pathognomonic for schizophrenia were to be found in reduced magnitude among schizoids. Referring to the prominent features found in these milder forms, Bleuler (1950) wrote:

Even in the less severe forms of the illness, indifference seems to be the external sign of their state; an indifference to everything—to friends and relations, to vocation or enjoyment, to duties or rights, to good fortune or to bad. (p. 40)

Applying the term *autism* to signify the characteristic detachment from reality and the predominance of the inner life among these individuals, Bleuler went on to note:

Autism is not always detected at the very first glance. Initially the behavior of many patients betrays nothing remarkable. It is only on prolonged observation that one sees how much they always seek their own way, and how little they permit their environment to influence them. (p. 65)

The foundations of the schizoid disposition were also formulated by Bleuler's erstwhile student and subsequent colleague Carl Jung (1921/1923) in his concept of "introversion." Describing the shut-in-ness of schizoids, Jung writes:

They are mostly silent, inaccessible, hard to understand . . . They neither shine nor reveal themselves. Their outward demeanor . . . is inconspicuous . . . with no desire to affect others, to impress, influence, or change them in any way . . . which may actually turn into a disregard for the comfort and well-being of others. One is distinctly aware then of the movement of feeling away from the object. (p. 247)

Despite Bleuler's seminal contributions to the schizophrenic concept, as well as Jung's to that of the introversive attitude, it was Ernst Kretschmer

(1925) who introduced the most subtle refinements of the schizoid character portrayal. Distinctions first posited by him closely parallel subsequent discriminations in theory (Millon, 1969) and are an important forerunner of the DSM-III and DSM-IV differentiation between schizoid and avoidant types. Because of the originality of this demarcation, as well as the descriptive clarity and clinical astuteness of his text, more than the usual attention is devoted here to his contributions.

Although Kretschmer noted that schizoids exhibit certain "peculiarities of character" in mixed or "different relative proportions," he identified two relatively distinct subgroups at the extremes, what he termed the "hyperaesthetic" and the "anaesthetic" schizoid types. The former group, those at the hyperaesthetic extreme, are essentially equivalent to what the DSM-III and DSM-IV have labeled the "avoidant personality." This syndrome is described more fully in Chapter 7. For comparative purposes, however, a few phrases are quoted from Kretschmer (1925) to convey how this type contrasts with the highly anaesthetic types, termed the "schizoid personality" in the DSM. Kretschmer portrayed the extreme hyperaesthetic as follows:

Timid, shy, with fine feelings, sensitive, nervous, excitable. . . .

Abnormally tender, constantly wounded . . . "all nerves.". . .

[hyperaesthetics] feel all the harsh, strong colors and tones of everyday life . . . as shrill, ugly . . . even to the extent of being psychically painful. Their autism is a painful cramping of the self into itself. They seek as far as possible to avoid and deaden all stimulation from the outside. (pp. 155–161)

Descriptively, and in contrast to the hyperaesthetic-avoidant, Kretschmer (1925) portrayed the extreme anaesthetic-schizoid personality as follows:

We feel that we are in contact with something flavorless, boring. . . . What is there in the deep under all these masks? Perhaps there is a nothing, a dark, hollow-eyed nothing—affective anemia. Behind an ever-silent facade, which twitches uncertainly with every expiring whim—nothing but broken pieces, black rubbish heaps, yawning emotional emptiness, or the cold breath of an arctic soullessness. (p. 150)

Kretschmer's descriptive language is so colorful as to mislead us into feeling that we are reading about a lively and exciting personality rather than one devoid of affect and interpersonally numbing. Relating the characteristic social indifference and introversiveness of the anaesthetic schizoid, Kretschmer (1925) wrote:

"Indifference" is a common schizoid variant of affective insensibility. It is an uninterestedness, which is ostentatiously manifested . . . The indifferent knows that he takes absolutely no interest in many things which are important to other people. (p. 172)

The autism of the predominantly anaesthetic . . . is unfeelingness, lack of affect response to the world about him, which has no interest for his emotional life, and for whose own rightful interests he has no feeling. He draws himself back into himself because he has no reason to do anything else, because all that is about him can offer him nothing. (p. 162)

Characterizing the lack of vitality, spark, or liveliness among the schizoid, Kretschmer went on to say:

The commonest type in our pre-psychotic material is that in which one finds affective lameness. . . . The term "affective lameness" has a close connection with popular speech, which describes those people as "lame (contorted)," in whose behavior it is clearly manifest that the most outstanding symptom is a psychomotor one. . . . One could have wished that he were livelier. "He is a bit tepid." "He is absolutely lacking in life and temperament." Such are the commonest descriptions of young men suffering from affective lameness. This lack of liveliness, of immediately reacting vivacity of psychomotor expression, is found also in the most gifted members of the group. . . .

"Lameness" implies . . . the loss of immediate connection between the emotional stimulus and the motor response. It is for this reason that with the "comfortable" person we always have a feeling that we are in emotional rapport, even when he says nothing, while the "lame" appears to us strange, unsympathetic . . . because we often cannot read in his face, or in his movements, the expression of what he is feeling, or, above all, the adequate reaction to what we are doing and saying to him. The essential quality . . . is that he can stand there with a puzzled face and hanging arms . . . in a situation

that would electrify even one of the "comfortables." (pp. 169–170)

They are . . . devoid of humor, and often serious, without exhibiting either sorrowfulness or cheerfulness.

The expression "dullness" denotes [their] passive lack of feeling . . . a phlegmatic state, which may be distinguished . . . by the lack of warm, emotional responsiveness toward mankind. (pp. 172–173)

Kretschmer considered both anaesthetic and hyperaesthetic tendencies to coexist in many individuals as a tension that often appeared on the surface as quietly restrained, but overlying a deeper sensitivity. In this regard, he anticipated the views held prominently by those of a psychoanalytic persuasion. As Kretschmer (1925) put it:

As soon as we come into close personal contact with such schizoids, we find, very frequently, behind the affectless numbed exterior . . . a tender personality-nucleus with the most vulnerable nervous sensitivity. (p. 153)

Reflecting the seminal contributions of Bleuler and Kretschmer, Eugen Kahn formulated an intricately structured framework for the temperamental substrates of various psychopathic (personality) types. Describing the "athymic" temperament and its varieties, Kahn portrays the features of what we would term today as the schizoid personality. Thus, Kahn (1931) wrote as follows:

[They] are striking first of all for the poverty and slowness of their motor, They are characterized by a marked inertia and it is occasionally difficult to get them in motion.

[These persons] are indifferent, inexcitable, and unmoved, but usually do not give the impression of coldness . . . The affective resonance is either present in a very slight degree or completely lacking. (pp. 191–197)

To Kretschmer, the root of the schizoid's "affective lameness" could be traced to constitutional temperament, a view shared by Bleuler and Kahn. In contrast, psychoanalytic thinkers acquainted with this personality were, as expected, inclined to locate its origins in troublesome childhood events. However, and unlike most of their "character" types, early analytic theorists did not trace or derive the schizoid pattern from a particular stage of libidinal or psychosexual

development. Nevertheless, several analytically oriented theorists—notably Karl Menninger, W. Reich, W. R. D. Fairbairn, Helene Deutsch, and D. W. Winnicott—each described an analogous pattern in the 1930s and early 1940s in terms of psychoanalytic metapsychology.

Influenced by Kretschmer, Menninger (1930) undertook a detailed analysis of several personality types, among them a subgroup he termed the schizoid, described as follows:

Reduced to its simplest terms, the common tendency of the members of this group is an inability to get along well with other people. . . . They maintain one kind of front for the world to look at if it cares (they don't care), but the real self, having looked at the world and renounced it, retreats into an inner unseen life. . . . They may make gestures, go through the motions . . . but the "pane of glass is always there." They never really make lasting contacts.

Most of them are more or less seclusive, quiet, reserved, serious-minded, unsociable, eccentric; . . . others are dull, apparently (not really) stupid, indifferent, often quite pliable, but more often very stubborn. (p. 79)

As with Farrar, Menninger sought to divide the schizoid into several subvarieties, five of which capture qualities akin to those we would judge today to be part of the syndrome, broadly conceived. Among these are the seclusive type, encompassing those who prefer to be alone and "did never care to mix with people"; the hard-boiled variety who ensure keeping their distance by being insensitive, heartless, and ruthless; the artistic variety, a detached other-worldly type who "submits to us fragments of their inner world"; the apparently stupid type who lack interest in their surroundings, take little part in social affairs, and manifest little or no initiative; the grouchy variety, containing those who erect a barrier to ensure seclusion.

In another significant paper of the 1930s, Kasanin and Rosen (1933) described their study of a group of schizoid patients who possessed personality traits such as having few friends, preferring solitary amusements, and being shy followers in groups, close-mouthed and extremely sensitive (although few patients exhibited all these features).

A key early personality theorist, Wilhelm Reich (1933), stressed the characteristic of what he called "psychic contactlessness" for the schizoid person. Reich, as with other psychoanalytic theorists of his time, saw conflicting elements underlying what he termed "schizoid depersonalization." Describing these individuals, he wrote:

At the top of the list we have the feeling of inner isolation. This feeling is sometimes present in spite of an abundance of social and professional relationships. In other cases, we meet with a feeling described as "inner deadness." There can be no doubt that . . . a schizoid depersonalization belongs to this group . . . when patients complain about being estranged, isolated, or apathetic, their feeling can be traced back to this contradiction between the object-libidinal current and the tendency to escape into oneself. Cleavage and ambivalence are direct manifestations of this paradox: The apathy is the result of the equilibrium created by the two opposing forces. (p. 313)

A major founder of the object-relations school of analysis, Fairbairn (1940/1952) stressed the role of depersonalization, derealization, and disturbances of the reality-sense in a range of syndromes he variously termed schizoid "characters," "types," "states," and "personalities." These persons sense themselves as "artificial," as having the feeling that a "plate-glass" exists between them and others, as experiencing a strange unfamiliarity with familiar persons and, conversely, as experiencing familiarity or déjà vu with unfamiliar persons or situations. Among their prominent clinical characteristics are "an attitude of isolation and detachment, and a preoccupation with inner reality." Of special note to Fairbairn is their "difficulty over giving in the emotional sense" (p. 15), which they cope with by "playing roles" and by "exhibitionism." To Fairbairn:

The significance of the exploitation of exhibitionism as defense lies in the fact that it represents a technique for giving without giving, by means of a substitute of "showing" for giving. (p. 16)

Especially significant to the schizoid pattern is their inability to perceive others as worthy of their empathy or love. This stems not only from their unwillingness to part with what little love they themselves possess, but because they feel that love "is too dangerous to release upon [their] objects" (p. 15). In line with his view that the root of the difficulty is traceable to oral libidinal strains, Fairbairn asserted that schizoids experience an unsatisfactory emotional relationship with their

parents and particularly with their mothers. . . . the type of mother who is specially prone . . . is the mother who fails to convince her child by spontaneous and genuine expressions of affection that she herself loves him as a person (1940, p. 13).

As a consequence of such an upbringing, schizoids are incapable of either giving love or being loved. Using his analytic terminology, Fairbairn stated that they have learned to keep their libidinal objects at a distance, "depersonalizing the object and de-emotionalizing the object-relationships" (p. 15).

Deutsch described a group of highly similar schizoid types. Even more clearly than Fairbairn, she considered the central feature of experience to have been the impersonality and formality of the child's early relationships. Labeled the "as if" type, these personalities learn how to act with others but are devoid of the feeling and relatedness that usually are part of these actions. Deutsch (1942) wrote:

The way of feeling and manner of life of this type forces on the observer the inescapable impression that the individual's whole relationship to life has something about it which is lacking in genuineness and yet outwardly runs along "as if" it were complete. (p. 302)

In detailing her portrayal of this personality, Deutsch stated:

The individual's emotional relationship to the outside world and to his own ego appears impoverished or absent . . . there are individuals who are not aware of their lack of normal affective bonds and responses, but whose emotional disturbance is perceived . . . only by those around them. (p. 301)

As both Bleuler and Fairbairn had noted earlier, schizoids often appear quite "normal" upon first impression. Over time or upon closer inspection "the lack of real warmth brings such an emptiness and dullness to the emotional atmosphere" (p. 302) that relationships simply cannot last in any meaningful or rewarding sense. Deutsch (1942) described this quality as follows:

All the expressions of emotion are formal. . . . all inner experience is completely excluded. It is like the performance of an actor who is technically well-trained but who lacks the necessary spark to make his impersonations true to life. . . .

Outwardly he conducts his life as if he possessed a complete and sensitive emotional capacity. To him there is no difference between his empty forms and what others actually experience. . . . The apparently normal relationship to the world . . . [is] a mimicry . . . despite the absence of object cathexis.

Further consequences of such a relation to life are a completely passive attitude to the environment with a highly plastic readiness to pick up signals from the outer world and to mold oneself and one's behavior accordingly.

Another characteristic . . . is that aggressive tendencies are almost completely masked by passivity, lending an air of negative goodness. (pp. 303–305)

In later years, Grinker, Werble, and Drye (1968), in research into so-called borderline syndromes, identified one subgroup whose characteristics clustered in accord with Deutsch's "as if" type. Among the notable features Grinker et al. uncovered were:

bland and adaptive behavior. . . . here was little evidence of negative behavior or affect . . . but what is also missing is manifestation of positive affect—in fact there is no evidence of love for anybody or anything. Furthermore, there is no indication of a well-developed sense of self-identity. (p. 87)

An early paper by Asperger (1944) characterized a form of pathology seen primarily in young children that appears in many of its features to portray the schizoid. Among its prime symptoms are the following: abnormalities of gaze, poverty of gesture and expression, unusual voice production which may or may not be present; autistic intelligence (when intelligent, they develop inventive world views and are attracted to mathematics and the natural sciences; when dull they function like automata); social adaptation impaired, with a lack of feeling for others, a solitariness, and an insistence on following their own inclinations. Tracing these youngsters over a 10-year period led Asperger to hypothesize that these features persist into adulthood. A lack of a well-developed sense of identity is central to Winnicott's (1945, 1956) formulation of what he termed "false self" personalities, a character type similar in its features to those described by Kretschmer, Fairbairn, and Deutsch. Winnicott portrayed this unfeeling and detached person as follows:

In the cases on which my work is based there has been a true self, hidden and protected by a "false self." This false self is no doubt an aspect of the true self. It hides and protects it, and it reacts to the adaptation failures and develops a pattern corresponding to the pattern of environmental failure. In this way the true self is not involved in the reacting, and so preserves a continuity of being. This hidden true self suffers an impoverishment, however, that results from a lack of experience. The false self may achieve a deceptive false integrity, that is to say a false ego-strength. . . . The false self cannot, however, experience life, and feel real. (1956, p. 387)

Note should be made of the ideas formulated by Melanie Klein (1946), another major theorist of the British school of object-relations thinking. In her papers on "schizoid mechanisms," she proposed the concept of "splitting" as a central construct of early development; this concept has come to serve as a major theme in subsequent psychoanalytic writings of the object-relations school. As with other analysts both in the mid-1940s and subsequently, the so-called schizoid was seen as an individual who split off very intense emotional experiences from ongoing life events; in this regard the schizoid character appears more like what we are currently labeling the Avoidant Personality Disorder. She writes that splitting is essentially a defensive maneuver against infantile persecutory anxieties, a means by which the infant is able to maintain cohesion by expelling into the outer world images of self that were unacceptable to itself. By what is called "projective identification," the infant clears itself of contradictory self-images but as a consequence creates frightening external persecutors, whence we observe an intense fear of others that appears beneath the surface of an apparently cool and composed outer presentation.

CONTEMPORARY PROPOSALS

H. Guntrip (1952) and R. Laing (1960), more recent followers of the object-relations and self-theory traditions of British psychoanalysis, have further elaborated Fairbairn's and Winnicott's notions of the "schizoid" personality. Both are exceptionally articulate. For example, Guntrip (1952) portrayed the schizoid as follows:

Complaints of feeling cutoff, shutoff, out of touch, feeling a part or strange, of things being out of focus or unreal, of not feeling one with people, or of the point having gone out of life, interest flagging, things seem futile and meaningless, all describe in various ways this state of mind. Patients usually call it "depression," but it lacks the heavy black, inner sense of brooding, of anger and of guilt . . . in classic depression.

External relationships seem to have been emptied by a massive withdrawal of the real libidinal self. Effective mental activity has disappeared into a hidden inner world; the patient's conscious ego is emptied of vital feeling and action, and seems to have become unreal . . . merely reporting [inner activities] as if it were a neutral observer, not personally in the inner drama of which [the patient] is a detached observer. The attitude to the outer world is the same: noninvolvement and observation at a distance without any feeling, like that of a press reporter describing a social gathering of which he is not a part, in which he has no personal interest, and by which he is bored. (p. 86)

Laing (1960) added to the false-self theme proposed by Winnicott and also portrayed the sense of schizoid detachment and impassivity:

In the schizoid condition here described there is a persistent scission between the self and the body. What the individual regards as his true self is experienced as more or less disembodied, and bodily experience and actions are in turn felt to be part of the false-self system. . . .

This detachment of the self means that the self is never revealed directly in the individual's expressions and actions, nor does it experience anything spontaneously or immediately. The self's relationship to the other is always at one remove. The direct and immediate transactions between the individual, the other, and the world, even in such basic respects as perceiving and acting, all come to be meaningless, futile, and false. . . .

The final effect is an overall experience of everything having come to a stop. Nothing moves; nothing is alive; everything is dead, including the self. The self by its detachment is precluded from a full experience of realness and aliveness. (pp. 82–87)

Picking up on Deutsch's concept of "as if," Arieti (1955) has proposed that the schizoids' insensitivity is a defense against their profound vulnerability to the pain of rejection. This vulnerability is so successfully repressed that no

longer is there any pain or social longing. Arieti's formulation of the dynamics of the schizoid may be more applicable to the DSM-III conception of the avoidant personality. In a thoughtful review of the literature, Nannarello (1953) concluded that the essential features of the schizoid were best summarized as uncomfortable feelings of inadequacy, a desire to withdraw from people, and a tendency toward autistic thinking.

Another analyst of the object-relations persuasion, M. Khan (1960) stressed the close relationship between mother and child as crucial to the development of the schizoid personality; again, we should note that Khan may be talking about what is now referred to as the avoidant personality. According to Khan, the mother of the future schizoid failed in her responsibility to serve as a "protective-shield," hence leading to "cumulative trauma." Concurrently, through acts of excessive indulgence she maintains a deep attachment to the child, what he terms a "symbiotic omnipotence" that essentially discourages the child's future attachment to others. The resulting effect results in an adult schizoid personality, who displays pseudocompliance, self-sufficiency, withdrawal, autoeroticism, an ability to mobilize help from others, feelings of omnipotence, and what Khan terms an "expectancy of oversensitive rapport."

Kernberg (1967, 1970) has offered thoughts that are consonant with the object-relations point of view, noting that splitting is the major defensive mechanism utilized by the schizoid. He views these individuals as having difficulty in understanding themselves owing to the conflicting elements of their inner personality. Seen as one variant of the borderline personality organization, their inner worlds, according to his proposals, are populated by contradictory self-images, one set composed of idealized or frightening aspects of internalized others and another split into both shameful and exalted self-images. As a result, there is a persistent state of subjective unreality and identity diffusion, which leads to chronic feelings of inner emptiness.

Other views generated by those of a psychoanalytic orientation have sought to reason along the lines expressed by earlier figures of the object-relations school. Most persuasive in this realm are the clinical hypotheses formulated by Akhtar (1987) who has drawn on a rich diversity of psychoanalytic precursors in presenting his argument. Separating clinical features into those that are overt from those that are covert, Akhtar (1992) states that the schizoid:

is overtly detached, self-sufficient, absentminded, uninteresting, asexual, and idiosyncratically moral, while covertly exquisitely sensitive, emotionally needy, acutely vigilant, creative, often perverse, and vulnerable to corruption. (pp. 141–142)

Turning to an entirely different perspective, that of psychopharmacologic research, D. F. Klein (1970, 1977) suggested that the traditional schizoid syndrome confuses two distinct personality categories. Of note is the correspondence between Klein's specific suggestion in this regard and the differentiation Kretschmer made some 45 years earlier between hyperaesthetic and anaesthetic schizoids. Klein (1970) wrote:

I believe the DSM-II schizoid personality . . . confuses two quite separate groups of people: the shy, socially backward, inept, obedient person who is fearful and therefore isolated but appreciates sociability and would like to be part of the crowd; and there is the asocial, eccentric, (imperceptive and undiplomatic) person who seeks to be alone and has difficulty in relationships with his peers, frequently resulting in social ostracism and scapegoating. (p. 189)

The former group—the shy, fearful type, who appreciates sociability—parallels Kretschmer's extreme hyperaesthetic and corresponds in several respects to the DSM-III and IV avoidant personality. Similarly, the asocial and imperceptive type, who has difficulty in relating with peers, possesses qualities akin to Kretschmer's high anaesthetic and to the DSM-III schizoid characterization. A theoretically derived distinction that also results in two "schizoid" variants was formulated by Millon (1969) and proposed as a typological framework for the DSM-III personality subcommittee. Labeled the "passive-detached" and "active-detached" patterns, or alternatively the "asocial" and "avoidant" personalities, they are analogous to the differentiation proposed by Kretschmer between anaesthetics and hyperaesthetics. The text and criteria described in later paragraphs served in 1975 as the initial working draft for the DSM-III schizoid (asocial) personality; Chapter 7 includes a comparable text and criteria for the avoidant personality. The key element of this proposal was to separate those individuals who were intrinsically deficient in their capacity to experience deep emotions and interpersonal attachments and sensitivities from those who were exceedingly sensitive and needy, but attempted to damp down these feelings so as to not be unduly distressed by the failure to have them appreciated and fulfilled by others. Hence, in Millon's view, the psychoanalytic position, although correct, characterizes the psychic state of those patients we now call the avoidant personality.

Beginning with the publication of the DSM-III, numerous investigators turned their attentions to the personality disorders, seeking to provide frameworks for understanding them from diverse theoretical viewpoints. Each of the following thinkers is an active and creative contributor to the field; their proposals continue to evolve as we write.

Of considerable promise has been the extension of cognitive-behavioral theories to the realm of personality study. Most encouraging in this regard is the work of Aaron Beck and his associates (Beck & Freeman, 1990b). In their description of the schizoid, they write:

Not surprisingly, individuals with schizoid personality disorder consider themselves to be observers rather than participants in the world around them. They see themselves as self-sufficient loners. Others often view them as dull, uninteresting, and humorless.

Schizoids also have a cognitive style characterized by vagueness and poverty of thoughts . . . Such a cognitive style further contributes to the lack of emotional responsiveness, since cues that produce affect are not perceived and are unlikely to result in emotions. (p. 125)

As is well known, Beck's primary contribution lies in the realm of cognitive distortions and dysfunctions; hence, in referring to the beliefs that are most notable among schizoids, he writes (Beck & Freeman, 1990b):

Their core beliefs consist of notions such as "I am basically alone," "Close relationships with other people are unrewarding and messy," "I can do things better if I'm not encumbered by other people," "Close relationships are undesirable because they interfere with my freedom of action."

The conditional beliefs are "If I get too close to people, they will get their hooks into me," "I can't be happy unless I have complete mobility." The instrumental beliefs are "Don't get too close," "Keep your distance," "Don't get involved." (p. 51)

Drawing impressive deductions from her interpersonal model, Benjamin (1993a) comments on a problematic and frequently observed feature of the schizoid:

There are no fears of or wishes about others. The baseline position involves active and passive autonomy. Underdeveloped in social awareness and skills, the schizoid nonetheless has instrumental skills, and can meet expectations of formal social roles (parent, boss, employee). He or she may be married but does not develop intimacy. There may be an active, but not necessarily bizarre, fantasy life. (p. 346)

Formally correct, but lacks skills in sending and receiving social cues. If brought to couples therapy, for example, he or she is perplexed about what the problem might be. He or she lacks the capacity to understand the spouse's wish for more intimacy. Seems like an interpersonal "black hole"—signals disappear forever without leaving a trace.

People with this pattern would logically not define themselves as patients and . . . present themselves for treatment. They are socially withdrawn; do not want to make social connections; and do not suffer from anger, fear or depression. (p. 349)

The rapidly developing support in some quarters for what has come to be known as the five-factor model (Costa & Widiger, 1993) has lent itself to rather inventive analyses of each of the personality disorders. Using the facets of each of the five factors as a basis for decoding the attributes of the schizoid, Costa and Widiger describe this personality as:

Typically loners, isolated and withdrawn from others . . . emotionally and socially detached.

Schizoid involves excessive introversion, particularly the facets of excessively low warmth, . . . low gregariousness, . . . and low positive emotions. . . . One would also expect low excitement seeking . . . Anhedonic traits of appearing indifferent to the praise or criticism, emotional coldness, detachment, and flattened affectivity will also suggest low self-consciousness and low openness to feelings. (p. 43)

In line with the more quantitative approach of the five-factor model is the work of Livesley (1986). What is most notable is Livesley's effort to quantify the judgments of experienced clinicians in rating the prototypal traits of various personality disorders. As expected, the characteristics recorded most frequently were; lonely, detached, withdrawn, seclusive; desires minimal

attachments; inability to establish social relationships; poor interpersonal skills; introverted; restricted affectivity; and aloof.

As indicated in earlier chapters, both Larry Siever (Siever & Davis, 1991) and C. Robert Cloninger (1986, 1987, 1993) have proposed innovative models for explicating the personality disorders. Although Siever has articulated neurobiological substrata undergirding the schizoid/schizotypal spectrum, it is Cloninger who has specified theoretically based distinctions differentiating the attributes of the schizoid and schizotypal. Using his framework of major brain systems and the stimulus-response characteristics they subserve as his model, Cloninger notes:

Schizoid individuals are highly resistant to social pressures to conform to the wishes of others because they are socially detached (low reward dependence), self-confident (low harm avoidance), and rigid (low novelty seeking). In addition, schizoid individuals are described as self-effacing because they prefer privacy and have a restricted ability to express warm feelings. I have recommended that the term imperturbable schizoid be used to make clear the more restrictive definition suggested. (1987, p. 585)

The concept of establishing clear diagnostic criteria for each of the personality disorders was first formulated in Millon's text of 1969. What is now referred to as the schizoid personality was labeled the "passive-detached" pattern and identified as the "asocial personality." That early text stated the criteria for four clinical domains as follows:

Four interrelated features stand out in the clinical picture: affectivity deficit *(emotional blandness; inability to experience intense feelings),* cognitive slippage *(obscurity and irrelevance in thought and communication that is inappropriate to the intellectual level),* complacent self-image *(lack of self-insight; unclear but untroubled concept of self)* and interpersonal indifference *(minimal interest in social relationships). (p. 226)*

Using the preceding criteria and their associated textual descriptions as a guide, Millon drafted the following text as the initial draft to be considered by the DSM-III Task Force, of which he was a member, in their preliminary discussions of the personality disorders:

This pattern is typified by a rather quiet, colorless and impassive style of interpersonal behavior. Affectionate needs are markedly limited and desires for communication and close relationship with others are minimal. There is little capacity for experiencing pleasure and a pervasively bland emotional tone characterizes daily life. This introversive and apathetic pattern covaries with a general lack of vitality and motoric spontaneity, deficits in stimulus-seeking behavior, impoverished social sensibilities and a notable cognitive vagueness regarding interpersonal matters.

Since adolescence or early adulthood at least 3 of the following have been present to a notably greater degree than in most people and were not limited to discrete periods nor necessarily prompted by stressful life events.

1. *Affectivity deficit (e.g., exhibits intrinsic emotional blandness; reports weak affectionate needs and an inability to display enthusiasm or experience pleasure).*

2. *Mild cognitive slippage (e.g., evidences impoverished and obscure thought processes inappropriate to intellectual level; social communication often tangential and irrelevant).*

3. *Interpersonal indifference (e.g., possesses minimal "human" interests; is satisfied with and prefers a peripheral role in social and family relationships).*

4. *Behavioral apathy (e.g., ease of fatigability, low energy and lack of vitality; displays deficits in activation, motoric expressiveness and spontaneity).*

5. *Perceptual insensitivity (e.g., reveals minimal introspection and awareness of self; impervious to subtleties of everyday social and emotional life).*

Following extended discussions, the originally proposed label for the DSM-III syndrome "asocial personality" was replaced with the designation "introverted personality." The term "asocial" had been preempted by the *International Classification of Diseases,* ninth edition (ICD-9), as an alternative label for the antisocial personality; confusion, especially in Europe, was thought inevitable. The substitute designation "introverted" was dropped in its turn because of objections from Jungian analysts. Finally, the label "schizoid" was reintroduced despite strong disagreements by members of the committee to the effect that this term conveyed

different meanings in prior manuals, and that it would result in confusions with a new syndrome that had imprudently been labeled "schizotypal personality."

The following text and criteria were proposed at an intermediate phase of the committee's work:

The essential features are a profound defect in the ability to form social relationships and to respond to the usual forms of social reinforcements. Such patients are characteristically "loners," who do not appear distressed by their social distance and are not interested in greater social involvement. Affectionate needs are markedly limited and there appears to be little capacity for experiencing pleasure.

Deficits in stimulus-seeking are notable and these patients frequently maintain solitary interests and hobbies. The characteristic introversive pattern frequently covaries with a general lack of vitality and motor spontaneity. Habits of speech typically are slow and monotonous with few rhythmic or expressive gestures. A pervasively bland emotional tone characterizes daily life as does a lack of self-reflection and introspection.

At least 3 of the following are characteristic of the patient's long term functioning and are not limited to discrete periods.

A. *Social relationship deficits (e.g., has few friends or close bonds with others).*

B. *Interpersonal indifference (e.g., has minimal desire for social involvement and is unresponsive to praise or criticism).*

C. *Anhedonia (e.g., exhibits weak affectionate needs and is unable to readily experience pleasure or enthusiasm).*

D. *Behavioral apathy (e.g., displays low energy, motivation, or stimulus-seeking behavior).*

E. *Minimal self-reflection (e.g., rarely examines self-motives or personal relationships).*

Notable in the preceding was an effort to include clinical features in several significant domains, (e.g., interpersonal, affective, behavioral, and cognitive). These and additional domains will be articulated and detailed in later sections. By contrast, and as noted in earlier chapters, the DSM-III, as well as recent ICDs, retained overlapping criteria and failed to encompass the full range of useful clinical realms. In both the DSM-III-R and DSM-IV, however, a more complete portrayal was achieved, though still limited in clinical range and depth. Emphases shifted in various ways to aid in making more refined distinctions as well as to provide a reasonable empirical basis to the criteria that were retained.

The *International Classification of Diseases,* tenth edition (ICD-10), has been modeled in part to coincide with the multiaxial system and diagnostic criteria formats of recent DSMs. Not all of the DSM's personality disorders are included in the recent ICD, but the schizoid is one that has been. The following are paraphrasings of the diagnostic criteria contained in this classification for the schizoid: few activities give pleasure; displays detachment, emotional coldness, or flattened affect; has limited capacity to express warm or tender affects, as well as to express angry feelings; seems indifferent to either praise or criticism; has little interest in having sexual experiences with another person; chooses solitary activities almost always; excessively preoccupied with fantasy and introspection; neither desires nor has close friends or confiding relationships; shows marked insensitivity to prevailing norms and conventions.

The DSM-IV organizes its conception of the schizoid with a primary focus on two clinical domains. The primary area is in the interpersonal sphere; some five different criteria are enumerated, notably a deficiency in the desire to be part of a family or other close social group; a preference for choosing solitary activities (ones that do not include interaction with others); minimal or limited interest in having sexual experiences; the presence of few or no close friends or confidants; a seeming indifference to the praise or criticism of others. The second domain given a central role in the schizoid portrayal pertains to the mood domain. Two criteria are noted, specifically a reduced ability to experience pleasure in both physical and interpersonal realms; and a tendency to exhibit emotional coldness, flattened affectivity, as evident in limited facial expressions, minimal social gestures, and a failure to experience strong feelings.

As will be discussed in the next several pages, the restriction in the DSM-IV to the interpersonal and mood domains limits the range of possible useful criteria to a rather narrow band. Relevant though these domains are, the schizoid manifests a much wider scope of domain characteristics than has been included in the DSM-IV (e.g., self-image, cognitive style, intrapsychic structural features).

Although derived from the authors' theoretical schema, an empirically and numerically derived set of factors comprising the distinguishable and partially separable traits of the schizoid personality has been developed and will be recorded in subsequent research papers. Next, however, are a few words describing the evolutionary model and theory as it pertains to the schizoid personality prototype. Before proceeding it may be useful for the reader to conceive each personality or personality disorder as a style of ecological adaptation deriving from the interplay of biological dispositions and early learning. For some persons, such as the schizoid, there may be a constitutional incapacity to experience all forms of affect, a disability, if you will, in sensibility feelings, a defect in responsiveness to even ordinary emotive sensations, a numbness to most promptings, good or bad, internal or external. This deficiency in affective sentiments and motivation results in their characteristic behavioral impassivity and interpersonal indifference.

The polarity schema for the schizoid (Figure 6.1) shows that they possess a marked deficiency in the capacity to experience both psychic pleasure (enhancement) and pain (preservation). In other words, they are unmotivated to seek out joy and gratification, are unable to view life enthusiastically, and also, they experience none of the distressing affects of life, such as sadness, anxiety, and anger. As a consequence of these deficiencies, schizoids have little motivation to seek out rewards or to distance themselves from

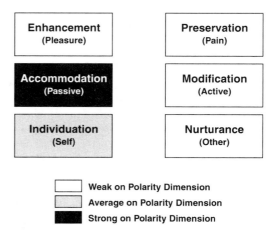

SCHIZOID PROTOTYPE

Figure 6.1   Status of the schizoid personality prototype in accord with the Million Polarity Model.

potentially discomforting experiences; the result is a rather passive (accommodating) individual, who is ill-disposed to modify life circumstances or to participate actively in life's events. Owing to these deficiencies and inclinations, there is little motivation to become involved in the affairs of others (nurturance). Hence, by default, if nothing else, they tend to be self-involved (individuated). The deductive model presented in this figure reflects the manner in which the theory formulates a personality disorder; it is essentially the same procedure by which Costa and Widiger articulate the components of these disorders using quantitatively derived five factors as their model, as well as the manner in which Cloninger does likewise employing his biologically anchored tripartite schema of harm-avoidance, novelty-seeking, and reward-dependence. The key distinction between Millon's model and those of a quantitative or neurobiological character is its grounding in a theory that transcends the particular forms of expression in which personality disorders manifest themselves (lexical, biochemical). Rather, it is anchored to the deeper elements of nature, as found in principles that apply to all the major disciplines of science.

A useful summary of the major historical contributors is represented in Figure 6.2.

CLINICAL FEATURES

Perhaps it is not necessary to say, but there are many variations to be seen in individuals diagnosed with the same label. Desirous though it may be to find that everyone given the same designation displays the same pattern of behaviors, feelings, and thoughts, the reality is that numerous and variegated forms might be comfortably subsumed under the same label. It would not be judicious to lead the naive reader into believing that a single pattern of features typifies each of our categorical classes. In the following sections, we will attempt to describe the many varieties of the prototypal personality disorders, because we are convinced, for the most part, that each prototypal personality is largely an extension or more extreme variant of normal types that exhibit similar features. After presenting the schizoid's eight prototypal clinical domains, we will begin our presentations in this and in later chapters with what we term "normal styles." Following this, we will describe a number of "childhood syndromes." Lastly, we will provide a brief review of a number of adult variants that have at their center a core set of features that deserve the designation of the personality disorder under review; however, they exhibit enough variation on the theme to justify describing them with terms that characterize those more or less distinctive qualities. We will refer to them as "adult subtypes."

PROTOTYPAL DIAGNOSTIC DOMAINS

With the foregoing as a background, this section details the clinical characteristics of the core group of *prototypal* schizoids in a more explicit and systematic fashion. Reference should be made

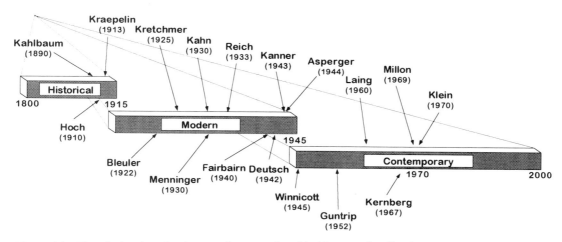

Figure 6.2 Historical review of major contributors to the schizoid personality disorder.

TABLE 6.1 Clinical Domains of the Schizoid Prototype

Behavioral Level

(F) Expressively Impassive. Appears to be in an inert emotional state, lifeless, undemonstrative, lacking in energy and vitality; is unmoved, boring, unanimated, robotic, phlegmatic, displaying deficits in activation, motoric expressiveness, and spontaneity.

(F) Interpersonally Unengaged. Seems indifferent and remote, rarely responsive to the actions or feelings of others, chooses solitary activities, possesses minimal human interests; fades into the background, is aloof or unobtrusive, neither desires nor enjoys close relationships, prefers a peripheral role in social, work, and family settings.

Phenomenological Level

(F) Cognitively Impoverished. Seems deficient across broad spheres of human knowledge and evidences vague and obscure thought processes, particularly about social matters; communication with others is often unfocused, loses its purpose or intention, or is conveyed via a loose or circuitous logic.

(S) Complacent Self-Image. Reveals minimal introspection and awareness of self; seems impervious to the emotional and personal implications of everyday social life, appearing indifferent to the praise or criticism of others.

(S) Meager Objects. Internalized representations are few in number and minimally articulated, largely devoid of the manifold percepts and memories of relationships with others, possessing little of the dynamic interplay among drives and conflicts that typify well-adjusted persons.

Intrapsychic Level

(F) Intellectualization Mechanism. Describes interpersonal and affective experiences in a matter-of-fact, abstract, impersonal, or mechanical manner; pays primary attention to formal and objective aspects of social and emotional events.

(S) Undifferentiated Organization. Demonstrates an inner barrenness, a feeble drive to fulfill needs, and minimal pressures either to defend against or resolve internal conflicts or cope with external demands; internal morphologic structures may best be characterized by their limited framework and sterile pattern.

Biophysical Level

(S) Apathetic Mood. Is emotionally unexcitable, exhibiting an intrinsic unfeeling, cold and stark quality; reports weak affectionate or erotic needs, rarely displaying warm or intense feelings, and apparently unable to experience most affects—pleasure, sadness, or anger—in any depth.

(F) = Functional domain.
(S) = Structural domain.

to the adjoining Table 6.1, and to similar tables in later chapters. These tables summarize and highlight the different domains that characterize the prototype of each personality disorder. Figure 6.3 presents these same clinical domains, but highlights their relative *salience* among schizoid personalities; for example, unengaged interpersonal conduct and apathetic mood/temperament are the two most prominent or characteristic features that distinguish the schizoid prototype.

Expressive Behavior: Impassive

Most characteristic of schizoids is their lack of demonstrativeness, and their deficits in energy and vitality. They appear to the observer to be unanimated and robotic; many display marked deficits in activation and spontaneity. Speech among schizoids typically is slow and monotonous, characterized by an affectless vacancy and obscurities that signify either inattentiveness or a failure to grasp the emotional dimensions of human communication. Movements are lethargic and lacking in rhythmic or expressive gestures. They rarely "perk up" or respond alertly to the feelings of others; they are not intentionally unkind, however. They seem invariably preoccupied with tangential and picayune matters, rather passively detached from others and drifting along quietly and unobtrusively, as if in a world of their own.

Individuals of this cast evidence underresponsiveness to all forms of stimulation. Events that normally provoke anger, elicit joy, or evoke sadness in others seem to fall on deaf ears. There is a

SCHIZOID PROTOTYPE

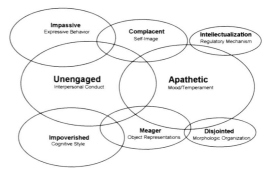

Figure 6.3 Salience of personologic domains in the schizoid prototype.

pervasive imperviousness to emotions, not only to those of joy and pleasure. Feelings of anger, depression, or anxiety rarely are expressed. This apathy and emotional deficit are cardinal signs of the schizoid syndrome. Their generalized inability to be activated and aroused may be exhibited in a wide-ranging lack of initiative and the failure to respond to most reinforcements that prompt others into action. Thus, they are not only unmoved by emotional stimuli but seem to possess a general deficiency in energy and vitality. When they do become involved, it tends toward mental activities, such as reading or television watching, or toward physical activities that call for minimal energy expenditures, such as sketching, watch repairing, computer surfing, and the like.

Interpersonal Conduct: Unengaged

For the most part, schizoids seem interpersonally indifferent and remote, failing to be responsive to the emotions and behaviors of others. They prefer solitary activities, exhibit few interests in the lives of others, and tend to fade into the social background, either unobtrusive in their presence or seemingly aloof. This appears to be their preference, that of maintaining a peripheral role in most interpersonal settings, neither desiring nor enjoying any close relationships. The inability of schizoids to engage in the give-and-take of reciprocal relationships may readily be observed. They are rather vague and disengaged from group interactions, appearing to be involved in their own world of preoccupations. It is even difficult for them to mix with others in pleasant social activities, let alone those demanding leadership. When relating to others in a mandatory setting, as in school or work, their social communications are expressed not in a peculiar or irrational way but in a perfunctory, formal, and impersonal manner.

For the same reasons that they fail to develop intrapsychic mechanisms, schizoids also tend not to learn complex interpersonal coping maneuvers. Their drives are meager and they lack the intense personal involvements sometimes conducive to painful emotional conflicts. This is not to say that they possess no drives or discords, but that those they do experience are of mild degree and of minor consequence. One of the distinctions of the schizoid personality, then, is the paucity (rather than the character or direction) of their interpersonal coping. If any factor in their generally feeble hierarchy of motives can be identified, it is their preference for remaining socially detached. This is not a driving need of theirs, as it is with the avoidant personality, but merely a comfortable and preferred state. When social circumstances press them beyond comfort, they may simply retreat and draw into themselves. Should social discord or demands become intense or persistent, they may revert to more severe coping reactions and display various pathological disorders such as seen in acute schizophrenic syndromes.

Cognitive Style: Impoverished

The thought processes of the schizoid tend, in general, to be rather deficient, not only in most spheres of human interest, but especially so with regard to social and personal life. Not uncommonly, their communications with others seem unfocused, conveyed in a loose or circuitous way, and occasionally wandering off the track, losing their purpose or intention. Schizoid personalities rarely are introspective because the satisfactions to be found in self-evaluation are minimal for those who are incapable of experiencing deep emotions. This diminished introspectiveness, with its attendant lowering of insight, derives from another feature of the schizoid pattern. They display a vagueness and impoverishment of thought, a tendency to skim the surface of events, and an inability to convey articulate and relevant ideas regarding interpersonal phenomena.

Some schizoids may exhibit a form of "tonal agnosia" in which the expressive qualities of both their own voice and those of others are markedly reduced. While words and language are technically understood, these patients are largely incapable of "reading" the intent and expressiveness which transcends the mere verbal constructions themselves. The emotion-laden qualities which suffuse the formal structure of communication are missed in great measure. Many may grasp grammatical and mathematical symbols with infallible precision, but fail to comprehend the grimaces, gestures, and voice timbre which enrich human-to-human communication.

Their style of amorphous communication may be related to another trait, referred to here as "defective perceptual scanning." It is characterized by a tendency to miss or blur differences and to overlook, diffuse, and homogenize the varied elements of experience. Instead of differentiating events and sensing their discriminable and distinctive attributes, schizoids tend to mix them up, intrude extraneous or irrelevant features, and perceive them in a somewhat disorganized fashion. This inability to attend, select, and regulate one's perceptions of the environment seems, once again, to be especially pronounced with social and emotional phenomena.

Self-Image: Complacent

The schizoid appears emotionally impervious to the character of social transactions, revealing little awareness in or interest in the personal lives of others, as well as in their own lives. They are not only indifferent to the meaning of what others convey to them, such as praise or criticism, but they exhibit little or no tendency to look into their personal feelings and attitudes. To the extent that they look inward, schizoid personalities characterize themselves as bland persons who are reflective and introversive. Most seem complacent and satisfied with their lives and are content to remain aloof from the social aspirations and competitiveness they see in others. Self-descriptions, however, tend to be vague and superficial. This lack of clarity does not indicate elusiveness or protective denial on their part but rather their deficient powers to reflect on social and emotional processes. Interpersonal attitudes are no less vague and inarticulate. When adequately formulated, schizoids perceive themselves to be somewhat reserved and distant, lacking in much concern or care for others. Rather interestingly, they are able to recognize that others tend to be indifferent to them and their needs.

Object-Representations: Meager

The past experiences embedded as a template in the mind of most schizoids appear to be few in number and diffusely articulated. In contrast to those of other personalities, these imprinted memories seem to be devoid of specificity and clarity. They also possess little of the dynamic interplay among drives, impulses, and conflicts that is found among well-adjusted persons. Owing to the feeble manner in which they experience events and persons, relatively little imprints strongly in their minds. Low in arousal and in emotional reactivity, as well as relatively imperceptive and therefore inclined to blur distinctions, their inner life remains largely homogeneous, undifferentiated, and

unarticulated. Lacking the natural variety of experiences that compose the minds of most people, schizoids are unable to engage in dynamic interplay, nor are they able to change and evolve as a consequence of their intrapsychic interactions.

Regulatory Mechanisms: Intellectualization

Schizoids describe the interpersonal and affective character of their experiences and memories in a somewhat impersonal and mechanical manner. They tend to be abstract and matter-of-fact about their emotional and social lives; when they do formulate a characterization, they pay primary attention to the more objective and formal aspects of their experiences rather than to the personal and emotional significance of these events. Schizoids engage in few complicated unconscious processes. Relatively untroubled by intense emotions, insensitive to interpersonal relationships, and difficult to arouse and activate, they hardly feel the impact of events and have little reason to devise complicated intrapsychic defenses and strategies. They do harbor segments of the residuals of past memories and emotions, but, in general, their inner world lacks the intensities and intricacies found in all other pathological personalities.

Morphologic Organization: Undifferentiated

As indicated in prior paragraphs, the inner world of the schizoid is largely desolate, devoid of the complex emotions, conflicts, and cognitions that are harbored even in most normal persons. Their inner world is barren. There are minimal drives to fulfill their needs; likewise, they experience minimal pressure to resolve their internal conflicts or to deal with external demands. More than any other personality, excluding perhaps the schizotypal, the structural composition of their intrapsychic world is highly diffuse and dynamically inactive.

Mood/Temperament: Apathetic

Perhaps the most striking and fundamental element of schizoids is their intrinsic deficiency in affective sensibility. Not only do they report few, if any, affectionate or erotic needs, but they appear unable to experience these major affective states—pleasure, sadness, or anger—to any degree. They are emotionally unexcitable, exhibit the weakest level of feelings, and seem to go through life in a cold and stark manner. We are also likely to see among schizoids a wide-ranging alexithymia, a deficiency in the range and subtlety of emotionally-related words. Since our habits of language represent, in part, symbols of our realities, the lack of the schizoids' affective sensibilities may become evident in a parallel decrement in their emotive terminology, and hence their alexithymia.

PROTOTYPAL VARIANTS

Before presenting the descriptive text on clinical domains that elaborates the more cryptic statements of Table 6.1, we will outline some of the variants of the schizoid prototype. As noted previously, this is done to convey to the reader that no single pattern or uniform constellation of features represents each of the categorized personality disorders. We find, for example, that there are some close-to-normal schizoids, others that show schizoid characteristics in childhood, as well a number of different variants within the adult schizoid group. Beyond these, in a later section, Comorbid Disorders, we will see how the schizoid covaries with other personality disorders, creating thereby still more intermixtures around the core schizoid prototype.

Normal Styles

As with most personality disorders (the exception likely to be the schizotypal, borderline, paranoid) the pattern of characteristics seen in the pathological form may also be seen in milder form among individuals who may be considered within the normal range. Hence the schizoid prototype can be considered dimensional, that is, distributed on a continuum of severity from normal at one end to seriously pathological at the other.

In this section, we will briefly characterize those at the so-called normal end of the continuum. For example, Oldham and Morris (1990) describe what they speak of as the "solitary style," self-contained individuals who require no one else to guide them, to admire them, to provide emotional sustenance, to entertain them, or to share their experiences. Although they may become involved with others, at heart they find greatest comfort, reassurance, and freedom with themselves.

Another description drawn from the Millon Index of Personality Styles (Millon, Weiss, Millon, & Davis, 1994) refers to the normal schizoid

pattern as "retiring." A quote from the inventory's manual follows:

Their needs to give and receive affection and to show feelings tend to be minimal. They are inclined to have few relationships and interpersonal involvements, and do not develop strong ties to other people. They may be seen by others as calm, placid, untroubled, easygoing, and possibly indifferent. Rarely expressing their inner feelings or thoughts to others, they seem most comfortable when left alone. They tend to work in a slow, quiet, and methodical manner, almost always remaining in the background in an undemanding and unobtrusive way. Comfortable working by themselves, they are not easily distracted or bothered by what goes on around them. Being somewhat deficient in the ability to recognize the needs or feelings of others, they may be seen as socially awkward, if not insensitive, as well as lacking in spontaneity and vitality. (p. 31)

Childhood Syndromes

Early in the 1940s, two child psychiatrists, Leo Kanner and Heinz Asperger, almost simultaneously, utilized the term "autism" to characterize rather similar children. Kanner's ideas (1943) quickly drew the attention of many psychologists and psychiatrists whereas Asperger's work (1944) remained essentially unknown until it was translated into English in 1991. Some small differences were recorded and these may be significant to our understanding of these childhood syndromes. Nevertheless, these youngsters showed rather striking features in common according to these theorists. According to Kanner and Asperger, the key feature was the mental aloneness of these youngsters, their tendency to disregard or ignore most stimuli that come from the outside world, especially in regard to people. Other features according to Kanner were their narrow preoccupations, their intense focus on unusual objects and activities in which they appear totally preoccupied and fascinated. Asperger considered their failure to make eye contact to be central. There is a poverty of facial expression and gestures as well as a tendency to follow their own impulses, regardless of the requirements of their surrounding environments. If language develops, it tends to be odd in character, typified by clichés, formulaic speech, or empty chatter. A notable distinction was Asperger's belief that these children could ultimately become normalized; by contrast, Kanner felt that their prognosis was likely to be an "unmitigated disaster." Another difference was Asperger's belief that the disorder represented a biological defect of affective-interpersonal contact, whereas Kanner implied that it was a psychogenic disorder, a result of problematic parenting, most particularly that of a remote "refrigerator mother."

Mention should be made of the brief tenure of a designation "schizoid disorder of childhood or adolescence," which was introduced into the DSM-III. Although its characterization has been subsumed under the schizoid personality label in the DSM-IV, the features noted for the disorder are worth mentioning. For example: a defect in the capacity to form social relationships; no apparent distress resulting from their isolation; little desire for social involvement; general avoidance of nonfamilial social contacts; no pleasure from peer interactions; a preference for being "loners."

The DSM-IV in its listing of autistic disorders characterizes it as highly similar to Asperger's disorder in that both give evidence of impairments in social interaction, as manifested by deficiencies in nonverbal behavior (such as eye-to-eye gaze, facial expression), a lack of social or emotional reciprocity, and an impaired sense of pleasure in other people's happiness. Those evidencing the autistic disorder also possess marked impairments in communication that are not present among those with Asperger's syndrome; likewise, autistic children manifest delays in cognitive development that those with Asperger's do not. Thus, autistic youngsters exhibit notable impairments in the ability to initiate or sustain social conversations and lack the ability to engage in spontaneous and social imitative play.

According to Wolff and Barlow (1970) the mothers of autistic children often describe them as "remote," "lacking in feeling," and "strange." These children were either withdrawn and uncommunicative or, if fluent, expressed themselves with metaphorical language.

Separating out the characteristics of the autistic from those of Asperger's syndrome is a difficult task indeed. In our judgment, it may be useful to differentiate the autistic youngster as one with a fundamental incapacity to attach and relate interpersonally, likely attributable to neurological or constitutional dysfunctions. By contrast, those assigned the Asperger's syndrome appear to be constitutionally oversensitive youngsters who possess communicative skills but have protectively drawn into themselves as a defensive position owing either to their hypersensitivity or to severely problematic interpersonal experiences. In this regard, they are perhaps seen best as early and extreme forms of the avoidant personality disorder.

In 1969, Millon wrote the following to characterize autistic youngsters. In contrast to those with Asperger's syndrome, autistic youngsters appear to exhibit in extreme form features seen to a lesser degree among schizoid personalities. He states:

These infants seem totally unresponsive to human stimulation; however, they demand a consistency and sameness in their physical environment and display an intense preoccupation with inanimate objects. Their impenetrable aloneness and their apparent inner emotional vacuum (may be summarized well by their) social isolation and a lack of personal identity.

Another characteristic of these children is their gross insensitivity to pain, further evidence of their affectivity deficit. Also notable is their tendency to engage in self-mutilating behaviors, such as head-knocking and hand-biting; this may reflect a desperate need for external stimulation to overcome what may be an extreme deficit in sensory receptivity. (p. 348)

In the discussion on childhood variants of the avoidant personality in Chapter 7, we will discuss youngsters who seem to be more akin to Asperger's syndrome, in that they are disposed to withdraw from their environment, but do so owing to an excessive degree of sensitivity. The pedagogical distinction between these two "pure types" may be difficult to discriminate overtly, but it is important that we conceptually locate them initially at different points on a continuum from passive-detachment at the one end to active-detachment at the other.

Adult Subtypes

The prototypes that constitute the body of the personality disorder chapters in this text represent derivations based essentially on *theoretical deduction.* They are given their descriptive characterizations from the vast literature provided by earlier clinicians and theorists, as well as from the texts of the DSM-III, III-R, and IV. What is presented is, in great part, a series of "ideal" or pure textbook conceptions of each disorder.

There are numerous variations, however, of these prototypal personality disorders, divergences from the theoretically derived prototype that represent the results of empirical research and clinical experience. Although it is our belief that the deeper or underlying laws that give shape to each of the personality prototypes are best understood in terms of theory, it is wise to recognize that there are fruitful, nontheoretical sources where such information has been and can be gathered (Millon, 1987a).

In this Adult Subtypes section, as well as in subsequent parallel sections in other chapters, we will describe variations on the core prototypal personality pattern that research and clinical observation suggests be included in our thinking about each personality disorder. We know that there is no single schizoid (or avoidant, or depressive, or histrionic) type. Rather, there are several variations, different forms in which the core or prototypal personality, expresses itself. Some reflect the workings of constitutional dispositions that life experience subsequently reshapes and impacts in different ways, taking divergent turns and producing moderately different psychological characteristics. The course and character of life experiences are complexly interwoven; numerous influences have simultaneous or sequential effects, often producing a mixture of patterns of different personality prototypes in the same person.

For these and other reasons, clinicians and students in our field must learn, not only the pure prototypal personalities, but the alternates and mixtures that are seen in clinical reality. This section, therefore, describes a number of these variations, or what we have termed "subtypes." They reflect mixtures, they reflect pure and mixed patterns of learning and experience, they reflect consistent inclinations of a specific type, and they reflect conflict resolutions in which overt patterns appear quite different from that which is covert or unconscious. The authors believe strongly that the reader should acquire increasing sophistication in the realm of personality *subtypes* as well as personality *prototypes*.

Numerous paths may eventuate in a schizoid personality disorder. We will briefly describe several of these in this section, as well as elaborate some aspects of their developmental course in later paragraphs.

The Languid Schizoid

As with other schizoids, the pattern we are calling *languid* can be traced either to life experiences or to inherent disabilities. Here we are likely to find some individuals who have been subjected to

marked stimulus impoverishment in the sensori-motor-autonomy stage, leading to the underdevelopment of relevant neural substrates. Among these, it is a failure to receive "psychic nourishment" requisite to the stimulation of their inherent activation and pleasurable potentials. For others, these deficits may stem from an inborn deficiency. What we see clinically among these persons is a mixed pattern that reflects a core schizoid makeup that has been interpenetrated with features of the depressive personality.

What is most notable in languid schizoids is the poverty in slowness of their activation level. Most are characterized by a marked inertia; rarely, do we see them engaged in any form of vigorous and energetic actions. They seem either too comfortable or too lazy, unable to rouse themselves to meet their responsibilities, or to engage in even the simplest of pleasurable activities. Perhaps their nature is intrinsically phlegmatic, especially when the tempo of their behavior is uniformly slow.

A distinction should be made between the languid and the affectless schizoids. Although the languid persons are accustomed to react slowly in all matters, including affectively, their affective capacities are neither shallow nor totally deficient. Some possess a reasonable measure of sentimentality, but rarely is it of considerable depth nor is it readily expressed.

As noted elsewhere (Millon, 1969), the lifestyle of these patients is typified by a quiet, colorless, and dependent way of relating to others. Their introversive pattern covaries with a general lack of vitality, deficits in social initiative and stimulus-seeking behaviors, impoverished affect, and a cognitive vagueness regarding interpersonal matters. Fatigability, low energy level, and weakness in motoric expressiveness and spontaneity are their most notable features.

These patients are inclined to possess an image of being a weak and ineffectual person. Life is experienced as uneventful, with periods of passive solitude interspersed with feelings of emptiness. There is a general deficiency in the expression of affection, which, in addition to their deficient energy level, may stem from an anhedonic inability to display enthusiasm or experience pleasure. Most evidence a tendency to keep to a simple, repetitive, and dependent life pattern.

The Remote Schizoid

Another set of difficulties that can result in the isolated and withdrawn schizoid pattern may be spoken of as the *remote subtype.* Youngsters subjected to intense parental/family hostilities and rejection very early in life may protectively withdraw in a manner so extreme as to reduce their original potential to feel and relate to the external world. Defensive maneuvers of this intensity and youth can be so severe as to make the child incapable of subsequent feeling and relating. We believe this to be an unusual adaptive maneuver, but a possibility nevertheless. The sequence just described is more likely to eventuate in an avoidant rather than a schizoid personality disorder. Here youngsters are quite capable of desiring relationships and feeling emotions intensely but have learned that such desires and emotions result in extreme anguish and disillusionment. Hence, they do not lack the capacity to feel and to relate to others, as do other schizoids, but have protectively damped down these emotions and wishes to such an extent as to be possibly unaware of them. Depending on the time and intensity of these overwhelming negative experiences, the child may exhibit signs that are more like the intrinsically deficient schizoid than the protectively avoidant pattern: most of these youngsters, we believe, retain the wish for affective bonding, but are deeply convinced that it will not be forthcoming. Nevertheless, what we see when we examine the more moderately severe *remote* personalities is a commingling of both core schizoid and avoidant features.

Very severe *remote* schizoids give evidence of features similar to the schizotypal personality; they manifest high scores on an assessment instrument such as the MCMI-III on both the schizoid and schizotypal scales. Many are seen among the homeless, as chronically institutionalized residents of half-way houses, and in such long-term outpatient settings as VA mental hygiene clinics. A marked deficit in social interest is notable, as are frequent behavioral eccentricities, occasional autistic thinking, and depersonalization anxieties. At best, they are likely to have acquired a peripheral but dependent role in social and family relationships. Both stem from low self-esteem and inadequacies in autonomy and social competence. These patients remain detached observers of the passing scene, are characteristically self-belittling, and possess self-images of being unloved and inadequate. Rather than venturing outward, they are increasingly remote from others and from sources of potential growth and gratification. Life is uneventful, with extended periods of solitude interspersed with occasional feelings of being disembodied, empty, and depersonalized. There is a tendency to follow a meaningless, ineffectual, and idle pattern,

drifting aimlessly and remaining on the periphery of social life.

A high proportion of these schizoids earn a very meager livelihood, quite frequently living a disengaged or parasitic lifestyle. Most are generally not adapted to functioning independently. Some give the impression of possessing a weakness of will or a deficient intellectual endowment; neither of these need be present, however. A goodly number of them appear asexual or have minimal sexual needs. When inclined to work, they are typically found in subordinate positions, becoming peripheral day laborers or municipal workers. Many are totally dependent on public support and welfare.

The Affectless Schizoid

In what may best be termed *the affectless schizoid type*, we believe that the isolated, emotionally detached, and nonsocially communicative features of this personality are likely to be a consequence in part of constitutional deficiencies. Perhaps these individuals have marked neurological deficits in those regions of the nervous system that subserve the capacity to relate with warmth and sensitivity to other humans, some lesion perhaps or structural aplasia in relevant systems (e.g., limbic). Here we are dealing with persons who are at the lower end of the normal distribution of affective sensibility; as noted, this diminished capacity is probably attributable largely to inborn limitations. Given these spiritless and emotionally diminished qualities, affectless schizoids are likely to show up clinically as possessing features that interweave with those seen in compulsive personalities.

Affectless schizoids should be distinguished conceptually from *schizotypal* personalities, where the primary defect is essentially a social/cognitive one. More precisely, in the latter syndrome there is a marked constitutional weakness in the capacity to accurately understand the meaning of human communications. In this schizoid, we see an "affective lameness"; in the schizotypal, we see a "cognitive dysfunction." Both defects usually result in marked social difficulties, the first owing to an incapacity to connect or resonate to others affectively, and in the latter an inability to cognitively grasp the meaning or fathom the interpersonal logic of their thoughts and behaviors.

A few words should be said to distinguish the *languid* from the *affectless* schizoid subtypes. In the languid, we see a primary slowness and ponderousness in energy and activation. Their deficits are largely motoric, evident in their slow movements, ready fatigue, and lack of initiative and drive. In the affectless, the deficiency is not motoric and behavioral, but is in the sphere of emotion and feeling. They seem unable to activate their affect; they are affectively lame, not energetically lame. Languids are torpid, phlegmatic, unmoved, look weary and depressed; the affectless are unexcitable, unperturbed, cold, look restrained and dispassionate.

In former years (e.g., Kraepelin, Bleuler, Schneider), deficiencies of an affective character were often judged to underlie the "moral insanities." Possessing a social insensibility was assumed to give rise to amoral behaviors. Such relationships do occur with certain temperamental and experiential backgrounds, but the incapacity to experience praise or blame and an emotional indifference to friends and strangers alike do not necessarily result in moral depravity, no less criminality. What we see in the affectless schizoid is simply an inability to activate any intense emotions, be they social or antisocial in character. There is minimal warmth, but there is also minimal anger and hostility.

The Depersonalized Schizoid

This variant of the schizoid is notable by the individual's dreamily distant qualities. Upon initial observation, one might think that these schizoids are enjoying the contemplation of some inner vision, some inner reality that draws them more and more into their isolated state. As with other schizoids, they are extremely inattentive and disengaged from the real world. But more than the others, they have not only deteriorated into a state of obliviousness, appearing as if they were preoccupied inwardly but, in fact, they are preoccupied with nothing in particular. Though present in the world of others, they appear to be staring into empty space, relating neither to the actions and feelings of others, nor to those that emanate from within themselves. These features bring this schizoid into a close amalgamation with the schizotypal personality such that many of their characteristics blend and unite.

As with many others who experience depersonalization, these schizoids are very much "outside observers," viewing themselves as distant objects, disembodied and vacant as phenomena unconnected to their own feelings and thoughts. They have drifted into a state in which they ignore not only external phenomena but those that emanate from within themselves. Disconnected from whatever is tangible and real in the world, including their own corporeal being, they are also *not* preoccupied with their own imagination and fantasies.

They are much like sleepwalkers who have a physical presence but are totally unaware of what they are doing and what they are thinking or feeling.

Despite their inward turning, thoughts and feelings are little more than a diffuse vagueness, an unclear and fuzzy set of disconnected ideas, an inchoate woolgathering, if you will. Not only are their internal processes undefined and diffuse, but their obscurity and their inability to relate leads others to sense increasingly that something is missing within them. Not only are they a million miles away, unrelated and unfocused in their human interactions, but their inner world appears equally distant and obscure, if not largely absent.

COMORBID DISORDERS AND SYNDROMES

Before detailing the disorders that frequently accompany the schizoid personality, it may be useful to reiterate an earlier discussion in Chapter 1 concerning distinctions between personality disorders and clinical syndromes.

Essentially, the behaviors that typify personality persist as permanent features of the individual's way of life and seem to have an inner autonomy; they exhibit themselves with or without external precipitants. In contrast, the behaviors that characterize Axis I clinical syndromes arise as a reaction to stressful situations and tend to be transient; they are of brief duration, subsiding or disappearing shortly after these conditions are removed. The clinical features of personality are highly complex and widely generalized, with many attitudes and habits exhibited only in subtle and indirect ways. In contrast, clinical syndromes tend to be characterized by isolated and dramatic behaviors that often simplify, accentuate, and caricature the more prosaic features of the patient's personality. They stand out in sharp relief against the background of more enduring and typical modes of functioning. Furthermore, personality traits feel "right" to the patients. They seem to be part and parcel of their makeup. In contrast, clinical syndromes often are experienced as discrepant, irrational, and uncomfortable. The behaviors, thoughts, and feelings of disorders seem strange and alien not only to others but to the patients themselves. They often feel as if they were driven by forces beyond their control.

It is our contention that a full understanding of Axis I clinical syndromes requires the study of Axis II personalities. Clinical syndromes are usually an outgrowth of deeply rooted sensitivities and coping strategies. The events a person perceives as threatening or rewarding, and the behaviors and mechanisms he or she employs in response to them, reflect a long history of interwoven biogenic and psychogenic factors that have formed the person's basic personality pattern.

Several qualifications should be noted lest the discussion imply an overly simplified relation between Axis I and Axis II syndromes. First, clinical syndromes do not arise in one personality pattern only. Second, in many cases several Axis I clinical syndromes may be simultaneously present because they reflect the operation of similar coping processes. Third, symptoms are likely to be transient because their underlying functions wax and wane as the need for them changes. And last, Axis I symptoms should, in large measure, be interchangeable, with one symptom appearing dominant at one time and a different one at another.

Although Axis I clinical syndromes often covary and are frequently interchangeable, we would expect some measure of symptom dominance and durability among different Axis II personalities. No one-to-one correspondence should be expected, of course, but differences in lifelong vulnerabilities and coping habits should lead us to anticipate that certain personalities would be more inclined to exhibit certain symptoms than others. In the compulsive personality, for example, where ingrained mechanisms such as reaction formation and undoing have been present for years, we would expect the patient to display symptoms that reflect these mechanisms. Similarly, histrionic personalities should exhibit the more dramatic and attention-getting symptoms since exhibitionistic histrionics have characterized their coping behaviors.

There are reasons not to overstate the correspondence between personality and clinical syndromes. Thus, symptoms that are often indistinguishable from those exhibited by pathological personalities arise also in normal persons. More importantly, there are endless variations in the particular experiences to which different members of the same personality syndrome have been exposed. To illustrate, compare two individuals who have been "trained" to become dependent personalities. One was exposed to a mother who was chronically ill, a pattern of behavior that brought her considerable sympathy and freedom from many daily burdens. With this as the background, the patient in question followed the model observed in the mother when faced with undue anxiety and threat, and thereby displayed hypochondriacal symptoms. A second dependent

personality learned to imitate a mother who expressed endless fears about every kind of event and situation. In this case, phobic symptoms arose in response to stressful and anxiety-laden circumstances. In short, the specific symptom "choice" is not a function solely of the patient's personality, but may reflect particular and entirely incidental events of prior experience and learning. This section describes the Axis I and Axis II disorders that co-occur with the personality pattern under review. Considerations relevant to differential diagnoses will be discussed in a later section.

As noted previously, objective precipitants in Axis I clinical syndromes often play a secondary role to those that exist internally. It is the patients' anticipatory sensitivities that dispose them to transform innocuous elements of reality so that they are duplicates of the past. As in a vicious circle, this distorted perception stirs up a wide range of associated past reactions. To specify the source of an Axis I disorder, then, we must look not so much to the objective conditions of reality, though these may in fact exist, as to the deeply rooted personality vulnerabilities of the patient.

Identifying these sensitivities is a highly speculative task because no one can specify exactly what goes on intrapsychically. The best we can do is to make theoretically and clinically informed guesses as to which attitudes in each of the major personality types are likely to give rise to the vulnerability. There is no single cause for Axis I clinical syndromes, even in patients with similar personalities. Moreover, not only do triggering precipitants differ from patient to patient, but different sensitivities may take precedence from one time to another within a single patient. The discussion proceeds with these cautions in mind.

Axis II Comorbidities

Patterns of comorbidity for the schizoid (SZD) are fairly consistently obtained with most methods and populations. As can be seen from Figure 6.4, the most prevalent association may be found between the SZD and the avoidant (AVD) personality; here co-diagnoses occur in 30% to 35% of cases. Almost as prevalent is the concurrence of SZD and schizotypal (SZT) personality disorders, where covariation appears in approximately 25% to 30% of the cases. As with all sources of prevalence data, there is a high degree of variability in comorbidity statistics. Whether these SZD, AVD, SZT results reflect intrinsic commonalities, or stem from the eye of the beholder owing to a

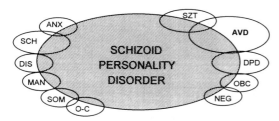

Figure 6.4 Comorbidity between schizoid personality disorder and other DSM Axis I and Axis II disorders.

belief in their joint association with the schizophrenic syndrome (or even to confusions stemming from the similarity in their names) cannot be ascertained. Figure 6.4 also records modest levels of SZD comorbidity with dependent (DPD), obsessive-compulsive (OBC), and negativistic (NEG) disorders.

The reader should refer back to the Adult Subtypes section (Languid, Affectless, etc.). In great measure, these subtypes reflect fusions between the basic schizoid prototype and other personality disorders.

Axis I Comorbidities

Complicated intrapsychic processes are not characteristic of the DSM-IV schizoid personality. As described earlier, these individuals lack the affective intensity to activate those defensive mechanisms that makeup unconscious dynamics. Consequently, schizoids exhibit few of the intricate coping maneuvers and experience few of the symbolic clinical syndromes usually recorded on Axis I.

Anxiety Syndromes (ANX).   In common with all pathological personalities, schizoids experience anxiety disorders. However, and in consonance with their flat and colorless style, intense emotionality is rarely exhibited, and states of chronic anxiety are almost never found. Nevertheless, two diametrically opposite sets of circumstances may prompt a flare-up of acute anxiety or panic disorder: excessive stimulation or persistent understimulation. Schizoids may "explode" when they feel encroached upon or when faced with unusual social demands and responsibilities. Similar consequences may follow from marked understimulation. Here, the schizoid experiences feelings of depersonalization, a sense of emptiness and nothingness, and a state of self-nonexistence,

stagnation, barrenness, and unreality that becomes frightfully overwhelming and unbearable.

Manic Syndromes (MAN).   Along similar lines, schizoids may exhibit brief and rather frenzied episodes of manic excitement in an attempt to counter the anxieties of depersonalization. Here, for but a fleeting period, they burst out of their characteristic retiring and unsociable pattern and into a frantic and bizarre conviviality. The wild, irrational, and chaotic character of their exuberance tends to run but a brief, if erratic, course before collapsing into their more typically subdued and inexpressive state.

Obsessive-Compulsive Syndromes (OC).   Extended social isolation, with its consequent periods of "empty" rumination, often results in obsessive thinking, which the schizoid may be unable to block from conscious intrusion. Most of these thoughts are meaningless (e.g., "where did I see a chair with one leg?") and experienced without emotion but, nonetheless, may be so persistent and distracting as to upset the routine of daily activities. Some recurrent thoughts may become tension laden, pertain to forbidden impulses or prohibited desires and, hence, evoke feelings of shame, disgust, or horror. The more desperately these patients try to rid themselves of these repugnant ideas, the more persistent and tormenting they may become. For example, a passing thought of poisoning a wayward wife may become fixed in a husband's mind; no matter how much he seeks to distract his attention from it, the thought returns time and again.

Dissociative Syndromes (DIS).   As already noted, depersonalization disorders are rather common among schizoids. As an extension or elaboration of their more characteristic state, these patients often experience altered perceptions of themselves and a sense of self-estrangement, including feeling "mechanical," distant, and disembodied. Trancelike states akin to estrangement also occur, but here the patients' awareness is merely dimmed. They may report being in a "twilight" dream world, totally immersed in inner events, and entirely oblivious to their surroundings.

As a function of their habitual lack of interest in the events of everyday life, schizoids often fail to acquire a coherent and well-integrated core of attitudes necessary for organizing an "inner identity." Empty or devoid of a past, deficient in "psychic" cohesion, and insensitive to external promptings, they are subject to the kind of splitting or disintegration that inclines them to dissociative states.

Somatoform Syndromes (SOM). Although only modestly prevalent, hypochondriacal disorders will become prominent and salient features when they do occur in schizoids. Noted by the presence of prolonged periods of weariness and exhaustion, undiagnosable physical sensations, and persistent insomnia, these patients may fall into a state of diffuse irritability and report pains in different, unconnected, and changing regions of the body. Phenomenologically, these schizoids report experiencing a heaviness and a drab monotony to their lives. Despite this lethargy, they become fixated, exquisitely attuned to some facet of normal physiology, or uncharacteristically concerned with a minor change in their bodily functioning. These preoccupations seem to reflect a need on their part to "latch on" to something tangible about themselves that will assure them they do, in fact, exist and are not insubstantial or disembodied.

Schizophrenic Syndromes (SCH). As noted earlier, schizoids may exhibit brief frenzied states of manic excitement; for similar reasons, they may succumb to other transient episodes, best diagnosed as brief reactive psychoses and schizophreniform disorders. The frenetic quality of their behavior is still prominent but, in contrast to the manic phase, exhibits significant elements of apprehension and agitation. Periods diagnosable as disorganized (hebephrenic) schizophrenia may also occur; here, the patient evidences a blend of irrational thinking and flat affect, punctuated every now and then by panicky outbursts and bizarre emotions. Phases of catatonic schizophrenia are also seen in these personalities. At these times, patients appear motivated by a desire to withdraw from external provocation rather than by a need to control untoward impulses, not that the latter should be overlooked as a factor. Faced with derogation and humiliation, schizoids may draw tightly into their shells, resistant to any form of stimulation that may demand that they think or feel. The grimacing and giggling often observed at these periods is a clue to their chaotic fantasy world.

The most characteristic feature of psychotic-level schizoid behavior is their profound lethargy and indifference to their surroundings. If they move, it is listlessly, languidly; they are perhaps best described as stuporous. Clothes droop as on a hanger, and their faces are lifeless and masklike. At best, speech is slow, labored, whispered, or totally inaudible. Passively withdrawn and unresponsive, they do not participate or feel involved, perceiving events and things about them as unreal and strange. There is a characteristic emotional poverty, compounded by a dreamy detachment, a tendency to stand immobile or fixed in one place. Many sit habitually in a cramped, bent-over, and peculiar position, to which they return repeatedly if they are distracted or dislodged. Others not only show the typical lack of initiative but display an automatic obedience to the requests of others, even when these directives could result in severe physical discomfort or danger. Some become so profoundly detached that they fail to register or react to painful stimuli.

DIFFERENTIAL DIAGNOSES

Differential diagnosis is no longer the important issue it has been in the past because overlapping syndromes are not only recognized but encouraged in the multiaxial DSM format; this is especially true in Axis I and Axis II combinations.

The prime Axis I clinical syndrome that may require differentiation from the schizoid personality is likely to be *depersonalization disorder.* In general, the breadth and number of traits involved and the specific features of interpersonal "coolness" and social indifference should help distinguish the personality syndrome from the more narrow and transient nature of the symptom disorder.

Differentiations between schizoid personality and various *schizophrenic disorders* may not be necessary when overlapping symptoms are observed; both should be registered on their respective axes where appropriate. Where distinction rather than covariance is the issue, the centrality of delusions, hallucinations, and disordered thinking to the schizophrenic diagnosis clearly sets it apart from the more prosaic and nonpsychotic features of the schizoid.

Turning to Axis II personality syndromes, diagnostic difficulties are likely to be encountered most often by clinicians seeking to distinguish schizoid, schizotypal, depressive, and avoidant personalities. Differentiations among these syndromes will become less troublesome as the reader progresses through this text. A few words are in order in the interim.

First, *schizotypal* personalities are more dramatically eccentric than schizoids, who are characteristically flat, colorless, and dull. Schizotypals exhibit several classic schizophrenic signs, though not delusions or hallucinations. Notable among these features are ideas of reference, suspiciousness, magical thinking, and odd speech—as well as the social isolation and restricted or cold affect that they share with the schizoid. Of course, schizoid and schizotypal characteristics will covary. The qualities of both syndromes frequently intermesh when schizoids begin to decompensate and are treated in institutional settings where they may observe and then adopt a variety of odd and peculiar mannerisms through modeling and vicarious learning.

Second, diagnostic differentiations between schizoid and *avoidant* personalities are difficult to make on initial observations because both tend to be socially hesitant and unresponsive. A nonempirical source of difficulty in this regard may arise among clinicians who consider all "bland exteriors" to signify an adaptive or defensive emotional blunting and withdrawal consequent to repressed childhood disappointments, conflicts, and anxieties. This theoretical assumption does not apply to the formulations of the schizoid as conceived in the DSM. Though presented atheoretically insofar as etiology is concerned, the DSM-IV schizoid is seen as not conflicted, nor suffering either ambivalence or deep disillusion; this patient's affectless and detached qualities stem from inherent deficits. For those who hold to the conflict, disillusion, and defense models, the avoidant personality designation represents the syndrome that derives from experiences of early rebuff or affectional deprivation. Avoidant types desire affect and social acceptance, whereas the similarly appearing schizoid is intrinsically unresponsive and indifferent to them. Avoidants may appear coolly detached, but they actually are restrained and fearful lest their intense desires be met with further rejection and humiliation. More is said about this distinction between the passively and actively detached types in Chapter 7.

Distinctions with the new *depressive* personality may be required by virtue of their comparable lack of joyful expressiveness and pleasurable reactivity. Both schizoids and depressives appear flat, colorless, and unreactive to external circumstances. The key difference lies in that the depressives can experience deep feelings, but almost entirely of a sad and unhappy character. As soon as they begin to voice their concerns, it should be evident whether one is dealing with a depressive individual or a schizoid. Schizoids may also need

to be differentiated from *paranoid* personalities, in that both evidence social isolation and restricted affect. The schizoid, however, does not manifest the suspiciousness and semidelusional ideation found among paranoid personalities.

There is a commonality also to be found with *obsessive-compulsive* personalities. Both schizoids and compulsives evince an emotional restrictiveness and a preoccupation with concrete and impersonal tasks. However, compulsives demonstrate strong feelings when provoked by troublesome circumstances; they also desire and are capable of social and personal intimacies that schizoids do not exhibit.

ASSESSING THE SCHIZOID: A CASE STUDY

In these and parallel sections in future chapters, we will briefly outline some of the clinical response features seen in the personality disorder under discussion as they appear in a number of the major current assessment instruments. We will not summarize the typical results of the majority of assessment tools reviewed in Chapter 4. These instruments are specifically geared to the identification of each of the personality disorders, and it should be expected that the relevant scale would be the most elevated.

Our primary emphasis in this section, although brief, will be on the most established psychological tests in use today. Our purpose here is merely to note the features of these instruments that are suggestive of characteristics among the various personality disorders under discussion. Specifically, we will note some of the clinical signs found in the Rorschach, the Thematic Apperception Test (TAT), and the MMPI.

The major portion of this and future sections will comprise a brief case history of a patient known to the senior author in his past clinical work. Following the case summary, an MCMI-III profile of scale scores and segments of the interpretive report associated with this patient will be presented.

The Rorschach data of the schizoid will likely include a rather small number of responses, including occasional rejections. Very few color responses are usually present; vague responses and odd descriptions are also typical. Both *M* scores and Animal Content responses tend to be high; reaction times are often slow. Similarly, the TAT response record is usually quite limited both in scope and in interest; by the latter, we mean that both the characterizations and themes presented by schizoids are quite bland and undeveloped, a not surprising pattern.

Not infrequently, the basic MMPI scales look close to normal among schizoids who are fairly well integrated within their social community. Scale 0 tends to be high, indicating their introversive tendencies. Particularly affectless and interpersonally disengaged schizoids often exhibit high scores on Scale 2, indicative of their anhedonic qualities. When unusually stressed, scores on Scale 8 are likely to be high. Profiles of an 1-8 character are not unusual.

The following case illustrates a typical schizoid personality.

Case 6.1

Harriet S., Age 22, College Junior, Unmarried

Harriet was an extremely pretty, petite brunette, who personified the young college coed in appearance. She sought counseling on the urging of her dormitory roommate because both felt she might have latent homosexual tendencies; this concern proved unjustified, but other characteristics of a pathological nature clearly were evident.

Harriet rarely enjoyed herself on dates; not that she found herself "disgusted" or "repelled" with necking and petting, but she simply "didn't experience any pleasure" in these activities (affectivity deficit). She went out of her way to avoid invitations to parties, preferring to stay in her room, either watching TV or working at her studies. She was an excellent student, majoring in geology and hoping for a field career in forestry, petroleum research, or archaeology.

Harriet was viewed as rather distant and aloof by her classmates. She rarely engaged in social activities, turned down an opportunity to join a sorority, and had no close friends; in fact, she had few friends at all, except for her roommate and one girl back home. Despite her good looks, she was asked to date infrequently; when she did date, it usually was a one- or two-date affair in which either the boy failed to ask again or she refused to accept the invitation. The little reputation she had on campus was that she was a "cold fish" and "a brain," someone who would rather talk about her

courses and career plans than dance, drink, and be merry.

One relationship with a boy lasted several months. He seemed to be a quiet and introversive young man who joined her in taking hikes, in demeaning the "childish" behaviors of their classmates, and in discussing their mutual interest in nature, trees, and rock formations. Their relationship faltered after 10 to 12 outdoor hiking dates; they seemed to have nothing more to say to each other. Harriet would have liked to continue this friendship, but she experienced no dismay over its termination (interpersonal indifference).

Further explorations showed that Harriet rarely experienced either joy, dismay, or anger. She seemed content to "let matters ride along," sitting on the sidelines while others became perturbed, ecstatic, or hostile about "silly little things between them." This viewpoint, however, reflected less a well-reasoned philosophy of life than an inability to grasp "what it is that got people so excited." In describing her few relationships, past and present, she seemed to be vague, superficial, and naive, unable to organize her thoughts and tending to wander into irrelevancies such as the shoes certain people preferred or the physical characteristics of their parents (cognitive slippage).

The MCMI-III provides a wide range of data on cases such as that of Harriet. Figure 6.5 encompasses all the scale scores of this schizoid personality. The following segments of the interpretive report characterize in some detail the personality configuration and clinical syndromes of this case.

Interpretive Summary

The MCMI-III profile of this woman suggests a subdued, inexpressive, dependent way of relating to life. She probably shows a marked deficit in social interest as well as frequent behavioral eccentricities, depressive-like thinking, and depersonalization anxieties. This intense, introversive pattern may coexist with a general lack of energy and a deficit in social initiative. She seems to evince little stimulus-seeking behavior, exhibits inappropriate or impoverished affect, and displays confusion or a metaphorical quality in her interpersonal thinking. Although she probably prefers a peripheral role in her family relationships, she is also likely to possess a strong, conflicting need to

CATEGORY		SCORE		PROFILE OF BR SCORES				DIAGNOSTIC SCALES
		RAW	BR	0 60	75	85	115	
MODIFYING	X	103	64					DISCLOSURE
INDICES	Y	8	39					DESIRABILITY
	Z	19	76					DEBASEMENT
	1	19	99					SCHIZOID
	2A	12	75					AVOIDANT
	2B	5	32					DEPRESSIVE
	3	18	95					DEPENDENT
CLINICAL	4	5	23					HISTRIONIC
PERSONALITY	5	4	22					NARCISSISTIC
PATTERNS	6A	6	62					ANTISOCIAL
	6B	3	36					AGGRESSIVE (SADISTIC)
	7	10	40					COMPULSIVE
	8A	13	74					NEGATIVISTIC
	8B	9	82					MASOCHISTIC
SEVERE	S	6	61					SCHIZOTYPAL
PERSONALITY	C	17	87					BORDERLINE
PATHOLOGY	P	3	45					PARANOID
	A	8	78					ANXIETY DISORDER
	H	8	63					SOMATOFORM DISORDER
CLINICAL	N	6	62					BIPOLAR MANIC DISORDER
SYNDROMES	D	9	60					DYSTHYMIC DISORDER
	B	4	62					ALCOHOL DEPENDENCE
	T	2	60					DRUG DEPENDENCE
	R	8	64					POST-TRAUMATIC STRESS
SEVERE	SS	12	68					THOUGHT DISORDER
SYNDROMES	CC	12	75					MAJOR DEPRESSION
	PP	0	0					DELUSIONAL DISORDER

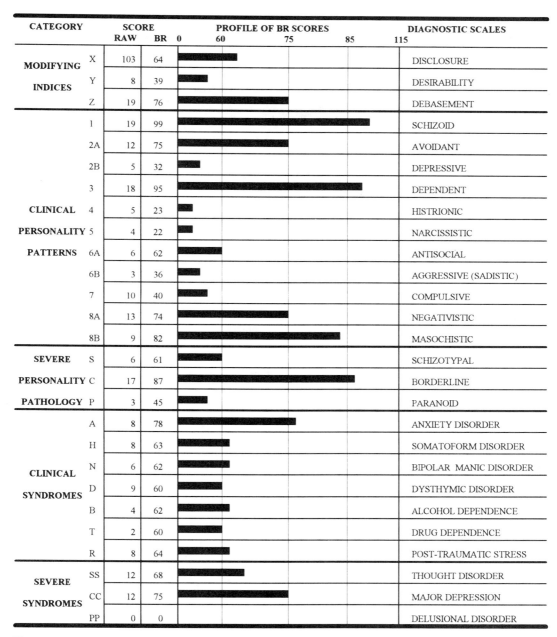

Figure 6.5   Millon Clinical Multiaxial Inventory-III.

depend on others. Both of these derive from her low self-esteem and her deficiencies in autonomous behavior.

It is probable that this woman is a detached observer of the passing scene. She is probably self-belittling and sees herself as being weak and ineffectual. Rather than expose herself to the outer world, she is likely to retreat, becoming increasingly remote from potential sources of opportunity and gratification. Life proceeds in an uneventful way for much of the time. Her extended periods of solitude may be interspersed with feelings of being disembodied, empty, and depersonalized. Ideas of reference may also occur on occasion. For the most part, she probably follows a meaningless, ineffectual, idle life pattern, generally remaining on the periphery of social activities.

It is possible that her thoughts have an unfocused and bizarre quality at times, particularly in regard to emotional and interpersonal matters. Her likely estrangement from others may have led her to lose touch with reality. Social communication may be odd, strained, self-conscious, and tangential, which further alienates her from others. Her inability to express affection may stem from her chronic isolation and her failure to experience any source of pleasure in her life. She may exhibit a chronic, mild dysthymia that is occasionally mixed with ill-defined anxiety.

Most likely this woman prefers a simple, repetitive, dependent life in which she can avoid self-assertion and remain indifferent to normal social aspirations. Disengaged from and uninterested in most of the rewards of human relationships, she may appear to others as an unobtrusively strange, disconnected, lifeless person. By restricting her social and emotional involvements, she probably perpetuates her pattern of isolation and dependency on others.

Daily feelings of dejection, apathy, and pessimism characterize this socially uncomfortable and lonely woman. A recurrent pattern of thoughts of death and of feeling blue, downhearted, unworthy, and unattractive suggests a major depression. Preoccupied with self-doubts and the perception of being physically unattractive, this shy and sad woman has periodic thoughts of suicide. In reaction to her deep sense of personal frustration and unhappiness, she is intropunitive, self-demeaning, and hypersensitive to her own shortcomings. She may evince a diminished capacity for pleasure that may be accompanied by sleep difficulties and a poor appetite that may indicate an anorexic pattern. She is not likely to yearn for acceptance and affection from others.

PATHOGENIC DEVELOPMENTAL BACKGROUND

Despite the long history and diverse methods that have been employed in researching the variants of the "schizophrenic spectrum," few data show up with sufficient consistency to be useful in identifying definitive "causes." Taken in concert, however,

these data provide a basis, at least, for speculating about some of the background characteristics that may be expected to be found in these individuals.

HYPOTHESIZED BIOGENIC FACTORS

The role of biophysical structures and processes in psychopathology is largely speculative. Given our current state of knowledge, it would be presumptuous to assert with any degree of confidence that we have conclusive evidence implicating any of the biogenic influences to be hypothesized. The available research data often are contradictory, nonapplicable, or based on poorly designed studies. With this caveat in mind, let us advance a few of the more plausible biogenic hypotheses.

Heredity

Since children inherit many overt physical features from their parents, it would seem safe to assume that features of internal morphology and physiochemistry may similarly be inherited. Extrapolating further, it would seem plausible that parents who are biologically limited in their capacity to experience intense emotions, or to be vigorous and active, possess certain associated structural and physiological deficiencies that they may transmit genetically to their children. What we are proposing, then, is that the schizoid pattern may arise because an individual is at the low end of a genetically based continuum of individual differences in neurological structures and physiochemical processes that subserve affectivity, interpersonal sensitivity, activation, and so on. Support for this speculation may be extracted from a variety of genetic studies, especially in the field of schizophrenia. However, to select data to fit these conjectures would be borrowing specious evidence for what should be viewed as a frankly speculative hypothesis.

Passive Infantile Reaction Pattern

We believe that a substantial number of adult schizoid personalities displayed in infancy and early childhood a low sensory responsivity, motor passivity, and a generally placid mood. They may have been easy to handle and care for, but it is likely that they provided their parents with few of the joys associated with more vibrant and expressive youngsters. As a consequence of their undemanding and unresponsive nature, they are likely to have evoked minimal stimulation and overt expressions of affectivity from their caretakers; this deficit in sheer physical handling may have compounded their initial tendencies toward inactivity, emotional flatness, and general insipidity.

Ectomorphic Body Structure

Numerous theorists have proposed that individuals with thin and fragile body builds typically are shy and introversive. It is debatable, however, as to whether this correlation can be attributed primarily to an intrinsic genetic linkage between these physical and psychological traits. A more plausible interpretation suggests that persons who possess the frail ectomorphic build tend to conserve their energies and lack the physical competencies, resilience, and mechanical wherewithal to engage in vigorous, assertive behaviors. Given these physical limitations, they may learn quickly to become indifferent to, and to avoid, emotionally charged situations and physically demanding activities.

Neurological Deficits in the Limbic or Reticular Systems

Defects in either the limbic or reticular regions of the brain may result in the development of a schizoid pattern. However, given the mild form of this personality impairment, it is probable that the correlated biophysical impairment is not that of tissue damage but of a numerical sparseness of neural cells, or a thinly dispersed branching system emanating from these regions.

Congenital aplasia of any of the centers of the limbic system may give rise to an affectivity deficit. Because the subregions of this complex anatomical system may be differentially impaired, no two persons will possess identical affectivity characteristics; for example, some schizoid personalities may exhibit the consequences of deficiencies in the "pleasure" center, whereas others may display behaviors associated with an underdeveloped "aversive" center, and so on.

The phlegmatic character of the schizoid pattern may derive from deficits in the reticular system as well. Though our understanding of the diverse functions carried out by this widely branched system is far from complete, we do know that it subserves arousal and activation. Thus, a feebly branched reticular formation may account

for the mild lethargy and lack of alertness that characterizes the schizoid personality.

The view that the reticular system is a major relay station for intrabrain circuitry is unverified but plausible. If this hypothesis is correct, dysfunctions in the reticular system may give rise to chaotic interneuronal transmissions, and these neurological defects may lead, in turn, to deficient emotional learnings; for example, in so disorganized a system, the emotional dimension of an experience may be circuited peculiarly and simply fail to be anchored to the intellectual awareness of that experience. As a consequence of these "discoordinations," the person may possess only an intellectual grasp of human relationships and may obscure them with irrelevant associations. This cognitive slippage, or breakdown in reticular coordination, may account, then, for deficient and irrational connections between normally associated emotions and cognitions.

Parasympathetic System Dominance

The activation and affectivity deficits of the schizoid personality may stem from an adrenergic-cholinergic imbalance in which the parasympathetic division of the autonomic nervous system is functionally dominant. The inhibitory effects on alertness and arousal of this dominance could well account for underresponsiveness, apathy, and emotional flatness.

Neurohormonal Synaptic Dyscontrol

Hypotheses implicating neurohormonal disturbances also are plausible; specific attention may be drawn to the role of these chemicals in maintaining synaptic control. Excesses or deficiencies in acetylcholine and norepinephrine may result in the proliferation and scattering of neural impulses, or in the inhibition of efficient neural sequences. Any form of chemically induced synaptic dyscontrol may give rise to either or both the cognitive slippage or affectivity deficits that characterize the schizoid pattern.

In summary then, several biogenic factors may contribute to a developmental course leading to schizoid personality patterns. Acceptance of the role of these hypothesized biogenic factors in no way precludes the fact that equivalent effects can be produced purely by psychogenic forces. In fact, no personality pattern can be attributed to biogenic factors alone. Clinical personality syndromes evolve through a lengthy chain of inter-acting biogenic and psychogenic determinants; the specific weight assigned to the various contribu-tory agents will differ from case to case.

CHARACTERISTIC EXPERIENTIAL HISTORY

The number and variety of influences that shape personality are legion. Dismayed by the infinite diversity of these determinants, some theorists have avoided assigning more weight to some influ-ences than to others; this evasion is unfortunate. Assuming that we have some grasp of the princi-ples by which behavior is learned, we should be able to infer, with some measure of accuracy, the kinds of antecedent conditions that are likely to give rise to these behaviors.

Despite the paucity of well-designed empirical research in this field, there is sufficient reason to believe that the following psychogenic hypotheses have merit as plausible conjectures.

Stimulus Impoverishment during the Sensory Attachment Stage

A lack of functional stimuli normally provided by the infant's caretakers may set the stage for various maturational and learning deficits. Insufficient in-take of stimulus nourishment during the first year of life is likely to result in the underdevelopment of the neural substrate for affectivity and in a defi-cient learning of interpersonal attachments.

Constitutionally unresponsive infants who have a built-in stimulus barrier, or who evoke few reac-tions from their environment, may experience a compounding of their initial activation and sen-sory deficits. Such children receive little attention, cuddling, and affection from their parents and, as a consequence, are deprived of the social and emo-tional cues requisite to learning human attachment behaviors. Although they may provide stimulation for themselves, this is likely to take the form of inanimate objects (dolls, blankets, blocks), thereby resulting in the acquisition of attachments to things rather than to people. Because of these in-born sensory or energy deficits, then, these infants are likely to be deprived of stimuli necessary for the maturation of the "emotional" brain centers, and the learning of human attachment behaviors.

These same consequences may develop in in-fants with entirely normal constitutional capaci-ties and dispositions. Thus, an average infant reared with minimal human interaction, either in an impersonal atmosphere or with cold and un-affectionate parents, will be deprived of early sensory stimulation necessary for normal devel-opment; these youngsters are likely to acquire the interpersonally detached and affectless sympto-matology of the schizoid pattern.

Formal or Impassive Family Atmospheres

Children learn to imitate the pattern of interper-sonal relationships to which they repeatedly are exposed. Learning to be stolid, reticent, and un-demonstrative can be an incidental product of ob-serving the everyday relationships within the family setting. Families characterized by inter-personal reserve, superficiality, and formality, or possessing a bleak and cold atmosphere in which members relate to each other in an aloof, remote or disaffiliated way, are likely breeding grounds for schizoid children, who evidence deeply in-grained habits of social ineptness or insensitivity.

Fragmented or Amorphous Family Communications

A brief excerpt from Deutsch's study of the "as if " personality effectively captures the essence of the experiential history of many schizoids. The case described is that of the only child of "one of the oldest noble families in Europe" and portrays the character of the relationship between parent and child that was "quite in accordance with tradition." The child's care and training were delegated to "strangers." Deutsch wrote:

On certain specified days of the week she was brought before her parents for "control." At these meetings there was a formal check of her educa-tional achievements, and the new program and other directions were given her preceptors. Then after a cool, ceremonious dismissal, the child was returned to her quarters. She received no warmth and no tenderness from her parents, nor did pun-ishment come directly from them. This virtual separation from her parents had come soon after her birth. Perhaps the most inauspicious compo-nent of her parents' conduct, which granted the child only a very niggardly bit of warmth, was the fact and this was reinforced by the whole program of her education that their sheer existence was strongly emphasized, and the patient was drilled in love, honor, and obedience towards them without ever feeling these emotions directly and realistically.

In this atmosphere, so lacking in feeling on the part of the parents, the development of a satisfactory emotional life could scarcely be expected in the child. (1942, p. 306)

To relate effectively to others requires the capacity to focus on what others are experiencing and communicating, and to convey appropriate and relevant reactions in response. Some individuals fail to learn how to attend and interpret the signals that others communicate, or fail to learn how to respond in meaningful and rational ways. Learning the skills of interpersonal communication is a requisite to shared social behaviors; without them, the individual cannot function effectively with others, and will appear detached, unresponsive, cold, and insensitive—traits that we have assigned to the schizoid pattern.

Family styles of communicating in which ideas are aborted, or are transmitted in circumstantial, disjunctive, or amorphous ways, are likely to shape the growing child's own manner of communication; in short, the child's pattern of relating to others will assume the vague and circumstantial style of the family. Moreover, exposed to disrupted, unfocused and murky patterns of thought, the child will, both by imitation and by the need to follow the surrounding illogic, learn to attend to peripheral or tangential aspects of human communication—to signs and cues that most people would view as irrelevant and distracting. This way of attending to, of thinking about and reacting to events, if extended beyond the family setting, will give rise to perplexity and confusion on the part of others. As a consequence, a vicious circle of disjointed and meaningless transactions may come to characterize the child's interpersonal relations, leading to further isolation and social distance. Together, these events will foster increased cognitive obscurities and emotional insensitivities, traits that characterize the schizoid and schizotypal patterns.

SELF-PERPETUATION PROCESS

What does the future hold for the schizoid? This section explores personality features that are themselves pathogenic, that is, foster increments in the individual's difficulties. Also touched upon are some of the therapeutic steps that might help reverse these trends.

The impassivity and lack of color of schizoids enable them to maintain a comfortable distance from others. But their preferred state of detachment is itself pathogenic, not only because it fails to elicit experiences that could promote a more vibrant and rewarding style of life but because it fosters conditions that are conducive to more serious forms of psychopathology. Among the more prominent factors that operate to this end are the following.

Impassive and Insensitive Behavior

The inarticulateness and affective unresponsiveness that characterize schizoids do little to make them attractive to others. Most persons are not inclined to relate to schizoids for any period, tending to overlook their presence in most settings and, when interacting socially, doing so in a perfunctory and unemotional way. Although the fact that others consider them as boring and colorless suits the asocial predilections of schizoids quite well, this preference for remaining apart and alone only perpetuates and intensifies their tendencies toward detachment.

Diminished Perceptual Awareness

The schizoid personality not only is socially imperceptive but tends to "flatten" emotional events by blurring and homogenizing experiences that are intrinsically distinct and varied. In effect, these personalities project their murky and undifferentiated cognitions on discriminable and complex social events. As a consequence of this perceptual diffusiveness, they preclude the possibility of learning from experiences that could lead them to a more variegated and socially discriminating life.

Social Inactivity

Passively detached schizoids perpetuate their own pattern by limiting severely their social contacts and emotional involvements. Only those activities required to perform their jobs or fulfill their family obligations are pursued with any diligence. By shrinking their interpersonal milieu, they preclude new experiences from coming to bear on them. This is their preference, but it only fosters their isolated and withdrawn existence by excluding events that might alter their style.

THERAPEUTIC INTERVENTIONS

The prognosis for this moderately severe personality is not promising. Many appear limited by a constitutional incapacity for affective expression and physical vigor. These liabilities may be inborn or acquired as a consequence of early experience. Regardless of their origin, however, the affectivity and interpersonal deficits found in these individuals are chronic and pervasive features of their personality makeup. Coupling these ingrained traits with the characteristic lack of insight and poor motivation for change, we can only conclude that the probability is small that they will either seek or succeed in a course of remedial therapy. If their deficits are mild and if the circumstances of their life are favorable, they will stand a good chance, however, of maintaining adequate vocational and social adjustments. Given their lack of intrinsic motivators, the role of contextual factors in mobilizing therapeutic progress is paramount.

STRATEGIC GOALS

The styles that schizoids have developed to cope with the events of their everyday life are a result, in great measure, of deficits in their intrinsic capacities to experience painful and pleasurable emotions. The impact of early learning may have further weakened these dispositions over time, continuing to color all subsequent events and thereby perpetuating the initial maladaptive patterns.

Reestablishing Polarity Balances

As noted in previous pages, the coping strategy that characterizes the schizoid's mode of relating to his/her environment can best be described as passively detached. Not only do they appear to lack the capacity to experience pleasure or pain, but they do not obtain gratification from either self or others. A major treatment goal of personologic therapy with this disorder is the enhancement of pleasure, particularly to overcome the imbalance in the pain-pleasure polarity. Moreover, their passively detached nature places them near the extreme end on the active-passive polarity. This latter imbalance warrants therapeutic efforts directed toward strengthening the active end of the continuum.

Countering Perpetuating Tendencies

When schizoids do come to the attention of a therapist, the latter's initial efforts are best directed toward combating their withdrawal tendencies. A major therapeutic goal is to prevent the possibility that they will isolate themselves entirely from the support of a benign environment. The therapist should seek to ensure that they continue some level of social activity to prevent them from becoming lost in fantasy preoccupations and separated from reality contacts. However, efforts to encourage a great deal of social activity are best avoided since their tolerance in this area is limited. Further therapeutic strategies should be oriented toward enhancing their perceptual awareness and countering their underresponsiveness to the environment. Schizoids typically display an emotional inattentiveness to others that needs to be addressed. Increasing affectivity will in turn promote more variegated social experiences.

Modifying Domain Dysfunctions

Primary domain dysfunctions can be seen in both the interpersonal conduct and mood/temperament domain. Providing the patient with an opportunity for social interaction can foster improvements in the interpersonal domain and lessen social isolation. Targeting the mood/temperament domain will involve activating the patient's characteristically dull mood and increasing the capacity to experience pleasurable affective states. Deficits in activation are also observed in expressive behavior. Improvements in this area would consist of elevating the energy level and enhancing the expressive abilities. Schizoids' cognitive style is rather vague and lacks richness. Intervention necessitates bringing clarity to their thought processes, helping them attend to both internal and external processes without losing focus.

Secondary dysfunctions can be seen across several other domains. Their self-image, object-representations, regulatory mechanisms, and morphologic organization all lack complexity and depth. By expanding their behavioral and social repertoire and simultaneously improving their ability to attend to different stimuli, a groundwork may be provided for improving these remaining domains.

TACTICAL MODALITIES

To accomplish the preceding goals, a variety of therapeutic modalities can be employed targeting the clinical domain dysfunctions. These techniques should then be combined and put in sequence to promote maximal growth. Because each individual possesses a unique constellation of attributes, a thorough assessment of the saliences of the clinical domains should be conducted. The following formulations are not foolproof, and the therapist needs to be aware of the potential stumbling blocks and resistances that may loom up.

Domain-Oriented Techniques

Techniques of *behavioral modification* appear to be of limited value other than to reinforce some social skills. Because schizoids commonly lack full awareness of customary ways of behaving in social spheres, social skills training and other more directive and educative measures may be employed to build a more appropriate interpersonal behavioral repertoire. Beck and Freeman (1990b) suggest setting up a hierarchy of social interaction goals that the patient may want to accomplish. Role playing and in vivo exposure can then be utilized to practice these skills. Audioplayback devices can be of some benefit in allowing patients to monitor their monotone speech. Videotaping can similarly be used in helping patients identify more subtle nuances in their own behavior.

A critical limitation of operant techniques is that few external sources of reinforcement can be identified since these patients appear to have a limited capacity to experience consequent events as either rewarding or punishing. Affection and recognition, which serve as potent reinforcers for most people, are not valued. An attempt should be made to carefully analyze the patient's behavioral repertoire and past history of reinforcement to identify any operant reinforcers that might be activated at this time. Behavioral change can at times be brought about by encouraging environmental modifications that may include occupational adjustments or a change in living situation.

Interpersonal techniques may prove problematic because a key element in interpersonal treatment is the therapeutic relationship, a feature in the schizoid's asocial world that possesses little value. Transference reactions are less likely to occur but, if present, may only recapitulate earlier maladaptive interpersonal patterns. The therapist's empathic stance and continued acceptance of the patient may facilitate rapport building. This may prove more fruitful than an insight-oriented approach, the latter seeking with minimal success to analyze the patient's mode of interacting in the session.

By providing a supportive and trusting environment, the therapist can facilitate collaboration.

The dyadic relationship can be used as a forum for practicing recently acquired interpersonal and social skills. Here the therapist can function as a mirror, enabling the patient to gain a closer look at the self, providing a measure for confirmation and elaboration of inchoate self-schemas.

Attempts to *cognitively* reorient the patient's attitudes may be useful for developing self-insight and for motivating greater interpersonal sensitivity and activity. The schizoid's cognitive style is markedly impoverished. Homework assignments, such as having the patient keep a daily record of dysfunctional beliefs, can help identify automatic thoughts and assist in disambiguating vague cognitions. Identified automatic thoughts typically center around negative cognitions about themselves, their preference for solitude, and the feeling that they are detached observers in life (Beck et al., 1990). These records can also help patients identify their emotions, gradations in intensity, and how their emotional states affect their interactions with others (Will, 1994).

As Young and Lindeman (1992) note, it is through interpersonal experience that schemas are developed and maintained. In the case of the schizoid, the absence of interpersonal experience may have contributed to the observed poverty of cognitions and their characteristic low complexity of self and other object-representations. Another drawback is that therapists frequently use affective techniques to trigger schemas. The tendency of these patients to intellectualize only serves to reduce the likelihood that arousal of emotions allows access to schemas. The automatic thoughts and schemas that revolve around beliefs that they are better off alone and that relationships have nothing to offer them can be explored. It is worthwhile for the therapist and the patient to examine both the functional and dysfunctional aspects of isolation in the patient's life. A realistic goal formulation, on which the therapist and the patient can agree, should be determined. For example, the schizoid is often unable to recognize and articulate subtleties of reinforcement. Cognitive methods developed in conjunction with the therapist can assist the patient in identifying gradations of enjoyment obtained from a variety of experiences.

If an interest is displayed in developing interpersonal relations and skills, *group* methods may prove useful in encouraging and facilitating the acquisitions of constructive social attitudes. In this setting, schizoids may begin to alter their self-image and increase the motivation and skills for a more effective interpersonal style. Group settings are also uniquely suited for triggering schemas of an interpersonal nature. The patient is provided with the opportunity to test the accuracy of the schemas as feedback from the other group members is readily available. The therapist will have to be extremely cautious not to expect the same degree of participation from the schizoid group member. Being in a group setting may place interactional demands on the client that might initially cause a great deal of anxiety.

It is not unlikely that schizoids come in for therapy at the request of family members. A decision may be made to involve other members of the family system in the therapeutic process. In some cases, *family* and *marital* therapy are best directed to educating the family members with regards to their relative's potential for change. Adjusting their expectations may in turn facilitate improvements when there is more tolerance and less intrusion in the schizoid's privacy by family members. Moreover, family members can be instrumental in cultivating reform by assisting in environmental modifications and by allowing the patient to explore newly learned social skills and modes of interacting. An in-depth assessment of the family system may, however, reveal maladaptive patterns that have over time perpetuated the personality pattern. Potential capacities for self-remediation that may have existed within the patient may have been squelched, thereby reinforcing this schizoid's image as a developmental failure.

For different reasons, little may be expected of *psychoanalytic* approaches because schizoids possess a relatively uncomplicated world of intrapsychic emotions and defenses. They are not very psychologically minded and frequently lack the desire to explore their inner world. In those few cases where analytically oriented psychotherapy may be indicated, the therapist will have to take a more active role than usual. Interventions should be directed to exploring the patient's internal object-relations. Being in therapy can provide a positive, stable relational experience that can then be internalized (Gabbard, 1994). This new sense of relatedness may result in the patient feeling more at ease revealing possible hidden aspects of the self. As a result, a greater awareness of the self may ensue. Enriching internal representations of self and others, increasing reality contacts, and enhancing the sense of self are primary therapeutic goals.

At the behavioral level, deficiencies are exhibited in the expressive act domain. When therapy is

first initiated, their low energy level and activation deficits may render the therapeutic process ineffectual. *Psychopharmacological* treatment may be called for. Trial periods with a number of stimulants can be explored to see if they perk up energy and affectivity. These should be used with caution, however, because they may activate feelings and drive states the patient's impoverished defensive structures and cognitive schemas are ill equipped to handle.

It may be useful to review the major strategies and tactics as depicted in Figure 6.6.

Potentiated Pairings and Catalytic Sequences

To prevent dropout, the patient must perceive therapy as offering something of value. Therapeutic efforts with schizoids may require psychopharmacological intervention at the onset to activate arousal systems and thereby counter their inability to experience affect or energy. This may in turn facilitate the use of other interventions that necessitate a certain amount of motivation and commitment. Such intervention can, however, be seen by the patient as a quick-fix resulting in premature termination. It may be necessary to enhance the therapeutic relationship before deciding on pharmacotherapy. The complaints that these patients do not get enjoyment out of activities and interpersonal relations can be addressed cognitively at first. Behavioral methods may be used more fruitfully after the patient's experiential repertoire has been increased or when the patient has attained a deeper level of experiencing. Group therapy can be used concurrently with individual psychotherapy but

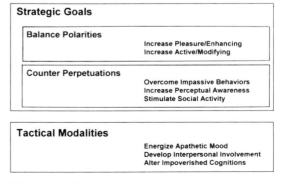

Figure 6.6 Therapeutic strategies and tactics for the prototypal schizoid personality.

only after the patient's desire as well as capability for social interaction has been adequately assessed. Family or marital approaches may be used conjointly and can complement individual therapy.

Resistances and Risks

The impoverished and globally undifferentiated phenomenology of the schizoid is itself a profound form of "passive resistance." Once in therapy, schizoids are not very likely to value the therapeutic relationship and may actually see the therapist as intrusive and hence shy away from therapy (Beck & Freeman, 1990b). A continuous risk is the possibility that they will drop out of therapy and revert back to their prior isolated and detached lifestyle. Even if impressive progress is made within a particular session, generalization of insight or behavior may not occur if the patient

simply goes home to a solitary existence. Booster sessions to prevent regressions such as these are especially wise following termination.

Another danger is that the therapist may find interacting with such a patient unrewarding. Feelings such as frustration, helplessness, boredom, and impotence may be experienced. Therapists need to be keenly aware that progress made with some schizoids will consist of the ability for them to derive greater satisfaction from solitary activities and will not necessarily reduce social isolation. Even though strengthening social connectedness is a primary goal in therapy, group methods and other more interactive forms of therapy may be contraindicated. If the therapist is not careful in determining the patient's social skill level and desire for social involvement, the premature push toward interacting with others may cause discomfort, which may, in turn, reinforce existing beliefs that one is better off alone.

CHAPTER 7

Avoidant Personality Disorders: The Withdrawn Pattern

Being "socially detached" can arise from numerous pathogenic sources and unfold through divergent developmental lines. One group of pleasure-deficient individuals, the schizoid personality discussed in the previous chapter, is noted by its passive detachment. These persons lack the affective capacity necessary for successful social relationships. Because of their deficits, they fail to respond to the usual incentives and punishments that both activate interpersonal behavior and stimulate socially relevant and mutually rewarding communications.

In terms of surface behavior, a second group, referred to as the "avoidant personality," appears very much like the first. Closer inspection, however, reveals that these "actively" detached persons are quite *dissimilar* from the passive type. They are oversensitive to social stimuli and are hyperreactive to the moods and feelings of others, especially those that portend rejection and humiliation. Their extreme anxiety not only intrudes into their thoughts and interferes with their behaviors but also distracts them from pleasurable or life-enhancing pursuits, and disposes them to distance themselves from others as a protection against the psychic pain they anticipate.

The distinction drawn here between passively detached (schizoid) and actively detached (avoidant) personality types corresponds closely to data generated in studies of schizophrenia that consistently uncover two contrasting sets of characteristics. Some researchers reviewing their data suggest that schizophrenic patients are distinguished best by a number of deficits, their *underarousal,* undermotivation, and insensitivities. Others assert with equal conviction and support that these patients are best characterized by their excessive reactivity, that is, *overarousal,* overmotivation, and hypersensitivity.

The senior author's own theoretical work (Millon, 1969) has led him to the conclusion that both

sets of seemingly contradictory findings are correct, if viewed in terms of the distinction between active and passive detachment. Both detached patterns, passive (schizoid) and active (avoidant), are disposed toward the more severe schizophrenic disorders. Although the overt symptomatologies of the active and passive styles are highly similar, especially upon initial examination, their constitutional dispositions, experiential histories, and basic styles and strategies are quite distinct. One group—the passive, or *schizoid*—will display chronic underreactivity, affectivity deficit, cognitive slippage, and interpersonal indifference; whereas the other—the active, or *avoidant*—will show up as chronically overreactive and hyperalert, with affective disharmony, cognitive interference, and interpersonal distrust among their major features. The authors believe that the reason researchers have consistently turned up paradoxical and contradictory results in schizophrenia can be traced, in great measure, to their failure to recognize that a basic distinction exists between actively and passively detached personalities. The features of the pleasure deficient *schizoid* were elaborated in Chapter 6. The pleasure deficient and actively detached *avoidant* personality is the prime focus in this chapter.

HISTORICAL ANTECEDENTS

The label avoidant personality is new, having been coined by Millon (1969) as a descriptive designation for individuals distinguished best by their active, as opposed to passive, aversion to social relationships. Personality features of a cast similar to the avoidant have been scattered through the clinical literature, most frequently in conjunction with conceptions of the schizoid personality and in descriptions of phobic character traits. Although this literature is quite slim, an attempt is made here to identify a number of these historic parallels. Before doing so, it should be noted that the mistrustful interpersonal style of the avoidant and the characteristic developmental history of parental deprecation represent features that have been ascribed, notably by analytic theorists, to a broad range of other personality disorders—for example, to the schizoid character by Fairbairn (1940/1952) and, more recently, to the narcissistic personality by Kohut (1971). This chapter, however, is concerned with those authors whose conceptions of both the phenomenology and pathogenic background of the personality types they have studied appear to be clear forerunners of the DSM-IV avoidant pattern. Because the history of the avoidant conception is essentially a modern one, we will begin our discussions with essentially modern formulations rather than those from the 19th century and earlier.

MODERN FORMULATIONS

The first portrayal that approximates the actively detached character of the avoidant was described in 1911 by Bleuler in his initial formulation of the schizophrenic concept. Discussing several of the contrasting routes that often lead to the psychotic syndrome, Bleuler (1950) recorded the early phase of certain patients as follows:

There are also cases where the shutting off from the outside world is caused by contrary reasons. Particularly in the beginning of their illness, these patients quite consciously shun any contact with reality because their affects are so powerful that they must avoid everything which might arouse their emotions. The apathy toward the outer world is then a secondary one springing from a hypertrophied sensitivity. (p. 65)

Another early description that coincides in certain respects with the avoidant trait constellation was presented by Schneider (1923/1950) in his conception of the aesthenic personality. Although aesthenics are noted best by their extraordinary attention to and hypochondriacal concern with bodily functions, this basic preoccupation extends into the psychic realm as well. Schneider described this feature as follows:

Just as the aesthenic patient no longer takes his bodily functions for granted so he loses the normal, carefree attitude to psychic functions. . . . All this is due in the first place to the chronic habit of self-investigation. . . . Psychic functioning as with bodily function becomes interfered with and starts to falter. . . . Feelings do not seem genuine, relationships appear lifeless and void. . . .

All human activity needs a certain psychic half light or chiaroscuro if it is to be experienced as an integral part of the self. Actions tend to disintegrate if full attention is focused on them in the same way as the body ceases to function smoothly if it is subjected to too much conscious interference. (p. 141)

Reflecting on observations made by Kretschmer concerning aesthenics, Schneider noted that these patients also fail to relax after reacting to an experience though they may personally be no longer oppressed by it. A disturbed emotional undertow persists or the situation is deliberately prolonged. Schneider's descriptions range across a wide number of psychopathological personalities. Similarly akin to our current characterizations of the avoidant personality is his depiction of what he terms:

The insecure self-distrusting psychopaths . . . a deeply rooted, inner insecurity and the lack of any robust self-confidence. Such traits are not easy to detect. The inner tangles and panics of these uncertain, self-mistrusting personalities are sometimes tightly concealed from the world outside. . . . This type is continually ridden with bad conscience and are the first to blame themselves for anything that goes wrong . . . They are people forever dissatisfied with themselves through life. (p. 21)

Turning more directly to the observations of Kretschmer (1925) leads to the first series of descriptions that presaged the avoidant personality in the majority of its elements. As discussed in the preceding chapter, Kretschmer identified two polarities of sensitivity among those with the schizoid temperament: the anaesthetic and the hyperaesthetic. Those whose constitutional dispositions cluster at the anaesthetic pole correspond closely to the DSM-IV schizoid, described in detail in Chapter 6. It is the group that Kretschmer located at the hyperaesthetic end of the continuum, which exhibits sensibilities that foreshadow and exemplify the avoidant pattern. Kretschmer's own words illustrate his portrayal:

In the hyperaesthetic type, there often develops a sharp antithesis: "I" and "The external world." There is a constant excited self-analysis and comparison: *"How do I impress people? Who is doing me an injury? In what respect have I to forgive myself something? How shall I get through?" This is particularly true of gifted, artistic natures. . . . They are men who have a continual psychic conflict, whose life is composed of a chain of tragedies, a single thorny path of sorrow. . . .*

[Here] we find the qualities of nervousness, excitability, capriciousness, anxiousness, tenderness, and, above all, sensitive susceptibility. . . . He behaves shyly, or timidly, or distrustfully, or as if he were pushed in to himself. He complains of nerve troubles. He keeps anxiously away from all coarse games and brawls. . . .

They are not restful in spirit, but, under the covering of a sulky silence, there always glimmers a spark of inner tension, which has the character of a complex, and springs from the accumulation of all the little everyday unpleasantness of office and family life; which get heaped up inside, which cannot be overcome, and which cannot be spoken out. (1925, pp. 167–174)

The key phrase depicting Kretschmer's hyperaesthetic, and one equally central to an understanding of the avoidant personality, was stated by him thus: "They seek as far as possible to avoid and deaden all stimulation from the outside" (p. 161). How sharply this differs from the anaesthetic, or DSM-IV schizoid, who Kretschmer depicted as possessing "a certain psychic insensitivity, dullness . . . lack of spontaneity [and] affective imbecility" (p. 156).

In a major and thoughtfully detailed work, Kahn (1931) outlined features very much in keeping with our current conception of the Avoidant prototype. In describing what he terms the *passive autist*, Kahn writes:

He is unable to really experience himself as well as others and he remains always caught in a kind of fragmentary experience. He fails to assert himself completely and he cannot submit because fundamentally he seeks but one goal: ego-protection, the protection of his own personality which he always feels to be weak and beset on all sides. His goal direction is impotence and resentment: Refusing to act and to face the perils of the environment he prefers to live outside the struggle of life as on a well-protected island. (p. 267)

Conceived as a formal entity, traditional psychoanalytic theorists have used the schizoid label to represent that which we term today as the avoidant personality. Descriptively, both Reich (1933) and Menninger (1930) addressed what we would now consider to be characteristics of the avoidant personality. For example, Reich spoke of the following type:

The character erects itself as a hard protective wall against the experiencing of infantile anxiety and thus maintains itself, notwithstanding the great forfeiture of joie de vivre *which this entails. If a patient having such a character enters analytic treatment because of some symptom or other, this protective wall continues to serve . . . and it soon becomes apparent that nothing can be accomplished until the character armor, which conceals and consumes the infantile anxiety, has been destroyed. (pp. 82–83)*

In a similar fashion, Menninger (1930) addressed a character type also akin to what we speak of today as the avoidant personality. He terms them "isolated personalities," describing their features as follows:

Among the personality types prone to failure in social adjustments . . . analysis discovers that these are really of two sorts. Some are "temperamentally" unsocial and really prefer to be left out of it. . . . The other group is made up of wistful "outsiders" who long to dive into the swim and either don't know how or are held back by restraining fears which have been inculcated . . .

The former are called schizoid. . . . The latter deserve a technical designation, and I have suggested the use of the name "isolated personalities." They are those who have been artificially withheld from human contacts to the point of developing curious deficiencies, mannerisms, attitudes, oddnesses, which serve to preclude their absorption or amalgamation into the group when, later, opportunities develop. . . . Many people do suffer constantly and sometimes acutely with feelings of inadequacy, diffidence, self-dissatisfaction, so-called hypersensitivities, and a pervading discouragement because of such feelings. (pp. 64, 71)

The formulations of Fairbairn, Winnicott, Arieti, Guntrip, and Laing, using labels such as "schizoid" and "false-self," correspond in several major respects to the developmental history and socially detached character of the avoidant type. Reference may be made to their views presented in Chapter 6, and readers of their writings will no doubt find that their descriptions closely parallel those of the DSM-IV avoidant.

Along similar lines, the notion of a "phobic character" has been touched upon by a number of classically oriented analysts. Fenichel (1945), for example, wrote: "Phobic characters" would be the correct designation for persons whose reactive behavior limits itself to the avoidance of the situations originally wished for (p. 527).

Rado, a major contributor to the classical analytic school, described a subgroup of his "overreactive disorders" as follows:

I use the phrase phobic avoidance *since phobia is the avoidance mechanism.*

The . . . characteristic of the phobic avoidance mechanism is that it tends to spread, to reinforce one set of precautionary measures, to reinforce safeguards of the first order by new safeguards of the second order, the third order, and so forth. The more precautionary measures are introduced, the more the conditions of anxiety move along. (1969, p. 182)

MacKinnon and Michels (1971), adhering to a relatively traditional analytic model, set forth a number of features of what they term "phobic character traits." They wrote:

Far more common than the symptomatic phobia is the use of avoidance and inhibition as characterological defenses. . . . [It] is recognized as defensive avoidance only when the person's life situation exposes his inhibition as maladaptive. . . .

The individual is preoccupied with his security and fears any possible threat to it, constantly imagining himself in situations of danger while pursuing the course of greatest safety. (p. 149)

Breaking from the orthodox analytic mold, Horney (1945) proposed a personality characterization that she termed the "detached type" and described as exhibiting an interpersonal style of "moving away from people." The following excerpts illustrate her portrayal of this "interpersonally avoidant" and "actively detached" pattern:

There is intolerable strain in associating with people and solitude becomes primarily a means of avoiding it. . . .

What is crucial is their inner need to put distance between themselves and others. . . . They draw around themselves a kind of magic circle which no one may penetrate. . . .

All the needs and qualities they acquire are diverted toward this major need for not getting involved. . . .

A . . . precarious way to maintain self-sufficiency is by consciously or unconsciously restricting one's needs. . . . the underlying principle here is never to become so attached to anybody and anything so that he or it becomes indispensable. . . . Better to have nothing matter much.

His goals are negative: He wants not to be involved, not to need anybody, not to allow others to intrude on or influence him.

There is a general tendency to suppress all feeling, even to deny its existence. (1945, pp. 73–82)

In subsequent writings, Horney (1950) elaborated a variety of "neurotic solutions" to conflict. Among the characteristics that typify the detached style are self-hate and self-contempt, which Horney (1945) aptly described as follows:

On little or no provocation he feels that others look down on him, do not take him seriously, do not care for his company, and in fact, slight him. His self-contempt adds considerably to the profound uncertainty he has about himself, and hence cannot but make him as profoundly uncertain about the attitudes of others toward him. Being unable to accept himself as he is, he cannot possibly believe that others, knowing him with all his shortcomings, can accept him in a friendly or appreciative spirit.

What he feels in deeper layers is much more drastic, and may amount to an unshakable conviction that others plainly despise him. (p. 134)

Turning to entirely different quarters, several biologically oriented researchers have referred to syndromes that are also akin to the avoidant. On the basis of his early genetic family studies, Kallmann (1938), for example, came to speak of certain patients as suffering "schizoidia," describing them as exhibiting "autistic introversion, emotional inadequacy, sudden surges of temperament and inappropriate motor responses to emotional stimuli" (p. 162). Similarly, Kety, Rosenthal, Wender, and Schulsinger (1968), in their discussions of the "schizophrenic spectrum," spoke of their fourth and final subgroup as possessing attributes similar to Kretschmer's "schizothymics," a familial disposition to schizophrenia characterized by clinical features such as "nervousness," "shyness," and "sensitivity."

CONTEMPORARY PROPOSALS

A recent, and analytically oriented, theory that deals with the origins of schizophrenia describes the syndrome as possessing features that are prominent in the DSM-III avoidant personality. Set within an object-relations framework, Burnham, Gladstone, and Gibson (1969) attributed the primary clinical symptomatology of this group to what they termed the "need-fear dilemma"; they expressed the concern of this patient as follows:

He has an inordinate need for external structure and control. He requires others to provide the organization and regulation which he is unable to provide for himself. . . . [His] very psychological existence depends on his maintaining contact with objects, whether as individuals or as part of a social structure. . . .

The very excessiveness of his need for objects also makes them inordinately dangerous and fearsome since they can destroy him through abandonment. Hence he fears and distrusts them.

[Among] efforts to avert or alleviate the pain of his need-fear dilemma [is] . . . object avoidance. . . .

Avoidance takes various forms. In one form the person becomes quietly withdrawn and seemingly detached, unresponsive, and disinterested in others. . . .

Withdrawal may be the patient's way of trying to maintain extremely tenuous internal equilibria by limiting potentially disruptive object contacts. . . . Attempts by others to engage him in interaction are regarded as intrusions which carry the threat of disorganization. His usual reaction is either a deepening of the gulf of unresponsiveness or an abrupt outburst of rage. (pp. 27–31)

A more recent perspective on the avoidant personality has been developed by Aaron Beck and his associates (1990b), providing insights into the erroneous assumptions and expectations of the disorder. Beck offers the following characterization in line with his cognitive approach to the avoidant personality:

Their low tolerance for dysphoria prevents them from developing methods for overcoming their shyness and asserting themselves more effectively. Since they are introspective and monitor feelings continually, they are acutely sensitive to their feelings of sadness and anxiety. Ironically, despite their hyperawareness of painful feelings, they shy away

from identifying unpleasant thoughts—a tendency that fits in with their major strategy and is labeled "cognitive avoidance." (p. 44)

Avoidant patients have several long-standing dysfunctional beliefs or schemas that interfere with their social functioning. These beliefs may not have been fully articulated, but reflect patients' understandings of themselves and others. As children, they may have had a significant person (parent, sibling, peer) who was highly critical and rejecting of them. They developed certain schemas from interactions with that person, such as "I'm inadequate," "I'm defensive," "I'm unlikable," "I'm different," "I don't fit in." They also developed schemas about other people: "People don't care about me," "People will reject me." Not all children with critical, rejecting significant others, however, become avoidant. Avoidant patients must make certain assumptions to explain the negative interactions: "I must be a bad person for my mother to treat me so badly," "I must be different or defective—that's why I have no friends," "If my parents don't like me, how could anyone?" (p. 261)

Enriching our understanding of the avoidant further is the work of Lorna Benjamin (1993a). The perspective that she brings to bear is essentially an interpersonal one. Commenting on the avoidant from this orientation, Benjamin writes:

There is intense fear of humiliation and rejection. To avoid expected embarrassment, the AVD withdraws and carefully restrains himself or herself. He or she intensely wishes for love and acceptance, and will become very intimate with those few who pass highly stringent tests for safety. Occasionally, the AVD loses control and explodes with rageful indignation. (p. 297)

Expects to be degraded and humiliated by people, and so he or she refuses any assignments that might involve increased interpersonal contact and the associated likelihood of mockery, or the possibility that someone might say, "I don't want to deal with this (avoidant) person." (p. 300)

Employing the factor analytic methodology to the study of personality disorders, Costa and Widiger (1993) have provided a latent mathematical model as a means of making explicit the underlying trait combinations from which the various disorders may be derived. In addressing the features that underlie the avoidant personality, Costa and Widiger point to the following trait combinations:

From the perspective of the FFM, AVD involves (a) introversion, particularly the facets of low gregariousness (no close friends, avoids significant interpersonal contact, and unwilling to get involved with others); low excitement seeking (exaggerates potential dangers, difficulties, or risks in doing anything outside of normal routine); low activity (avoidance of social and occupational activities, and canceling of social plans); and low assertiveness; and (b) neuroticism, particularly the facets of vulnerability, self-consciousness, and anxiety (e.g., easily hurt by criticism and disapproval). (p. 49)

An explicitly biological formulation was formulated in Klein's (1970) differentiation of two schizoid subtypes. The first he believes is aptly labeled as such in the DSM; it is noted by an intrinsic asocial inclination that is experienced as ego-syntonic. The second type, quite similar in its sensitivities to the DSM avoidant, Klein described as:

The shy, socially backward, inept, obedient person who is fearful and therefore isolated but appreciates sociability and would like to be part of the crowd . . . seems to have an emotional state compounded of anticipatory anxiety [and] low self-esteem. (p. 189)

A more current formulation based on Siever and Davis's (1991) perspective on the personality disorders has led them to propose several core psychobiological predispositions, one of which is referred to as "anxiety/inhibition." They write as follows:

Anxiety/inhibition may be defined as the subjective and physiological concomitants of anticipation of future danger or aversive consequences of current behavior, e.g., punishment. Pathological anxiety may be based on an excessive sensitivity to punishment. The anxious individual is thus more ready to interpret environmental events as threatening and manifests an excessive reaction to stimuli that others may find relatively innocuous. (p. 1652)

Mastery of anxiety is required for the child to venture out beyond familiar and comfortable surroundings and explore the environment. How would children with a very low threshold for anxiety meet this challenge? Such children would tend to be shy, inhibited, and fearful and would experience difficulty in forming new relationships or mastering new situations. As a result, they may be more dependent on familiar caretakers and avoid

novel situations. They might also be more apprehensive of potential negative consequences of their behaviors and be less able to arrive at action-oriented solutions to interpersonal conflicts or dilemmas. The inhibition could interfere with their learning the more realistic and often beneficial outcomes of more assertive behaviors. Fearful children may be more likely to experience anxiety and inhibition in potentially conflictual situations involving the expression of aggression such as competitive activities with peers. (p. 1655)

The diversity of syndromes posited in the past that parallel important clinical segments of the avoidant personality should be a testament to its validity as a clinical entity, despite its recency as a formal and official designation. Only time will tell whether it is best conceived in purely descriptive terms or through notions such as temperament (Kretschmer), developmental conflict (Horney), or early object anxiety (Burnham).

As conceived in the DSM-III, the avoidant personality had its origins in a biosocial-learning theory and was described as the personality pattern representing an active-detached coping style. Four criteria were proposed in *Modern Psychopathology* (Millon, 1969) to characterize the central traits of this personality type; they are listed in the following paragraph:

The dominant features of the pathological personality we have termed the avoidant pattern may be summarized in these four traits: affective disharmony *(confused and conflicting emotions),* cognitive interference *(persistent intrusion of distracting and disruptive thoughts),* alienated self-image *(feelings of social isolation; self-rejection), and* interpersonal distrust *(anticipation and fear of humiliation and betrayal). (p. 234)*

In accord with the preceding formulation, the following clinical features and diagnostic criteria were presented by Millon in 1975 as the initial working draft of the avoidant syndrome for the personality subcommittee of the DSM-III Task Force:

This pattern is typified by an apprehensive and fearful mistrust of others. There is a depreciation of self-worth, a marked social awkwardness and a general distancing from interpersonal closeness. Desires for affection may be strong, but are self-protectively denied or restrained. Recurrent anxieties and a pervasive mood disharmony characterize the emotional life. Thought is periodically distracted

*and confused and there is an overalertness to poten-
tial social derogation that is intensified by tendencies to distort events in line with anticipated
rejection.*

*Since adolescence or early adulthood at least 3
of the following have been present to a notably
greater degree than in most people and were not
limited to discrete periods nor necessarily prompted
by stressful life events.*

1. *Affective dysphoria (e.g., notes a constant
   and confusing undercurrent of tension, sadness and anger; exhibits vacillation between
   desire for affection, fear and numbness of
   feeling).*

2. *Mild cognitive interference (e.g., relates
   being bothered and distracted by disruptive
   inner thoughts; irrelevant and digressive
   ideation upsets effective social communication).*

3. *Alienated self-image (e.g., describes life as
   one of social isolation and rejection; devalues self and reports periodic feelings of
   emptiness and depersonalization).*

4. *Aversive interpersonal behavior (e.g., tells of
   social pan-anxiety and distrust; protectively
   seeks privacy to avoid anticipated social
   derogation).*

5. *Perceptual hypersensitivity (e.g., vigilant
   scanning for potential threats to self; overin-
   terprets innocuous behaviors as signs of
   ridicule and humiliation).*

Following several committee discussions, a
number of modifications in the diagnostic criteria
were proposed and, with notable exceptions,
served as the principal components of the final
DSM-III draft:

A. *Excessive social withdrawal (e.g., distances
   self from close personal attachments; engages in peripheral social and vocational
   roles).*

B. *Hypersensitivity to rejection (e.g., apprehensively alert to signs of social derogation; interprets innocuous events as ridiculing).*

C. *Contingent personal relationships (e.g., is
   self-protectively unwilling to enter into relationships unless given unusually strong guarantees of being uncritically accepted).*

D. *Low self-esteem (e.g., devalues self-achievements and is overly dismayed by personal
   shortcomings).*

E. *Emotional dysphoria (e.g., experiences a
   confusing mixture of feeling tense, sad,
   angry, and lonely).*

The DSM-III-R modified the characterization
presented in the DSM-III in an effort to portray
the disorder as akin to the psychoanalytic description of a phobic character type. In so doing, several
features central to the DSM-III characterization
were deleted (e.g., low self-esteem); other features
were added to strengthen the phobic qualities ostensibly typifying the avoidant personality type.
These changes proved problematic and were essentially reversed in the DSM-IV, as well as in the
ICD-10.

Following the line of official classifications
from the DSM-III-R to that of the ICD-10, we find
that the category under discussion is referred to as
the "anxious (avoidant) personality disorder," giving prominence thereby to the presence of a strong
element of anxiety underlying the portrayal. Despite this characterization, the criteria enumerated
place heavy emphasis on the interpersonal aspects
of the clinical picture. In their description, the anx-
ious/avoidant is portrayed as possessing persistent
and pervasive feelings of apprehension and tension;
a belief that one is personally unappealing, socially
inept, or inferior to others; an excessive preoccupation with being criticized or rejected socially; an
unwillingness to become involved with others unless certain of being liked; a tendency to restrict
one's life to ensure physical security; and an avoidance of activities that involve significant interpersonal contact owing to a fear of criticism,
disapproval, or rejection. Assumed in the preceding
is a hypersensitivity to signs of humiliation and
embarrassment.

The DSM-IV parallels the diagnostic criteria
outlined for the ICD-10. The general characterization is briefly noted by a pattern of social
inhibition, feelings of inadequacy, and an oversensitivity to negative evaluations. As in the ICD,
there is a heavy emphasis on features that manifest themselves in the interpersonal domain. Four
Interpersonal criteria include the following: an
avoidance of activities that involve appreciable interpersonal contact owing to fears of criticism,
disapproval, or rejection; a disinclination to become involved with new persons unless they are
certain to like and accept the avoidant without
criticism; a hesitation to relate intimately unless
there is assurance of uncritical acceptance and
minimal likelihood of being shamed or ridiculed,
and despite desires to relate, the maintenance of

distance as a means of diminishing the possibility of disapproval and derision. Two criteria relate to a problematic Self-image domain, notably feelings of inadequacy and low self-esteem; and the perception that one is socially inept, as well as personally unappealing or inferior to others. Finally, there is a Mood characterization noted in one criterion: a tendency to exaggerate the potential dangers of rather ordinary circumstances, a reluctance to take personal risks lest they prove embarrassing, and a restricted lifestyle resulting from a need for certainty and security.

We can review the features of the avoidant personality prototype using the theoretical model of polarities by examining Figure 7.1. As discussed in Chapter 6, we may best conceive the polarity model as a framework of ecological adaptations that represent styles of dealing with life circumstances based on constitutional dispositions and early learning. Personalities that are termed "disordered" represent different forms of *mal*adaptation, modes of ecological functioning that are not only pathological, but also pathogenic. In some persons, such as the avoidant type, we may find an inborn sensitivity to "pain," a biologically based extreme fearfulness, even in relatively benign circumstances, a tendency to feel anxiously disrupted when facing potential or actual physical or psychic stress. No less likely in the history of otherwise normally endowed youngsters we may find a fearful reactivity when the child had been repeatedly exposed to threatening life circumstances, such as having been reared by rejecting and hostile parents. As a result there may be a deficiency in the capacity to experience the pleasures of life, the joys, the rewards, the means by which life is enhanced and extended. Conversely, we may see an overconcern and preoccupation with activities that center on the preservation of life, that is, avoiding the sadness and the anxiety that is generated as emotional responses to psychic pain. What is central here is a hyperalertness to the possibility that life will likely get worse rather than better. On the one hand, there is a focus on preserving oneself, and on the other, an inattention to experiences that can make life more gratifying and pleasurable. On the second pair of polarities, we see an excessive utilization of the active mode of adaptation (modifying one's ecological niche). Interpretively, this signifies a necessary element in preserving life, a hypervigilant awareness and avoidance of events that may portend rejection, denigration, humiliation, and failure. At the third polarity level, the role of self versus others is of minimal consequence: They are only background factors in orienting and motivating the life of the avoidant. In effect, the central features of the avoidant personality are most clearly seen in their hyperalertness and reactivity to the possibility of psychic pain.

A useful summary of the major historical contributors is represented in Figure 7.2.

CLINICAL FEATURES

The following sections outline the major domains that provide useful information in diagnosing the prototypal variant of the avoidant personality.

Prototypal Diagnostic Domains

Avoidant personalities are acutely sensitive to social deprecation and humiliation. They feel their loneliness and isolated existence deeply, experience being "out of things" as painful, and have a strong, though often repressed, desire to be accepted. Despite their longing to relate and to be active participants in social life, they fear placing their welfare in the hands of others. Their social detachment does not stem, therefore, from deficit drives and sensibilities, as in the schizoid personality, but from an active and self-protective restraint.

AVOIDANT PROTOTYPE

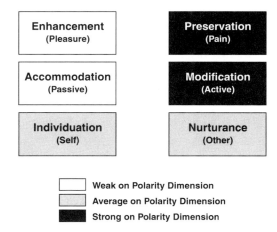

Figure 7.1   Status of the avoidant personality prototype in accord with the Millon Polarity Model.

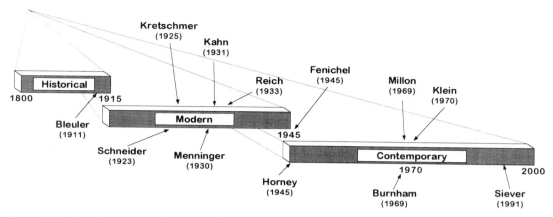

Figure 7.2 Historical review of major contributors to the avoidant personality disorder.

Although experiencing a pervasive estrangement and loneliness, they dare not expose themselves to the defeat and humiliation they anticipate. Because they cannot express their affective feelings overtly, they cumulate and are often directed toward an inner world of fantasy and imagination. The avoidant's need for affect and closeness may pour forth in poetry, be sublimated in intellectual pursuits, or be expressed in sensitively detailed artistic activities.

Isolation and protective withdrawal result in secondary consequences that further compound the avoidants' difficulties. Their obviously tense and fearful demeanor often elicits ridicule and deprecation from others. Expressions of self-doubt and anxious restraint leave them open to persons who gain satisfaction in taunting and belittling those who dare not retaliate. The additional humiliation they experience thereby not only confirms their mistrust of others but reactivates the wounds of the past.

With this précis in mind, the domains of clinical data that help diagnose the avoidant pattern will be detailed next (see Table 7.1 and Figure 7.3).

Expressive Behavior: Fretful

The pervasive sense of unease and disquiet is what is most observable about avoidants. They evince a constant timorous and restive state, overreacting to innocuous experiences, hesitant about relating to events that may prove personally problematic, and anxiously judging these events as signifying ridicule or rejection from others. The speech of avoidants is generally slow and constrained. They

exhibit frequent hesitations, aborted or fragmentary thought sequences, and occasional confused and irrelevant digressions. Physical behaviors tend to be highly controlled or underactive, although marked with periodic bursts of fidgety and rapid staccato movements. Overt expressions of emotion are typically kept in check, but this underresponsiveness overlays deep tension and disharmony. They exert great restraint, not only in the control of anxiety, but in controlling feelings of confusion and in subduing the upsurge of anger.

Interpersonal Conduct: Aversive

Avoidants distance from situations that may involve them in close personal relationships; they are strongly disinclined to become intimate unless they are certain that they will be liked and fully accepted. There is a long history of maintaining distance from others and of preferring privacy so as to avoid being shamed and humiliated. They report an extensive history of rejection, leading them to acquire a general distrust of others and a broad social pananxiety. A shy and apprehensive quality characterizes avoidants. They are not only awkward and uncomfortable in social situations but seem to shrink actively from the reciprocal give-and-take of interpersonal relations. They often impose a strain upon others in face-to-face interactions. Their discomfort and mistrust often take the form of subtle testing operations, that is, guarded maneuvers by which they check whether others are sincere in their friendly overtures or are a deceptive threat to their security. Most observers who have only passing contact with

TABLE 7.1   Clinical Domains of the Avoidant Prototype

Behavioral Level

(F) Expressively Fretful. Conveys personal unease and disquiet, a constant timorous, hesitant, and restive state; overreacts to innocuous events and anxiously judges them to signify ridicule, criticism, and disapproval.

(F) Interpersonally Aversive. Distances from activities that involve intimate personal relationships and reports extensive history of social pananxiety and distrust; seeks acceptance, but is unwilling to get involved unless certain to be liked, maintaining distance and privacy to avoid being shamed and humiliated.

Phenomenological Level

(F) Cognitively Distracted. Warily scans environment for potential threats and is preoccupied by intrusive and disruptive random thoughts and observations; an upwelling from within of irrelevant ideation upsets thought continuity and interferes with social communications and accurate appraisals.

(S) Alienated Self-Image. Sees self as socially inept, inadequate, and inferior, justifying thereby his or her isolation and rejection by others; feels personally unappealing, devalues self-achievements, and reports persistent sense of aloneness and emptiness.

(S) Vexatious Objects. Internalized representations are composed of readily reactivated, intense, and conflict-ridden memories of problematic early relations; limited avenues for experiencing or recalling gratification, and few mechanisms to channel needs, bind impulses, resolve conflicts, or deflect external stressors.

Intrapsychic Level

(F) Fantasy Mechanism. Depends excessively on imagination to achieve need gratification, confidence building, and conflict resolution; withdraws into reveries as a means of safely discharging frustrated affectionate, as well as angry impulses.

(S) Fragile Organization. A precarious complex of tortuous emotions that depend almost exclusively on a single modality for its resolution and discharge (i.e., avoidance, escape, and fantasy); hence, when faced with personal risks, new opportunities, or unanticipated stress, few morphologic structures are available to deploy and few backup positions can be reverted to, short of regressive decompensation.

Biophysical Level

(S) Anguished Mood. Describes constant and confusing undercurrent of tension, sadness, and anger; vacillates between desire for affection, fear of rebuff, embarrassment, and numbness of feeling.

(F) = Functional domain.
(S) = Structural domain.

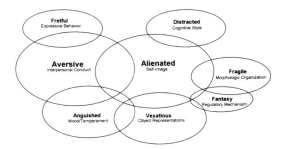

Figure 7.3   Salience of personologic domains in the avoidant prototype.

avoidant personalities tend to see them as timid, withdrawn, or perhaps cold and strange—not unlike the image conveyed by the schizoid personality. Those who relate to them more closely, however, quickly learn of their sensitivities, their touchiness, evasiveness, and mistrustful qualities.

Interpersonally, avoidants are best characterized as actively detached personalities; they are guided by the need to put distance between themselves and others—to minimize involvements that can reactivate or duplicate past humiliations. Privacy is sought and they attempt to eschew as many social obligations as possible without incurring further condemnation. Any event that entails a personal relationship with others, unless it assures uncritical acceptance, constitutes a potential threat to their fragile security. They may deny themselves even simple possessions to protect against the pain of loss or disappointment. Efforts to comply with the wishes of others, no less to assert themselves, may have proved fruitless or disillusioning. Appeasement may have resulted in a loss of what little personal integrity they may have felt they still possessed, leading only to feelings of greater humiliation and disparagement. The only course they have learned that will succeed in reducing shame and humiliation is to back away, draw within themselves and keep a watchful eye against incursions into their solitude.

In sum, these personalities avoid the anguish of social relationships by distancing themselves and remaining vigilant and alert to potential threat. This actively detached coping style contrasts markedly with the strategy of passively detached schizoids, who are perceptually insensitive to their surroundings. Avoidants are overly attentive and aware of variations and subtleties in their stimulus world. They have learned in the past that the most effective means of avoiding social rejection and deprecation is to be hyperalert to cues that forewarn their occurrence. By decreasing their relationships and diminishing their importance, they can minimize the hazards they fear surround them.

Cognitive Style: Distracted

It is characteristic of avoidants to scan their environment for potential threats. Also problematic is their preoccupation with intrusive and disruptive inner thoughts that seem to flood their efforts at maintaining psychic control. This upwelling from within of seemingly random and irrelevant feelings and ideas will often upset the continuity of their thoughts and interfere with their social communications. The avoidant personality is hyperalert to the most subtle feelings and intentions of others. These individuals are "sensitizers," acutely perceptive observers who scan and appraise every movement and expression of those with whom they come into contact. Although their hypervigilance serves to protect them against potential dangers, it floods them with excessive stimuli and distracts them from attending to many of the ordinary yet relevant features of their environment. Avoidants contrast markedly to schizoids, who appear devoid of the ability to register extraverbal cues (intonation, expressive gestures) of human communication, what we would term "tonal agnosia." These patients are typically extraordinarily sensitive to the subtleties of tone and feeling, hyperalert to the meaning of emotive utterances, such as voice inflections and facial grimaces, as well as possessing an infallible ear for vocal cadences and nuances, especially those which are judgmental or potentially derogatory.

Thought processes are not only interfered with by this flooding of irrelevant environmental details but are complicated further by inner emotional disharmonies that intrude and divert the avoidants' attentions. Combined with extraneous perceptions, these intrusive feelings upset their cognitive processes and diminish their capacity to cope effectively with many of the ordinary tasks of life. This cognitive interference is especially pronounced in social settings, where avoidants' perceptual vigilance and emotional turmoil are most acute.

Self-Image: Alienated

For the most part, avoidants see themselves as socially inept and inferior. Their self-evaluations judge them as personally unappealing and interpersonally inadequate, and they devalue whatever achievements they have attained. Most fundamentally, they find valid justifications for their being isolated, rejected, and empty. Avoidants describe themselves typically as ill at ease, anxious, and sad. Feelings of loneliness and of being unwanted and isolated are often expressed, as are fear and distrust of others. People are seen as critical, betraying, and humiliating. With so trouble-laden an outlook, avoidants understandably show interpersonal aversiveness in their social behavior.

Disharmonious emotions and feelings of emptiness and depersonalization are especially noteworthy. Avoidant personalities tend to be excessively introspective and self-conscious, often perceiving themselves as different from others, and they are unsure of their identity and self-worth. The alienation they feel with others is paralleled, then, by a feeling of alienation from themselves. They voice futility with regard to the life they lead, have a deflated self-image, and frequently refer to themselves with an attitude of contempt and derision more severe than they hear from others.

Object-Representations: Vexatious

The internalized residue of the past that inheres within the mind of the avoidant comprises intense, conflict-ridden memories of problematic early relationships. These can be readily reactivated with minimal promptings. Moreover, there are limited recollections of a more rewarding nature to draw on or to dispose one to perceive the world in an optimistic fashion. Owing to the pervasiveness of these troublesome memories, there are few opportunities to develop effective and satisfying means to bind one's impulses, to resolve one's conflicts, or to deflect external stressors. Avoidants are trapped in the worst of both worlds, seeking to avoid both the distress that surrounds them and the emptiness and wounds that inhere within them. This latter feature is especially significant to an understanding of the avoidant for it signifies that turning away from one's external environment brings little peace and comfort. Avoidants find no solace and freedom within themselves. Having internalized the pernicious attitude of self-derogation and deprecation to which they were exposed in earlier life, they not only experience little reward in their accomplishments and thoughts but find instead shame, devaluation, and humiliation. In fact, they may feel more pain being alone with their despised self than with the escapable torment of others. The immersion of self in the individual's own thoughts and feelings is the more difficult experience because a person cannot physically avoid the self, cannot walk away, escape, or hide from his or her own being. Deprived of feelings of worth and self-respect, these persons suffer constantly from painful thoughts about their pitiful state, their misery, and the futility of being themselves. Efforts that are even more vigilant than those applied to the external world must be expended to ward off the painful ideas and feelings that well up within them. These aversive signals are especially anguishing since they pervade every facet of the avoidants' makeup. It is their entire being that has become devalued, and nothing about them escapes the severe judgment of self-derision.

Regulatory Mechanisms: Fantasy

The avoidant's prime, if not sole, recourse is to break up, destroy, or repress these painful thoughts and the emotions they unleash. These personalities struggle to prevent self-preoccupations and seek to intrude irrelevancies by blocking and making their normal thoughts and communications take on different and less significant meanings. In effect, and through various intrapsychic ploys, they attempt to interfere actively with their own cognitions. Similarly, the anxieties, desires, and impulses that surge within them must be also restrained, denied, turned about, transformed, and distorted. Thus, they seek to muddle their emotions also, making their affective life even more discordant and disharmonious than it is typically. To avoidants, it is better to experience diffuse disharmony than the sharp pain and anguish of being themselves. Despite their efforts at inner control, painful and threatening thoughts and feelings will periodically break through, disrupting more stable cognitive processes and upsetting whatever emotional equanimity they are able to muster.

Apart from destroying their inner cognitions, avoidants depend excessively on fantasy and imagination to achieve a measure of need gratification, to build what little confidence they may have in their self-worth, and to work out what few methods they can for resolving conflicts. Avoidants

experience their feelings deeply and hence must use their daydreams and reveries as a means of dealing with their frustrated affectionate needs and discharging their resentful and angry impulses. But fantasies also prove distressing in the long run because they point up the contrast between desire and objective reality. Repression of all feelings is often the only recourse, hence accounting for the avoidant's initial appearance of being flat, unemotional, and indifferent, an appearance that belies the inner turmoil and intense affect these persons truly experience.

Morphologic Organization: Fragile

The intraspychic structure of the avoidant is composed of a precarious complex of tortuous emotions, each of which can be reactivated and can overthrow the fragile psychic controls of these patients. What holds the structure together is a reliance, excessive in its use, of avoidance, escape, and fantasy. When faced with personal risks or unanticipated stress, the avoidant possesses few morphologic structures or dynamic mechanisms to deal with these difficulties. Similarly, there are few backup positions to which the avoidant can revert, short of regressive decompensation. Protecting the self from real and imagined psychic pain is a paramount goal in these personalities. Avoiding situations that may result in personal humiliation or social rejection is the guiding force behind their interpersonal relationships. Of equal threat is the avoidant's own aggressive and affectional impulses. These are especially distressing since these persons fear that their own behaviors may prompt others to reject and condemn them. Much intrapsychic energy is devoted to mechanisms that deny and bind these inner urges.

Avoidant personalities are beset by several notable conflicts. The struggle between affection and mistrust is central. They desire to be close, show affection, and be warm with others, but they cannot shake themselves of the belief that such actions will result in pain and disillusion. They have strong doubts concerning their competence and, hence, have grave concerns about venturing into the more competitive aspects of our society. This lack of confidence curtails their initiative and leads to the fear that their efforts at autonomy and independence will only fail and result in humiliation. Every route toward gratification seems blocked with conflicts. They are unable to act on their own because of marked self-doubt; on the other hand, they cannot depend on others because they mistrust them. Security and rewards can be obtained, then, neither from themselves nor from others; both provide only pain and discomfort.

Mood/Temperament: Anguished

Avoidants describe their emotional state as a constant and confusing undercurrent of tension, sadness, and anger. They feel anguish in every direction they turn, vacillating between unrequited desires for affection and pervasive fears of rebuff and embarrassment. Not infrequently, the confusion and dysphoria they experience leads to a general state of numbness. As noted, avoidant personalities have a deep mistrust of others and a markedly deflated image of their own self-worth. They have learned to believe through painful experiences that the world is unfriendly, cold, and humiliating, and that they possess few of the social skills and personal attributes by which they can hope to experience the pleasures and comforts of life. They anticipate being slighted or demeaned wherever they turn. They have learned to be watchful and on guard against the ridicule and contempt they expect from others. They must be exquisitely alert and sensitive to signs that portend censure and derision. And, perhaps most painful of all, looking inward offers them no solace because they find none of the attributes they admire in others.

Their outlook is therefore a negative one: to avoid pain, to need nothing, to depend on no one, and to deny desire. Moreover, they must turn away from themselves also, away from an awareness of their unlovability and unattractiveness, and from their inner conflicts and disharmony. Life, for them, is a negative experience, both from without and from within.

The hyperarousal of avoidants may reflect a biophysical sensory irritability or a more centrally involved somatic imbalance or dysfunction. Using a different conceptual language to refer to this biophysical speculation, it might be hypothesized that these individuals possess a constitutionally based fearful or anxious temperament, a hypersensitivity to potential threat. The conjectures suggested here may be no more than different conceptual approaches to the same thesis; for example, a fearful temperamental disposition may

simply be a behavioral term to represent a biophysical limbic system imbalance.

A few speculations of an anatomic and biochemical nature may be in order. For example, avoidant personalities may experience aversive stimuli more intensely and more frequently than others because they possess an especially dense or overabundantly branched neural substrate in the "aversive" center of the limbic system. As will be described in slightly greater detail in the section on Hypothetical Biogenic Factors, another plausible speculation for their avoidant tendencies is a possible functional dominance of the sympathetic nervous system. Thus, excess adrenaline owing to any one of a number of autonomic or pituitary-adrenal axis dysfunctions may give rise to the hypervigilant and irritable characteristics of this personality. Imbalances of this kind may lead also to the affective disharmony and cognitive interference found among these patients. Deficiencies or excesses in certain brain neurohormones may facilitate rapid synaptic transmission and result in a flooding and scattering of neural impulses. Such individuals will not only appear overalert and overactive but may experience the avoidant's characteristic cognitive interference and generalized emotional dysphoria.

Prototypal Variants

As in prior and future chapters, we will recognize and present in some detail several variations of the basic avoidant personality prototype. These differentiations underscore that there is no single, pure textbook type of any of the personality disorders. Although core prototypal features are present that are shared in common, it is important to note that these deep commonalities can manifest themselves, not only in a diversity of pathological forms, but also in normal and childhood patterns of behavior.

Normal Styles

"Normal" avoidants are not people that we generally deal with in everyday transactions. Though their characteristics may not reach the level of severity that justify the label "disorder," they do evidence the central features of this personality style, that of hypersensitivity and distancing from relationships in which their status is unsure or questionable. What we see in these individuals is an alertness to the possibility of rejection, a general shyness and a lowered sense of self-esteem. Yet, many of these somewhat shy and hesitant individuals, when placed in functions or settings that are congenial to their lifestyle, are able to carry out their social and vocational responsibilities with considerable competence. In the following passage, Oldham and Morris (1990) variously characterize the "vigilant" and the "sensitive" styles:

Nothing escapes the notice of the men and women who have a Vigilant personality style. These individuals possess an exceptional awareness of their environment. Their sensory antennae, continuously scanning the people and situations around them, alert them immediately to what is awry, out of place, dissonant, or dangerous, especially in their dealings with other people. (p. 151)

Sensitive people come into possession of their powers when their world is small and they know the people in it . . . These men and women—although they avoid a wide social network and shun celebrity—can achieve great recognition for their creativity. Nestled in an emotionally secure environment, with a few dear family members or friends, the Sensitive style's imagination and spirit of exploration know no bounds. With their minds, feelings, and fantasies, Sensitive people find freedom. (p. 173)

Another characterization of the avoidant style may be found in Millon et al. (1994), where the primary features are a "hesitating" pattern of social relatedness, an unsureness of one's acceptance, and a general feeling of unease and self-consciousness. Despite the features noted, these hesitating-avoidant individuals may function competently in secure settings. The following quote depicts the pattern well:

These persons have a tendency to be sensitive to social indifference or rejection, to feel unsure of themselves, and to be wary in new situations, especially those of a social or interpersonal character. Somewhat ill at ease and self-conscious, these individuals anticipate running into difficulties in interrelating and fear being embarrassed. They may feel tense when they have to deal with persons they do not know, expecting that others will not think well of them. Most prefer to work alone or in small groups where they know that people accept them. Once they feel accepted, they can open up, be

friendly, be cooperative, and participate with others productively. (p. 32)

Childhood Syndromes

It has been apparent for several decades that there are children who manifest attributes akin to schizophrenia, that is, demonstrate the confused thinking and the tendency to withdraw from interpersonal contact. In most quarters, these youngsters have been given the label "childhood schizophrenia." A few decades ago, however, these cases were categorized and referred to as "isolated personalities" (Group for the Advancement of Psychiatry, 1966). In the DSM-II these very same traits were labeled "withdrawing reaction of childhood," noted as possessing the following descriptive features:

This disorder is characterized by seclusiveness, detachment, sensitivity, shyness, timidity, and general inability to form close interpersonal relationships. The diagnosis should be reserved for those who cannot be classified as having schizophrenia and whose tendencies toward withdrawal have not yet stabilized enough to justify the diagnosis of schizoid personality. (p. 348)

With the advent of DSM-III, the disorder was entitled "Avoidant disorder of childhood or adolescence." Here the primary features were listed as persistent and excessive shrinking from stranger contact; a desire for affection and acceptance, and a generally warm relationship with family members; and distancing behavior that interferes with social/peer relationships.

In DSM-IV, the avoidant characterization for childhood and adolescence was dropped in favor of its inclusion in the adult personality disorder of the same name. Nevertheless, in DSM-IV there remain some features that come close to the characterizations of a childhood avoidant disorder. Specifically, in the "reactive-attachment disorder: inhibited type," we find the following description:

persistent failure to initiate or respond in a developmentally appropriate fashion to most social interactions, as manifest by excessively inhibited, hypervigilant, or highly ambivalent and contradictory responses (e.g., the child may respond to caregivers with a mixture of approach, avoidance, and resistance to comforting, or may exhibit frozen watchfulness). (1994, p. 116)

More precise and accurate characterizations were made in descriptions by the Group for the Advancement of Psychiatry (1966), where these child categories were listed as "overly-inhibited personalities." The DSM-II classification was labeled "over-anxious reaction of childhood," and was described as follows:

This disorder is characterized by chronic anxiety, excessive and unrealistic fears, sleeplessness, nightmares, and exaggerated autonomic responses. The patient tends to be immature, self-conscious, grossly lacking in confidence . . . and apprehensive in new situations and unfamiliar surroundings.

As noted in Chapter 6, we drew a distinction between the features of those labeled Autistic from those possessing what has been called Asperger's syndrome. The former appear to characterize youngsters who are constitutionally deficient in the capacity to experience affect, whereas the latter may result from those who are extraordinarily sensitive to emotional stimuli. Overwhelmed by their environment, Asperger youngsters may withdraw to protectively dampen their sensitivities, hence appearing overtly not unlike Autistics, who begin life with an already diminished sensitivity. Autistic children may never be able to acquire the capacity for deeper feelings. By contrast, Asperger children, given calm and caring nurturance, may gradually grow out of their shell. Should their care be other than gentle, however, they may remain cautiously withdrawn and fearful, not unlike the features seen in adult Avoidant personalities.

In 1969, Millon referred to these impairments as "infantile and child threctics" to represent the extraordinary fearfulness and vulnerability to threat that typified these youngsters. In the very first months of life, these youngsters display an excruciating sensitivity to stimulation, whimpering or crying at the slightest noise and movement; parents invariably report them to be markedly colic and difficult to schedule. Their tenseness and hyperirritability proves extremely discouraging and exasperating to their caretakers, often setting off a chain of parental reactions that intensifies the child's established pathological disposition. The etiologic basis for what we have termed *threctism* may also be viewed as a quantitatively more extreme but qualitatively comparable set of conditions as those that give rise to adult avoidant personality.

In primary or infant threctism, we observe infants who evidence extraordinary tension and fearfulness in the first months of life. In these cases, we infer the presence of either unusual sensory sensitivities, overendowed neural pain centers or aberrant structures of neural integration; such inferences, however, rest on the assumption of a benevolent caretaking environment during infancy. For these youngsters, attachment learning may be disrupted by the intensity, flooding, or disjunctiveness of sensory impressions; thus, these infants must set up a protective barrier against what they sense to be an overwhelming influx of external stimuli.

With less severe biological dispositions, threctic children need not necessarily develop serious pathology. If they possess parents who are exquisitely alert to their child's sensitivities, and thereby handle the infant with great care, the child's impairment may be surmounted and allow the acquisition of appropriate human attachments; thus, despite an inborn threctic disposition, the child's development may take a healthy turn under proper environmental conditions.

The etiology of a secondary or childhood threctism is essentially psychogenic. These infants appear to possess normal sensibilities at birth, but are exposed in the very first months to extremely intense and painful sensory stimulation. To handle this stimulation, the infant protectively diminishes contact with the world by reducing sensory awareness; diagnosis of these cases should be based on evidence of particularly harsh or chaotic early environments. Many of these children acquire some form of attachment behavior; they discover a small sphere within their environment, usually neutral inanimate objects, which they draw on repetitively as a "safe" source of sensory stimulation.

In general, these youngsters display their pathology at a somewhat later age than primary threctics. However, in cases of extremely harsh early handling, the pathological pattern may already be manifest at the age of 1 or 2 years. Other less severely treated youngsters may not develop the full-blown disturbance until 7 and 10 years of age.

In what he has called the "inadequacy syndrome," Millon (1969) describes the avoidant constellation as seen in adolescence. These youngsters are characterized by low self-esteem, an awkward self-consciousness, a timorous and hesitant manner in social situations, and a tendency to view themselves as incompetent, unattractive, clumsy or stupid. These youngsters feel that they cannot "make the grade," become a part of the peer in-group or be sought after and valued in the competi-tive give-and-take that characterizes adolescent relationships. They dread facing the social respon-sibilities and expectations that society has estab-lished for their age group and are fearful that they will falter in finding a mate, getting a job and so on. In short, they lack the confidence that they can function and be accepted on their own.

These youngsters do not question or reject the established values and goals of the larger society; they very much wish to achieve them and be consid-ered "regular guys" or attractive girls. However, they experience repeated failures in their quest and slip into increasingly more isolated behaviors, pre-occupying themselves with watching TV, day-dreams of glory and other forms of fantasy escape. In these, they see themselves as the football hero or as the girl with all the boys flocking about her. The more desirous they are of these conventional goals, the more envious they become of those who appear to possess them and the more often they view them-selves as inadequate, unattractive, and forlorn.

Adult Subtypes

Avoidant characteristics often acquire subsidiary features as they begin to withdraw socially and experience critical and unsupportive responses from others. Research utilizing the MCMI (Millon, 1977, 1987, 1994) shows that profiles including the avoidant pattern are shared most often with schizoid, dependent, depressive, nega-tivistic, schizotypal, and paranoid personalities. When they begin to exhibit some of these associ-ated personality features, the moods and actions that these patients manifest will provoke reac-tions that give a different coloration from the original traits that characterized the avoidant at the start. Insidiously developing features com-bine with the avoidant pattern and express them-selves in a number of the subtypes discussed next.

The Conflicted Avoidant

More than is typical of the "ordinary" avoidant, the behavior of these notably conflicted personalities is the struggle they face between desiring detach-ment from others and fearing to be independent. *Conflicted avoidants* would like to be close and show affection but anticipate experiencing in-tense pain and disillusionment. Complicating the concern about venturing into close relationships is

a markedly deflated self-esteem. Thus, any effort to make a go at independence is constrained by the fear that it will fail and result in humiliation. Al-though they have no alternative but to depend on supporting persons and institutions, this behavior overlies deep resentments. Others have either turned against these avoidants or disapproved their efforts to achieve autonomy. They are often petu-lant and negativistic, and on occasion will attack others for failing to recognize their need for affec-tion and nurturance. The dependency security they seek is seriously jeopardized under these circum-stances. To bind their conflictful feelings and anger, and thereby protect against humiliation and loss, they become anxious and withdrawn, experi-encing a persistent and pervasive dysphoric mood. As evident from the foregoing, we should expect to find that the unresolvable angst of these conflicted individuals often results in a blending of core avoidant features with those seen among negativis-tic personalities.

The discontent, outbursts, and moodiness of conflicted avoidants frequently evoke humiliating reactions from others, and these rebuffs only serve to reinforce self-protective withdrawal. Every av-enue of gratification seems trapped in conflict. They cannot act alone because of marked self-doubts. On the other hand, they cannot depend on others because of a deep social mistrust. Disposed to anticipate disappointments, they often precipi-tate disillusionment through obstructive and nega-tive behaviors. They report feeling misunderstood, unappreciated, and demeaned by others; voice a sense of futility about life; have a deflated self-image; and frequently refer to self with contempt and deprecation. A depressive tone and anxious wariness are everpresent, evident in erratic and conflictful displays of moodiness.

Unable to muster the wherewithal to overcome deficits, and unable to achieve the support desired from others, conflicted avoidants remain embit-tered and conflicted, disposed to turn against the self, expressing feelings of unworthiness and use-lessness. Expecting to be slighted or demeaned, they have learned to be watchful and on guard against the ridicule and contempt they anticipate from others. Looking inward offers them no solace because they see none of the attributes admired in others in themselves. This awareness intrudes on their thoughts and interferes with effective behav-ior, upsetting their cognitive processes and dimin-ishing their capacity to cope effectively with ordinary life tasks. During periods when stresses are minimal, they may deny past resentments and attempt to portray an image of general well-being and contentment. These efforts, however, give way readily under the slightest of pressures.

Anticipating rejection and deprecation, they frequently jump the gun with impulsive hostility. What is seen is a cyclical variation of constraint followed by angry acting-out, followed in turn by remorse and regret. These erratic emotions not only are intrinsically distressing but upset their capacity to cope effectively with everyday tasks. Unable to orient emotions and thoughts logically, they may at times become lost in personal irrelevancies and autistic asides. This inability to order ideas and feelings in a consistent and relevant manner only further alienates conflicted avoidants from others.

The Hypersensitive Avoidant

In what may be termed the *hypersensitive avoidant,* we see many of the general features characteristic of the basic personality core, but in an accentuated form. The behavior of these patients is characterized by a high-strung and prickly manner, a hyper-alertness to signs of rejection and abuse, and an excessive weariness that leads to a peevish and wary attitude toward their environment. As such, these hypersensitive individuals display a fusion of basic avoidant characteristics permeated with features more central to the paranoid personality.

In addition to their pervasive apprehensiveness, there are intense and variable moods that are noted by prolonged periods of edginess and self-deprecation. The expectancy that people will be rejecting and disparaging may precipitate profound gloom at one time, and irrational negativism, another. At times, despite a longing to relate and be accepted, hypersensitive avoidants constrain their needs, protectively withdraw from threats to their fragile emotional balance, and maintain a safe distance from any emotional involvements. Retreating defensively, they may become remote from others and from needed sources of support. A surface apathy may be exhibited in these efforts to damp down or deaden excess sensitivities. Nevertheless, intense contrary feelings occasionally break through in peevish and immature outbursts.

Thin-skinned and deeply resentful, hypersensitive avoidants find it difficult to bind their anger toward the persons who have seemed to be unsupportive, critical, and disapproving. The little security that these avoidants possess, however, is threatened when these bristly feelings and resentments are discharged. Easily offended, but desiring to protect against further loss, they make repeated efforts to resist expressing anger, albeit unsuccess-fully. When not withdrawn and drifting in peripheral social roles, they are unpredictable, irritably edgy, and negativistic, engaging at times in wrangles and disappointments with others, vacillating between moments of being agreeable, sullenly passive, and irritably angry. These difficulties are frequently complicated by genuine expressions of guilt and contrition that are mixed with feelings of being misunderstood, unappreciated, and demeaned by others.

Hypersensitive avoidants have learned to be watchful, on guard against ridicule, and ever-alert to signs of censure and derision. They detect the most minute traces of annoyance expressed by others and make the molehill of a minor and passing slight into a mountain of personal ridicule and condemnation. They have learned that good things don't last, that affection will capriciously end, followed by disappointment and rejection.

The Phobic Avoidant

Phobic syndromes are seen among many and diverse personality types. Some are active and energetic, expressing their fears in rapid and dramatic ways. Those who are more constrained may show a motor restlessness, a general worrisomeness about being exposed as being weak and inadequate. Personalities of a more irritable nature seem perennially on edge even when feared objects are not present; their imagination does not permit them a moment of rest or refuge. Others, perhaps of a more compulsive variety, seek to bury their anxieties behind their public reserve but, under close observation, can be seen as tense and anxious. Among the avoidants, there are individuals who rarely achieve freedom from their state of generalized anxiety. Seeking to limit the many sources of their anguish, they are disposed to find highly specific phobic precipitants which, though fewer in number, almost invariably overwhelm their defenses and undo their psychic controls.

When faced with the phobic object, these avoidant personalities may also experience a feeling of powerlessness against forces which seem to surge from within themselves, an intense and panicky feeling of terror and disorganization. A rush of irrational impulses and bizarre thoughts may carry them away. More typically, however, there is an inability to focus, a loss in the ability to distinguish the safe from the unsafe, or the relevant from the irrelevant. This distress may continue to mount as they become self-consciously aware of their growing tensions and their inability to surmount these feelings.

Phobic avoidants are usually a mixture of dependent and avoidant personalities. Both personality types are very desirous of close personal relationships, but avoidants fear or do not trust others. Dependents are not only desirous of intimate relationships, but need them and dread their loss. When facing the possibility of such loss, the anxieties of dependents become intense, even overwhelming, mirroring the everyday state in which avoidants live. Mixed avoidant/dependents hesitate to exhibit these fears, lest they precipitate that which they dread. Instead of feeling trapped between desire and loss, these mixed types turn their attentions to finding a symbolic substitute, some object or event onto which they can displace and funnel their anxieties. These phobic objects enable them to redirect and discharge their fears, while neither being conscious of them, nor having to deal with them forthrightly. Moreover, by maintaining a distance from their trivial phobic replacement, they can now tolerate "the loss of" the symbol that serves as a substitute for what they desperately wish to keep. It is this anxious and dependent personality fusion that we have termed the *phobic avoidant.*

As just noted, the phobic experience is likely to signify a psychic displacement and condensation of avoidants' internal and generalized anxiety onto a symbolic external object. They do not neutralize or dilute their omnipresent anxiety but merely divert it into a well-circumscribed and potentially avoidable external source. In this way, they may block from conscious awareness the deeper and hidden intrapsychic reason for their anxiety. Whereas this mechanism works for most other personality types, it is only partially successful in the *phobic avoidant.* Here, in particular, the objects or events to which the phobic response is displaced have a clear symbolic significance. Whereas externalization enables most patients to cope with the experience of anxiety, avoidant phobics do so with limited success in that the symbolic object often directly represents the more pervasive sources of their anxiety. Thus, avoidant phobics may be especially prone to experience "social phobias," a fear of being exposed and humiliated in public settings. As we know, the primary source of avoidants' anxieties is their anticipation and fear of personal rejection and humiliation.

In contrast with other personalities, the phobias of avoidants tend to be private affairs. For them, the symptom is frequently not designed to solicit social attention and support, because many of these personalities are convinced that such attentions will only bring forth ridicule and abuse. Dreading further social humiliation, they frequently search out tangential and innocuous external objects so as to keep their phobias hidden and personal. Nevertheless, among these avoidants, there may be much to be gained by fearing something explicit and defined. Although most would desire to shroud their phobia in a measure of secrecy, lest they be further humiliated, where possible they may also attempt to use their distress to gain a degree of protection and security among those who are partially supportive. In this way, these avoidants may successfully distance from anxiety-producing situations, while also having a degree of forbearance from others.

For other phobic avoidants, the process of finding a phobic object may represent a "cry for compassion," a desire to locate little, self-created fears, and to make instrumental use of them for deterring the rejection and abandonment threats of otherwise nonsupportive persons. Although the "phobic character" is viewed in the analytic literature as signifying a fear of the "desired object," this intrapsychic reversal is likely to apply to personalities other than the avoidant.

The Self-Deserting Avoidant

As with other personalities of this type, *self-deserting avoidants* draw more and more into themselves as a means of avoiding the discomforts of relating to others. In so doing, they find themselves increasingly aware of the psychic contents of their inner world. Whereas they may have used fantasy initially to make their life more bearable, fantasies often bring no surcease. They begin to recognize that turning inward only centers their thoughts on the misery of their lives and the pain and anguish of past experiences. Although spared the difficulties of public exposure and personal humiliation, they have not been successful in avoiding their inner sorrows and torment. There are moments, of course, when their fantasies provide them with fulfilling images and longings, but these become fewer and fewer over time.

Increasingly confused about where to turn, self-deserting avoidants feel like melancholy outsiders, not only lacking in intimate and warm relationships but also having a minimal self-value. What we see in this process is the merging of avoidant and depressive personality features, an amalgamation of social aversion and self-devaluation. Although self-deserting avoidants thus create a protective barrier from their "real" world, the inner world into which they have withdrawn proves to be no less problematic and disparaging. Totally interiorized, they can no longer escape from what made them draw into themselves in the first place. Subject to their own inescapable fantasies, their anguish mounts increasingly. More and more they cannot tolerate themselves, and more and more they seek to undo their self-conscious awareness.

Seeking to ensure that nothing will get to them, self-deserting avoidants not only distance from the outer world but increasingly block awareness from their own thoughts and feelings. They are now self-abandoning, becoming increasingly neglectful of their very being, jettisoning both their psychic and physical well-being, perhaps becoming increasingly incompetent, exerting themselves minimally, and ultimately failing to fulfill even the barest of acts of self-care. Some self-deserting avoidants are plunged into despair and driven toward suicide, deserting their own selves to jettison the anguish and horror within. Others regress into a state of affect-lessness, an emotional numbness in which they become completely disconnected from themselves. This disconnection and self-desertion grows into an habitual way of life, a way of remaining in flight from both their outer and inner realities.

This flight from cognitive self-awareness may result in a splitting of consciousness, a breaking up into parts of what was once interconnected, a now random set of exchangeable pieces. It is at this point of self-fragmentation and cognitive disorganization that we see the blending of the avoidant style and the schizotypal structure. As these regressions and fragmentations proceed, self-deserting avoidants first become outside spectators, observing from without the drama of their transformation. They are partially connected to both themselves and others by virtue of remaining non-participant onlookers.

Comorbid Disorders and Syndromes

As in Chapter 6, this section discusses the several Axis I syndromes and Axis II disorders that frequently exist concurrently with the personality disorder under review. The comorbidities of the avoidant personality (AVD) are among the most frequent of the personalities; hence our discussion here will be more extensive than usual. Problems of differential diagnosis will be discussed in a subsequent section.

Axis II Comorbidities

As can be seen in Figure 7.4, the AVD is associated with eight or so different comorbid personality disorders that deserve notation. The overlap is greatest with the schizoid (SZD), depressive (DPS),

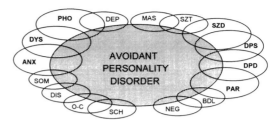

Figure 7.4 Comorbidity between avoidant personality disorder and other DSM Axis I and Axis II disorders.

dependent (DPD), and paranoid (PAR) personalities; also noted are correspondences with the masochistic (MAS), schizotypal (SZT), borderline (BDL), and negativistic (NEG) patterns. Reference should also be made to the AVD Adult Subtypes section (e.g., Conflicted, Hypersensitive). These subtypes reflect partial comorbidities with the basic avoidant prototype.

Axis I Comorbidities

As noted previously, AVD types are among the most vulnerable of the personality patterns to Axis I clinical syndromes; they not only exhibit more of them but experience them more frequently and intensely than almost all other types, with the possible exception of the borderline personality in whom these symptoms often achieve the characterological quality of chronicity. Because the Avoidant designation is among the newest of the official personality syndromes, its concomitant clinical syndromes are elaborated more fully than usual.

Anxiety Syndromes (ANX).   The most common of the avoidant's symptoms is the *generalized anxiety disorder,* typically seen for prolonged periods and consisting of moderately intense and widely exhibited apprehensions. The interpersonal abilities of avoidants are barely adequate to the social strains and challenges they must handle. As such, they characteristically seem on edge, unable to relax, easily startled, tense, worrisome, irritable, preoccupied with calamities, and prone to nightmares; and they have poor appetites and suffer fatigue and intangible physical ailments. Some avoidants "adjust" to this pervasively uncomfortable state, but their lives are thereby limited and impoverished, restricted by the need to curtail their activities and relationships to just those few they can manage. Phenomenological apprehension is the most notable symptom voiced by these patients. They often report a vague and diffuse awareness that something dreadful is imminent; the experience is compounded because they are unsure what it is that they dread and from where the danger may arise. This feeling of impending disaster periodically reaches intense proportions, as in an acute panic disorder. Frequently, avoidants will be precipitated into anxiety as a consequence of social encroachment. Their histories have made them hypersensitive to social derogation and humiliation. Not only have they acquired a marked distrust of others, but they lack the self-esteem to retaliate against insult and derision. When repeated deprecations occur, reactivating past humiliations and resentments, avoidants are unable to respond or fear responding as they would like. As a consequence, their frustration and tension may mount, finally erupting into an acute panic.

Phobic Syndromes (PHO).

Phobic Syndromes (PHO). *Social phobias,* of course, are so deeply ingrained and pervasive a part of the avoidant that it is difficult to say where the personality trait ends and where the phobic symptom begins. Nevertheless, avoidant personalities may have particular phobic feelings about specific settings or persons that are of substantially greater magnitude than they possess toward most interpersonal situations. Avoidants tend to keep their phobias to themselves. For them, the phobic symptom does not serve as a means of soliciting social attention, as it does in dependents or histrionics, because they are convinced that such attentions will bring forth only ridicule and abuse. As with anxiety, phobias are an expression, albeit a symbolic one, of feeling encroached on or of being pressured by excessive social demands. Crystallized in phobic form, these patients have an identifiable and circumscribed anxiety source that they can then actively avoid. In a similar manner, phobic symptoms may enable avoidants to redirect feelings of resentment that they dare not express toward the "true" object of these feelings. Dreading social rebuke, avoidants will seek some innocuous external source to keep their resentments in check. Through displacement and condensation, the selected phobic object may come to represent a symbolic, yet "real," basis for their anxieties and resentments.

Obsessive-Compulsive Syndromes (OC). Obsessive or compulsive preoccupations may serve to distract patients from reflecting on their "true" misery. Similarly, they may serve to counteract feelings of estrangement or depersonalization by providing patients with thoughts and behaviors that assure them there is some tangible reality to life.

Moreover, these ruminations and activities fill up time and distract their attention from anticipated social derision. For example, a 30-year-old severely avoidant man made a 360-degree turn each time he walked through a door. He believed that this act would change his personality, which, in turn, would disincline those he subsequently met from ridiculing him. Ritualistic behaviors such as these often signify a bizarre method of controlling socially condemned thoughts and impulses. Thus, this same patient put the index finger of his right hand to his lips, and then placed both hands in the back pockets of his trousers whenever he felt the urge to speak obscenities or fondle the breasts of women passersby.

Somatoform Syndromes (SOM). Avoidant personalities exhibit *hypochondriacal syndromes* to achieve a variety of different coping goals, such as countering feelings of depersonalization. They may become alert to bodily sounds and movements to assure themselves that they are "real" and alive. In more severe states, and because of their habitual social isolation and self-preoccupations, these bodily sensations may become elaborated into bizarre and delusional experiences. Discomforting bodily sensations may be used also as a symbolic form of self-punishment, representing the disgust, if not hatred, that some avoidants feel toward themselves. Fatigue in these personalities may be seen as an extension of the avoidant's basic detachment strategy. Thus physical inertia can serve instrumentally as a rationalization to justify withdrawal from social contact.

A wide variety of *conversion disorders*—ranging from minor tics, generalized sensory anesthesias, and motor paralyses to the total loss of vision or hearing—may be exhibited by avoidant personalities. These symptoms do not occur frequently, however, since these patients wish to avoid situations that promote attention. Nevertheless, when they are unable to avoid social pressure or deprecation, and fear expressing their dismay directly or overtly, they may bind their anxieties into conversion symptoms. These symptoms are most likely to occur in response to strong impulses of counterhostility that must be contained. Specifically, symptoms such as loss of vision and hearing may be understood if seen as an extension of their habitual avoidance strategy. By eliminating their sensory awareness, they no longer see or hear others deriding them. A severance of body functions, such as in sensory anesthesias or motor paralyses, may reflect the condensation and displacement of depersonalization anxieties. Thus, rather than experience a sense of nothingness, avoidants may crystallize and contain this dreadful feeling by attaching it to one part of the body. Conversion symptoms may also reflect self-repudiation. Viewing themselves with derision and contempt, avoidants may utilize conversion as an expression of self-rejection. By disconnecting some part of themselves, they symbolize their desire to disown their body. Some conversion patients evidence *la belle indifference*—a lack of concern about their bodily symptoms. Although this indifference to illness does occur, it is by no means typical of all conversion patients and would be expected among those who do not wish to draw attention to their ailment. For this reason, it is found in avoidant personalities who have serious concerns as to how others will react to their infirmity.

Dissociative Syndromes (DIS). As noted repeatedly, avoidant personalities experience frequent and varied forms of dissociative disorder. Feelings of estrangement may arise as a protective maneuver to diminish the impact of excessive stimulation or the pain of social humiliation. These symptoms may also reflect the patient's devalued sense of self. Thus, without an esteemed and integrated inner core to which experience can be anchored, events often seem disconnected, ephemeral, and unreal. Self-estrangement may also be traced to avoidants' characteristic coping maneuver of cognitive interference, which not only serves to disconnect normally associated events but deprives these persons of meaningful contact with their own feelings and thoughts. Experiences of amnesia may also arise occasionally as an expression of self-rejection. To be oneself is not a cheerful prospect for these persons, and life may be started anew by the act of disowning one's past identity. Brief frenzied states in which frustrated and repressed impulses are discharged may be commonly found in these patients, especially at advanced levels of severity.

Depressive Syndrome (DEP). Given their detached style, we might think that avoidants would not be among those who display affective disorders. This belief would be consistent with their characteristic effort to flatten emotions and suppress or otherwise interfere with feelings. Despite their efforts in this regard, these patients often experience *major depressions,* feeling a deep sadness, emptiness, and loneliness. Many express a yearning for the affection and approval they have been denied. Added to this melancholic tone is the contempt these patients feel for themselves and the self-deprecation they experience for their

unlovability, weaknesses, and ineffectuality. Though hesitant to display this self-contempt before others, lest it invite a chorus of further derision, tactful probing will readily elicit both the self-deprecatory comments and the genuinely felt moods of futility and dejection. Repetitive *dysthymic* periods, particularly of a quiet, despondent nature, are also among their more notable Axis I syndromes.

Schizophrenic Syndromes (SCH). Among the more severe or psychotic disorders, *disorganized schizophrenic* episodes signify a surrendering by the avoidant of all coping efforts. Although every pathological pattern may exhibit this disorder, it is an active coping maneuver in some personality types, thereby increasing the likelihood of its occurrence. Moreover, some personalities are more disposed than others to surrender their controls and thus to collapse into a fragmented state. Avoidant personalities are among those especially inclined to this disorder, not only because they are easily overwhelmed by external and internal pressures but because disorganization is an extension of their characteristic protective maneuver of interfering with their cognitive clarity. By blocking the flow of thoughts and memories, they effectively distract themselves and dilute the impact of painful feelings and recollections. Disorganized (hebephrenic) schizophrenia may arise, then, as a direct product of either intolerable pressures or self-made confusions, or both. The upshot is a clinical picture of forced absurdity and incoherence, and a concerted effort to disrupt cognitive logic and emotional stability.

Catatonic schizophrenic disorders signify a protective withdrawal, a retreat into indifference, and a purposeful uninvolvement and insensitivity to life so as to avoid the anguish it has produced. By disengaging themselves totally, avoidants need no longer feel the painful emotions they experienced before, no longer suffer the discouragement of struggling fruitlessly, and no longer desire and aspire, only to be frustrated and humiliated again. Faced with a sense of hopelessness and futility, severely troubled avoidants have given up, have become uncaring, neutral, flat, impassive, and "dead" to everything. This shutting off of emotions and the retreat into indifference are protective devices that can be employed easily by all individuals who have been overwhelmed by a sense of hopelessness and futility. Despite its ease as a coping maneuver, it appears with significantly greater frequency among avoidants whose lifelong strategies dispose them to emotional detachment and withdrawal. It is a "logical" extension then of their personality style. Unable to handle substantial overstimulation—be it from unexpected responsibilities, objective threat, or reactivated anxiety—they may overemploy their characteristic coping strategies and withdraw into a catatonic stupor, an impassive, unresponsive, and unfeeling state. Avoidant personalities can usually be identified at these times by their total muteness and their complete "tuning out" of the world, traits that result in an inner void and a picture of masklike stupor. At other times, a catatonic rigidity becomes the prominent feature, a purposeful recalcitrance and manifest uncooperativeness. Beneath the quiet and restrained exterior, however, lies a seething but controlled hostility. These avoidants are not only mute and immobile, then, but bullheaded and adamant about remaining in certain fixed and preferred positions, opposing all efforts to alter them. This rigidity is manifested in their body tension, with fists clenched, teeth gritted, and jaw locked tight and firm. Breaking periodically through this physical immobility may be stereotyped repetitive acts, bizarre gestures, grimaces, and peculiar tics, grins, and giggles. Every now and then inner impulses and fantasies may emerge briefly in a catatonic excitement, often discharged or enacted in strange, symbolic expressions. Obviously, there are active, though confused, thoughts and emotions churning beneath the passive catatonic exterior.

Severely disturbed avoidants may also show periods of *paranoid* schizophrenia, with their unsystematic and incoherent delusions. Distortions of reality are almost an inevitable consequence of prolonged periods of marked social isolation. In addition, brief delusional formations may develop if these patients are faced with severe depersonalization feelings or are thrust into situations of excessive responsibility and stimulation. These delusions are usually bizarre and nonsensical.

DIFFERENTIAL DIAGNOSIS

As with the DSM-IV schizoid personality, the avoidant syndrome may frequently be confused with similar disorders until clinicians have had adequate time and numerous cases to which to apply its criteria.

As far as Axis I distinctions are concerned, the only differentiation that may cause substantive difficulty is that between the avoidant personality and social phobias. They do overlap and may be simultaneously diagnosed. There are two prime distinctions. First, there is a pervasiveness and diffuseness to the personality's socially aversive behaviors, in contrast to the specificity of the phobic object and the intensity of the phobic response. Second, unless it covaries with the avoidant syndrome, the phobic symptom is not associated with the broad range of traits that characterize the personality, such as "low self-esteem," the "desire for acceptance," and so on.

In differentiating between avoidant and other Axis II personality syndromes, predicaments may occur in separating avoidants from schizoids, schizotypals, dependents, and paranoids.

As noted earlier, avoidant personalities desire social acceptance and feel their isolation deeply, whereas the *schizoid* is genuinely indifferent to social matters and is intrinsically blunted emotionally.

Schizotypal personalities differ from avoidants in their obvious eccentricities, such as their odd speech, ideas of reference, and so on—essentially the features of schizophrenia without the presence of delusions or hallucinations; avoidants lack these dramatic peculiarities and bizarre behaviors, exhibiting instead the anticipation of humiliation, a fear of interpersonal rejection, a need for love, lack of self-esteem, and the desire for social acceptance.

Paranoid personalities share many features with avoidant types, notably a suspiciousness and fearfulness of a threatening environment. Here again, the avoidant's loneliness and hyperalertness stem from an intense sense of personal devaluation and low self-esteem. By contrast, the paranoid's reluctances derive from a desire to maintain autonomy and an expectation of malice and deceptiveness of others. No less characteristic is the paranoid's typical anger and abrasive manner.

Both avoidant and *dependent* personalities exhibit feelings of personal inadequacy; they differ in that dependents respond to criticism by increasing their submissiveness and by exhibiting a willingness to maintain relationships at all costs, whereas avoidants withdraw and distance further from those who express such negative evaluations.

ASSESSING THE AVOIDANT: A CASE STUDY

Extensive research literature on assessment signs of the avoidant personality have not been sufficient to permit definitive statements. Nevertheless, there are a few test response patterns that might be noted as probable.

On the Rorschach, avoidants give evidence of their distancing inclinations by a frequent preoccupation with minor details, suggestions of suspiciousness and hesitation in both the content and location of their responses. Movement responses, for example, tend to be frozen or signify a protective distancing activity. Popular responses are often frequent, although more severe avoidant types are likely to include weak or inadequate animal figures that are subject to being hurt or killed. The TAT produces story lines signifying anxiety and the anticipation of rejection between characters. A high degree of variability in story length may be anticipated, with some highly elaborated and obviously personal in nature, whereas others, perhaps those reminiscent of unusually painful past experiences are quickly dispensed with or rejected.

MMPI scores usually show Scale 0 to be very high, signifying the avoidant's habitual social withdrawal; Scale 6 may also be high owing to the perceptual hypervigilance of these personalities. Similarly, profiles of a 2-7/7-2 configuration are not uncommon. Where the pathology is more severe, Scale 8 is often high, whereas Scale 9 may be low.

The following case history presents the pathogenic course of an avoidant personality; the parallel MCMI-III profile (Figure 7.5) and interpretive segments illustrate features that typify the disorder.

CASE 7.1

Donald F., Age 18, High School Junior

Donald's father was an aggressive and financially successful physician, noted within his specialty as the originator of an important surgical procedure; his mother was a rather shy and retiring woman who had been a high school teacher before her marriage. Donald had two brothers, one older and one younger than himself.

From the very first, Donald seemed an unusual baby. He cried incessantly, was difficult to feed and impossible to fit into any schedule of management and care. Colic persisted well into the latter half of his first year. He continued to be easily upset; at 8 months, he cried at the sight of anyone other than his mother, and this persisted well into his second year.

His father was easily exasperated with Donald, especially when the boy failed to stand and walk at the age of 10 months; Donald did not walk at all until 20 months of age, and evidenced a wide variety of other developmental lags in speech and motor performance.

Although his mother sought to compensate for the obvious rejection Donald experienced at the hands of his father, her efforts and tolerance diminished sharply with the birth of her third child. Throughout his early years, Donald constantly was compared with his older brother, a robust youngster who was assertive and cheerful in manner, and who matured rapidly in all spheres of motor and cognitive functioning. The advent of the third son in the family, a child who showed signs of progressing in a manner similar to the first, further categorized Donald as the "slow and difficult one."

Donald's performance in school was well above average, but far below his father's expectations and his brother's achievements. Although his father's taunting took on a joking tone, he managed, quite effectively, to humiliate and deprecate him. Donald remained an isolate within his home, and a fearful, quiet and socially withdrawn adolescent among his peers at school.

The following profile (Figure 7.5) reflects the MCMI-III scores of an avoidant personality such as Donald. Segments of the interpretive report are noted as well.

INTERPRETIVE SUMMARY

The MCMI-III profile of this man may best be characterized as fearful, depressive, socially shy, and self-effacing. Hesitant about self-assertion, he may have learned to lean on others for security, and he assumes the role of a submissive and self-sacrificing partner in close relationships. Exceedingly insecure and vulnerable if separated from those who provide support, he may place himself in inferior or demeaning positions, permitting others to be exploitive and abusive. In fact, he may occasionally seek out relationships in which he will suffer. He resents those who fail to appreciate his intense needs for affection and nurturance; however, because his security is threatened when these resentments are expressed, he may hesitate discharging any negative feelings and does so only infrequently and indirectly. Ever fearful of rebuff, he may withdraw voluntarily from painful social relationships or try

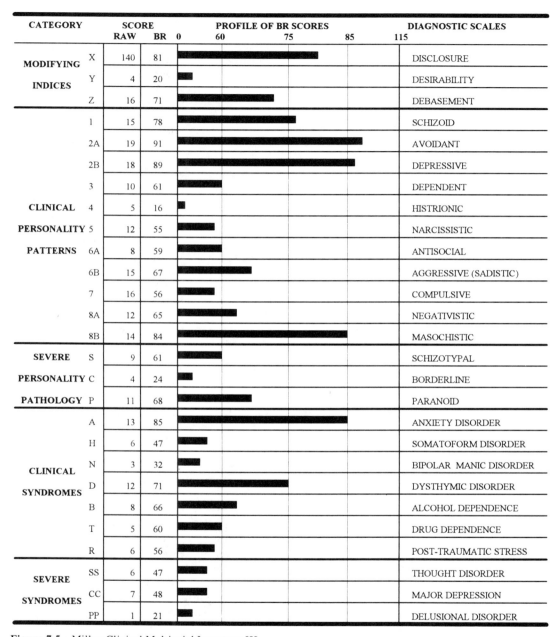

CATEGORY		SCORE RAW	BR	PROFILE OF BR SCORES 0 60 75 85 115	DIAGNOSTIC SCALES
MODIFYING INDICES	X	140	81		DISCLOSURE
	Y	4	20		DESIRABILITY
	Z	16	71		DEBASEMENT
CLINICAL PERSONALITY PATTERNS	1	15	78		SCHIZOID
	2A	19	91		AVOIDANT
	2B	18	89		DEPRESSIVE
	3	10	61		DEPENDENT
	4	5	16		HISTRIONIC
	5	12	55		NARCISSISTIC
	6A	8	59		ANTISOCIAL
	6B	15	67		AGGRESSIVE (SADISTIC)
	7	16	56		COMPULSIVE
	8A	12	65		NEGATIVISTIC
	8B	14	84		MASOCHISTIC
SEVERE PERSONALITY PATHOLOGY	S	9	61		SCHIZOTYPAL
	C	4	24		BORDERLINE
	P	11	68		PARANOID
CLINICAL SYNDROMES	A	13	85		ANXIETY DISORDER
	H	6	47		SOMATOFORM DISORDER
	N	3	32		BIPOLAR MANIC DISORDER
	D	12	71		DYSTHYMIC DISORDER
	B	8	66		ALCOHOL DEPENDENCE
	T	5	60		DRUG DEPENDENCE
	R	6	56		POST-TRAUMATIC STRESS
SEVERE SYNDROMES	SS	6	47		THOUGHT DISORDER
	CC	7	48		MAJOR DEPRESSION
	PP	1	21		DELUSIONAL DISORDER

Figure 7.5 Millon Clinical Multiaxial Inventory-III.

to convince himself that martyrdom is a worthy state, all in an effort to prevent himself from venting his anger directly.

Depressive feelings, loneliness, and isolation may be increasingly experienced. His underlying tension and emotional dysphoria may be present in disturbing mixtures of anxiety, sadness, and guilt.

His insecurity and his fear of abandonment account for what may appear at times to be a quiet, submissive, and benign attitude. Aside from his occasional expressions of resentment, he may be extremely conciliatory, placating, and even ingratiating. By acting weak, expressing self-doubt, depriving himself, communicating a need for assurance and direction, and displaying a desire to submit and comply, he hopes to evoke nurturance and protection. By submerging his individuality, focusing on his worst features and lowly status, subordinating his personal desires, and submitting at times to abuse and intimidation, he hopes to avoid total abandonment.

His frequent complaints of inadequacy, fatigability, and illness may reflect an underlying mood of depression. Under these circumstances, simple responsibilities demand more energy than he can muster. Life may be referred to as empty with constant feelings of weariness and apathy. By withdrawing, being melancholy and self-abnegating, or restricting his social involvement to situations in which he may be exploited or abused, he precludes new, potentially favorable experiences from redirecting his life.

Consistent with his pervasive discontent and sadness, this insecure and troubled man reports suffering from a variety of symptoms that constitute an anxiety disorder. In addition to palpitations, distractibility, jittery feelings, and restlessness at one moment and exhaustion the next, he may experience presentiments of tragic outcomes as well as periodic panic attacks and agoraphobia. Expecting the worst to happen, he not only looks for confirmation but also may precipitate events that generate self-defeating stressors that further intensify his anxieties.

PATHOGENIC DEVELOPMENTAL BACKGROUND

As stated previously, personality represents the individual's pervasive style of functioning and arises as a consequence of the intricate and sequential interplay of both biological and psychological influences. As in earlier chapters, this section outlines several of the more plausible biogenic and psychogenic factors that underlie the development of the personality under review. Note again that the influences hypothesized here are neither necessary, sufficient, mutually exclusive, nor even contributory causes in all cases. They are posited as reasonable conjectures; any number of combinations of these determinants may shape the course of pathological personality development.

HYPOTHESIZED BIOGENIC FACTORS

As noted earlier, propositions implicating biophysical determinants are highly speculative, given our present state of knowledge. Let us note, further, that the following hypotheses represent, in several circumstances, different conceptual approaches to the same thesis (e.g., a threctic reaction pattern may simply be a behavioral term to represent a biophysical limbic system imbalance).

Heredity

Genetic predispositions to avoidant behavior cannot be overlooked, despite the lack of empirical data. Many structural elements and physiological processes compose the biophysical substrate for those complex psychological functions we refer to as affective disharmony, interpersonal aversiveness and so on. It would be naive to assume that these biophysical substrates do not vary from person to person, or that they are not influenced in part by heredity. Studies that demonstrate a higher than chance correspondence within family groups in social apprehensiveness and withdrawal behavior can be attributed in large measure to learning, but there is reason to believe, at least in some cases, that this correspondence may partially be assigned to a common pool of genotypic dispositions within families. The particular regions that may be involved in these ostensive genetic dispositions will be noted in several of the following sections.

Threctic Infantile Reaction Pattern

Infants who display hyperirritability, crankiness, tension, and withdrawal behaviors from the first days of postnatal life may not only possess a constitutional disposition toward an avoidant pattern but may prompt rejecting and hostile attitudes from their parents. Frightened and hypertense babies, who are easily awakened, cry, and are colicky rarely afford their parents much comfort and joy. Rather, such infants typically induce parental weariness, exasperation, and anger; these attitudes and feelings in turn may shape a stereotype of a troublesome, whining, and difficult-to-manage child. In these cases, an initial biophysical tendency toward anxiety and withdrawal may be aggravated further by parental rejection and deprecation.

Slow or Irregular Maturation

Delayed or uneven maturation in any of the major spheres of sensory, sensorimotor, or cognitive functioning may be conducive to psychopathology. Developmental immaturities and integration deficits may signify an impaired biophysical substrate that can limit the child's capacity to cope adequately with the normal tasks of each developmental stage. These intrinsic deficiencies often are compounded by the child's self-conscious awareness of these inadequacies. Of equal if not greater import in compounding these deficits are parental reactions to the child's atypical development. Parents who expect their children to progress well and rapidly through the usual developmental sequence may experience considerable anxiety and dismay over deviations and failures they observe. Inadequate achievements often result in parental condemnation and ridicule, which will evoke in the child feelings of social alienation and low self-regard.

Limbic Region Imbalances

Quite possibly, avoidant personalities experience aversive stimuli more intensely and more frequently than others because they possess an especially dense or overabundantly branched neural substrate in the aversive center of the limbic system. An excellent follow-up study was carried out by Kagan (1989) with 2-year-old children who evinced extremes in either behavioral restraint or spontaneity in unfamiliar contexts. These children were followed until they were 7 years of age. The majority of the restrained group remained quiet and socially avoidant, whereas those who were spontaneous became talkative and interactive. Group differences in peripheral physiological reactions suggested that inherited variations in arousal thresholds may be associated with selected limbic sites that, in turn, may undergird shyness in childhood and more marked social avoidance in adulthood.

Individual differences in brain anatomy are often well demonstrated and plausible neurologically, but we must recognize that speculations attributing complex forms of clinical behavior to biophysical variations are not only conjectural but rather simplistic. Even if clear-cut differences in biological aversiveness are found, the psychological form and content of these tendencies would take on their specific character only as a function of the individual's particular life experiences and learnings.

Sympathetic System Dominance

Another plausible speculation for the threctic or aversive feature of the active-detached avoidant pattern centers on a presumed functional dominance of the sympathetic nervous system. Excess

adrenaline resulting from any one of a number of possible dysfunctions, either in the autonomic system or in the pituitary-adrenal axis, may give rise to the hypervigilance and irritability characteristic of the avoidant personality. Imbalances of this kind also may account for the affective anguish and cognitive distraction found among these patients.

Although hypotheses implicating adrenal involvement lend themselves more readily to experimental test than those pertaining to the limbic system, no adequately designed studies have been executed to this date, and these hypotheses remain essentially speculative.

Neurohormonal Synaptic Acceleration

Deficiencies or excesses in any of the various neurohormones may facilitate rapid synaptic transmission, resulting in the flooding and scattering of neural impulses. Such individuals not only will appear overalert and overactive but may experience cognitive distractability, social anxiety, and a generalized emotional disharmony. Let us briefly note the rationale for these effects.

First, uninhibited neural transmission may generate many pathological consequences; it can make normally discriminable stimuli functionally equivalent, allow irrelevant impulses to intrude on logical associations, diminish the control and direction of thought and permit the emergence of inappropriate memory traces—in short, it can result in a marked interference with normal cognitive processes.

Second, a lowering of normal resistance at the synapse, with its attendant flooding of impulses, may give rise to anxiety under conditions of normal stimulation. For example, individuals subjected to this impairment may be overwhelmed, overexcited, and overaroused by experiences that most people take in stride. What we observe as anxiety readiness and interpersonal aversiveness in the avoidant's active-detached pattern may be a protective maneuver to counteract a biologically based inability to control stimulus input and to coordinate impulse transmission. Along similar lines, the affective disharmony of the avoidant may be a product of the inability to inhibit the intrusion of discordant memories and emotions.

CHARACTERISTIC EXPERIENTIAL HISTORY

Attempts to list and detail the infinite number of life experiences that may shape the development of an avoidant pattern would be not only futile but misleading. It is not so much the particulars of the timing, setting, or source of these experiences that make them important but rather the significance of the message they convey to the individual. These diverse experiences possess one central theme in common: They serve to depreciate the individual's self-esteem through either explicit or implicit signs of rejection, humiliation, or denigration. Repeated exposure to such events will not only foster an image of deflated self-worth but will tend, ultimately, to produce the affective disharmony, cognitive interference, and interpersonal distrust characteristic of the active-detached personality. We will elaborate two of the primary sources of these derogating experiences in the following sections.

Parental Rejection and Deprecation

Normal, attractive, and healthy infants may encounter parental devaluation, malignment, and rejection. Reared in a family setting in which they are belittled, abandoned, and censured, these youngsters will have their natural robustness and optimism crushed, and acquire in its stead attitudes of self-deprecation and feelings of social alienation. We can well imagine the impact of these experiences in the case of Donald F. who was not especially robust and competent to start with.

The consequences of parental rejection and humiliation are many and diverse. In the following discussion we will outline them as they might arise during the neuropsychological stages of development.

1. Parents who handle their infants in a cold and indelicate manner during the sensory attachment stage will promote feelings of tension and insecurity on the part of their offspring. These infants will acquire a diffuse sense that the world is harsh, unwelcoming, and discomforting. They will learn, in their primitive and highly generalized way, to avoid attaching themselves to others; they will acquire a sense of mistrust of their human surroundings and, as a result, feel isolated, helpless, and abandoned.

In self-protection, these youngsters may learn to "turn off" their growing sensory capacities so as to diminish the discomfort they experience. By so doing, however, they may set the stage for a long-standing and generalized habit of stimulus withdrawal.

2. Parents who scorn, ridicule, and belittle their offspring's first stumbling efforts during the sensorimotor-autonomy stage will diminish markedly feelings of self-competence and the growth of confidence (e.g., the experience of Donald F. at the hands of his father). Although normal language skills and motor control may develop, such youngsters will often utilize these aptitudes in a hesitant and self-doubting manner. They may accept as "valid" their parents' criticisms and derogations; in time, they may come to disparage and revile themselves just as their parents had done.

Harsh self-critical attitudes have far-reaching and devastating consequences. By belittling their own worth, people cannot turn to themselves to salve their wounds or gain the rewards they cannot obtain elsewhere. Thus, as a consequence of self-derogation, avoidants not only fail to obtain positive reinforcements from others but cannot obtain them from within. They are caught in a web of social *and* self-reproval; they, themselves, have become the agent of negative reinforcement. Thus, in referring to himself, Donald F. would characteristically comment first on his stupidity and ineptness, and then note how his father and brothers were so much more able intellectually and socially. A cardinal feature of the active-detached pattern, that of self-alienation, has taken root.

3. The roots of self-deprecation begun in the *sensorimotor-autonomy* stage take firmer hold as youngsters progress into the next two periods: *pubertal/gender identity* and *intracortical-integration*. The image of being a weak, unlovable, and unworthy person takes on a strong cognitive base. The child becomes increasingly aware of him- or herself as an unattractive, pitiful person, who deserves to be scoffed at and ridiculed. Little effort may be expended to alter this image because nothing the youngster attempts can succeed, given the deficits and inadequacies he or she sees within.

Peer Group Alienation

Signs of avoidant behavior usually are evident well before children begin to participate in the give-and-take of peer relationships, school and athletic competitions, heterosexual dating with its attendant anxieties, and so on. These early signs may reflect the operation of constitutional dispositions, or attitudes and habits conditioned by the circumstances of family life. Whatever its origins, many school-age children already possess the social hesitations and aversive tendencies that will come to characterize them more clearly in later life.

But for many other youngsters, the rudiments of social withdrawal and self-alienation have developed only minimally when they first encounter the challenges of peer-group activities. For them, the chances of enhancing their competencies and for developing the requisite skills for effective social adaptation remain good, unless they experience rejection, isolation, or the devastating ridicule that often can be meted out by agemates. Such is often the case with avoidant youngsters who come into the *pubertal-gender identity* stage. As the child ventures to meet his peers at school, on the playground, on the athletic field, at school dances, and so on, he is exposed to a variety of challenges that may wear down his sense of self-competence and self-esteem. Many such youngsters will be shattered by daily reminders of their scholastic ineptitude, some will be ridiculed for deficits in athletic prowess, others will be humiliated and experience cruel derogation at the hands of their peers because of physical unattractiveness and their lack of allure, vitality, and so on. Unable to prove themselves in any of the myriad intellectual, physical, or social spheres of peer competition, they may not only be derided and isolated by others but become sharply critical toward themselves for their lack of worthiness and esteem. Their feelings of loneliness and rejection now are compounded further by severe self-judgments of personal inferiority and gender unattractiveness. They are unable to turn either to others for solace and gratification or to themselves.

Many of these youngsters not only accept their plight but compound it by identifying with a weak and ineffectual parent. Still seeking love and affection, they imitate an unwholesome parental model, and thereby seal their fate. By abdicating their individual identities for the dubious comforts and rewards of parental identification, they subvert their own growth, and undermine whatever possibilities they may have had for finding a more satisfying style of life. They now copy the insecurities and inadequacies of their sorrowful parental prototype, learning to display the same social deficits and ineffectualities they observe.

SELF-PERPETUATION PROCESSES

The coping style employed by the avoidant personality is not a matter of choice. It is the principal, and perhaps only, means these individuals have found effective in warding off the painful humiliation experienced at the hands of others. Discomforting as social alienation may be, it is less distressing than the anguish of extending themselves to others, only to be rebuffed or ridiculed.

Distance guarantees a measure of safety; trust only invites disillusion.

The coping maneuvers of avoidants prove self-defeating. There is a driven and frightened quality to their behaviors. Moreover, avoidants are adaptively inflexible because they cannot explore alternative actions without feeling trepidation and anxiety. In contrast to other personalities, the avoidant coping style is essentially negative. Rather than venturing outward or drawing on what aptitudes they possess, they retreat defensively and become increasingly remote from others and removed from sources of potential growth. As a consequence of their protective withdrawal, avoidants are left alone with their inner turmoil, conflicts, and self-alienation. They have succeeded in minimizing their external dangers, but they have trapped themselves in a situation equally devastating. Several behaviors that foster and intensify the avoidant's difficulties are noted here.

Active Social Detachment

Avoidant personalities assume that the experiences to which they were exposed in early life will continue forever. Defensively they narrow the range of activities in which they allow themselves to participate. By sharply circumscribing their life, they preclude the possibility of corrective experiences that might lead them to see that all is not lost and that there are kindly persons who will neither disparage nor humiliate them.

A further consequence of detaching themselves from others is that they can become preoccupied with their own thoughts and impulses. Limited to the inner world of stimuli, they will reflect and ruminate about the past, with all the discomforts it brings forth. Because their experiences have become restricted largely to thinking about past events, life becomes a series of duplications. As a consequence, avoidants are left to relive the painful experiences of earlier times rather than be exposed to new and different events that might alter their outlook and feelings. Moreover, these self-preoccupations serve only to further widen the breach between themselves and others. A vicious circle may take hold. The more they turn inward, the more they lose contact with the typical interests and thoughts of those around them. They become progressively more estranged from their environment, increasingly out of touch with reality and the checks against irrational thought provided by social contact and communication. Away from the controls and stabilizing influences of ordinary human interactions, they begin to lose their sense of balance and perspective, often feeling puzzled, peculiar, unreal, and "crazy."

Suspicious and Fearful Behaviors

Detached and mistrustful behaviors not only establish distance from others but evoke reciprocal reactions of disaffiliation and rejection. An attitude that communicates weakness, self-effacement, and fear invariably attracts those who enjoy deprecating and ridiculing others. Thus, the hesitant posture, suspicious demeanor, and self-deprecating attitudes of the avoidant will tend to evoke interpersonal responses that lead to further experiences of humiliation, contempt, and derogation—in short, a repetition of the past. Any apparent sensitivity to rebuff or obviously fearful and unassertive style will tend to evoke ridicule from peers, an experience that will only reinforce and intensify this personality's aversive inclinations.

Emotional and Perceptual Hypersensitivity

Avoidant personalities are painfully alert to signs of deception, humiliation, and deprecation. As noted in an earlier case presentation, these patients detect the most minute traces of indifference or annoyance on the part of others and make the molehills of minor and passing slights into mountains of personal ridicule and condemnation. They are incredibly sensitive instruments for picking up and magnifying incidental actions and for interpreting them as indications of derision and rejection. This hypersensitivity functions well in the service of self-protection but fosters a deepening of the person's plight. As a result of their extensive scanning of the environment, avoidants actually increase the likelihood that they will encounter precisely those stimuli they wish most to avoid. Their exquisite antennae pick up and transform what most people overlook. In effect, their hypersensitivity backfires by becoming an instrument that brings to their awareness, time and again, the very pain they wish to escape. Their defensive vigilance thus intensifies rather than diminishes their anguish.

Intentional Interference

Avoidants must counter the flood of threatening stimuli that they register as a consequence of their emotional and perceptual hypersensitivities. To assure a modicum of personal tranquillity, they engage constantly in a series of cognitive reinterpretations and digressions. They may actively block, destroy, and fragment their own thoughts, seeking to disconnect relationships between what they see, what meanings they attribute to their perceptions, and what feelings they experience in response. Defensively, then, they intentionally destroy the clarity of their thoughts by intruding irrelevant distractions, tangential ideas, and discordant emotions. This coping maneuver exacts its price. By upsetting the smooth and logical pattern of their cognitive processes, avoidants further diminish their ability to deal with events efficiently and rationally. No longer can they attend to the most salient features of their environment, nor can they focus their thoughts or respond rationally to events. Moreover, they cannot learn new ways to handle and resolve their difficulties because their thinking is cluttered and scattered. Social communications also take on a tangential and irrelevant quality, and they may begin to talk and act in an erratic and halting manner. In sum, in their attempt to diminish intrusively disturbing thoughts, they fall prey to a coping mechanism that further aggravates their original difficulties and ultimately intensifies their alienation from both themselves and others.

THERAPEUTIC INTERVENTIONS

Avoidant personalities are among the most frequent disorders that therapists encounter in their offices. As is evident from the preceding discussions, the prognosis for the avoidant personality is often quite poor. Not only are these persons' habits and attitudes pervasive and ingrained, as are all personality patterns, but many are trapped in environments that provide them with few of the supports and encouragements needed to reverse their lifestyles. Therapists with avoidant clients will be challenged not only to keep them in therapy but also to get beyond these patients' tendency to reveal only that which they believe will restrain the therapist from thinking ill-well of them. If the therapist manages to gain a client's trust, however, a strong alliance can be forged, and progress can be made—given enough time, patience, and conscientious use of interventions.

STRATEGIC GOALS

Therapeutic intervention with avoidant patients has as its ultimate aim to reestablish balance within the pleasure-pain and active-passive polarities. The asymmetrical focus within these domains leads to a clinical picture characterized by overly active avoidance of perceived threatening situations. Active search for psychic enhancement (pleasure) is notably absent. Therapeutic strategies need to be aimed at countering the patient's tendencies to perpetuate a pattern of social withdrawal, perceptual hypervigilance, and intentional cognitive interference. Clinical work targeting the most salient of the domain dysfunctions can help alter the alienated self-image, aversive interpersonal conduct, vexatious object-representations, and anguished mood that characterize these patients' psychic state.

Reestablishing Polarity Balances

Like the schizoid, the avoidant patient has marked difficulty experiencing pleasure. Unlike the schizoid, however, who has a lowered capacity to experience emotional distress as well as pleasure, the avoidant is hyperresponsive to anxiety-provoking stimuli. The avoidant personality's primary aim of avoiding humiliating interpersonal experiences precludes being exposed to interactions in which the yearned for affection can occur. Active withdrawal from situations they fear may be hurtful ensures that avoidants will rarely express their wishes even in nonintimate relationships. This leads to frustration of goals in general, as well as to feelings of loneliness. Typically, in their determination to avoid rejection and pain, avoidant personalities preclude from their repertoire of behaviors interactions that might result in personal gratification.

A major therapeutic goal would thus be to increase avoidant patients' active focus on pleasurable stimuli, and to decrease their active avoidance of potentially painful stimuli.

Countering Perpetuating Tendencies

The characteristic active social detachment that avoidants employ as a defense against experiencing rebuff and criticism actually ensures that they experience no social interaction that serves to disconfirm their pessimistic expectations. An understanding of how their own actions solicit the very reactions from others that they so fear can help avoidants appreciate that they need to control their suspicious and fearful expectancies and behaviors in order for normal interaction to take place. Increased social contact can lead to nonthreatening encounters that can help reorganize

their extreme schemas. Therapeutic intervention can provide patients with self-understanding, social skills, and the means to control or tolerate their symptoms of anxiety to help assure that their fledgling efforts to reach out for rewarding interaction will be successful.

The wood that feeds the fire of withdrawal and suspicious behaviors is the very emotional and perceptual hypersensitivity that avoidants develop as a defense against potentially painful interactions. As their sensitivity escalates, all positives are seen as true positives. Their subjective identification of threat skyrockets so that avoidants spend much time and emotional energy avoiding and processing nonexistent personal assaults. An understanding of normal human behavior, and the ability to differentiate between real, incidental, and imagined threats can allow more normal living to occur. Internal reference points according to which they can judge their own behavior need to be established so that they do not feel at the mercy of others' often unpredictable and irrational responses.

Once the avoidants' hypersensitivities are reduced, they can begin to decrease their use of intentional cognitive interference as a defense against their (often misguided) painful conclusions about others' reactions. More realistic thought processes allow them to deal more effectively with their environments, learn from their surroundings, and to communicate more profitably. Positive social interaction may serve, in turn, to further distract avoidants from the thoughts and impulses that preoccupy them. No longer limited to their inner world of impulses, they have material other than their past pain to ponder, and can develop more normative and adaptive attitudes toward their lives, allowing them to communicate with others and to feel less "unusual."

Modifying Domain Dysfunctions

The avoidant's predisposition and/or learning history lead to a clinical picture dominated by primary disturbances in self-image, interpersonal conduct, object-representations, and mood/temperament. The self is perceived as socially inept and self-achievements are devalued. The emotional suffering that accrues from social isolation and perceived rejection is seen as a justified natural consequence of personal inadequacy. Feelings of aloneness, and even depersonalization, are often reported. Increased social contact, assertiveness, improved social skills, and exploratory client-centered therapy can all direct the avoidant toward an improved self-image.

Aversive interpersonal conduct leads the avoidant to maintain social distance in the hope that privacy will ensure protection against anticipated humiliation and derogation. Cognitive, interpersonal, and other exploratory therapies can help the avoidant rework aversive schemas. Behavior modification programs may prove invaluable in providing avoidants with necessary social skills and incipient self-confidence. Together, these interventions help create more realistic and optimistic mental schemas about human relationships to replace the vexatious object representations that characterize their mental framework. Pharmacological intervention can also be considered to help ease anxiety that interferes with personal growth, effectively lowering the threshold at which avoidants may be cajoled into taking initiative with respect to their own lives.

Avoidants also need to learn to control their fretful expressive behavior in favor of a more relaxed and confident style that promotes rewarding relationships. Their distracted cognitive style interferes with fluid thinking and spontaneous communication. On an intrapsychic level, avoidants rely too heavily on fantasy as a regulatory mechanism to cope with environmental stress. Neither reveries nor isolation will promote adaptive resolution of problems, or help strengthen the fragile morphologic organization of their coping system.

TACTICAL MODALITIES

Therapists working with avoidant patients must keep in mind that the avoidant will be hesitant to share feelings of shame or inadequacy with the therapist for fear of rejection. The best way to counter such client apprehension is with freehanded empathy and support. Benjamin (1993a) points out that many avoidants find it particularly difficult to discuss maltreatment within their childhood family, as well as any negative feelings they have toward family members. This arises from the pressure many avoidants feel to be loyal to the family and its members, and from the accompanying transmitted belief that outsiders are "dangerous" and not to be trusted. Continued support and understanding are the therapist's only recourse against even this resistance. A protective, sanctuarylike therapeutic environment is the only one that is likely to draw the avoidant out of his or her shell.

Domain-Oriented Techniques

Considering therapy from the viewpoint of formal technique, a first approach would be to assist the patient in arranging a more rewarding environment that facilitates opportunities to enhance feelings of self-worth. In the beginning, *supportive* therapeutic approaches of this type may be all avoidant patients can tolerate until they are capable of dealing comfortably with their more painful feelings. Early supportive therapy is necessary, then, but not sufficient, to produce therapeutic change.

At the behavioral level, avoidants manifest both aversive interpersonal conduct, and fretful expressive behavior. *Behavior modification* may prove useful as a way to learn less fearful reactions to formerly threatening situations; in general in vivo exposure is considered more effective than desensitization for symptoms of social anxiety. Before actually engaging in social interaction exercises, avoidant patients can be assigned preliminary *cognitive* tasks such as self-monitoring of their withdrawal behavior, to help clarify their inclination to avoid certain people or social situations. They can also be asked to keep a log of their self-deprecatory self-statements and physiological arousal. Anxiety-management training can be very helpful. If past avoidant behavior has resulted in a failure to acquire critical social skills, then behavioral rehearsal will often improve assertiveness and behavioral fluidity. Once these tasks have been accomplished, hierarchical grading of social tasks in regard to anxiety-provoking potential (talking to a mail carrier vs. engaging in conversation with one's boss) can help organize the sequence of homework assignments. It is very important not to rush the patient through these steps. Initial success is critical in shifting the balance toward a more active stance with regard to procuring interpersonal pleasure and correcting aversive interpersonal conduct.

The preceding techniques are especially useful short-term adjunct interventions. More lasting change, however, requires additional techniques. *Interpersonal* therapy represents a prolonged effort toward healing through a "corrective emotional experience" with the therapist that ideally will generalize to contexts outside the therapy hour as the patients learn that they can succeed in the chances they take within treatment. The interpersonal approach outlined by Benjamin (1993a) suggests a general sequence of strategic intervention the authors have found to be clinically effective.

Once the patient's trust is gained through supportive reassurance and protection, the therapist can move the patient toward more functional behaviors by refusing to support avoidance and by encouraging assertive behavior. Examination of the effects of his or her own behavior can help the avoidant sacrifice the safety of problematic patterns for the possibility of achieving enhancing experiences through more "risky" behavior such as giving up a triangular relationship despite opening himself or herself up to the mercy of the whims of only one person with nowhere to turn for comfort. For example, a secret lover who provides comfort and is protective when a spouse is angry or withdrawn may be given up in favor of improving the relationship with the spouse.

Family or *couple* therapy can be very helpful for a patient who is caught in a social environment that unwittingly supports avoidant behaviors. If the therapist is careful not to allow "trashing" in the name of communication to occur during the sessions, these techniques can help speed the healing process for the patient (Benjamin, 1993). *Group* approaches allow for forced exposure to strangers in an atmosphere of acceptance, and can help patients overcome painful social embarrassment in most therapeutic groups. Patients should not be forced into interacting, but rather should be allowed to observe from the sidelines until they feel ready to risk exposure. In groups that emphasize behavioral approaches, patients also have a unique opportunity to acquire and practice behavioral and social skills.

Avoidant patients can also profit from methods of *cognitive reorientation* designed to alter erroneous self-attitudes and distorted social expectancies. In an effort to change the dysfunctional schemas that underlie avoidant behavior, cognitive therapy focuses largely on clarifying for the patient his or her pattern of "automatic thoughts" within the therapeutic relationship. This helps patients discover thinking errors they commit in everyday life that contribute to their dysphoria and self-defeating behaviors. Honest discussion of patients' feelings toward the therapist and their fears regarding the relationship are the primary tools. As patients realize that the therapist (who serves as a mirror for other relationships) will not reject, abandon, or denigrate them despite exposure, they start to reformulate automatic thinking patterns and reestablish a measure of balance within their personality structure. In working toward this end, Beck and Freeman (1990b) suggest that patients can rate their therapist's feedback on a scale ranging from 0% to 100%, and thus monitor

their own trust in the therapist, as well as in the feedback provided. Beck suggests that patients and therapists engage in experiments to evaluate the validity of their distorted cognitive schemas and automatic thoughts. For example, the therapist can ask the patient if there is anything that the patient cannot disclose. Frequently the patient may express hesitation in responding, but that can be examined and his or her fears confronted. The patient's fantasies about negative and rejecting therapist response can be discussed, and more realistic possibilities can be explored.

Psychodynamic theories frame avoidant behavior as being driven by the shame of not measuring up to one's ego ideal, of being weak, defective, even disgusting. Treatment emphasizes a strongly empathic understanding of the patient's experience of humiliation and embarrassment due to exposure both in front of the therapist and in their daily lives. Childhood memories are analyzed to clarify the roots of the disorder. Confrontation of feared situations is encouraged, as is detailed exploration of anxiety-provoking fantasies, particularly in the context of transference toward the therapist. These deeper and searching procedures of psychodynamic therapies can be useful in reconstructing unconscious anxieties and mechanisms that pervade all aspects of patients' behavior, and of the communication style that contributes to or intensifies the avoidant's problems. If social hypersensitivity is severe, and the fear of rejection and denigration puts the patient at risk for extreme behavioral withdrawal or termination of treatment, possible benefits of *psychopharmacological* intervention can be evaluated. MAO inhibitors may be considered as a possible adjunct to behavioral, as well as other forms of treatment. This medication has been found to be effective at times in controlling the symptoms of social phobia, and may allow the patient to experience a measure of initial success with behavioral intervention. Beta-blockers may also be helpful in controlling symptoms of autonomic excitation such as sweating, trembling, and blushing without a direct psychoactive effect. Brief episodes of panic may be controlled with benzodiazepine anxiolytics. Serotonin uptake-inhibitor antidepressant medications may also prove to be effective in this regard.

It may be useful to review the major strategies and tactics depicted in Figure 7.6.

Potentiated Pairings and Catalytic Sequences

Any intervention plan that is opted for by the therapist is at risk for failure if the initial stages

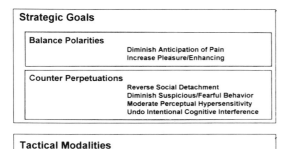

Figure 7.6 Therapeutic strategies and tactics for the prototypal avoidant personality.

of the therapeutic interaction are not primarily supportive and aimed at fostering trust toward the therapist. With trust established, the therapist can help the patient arrange for a rewarding environment and facilitate the discovery of opportunities that would enhance self-worth. With continued therapy, the therapist can gradually shift to a slightly more confrontational style within the framework of a cognitive, interpersonal, psychodynamic, or behavioral intervention. In the course of any long-term individual exploratory psychotherapy aimed at helping the patient get at the roots of dysfunctional patterns, it is often advisable to make concomitant use of shorter-term behavioral techniques. More withdrawn patients can thus acquire the skills necessary for initial experiences of social success that instill hope and foster the motivation needed to tolerate the more painful aspects of therapy. Group therapy can be considered as a more benign and accepting social forum than avoidants normally encounter for learning new attitudes and skills. Favorable response to anxiolytic medication may also allow highly symptomatic patients to tolerate new situations and more proactive social behavior. Especially in the initial stages, selectively combined interventions allow for positive reward gained by interacting socially in previously unthinkable ways, and for the formation of new schemas about self and others without the failure-inducing disruption caused by overwhelming anxiety.

After initial success with behavioral, interpersonal, or cognitive therapy, some patients may profit from family or couple therapy. These interventions are indicated for individuals who are embedded in social contexts that unwittingly help maintain the patient's avoidant behavior, and

whose treatment may be facilitated by the development of a more supportive environment. As is suggested by Beck and Freeman (1990b), the therapist should work with the patient on a program designed to prevent relapse. Ongoing behavioral goals include establishing and improving friendships, behaving in appropriately assertive ways in different social contexts, and trying new experiences. These help maintain motivation and give patients a chance to monitor their own behavior. Patients can be taught to use anxiety as a signal to check for maladaptive automatic thoughts, to keep logs of avoidance-producing thinking and discrediting evidence against their own irrational beliefs, to plan strategies ahead of time for difficult situations, and to call the therapist for a booster session if all else fails.

RESISTANCES AND RISKS

Because of their basic mistrust of others, avoidants are unlikely to be motivated either to seek or to sustain a therapeutic relationship. Should they agree to treatment, they will probably engage in maneuvers to test the sincerity and genuineness of the therapist's feelings and motives. Most often, they will terminate treatment long before remedial improvement has occurred. This tendency to withdraw from therapy stems not only from their doubts and suspicions regarding the therapist's integrity, and their fear of social rejection and disapproval by the therapist, but also from their unwillingness to face the humiliation and anguish involved in confronting painful memories and feelings. They sense intuitively that their defenses are weak and tenuous and that to face directly their feeling of unworthiness, no less their repressed frustrations and impulses, will simply overwhelm them, driving them into unbearable anxieties and even to (as they fear) "insanity."

To add to these fears, the potential gains of therapy may not only fail to motivate the avoidant but may actually serve as a deterrent, reawakening what these personalities view as false hopes, reminding them of the dangers and humiliations they experienced when they tendered their affections to others but received rejection in return. Having found a modest level of comfort by detaching themselves from others, they would rather let matters stand, keep to the level of adjustment to which they are accustomed, and not "rock the boat" they have so tenuously learned to sail.

When an avoidant enters a therapeutic relationship, the therapist must take great pains not to push matters too hard or too fast. Among other things, the patient may feel he or she has but a fragile hold on reality. The therapist should seek, gently and carefully, to build a sense of genuine trust. Gradually, attention may be turned to the patient's positive attributes, addressing these as a means of building confidence and enhancing feelings of self-worth. Therapy is likely to be a slow and arduous process, requiring the reworking of long-standing anxieties and resentments, bringing to consciousness the deep roots of mistrust, and, in time, enabling the patient to reappraise these feelings more objectively. On the other hand, astute therapists also have to take care that their warm empathic behavior does not result in the patient regarding the therapeutic relationship as so satisfying that it becomes an end in itself rather than a base for learning and venturing into other relationships. Therapists must also keep in mind throughout the therapeutic process that the patient's intellectual "understanding" of problems is not enough to solve them; behavioral progress must not be neglected (Benjamin, 1993a).

CHAPTER 8

Depressive Personality Disorders: The Giving-Up Pattern

It has often been said that depression is the equivalent of the common cold in psychopathology, "a ubiquitous infliction to which most of us are subject from time to time" (Coyne, 1986, p. 1). Numerous problems stem from this ubiquity. For example, where does depression begin, and how shall it be differentiated from normal sadness and dejection: Is it an endogenous disease process, an extreme variant of unhappiness generated by environmental circumstances? Does it show periodicity or is it a continuous process? Is it an intrinsic part of a personality pattern, or an episodic clinical syndrome that waxes and wanes for reasons unknown? As Coyne has stated in the introduction to his papers on depression:

Increasingly, theoretical statements about the nature of depression start with an acknowledgment of its heterogeneity and the complexity and interdependence of causal factors now presumed to play a role in it. Yet beyond that, authors tend to lapse into a singular frame of reference that is predictable from their discipline and their indoctrination.

The study of depression is thoroughly fragmented and efforts at integration have been few and generally feeble and unsatisfactory. Investigators in genetics, biochemistry, experimental psychopathology, and epidemiology generally do not stay abreast of developments in other fields that have direct bearing on their own work. (p. 19)

The elucidation of the comorbidity of personality traits/disorders and mood disorders is of both theoretical and clinical importance. Major depression is among the most common reasons for seeking psychiatric help and hospitalization in the general population. Clarification of the interrelationship between personality and depressive symptomatology can have important implications in psychotherapeutic and psychopharmacological interventions. An increased understanding of this

relationship can also help clarify the heterogeneous nature of depressive illness and better delineate the ways in which these syndromes and personality disorders interact and modify each other. A summary of these possible relationships may be useful as an introduction to this chapter. This review of the many ways in which personality and clinical syndromes may become intertwined is applicable not only to depressive disorders, but to all Axis II/Axis I interactions; the reader may wish to go back and examine earlier chapters with these considerations in mind, as well as to keep them in mind when reading later chapters.

- *Characterological Predisposition Hypothesis.* The most popular approach in both theory and research, the dispositional hypothesis, suggests that characterological disorders are primary, with depression being a secondary feature of the pathology. It is postulated that particular features of a personality style (e.g., ineffective coping mechanisms, maladaptive self-defeating behaviors, alienation of others) may render an individual vulnerable to specific psychosocial stressors (e.g., abandonment, rejection, loss of prestige).

- *Complication Hypothesis.* In contrast to the characterological predisposition hypothesis, the complication thesis postulates that it is the experience of depressive disorder that influences personality, not the other way around. Such changes in personality may be limited to the duration of the depressive episode, appear only as a short-term alteration immediately following the episode, or in the case of recurring depressive episodes, develop into a long-term or chronic alteration. These changes in personality may include the person's perception of self and the environment, and/or the person's style of interacting with others. Commonly recognized postmorbid personality features include res-ignation, insecurity, or pessimism (Phillips, Gunderson, Hirschfeld, & Smith, 1989).

- *Attenuation Hypothesis.* Also known as the "subclinical approach" (Hirschfeld & Cross, 1987), this hypothesis presumes that person-ality disorders are an attenuated or alterna-tive expression of the disease process that underlies the depressive disorder. As such, certain personality traits (e.g., cyclothymia) may be viewed as milder manifestations of the full-blown mood disorder. Both the per-sonality disorder or its set of traits, as well as those of depression, are seen to rise from the same genetic or constitutional origins.

- *Coeffect Hypothesis.* The hypothesis states that depression and personality occur to-gether as a result of a common third variable (e.g., traumatic childhood), even though they do not share a common psychobiological ori-gin. In this sense, neither the personality dis-order nor the depressive disorder give rise to the other.

- *Modification Hypothesis.* Also known as the "pathoplasty approach," this hypothesis puts considerations of etiology and pathogen-esis aside, proposing merely that personality features will substantially influence not only the manner in which depression is presented clinically, but also responsivity to treatment and the prognosis of the depressive episode. Depending on the premorbid personality style, depressive symptoms such as hopeless-ness, helplessness, and self-deprecation may come to serve a variety of secondary goals. Among these added gains of depression are the eliciting of nurturance from others, an ex-cuse of avoiding unwanted responsibilities, a rationalization for poor performance, or a method for safely (albeit indirectly) express-ing anger toward others. Partly determined by the gains received, depressive symptoms may take the form of dramatic gestures, irritable negativism, passive loneliness, or philosophi-cal intellectualizations.

- *The Orthogonal Hypothesis.* This hypothesis suggests that whereas personality disorders and depression are fundamentally indepen-dent entities, they frequently co-occur be-cause both are, in effect, common conditions. This notion relates to the influence of high prevalence or base rates; separate conditions that have high probabilities of occurring in a given population or setting will tend to be diagnosed together more often than those that are infrequently encountered within that pop-ulation or setting.

- *Overlapping Symptomatology Hypothesis.* According to this hypothesis, the observed comorbidity of personality disorders and depression is largely artifactual in that it re-sults from overlapping criteria sets em-ployed to diagnose each of the disorders. The influence of classification methods on comorbidity has been the subject of much recent research. Proponents of the overlap-ping symptomatology hypothesis cite the frequent inclusion of maladaptive affectiv-ity as being diagnostically relevant to a number of personality disorders, particu-larly those from the "dramatic-erratic" per-sonality cluster of DSM-III-R (Farmer & Gray, 1990). Such overlap may result in the assignment of two or more independent di-agnoses on a multiple axis for what is in fact a single disorder.

- *Heterogeneity Hypothesis.* This final hypothe-sis postulates that several different sources contribute to the signs and symptoms of depression and personality disorders. Various configurations of genetic/constitutional fac-tors in conjunction with environmental variables may combine to produce differing vulnerabilities to expressions of depression or personality pathology. A heterogeneous popu-lation arises from these various combinations including a subset of individuals who evidence both symptoms of personality disorder and depression. The heterogeneity hypothesis is most consistent with Millon's (1969, 1981, 1986) biopsychosocial conceptualization of personality and psychopathology.

The construct of a depressive personality disor-der was extensively discussed in the DSM-IV Per-sonality Work Group. It was concluded that the depressive personality be included as an enduring type of psychological disorder that evinces a rela-tively early onset, demonstrates a fairly stable and long-term course, and exhibits its many features across diverse situations over time.

In prior DSMs, the notion of a personality vari-ant of depressive character was conceptualized in part by the introduction of a construct termed *dys-thymic disorder* (previously, the depressive neuro-sis). However, it was soon recognized that the dysthymic construct was rather heterogeneous, necessitating differentiations into primary and secondary, as well as early and late-onset subtypes. Furthermore, the criteria employed for dysthymia emphasized mood symptomatology rather than a diverse set of personality traits. Moreover, the symptoms elaborated in the dysthymic category were largely of a somatic or vegetative character, rather than cognitive or interpersonal in nature. The desire was expressed that a depressively centered disorder be introduced whose symptoms were less severe, more social in character, and more prolonged, if not lifelong, compared with those encompassed in the dysthymic diagnosis. The introduction of the *self-defeating/masochistic* disorder was provisionally made in part to achieve these goals. Not only has the self-defeating/masochistic personality disorder been dropped from the most recent manual, a decision not shared by the authors of this book, but the depressive symptomatology it encompassed required that its features be intentionally provoked by others in response to the individual's desire to elicit punitively rejecting responses. Because of this focus, as well as other reasons, it was decided to introduce criteria, albeit provisionally, that represent a purer or prototypal variant of a *depressive personality disorder.* To elaborate on this disorder, we have chosen to include the depressive prototype in the present chapter, which we believe to be consistent with theory, clinical observation, and an extensive literature over the past many centuries.

HISTORICAL ANTECEDENTS

The history of depression in its manifold forms has been known to humankind since earliest recorded history. It has remained an enigma, however. The overt manifestations of the disorder are obvious to even the simplest of minds. Yet its underlying causes and shifting expressions are debated to the present time, as evident in intense discussions during the most recent DSM and ICD formulations. Does it covary with mania, is there an irritable, explosive component associated with it, does it wax and wane, is there a continuous chronic state with moments of greater and lesser intensity, is it an adaptive reaction to life circumstances, or a constitutionally based temperament with genetic origins? Through the ages, clinicians, theorists, and empiricists have sought answers to questions such as these.

Hippocrates gave the first formal medical description of depression, referring to it as melancholia. Empedocles initially proposed the four-elements model that served as the basis of the

physiological doctrines of Hippocrates. These four elements—fire, water, air, and the earth—were manifested in many spheres of life. As expressed in the human body, this model became the groundwork for the four humors, heat (blood), dryness (phlegm), moisture (yellow bile), and cold (black bile), found respectively and most prominently in the heart, brain, liver, and spleen. When these humors were balanced, the individual was in a healthful state; when unbalanced, illness occurred.

The predominance of black bile served as the substrate for melancholia. Although Hippocrates may have been the first to provide a medical description of depression, it was Aretaeus who presented a complete and very modern portrayal of the disorder. Moreover, Aretaeus proposed that melancholia was best attributed to psychological causes, having nothing to do with bile, or other bodily humors. Further, he was the first to recognize the covariation between manic behaviors and depressive moods, antedating the views of many clinical observers in the 16th and 17th century. Aretaeus wrote as follows:

The characteristic appearances, then, are not obscure; for the patients are dull or stern, dejected or unreasonably torpid, without any manifest cause: such is the commencement of melancholy. And they also become peevish, dispirited, sleepless and start up from a disturbed sleep. . . . But if the illness becomes more urgent, hatred, avoidance of the haunts of men, vain lamentations are seen; they complain of life and desire to die. (Quoted in Lewis, 1934)

A layperson, Robert Burton (1621) wrote a most impressive, if wandering work entitled *Anatomy of Melancholy* even though it was preceded by other works on melancholia in the 16th century. Sir William Osler judged Burton's immense and erudite work as the most significant medical treatise written by a layperson. It served as a guide to understanding melancholia for the next two centuries. As noted in Chapter 18 "Borderline Personality Disorders," it stimulated ideas concerning one or another of the several variants of depressive disorder, most notably the writings of Bonet, Schacht, and Herschel who, in turn, laid the groundwork for 19th-century French and German clinicians such as Baillarger, Falret, Feuchtersleben, Greisinger, and Kahlbaum. To illustrate, Feuchtersleben wrote (1847):

Here the senses, memory, and reaction give way, the nervous vitality languishes at its root, and the vitality of the blood, deprived of this stimulant, is languid in all its functions. Hence the slow and often difficult respiration, and proneness to sighing. . . . When they are chronic, they deeply affect vegetative life, and the body wastes away. (p. 135)

Kahlbaum (1882) was firm in the belief that mania and melancholia were a single disease that manifested itself in different forms and combinations over time. He termed the milder variant of these patterns *cyclothymia*.

Kraepelin (1896) borrowed heavily from his German predecessor Kahlbaum's formulations but separated the "personality" and "temperament" variants of cyclothymia from the manifest or clinical state of the disease. Nevertheless, he proposed the name *maniacal-depressive insanity* for "the whole domain of periodic and circular insanity," including such diverse disturbances as "the morbid states termed melancholia and certain slight colorings of mood, some of them periodic, some of them continuously morbid" (p. 161).

Like Kahlbaum, Kraepelin viewed "circular insanity" to be a unitary illness. Moreover, every disorder that gave evidence of mood disturbances—however regular or irregular; whatever the predominant affect, be it irritability, depression, or mania—was conceived by him to be a variant or "rudiment" of the same basic impairment. To Kraepelin, the common denominator for these disturbances was an endogenous metabolic dysfunction that was "to an astonishing degree independent of external influences" (p. 173).

In the eighth edition of his monumental *Psychiatrie* (1909–1915), Kraepelin began to formulate a number of subaffective personality conditions that are quite comparable to current depressive personality criteria. Thus, Kraepelin (1921) wrote:

There are certain temperaments which may be regarded as rudiments of manic-depressive *insanity. They may throughout the whole of life exist as peculiar forms of psychic personality, without further development; but they may also become the point of departure for a morbid process which develops under peculiar conditions and runs its course in isolated attacks. Not at all infrequently, moreover, the permanent divergencies are already in themselves so considerable that they also extend into the domain of the morbid without the appearance of more severe, delimited attacks. (p. 118)*

As was typical of his time, Kraepelin considered the disorder to be characterized by an inborn temperamental disposition characterized

"by a permanent gloomy emotional stress in all experiences in life" (p. 118). According to him, "the morbid picture is usually perceptible already in *youth*, and may persist without essential change throughout life" (p. 123). Kraepelin describes this persistent lifelong temperamental disposition in the following quotes:

Mental efficiency may be good, yet the patients, as a rule, have to struggle with all sorts of internal obstructions, which they only overcome with effort; they, therefore are easily fatigued. Moreover, they lack the right joy in work. Although they are often ambitious and strive upward with success, they yet do not find complete, lasting satisfaction in their work, as they keep in view the mistakes and deficiencies of their achievements, as well as the approaching difficulties, rather than the value of the thing accomplished. Therefore, difficulties and doubts very easily press upon them, which make them uncertain in their activity and occasionally force them to repeat the same piece of work again and again . . . Every moment of pleasure is embittered to them by the recollection of gloomy hours, by self-reproaches, and still more by glaringly portrayed fears for the future.

Many patients are constantly tormented by a certain *feeling of guilt, as if they had done something wrong, as if they had something to reproach themselves with. Sometimes the things are real, but very remote or quite insignificant, with which this tormenting uncertainty is connected.*

But it is especially their lack of self-confidence *which prevents them from cultivating personal relations. Compared with other people who are perhaps otherwise far beneath them, they appear to themselves awkward, boorish, foolish; they do not get rid of the tormenting feeling that they are continually exposing their weak spot, that the people around them look at them over the shoulder, that their presence is not desired. (pp. 119–122)*

MODERN FORMULATIONS

Continuing in the tradition of positing a depressive temperament set out most clearly in Kraepelin's work at the turn of the century, both Kurt Schneider and Ernst Kretschmer extended the notion of temperament in somewhat different directions. To Schneider (1923/1950), who termed these individuals *depressive psychopaths*, the essential element was a persistent sense of gloom. Unlike Kraepelin, however, as well as his contemporary Kretschmer,

Schneider considered the depressive personality to be an extreme variant of normal personality traits, rather than a facet or expression of major affective (manic-depressive) disorder. In line with German psychiatric tradition, however, he considered inborn constitutional dispositions to be at its core, with experiential factors playing only a modifying role. In his usual perceptive and succinct way, Schneider portrayed the disorder as follows:

The basic common characteristic of depressives is the constant pessimism or at any rate their very skeptical view of life, which they seem to reject yet at the same time seem to love in a rather dismal way. They tend to take everything seriously and have no capacity for frank enjoyment. They are prone to "see through" things and usually find something imperfect. They are apt to deplore the past and fear the future. They have little heart for their own purposes and are deeply distrustful. They are distracted by daily worries, hypochondriacal fears, self-analysis, doubt over life itself. Bogies of all description haunt them and they suffer a good deal from unhappy experiences and many crises. (pp. 79–80)

In his book *Physique and Character* (1925), Kretschmer follows the main line of thought originally proposed by Kraepelin to the effect that the manic and depressive qualities covary: In this regard he differed from his contemporary Schneider. Selecting the term *cycloid* to reflect this pattern of combined temperaments, Kretschmer perceived the depressive component to be a mixture of inborn chemical dispositions that exhibit themselves with depression at one end and mania at the other. In his experience with patients, Kretschmer records that he comes across those with primary hypermanic temperaments far more often than those he terms constitutional depressives. As in his formulation of the schizoid temperament, where patients may show varying proportions of the asthenic and hyperaesthetic temperament, Kretschmer notes that hypomanics are likely to possess a small depressive component, whereas those of a melancholic temper will likewise give occasional evidence of a "vein of humor." This relation between hypomanic and melancholic elements in cycloid personalities is called diathetic or mood proportion. Kretschmer describes aspects of the melancholic as follows:

Tears come easily to his eyes, he can't get over even quite little things, and he grieves longer and deeper than other people over sad situations. That is to say: In the case of such individuals, it is not that the temperament itself is sad, but only that it is more easily roused by sad conditions. And what is particularly significant is this: In difficult, responsible positions, when there is any danger, in thorny, exasperating situations, and in sudden precarious crises in business, they are not nervous, irritated, or agitated, like the average man, and particularly like a great many schizophrenes. But they are unhappy. They cannot see any distance ahead, everything stands like a mountain in front of them. (p. 130)

Continuing in the tradition of Kraepelin's temperament notions, Kahn (1931) describes the "gloomy" personality as follows:

Peculiar to them is " a constantly gloomy feeling tone in all life experiences" (Kraepelin). They have a serious attitude toward life, take everything hard, and are unable to throw things off; brooding was invented for them. As genuine pessimists they see the future dark and dangerous before them. Overestimating all difficulties they tend in general to underestimate themselves, to feel themselves insufficient, and they lack self-confidence and security. Here character elements are evident. In their sad mood and their insecurity they are often easily wounded and appear not infrequently exaggeratedly sensitive because they adjust very slowly to their experiences (Verhaltung—restraint—in Kretschmer's sense).

Many of the gloomy have an affective resonance of unusual depth, are compassionate and kind. It is almost as if the familiarity with suffering which marks their own nature had made them particularly sensitive to the suffering of others. There are gloomy persons of a deep affectivity who conceal their resonance in order to protect themselves. (pp. 212–213)

Turning the clock back to an earlier period of this century, Adolph Meyer (1951) initially welcomed the then new Kraepelinian classification system in 1902, adopting segments of its formulations, as evident in the following quote:

1. *Constitutional depression: a pessimistic temperament that is inclined to see the dark side of everything and is led to gloominess and despondency upon slight provocation.*

2. *Simple melancholia proper: an excessive or altogether unjustified depression, often accompanied by defective sleep, precordial pain or uneasiness; a susceptibility for the unpleasant and wearing aspect of things*

only, and a feeling of a self-deprecation, of sinfulness, without insight into the unwarranted morbid nature of the condition. The patient feels himself too bad to live or to be treated kindly.

3. Other forms are characterized by prolonged "neurasthenic" malaise and a feeling of depression (frequently over moral matters).

Clinical experience and experimental psychology show that there are undoubtedly several distinct disease processes which account for the differences of the above types. But definite statements as to their nature and concerning the pathological anatomy seem as yet premature (pp. 566–568).

Meyer soon became disillusioned with the Kraepelinian approach, essentially his fatalistic view of illness and his strictly deterministic prognosis and outcome for those of a depressive temperament. Meyer turned to a view increasingly shared by those of a psychoanalytic persuasion, that is, discarding the disease model and viewing psychiatric disorders, not as fundamentally organic conditions, but rather a consequence of environmental factors and life events.

Initially sympathetic to Freud's theories, Meyer soon became critical of the "mysticism" and "esoteric" nature of psychoanalysis. Despite his break from Freud's metapsychology, Meyer shared a common view regarding the role of life experiences as central to the emergence of all psychiatric disorders.

Psychoanalytic models of depression began with a key paper by Karl Abraham (1911), Approaching the "manic-depressive insanities" and their allied conditions from a developmental perspective, Abraham's view was that depression results from the inward turning of aggression. In this formulation, retroflexed anger is initially directed toward a desired/loved person who has thwarted the individual's need for dependency and love. Because the loved object has become internalized as part of oneself, the patient himself unwittingly becomes the target of the anger he feels. Taken to the extreme, the process results in self-destructive if not suicidal feelings.

In contrast to the clinical richness of descriptive psychiatry, as seen in the writings of Kraepelin and his disciples, Abraham continues the psychoanalytic model of searching for the causes and dynamics of the disorder. Following his mentor Freud, he begins a long process designed to explicate the underlying forces that give rise to the overt phenomenology of depression. Thus, Abraham speaks of the source of depression as follows (1911):

It is derived from an attitude of the libido in which hatred predominates. This attitude is first directed against the person's nearest relatives and becomes generalized later on. It can be expressed in the following formula: "I cannot love people; I have to hate them."

The pronounced feelings of inadequacy from which such patients suffer arise from this discomforting internal perception. If the content of the perception is repressed and projected externally, the patient gets the idea that he is not loved by his environment but hated by it (again first of all by his parents, etc., and then by a wider circle of people). This idea is detached from its primary causal connection with his own attitude of hate, and is brought into association with other—psychical and physical—deficiencies. It seems as though a great quantity of such feelings of inferiority favoured the formation of depressive states.

Thus, we obtain the second formula: "People do not love me, they hate me . . . because of my inborn defects. Therefore I am unhappy and depressed." (pp. 144–145)

Freud's 1917 paper *Mourning and Melancholia* interprets the essence of depression to be less a matter of anger toward self than a matter of loss internal to self. What is lost is not some external reality but some significant part of one's own ego. Contrasting the concept of mourning, a reality-based loss, with that of melancholia, an ego loss, Freud writes (1917/1925):

The distinguishing mental features of melancholia are a profoundly painful dejection, cessation of interest in the outside world, loss of the capacity to love, inhibition of all activity, and a lowering of the self-regarding feelings to a degree that finds utterance in self-reproaches and self-revilings, and culminates in a delusional expectation of punishment. This picture becomes a little more intelligible when we consider that, with one exception, the same traits are met with in mourning. The disturbance of self-regard is absent in mourning; but otherwise the features are the same. Profound mourning, the reaction to the loss of someone who is loved, contains the same painful frame of mind, the same loss of interest in the outside world.

In mourning we found that the inhibition and loss of interest are fully accounted for by the work of mourning in which the ego is absorbed. . . . The melancholic displays something else besides which is lacking in mourning—an extraordinary diminution in his self-regard, an impoverishment of his ego on a grand scale. In mourning it is the world which has become poor and empty; in melancholia it is the ego itself. The patient represents his ego to us as worthless, incapable of any achievement and morally despicable; he reproaches himself, vilifies himself and expects to be cast out and punished. He abases himself before everyone and commiserates with his own relatives for being connected with anyone so unworthy. (pp. 50–51)

Starting with Abraham's theory as a base, Freud's subsequent writings introduced a number of features of melancholia that were given primacy by later followers, notably characteristics such as (a) a marked deflation of self-esteem, (b) self-accusations, and (c) an almost delusional need for self-punishment.

Rado (1928, 1969) drew on the role of rage and self-punishment as central to the self-abusive behaviors seen in depressive characters. To Rado, depressively disposed individuals have an intense craving for love and approval. However, simultaneous with this need are intense ambivalences toward the object of love. To control against the expression of hostility, there is an intense sense of guilt. Self-punishment is seen as an expiatory act, a plea for forgiveness for the rage that one feels internally. Remorseful self-abuse and expiation is seen by Rado as the key element in depression. Rado phrases this formulation as follows (1928):

The most striking feature in the picture displayed by the symptoms of depressive conditions is the fall in self-esteem and self-satisfaction. The depressive neurotic for the most part attempts to conceal this disturbance; in melancholia it finds clamorous expression in the patients' delusional self-accusations and self-aspersions, which we call "the delusion of moral inferiority." (p. 421)

Summing up several elements of the psychoanalytic approach to the depressive character are the writings of Menninger. In describing the psychological mechanisms of melancholia, Menninger comments (1930):

It happens to people who, because of childhood experiences, are particularly incapable of bearing such a loss and react to it, therefore, terrifically. They react to it in a double way, first by feeling

that their ego has been impoverished, that there is no use in living, or that they are not worthy to live, and at the same time reproaching or attacking themselves as if they were guilty of something connected with the loss of this loved object. It has been found that they feel this way because the unconscious hate concealed in the feelings of love for the lost object is now reflected upon themselves so that they attack the loved person, as it were, for having gone away and at the same time punish themselves for this attack and hatred. (p. 121)

Deviating slightly from the core views of depressive characterizations formulated by her analytic colleagues, Horney (1945) portrays the disorder as one of "hopelessness." In portraying individuals in this fashion, Horney stresses not so much the causality of the depressive pattern, but rather its outlook and future perspectives. She writes:

Any minor failure may plunge him into a depression because it proves his general unworthiness—even when it is due to factors beyond his control. Any harmless critical remark may set him worrying or brooding, and so on. As a result, he is ordinarily more unhappy and discontented than the circumstances warrant.

This situation, bad enough as it stands, is aggravated by further consideration. Human beings can apparently endure an amazing amount of misery as long as there is hope; but neurotic entanglements invariably generate a measure of hopelessness, and the more severe the entanglements the greater the hopelessness. (pp. 179–180)

CONTEMPORARY PROPOSALS

In Fenichel's systematic survey of the psychoanalytic literature, he states that the minor as well as the more serious melancholic forms of depression have in common a decrease in self esteem. To him, a slightly sad person needs "consolation, narcissistic supplies" from the desired external object. A severely depressed individual becomes disturbed when these vital supplies are lacking. As Fenichel states (1945):

Depression is based on the same predisposition as addiction and pathological impulses. A person who is fixated on the state where his self esteem is regulated by external supplies or a person whose guilt feelings motivate him to regress to this state vitally needs these supplies. He goes through this world in a condition of perpetual greediness. If his narcissistic needs are not satisfied, his self-esteem diminishes to a danger point. (p. 387)

Blending the views of Horney and Fenichel are the contributions of Edward Bibring (1953). Depression is seen here as an independent state of the ego that is unrelated to the vicissitudes of retroflexed anger. Helplessness and loss of self-esteem are the focal points in Bibring's formulation. Depression is especially a vulnerability of the overambitious or the conventional, and arises when one is unable to live up to one's ego ideals, whether it is to be simply worthy and lovable, or to be strong and superior. Bibring writes:

In all instances, the depression accompanied by a feeling of being doomed, irrespective of what the conscious or unconscious background of this feeling may have been: In all of them a blow was dealt to the person's self-esteem, on whatever grounds such self-esteem may have been founded. From this point of view, depression can be defined as the emotional expression (indication) of a state of helplessness and powerlessness of the ego, irrespective of what may have caused the breakdown of the mechanisms which established his self-esteem. (p. 163)

In a particularly perceptive essay on masochism, Bieber (1974) describes an experiential basis for the phenomenon in a manner that is less psychoanalytic than it is social-learning. He writes:

. . . a basic principle of masochism: self-inflicted injury wards off threats believed to be even more injurious. . . . When children are given nonambivalent parental affection only when ill, injured, or failing in some respect, it would appear . . . that the victim will likely evolve masochistic coping behavior. (p. 325)

Continuing the analytic tradition in its finest sense, Kernberg (1988) has formulated a rich and detailed taxonomy regarding the personality disorders, including a type he refers to as the depressive-masochist; more will be said about this personality in Chapter 16. For the present, it should be noted that Kernberg's views correspond closely to the description of "moral masochism" in the psychoanalytic literature. A brief quote will suffice:

The sense of being rejected and mistreated in reaction to minor slights may lead these patients to unconscious behaviors geared to making the objects of their love feel guilty . . . ; consequent actual rejection from others may spiral into severe problems in intimate relations and may also trigger depression connected to loss of love. (p. 1089)

Brief reference should be made to the work of Bowlby (1969, 1973, 1980) who presented the notion that two fundamental personality variants experience the intensity of "loss" to an extent that produces a deep feeling of depression. Thus, Bowlby describes those who are "anxiously attached," at the one extreme versus those who are "compulsively self-reliant" at the other. According to Bowlby, excessive self-reliance is merely a defensive action against the experience of early loss and frustration, a response against the possibility of being drawn into dependency and caretaking roles for others. By contrast, those who are "anxiously attached" seek interpersonal closeness at almost any cost, becoming increasingly dependent on these figures for their security, and resulting in a deeper concern about the stability about these relationships. This contrast of two depressively inclined character patterns is seen more clearly in the work of Beck (1983) and Blatt and Schichman (1983).

A model paralleling both Bowlby's and Beck's depressive character structures, but one more in line with psychoanalytic metapsychology has been proposed by S. Blatt (1974), who formulates his notions as follows:

A character style in which there is unusual susceptibility to dysphoric feelings, a vulnerability to feelings of loss and disappointment, intense needs for contact and support, and a proclivity to assume blame and responsibility and to feel guilty.

While types of depression are probably interrelated on a continuum, a simple or "anaclitic depression" . . . describes an infantile type of object choice in which the mother is sought to soothe and provide comfort and care. This type of depression results from early disruption of the basic relationship with the primary object and can be distinguished from an "introjective depression," which results from a harsh, punitive, unrelentingly critical superego that creates intense feelings of inferiority, worthlessness, guilt, and a wish for atonement. (1974, pp. 109, 114)

Although originally trained in the psychoanalytic mold, A. T. Beck has moved increasingly in the direction of a cognitive model for understanding personality and depression (Beck, 1976, 1983; Beck & Freedman, 1990b). Like Bibring, Beck proposes that helplessness and hopelessness lie at the center of depressed personalities. In his theoretical model, Beck postulates the presence of underlying irrational schemas that derive from early developmental experiences. Two such schemas related to personality styles are detailed (Beck, 1983). The first he terms *sociotropy,* characterized by dysfunctional beliefs associated with the need for love and approval (e.g., I am worthless if everyone doesn't love me). The second personality schema is termed autonomy and is characterized by deep perfectionistic beliefs (e.g., If I make a mistake, I am a worthless person). Although Beck does not view these two cognitive schemas to be fixed personality types themselves, one may dominate an individual's cognitive functioning to a marked extent and ultimately produce exaggerated perceptions and emotional responses. Beck writes:

Sociality *(sociotropy) refers to the person's investment in positive interchange with other people. This cluster includes passive receptive wishes (acceptance, intimacy, understanding, support, guidance); "narcissistic wishes" (admiration, prestige, status); and feedback—validation of beliefs and behavior. The individual is dependent on these social "inputs" for gratification, motivation, direction, and modification of ideas and behavior. The motif of this cluster is "receiving."*

Individuality *(autonomy) refers to the person's investment in preserving and increasing his independence, mobility, and personal rights; freedom of choice, action and expression; protection of his domain; and defining his boundaries. The person's sense of well-being depends on preserving his integrity and autonomy of his domain; directing his own activities; freedom from outside encroachment, restraint, constraint, or interference; and attaining meaningful goals. The motif of this cluster is "doing." (p. 272)*

According to Beck, personality and depression differ in that the schemas operate more continuously in those with depressive personality disorders, but are more intermittent and latent in those with simple depressions.

Another highly inventive model of personality disorders is grounded in a well-articulated interpersonal model by Lorna Benjamin (1974, 1993a,

1993b). In her effort to fuse a relationship between personality and depression, Benjamin focuses on two central elements; helplessness and self-criticism. Social withdrawal and interpersonal disengagement may also be present, but Benjamin considers them a secondary reaction or defense against more fundamental tendencies. And in contrast to recent temperament-neurobiological models, Benjamin gives primary emphasis to early experiences and social learning. In her recent analysis of the depressive pattern, Benjamin writes (1993):

I expect that depression follows the patient's perception that he or she is helpless, trapped, blocked, overwhelmed, and without recourse. I also believe that depression is likely to be manifested when there is a perceived loss of an attachment object, or when there is an event that enhances self-criticism.

Measures of these predispositions toward helplessness, self-criticism, and sensitivity to object loss can be considered indices of aspects of "personality" that are relevant to depression.

A person can feel helpless or self-critical or abandoned because of a predisposition, a reaction to overwhelming external circumstance, or some interaction between the two. The predisposition may be determined by genetics or experience or both. To separate the "broken brain" version of the predisposing model from the "environmentally programmed" version of the predisposing model, one would need to engage in very careful sequential analysis of the development of a person's view of himself or herself and the environment. (pp. 124–125)

Owing to the recency of the DSM-IV depressive personality characterization, most factor analytic theorists on the contemporary scene have not had an opportunity to formulate their conceptions of the disorder in line with their clinical models. Nevertheless, these methodologies have been applied, albeit tentatively, in the inventive analysis of Costa and Widiger (1994). In their effort to decode the underlying or latent traits that combine to give rise to the depressive personality, these authors recognize difficulties in separating the depressive from the masochistic (self-defeating) types. They write:

The DPS proposal is quite similar to that of SDF, but it does involve an elimination of the features of low conscientiousness and most of the features of agreeableness. Only one of the diagnostic criteria

for DPS involves low agreeableness (negativistic, critical, and judgmental of others). The DPS criteria are then largely confined to neuroticism and in particular to the one facet of trait depression (dejection, gloomy, cheerless, low self-esteem, feelings of inadequacy, self-blaming, brooding, pessimistic and guilty). (p. 53)

Although a contemporary of the preceding authors, Donald Klein (Klein & Davis, 1969; Klein et al., 1980), a noted psychopharmocological psychiatrist, has played a major role in contemporary thinking concerning the biological substrates of various character and personality disorders. Klein makes a series of subtle distinctions that are worthy of note in approaching the depressive personality disorder. The separation he draws relates to whether the individual is capable of pleasurable experiences or whether this capacity is totally lacking. Thus, in what he terms "the endogenous depressive group" pathological states result from an intense nonreactive and pervasive impairment in the ability to experience pleasure or respond affectively to anticipation. As Klein states it:

This key inhibition of the pleasure mechanism results in a profound lack of interest and investment in the environment, often associated with inability to enjoy food, sex, or hobbies. (Klein et al., 1980, p. 234)

The second category is termed the *characterological dysphoric.* Here, the individual is capable of experiencing pleasure but it is overwhelmed by a preoccupation with pervasive unhappiness. As Klein et al. (1980) put it:

Chronic dysphorics are constantly dissatisfied and describe severe subjective distress, unhappiness, and apathy. By chronic it is meant that this is not a phasic disorder, but a predominant characteristic of most of the patient's adult life.

Chronic dysphorics often maintain a facade of chronic unhappiness when confronted with interested or sympathetic observers. However, under some social circumstances, they participate in an active, outgoing, friendly, and pleasurable manner. A particularly favorable environment for this affective shift is the company of the similarly afflicted or admiring, subservient friends. Here, sad tales of lifelong distress may be zestfully related. (p. 247)

The biological orientation of recent years concerning a depressive character structure has been carried out most impressively by Hagop Akiskal and associates (1981, 1983, 1984, 1992). As a consequence of his research, particularly those related to treatment outcome, Akiskal believes that the characterological depressions may be divided into two broad categories: subaffective dysthymics and character spectrum disorders. He summarizes a vast body of biological indicators in the following manner (1980):

Our data suggest the existence of a heterogeneous group of chronic depressions. Even when those depressions accompanying unipolar and disabling nonaffective illnesses are excluded, we are still left with at least two types of characterological depressions. "Subaffective dysthymias" have affinity to primary affective illness (both unipolar and bipolar); and "character spectrum disorders" consist of a broad array of personality disorders with secondary dysphoria. (p. 783)

In his recent studies of the character spectrum concept, Akiskal proposes a multicausal etiologic schema in which affective personality traits are viewed as mediating variables that link deeper biological dispositions to environmental risk factors. As he sees it, these temperamental dispositions are subclinically active on a continuous basis but are easily triggered by environmental challenges.

In later publications on the affective temperaments, Akiskal (1984, 1992) writes of subaffective dysthymics, subaffective cyclothymics, and subaffective borderlines. The first group demonstrates as primary features what might be characterized as a depressive personality, exhibiting Schneiderian traits such as passivity, assertiveness, pessimism, anhedonia, self-criticism, brooding, and inadequacy preoccupations. In referring to the cyclothymic segment of the spectrum disorder, he refers to the presence of tempestuous relationships, drug or alcohol use, instability, irritable qualities, explosive outbursts followed by guilt, and erratic work habits. In the subaffective borderline disorder, he speaks of consistent instability, vulnerability to object loss, substance abuse, and the presence of histrionic and antisocial features.

In line with the notion that significant elements of temperament influence the character of personality, the work of Larry Siever (Klar & Siever, 1985; Siever & Davis, 1991) would be well worth noting. In Siever's conception of *affective instability,* defined "as a predisposition to marked, rapidly reversible shifts in affective states that are extremely sensitive to meaningful environmental events" (Siever & Davis, 1991, p. 1651), he proposes a common core liability for a variety of affective disorders. The causal mechanism for this vulnerability is a cholinergic dysfunction, as indicated in variety of biological markers. Noradrenergic dysregulations are posited as the mechanism underlying the classical vegetative symptoms of an autonomous endogenous depressive temperament. Those with this core affective sensitivity are inclined to become dysthymic or cyclothymic, depending on their developmental history. Given certain patterns of early life experience, this vulnerability may be shaped into a persistent depressive pathology. Siever and Davis describe this temperament-experience interaction as follows:

Affective states may also powerfully color the way in which the world is experienced, encoded internally, and retrieved from memory. Thus, the way in which developing children perceive themselves in relation to others may depend in part on their affective state.

Affectively unstable children might be expected to be more sensitive to transient frustrations and separations throughout their development, thus impairing their mastery of these inevitable concomitants of normal development and distorting their self-image and affective perception of others . . . Their appraisal of themselves and others may be powerfully influenced by intense, recurrent dysphoric feelings, so that many tend to experience themselves in the context of the negative feelings of separation as "defective" and their caretakers as abandoning or frustrating. (p. 1655)

Another recent model anchored to a neurobiological theory of personality has been formulated by C. R. Cloninger (1986, 1987, 1993). In his elegant construction, Cloninger does not specifically address the concept of a depressive temperament or personality, although the implications of such inclinations are articulated in a broad model that encompasses both anxiety and affective disorders. As described in Chapter 2, Cloninger proposes that anxiety, affective, and personality disorders are anchored to a fundamental set of heritable traits (novelty seeking, harm avoidance, reward dependence), each of which derives from a neurobiological substrate (dopaminergic, serotonergic, and noradrenergic, respectively). It is the interaction of these heritable traits that give shape to the development of personality by influencing a wide range of experiential processes such as learning, cognition, mood, and general adaptation. It should be noted, however, that Cloninger proposes the presence of an autonomous affective

disorder that is related neither to personality nor environmental stressors. How the elements of his theory can be interwoven to generate a depressive personality or character type remains an open question in Cloninger's model.

Although the syndrome labeled "dysthymia" was seen by some as a concept akin to a depressive personality disorder, neither the DSM-III nor the DSM-III-R came to grips with the need to include a composite of several non-mood-related traits to justify conceiving the syndrome as a personality type; hence, in effect, and as a formality, neither DSM included the depressive personality disorder in their descriptive manual. The inclusion of the self-defeating personality in the Appendix of DSM-III-R served tangentially to encompass features similar to what is now termed the depressive personality; in fact, a number of thoughtful clinicians have spoken of them as a joint syndrome (e.g., the depressive-masochistic character) (Kernberg, 1984). Despite their characterological overlap, they have been considered by most theorists as two conceptually distinct prototypes, as we have formulated them in this text. Moreover, it was not the intent of the DSM-III-R developers to introduce the self-defeating type as an alternate or substitute for a depressive personality disorder. An explicit and detailed discussion regarding the personality characteristics of the latter category did not take place until the developmental phases of the DSM-IV. Despite extensive debates and disagreements, notably the fear that this category might incline clinicians not to employ potentially effective psychopharmacological agents with a personality disorder, a decision was made to introduce the personality variant of the depressive spectrum into the Appendix of the official manual.

The essential feature of this DSM-IV disorder is a pervasive pattern of depressive cognitions and behaviors. Several clinical domains are included among the diagnostic criteria. Mood is central, of course, summarized in one criterion: affect dominated by feelings of dejection, gloominess, cheerlessness, and joylessness. Three cognitive criteria are recorded: a tendency toward brooding and worry, dwelling persistently on negative and unhappy thoughts; pessimism, as seen in doubts that things ever improve, always anticipating the worst; a proneness to feelings of guilt and remorse, as seen in severe self-judgments for shortcomings and failures. Self-image criteria are likewise included, notably beliefs of personal inadequacy, worthlessness, and low self-esteem: being self-critical, self-blaming, and self-derogatory. The sole interpersonal criterion signifies an extension of self-attitudes redirected toward others, namely; negativistic, critical, and harshly judgmental of others.

Notable was the decision of the ICD-10 committee not to include a depressive character type in their personality disorders listing (features of similar cast are to be found in the ICD category of "affective personalities," a section subsumed under the mood disorders).

Millon (1994) has recently outlined some of the key features of the disorder in terms of his polarity schema. The clinical derivations of this formulation make up the major body of this chapter. Figure 8.1. portrays the polarity model; the text of the chapter outlines the elements of the disorder in terms of its clinical domains, predisposing background, and therapeutic interventions. A brief summary of the clinical characteristics of the disorder is noted next, following which the features of the polarity model will be portrayed:

Characteristics include glumness, pessimism, lack of joy, the inability to experience pleasure, and motoric retardation. There has been a significant loss, a sense of giving up, and a loss of hope that joy can be retrieved. Notable is an orientation to pain, despair regarding the future, a disheartening and woebegone outlook, an irreparable and irretrievable state of affairs in which what might have been is no longer possible.

DEPRESSIVE PROTOTYPE

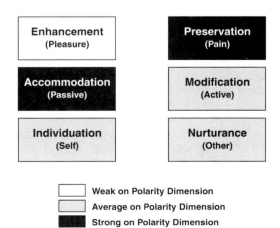

Enhancement (Pleasure)	**Preservation** (Pain)
Accommodation (Passive)	**Modification** (Active)
Individuation (Self)	**Nurturance** (Other)

☐ Weak on Polarity Dimension
▨ Average on Polarity Dimension
■ Strong on Polarity Dimension

Figure 8.1 Status of the depressive personality prototype in accord with the Millon Polarity Model.

This personality experiences pain as permanent with pleasure no longer considered possible. What experiences or chemistry can account for such persistent or pervasive sadness? Clearly, there are biological dispositions to take into account. The evidence favoring a constitutional predisposition is strong, much of it favoring genetic factors. The thresholds involved in permitting pleasure or sensitizing one to sadness vary appreciably. Some individuals are inclined to pessimism and a disheartened outlook. Similarly, experience can condition a hopeless orientation. A significant loss, a disconsolate family, a barren environment, and hopeless prospects can all shape the depressive character style. (Millon, 1994, p. 11)

If we review the theoretically generated polarity model, as illustrated in Figure 8.1, we should note a strong representation in both the *preservation* polar extreme and the *accommodating* ecological adaptation style. This signifies, first, an overconcern with pain and anguish, and second, that the person has "given up," essentially succumbing to what is judged to be the inevitability of continuing suffering and misery. Despite important similarities, this depressive pattern contrasts in significant ways from the schema representing the avoidant personality. In both personality disorders, there is an adaptive focus on preservation and pain reduction; similarly, in both disorders there is an inattention to the pleasures and gratifications that could enhance life. The core distinction in ecological adaptation is that the avoidant actively seeks to minimize pain by anticipating its eventuality and taking steps to distance from or avoid that possibility. By contrast, the depressive no longer attempts to avoid the anguish and despair of life. Rather, he or she has accepted it as if it were inevitable and insurmountable. Depressives remain passive, resigned to the distressing realities that they have suffered, no longer seeking to eschew it, but to surrender to it.

A review of the major historical contributors is given in Figure 8.2.

CLINICAL FEATURES

Several aspects of the depressive personality can be usefully differentiated for preliminary diagnostic purposes. The first phase of this assessment process attempts to delineate eight prototypal

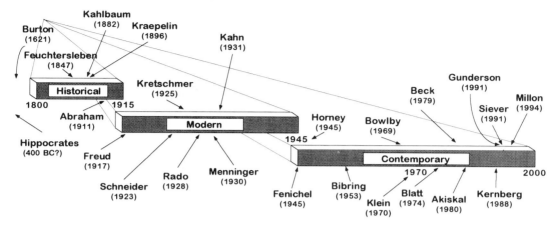

Figure 8.2   Historical review of major contributors to the depressive personality disorder.

domains in which the clinical features of the depressive can be separately analyzed and described.

PROTOTYPAL DIAGNOSTIC DOMAINS

As in all of the chapters of this text, we have sorted the various components of each disordered personality's traits and characteristics into eight domains, beginning with those that manifest themselves in the overt behavior of the individual to those that are essentially hidden from observation but may be discerned inferentially and measured biologically (see Table 8.1 and Figure 8.3).

Expressive Behavior: Disconsolate

It is difficult not to recognize the disconsolate appearance of depressive personalities. Their posture conveys a deeply forlorn and heavyhearted quality. Their speech is somber, woebegone, if not grief stricken in its character of expression. The tone of their voice seems irremediably dispirited and discouraged, and they portray a visual image of unresolvable hopelessness and wretchedness.

It can be said unquestionably that the depressive shows little initiative or spontaneity. Although answering questions posed in the interview process, depressives tend not to offer information on their own; moreover, what they do say has little variety. For the most part, speech is halting and uncertain. There is a slow, draggy element to all aspects of the depressed expressive behavior. Responses and movements take a long time, and even among those who are inclined to be agitated and

irritable, there is a marked reduction in purposeful or intentional behaviors. Much of their activity appears as if it were portrayed in slow motion.

Interpersonal Conduct: Defenseless

Depressive personalities evince a constant state of feeling vulnerable, assailable, and unprotected. They act as if they were defenseless and unshielded and, hence, beseech others to be protective and nurturant. Always fearing abandonment and desertion, their interpersonal behaviors are either one of two basic varieties, that of an unprotected and inadequate individual who passively withdraws from others, or a needy and demanding person who seeks others to provide assurances of affection and steadfastness.

First and foremost, the moods and complaints of the depressive are designed to summon nurturant responses from others. He recruits from both family and friends reassurances of his lovability and value to them, and seeks to gain assurances of their faithfulness and devotion to him. As with many other personality disorders, the depressive's symptoms may serve as an instrument for avoiding unwelcome responsibilities. This is especially effective with these personalities because they openly admit their worthlessness and are able to demonstrate their general sense of helplessness for all to see. In this regard, their impairment serves also as a rationalization for their indecisiveness and their failures. Here, their complaints may be colored with subtle accusations, claims that others have not been sufficiently supportive of them, thus fostering further

TABLE 8.1 Clinical Domains of the Depressive Prototype

Behavioral Level

(F) Expressively Disconsolate. Appearance and posture conveys an irrelievably forlorn, somber, heavy-hearted, woebegone, if not grief-stricken quality; irremediably dispirited and discouraged, portraying a sense of permanent hopelessness and wretchedness.

(F) Interpersonally Defenseless. Owing to feeling vulnerable, assailable, and unshielded, will beseech others to be nurturant and protective; fearing abandonment and desertion, will not only act in an endangered manner, but seek, if not demand assurances of affection, steadfastness, and devotion.

Phenomenological Level

(F) Cognitively Pessimistic. Possesses defeatist and fatalistic attitudes about almost all matters, sees things in their blackest form and invariably expects the worst; feeling weighed down, discouraged, and bleak, gives the gloomiest interpretation of current events, despairing as well that things will never improve in the future.

(S) Worthless Self-Image. Judges oneself of no account, valueless to self or others, inadequate and unsuccessful in all aspirations; barren, sterile, impotent, sees self as inconsequential and reproachable, if not contemptible, a person who should be criticized and derogated, as well as feel guilty for possessing no praiseworthy traits or achievements.

(S) Forsaken Objects. Internalized representations of the past appear jettisoned, as if life's early experiences have been depleted or devitalized, either drained of their richness and joyful elements, or withdrawn from memory, leaving one to feel abandoned, bereft, and discarded, cast off and deserted.

Intrapsychic Level

(F) Asceticism Mechanism. Engages in acts of self-denial, self-punishment, and self-tormenting, believing that one should exhibit penance and be deprived of life's bounties; not only is there a repudiation of pleasures, but there are harsh self-judgments, as well as self-destructive acts.

(S) Depleted Organization. A scaffold for morphologic structures that is markedly weakened, with coping methods enervated and defensive strategies impoverished, emptied, and devoid of their vigor and focus, resulting in a diminished, if not exhausted capacity to initiate action and regulate affect, impulse, and conflict.

Biophysical Level

(S) Melancholic Mood. Typically woeful, gloomy, tearful, joyless, and morose; characteristically worrisome and brooding; the low spirits and dysphoric state rarely remit.

(F) = Functional domain.
(S) = Structural domain.

DEPRESSIVE PROTOTYPE

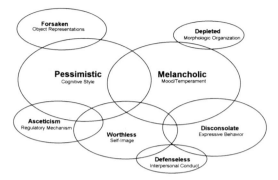

Figure 8.3 Salience of personologic domains in the depressive prototype.

their sense of futility and hopelessness. Overt expressions of hostility, however, are rarely exhibited because they fear that such actions will prove offensive and lead others to rebuke or reject them. As a result, anger and resentment are discharged only in subtle or oblique forms. Depressives often do this by overplaying their helplessness and ineffectuality, not only creating guilt in others thereby, but causing them no end of discomfort as they attempt to meet the patient's seemingly justified need for care and nurturance.

Depressives crave the love and support of others, but fail to reciprocate in ways that either gratify others or reinforce a positive relationship. The depressive's clinging behaviors, self-preoccupation, and devious coping maneuvers may ultimately evoke annoyance and exasperation from others. Under these circumstances, depressives may be persistent in soliciting the sympathy they desperately need. Failing in this regard, they may turn inward into bitter silence and guilty self-reproach. Protestations of guilt and self-condemnation may not only come to the fore, but may be unrelieved and pervasive.

Cognitive Style: Pessimistic

Depressives see life in its blackest form, and invariably expect that the worst will happen. They give the gloomiest of interpretations about events, despairing that things will ever improve in the future. They feel weighed down, discouraged, and bleak, possessing a pessimistic, defeatist, and fatalistic attitude about almost all matters. To make matters worse, depressives seem totally preoccupied with themselves and their plight, obsessively worrying about their misfortunes, both past and present.

Not only are depressives filled with remorse for their felt inadequacies, but they occasionally imagine fantasied resolutions to their difficulties that involve some magical event or omnipotent force. At heart, however, they have little hope that any solution can ever be found. Their communications with others are stereotypical and grayishly colored. Efforts may be made to fight back depressive feelings and thoughts by consciously diverting ideas and preoccupations away from one's depressive moods. For the most part, these new ruminations are replaced by equally troublesome ones. There is a tendency to reactivate and then to brood over minor incidents of the past. Thoughts and feelings that are *not* part of the depressive's preoccupations are as clinically significant as are those with which they are preoccupied. Retrospective falsification is not uncommon; few of the pleasures of the past are remembered, only those of a painful and distressing nature.

Depressives believe that their present state is irreversible and that any attitude other than pessimism or gloom is merely illusory. In what has been termed the "helplessness-hopelessness" outlook, these patients assume that they are unable to help themselves and are unlikely to be helped by outside forces as well (Engel, 1968). Most personalities can endure an astounding degree of misfortune, as long as they believe that there is hope for them. In the depressive, the pessimistic schemas that repeatedly shape their thoughts generate increasing levels of hopelessness, such that they are unable to imagine or plan conditions that could make things better. For the depressive, life seems to create an ever deeper well of hopelessness.

Self-Image: Worthless

Depressives tend to feel guilty for possessing no praiseworthy traits or achievements. They regard themselves to be valueless to self and others, inadequate and unsuccessful in all aspirations of a meaningful life. Not only do they view themselves as sterile, impotent, and of no consequential value, but they judge themselves also as reproachable, if not contemptible—as persons who *should* be criticized and derogated.

Almost any minor failure can plunge moderately unhappy depressives into a more severe state of disconsolation; such an event only proves further their state of unworthiness. Similarly, a rather harmless critical remark may set into motion obsessive worrying and brooding, further intensifying their sense of worthlessness. Even when matters are going well, there remains a deep sense of personal inadequacy, a feeling of being deficient in a host of attractive qualities, such as being popular, intelligent, physically appealing, and so on. Should adverse experiences occur, depressives will attribute its cause to some deficiency within themselves, thereby criticizing themselves for possessing the alleged defect. When difficulties become increasingly problematic, depressives are prone to blame themselves for circumstances that have no connection to them. They believe that they are incapable of taking the initiative and making decisions, reflecting their fear that they will make the wrong move or display their inadequacies for others to see.

Many depressive personalities reach so deep a level of self-denigration that they begin to take pity on themselves. When feelings of hopelessness and self-sympathy reach so low a state, there is a possibility that constructive outcomes may follow. In certain cases, depressives may feel that they have "paid their price" by sinking to the bottom of life, and that they can go no deeper into their depression than they have. Now may be a time for renewal, for an inner salvation that may be worth pursuing. On the other hand, it is at these times also that a formidable danger of self-destructiveness may take hold as well.

Object-Representations: Forsaken

We use the term object-representations to represent a series of silent, inner assumptions about the character of significant others, as well as life in general. It relates to unconscious premises that give shape to how the individual interprets the transient events of everyday life. It comprises distinctly personal expectations and assumptions that are used to selectively interpret and integrate significant experiences, and contains unarticulated rules and dispositional inferences that serve both to accurately interpret observations, as well as to repetitively and erroneously distort them.

In the phenomenologically oriented world of cognitive modes (Millon et al., 1994) that are referred to with terms such as schemas, these dispositional sets relate to how events are screened, differentiated, and interpreted, largely in a conscious manner. But there is an unconscious matrix of schemas as well that refer to significant intrapsychic structures which also selectively categorize and evaluate experiences beneath the level of awareness. It is these latter schemas that we refer to when we speak of object-representations, an unconscious tendency to mold perceptions and cognitions in line with inner templates that were given shape and character earlier in life. These templates may remain inactive for periods of time, but become energized and prominent when stimulated by relevant reality experiences. Activated, they transform what is actually happening in reality so as to make it fit the unconscious template of expectancy and assumption. In the depressed, this template saturates ongoing experiences and thoughts with a pessimistic and negativistic tone.

In effect, the content of the depressive's inner world appears to be devitalized, jettisoned, or depleted. It appears overtly drained of its richness or joyful elements. What good things happened in the past, what happy memories and fulfillments may have been experienced, appear to have been withdrawn from memory, leaving the depressive feeling forsaken, perhaps abandoned and bereft, perhaps discarded and cast off.

Regulatory Mechanisms: Asceticism

The dynamic processes of the intrapsychic world of the depressive have as their primary goal the fulfillment of a belief that one should experience penance and be deprived of life's bounties. Through the ascetic mechanism, depressives maneuver their inner world to achieve self-denial, self-punishment, and self-tormenting. Not only is there a diminution or repudiation of pleasurable memories, but those that persist are transformed into their opposite through harsh self-appraisals and, if need be, self-destructive acts.

With so punitive an attitude toward self, depressives allow themselves minimal pleasure, if any, and constantly appraise their own actions to determine whether they have attained more joy and satisfaction than they deserve. Driven by the feeling that they deserve less rather than more, they may give up totally on themselves and abdicate from life altogether. In a sense, they have adopted a mechanism of "playing dead" as a means of remaining alive. Self-abdication and total resignation from life have become intrapsychic maneuvers to permit them to avoid total annihilation by suicide, an act of self-jettisoning that lies but a moment ahead.

Morphologic Organization: Depleted

The overall scaffold for the intrapsychic structures of the depressive appears markedly weakened, unable to withstand much stress without decompensating. Coping methods are enervated and dynamic strategies seem impoverished. These forces that maintain psychic cohesion appear to have been emptied or devoid of focus and vigor. As a consequence, the depressive shows a diminished, if not exhausted capacity to initiate overt action or to regulate internal affects, impulses, and conflicts.

To protect against these feelings of inner ineffectuality, depressives struggle intrapsychically to keep their distressing feelings at as low a level as possible, to keep them out of awareness, and to ignore both their origins and their current realities. By structuring the inner world in this manner, depressives can minimize the experience of psychic pain. Moreover, they may succeed in isolating their affect to such an extent that they manifest only the overt appearance and complaints of depression, without experiencing its emotional undertone. In a rather circuitous manner, it is at these times that we often find the patient inclined to self-destruction and suicide. Drained of feeling and life, these depressives may conclude that there is little meaning to life and that they can no longer control and direct it. Perhaps it is only when they act to kill themselves that they can regain the feeling of competence and autonomy. The occasionally observed phenomenon of improved mood just prior to taking one's own life is related to this defensive maneuver. Should the preceding sentence be erroneously interpreted, let us note that suicide more commonly occurs when these patients seek to escape from painful or humiliating life circumstances.

Mood/Temperament: Melancholic

Depressives are characteristically gloomy, morose, and tearful. Brooding and feeling inescapably worried, with low spirits and a woeful and joyless mood, their pervasive dysphoric state may persist at a moderate level in severity, remitting only on rare occasions. Their self-denigration and habitual gloom are so deeply ingrained that they have become intrinsic parts of their personality structure. Although certain subtypes may emphasize one or another aspect of the depressive constellation of symptoms—sad feelings, anguish, irritability, guilt, emptiness, longing— it is clear that these patients have a diminished interest in life, few appetites for joy and close-ness, and although they go through the motions of relating, eating, sexualizing, even play, they do so with but little enthusiasm. Their temperamentally based inertia and sadness may undermine what-ever capacity they may have had to smile and enjoy the humor and pleasures of life.

Further reinforcing the belief that there are physiological underpinnings to this temperamental disposition are the variety of vegetative functions they display, even lowered metabolic rates and slowed gastrointestinal functions. Most commonly, complaints include difficulty in sleeping, early morning awakening, fatigue, diminished libido and appetite, as well as various bodily aches and pains. For some, the dysregulation of the hormonal sub-strates of mood are such that they may, for brief periods of time, become euphoric and socially dri-ven, almost to the point in some of crossing the threshold to hypomania. More often, however, we are likely to observe a persistent dysthymic or melancholic temperament.

PROTOTYPAL VARIANTS

Variations can be seen in all personality disorders, some more clearly differentiated, others adhering closely to the core prototypal pattern. Of interest are not only these adult pathological variations, but the more-or-less normal types, as well as the frequently observed childhood syndromes.

In our judgment, normality and depression-as-personality are rarely seen. What we do see are so-called normal individuals who exhibit depres-sionlike periods (e.g., mourning, grief, dejection), usually in response to external precipitants (e.g., death, divorce, job loss). Thus, "normal depres-sion" is rarely a personality disorder, but a tempo-rary and externally induced state of affairs. With these factors in mind, we will now discuss child-hood forms of a pervasive and enduring depressive character.

Childhood Syndromes

The problematic nature of depression in children may be seen by the contrast between two distin-guished analysts some two or three decades ago. According to Mahler (1967):

We know that the systematized affective disorders are unknown in childhood. It has been conclusively

established that the immature personality structure of the infant or older child is not capable of produc-ing a state of depression as that seen in the adult. (p. 342)

By contrast, the work of Rene Spitz (1965) sug-gests that some infants develop severe depression-like reactions upon maternal separation. Spitz reported weepy, withdrawal, and lethargic behav-iors, what he termed "anaclitic depression," a pat-tern noted by weight loss, frozen facial expressions, and a faraway gaze. Bowlby (1958) has likewise re-ferred to the characteristics of children separated from their mothers as a serious form of infant dis-turbance; avoiding the depressive term for such behaviors, Bowlby calls these reactions "mourning secondary to separation." Reviewing the literature over the preceding decades, Mendelson (1974) con-cludes that childhood depression theorists have shown a marked lack of clinical familiarity with the subject material they have freely discussed and elaborated. To him:

It would seem that in no other area of the psycho-analytic literature on depressives are the theoreti-cal papers so far removed from the observations that any clinician can make in the course of his daily practice. (p. 165)

In attempting to explain the ostensive low prevalence of childhood depression, some clini-cians assert that these low frequencies may be a consequence of children's inability to verbalize or articulate the deeper moods they experience. In contrast to the obvious motoric hyperactivity of many disturbed children, young depressives do not manifest an easily observable set of charac-teristics; rather, their depressive feelings must be inferred from their subdued behaviors and inex-pressive facial features.

Summarizing the characteristics of depressive symptoms found in children, Sandler and Joffe (1965) record the following as typical of the per-vasively melancholic child, a description not un-like what we would term a childhood syndrome. Included are:

1. An appearance of being sad and unhappy.
2. A social withdrawal and lack of interest.
3. An attitude of discontent, with little capacity for pleasure.

4. A sense of feeling unloved or rejected, with a consequential distancing from those who have been disappointing.

5. An unwillingness to accept comforting overtures from others.

6. A general tendency toward "oral passivity."

7. The presence of insomnia or other sleep disturbances.

8. Occasional autoerotic activities.

9. Difficulty in maintaining therapeutic contact.

In reviewing the durability and persistence that typifies a pathology of personality, Arieti and Bemporad (1978) describe the changes in depressive symptomatology among older adolescents in the following:

Repeatedly rejected children are reacting to their own belief that they are unlovable rather than only to the immediate pain to the rejection. Therefore, depression at this stage takes on a more cognitive, evaluative characteristic and in this sense is no longer the immediate, stimulus-bound sadness of the younger child. . . . Behavior is scrutinized and evaluated in terms of the self. This cognitive aspect causes older children to remain depressed regardless of changes in external circumstances. (p. 196)

Brief mention should be made of the characteristics of depressive children who become suicide attempters (Mattson, Sesse, & Hawkins, 1969). Most notable among these syndromes is:

(1) sustaining a recent death or desertion by a significant figure, (2) experiencing marked self-depreciation, (3) a cry for help when exposed to overwhelming stress, (4) the emergence of revengeful anger as a means of manipulating or controlling others, (5) slipping into a psychotic state with an inclination to act-out and possess delusional beliefs, and (6) risky flirtations with death as a means of retribution or soliciting peer-approval.

Adult Subtypes

Despite its recency as a formal DSM classification, the history of depressive syndromes is a long and rich one, many elements of which can be drawn on for the following personality presentations. Some exhibit their depressive mood with displays of dramatic gesture and pleading commentary; others are demanding, irritable, and cranky. Some verbalize

their thoughts in passive, vague, and abstract philosophical terms. Still others seem lonely, quietly downhearted, solemnly morose, and pessimistic. Common to all, however, is the presence of self-deprecatory comments, feelings of apathy, and marked discouragement and hopelessness. Their actions and complaints usually evoke sympathy and support from others, but these reassurances provide only temporary relief from the prevailing mood of dejection.

The Ill-Humored Depressive

In these personalities, well described by Kraepelin and Schneider, we see a constant barrage of complaints, irritability, and a sour grumbling discontent, usually interwoven with hypochondriacal preoccupations and periodic expressions of guilt and self-condemnation. Their habitual style of acting out their conflicts and ambivalent feelings becomes more pronounced, resulting in extreme vacillations between bitterness and resentment, on the one hand, and intropunitive self-deprecation on the other. Self-pity and bodily anxieties are extremely common and may serve as a basis for distinguishing them from other depressive types. A review of empirical and clinical studies suggests that the characteristics of these depressives interweave with features seen most commonly among negativistic personalities.

Although not invariably gloomy, these *ill-humored depressives* find pleasure in nothing and appear contented with nothing, taking out their grumbling negativism, not so much in a nagging and dissatisfied attitude toward others, but directing their ill disposition against themselves. They exhibit a mood composed of irritability, anxiety, and self-flagellation. There is a self-tormenting quality, a kind of scolding and hypochondriacal attitude, an extreme preoccupation with themselves and an annoying insistence that others hear their complaints and troubles. As Kretschmer has described them, they appear cold and selfish, irritable and critical, rejoicing in the failures of others, and never anticipating or wishing others the rewards and achievements of life.

For limited time periods, there may be an incessant despair and suffering, an agitated pacing to and fro, a wringing of hands, and an apprehensiveness and tension that are unrelieved by comforting reassurances. In some cases, the primary components are hostile depressive complaints and a demanding and querulous irritability in which these personalities bemoan their sorry state and their desperate need for attention to their manifold physical illnesses, pains, and incapacities.

The Voguish Depressive

Both Schnieder and Kraepelin noted a tendency of certain depressives to display vanity and voguishness. To these personalities, suffering is seen as something noble, permitting them to feel special, if not elitist. They, thereby, acquired a philosophical refuge that could enable them to ponder "the bitterness of earthly life." Some of these *voguish depressives* display an aesthetic preoccupation, a way of dressing and living that gives stature to their unhappy moods. They philosophize about their "existential sadness" or the alienation that we all share in this "age of mass society." This use of fashionable language provides them with a bridge to others. It gives them a feeling of belonging during times when they are most isolated from the attachments they so desperately seek. As such, these depressives are often seen to exhibit histrionic personality characteristics and, to a lesser extent, those of the narcissistic personality.

Moreover, their pseudosophistication about up-to-date matters not only enables them to rationalize their personal emptiness and confusion but also allows them to maintain their appeal in the eyes of "interesting" people. By adopting currently popular modes of disenchantment, they reinstate themselves as participants of an "in" subgroup and thereby manage to draw attention to themselves. These feeble signs of social attachment also provide a means for overcoming their deep sense of loss and isolation. However, should their expressions of connectedness fail to fulfill their attachment needs, they are likely to be quickly withdrawn and replaced with soulful declarations of guilt and hopelessness.

The Self-Derogating Depressive

Feelings of helplessness and futility readily come to the fore when these *self-derogating depressives* are faced either with burdensome responsibilities or the anticipation of social abandonment. The actual loss of a significant person almost invariably prompts severe dejection, if not a psychotic depression. Anticipation of abandonment may prompt these patients to admit openly their weaknesses and shortcomings as a means of gaining reassurance and support. Expressions of guilt and self-condemnation typically follow because these verbalizations often successfully deflect criticism from others, transforming their threats into comments of reassurance and sympathy.

Guilt may arise as a defense against the possible expression of resentment and hostility. These self-derogating depressives usually contain their anger because they dread provoking the retribution of abandonment and isolation. To prevent this occurrence, they turn inward whatever aggressive impulses they feel, discharging them through self-derisive comments and verbalizations of guilt and contrition. This maneuver not only tempers the exasperation of others, but often prompts others to respond in ways that make the patient feel redeemed, worthy, and loved. Hence, self-derogation serves not only to express one's feelings, but also to solicit support from others.

Self-derogating personalities have managed to gain a measure of control over their feelings of loss and anger. This they have done by turning their feelings inward, that is, by diminishing their own self-worth and taking out their hatred on themselves. Thus, they persist in voicing guilt and self-disparagement for their failures, guilt-ridden actions of the past, as well as other shameful feelings and thoughts. Through their self-derogating depressive personality style, they manage to cloak whatever contrary impulses they may have felt toward others, seek redemption and ask absolution for their past behaviors and forbidden inclinations. Moreover, their self-derogating style solicits support and nurturance from others. In a more subtle way, it also serves as a devious means of venting their hidden resentment and anger. Their state of helplessness and their protestations of self-derogation make others feel guilty and burden them with extra responsibility and woes. As should be evident from the foregoing, we may identify a fusion between depressive and masochistic features among these individuals. In these interfused personalities, we find features that have been thoughtfully described by Kernberg (1988a) and others as "depressive-masochistic" characters.

These maneuvers become problematic themselves in that the depressive is now increasingly dismayed and disillusioned as he or she becomes aware of having wasted much of life, missing opportunities and falling far behind peers. Not only is the person ashamed, but may come to envy others who appear to be so much more successful and achieving. Self-derogation has only intensified a sense of worthlessness. It has prevented the depressive from exploring his or her life wisely, as well as finding a better route to make life more worthwhile. The individual's own actions have diminished whatever hopes he may have had. The depressive feels not only a sense of loss for what might have been, but also a sense of self-alienation, often sinking into a depressive paralysis in which the person is unable to function.

The Morbid Depressive

A depressive paralysis is what comes to characterize the *morbidly depressive personality,* a style that frequently blends into Axis I clinical depressions. These morbid types experience deep feelings, contrasting markedly with the emotional flatness of certain schizoids. The gloom and profound dejection are clearly conveyed as these patients slump with brow furrowed, body stooped, and head turned downward and away from the gaze of others, held in their hands like a burdensome weight. Various physical signs and symptoms further enable us to distinguish these disorders from other depressive personality subtypes. Many of these morbid depressives lose weight and look haggard and drained. Not uncommonly, they follow a characteristic pattern of awakening after 2 or 3 hours of sleep, turn restlessly, have oppressive thoughts, and experience a growing dread of the new day. Notable, also, is the content of their verbalizations, meager though they may be, reporting a vague dread of impending disaster, feelings of utter helplessness, a pervasive sense of guilt for past failures and a willing resignation to their hopeless fate. Most typically, we will find features of the dependent personality permeating the psychic makeup of this basic *morbid* depressive personality subtype. It is their deep and pervasive sense of personal incompetence that makes dependents feel incapable of coping; moreover, given their habitual style, they do not even hope to be able to deal with their current troubled state, hence resulting in the profound dejection and morbidity. By contrast, other personalities that covary with the depressive possess sufficient feelings of competence and self-worth to enable them, at the very least, to believe that they *may* ultimately cope with the difficulties they experience.

When not in a deep phase of gloom, these morbid depressives evince a withering self-contempt. They demean everything about themselves, seeing only the worst in what they have done, caught in an obsessive pessimism, a relentless negativism in which it seems that nothing can get better. They speak of being outcasts, sacrificial victims, suffering forevermore by what life has done to them and what they have done to themselves. Feeling permanently dislocated and unworthy, they "know" that others are as contemptuous of them as they are of themselves. They experience "the black dog," a sense of inner darkness that drains whatever hope they may have had or wished for into a vacuous hole. The mood is one of despondency and helplessness, a state akin to what other personalities exhibit when experiencing a clinical depressive syndrome. But for the morbidly depressed, despair is a persistent and unrelenting state, so much so that it pervades every fabric of their psychic makeup.

The Restive Depressive

These depressive personalities often covary with avoidant personalities, creating a pattern of characteristics that reflect the features of both. Typically anguished and agitated, these mixed personalities exhibit a wrought-up despair, vacillating between fretfulness and confusion at one time, and dysphoria and despair the next. They evidence a perturbed discontent as they think about the anguish others have caused them, venting little of the displeasure and vexation they feel. Should they ventilate their disquieted and unsettled moods, they invariably will restrain their acts of irritability and disillusionment by turning them inward, manifesting a despondency and sour disaffection with themselves. These shifting and vacillating attitudes serve to discharge their tensions and relieve them of their deep unhappiness and resentfulness. Nervous, fretful, distracted, these *restive depressives* manifest a sequence of brittle moods—usually short-lived and intense—affects and attitudes that ultimately become increasingly self-destructive.

Unable to get a clear hold on their feelings, their self-destructive acts may be expressed either directly through violent suicide or through insidious behaviors such as severe alcohol or drug abuse. As they despair that anything in life can ever become rewarding again, they feel they must do something to express their deeply pessimistic view of both life and themselves. Feeling defeated and helpless, seeing no way to restore their participation in the good life, many of these restive types conclude that they must rid themselves of the inescapable suffering they experience.

Suicidal acts are not merely a means to bring attention to oneself, but a way out, a final solution to the everpresent problems they face, a way to eliminate once and for all a persistent and painful existence. Self-destruction also serves to retaliate against others for not having cared enough. It is a form of retribution, of inflicting pain on others without being either overtly hostile or having to feel guilt after the act. It is the only aspect of their lives that they can master. Self-annihilating though it may be, suicide becomes the final act that demonstrates they can control their lives.

COMORBID DISORDERS AND SYNDROMES

This section attempts to note a number of the covariant or comorbid syndromes and disorders of the newly formulated depressive personality of DSM-IV. As in previous chapters, we will attempt to identify its most frequent Axis II and Axis I comorbidities. These are outlined in Figure 8.4.

Axis II Comorbidities

Given the recency of the depressive personality as an official designation, there is little research available to guide our choice of covariant personality disorders. The following notations are highly speculative therefore, based on theoretical deduction rather than empirically derived prevalence data. As conceived in this fashion, the primary covariations are likely to be found with the avoidant (AVD) and masochistic (MAS) patterns. Also noteworthy are correspondences with the dependent (DPD), borderline (BDL), and negativistic (NEG) personalities.

Axis I Comorbidities

The primacy of depressive symptomatology in these personalities may override the presence of numerous clinical syndromes that might otherwise be manifested. Many of these chronically depressed individuals also evidence mood swings that cross into *major depressive* disorders. Some also give evidence of a quasi-cyclical pattern in which *brief manic episodes* may be expressed. Although the majority are quietly passive and unassertive, a small minority also exhibit a concurrent *general-*

ized anxiety, some of whom also experience *panic* reactions. Focused *phobic* disturbances are often evident as well. It is not uncommon for *somatization* disorders to run concurrently with depressive traits over extended periods. These individuals experience numerous vegetative symptoms, and a preoccupation with these bodily symptoms may be expected as a comorbid feature. Those exhibiting this hypochondriacal feature often believe that they are not getting adequate medical care, resulting in a history of multiple complaints and repeated diagnostic procedures, adding further to their becoming a psychic invalid.

DIFFERENTIAL DIAGNOSES

As should be obvious by the commonality in their label, depressive personalities are difficult to differentiate from *dysthymic* and *major depressive* disorders; this is especially evident when the dysthymic disorder is of an extended duration. The essential distinction is that the depressive personality should be demonstrated in childhood or adolescence; the depressive symptomatology should be observable before it is manifested in adult pathology. Similarly, the personality disorder may be differentiated from major depressive episodes by virtue of the latter's rapid onset and intensity. Nevertheless, covariations are to be expected. Perhaps most important is the presence among depressive personalities of a wide range of characteristic cognitive, intrapsychic, and interpersonal traits that emerge as a consequence from long-standing periods of unhappiness and sadness. Hence, early onset, extended and moderate clinical symptomatology, as well as the presence of multiple trait characteristics should help in differentiating the preceding disorders.

Depressive personalities overlap considerably with a number of other Axis II syndromes, notably the masochistic, schizoid, avoidant, negativistic, and borderline.

Separating the depressive and *masochistic* individuals has been a clinical issue for many therapists and theorists. As noted previously, some authors refer to a constellation termed the "depressive-masochistic" character (Kernberg, 1988). Distinctions between them have been alluded to in earlier sections of this chapter. The prime differentiating element is the depressives' feeling of hopelessness and the inevitability of their affective state. By contrast, masochists, though evidently discontent and unhappy, take pains to participate

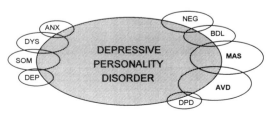

Figure 8.4 Comorbidity between depressive personality disorder and other DSM Axis I and Axis II disorders.

in their environment, either by seeking to please or submit to others, or to manipulatively "create" their own misfortunes and misery.

Both *schizoids* and depressives lack the ability to experience pleasure, to feel joy and to respond to the positives in their lives. However, schizoids are *intrinsically* incapable of experiencing any emotion to a significant degree, both psychic contentment and discontentedness. By contrast, depressives not only can feel intensely but are overly reactive to the unhappiness they experience in life.

The distinction between the *avoidant* and the depressive has been touched on previously. Although both personalities experience a considerable measure of life's unhappiness and discouragement, avoidants take an active role in eschewing the precipitants of their discontent; depressives give up, accepting their miserable state as inevitable and irreversible.

Negativistic personalities share a number of features in common with depressives, notably their pessimism, their feelings of personal misfortune, and the sense of being misunderstood and devalued. However, depressives are more persistently self- rather than other-derogating, more consistently gloomy and melancholy rather than irritable and angry, and more prone to feel guilty and hopeless rather than sullen and resentful.

Difficulties arise at times in differentiating between *borderline* and depressive personalities owing to the high frequency with which borderlines manifest depressive symptomatology. However, borderlines "fight-back," reacting angrily and energetically, if erratically, to their fate, whereas true depressive personalities, as just noted, submit to its inevitability, passively sinking into their state of gloom and melancholy.

ASSESSING THE DEPRESSIVE: A CASE STUDY

As in the preceding chapters, a brief summary will be presented of the depressive personality's likely test response patterns on several standard and well-established psychometric instruments. It features a case study of a depressive personality, a detailed MCMI profile, and an interpretive report.

Notable among depressives are the small number of responses given to the Rorschach, frequently less than 15; similarly, several cards may be rejected and others may produce long reaction times. Content often reflects the patients' low sense of self-worth and feelings of inadequacy in

handling the Rorschach. The percentages of pure *F* responses and popular responses are high. The use of shading or the color black are also common. On the low side are chromatic colors, and *M* and *W* responses. Stories on the TAT tend to be brief and mundane, often merely a description of the card's characters rather than a thematic story. When stories are portrayed, they tend to present themes of sadness and loss.

Not surprisingly, Scale 2 on the MMPI is most typically elevated among depressive personalities. High point codes incorporating 2-7, 3-2, and 2-8 are frequent. If Scale 8 is high, it may suggest a possible borderline level of severity, with agitated depressive and self-destructive features notable. The inclusion of a high Scale 4 in the configuration also suggests borderline elements or negativistic personality features. High point 2-0 codes are suggestive of a long-term depressive pattern in which positive affects (e.g., anhedonia) are notably lacking.

The following case summarizes the developmental background of a depressive personality disorder. It includes an MCMI-III profile (Figure 8.5) and an interpretive report.

CASE 8.1

Minerva T., Age 32, Married, Two Children

Minerva was a housewife with a lifelong depressive pattern that periodically deteriorated into a bipolar level of functioning following progressively severe conflicts with her physician husband who made greater demands of independence and sociability on her part than she could comfortably handle. In the early years of her marriage, Minerva sought to fulfill his expectations by becoming involved in country club activities and entertaining his professional associates. The success of these efforts was short-lived, and as a consequence, she became increasingly depressed and self-deprecating.

Inquiries into her early history indicated that Minerva had several episodes in which her depressive moods were exacerbated. Recalling her early life, Minerva recognized that she had always been a "sad little girl" who had kept to herself for fear that her friends would disapprove of her moods and humiliate her. She always saw herself as unattractive or gloomy—someone who could not be liked owing to her temperament and outlook. Nevertheless, Minerva was able to function quite well in school, achieving high grades

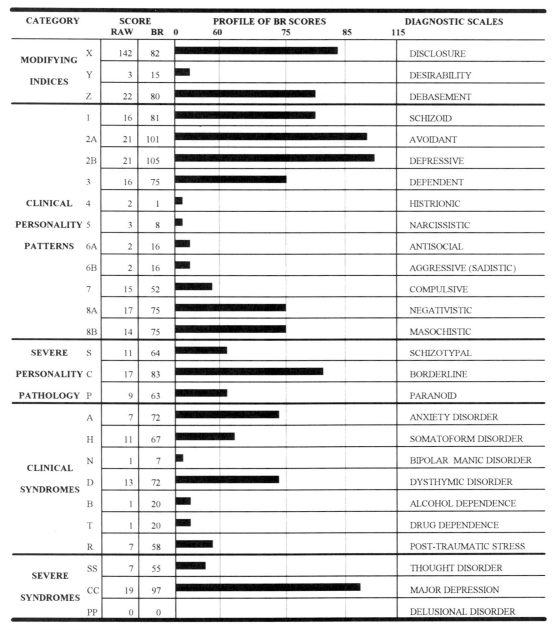

CATEGORY		SCORE		PROFILE OF BR SCORES				DIAGNOSTIC SCALES
		RAW	BR	0 60	75	85	115	
MODIFYING INDICES	X	142	82					DISCLOSURE
	Y	3	15					DESIRABILITY
	Z	22	80					DEBASEMENT
CLINICAL PERSONALITY PATTERNS	1	16	81					SCHIZOID
	2A	21	101					AVOIDANT
	2B	21	105					DEPRESSIVE
	3	16	75					DEPENDENT
	4	2	1					HISTRIONIC
	5	3	8					NARCISSISTIC
	6A	2	16					ANTISOCIAL
	6B	2	16					AGGRESSIVE (SADISTIC)
	7	15	52					COMPULSIVE
	8A	17	75					NEGATIVISTIC
	8B	14	75					MASOCHISTIC
SEVERE PERSONALITY PATHOLOGY	S	11	64					SCHIZOTYPAL
	C	17	83					BORDERLINE
	P	9	63					PARANOID
CLINICAL SYNDROMES	A	7	72					ANXIETY DISORDER
	H	11	67					SOMATOFORM DISORDER
	N	1	7					BIPOLAR MANIC DISORDER
	D	13	72					DYSTHYMIC DISORDER
	B	1	20					ALCOHOL DEPENDENCE
	T	1	20					DRUG DEPENDENCE
	R	7	58					POST-TRAUMATIC STRESS
SEVERE SYNDROMES	SS	7	55					THOUGHT DISORDER
	CC	19	97					MAJOR DEPRESSION
	PP	0	0					DELUSIONAL DISORDER

Figure 8.5 Millon Clinical Multiaxial Inventory-III.

and an occasional award. This continued throughout her college years, a period when she found herself capable of being seen as an attractive and competent young person. Minerva became involved with a young instructor at the university, permitting herself for the first time in her life to let her emotions play out freely. Unfortunately, this affair was short-lived and Minerva felt humiliated, drawing into herself and experiencing another brief but severe depression, necessitating a 3-week stay at a local general hospital. It was on this occasion that she met her future husband, a young intern who was drawn to Minerva owing to her intellectual abilities and diverse interests in life. Although Minerva hesitated moving forward toward marriage, fearing that she was "genetically inferior" and would likely produce depressive children, she assented and was married shortly after graduation. Not long after the birth of her first child, she succumbed to a postpartum depression, lasting several months, which was followed by several more episodes of severe depression.

Rather than support her during these periods, her husband became all the more critical and exasperated. In time, Minerva's attempts to "brighten up" were less frequent and more abbreviated; she became more clinging and depressed, with periodic breaks that were severe enough to justify repeated institutionalizations. On her return home from these brief hospital stays, Minerva would be jovial and enthusiastic about "asserting" herself again. Usually in less than a month or two, however, she would regress once more to her dependent and disconsolate state, beginning the cycle anew, only to be rehabilitated and sustained by a number of the newer antidepressive medications.

INTERPRETIVE SUMMARY

The MCMI-III profile of this troubled woman suggests a pervasive apprehensiveness, intense and variable moods, prolonged periods of dejection and self-deprecation, and episodes of withdrawn isolation or unpredictable anger. A long-standing expectation that others will be rejecting or disparaging precipitates profound gloom, self-defeating and self-abnegating behavior, and irrational negativism. Vacillation in mood is exhibited between desires for affection, self-destructive acts, fear, and a general numbness of feeling. Despite her longing for warmth and acceptance, she withdraws to maintain a safe distance from close psychological involvement. Retreating defensively, she not only becomes remote from her much-needed and desired sources of support but also impulsively seeks self-sabotaging pursuits.

Surface apathy may characterize her efforts to conceal her excess sensitivity. Behind this front of restraint may be intense contrary feelings that break through in displays of temper toward those whom she sees as being unsupportive, critical, and disapproving. The little security that she possesses, however, is threatened when these resentments are expressed. Therefore, to protect against further loss, she attempts to conceal or resist expressing anger, albeit unsuccessfully.

There are times of contrition when she may engage in expiatory self-damaging acts and suicidal gestures. Thus, when she is not withdrawn and drifting aimlessly in peripheral social roles, she may behave in an unpredictable manner, impulsively falling into troublesome situations. Innumerable wrangles and disappointments with others may occur as she vacillates between self-denial, sullen melancholy, self-destructive activities, and explosive anger. Frequently, these behaviors are interspersed with genuine expressions of guilt and contrition that are then mixed with feelings of being misunderstood, unappreciated, and demeaned by others. Not atypically, she may intentionally provoke condemnation through her sad and inconsistent behavior and then accuse others of having mistreated her.

There is a sense of low self-worth in this woman such that she cannot help but painfully contemplate the pitiful and futile state of her identity. A tendency toward extreme introspection may compound her identity problem. The alienation that she feels from others may very well be paralleled by feelings of alienation from herself, adding to her undercurrent of tension, sadness, and anger.

For some time now she has learned to expect ridicule and derision. She appears to detect the most minute traces of indifference expressed by others and interprets a minor slight as contempt and condemnation. Life has taught her that good things do not last and that overtures of affection end in disappointment and rejection. Anticipating disillusionment, she may undermine potentially positive opportunities with impulsive hostility. A cyclical variation may be observed as her efforts at emotional constraint are followed by impulsive outbursts that in turn are followed by remorse and regret. These erratic emotions are not only intrinsically distressing but also upset her limited capacity to cope with everyday tasks. Unable to orient her emotions and thoughts logically, she may drift occasionally into personal irrelevancies and autistic asides. Her inability to communicate ideas and feelings in a relevant manner further alienates her from others.

The self-demeaning comments and feelings of inferiority that mark this woman's major depression are part of her overall and enduring characterological structure, a set of chronic self-defeating attitudes and depressive emotions that are intrinsic to her psychological makeup. Feelings of emptiness and loneliness and recurrent thoughts of death and suicide are accompanied by expressions of low self-esteem, preoccupations with failures and physical unattractiveness, and assertions of guilt and unworthiness. Although she complains about being aggrieved and mistreated, she is likely to assert that she deserves anguish and abuse. Such self-debasement is consonant with her self-image, as is her tolerance and perpetuation of relationships that foster and aggravate her misery.

PATHOGENIC DEVELOPMENTAL BACKGROUND

As is true with most personality disorders, many readers tend to see the role of biogenic or constitutional factors in depression as contrasting with those of a psychogenic nature. There is no opposition or contradiction between these two perspectives. They have been separated for pedagogical purposes, not because we believe them to be independent sources of influence. They are intrinsically and complexly interwoven, such that biological dispositions can themselves be enlarged by experience and may then be precipitated into manifest clinical form by environmental causes.

The inclination to experience a troubled life with depressive symptomatology is not necessarily maladaptive in all of its aspects. Such inclinations signify an ability to communicate helplessness and dependency, which elicit nurturing attention and care. Hence, the disposition to become depressed may have been selectively reinforced to serve an important function in the course of evolution. Problematic in certain regards, this temperamental disposition may have enhanced the likelihood that those who deeply suffer the "slings and arrows" of life will likely elicit protective care to a greater extent than those who are incapable of expressing such feelings. In sum, depressiveness may not only stem from a fusion of biogenic and psychogenic sources, but reflect qualities that enhance individual survival.

Hypothesized Biogenic Factors

The role of biogenic factors in depressive disorders has been studied throughout history (e.g., Burton, 1621) and in a number of different modern ways. Contemporary studies suggest that genetic and neurochemical factors play a distinct though modest role in various depressive personality subtypes. Work in population and family studies, specifically research focused on twins and adoptees, suggest several biological markers of a depressogenic

inclination. However, evidence gathered in numerous family studies indicates considerable heterogeneity among depressive personality disorders and their clinical syndromes. This work suggests that there are numerous heterogeneous subtypes that may not differ genotypically; on the other hand, there may be genotypically distinct types that do not differ phenotypically.

As is true with many other personality disorders, genetic studies cannot yet delineate a clear path to overt depression (e.g., consistent hormonal abnormalities have not been found). Nevertheless, there is a strong suspicion that the "depressive spectrum" includes relationships between autonomic dysfunctions, electromyographic responses, sleep disorders, and the like. Each of these moderately reliable findings suggests that biophysical substrates are present. Similarly, neurochemical hypotheses are given strong support owing to the responsivity of depressive patients to specific psychopharmacological agents (e.g., serotonin uptake inhibitors). All in all, there are more pieces of circumstantial biogenic evidence for the depressive than found in almost all other personality disorders. Nevertheless, these studies remain tenuous and unreliable, though supportive of a significant role to be elaborated in future work.

Characteristic Experiential History

Owing to the recency of the construct depressive personality disorder, little of a substantial character has been researched or even clinically hypothesized about this form of pathology. Nevertheless, as evidenced in the sections Modern and Contemporary Proposals, researchers have speculated about which factors are likely to give rise to depression, broadly conceived (i.e., not only its character variant). In what follows, we will attempt to distill some of the proposed elements that may play a significant part in shaping the experiential course that leads to the prototypal depressive personality pattern.

Early Loss of Emotional Support

It appears that depressive affect may be grounded at a very early stage in development, termed the *sensory-attachment stage*. It is at this time that children acquire experiences, through parental feeling and behavior, that their environment is receptive and caring or indifferent and distant. During this period, children learn to discriminate pleasurable experiences from painful ones. Fundamental feelings of security and attachment result from an adequate level of sensory gratification and nurturance. However, a failure to experience clear and unequivocal signs of warmth and acceptance at the sensory level may create fundamental feelings of insecurity, emotional detachment, and isolation.

A distinction should be made between the experiences of the depressively prone from the avoidantly prone child. In the depressive, we see parental distancing or indifference; in the avoidant, we see rejection and devaluation. Depressive infants lack experiences of warmth and closeness; avoidant infants experience parental interaction, but it is of a deprecating and belittling nature. Depressive children learn to give up because their efforts to bring forth the deficient warmth are unsuccessful. Avoidant children learn to actively withdraw and not seek additional parental interactions because they are painful rather than merely indifferent.

The extremes of infantile depressive feelings are perhaps best described in the work of Spitz (1946) in his characterization of the syndrome labeled "hospitalism," an infantile disorder characterized by sadness, weepiness, loss of appetite, insomnia, environmental withdrawal and, on occasion, death. Of course, Spitz's cases were extraordinary in that they referred to infants who were almost entirely isolated and deprived of maternal relatedness.

The origins of depressive withdrawal are found not only in extraordinary circumstances such as those associated with total parental disengagement or death, but may be seen in lesser form among infants who lack important experiences of warmth and parental responsiveness. This may be seen in the less problematic parent-child relationships reported in the work of Bowlby (1969) and of Mahler (1975). Both recount circumstances in which the child is unable to experience the affection and consistent support of a significant maternal-like person. Bowlby's work describes studies of children and lower animals faced with troublesome separations from parental-like figures. Following initial protests and efforts to search for and retrieve the lost objects, the child gives up and withdraws into what Bowlby describes as despair and disorganization. Withdrawn and inactive, such children learn to make few demands on their environment, become emotionally detached rather than attached, conserve their energies, develop a generalized sense of hopelessness and, owing to their limited capacities and immaturity, feelings of helplessness.

As noted, children need not have experienced total loss for this sequence of detachment and depression to ensue. Sometimes it is not the lack of mother's warmth, but incidental circumstances of life in which the normally expected level of attention and care could not be available. What is most significant is not the specific character of actual loss, but the emergence of the child's *feeling* of loss and isolation, and the consequent failure of his or her efforts to call attention to self that proves of no help. Such children experience in the sensory-attachment stage not only that they are in a precarious position, but learn that efforts to elicit needed emotional security and warmth will be insufficient, if not futile. Thus, even moderate signs of parental indifference and coldness can result in these children's broad disposition to feel helpless, isolated, and forever unsure that they can elicit needed affection and support. There remains a deeply embedded, persistent, and ongoing craving for security and warmth from parental figures (who represent the world at large at this stage) that is intensified with every event that reinforces this sense of isolation and hopelessness. In effect, what has been established is a fundamental and everpresent template for later feelings of helplessness and depressiveness.

Trained Helplessness

The foundations for a depressive personality disposition may also be traceable to the second neuropsychological stage, that termed *sensorimotor-autonomy*. It is usually at this period that the children's initial capacities to do things on their own, to maneuver within the world with confidence and assertiveness, begin to take hold. However, as Mahler and her associates have so ably pointed out, the establishment of "separateness" and "individuation" can be undermined by parental attitudes, with consequential feelings of diminished competence and persistent dependency on the child's part.

Barring earlier problematic experiences, most toddlers begin to assert a measure of independence from their mothers, experiencing a sense of elation and triumph over newly achieved competencies in locomotion and speech. Inevitably, these forms of sensorimotor mastery run into occasional failures as children exercise their newfound abilities. Whatever the source may be, parental disapproval and deprecation will at these times puncture the young child's growing sense of confidence and competence. Should self-esteem be injured severely thereby, should the parent take over and show the child repeatedly that the parent can always do things "better," should the parent be critical and demeaning repetitively, the child will, in any of these circumstances, become seriously disappointed in his or her self, developing a deep feeling of fundamental ineptitude and helplessness. To be both overprotected and deprecated at the same time will result in a sense of ineffectuality, inadequacy, and defenselessness. As a result of this "learned helplessness," we see the emergence of a basic passivity and a strong, negative evaluation regarding the child's capacity ever to manage the world.

This sequence of events has similarities to that experienced by the future dependent child. However, in the dependent-prone youngster, the parental attitude is one of not wishing to "lose their baby"; parents restrict the toddler's ventures out of fear that their child might be overtaxing his or her abilities; such parents make no demands for self-responsibility and discourage children's impulse to go it on their own. The wish to "leave it to mother" is based on love and care, however, not on deprecation and devaluation, its source from among future depressives. In this latter case, the future depressive is derogated and humiliated, made to feel inadequate and insufficient, repetitively denigrated by parental devaluations. Such youngsters not only fail to function adequately on their own and hence feel helpless, but through parental disparagement believe they can never possess the competencies to do so and thus feel hopeless.

Reinforcing Sadness as an Identity

Given the preceding as a base, youngsters who are prone to depression approach adolescence with serious doubts concerning their potential appeal as a member of their gender. Anticipating disinterest or derogation from their peers, these youngsters cannot retreat to their homes seeking acceptance and understanding. Devaluing themselves and expecting to be further devalued by all segments of their social world, they turn inward to minister and pamper themselves, disinclined to venture forth to be further alienated and derided in peer-group relationships. Their lack of confidence in themselves, and in what they will elicit interpersonally, further reinforces the belief that they are unattractive persons who will be further humiliated by others.

Typically, many of these youngsters find themselves adopting a public role of acting sorrowful and easily pained. Their overt expressions of loneliness and pitifulness often serve, at least initially, to solicit attention and reinforcements from well-intentioned others, in the form of public signs of empathy and care. As a consequence of this attention and the wish of concerned others to help them overcome their sad state, they experience many surprisingly new reinforcements for their depressive behaviors. Such positive responses prove successful and highly rewarding, at least in the short run, often bringing them out of their unhappy state, albeit in the role of a pitiable and ineffectual person. A continuing depressive role will become increasingly aversive to others, however, leading them eventually to avoid their sorrowful peer, resulting further in embedding the depressive-prone youngster's sense of general unappeal and gender inadequacy.

Loss of Self

The preceding stages that often undergird the development of a depressive character structure may be further reinforced by difficulties during the *intracortical-integrative* stage. Central to this period is the emergence of a clear and cohesive sense of self, an inner representation of who the person is and who the person may wish to be. Such self-image representations may be either highly accurate or grossly distorted. What we find among depressive personalities is a judgment that one is valueless and worthless, inadequate and unsuccessful in all aspirations, a barren, sterile, impotent person who is both inconsequential and reproachable.

How does this sense of possessing few or no praiseworthy traits or achievements come to pass? Primary in this regard is the continuing feeling of not being loved, perhaps, more important, not ever being lovable. It is during and immediately post puberty and into early maturity that the mental image of "self" comes to be firmly embedded. As a consequence of earlier deprecations of self by others, followed by having fallen short during puberty, a sharp schism between self-image and "ego-ideal" becomes established; that is, the values and aspirations one desired for oneself are no longer possible to achieve. The split between reality and ideal is irremediable.

It is the disparity between being and what might have been that the depressive believes has been severed forever. No cohesion can take place, no integration can occur between one's real self and one's ideal self. This everpresent cleavage in one's psychic makeup results in a sense of emptiness and loss, a loss not of others, not of parts of self, but of the very essence of self. Again, depressives feel helpless and hopeless about overcoming this schism. It remains an undercurrent that persists in creating gloomy moods and depressive cognitions.

Depressively prone youngsters not only allow themselves little pleasure, but are self-punitive and self-sadistic. Increasingly distressing though introspection may be, these children continue to find the reality of self to be despicable and condemnable. Wherever they go, the despised self is inherent, an everpresent and condemned existence. Such introspection disrupts their cohesion and uncovers a fragile psychic state that produces a chronic series of depressogenic feelings, experiences, and relationships.

SELF-PERPETUATION PROCESSES

It must be said again that chronic depressive moods often reflect the persistence of internal mood dysregulations, continuing states of unhappiness and sadness that are driven primarily by long-term neurobiological defects and deficiencies. Not that biological forces can display themselves manifestly without being interwoven with psychological influences, but when biogenic dysfunctions are markedly persistent and penetrant, the role of psychological factors will play a lesser role than otherwise. Our current state of knowledge does not allow us to differentiate conditions that have stronger or lesser biological components.

Re-Creating Experiences of Suffering

Pessimistic and self-devaluing schemata influence how information and relationships are processed by depressive individuals. Retrospective recall and future anticipations are all colored by cognitive distortions and expectancies that further reinforce their unhappy state. As noted previously, depression often recruits support and nurturance; it deflects criticism and condemnation, and serves as a means of distancing from others and avoiding responsibilities about which one feels ambivalent or negative. As with the masochist, many depressives want to suffer, perhaps to suffer more than is warranted by the instrumental goals they seek to achieve.

How perverse a strategy this can be. Depressives exaggerate their misery and submerge themselves in feelings of helplessness, unhappiness, and unworthiness. One cannot help but be struck by the fact that these self-inflicted wounds deepen the abyss of misery of these persons. Again and again, depressives magnify minor disadvantages and failures into signs of irrevocable humiliation. As a result of these acts of self-generated despair, depressives greatly impair their ability to experience a measure of life's joy and contentment. They thereby sink into feeling helpless, needing others to care for their needs and take responsibility for their actions. Although there are advantages to disconsolation and defenselessness, these depressives have made their already problematic situation even more tormenting. In time, fewer and fewer advantages of depression are to be gained; no persons are around to be impressed, no more sympathy is forthcoming, and there are no triumphs in asserting one's will. Life dwindles to a state of nothingness and loses segments of its reality. By exaggerating their claims, depressives drive others away. Increasingly, the feelings of misery and unworthiness begin to lose a sense of reality; even the sting of depressive pain is gradually lulled and narcotized into a feeling of emptiness.

Self-Accusatory Attitudes

Although the overt expression of contrition and guilt may serve to deflect further condemnation by others, depressives further reinforce their own sense of unworthiness and despicability by these attitudes. Self-accusations, by which depressives invalidate their own worth, are acts of self-derogation in which the individual becomes his or her own worst enemy. Thus, in seeking to avoid the torment of others, depressives become their own persecutor, a critical, suspicious, and clever oppressor who knows exactly what to demean within the self to experience a measure of relief and expiation.

At some level, depressives are aware that their retroflected rage is but a facade, a clever device to mislead environmental tormentors, real or imagined. Thus, they must pursue their self-assault all the more severely and punish themselves deeply, not only as an act of contrition, as it may appear on the surface, but for the failure once again to be forthright and competent, that is, to say what they believe and to stand on their own. They have failed to deal again with their buried resentment toward parents and their disappointment in self. Their conscious remorse is recognized as a mockery of the deep and lifelong roots of helplessness and unworthiness. Elements of self-rage may be seen in the refusal to eat, the inability to engage in sex, and the general incapacity to feel any pleasure. They may be left with only one form of self-mastery and expiatory self-punishment—suicide.

Reinforcing Feelings of Hopelessness

The mere act of hopelessness, the ultimate product of a history of failure in eliciting care and affection, is a self-fulfilling process that not only signifies the future persistence of failure, but alienates depressives increasingly from the self. Concluding that they are unable to be the active master of their fate, they lose so much faith in self that they give up, unwilling even to try to make matters better, to seek what is desirable and, hence, to fall into a state akin to what Kierkegaard termed a "psychic death." The vicious circle has continued; these patients have lost not only the hope of what could be, but of the very sense of self.

THERAPEUTIC INTERVENTIONS

Most individuals with a depressive personality disorder accept their chronic dysphoria and feeling of hopelessness as an inevitable life condition, and come into therapy only after a significant other insists that something needs to be done. Sometimes, a major life trauma pushes them into treatment. A therapist may at first focus on the present symptoms and conclude that the patient is suffering from a severe bout of depression, only to later realize that the patient describes having felt this way since childhood or adolescence. Such patients may consider their feelings to be justified by life circumstance or personal failings, and deny any hope that they may eventually feel better; years of experience have taught depressives that even when things look relatively bright, feelings of despair lurk right around the corner.

Many individuals with a depressive personality disorder respond to psychopharmacological intervention; a therapist would do well to consider antidepressants as a first inroad into alleviating the patient's suffering. Many patients, however, who respond to medication nonetheless continue to be skeptical about the durability of newfound improvements, having previously experienced short-lived periods of comfort. To support and consolidate gains, the therapist needs to help the patient overcome the maladaptive personality characteristics and patterns of behavior that inevitably develop as a result of the patient's chronic

depression. Whereas overt depressive symptomatology, including downcast mood and vegetative signs, may disappear after administration of an appropriate medication, more covert personality factors may be less affected. Interpersonal behavior, self-concept, cognitive schemas, and expectancies that have been shaped by past depressive experience need to be replaced by more adaptive variants in order not to hinder the patient's optimal functioning or even undermine affective and energy gains.

Some patients do not respond to medication and thus have a more challenging road to travel on the way to recovery. In these cases, the patient and therapist will have to rely directly on behavioral, cognitive, interpersonal, and/or other interventions to improve affect and increase pleasure as well as to reconstruct the patient's personality.

STRATEGIC GOALS

A course of therapeutic intervention for a depressive patient should aim to accomplish several parallel yet intertwined goals. The depressive's characteristic passivity needs to be replaced with more active interaction with the environment, and the affective and cognitive emphasis on pain needs to be shifted to a focus on pleasure. Unlike avoidants, who actively withdraw from potentially distressing situations, depressives have come to accept pain as unavoidable, hence their helpless immobility. Increased anticipation of pleasure could help encourage depressives to be more proactive regarding their environment. Subsequent experiences with success can help alter depressives' pessimistic cognitive style, expectations, and melancholic mood. Cognitive interventions that attack the dysfunction within these domains directly can support the personality changes that result from new experiences with the environment, and hence ultimately help restore these patients' lost sense of self-worth.

Reestablishing Polarity Balances

The hallmark of the depressive personality is his or her psychic pain and sense of hopelessness about improving the quality of life. Cognitive-behavioral interventions that encourage the patient to interact in more adaptive ways with the environment can help sensitize the patient to experiences of success and pleasure, hence resulting in increased balance on the pain-pleasure polarity. A lessened sense of helplessness and strengthened motivation for rewarding experiences also indirectly foster more active coping strategies. These shift the patient away from the depressogenic passive end of the active-passive dimension.

Modifying Domain Dysfunctions

The crux of the depressive personality's dysfunction rests in the interaction of a pessimistic cognitive style and a deeply entrenched melancholic mood. The time-tested conviction that efforts to manipulate the environment or one's mood are futile ensures that the depressive will be ineffectual in efforts to plan for change. Even on those occasions when he or she overcomes feelings of inadequacy and hopelessness in an attempt to secure some reward from the environment, a resistant melancholic mood and negative interpretational bias interfere with the enjoyment of life's simple pleasures and small victories.

Psychopharmacological intervention often is a useful first inroad into the depressive's difficulties. Most depressives respond moderately well to medication, providing them with increased energy and a first inkling of optimism. With this renewed sense of hope, patients may be open to exploring and working toward changing attitudes and behaviors that contribute to the depressive pattern. Patients can be taught that helpless interpersonal behavior alienates even the most well-meaning others, attracts individuals with sadistic and exploitive tendencies, or even brings out such tendencies in "regular" folks. Social skills training can teach patients to replace disconsolate expressive behavior and defenseless interpersonal conduct with more assertive and appealing alternatives. Planning tasks by breaking them up into small manageable steps can also help provide depressives with successes that, along with improved quality of social interactions, can increase their sense of self-efficacy and help bolster their worthless self-image.

Improvements in these latter domains can serve to encourage the depressive to reclaim forsaken object-representations and dare to hope for (and hence find reason to work toward) something better than disappointment and failure. Increased subjective experience of pleasure can also help rejuvenate the personality's depleted morphologic organization and render coping mechanisms a little more vital and productive than previously. Although depressives start out believing they can feel comfortable with only a self-denial pattern of existence,

effective coping can, in fact, begin to occur as soon as hope becomes a part of their repertoire.

Countering Perpetuating Tendencies

The depressive's pessimistic expectations, lack of a sense of self-worth, and melancholic mood all serve to ensure that environmental conditions continue to reinforce the person's usual pattern of feeling, thinking, and behaving.

As depressives appraise their future, pessimistic expectations far outweigh hopes for success and satisfaction. Rather than exert themselves in vain and admit the possibility of further crushing failures and disappointments, depressives passively resign themselves to bear the burden of their fate. Depressives respond halfheartedly to opportunities to improve their lot, further entrenching their hopelessness and self-reproach. Experiences of success are not likely under such circumstances. Their low self-esteem and self-inflicted lack of success suggest that even if there was a road out of this empty, cold world, depressives would not be capable of navigating around the obstacles. Believing themselves to lack the capacity to make improvements, they may turn, in the hope of salvation, to others. Others may react to the disconsolate and defenseless behavior of depressives with initial support but, in time, often withdraw because of their feelings of frustration. Aware of the effect their melancholic mood has on others, yet feeling unable to behave in a more energetic and optimistic way, depressives find their pessimistic expectations fulfilled and their poor self-image reinforced. They may vow ever more forcefully to keep to themselves to avoid further pain.

The vicious circle fueled by the depressive's pessimistic expectations can be interrupted by confronting pessimism directly, by cognitive interventions that challenge assumptions, and by behavioral "experiments." Even a trickle of motivation, for some more easily mastered with the help of antidepressants, can help patients alter their depressogenic interpersonal habits, especially with social skill and assertiveness training. Tasks can be broken down into easily accomplished small steps thus exposing patients to success. Feelings of self-efficacy can bolster the self-image of patients, and supportive antidepressants may help to further lift melancholia. Cognitive techniques can teach patients to search for objective feedback in their environment, rather than to rely solely on emotional reasoning. Problem-solving skills allow patients to generate alternative plans in cases of genuine disappointment or failure, thus preventing them from sinking again into apathetic despair.

TACTICAL MODALITIES

In building a relationship with a depressive patient, the therapist needs to carefully balance a supportive position that satisfies the patient's dependency needs against encouraging helplessness. Whereas most depressive patients claim to expect nothing but more unhappiness for their future, many in fact harbor a secret hope that the therapist has a magical solution that will put an end to their feelings of misery and incompetence. Patients with a depressive personality disorder have probably spent most of their time believing that life is an exhausting struggle that yields no rewards, at best, and metes out disappointments and punishments as a matter of course. These patients realize that life is not so cloudy for all their peers and often subconsciously hope that the therapist holds the secret to joy and vitality. Whereas depressives dare not risk openly assuming that such a wish could be realized, for fear of another devastating disappointment, the therapist will often receive both subtle and overt clues about patients' dependent wishes. Although the therapist will likely feel pressure to ease the patients' distress and pain, it is not advisable to assume too omnipotent a "helping" position. The therapist, however, must impart hopefulness and optimism about the possibility of achieving improved functioning and affect, while making clear that the patient must engage in a lot of collaborative work with the therapist to arrive at realistic but promising solutions. Although the patient may wish for a "magic helper," the therapist should emphasize developing the depressive's sense of self-efficacy and problem-solving ability.

In the beginning stages of therapy, satisfying too few of the patient's dependency needs may cause him or her to feel that the therapist is not interested or caring; this may increase the depressive's sense of futility. With very depressed patients, the therapist may have to do more than the usual amount of work to keep the session going. Many such patients feel embarrassed, incompetent, guilty, and misunderstood. They may also lack the confidence or energy to express this. Pushing patients too quickly, or even assuming a "cheerful" position may give the impression that the depressive affect will not be tolerated, resulting in feelings of shame that may lead patients to terminate

therapy. The truly therapeutic relationship is one in which the therapist can provide empathic support while conveying confidence in the patient's capacity to learn to care for him- or herself.

Domain-Oriented Techniques

What should be the focus of the therapeutic program? A useful initial approach with the depressive, as with all personality disorders, is the therapist's willingness to adopt a supportive attitude. After having lived with and accepted the inevitability of depressive symptoms since childhood or adolescence, the patient usually enters therapy at a time of crisis or when a relationship appears to be threatened by the patient's gloomy outlook and behavior. The first goal is to alleviate the patient's pain and to establish a solid and realistic therapeutic alliance. MacKinnon and Michels (1971) encourage the therapist to enhance the patient's defenses in order to shield the person against excessive pain. If the patient has suffered a recent interpersonal loss, the therapist can attempt to stand in for the lost figure until the patient stabilizes enough to regain some motivation and hope.

The second objective of supportive therapy is to protect the patient from self-injury. The therapist must be careful to clarify the consequences of irrational, self-defeating decisions. The therapist, although unable to make decisions for the patient directly, can encourage the patient to "wait till feeling better," thereby conveying concern (in itself therapeutic) and the attitude that improvement is expected. In order not to undermine the patient's self-confidence and self-efficacy, it is to be emphasized that the "sick" role and the therapist's advice are only temporary.

Depressive patients often suffer from excessive guilt. The therapist's acknowledgment of the burden of guilt, and reassurance that the depressive has suffered enough can help patients believe that "forgiveness" is possible, and that they finally deserve to build a better life. Some patients feel guilt about being a burden to their family by not functioning adequately at work or in other roles. Anger at others may be denied because of such guilt, serving only to increase symptoms and interfere with relationships. Encouraging the patient to acknowledge and work through anger can be helpful. Once the patient and therapist have developed a solid alliance and the patient has realistic expectations about the advantages of working toward changes, other interventions can be initiated.

Designing a useful *behavioral* intervention for the depressive patient begins with a careful analysis of the patient's interactions with the environment. Pleasant and unpleasant events need to be identified, as do problematic patterns of behavior. By keeping a record of daily events and moods, interventions to help change depressogenic activities can be devised. Once goals have been agreed on, it is often useful for patients to choose specific reinforcers that they can employ to reward themselves when they have carried out planned assignments successfully. Interventions usually fall into one of three categories: changes in the environment (e.g., changing jobs, going to the movies), teaching new interaction skills (e.g., assertiveness training, modeling), and increasing pleasure-related actions (e.g., relaxation and pleasure training). Patients are encouraged to engage in activities that they enjoy, particularly ones that activate positive moods; they may also be taught to set time aside daily for rewarding activities. Some behavioral intervention programs include the patient's significant others to encourage communication and facilitate social interaction.

Cognitive techniques for treating depressive personality disorders make much use of behavioral tactics as well. Combining the two approaches is a powerful medium through which to change the patient's behavior and environmental consequences, and to alter depressogenic attitudes. The cognitive approach emphasizes directly challenging the patient's depressogenic assumptions through logical reasoning as well as with environmental "data." By keeping track of events, thoughts, and moods, depressive patients can learn how much of their dysphoria is related directly to their appraisal of their environment and of themselves, as well as to their subsequent negative self-talk. Once negative automatic thoughts have been identified, they can be evaluated and modified. When patients have depressogenic thoughts, they may learn to ask themselves such questions as "What's the evidence?" "Is there any other way to look at it?" "How could alternative (less pessimistic) explanations be tested?" and "What can I do about it (to make it better)?" (Beck & Freeman, 1990b). The tacit beliefs on which automatic thoughts rest also need to be identified and altered for lasting change to occur and for negative thoughts not to resurface in a new form. Dysfunctional cognitive habits such as overgeneralization, arbitrary inference, emotional reasoning, and dichotomous thinking can be confronted directly, allowing patients to alter their thinking and the maladaptive behaviors that logically result from faulty thought processes. A basic strategy is to help patients realize that their thoughts are inferences about the world, and not facts. Predictions can then be made, and experiments devised to test their validity.

Behavioral exercises are used mainly as an extension of cognitive change techniques, for example, to show that optimistic appraisals of situations are justified and can be achieved. Activities can be planned to test assumptions, as well as to provide the patient with positive experiences. Cognitive rehearsal techniques can help a patient accomplish goals by imagining the steps, predicting "obstacles" and conflicts, and figuring out ways to overcome them.

Interpersonal approaches emphasize the place of the social environment in the development and maintenance of symptoms. The steps involved in treatment include reviewing symptoms and describing their usual course. Treatment is outlined, and the therapist declares the patient to have an "illness" that can be treated with his or her cooperation. Interpersonal problems are worked out in the course of therapy. Developing positive relationships can alleviate depressive symptoms by providing the patient with support, pleasure, and hope.

Depressive symptoms may be related to problems found in one or more of four general areas of dysfunction: grief overreactions, interpersonal disputes, role transitions, and interpersonal deficits. If the difficulty is a feeling of loss from a grief overreaction, or a strong sense of generalized deprivation, then therapy may focus on facilitating the delayed mourning process and helping the patient substitute new relationships and interests for those that have been lost or are chronically missing. If interpersonal disputes are the issue, a plan of action and effective communication are emphasized. For patients who are having difficulties adapting to new roles, emphasis is placed on regarding the role more positively, and on mastering skills needed to function effectively in the new capacity. Patients who have interpersonal deficits need to identify past positive relationships on which to base future ones, to practice skills, and to search new promising situations and people.

A number of strengths associated with *group* approaches to treatment of depressive disorders have been pointed out by numerous clinicians. In group therapy, depressive patients come to realize that others experience difficulties similar to their own, and that they are not alone in their vulnerability. This realization can be therapeutic in itself. Participants can be encouraged to assist each other in solving difficulties and overcoming problems, thus helping them bolster their waning sense of self-worth and interpersonal competence. Witnessing improvement in their fellow group members' outlook can reinforce the very tenuous hope patients have for improved functioning, and help build the motivation needed to make adaptive changes. The group format also allows for role-playing, multiparticipant discussions and behavioral interventions. Patients that lack social skills can experience corrective feedback about maladaptive behaviors. Positive reinforcement from a supportive group can give the patient confidence to experiment with new behaviors outside the therapy after practicing with members.

Family and *couples* approaches to treating a depressive's interpersonal relationship and functioning difficulties can focus on several areas of dysfunction. The reaction of the patient's spouse and of other family members who contribute to the patient's depressive tendencies, can be explored so as to improve the patient's overall functioning. Family members can learn about helpful ways to react to symptomatic behavior. The patient's or other family members' cognitive patterns may contribute to the depressive's pathogenesis. Distortions in problem definition, in expectancies for the self and spouse, in beliefs about change, and in attributions for behavior can be exposed and altered. Behavioral interventions can be conducted with the spouse and/or other family members to increase the patient's social skills, and to demonstrate the advantages of more adaptive interaction strategies. Hostile interactions can be reduced. Often a lack of intimacy with the patient's spouse precipitates, exacerbates, or maintains symptomatology. Teaching the couple to interact in supportive and comforting ways can alleviate acute symptoms, and help the depressive patient replace maladaptive schemas with better attitudes and coping mechanisms.

Psychodynamic approaches that involve short-term therapy are currently based on one of two premises. The first is that depression is largely caused by disturbed interpersonal relations; childhood experiences of disappointment with significant others predispose individuals to replicate depressogenic patterns. The second premise is that depressive patterns reflect difficulties in adaptive functioning that are related to inadequate self-esteem. A perceived discrepancy between aspirations and reality or what had once been and what is now (loss), is hypothesized to cause depressive symptomatology.

Analyzing the patient's transference toward the therapist and examining the patient's developmental interpersonal history as the source of maladaptive emotional and cognitive distortions are the crux of dynamic treatments. The process may be divided into stages. First, the therapist and patient search for persistent and problematic remnants of childhood interpersonal functioning, as it presents in the relationship between them. The second phase involves the patient working on relinquishing defenses, beliefs, and patterns that have been identified, and replacing them with more realistic and functional modes of behavior. Dreams, relationships, and feelings are all analyzed and traced to their origins. A new, mature appraisal of the patient's history and context can then help protect against continued depressive symptomatology. Healing is also promoted by supportive empathy, direct advice (when appropriate), and a positive relationship experience with the therapist.

Psychopharmacological intervention can greatly help depressives live normal lives by uplifting their melancholic mood state. Although antidepressants may not restructure the fundamental nature of the patient's personality, it certainly can help the patient feel more optimistic and energetic enough to take risks in experimenting with new behaviors. The many antidepressants available on the market have different side-effect and contraindication profiles; careful evaluation of the patient's history and sensitivities can help in deciding which one is appropriate. It is also important for the therapist to emphasize that there is a lag between onset of medication administration and its psychoactive effects, in order to guard against the patient becoming discouraged during the usual 2- to 6-week delay.

A review of the major strategies and tactics is shown in Figure 8.6.

Potentiated Pairings and Catalytic Sequences

The first inroad to be considered by the therapist when planning a treatment strategy for someone with depressive personality disorder is usually pharmacological intervention with antidepressants. Although not every patient is willing to take medication, and although several different medications may need to be prescribed before an optimal one may be found, a great many depressive patients

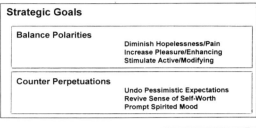

Figure 8.6 Therapeutic strategies and tactics for the prototypal depressive personality.

report that they feel as though a cloud has been lifted once they take an effective drug.

For patients who take medication (as well as for those who do not), a useful initial approach is a supportive one. Alleviating the patient's pain, offering empathic understanding, and protecting the person against bad decisions, can do much to inspire the patient's hope and motivation.

Behavioral intervention may next be employed, as well as combined with personality-reforming techniques, whether cognitive, interpersonal or dynamic. Behavioral changes can help open up new experiences and reinforce more adaptive patterns. More thoroughgoing analyses of the patient's life and difficulties can help change the fabric of depressogenic attitudes and actions, thereby immunizing the patient against relapse during times of stress.

If the therapist deems adjunct family or couples intervention to be appropriate, it can begin as soon as the patient and therapist feel ready. Similarly, participation in a supportive group for depressive individuals can be of benefit for several reasons. Although the therapist may be idolized or suspected of being supportive out of professional duty, other group members can be regarded as peers. Patients often feel less isolated and genuinely hopeful when they meet others in similar situations who experience improved moods and lives.

An important aspect of achieving successful intervention with depressive personalities is focusing on major episodes and relapse prevention. Patients should be advised of the frequency with which most people reexperience intense dysphoric periods, and should be taught strategies for feeling better and keeping active. Booster sessions can be recommended to keep patients functioning at an

optimal level. Patients who are on medication need to be monitored regularly.

RISKS AND RESISTANCES

The high success rate of antidepressants for treating symptoms of depressive personality disorder may lead some therapists to be prematurely reassuring that difficulties will quickly abate. Some patients who fail to respond to medication may feel pressure to do so, and internalize the lack of pharmacological success as a personal failure or as confirmation that they are a hopeless case. The little motivation they had to try to improve their lot may be undone, rendering potentially helpful cognitive, behavioral, or interpersonal interventions impossible to utilize. Some patients need to try several different medications before finding one they respond to favorably. It should be understood that disappointed initial optimism can confirm patients' skepticism and make them unwilling to experiment with alternatives.

Other difficulties can arise from the depressive patient's need to find a magic solution and the therapist's willingness to provide it. Some patients may interpret their therapist's confidence as the promise of a powerful helper, and attribute improvements in their condition to his or her skill and knowledge, increasing their sense of dependency on the therapist rather than their sense of self-efficacy. Still others may attribute past difficulties to a "chemical imbalance" and, encouraged by their therapist's optimistic outlook, spring into new activities and relationships without having compensated for years of interpersonal and cognitive deficits. Therapists need to keep in mind that improved affect does not necessarily imply that the patient has acquired the skills needed to successfully tackle added responsibilities and to deal with the consequences of more risky interpersonal behavior. Patients may become too bold, and thereby "get in trouble." Engaging in activities that carry great emotional risks and experiencing failure before new schemas and patterns have time to develop can send the patient into a renewed crisis of despair about the futility of both life and treatment.

Encouraging patients to make the most adaptive use of increased enthusiasm and energy, and helping them develop the skills needed for more socially rewarding and personally contented lives will be productive goals. The therapist must be mindful that long-standing interpersonal patterns will have to be addressed and changed for the patient to maintain improvements and that old cognitive schemas will need more than pharmacological intervention in order to change. Patients should be warned that bad times and moods inevitably will come again, and they should be prepared to deal with them effectively, thereby preventing full relapse. Some patients may be so apprehensive about falling back into their previous state of despair that they do not truly appreciate their improved affect, and are unwilling to experiment with new behavior for fear of negative consequences. The therapist must strike a therapeutic balance between being encouraging and optimistic on the one hand, yet urging caution on the other, emphasizing that recovery is a process, and making no unrealistic promises about the possibility of future perfection and happiness.

PART III

INTERPERSONALLY-IMBALANCED PERSONALITIES

CHAPTER 9

Dependent Personality Disorders: The Submissive Pattern

This chapter begins our discussion of what we have termed the "imbalanced personality styles"; included in this category are the dependent, histrionic, narcissistic, and antisocial disorders. What justifies unifying them is that their ecological orientation is heavily weighted in one or the other direction of the *self-other* polarity. They are either strongly disposed to orient themselves toward fulfilling the needs and desires of *others*—the dependent and histrionic patterns—or conversely, are overly inclined to meet their own, *self*ish wishes and aspirations—the narcissistic and antisocial.

To center one's attentions and activities almost exclusively to gain the approval or nurturance of others is a clear form of *imbalance,* a placing of oneself in a secondary position by depending on others or arranging one's life to fulfill "their" wishes. Similarly, a disinclination to value others, and to be satisfied only when meeting one's own needs and desires is an equally problematic form of *imbalance.* In both cases, self-oriented or other-oriented, there is no pleasure or life-enhancing deficiency, as in the three personality disorders discussed in the immediately preceding chapters. Thus the schizoid, avoidant, and depressive personalities either lack the capacity or the inclination to enhance life's potentials, that is, to seek or to experience pleasure. By contrast, the four personality disorders that make up this section have ample capacity to experience pleasure and enhance their lives. However, by being either self- or other-inclined, they orient their life-rewarding and life-preserving activities solely in one direction.

Both *dependent* and *histrionic* personalities are distinguished from other personality patterns by their marked need for social approval and affection, and by their willingness to live in accord with the desires of others. The "centers of gravity" of both dependents and histrionics lie in others, not in themselves. They adapt their behavior to please those to whom they are attached, and their search

for love leads them to deny thoughts and feelings that may arouse the displeasure of others. They avoid placing themselves first lest their actions be seen as unpleasant or repugnant. Both personality types feel paralyzed when alone and need repeated assurances that they will not be abandoned. Exceedingly sensitive to disapproval, they may experience any form of disinterest or criticism as devastating.

Dependents and histrionics do differ, however. Dependents take an ecologically *passive* stance, leaning on others to guide their lives, encouraging others to take the initiative, to arrange the dependent's life circumstances, and to be available to nurture and protect them. Moreover, dependent personalities *need* others to manage their lives. By contrast, histrionics are *active,* taking the initiative to arrange and to modify the ecological circumstances of their lives, ensuring first and foremost that the attentions and approval they need from others will be forthcoming. They do not sit passively, waiting for the competencies and skills of others to give shape to their lives. They do not cling or seek nurturance, as does the dependent personality. Rather, the principal goal is securing attention and approval, a means to avoid disinterest and abandonment. In contrast to the dependent, they possess the will and the ability to take charge of their lives; however, they are deeply insecure, unsure of whether they are desirable, if not truly loved.

Dependent personalities have a notable tendency to denigrate themselves and their accomplishments. What self-esteem they possess is determined largely by the support and encouragement of others. Unable to draw on themselves as a major source of comfort and gratification, they must arrange their lives to ensure a constant supply of nurturance and guidance from their environment. However, by turning exclusively to external sources for sustenance, dependents leave themselves open to the whims and moods of others. Losing the affection and protection of those on whom they depend leads them to feel exposed to the void of self-determination. To protect themselves, dependents quickly submit and comply with what others wish, or make themselves so pleasing that no one could possibly want to abandon them.

Dependents are also notably self-effacing, obsequious, ever-agreeable, docile, and ingratiating. A clinging helplessness and a search for support and reassurance characterize them. They tend to be self-depreciating, feel inferior to others, and avoid displaying initiative and self-determination. Except for needing signs of belonging and acceptance, they refrain from making demands on others. They deny their individuality, subordinate their desires, and hide what vestiges they possess as identities apart from others. They willingly take a submissive role in the hope of avoiding isolation, loneliness, and the dread of abandonment. Paralyzed and empty if left on their own, they feel the need for guidance in fulfilling even simple tasks or making routine decisions.

Many dependent individuals search for a single, all-powerful "magic helper," a partner in whom they can place their trust and depend on to protect them from having to assume responsibilities or face the competitive struggles of life alone. Supplied with a nurturant partner, they may function with ease, be sociable, and display warmth, affection, and generosity. Deprived of this support, they withdraw into themselves and become tense, despondent, and forlorn.

Despite the well-known prevalence of this personality pattern, there was only passing reference to it in the DSM-I and no provision at all in the DSM-II. The closest approximation in the DSM-II, though far from sufficient in either scope or clarity, was the "inadequate personality." The DSM-III and DSM-IV took cognizance of this important syndrome and gave it the status of a separate and major personality disorder. Before elaborating the clinical picture of the DSM dependent personality it will be useful and illuminating to briefly review formulations of a parallel nature that have been published by early as well as contemporary clinical theorists.

HISTORICAL ANTECEDENTS

Although their writings are of the 20th century, the conceptions of both Kraepelin and Schneider are more typical of earlier times; hence we will list them briefly under the designation "historical antecedents." The features of passively allowing others to assume responsibility and the characteristic receptivity to external influence were first described under the labels of the "shiftless" type by Kraepelin (1913) and the "weak-willed" personality by Schneider (1923/1950). Both theorists made little reference to the need for and the seeking of external support that typify dependent patients, stressing instead "their irresoluteness of will" and the ease with which they can be "seduced" by others. Schneider noted, "as far as their pliable natures will allow they are responsive to good influences, show regret for their lapses and display good intentions" (p. 133). Kraepelin considered these types to be a product of delayed maturation, a position that we are inclined to share. However, we do not agree with the following judgment of Kraepelin and Schneider that these individuals are readily "exploited to no good end," and "minimally competent to handle their affairs." To these early theorists, the "shiftless and weak-willed types" are easy prey to "bad notions" and ready targets for social forms of misconduct such as addiction and thievery.

MODERN FORMULATIONS

A distinct shift from the notion that these personalities were potentially immoral characters was taken by psychoanalytic theorists who were also writing in the first three decades of this century. Evolving their formulations in line with libidinal or psychosexual stage theory, both Freud and Abraham gradually constructed the "oral character" type, subsequently divided into two variants with appreciably different early experiences. Specifically, one was termed the "oral-sucking" or "oral-receptive" character, stemming from an early history of unusual gratification during nurturant feeding and weaning, versus "oral-pessimists" or "oral-sadistic" characters, whose early experiences were notably frustrating in nature; this latter variant will be discussed in Chapter 15, which deals with the negativistic (passive-aggressive) personality. Most clearly presented by Karl Abraham (1924/1927a), he describes the "oral-receptive" precursor of the DSM-III dependent personality as follows:

According to my experience we are here concerned with persons in whom the sucking was undisturbed and highly pleasurable. They have brought with them from this happy period a deeply rooted conviction that everything will always be well with them. They face life with an imperturbable optimism which often does in fact help them to achieve their aims. But we also meet with less favourable types of development. Some people are dominated by the belief that there will always be some kind person—a representative of the mother, of course—to care for them and to give them everything they need. This optimistic belief condemns them to inactivity . . . they make no kind of effort, and in some cases they even disdain to undertake a bread-winning occupation. (pp. 399–400)

Elaborating on this early statement, Fenichel (1945) highlighted other prime traits of the oral character, particularly those individuals who have experienced deprivation at this stage:

If a person remains fixated to the world of oral wishes, he will, in his general behavior, present a disinclination to take care of himself, and require others to look after him. . . . The behavior of persons with oral characters frequently shows signs of identification with the object by whom they want to be fed. Certain persons act as nursing mothers in all their object relationships. They are always generous and shower everybody with presents and help. (p. 489)

Sullivan (1947), although drawing from a different theoretical framework than libidinal theory, described in his "inadequate" personality a series of characteristics that correspond in many respects to the current DSM-IV criteria:

Some of these people have been obedient children of a dominating parent. They go through life needing a strong person to make decisions for them. Some of them learned their helplessness and clinging vine adaptation from parental example. (p. 84)

Perhaps the closest parallel to the DSM dependent personality is found in the descriptive features of the "compliant" type as formulated by Karen Horney (1945):

He shows a marked need for affection and approval and an especial need for a "partner"—that is, a friend, lover, husband or wife who is to fulfill all expectations of life and take responsibility for good and evil. . . .
This type has certain characteristic attitudes toward himself. One is the pervasive feeling that he is weak and helpless—a "poor little me" feeling. . . . A second characteristic grows out of

his tendency to subordinate himself. He takes for granted that everyone is superior to him. . . . The third feature . . . is his unconscious tendency to rate himself by what others think of him. His self-esteem rises and falls with their approval or disapproval, their affection or lack of it. (pp. 49–50)

A similar set of traits was provided by Erich Fromm (1947) in his characterization of the "receptive orientation":

In the receptive orientation a person feels "the source of all good" to be outside, and he believes that the only way to get what he wants—be it something material, be it affection, love, knowledge, pleasure—is to receive it from that outside source. . . .
They are dependent not only on authorities for knowledge and help but on people in general for any kind of support. They feel lost when alone because they feel that they cannot do anything without help. This helplessness is especially important with regard to those acts by which their very nature can only be done alone—making decisions and taking responsibility. (pp. 62–63)

As noted earlier—and quite surprisingly given its extensive reference in the literature—the dependent personality syndrome was accorded only brief mention in the DSM-I, noted as a subvariant of the passive-aggressive disorder, and it was totally overlooked in the DSM-II. Features of dependency were most closely represented in the *inadequate* personality disorder, but these failed to provide either a comprehensive or coherent picture of the clinical type. For reference purposes, the salient aspects of the inadequate personality were noted as follows:

This behavior pattern is characterized by ineffectual responses to emotional, social, intellectual and physical demands. While the patient seems neither physically nor mentally deficient, he does manifest inadaptability, ineptness, poor judgment, social instability and lack of physical and emotional stamina. (p. 44)

CONTEMPORARY PROPOSALS

There are major themes to be found in current object-relations and attachment theory that lay the groundwork for conceptions of the dependent personality, notably those found in Mahler and her associates (1975) and Bowlby (1969, 1980). Important themes that stress the acquisition of dependency behaviors have also been proposed by Heathers (1955), Gewirtz (1972), and Bandura (1977). A recent analysis relating attachment behaviors to the dependent personality style has been presented by Livesley, Schroeder, and Jackson (1990). The ensuing quote differentiates attachment from dependency as follows:

[Attachment is] any form of behavior that results in a person attaining or retaining proximity to some preferred individual, who is usually conceived as stronger and/or wiser. Dependency behaviors, in contrast, are not directed toward a specific individual, nor are they concerned with promoting the feelings of security that arise from proximity to attachment figures. Instead, they are more generalized behaviors designed to elicit assistance, guidance, and approval [from others]. (p. 132)

The recent work of Beck and his associates (1990b) on the personality disorders extends into a new sphere what Beck previously contributed to the understanding and treatment of depression and other emotional disorders. Applying his insights into the cognitive dysfunctional beliefs of the dependent personality disorder, Beck notes:

DPD can be conceptualized as stemming from two key assumptions. First, these individuals see themselves as inherently inadequate and helpless, and therefore unable to cope with the world on their own. They see the world as a cold, lonely, or even dangerous place that they could not possibly handle alone. Second, they conclude that the solution to the dilemma of being inadequate in a frightening world is to try to find someone who seems able to handle life and who will protect and take care of them. They decide that it is worth giving up responsibility and subordinating their own needs and desires in exchange for being taken care of. (p. 290)
In terms of hierarchy of beliefs, their core belief is likely to be "I am completely helpless," or "I am all alone." Their conditional beliefs are "I can function only if I have access to somebody competent," "If I am abandoned, I will die," "If I am not loved, I will always be unhappy." The instrumental level consists of imperatives such as "Don't offend the caretaker," "Stay close," "Cultivate as intimate

a relationship as possible," "Be subservient in order to bind him or her." (p. 45)

Drawing on the insightful works of Horney and Fromm was the controversial proposals made by Timothy Leary. At the time, Leary (1957) and his associates outlined the first systematic appraisal of personality disorders from an interpersonal perspective. Leary describes what he called the "docile-dependent" personality type, as follows:

The moderate form of this security operation is expressed as a respectful or poignant or trustful conformity. In its maladaptive intensity it is manifested as a helpless dependency. These subjects in their interpersonal reflexes avoid the expression of hostility, independence, and power.
Human beings utilize these security operations because they found that they are least anxious when they are outwardly relying on or looking up to others. . . . These persons . . . seem to go out of their way to pull sympathy, help, and direction from others; who use their symptoms to communicate a helpless, painful, uncertain, unfrightened, hopeful, dependent personality. (pp. 292, 293)

Extending the ideas posited by Leary and his associates some years earlier, Benjamin has refined the interpersonal perspective on personality disorders in her recent works. Describing aspects of the dependent personality disorder, Benjamin (1993a) writes:

The baseline position is of marked dependentness to a dominant other person who is supposed to provide unending nurturance and guidance. The wish is to maintain connection to that person even if it means tolerating abuse. The DPD believes that he or she is instrumentally incompetent, and this means that he or she cannot survive without the other dominant person. (pp. 228, 229)

Of potential recent interest are factor analytic studies of personality types and traits. For example, in a series of cross-validated projects designed to assess the factorial unity of certain presumed psychoanalytic types, Lazare, Klerman, and Armor (1966, 1970) identified the following characteristics as covarying to a high degree in what they termed the "oral factor": dependence, pessimism, passivity, self-doubt, fear of sexuality, and suggestibility. Along similar lines, Walton and Presley (1973a, 1973b) rated a population of patients on an inventory of personality traits and extracted a major component that they labeled "dependentness"; it was composed of the following items: timidity, meekness, dependentness, intropunitiveness, indecisiveness, and avoidance of competition. In noting possible parallels to this component in the clinical literature, Walton and Presley referred to the "obviously related" dependent personality, a classification well known to practicing professionals but one that did not appear in either the DSM-II or the ICD system.

As noted in prior chapters, the five-factor model has become the primary framework representing the statistical approach to the study of personality and its disorders. Notable in this regard has been the work of Costa and Widiger (1993) in which a systematic effort has been made to articulate the trait substrates of the personality disorders. As regards the dependent personality, they write:

DEP represents primarily an extreme variant of agreeableness with high levels of neuroticism and low assertiveness. Dependent individuals are characterized by a marked need for social approval and affection and will sacrifice many of their own needs, values, options, pleasures, and other goals to live in accord with the desires of others. (p. 50)

Few biologically grounded proposals have been made regarding the dependent personality. Cloninger (1987a) has proposed that this personality may be characterized, utilizing his theoretical model, by low novelty seeking, high harm avoidance, and high reward dependence. Given this combination, Cloninger suggests this personality would be highly submissive, deferential, ingratiating, and highly sensitive to criticism, frustration, and punishment, a picture quite consistent with the dependent personality disorder.

Millon (1969) drew upon his theoretically derived passive-dependent personality pattern to list a series of four basic criteria to characterize what we now term the "dependent personality" (referred to by him at that time as the submissive personality):

We shall label the central traits of the passive-dependent personality as follows: gentle affectivity *(having kind, soft and humanitarian impulses),* cognitive denial *(showing a Pollyanna-like refusal to admit discomforting thoughts),* inadequacy self-image *(viewing oneself as inferior, fragile and unworthy) and* interpersonal compliance *(willing to submit and oblige to others). (p. 244)*

Millon provided the following descriptive features and criteria in 1975 as the initial working draft for the personality subcommittee of the DSM-III Task Force:

This pattern is typified by a passive-dependency, general social naïveté and a friendly and obliging temperament. There is a striking lack of initiative and competitiveness, self-effacement of aptitudes and a general avoidance of autonomy. Appeasing and conciliatory submission to others is notable, as is a conspicuous seeking and clinging to supporting persons. Except where dependency is at stake, social difficulties are cognitively denied or neutralized by an uncritical and charitable outlook.

Since adolescence or early adulthood at least 3 of the following have been present to a notably greater degree than in most people and were not limited to discrete periods nor necessarily prompted by stressful life events.

1. *Pacific temperament (e.g., is characteristically docile and noncompetitive; avoids social tension and interpersonal conflicts).*

2. *Interpersonal dependentness (e.g., needs a stronger, nurturing figure, and without one feels anxiously helpless; is often conciliatory, placating, and self-sacrificing).*

3. *Inadequate self-image (e.g., perceives self as weak, fragile and ineffectual; exhibits lack of confidence by belittling own aptitudes and competencies).*

4. *Pollyanna cognitive style (e.g., reveals a naive or benign attitude toward interpersonal difficulties; smoothes over troubling events).*

5. *Initiative deficit (e.g., prefers a subdued, uneventful and passive life style; avoids self-assertion and refuses autonomous responsibilities).*

In a second draft revision of the criteria, Millon (1977) wrote the following list for review by his DSM-III Task Force associates:

A. *Excessive dependency (e.g., displays a chronic and conspicuous need for supporting or nurturant persons).*

B. *Isolation anxiety (e.g., cannot tolerate being alone for more than brief periods).*

C. *Lack of confidence and initiative (e.g., perceives self as weak, belittles aptitudes and is noncompetitive).*

D. *Dependent and socially conciliatory (e.g., avoids self-assertion, is self-sacrificing and Pollyanna-like).*

E. *Abdication of responsibilities (e.g., seeks others to assume leadership and direction for one's affairs).*

The shift from DSM-III to DSM-III-R in the dependent personality disorder was a modest but significant one. The core characterization referring to a lack of self-confidence was dropped from the criteria owing to the belief that this feature had little diagnostic specificity. Diagnostic specificity is an important consideration if one wishes to differentiate disorders rather than describe them. Specificity in this case may be less important than the recognition of a central feature of the disorder which, in our judgment, is crucial to the understanding of the dependent. In fact, it underlies a wide range of behaviors manifested by dependent persons (e.g., the need to seek others to serve as nurturers and supporters).

The ICD-10 has drawn on most of the characterizations listed in the DSM-IV criteria. Among these are such features as encouraging others to make most important life decisions: subordination of one's own needs to those on whom one is dependent, with unnecessary compliance to one's wishes: an unwillingness to make normal demands upon persons upon which one depends: considerable discomfort when helpless and alone owing to exaggerated fears of one's inability to take care of oneself: preoccupation with fears of being abandoned by those on whom one depends: and limited capacity to make decisions without excessive advice and reassurance from others. Associated features may include perceiving oneself as incompetent, helpless, and lacking in stamina.

Central to the DSM-IV characterizations is a pervasive need to be taken care of, resulting in dependent and clinging behaviors, as well as fears of separation. Among the eight listed diagnostic criteria, five express difficulties within the Interpersonal domain, two relate to problematic Self-image manifestations, and one relates primarily to the Cognitive sphere. In the Interpersonal realm, the following features serve as separate criteria: difficulties in making ordinary or everyday decisions without excessive advice and reassurance: an inclination to passivity by allowing others, often a single other person, to assume responsibility for most areas of life: difficulty in voicing independent views or expressing disagreement with significant others owing to a fear of losing their support or approval: a willingness to go to unusual lengths to obtain nurturance and support, even to undertaking unpleasant tasks; and an urgent seeking for relationships to supplant one that may have been terminated. A single Cognitive criterion is recorded, notably an unrealistic and excessive preoccupation with fears of being abandoned and thereby being left alone to take care of oneself. Finally, the two criteria that relate to the Self-image domain include a lack of self-confidence in one's self (rather than a lack of motivation or energy), resulting in an inability to initiate projects or to undertake independent tasks; and having exaggerated fears of not being competent to take care of oneself, resulting in feelings of helplessness and discomfort when alone.

We next turn to the dependent personality as interpreted by Millon's Polarity model; Figure 9.1 outlines the major motivational elements that undergird the ecologically adaptive style of this personality prototype. As with the majority of other personalities, the role of the enhancement (pleasure) and preservation (pain) polarities are of only modest significance. This minimal role was not found in the case of the schizoid, avoidant, and depressive personality patterns; here, the pleasure domain was notably deficient and the pain domain was prominent. In the dependent personality, primary attention may be found in the *other* (nurturant) and the *passive* (accommodating) polarities. Dependents share with the histrionic personality style a major ecological commitment to an other-oriented direction; both seek support, attention,

DEPENDENT PROTOTYPE

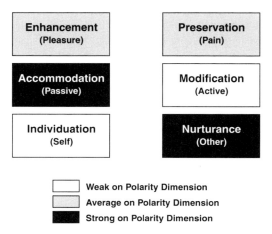

Figure 9.1   Status of the dependent personality prototype in accord with the Millon Polarity Model.

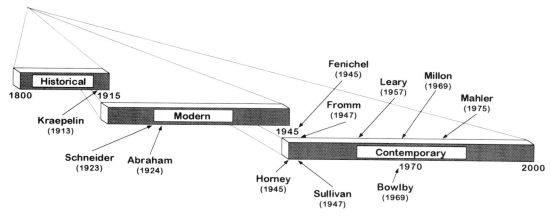

Figure 9.2   Historical review of major contributors to the dependent personality disorder.

and protection from others. However, for the dependent personality pattern, there is also an adaptive style of searching for guidance and support from others, a need to have them not only provide nurturance and protection but also to guide and show them how and when to achieve these security goals. This contrasts with the actively oriented ecological style of the histrionic personality, who arranges his or her life circumstances by making things happen. Histrionics may need others for attention and approval but are unwilling to accept the possibility that these might not be forthcoming; hence, they arrange and manipulate events, rather than wait for others to do it for them. Histrionics take active steps to achieve their goals effectively and reliably. By contrast, dependents entrust all to others, being passive, loyal, trustworthy and dependable, but lacking in initiative and competence.

A chronology of the major historical contributors is shown in Figure 9.2.

CLINICAL FEATURES

In the following sections, we will draw on theory, clinical literature, and the DSMs to provide both the structure and details of the dependent personality pattern.

PROTOTYPAL DIAGNOSTIC DOMAINS

Although the following analysis is separated into eight domains, the traits described should be seen as forming a coherent picture (Table 9.1). Congruity among the eight descriptive realms of behavior, phenomenological report, intrapsychic processes, and biophysical temperament should be expected because a distinguishing characteristic of a personality trait is its pervasiveness— its tendency to operate in numerous spheres of psychological functioning. It should not be surprising, therefore, that each section provides a clinical impression similar to the others (see also Figure 9.3).

Expressive Behavior: Incompetent

One of the most notable features of dependents is their lack of self-confidence, a characteristic apparent in their posture, voice, and mannerisms. They tend to be overly cooperative and acquiescent, preferring to yield and placate rather than be assertive. Large social groups and noisy events are abhorrent, and they go to great pains to avoid attention by underplaying both their attractiveness and their achievements. They are often viewed by friends as generous and thoughtful, and at times as unduly apologetic and obsequious. Neighbors may be impressed by their humility, cordiality, and graciousness, and by the "softness" and gentility of their behavior.

Beneath their warmth and affability may lie a plaintive and solemn quality, a searching for assurances of acceptance and approval. These needs may be especially manifest under conditions of stress. At these times, dependents are likely to exhibit overt signs of helplessness and clinging behaviors. They may actively solicit and plead for attention and encouragement. A depressive tone will often color their mood, and they may become overtly wistful or mournful. Maudlin and sentimental by

TABLE 9.1   Clinical Domains of the
Dependent Prototype

Behavioral Level

(F) Expressively Incompetent. Withdraws from
adult responsibilities by acting helpless and seeking
nurturance from others; is docile and passive, lacks
functional competencies, and avoids self-assertion.

(F) Interpersonally Submissive. Needs excessive
advice and reassurance; subordinates self to stronger,
nurturing figure, without whom may feel anxiously
alone and helpless; is compliant, conciliatory and placating, fearing being left to care for oneself.

Phenomenological Level

(F) Cognitively Naive. Rarely disagrees with others
and is easily persuaded, unsuspicious, and gullible;
reveals a Pollyanna attitude toward interpersonal difficulties, watering down objective problems and smooth-
ing over troubling events.

(S) Inept Self-Image. Views self as weak, fragile,
and inadequate; exhibits lack of self-confidence by
belittling own attitudes and competencies, and hence
not capable of doing things on one's own.

(S) Immature Objects. Internalized representations
composed of infantile impressions of others, unsophisticated ideas, incomplete recollections, rudimentary
drives and childlike impulses, as well as minimal competencies to manage and resolve stressors.

Intrapsychic Level

(F) Introjection Mechanism. Is firmly devoted to
another to strengthen the belief that an inseparable
bond exists between them; jettisons independent views
in favor of those of others to preclude conflicts and
threats to relationship.

(S) Inchoate Organization. Owing to entrusting others with the responsibility to fulfill needs and to cope
with adult tasks, there is both a deficient morphologic
structure and a lack of diversity in internal regulatory
controls, leaving a miscellany of relatively undeveloped
and undifferentiated adaptive abilities, as well as an
elementary system for functioning independently.

Biophysical Level

(S) Pacific Mood. Is characteristically warm, tender, and noncompetitive; timidly avoids social tension
and interpersonal conflicts.

(F) = Functional domain.
(S) = Structural domain.

disposition, they may also become excessively conciliatory and self-sacrificing in their relationships.

Interpersonal Conduct: Submissive

What interpersonal behaviors do dependents use
to manipulate their environment, and how do they
arrange their relationships to achieve their aims?

DEPENDENT PROTOTYPE

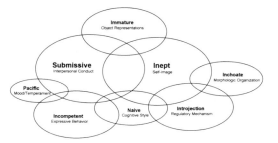

Figure 9.3   Salience of personologic domains in the
dependent prototype.

A major problem for dependent individuals is
that they not only find little reinforcement within
themselves but feel that they are inept and stumbling, and thus lacking in the skills necessary to
secure their needs elsewhere. As they see it, only
others possess the requisite talents and experience
to attain the rewards of life. Given these attitudes,
they conclude that it is best to abdicate self-
responsibility, to leave matters to others, and to
place their fate in others' hands. Others are so
much better equipped to shoulder responsibilities,
to navigate the intricacies of a complex world, and
to discover and achieve the pleasures to be found in
the competitions of life.

To achieve their goals, dependent personalities
learn to attach themselves to others, to submerge
their individuality, to deny points of difference, to
avoid expressions of power, and to ask for little
other than acceptance and support—in other words,
to assume an attitude of helplessness, submission,
and compliance. Moreover, by acting weak, expressing self-doubt, communicating a need for assurance, and displaying a willingness to comply and
submit, dependents are likely to elicit the nurturance and protection they seek.

Cognitive Style: Naive

It is characteristic of dependents to limit awareness
of self and others to a narrow sphere, well within
comfortable boundaries. They constrict their world
and are minimally introspective and Pollyanna-like
with regard to difficulties that surround them.
From an introspective view, dependent personalities tend to be naive, unperceptive, and uncritical.
They are inclined to see only the "good" in things,
the pleasant side of troubling events.

Self-Image: Inept

Dependents view themselves as weak and inadequate individuals, fragile when feeling alone or abandoned, and generally incapable of doing things on their own without the support or guidance of another. Not only do they lack a sense of self-confidence, but for reasons noted previously, they have a tendency to belittle their own competencies, beliefs and achievements. Dependents not only see themselves to be of limited value to others but prefer this image because few demands are made of inadequate persons, who are therefore often able to solicit the support and protection they desire.

From another perspective, dependents see themselves as considerate, thoughtful, and cooperative, disinclined to be ambitious and modest in their aspirations. Closer probing, however, is likely to evoke marked feelings of personal inadequacy and insecurity. Dependents tend to downgrade themselves, claiming to lack abilities, virtues, and attractiveness. They are disposed to magnify their failures and defects. When comparing themselves with others, they minimize their attainments, underplay their attributes, note their inferiorities, and assume personal blame for problems they feel they have brought on others. Of course, much of this self-belittling has little basis in reality. Clinically, this pattern of self-deprecation may best be conceived as a strategy by which dependents elicit assurances that they are not unworthy and unloved. Hence, it serves as an instrument for evoking praise and commendation.

Object-Representations: Immature

If one is able to examine the inner world of the dependents' representations of significant others, one is likely to see that these images are childlike, if not infantile in character. The content of their intrapsychic world seems to be composed of unsophisticated ideas, of incomplete recollections, and of rudimentary aspirations. Persons are seen as they may have been years before (e.g., as parents were when the patient was a child). Most other personality types hold mixed images of the past; although initially infantlike or childlike, the overlays of subsequent experiences give them a completeness, such that later impressions become part of the overall picture. For the dependent, however, there is a fixation on the past, with prominence given to more youthful impressions.

Dependents must be more than childlike if they are to secure and retain their hold on others. They must be admiring, loving, and willing to give their "all." Only by internalizing the role of the totally submissive and loyal can they be assured of evoking consistent care and affection. Fortunately, most dependents have learned through parental models how to behave affectionately and admiringly. Most possess an ingrained capacity for expressing tenderness and consideration, essential elements in holding on to their protectors. Also important is that most dependents have learned the "inferior" role well. They are able, thereby, to provide their "superior" partners with the feeling of being useful, sympathetic, stronger, and competent—precisely those behaviors that dependents seek in their mates. From many sources, then, dependent personalities have learned interpersonal strategies that succeed well in achieving the goals they seek.

Regulatory Mechanisms: Introjection/Denial

The inadequacies that dependents see within themselves may provoke feelings of emptiness and the dread of being alone. These terrifying thoughts are often controlled by introjection, a process by which they internalize the beliefs and values of another, imagining themselves to be one with, or an integral part of, a more powerful and supporting figure. By allying themselves with the competencies of their partners, they can avoid the anxieties evoked by the thought of their own impotence. Not only are they uplifted by illusions of shared competence, but through incorporation they may find solace in the belief that the attachments they have constructed are firm and inseparable.

Denial mechanisms also characterize the dependent's defensive style. This is seen most clearly in the Pollyanna quality of dependents' thoughts. Dependents are ever-alert to soften the edges of interpersonal strain and discomfort. A syrupy sweetness may typify their speech, and they may persistently cover up or smooth over troublesome events. Especially threatening are their own hostile impulses; any inner feeling or thought that might endanger their security and acceptance is quickly staved off. A torrent of contrition and self-debasement may burst forth to expiate momentary transgressions.

Morphologic Organization: Inchoate

The dependent has entrusted to others the capabilities and responsibilities for dealing with life's tasks. As a consequence, the morphologic structure of the dependent's intrapsychic world has not developed an adequate diversity of regulatory controls. What exists in this realm are either "borrowed" competencies through introjection, or a melange of relatively underdeveloped and undifferentiated coping abilities. Although able to function adequately when allied or closely connected to others who can "function" for them, dependents are only weakly effective when coping on their own.

By acting in a weak and inferior manner, dependents effectively free themselves of the responsibilities they know they should assume but would rather not. In a similar manner, self-depreciation evokes sympathy and attention from others, for which dependents are bound to feel guilt. Maneuvers and conflicts such as these are difficult for dependents to tolerate consciously. To experience comfort with themselves, dependents are likely to deny the feelings they experience and the deceptive strategies they employ. Likewise, they may cover up their obvious need to be dependent by rationalizing their inadequacies, attributing them to some physical illness, unfortunate circumstance, and the like. And to prevent social condemnation, they are careful to restrain assertive impulses and to deny feelings that might provoke criticism and rejection.

Dependents' social affability and good-naturedness not only forestall social deprecation but reflect a gentility toward the self, a tender indulgence that protects them from being overly harsh with their own shortcomings. To maintain equilibrium, they must take care not to overplay their expressions of guilt, shame, and self-condemnation. They are able to maintain a balance between moderate and severe self-deprecation by a Pollyanna tolerance of the self, "sweetening" their own failures with the same saccharine attitude that they use to dilute the shortcomings of others.

Mood/Temperament: Pacific

When matters are progressing well in their lives, dependents tend to be warm, tender, and noncompetitive, timidly avoiding social tensions and interpersonal conflicts. However, this pacific mood gives way under conditions of rejection and abandonment, a time period when dependents are likely to seek counseling or therapy. Underneath their initial Pollyanna veneer, these troubled dependents can no longer feel the joy of living. Once they "let down their hair," they will report deep feelings of insecurity, pessimism, discouragement, and dejection. Whatever their "suffering" may have been before, it is no longer done in silence, away from

those for whom they had to appear pleased and content with life. Now that life has taken a turn for the worse, their underlying insecurities become evident in gloomy and tearful emotions.

PROTOTYPAL VARIANTS

As in prior and later chapters, we will describe a series of variations of the prototypal dependent in the following paragraphs, beginning with what we have termed "normal styles."

Normal Styles

Dependent individuals have historically been found in all traditional cultures, persons whose roles are clearly defined as providing service to others, expected to act in a self-abnegating manner, and exhibiting a public posture of low self esteem. Even in our own Western culture, in the latter part of the 20th century, there remain many settings where women play an inferior and subjugated role. Since the advent of the feminist movement, however, women no longer should nor are they willing to accept the status of second-class citizens. Despite this important advance, the role of dependent ministering to the wishes of others remains a pervasive cultural style throughout much of the undeveloped world, both for women and men.

Apart from the impact of culture in shaping this style of life for many of its citizens, there are those who are disposed to assume this role by virtue of the specifics of their individual experiences, not those imposed on them by society.

Oldham and Morris (1990) describe normal dependents as expressing the "devoted style," characterizing them by the fact that they "care" and that they are extremely solicitous and concerned for the welfare of others before themselves.

A slightly different portrayal of the normal Dependent style is presented by Millon et al. (1994) in referring to those individuals whose scores on the MIPS "agreeing" scale are at the high end of the dimension:

These persons represent an accommodating, participatory, compromising, and agreeing pattern of behavior. Their congenial obligingness is voluntary rather than being coerced or being a product of self-derogation. Those who fit this pattern are notably cooperative and amicable. Disinclined to upset others, they are willing to adapt their preferences to be compatible with those of others.

Trusting others to be kind and thoughtful, they are also willing to reconcile differences and to achieve peaceable solutions, as well as to be considerate and to concede when necessary. Cordiality and compromise characterize their interpersonal relationships. (p. 34)

Among the healthy dependent varieties, we find individuals who are capable of empathizing with others, willingly giving of themselves and possessing a great capacity for caring and sustained love for others. They are among the most trusting of individuals, communicating unquestioned acceptance of others. They are modest and gentle in their demeanor, comfortable sanctuaries for those who seek peace and solace.

Notable is their uncritical and unthreatening manner. They do not set unattainable standards for either themselves or for those whom they value. Easy to please, they demand little from others, are totally uncritical, and invariably gracious, even to those they may dislike. Altruistic and unselfish, their love is unconditional, extended with no strings attached. Most have deep reservoirs of good will and are invariably pleased by the good fortunes of others. Despite the high esteem in which they are held for their modesty and goodwill, the more that people value them, the more humble they become and the less they want. They are as close to what one thinks of as saints, but are simply pleased to be thought of as good, and would be embarrassed to be acknowledged as special. Charitable in giving of themselves, they put a positive light on all life events and stress the virtues and good they find in others.

Childhood Syndromes

In 1952, Margaret Mahler coined the term "childhood symbiosis," a pattern of behavior that closely parallels the adult Dependent Personality disorder, although in more severe form and at an earlier stage of development. Problematic as this syndrome was seen, it is usually less serious in its level of pathology and occurs with somewhat lesser frequency than either autism, Asperger's syndrome, or threctism. Perhaps this is because the symbiotic child has gained the rewards of a close personal relationship.

In the DSM-III, the label "separation-anxiety disorder" was introduced to portray the features seen in these youngsters. What was judged essential in the clinical picture was the predominance of anxiety on separation from major attachment figures. Also notable were unrealistic worries about possible harm to significant figures, or an unrealistic concern that some calamitous event would separate the child from these attachments. Also present were refusals to go to school, an unwillingness to go to sleep away from home, repeated nightmares, and social withdrawal or sadness when not with the attachment figure. These same themes are also seen as diagnostic criteria in DSM-IV.

As noted, there is an unusual attachment to the caretaking figure; the child brooks no separation and may be overwhelmed by panic should the mother leave. This contrasts markedly to autistic and threctic children, who seem indifferent to the presence of others or relieved when left alone. Parents describe symbiotic youngsters as extremely immature and fearful, as "cry-babies" who cling like appendages, unwilling or unable to stand and do things on their own (these clinical symptoms do not usually draw notice until the second stage of neuropsychological development when the child fails to assume autonomous behaviors; they generally come to attention, then, between the ages of 2 and 4).

Moderately impaired youngsters with similar features may properly be regarded as "child-symbiosis: moderate severity"; mild cases of overattachment at this age do not signify pathology because most of these youngsters "grow out of" the habit. A pattern similar to the moderate form of symbiosis was described in the 1966 report of the Group for the Advancement of Psychiatry (GAP) under the label "overly dependent personalities." These cases may be difficult to differentiate from the moderately severe form of "childhood threctism" in that both groups of youngsters exhibit extreme apprehension; the threctic child, however, is pervasively anxious and tense whereas the symbiotic child is so only when parted from the person(s) to whom he or she is attached.

As we view it, the *symbiotic* child experiences a morbid parental attachment, producing marked separation anxieties, and a failure to acquire autonomous competencies; the child not only struggled to retain the symbiotic unity of the first developmental stage, but was incapable of functioning alone. Excessive dependency may have had its basis in a constitutional threctic temperament, a biophysically based vulnerability to threat and anxiety. Parents who responded to their youngsters' pathetic fearfulness by coddling and overprotecting them set the stage for learning intense attachments. Furthermore, the constitutional fearfulness of these children disposed them to avoid venturing into the unknown, thereby further reinforcing their dependencies. At some critical period, such as when the child was enrolled in nursery school or when a new sibling was born, the severe nature of this dependency attachment was brought into sharp relief.

No constitutional disposition need have existed, however, to have encouraged the development of excessive attachment and dependency behaviors; parental anxieties and an overprotective style of childhood management may have fostered the same condition. Here, too, the problem often first becomes manifest when the youngster panics at periods of separation or forced independence. As Mahler (1968) has pointed out, this troubled pattern can be seriously exacerbated if the maternal figure manifests ambivalence about permitting the child to become increasingly autonomous of her control or oversight.

Adult Subtypes

Although all combinations are possible theoretically, experience and research show that only certain personality types tend to overlap or coexist with the dependent disorder. This discussion draws on the evidence of several statistical cluster studies to supplement what theoretical deduction and observation suggest as the most prevalent personality mixtures. Also included are patterns that reflect differences in the pathogenic background of the various personality subtypes.

The Disquieted Dependent

This adult subtype is likely to be prevalent in settings that minister to ambulatory chronic patients who are sustained in a dependent and largely parasitic state by virtue of institutional rewards and requirements. As with other dependent varieties, their behavior may be characterized as submissively dependent, self-effacing, and noncompetitive. Others are leaned on for guidance and security, and a passive role is assumed in relationships. These dependents, however, give evidence of intense apprehensiveness and fearfulness that overlie a sulking lack of initiative and an anxious avoidance of autonomy. Hence, the *disquieted* dependent reflects a commingling of the basic dependent style with that of the avoidant personality.

We may summarize some of their more distinctive features by noting that *disquieted dependents* are restlessly perturbed, seem easily disconcerted and fretful, experience a general sense of dread and foreboding; but as with other dependents, they are apprehensively vulnerable to fears of abandonment and experience a sense of loneliness unless they are near nurturing figures or accessible to supportive institutions.

These personalities are exceedingly dependent, not only in needing attention and support from others to maintain equanimity, but in being especially vulnerable to separation from those who provide support. Anguished and fearful of loss, they may ventilate their tensions through outbursts of anger directed toward others for having failed to appreciate their needs for security and nurturance. The very security that these patients so desperately need is completely undone, however, when resentments are expressed.

Disquieted dependents are not only apprehensive but have acquired a pattern of withdrawing from social encounters. Further, they have built a tight armor to damp down and deaden excessive sensitivity to rejection. Loneliness and isolation are commonly experienced. Despite their efforts to be pleasant and agreeable, as dependents often are, they experience an underlying tension and emotional dysphoria, expressed in disturbing mixtures of anxious, sad, and guilt-ridden feelings. Insecurity and fears of abandonment underlie what may appear on the surface to be a quiet, dependent, and benign attitude toward difficulties. Despite past rebuff and fears of isolation, the disquieted dependent continues to evidence a clinging helplessness and a persistent search for support and reassurance. Complaints of weakness and easy fatigability may reflect an underlying mood of depression. Having experienced continuing rebuff from others, the patient may succumb to physical exhaustion and illness. Under these circumstances, simple responsibilities demand more energy than the patient can muster. The individual expresses the feeling that life is empty but heavy, experiencing a pervasive sense of anxiety and fatigue.

The Accommodating Dependent

The *accommodating dependent's* behavior is best characterized by a submissiveness, a high degree of agreeableness and a leaning on others for affection, nurturance, and security. The fear of being abandoned leads this personality to be overly compliant and obliging. Some of these individuals handle their fears by being socially gregarious and superficially charming, often evident in the seeking of attention and in self-dramatizing behaviors. We will describe such personalities as the *appeasing histrionic,* to be discussed in Chapter 10. These individuals possess an unusual knack for placating and conceding; as basic histrionics, they comfortably exhibit gregarious, charming, and self-dramatizing behaviors. Both accommodating dependents and appeasing histrionics are gracious, neighborly, benevolent, compliant, eager to please, that is, obliging and agreeable in their relationships with others. What differentiates them is the strong tendency of accommodating subtypes to be self-sacrificing, their ability to adopt not only a submissive style, but to play the role well of inferior and subordinate to others. In this regard, we see in these individuals a basic amalgamation between the dependent and masochistic personality styles.

The accommodating dependent reveals a naive attitude toward interpersonal problems. Critical thinking rarely is evident and most cognitive knowledge appears to be almost entirely undeveloped and immature. There is an effort to maintain an air of pleasantry and good spirits, a denial of all disturbing emotions, covering inner disharmonies by short-lived distractions. In part, this may stem from a tendency to be genuinely docile, softhearted, and sensitive to the desires of others. These individuals are more than merely accommodating and docile in efforts to secure dependency needs. They are admiring and loving, giving all to those upon whom there is dependence. They have also learned to play the inferior role well, providing partners with the rewards of feeling useful, sympathetic, stronger, and more competent. There is often an active solicitousness of praise, a willingness to demean oneself, and a tendency to be self-sacrificing and virtuous.

In what way do these compliant and good-natured individuals prove to be a problem to others? They always have a smile and a friendly word; they are responsive and agreeable, whatever others might request; accommodating dependents are always willingly obliging. Difficulties arise in that these individuals always say yes, but rarely follow through in fulfilling those requests. Unsure of themselves and in many ways deficient in their competencies, these dependents lack the wherewithal to achieve what others expect of them. Adult activities call for more than good-natured agreeableness. They require concerted attention, a capacity to execute, not only difficult tasks, but even those that may be enjoyable and mutually rewarding.

All that really matters to accommodating dependents is that others like them, are pleased by them, and are willing to accept their smiles and goodwill as sufficient. Fearing that they may fail to receive acceptance and approval by attempting any "real actions" on their part, that is, by seeking to execute adultlike responsibilities, they restrain themselves from demonstrating their weaknesses and inefficiencies, reverting again and again to sociable pleasantries. Fearing conflict and rejection, stuck with their overpowering need to be liked and accepted, they are unable to follow through on any realistic commitments, lapsing once more to their friendly and ever-promising front.

As noted previously, the accommodating dependent is similar to the appeasing histrionic personality in that both seek harmony with others, if necessary at the expense of their internal values and beliefs. Similarly, both are likely to actively avoid all situations that may involve personal conflict. However, to minimize distressing relationships, accommodating dependents avoid self-assertion and abdicate autonomous responsibilities, preferring to leave matters in the hands of others. By contrast, histrionics take an active posture, maneuvering and manipulating their life circumstances, rather than passively sitting by. Both types, however, owing to their preoccupation with gaining external approval, may be left without an inner identity. *Accommodating* and *appeasing* personalities value themselves not in terms of their intrinsic traits, but in terms of their relationships with others. By submerging or allying themselves with the competencies and virtues of others, these personalities not only are bolstered by the illusion of shared competence but find solace in the belief that bonds so constructed are firm and inseparable.

As noted, accommodating dependents feel helpless when faced with responsibilities that demand autonomy or initiative. The loss of a significant source of support or identification may prompt severe dejection. Under such conditions of potential rejection or loss, they will openly solicit signs of reassurance and approval. Guilt, illness, anxiety, and depression are frankly displayed because these tend to deflect criticism and transform threats of disapproval into those of support and sympathy. When dependency security is genuinely threatened, the accommodating personality will manifest an anxious depressiveness covarying with other, more extreme reactions.

The Immature Dependent

There is reason to believe that maturation does not follow a predetermined course in all individuals; moreover, persons differ in the speed in which certain processes develop. Similarly, there is evidence to indicate that not all persons mature in all their capacities and functions to the same level. For example, in the intellectual realm, there are persons who appear extraordinarily talented in mathematics and music at a very early age; conversely, there are those who never achieve even a modest level of accomplishment at any point in their life in these same realms. Individual differences in the level and rapidity of maturational development is widespread across all attribute domains.

The preceding discussion also applies to the maturation of adultlike characteristics and capabilities. Some persons remain childlike throughout their lives. They prefer childhood activities, find great satisfaction relating to children, and seem either incapable of, or to abhor activities we assume are normal features of adult activity and responsibility. These persons are not only dependent because they are childlike in their outlook and competencies, but also because they seem *satisfied* to remain childlike in their activities and orientation. It is these individuals whom we refer to as *immature dependent personalities*. In describing these immature dependent subtypes, we might say that they are undeveloped, inexperienced, unsophisticated, unformed, and unversed. Pleased and satisfied with themselves in not assuming adult roles and responsibilities, they are also incapable of doing so owing to their half-grown or childlike level of maturity.

Whether they are so disposed by constitutional predilections or reinforced in early life to prefer a childlike existence cannot be determined by present scientific means. Whatever its origins, these personalities seem to prefer, feel protected by, or find their greatest satisfactions in remaining oriented to the world of childhood and adolescence. To remain undeveloped is to find a more tranquil existence than found in adulthood with its demands, strivings, competition, and responsibilities. Some of these immature dependents may simply lack ambition and energy, hence making the expectancies of adulthood overwhelming and frightening. Others appear to be overly passive and easygoing, undeveloped in the acquisition of autonomous behaviors and the confidence-building crucial in the second stage of neuropsychological development. Many appear to lack a strong gender identity and to find the assumption of adult roles to be somewhat distasteful or frightening.

For the most part, these individuals are pleasant and sociable—as long as they are permitted to remain pre-adult in their preferences and activities. These individuals can become quite problematic to others who expect more of the dependents or demand that they "mature" and get down to the business of life. Unfortunately, the business of life implies being and acting like an adult. To dependents' troubled parents or spouses, these behaviors are often seen as signs of irresponsibility and neglectfulness.

The Ineffectual Dependent

The *ineffectual dependent* type shows similarities to the *languid schizoid* pattern. Both styles exhibit a general lack of vitality, low energy level, fatigability, and a general weakness in expressiveness and spontaneity. Hence, we are likely to see with some frequency that ineffectual dependents reflect the intermingling of both basic dependent and schizoid characteristics. However, the languid schizoid is motorically and affectively deficient. Moreover, thought processes among purer schizoid personalities, though not markedly deficient, appear unfocused, particularly with regard to interpersonal matters. Schizoid languid types also show a deficiency in the expression of affect, a defect stemming in all probability from an anhedonic temperament, inclining them to be persistently aloof from life's social interactions. By contrast, *ineffectual dependents* do not want to be isolated from close personal relationships. Although seeking to be close and caring, these dependent types lack drive and staying power, are deficient in their adultlike skills, and seem simply unwilling to pursue solutions to end even minor problems.

What ineffectual dependents possess is a desperate need to lead a totally untroubled life and to be free of any and all responsibilities. There is a fatalism about them, a willingness to ignore the difficulties they may face by simply refusing to deal with them, to tune them out, or let them be. They seem resigned and not unhappy to accept their ineffectual fate—except for one thing, that of being nurtured and protected by others. However, other than seeking peace and amity with others at any price, these dependents are unwilling to face life's difficulties squarely. They fall to such a level as to be unable to deal with any and all difficulties. If possible, they would like to turn their backs on what they see as a demanding world, or to bury their heads as far as they can in the sand. Not wanting to deal with reality, they resist all pressures that might intrude on them, sleepwalking through their lives, increasingly disengaged and dependent. They cling to others in a childlike manner, even for the most basic requirements of everyday survival. What is seen as most prominent is their total malleability and lack of will.

The Selfless Dependent

Selfless dependents not only subordinate themselves to others, a characteristic shared by other dependent personalities, but merge themselves totally with another such that they lose themselves in the process. These dependents willingly give up their own identity as independent human beings to acquire a more secure sense of significance, identity, emotional stability, and purpose in life. As the process of total identification with another becomes established and integrated, these individuals fail increasingly to develop any of their own, personally distinctive, potentials. And as their own sense of self becomes a less significant part of their being, whatever they do is done almost entirely in the service of extending the status and significance of another, be it a person or an institutional entity.

Whatever impulses and potentials that might have existed for them as independent persons are denied or dissociated. They have become fully merged, as if they had no self, were nonbeings, except for their coupling with another person. Their existence has *not* been denied, as occurs in some cases of the ineffectual dependent style, but becomes an extension of whomever they are now a part. So fused and entwined, they may act at times in ways quite divergent from what has been characteristic of them. Thus, they may exhibit an air of confidence and self-assurance, but only as it reflects the achievements and powers of the person or institution to which they are united. Thus, they have not lost a sense of self-worth. Rather, by virtue of their alliances, they have acquired and assumed that they themselves now possess many of the qualities that inhere intrinsically in those with whom they have identified.

Many *selfless dependents* feel fulfilled by their associations. Not only do they willingly submit to the values and beliefs of their significant attachments, but their very sense of being depends on it. The more they are fused with the idealized object, the more attached they are emotionally, and the more they feel that they themselves exist as persons who have significance in the world. For example, there are many mothers who live for their children or submerge themselves totally within the lives of their husbands. Although they may have gone overboard in their identifications, losing too much of themselves by so doing, these selfless dependents feel vitalized and valuable by virtue of these joinings. They have given totally of themselves and have embraced fully the actions and values of another, naively displacing their very selves for that person's sake.

Owing to the insecurities that result from their loss of self, and the vulnerable position in which they have placed themselves, these dependent personalities are likely to have acquired some of the features of the depressive personality. Although no actual loss may have occurred in the past, these dependents have learned to live on the edge of such possibilities. Experiencing the loss and consequent hopelessness that would ensue from such an eventuality, elements of a depressive character would have infused into their basic dependent style, interjecting expectancies and reactions that would have occurred had these losses become reality.

COMORBID DISORDERS AND SYNDROMES

This section briefly discusses the prime Axis I and Axis II disorders that often covary with the personality syndrome under review. The comorbidities associated with the dependent personality disorder are outlined in Figure 9.4. Although abbreviated, it should be self-evident which disorders and syndromes overlap frequently.

Axis II Comorbidities

As noted in previous chapters, features of other personalities often fuse with the dependent personality prototype, as seen in various Adult Subtypes (e.g., immature, ineffectual). It would be of interest, however, to visually represent which Axis II disorders have, in fact, been found empirically to covary with the dependent personality. As seen in Figure 9.4, the highest degree of correspondence for the dependent personality is found with the avoidant (AVD) and masochistic (MAS) personality types. Lesser comorbidities are seen with the histrionic (HIS) and the depressive (DPS). Not

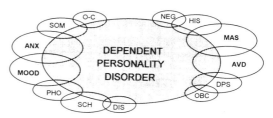

Figure 9.4 Comorbidity between dependent personality disorder and other DSM Axis I and Axis II disorders.

to be overlooked also are minor degrees of concurrence with obsessive-compulsive (OBC) and negativistic (NEG) personality types.

Axis I Comorbidities

In addition to identifying the most frequent accompanying Axis I difficulties, we will describe the more common sensitivities and vulnerabilities that dispose dependent personalities to exhibit these syndromes. Further, note will be made of several of the hypothesized dynamics and secondary gains that characteristically occur among these personalities when they exhibit the Axis I disorder under discussion.

Anxiety Syndromes (ANX). Dependent personalities are extremely vulnerable to anxiety disorders, especially those referred to as separation anxieties. Having placed their welfare entirely in the hands of others, they expose themselves to conditions that are ripe for generalized anxieties. There may be an ever-present worry of being abandoned by their sole benefactor and left alone to struggle with their meager competencies. Another factor that may give rise to *panic anxiety* attacks is the anticipation and dread of new responsibilities. Their sense of personal inadequacy and the fear that new burdens may tax their limited competencies (thereby bringing disapproval from others) may precipitate a dramatic change from calmness to marked anxiety. Because anxious displays often serve to evoke nurturant and supporting responses from others, an anxiety disorder may come to be used as a tool that enables the dependent to avoid the discomforting responsibilities of autonomy and independence.

Phobic Syndromes (PHO). Dependent personalities develop phobic disorders when their security is threatened or when demands are made that exceed their feelings of competence. They avoid responsibility, especially actions requiring self-assertion and independence. To ensure the safety of their dependency, they will quickly displace or transform any thought or impulse that may provoke rebuke. *Social phobias* are not uncommon among these personalities. Not only do phobic symptoms externalize anxiety and avoid threats to security, but by anchoring inner tensions to tangible outside sources, dependents prompt others to come to their assistance. For these reasons, dependents are especially vulnerable to *agoraphobic attacks.* These anticipatory fears of leaving familiar and secure settings, most frequently one's home, serve well as a means of soliciting care and protection. Thus, the phobic maneuver achieves secondary gains that are fully consonant with the patient's basic dependent orientation.

Obsessive-Compulsive Syndromes (O-C). Often preoccupied with self-doubts, dependent personalities may be subject to a variety of obsessive-compulsive disorders. These symptoms usually stem from reactivated feelings of inadequacy and are precipitated by situations calling for independence and responsibility. At these times, they are likely to weigh interminably the pros and cons of the situation and thereby endlessly postpone any change in their dependent status. Obsessional thoughts and compulsive acts may also arise in response to feelings of separation anxiety or repressed anger. Here, coping is an aid (through reaction formation or undoing) in countering tensions that stem from the isolation or discharge of security-jeopardizing impulses. These symptoms often take the form of "sweet" thoughts and approval-gaining acts.

Somatoform Syndromes (SOM). Dependent personalities may develop somatoform disorders as a means of controlling the upsurge of forbidden impulses. More commonly, these symptoms promote the avoidance of onerous responsibilities and help recruit secondary gains such as sympathy and nurturance. By displaying physical helplessness, dependents often succeed in eliciting the attention and care they need. *Conversion* symptoms may be a form of self-punishment for feelings of guilt and worthlessness. Dependents tend, however, not to be too harsh with themselves. Their conversion symptoms are likely to take the form of relatively mild sensory anesthesias such as a generalized numbness in the hands and feet. It is notable that their symptoms often are located in their limbs, a way perhaps of demonstrating to others that they are disabled and, therefore, incapable of performing even routine chores.

Among the principal goals of *hypochondriacal* and *somatization* disorders are dependents' desires to solicit attention and nurture from others and to evoke assurances that they will be loved and cared for, despite weaknesses and inadequacy. By their illness, dependents divert attention from the true source of their dismay, the feeling that others are showing little interest and paying little attention to them. Without complaining directly about their disappointment and resentment, dependents still manage through their physical ailments to attract and rekindle the flagging devotions of others. Not to be overlooked also is that illness complaints may be employed to control others, make them feel guilty, and thereby retaliate for the disinterest and mistreatment dependents may feel they have suffered. In some cases, pain and nagging symptoms represent a form of self-punishment, an attack on oneself that is disguised in bodily ailments and physical exhaustion.

Factitious Syndromes (FAC).   Because dependent personalities have been well trained to view themselves as weak and inadequate, it would not be unlike them to readily assume the role of the patient and, hence, be disposed to factitious disorders. Overdependency and excessive parental solicitousness may have taught them as children to protect themselves, not to exert their frail capacities or assume responsibilities that may strain their delicate bodies. Any source of tension, be it externally precipitated or based on the control of forbidden impulses, may lead to an anxious conservation of energy. Having learned that frailty and weakness elicit protective and nurtural reactions from others, dependents may allow themselves to succumb to physical exhaustion or illness as a device to ensure these desired responses. It is not unlikely that genuinely felt guilt may be stirred up when dependents recognize how thoughtless and ineffectual they have been in carrying out their responsibilities. But here again, physical weariness and bodily illness come to the rescue as a rationalization to exempt them from assuming their share of chores.

Dissociative Syndromes (DIS).   Although infrequent, dependent personalities may develop dissociative disorders. These dreamlike trance states may occur when they are faced with responsibilities that surpass their feelings of competence. Through this process, the dependent effectively fades out of contact with threatening realities. Amnesic episodes, however, are likely to be rare since they would prompt to intensify existent separation anxieties. Repetitive somnambulistic states may not be as uncommon. Here dependents may vent minor forbidden impulses or seek to secure affect and nurture. Brief, frenzied actions may arise if the patient is in a decompensated state. Here dependents may feel an upsurge of intense hostile impulses that can threaten their dependency security. By these means, contrary feelings are discharged without the patient knowing it and therefore without having to assume blame. Irrational acts such as

these are so uncharacteristic of this personality that these behaviors are seen by others as a sure sign of sickness, thereby eliciting support (rather than rejecting) responses.

Mood Syndromes (MOOD).   Because dependent personalities are especially susceptible to separation anxiety, feelings of helplessness readily come to the fore when they anticipate abandonment. The actual loss of a significant person is very likely to prompt any number of affective disorders, including a *major depression.* Actual abandonment may prompt the dependent to plead for reassurance and support. Expressions of guilt and self-condemnation are not uncommon because these verbalizations often deflect criticisms and transform threats into sympathy. Guilt may be employed as a defense against outbursts of resentment and hostility. Dependents usually contain their anger since they dread provoking retribution. To prevent this, dependents typically turn their aggressive impulses inward, discharging them through self-derisive comments, guilt, and contrition. Here we may see the development of chronic states of *dysthymia.* These less severe depressive periods not only temper the exasperation of others but often prompt them to respond in ways that make the patient feel redeemed and loved.

On occasion, dependent personalities exhibit a marked, although usually temporary, reversal of their more subdued and acquiescent style. In these cases of *bipolar disorder,* with their unusual *manic* episodes, the happy-go-lucky air, boundless energy, and buoyant optimism are merely a front, an act in which they try to convince themselves as well as others that "all will be well." What we see at these times is a desperate effort to counter the beginning signs of hopelessness and depression, a last-ditch attempt to deny what they really feel and to recapture the attention and security they fear they have lost.

Schizophrenic Syndromes (SCH).   Dependent personalities succumb on rare occasion to *schizoaffective* disorders. Here we often see a coloring of sadness that draws others to, rather than away, from the patient. The tone of inner softness reflects an inclination to acquiesce to the wishes of others in the hope of maintaining some measure of affection and support from them. It is in dependent patients that we often see the cataleptic waxy flexibility of the *catatonic* disorder. This willingness to be molded according to the desires of others signifies the personality's complete abandonment of self-initiative and its total dependence and sub-mission to external directives. At the heart of these patients' passive accuiescence is the deep need that dependents have to counter their separation anxieties and to avoid actions that might result in disapproval and rejection.

DIFFERENTIAL DIAGNOSES

Since multiple diagnoses among mental disorders are not only possible but encouraged by the DSM-IV multiaxial schema, the importance of differen-tial diagnosis, so central to conventional medical assessment, has clearly diminished. Despite its lessened role, there are justifications for insisting on clear differentiation among disorders. The main reason is to reduce diagnostic confusion, not to sep-arate syndromes that naturally overlap. Diagnostic clarity is important because it bears on the nature and goals of treatment. For example, if a dependent personality style accounts for a particular set of symptoms more accurately than a transient or situationally specific agoraphobia, the therapist will likely decide that cognitive or intrapsychic, rather than behavioral, methods are most suitable to the case.

Few problems should be encountered when sep-arating personality syndromes from disorders listed under Axis I. Because multiaxial diagnosis requires a listing of impairments from both Axis I and Axis II, the task should not be primarily that of differentiating between these two spheres but of finding which categories in the first axis covary with which categories in the second. Nevertheless, if the behaviors under scrutiny give evidence of having been lifelong, then they should be identi-fied as representing a personality disorder, rather than a clinical syndrome. Similarly, if pathologi-cal features manifest themselves across a wide va-riety of settings and circumstances, rather than being limited to specific situations, then a person-ality diagnosis is again the likely correct one.

There are two Axis I syndromes that present more than the usual level of differential diagnostic difficulty with the dependent personality. The first of these potentially confusing classifications is *dysthymic disorder;* the second is *agoraphobia.*

In the first of these syndromes, the problem centers on the so-called stability, or long-standing nature, of the Axis I category; *dysthymia* requires an extended period of time. However, the descrip-tive criteria for this diagnosis focuses almost exclusively on the patient's depressed mood and fails to include the diverse clinical traits that com-prise the dependent personality complex. Of course, the Axis I dysthymic disorder may be diag-nosed as concurrent with the Axis II dependent personality.

As far as *agoraphobia* is concerned, the issue is essentially one of duration and pervasiveness of symptomatology. Quite typically, the symptoms of agoraphobics are situationally specific and arise episodically. Moreover, the dependent's hesitations in assuming responsibility and autonomy take a passive form, whereas agoraphobics are insistent and demanding of the support of others. Addition-ally, the dependents' interpersonal submissiveness and feelings of inadequacy are characteristics that are not found in most patients who have an agora-phobic fear of being alone or in unprotected situa-tions. Again, where appropriate, the simultaneous diagnosis of an agoraphobic Axis I disorder and a dependent Axis II personality is available to the clinician.

Turning to Axis II diagnostic discriminations involving the dependent personality, we find that confusions are made most often with the three per-sonality patterns with which they frequently over-lap with histrionic, masochistic, and the avoidant.

The key features differentiating the dependent from the *histrionic* are the passivity, submissive-ness, self-effacement, and docility of the former, in contrast to the actively manipulative, gregari-ous, charming, and frequently seductive, attention-getting behaviors of the latter.

As far as differentiating *avoidant* from depen-dent personalities, the primary distinction relates to matters of trust; both have strong needs for af-fection and nurturance, but the avoidant fears and strongly doubts the good faith of others, anticipat-ing instead both rejection and humiliation, and thereby seeks to withdraw from close relation-ships; the dependent, in contrast, is not only recep-tive to others and willing to rely on their goodwill but has learned to anticipate gratifying conse-quences when turning to them.

The inclusion of the *masochistic* personality among the major disorders in this text may lead to diagnostic difficulties. Both dependents and masochists are self-effacing and adopt rather sub-missive roles in their relationships. The difference is in part a matter of degree, but beyond that the motives that drive their behaviors, and the self-defeating qualities of the masochist aid in making discriminations. The dependent's alliance with others has been a good one inasmuch as others have historically been supporting and nurturing. The dependents' confidence is weak by virtue of actual deficiencies in their capacity to function maturely. By contrast, masochists may be fully competent, but they either demean that competency, or undo what they are capable of. Thus, masochists create difficulties for themselves owing to their fear that success will result in rejection or depreciation. Similar though they may be, their motives and their anticipations about their relation to others differ significantly.

Occasional difficulties may arise in drawing the line between decompensated dependent personalities and personalities diagnosed in accord with DSM-IV criteria as *borderline* types. The degree of overlap may be substantial, and further, if viewed longitudinally, borderline patients may be understood best as progressively impaired or deteriorated variants of other personality types, such as the dependent. Not only do the severe features of the borderline overlap and shade into personality types that are characteristically less impaired, but these features often reflect the insidious and progressive disintegration of formerly adaptive functions. For purposes of differential diagnosis it would appear most apt, where the collapse of coping and self-control has advanced significantly, to apply the label of borderline. However, it is the author's view that a double entry, including both borderline and dependent diagnoses, would be more suitable and informative in that it would convey simultaneously the long-term and characteristic dependent style, and the more recent and deteriorated level to which this style has regressed structurally.

ASSESSING THE DEPENDENT: A CASE STUDY

A few words should be said at the outset concerning the test response pattern of this personality on several of the major assessment tools in use today.

The dependent's high degree of conventionality and desire to please appears to produce responses on the Rorschach that are consonant with expectations. Keeping within safe boundaries, dependents seem to focus primarily on the *D* and *Dd* areas, as well as providing few *W* and *dd* responses. As anticipated, there is a high frequency of popular responses and a high *F+* percent. Movement responses seem to be associated most frequently with animals rather than humans. Although not invariable, dependents provide a greater number of responses than average.

The story themes and character descriptions on the TAT cards are likewise consonant with expectations. Elaborations seem to be centered on the activities of portrayed children and considerable detail is given to the feelings and behaviors of younger persons. As with avoidants, dependent personalities have a tendency to limit their thematic developments on cards that evoke feelings of anxiety and insecurity. Despite their denial needs, themes related to loss of significant figures may be described and elaborated; clinicians should inquire along these lines where appropriate.

On the MMPI, there appears to be a high frequency of elevated Scale 3 and Scale L scores. Profile 2-7/7-2 is quite frequent in dependents who are currently experiencing an Axis I Anxiety or Dysthymic disorder. Both Scale 4 and Scale 9 are typically at the low end of the distribution; these latter diminished scores reflect their docility, lack of initiative, and general passivity.

The following case, with accompanying MCMI-III profile and interpretive report, illustrates a long-standing dependent personality pattern.

CASE 9.1

Anthony L., 57, Married

Mr. L. was a rather short, thin, and nicely featured but somewhat haggard man who displayed a hesitant and tense manner when first seen by his physician. His place of employment for the past 22 years had recently closed and he had been without work for several weeks. He appeared less dejected about the loss of his job than about his wife's increasing displeasure with his decision to "stay at home until something came up." She thought he "must be sick" and insisted that he see a doctor; the following picture emerged in the course of several interviews.

Mr. L. was born in Europe, the oldest child and only son of a family of six children. His mother kept a careful watch over him, prevented him from engaging in undue exertions and limited his responsibilities; in effect, she precluded his developing many of the ordinary physical skills and competencies that most youngsters learn in the course of growth. He was treated as if he were a treasured family heirloom, a fragile statue to be placed on the mantelpiece and never be touched for fear he might break. Being small and unassertive by nature, he accepted the comforts of his role in a quiet and unassuming manner.

A marriage was arranged by his parents. His wife was a sturdy woman who worked as a seamstress, took care of his home and bore him four children. Mr. L. performed a variety of odds-and-ends jobs in his father's tailoring shop. His mother saw to it, however, that he did no "hard or dirty work," just helping about and "overlooking" the other employees. As a consequence, Mr. L. learned none of the skills of the tailoring trade.

During the ensuing years, he obtained employment at a garment factory owned by his brothers-in-law. Again he served as a helper, not as a skilled workman. Although he bore the brunt of essentially good-humored teasing by his co-workers throughout these years, he maintained a friendly and helpful attitude, pleasing them by getting sandwiches, coffee, and cigarettes at their beck and call. In the process of serving the needs of others, Mr. L. gradually developed the habit of sharing occasional drinks before the day's work was done. The habit persisted and grew into a major issue concerning alcoholism that has waxed and waned over the years.

Mr. L. was never troubled by his "failure" to mature and seemed content to have others take care of him, even though this meant occasional ridicule and humiliation. His present difficulty arose when the factory closed. Lacking the wherewithal of a skilled trade and the initiative to obtain a new position, he "decided" to stay at home, quite content to remain dependent on others.

Figure 9.5 provides a MCMI-II personality profile outlining the BR scores for a dependent personality pattern akin to the case of Anthony, following which the instrument's interpretations are likewise reported.

INTERPRETIVE SUMMARY

The MCMI-III profile of this man suggests that he is fearfully dependent, socially anxious, self-demeaning, and dejected. Hesitant about asserting himself, he may lean on others for guidance and security. He may strive to assume a passive and self-sacrificing role in many relationships and settings. His lack of initiative, avoidance of adult forms of autonomy, and willingness to accept undeserved blame and criticism may be notable. Unusually dependent and insecure, he may feel vulnerable if he

does not receive support from those who usually provide it. Despite his dependency and his inclination to permit others to exploit him, he is likely to resent those on whom he must lean because they are often abusive and inconsiderate, and he occasionally expresses anger toward them. He typically discharges this anger in an indirect manner, however, because his security is threatened by any expression of resentment. Fearful of rebuff by others, he may withdraw from what he experiences as painful social relationships to prevent himself from expressing resentment.

An underlying tension and emotional dysphoria are usually manifested in disturbing mixtures of anxiety, anger, and guilt. His insecurity and his fear of being left to his own devices may underlie a superficial quiet, nondisclosing, and benign attitude toward his problems. Apart from extended periods of dejection and helplessness, he is extremely conciliatory and even ingratiating. He hopes to evoke support and protection by acting weak and depressive, by expressing self-doubt, by communicating a need for assurance and direction, and by displaying a desire to submit and comply. Moreover, by submerging his individuality, subordinating his personal desires, and submitting at times to abuse and intimidation, he hopes to avoid humiliation and rejection.

This man's reported feelings of apathy and weakness and his tendency to succumb easily to physical exhaustion and illness may reflect a persistent and chronic dysthymia. Simple responsibilities may demand more energy than he can muster, and he may describe his life as empty. By acting incompetent and hopeless, by withdrawing, behaving in a selfless manner, and restricting his emotional involvement to occasional abusive and exploitive situations, he precludes new, potentially favorable experiences for reorienting his life.

Evidence indicates that recurrent periods of alcoholism are a major problem for this troubled man. Anxious, lonely, and socially apprehensive, he may find alcohol to be a useful lubricant that reduces tensions, stirs fantasies of enhanced esteem, and permits the quick dissolution of psychic pain. By disconnecting his preoccupation over social rejection and isolation, alcohol serves to undo his sense of alienation, to bolster his diminished self-confidence, and to provide a respite from the anguish and frustration that characterize much of his life.

A pattern of dysthymia is an integral part of this man's characterological structure. He exhibits a cluster of chronic general traits in which feelings

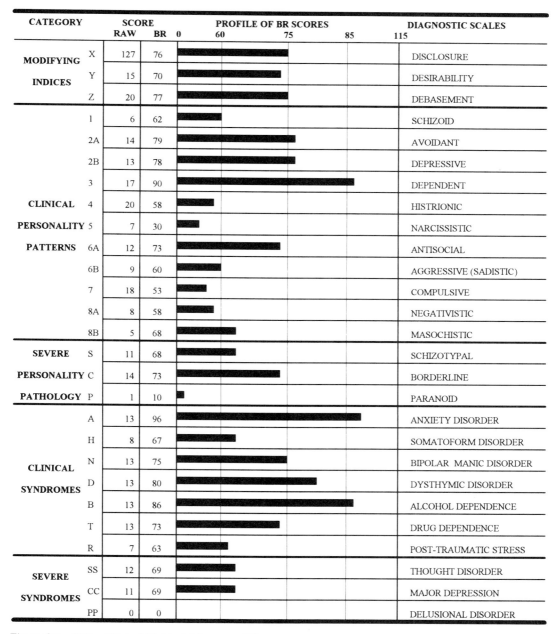

CATEGORY		SCORE		PROFILE OF BR SCORES				DIAGNOSTIC SCALES
		RAW	BR	0 60	75	85	115	
MODIFYING INDICES	X	127	76					DISCLOSURE
	Y	15	70					DESIRABILITY
	Z	20	77					DEBASEMENT
CLINICAL PERSONALITY PATTERNS	1	6	62					SCHIZOID
	2A	14	79					AVOIDANT
	2B	13	78					DEPRESSIVE
	3	17	90					DEPENDENT
	4	20	58					HISTRIONIC
	5	7	30					NARCISSISTIC
	6A	12	73					ANTISOCIAL
	6B	9	60					AGGRESSIVE (SADISTIC)
	7	18	53					COMPULSIVE
	8A	8	58					NEGATIVISTIC
	8B	5	68					MASOCHISTIC
SEVERE PERSONALITY PATHOLOGY	S	11	68					SCHIZOTYPAL
	C	14	73					BORDERLINE
	P	1	10					PARANOID
CLINICAL SYNDROMES	A	13	96					ANXIETY DISORDER
	H	8	67					SOMATOFORM DISORDER
	N	13	75					BIPOLAR MANIC DISORDER
	D	13	80					DYSTHYMIC DISORDER
	B	13	86					ALCOHOL DEPENDENCE
	T	13	73					DRUG DEPENDENCE
	R	7	63					POST-TRAUMATIC STRESS
SEVERE SYNDROMES	SS	12	69					THOUGHT DISORDER
	CC	11	69					MAJOR DEPRESSION
	PP	0	0					DELUSIONAL DISORDER

Figure 9.5   Millon Clinical Multiaxial Inventory-III.

of uselessness, dejection, pessimism, and discouragement are intrinsic components. Preoccupation with concerns over his social adequacy and personal worthiness, pervasive self-doubts, and feelings of guilt are all part of a constellation of long-term features of this man's psychological makeup. His reports of feeling aggrieved and mistreated are consistent with his belief that he deserves the anguish and abuse he experiences. Consonant with his intrapsychic dynamics, he may regularly set in motion conditions that further aggravate his misery.

PATHOGENIC DEVELOPMENTAL BACKGROUND

The discussion now turns to hypotheses concerning the developmental background of dependent traits. Before listing a number of influences that ostensibly shape the dependent pattern, we should reiterate three points. First, most hypotheses in psychopathology are conjectural. Second, a role ascribed to constitutional or biological determinants in no way precludes comparable effects of learning and experience. Third, biogenic and psychogenic factors interact; they are separated here only for pedagogical purposes

HYPOTHESIZED BIOGENIC FACTORS

Heredity

The thesis that dispositions to behavior may in part be rooted in genetic factors is no less plausible in the passive-dependent pattern than in any other; convincing empirical evidence is lacking, however. Similarities among members of a family group suggest the operation of hereditary determinants, but these findings may reflect environmental influences as well.

Despite the paucity of concrete data and the unquestioned influence of learning, common sense tells us that an individual's inherited biological machinery may incline the person to perceive and react to experiences in ways which result in learning a passive and dependent style of behavior. Dependency per se is never inherited, of course, but certain types of genetic endowments have high probabilities of evolving, under normal life experiences, into dependent personality patterns.

Melancholic or Threctic Infantile Reaction Patterns

If the assumption is correct that one's constitutional makeup is moderately consistent throughout life, it would seem reasonable to conclude that many adult dependents would have displayed a tendency to moroseness and fearfulness in infancy and early childhood. A soft, gentle, and somewhat sad or solemn quality may have characterized their early moods. Similarly, they may have shown a reticence, a hesitance to assert themselves, a restraint in new situations and a fear of venturing forth to test their growing capacities.

Early biophysical dispositions elicit distinctive reactions from parents. A gentle but sad and fearful infant is likely to evoke warmth and overprotectiveness from a concerned mother. Such children invite excessive care and compassion from others, which in turn may result in their learning to be overly dependent and comfortable with their caretakers. Rather than overcoming their initial dispositions, the reactions they draw from others may lead them to be even less assertive and venturesome than they otherwise would have been.

Ectomorphic or Endomorphic Body Build

Competencies for independent behavior and initiative depend in large measure on physical stamina, strength, and agility. Deficits in muscularity and vigor may result in a delayed achievement of these competencies, and a consequent tendency to depend on others to assume normal tasks and responsibilities. Heavy and cumbersome youngsters (endomorphic), or youngsters who are frail and easily fatigued (ectomorphic), are less capable and, therefore, less disposed to assert themselves or to experience success in independent actions than physically more well-endowed youngsters.

Neurological Imbalances between Reticular and Limbic Systems

A somewhat intricate pattern of neural organization may be hypothesized to account for the disposition to develop a dependent personality. Conceivably, reticular arousal mechanisms may be sluggish and inactive in these individuals, giving rise to deficit coping reactions under conditions of stress. At the same time, they may be overly endowed in those regions of the limbic system associated with the experience of fear, pain, and sadness.

Given these two neural characteristics, such persons may experience considerable stress even with minor discomforts, and learn to turn to others for assistance. Their limbic attributes cause them to feel difficulties intensely; their reticular attributes prevent them from mustering the reactive powers to cope with these difficulties. In an environment with thoughtful and protective caretakers, such children quickly will learn to depend on others to execute the defensive actions they cannot manage on their own. The reinforcement they receive by turning to others to cope with stress "binds" them to the caretakers and to the protection they provide. These children may drift increasingly, as a consequence, toward greater and greater dependency attachments.

Adrenal Dysfunctions

The speculative thesis proposed regarding the effects of neurological imbalances may be applied equally well to physiochemical impairments or variations. It may be conjectured, for example, that adrenal reactivity to stress is more than sufficient for short periods, but is rapidly depleted before adequate restitutive mechanisms can be mustered. Thus, the individual will experience intense emotional turmoil but lack sustained adrenal reactions necessary for effective coping responses. Experiencing threat but unable to follow through effectively, the individual learns to lean on others either for protection from or resolution of distress.

CHARACTERISTIC EXPERIENTIAL HISTORY

It would not be difficult to enumerate a score of influences that might contribute to the development of the dependent pattern. We have chosen the determinants to be described here because they arise often in the history of these individuals and appear to have carried weight in initiating, as well as in shaping, their personality style. Each of these factors contributed, first, to the development of excessive attachment learning and, second, to the avoidance of independent behaviors.

Parental Attachment and Overprotection

Every infant is helpless and entirely dependent upon caretakers for protection and nurturance. During the first few months of life, children acquire a vague notion of which objects surrounding them are associated with increments in comfort and gratification; they become "attached" to these objects because they provide positive reinforcements. All of this is natural. Difficulties arise, however, if the attachments children learn are too narrowly restricted, or so deeply rooted as to deter the growth of competencies by which they can obtain reinforcements on their own. Let us follow the course of these pathological attachments through the four stages of neuropsychological development.

Stage 1. Sensory-Attachment. The first stage of neuropsychological development, referred to as sensory-attachment, serves as a foundation for future growth. Supplied with adequate amounts of beneficent stimulation, children are likely to develop both interpersonal sensitivity and trust.

What may go wrong that leads to a pathological dependent pattern? It seems plausible that infants who receive an adequate amount of reinforcing stimulation but obtain that stimulation almost exclusively from one source, usually the mother, will be disposed to develop dependent traits. They experience neither stimulus impoverishment nor enrichment but are provided with stimuli from an unusually narrow sphere of objects. As a consequence of this lack of variety, the infant will form a singular attachment, a fixation if you will, on one object source to the exclusion of others.

Any number of factors may give rise to this exclusive attachment. Unusual illnesses or prolonged physical complications in the child's health may prompt a normal mother to tend to her infant more frequently than is common at this age. On the other hand, an excessively worrisome and anxious mother may be overalert to real and fantasied needs she sees in her normal child, resulting in undue attention, cuddling, and so on. Occasionally, special circumstances surrounding family life may throw the infant and mother together into a "symbiotic" dependency.

Stage 2. Sensorimotor-Autonomy. Infants who retain their exclusive attachment to the mother during the second neuropsychological stage, that known as sensorimotor-autonomy, will have their earlier training in dependency behaviors strengthened and perpetuated. However, there are many youngsters who were not especially attached to their mothers in the first stage who also develop the dependent pattern; experiences conducive to the acquisition of dependency behaviors can arise independently of an initial phase of exclusive maternal attachment.

The sensorimotor-autonomy stage is distinguished by opportunities to learn skills essential to the emergence of competence and independent behaviors. Circumstances that deter the development of these competencies can foster dependency. What conditions, distinctive to this period, result in the learning of these behaviors?

Not uncommon among these is the child's own deficit talents and temperamental disposition, such as physical inadequacies, fearfulness of new challenges, anguish when left alone, and so on. Some children, by virtue of constitutional temperament or earlier learning, elicit protective behaviors from others; their parents may have unwillingly acceded to overprotective habits because the child "forced" them to do so. Similarly, children who have suffered prolonged periods of illness may be prevented from exercising their maturing capacities either because of realistic physical limitations or as a result of the actions of justifiably concerned parents.

Barring the operation of constitutional dispositions and physical deficits, average youngsters in this stage will assert their growing capacities, and strive to do more and more things for themselves. This normal progression toward self-competence and environmental mastery may be interfered with by excessive parental anxieties or other harmful behaviors; for example, parents may discourage their son's independence for fear of losing "their baby"; they place innumerable barriers and diverting attractions to keep him from gaining greater autonomy. These parents limit the child's ventures outside the home, express anxiety lest he strain or hurt himself, make no demands for self-responsibility and provide him with every comfort and reward so long as he listens to mother. Rather than let him stumble and fumble with his new skills, his parents do things for him, make things easier, carry him well beyond the walking stage, spoon feed him until he is 3, tie his shoelaces until he is 10, and so on. Time and time again he will be discouraged from his impulse to "go it alone."

Ultimately, because of the ease with which he can obtain gratifications simply by leaning on his parents, he will forego his feeble efforts at independence; he never learns the wherewithal to act on his own to secure the rewards of life; he need not acquire any self-activated instrumental behaviors to obtain reinforcements; all he need do is sit back passively, and "leave it to mother."

Stage 3. Pubertal/Individuation-Nurturance.
Let us briefly elaborate some factors that dispose the child to the dependent pattern in the third neuropsychological stage, that termed pubertal/individuation-nurturance. The major theme to be noted here concerns events or relationships that lead individuals either to believe that they cannot compete with others or to learn that a dependent rather than an assertive role will assure less discomfort and greater reward.

A family situation in which the youngster is exposed to a more aggressive, competent, or troublesome sibling may set the stage for learning a dependent personality style. For example, the presence of a more assertive and competent sibling may

result in unfavorable self-comparisons; similarly, a hostile and difficult-to-manage sibling may invite a child to adopt the "good boy" image, one who, in contrast to his sibling, listens to mother, and acquiesces to her every mood and wish so as to gain comparative favor; in a third family, a girl who repeatedly experiences the lashing out of an angry and jealous sibling may run so often for parental cover that she learns to cling to them rather than confront the world on her own. Should the sibling display all of these troubling features—greater competence, unmanageability, and a hostile acting out of jealousy—the likelihood is rather high that the child exposed to these qualities will develop both the sweet dependent strategy and the dependent inadequacy role.

Similar difficulties conducive to dependency may be generated in experiences with the individual's peer group. Feelings of unattractiveness and competitive inadequacy, especially during adolescence, may result in social humiliation and self-doubt. These youngsters, however, are more fortunate than the active-detached adolescent because they usually can retreat to their home where they will find both love and acceptance; in contrast, active-detached youngsters receive little solace or support from their family. Although the immediate rewards of affection and refuge at home are not to be demeaned, they may, in the long run, prove a disservice to children, who ultimately must learn to stand on their own.

Stage 4. Intracortical Initiative.
Parental pampering and overprotection, continued into the fourth neuropsychological stage, intracortical initiative, often have a devastating effect upon children's growing self-image. First, they may fail to develop a distinct picture of themselves apart from the caretaker. Their excessive dependence on others for the execution of everyday tasks of life has denied them the opportunity to do things for themselves, to form an impression of what they are good at and who they are. Failing to break their symbiotic dependency on their mother deprives them of experiences by which they can discover attributes that distinguish them as individuals.

Second, it is implicit in parental overprotection that the children cannot take care of themselves. Pampered children are apt to view themselves as their parents do, as needing special care and supervision because they are incompetent, prone to illness, oversensitive and so on; their self-image mirrors this parental image of weakness and inferiority.

Third, when such children are forced to venture into the outside world, they find that their sense of inferiority is confirmed; objectively they are less competent and mature than others of their age. Unsure of their identity and viewing themselves to be weak and inadequate, they have little recourse but to perpetuate the early pattern by turning to others again to arrange their life and to provide for them.

More women than men develop the dependent pattern. Some theorists attribute this fact to an inherent dependent disposition on the part of the female sex. Equally plausible is the thesis that the cultural roles that are sanctioned in most societies reinforce the learning of dependent behaviors among women.

SELF-PERPETUATION PROCESSES

It may appear strange, even paradoxical, that the genuine affection and acceptance experienced in childhood by dependent personalities should dispose them to pathology. For most of these individuals, childhood was a time of warmth and security, a period marked by few anxieties that were not quickly dispelled by parental attention and care. Too much of a good thing, however, can turn bad. Excessive parental shielding may establish habits and expectancies that are detrimental in the long run because they ill prepare the children to cope on their own with life. Accustomed to support from others and ill-equipped without them, dependents stand implanted, rooted to the deep attachments of their childhood. Unable to free themselves from their dependence, they face the constant danger of loss, dread desertion, and fear the abyss into which they will fall if left on their own. Beneath their pleasant and affable exterior, then, lies an extreme vulnerability, a sense of helplessness, and a fear of abandonment. Dependents' lack of resources and their self-doubts compel them to seek safe partners, trustworthy figures "like mother," who can be depended on to assure them that they are loved and will not be deserted.

What does the future usually hold for dependents, how and why do they remain fixed in their ways, and what approaches are best when intervening therapeutically? These questions are addressed, albeit briefly, in the final section of the chapter.

Dependent personalities, despite claims of ineptness and inadequacy, employ an ecologically adaptive style, an interpersonal coping strategy that recruits the nurture and support they need. Moreover, it is a style that forestalls their sinking into deeper levels of psychopathology. By soliciting attention and affection, dependents remain in close touch with the real world and are exposed constantly to social relationships that keep them from straying too far into subjective distortion. Although dependency behaviors protect against the pernicious and decompensating effects of social withdrawal and autistic distortion, the problem remains that this once adaptive strategy persists far beyond its origins and ultimate utility. More importantly, it leads the person into self-defeating vicious circles. A brief review follows of some of the features that aggravate the dependent's characteristic inadequacies.

Self-Deprecation

Dependents not only observe real deficits in their competence, but they deprecate what virtues and talents they may possess. This prevents others from expecting them to assume responsibilities they would rather avoid. Successful as a shield against discomfort and in protecting their dependency needs, these actions are carried out at the cost of demeaning their own self-respect. Their rationalizations of inadequacy, offered for the benefit of others, have an impact on their own person. Each time dependents announce their defects, they convince themselves as well as others and thereby deepen their self-image of incompetence. Trapped by their own persuasiveness, they further reinforce their belief in the futility of standing on their own, and they are, hence, likely to try less and less to overcome their inadequacies. Their strategy has fostered a vicious circle of increased helplessness and dependency.

Avoidance of Adult Activities

Dependents' sense of inadequacy, fear of failure, and hesitation about antagonizing others cause them to refrain from activities that may facilitate a more mature and independent life-style. For example, despite ample opportunities to learn skills and to assume more "manly" roles, some dependent men shy away from these "threats," fear they could never succeed, and prefer instead to remain inept but good-natured and easy to get along with. Self-imposed restrictions will diminish short-term embarrassments and anxieties associated with failure, but they also diminish the probability that the dependents will acquire competence and confidence that will enable them to function more maturely. By making themselves less accessible to growth opportunities, they effectively preclude further maturation, and, hence, become ever more needful of others.

Clinging Social Behaviors

Although dependents appease others and apologize for their incompetence, their need for affection and assurance that they will not be abandoned may become so persistent as to exasperate and alienate those on whom they lean most heavily. Of course, exasperation and alienation on the part of others only serve to increase the dependents' neediness. As the vicious circle persists, they may become more desperate, more ingratiating, and more urgently pleading and clinging, until they become "millstones around their partner's necks." Wearying of demands to prove fealty and love, the stronger partner may openly express annoyance, disapproval, and, finally, rejection. Seriously rebuffed, a cycle of decompensation may begin or take on an increased pace. Overt expressions of self-blame, self-criticism, and self-condemnation may come to the fore. Fearful of expressing hostility, lest this result in further loss, dependents are likely to turn these feelings inward first, to reproach themselves for their shortcomings and, second, to promise to be "different" and redeem themselves for their past mistakes. The "new leaf" they plan to "turn" takes the form of promises of greater competence and less dependence—aspirations that run counter to their lifelong personality style. These goals rarely are achieved, and at this point we often see the emergence of a serious symptom disorder such as a major depression.

THERAPEUTIC INTERVENTIONS

Despite the possibilities of decompensation just noted, the prognosis for the dependent pattern is relatively good. Dependents are likely to have had a supporting relationship with at least one parent and this provides them with a reservoir of security and a feeling of being loved and wanted. Each of these positive emotions will sustain a dependent through difficult periods. Additionally, affectionate parents serve as models for imitative learning, equipping dependents with reciprocal habits of affection and generosity. As noted earlier, dependency needs assure interpersonal contact, thereby forestalling the potentially decompensating effects of self-preoccupation and subjective distortion.

STRATEGIC GOALS

The dependent's developmental history and early learning experiences have profoundly influenced his or her current personality pattern. The submissive dependence on others pervades all clinical domains and has resulted in an imbalance in the polarities. Because this personality style is so ingrained and others have learned to react to the dependent in a predetermined manner, the pattern perpetuates itself. Making the dependent's life more balanced by targeting the weaker areas constitutes a major therapeutic goal for this disorder.

Reestablishing Polarity Balances

Dependents have learned that the source of pleasure and the avoidance of pain is found externally. Dependents define themselves in terms of others and therefore seek nurturance from others. Given their often extreme reliance on their partners, alteration of the other-self polarity would involve countering the belief that their fate is dependent on others and fostering the self-focus as well as a diversification of coping strategies. To gain support and nurturance, dependents have learned to wait in a passive manner for others to take the lead. In the passive-active polarity, one of the main goals of therapy would be to increase their active involvement in pursuing need-satisfaction without excessive support from others.

Countering Perpetuating Tendencies

The dependent's deep-seated feelings of incompetency must be addressed in therapy because they contribute to the failure to develop a more independent lifestyle. Increasing self-perceptions of adequacy will provide the dependent with the courage to engage in a wide variety of social experiences and hence will preclude the possibility of social withdrawal and isolation. A consequence of this improvement will be a lesser need for others to provide a more stable sense of security. A decrease in clinging behaviors will help interrupt the dependent perpetuating pattern because rejection by significant others and the internalization of failure become less likely.

Additional perpetuating factors have probably reflected childhood social stereotypes in which others have learned to selectively perceive only the person's dependent attributes and ignore efforts at independence. Changing the expectations of significant others leads to a broad range of social experiences that are essential for change.

Modifying Domain Dysfunctions

Most notable in dependents are their deficiencies in the self-image and interpersonal conduct domain. Targeting feelings of inadequacy and fostering the development of a more competent sense of self should be considered primary goals of therapy. This will be facilitated if a concurrent attempt is made to reduce the submissive behavior that characterizes their interpersonal style. Expressively, dependents lack functional competencies, and their passivity diminishes opportunities for more diverse experiences that might promote feelings of adequacy. Therapy should further attempt to counter the naive cognitive style that emerges when dependents are confronted with interpersonal difficulties and problematic events. Helping dependents assess the validity of their beliefs about the consequences of assertive and autonomous behavior, and engaging patients in reality testing will clear the way for changes in this domain.

Intrapsychically, dependents defend against stress by employing introjection as a primary mechanism. They deal with their feelings of ineptness by identifying with others. This gives them a false sense of security and protects them from exposing their own relatively undeveloped adaptive style. By promoting self-control, independent thinking, and a more active attempt at acquiring mature skills, the therapist can foster improvement. Helping dependents to establish an independent personal identity will also require replacing the internalized representations of others with more realistic mature ones of their own.

TACTICAL MODALITIES

To facilitate improvements in the areas just noted, the therapist can opt to use a variety of techniques. These must be chosen and synchronized in such a manner as to allow for the optimal acquisition of independent and autonomous skills, while at the same time to encourage movement between

self and others. Invariably, resistance will be encountered along the way, and an understanding of the nature of these obstacles and when they are likely to occur, will assist in treatment planning.

Domain-Oriented Techniques

Behaviorally, dependents are rather passive and unsure of themselves, often waiting for others to provide support and guidance. *Behavioral* techniques can be employed after a "functional analysis" of behavior has been completed. This will bring to light the problem areas in the patient's life and target the avoidance behaviors that reinforce the maintenance of this pattern. A functional analysis of the dependent's style will reveal that although the immediate consequences of clinging behavior may be positive, long-term effects can run exactly counter to the desired effect and result in hostility from others.

With proper guidance, however, dependents can start to recognize the patterns of their dependency, including the events and cognitions that prompt their behavior. Setting up an anxiety hierarchy of independent and assertive behaviors for gradual implementation is a good place to begin. Both role playing and modeling can provide the patient with basic skills for a new repertoire of behaviors. Before attempting this, it is critical to assess whether the patient actually lacks functional competencies. If this appears to be the case, some remedial training of appropriate skills should be considered. In session, reinforcement and feedback can be provided immediately contingent on appropriate behavior. Gradual exposure can move from in-therapy situations to external settings, such as the home, social gatherings, and work, fostering generalization and maintenance of the newly acquired competencies. While the patient is working on the hierarchy, anxiety levels may temporarily rise. Teaching patients anxiety-reducing skills, such as breathing techniques and deep muscle relaxation, can help them feel more at ease and can additionally increase their tolerance for anxiety.

The reluctance of dependents to stand up for themselves can be targeted with assertiveness training, and by specifically teaching the patient skills that allow the expression of negative feelings in a constructive way. Complementary techniques include communication skills training and role playing. Role playing can accomplish two goals. It provides the therapist with a more adequate sense of the patient's relationships with others and can thus be quite revealing; additionally, it allows the patient to practice increasingly assertive behaviors.

Teaching self-management techniques and behavioral contracting can be most helpful with dependents in bolstering self-reliance. Initially, the therapist will want to provide guidance when writing self-contracts to ensure that they are fair and manageable. The key to successful behavioral management here is appropriate reinforcement of the target goal, that is, increasingly independent behavior.

Interpersonal techniques can be useful in treating dependents, not only because they are receptive to treatment, but also because they are disposed to seek assistance wherever they can, especially in close interpersonal relationships. The strength and authority of the therapist comforts them with a feeling of assurance that an all-powerful person will come to their rescue when needed, and provide them with the kindness and helpfulness they crave. Moreover, the task of unburdening their woes to a therapist calls for little effort on their part. Although they may lack accurate insight into their difficulties, dependents will provide ample data to lead the therapist to uncover the origins of their problems. Furthermore, dependents are disposed to trust others, especially therapists to whom they are likely to attribute great powers and the highest of virtues.

It is very important that the relationship between the therapist and dependent patients not reestablish the dominance-submission pattern that has characterized their history. Interpersonally, dependents need to learn to separate and differentiate the self from others, thereby becoming increasingly autonomous. The therapist can help patients explore their long-standing patterns of interacting, and how these have maintained their inadequate behaviors. Analysis of dependent behaviors displayed in session may further shed light on the dynamics of this mode of interacting. The therapist, at times, may wish to communicate personal reactions to provide the patient with valuable feedback. Benjamin (1993a) points out that dependents have a restricted view of their interpersonal world and do not consider the possibility of being in charge or in control.

Beck and Freeman (1990b) also note that these patients show dichotomous thinking with respect to independence, believing either that one is completely dependent and in need of help or totally independent and alone. There do not appear to be gradations. This may contribute to a belief that the goal of therapy is independence and con-

sequently isolation. The patient's unrealistic expectations about the consequences of displaying more independent behavior can be addressed cognitively by helping the patient place a variety of behaviors on a continuum from dependence to independence.

Although there are a multitude of *cognitive* techniques the therapist may elect to use, the fundamental goal of cognitive therapeutic tactics is to bolster the dependent's self-image and encourage the use of a more active problem-solving approach in dealing with life's problems. In the course of therapy, their distorted thoughts are identified, monitored, and subsequently challenged.

Initially, dependents will likely look to the therapist to provide them with answers and to tell them what to do. Guided discovery and Socratic-type questioning can help the patient arrive at a greater understanding of what is transpiring (Beck & Freeman, 1990b). The therapist can further this course by asking patients to record their perceptions and feelings about problematic events. In this manner, the patients can monitor situations that occur during the week and start gaining more insight into their automatic thoughts and associated emotions. Particular attention should be paid to the sequence of events and their consequences, including reactions from significant others. This will highlight the sustaining nature of their dysfunctional style.

Working on identifying maladaptive and perpetuating patterns will soon bring to light the automatic and demeaning thoughts of the dependent personality. Cognitively, dependents are best described as naive and rather gullible. They tend to smooth over events that others would consider disturbing. Because they see themselves as unable to manage without the assistance of others, they may have developed this naive cognitive style and Pollyana attitude to avoid interpersonal conflict and the expected repercussions that ensue. Therapy should assist the patient to substitute passive cognitions with active ones, and an improving self-image for an inept one.

Once dependents develop a more realistic perception of their internal and external environment, there will be less need to suppress or minimize resentments and interpersonal conflict. Successfully challenging automatic beliefs and maladaptive schemas is a primary part of this process. The therapist may initially need to provide direct assistance in identifying more rational responses and exploring alternative modes of interacting, but at some point in therapy, the patient must be encouraged to actively explore the consequences of alternative behaviors.

The therapist may wish to use some Gestalt techniques to facilitate schema changes at the emotional level, while simultaneously working on developing problem-solving skills. One such approach, the two-chair technique, allows for the expression of feeling without having to fear the consequences. The dependent can work on one part of the conflict while sitting on one chair and then switch chairs to play the role of "adversary." The reversal technique may be especially suited to practice assertiveness skills, making the transition to facing the actual person less abrupt. The dependent can be instructed to act out the part of an uncompromising obstinate person. A good deal of emphasis should be placed on the feelings experienced during these exercises. Suggesting that the patient write letters can further cultivate expression of emotion.

Beck and Freeman (1990b) suggest setting very clear and specific goals early on in treatment, since progress toward these goals would constitute evidence of personal growth. The goals can further be broken down into concrete manageable components, so each successive approximation to the desired behavior is an accomplishment in itself, serving thereby as a reinforcement.

The dependent's automatic thoughts are likely to interfere with progress in therapy and will be evidenced by complaints of not being able to complete homework assignments or exercises. The therapist can use this resistance productively by asking the patient to test the validity of these thoughts through in-session reality testing. Emerging feelings of anxiety may produce resistance tactics, but a moderate degree of anxiety is necessary at times for change to occur.

Group therapy may be particularly suited as an arena for learning autonomous skills and as an aid to the dependent's growth of social confidence. In this setting, patients can learn to assert themselves, while receiving feedback that others will not abandon them when they display confidence and make independent decisions. Depending on the patient's level of motivation and potential for growth, either a supportive problem-solving group or a more insight-oriented group may be appropriate. In the dyadic relationship between the therapist and the dependent, some regressive behaviors may be elicited, as well as negative transferences that may be counterproductive to therapeutic progress. In contrast, the group offers the advantage that when dysfunctional patterns are reactivated,

feedback comes from "equals." There is a good likelihood that constructive interactions will occur between the dependent and group members. Another advantage of the group setting is that abandonment issues may be less frequent because the dependent is not solely reliant on the therapist for nurturance.

Family or *couples* therapy may be helpful, especially in those cases where the family system is instrumental in maintaining the dependent pattern. The family can play an important role in facilitating behavior change by not excusing the dependent from assuming adult responsibilities. The role of societal and cultural factors, however, must be kept in mind when working with dependents and their families. Independent and assertive behavior may not be sanctioned by a large segment of the system. When work on interpersonal relationships is contraindicated because of these prohibitions, other options such as environmental change may be explored to maximize growth and minimize continued dependence. Encouraging the development of outside interests, for example, may open the door to myriad opportunities the dependent would never have considered for fear of endangering his or her relationships with significant others.

To rework deeper object attachments and to construct a base for competency strivings, it may be necessary to utilize *psychodynamic* approaches. The therapist-client relationship can be the basis for a corrective emotional experience. The patient can gradually start to internalize healthy components of this relationship, thereby replacing the immature representations currently existing. Gabbard (1994) comments on the importance of exploring the unconscious factors that might contribute to the dependence. He states that a submissive clinging stance toward others may have different meanings for each dependent; for some it may be a defense against hostility, for others it is a way to avoid the reactivation of traumatic experiences. Exploring the dependent's past separations and their impact is recommended. A decreased but healthier intimacy with parents will ensue as a more realistic perception of the parents emerges. With more seriously impaired personalities, the goal of therapy may be to bypass total independence and instead gear therapy toward helping them substitute dependency on the original family with a less severe dependency on the marital partner (Stone, 1993). The therapist can serve as a temporary transitional object.

It is not unlikely that during the course of therapy, some relationships will come to an end;

ultimately so will the therapeutic relationship. As with other losses, some grief work may be necessary.

As the exposure to mature relationships starts to increase, the therapist's interventions may address the dependent's lack of diversity in internal controls and regulatory mechanisms. Dependents will often subordinate their own needs to those of others because they fear being deprived of a supporting relationship. Moreover, their low self-esteem leads them to place excessive value on others. As a result, the dependent's primary defense mechanism is introjection. Because they have always relied on others to take care of them and solve their problems, dependents have not pursued the development of independent skills. Their deficient morphologic structure can be targeted by focusing on gradually building skills and on self-management, thereby increasing the dependent's coping abilities.

Psychopharmacological treatment, notably certain antidepressants and antianxiety agents, may occasionally prove useful in treating dependents, who are often plagued by fatigue, lethargy, and diffuse anxieties that incline them to postpone efforts at independence. These agents may be used to promote vigor and alertness. Anxiety may temporarily escalate when the patient is experimenting with increasingly autonomous behaviors because the threat of rejection or abandonment is perceived to be all too real. Restoring the patient's anxiety levels to normal limits may be facilitated by relaxation training. In severe cases, when extreme separation anxiety and possible panic attacks are present, tricyclic antidepressants and MAOIs may be considered, with appropriate consultation and follow-up. Special care should be taken not to allow the patient to become overreliant on medication, as well as to avoid medication with possible addictive properties.

Figure 9.6 presents a review of the major strategies and tactics.

Potentiated Pairings and Catalytic Sequences

Dependent personalities inevitably enter therapy soliciting active assistance from the therapist. As previously mentioned, the dependent is likely to feel positive about therapy and its prospects for providing nurturance, support, and guidance. Engaging the patient in therapy and establishing a long-term therapeutic alliance can be accomplished by initially giving the patient more directive feedback and engaging in acute problem

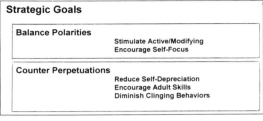
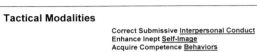

Figure 9.6 Therapeutic strategies and tactics for the prototypal dependent personality.

solving. As Beck and Freeman (1990b) note, it may be wise to allow some dependence in the treatment, as long as the therapist consistently works to wean the patients away from that dependence. According to these authors, progress in therapy from dependence to autonomy can be fostered by changing the structure of therapy itself. Sessions can move from the therapist providing the structure and being more directive to the patient dictating the agenda. Moving from individual to group therapy can additionally serve to reduce the patient's dependence on the therapist. When a trusting relationship has been formed, the therapist can make use of interpersonal reinforcement to encourage the patient to experiment with increasingly independent behaviors. If a significant degree of anxiety is present, therapy may be largely confined to more supportive methods until relief occurs. Psychopharmacological intervention may then also be considered.

Cognitive and behavioral techniques are best used concurrently to deal with the almost inevitable resistance to giving up dependent behaviors. At the domain level, it will become evident that once they successfully start to build autonomous skills, dependents' view of themselves as capable, effective human beings will be enhanced. With the aid of behavioral experiments, they should gradually acquire competencies to rectify their expressive and organizational deficits. No longer "incompetent," dependents will see in time that abandonment and rejection are not imminent, thereby reducing the need for interpersonal clinging and introjection. Improvements in their self-image will in turn serve to increase the chances they will attempt new behaviors and thereby acquire significant functional competencies.

RESISTANCES AND RISKS

The dependent's receptiveness and the auspicious beginning of therapy may create a misleading impression that future progress will be rapid. Quite naturally, these patients will seek a dependent relationship with their therapist. Despite promises to the contrary, they will resist efforts to guide them into assuming independence and autonomy. Their goal is to elicit more nurturance and help from the therapist. All this is to be expected because their dependence is quite ego-syntonic. Assisting them in relinquishing their dependency habits will prove a slow and arduous process. Building an image of competence and self-esteem must proceed one step at a time through a program of strengthening attributes and dislodging the habit of leaning onto others.

The therapist may get caught up in their patients' attempts to elicit support. After a while, excessive dependence can be exasperating. Resulting countertransference feelings of annoyance may lead to rejection once again, which in turn will intensify the dependency and clinging behaviors (Stone, 1993). Countertransference may also take the form of the therapist allowing the patient to become emotionally dependent on him or her, resulting in reduced efforts at gaining independence. If attempts at autonomy, however, are pushed too hard initially, the anxiety may result in premature dropout.

Another potential caveat stems from the dependent's search for approval. Observed behavior changes, such as enhanced assertiveness, may be confined to sessions with the therapist and not exhibited elsewhere. It is important to evaluate to what degree behavior change actually has occurred outside the therapy setting. If the patient's environment continues to foster or maintain dependency, what appears to be progress in the therapy room may not have generalized to his or her dysfunctional world.

The therapist and patient should come to an understanding of the goals of therapy. Especially when resistance is encountered, reconceptualization of the dependent's therapeutic objectives may be useful. Progress in therapy may be impeded by the dependent's basic belief that he or she is inadequate. The patient may feel incompetent to utilize treatment efficiently and may attribute progress made to the therapist rather than to the self. Yet another potential factor that may strengthen the belief that success is attributable to external sources is reliance on medication.

Neither the therapist nor the patient must forget that the ultimate goal is not necessarily complete independence, but rather the flexibility to move between self-reliance and a healthy mutual dependence.

CHAPTER 10

Histrionic Personality Disorders:
The Gregarious Pattern

Dependent and histrionic personalities share important traits. Both turn to others for protection and the rewards of life. Beneath the social affability that characterizes them lies an intense need for attention and affection. They require constant affirmation of approval and acceptance, are vulnerable to the moods and attitudes of those on whom they depend, and often experience a sense of helplessness when anticipating disinterest from others or when threatened with desertion.

Chapter 9 described dependent personalities, who not only find security through the support of others but who turn passively to them in the hope that they will be kind enough not only to bestow approval and affection, but to take care of them. This passivity in seeking guidance and nurturance contrasts markedly with the more active and manipulative style of the histrionic personality. Histrionics are no less dependent on others for attention and affection but, in contrast to dependents, take the initiative in assuring that these reinforcements will be forthcoming. Rather than placing their fate in the hands of others, and thereby having their approval needs in constant jeopardy, histrionic personalities actively solicit the interest of others through a series of seductive ploys that are likely to assure receipt of the attention and interest they need. Toward these ends, histrionics develop an exquisite sensitivity to the moods and thoughts of those they wish to please. This hyperalertness enables them to quickly assess what maneuvers will succeed in attaining the ends they desire. This extreme "other-directedness," devised in the service of achieving approval, results, however, in a lifestyle characterized by a shifting and fickle pattern of behaviors and emotions. Unlike dependent personalities, who anchor themselves usually to only one object of attachment, the histrionic tends to be lacking in fidelity and loyalty. The dissatisfaction with single attachments, combined with a need for constantly replenished stimulation and attention, results in a seductive, dramatic, and capricious pattern of personal relationships.

This well-known syndrome, missing entirely in the official 1952 nosology, was reinstated in the DSM-II, though under the archaic label of the "hysterical personality." A less controversial and more appropriate appellation, that of "histrionic personality disorder," was officially introduced in the DSM-III and continues as its designation in the DSM-IV.

HISTORICAL ANTECEDENTS

As just noted, the designation *histrionic personality* achieved recognition as an official classification for the first time in the formal listings of the DSM-III, published in 1980. The term replaced that of hysterical personality, a syndrome whose origins in the word *hysteria* can be traced to the early days of both the Egyptians and the Greeks. During ancient times, it was used to represent the womb and signified excessive emotionality exhibited by women at the time of their menses; the womb ostensibly traveled throughout the body and often settled in the brain, where it led to the overexcited behaviors referred to as hysterical.

During medieval times, emotional behaviors and erotic desires of women were vigorously suppressed by the church, which viewed such inclinations as dangerous and lustful, even responsible for failures and impotence among men. Serving as a guide for the church during the Inquisition, two German monks, Kramer and Sprenger, published the *Malleus Maleficarum* (1496), a religious tract that provided a rationale for persecuting "witches." Opposing views regarding the condemnation of women possessing hysteria were written during the 16th century by Bodin, Weyer, and Jorden. By the late 17th century, Willis (1668) suggested that the affliction was associated with the brain and not with a traveling womb. Nevertheless, in the late 18th century, Pinel, renowned for his humane approach to the mentally disordered, persisted in the view that women demonstrated intense emotional reactions at the time of their period, recommending early marriage and frequent pregnancies as a solution to this disorder. A useful review of this early period has been written by Ey (1982).

The first *psychosocial* descriptions of what we now refer to as the histrionic personality were written in the mid-19th century. Ernst von Feuchtersleben (1847) depicted women disposed to hysterical symptoms as being sexually heightened, selfish, and "overprivileged with satiety and boredom." Attributing these traits to the unfortunate nature of female education, he wrote: "It combines everything that can heighten sensibility, weaken spontaneity, give a preponderance to the sexual sphere, and sanction the feelings and impulse that relate to it." Less oriented to matters of sexuality, Wilhelm Griesinger (1845/1867), the major psychiatric nosologist of mid-19th-century Germany, wrote that hysterical women displayed an "immoderate sensitiveness, especially to the slightest reproach [in which there is a] tendency to refer everything to themselves, great irritability, great change of disposition on the least, or even from no, external motive." Among other distinguishing characteristics, according to Griesinger, were their volatile humor, their senseless caprices, and their inclination to deception, prevarication, jealousy, and malice.

Going beyond the descriptive eloquence of his contemporaries, Briquet (1859) rejected the historic view that men could not develop hysteria. He was also quite clear in pointing to psychological influences that could play a significant role in the symptomatological expression of the disorder. Briquet referred to painful emotional states, such as sadness and fear, as elements in precipitating the disorder. Moreover, he mentioned untoward developmental experiences as playing a pathogenic role (e.g., bad parental treatment, spousal abuse, unfavorable employment, or business failures). Recognizing that only a small subset of those subjected to these psychosocial experiences develop the hysterical syndrome, Briquet proposed that the notion of *predispositions* be considered as a pathogenic factor.

Further recognition of the place of psychobiological influences, other than ostensive menstrual factors, arose as a result of the striking role played by Charcot's use in the 1870s and 1880s of hypnosis to alleviate conversion hysterical symptoms.

Not the least of those who were impressed by the power of this new tool was a young attending neurologist by the name Sigmund Freud. Carrying the hypnotic procedure into his clinical work with Breuer, they published their first scientific paper in 1893. Here, they not only showed the efficacy of the hypnotic procedure in bringing repressed emotions into the open, but thoroughly elucidated the role of unconscious psychic phenomena, including the place of sexual traumas and conflicts in the hysterical syndrome.

Classificatory theorists of *personality* at the turn of the century were not concerned with clinical entities per se. However, their speculative models enabled them to derive character types that corresponded closely to the prime features of the "histrionic." As noted briefly in Chapter 2, Ribot (1890) formulated an "emotional" type characterized by an active disposition and extreme impressionability; along similar lines is Queyrat's (1896) active-emotional "passionate" type. Heymans and Wiersma's (1906–1909) "choleric" character is noted by active, emotional, and external susceptibility; the same descriptive features are to be found in McDougall's "fickle" temper (1908/1932). Hirt (1902), seeking to connect the classical four humors to psychiatric populations, assigned extremes in the sanguine temperament to the hysterical type, depicting them as superficially excitable, enthusiastic, unreliable, attention craving, and vain.

Two major strands of thinking concerning personality types emerged in the early 20th century. On the one hand were the classical descriptive psychiatrists such as Kraepelin, Bleuler, Kretschmer, and Schneider; on the other were those of a psychoanalytic persuasion, notably Freud, Abraham, and Reich. Despite their chronological overlap, they are separated here for purposes of considering their views of the so-called hysterical personality.

Kraepelin (1904) provided a variety of different portraits of the hysterical type, noting as characteristic their delight in novelty, enthusiasm, vivid imagination, great excitability, mood lability, romantic preoccupation, capriciousness, and impulsiveness. In his classic lectures on psychiatry, published first in 1904, he provided the following delineation of a seriously disturbed hysterical patient:

The emotional sympathies of the patient are more and more confined to the selfish furthering of her own wishes. She tries ruthlessly to extort the most careful attention from those around her ... is extremely sensitive to any supposed neglect, is jealous . . . and tries to make [others] give in to her by complaints, accusations, and outbursts of temper. The sacrifices made by others . . . only serve to pave the way for new demands. To secure the sympathy of those around her, she has recourse to . . . histrionic exaggeration. (p. 253)

A similar description was formulated by Pierre Janet (1901), another student of Charcot's, in his list of the "stigmata" of hysteria; included here were the characteristic exhibitionistic, flamboyant, and demanding behaviors.

MODERN FORMULATIONS

According to Karl Jaspers (1925), the essential feature of this personality was the "attempt to seem more than one is." Tracing the evolution of the disorder, Jaspers noted that the more self-deception and histrionics crept in, the more there was a loss of contact with genuine feelings; ultimately, nothing was left but "counterfeit demonstrativeness." As Jaspers elaborates:

The hysterical personality feels the need to appear before others more than it is, to experience more than it is capable of experiencing. In place of the original genuine experience with its natural expression there enters in a fictitious, acted forced experience. This experience must not be consciously fictitious but it is characterized by the ability (the true hysterical gift) of the person concerned, to live entirely in its own theatre, to be completely carried away at the moment, thus bearing an air of genuineness. (p. 389)

Schneider (1923/1950) assigned the label "attention-seeking" (*Geltungsbeduerftig*) as a substitute for hysterical, claiming that the latter term implied a moral judgment and had acquired too broad and vague a meaning; a central feature in Schneider's account of these personalities was their proclivity to exaggeration and pathological lying, employed in the service of making themselves appear more interesting or attractive to others. Also described by Schneider are a group of "hyperthymic" personalities whose features are likewise subsumed under the current notion of a histrionic character. He describes them as follows:

Active, equable and great optimists. Often however, they are shallow, uncritical, happy-go-lucky, cocksure, hasty in decision, and not very

dependable. [Quoting Kant, he states that they are] of a lighthearted, sanguine temperament . . . carefree, hopeful, chasing one thing after another and promising beyond its capacity . . . it produces sociable, merry and witty people who play with life. (p. 70)

An especially apt and colorful summary of the features of the hysterical character was written by Kretschmer (1926). In many of its details it could be substituted for the descriptive text written for the DSM III:

Another lively and overidealistic psychic sexuality with prudish rejection physical correlate, a rapidly vanishing lean of feelings, enthusiasm for impressive persons, a preference for what is loud and lively, a theatrical pathos, an inclination for brilliant roles, to dream themselves into big purposes in life, the playing with suicide, the contrast between enthusiastic self-sacrificial abandonment and a naive, sulky, childish egotism, and especially a mixture of the droll and tragic in their way of living. (p. 26)

Before moving on to the evolving formulations of Freudian psychoanalytic theory, we will take a brief excursion to characterizations by Jung and Adler that conform in several respects to the histrionic style. Specifically, in his "extroverted-intuitive" type, Jung conceived a set of features that correspond closely to the hysterical personality as described in his day. Jung (1921) wrote as follows:

There is a marked dependence on external situations . . . he has a keen nose for anything new in the making. Because he is always seeking out new possibilities, stable conditions suffocate him. He seizes on new objects or situations with great intensity . . . only to abandon them cold-bloodedly, without any compunction . . . as soon as their range is known. (p. 368)

Adler's (1964) "passive-constructive" lifestyle also depicts traits characteristic of the histrionic, notably attention seeking, behaving in a charming manner, and wishing to be recognized as special even if one has few achievements to deserve it.

As evident from the preceding paragraphs, psychiatrists and psychologists began to write about the traits of so-called hysterical characters as early as the mid-1800s. Although psychoanalytic theory had its origins in Freud's explication of the hysterical symptom, it was not until 1932 that he elucidated his views on the hysterical character. Similarly, and despite Abraham's signal role in formulating the concepts of oral and anal characters in early 1920s, Freud's interest focused on the relationship between libidinal development and hysterical symptoms, not on hysterical character traits. Fritz Wittels (1930) was the first analyst to provide a systematic description of the hysterical structure; he asserted that despite important relationships connecting the hysterical symptom and the hysterical character, a significant segment of character operates independent of the symptom. Further, and in contrast to Abraham who anchored the hysteric symptom to phallic-stage failures, Wittels (1930) ascribed the formation of character to fixations at the infantile or pregenital level. He wrote as follows:

The hysterical character never frees itself from its fixation at the infantile level. Hence it cannot attain its actuality as a grown-up human being; it plays the part of a child, and also of the woman. The hysteric person has no actuality, she confuses fantasy and reality. (p 187)

In Freud's (1931/1950) paper on "libidinal types," he spoke of those cases in which the id has become predominant as the "erotic" character. In his discussion of parallels between libidinal and character structures, he stated: "It seems easy to infer that when persons of the erotic type fall ill they will develop hysteria" (p. 250). To Freud, the distinguishing motive that governs the behavior of hysterics is the "dread of loss of love," which results in becoming "particularly dependent on those who may withhold their love from them" (p. 250).

As noted in Chapter 2, it was Reich (1933/1949) who provided the first solid underpinnings to the psychoanalytic theory of character formation. In portraying what he termed the "outstanding characteristics" of the hysterical types, he wrote as follows:

Disguised or undisguised coquetry in gait, look, or speech betrays, especially in women, the hysterical character type. In the case of men, besides softness and excessive politeness, a feminine facial expression and a feminine bearing also appear.

We find fickleness of reactions, i.e., a tendency to change one's attitudes unexpectedly and unintentionally; a strong suggestibility, which never appears alone but is coupled with a strong tendency to reactions of disappointment. An attitude

of compliance is usually followed by its opposite, swift deprecation and groundless disparagement. (pp. 204–205)

CONTEMPORARY PROPOSALS

Otto Fenichel (1945), a major scholar of psychoanalytic thought, has reinforced and added to Reich's formulations in describing the hysterical characters as:

Persons who are inclined to sexualize all nonsexual relations, toward suggestibility, irrational emotional outbreaks, chaotic behavior, dramatization and histrionic behavior, even toward mendacity and in its extreme form, pseudologic phantastica. . . .

The histrionic quality . . . is a turning from reality to fantasy and probably also an attempt to master anxiety by "acting" actively what otherwise might happen passively . . . hysterical "acting" is . . . directed toward an audience. It is an attempt to induce others to participate in the daydreaming. (1945, pp. 527–528)

Although both Sullivan (1947) and Horney (1950) described personality types akin to the classical hysterical character, it was Fromm (1947) among the neo-Freudian social theorists who captured its modern variant most acutely in his delineation of the "marketing orientation."

Success depends largely on how well a person sells himself on the market, how well he gets his personality across, how "nice a package" he is; whether he is "cheerful," "sound," "aggressive," "reliable," ambitious. . . .

Since success depends largely on how one sells one's personality, one experiences oneself as a commodity. . . . A person is not concerned with his life and happiness, but with becoming salable.

In the marketing orientation man encounters his own powers as commodities alienated from him. He is not one with them but they are masked from him because what matters is not his self-realization . . . but his success in the process of selling them. Both his powers and what they create become estranged . . . something for others to judge and to use; thus, his feeling of identity becomes as shaky as his self-esteem; it is constituted by the sum total of roles one can play: "I am as you desire me."

The premise of the marketing orientation is emptiness, the lack of any specific quality which could not be subject to change. . . . The marketing personality must be free, free of all individuality. (pp. 69–78)

A fine paper by Chodoff and Lyons (1958), which summarized the history and contrasted the hysterical symptom with the hysterical character, furnished a brief description that has been referred to time and again in the literature. Following a listing of cardinal qualities, they summarized:

The hysterical personality is a term applicable to persons who are vain and egocentric, who display labile and excitable but shallow affectivity, whose dramatic, attention-seeking and histrionic behavior may go to the extremes of lying and even pseudologic phantastica, who are very conscious of sex, sexually provocative yet frigid, and who are dependently demanding in interpersonal situations. (p. 736)

Within psychoanalytic circles, views concerning the development and varieties of hysterical character remain controversial. A seminal paper by Marmor (1953) has raised questions concerning whether the psychosexual origin of its formation is primarily oral rather than phallic; Easser and Lesser (1965) and Kernberg (1967), although adhering to the classical themes of earlier writers, suggest several differentiations within the hysterical character spectrum.

In a particularly apt analysis of the hysterical personality, Easser and Lesser summarized a group of hysterics whom they referred to as "hysteroids":

Presenting problems revolved in the main around sexual behavior and the real or fantasied sexual object. They all complained of disillusionment and dissatisfaction with their lovers. This followed the shattering of a romantic fantasy. . . .

All expressed concern over their passionate sexuality and their fear of the consequence of such passion. The fear of their sexual passion was multi-determined. . . .

Not one of this group lacked long-term friendships, social and cultural interests. Although all were apprehensive with strangers and in strange situations, they became rapidly and successfully involved. Nonetheless, they failed to gain confidence after repeated success. . . . They obtained pleasure in entertaining others and assumed the role of hostess with graciousness, so long as they held the center of the stage, through integration and seductiveness as a rule, through temper tantrums

when necessary. These traits make the hysteric a warm but often trying friend. . . .

There was a marked difference in their behavior within the family group and outside it. At home, especially with their mothers, a marked regression occurred. Self-reliance, assertion, and competitiveness diminished and inhibition replaced social vigor. (pp. 393–394)

Consistent with his restructuring and differentiation of character types, Kernberg (1975, 1984) has brought attention to variations in this personality in several of his essays. For example, he seeks to maintain a distinction between the classic hysterical personality and the more contemporary histrionic type. Thus, he places the traditional hysterical variant at a "higher" level of adaptation and psychic structure, whereas he uses the histrionic construct to represent "lower" levels of psychic functioning. Also differentiated are the clinical forms of expression in these two levels that distinguish male and female variants. Among the hysterical category, he speaks of women as being dramatic:

. . . but their display of affects is controlled and has socially adaptive qualities. The way they dramatize their emotional experiences may give the impression that that their emotions are superficial, but exploration reveals otherwise . . . They are not inconsistent or unpredictable in their emotional reactions. They lose emotional control only selectively, vis-à-vis a few closely related persons concerning whom they have intense conflicts, especially of a sexual and competitive nature. (p. 3)

Making further significant differentiations, Kernberg recognizes that the same deeper personality structure may express itself in a variety of ways. Thus, in the following, Kernberg describes how the hysterical variant manifests itself among men:

Several patterns of disturbances in their sexual adaptation characterize men with hysterical personality. One pattern is characterized by a pseudo hypermasculine quality, a histrionic accentuation of culturally accepted masculine patterns. . . . A related, though superficially an apparently contrasting pattern is that of a seductive, subtly effeminate, infantile sexual behavior that combines flirtatiousness and heterosexual promiscuity with a dependent, childlike attitude toward women. (p. 4)

Seeking to clarify the distinction between the syndromes of hysterical and histrionic personality disorders, as conceived by contemporary psychoanalytic thinkers, Gabbard (1994) writes as follows:

The histrionic personality is more florid than the hysterical in virtually every way. . . . Greater lability of affect, more impulsivity, and a more overt seductiveness are all hallmarks. The sexuality of these patients is often so direct and unmodulated that it may actually "turn off" members of the opposite sex. . . .

By contrast, persons who have true hysterical personality disorder may be much more subtly dramatic and exhibitionistic, and their sexuality may be expressed more coyly and engagingly. In addition . . . a sizable group of high level hysterics are not dramatic or flamboyant at all. . . .

Patients with hysterical personality disorder are often reasonably successful at work and demonstrate ambition as well as constructive competitiveness. This active mastery can be juxtaposed with the aimless, helpless, dependent quality that keeps histrionic patients from succeeding. . . .

Hysterical patients can tolerate separation from their love objects even though they may identify those relationships as their main area of difficulty. Histrionic patients, on the other hand, are often overwhelmed with separation anxiety when apart from their love objects. (pp. 559–660)

Another major psychoanalytic thinker is the psychologist David Shapiro (1965, 1981), who has sought to bridge aspects of the analytic model with that of cognitive psychology. Focusing on the defects of "cognitive style," Shapiro provides a series of insightful analysis of several of the major personality disorders, or what he has termed "character styles." In his perceptive analysis of the histrionic (hysterical) personality, Shapiro notes the following (1965):

I am suggesting that hysterical cognition in general is global, relatively diffuse, and lacking in sharpness, particularly in sharp detail. In a word, it is impressionistic. *In contrast to the active, intense, and sharply focused attention of the obsessive-compulsive, hysterical cognition seems relatively lacking in sharp focus of attention; in contrast to the compulsive's active and prolonged searching for detail, the hysterical person tends cognitively to respond quickly and is highly*

susceptible to what is immediately impressive, striking, or merely obvious. (pp. 111–112)

It is my interest, however, to point out that they are aspects of a general mode of cognition. The first of these is the hysterical incapacity for persistent or intense intellectual concentration; the second is the distractibility or impressionability that follows from it; and the third is the nonfactual world in which the hysterical person lives. (p. 113)

As noted previously, Aaron Beck and Freeman (1990b) have extended their work on depression to a wide range of disorders, including those of personality. Following his cognitive model, Beck describes the erroneous beliefs and dysfunctional self-views in the following passage:

They view others favorably as long as they can elicit their attention, amusement, and affection. They try to form strong alliances with others, but with the proviso that they be at the center of the group and that others play the role of attentive audience.

Conditional beliefs include the following: "Unless I captivate people, I am nothing," "If I can't entertain people, they will abandon me," "If people don't respond, they are rotten," "If I can't captivate people, I am helpless." (p. 50)

When they don't get their own way, however, they believe they are being treated unfairly, and they try to coerce compliance or get even by having temper tantrums. Their tolerance for frustration is low, and they may resort to crying, assaultive behavior, and suicidal gestures to get their way or to "punish" the offender. (p. 51)

They conclude that, since they are incapable of caring for themselves, they will need to find ways to get others to take care of them. Then they actively set about seeking attention and approval, in order to find ways to insure that their needs are sufficiently met by others.

Since other people are seen to hold the key to survival in the world, histrionic patients tend also to hold the basic belief that it is necessary to be loved by virtually everyone for everything they do. This leads to a very strong fear of rejection. Even entertaining the notion that rejection is possible is extremely threatening to these individuals, since this reminds them of their tenuous position in the world. Any indication of rejection at all is devastating, even when the person doing the rejecting is not actually that important to a patient. Feeling basically inadequate, yet desperate for approval as their only salvation, people with HPD cannot relax and leave the acquisition of approval to chance. Instead, they feel constant pressure to seek this attention in ways they have best learned to achieve them. (pp. 215, 216)

Picking up the major themes of earlier interpersonal theorists such as Horney and Sullivan, Leary articulates a detailed model of the histrionic type in what he terms "the cooperative-overconventional" personality, individuals who demonstrate unusual extroverted friendliness and sociability and a striving to be liked and accepted. Leary (1957) states:

Individuals who rigidly and inappropriately express agreeable, affiliative behavior are diagnosed as overconventional personalities. These are the persons who cannot tolerate any critical or strong or guilty behavior in themselves. They continually strive to please, to be accepted, to establish positive relations with others.

Gross misperceptions of social reality characterize their approach. They just cannot see hostility or power in themselves. They avoid feelings of depression. A rigid overoptimism is quite typical. They often misperceive the interpersonal behavior of others and tend to saturate all their social exchanges with affiliative motifs. (p. 304)

The overconventional person apparently has learned that he can reduce anxiety and gain heightened self-esteem by means of optimistic blandness. He has discovered that acceptance and approval from others can be won by means of friendly operations. He feels safe, comfortable, secure when he is employing these protections. (p. 305)

One of the major adherents to the interpersonal school that Horney, Sullivan, and Leary helped to establish is L. Benjamin (1974, 1993a). In her insightful analysis of the histrionic personality style, Benjamin provides a general characterization, as well as one specific to this individual's interpersonal behavior. In her most recent work, Benjamin (1993a) writes:

There is strong fear of being ignored, together with a wish to be loved and taken care of by someone powerful, who nonetheless can be controlled through use of charm and entertainment skills. The baseline position is of friendly trust that is accompanied by a secretly disrespectful agenda of forcing delivery of the desired nurturance and love.

Inappropriate seductive behaviors and manipulative suicidal attempts are examples of coercions. (p. 173)

Sees others as strong and able to provide whatever is needed whenever it is needed. Has no interest in developing competence at tasks. Counts on being attractive to someone powerful who can take care of things. Uses anger to coerce compliance if others do not immediately provide what is wanted and needed. (p. 177)

Note should be made of the early factor analytic studies by Lazare, Klerman, and Armor (1966, 1970) and by Walton and Presley (1973a, 1973b). The latter study uncovered a small group of traits that paralleled those assigned to the traditional hysterical personality category, notably ingratiation, need for attention, excessive emotional display, unlikability, and insincerity. In a cross-validation investigation to confirm and elaborate earlier findings, Lazare et al. noted that only four of seven traits that are classically associated with the hysterical character clustered together as anticipated. Traits that held up as strongly as predicted were emotionality, exhibitionism, egocentricity, and sexual provocativeness; those clearly failing to do so were suggestibility and fear of sexuality; the trait of dependency fell into an intermediary position. Among the unanticipated characteristics uncovered in the hysterical cluster were aggression, oral expression, obstinacy, and rejection of others. On the basis of these latter findings, Lazare et al. concluded that their "hysterical" population may have corresponded to the "infantile" personality described by Kernberg (1967), a type characterized as a primitive or regressed hysterical variant.

In an effort to systematize the use of factor analytic techniques as a means of identifying fundamental trait dimensions related to the personality disorders, reference must be made to the recent studies by Costa and Widiger (1994). In describing the histrionic personality, they write:

HST largely represents an extreme variant of extraversion. Extraversion involves the tendency to be outgoing, talkative, and affectionate (high warmth); to be convivial; to have many friends; and to actively seek social contact (high histrionicness); to be assertive and dominant (high assertiveness); to be energetic, fast-paced, and vigorous (high activity); to be flashy; to seek strong stimulation; to take risks (high excitement seeking); and to be high spirited, buoyant, optimistic, and joyful (high positive emotions). (p. 47)

At an entirely different level, Donald Klein, a psychopharmacologically oriented theorist (1967, 1971, 1972, 1975), has suggested that the hysterical personality as formulated in the DSM-II was an amalgam of three subgroups that respond differently to psychotropic drugs: the histrionic, the emotionally unstable, and what he termed the "hysteroid dysphoric." Ncting that cross-sectional distinctions are difficult to draw, and that diagnosis often requires prolonged longitudinal study, Klein nevertheless identified several key factors to delineate their respective characters. All three variants give evidence of the classical signs of lability, vanity, and dependency; but the "histrionic" is noted especially by "role-playing and symptom imitation . . . symptoms may not be the direct external manifestations of intolerable affective states but rather may be environmentally oriented, learned manipulative devices" (1972, p. 355). Klein contrasted them to the "emotionally unstable" type who are predominantly:

. . . female adolescents whose mood disorder consists of short periods of tense, empty unhappiness, accompanied by inactivity, withdrawal, depression, irritability and sulking, alternating suddenly with impulsiveness, giddiness, low frustration tolerance, rejection of rules and shortsighted hedonism. (1972, p. 356)

Last, in portraying the "hysteroid dysphoric," Klein (1972) wrote:

They are fickle, emotionally labile, irresponsible, shallow, love-intoxicated, giddy and shortsighted. . . . Seductive, manipulative, exploitative and sexually provocative, they think emotionally and illogically. Easy prey to flattery and compliments . . . they are possessive, grasping, demanding, romantic . . . when frustrated or disappointed, they become reproachful, tearful, abusive and vindictive . . . Rejection sensitivity is perhaps their outstanding common clinical feature. (p. 237)

Whether Klein's distinctions merely represent different expressions of the same basic syndrome or are types deserving clear differentiation on the basis of their response to psychopharmacologic agents, as Klein contends, cannot be gauged at this time. Regardless, they are illuminating and effective portrayals of classical hysterical characters.

Another neurobiologically oriented theorist is Cloninger (1987a), who derives his concept of the histrionic personality on the basis of his formulation of character traits associated with three major brain systems. His description of this personality is as follows:

Histrionic personality is defined here in terms of the basic response patterns of high novelty seeking, low harm avoidance, and high reward dependence, which are associated with the second-order traits of being impulsive, gullible or emotionally vulnerable, and narcissistic. This corresponds closely to the DSM-III and ICD descriptions of histrionic or hysterical personality. These traditional groups are also characterized by their narcissistic traits (dramatic, attention-seeking, self-indulgent, vain), vulnerability and emotional dependence (dependent, seeking reassurance, warm, and charming), and impulsive-aggressive traits (craving for activity and excitement, angry outbursts, and suicidal behavior). (p. 584)

Moving to other recent work, Millon, using his theoretically derived histrionic personality pattern as a basis (1969), summarized the distinguishing features of the *"gregarious-histrionic"* type in the following descriptions and diagnostic criteria:

Using the format of characteristics which has served to summarize the principal features of previous personality patterns, the following distinguishing attributes may be noted in the histrionic pattern: labile affectivity (uncontrolled and dramatic expression of emotions), cognitive dissociation (failure to integrate learnings; massive repression of memories), sociable self-image (perception of self as attractive, charming and affectionate) and interpersonal seductiveness (a need to flirt and seek attention). (1969, p. 253)

In line with the preceding criteria, Millon wrote the following initial working draft in 1975 as a member of the DSM-III Task Force personality subcommittee:

This pattern is typified by a histrionic, facile and superficially charming social lifestyle. There is a persistent seeking of attention, stimulation and excitement, usually expressed in seductive, immaturely exhibitionistic and self-dramatizing behaviors. Interpersonal relationships are characteristically shallow, frivolous and fleeting. A general intolerance of delay and inactivity often results in impulsive and over-reactive behaviors. Thought processes are typically insubstantial, unreflected and scattered. Highly labile emotions are notable by their easy and short-lived enthusiasms followed by rapid boredom. Since adolescence or early adulthood at least 3 of the following have been present to a notably greater degree than in most people and were not limited to discrete periods nor necessarily prompted by stressful life events.

1. *Fickle affectivity (e.g., displays short-lived, dramatic and superficial affects; reports tendency to be easily excited and as easily bored).*

2. *Sociable self-image (e.g., perceives self as stimulating and charming; attracts fleeting acquaintances and enjoys rapidly-paced social life).*

3. *Interpersonal seductiveness (e.g., actively solicits praise and manipulates others to gain attention and approval; exhibits self-dramatizing and childishly exhibitionistic behaviors).*

4. *Cognitive dissociation (e.g., integrates experiences poorly which results in scattered learning and unexamined thought; reveals undependable, erratic and flighty judgment).*

5. *Immature stimulus-seeking behavior (e.g., is intolerant of inactivity, leading to unreflected and impulsive responsiveness; describes penchant for momentary excitements, fleeting adventures and short-sighted hedonism).*

A revision of the preceding emerged following committee discussion; the focus shifted somewhat and resulted in these recommended criteria:

A. *Persistent attention-seeking (e.g., socially seductive and childishly exhibitionistic as a means of soliciting praise and approval).*

B. *Interpersonally demanding (e.g., insistent on getting own way by manipulating others to achieve ends).*

C. *Overly reactive and intensely expressed affect (e.g., displays short-lived, dramatic and superficial emotion; is easily excited and quickly bored).*

D. *Socially histrionic (e.g., pursues active social life and is successful in attracting fleeting acquaintances).*

E. *Immature stimulus-seeking (e.g., penchant for momentary excitements, impulsively adventurous, and short-sighted hedonism).*

The final criteria reflect further modifications, but the classic distinguishing features remain close to what has been written for well over 100 years.

Included in the minor changes introduced in the DSM-III-R was the elimination of a criterion from the DSM-III that referred to the manipulative use of suicidal threats, gestures, or attempts; this criterion was deleted in order to better differentiate the histrionic from the borderline personality. It had not been recommended as one of the characteristic features in the initial DSM-III formulations of the histrionic personality disorder.

The ICD-10 includes a histrionic disorder and characterizes the personality in the following manner: the presence of self-dramatization, theatricality, and the exaggeration of emotional expression; a high degree of suggestibility, noted by the ease with which they are influenced by others and by circumstances; affective shallowness and lability; persistent seeking of excitement, appreciation by others, and activities designed to achieve the center of attention; inappropriately seductive appearance and behaviors; an overconcern with physical attractiveness. Associated features often include egocentricity, self-indulgence, and manipulative behavior designed to achieve one's own needs. Owing to the exclusion of the narcissistic personality disorder, a major component of the DSM-III and the DSM-IV, the ICD-10 characterization of the histrionic includes features that would otherwise be a part of the narcissistic disorder. As discussed at international meetings, the decision of the ICD-10 committee was based on a lack of support for the presence of narcissistic personality styles in both Europe and Asia. Perhaps the impact of the American lifestyle has not reached the proportions in cultures and societies other than those in the United States to achieve significant prevalence levels.

The DSM-IV follows the criteria outlined in DSM-III and DSM-III-R, grouping the features enumerated into four clinical domains. Most prominent are those that relate to Interpersonal Conduct where four criteria are listed: discomfort in situations in which the person is not the center of attention; social interactions typified by inappropriately sexually seductive behaviors; consistent use of physical appearance to draw attention to oneself; and incidental relationships considered to be more intimate than they are. Two Cognitively relevant criteria are also specified: a style of speech that signifies a superficially impressionistic view of the world, (e.g., opinions are vague and diffuse, usually without supporting facts and details); a high degree of suggestibility (e.g., opinions and feelings are easily influenced by others and by current fads). A significant Behavioral criterion is included, namely: self-dramatization, theatricality, and the excessive public display of emotions (e.g., temper tantrums). Finally, a significant Mood criterion is noted: displays highly labile, rapidly shifting, and a facile, but shallow expression of emotions.

We next review the evolutionary model and theory. The polarity schema to characterize the histrionic personality is presented in Figure 10.1. The elements that stand out are an ecological focus on others (nurturance) and on activity (modification). As is typical in most personality disorders, both the pain and pleasure polarities are not notably significant.

In a manner similar to the dependent personality, the histrionic's adaptive style is centered on relationships with other persons. However, the dependent and the histrionic differ markedly in their mode of adaptation; histrionics actively manipulate the environment to achieve their ends; by contrast, dependents are passive, not only in that they accommodate to the environment, but that they look to others to guide and nurture them. Histrionics engage in a variety of interpersonal maneuvers to ensure that others are attentive and approving, even desirous of and willingly offering tribute to them.

Dependents not only seek but need others to care for and nurture them, as well as to provide them with guidance. By contrast, histrionics are actively involved in giving to and even nurturing others. These latter behaviors are not altruistic, but a means of soliciting and ensuring reciprocal approval and esteem. It is the active-modifying stance that the histrionic takes to assure a continuous supply of admiration and fulfillment that distinguishes his or her style of behavior. Should this supply of reciprocal gratification fail to be forthcoming, the histrionic will quickly jettison the "defective" partner, turning without much ado to locate another who will supply these needs.

A useful summary of the major historical contributors is represented in Figure 10.2.

CLINICAL FEATURES

The following sections should aid the reader in outlining a cognitive map, so to speak, of the prototypal histrionic personality disorder (see also Table 10.1 and Figure 10.3).

PROTOTYPAL DIAGNOSTIC DOMAINS

Histrionic personalities often demonstrate, albeit in caricature and mild pathological form, what our society tends to foster and admire in its members—to be well liked, successful, popular, extroverted, attractive, and sociable. Beneath this surface portrayal we often see a driven quality, a consuming need for approval, a desperate striving to be conspicuous and to evoke affection or attract attention at all costs. Despite the frequent rewards these behaviors produce, they stem from needs that are pathologically inflexible, repetitious, and persistent. In this section, the histrionic picture is detailed in line with the four spheres of clinical observation and analysis employed in Chapter 9 for description of the dependent personality.

Expressive Behavior: Dramatic

Although not unique, there are distinctive aspects to the expressive behaviors of histrionics. They are overreactors, relating at times in a volatile and a

HISTRIONIC PROTOTYPE

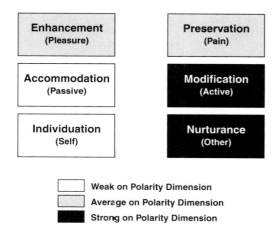

Figure 10.1 Status of the histrionic personality prototype in accord with the Millon Polarity Model.

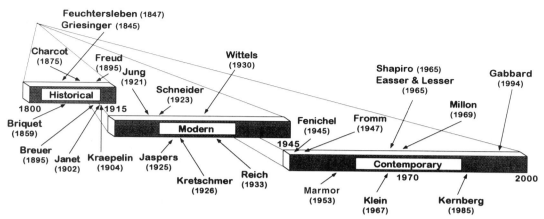

Figure 10.2   Historical review of major contributors to the histrionic personality disorder.

provocative manner, but usually displaying themselves in an engaging and theatrical manner. They show a tendency to be intolerant of inactivity, resulting in impulsive, capricious, and highly emotional behaviors. Similarly, there is a penchant for momentary excitements and hedonic ventures. Histrionic personalities often impress one at first meeting by the ease with which they express their thoughts and feelings, by their flair for the dramatic, and by their capacity to draw attention to themselves. These exhibitionistic and expressive talents are manifested, however, in a series of rapidly changing, short-lived, and superficial affects. Histrionic personalities tend to be capricious, easily excited, and intolerant of frustration, delay, and disappointment. Moreover, the words and feelings they express appear shallow and simulated rather than deep or real.

Interpersonal Conduct: Attention-Seeking

Histrionics are more than merely friendly and helpful in their relationships; they are actively solicitous of praise, "market" their appeal, and are often entertaining and sexually provocative. Because affection and attention are primary goals, histrionics engage in a variety of maneuvers to elicit a favorable response. Women may behave in a charming or coquettish manner; men are typically generous in praise and, on occasion, overtly seductive. Both men and women often display an interesting mixture of being carefree and sophisticated, on the one hand, and inhibited and naive, on the other. In the sphere of sexuality, for example,

many histrionics are quite at ease while "playing the game" but become confused, immature, or apprehensive once matters get serious.

Characteristically, histrionics are unable to follow through and sustain the initial impression of goodwill and sophistication they convey. Social life is one in which there are "many acquaintances but few friends." In most areas of personal activity, they put up a good show at the start but often falter and withdraw when depth and durability in relationships are required.

It is toward the end of achieving these goals and avoiding these fears that histrionics have learned to manipulate others to their suiting. More than merely agreeable and friendly, they "sell" themselves by employing their talents and charm to elicit recognition and esteem. This is done by presenting an attractive front, by seductive pretensions, by a dilettante sophistication, and by a show of postures and acts to impress and amuse others. Displays and exhibitions, dramatic gestures, attractive coiffures, frivolous comments, clever stories, and shocking clothes, all are designed not to "express themselves" but to draw interest, stimulation, and attention. In short, histrionics use themselves as a commodity with a bag of tricks, a conspicuous "personality" that corners all the attention of those with whom they come into contact.

Histrionic personalities not only acquire skill in sensing what is salable or will "get across" to others, but they learn to be alert to signs of potential hostility and rejection. This hypervigilance enables them to quickly adapt their behaviors to minimize indifference and disapproval. Their interpersonal

TABLE 10.1   Clinical Domains of the
Histrionic Prototype

Behavioral Level

(F) Expressively Dramatic. Is overreactive,
volatile, provocative, and engaging, as well as intolerant of inactivity, resulting in impulsive, highly emotional, and theatrical responsiveness; describes
penchant for momentary excitements, fleeting adventures, and short-sighted hedonism.

(F) Interpersonally Attention-Seeking. Actively
solicits praise and manipulates others to gain needed
reassurance, attention, and approval; is demanding, flirtatious, vain, and seductively exhibitionistic, especially
when wishing to be the center of attention.

Phenomenological Level

(F) Cognitively Flighty. Avoids introspective
thought, is overly suggestible, attentive to fleeting
external events, and speaks in impressionistic generalities; integrates experiences poorly, resulting in scattered learning and thoughtless judgments.

(S) Gregarious Self-Image. Views self as sociable,
stimulating, and charming; enjoys the image of attracting acquaintances by physical appearance and by pursuing a busy and pleasure-oriented life.

(S) Shallow Objects. Internalized representations
are composed largely of superficial memories of past
relations, random collections of transient and segregated affects and conflicts, as well as insubstantial
drives and mechanisms.

Intrapsychic Level

(F) Dissociation Mechanism. Regularly alters and
recomposes self-presentations to create a succession
of socially attractive but changing facades; engages in
self-distracting activities to avoid reflecting on and
integrating unpleasant thoughts and emotions.

(S) Disjointed Organization. There exists a
loosely knit and carelessly united morphologic structure in which processes of internal regulation and
control are scattered and unintegrated, with ad hoc
methods for restraining impulses, coordinating
defenses, and resolving conflicts, leading to mechanisms that must, of necessity, be broad and sweeping
to maintain psychic cohesion and stability and, when
successful, only further isolate and disconnect
thoughts, feelings, and actions.

Biophysical Level

(S) Fickle Mood. Displays rapidly shifting and shallow emotions; is vivacious, animated, impetuous and
exhibits tendencies to be easily enthused and as easily
angered or bored.

(F) = Functional domain.
(S) = Structural domain.

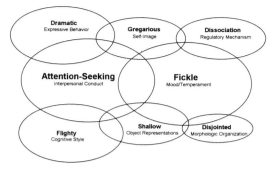

HISTRIONIC PROTOTYPE

Figure 10.3   Salience of personologic domains in the
histrionic prototype.

facility extends, therefore, not only to evoking
praise but to avoiding rejection. By paying close attention to the signals that people transmit, histrionics can fashion their reactions to conform with the
desires of others. Then they need not fear indifference or desertion because they are always ready to
maneuver themselves to do things that correspond
to the wishes and expectations of others.

Despite the charm and talent for pleasing others, the histrionic fails to provide them with genuinely sustained affection. All that histrionic
personalities offer in return for the approval they
seek are fleeting and often superficial displays of
affection.

Cognitive Style: Flighty

Histrionics are inclined to avoid introspective
thought. Lacking an integrated sense of self, owing
to their exteroceptive orientation, they are overly
suggestible, are excessively attentive to fleeting
and superficial events, and integrate their experiences poorly. This has resulted in a widely scattered but shallow pattern of learnings, as well as a
tendency to speak in impressionistic generalities
and to come to essentially thoughtless judgments.
The preoccupation of histrionic personalities with
external rewards and approvals often leaves them
bereft of an identity apart from others. They describe themselves not in terms of their own traits
but in terms of their relationships and their effects
on others. Histrionics behave like "empty organisms" who react more to external stimuli than to
promptings from within. They show an extraordinary sensitivity to the thoughts and moods of those

from whom they desire approval and affection. This well-developed radar system serves them well, for it not only alerts them to signs of impending rejection but enables them to manipulate the object of their designs with consummate skill.

This orientation toward external stimuli leads histrionics to pay fleeting, impressionistic, and scattered attention to details, and accounts in part for their characteristic distractible and flighty behaviors. The susceptibility of histrionics to transient events parallels their superficial cognitive style, their lack of genuine curiosity, and their inability to think in a concentrated and logical fashion. Habits of superficiality and dilettantism may represent an intellectual evasiveness and a desire to eschew troublesome thoughts or emotionally charged feelings. Part of the flightiness of histrionic personalities derives from an avoidance of potentially disruptive ideas and urges, especially those that might bring to awareness their deeply hidden dependency needs. For these and other reasons, they "steer clear" of self-knowledge and depth in personal relationships. In effect, histrionics dissociate themselves from thoughts, from people, and from activities that might upset their strategy of superficiality.

Self-Image: Gregarious

Histrionic personalities view themselves as sociable, friendly, and agreeable people. They consider themselves to be stimulating and charming, well liked by others and able to be quite successful in terms of creating an exciting and interesting lifestyle. They value the capacity to attract acquaintances, particularly by physical appearance, and by the creation of a busy and pleasure-oriented context for their social life. Many lack insight, however, failing to recognize, or to admit recognizing, their deeper insecurities, their desperate need to draw attention to themselves and to be well liked. Signs of inner turmoil, weakness, depression, or hostility are almost invariably denied, suppressed so as not to be part of their sense of self.

Object-Representations: Shallow

Most persons seek stimulation, attention, and approval, but it is only the histrionic personality who possesses an insatiable striving for these experiences, who feels devoid of an inner self and seeks constant nourishment to fill that void. Lacking a core identity apart from others, histrionics must draw nurture from those around them. It is others who supply the sustenance of life without which the histrionic will feel a deep vacancy, a fear of collapse, and a falling apart in disarray or into the empty chasm that exists within them. The internalized objects of the histrionic's intrapsychic content are composed largely of superficial memories of past relationships. Owing to the facile manner in which histrionics attach themselves to others, their inner world is composed of a random collection of transient and unconnected affects, a template of insubstantial relationships, impulses, and memories. It is the scattering and incidental character of these inner templates that leads the histrionic to become evermore dependent on external stimulation and approval. How do histrionics manipulate their inner world to assure the stimulation and approval they require?

It may be useful before proceeding to note again that the interpersonal behaviors of most pathological personalities do not usually appear strikingly different from that seen among normal individuals. Their distinction lies not so much in their uniqueness or bizarreness but in their inflexibility and persistence.

Histrionics are often successful in accomplishing their aims of eliciting stimulation and captivating the attentions of others. Their strategies are considered pathological because they fail to limit their manipulations to situations in which they are appropriate. Rather, they are applied indiscriminately and persistently, seeking to attract the attentions of insignificant persons in unsuitable circumstances. Histrionics' need for recognition and approval appears insatiable. As soon as they receive attention from one source, they turn their unquenchable thirst for approval to others. The histrionic is a bottomless pit into which esteem and tribute may be poured. Equally important is the observation that a failure to evoke attention and approval often results in dejection and anxiety. Signs of indifference or neutrality on the part of others often are interpreted as rejections and result in feelings of emptiness and unworthiness.

Having failed throughout life to develop the richness of inner feelings and lacking resources from which they can draw, histrionics have difficulty in maintaining a full, meaningful, and stable relationship with another. At some level, they also sense the disparity that exists between the favorable but superficial impression they give to others and their real lack of inner substance. As a result, they are likely to shy from prolonged contact with others for fear that their fraudulence will be uncovered. In sum, the facile emotions of histrionics are shallow, fleeting, and illusory; not only are they unable to sustain close relationships, but they quickly abandon what few they may have had before the "truth" be known.

Regulatory Mechanisms:
Dissociation/Repression

As already noted, histrionics actively seek to avoid introspection and responsible thinking. Not only are they characteristically attuned to external rather than internal events, but their lifelong orientation toward what others think and feel has prevented them from learning to deal with their own inner thoughts and feelings. As a consequence, they lack intrapsychic skills and must resort to gross mechanisms to handle unconscious emotions. What they have learned best is to simply seal off, repress, or dissociate entire segments of memory and feeling that may prompt discomfort. As a result, much of their past is a blank, devoid of the complex reservoir of attitudes and emotions they should have acquired through experiences. Histrionics regularly alter and recompose their self-presentations to create a succession of socially attractive but changing facades. By disconnecting their true selves from the theatrical pose they present to the world, they can distract themselves sufficiently to avoid reflecting on and integrating the emptiness that inheres within them or the painful thoughts and emotions that otherwise surge up into consciousness.

To the degree that histrionics possess an inner world of thought, memory, and emotion, they try to repress it and to keep it from intruding into their conscious life. This they do for several reasons. First, their own sense of worth depends on the judgment of others; there is no reason to explore the inner self, for they alone cannot appraise their personal value or provide acceptance or approval. Second, by turning attentions inward histrionics distract themselves from attending to the outer world. This divided attention can prove troublesome since they feel they must be ever alert to the desires and moods of others.

The contrast between their pretensions and objective reality leads histrionics to repress not only one or two deficiencies within themselves but all of their inner self; it is the triviality of their entire being, its pervasive emptiness and paucity of

substance, that must be kept from awareness. Repression is therefore applied across the board; it is massive and absolute.

Morphologic Organization: Disjointed

The morphologic structure and organization of the histrionic's inner world is loosely knit and carelessly united. Internal controls and regulations are scattered and unintegrated, with ad hoc methods used to restrain impulses, coordinate defenses, and resolve conflicts. Regulatory mechanisms must, of necessity, be broad and sweeping to maintain overall psychic stability and cohesion. Of course, when successful, these efforts only undermine psychic coherency by further disconnecting and isolating this personality's thoughts, feelings, and actions.

Having deprived themselves of past learnings, histrionics are less able to function on their own and thereby perpetuate their dependency on others. Moreover, to compensate for the void of their past, and for the guidance these learnings could provide, they remain locked into the present. In short, the intrapsychic world of the histrionic personality not only remains skimpy and insubstantial, but their preoccupation with external immediacies has led to a further impoverishment of what little richness and depth they may possess.

To preserve their exteroceptive vigilance, they must reduce "inner" distractions, especially those that may be potentially disturbing. Histrionics seek actively to blot out any awareness of the barrenness of their intrapsychic world. This inner emptiness is especially intolerable because it points to the fraudulence that exists between the impressions they seek to convey to others and their true cognitive sterility and emotional poverty.

Mood/Temperament: Fickle

The biological underpinnings of the histrionic personality may not be too difficult to infer. Conceived in temperamental terms, histrionic behavior suggests both a high level of energy and activation, and a low threshold for autonomic reactivity. Histrionics tend, in general, to be quick and responsive, especially with regard to the expression of emotions. Feelings of both a positive and negative variety come forth with extreme ease, suggesting either an unusually high degree of sensory irritability, excessive sympathetic activity, or a lack of cortical inhibition. No single temperament label readily captures the highly fickle, intense, erratic, and wide range of emotions to which they are disposed.

It would seem reasonable that histrionic adults would have displayed a high degree of emotional responsiveness in infancy and early childhood. This inference derives from the facts that constitutional traits are essentially stable throughout life and that active and responsive children are likely to foster and intensify their initial responsiveness by evoking stimulating reactions from others.

Prototypal Variants

We will next present some of the many forms in which the basic histrionic style manifests itself, beginning with normal variants, then childhood syndromes, and finally the several subtypes found clinically among adults.

Normal Styles

Our society is one in which friendliness and general sociability is usually rewarded and viewed in favor. That is not the case necessarily in other cultures. People who are expressive and histrionic are sometimes viewed with suspicion, perhaps seeming overly superficial and nonsubstantive. What we look for in identifying a Histrionic Personality Disorder are qualities that derive primarily from the special circumstances of the individuals upbringing and experience, not those that can be attributed to the forces and values of the larger society. When we think of a histrionic personality *style,* not a disorder, we should suspect that both cultural and unique life experiences have coalesced, a pattern of behaviors that stems from both the specifics of the individual's past and the impact of social influences.

In portraying what they term the "dramatic style," Oldham and Morris (1990) refer to persons who have been granted the gift of strong feelings with which they color the lives of those around them. These personalities fill their life with excitement, their laughter, their flamboyance and sensitivity, each of which can often lift the spirits of those with whom they live and work.

Another characterization of the normal histrionic pattern may be seen in the "Outgoing" style described by Millon et al. (1994), one that focuses on the sociability rather than the theatrical aspects of this type:

Histrionic persons go out of their way to be popular with others, have confidence in their social abilities, feel they can readily influence and charm others, and possess a personal style that makes people like them. Most enjoy engaging in social activities, and like meeting new people and learning about their lives. Talkative, lively, socially clever, they are often dramatic attention-getters who thrive on being the center of social events. Many become easily bored, especially when faced with repetitive and mundane tasks. Often characterized by intense and shifting moods, histrionic types are sometimes viewed as fickle and excitable; on the other hand, their enthusiasms often prove effective in energizing and motivating others. Inclined to be facile and enterprising, outgoing people may be highly skilled in manipulating others to meet their needs. (p. 32)

In sum, normal histrionic types are seen as friendly and charming; they seek the attentions of others and almost invariably convey an air of well-being and self-enjoyment. These persons possess a genuine warmth and social attractiveness. Most see themselves as cheerful and optimistic persons whose goal in life is to always be happy and to experience periodic euphoric states. There is a joie de vivre, a joy in life that often stimulates others into feeling equally exuberant. Many act and think like adolescents, even into their middle and older years. They are often resilient, possess a capacity to overcome life's setbacks and disappointments, rarely letting problems and difficulties get them down. Their outlook is strongly affirmative, invariably open to new possibilities, and joyfully surprised by the potentials in new experiences.

Childhood Syndromes

There is little evidence that highly sociable, dramatically expressive youngsters are viewed in our society as problematic; this would not be the view, of course, in cultures where emotional expressiveness and theatricality are viewed as distasteful, if not repugnant (e.g., as in many Asian societies). In the clinical literature, we likewise find little to support the clinical significance of childhood histrionic behaviors. Nevertheless, there is a related subcategory in the DSM-IV labeled *reactive-attachment disorder: disinhibited type.* It states as its primary feature "diffuse attachments as manifested by indiscriminate sociability, as evident in a marked inability to exhibit appropriate and selective attachments." Whether this characterization is a precursor of later styles of histrionic behavior with its indiscriminate search for attention and approval has not been thoroughly examined either theoretically or empirically.

Adult Subtypes

As noted in previous chapters, this section draws on extensive clinical observations, as well as research on cluster and factor analyses that provide an empirical base for determining variants and coexisting personality disorders. The following sections illustrate clinical syntheses of these personality subtypes.

The Theatrical Histrionic

The *theatrical histrionic* is a caricature of the basic histrionic—dramatic, romantic, attention-seeking. As Fromm recognized in his description of the "marketing orientation," there are individuals who live life as if they were commodities, objects for sale. No characteristic of oneself is seen as intrinsic—as a stable and fundamental aspect of the self. It is the appearance of things that is everything. These personalities transform themselves into something synthesized, something that appears in ways other than it really is. This readily devised image is projected on the world, shifting from time to time as the occasion calls for. Theatrical histrionics package themselves to meet the expectations of others as closely as possible. They are chameleons of sorts, changing their colors and shadows to fit whatever environment in which they find themselves. We may describe this variant of the histrionic as affected and mannered, one who "puts on" striking and eye-catching postures and clothes, markets his or her appearance to others, and simulates desirable and dramatic poses that are fabricated or synthesized to create an appealing image of self.

Problems arise as a consequence of these flexible images of self. Despite the charm and adaptiveness of these maneuvers and the ability to simulate all types of roles and characters, the theatrical histrionic is left with a sense of inner emptiness. No intrinsic quality can be seen, merely a set of mirrors that reflect what would be pleasing and attractive to others. Everything is simulated and expedient, all is pragmatic and marketable. These personalities are superb manipulators of symbols that mimic reality.

Several varieties of the theatrical type are seen in society. The most visible caricatures are women who encase themselves in bright jewelry, sexy clothes, and appealing perfumes. They spend much of their time putting on makeup, trying on different clothes, and reading fashion magazines. The parallels among men are the great raconteurs and joke-tellers; also notable are those who spend an inordinate amount of time "working out," trimming and shaping their bodies to fit the latest model of the virile and vigorous man.

There are the romanticized types who complain of being disillusioned with their spouses or lovers. Living in a fantasized world of romantic aspirations, they seek to seduce and conquer those of the opposite sex. They seek to become femme fatales, bon vivants, or casanovas. By whatever means possible, they display themselves, acting as if they were lures to attract the most attractive prize available to them. They become similar to the ornaments worn on their body, a clever device to seduce the unsophisticated. Interestingly, persons of the same gender quickly size up the superficial ploys engaged in by the theatrical histrionic. Women quickly spot these behaviors and decoys; men are not as discerning, but also come to recognize the deceptive smile, the coy look, and the humorous comment. This histrionic's mode of operation is patently obvious, except to those who are in the process of being admired and seduced.

The Infantile Histrionic

This personality variant often demonstrates a compound of histrionic and borderline personality features. It is akin to what Kernberg (1967) has referred to as the "infantile personality," noted by labile and diffuse emotions, childlike pouting, and demanding-clinging behaviors, as well as a crude and direct sexual provocativeness. In certain ways, this adult subtype might be spoken of as a primitively developed and poorly organized histrionic. Descriptively, we might characterize the infantile histrionic as labile, high-strung, and inclined to express volatile emotions. They display a childlike hysteria, typified by a pouting and demanding attachment to others; they fasten and clutch to significant others, seemingly fused to them, if not clinging and "hanging on."

The infantile histrionic's behavior is typified by marked dependency needs, deep and varying recurring moods, prolonged periods of moodiness and self-deprecation, as well as episodes of high energy and impulsive, angry outbursts. There is an anxious seeking for reassurance from others to maintain equanimity. An intense fear of being abandoned leads the infantile histrionic to be overly compliant at one time, profoundly gloomy the next, behave with negativistic outbursts and tantrums, and then to engage in sexually provocative behaviors. Some see this person as submissive and childlike, and others as unpredictable, irritable, and irrational. The patient often portrays conflicting emotions simultaneously, notably love, rage, and guilt. There appears to be an affective-activity equilibrium that is in constant jeopardy. As a consequence, the patient vacillates between being tense and high-strung, manipulative, and moody, and is particularly sensitive to the pressures and demands of others. Vacillation between moments of childlike agreeableness, acting in an enticing and tempting manner, and being sullen or pouty is typical and frequent.

These infantile types often complain bitterly about the lack of care expressed by others and of being treated unfairly, behaviors that keep others constantly on edge, never knowing if they will be reacted to in a cooperative or a sulky manner. Although occasionally making efforts to be obliging, if not seductive, the patient frequently precipitates interpersonal difficulties by constantly doubting the genuineness of interest others may express. These irritable and childlike testing maneuvers frequently exasperate and alienate those on whom the patient depends. Not uncommonly, these histrionics will exhibit seductive and clinging behaviors. However, others may have grown increasingly weary of these behaviors, leading the patient to react by vacillating erratically between expressions of gloomy self-deprecation, behaving in a sexually provocative manner, and being petulant and bitter. The struggle between childlike acquiescence and adult self-assertion constantly intrudes into the patient's life. The inability to regulate sexual impulses and emotional controls, the feeling of being misunderstood, and the unpredictable moods expressed, all contribute to innumerable wrangles and conflicts with others and to a persistent tense, resentful, and emotional tone.

The Vivacious Histrionic

A frequent association has been found between histrionic and hypomanic features. Prevalence data indicate that this covariation occurs with considerable frequency in settings such as drug treatment programs, marital counseling clinics, and centers for handling female youth offenders.

In addition to the high level of energy and vigor that typifies hypomanic types, these histrionic personalities tend to be clever, charming, flippant, and capable of weaving fanciful images that intrigue and seduce the naive. Given these latter characteristics, it should not be surprising that these vivacious histrionics also exhibit a variety of narcissistic personality traits.

Driven by a need for excitement and stimulation, this energetic and driven *vivacious histrionic* amalgam acts impulsively, is unable to delay gratification, and evidences a penchant for momentary excitements and fleeting adventures, with minimal regard for later consequences. These individuals are notably thrill seeking, easily infatuated, and overly, but transiently, attached to one thing or person following another. We might describe these histrionics with the following adjectives: vigorous, bubbly, spirited, brisk, and impulsively expressive. They are restlessly energetic, ebullient, seeking momentary playful and joyful adventures, without imposing constraints on where and when these are to be pursued.

For the most part, vivacious histrionics tend to be overly cheerful, of a lively and spirited nature, disposed to live life to the fullest in a brisk and vigorous way. They are persons who are distinguished by the animated nature of their movements, by their ill disposition to sit still and relax for any period of time. They always seem to be on the go, gesticulate freely and in a highly expressive manner, enjoy their conversations, and produce their ideas in a quick tempo. They race their physical and psychic engines, exhibiting vigor in their movements, as in all other aspects of their behaviors and thoughts. For the most part, they are quite cheerful, although inclined to be rather superficial in the topics they discuss. They move from one thing to another, often in a joyous and joking manner. Most view things from an optimistic and cheerful perspective; serious and problematic matters tend to be overlooked.

Vivacious histrionics often lack social dependability, exhibiting a disdain for the effects of their behaviors, as they pursue one restless chase or satisfy one whim after another. There may be a capricious disregard for agreements hastily assumed, and a trail may be left of broken promises and contracts, squandered funds, distraught employers, and so on. Lacking inner substance and self-discipline, tempted by new and exciting stimuli, and skilled in attracting and cheerfully seducing others, such vivacious histrionic personalities may travel an erratic course of flagrant irresponsibility and leave in their wake the scattered debris of seductive and once promising hopes.

The Appeasing Histrionic

The desire to please another, to make the person like them, to approve of them, to tell them that what they are doing is good, is the major driving force that motivates these *appeasing histrionic* subtypes. Approval from others is their supreme goal. Not only do these histrionics want to demonstrate that they love everybody and will do anything for them, but appeasing personalities want everyone to praise and commend them in return. The search for reciprocal recognition and approval compels and justifies everything they do. Appeasing histrionics show an unusual knack for pleasing people, for being thoughtful about their wishes, for making them become friends rather than mere acquaintances. What is most distinctive about these histrionics is the need on their part to placate others, to try to mend schisms that have taken place, and to patch up or smooth over troubling matters. They moderate conflicts by yielding, compromising, and conceding to the wishes of others and are ready to sacrifice themselves for approval and commendation. The configuration of characteristics that typify this appeasing type often encompasses an admixture of histrionic, dependent, and compulsive features.

Alert to every sign of potential indifference, appeasing histrionics quickly anticipate and avoid what may be seen as unfavorable; rather, they appraise matters and then enact what would make them most appealing in the eyes of others. They wish to be faultless pleasers, invariably seen as well-intentioned, not only in a superficial and momentarily obliging way, but through acts of genuine goodwill that others cannot help but appreciate. They are magnificent flatterers, willing to sacrifice any and all signs of integrity to evoke praise and good will.

As youngsters, many of these individuals experienced a never-satisfied mother or father, a person who found nothing about their child that pleased them, nothing that was seen as appealing or attractive or right. Such a parent kept goading the child to *prove* that he or she was virtuous, competent, beautiful, and loving. And such youngsters strove fruitlessly to appease the unappeasable, to placate the unplacable, and now find themselves investing much of their lives searching for ways to elicit admiration and respect, some small measure of praise, which is likely to be faint, if at all forthcoming.

Beneath their surface affability, appeasing histrionics feel, at heart, that they are worthless or problem persons, marked early in life as inferior or troublesome, consigned to a self-image of being profoundly inadequate, unloved, and unlovable. They desperately try to compensate for their deficiencies, invariably look for ways in which they can gain some measure of appreciation. But the unrelenting and acidlike rain of a parent's early depreciation and criticism, the sense of belittlement and dissatisfaction, remains deeply embedded, a feeling of unworthiness that can never be corrected. Admonished repeatedly not to do this or to make sure to do that, the appeasing histrionic's outlook on life reflects an endless search for signs of warm regard and praise. No matter what the appeasing personality tries to do, there is nothing that will or can achieve these goals. Despite the hidden hostility felt toward the unappeasable parent, it is kept at bay, deeply suppressed, while this personality's yearning for favorable signs of affection continues to gnaw painfully within.

The Tempestuous Histrionic

The *tempestuous histrionic's* behavior is typified by a high degree of emotional lability and short periods of impulsive acting out, alternating with depressive complaints, moodiness, and sulking. Notable also are a hypersensitivity to criticism, a low frustration tolerance, immature behaviors, short-sighted hedonism, and a seeking of excitement and stimulation. Emotions surge readily to the surface, untransformed and unmoderated, evident in a distractible, flighty, and erratic style of behavior. Whatever inner feelings—guilt, anger, or desire—may be sensed, they spill quickly to the surface in pure and direct form.

The tempestuous histrionic is frequently out of control, overly reactive to minor provocations, and acts out in a stormy, impassioned, and turbulent manner. When not overly wrought up, they exhibit moody complaints and sulky behaviors, but quickly revert to an angry and inflamed response to minor events. As with other personalities, each subtype of the histrionic exhibits a commingling of the basic personality interpenetrated with features found more typically in other personality styles. In the case of the tempestuous histrionic, we see many features of the negativistic personality and severe forms show characteristics of the borderline, as well.

Moods tend to be brittle and variable among these tempestuous types, with periods of high excitement and affability alternating with a leaden paralysis, fatigue, oversleeping, overeating, and an overuse of alcohol. This personality displays short-lived, dramatic, and superficial affects, reporting a tendency to be easily excited and then quickly bored. Mood levels are highly reactive to external stimulation. Feelings of desperation or euphoria are expressed dramatically and more intensely than justified by the situation. The patient behaves by fits and starts, shifting capriciously down a path that appears to lead nowhere, often precipitating wrangles with others and disappointments for self.

As noted in earlier pages, Klein's (1972) descriptions of the "hysteroid dysphoric" characterize an affectively labile and shallow personality, seductive and sexually provocative, frequently love intoxicated and giddy, inclined to think emotionally and illogically. Their behaviors are precipitous and enacted in an impetuous and excited way, often creating social turbulence and stormy relationships. Despite their desire to be liked, these personalities generate chronic and repeated conflicts with others. They often behave like children—demanding, self-centered, and uncontrolled. They seem unable to put effective limits on their emotionally impulsive and irritable behaviors, often flying off the handle and succumbing to temper tantrums.

Cut off from needed external attentions, tempestuous histrionics may engage either in a frantic search for approval, become easily nettled and contentious, or become dejected and forlorn. There may be extreme cyclical swings, alternating periods of simulated euphoria and illusory excitements, intermingled with moments of hopelessness and self-condemnation. Also frequent are angry and depressive complaints, usually to the effect that others misunderstand them and that life has been full of disappointments. Over time, these personalities may become less and less histrionic in their behaviors and more and more disgruntled, critical, and envious of others, grudging their good fortunes with a jealous, quarrelsome, and irritable reaction to minor slights. They may come to be preoccupied with bodily functions and health, overreact to illness, and voice unreasonable complaints about minor ailments. These symptoms may be displayed exhibitionistically to regain lost attention and support.

The Disingenuous Histrionic

The *disingenuous histrionic's* behavior is typified by a veneer of friendliness and sociability. Although making a superficially good impression on acquaintances, a more characteristic unreliability, impulsive tendencies, and deep resentments and moodiness are seen frequently among family members and other close associates. A socially facile lifestyle may be noted by a persistent seeking of attention and excitement, often expressed in seductive behaviors. Relationships are shallow and fleeting, frequently disrupted by caustic comments and impulses that are acted on with insufficient deliberation.

This personality is frequently seen as irresponsible and undependable, exhibiting short-lived enthusiasms and immature stimulus-seeking behaviors. Notable also among these disingenuous histrionics is a tendency to be contriving and plotting, to exhibit a crafty and scheming approach to life, a tendency to be insincere, calculating, and occasionally deceitful. Not likely to admit responsibility for personal or family difficulties, this histrionic manifests a cleverly defensive denial of psychological tensions or conflicts. Interpersonal difficulties are rationalized and blame is projected on others. Although egocentrically self-indulgent and insistent on attention, the disingenuous type provides others with minimal loyalty and reciprocal affection. From the foregoing picture, it should be evident that this histrionic subtype shares many of the characteristics typically seen among antisocial personalities.

This variant of the histrionic is more egocentric and deceitful than most histrionics. They are more willful and insincere in their relationships, doing everything necessary to obtain what they need and want from others. Also in contrast to other histrionics, they seem to enjoy confrontations, gaining a degree of gratification in the excitement and tension that conflicts engender. They can be quite calculating and guileful if someone has what they want, be it the attentions of a person or something tangible and material. What has happened is that their need for the approval of others gradually erodes over time and is replaced by the means they employ to achieve approval. In effect, what is now most prominent is the style of being manipulative and cunning, that is, controlling others fully.

Disingenuous histrionics recognize that gaining the attention and praise of others did not come without a price. Moreover, they know that the attention and commendation of others did not come willingly, but was evoked as a consequence of their own plotting and scheming behaviors. Beneath the surface, their greatest fear is that no one would care or love them, unless they made them do so. Despite this recognition, these histrionics attempt to persuade themselves that they are basically well intentioned, that their insincerely motivated scheming is appreciated for its intrinsic worth. Throughout these mixed internal messages, nevertheless, disingenuous histrionics persist in seeking what is most important to themselves, always angling and maneuvering to acquire it. These histrionics are no less self-deceptive regarding their motives than are those whom they deceive.

Disingenuous persons are often fearful that others may see them as indecisive or softhearted. When mildly crossed, subject to minor pressures, or faced with potential embarrassment, these histrionics may be quickly provoked to anger, often expressed in a revengeful or vindictive way. The air of superficial affability is extremely precarious and they are ready to depreciate anyone whose attitudes touch a sensitive theme. Although infrequent, when the thin veneer of sociability is eroded there may be momentary upsurges of abuse and rage.

COMORBID DISORDERS AND SYNDROMES

The following brief discussion concerns the major varieties of both Axis I syndromes and Axis II disorders that frequently coexist with the personality type under review. Equally important, in the authors' judgment, is the opportunity these parallel presentations in Chapters 6 through 19 provide for elaborating the distinctive manner and form in which each personality pattern expresses the clinical syndromes they have in common. For example, experienced clinicians know, and Chodoff and Lyons (1958) have shown, that "hysterical conversion" symptoms are found as frequently among nonhistrionic as among histrionic personalities. Clinical syndromes signify different vulnerabilities and coping responses in different personality styles; there is value, therefore, in elaborating their interface.

Axis II Comorbidities

Figure 10.4 portrays the pattern of relationships between the histrionic (HIS) personality prototype and a number of other Axis II disorders (as well as Axis I syndromes). The previous section on Adult Subtypes also provides useful insights into the clinical features of other personality disorders that often fuse with the basic histrionic prototype; these should be referred to as a guide to additional variations of the histrionic style. As can be noted in Figure 10.4, the greatest level of comorbidity is found with the narcissistic (NAR) personality pattern. Other strong associations are with the dependent (DPD), borderline (BDL), and antisocial (ATS) personality patterns. Similarly, modest overlaps or combinations with the negativistic (NEG) and compulsive (OBC) patterns should be noted.

Axis I Comorbidties

This section turns to those Axis I disorders to which the histrionic personality is most susceptible, identifying not only the manner in which the various symptoms are manifested but also the probable dynamics and secondary gains with which they are typically associated.

Anxiety Syndromes (ANX). Histrionics are vulnerable to *separation anxieties* to only a slightly lesser extent than are dependent personalities. The conditions that give rise to these feelings, however, are quite different. Histrionics promote their own anxieties by their tendency to seek diverse sources of support and stimulation. Moreover, they quickly get bored with old attachments and excitements. As a consequence, they frequently set themselves up to be isolated and alone, stranded for extended periods with no one to lean on and nothing to be occupied with. During these empty times, they feel at

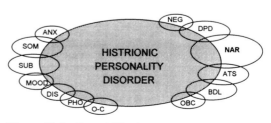

Figure 10.4   Comorbidity between histrionic personality disorder and other DSM Axis I and Axis II disorders.

loose ends and experience a marked restlessness and generalized anxiety until some new romance or excitement attracts their interest. Histrionic patients experience genuine discomforts during these vacant periods, but they tend to overdramatize their distress as a means of soliciting attention and support. The use of exhibitionistic displays of anxiety as an attention-getting tool is notable.

Phobic Syndromes (PHO). Histrionics exhibit phobic symptoms somewhat less frequently than dependent personalities. Feelings of emptiness and aloneness may be symbolized and transformed into brief *agoraphobias.* Similarly, an upsurge of socially unacceptable aggressive impulses may serve to prompt the formation of a protective or neutralizing phobic symptom. Symptoms such as these are also displayed exhibitionistically, that is, utilized as dramatic vehicles to gain attention and support from others. Histrionics are likely to be quite open about their symptom, in contrast to most other personalities with phobic problems. In essence, they will often try to get as much attention gaining mileage out of their discomforts as they can.

Obsessive-Compulsive Syndromes (O-C). Obsessional symptoms occur infrequently among histrionics. However, as a consequence of their lack of a cohesive personality organization, their thoughts and emotions may become scattered and disconnected. These unconnected or free-floating obsessional thoughts illustrate a variant of the dissociative thesis first posited by Janet (1901). Contributing further to these symptoms is the tendency of these patients to exhibit dramatic emotion in response to matters of minimal significance; similarly, but conversely, they are inclined to discuss serious problems with an air of cool detachment. The ease with which intense affects and ideas can be isolated from one another contributes to the emergence of seemingly unconnected and unanchored obsessive symptoms. The poor psychic integration of histrionics means that with little strain or tension they can disconnect an emotion from its associated content. Not infrequently, histrionics report experiencing a "free-floating" erotic emotion or sexual impulse, without an external precipitant or focus. In parallel fashion, they often speak of hostile thoughts that obsessively preoccupy them but lack normally associated feelings of anger. Which behavior or emotion will be expressed and which will be repressed is usually determined by their goal of seeking social approval and minimizing social rebuke; for

example, histrionics rarely vent hostility but often manifest unfeeling seductive behaviors.

Somatoform Syndromes (SOM). Histrionic personalities openly and dramatically exhibit *conversion symptoms.* This is consistent with their desire to attract attention to themselves. Among the more common conversions in this personality are mutism and persistent laryngitis, which usually serve to protect against an unconscious impulse to verbalize hostile thoughts that may provoke social reproval. Moreover, these symptoms are quite eye-catching and enable the patients both to dramatize their plight and to draw the total attention of others to their only means of communication, gesticulation and pantomime.

Histrionics also utilize *hypochondriacal* and *somatization* symptoms as instruments for attracting attention and nurture. To be fussed over with care and concern is rewarding for most individuals. In histrionics, it is like a drug that is needed to sustain them. When histrionics feel a sense of emptiness and isolation, they desperately seek a diet of constant concern and approval. To be ill is a simple solution because it requires little effort yet produces guaranteed attention. Thus, if nothing else "works," *factitiously* created symptoms may be depended on as a means of achieving these ends. Moreover, if life becomes humdrum and boring, physical ailments not only evoke attention from others but provide a new preoccupation and source of stimulation. *Psychogenic pains* and aches are another form of preoccupation and stimulation to fill the empty moments. Only rarely, however, do histrionics display somatic fatigue—this symptom runs counter to their active stimulus-seeking style. They prefer to use obvious and dramatic complaints to draw attention to themselves for these behaviors enable them to continue to participate actively in social affairs.

Dissociative Syndromes (DIS). The lack of an integrated personality organization among histrionics makes it difficult for them, even in normal times, to unify the disparate elements of their lives. During periods of strain and discord, this integrative deficiency may result in the development of a dissociative disorder. *Psychogenic fugue* states may not be uncommon; they usually take form in a search for attention and stimulation when the person feels unwanted or otherwise deprived. Daytime *depersonalization* episodes are unusual, however, because histrionic patients seek to be alert to their environment. Also rare

are *psychogenic amnesia* and *multiple personality states.* When they do occur, these symptoms usually signify the histrionic's attempt to break away from a confining and stultifying environment. Faced with internal psychic poverty and external boredom or constraint, histrionics may seek the gains of a more exciting and dramatic life in which they can achieve the attention and approval they crave.

Substance Use Syndromes (SUB). In a logic that is not dissimilar to that which activates their tendency to drift off into fugue states, histrionics may become involved in the excessive use of drugs or alcohol, substances that free them up from the constraints they may feel, or enable them to act out in ways that are congenial to their stimulus-seeking tendencies. Through these vehicles of self-transformation, they are not only able to regain a feeling of well-being, but also to bolster a flagging sense of self-worth, even omnipotence. Moreover, should they be placed in settings in which they are restrained, they are able through substance use to disinhibit otherwise controlled impulses, without assuming personal responsibility or guilt.

Mood Syndromes (MOOD). Histrionic personalities characteristically overplay their feelings of *dysthymic* disorder, expressing them through dramatic and eye-catching gestures. This is in contrast to the flat and somber picture typically seen in the dependent, and to the tense and guilt-ridden quality seen, for example, among compulsive and passive-aggressive personalities. The exhibitionistic display of mood is a natural outgrowth of their basic style of actively soliciting attention and approval. Episodes of milder depression in histrionics are usually prompted less by a fear of abandonment than by a sense of emptiness and inactivity. It arises most often when they feel stranded between one fleeting attachment and another or between one transitory excitement and the next. At these times of noninvolvement, histrionics sense a lack of direction and begin to experience a fearful void and aloneness. Depressive complaints tend to be expressed in popular jargon.

Histrionics are likely to evidence agitated rather than retarded *major depressions.* The primary precipitant tends to be anticipated losses in dependency security. Histrionics may wail aloud and make well known their feelings of helplessness and abandonment, all in the hope of soliciting support and nurture. Their agitation does not reflect an internal struggle, as in more ambivalent personality types, but is a direct and simple expression of the worrisome apprehension they seek to resolve.

Among other Axis I symptoms to which histrionics are particularly susceptible are *bipolar disorders* and *cyclothymic disorders;* these syndromes are consistent with their characteristic socially histrionic and exuberant style. Confronted with severe separation anxieties or anticipating a loss of social approval, histrionic personalities may intensify their habitual behavior pattern until it reaches the forced and frantic congeniality we term *manic* or *hypomanic.* Here we may observe a frenetic search for attention, a release of tension through hyperactivity, and an effort to stave off the growing feeling of depressive hopelessness.

DIFFERENTIAL DIAGNOSTIC SIGNS

In earlier chapters several reasons were presented for a decreased concern over matters of differential diagnosis. Essentially, the multiaxial format of DSM-IV encourages the recording of overlapping diagnoses within each axis and, more importantly, it *requires* the listing of impairments from both Axis I and Axis II. Multiple diagnoses notwithstanding, there are areas in which diagnostic confusions can occur because the issue is *not* overlap but a matter of distinguishing among fundamentally different processes that appear similar on the surface. Several such disorders and syndromes will be discussed in this section.

Among the Axis I clinical syndromes, overlap with the *cyclothymic disorder* may become a problem under certain circumstances. Hypomanic periods, as observed in these disorders, are found among numerous personality types other than the histrionic and for this reason distinctions may be needed. The symptoms of elevated, expansive, and irritable mood are notable in both syndromes, but there is an urgency, restlessness, and intensity about the hypomanic phase of cyclothymia that does not typify the everyday behaviors of the histrionic. Similarly, as a personality pattern, the histrionic has learned to behave in a reasonably skillful social manner, histrionicly maneuvering and manipulating others in a way that is usually seen as attractive rather than infantile and desperate. Although occasionally inappropriate, the usual pattern of the histrionic's lifestyle is adaptive in that it does not interfere with routine social and occupational functioning, as does the behavior and mood of the cyclothymic disorder.

Turning to Axis II discriminations, superficial similarities between histrionics and *narcissists* in their desire to be the center of attention, in behaving exhibitionistically, and in their characteristic buoyant (if fickle) moods lead frequently to initial differential diagnostic difficulties. Of course, these two personality patterns may, and frequently do, coexist. A clear distinction, rather than a multiple diagnosis, should be made when warranted, however. The essential difference is found in the relative dominance or centrality of seeking dependence on others versus independence from others. Histrionics seek close, if not necessarily enduring, relationships and are willing to subscribe to popular fads and conventions, as well as act fragile and needy if these behaviors give promise of attention and favor. Narcissists disdain acts of dependency, seek recognition for their superiority, are lacking in social empathy, turn away from group fashions and regulations, acting as if they were above the responsibilities of shared social life. Rather than being on the "in" or seeking to "outdo" others in identifying with social styles, as do histrionics, narcissists avoid and depreciate such "demeaning" behaviors. Their style interpersonally is exploitive rather than seductive, as in the histrionic. Furthermore, narcissists struggle to convey a consistently cool and nonchalant air rather than displaying the histrionic's short-lived and dramatic moods.

Commonalties also exist with several variants of the *antisocial* personality disorder. There is a tendency on both parts to be impulsive, seductive, and manipulative. The histrionic, however, is manipulative as a means of gaining attention and nurturance, whereas antisocials manipulate others to gain profit and power. Histrionics are excessively dramatic in their behaviors and emotions and, in contrast to antisocials, do not engage in socially repugnant and illegal behaviors.

Similarities with the *borderline* personality may prove problematic as well, although many borderlines evidence a more severe form of histrionicism reflecting a structurally defective pattern of dysfunctions. Whereas both borderlines and histrionics exhibit rapidly shifting or labile emotions, it is only the borderline where we see angry disruptions, self-destructive behaviors, identity disturbances, and periodic feelings of emptiness and aloneness.

The overlap between histrionic personalities and *dependents* is also notable in that both look excessively to others to provide them with guidance and praise. Dependents, however, are passive, cling to others, and await their advice and support.

By contrast, histrionics are active in soliciting the approval they seek, seducing others with exaggerated emotions and dramatic behaviors to effect the consequences they seek.

ASSESSING THE HISTRIONIC: A CASE STUDY

As in previous chapters, a brief note will be made of the histrionic's performance on the major assessment tools employed by clinicians today. Owing to their denial tendencies and their high need for being viewed as desirable, their Rorschach protocols produce a rather modest number of responses, a surprising finding among these otherwise active and highly expressive personalities. Despite their efforts to constrain exposing themselves in this ambiguous task, histrionics invest considerable emotionality in describing the ink blots. Thus, there is a dramatic character to what they do portray, and side comments are voiced regarding their reactions to the task at hand. Animal content and sexual responses are not uncommon. In general, both W and dd responses are infrequent. Responses to both shading and color are highly variable in these patients, some giving many such responses, and others very few.

The TAT provides considerable information, unless the histrionic is self-protective and defensive against exposing less-than-attractive traits to the observing clinician. When histrionics are not inclined to deny or protect themselves, their story themes tend to be dramatic, although they are not likely to be inventive and original; for example, story lines may be borrowed from current TV shows or popular movies. Story characters will likely be portrayed with superficial emotions, and themes that relate to the histrionic's current psychological difficulties may be avoided.

The MMPI provides several leads suggestive of the histrionic personality pattern. Because histrionics are not likely to enter treatment unless they are experiencing significant distress in their current life situation, they frequently score high on Scale 2 and Scale 3: when their current difficulties are prominent, Scale 3 is likely to be the higher. Also common are 3-9/9-3 profiles, which appear to reflect the intensely active and emotional qualities of this personality. Scale 4 often combines with the preceding 3-9 configuration, further signifying the egocentric irresponsibility that typifies some histrionic subtypes. Among histrionics who are experiencing considerable anxiety in their current life situation, high scores on Scale 7 may be expected. In general, Scales L, F, and K tend to be within the normal range, whereas Scale 5 may be elevated in men and Scale 0 will be notably low.

The following case illustrates a number of the major features of histrionics, following which will be a presentation of an MCMI-III profile and its associated interpretive meaning (Figure 10.5).

Case 10.1

Mary Lou, Age 37, Divorced, Remarried, One Child

Mary Lou, an attractive and vivacious woman, sought therapy in the hope that she might prevent the disintegration of her third marriage. The problem she faced was a recurrent one, her tendency to become "bored" with her husband and increasingly interested in going out with other men and reverting to an earlier period of serious alcoholism. She was on the brink of "another affair" and decided that before "giving way to her impulses again" she had "better stop and take a good look" at herself. The following history unfolded over a series of therapeutic interviews.

Mary Lou was four years older than her sister, her only sibling. Her father was a successful and wealthy business executive for whom children were "display pieces," nice chattels to show off to his friends and to round out his "family life," but "not to be troubled with." Her mother was an emotional but charming woman who took great pains to make her children "beautiful and talented." The girls vied for their parents' approval. Although Mary Lou was the more successful, she constantly had to "live up" to her parents' expectations in order to secure their commendation and esteem.

Mary Lou was quite popular during her adolescent years, had lots of dates and boyfriends, and was never short of attention and affection from the opposite sex. She sang with the high school band and was a cheerleader, an artist on the school newspaper, and so on. Rather than going to college, Mary Lou attended art school where she met and married a fellow student—a "handsome, wealthy ne'er-do-well." Both she and her husband began "sleeping around" by the end of the first year, and she "wasn't certain" that her husband was the father of her daughter. A divorce took place several months after the birth of this child. Soon thereafter she met and married a man in his 40s who

gave both Mary Lou and her daughter a "a comfortable home, and scads of attention and love." It was a "good life" for the four years that the marriage lasted.

Mary Lou "knocked about" on her own for the next two years, partying and drinking heavily, as well as being occupied for a short period as a call girl. This came to a sharp halt when she met her present husband, a talented writer who "knew the scoop" about her past. Mary Lou felt that she had attained what she wanted in life and did not want to spoil it owing to her continuing indulgence in alcohol. Her husband was a strong, mature man who "knew how to keep her in check." She herself had an interesting position as an art director in an advertising agency, and her daughter seemed finally to have "settled down" after a difficult early period. Mary Lou feared that she would not be able to control her tendency to "get involved," with either men or alcohol, and turned to therapy for assistance.

Interpretive Summary

The MCMI-III profile of this woman suggests a veneer of friendliness and sociability, yet shows contempt for conventional morals. Although she is able to make a good impression on casual acquaintances, she displays a characteristic impulsiveness, restlessness, and moodiness, especially to family members and close associates. Likely to be untrustworthy and unreliable, she may persistently seek excitement and engage in self-dramatizing behavior. Her relationships tend to be shallow and fleeting, and she may fail to meet her responsibilities. Her communications may be characterized at times by caustic comments and callous outbursts, and she may act rashly, using insufficient deliberation and poor judgment. Seen by some as irresponsible and undependable, she may exhibit short-lived enthusiasm followed by disillusionment and resentment.

This woman is unlikely to admit responsibility for personal or family difficulties. She may have an easily circumvented conscience and may be quite facile in denying the presence of psychological tension or conflict. Interpersonal problems are frequently rationalized, especially those that she engenders, and blame may readily be projected onto others. Self-indulgent and insistent on getting her way, she may reciprocate the efforts of others with only minimal loyalty and consideration. The

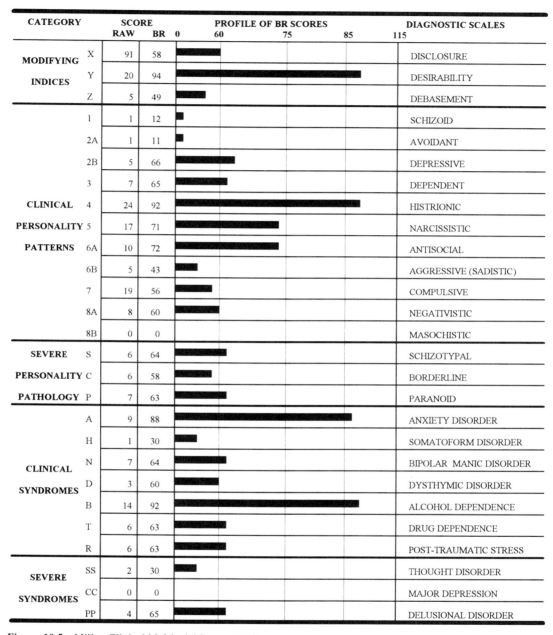

CATEGORY		SCORE RAW	BR	PROFILE OF BR SCORES 0 60 75 85 115	DIAGNOSTIC SCALES
MODIFYING INDICES	X	91	58		DISCLOSURE
	Y	20	94		DESIRABILITY
	Z	5	49		DEBASEMENT
CLINICAL PERSONALITY PATTERNS	1	1	12		SCHIZOID
	2A	1	11		AVOIDANT
	2B	5	66		DEPRESSIVE
	3	7	65		DEPENDENT
	4	24	92		HISTRIONIC
	5	17	71		NARCISSISTIC
	6A	10	72		ANTISOCIAL
	6B	5	43		AGGRESSIVE (SADISTIC)
	7	19	56		COMPULSIVE
	8A	8	60		NEGATIVISTIC
	8B	0	0		MASOCHISTIC
SEVERE PERSONALITY PATHOLOGY	S	6	64		SCHIZOTYPAL
	C	6	58		BORDERLINE
	P	7	63		PARANOID
CLINICAL SYNDROMES	A	9	88		ANXIETY DISORDER
	H	1	30		SOMATOFORM DISORDER
	N	7	64		BIPOLAR MANIC DISORDER
	D	3	60		DYSTHYMIC DISORDER
	B	14	92		ALCOHOL DEPENDENCE
	T	6	63		DRUG DEPENDENCE
	R	6	63		POST-TRAUMATIC STRESS
SEVERE SYNDROMES	SS	2	30		THOUGHT DISORDER
	CC	0	0		MAJOR DEPRESSION
	PP	4	65		DELUSIONAL DISORDER

Figure 10.5   Millon Clinical Multiaxial Inventory-III.

clinician may wish to corroborate these hypotheses as well as those that follow.

When this woman's wishes are not fulfilled, when she is subjected to minor pressures, or when she is faced with potential embarrassment, she may be inclined to abandon her responsibilities, possibly with minimal guilt or remorse. Unfettered by the restrictions of social conventions or the restraints of personal loyalties, she may be quick to free herself from encumbrances and obligations. Superficial affabilities may collapse easily, and she is likely to jettison those who challenge her autonomy or beliefs. Although infrequent, her temper outbursts may turn into uncontrollable rage. More typically, she may simply be impetuous and imprudent, throwing caution to the wind, driven by a need for excitement and an inability to delay gratification, with minimal regard to consequences. Adventure-seeking, she may restlessly chase one capricious whim after another and is likely to travel an erratic course of irresponsibility, delighting in defying and challenging social conventions. There is reason to think that she may have a poor prognosis for staying out of trouble.

Strong indications exist that this woman has an alcoholic disorder, quite likely as one facet of a more pervasive substance-abuse syndrome. Drinking is an extension of her general self-centered and stimulus-seeking lifestyle. Though exploitive and hedonistic, she may enjoy the superficial and somewhat adolescent camaraderie of drinking buddies. In addition to its consonance with her overall self-indulgent, somewhat immature, and pleasure-seeking style, drinking provides an outlet for a variety of oppositional attitudes and resentments, such as antiauthority feelings, resistance to adhering to establishment-oriented social ideals, and rejection of family constraints and expectations.

PATHOGENIC DEVELOPMENTAL BACKGROUND

As noted in the introduction to a parallel section in Chapter 6, the influences posited here as significant in forming the histrionic personality must be understood to be conjectural. Further, the distinction made in grouping these influences into biogenic and experiential sections is merely pedagogical; the pattern of determinants is not only interactive but is reciprocal and sequentially interconnected. With these caveats, discussion of the topic proceeds.

HYPOTHESIZED BIOGENIC FACTORS

The role of constitutional dispositions in this, as in most other patterns, is highly speculative. The following hypotheses have the merit of plausibility.

Heredity

The role of heredity cannot be overlooked in searching for the biological origins of the histrionic pattern. The neural and chemical substrate for tendencies such as sensory alertness and autonomic or emotional reactivity may logically be traced to genetic influences. Evidence demonstrating a high degree of family correspondence in these traits is suggestive of physiological commonalities but can be explained also as a function of experience and learning. The need for research is obvious, not only in establishing factually the presence of family correspondence but in tracing the manner in which such alleged genetic factors unfold and take shape as psychological traits.

Hyperresponsive Infantile Reaction Patterns

As noted earlier in the chapter dealing with the mood/temperament domain, histrionics are likely to have displayed a high degree of alertness and emotional responsiveness in infancy and early childhood. Not only are constitutional traits essentially stable throughout life, but active and responsive children will tend to foster and intensify their initial responsiveness by evoking varied and stimulating reactions from others.

Neurological Characteristics

Among the possible sites that may be posited for the high emotional responsivity of the histrionic are the limbic and reticular systems. A neurally dense or abundantly branched limbic region may account for the intensity and ease with which emotions are expressed. A low threshold for reticular activation, stemming from any number of idiosyncratic features of that region, may underlie part of the excitability and diffusive reactivity typical of the histrionic personality.

Physiochemical Characteristics

Ease of sympathetic arousal and adrenal reactivity may be rooted in the individual's constitutional makeup; this can result in the heightened and labile ems emotions seen among histrionics. Similarly, neurochemical imbalances may facilitate a rapid transmission of impulses across synaptic junctions, resulting in the tendency of these patients to be distractible and excitable.

The preceding biogenic hypotheses must be viewed as highly conjectural. Even if evidence can be adduced in support of these notions, the question will remain as to why some persons who possess these constitutional characteristics become histrionics whereas others develop different pathological patterns, and most remain essentially normal.

CHARACTERISTIC EXPERIENTIAL HISTORY

Biogenic influences appear less relevant in the development of the histrionic pattern than in some of the personality types previously described. It is logical, then, to focus our attention on psychological experience and learning as the primary etiologic variables.

Stimulus Enrichment and Diversity in the Sensory-Attachment Stage

Constitutionally alert and responsive infants will experience greater and more diverse stimulation in the first months of life than dull and phlegmatic infants. As a consequence of these early stimulus gratifications, their tendency is reinforced to look outward to the external world for rewards rather than inward into themselves. In a similar manner, normally alert infants may develop this exteroceptive attitude if their caretakers, by virtue of sensory indulgence and playfulness, expose them to excessive stimulation during the sensory-attachment stage.

Both dependents and histrionics exhibit a focus on external rather than internal sources of reinforcement. But there is a basic difference between them that may be traced in part to differences in the diversity, intensity, and consistency in early sensory-attachment learning.

Dependents appear to have received their enriched stimulation from a single, perhaps exclusive, source that provided a consistent level of gratification. In contrast, histrionics appear to have been exposed to a number of different sources that provided brief, highly charged, and irregular stimulus reinforcements. For example, the histrionic may have had many different caretakers in infancy (parents, siblings, grandparents, foster parents) who supplied the child with intense, short-lived stimulus gratifications that came at irregular or haphazard intervals. Such experiences may not only have built a high level of sensory capacity, which requires constant "feeding" to be sustained, but may also have conditioned the infant to expect stimulus reinforcements in short concentrated spurts from a melange of different sources. (We may note parenthetically that irregular schedules of reinforcement establish deeply ingrained habits that are highly resistant to extinction.) Thus, the persistent yet erratic dependency behaviors of the histrionic personality may reflect a pathological form of intense stimulus seeking that can be traced to highly charged, varied, and irregular stimulus reinforcements associated with early attachment learning.

The shifting from one source of gratification to another so characteristic of histrionics, their search for new stimulus adventures, their penchant for creating excitement and their inability to tolerate boredom and routine, all may represent the consequences of these unusual early experiences.

Parental Control by Contingent and Irregular Reward

In addition to differences in the variety, regularity, and intensity of stimulus enrichments in the sensory-attachment stage, the experiences of the histrionic child may be distinguished from those of the dependent both during and after the sensorimotor-autonomy stage.

Dependent children continue to receive attention and affection from their caretakers *regardless of* their behavior; it is *not* necessary for them "to perform" in order to elicit parental nurturance and protection. As a consequence of sitting idly by and passively waiting for their parents to tend to their needs, they fail to develop adequate competencies and autonomy.

Histrionic children, in contrast, appear to learn that they must engage in certain sanctioned behaviors, and must satisfy certain parental desires and expectations in order to receive attention and affection.

What are the conditions of learning that shape these strategies into the histrionic form? They seem to be characterized by the following three features: minimal negative reinforcement (e.g., parents rarely criticize or punish); positive reinforcement contingent on performance of parentally approved behaviors (e.g., favorable comments are conveyed only if the youngster "was pretty" or "performed"); and irregularity in positive reinforcement (e.g., parents often fail to take cognizance of "productions" even when attempts are made to attract their attention). Stated in conventional language, the parents of the future histrionic rarely punish their children and distribute rewards only for what they approve and admire, but often fail to bestow these rewards even when the child behaves acceptably.

This pattern of experiences has three personality consequences: strategies designed to evoke rewards, a feeling of competence and acceptance *only* when others acknowledge one's performances, and a habit of seeking approval for its own sake. All

three of these traits are characteristic of the histrionic personality. Let us detail their development:

1. Children who receive few punishments and
many rewards will develop a strong and innambiva-
lent inclination to relate to others. If they learn that
the achievement of rewards is dependent on fulfilling the expectations and desires of others, they will
develop a set of instrumental behaviors designed to
please others and thereby elicit these rewards.
However, if these strategies succeed sometimes but
not always (i.e., are irregularly reinforced), children will persist in using them, or variations of
them, well beyond all reason, until they do succeed,
which eventually they will. In other words, these
instrumental behaviors will not easily be extinguished, even if they fail much of the time.

2. As a consequence of this pattern of experiences, the child will become actively rather than
passively oriented toward others and will learn to
look to others rather than to self for rewards. The
pleasing behavior is only a preliminary, and *not* a
sufficient condition for achieving reinforcements;
the same behavior on their part will elicit a reward
one time but fail, another. Although the child acts
at all times to please and perform for others, it is
always *they* who determine whether and when to
give a reward. The child awaits their judgment as to
whether behavioral efforts will bring recognition
and approval; as a consequence, it is they who define the adequacy of the behavior—competence is
judged by the reaction of others, not by the child's
own efforts or behaviors.

3. Because favorable recognition of competence
occurs only irregularly, that is, not every time the
child performs "proper" acts, he or she is never
sure of adequacy and, therefore, continues to look
to others, even after repeated failures to evoke a favorable response. Because of the irregularity of reinforcement, then, the search takes on a "life of its
own"; the habit of soliciting signs of approval becomes so firmly established that it eventually is
pursued for its own sake.

Histrionic Parental Models

Two features of family life often contribute to the
development of the histrionic pattern—histrionic
parental models, and sibling rivalry. Let us look
into the first attribute.

There is little question that children learn,
quite unconsciously, to mimic what they are exposed to. The prevailing attitudes and feelings,
and the incidental daily behaviors displayed by

family members serve as models that growing
children imitate and take as their own long before
they are able to recognize what they are doing or
why. This process of vicarious learning is made
especially easy if parental behaviors and feelings
are unusually pronounced or dramatic. Under
these circumstances, when parents call attention
to themselves and create emotional reactions in
their child, the child cannot help but learn clearly
how people behave and feel. Thus, many female
histrionics report that they are "just like mother,"
emotionally labile women "bored to tears with
the routines of home life," flirtatious with men,
and clever and facile in their dealings with people. The presence of a histrionic parent who exhibits feelings and attitudes rather dramatically,
provides a sharply defined model for vicarious
and imitative learning.

Sibling Rivalry

Children who struggled long and hard to capture
the attention and affection of their parents under
conditions of sibling rivalry often continue to utilize the devices that led to their periodic successes
long after the rivalry ceased in reality. Not only
are these behaviors reactivated when they seek attention in the future, but they often misperceive
innocuous situations (perceptive distortion) and
recreate competitive situations (repetition compulsion) in such ways as to bring forth the strategies they learned in the past. If the child learned to
employ cuteness, attractiveness, and seduction as
a strategy to secure parental attention, these interpersonal behaviors may persist, and take the form
of a lifelong histrionic pattern.

Ease of Interpersonal Attraction

Esthetically appealing girls and likable or athletic
boys need expend little effort to draw attention
and approval to themselves. Their mere "being" is
sufficient to attract others.

Rewarding as these experiences may be in
building up a high sense of self-esteem, they have
their negative consequences. These persons become excessively dependent on others because
they are accustomed to approval and have learned
to expect attention at all times. They experience
considerable discomfort, then, when attention fails
to materialize. In order to assure the continuation
of these rewards, and thereby avoid discomfort,
they learn to "play up" their attractiveness. For example, the formerly pretty young girl, in order to

elicit the attention and approval that came so readily in youth, goes to great pains as she matures to remain a pretty woman. Similarly, the formerly successful young athlete struggles to keep his muscular and trim figure as he progresses into middle life. Both of these attractive individuals may have failed to acquire more substantial talents in their youth because they needed none to elicit social rewards. What we observe in their later life, then, is a childish exhibitionism and an adolescent, flirtatious and seductive style of relating, both of which characterize the histrionic personality.

Shifting Standards and Values

People can be the masters of their fate only if they possess a personal identity, a sense of self-competence and self-sufficiency based on a framework of internal standards and values. They cannot initiate actions independently of others, nor navigate their own course unless they have a coherent set of goals and aspirations to guide them through changing tides and the buffeting of distracting events.

What happens if a person knows few fixed points of reference, has been exposed to shifting standards and has no stable anchor or reliable rudder by which to orient him- or herself?

In our massively complex and ever-changing society, more youngsters than ever before grow up devoid of a set of firm and stable standards by which they can guide their lives. Not only are there more things to master and more variety and change to contend with, but children today are provided with less direction than they were years ago.

Of course, not every child raised in our society is plagued with such ambiguity. Most are imbued with unalterable beliefs, rules of conduct, and sanctioned goals. Although the straight and narrow path rarely is adhered to anymore, most parents do establish clear boundaries and standards to assure against major digressions.

But there are many parents who fail to provide their children with a consistent or stabilizing set of values. Some fail because they are intellectually committed to a laissez-faire policy; others are confused and vacillating themselves; a third group is so preoccupied with their own lives that they have little time or inclination to guide their child's development. Whatever the reason, some children are left to fend for themselves, to discover their own direction in the complex and changing world that surrounds them. These children find no clarity or consistency elsewhere. They are exposed to one set of values here and another, entirely contradictory,

set there; what seems right one day, doesn't the next. In short, they find no firm footing anywhere.

Such children learn that the best course of action is to size up each situation as they face it, and guide themselves in accord with the particular demands of that situation, and no other. Rather than acquire a set of uniform and rigid standards, they must acquire flexibility, an adaptiveness to changing circumstances. To be committed for long or to believe in anything wholeheartedly, is foolish—events change and one must be ready to adjust to them.

Such youngsters never establish a firm image of their personal identity, an internal and stable set of beliefs to which they are committed as their own. Personal identity is diffuse; life progresses, not with an internal gyroscope but with a radar system oriented and sensitive to the changing values and expectations of others. Unsure of their beliefs, or even who they are, these children must be hyperalert and hyperadaptive to their environment. They shift aimlessly from one brief and fleeting course of action to another and seem dilettante, restless, and capricious, all of which are traits that characterize the histrionic pattern.

SELF-PERPETUATION PROCESSES

We all engage in automatic and persistent behaviors that are "senseless" if viewed in terms of their objective utility. The difference between the persistent behaviors we consider normal and those that are pathological is that "normal" senseless and repetitive acts do not create problems or intensify existent ones. Pathological behaviors, no matter what their immediate utility, ultimately foster new difficulties and perpetuate old ones. This section considers aspects of histrionic behaviors that foster these consequences. Each of the three characteristics of the histrionic pattern discussed in this section tends to set up vicious circles that promote new problems.

External Preoccupations

This chapter has already recorded the observations that histrionics orient their attention to the external world and that their perceptions and cognitions tend to be fleeting, impressionistic, and undeveloped. This preoccupation with incidental and passing details prevents experiences from being digested and embedded within the individual's inner world. In effect, histrionics show little integration and few well-examined reflective processes that intervene between perception and action; behaviors are emitted before they have been connected and organized by the operation of memory and thought. The disadvantages of this hyperalertness to external stimuli may outweigh its advantages. Unless life events are digested and integrated, the individual gains little from them. Interpersonal transactions and learnings pass through the person as if he or she were a sieve. There is little opportunity to develop inner skills and few memory traces against which future experience can be evaluated. Indiscriminate and scattered responsiveness leaves the person devoid of an inner reservoir of articulated memories and a storehouse of examined ideas and thoughts. In short, an excessive preoccupation with external events perpetuates the histrionic's "empty shell" and further fosters dependence on others as the only source of guidance.

Massive Repression

The tendency of histrionics to seal off, repress, and make inaccessible substantial portions of their meager inner life further aggravates their dependence on others. By insulating their emotions and cognitions from the stream of everyday life, histrionics deny themselves opportunities to learn new alternatives for their behavior, to modify their self-image, or to become more genuinely skillful and knowledgeable persons. As long as they block the merger that should occur between new and old experiences, they are likely to remain stagnant, unaltered, and impoverished. Deprived of opportunities to learn and grow, they will further perpetuate the vicious circle of dependency on others. As a consequence, the histrionic progresses little beyond childhood and retains the values and modes of behavior of an adolescent.

Superficial Social Relationships

The histrionic personality requires a retinue of changing events and people to replenish the need for stimulation and approval. Thus, as life progresses, histrionics move capriciously from one source to another. One consequence of these fleeting and erratic relationships is that histrionics can never be sure of securing the affection and support they crave. By moving constantly and by devouring the affections of one person and then another, they place themselves in jeopardy of having nothing to tide them over the times between. They may be left high and dry, alone and abandoned with nothing to

do and no excitement with which to be preoccupied. Cut off from external supplies, histrionics are likely either to engage in a frantic search for stimulation and approval or to become dejected and forlorn. They may proceed through cyclical swings, alternating moments of simulated euphoria and excitement with longer periods of hopelessness, futility, and self-condemnation. Should deprivation be frequent or prolonged, the probability is high that these personalities will display the signs of a clear and serious affective disorder.

Despite their lack of well-developed inner resources, histrionics have a reasonably good prognosis because they possess motivation and skills for maintaining satisfactory interpersonal relationships. Given their desire to relate to others and their facility for eliciting attention and approval, the probability is slight that they will succumb to prolonged pathology.

THERAPEUTIC INTERVENTIONS

Histrionics rarely seek therapy. When they do, they usually have experienced a period of social disapproval or deprivation, and hope that the therapist will help fill the void. Often, when the patient's social environment returns to its baseline level of reward the patient will terminate therapy, regardless of whether any therapeutic shift in personality structure has taken place. For this reason, it is a good idea for the patient and therapist to establish very specific treatment goals. This approach helps the patient remain motivated to stay in therapy despite rather vague presenting complaints such as boredom, restlessness, discontent, and loneliness. The histrionic personality also often reports a growing disaffection with his or her mate, a feeling that the vitality that supposedly characterized earlier years together has now palled. Sexual interest may have faded, and the frequency of relations may have dropped due to impotence or frigidity. As disaffection intensifies, conflicts and tension rise, prompting the patient to feel not only a sense of loss but of rejection and hostility from his or her mate. Life feels as if it has taken on a purposeless and meaningless quality. The patient may begin to dramatize this plight, feeling that every recourse is hopeless and futile.

STRATEGIC GOALS

In planning a therapeutic intervention program, the ultimate goal is to correct the tendency of histrionics to fulfill all their needs by focusing on others to the exclusion of self. This requires a shift not only on the self-other but on the active-passive polarities as well. Specific interventions aimed at reversing problem-perpetuating behavioral tendencies and at modifying personologic domain dysfunctions must be chosen according to the individual case.

Reestablishing Polarity Balances

Histrionic personalities operate from the basic premise that they are incapable of handling a large number of life's demands, and need someone truly competent and powerful to do so for them. In their effort to ensure that someone with these attributes is in fact around and willing to take care of those responsibilities histrionics must spend their emotional and mental energy focusing on others. They must keep a close vigilance of the "rescuer," so that at any sign of displeasure or potential rejection, they can placate the significant other and thus secure survival. In addition, the rescuer must be charmed and impressed enough to supply a generous dose of rewards, including praise and admiration, without which histrionics become anxious and depressed. These efforts, despite coming naturally to histrionics, are demanding enough that there is little resource left with which to examine their own internal state. Ironically, success at these goals obviates the need to develop instrumental competence.

To reestablish balance within the self-other polarity, histrionics must learn to turn inward and away from others as a means of gratification and to accomplish instrumental goals. In terms of overall adaptation, it would also serve histrionics well to shift away from their persistent attempts to ensure that the environment does indeed yield sought-for gratification, and learn to channel time and energy in more profitable ways. As they become more passive in relation to their social environment, and overcome the anxiety of giving up full control over the script of their social lives, histrionics may come to enjoy the element of surprise that comes with not having to orchestrate every social interaction.

Countering Perpetuating Tendencies

In an attempt to evade the anxiety that accompanies internal exploration, histrionics engage in massive repression of their unsettled inner lives. Rather than face the existential anxiety that is an inevitable consequence of a deep appreciation of the nature of life, histrionics adopt a protective superficiality. Whatever anxieties do penetrate the shallow surface from the repressed realm of deeper experience are kept at bay through a fantasy of fusion with a powerful other. These strategies, however, involve blocking those very cognitions and emotions that would allow histrionics to process stimuli in an adaptive way. In the case of the histrionic, the lack of fruitful mental processing does not generally involve any kind of thought disorder; distraction is the histrionic's dysphoria-avoiding secret. A constant stream of social "excitement" and engaging (if trivial) external preoccupations must be maintained to keep histrionics from facing the hollow inner turmoil they so dread. Such a strategy requires that histrionics be adept at creating interpersonal drama and approval. When a relationship inevitably moves past the initial high and into the reality of interpersonal differences that need to be worked out, histrionics must quickly secure approval and admiration in order not to fall prey to despair. Moving onto a new relationship provides another opportunity for a honeymoon period but ensures that relationships do not get past a superficial level of intimacy, leaving histrionics without solid relationships to provide support and understanding during inevitable lapses of high drama in their social lives.

In working with a histrionic, a therapist will probably find that the patient thwarts all attempts to examine thoughts and feelings. Patiently guiding the histrionic down the road to self-discovery can prove extremely helpful in reversing maladaptive patterns. If histrionics can bear to face their anxieties, they can also be convinced to give up the external preoccupations that distract them from the processing of stimuli. Allowing the mind to perform logical cognitive operations can begin to change their impressionistic and underdeveloped schemas about causal relationships between events, thoughts, and feelings. Focusing on such previously unexamined matters can result in the integration of past experiences. These, in turn, should lead to learning and the flexibility to engage in alternate and less adolescentlike forms of coping behavior as well as the development of a more mature level of personal independence. Self-examination can also help histrionics see the long-term futility of relationship-hopping and how it serves to deprive them of the very security they crave. Then they can grasp the value of trying to develop skills to deal with less gratifying aspects of relationships, and to tolerate not always being center stage as the price for long-term intimacy.

Modifying Domain Dysfunctions

The most salient disturbances in the prototypical histrionic personality are in the mood, interpersonal conduct, expressive behavior, and cognitive domains. Histrionics exhibit fickle mood and temperament. They overreact to environmental events, displaying dramatic but shallow emotional reactions that often lead them to behave in a less than ideal way. Constantly on an emotional see-saw between enthusiasm and irritation (anything is better than boredom), they rarely have the emotional tranquillity necessary to encourage the development of adaptive behavior. Probably one of the earliest ways to reduce their emotional hyperreactivity is to focus therapeutic sessions on their flighty cognitive style. Because histrionics habitually avoid introspection and obsess about external events, cognitive approaches can help them learn to integrate experiences and thus forge rational schemas with which to process stimuli more completely and meaningfully. Exploratory therapy, behavioral experiments, group therapy, and cognitive exercises all can help histrionics give up a lifestyle characterized by impulsive behavior and thoughtless judgment.

The flirtatious interpersonal behavior that is the hallmark of the histrionic personality inevitably produces long-term problems despite its short-term rewards. Whereas histrionics initially easily seduce and manipulate other people, ultimately they perceive the histrionics as shallow and flighty. Rarely do they experience the satisfaction of genuine intimacy and appreciation for the person they are. Once again, work in the cognitive domain can help histrionics see the advantages of limiting exhibitionistic and seductive behaviors to only those few social contexts in which they are appropriate. Behavior modification can be particularly helpful in teaching alternate behavior skills, such as more assertive communication. Because histrionics are resistant to giving up the colorful style of their demonstrative behavior that has gained them so much attention, they should be taught to discriminate when it is appropriate and when it will lead only to long-term complications and an unfavorable shallow impression. Similar interventions can prove invaluable in modifying the theatrical overresponsiveness the histrionic uses in an attempt to ward off boredom by creating momentary adventures.

The histrionic self-image is gregarious. The self is seen as charming and oriented toward a full and pleasurable social life. This would not be problematic in and of itself; the fact is that histrionics do not know how to define themselves without reference to others. Lack of a personal identity leaves histrionics open to despair when left alone. Defining a personal identity is a major therapeutic objective. Part of this work can involve examining the historical antecedents of the development of their shallow object-representations schema, and helping histrionics see that human interactions, emotions, and conflicts can be integrated in logical, meaningful, and cohesive ways.

Intrapsychically, the histrionic tries to avoid stress by using dissociation as a regulatory mechanism, altering self-presentations to create a favorable response when one "persona" fails. Distraction is used to avoid painful internal experiences, even if personal identity and self-understanding must be sacrificed. Consequently, the morphologic organization of their mental coping and processing schemas and structures is weak and lacking cohesion. Without allowing themselves to think about stimuli, histrionics ensure that new behavioral strategies cannot be developed; coping will be inflexible and lack logical cohesion mirroring the morphologic structure from which it stems. A therapeutic goal would be to emphasize this fact, so that histrionics can make informed decisions about behavior patterns. Many patients would indeed like to develop a stronger and less reactive sense of self.

TACTICAL MODALITIES

Most histrionic patients tend to view the therapist as a "magical" and omniscient helper who has the power to solve all the patient's problems. Chances are good that the patient will try to "charm" the therapist with entertaining stories and good looks, or pull for attention and nurturing with a dramatic show of distress. Two main problems arise when the therapist gives in to the patient's dependency. First, the patient learns neither self-sufficient behaviors nor how to make decisions, and second, the patient eventually discovers that the therapist's caretaking capacity is indeed not superhuman, and possibly terminates therapy prematurely due to anxiety and disappointment over this inevitable discovery. It is no easy task, however, for the therapist to consistently reinforce independent and assertive behaviors in the face of the histrionic's well-practiced emotionally seductive and compelling help-seeking style.

Domain-Oriented Techniques

Behavioral interventions can initially be most useful in relieving symptoms of emotional distress in histrionic patients; relaxation training and problem-solving strategies are particularly helpful in this regard. More long-term objectives of changing coping styles involve an array of case-specific cognitive-behavioral experiments that allow patients to challenge their assumptions about their fundamental lack of capacity to care for themselves. Assertiveness training can provide histrionics with behavioral alternatives to the manipulative seductive ploys they use to procure their wants and needs. Encouraging patients to do just that of which they are the most afraid, in small and controlled steps while carefully monitoring their reactions can lead to the acquisition of behavioral and coping skills that foster lasting changes in self-efficacy.

Although *behavior therapy* might be sufficient to help overcome some of the dysfunctional maneuvers and the shallowness that histrionics employ to avoid their deep abandonment fears, these individuals will require more searching therapeutic interventions to improve. For therapy to be successful in the long run, histrionics must come to tolerate the very existential anxiety they so successfully, but superficially, have learned to defend against. The process, however, necessitates that histrionics be able to tolerate the identity crisis that inevitably accompanies the examination of long-term core conflicts and deep-seated anxieties. In the outline of her *interpersonal* therapeutic approach, Benjamin (1990a) suggests that histrionics can be supported through this process by warm sympathy toward the patient's observing ego (the part of the patient that can rationally understands how certain behaviors can lead to problems) with whom the therapist can "gang up" against the "enemy"—that part of the patient that feels compelled to keep acting out damaging histrionic patterns.

Interpersonal therapy also makes use of concrete problems and relationships as a springboard from which to examine dysfunctional patterns. Alternate behaviors are actively recommended. Benjamin summarizes the histrionic position as one in which interpersonal relationships are dominated by an overtly expressed friendly trust, accompanied by a disrespectful covert agenda of forcing nurturance and love from a powerful other. Seductive and manipulative behaviors are the means to the histrionic's coercive ends. Addressing transference issues directly through questions concerning the patient's feelings about the therapy and

therapist are suggested. Revealed reactions can then be connected back to earlier history and the self-perpetuating quality of these patterns can be explored. Delineating the differences between social and therapeutic relationships (differences in reciprocity, expectations) can be used to counter romantic transference reactions.

As difficult as it is to convince histrionics to engage in self-exploratory and logical cause and effect analysis, the patient's need for approval can be taken advantage of in the initial stages of therapy by using approval and appreciation of strengths to reinforce the patient's tentative efforts. Although direct advice-giving is rarely profitable, helping the patient analyze the reasons for and consequences of life choices can be invaluable. Confrontation of the dependency wish and acceptance that it inevitably cannot be satisfactorily fulfilled represents a therapeutic milestone on the road to developing a more adaptive personality structure. Once this goal is achieved, some histrionics can independently go on to make lasting changes in their lives. Others may need ongoing support as they explore new avenues to developing an identity.

Interpersonal therapists often suggest that *couples* therapy can be useful particularly for pairs whose personality styles are complementary, as has been clinically noted to be commonly the case. Histrionics often become involved with overcontrolled compulsives; intervention that focuses on role reversal can lead to more balanced personality styles as new behaviors are integrated into cognitive schemas. *Group* intervention approaches may be most efficacious with histrionic patients. Having an opportunity to observe individuals with similar interpersonal patterns can provide the patient with a mirror that fosters better understanding of the impact of their own behavior on others. Multiple perspectives on the self afforded by group members can encourage patients to integrate diverse information and bolster object-representation schemas. As the group members' acquaintance with each other deepens through the process of mutual sharing and appraisal, it is doubtful that the group will continue to accept dramatic and flirtatious behavior as a substitution for genuine sharing. Group approval and encouragement of appropriate assertive behaviors and simultaneous disregard for histrionic displays can serve as powerful reinforcers that help bring about change, as long as the patient does not feel so threatened by being challenged that he or she drops out of the group.

The procedures of *cognitive* reorientation may also prove useful in helping histrionics gain insight into their patterns, and in building a richer inner life that would decrease their dependence on others for identity and reinforcements. In the *cognitive* therapy approach outlined by Beck and Freeman (1990b), the initial challenge for the therapist is to be able to maintain the patience needed to help histrionics process and perceive environmental stimuli in ways that are largely characterologically unnatural to them. Persisting despite frustration is key to successful treatment; learning the very process of cognitive therapy itself can ultimately prove to be the histrionic's greatest new tool, as new cognitive processing skills lead to novel interpretations of the environment that foster increases in independent competent behavior. The authors point out that it is especially important for the therapist to consistently reinforce assertive and competent responses, so as not to encourage the dependent patterns that so often bring long-term distress despite immediate reinforcement. Because of histrionics' lack of attention to detail, setting up specific goals with them can sometimes be difficult. However, insisting that histrionics establish very clear ideas about their therapeutic objectives (how their lives will be different) can help ensure that the goals are meaningful to the patient and that termination "by boredom" is less likely.

In terms of specific interventions, the authors suggest that the first step is to help patients identify their dysfunctional automatic thoughts. Histrionics have trouble with this task; they are not adept at processing environmental events, the thoughts they have, and the feelings conjured by them in logical and detailed ways. Learning this skill, however, allows clients to focus on their emotions and desires, identify cognitive distortions, and discover accurate causal relationships between environmental, cognitive, and emotional events. Another great advantage of focusing on learning to identify the relationship between automatic thoughts and behavior is that patients can learn to stop and try to figure out what thoughts they are having before reacting, thus learning to control their impulsivity. Learning to analyze these relationships in terms of a means-ends analysis can help make histrionics aware of behavioral consequences. These new insights can help persuade histrionics to undertake behavioral experiments in which they "try on" different behavioral styles for effect.

One of the major behavioral changes cognitive therapy aims to support is increased assertiveness and decreased manipulation. Helping histrionics identify their wants is a necessary first step in facilitating their assertive communication about them to others. Identifying desires can be seen as part of a larger process of discovering a sense of identity; most histrionics spend so much time focusing on others to get their attention and approval, modifying their behavior to impact on each particular individual, that they hardly know who the fundamental "I" in their "personality" is. The authors suggest that making lists of things that the patient knows about him- or herself, even as basic as favorite colors and foods, is a good way to begin building a self-concept. Another important goal toward the end of increasing assertiveness is to decrease the histrionic's fear of rejection. Histrionics become paralyzed by the possibility of a relationship ending, and often are convinced that straightforward assertive behavior (as opposed to the "irresistible" cute, coy, or dramatic ploys they usually depend on) will be easier for others to turn their back on. The possibility of a rejection can be cognitively handled in therapy by imagining what life was like before a particular relationship, and how the patient could manage to survive in the future if a particular relationship were to end.

Psychodynamic therapies tend to be based on the premise that patients need to grasp the familial origins of their desire to have all their needs met by a significant powerful other. The assumption is that excessive dependency is unresolved and often unconscious, and that it needs to be brought to light. Techniques include analyzing manipulative behavior and its subconscious as well as conscious goals. The futility of the histrionic's efforts needs to be made clear: It is impossible to have all of one's needs met by someone else without being prepared to tolerate loss of self-respect. These issues can all be worked on within the framework of the inevitable transference reaction. Current psychodynamic thinking frames patients' reactions toward the opposite-sex therapist in terms of their goal of manipulating the therapist to satisfy all their needs. These goals spring from the unconscious dependent fantasy relationship of patients with their opposite-sex parent; nurturance—not sexual gratification—is considered the true goal of even sexually provocative behavior.

Although the classic psychodynamic therapist stance of neutrality and refusal to provide direct advice is successful with a large number of patients, those with very pronounced ego-weaknesses may suffer from this particular therapist style.

Weaker patients may decide that the therapist is withholding not because of the desire to communicate a lack of omniscience, but rather out of principle, and try to extract these responses from the therapist at all costs. The ensuing transference drama can be more disruptive to therapy than an interested and sympathetic, if noncommittal, response to pleas for advice. Examination of such requests can in fact be used to point out to the patient what one can reasonably expect from other people. No intervention plan is complete without providing the patient with alternate behavioral possibilities and an understanding of their possible advantages over current patterns.

Psychopharmacological intervention with histrionics tends to be limited to dealing with episodes of depression. When histrionics with depression come to the attention of a therapist, the degree to which symptoms are biologically based and to which they are a means to secure therapist attention need to be evaluated, and the possible advantages of taking antidepressant medication as a complement to psychotherapy can be considered.

A review of the major strategies and tactics is given in Figure 10.6.

Potentiated Pairings and Catalytic Sequences

A first therapeutic step might be to curtail the patient's tendency to overemotionalize and thereby aggravate his or her distraught feelings. Relaxation training and "cause and effect" thinking skills can be useful adjuncts to the initial phases of long-term exploratory therapies. If a histrionic presents with depression that is evaluated to be

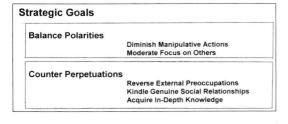

Figure 10.6 Therapeutic strategies and tactics for the prototypal histrionic personality.

endogenous and interfering with adaptive functioning, antidepressant medication can be considered as a support to psychotherapy. However, the therapist must establish a solid alliance and specific goals before prescribing medication because there is always the risk that as soon as histrionics feel better they will terminate therapy regardless of whether changes have been made.

Clients whose familial or couple environment encourage their patterns would do well to participate in specific family or couple interventions as an adjunct at some point in their individual therapy. Group therapy can also help histrionics by exposing them to others with similar behavior patterns that they sometimes resist seeing in themselves, and gives them the opportunity to be rewarded for appropriate behavior from a group of people. Because others are the most powerful reinforcers for histrionics, this forum can potentially show rapid results.

RESISTANCES AND RISKS

A therapist whose own sense of identity and self-worth are largely satisfied by being very helpful to others may easily be manipulated into playing the "savior" role and actually repeat the patient's maladaptive experiences of significant others. Other therapists may find the flighty histrionic style annoying; hypervigilant histrionics are apt to sense the disapproval and in fact regress further into their manipulative, theatrical ways. Therapists need to make a real effort at empathy lest their intervention efforts be jeopardized. On the other hand, empathy should not imply playing the histrionic's game. Despite the entertaining and charming communication style, it is important for the therapist to maintain sober and respectful attention. The playful banter that is often therapeutically helpful with other personality styles can reinforce histrionics' belief that one is always on display and must charm significant others to get attention and approval. A more serious attention, particularly a stance of respect toward the patient, helps provide the histrionic with alternate interaction schemas.

Some histrionics will fear the possibility of becoming drab and dull even as they see the advantages of becoming "deeper" and adopting a more premeditated behavioral style. It is a better idea to encourage more constructive expression of the histrionic's natural dramatic flair (often it can be used to advantage by enlisting the dramatic persona to work with the therapist against maladaptive cognitions and behaviors) than to endorse a complete suppression of such tendencies, which may lead to termination.

One of the frustrations a therapist might feel when working with histrionics is their tendency to have "pseudo-insights." Just when the therapist is sure that the therapy has come to a breakthrough, the vague and forgetful style of the histrionic leads to rapid disintegration of apparent gains. The tendency of the patient to want to make the therapist feel important in the hopes of thereby securing special treatment also often leads to enthusiastic agreement with the therapist, despite the lack of real internalization of the issues. Patience on the part of the therapist is a must if disappointment in pseudo-progress is not itself to become disruptive.

CHAPTER 11

Narcissistic Personality Disorders: The Egotistic Pattern

Although equally "imbalanced" in the self-other polarity, albeit in the direction of self rather than other, certain personalities are completely opposite in their orientation to dependent and histrionic personalities, who look to others to provide the reinforcements of life. Both the narcissistic and antisocial patterns (described in this and the next chapter) turn inward for gratification, having learned to rely on themselves rather than others for safety and self-esteem. Weakness and dependency are threatening. Because both narcissists and antisocials are preoccupied with matters of personal adequacy, power, and prestige, status and superiority must always be in their favor. They fear the loss of self-determination, proudly display their achievements, and strive to enhance themselves and to be ascendant, stronger, more beautiful, wealthier, and more important than others. In sum, it is what they think of themselves, not what others say or can provide for them, that serves as the touchstone for their security and contentment.

The independent personality style has been divided into two subtypes in earlier writings (Millon, 1969): the passive-independent, or narcissistic personalities, who are confident of their self-worth and who feel they need be merely themselves to justify being content and secure; and the active-independent, or antisocial personalities, who struggle to "prove" themselves, who insist on their rights and will be harsh and ruthless when necessary to retaliate or gain power over others. For the narcissistic type, self-esteem is based on a blind and naive assumption of personal worth and superiority. For the antisocial type, it stems from distrust, an assumption that others will be humiliating and exploitive. To these personalities, whose independence from others takes on an active and angry character, self-determination is a protective maneuver; it is a means of countering, with their own power and

prestige, the hostility, deception, and victimization they anticipate from others. Although both passive (narcissists) and active-independents (antisocials) devalue the standards and opinions of others, finding gratification primarily within themselves, their life histories and the strategies they employ for achieving their needs are substantially different.

This chapter focuses on the narcissistic personality, a character pattern that has gained considerable recognition in the past two decades. Rather sadly, it has grown into a diagnostic fad among certain groups of mental health professionals, notably those of a psychoanalytic persuasion. This shift in status from a largely unknown clinical entity to a paramount and perhaps second most prevalent personality syndrome diagnosed in several analytic centers is less a commentary on our times (Lasch, 1978) than on the fervor characterizing insular schools of thought that may be undergoing popular decline or serious external appraisal (Millon, 1967). In the opening paragraphs of a work describing the narcissistic personality more than 25 years ago, the author wrote as follows:

This rather fascinating pattern, though well known in contemporary life, and depicted so well in literary writings, has been given but scant theoretical and clinical attention. For example, the recent DSM-II has no diagnostic category that approximates the clinical features of this personality type. (1969, p. 261)

Drafted initially in 1966, and updated just prior to publication, this statement could not be written today, except facetiously. Analytic theorists Otto Kernberg and Heinz Kohut have carried many of their colleagues along a path that has promised a renewed vitality for psychoanalytic theory and therapy; it is the construct of narcissism (and borderline) that serves as the cornerstone of this enthusiastic revival. Fortunately, the concept of a narcissistic personality syndrome does not stand or fall on the vagaries of the future of psychoanalysis. As formulated in this chapter, the syndrome is well ensconced in the DSM-III and reflects the thinking, not only of Kernberg and Kohut but of biosocial and learning theories such as utilized by the authors; its viability is more solidly rooted than its current faddish character might suggest.

The label "narcissistic" connotes more than mere egocentricity, a characteristic found in all individuals who are driven primarily by their needs and anxieties. More particularly, narcissism signifies that these individuals overvalue their personal worth, direct their affections toward themselves rather than others, and expect that others will not only recognize but cater to the high esteem in which narcissists hold themselves. This form of self-confidence and self-assurance is conducive to success and the evocation of admiration in our "other-directed" society. It falters as a lifestyle, however, if the person's illusion of specialness is poorly founded in fact or if the supercilious air is so exaggerated as to grate on and alienate significant others.

In contrast to the antisocial personality, the self-centeredness of the narcissist is not anchored to feelings of deep distrust and animosity. Narcissistic individuals are benignly arrogant. They exhibit a disdainful indifference to the standards of shared social behavior and feel themselves above the conventions of the cultural group, exempt from the responsibilities that govern and give order and reciprocity to societal living. It is assumed that others will submerge their desires in favor of the narcissists' comfort and welfare; they operate on the fantastic assumption that their mere desire is justification for possessing whatever they seek. Thus, their disdainfulness is matched by their exploitiveness, their assumption that they are entitled to be served and to have their own wishes take precedence over others, without expending any effort to merit such favor. In short, narcissists possess illusions of an inherent superior self-worth and move through life with the belief that it is their inalienable right to receive special considerations.

Although the status of the narcissistic personality achieved official recognition in the 1980 DSM-III manual (it has yet to do so in the ICD-10), its origins can be traced back about one century, to which period we turn next.

HISTORICAL ANTECEDENTS

Havelock Ellis (1898/1933) first gave psychological significance to the term *narcissism* by conceptualizing it as autoeroticism, that is, sexual gratification without stimulation or evocation by another person. Paul Nacke (1899) used the term in a similar manner, applying it to the perversion of being preoccupied with the sight and pleasures of one's own body in a manner usually reserved for those of the opposite sex. In 1908, J. Sadger extended the concept to other so-called perversions, notably that of homosexuality.

Although Freud (1900) did not use the term narcissism to represent an important observation he noted in his investigation of dreams, he reports the following as a likely basis for the personality traits of these individuals:

I have found that people who know that they are preferred or are favored by their mother give evidence in their lives of a peculiar self-reliance and an unshakeable optimism which often seem like heroic attributes and bring actual success to their possessors. (p. 398)

More will be said in later sections about Freud's view of the favorable experiences that typify the narcissist's relationship with his or her mother, and the contrasting position of a problematic relationship that is held by most contemporary analytic theorists of the narcissistic personality.

MODERN FORMULATIONS

Freud's (1910/1957, 1911/1925) first explicit formulation of narcissism conceived it as a normal phase of development standing midway between autoeroticism and object-love. During this transitory period, initially diverse and unconnected autoerotic sensations were fused into what was experienced as one's body, which then become a single, unified love-object. In 1914 Freud aligned narcissism with libido theory and proposed that it ultimately matured and diffused into object relationships. Shortly thereafter he reformulated his thinking on the developmental sequence and spoke of the autoerotic phase as the "primary narcissistic condition." This first phase became the initial repository of libido from which emerged not only the love of self but love in general. In time narcissism was conceived by

Freud as a universal developmental process that continued through life but unfolded through sequential stages. He recognized that difficulties may arise in this normal, sequential progression. First, there may be failures to advance from libidinal self-love to object-love, and, second, "peculiarities" may occur in the way the person expresses narcissistic love. Freud (1914/1925) described this latter difficulty as follows:

We have found, especially in persons whose libidinal development has suffered some disturbance, as in perverts and homosexuals that in their choice of love-object they have taken as their model not the mother; but their own selves. They are plainly seeking themselves as love-object and their type of object choice may be termed narcissistic. (p. 45)

In this only major paper devoted exclusively to narcissism, Freud (1914/1925) suggested that in certain cases—notably among "perverts and homosexuals"—libidinal self-centeredness stems from the child's feeling that caretakers cannot be depended on to provide love reliably. Either rebuffed by their parents or subjected to fickle and erratic attention (seductive one moment and deprecating the next) these children "give up" as far as trusting and investing in others as love-objects. Rather than rely on the capriciousness of others or risk their rejection, these youngsters avoid the lasting attachment they achingly desire and decide instead that it is only themselves they can trust and therefore love.

In light of current debates within psychoanalytic circles, it is important to note that the developmental origin of the term narcissism described here was only one of several concepts that Freud posited as the source of libidinal self-cathexis. Moreover, the paper was not written for the purpose of formulating either a narcissistic personality type or a narcissistic character structure. Rather, Freud's interest lay in exploring and elaborating variations in both the development and the nature of libidinal cathexis. As far as clinical syndromes were concerned, he referred in this paper to characteristics observed among paraphrenics (paranoid schizophrenics), megalomaniacs, and hypochondriacs. When Freud wrote, for the first time in 1931, of a narcissistic libidinal type, he described this individual as follows:

The main interest is focused on self-preservation; the type is independent and not easily overawed.

. . . People of this type impress others as being "personalities"; it is on them that their fellow men are specially likely to lean; they readily assume the role of leader, give a fresh stimulus to cultural development or break down existing conditions. (p. 249)

What is striking in this quote is Freud's characterization of the narcissist's strength and confidence, especially since it contrasts so markedly with the low self-esteem, feelings of emptiness, pain, and depression that certain of his recent disciples (Forman, 1975; Kohut, 1971) attribute to this personality. Disparities in characterizations such as these often arise as a consequence of shifts in Freud's formulations from one period to another over his productive and long career. In this case, it can be traced to the fact that Freud identified several origins of narcissistic self-cathexis, only one of which is the type of parental caprice and rejection that may lead to feelings of emptiness and low self-esteem. As evident from earlier excerpts, and as later elaborated further, Freud's description of the narcissistic libidinal type, brief though it is, corresponds much more closely to the DSM-III portrayal of the narcissistic personality than do several contemporary characterizations that trace their antecedents to either parental rebuff or unreliability. Relevant to this issue is a quote of Freud's reproduced later in the chapter suggesting that narcissistic self-investment is more likely to be a product of parental overvaluation than of parental devaluation.

Moving back somewhat to the 1920s, we find three analytically oriented theorists who addressed the concept of a narcissistic personality. Wilhelm Reich claimed to have first formulated what he termed the "phallic-narcissistic" character at a Vienna Psychoanalytic Society meeting in 1926, although Waelder (1925) made reference to narcissistic personality features in an earlier paper focusing on the mechanisms of the psychotic process. He described a case evincing an air of condescending superiority, a preoccupation with self, a lofty regard for his own intellectual capabilities, and a lack of empathy for others. Waelder characterizes these features as follows:

He was a young scientist of unusual ability and originality, whose mental constitution showed signs of narcissism and psychotic characteristics. His attitude towards those around him was one of marked superiority, which certainly had some actual foundation in his intellectual gifts. He had the least possible capacity for inner adaptation to other people. He felt different from mankind in general; he was perfectly able to understand others intellectually, but their nature seemed to him alien. In his mind he was independent of the opinion of most people (he made an exception to a few individuals whom he esteemed highly), and his chief problem in life was the fostering of his own self-respect, an attitude which determined most of his mental sensations. (p. 264)

Even earlier than Waelder's publication was Andreas-Salome's (1921) paper on the "dual orientation of narcissism." In this work she anticipated the division that developed in the 1960s, exemplified in the theoretical writings of Kernberg and Kohut. Although she recognized that difficulties ensue from failures in "object-cathexis of the libido," resulting in compensatory narcissistic adaptations, she also spoke of the "fact" that narcissistic processes are not limited to a single early phase of libidinous development, but "remains as a kind of fundamental continuity" throughout development; in the former, she anticipates the Kernbergian model, in the latter, that of Kohut.

A comprehensive exposition of Reich's general theory was published in 1933. It characterized a narcissistic type as follows in a subsequent English translation:

The typical phallic-narcissistic character, on the other hand, is self-assured, sometimes arrogant, elastic, energetic, often impressive in his bearing.

The most pronounced types tend to achieve leading positions in life and are ill suited to subordinate positions among the rank and file.

If their vanity is offended, they react with cold disdain, marked ill-humor, or downright aggression. Their narcissism, as opposed to that of other character types, is expressed not in an infantile but in a blatantly self-confident way, with a flagrant display of superiority and dignity. (1949, pp. 217–218)

Notable is the close correspondence between Reich's depiction and Freud's (1931/1950) formulation of the narcissistic libidinal type; both provide clear descriptions that anticipate the text of recent DSMs. In contrast to both Freud and more contemporary analytic theorists, Reich attributed the origins of narcissism to fixations at the libidinal phallic stage and conceived it as a compensation and wish-fulfilling reaction to conflicts associated with the castration complex.

Significant shifts in emphasis among psychoanalytic thinkers began in the mid-1930s and resulted in the emergence of a series of new orientations. Spawned at that time were neo-Freudian schools of ego, self, object relations, and social theory.

Karen Horney (1939), the prime social theorist of psychoanalysis, addressed the concept of narcissism in an important early book, formulating the central features of the personality type as follows:

If narcissism is considered not genetically but with reference to its actual meaning it should, in my judgment, be described as essentially self-inflation. Psychic inflation, like economic inflation, means presenting greater values than really exist. It means that the person loves and admires himself for values for which there is no adequate foundation. Similarly, it means that he expects love and admiration from others for qualities that he does not possess, or does not possess to as large an extent as he supposes. (pp. 89–90)

CONTEMPORARY PROPOSALS

Although not addressing a narcissistic character structure directly, Fenichel (1945) described what he referred to as the "Don Juans" of achievement. Developing this theme in recounting a case of his, Fenichel extrapolated to a general portrayal of these individuals, noting that they had considerable success but no inner satisfaction. Racing from one achievement to another, they seemed driven by their overwhelming narcissistic needs. Because these needs were deeply embedded in childhood, the individual could never resolve or fulfill them. In time, these persons ultimately realize that their repetitive searches for fulfillment only served the purpose of concealing their deeper feelings of emptiness. Unsure of their real self-worth, actual, substantive achievements prove to be gratifying only temporarily.

A similar depiction of the narcissistic personality was proposed by Tartakoff (1966) in his description of individuals with a "Nobel Prize Complex." As in the case described by Fenichel, these individuals have an intense need to achieve great wealth or great recognition, such as the coveted Nobel Prize. Many such individuals may have been unusually talented or successful in their early years, thought of as being the best or the first among their peers, the "chosen one" by virtue of their extraordinary gifts. Frequently only children, they carry within them a high sense of confidence, but under the press of upsetting realities, they may become less sure of their worth and, hence, must revert to fantasies and illusions about their specialness.

The recent growth of interest in narcissism among orthodox analytic thinkers may be traced to notions presented in the early 1960s by A. Reich (1960), E. Jacobson (1964), H. Nagera (1964), and H. Rosenfeld (1964).

A. Reich (1960), in discussing pathological forms of self-esteem regulation, brings to the foreground several unattractive features of the narcissist's effort to compensate for a deeper sense of inadequacy:

We must take into account the aggressive components of the narcissistic exhibitionistic strivings. Self-conscious people seek to undo feelings of inadequacy by forcing everyone's attention and admiration upon themselves, but they fail in this defensive attempt. They feel that attention is indeed focused on them in a negative way: as though others, instead of being dazzled, were discerning the warded-off "inferiority" behind the false front. The exhibitionistic drive contains contempt for those whose admiration is needed. (p. 58)

Taking a different tack, Rosenfeld (1964) wrote the following in his description of the narcissist:

[This] patient . . . feels that he is loved by everyone, or demands to be loved by everyone, because he is so lovable. All these patients seem to have in common the feeling that they contain all the goodness which would otherwise be experienced in a relationship to an object. We usually encounter simultaneously a highly idealized self-image . . . and anything interfering with this picture is rigorously defended against and omnipotently denied. (p. 333)

The most enthusiastically received revisions in psychoanalytic thought by far are those formulated by Otto Kernberg (1967, 1970) and Heinz Kohut (1966, 1968, 1971). The author has neither the space nor the inclination here to trace the circuitous labyrinths through which their metapsychological assertions wind their way. Nor is the clinical utility of their views confirmed by debates

that have filled recent analytic journals. Nonetheless, a reasonably detailed synopsis of their major themes is in order.

Kernberg, in his restructuring of a diagnostic framework for characterology, deemphasized the psychoanalytic classification schema that has traditionally been based on libidinal development. Stage sequences are referred to as a means of identifying levels of instinctual maturation (e.g., pregenital, genital). The vicissitudes of maturation give rise to the clinical features, defensive operations, level of severity, prognosis and, most centrally, the structural integration or organization that is likely to characterize the individual's personality. Employing his framework of levels of structural organization as a model for constructing "a psychoanalytic classification of character pathology," Kernberg (1967) described the features of the narcissist as follows:

These patients present an unusual degree of self-reference in their interactions with other people, a great need to be loved and admired by others, and a curious apparent contradiction between a very inflated concept of themselves and an inordinate need for tribute from others. Their emotional life is shallow. They experience little empathy for the feelings of others, they obtain very little enjoyment from life other than from the tributes they receive from others or from their own grandiose fantasies, and they feel restless and bored when external glitter wears off and no new sources feed their self-regard. They envy others, tend to idealize some people from whom they expect narcissistic supplies, and to depreciate and treat with contempt those from whom they do not expect anything (often their former idols). In general, their relationships with other people are clearly exploitative and sometimes parasitic. It is as if they feel they have the right to control and possess others and to exploit them without guilt feelings—and behind a surface which very often is charming and engaging, one senses coldness and ruthlessness. Very often such patients are considered to be "dependent" because they need so much tribute and adoration from others, but on a deeper level they are completely unable really to depend on anybody because of their deep distrust and depreciation of others. (p. 655)

Kernberg asserted that the haughty and grandiose constellation of behaviors that characterizes the narcissist is a defense against the projection of "oral" rage that, in turn, stems from the narcissist's incapacity to depend on "internalized good objects." In this etiologic formulation, Kernberg claimed that the experiential background of most narcissists includes chronically cold parental figures who exhibit either indifference or covert, but spitefully aggressive, attitudes toward their children. At the same time, the young, future narcissist is often found to possess some special talent or status within the family, such as playing the role of "genius" or being the "only child." This quality of specialness serves as a refuge, at first only temporarily but ultimately an often-returned-to haven that reliably offsets the underlying feeling of having been unloved by the vengefully rejecting parent.

Kohut's views are more difficult to summarize than those of Kernberg, perhaps as a consequence of their greater originality. Despite having been written in esoteric, if not obscure, psychoanalytic jargon and having been formulated in an ingenious, if at times ponderous and tautological fashion, Kohut's work has attracted numerous disciples. Fortunately, a score of "interpreters" have sought to elucidate his metapsychological assertions, which many consider among the more imaginative advances in recent analytic theory (Forman, 1975; Gedo & Goldberg, 1973; Palombo, 1976; Wolf, 1976).

Kohut rejects the traditional Freudian and Kernbergian thesis that narcissistic self-investment results from a defensive withdrawal of object-love attachments following a pattern of chronic parental coldness or vengeful spite. This classical view contends that narcissism is a result of developmental arrests or regressions to earlier points of fixation. Thus, the future narcissist, according to standard analytic metapsychology, regresses to or fails to progress through the usual developmental sequence of initial undifferentiated libido, followed by autoeroticism, narcissism, and, finally, object-love. It is not the content as such but the sequence of libidinal maturation that Kohut challenges. His clinical observations have led him to assert that the primitive narcissistic libido has its own developmental line and sequence of continuity into adulthood. That is, it does not "fade away" by becoming transformed into object-libido, as contended by classical theorists, but unfolds into its own set of mature narcissistic processes and structures. In healthy form, for example, these processes might include behaviors such as humor and creativity; similarly, and most significantly, it is through this narcissistic developmental sequence that the cohesive psychic structure of "self" ultimately emerges.

Pathology in narcissistic development, according to Kohut, occurs as a consequence of failures to integrate one of two major spheres of self-maturation, the "grandiose self" and the "idealized parental imago." Confronted by realistic shortcomings that undermine early feelings of grandiose omnipotence, or subsequently recognizing the equally illusory nature of the idealized powers they have attributed to their parents, these children must find a way to overcome their "disappointments" so as not to "fragment." If disillusioned, rejected, or experiencing cold and unempathic care at the earliest stages of self-development, serious pathology, such as psychotic or borderline states, will occur. Trauma or disappointment at a later phase will have somewhat different repercussions depending on whether the difficulty centered on the development of the grandiose self or on the parental imago. In the former, the child will fail to develop the sense of fulfillment and self-confidence that comes from feeling worthwhile and valued; as a consequence, these needs will "split off" and result in the persistent seeking of narcissistic recognition through adulthood. Along the second line of self-development, children who are unable to idealize their parents because of the latter's indifference or rejection will feel devastated, depressed, and empty. Through adulthood, they will seek idealized parental surrogates who, inevitably, will fail to live up to the omnipotent powers the narcissists hoped to find within them. In their desperate search for an ideal that is greater than themselves, they are often led to behave in a weak and self-effacing manner that will enable others to overshadow them.

What is notable is that Kohut's is a developmental theory of self and not a personality characterization. Nevertheless, it leads to a clinical picture that is at variance with those of Freud, Kernberg, and the DSM-III and IV. The features that emerge from Kohut's descriptions have been summarized by Forman (1975). Listed among the more prominent are (a) low self-esteem, (b) tendencies toward periodic hypochondriasis, and (c) feelings of emptiness or deadness. To illustrate their contrasting views, for example, the episodic depression that Kohut finds so characteristic of narcissistically injured persons is not seen by Kernberg to be a true depression at all. Rather, Kernberg contends that when "narcissists" feel seriously disappointed or abandoned they may appear depressed on superficial examination, but they are, in fact, smoldering with constrained anger and revengeful resentment.

It is not only in psychoanalytic circles that narcissism has acquired its faddish status and intellectual fascination. We appear to be witnessing the "me" generation, a subculture immersed in what has been popularly described as "our narcissistic society." Fortunately, the validity of the narcissistic personality as a conceptual entity does not rest solely on the speculations of analytic theory nor the passing character of contemporary lifestyles.

Recent and insightful characterizations of various narcissistic types have been presented by Adler (1981, 1986), Bursten (1973b, 1982), and Cooper (1981, 1989).

Bursten (1973b) has sought to distinguish four personality variants within the narcissistic grouping, speaking of them as the craving, paranoid, manipulative, and phallic types. He refers to the craving variety as "clinging, demanding, often pouting and whining" (p. 290). Those labeled paranoid narcissists correspond with general descriptions of the paranoid personality. Manipulative narcissists encompass a large segment of what are referred to as antisocial personalities in the DSM. The fourth subtype, phallic narcissists, describes patients who are exhibitionistic, reckless, cold, and arrogant. In seeking to contrast borderline from narcissistic personalities, Bursten makes reference to the distinction as bearing on the cohesiveness of self. Elaborating this distinction, he speaks of the narcissistic personality as comprising (1982):

. . . a group of people whose sense of self is sufficiently cohesive that they do not suffer from these types of fragility problems. The striking feature of this cluster of personality types centers around self-esteem. They maintain an intense interest in themselves and harbor both grandiose fantasies, albeit not to a delusional extent, and the need to associate with powerful figures. When one frustrates their vanity or their need for an ideal "parent," they become dysfunctional—they suffer severe disappointment, depression, rage, and hypochondriasis. They may even have fleeting episodes of confusion, but such mental disintegration is very brief and does not have the prominence and the persistence of people whose personalities fall in the borderline cluster. Elsewhere, I have theorized that the cohesiveness of their sense of self is maintained by the intensity of their narcissistic focus on themselves. (p. 414)

Drawing on Bursten's conceptions of self-cohesiveness, Adler (1981) elaborates further on the continuum of narcissistic and borderline personalities:

Borderline patients have serious difficulties in maintaining stable self-object transferences as well as a sense of self-cohesiveness. . . .

Patients with narcissistic personality disorders on the upper end of the continuum are able to maintain self-cohesiveness, except for transient fragmentation. . . . These fragmentation experiences can often be examined in the therapeutic situation without serious disruption. . . . Finally, patients with a narcissistic personality disorder do not experience the feelings of aloneness experienced by borderline patients.

From the borderline patient capable of a serious regression at one end of the continuum to the patient with a stable narcissistic personality disorder at the other end, we can evaluate our patients using . . . cohesiveness of the self, self-object transference stability, and the achievement of mature aloneness. (pp. 47–48)

Cooper (1984, 1988, 1989) has written extensively on different facets of the narcissistic character, describing aspects of its development, the central role of an integrated self-image, and its intertwining with masochisticlike tendencies. In each sphere, his insights have been unusually astute and his themes both scholarly and eloquently expressed. Speaking of the importance of an integrated self-image, Cooper (1984) writes:

A vital aspect of normal self-development is the achievement of an internalized, integrated self-image. (p. 46)

Different workers have referred to these integrative capacities and failures in a variety of ways. Kohut spoke of enfeebled selves lacking cohesion. Kernberg speaks of splits in self-representations. Erikson referred to identity diffusion, and Winnicott spoke of the False Self. Under many different headings, every investigator in this area has emphasized the core importance of the creation of a unified, coherent, integrated inner sense of self. (p. 47)

Describing the intermeshing of narcissistic and masochistic pathology, Cooper (1989) comments:

Frustrations of narcissistic strivings lead to reparative attempts to maintain omnipotent fantasies. . . . Self esteem takes on a pathological quality when an individual begins to derive satisfaction from mastery of his own humiliations. . . . A pattern of deriving pleasure out of displeasure has begun. This

pattern provides the groundwork for the later clini-
cal picture of . . . the "injustice collector." . . .

These individuals are basically narcissistic-
masochistic characters and their analysis regularly
reveals that narcissistic defenses of grandiosity and
entitlement are used to ward off masochistic tenden-
cies toward self-abasement and self-damage.
(p. 314)

Taking issue with the descriptively narrow formulations of the narcissistic personality in the
DSM, Cooper and Sacks (1991) offer the following comments:

The diagnostic features are a caricature, not a
clinical picture. The core issue is a conflict over
self-esteem in defense of self-inflation. This
grandiosity is more or less fragile or becomes
more or less pathologically unrealistic when
threats to self-esteem and self-representation are
present in the form of criticism, tasks beyond
one's capacity, etc.

These patients often have a slippery ethical sys-
tem, not out of an intent to exploit, but out of the
need to hide flaws and keep their defects secret.
Narcissistic characters also have frequent paranoid
tendencies, again arising out of the need to hide im-
perfections. The sense of needing to feel perfect is as
much a part of the picture as grandiosity, which is
an overt characteristic. (p. 3)

The sense of omnipotence and absolute self-
sufficiency seen in the illusions of narcissists are
traced to the fetal period by the French analyst
Grunberger (1979):

The hypothesis I am proposing is based on the
premise of a prenatal state of elation, the source of
all the various forms of narcissism. Though often
very different in their manifestations, these vari-
ants have a common denominator that always leads
back to the same prenatal origin. (p.12)

The fetus has often been described as existing
in an elative state that constitutes a perfect home-
ostasis, without needs, for, since needs are satis-
fied automatically, they do not have to be formed
as such. . . . It can provide the basis for certain
elaborations that appear later as distinctive nar-
cissistic states in so far as they are experienced in
a "pure" mode, that is, unconflicted (or without
guilt). (p. 14)

Magic omnipotence, the longing for autonomy,
and self-esteem (in a positive or negative form) are
frequently cited characteristics of the narcissist.
The fetus, it happens, is truly omnipotent and

sovereign (in his universe, which for him is one
and the same as the universe); he is autonomous,
knowing nothing other than himself. (p.15)

A thoughtful characterization of the inner world
of narcissists and their developmental origins has
been eloquently formulated by Miller (1981); she
comes to a conception that is similar to those presented by Andreas-Salome (1921) and Millon
(1969). As noted in previous pages, her view also
reflects one of the two origins of narcissistic
pathology proposed by Freud in his early seminal
paper on narcissism (Freud, 1914). Addressing the
role of overindulgence (rather than frustration) in
childhood, Miller recognizes that those who may
later become narcissists were not loved as persons
in their own right. Rather, they served to fulfill
parental longings, served to achieve glorification
for their parents' unrequited desire for glorification, and failed to be provided with the genuine
emotional acceptance necessary to develop an
authentic sense of self. A sense of loneliness is experienced in the home setting. As a result, these
children become narcissistically self-involved, lose
their empathic responsiveness and social spontaneity, and must compensate by fantasies of grandiose
achievements and acclaim. Achieved public recognition is not the same as genuine love; hence, such
achievements bring little self-acceptance and leads
the narcissist to become envious of those whose
inner lives are more genuinely fulfilled.

In a series of particularly insightful papers,
Akhtar and Thomson (1982) have sought to bring
the scattered literature on the narcissist into a multifaceted profile, including their characteristic
overt and covert features in six areas of psychosocial functioning. In a recent book, Akhtar (1992)
indicates that narcissists appear overtly grandiose,
exploitative, seductive, and articulate. Covertly,
however, they are doubt-ridden, envious of others,
chronically bored, corruptible, and unable to love.
Akhtar's format for differentiating the overt from
the covert is an extremely helpful distinction owing
to the disparity that exists among many narcissists
between their self-presentations and their intrapsychic doubts.

Another important contributor to the narcissistic personality literature is Gunderson (1983;
Gunderson & Ronningstam, 1991, Gunderson,
Ronningstam, & Smith, 1991). In summarizing
the features of the narcissist, he includes several
criteria (Gunderson & Ronningstam, 1991):

Narcissistic patients are usually talented and have
had sustained periods of successful academic,

employment, or creative achievement. This is frequently a source for their sense of superiority. It is also a reason why they are more apt to appear in private practice settings than in either institutions or clinics. . . .

Narcissistically disturbed patients reported histories in which they have reacted with hostility and suspicion to the perception of other people's envy toward them. They believe that because of envy other people have set out to hurt them, spoil their work, diminish their achievements, or criticize them behind their back. . . .

Feelings of devaluation or contempt may occur toward many people but are especially evident toward anyone who they believe has betrayed or otherwise disappointed them. These become sustained attitudes of dislike or dismissal. (pp. 114–115)

Another astute contemporary theorist, Stone (1993) further amplifies the divergent backgrounds and psychic states of the narcissist in the following:

Narcissistic traits can develop, curiously, when there are deviations from ideal rearing on either side: pampering or neglecting; expecting too much or too little. Excessive praise of a child . . . can give rise to . . . feelings of superiority, of being destined for greatness. . . . But compensatory feelings of a similar kind can arise where there has been parental indifference and neglect, for in this situation a child may develop an exaggerated desire for "greatness" by way of shoring up a sense of self-worth in the absence of the ordinary parental praise. Whereas the overly praised child may regard himself as better than he really is, the neglected child may present a dual picture: an outward sense of (compensatory) specialness covering an inward sense of worthlessness. (p. 260)

Several perspectives have been brought to bear on the concept of the narcissistic personality that deviate in major regards from classical psychoanalytic approaches. Notable among these are interpersonal theorists such as Leary and Benjamin, cognitively oriented thinkers spearheaded by Beck and associates (1990), as well as social learning theorists such as Millon (1969, 1981, 1990). We will turn first to contributors oriented by the view that interpersonal behavior lies at the heart of this disorder.

Timothy Leary (1957), a disciple of Horney and others of the social and interpersonal school of thought, extended their notions to what he terms "adjustment through competition." Leary speaks of this pattern as demonstrating a competitive self-confident narcissism, described in the following quotes:

In its maladaptive extreme it becomes a smug, cold, selfish, exploitive social role. In this case the adaptive self-confidence and independence become exaggerated into a self-oriented rejection of others. . . .

These individuals feel most secure when they are independent of other people . . . The narcissist puts . . . distance between himself and others—wants to be independent of and superior to the "other one." Dependence is terrifying. (p. 332)

The second group of . . . patients . . . are those whose self-regard has received a decent defeat. They often report the most colorful and fearful symptomotology . . . The superficial impression of depression or dependence is deceptive. Psychological testing or perceptive interviewing will reveal that the patients are not as anxious or depressed as they appear. What becomes evident is a narcissistic concern with their own reactions, their own sensitivities. The precipitating cause for their entrance to the clinic is usually a shift in their life situation, which causes frustration or a blow to their pride. (p. 335)

Following the interpersonal perspective of Leary are a number of interpersonally oriented theorists who drafted their model of various personality disorders in highly fruitful work. Notable among this group is Lorna Benjamin (1993a), who has formulated a complex analysis of the narcissistic character. In her recent work, she describes this personality as follows:

There is extreme vulnerability to criticism or being ignored, together with a strong wish for love, support, and admiring deference from others. The baseline position involves noncontingent love of self and presumptive control of others. If the support is withdrawn, or if there is any evidence of lack of perfection, the self-concept degrades to severe self-criticism. Totally lacking in empathy, these persons treat others with contempt, and hold the self above and beyond the fray. (p. 147)

[The narcissist] expects to be given whatever he or she wants and needs, no matter what it might mean to others. This does not include active deception, but rather is a consequence of the belief that he or she is "entitled." For example, the NPD would not set out to con a "little old lady" out of

her life savings; however, if she offered them, the NPD would accept such a gift without reflection about its impact on her. [He/She] will expect great dedication, overwork, and heroic performance from the people associated with him or her—without giving any thought to the impact of this pattern on their lives. (p. 150)

Contributing the insightful analysis of the narcissistic personality from a cognitive point of view, Beck and Freeman (1990b) provide the following proposals concerning this individual's distorted belief system:

The core narcissistic beliefs are as follows: "Since I am special, I deserve special dispensations, privileges, and prerogatives," "I'm superior to others and they should acknowledge this," "I'm above the rules."

Their main strategies consist of doing whatever they can to reinforce their superior status and to expand their personal domain. Thus, they may seek glory, wealth, position, power, and prestige as a way of continuously reinforcing their "superior" image.

Their main affect is anger when other people do not accord them the admiration or respect that they believe they are entitled to, or otherwise thwart them in some way. They are prone to becoming depressed, however, if their strategies are foiled. (p. 50)

NPD can be conceptualized as stemming from a combination of dysfunctional schemas about the self, the world, and the future. The early foundation of these schemas is developed by direct and indirect messages from parents, siblings, and significant others, and by experiences that mold beliefs about personal uniqueness and self-importance. . . . Narcissists regard themselves as special, exceptional, and justified in focusing exclusively on personal gratification; they expect admiration, deference, and compliance from others, and their expectations of the future focus on the realization of grandiose fantasies. At the same time, beliefs about the importance of other people's feelings are conspicuously lacking. Behavior is affected by deficits in cooperation and reciprocal social interaction, as well as by excesses in demanding, self-indulgent, and sometimes aggressive behaviors. (p. 238)

In their effort to identify the underlying trait dimensions of the major personality disorders, the five-factor theorists Costa and Widiger (1993),

note the following combination of characteristics in the narcissistic personality:

NAR is characterized primarily by traits of grandiosity, entitlement, arrogance, and exploitation and is evident from the perspective of the FFM primarily by low agreeableness. The narcissist is not particularly hostile (which is a facet of neuroticism) or even physically aggressive. Facets of low agreeableness include exploitation, conceit, self-centeredness, and arrogance, which clearly describe the narcissistic person. (p. 48)

In his early formulations of a biosocial learning theory of personality pathology, Millon (1969), provides a different foundation for deriving the behavioral constellation that typifies the narcissistic clinical pattern. Conceived neither in terms of libidinal regressions nor disappointments with formerly omnipotent parents, this formulation is relatively straightforward, tracing the origin of the narcissistic style to the unrealistic overvaluation by parents of the child's worth, that is, creating an enhanced self-image that cannot be sustained in the outer world. Unable to live up to their now internalized parental illusions of self-worth, narcissists will display a wide range of behaviors that typify this personality syndrome.

Criteria for the narcissistic personality were specified in this early work as follows:

The clinical features noted above suggests the following primary characteristics of the passive-independent pattern: elevated affectivity (buoyant, optimistic and carefree), cognitive expansiveness (boundless in imagination; facile in rationalizations), admirable self-image (egotistic; self-assured) and interpersonal exploitation (presumptuous in expectation of special considerations and good will). (p. 263)

The following excerpts present some of the features and diagnostic criteria as drafted by Millon in 1975 to serve as the initial working draft for the DSM-III personality subcommittee:

This pattern is typified by an inflated sense of self-worth, an air of supercilious imperturbability and a benign indifference to shared responsibilities and the welfare of others. A special status for self is taken for granted and there is little awareness that exploitive behavior is inconsiderate and

presumptuous. Achievement deficits and social ir-
responsibilites are justified and sustained by a
boastful arrogance, expansive fantasies, facile rationalizations and frank prevarications. Marked
rebuffs to self-esteem may provoke serious disruptions in the characteristic unruffled composure.
Since adolescence or early adulthood at least 3 of
the following have been present to a notably
greater degree than in most people and were not
limited to discrete periods nor necessarily
prompted by stressful life events.

1. *Inflated self-image (e.g., displays pretentious
   self-assurance and exaggerates achievements
   and talents; often seen by others as egotistic,
   haughty, and arrogant).*

2. *Interpersonal exploitiveness (e.g., divulges
   taking others for granted and using them to
   enhance self and indulge desires; expects
   special favors and status without assuming
   reciprocal responsibilities).*

3. *Cognitive expansiveness (e.g., exhibits immature fantasies and an undisciplined imagination; is minimally constrained by objective
   reality, takes liberties with facts and often
   prevaricates to redeem self-illusion.*

4. *Insouciant temperament (e.g., manifests a
   general air of nonchalance and imperturbability; except when narcissistic confidence is
   shaken, appears coolly unimpressionable or
   buoyantly optimistic).*

5. *Deficient social conscience (e.g., reports
   flouting conventional rules of shared social
   living, viewing them as naive or inapplicable
   to self; reveals a careless disregard for personal integrity and an indifference to the
   rights of others).*

Minor revisions of this draft were introduced
in 1977, resulting in the following recommended
criteria:

A. *Inflated self-esteem (e.g., exaggerates
   achievements and talents; displays pretentious self-assurance).*

B. *Interpersonal exploitiveness (e.g., uses others
   to indulge desires; expects favors without assuming reciprocal responsibilities).*

C. *Expansive imagination (e.g., exhibits immature and undisciplined fantasies; often prevaricates to redeem self-illusions).*

D. *Supercilious imperturbability (e.g., except
   when narcissistic confidence is shaken*

*appears nonchalant and coolly unimpres-
   sionable).*

E. *Deficient social conscience (e.g., flouts conventions of shared social living, reveals disregard for personal integrity and the rights
   of others).*

Modified in certain details, notably in specifying symptoms manifested when confidence in self
is shaken (e.g., rage, humiliation, unworthiness,
and emptiness), the central features of these criteria served to guide the final version.

The DSM-III-R followed the criteria for DSM-
III rather closely; however an item pertaining to
preoccupation with feelings to envy was added.

As noted previously, the ICD-10 does not
include a narcissistic personality disorder in its
taxonomy.

The DSM-IV continues the earlier DSM tradition of diverse diagnostic criteria, and groups the
nine listed attributes into four broad clinical domains. As with previously described personality
disorders, the Interpersonal domain takes precedence with five noted criteria: is interpersonally
exploitive, as evidenced by the habitual taking advantage of others; exhibits a lack of empathy, as
seen in an unwillingness or inability to identify
with the needs and feelings of others; is envious of
others and believes, as well, that others envy him or
her; seeks and requires excessive signs of admiration from others (e.g., fishes for compliments, preoccupied with how favorably one is judged); has
a sense of entitlement (e.g., is unreasonable in
expecting favorable treatment and automatic compliance with one's wishes). Two features within
the Self-image domain are notable: exhibits a
grandiose sense of self-importance by exaggerating
talents and achievements, as well as expecting to be
seen as superior despite limited achievements; believes that one is special and unique, assuming that
only few can understand or be associated with oneself. A notable criterion in the Cognitive domain is
also recorded: preoccupied with fantasies of unlimited success, power, beauty, or romanticized love
(this criterion may be equally indicative of a Regulatory or Ego mechanism). Lastly, a significant Behavioral criterion is noted: displays an arrogant,
snobbish, disdainful attitude, as well as haughty
and patronizing behaviors.

We turn, finally, to the characterization of the
narcissistic personality in accord with Millon's
ecological framework and its evolutionary model
of polarities, as portrayed in Figure 11.1. What is

NARCISSISTIC PROTOTYPE

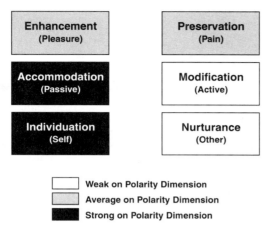

Figure 11.1 Status of the narcissistic personality prototype in accord with the Millon Polarity Model.

most notable in this chart is the primacy of both passive/accommodation and self/individuation in the narcissist's adaptive style. What this translates into is the narcissist's focus on self as the center of one's existence, with a comparable indifference to others (nurturance). Owing to an unusual developmental background, in which others overvalued the narcissists' self-worth by providing attention and tribute unconditionally, they fail to develop the motivation and skills ordinarily necessary to elicit these tributes. To them, merely being who they are is sufficient; one does not have

to do anything, no less achieve, to elicit signs of admiration and high self-esteem. Narcissists are passive, therefore, because they expect the rest of the world to do their bidding without reciprocal efforts.

Whereas narcissists assume that others will favor them without effort on their part, antisocial personalities make no such assumption at all. The active/modifying polarity is preeminent in the antisocial because they feel they have been mistreated and undervalued. They must actively usurp and take from others that which they assume will never be given them; nothing is voluntarily supplied by others. Whereas narcissists expect others to be freely forthcoming, antisocials expect nothing and hence must take what they can.

A useful summary of the major historical contributors is represented in Figure 11.2.

CLINICAL FEATURES

As in previous sections, we will attempt to provide a wide range of perspectives for observing and conceptualizing the traits of the narcissistic personality disorder.

PROTOTYPAL DIAGNOSTIC DOMAINS

This discussion will turn first to the typical characteristics of the narcissistic personality as organized in the eight clinical domains format (see Table 11.1 and Figure 11.3).

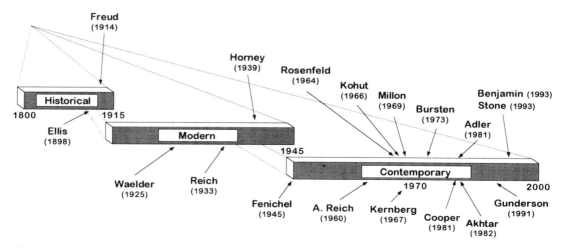

Figure 11.2 Historical review of major contributors to the narcissistic personality disorder.

TABLE 11.1   Clinical Domains of the Narcissistic Prototype

Behavioral Level

(F) Expressively Haughty. Acts in an arrogant, supercilious, pompous, and disdainful manner, flouting conventional rules of shared social living, viewing them as naive or inapplicable to self; reveals a careless disregard for personal integrity and a self-important indifference to the rights of others.

(F) Interpersonally Exploitive. Feels entitled, is unempathic and expects special favors without assuming reciprocal responsibilities; shamelessly takes others for granted and uses them to enhance self and indulge desires.

Phenomenological Level

(F) Cognitively Expansive. Has an undisciplined imagination and exhibits a preoccupation with immature and self-glorifying fantasies of success, beauty, or love; is minimally constrained by objective reality, takes liberties with facts and often lies to redeem self-illusions.

(S) Admirable Self-Image. Believes self to be meritorious, special—if not unique—deserving of great admiration and acting in a grandiose or self-assured manner, often without commensurate achievements; has a sense of high self-worth, despite being seen by others as egotistic, inconsiderate, and arrogant.

(S) Contrived Objects. Internalized representations composed far more than usual of illusory and changing memories of past relationships; unacceptable drives and conflicts are readily refashioned as the need arises, as are others often simulated and pretentious.

Intrapsychic Level

(F) Rationalization Mechanism. Is self-deceptive and facile in devising plausible reasons to justify self-centered and socially inconsiderate behaviors; offers alibis to place oneself in the best possible light, despite evident shortcomings or failures.

(S) Spurious Organization. Morphologic structures underlying coping and defensive strategies tend to be flimsy and transparent, appear more substantial and dynamically orchestrated than they are in fact, regulating impulses only marginally, channeling needs with minimal restraint, and creating an inner world in which conflicts are dismissed, failures are quickly redeemed, and self-pride is effortlessly reasserted.

Biophysical Level

(S) Insouciant Mood. Manifests a general air of nonchalance, imperturbability, and feigned tranquillity; appears coolly unimpressionable or buoyantly optimistic, except when narcissistic confidence is shaken, at which time either rage, shame, or emptiness is briefly displayed.

(F) = Functional domain.
(S) = Structural domain.

NARCISSISTIC PROTOTYPE

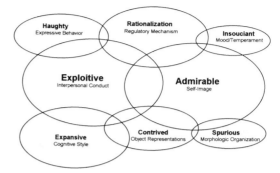

Figure 11.3   Salience of personologic domains in the narcissistic prototype.

Expressive Behavior: Haughty

It is not uncommon for narcissists to act in an arrogant, supercilious, and disdainful manner. There is also a tendency for them to flout conventional rules of shared social living. Viewing reciprocal social responsibilities as being inapplicable to themselves, they show and act in a manner that indicates a disregard for matters of personal integrity and an indifference to the rights of others. When not faced with humiliating or stressful situations, narcissists convey a calm and self-assured quality in their social behavior. Their seemingly untroubled and self-satisfied air is viewed by some as a sign of confident equanimity. Others respond to it much less favorably. To them, these behaviors reflect immodesty, presumptuousness, pretentiousness, and a haughty, snobbish, cocksure, and arrogant way of relating to people. Narcissists appear to lack humility and are overly self-centered and ungenerous. They characteristically, but usually unwittingly, exploit others, take them for granted, and expect others to serve them, without giving much in return. Their self-conceit is viewed by most as unwarranted; it smacks of being "uppity" and superior, without the requisite substance to justify it.

Interpersonal Conduct: Exploitive

As previously noted, narcissists feel entitled, expecting special favors without assuming reciprocal responsibilities. Not only are they unempathic, but they take others for granted, are shameless in the process, and use others to enhance their own personal desires. Unfortunately for them, narcissists must come to terms with living in a world composed of others. No matter how preferred their fantasies may be, they must relate and deal with all the complications and frustrations that real relationships entail. Furthermore, no matter how satisfying it may be to reinforce oneself, it is all the more gratifying to arrange one's environment so that others will contribute their applause as well. True to their fashion, narcissists will seek to accomplish this with minimal effort and reciprocity on their part. In contrast to the dependent personality, who must submit and acquiesce to evoke favorable rewards, or the histrionic, who must perform and be attractive to win praise from others, narcissists are likely to contribute little or nothing in return for the gratifications they seek. In fact, some narcissists assume that others feel "honored" in having a relationship with them, and that others receive as much pleasure in providing them with favors and attention as the narcissist experiences in accepting these tributes.

It should not be surprising that the sheer presumptuousness and confidence exuded by the narcissist often elicits admiration and obedience from others. Furthermore, narcissists typically size up those around them and quickly train those who are so disposed to honor them; for example, narcissists frequently select a dependent mate who will be obeisant, solicitous, and subservient, without expecting anything in return except strength and assurances of fidelity. It is central to narcissists' interpersonal style that good fortune will come to them without reciprocity. Because they feel entitled to get what they wish and have been successful in having others provide them with comforts they have not deserved, narcissists have little reason to discontinue their habitual presumptuous and exploitive behaviors.

Cognitive Style: Expansive

For the most part, narcissists exhibit an undisciplined imagination, and seem preoccupied with immature and self-glorifying fantasies of success, beauty, or romance. Although nondelusional, narcissists are minimally constrained by reality. They also take liberties with facts, embellishing them, even lying, to redeem their illusions about their self-worth. Narcissists are cognitively expansive. They place few limits on either their fantasies or rationalizations, and their imagination is left to run free of the constraints of reality or the views of others. They are inclined to exaggerate their powers, to freely transform failures into successes, to construct lengthy and intricate rationalizations

that inflate their self-worth or justify what they feel is their due, quickly depreciating those who refuse to accept or enhance their self-image.

Self-Image: Admirable

Narcissists feel justified in their claim for special status, and they have little conception that their behaviors may be objectionable, even irrational. Narcissists believe that they are special, if not unique persons that deserve great admiration from others. Quite frequently, they act in a grandiose and self-assured manner, often without commensurate achievements. Although they expect to be seen as meritorious, most narcissists are viewed by others as egotistic, inconsiderate, and arrogant. Their self-image is that they are superior persons, "extraspecial" individuals who are entitled to unusual rights and privileges. This view of their self-worth is fixed so firmly in their minds that they rarely question whether it is valid. Moreover, anyone who fails to respect them is viewed with contempt and scorn.

It is not difficult to see why the behaviors of the narcissist are so gratifying to them. By treating themselves kindly; by imagining their own prowess, beauty, and intelligence; and by reveling in their "obvious" superiorities and talents, they gain, through self-reinforcement, the rewards that most people must struggle to achieve through genuine attainments. Narcissists need depend on no one else to provide gratification; they always have themselves to "keep them warm."

Object-Representations: Contrived

The internalized representations of past experiences are deeply embedded and serve as a template for evaluating new life experiences. For narcissists, these object-representations are composed far more than usual of illusory and changing memories. Problematic past relationships are readily refashioned so as to appear entirely consonant with the narcissists' high sense of self-worth. Unacceptable impulses and deprecatory evaluations are quickly transformed so as to enable these individuals to maintain their preferred and contrived image of both themselves and their past. Fortunately for most narcissists, they were led by their parents to believe that they were invariably lovable and perfect, regardless of what they did and what they thought. Such an idyllic existence could not long endure; the world beyond home is seldom so benign and accepting. As a consequence, the narcissist must transform the less palatable aspects of the past so they are consistent with what the person wishes they were rather than what they were in fact.

Regulatory Mechanisms: Rationalization/Fantasy

What happens if narcissistics are not successful, if they face personal failures and social humiliations? What if realistic events topple them from their illusory world of eminence and superiority? What behaviors do they show and what mechanisms do they employ to salve their wounds?

While they are still confident and self-assured, narcissists deceive themselves with great facility, devising plausible reasons to justify their self-centered and socially inconsiderate behaviors. With an air of arrogance, narcissists are excellent at rationalizing their difficulties, offering alibis to put themselves in the best possible light, despite evident shortcomings or failures on their part.

If rationalizations fail, they will likely become dejected, shamed, and feel a sense of emptiness. Narcissists will have little recourse other than to turn for solace to their fantasies. In contrast to the antisocial personality (described in Chapter 12), most narcissists have not learned to be ruthless, to be competitively assertive and aggressive when frustrated. Neither have most acquired the seductive strategies of the histrionic to solicit rewards and protections. Failing to achieve their aims and at a loss as to what they can do next, they are likely to revert to themselves to provide comfort and consolation. It is at these times that their lifelong talent for imagination takes over. These facile processes enable them to create a fanciful world in which they can redeem themselves and reassert their pride and status. Because narcissists are unaccustomed to self-control and objective reality testing, their powers of imagination have free rein to weave intricate resolutions to their difficulties.

What the narcissist is unable to work out through fantasy is simply repressed, put out of mind and kept from awareness. As noted previously, narcissists invent alibis, excuses, and "proofs" that seem plausible and consistent, and convince them of their continued stature and perfection. Flimsily substantiated rationalizations are offered, but with a diminished air of confidence and authority. However, narcissists may never have learned to be skillful at public deception; they usually said and did what they liked without a care for what others thought. Their poorly conceived rationalizations may, therefore, fail to bring relief and, more seriously, may evoke scrutiny and deprecating comments from others. At these times, narcissists may be pushed to the point of employing projection as a defense, as well as to begin constructing what may become rather primitive delusions.

Morphologic Organization: Spurious

Narcissists suffer few conflicts; their past has supplied them, perhaps too well, with high expectations and encouragement. As a result, they are inclined to trust others and to feel confident that matters will work out well for them. As will be detailed in a later section, this sanguine outlook on life is founded on an unusual set of early experiences that only rarely are duplicated in later life.

The structural organization of narcissists' inner world for dealing with life tends to be quite flimsy and transparent to the discerning observer. From a surface view, one would assume that their personality organization is more substantial and dynamically orchestrated than it is in fact. Owing to the misleading nature of their early experiences (i.e., narcissists really did not have to do much to make the world work for them), these individuals have never developed the inner skills necessary to regulate their impulses adequately, to channel their needs skillfully, or to acquire strategies for resolving conflicts, overcoming failures, and regaining a genuine sense of competence after problematic experiences.

Reality bears down heavily at times. Even the routine demands of everyday life may be viewed as annoying incursions by narcissists. Such responsibilities are experienced as demeaning, for they intrude upon the narcissist's cherished illusion of self as almost godlike. Alibis to avoid pedestrian tasks are easily mustered because narcissists are convinced that what they believe must be true and what they wish must be right. Not only do they display considerable talent in rationalizing their social inconsiderateness, but they utilize a variety of other intrapsychic mechanisms with equal facility. However, because they reflect minimally on what others think, their defensive maneuvers are transparent, a poor camouflage to a discerning eye. This failure to bother dissembling more thoroughly also contributes to their being seen as cocksure and arrogant.

Unable to disentangle themselves from lies and inconsistencies, and driven by their need to maintain their illusion of superiority, they may begin to turn against others, accusing the latter of their own deceptions, their own selfishness, and their own irrationalities. It is at these, not very typical, times that the fragility and pathology of the narcissist becomes clearly evident. "Breakdowns" in the defensive structure of this personality, however, are not too common. More typically, the exploitive behaviors and intrapsychic maneuvers of narcissists prove highly adaptive and provide them with the means of thwarting serious or prolonged periods of dejection or decompensation.

Mood/Temperament: Insouciant

Roused by the facile workings of their imagination, narcissists experience a pervasive sense of well-being in their everyday life, a buoyancy of mood and an optimism of outlook—*except* when their sense of superiority has been punctured. Normally, however, affect, though based often on their semi-grandiose distortions of reality, is generally relaxed, if not cheerful and carefree. There is a general air of nonchalance, an imperturbability, a feigned tranquillity. Should the balloon be burst, however, there is a rapid turn to either an edgy irritability and annoyance with others or to repeated bouts of dejection that are characterized by feeling humiliated and empty. Shaken by these circumstances, the narcissist is likely to briefly display a vacillation between rage, shame, and feelings of emptiness.

PROTOTYPAL VARIANTS

Narcissistic features as we have conceived them can be found in both normal and childhood forms. No less varied are the several ways in which this personality style manifests itself in adult disorders. We will turn next to these variations of the prototypal narcissist.

Normal Styles

With the exception of the unusually well-to-do and those close to regal stature, the narcissistic personality style may be considered to be a pattern of behavior unique to the late 20th century. And even during this period, as writers such as Lasch (1978) have noted, it may be more or less distinctive to the upper and upper middle social classes of the United States. As conferences of an international character have demonstrated, narcissistic styles are not prevalent among clinical populations in most nations; the failure of the ICD-10 to include the narcissistic disorder attests to the preceding.

Nevertheless, in narcissistic societies such as ours, the center or fulcrum of life's activities have increasingly been focused on the achievement of personal gratification and self-enhancement. The descriptions that follow reflect this "normal" style of functioning; the body of this chapter comprises more severe extremes of this style. Portraying the normal narcissist as possessing "a self-confident style" Oldham and Morris (1990) write:

Self-confident individuals stand out. They're the leaders, the shining lights, the attention-getters in their public or private spheres. Theirs is a quality born of self-regard, self-respect, self-certainty—all those self words that denote a faith in oneself and a commitment to one's self-styled purpose . . . Many of them have the charisma to attract plenty of others to their goals. . . . Hitch on to their bandwagons, and you'll be well rewarded. (p. 79)

The following characterization, termed the "Asserting" pattern in Millon et al. (1994), portrays a rather similar picture to the preceding, stressing again the competitive and self-assured elements of this personality style:

An interpersonal boldness, stemming from a belief in themselves and their talents, characterizes these persons. Competitive, ambitious, and self-assured, they naturally assume positions of leadership, act in a decisive and unwavering manner, and expect others to recognize their special qualities and cater to them. Beyond being self-confident, they are audacious, clever, and persuasive, having sufficient charm to win others over to their own causes and purposes. Problematic in this regard may be their lack of social reciprocity and their sense of entitlement—their assumption that what they wish for is their due. On the other hand, their ambitions often succeed, and they typically prove to be effective leaders. (p. 32)

Given our dominant cultural orientation toward self-enhancement, it is often difficult to determine which self-focused traits indicate a narcissistic disorder and which are merely adaptive styles that fit societal modes. Where the line should be drawn between self-confidence and healthy self-esteem versus an artificially inflated and empty sense of self-worth is not always an easy task. The healthy narcissist should demonstrate, in addition to the usual characteristics of the personality type, social concerns and interpersonal empathy, a genuine interest in the ideas and feelings of others, and a willingness to acknowledge one's personal role in problematic interpersonal relationships. Where the disorder is present, we see a persistent insensitivity to others, a general social exploitiveness, and lack of reciprocity in everyday relationships.

Childhood Syndromes

The literature on narcissism has grown considerably in the past two decades. Yet the ICD-10 has not seen fit to include the narcissistic personality as a disorder in its most recent official classification because the disorder has not been judged prevalent enough outside the United States to justify a separate designation. Similarly, and despite the theoretical literature growth, little has been written about disturbances of a narcissistic variety in the research literature. Depending on one's orientation regarding the syndrome (i.e., whether one adheres to a compensatory narcissistic picture or a socially learned characterization), the origins and nature of the disorder can be quite disparate in its characterizations.

Those who follow the general psychoanalytic paradigm would be disposed to characterize the young narcissist as a troubled and rejected child, who has had to turn to self for affection and approval rather than be dependent on others for such admiration. Conversely, those disposed to a social learning model of narcissism would portray family environments as overly indulgent and admiring. Will the real narcissistic child please stand up? Despite the forgoing pessimistic comment, there is no reason to doubt that there are children who are obnoxiously self-indulgent and interpersonally exploitive, "little narcissists." Whether such youngsters can be described in early childhood as evidencing a pathology in their psychic makeup and behavior is questionable. At this early stage, an abundance of parental indulgence and care can set the stage for a high sense of self-esteem and confident social relationships. On the other hand, children who are abused and rejected and, hence, must turn to themselves for emotional nurturance, are, in our estimation, not likely to develop a narcissistic adult pattern. Rather, they are more prone, with this history, to become either antisocial, or avoidant, the former owing to their anger and desire to claim that which is their due, the latter as a protective withdrawal against anticipated further assault and deprecation.

Despite the foregoing commentary, there are distinguished psychoanalysts, such as P. Kernberg (1989), who follow the fundamental model of narcissistic disorder in accordance with the analytic interpretive framework. Thus, she notes that children with narcissistic disorders exhibit many pathological features found in adults with this disorder. In addition, these children demonstrate impaired peer interactions, pathology in play, and preoccupations with self-image. Also, she notes that these children often seek out friends who are not notably attractive, a means of enhancing their own comparative self-esteem, as well as a method for gaining attention and maintaining control.

Nevertheless, the reader may wish to look into the discussions on childhood syndromes in the avoidant (Chapter 7) and antisocial (Chapter 12) to gain a perspective on childhood disorders with problematic early experiences and their developmental consequences.

Adult Subtypes

Clinical experience and research employing the Millon Clinical Multiaxial Inventory (Millon, 1977, 1987c, 1994a) suggest several personality blends that incorporate distinct narcissistic features. A review of the developmental background of other narcissistic personalities contributes further to the variants described in the following paragraphs.

The Unprincipled Narcissist

The *unprincipled narcissist* has been seen more often these past two or three decades in drug rehabilitation programs, centers for youth offenders, and in jails and prisons. Although these individuals often are successful in society, keeping their activities just within the boundaries of the law, they enter into clinical treatment rather infrequently.

The behavior of these narcissists is characterized by an arrogant sense of self-worth, an indifference to the welfare of others, and a fraudulent and intimidating social manner. There is a desire to exploit others, to expect special recognitions and considerations without assuming reciprocal responsibilities. A deficient social conscience is evident in the tendency to flout conventions, to engage in actions that raise questions of personal integrity, and to disregard the rights of others. Achievement deficits and social irresponsibilities are justified by expansive fantasies and frank prevarications. Descriptively, we may characterize this narcissist as devoid of a superego, that is, evidencing an unscrupulous, amoral, and deceptive approach to relationships with others. More than merely disloyal and exploitive, these narcissists may be found among society's con men and charlatans, many of whom are vindictive and contemptuous of their victims. The features that are clearly seen in the unprincipled narcissist support the conclusion that these individuals are an admixture of both narcissistic and antisocial personality characteristics.

The unprincipled narcissist evidences a rash willingness to risk harm and is notably fearless in the face of threats and punitive action. Malicious tendencies are projected outward, precipitating frequent personal and family difficulties, as well as occasional legal entanglements. Vengeful gratification is often obtained by humiliating and dominating others. These narcissists operate as if they have no principles other than exploiting others for their personal gain. Lacking a genuine sense of guilt and possessing little social conscience, they are opportunists and charlatans who enjoy the process of swindling others. In a game narcissists enjoy playing, they outwit others and hold them in contempt owing to the ease with which they can be seduced. Relationships survive only as long as the narcissist has something to gain. People are dropped with no thought to the anguish they may experience as a consequence of the narcissist's careless and irresponsible behaviors.

In many ways, the unprincipled narcissist is similar to the *disingenuous histrionic*. They share a devious and guileful style, plotting and scheming in their calculations to manipulate others. However, the disingenuous histrionic continues to pursue the strong need for attention and love, characteristics not present in the narcissist where there is a basic self-centeredness and an indifference to the attitudes and reactions of others. The unprincipled narcissist preys on the weak and vulnerable, enjoying their dismay and anger; the histrionic, by contrast, seeks to hold the respect and affection of those they dismiss in the pursuit of love and admiration.

Unprincipled narcissists display an indifference to truth that, if brought to their attention, is likely to elicit an attitude of nonchalant indifference. They are skillful in the ways of social influence, are capable of feigning an air of justified innocence, and are adept in deceiving others with charm and glibness. Lacking any deep feelings of loyalty, they may successfully scheme beneath a veneer of politeness and civility. Their principal orientation is that of outwitting others, getting power and exploiting them "before they do it to you." They often carry a chip-on-the shoulder attitude, a readiness to attack those who are distrusted

or who can be used as scapegoats. A number of these narcissists attempt to present an image of cool strength, acting tough, arrogant, and fearless. To prove their courage, they may invite danger and punishment. But punishment only verifies their unconscious recognition that they deserve to be punished. Rather than having a deterrent effect, it only reinforces their exploitive and unprincipled behaviors.

The Amorous Narcissist

The distinctive feature of this narcissistic personality type is an erotic and seductive orientation, a building up of one's self-worth by engaging members of the opposite gender in the game of sexual temptation. There is an indifferent conscience, an aloofness to truth and social responsibility that, if brought to the *amorous narcissist's* attention, elicits an attitude of nonchalant innocence. Though totally self-oriented, these individuals are facile in the ways of social seduction, often feign an air of dignity and confidence, and are rather skilled in deceiving others with their clever glibness. These narcissists are skillful in enticing, bewitching, and tantalizing the needy and the naive. Although indulging their hedonistic desires, as well as pursuing numerous beguiling objects at the same time, they are strongly disinclined to become involved in a genuine intimacy. Rather than investing their efforts in one appealing person, they seek to acquire a coterie of amorous objects, invariably lying and swindling as they weave from one pathological relationship to another. The qualities just outlined are strongly suggestive of the observation that these narcissistic types possess numerous characteristics that are primary among histrionic personalities.

Although a reasonably good capacity for sexual athletics sustains the vanity of many individuals, narcissists or not, the need to repeatedly demonstrate one's sexual prowess is a preeminent obsession among amorous subtypes. Among these personalities are those whose endless pursuit of sexual conquests is fulfilled as effectively and frequently as their bewitching style "promises." Others, however, talk well, place their lures and baits extremely well—until they reach the bedroom door; maneuvering and seduction is done with great aplomb, but performance falls short. For the most part, the sexual exploits of the amorous narcissist are brief, lasting from one afternoon to only a few weeks.

Some amorous narcissists are fearful of the opposite sex, afraid that their pretensions and ambitions will be exposed and found wanting. Their sexual banter and seductive pursuits are merely empty maneuvers to overcome deeper feelings of inadequacy. Although they seem to desire the affections of a warm and intimate relationship, they typically feel restless and unsatisfied when they find it. Having won others over, they seem to need to continue their pursuit. It is the act of exhibitionistically being seductive, and hence gaining in narcissistic stature, that compels. The achievement of ego gratification terminates for a moment, but it must be pursued again and again.

Not infrequently, amorous narcissists leave behind them a trail of outrageous acts such as swindling, sexual excesses, pathological lying, and fraud. This disregard for truth and the talent for exploitation and deception are often neither hostile nor malicious in intent. These characteristics appear to derive from an attitude of narcissistic omnipotence and self-assurance, a feeling that the implicit rules of human relationships do not apply to them and that they are above the responsibilities of shared living. As with the basic narcissistic pattern, individuals of this subtype go out of their way to entice and inveigle the unwary among the opposite sex, remain coolly indifferent to the welfare of those whom they bewitch, whom they have used to enhance and indulge their hedonistic whims and erotic desires.

Caring little to shoulder genuine social responsibilities and unwilling to change their seductive ways, amorous narcissists refuse to "buckle down" in a serious relationship and expend effort to prove their worth. Never having learned to control their fantasies or to be concerned with matters of social integrity, they will maintain their bewitching ways, if need be by deception, fraud, lying, and by charming others through craft and wit. Rather than apply their talents toward the goal of tangible achievements or genuine relationships, they will devote their energies to construct intricate lies, to cleverly exploit others, and to slyly contrive ways to extract from others what they believe is their due. Untroubled by conscience and needing nourishment for their overinflated self-image, they will fabricate stories that enhance their worth and thereby succeed in seducing others into supporting their excesses. Criticism and punishment are likely to prove of no avail since these narcissists quickly dismisses them as the product of jealous inferiors.

The Compensatory Narcissist

Compensatory narcissists deviate in a fundamental way from other narcissistic subtypes as well as from the prototypal narcissist. The origins that undergird their overtly narcissistic behaviors derive from an underlying sense of insecurity and weakness, rather than from genuine feelings of self-confidence and high self-esteem. Beneath their surface pseudo-confidence, the posture they exhibit publicly, this narcissist is driven by forces similar to those who overtly display characteristics more akin to the negativistic and avoidant personalities.

The compensatory narcissist represents patients who are labeled "narcissistic" by those in the psychoanalytic community in that they have suffered wounds in early life. Many have been exposed to experiences akin to the negativistic, avoidant, and antisocial types. In essence, these personalities seek to make up or compensate for early life deprivations. They are similar to the antisocial, but compensatory narcissists seek to fill their sense of emptiness by creating an illusion of superiority and by building up an image of high self-worth, rather than by usurping the power and control that others possess or by accumulating material possessions.

Compensatory narcissists need others to fulfill their strivings for prestige. Their motive is to enhance their self-esteem, to obtain and to store up within the self all forms of recognition that will "glorify" their public persona. Much to the annoyance of others, these narcissists "act drunk" as they recount their successes and record for others to acknowledge all forms of even minor public recognition. In effect, these narcissists actively worship themselves; they are their own god. As this inflated and overvalued sense of self rises evermore highly, narcissists look down on others as devalued plebeians. More and more, they acquire a deprecatory attitude in which the achievements of others are ridiculed and degraded.

Life is a search for pseudo-status, an empty series of aspirations that serves no purpose other than self-enhancement. This search for these vacuous goals may begin to run wild, resting from its very foundation on an unsure sense of self-value that has but little contact with tangible achievements. Instead of living their own lives, they pursue the leading role in a false and imaginary theater. Nothing they achieve in this pursuit relates much to reality. Their tenacious aspirations for glory may impress the naive and the grateful, but they possess little of a genuine or objective character.

Should these pursuits lose their grounding in reality, becoming more and more an imaginary world, peopled with self and others as in a dream, compensatory narcissists begin to deceive themselves in a manner not unlike the *fanatic paranoid*. If we draw a line between these two personality subtypes, we would see that the compensatory narcissist strives for prestige in a world composed of real people. When reality recedes and fantasy comes more to the fore, we see the fanatic who acts out aspirations in solitude. One comes to the stage in front of others, be it in the form of exaggeration and boasting; the other stands alone in an inner world, a "pseudo-community," as Cameron (1963) has phrased it, where imagination has substantially replaced reality.

Owing to the insecure foundations on which their narcissistic displays are grounded, compensatory narcissists are "hypervigilant," to use a term employed by Gabbard (1994). What is meant here is they are exquisitely sensitive to how others react to them, watching and listening carefully for any critical judgment, and feeling slighted by every sign of disapproval. Although not delusional, as are their paranoid counterparts, these narcissists are prone to feel shamed and humiliated, especially hyperanxious and vulnerable to the judgments of others. They "know" that they are frauds at some level, pretenders who seek to convey impressions of being of higher standing than they know is truly the case. Despite this awareness, they do not act shy and hesitant, as would seem likely. Instead, they submerge and cover up their deep sense of inadequacy and deficiency by pseudo-arrogance and superficial grandiosity.

The Elitist Narcissist

Reich (1949) captured the essential qualities of what we are terming the *elitist narcissist* when he described the "phallic-narcissist" character as a self-assured, arrogant, and energetic person "often impressive in his bearing. . . . and are ill-suited to subordinate positions among the rank and file." As with the compensatory narcissist, elitist narcissists are more taken with their inflated self-image than with their actual self. Both narcissistic types create a false facade that bears minimal resemblance to the person they really are. Compensatory narcissists, however, know at some level that they are a fraud in fact, and that they put forth an appearance different from the way they are. By contrast, elitist narcissists, perhaps the purest variant of the narcissistic style, are deeply convinced of their superior self-image although it is grounded on few realistic achievements. To elitists, the appearance of things is perceived as objective reality; their inflated self-image is their intrinsic substance. Only when these illusory

elements to their self-worth are seriously undermined will they be able to recognize, perhaps even to acknowledge, their deeper shortcomings.

As a consequence of their sublime self-confidence, elitists feel quite secure in their apparent superiority. They achieve this in part by capturing the attentions of others and making them take note of the supposed extraordinary qualities. Most everything these narcissists do is intended to persuade others of their specialness, rather than to put their efforts into acquiring genuine qualifications and attainments. They feel privileged and empowered by virtue of whatever class status and pseudo-achievements they may have attained. Most are upwardly mobile, seeking to cultivate their sense of specialness and personal advantage by associating with those who may possess genuine achievements and recognition. Many elitists will create comparisons between themselves and others, turning personal relationships into public competitions and contests. Unrivaled in the pursuit of becoming "number one," the grounds for this goal are not determined by genuine accomplishments, but by the degree to which they can convince others of its reality, false though its substance may be.

As just described, many narcissistic elitists are social climbers who seek to cultivate their image and social luster by virtue of those with whom they are affiliated. To them, it is not the old chestnut of "guilt by association," but rather that of "status by association." Idolizing public recognition, narcissists of this type get caught in the game of one-upmanship, which they strive vigorously to win, at least comparatively. Status and self-promotion are all that matter to narcissistic elitists. To be celebrated, even famous, is what drives them, rather than to achieve substantive accomplishments. In whatever sphere of activity matters to them, they invest their efforts to advertise themselves, to brag about achievements, substantive or fraudulent, to make anything they have done appear to be "wonderful," better than what others may have done, and better than it may actually be.

By making excessive claims about themselves, these narcissists expose a great divide between their actual selves and their self-presentations. In contrast to many narcissists who recognize this disparity, elitists are convinced and absolute in their belief in self. Rather than backing off, withdrawing, or feeling shame when slighted or responded to with indifference, elitist narcissists speed up their efforts all the more, acting increasingly and somewhat erratically to exhibit deeds and awards worthy of high esteem. They may present grandiose illusions about their powers and future status; they may puff up their limited accomplishments; they may seek competitively to outdo those who have achieved in reality.

By the persistence and social intrusiveness of their behaviors, narcissistic elitists may begin to alienate themselves from others, and the admiration they seek. Insulating themselves from signs of painful indifference and psychic injury, they may try to distance or screen out negativistic and judgmental responses. Some may become overtly hostile, acquiring characteristics of the *querulous paranoid,* quickly losing the remaining elements of their former charm and cleverness, becoming increasingly contemptuous of those whom they feel are treating them so shabbily. Still believing themselves to be special persons, these elitists see little need to listen or follow the dictates of anyone else. They may begin to react with outright anger and irritability, convinced that they need no one. As these self-protective beliefs and actions gain in their defensive and negative tone, the elitist narcissist comes to be seen as an undesirable and embarrassing person, a touchy and inflated character whom others wish to shun.

COMORBID DISORDERS AND SYNDROMES

Following the sequence established in the prior chapters, attention turns next to the major Axis I and Axis II syndromes that covary with the personality under review. Note again that where personalities share a vulnerability to the same disorder, each manifests the characteristic symptoms in a somewhat distinctive way.

Axis II Comorbidities

As can be seen in Figure 11.4, several personality disorders often covary with the narcissistic (NAR) pattern. Most notable among these are the antisocial (ATS) and histrionic (HIS) variants. Also listed are covariations seen with the sadistic (SAD), paranoid (PAR), and negativistic (NEG) personality types. Features of these comorbid personalities and the basic narcissistic pattern often play a significant part in producing several of the Adult Subtypes described previously.

Axis I Comorbidities

Narcissistic personalities display a tendency to several of the major clinical syndromes listed in

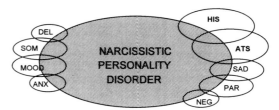

Figure 11.4 Comorbidity between narcissistic personality disorder and other DSM Axis I and Axis II disorders.

DSM-IV. A number of these will be noted in the following paragraphs.

Mood Syndromes (MOOD). *Dysthymic* disorder is perhaps the most common symptom disorder seen among narcissists. Faced with repeated failures and social humiliations, and unable to find some way of living up to their inflated self-image, narcissists may succumb to uncertainty and dissatisfaction, losing self-confidence and convincing themselves that they are, and perhaps have always been, fraudulent and phony. Kernberg (1975) has described this process of self-disillusionment well:

For them, to accept the breakdown of the illusion of grandiosity means to accept the dangerous, lingering awareness of the depreciated self—the hungry, empty, lonely primitive self surrounded by a world of dangerous, sadistically frustrating and revengeful objects. (p. 311)

Recounting the psychic consequences of the loss of stature in a national political figure, Kernberg (1975) described the steps of decompensation into a *major depression* as follows:

He became depressed and developed deep feelings of defeat and humiliation accompanied by fantasies in which his political opponents were gloating with satisfaction over his defeat. His depression diminished. He went into retirement, but gradually devaluated the areas of political science in which he had been an expert. This was a narcissistic depreciation of that in which he was no longer triumphant, which brought about a general loss of interest in professional, cultural and intellectual matters. His primary areas of professional and intellectual interests no longer seemed exciting and reminded him again of his failure. . . .

He experienced an increasing sense of estrangement which finally evolved into the recurrence of a

now severe, chronic depression, with a predomi-nance of impotent rage over mourning processes. *(pp. 311–312)*

Because depression is not experienced as con-sonant with the narcissist's self-image, it rarely endures for extended periods unless the psychic blow is irreparable, as in the case just described. Most typically, we observe rapid shifts in the character of the depressive symptomatology as narcissists succumb at first to their feelings of ap-athy and worthlessness, and then abruptly seek to retrieve their grandiose self-confidence and re-assert themselves. At one time, they may express their depressive mood dramatically; at other times, in a cranky and irritable manner; and at yet another, in a dreamy, vague, and philosophically abstract way. Not untypically, narcissists will uti-lize their mood as a rationalization for their in-creasing indecisiveness and failures. Here, their complaints are likely to be colored with subtle ac-cusations and claims that others have not sup-ported or cared for them, thus fostering their growing sense of futility and ineffectuality. As is more characteristic of the negativistic personal-ity, narcissists may vacillate for a brief period be-tween anxious futility and self-depreciation at one time and a bitter discontent and demanding attitude the next. A struggle ensues between vent-ing and curtailing the rage felt toward others sim-ply for being witness to their shame and humiliation. Moody and pessimistic complaints are not only genuinely expressed but are a useful outlet for mounting resentments. Moreover, de-pressively toned hostility often serves to intimi-date others, and it thereby functions as a form of retribution or vengeance for their failure to rescue the narcissist from his or her own deficiencies.

Anxiety Syndromes (ANX). Narcissistic person-alities do not characteristically exhibit anxiety disorders. However, anxiety may be manifest for brief periods until the patient cloaks or restrains the overt expression of these embarrassing feel-ings. The image of being weak conveyed by a pub-lic display of anxiety is anathema to narcissists. Rarely is it overt, tending instead to be neutral-ized or camouflaged by other symptoms such as touchy irritability and sudden resentments. Anxi-ety precipitants in narcissists usually relate to shame and failure such as might arise in a public disparity between their illusion of superiority and the specifics of reality.

Somatoform Syndromes (SOM). There is a rea-sonable likelihood that narcissists will exhibit *hypochondriacal* symptoms following the shame of a humiliating defeat or embarrassment. Unable to solicit the tribute they expect from others, nar-cissists become their own source of solicitude by nurturing their wounds symbolically. Their hypochondriacal concerns are a form of self-min-istering, an act of providing the affection and at-tention they can no longer obtain from others. As Fenichel (1945) has stated regarding hypochon-driasis: "Narcissistic withdrawal means a transfer of libido from object representations to organ rep-resentations" (p. 261). Not to be overlooked also among the secondary gains of these symptoms is their use as a rationalization for failures and shortcomings. Discomforting though it may be to admit to any frailty, it impugns narcissists' competence somewhat less if they can ascribe their "defeats" to a physical illness rather than to a self-implicating psychological shortcoming. Ad-ditionally, physical complaints are often a useful disguise for discharging anger and resentment. Discontent over their own inadequacies and too ashamed to express anger directly, narcissists may cloak their resentments by using their physical impairments as an excuse. Thus, they may become "household tyrants," not only by cre-ating guilt in others for the failure to attend to the needs of a "sick person" but by demanding that their claims for special status be instituted once again.

Delusional Syndromes (DEL). Under conditions of unrelieved adversity and failure narcissists may decompensate into paranoid disorders. Owing to their excessive use of fantasy mecha-nisms, they are disposed to misinterpret events and to construct delusional beliefs. Unwilling to accept constraints on their independence and un-able to accept the viewpoints of others, narcissists may isolate themselves from the corrective ef-fects of shared thinking. Alone, they may rumi-nate and weave their beliefs into a network of fanciful and totally invalid suspicions. Among narcissists, delusions often take form after a seri-ous challenge or setback has upset their image of superiority and omnipotence. They tend to exhibit compensatory grandiosity and jealousy delusions in which they reconstruct reality to match the image they are unable or unwilling to give up. Delusional systems may also develop as a result of having felt betrayed and humiliated. Here we may see the rapid unfolding of persecutory delusions and an arrogant grandiosity characterized by verbal attacks and bombast. Rarely physically abusive, anger among narcissists usually takes the form of oral vituperation and argumentativeness. This may be seen in a flow of irrational and caustic comments in which others are upbraided and denounced as stupid and beneath contempt. These onslaughts usually have little objective justification, are often colored by delusions, and may be directed in a wild, hit-or-miss fashion in which the narcissist lashes out at those who have failed to acknowledge the exalted status in which he or she demands to be seen.

DIFFERENTIAL DIAGNOSTIC SIGNS

Differentiations are not an issue between narcissism and Axis I syndromes. Short-lived hypomanic episodes often convey the confident ebullience frequently seen among narcissistic personalities, but narcissists lack the frenetic and driven quality of the manic disorder. Where they coexist, both may properly be diagnosed. Problems may arise owing to the frequent overlap of narcissistic and histrionic, antisocial, sadistic, and paranoid Axis II disorders.

The major sphere of confusion that may have some clinical import lies in differentiating narcissistic from *histrionic* personalities; as noted earlier, these patterns frequently merge into a single diagnostic blend. The major points of differentiation were drawn in Chapter 10 and need but minimal repetition here. Essentially, the distinguishing feature of narcissists is their desire to avoid dependence on others and to view themselves as "cool" and "above" the responsibilities of shared living. By contrast, histrionic personalities, though equally needy of recognition and tribute, can be warmly expressive, often seek close (if fleeting) relationships, and willingly subscribe to the conventions and fashions of social life, if these give promise of bringing the approval and attentions they desire.

Much has been written in the recent literature seeking to clarify similarities and differences between narcissistic and *borderline* personalities. This preoccupation reflects confusions that exist in the field concerning what these new syndromes constitute in the first place. As presented in contemporary psychoanalytic literature, both syndromes are formulated often as obscure matrices of intangible metapsychological concepts that lack clear clinical referents, often leading the less experienced clinician to conclude that they are quite similar and difficult to disentangle. No difficulty of this sort will exist among readers who review each set of diagnostic criteria spelled out in the DSM-IV. In brief, the similarities between these syndromes are minuscule, and each is clearly delineated and comprehensible, even to the clinical novice.

Differential problems may be faced in distinguishing narcissistic from *paranoid* personalities. In many cases, overlap may be considerable. According to Millon (1969) and Meissner (1979), paranoid personalities are frequently, though not invariably, advanced or more severe variants of the narcissistic personality, reflecting the progressive deterioration of formerly adaptive functions. More is said concerning this process of decompensation in later chapters. To this author, it appears that recording both diagnoses, when appropriate, will convey both the long-term narcissistic personality structure and the more recently evolved paranoid pattern to which the individual has deteriorated.

Difficulties arise in differentiating narcissistic and *antisocial* personalities, owing to their frequent comorbidity and similar characteristics. Both are independent, oriented to meet their own needs before those of others. However, narcissists passively exploit others, often gently and indirectly seducing them into viewing them as special and deserving. By contrast, antisocials are more obviously deceptive and antagonistic, actively usurping the powers that others possess, as well as the material gains they can provide for the antisocial.

Sadistic personalities exhibit some features akin to the narcissist in that both attempt to dominate others and to make them pay homage to their status. However, the narcissist does not manifest the impulsivity, the destructiveness, and cruel disdain for others that are typically seen among sadists.

ASSESSING THE NARCISSISTIC: A CASE STUDY

The response patterns of the narcissistic personality on several of the most frequently used clinical instruments will be briefly described before we present a formal case history and its associated MCMI-III clinical profile and interpretation.

The protocols produced by narcissistic personalities on the Rorschach tend to exhibit two contrasting patterns, the first being quite extensive in the number of responses given, the second rather limited in number. Narcissists who feel valued by the attending psychologist, confident in the extent to which the clinician will appraise them, will "show off," providing a high number of responses, although not notably detailed in their specificity. A high proportion of W responses is typical, each, however, of modest quality and of grandiose scope. This poor-quality response style is also likely to be seen in their M, FC and CF responses (e.g., color responses are of relatively poor or inadequate form). Special emphasis may be given to human movement responses, especially those that focus on attractive traits, either physical or mental in quality. When narcissistic individuals feel that the administering clinician is treating them "like everyone else," they are likely to provide the minimum number of responses they judge adequate to the task. Under these circumstances, there is a tendency to give a higher proportion than usual of F responses, with descriptive features voiced in a rather perfunctory manner.

The TAT cards elicit a similarly divided response pattern; some narcissists are expansive and others are constrained. Story themes that are distinctive to the narcissist tend to focus on the impressive achievements of the central characters, especially when these are of the respondent's gender. Content, however, tends to be rather skimpy in detail, except for the glory in which the character is portrayed. Not uncommonly, in an attempt to impress the clinician, side jokes and "shocking" comments are voiced, usually tangential to the themes presented in the stories.

The MMPI provides a number of suggestive guidelines for identifying narcissists. Scale 4 is often the most elevated, with either Scale 2 or Scale 9 as secondary elements. When Scale 2 is secondarily elevated, we are likely to see a narcissist whose sense of self-assurance has recently been undermined, which deflates self-esteem and provokes feelings of depression. When Scale 9 is part of the configuration—and if Scale 6 is also high—we are likely to be recording a strongly defensive attitude on the part of the narcissist, who is seeking to counteract criticisms and assaults upon self-worth. Thus, this latter configuration suggests a narcissist's effort to overcome signs of failure and weakness, as well as to possibly

indicate the early phases of paranoid suspiciousness and irritability.

CASE 11.1

Larry G., Age 35, Writer, Married, One Child

Larry came to the attention of a therapist when his wife insisted that they seek marital counseling. According to her, Larry was "selfish, ungiving, and preoccupied with his work." Everything at home had to "revolve about him, his comfort, moods, and desires, no one else's." She claimed that he contributed nothing to the marriage, except a rather meager income. He shirked all "normal" responsibilities and kept "throwing chores in her lap," and she was "getting fed up with being the chief cook and bottle-washer . . . tired of being his mother and sleep-in maid."

On the positive side, Larry's wife felt that he was basically a "good-natured guy with talent and intelligence." But this wasn't enough. She wanted a husband, someone with whom she could share things. In contrast, he wanted, according to her, "a mother, not a wife"; he didn't want "to grow up . . . he didn't know how to give affection, only to take it when he felt like it, nothing more, nothing less."

Larry presented a picture of an affable, self-satisfied, and somewhat disdainful young man. He was employed as a part-time ghost writer, but looked forward to his evenings and weekends when he could turn his attention to serious writing. He claimed that he had to devote all of his spare time and energies to "fulfill himself," to achieve expression in his creative work. His wife knew of his preoccupation well before they were married; in fact, it was his self-dedication and promise as a writer that initially attracted her to him. As Larry put it, "What is she complaining about . . . isn't this what she wanted, what she married me for?"

Hidden until the end of an extended series of clinical interviews were features of Larry's behavior that were not divulged in earlier phases of treatment. Alcoholism was an issue of increasing importance in his work, but especially in his relationship with his wife. He had participated in Alcoholics Anonymous, with no success. During a number of his alcoholic sprees (he would often disappear for several days), Larry would return home and abuse his wife, attacking her primarily verbally, although occasionally physically, as well. Larry accused his wife of being the cause of his failures as an author, of having seduced him into marrying her, of setting obstacles in his way, and not valuing the work that he showed her. Thus his narcissism was punctuated by explosive sadistic acts in which he would berate and deprecate everything that his wife had done. Following these outbursts, he would be contrite and sorrowful, stating that he was "terribly sorry" and would "never do that again."

Exploration of Larry's early history provided the following. Larry was an only child, born after his mother had suffered many miscarriages; his parents had given up hope of ever having a child until he came along, "much to their surprise and pleasure." His parents doted over him—he never assumed any household or personal responsibilities. He was given music and art lessons, discovered to have considerable talent in both and given free rein to indulge these talents to the exclusion of everything else. He was an excellent student won several scholarships and received much praise for his academic and writing aptitudes. To his family, he was "a genius at work"; life at home centered entirely around him.

Socially, Larry recalled being "pretty much of an isolate," staying home "drawing and reading, rather than going outside with the other kids." He felt he was well liked by his peers, but they may have thought him to be a "bit pompous and superior." He liked being thought of this way, and felt that he was "more talented and brighter" than most. He remained a "loner" until he met his wife.

His relationships with his occasional co-workers and social acquaintances were pleasant and satisfying, but he admitted that most people viewed him as a "bit self-centered, cold and snobbish." He recognized that he did not know how to share his thoughts and feelings with others, that he was much more interested in himself than in them and that perhaps he always had "preferred the pleasure" of his own company to that of others.

Figure 11.5 outlines the MCMI-III profile of a narcissistic personality style; it is followed by a presentation of segments of the associated interpretive report.

INTERPRETIVE SUMMARY

The MCMI-III profile indicates that this is an egocentric man who may be identified by an inflated sense of self-importance, resentful and arrogant attitudes, a socially intimidating manner, and a voiced pride in self-reliance and unsentimentality. He is competitive about his self-worth, and it is employed to compensate for past humiliation and failures. Deeply felt resentment may be projected outward, precipitating frequent squabbles, antagonism, and personal and family difficulties. In his opinion, others are belligerent and antagonistic, and thus he is justified in his defensive aggressiveness.

It appears that the guiding principle for this man may be to outwit others and to use them to enhance himself Constantly seeking recognition, admiration, and power, he may look to exploit others. Closeness and intimacy, displays of weakness, and a willingness to compromise may be seen by him as fatal concessions that can be avoided by acting cool, arrogant, and self-assured.

It would not be too hypothetical to record that he is self-centered and socially intolerant, aware of—but intentionally inconsiderate of—the feelings of others. He appears to expect special attention from others without intending to reciprocate. Although he is unlikely to pursue frank antisocial behavior, he may experience alcoholism or drug difficulties. His failures and social irresponsibility are typically justified with nonchalant indifference, boastful arrogance, even unvarnished prevarications.

Another likely hypothesis is that he is characteristically touchy and jealous, inclined to brood and harbor grudges, and prone to ascribe malicious tendencies to others. Easily provoked, he may express sudden, unanticipated abusiveness. Moreover, he may distort and magnify the incidental remarks of others into major insults and purposeful slanders. Much of his expansive and arrogant demeanor may be a posture and a fantasy of importance and potency rather than a reality, and it may be acted out only with safe partners and subordinates. Nevertheless, his desire to impress and intimidate others is deeply felt and appears to stem from his need to overcome his sense of inner weakness and to vindicate past injustices.

That this man experiences repeated episodes of alcohol abuse may be reliably assumed. These bouts may be prompted in part by the frustration and disappointment in his life. He is characteristically unpredictable, moody, and impulsive, and these behaviors may be intensified when he is drinking heavily. At these times, his brooding resentment breaks out of control, often resulting in stormy and destructive consequences. He may

CATEGORY		SCORE		PROFILE OF BR SCORES				DIAGNOSTIC SCALES
		RAW	BR	0　　　60	75	85	115	
MODIFYING INDICES	X	135	79					DISCLOSURE
	Y	18	84					DESIRABILITY
	Z	7	56					DEBASEMENT
CLINICAL PERSONALITY PATTERNS	1	7	63					SCHIZOID
	2A	6	69					AVOIDANT
	2B	3	55					DEPRESSIVE
	3	7	60					DEPENDENT
	4	22	68					HISTRIONIC
	5	27	103					NARCISSISTIC
	6A	20	88					ANTISOCIAL
	6B	21	85					AGGRESSIVE (SADISTIC)
	7	10	34					COMPULSIVE
	8A	17	80					NEGATIVISTIC
	8B	1	15					MASOCHISTIC
SEVERE PERSONALITY PATHOLOGY	S	2	37					SCHIZOTYPAL
	C	11	69					BORDERLINE
	P	9	63					PARANOID
CLINICAL SYNDROMES	A	3	57					ANXIETY DISORDER
	H	2	57					SOMATOFORM DISORDER
	N	6	59					BIPOLAR MANIC DISORDER
	D	3	57					DYSTHYMIC DISORDER
	B	17	99					ALCOHOL DEPENDENCE
	T	12	70					DRUG DEPENDENCE
	R	2	27					POST-TRAUMATIC STRESS
SEVERE SYNDROMES	SS	2	27					THOUGHT DISORDER
	CC	1	17					MAJOR DEPRESSION
	PP	3	60					DELUSIONAL DISORDER

Figure 11.5　Millon Clinical Multiaxial Inventory-III.

subsequently express genuine feelings of guilt and contrition, but the destructive and injurious effects of his behavior are likely to persist. Deep resentment that is restrained in his sober state may be unleashed in full force when he is drinking and manifests itself in irrational accusations and physical intimidation, if not brutality, toward family members. He may evince a self-destructive facet to his extropunitive hostility, and this serves to undermine both himself and others.

PATHOGENIC DEVELOPMENTAL BACKGROUND

An attempt is made in this section to trace some of the influences that are likely to have shaped the development of narcissistic traits. Primary consideration is given to propositions derived from social learning theory; analytic formulations have been extensively reviewed in the literature, and they are summarized earlier in the chapter.

HYPOTHESIZED BIOGENIC FACTORS

The role of biogenic influences in the narcissistic personality seems especially unclear. Although evidence adduced in support of biogenic determinants for most of the other personality patterns was largely of a speculative nature, there was some, albeit tenuous, logic for these speculations. In the case of the narcissistic pattern, however, where the existence of distinctive biophysical traits seems lacking, conjectures would have unusually weak grounding; thus, none will be proposed. Note should be made, however, that the self-oriented focus of the narcissist is found more frequently among males than females, a finding consistent with the evolutionary models.

CHARACTERISTIC EXPERIENTIAL HISTORY

Because biological sources provide little evidence for the development of the narcissistic personality, we must trace the roots of this pattern among psychogenic influences.

Parental Overvaluation and Indulgence

Whatever the reasons may be, some parents come to view their child as "God's gift to mankind." These parents pamper and indulge their youngsters in ways that teach them that their every wish is a command, that they can receive without giving in return, and that they deserve prominence without even minimal effort. It may be instructive to reproduce an excerpt from Freud's seminal paper "On Narcissism" to point up a central contributor to the development of narcissism. It signifies Freud's awareness that narcissism need not stem from rejection or disillusion, as Kernberg and Kohut contend, but may be a direct consequence of parental overvaluation. In describing these parents, Freud wrote:

They are impelled to ascribe to the child all manner of perfections which sober observation would not confirm, to gloss over and forget all his shortcomings. . . .

Moreover, they are inclined to suspend in the child's favour the operation of all those cultural requirements which their own narcissism has been forced to respect, and to renew in his person the claims for privileges which were long ago given up by themselves. The child shall have things better than his parents; he shall not be subject to the necessities which they have recognized as dominating life . . . restrictions on his own will are not to touch him; the laws of nature, like those of society, are to be abrogated in his favour; he is really to be the center and heart of creation. (p. 48)

Horney presented a similar developmental history in the following statement (1939):

Parents who transfer their own ambitions to the child and regard the boy as an embryonic genius or the girl as a princess, thereby develop in the child the feeling that he is loved for imaginary qualities rather than for his true self. (p. 91)

In short order, children with such experiences will learn to view themselves as special beings, and learn to expect subservience from others; they begin to recognize that their mere existence is sufficient to provide pleasure to others and that their every action evokes commendation and praise. Unfortunately, they fail to learn how to cooperate and share or to think of the desires and interests of others. They acquire little sense of interpersonal responsibility and few skills for the give-and-take of social life. The family world revolves about them. They are egotistic in their attentions and narcissistic in the expression of their love and affect.

Children who have been exposed repeatedly to acquiescent and indulgent parents will expect comparable treatment from others, and they learn to employ the presumptuous and demanding strategies that quickly elicited favored reactions when these were not immediately forthcoming from their parents. Thus, when their desires are frustrated, they need act only in one way—feel entitled and assume that their wishes will automatically be met.

Such youngsters learn not only to take others for granted and to exploit them for personal benefit, but they also learn to see others as weak and subservient. By their fawning and self-demeaning behaviors, the parents of future narcissists have provided them with an image of others as manipulable, docile, and yielding. This view not only enhances narcissists' image of their own specialness but serves to strengthen their inclination to exploit others. Seeing others as weak and submissive allows them to ride roughshod over their interests with impunity.

It may be useful to trace the effects of parental overvaluation through the stages of neuropsychological development.

Feelings of omnipotence begin shortly after birth but do not take hold in a meaningful fashion until the sensorimotor-autonomy stage. Every minor achievement of future narcissists is responded to with such favor as to give them a deluded sense of their own extraordinary self-worth. Extreme confidence in one's child need not be a disservice, if it is well earned. In the case of the future narcissist, however, a marked disparity will exist between the child's actual competence and the impression he or she has of it. Failures in parental guidance and control will play an important role during the intracortical-initiative stage. The child is encouraged to imagine, explore, and act without discipline and regulation. Unrestrained by the imposition of parental limits, the child's thoughts and behaviors may stray far beyond accepted boundaries of social reality. Untutored by parental discipline regarding the constraints of fear, guilt, and shame, the child may fail to develop those internal regulating mechanisms that result in self-control and social responsibility.

Only Child or First Male Status

Brief mention should be made of the high frequency with which the preceding parental conditions arise in the case of only children and among firstborn males in certain cultural/ethnic groups. Such children often are viewed by their parents as objects of special value. Not only are they often fawned over but they typically experience few of the restrictions and learn few of the responsibilities

of sharing acquired by youngsters with siblings or siblings given lesser status.

These comments suggest that the popular notion of "only children being spoiled" has some merit in fact; needless to say, only children need not be exposed to parental overvaluation and indulgence, nor is such exposure limited to those who are only children.

SELF-PERPETUATION PROCESSES

A major factor in the perniciousness of personality pathology is that its characterological behaviors are themselves pathogenic. Pathological personality patterns perpetuate themselves by setting into motion new and frequently more troublesome experiences than existed in the past. This section turns to a number of these self-perpetuating features.

As with all personalities, narcissists exhibit their style with persistence and inflexibility. They cannot alter their strategy because these patterns are deeply ingrained. Rather than modifying their behavior when faced with failure, they may revert more intractably to their characteristic style; this is likely to intensify and foster new difficulties. In their attempts to cope with shame and defeat, they set up vicious circles that only perpetuate their problems. Three of these are elaborated next.

Illusion of Competence

Narcissists assume that the presumption of superiority will suffice as its proof. Conditioned to think of themselves as able and admirable, they see little reason to waste the effort needed to acquire these virtues. Why bother engaging in such demeaning labors as systematic and disciplined study if one already possesses talent and aptitude? Moreover, it is beneath one's dignity to struggle as others do. Because they believe that they are well endowed from the start, there is no need to exert their energies to achieve what they already have. They simply assume that what they wish will come to them with little or no effort on their part.

Many narcissists begin to recognize in time that they cannot "live up" to their self-made publicity and fear trying themselves out in the real world. Rather than face genuine challenges, they may temporize and boast, but they never venture to test their adequacy. By acting in this way, they can retain their illusion of superiority without fear of disproof. As a consequence, however, narcissists paralyze themselves. Their unfounded sense of confidence and their omnipotent belief in their perfection inhibit them from developing whatever aptitudes they may in fact possess. Unwilling or fearful of expending the effort, they may slip increasingly behind others in actual attainments. Their deficits may become pronounced over time, making them, as well as others, increasingly aware of their shortcomings. Since the belief in their superiority is the bedrock of their existence, the disparity between their genuine and their illusory competence becomes extraordinarily painful. The strain of maintaining their false self-image may cause them to feel fraudulent, empty, and disconsolate. They may succumb to periodic depressions or may slip slowly into paranoid irritabilities and delusions.

Lack of Self-Controls

The narcissist's illusion of superiority and entitlement is but one facet of a more generalized disdain for reality. Narcissists are neither disposed to stick to objective facts nor to restrict their actions within the boundaries of social custom or cooperative living. Unrestrained by childhood discipline and confident of their worth and prowess, they may take liberties with rules and reality, and prevaricate and fantasize at will. Free to wander in their private world of fiction, narcissists may lose touch with reality, lose their sense of proportion, and begin to think along peculiar and deviant lines. Their facile imagination may ultimately evoke comments from others concerning their arrogance and conceit. Ill-disposed to accept critical comments about their "creativity" and needing to retain their admirable self-image, narcissists are likely to turn further to their habit of self-glorification. Lacking social or self-controls, however, their fantasies may take flight and recede increasingly from objective reality.

Social Alienation

Were narcissists able to respect others, allow themselves to value others' opinions, or see the world through others' eyes, their tendencies toward illusion and unreality might be checked or curtailed. Unfortunately, narcissists have learned to devalue others, not to trust their judgments, and to think of them as naive and simpleminded. Thus, rather than question the correctness of their own beliefs, they assume that the views of others are at fault. Hence, the more disagreement they have with others, the more convinced they

are of their own superiority and the more isolated and alienated they are likely to become. These ideational difficulties are magnified further by their inability to participate skillfully in the give-and-take of shared social life. Their characteristic selfishness and ungenerosity often evoke condemnation and disparagement from others. These reactions drive narcissists further into their world of fantasy and only strengthen their alienation. And this isolation further prevents them from understanding the intentions and actions of others. They are increasingly unable to assess situations objectively, thereby failing further to grasp why they have been rebuffed and misunderstood. Distressed by these repeated and perplexing social failures, they are likely, at first, to become depressed and morose. However, true to their fashion, they will begin to elaborate new and fantastic rationales to account for their fate. But the more they conjecture and ruminate, the more they will lose touch, distort, and perceive things that are not there. They may begin to be suspicious of others, to question their intentions, and to criticize them for ostensive deceptions. In time, these actions will drive away potential well-wishers, a reaction that will only serve to "prove" the narcissists' suspicions.

Deficient in social controls and self-discipline, the tendency of narcissists to fantasize and distort may speed up. The air of grandiosity may become more flagrant. They may find hidden and deprecatory meanings in the incidental behavior of others, becoming convinced of others' malicious motives, claims upon them, and attempts to undo them. As their behaviors and thoughts transgress the line of reality, their alienation will mount, and they may seek to protect their phantom image of superiority more vigorously and vigilantly than ever. Trapped by the consequences of their own actions, they may become bewildered and frightened as the downward spiral progresses through its inexorable course. No longer in touch with reality, they begin to accuse others and hold them responsible for their own shame and failures. They may build a "logic" based on irrelevant and entirely circumstantial evidence and ultimately construct a delusional system to protect themselves from unbearable reality.

THERAPEUTIC INTERVENTIONS

Despite the potential for serious decompensation, as previously described, most narcissists function successfully in society if they possess even a modicum of substance and talent to back their confidence. Difficulties arise only when a marked disparity exists between their presumptions and their actual competence. Narcissists' bountiful reservoir of self-faith can withstand considerable draining before it runs dry. A particularly painful blow to their pride, however, may precipitate a depressive disorder that causes intolerable and unaccustomed discomfort. Such an event may entail a severe occupational failure, an embarrassing loss of public esteem, or a sudden change of attitude on the part of a previously idolizing partner. The suffering endured as a result of the crisis is often perceived as exceptional in itself, and as deserving of professional attention. Once involved in treatment, however, narcissistic patients present resistances that make personality restructuring a difficult goal to realize. They persist in blaming others for all their difficulties, adopt a position of superiority over the therapist, and perceive any attempt at constructive confrontation as humiliating criticism. If comfort and regained confidence are the goals, however, these can often be achieved in only few sessions. The therapist can hold narcissists' initial interest by allowing them to focus attention on themselves, and by further encouraging discussions of their past achievements, the therapist may enable narcissists to rebuild their recently depleted self-esteem. Not infrequently, narcissists restore their self-confidence by talking about themselves, by recalling and elaborating their attributes and competencies in front of a knowing and accepting person.

STRATEGIC GOALS

Merely reestablishing former levels of functioning, however, especially rebuilding the narcissist's illusions of superiority, may prove over the long run to be a disservice to the narcissistic patient. Until more realistic self-evaluation is achieved, it is not likely that narcissists will be motivated to develop competencies and socially cooperative attitudes and behaviors that would lead to more gratifying and adaptive lives. If the capacity to confront their weaknesses and deficiencies is strengthened, patients may be able to acquire greater self-control, to become more sensitive and aware of reality, and learn to accept the constraints and responsibilities of shared social living.

Reestablishing Polarity Balances

Characteristic narcissistic confidence, arrogance, and exploitive egocentricity is based on a deeply ingrained, if sometimes fragile, self-image of superior self-worth. Achievements and manifest talents are often not proportional to the narcissist's presumptions of "specialness." The alternative to maintaining unsustainable beliefs of personal infallibility, that is, recognition of imperfections, limitations, and flaws, however, is tantamount to reconciliation with failure and utter worthlessness. For some narcissists, such unreal expectations for themselves stem from experiences in which otherwise doting parents became unsupportive or even abusive at the manifestation of "imperfection" in their child; others simply cannot conceive life among the "masses." As those around narcissists "dare" not to notice their special uniqueness, and then behave appropriately, narcissists turn away from attempting to secure comfort from "simpleminded" others. Instead, they increasingly rely on themselves as a source of rewards. Turning inward provides opportunity to pamper and ponder the self, and to fantasize about the great recognition that will come to shine on the narcissist one day. Thus narcissists, who start out high on the self-polarity, become increasingly less other-oriented with the passage of time.

In the mind of narcissists, others are the source of all troubles and difficulties, and are responsible for any failures to achieve fantasized goals. Not only do others have to make this up to the narcissist, but their natural inferiority dictates that they should attend to all the narcissist's whims and needs. The narcissist's exploitive egocentricity is not the two-faced, contract-breaking, means-to-an-end exploitiveness of the antisocial. Rather than actively planning, the narcissists' arrogance and snobbish sense of superiority lead them to believe that others owe them something, and their self-centered convictions of genuine entitlement result in the passive exploitation of others. The sense of superiority often results in a lack of goal-oriented behavior in general; narcissists simply believe that good things are their due, a natural by-product of their intrinsic specialness. This nonadaptive bias toward the passive end of the active-passive dimension often results in personal, social, and professional stagnation.

A main therapeutic goal in trying to increase a narcissist's other-orientedness and active goal-directed behaviors is to help him or her accept that while human imperfections are inevitable, they are not necessarily a sign of failure or worthlessness. If narcissists can appreciate the benefits (lack of pressure, decreased fear of criticism) of not needing to be infallible, they may be able to consider their part of the responsibility for any difficulties they may be having. Active problem-solving and improved interpersonal interaction is a worthy goal.

Modifying Domain Dysfunctions

The most salient narcissistic dysfunctions are manifested in the self-image and interpersonal conduct domains, and are expressed in the form of an admirable self-concept and unempathic, even exploitive treatment of others. At best, the narcissist confidently displays achievements and behaves in an entitled, and occasionally grating manner. Facts are twisted and the line between fantasy and reality becomes blurred as narcissists boast of unsupportable personal successes and talent; at the same time, interpersonal behavior moves toward the inconsiderate, arrogant, and exploitive. Others may express irritation at the nonsubstantiated grandiosity of narcissists' fantasies and at the inequitable nature of their social interactions. However, taking advantage of others to indulge desires and enhance a situation, with no consideration of reciprocal responsibilities, is considered justified owing to narcissists' sense of self-importance. As long as they maintain this self-schema, narcissists have little chance of finding motivation to effect changes in other areas. Thus, a first therapeutic intervention needs to focus on accepting a realistic self-image. As the cognitive foundation on which exploitive behavior is justified is weakened, interventions that increase empathic understanding and cooperative interactions can become the clinical focus. The possible advantages of these cognitive and behavioral modifications—warmer receptions from others and a more solid personal sense of efficacy—can then be integrated to encourage further development.

Successful intervention in the primary domains can lead to beneficial advances within secondary domains. Furthermore, resolving secondary domain dysfunctions therapeutically can also bolster progress in the more salient areas. Behavioral interventions, including role-playing, techniques of behavioral inhibition, modeling, and systematic desensitization, that elicit nonadulating therapeutic feedback can help extinguish haughty expressive behavior as well as exploitive interpersonal conduct. These can, in turn, result in more genuine interpersonal events that subsequently serve as useful counterexamples to unrealistic or contrived object-representations. Such exercises and the results they generate may set the groundwork for a more searching exploration of the patient's internalized schemas and their negative consequences. Illusory ideas and memories and pretentious attitudes can eventually be replaced with reality-based experiences and object-representations.

As the patient comes to grasp the nonadaptive nature of the expansive narcissistic cognitive style, preoccupation with immature fantasies may be decreased. As cognitive and behavioral dysfunctions come to be regulated, the narcissist's insouciant mood is also likely to be naturally tempered. Baseline nonchalance and buoyancy can be replaced with more context-appropriate feelings. The rage, shame, and emptiness that resulted from undeniable discrepancies between self-image and reality are often modified along with the patient's self-concept. In some cases, psychopharmacological intervention may be indicated if a resistant depression appears to be interfering with therapeutic progress.

Ultimately, therapeutic interventions in the preceding domains can have a beneficial effect on this personality's spurious morphologic organization. Flimsy defensive strategies can be replaced by stronger coping mechanisms, and the stress-reducing regulatory mechanism of rationalization can be given up for more realistic and growth-fostering inner and outer self-representations.

Countering Perpetuating Tendencies

Narcissists' characteristic difficulties almost all stem from their lack of solid contact with reality. The same disdain for objectivity prevents effective coping with subsequent troubles. The problem-perpetuating cycle begins with early experiences that provide noncontingent praise, teaching narcissists to value themselves regardless of accomplishments. Their inflated sense of self-worth causes them to conclude that there is little reason to apply any systematic effort toward acquiring skills and competencies when "it is so clear that" they already possess such obvious and valuable talents and aptitudes. Their natural gifts, they believe, are reason enough for them to achieve their goals and earn others' respect.

In time, narcissists come to realize that others, who are expending considerable effort to achieve goals, are moving ahead and receiving more recognition. Envious and resentful because the acknowledgment of what is "rightfully theirs" is being bestowed on others, narcissists intensify their boasting and air of superiority. Eventually, the prospect of actually going out in the world and risking humiliating failure for all to witness becomes untenable in the face of the grand illusions of personal competence narcissists feed to themselves and others.

The problems posed by narcissistic illusions of competence feed into and are exacerbated by social alienation and lack of self-controls. The conviction that they are entitled leads narcissists to harbor disdain for social customs and cooperative living. A lack of respect for others' opinions and feelings leads to a failure to integrate normative feedback about their behaviors and illusions. In fact, the conviction that others are simpleminded and naive causes narcissists to retreat further into their illusory and isolated world of fantasy at every hint of disapproval. Self-serving rationalizations of others' lack of adulation can escalate until complementary paranoid delusions of persecution and grandiose illusions become firmly entrenched. Were narcissists to possess some self-controls, their social isolation may not have such dire consequences. Internal reality testing, however, is as neglected as are external inputs. Rather than working to realize ambitions, narcissists—driven by conceit and threat of failure—push to retain their admirable self-image through fantasy. The regard for reality that would prevent narcissists from perpetuating their psychological and coping difficulties is notably absent.

Therapeutic intervention offers an inroad into the pathological cycle through the modification of the overblown self-image. As the self is appraised more realistically, perfection is seen as unattainable, and the need to employ self-discipline to achieve goals is understood, the narcissistic patient may come to recognize and accept his or her similarity to others. As the patient begins to make genuine efforts to improve the quality of life, an appreciation for others' hard work and achievements may develop and replace chronic envy and resentment. Intervention aimed directly at increasing empathic understanding can lead to a sensitivity to others' feelings that fosters motivation to adopt cooperative interpersonal behaviors. Toward this end, narcissists can choose to learn to tolerate and make use of constructive social feedback. Day-to-day successes can eventually provide the gratification that can bolster the patient's resolve not to perpetuate nonadaptive cognitive and behavioral strategies, and help control the impulse to escape into unproductive flights of fantasy. If social isolation is thus decreased, therapeutic work has led to difficult-to-realize modifications in the patient's deeply entrenched lifestyle.

TACTICAL MODALITIES

Working with narcissists is difficult for therapists who seek change in a patient's personality. Benjamin (1993a) notes that the patient's presumptions of entitlement and admiration may encourage the therapist to join the patient in mutual applause, while criticizing the rest of the world. Alternatively, the patient may maintain a stance of superiority. Neither kind of therapeutic alliance helps the patient achieve more adaptive functioning. Any confrontation of the narcissist's patterns will be experienced as criticism, however, and chances are high that the patient will choose to terminate therapy. Benjamin suggests that narcissists may consider changing their interpersonal habits if they are convinced that it will lead to a more favorable response from others. Overall, best therapeutic outcomes may come from honest interpretations presented in a tone of approval and acceptance. Good therapeutic gain will result when the patient internalizes the therapist's empathic acceptance of the patient's faults and deficits. As children, most narcissists were noncontingently praised for their "perfection," and may have been led to feel like utter failures when their inevitable lack of perfection was too apparent to be ignored. The therapist's attitude that faults are inevitable and perfectly human provides an opportunity for realistic self-evaluation of self-worth that was rarely provided in the typical narcissist's early learning history. Carefully timed self-disclosures of the therapist's reactions toward the patient can also potentially lead to substantial therapeutic gain. Such information can encourage the patient's insight into the negative impact of his or her habitual behaviors on others, and, if revealed with supportive skill, can foster motivation to modify these habits.

Domain-Oriented Techniques

Behavioral approaches to treating narcissistic behaviors (e.g., sexual exploitation) and destructive habits (e.g., overspending, not working) include contingency management and behavioral response prevention. Systematic desensitization of evaluation distress and role-play reversals that increase empathic understanding of others can also prove to be useful adjuncts to individual therapy.

Benjamin's *interpersonal* approach (1993a) suggests that achieving the first crucial therapeutic objective, the patient's recognition of problematic interpersonal patterns, is particularly challenging with narcissistic patients. While the therapist's empathic understanding is necessary in facilitating this process, the form of therapist statements needs to be carefully considered to prevent encouraging narcissistic tendencies inadvertently. Benjamin provides examples of more and less therapeutically effective statements in discussing a narcissistic patient and his dissatisfied wife. An example of a response that probably encourages a narcissistic schema is "You have been trying so hard to make things go well, and here she (your wife) just comes back with complaints." Benjamin notes that such a therapist response would probably enhance the patient's pattern of externalizing and blaming. A preferred alternative would be, "You have been trying so hard to make things work well, and you feel just devastated to hear that they aren't going as perfectly as you thought." The advantage of this latter response is that it encourages the patient to examine internal processes and reaction patterns.

Present habits become clearer when their functional significance is grasped. To this end, patients' patterns of emotional reactions such as envy and feelings of entitlement can be traced to early interactions with significant others. Internalized representations of these early figures continue to guide present functioning. As patients come to recognize which attitudes and behaviors are motivated by earlier "internalizations," they may become freer to modify them. An example provided by Benjamin considers a patient who expressed anger and envy about a friend's receipt of public acknowledgment of success. The therapist shifted the patient's focus to issues underlying the envy by asking the patient how his mother would react to such news. Further discussion helped clarify to the patient that his concern about her reaction of disappointment (real or internalized) supported his unpleasant envious feelings. Such insight can help the patient resolve to detach from internalized representations of such figures. Finally, it is noted that once the patient accepts that unattainable ambitions and maladaptive behaviors need to be given up in favor of more realistic and fruitful cognitive and interactive habits, the bulk of the therapeutic challenge may be well on its way; new learning may be a relatively easy undertaking thereafter.

Couples intervention can be a very effective way for the narcissist to learn to relate to another person in an empathic way. Benjamin points out that encouraging simple expressions of affect may serve to perpetuate rather than modify problems when working with a narcissist and his mate, particularly if the mate exhibits dependent or masochistic traits (often found to be the case).

Mates with these characteristics are prone to accept the narcissist's blame for the couple's difficulties. Instead, the complementarity of the partners' patterns needs to be confronted, and collaboration from both parties secured. Agreements about reallocation of household duties and funds can help the narcissist give up the "entitled" role. Role-plays and role-reversals can help teach narcissists empathic understanding that would make such transitions more palatable for them. Benjamin points out that in order for role-playing techniques to be successful, the narcissist's exact words and inflections must be used by the mate; failure at exact mirroring can lead to rage and withdrawal. Properly done, this technique can also hit home the fact that the patient is not always at the center of the mate's experiential field, which serves not only to decrease feelings of grandiosity and entitlement, but also to reduce the perception that every instance of the mate's failure to notice the narcissist is necessarily an insult.

Group approaches can be problematic, as the patient often experiences rage and counters with withdrawal at any hint of empathic failure from other group members or from the therapist. Systematically examining the patient's reactions can help provide the patient with insight, given that the therapist-patient relationship is strong enough for the patient to tolerate the stresses of the group setting. If the group can offer unanimous strong support, the patient is more likely to consider feedback about unappealing behavior patterns.

The *cognitive* approach to treating narcissistic personality disorder outlined by Beck and Freeman (1990b) suggests that while long-term treatment goals vary with each patient, they are likely to include "adjustment of the patient's grandiose view of self, limiting cognitive focus on evaluation by others, better management of affective reactions to evaluation, enhancing awareness about the feelings of others, activating more empathic affect, and eliminating exploitive behavior" (p. 248). Beck and Freeman suggest that general interventions should be tailored to what they refer to as the three narcissistic hallmarks of dysfunction: grandiosity, hypersensitivity to evaluation, and lack of empathy.

From a cognitive perspective, narcissists' tendency to overvalue themselves is based on faulty comparisons with others, whose differences from the self are overestimated. When the comparison obviously favors another, however, narcissists tend to undervalue the self to a disproportionate extent as well. Much of these extremes in thinking can be attributed to an all-or-nothing categorical style. The therapist aims to temper extreme dualistic thinking by endorsing more realistic middle-ground positions. Another useful technique is to encourage patients to make comparisons intrapersonally rather than using others as reference points, so that progress can be internally and more honestly gauged. Searching for personal similarities with others is another cognitive exercise that can lead to improved attitudes and empathic social behavior. Beck and Freeman also note that pervasive cognitive orientations can be modified by encouraging the patient to provide evidence for case-appropriate "alternate beliefs" which, if integrated, help reverse narcissistic tendencies. Examples of such therapeutic positions include "one can be human, like everyone else, and still be unique," "colleagues can be resources, not just competitors," "everyone has flaws," "feedback can be valid and helpful. It's only devastating if I take it that way," and "ordinary things can be very pleasurable."

Another recommendation is to encourage narcissistics to modify their fantasies. Rather than attempting to eliminate a deeply entrenched fantasizing habit, however, the typically unrealistic and unadaptive contents can be replaced with attainable gratifications and pleasures. An example provided suggests that fantasizing about singing a hit song in front of an audience of thousands can be replaced by imagining singing with a community choir. By focusing on the potential gratification of engaging in the activity itself, rather than on others' positive evaluation of the performance, more realistic fantasizing can serve as a covert rehearsal of adaptive and esteem-building behavior.

The flip side of the narcissistics' craving for recognition and adulation is their hypersensitivity to criticism and their defensive grandiosity. Systematic desensitization through exposure to a hierarchy of negative feedback can be effective in reducing troublesome responses. The therapist can utilize the visualization of coping strategies that enable the narcissist to deal effectively with constructive criticism. Additional exercises toward this end include learning how to decide whether a particular evaluative situation is important, and how to request specific feedback from others. This can reduce the time and energy distracted from more important tasks, anxiously pondering the opinions of others, even in situations of no consequence. Thought stopping can be used to intervene with this form of obsessive rumination.

In working toward the end of increasing the narcissist's empathy, three general stages of intervention may be recommended. First, the empathic deficit needs to be brought to light. The therapist can often be helpful by drawing attention to others' feelings. If necessary, instances of inconsiderateness or exploitation should be pointed out. In the second stage, the patient can actively imagine how others feel, often effectively accomplished by engaging in emotion-focused role-plays and role-reversals. Specific new beliefs regarding the significance of others' feelings can be explored and verbalized. Behaviors that are consistent with these beliefs can be devised and rehearsed, both in therapy and outside.

Psychodynamic approaches to restructuring the narcissistic personality are generally based on one of two basic approaches, the first proposed by Kernberg, the second by Kohut. Kernberg formulates narcissistic grandiosity to be a result of the child's rage at mother's indifference or rejections. Kohut sees the disorder as a developmental arrest caused by a maternal failure to validate her child's developing self-worth. Kernberg's clinical recommendations include confronting the patient's conscious and subconscious anger, examining negative transference toward the therapist, and addressing the patient's use of defenses such as splitting, projection, and projective identification. Kohut's model encourages the therapist to assume a sympathetic and accepting stance, while addressing the objective need for the patient to accept personal limitations.

Some narcissists present with a depression that appears to be more persistent than would be expected, given these patient's personality and circumstances. If symptoms such as chronic feelings of emptiness and sensitivity to rejection appear to be interfering with the realization of adaptive therapeutic change, the possible benefits of *psychopharmacological* intervention may be carefully evaluated.

The major strategies and tactics are reviewed in Figure 11.6.

Potentiated Pairings and Catalytic Sequences

The initial phase of therapy with a narcissistic patient needs to focus almost exclusively on building a supportive working alliance. Confronting the patient's maladaptive behaviors before trust and respect for the therapist are established is likely to lead to premature termination. Once this

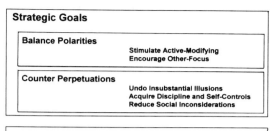

Strategic Goals

Balance Polarities
Stimulate Active-Modifying
Encourage Other-Focus

Counter Perpetuations
Undo Insubstantial Illusions
Acquire Discipline and Self-Controls
Reduce Social Inconsiderations

Tactical Modalities
Moderate Admirable Self-Image
Dismantle Interpersonal Exploitation
Control Haughty Behavior
Diminish Expansive Cognitions

Figure 11.6 Therapeutic strategies and tactics for the prototypal narcissistic personality.

foundation has been laid, intervention focus can turn to increasing the patient's insight into his or her behavior. The developmental history and functional significance of patterns can be explored, and undesirable consequences can be clarified. Working toward helping the patient integrate more adaptive behavioral and cognitive alternatives can then begin.

At this point, the therapist can consider several adjunct interventions. If resistant depression is judged to be interfering with functioning, and the therapist judges that alleviation of acute dysphoria will not lead to abandonment of more long-term reconstructive goals, pharmacological treatment should be carefully considered. If appropriate, group, couple, and/or family therapy may be useful concomitant approaches. Group intervention is more likely to lead to therapeutic gains if the group can provide strong support to offset the patient's tendency to withdraw at the first hint of illusion-shattering confrontation. Couple and family therapy provide an opportunity for behavioral exercises such as role-plays that increase empathy and sharpen insight into the problem-perpetuating nature of cognitive and behavioral habits specific to the patient's personal life. Guided negotiation with

significant others can help break complementary patterns that support narcissistic behavior, and lead to new interactions that provides gratification and bolsters the patient's motivation to continue working toward adaptive change.

RISKS AND RESISTANCES

Narcissists are not inclined to seek therapy. Their pride disposes them to reject the imperfection-confirming "weak" role of patient. Most are convinced they can get along quite well on their own. Often, a narcissist who accepts voluntary treatment will try to enlist the therapist to support the opinion that the patient's problems are largely the result of the imperfections and weaknesses of others. Alternatively, the narcissist may adopt a stance of superiority and discredit the therapist, or terminate treatment prematurely. In sum, narcissists will not accede to therapy willingly. Moreover, once involved, they will maintain a well-measured distance from the therapist, resist the searching probes of personal exploration, become indignant over implications of deficiencies on their part, and seek to shift responsibility for these lacks to others. The treatment setting may give witness to struggles in which narcissists seek to outwit the therapist and assert their dominance. Stone (1993) notes that much of the narcissistic patient's sarcasm, devaluation, and domination toward the therapist can be seen as a "test" of whether the therapist will respond in kind and therefore, like the patient's parents (who may have modeled the offensive behavior), is not to be trusted. Setting limits without resorting to an accusatory or attacking stance can prove to be invaluable aids in working with these patients. Great patience and equanimity are required to establish the spirit of genuine confidence and respect without which the chances of achieving reconstructive personality change become even slimmer.

CHAPTER 12

Antisocial Personality Disorders: The Aggrandizing Pattern

Independent personalities are identified by their inclination to turn to themselves as the primary source for fulfilling needs (Millon, 1969). A major distinction has been drawn, however, between those who are passively independent versus those who are actively independent. Passive-independents, or what the author and the DSM-IV have termed narcissistic personalities, are characterized by their sublime, if unjustified, self-confidence and their deeply rooted faith in themselves as superior human beings. In contrast, active-independents—what the author has designated as aggrandizing personalities and are labeled in the DSM-IV as antisocial personalities—are driven by a need to prove their superiority; strivings for independence stem not so much from a belief in self-worth as from a mistrust of others. These antisocial personalities have faith only in themselves and are secure only when they are independent of those who they fear may undo, harm, or humiliate them.

Prior to the DSM-IV characterization of "antisocial," the designation for this personality syndrome placed too great an emphasis on the delinquent, criminal, and other undesirable social consequences often found among these patients. Of course, some active-independent personalities are openly and flagrantly illegal in their social behavior and, therefore, may properly be spoken of as antisocial. Other individuals with essentially similar basic personalities, however, fit into the mainstream of society, displaying their characteristic traits through socially acceptable avenues. The author considers it a major regressive step that the DSM-III returned to an accusatory judgment rather than a dispassionate clinical formulation; what we had before us was but a minor variation of earlier, ill-considered, and deplorable notions such as "moral insanity"

and "constitutional psychopathic inferiority." Minor changes were introduced into DSM-IV that helped in part to remedy this negative valuation.

Only a minor subset of the antisocial personality pattern comes into conflict with the law. Many find themselves commended and reinforced in our competitive society, where tough, hard-headed realism is admired as an attribute necessary for survival. Most find a socially valued niche for themselves in the rugged side of the business, military, or political world. Complicating the characterization of the antisocial is the deletion of the sadistic personality as a separate clinical entity. Many of the antisocials are now seen as possessing as inherent traits features that should conceptually be segregated into the sadistic personality pattern; we have made this differentiation in the present text in a manner similar to its formulation in an appendix to the DSM-III-R. As will be read in Chapter 13, many of the characteristics attributed to the antisocial are now best conceived as features of the sadistic personality.

The senior author took strong exception to the narrow view of antisocial as "criminal" that had been promulgated in the DSM-III. A quote follows of a comment prepared by this author in 1978 in criticism of the draft version that served as the basis for the final text of the DSM-III antisocial personality:

I have never felt comfortable with the write-up for the antisocial personality disorder. I very much agree with those who contend that the focus given is oriented too much toward the "criminal personality" and not sufficiently toward those with similar propensities who have avoided criminal involvements. More importantly, the write-up fails to deal with personality characteristics at all, but rather lists a series of antisocial behaviors that stem from such characteristics. In that sense we have shifted the level of our focus in this disorder from that employed in describing all of the other personality disorders. The list comprising the antisocial diagnostic criteria is merely a sequence of picayunish specifics (e.g., thefts, three or more traffic arrests, etc.). These details make us delude ourselves that we are a mature empirical science when, in actuality, they derive from the data of one, highly biased research study. I would very much like to see a shift back from these narrow "empirical" details toward our "standard format." The semi-abstract criterion concepts of our standard format capture the underlying tone of the relevant trait or symptom we are addressing; we can record particular acts as illustrative examples.

It is these more general traits that I would like to see us list as diagnostic criteria. If there is some value in specifying particular illustrations to exemplify them, then, and only then, should we list such details.

HISTORICAL ANTECEDENTS

Because of its extensive and divergent literature, the following review of the antecedent concepts and theories of this personality pattern is more detailed than usual. Its origins and clinical characteristics have been formulated and reformulated innumerable times over the past two centuries. Throughout this checkered history, the notion of an antisocial character has served to designate a rather varied collection of behaviors that have little in common other than being viewed as repugnant to the social mores of the time. Despite disagreements concerning its nature and origins, few clinicians today will fail to "get the picture" when they hear the designations "sociopath" or "antisocial personality."

Descriptions of the features that now characterize the antisocial personality can be traced back to earliest times. Theophrastus, a student of Aristotle, was well known for his apt portrayal of personality characters. One of them, *The Unscrupulous Man*, corresponds closely to our current conception of the antisocial. As best as can be translated, he wrote:

The Unscrupulous Man will go and borrow more money from a creditor he has never paid. . . .When marketing he reminds the butcher of some service he has rendered him and, standing near the scales, throws in some meat, if he can, and a soup-bone. If he succeeds, so much the better; if not, he will

snatch a piece of tripe and go off laughing. (cited in Widiger, Corbitt, & Millon, 1991, p. 63)

Attention was drawn to the clinical features of this personality when psychiatrists at the end of the 18th century engaged in the age-old arguments concerning free will and whether certain moral transgressors were capable of "understanding" the consequences of their acts. It was Philippe Pinel (1801, 1806), referring to a form of madness known at the time as *la folie raisonnante,* who noted that certain patients engaged in impulsive and self-damaging acts, although their reasoning abilities were unimpaired and they fully grasped the irrationality of what they were doing. Describing these cases under the name *manie sans délire* ("insanity without delirium"), his description was among the first to recognize that madness need not signify the presence of a deficit in reasoning powers. As Pinel (1801) described it:

I was not a little surprised to find many maniacs who at no period gave evidence of any lesion of understanding, but who were under the dominion of instinctive and abstract fury, as if the faculties of affect alone had sustained injury.

Until Pinel forcefully argued the legitimacy of this psychopathological entity, it was universally held that all mental disorders were disorders of the mind; because mind was equated with reason, only a disintegration in the faculties of reason and intellect would be judged as insanity. Beginning with Pinel, however, there arose the belief that one could be insane *(manie)* without a confusion of mind *(sans délire).*

Benjamin Rush, the well-known American physician, wrote in the early 1800s of similar perplexing cases characterized by lucidity of thought combined with socially deranged behaviors. He spoke of these individuals as possessing an "innate, preternatural moral depravity" in which "there is probably an original defective organization in those parts of the body which are preoccupied by the moral faculties of the mind" (1812, p. 112). Rush appears to have been the first theorist to have taken Pinel's morally neutral clinical observation of defects in "passion and affect" and turned it into a social condemnation. He claimed that a lifelong pattern of irresponsibility was displayed by these individuals without a corresponding feeling of shame or hesitation over the personally destructive consequences of their actions. Describing the features characterizing this type, Rush (1812) wrote:

The will might be deranged even in many instances of persons of sound understandings . . . the will becoming the involuntary vehicle of vicious actions through the instrumentality of the passions. Persons thus diseased cannot speak the truth upon any subject. . . . Their falsehoods are seldom calculated to injure anybody but themselves. (p. 124)

As evident from the dates mentioned in the preceding paragraphs, the British alienist J. C. Prichard (1835)—credited by many as having been the first to formulate the concept of "moral insanity"—was, in fact, preceded in this realization by several theorists; nevertheless, he was the first to label it as such and to give it wide readership in English-speaking nations. Although he accepted Pinel's notion of *manie sans délire,* he dissented from Pinel's morally neutral attitude toward these disorders and became the major exponent of the view that these behaviors signified a reprehensible defect in character that deserved social condemnation. He also broadened the scope of the original syndrome by including under the label "moral insanity" a wide range of previously diverse mental and emotional conditions. All these patients ostensibly shared a common defect in the power to guide themselves in accord with "natural feelings"—that is, a spontaneous and intrinsic sense of rightness, goodness, and responsibility. Those afflicted by this disease were swayed, despite their ability to intellectually understand the choices before them, by overpowering "affections" that compelled them to engage in socially repugnant behaviors. As Prichard (1835) described it:

There is a form of mental derangement in which the intellectual functions appear to have sustained little or no injury, while the disorder is manifested principally or alone in the state of the feelings, temper or habits. In cases of this nature the moral or active principles of the mind are strangely perverted or depraved; the power of self-government is lost or greatly impaired and the Individual is found to be incapable, not of talking or reasoning upon any subject proposed to him, but of conducting himself with decency and propriety in the business of life. (p. 85)

The separation between insanity due to defects in reasoning versus those owing to defects in "natural affections" espoused by Prichard led to a major and long-standing controversy among British legal scholars and alienists. The discussion returns to this controversy after a few comments on the terminology of the day.

The word *moral* was imposed upon Pinel's concept by both Rush and Prichard. Pinel's syndrome signified the inability to restrain the affections (emotions) without a corresponding loss of reasoning; it was entirely neutral with regard to conventional notions of morality. Immersed in the British philosophical doctrine of "natural rights, which stressed both the state's and the individual's responsibility for social action, Rush and Prichard took Pinel's neutral clinical observation and transformed it into an entity consisting of moral censure and social depravity. In seeking to counter this intrusion of irrelevant philosophical and moralistic values upon clinical judgments, the distinguished British psychiatrist of the mid-19th century, Daniel Hack Tuke (1892), proposed that Prichard's label be dropped and the syndrome renamed "inhibitory insanity," thereby recapturing the essence and moral neutrality of Pinel's original formulations.

Prichard's entity of "moral insanity" has little in common as a clinical syndrome with contemporary notions of psychopathy or antisocial personality. So diverse a group of disorders were subsumed in Prichard's category that almost all mental conditions, other than mental retardation and schizophrenia, would be so diagnosed today. If we sorted the "morally insane" into contemporary categories, the syndrome would be depleted so severely as to leave but a minor fraction that could be characterized by current notions of antisocial behavior.

Prichard (1835) did make one important positive contribution in that he was the first theorist to have differentiated the prognosis of long-standing clinical traits from those that arise in response to transient stresses. He stated this original idea as follows:

When the disorder is connected with a strong natural predisposition, it can scarcely be expected to terminate in recovery. Such we must conclude to be the case in those instances in which the phenomena bear the appearance of an increase or exaltation of peculiarities natural to the individual, and noted as remarkable traits in his previous habits. If, however, this morbid state of mind has been the effect of any external and accidental cause, which admits of removal, or if the individual can be extracted from its influence or helped defend against it, there is reason to hope that the disorder will gradually subside. (p. 122)

The concept of moral insanity continued as a major source of contention and preoccupation in England for more than 70 years. In contrast to Daniel Hack Tuke, Henry Maudsley (1874), another leading British psychiatrist of the period, not only sided unequivocally with Prichard but contended that there existed a specific cerebral center underlying "natural moral feelings." His views concerning the morally insane were stated thus:

As there are persons who cannot distinguish certain colours, having what is called colour blindness, so there are some who are congenitally deprived of moral sense. (p. 11)

To the notion that there were cerebral deficits among the morally depraved were added several anthropological "stigmata," as proposed by Lombroso (1872–1887) and Gouster (1878). Dismissing the primitive physical anthropology, what is striking about Lombroso's exposition is how closely it corresponds to the thinking of current DSM criteria. Lombroso was explicit in proposing the idea of a "born delinquent," whereas the DSM-III only implies a similar notion. According to Lombroso, constitutionally disposed criminal types display a notably large and projective lower jaw, outstretched ears, retreating forehead, left-handedness, robust physique, precocious sexual development, tactile insensibility, muscular agility, and so on. Behaviorally, they are emotionally hyperactive, temperamentally irascible, impetuous in action, and deficient in altruistic feelings. Gouster's list of stigmata parallels other aspects of the DSM-III antisocial personality criteria. Most similar is the symptom cluster characterized by moral perversion from early life, as evidenced in headstrong, malicious, disobedient, irascible, lying, neglectful, and frequently violent and brutal behaviors; also noted are a delight in intrigue and mischief, and a tendency toward excesses in seeking excitement and passion.

Toward the end of the 19th century, German psychiatrists turned their attentions away from the value-laden theories of the English alienists and toward what they judged to be observational research. Prominent among this group was J. L. Koch (1891), who proposed that the label *moral insanity* be replaced by the term *psychopathic inferiority,* under which he included:

. . . all mental irregularities whether congenital or acquired which influence a man in his personal life

and cause him, even in the most favorable cases, to seem not fully in possession of normal mental capacity. (p. 67)

The term *psychopathic,* a generic label for all personality disorders until recent decades, was selected by Koch (1891) to signify his belief that a physical basis existed for these impairments. Thus, he stated:

They always remain psychopathic in that they are caused by organic states and changes which are beyond the limits of physiological normality. They stem from a congenital or acquired inferiority of brain constitution. (p. 54)

As with Prichard, Koch included a wide group of conditions in his category of psychopathic inferiorities, only a small portion of which would be considered within our current rendering of an antisocial or sociopathic syndrome. His subgroups of "psychopathic disposition" (*Zartheit*), noted by tension and high sensitivity; "psychopathic taint" (*Belastung*), seen clinically in those with peculiarities, egocentricities, and impulsive fury; and "psychopathic degeneration," manifested predominantly in borderline mental states, all rested on presumptive physical defects, none of which Koch admitted could be structurally or physiologically verified.

The concept of a "constitutionally inferior" type was introduced into American literature at the turn of the century by Adolf Meyer, shortly after his arrival from Germany. Although following Koch's ideas in the main, Meyer sought to separate psychopathic cases from psychoneurotic disorders, both of which were grouped together in Koch's "psychopathic inferiorities" classification. Meyer was convinced that the etiology of the neuroses was primarily psychogenic, that is, colored less by inherent physical defects or by "constitutional inferiorities." The line of distinction he drew between these groups remained clear and sharp for many years in American nosology. The label *inferiority,* however, did not fare as well since its deprecatory connotation was anathema to both the verbalized social values and medical practices of the day. "Constitutional psychopathic state" and "psychopathic personality" evolved as the two popular American designations through the first half of the 20th century.

It is necessary to step back again in this review to bring into sharper focus the fact that for the first three decades of this century the label *psychopathic* conveyed nothing more than Koch's contention that the individual's personality was physically rooted or constitutional. Further, the term *inferiority* implied nothing more, insofar as specific clinical characteristics were concerned, than the observation that these personalities deviated unfavorably from the norm. In time, the term took on a more specific cast, assuming the features connoted by the designation *moral insanity,* the historical precursor that Koch sought to escape. Recall that the meaning of the category *manie sans delire,* as originally formulated by Pinel, had nothing whatsoever to do with the value judgments ascribed to it by Prichard in his construction of moral insanity. Similarly, Koch's effort to obviate the moral pejoratives in Prichard's conception was slowly undermined as his designation gradually evolved to mean quite the opposite of what he intended. This fascinating transmutation of the meaning of a diagnostic label is not unique in the history of clinical science. Moreover, to add further insult to the injury of having *psychopathy* so misconstrued, Koch's intent that a physical etiology for these syndromes be clearly affirmed was undone in later years when the designation was changed to *sociopathy,* a means of signifying its now ostensive social origins. The shifting sands of our terminologies and theories in this field should give us good reason to question current formulations that appear to be throwbacks to earlier, discarded notions. Although the label "antisocial personality" may seem less pejorative than "constitutional psychopathic inferior," it does hark back to its ancestral forerunner, "moral insanity."

We pick up the threads of this historical review with the descriptions provided by Emil Kraepelin; the successive editions of his important text reflect the changing emphases given the psychopathic syndrome. In the second edition of this major work (1887), Kraepelin identified the "morally insane" as suffering congenital defects in their ability to restrain the "reckless gratification of . . . immediate egotistical desires" (p. 281). The fifth edition, in 1896, referred to these conditions as "psychopathic states" for the first time, asserting that these constitutional disorders display themselves as lifelong morbid personalities. The next edition, published in 1899, referred to psychopathic states as one of several forms of degeneration along with syndromes such as obsessions, impulsive insanity, and sexual perversions. Retaining the theme of degeneration in his

seventh edition of 1903–1904, Kraepelin now referred to these states as "psychopathic personalities," by which he meant:

Those peculiar morbid forms of personality development which we have grounds for regarding as degenerative. The characteristic of degeneration is a lasting morbid reaction to the stresses of life. (p. 547)

In 1905, Kraepelin identified four kinds of persons who had features akin to what we speak of today as antisocial personalities. First, were the "morbid liars and swindlers" who were glib and charming, but lacking in inner morality and a sense of responsibility to others; they made frequent use of aliases, were inclined to be fraudulent con men, and often accumulated heavy debts that were invariably unpaid. The second group included "criminals by impulse," individuals who engaged in crimes such as arson, rape, and kleptomania, and were driven by an inability to control their urges; they rarely sought material gains for their criminal actions. The third type, essentially referred to as "professional criminals," were neither impulsive nor undisciplined; in fact, they often appeared well mannered and socially appropriate but were inwardly calculating, manipulative, and self-serving. The fourth type, the "morbid vagabonds" were strongly disposed to wander through life, never taking firm root, lacking both self-confidence and the ability to undertake adult responsibilities.

By the eighth edition of his work (1909–1915), Kraepelin described psychopaths as deficient in either affect or volition. He separated them into two broad varieties, those of morbid disposition, consisting of obsessives, impulsives, and sexual deviants; and those exhibiting personality peculiarities. The latter group was differentiated into seven classes: the excitable (*Erregbaren*), the unstable (*Haltlosen*), the impulsive (*Triebmenschen*), the eccentric (*Verschobenen*), the liars and swindlers (*Luegner und Schwindler*), the antisocial (*Gessellschaftsfeinde*), and the quarrelsome (*Streitsuechtige*). Only the latter three possess features similar to current notions of the antisocial. As noted previously, liars and swindlers are "naturally cheats and occasionally thieves"; sexual offenses are common to them, and they are "uncertain and capricious in everything." The quarrelsome personality is "in constant trouble"; they think others are always against them and their judgment is "warped and unreliable." Last, antisocial personalities, the explicit and prime forerunners of our contemporary nomenclature, are:

the enemies of society . . . characterized by a blunting of the moral elements. They are often destructive and threatening . . . [and] there is a lack of deep emotional reaction; and of sympathy and affection they have little. They are apt to have been troublesome in school, given to truancy and running away. Early thievery is common among them and they commit crimes of various kinds. (Partridge, 1930, pp. 88–89)

MODERN FORMULATIONS

The details characterized by Kraepelin in the final edition of his monumental text are almost identical to the diagnostic criteria spelled out for the younger antisocial in the DSM-III. Were Kraepelin's views the final word? Apparently many of his contemporaries thought not.

K. Birnbaum (1914), writing in Germany at the time of Kraepelin's final edition, was the first to suggest that the term *sociopathic* might be the most apt designation for the majority of these cases. To him, not all delinquents of the degenerative psychopathic type were either morally defective or constitutionally inclined to criminality. Birnbaum asserted that antisocial behavior only rarely stems from inherent immoral traits of character; rather, it reflects most often the operation of societal forces that make the more acceptable forms of behavior and adaptation difficult to acquire. This social conditioning thesis did not become a prominent alternative in psychiatric circles until the later 1920s, largely gaining serious consideration through the writings of Healy and Bronner (1926) and Partridge (1930) in the United States. In the interim decades, psychopathy was conceived internationally in the manner most explicitly stated in the British Mental Deficiency Act of 1913; still wedded to Prichard's conception of moral insanity developed some 80 years earlier, it was judged a constitutional defect that manifested "strong vicious or criminal propensities on which punishment has had little or no deterrent effect."

Kraepelin's prime disciple in German psychiatry, Kurt Schneider (1923/1950), reinforced his mentor's thesis, stressing the observation that many were delinquent in youth and largely incorrigible. However, he stated that we should be mindful that in addition to those who progress

into criminal activity, many of this type may also be found in society at large. Moreover, Schneider observed that many of these individuals were unusually successful in positions of either political or material power.

Schneider (1923/1950) anticipated a number of contemporary problems concerning these "psychopaths," and referred to the views of alienists that preceded him by many decades, who faced similar issues. He writes:

. . . that the term moral insanity was likely to be much used in forensic medicine and dramatically urged all those concerned with the criminal law to watch out lest the pleas of moral insanity wrested the sword of justice from their hands.

It does not seem to us proper in Court cases to put forward a pleas of diminished responsibility in such personalities simply because this may be the only way to get admission into institutional custody. . . . It seems to us a functional matter of principle that judgments on the matter of culpability should not rest on considerations of legalistic expediency. (pp. 131–132)

Notable also was Schneider's division between a more *passive* affectionless variety (more like what we call today the schizoid type) from the more *active* antisocial type. In describing these "psychopathic" personalities, Schneider portrays these individuals as follows:

We mean personalities with a marked emotional blunting mainly but not exclusively in relation to their fellows. Their character is a pitiless one and they lack capacity for shame, decency, remorse and conscience. They are ungracious, cold, surly, and brutal in crime. . . . The social moral code is known, understood but not felt and therefore personality is indifferent to it. (p. 126)

In a review of the previous 50 years of research and theory on the "elusive category" of the psychopathic personality, the well-known British psychiatrist Sir Aubrey Lewis (1974) commented as follows:

These reveal a preoccupation with the nosological status of the concept . . . its forensic implications, its subdivisions, limits [and] the propriety of identifying psychopathic personality with antisocial behavior. The effect of reading solid blocks of literature is disheartening; there is so much fine-spun theorizing, repetitive argument, and therapeutic gloom. (pp. 137–138)

Seventy years ago, the same issues were in the forefront, notably whether the psychopathic personality was or was not synonymous with overt antisocial behavior. Partridge's (1930) detailed review of the conceptions of the psychopath then prevalent began as follows:

Ideas relating to psychopathic personality are scattered widely throughout psychiatric and criminological works. Much that has been written is somewhat incidental to the study of delinquency as a whole; some relate to the various types of mental disorders in which deviations of personality are involved. (p. 53)

In addressing the issue of whether psychopathy and antisocial behavior are one and the same, Partridge wrote:

There is comparatively little attention paid to [psychopathological] personality deviations which, though distinct, are not expressed in antisocial behavior.

   There is an assumption that at least some types of chronic misbehavior are the visible extensions, so to speak, of deep [personality] ledges. (p. 75)

In reporting on covariations found between diagnosed psychopathy and recorded histories of criminal or delinquent behavior, he noted:

The proportionate importance of the psychopath in the production of the total of delinquency has been given some attention. Some, we have seen, find a very large proportion of psychopathic personality in criminal groups or delinquents in general, some seem to find only a small one. (1930, p. 93)

In the conclusion of his analysis, Partridge wondered whether the tendency of nosologists to focus on antisocial behaviors, at the expense of the deeper personality structure and its nonsociopathic variants, simply reflects that these behaviors are "obvious." He wrote:

One reason why there has arisen confusion about the so-called psychopaths is that, in these cases, the personality deviations become apparent at an early age in a distinct form. . . . The main difference . . . being that the sociopathic forms are more objective, merely in their manifestations or

adjustment patterns—at least more fully revealed. (1930, pp. 98–99)

As the novel concepts and theories of psychoanalysis took root in the 1920s, preliminary and scattered notions concerning the character of psychopaths began to be published by clinicians oriented by this school of thought. Most were prompted to this task by an intriguing paper by Freud (1915/1925a) entitled "Some Character Types Met with in Psychoanalytic Work"; here Freud described "peculiar acts" that appear out of character for the individual. In exposing the dynamics of a subgroup of these cases, referred to as "criminality from a sense of guilt," Freud wrote:

Analytic work then afforded the surprising conclusion that such deeds are done precisely because they are forbidden, and because by carrying them out the doer enjoys a sense of mental relief. He suffered an oppressive feeling of guilt, of which he did not know the origin, and after he had committed a misdeed the oppression was mitigated. (p. 342)

This paper served as the impetus for a number of subsequent clinical reports by other analysts. Among those written in the early to mid-1920s was Aichhorn's "Wayward Youth," Reich's study the "Impulse Ridden Character," Abraham's analysis of the life and "History of an Impostor," and Alexander's conception of the "Neurotic Character."

Aichhorn (1925/1935) was perhaps the first to undertake an analytically based examination of delinquent behavior. Stressing the observation that surface controls imposed by treatment are rarely sufficient to withstand the unconscious forces of the patient, Aichhorn wrote:

When we look at dissocial behaviour, or symptoms of delinquency, as distinct from delinquency, we see the same relation as that between the symptoms of a disease and the disease itself. This parallel enables us to regard truancy, vagrancy, stealing, and the like as symptoms of delinquency, just as fever, inflammation, and pain are symptoms of disease. If the physician limits himself to clearing up symptoms, he does not necessarily cure the disease. The possibility of a new illness may remain; new symptoms may replace the old. . . . When a psychic process is denied expression and the psychic energies determining it remain undischarged, a new path of discharge will be found

along the line of least resistance, and a new form
of delinquency will result. (pp. 38–39)

Particularly sensitive to variations in the background of delinquent behaviors, Aichhorn asserts that either extreme indulgence and overvaluation or excessive harshness and depredation can set the groundwork for the child's renunciation of social values. Viewing these as defects of the superego, Aichhorn notes that these children are not disposed to internalize parental norms and will be inclined to seek immediate gratifications through impulsive behaviors.

Writing also in 1925, Abraham articulates his view of the development of antisocials in his analysis of "an impostor." In the following brief quote, he appears to join Aichhorn in recognizing conditions that give rise to narcissistic traits, on the one hand, and those of the antisocial, on the other:

We often come across the results of early pampering, which intensifies the child's demands for love to an extent which can never be adequately satisfied (narcissistic). Among delinquents (antisocial) we are more likely to come across a different fate of the libido in early childhood. It is the absence of love, comparable to psychological under-nourishment, which provides the pre-condition for the establishment of dissocial traits. An excess of hatred and fury is generated which, first directed against a small circle of persons, is later directed against society as a whole. (p. 304)

In what he first termed "instinct-ridden characters" and later revised as the "impulsive character," Reich (1925) asserted that the "superego" of these personalities failed to gain expression under the ego's unyielding controls, and subsequently could not adequately restrain the id's seduction when faced with instinctual temptations, hence resulting in the free expression of impulses. Contrasting the impulsive character from what he and others termed the "neurotic character" (essentially the compulsive personality), Reich writes as follows:

As we differentiated between the neurotic symptom and the neurotic character, we must now separate compulsive acts, in the sense of uncontrollable compulsive deeds, from the general behavior of the impulsive character. Whereas the former appears as a circumscribed foreign body within an otherwise ordered personality and is condemned by it, the . . . impulsive individual is . . . only rarely
recognized as pathological. . . . The actions of the impulsive individual never appear as senseless as do those actions of the compulsive neurotic and they are rationalized to a much greater degree. (pp. 251–252)

In commenting on papers presented by more traditional psychiatrists, Coriat, an American psychoanalyst, suggested in 1927 that the "constitutional psychopathic" was an antisocial character who fixated at infantile levels, had unresolved oedipal conflicts, and never learned to replace the ego ideals of childhood with the ego ideals of society. Partridge (1927), employing psychoanalytic concepts, perceived the demands of the psychopath as stemming from unfulfilled oral needs.

It was not until the work of Franz Alexander (1923, 1930, 1935), however, that the first assessment of psychopathy and criminal behavior was undertaken from a thoroughgoing psychoanalytic perspective. In Alexander's 1923 text *Psychoanalysis of the Total Personality,* he distinguished several levels of personality psychopathology; a similar thesis was presented in a 1930 paper, "The Neurotic Character." Four levels of pathology were proposed: neuroses, neurotic character, psychosis, and true criminality. They were arranged in this sequence to reflect diminishing levels of the ego's ability to restrain unconscious impulses, the neurotic displaying the greatest capacity and the criminal the least. The neurotic character was conceived by Alexander to be the underlying personality of psychopaths. To Alexander, neurotic characters act out their conflicts rather than transforming them intrapsychically. Alexander (1930) wrote:

They live out their impulses, many of their tendencies are asocial and foreign to the ego, and yet they cannot be considered true criminals. It is precisely because one part of such an individual's personality continues to sit in judgment upon the other . . . that his total personality is easily differentiated from the more homogeneous, unified and antisocial personality of the criminal. The singular and only apparently irrational drive to self-destruction met with in such people indicates rather definitely the existence of inner self-condemnation.

Their conduct arises from unconscious motives which are not directly accessible to their conscious personality. . . . Admonition, encouragement or punishment coming from the environment is as useless as his own resolution, "I am beginning a new life tomorrow."

A large proportion of such individuals, neurotically driven by unconscious motives, now to commit a transgression, then to seek punishment, sooner or later fall foul of the law. . . .

[Their] lives are full of dramatic action . . . something is always happening, as if they were literally driven by the demonic compulsion. . . . Here is where the adventurers belong whose manifold activities give expression to an underlying revolt against public authority. They always manage to be punished unjustifiably from their highly subjective point of view. (pp. 11–15)

Lest the analytic model of the psychopath be viewed as naive, it may be helpful to record a few excerpts from Alexander's study, *The Roots of Crime* (1935), indicating his thorough awareness that antisocial behaviors reflect an inextricable interplay among intrapsychic processes, social forces, and constitutional dispositions:

The chief difference between neurosis and criminal behavior is that in the neurosis the emotional conflict results in symbolic gratifications of unsatisfied urges, whereas in criminal behavior it leads to overt misdeeds. Those needs which are frustrated by economic conditions . . . cannot be satisfied as easily by the symbolic gratifications of phantasy as can the emotional tensions of love and hate. The emotional conflicts and deprivations of childhood, the resentments of parents and siblings, find a powerful ally in resentment against the social situation, and this combined emotional tension seeks a realistic expression in criminal acts and cannot be relieved by mere phantasy products that are exhibited in neurotic symptoms.

We found that criminality in some cases is a direct expression of a protest against certain deprivations, a reaction of spite against certain members of the family, the expression of jealousy, envy, hostile competition, all of which are strengthened by early sufferings or the lack of love and support on the part of adults. But, we must add, intense hostilities in such cases frequently create strong guilt feelings, which in turn lead to an unconscious need for punishment. . . .

Certain unacquired bases of the instinctive life (constitution), apart from the environmental influences, must be partly responsible for the fact that similar emotional conflicts may, depending on the make-up of the individual, result either in criminality or in neurosis. The introverted nature of the neurotic, his readiness to content himself with gratifications in phantasy and to renounce real

satisfaction, seems to be founded on some constitutional factor. And, on the other hand, certain individuals are characterized by a more robust, expansive instinctual life which contents itself only with outgoing behavior. (pp. 278–279)

The last paragraph is of special interest in that it presages, in almost exact detail, the views of later, vigorously antianalytic critics such as Eysenck, whose work is discussed shortly. Alexander was the first prominent psychoanalyst to invest a significant portion of his attention to antisocial behavior. Subsequent, similarly inclined writers (Allen, 1950; Bartemeier, 1930; Fenichel, 1945; Freidlander, 1945; Greenacre, 1945; Karpman, 1941; Levy, 1951; Wittels, 1937) also sought a rationale for the development of these behaviors with reference to intrapsychic processes and early parent-child relations.

A formulation similar to that presented by Alexander was made during this period by L. Bartemeier (1930), who wrote:

The neurotic character is more bold and daring than the neurotic personality. He does not allow society to intimidate him into mere phantasy but dramatizes his primitive impulses in real action. . . . He maintains a social spite against civilization and its restrictions. The life of such a person . . . is made up of socially ruthless indulgences and subsequent insistences upon punishment. These people only commit crime with emotional conflict while true criminals experience no such stress. (p. 516)

Wittels (1937) differentiated neurotic psychopaths from simple psychopaths; the former, fixated ostensibly at the phallic stage, fear their bisexual impulses, whereas the latter directly indulge their bisexuality. Karpman (1941) distinguished two variants of psychopathy also, the "idiopathic" and the "symptomatic." The former were judged to be the true psychopaths in that they were constitutionally guiltless, insensitive to the feelings of others, and disposed to acquisitiveness and aggression; moreover, no psychogenic history could be observed that would account for their antisocial inclination. Karpman's symptomatic group was composed of neurotics who "paraded" as psychopaths; they were akin to Alexander's neurotic characters and could not be considered true psychopaths because their actions stemmed from unresolved unconscious difficulties. Levy (1951) proposed another subdivision to represent what he saw as clearly different forms of early experience. Termed by Levy the "deprived psychopath" and the "indulged psychopath," they are similar in conception to Millon's (1969) distinction between "aggressive" and "narcissistic" sociopaths, the former being a product of a harsh upbringing; and the latter, of parental overvaluation.

A nonanalytic, yet incisive and thorough clinical characterization of the antisocial was provided by H. Cleckley in his book *The Mask of Sanity,* first published in 1941. Attempting to clarify problem terminologies and seeking to counter the trend of including ever more diverse disorders under the rubric of psychopathy, Cleckley proposed replacing the term with the label "semantic dementia" to signify what he viewed to be the syndrome's prime feature, the tendency to say one thing and to do another. More important than his proposal of a new nomenclature, which attracted little following, was the clarity of Cleckley's description of the psychopath's primary traits—guiltlessness, incapacity for object love, impulsivity, emotional shallowness, superficial social charm, and an inability to profit from experience. No less significant was Cleckley's assertion that these personalities are found not only in prisons but in society's most respected roles and settings. Cleckley (1941) illustrated this thesis with several examples of successful businesspeople, scientists, physicians, and psychiatrists. He wrote as follows:

In these personalities . . . a very deep seated disorder often exists. The true difference between them and the psychopaths who continually go to jails or to psychiatric hospitals is that they keep up a far better and more consistent outward appearance of being normal.

The chief difference . . . lies perhaps in whether the mask or facade of psychobiologic health is extended into superficial material success. (pp. 198–199)

CONTEMPORARY PROPOSALS

A passage concerning the evolving history of psychopathy, written by Cameron and Magaret in the early 1950s, is as apt today as it was then (1951):

The residue of this tortuous and perplexing historical development is unfortunately still with us. For example, the popular labels for social deviation now . . . seem merely to be a restatement of the outmoded category of "constitutional psychopathic inferiority." They do not refer to new concepts. Moreover, the accounts of psychopathic behavior given by present-day behavior pathologists are still likely to be accusations rather than descriptions. The evaluative attitudes of nineteenth-century psychiatry continue to tinge our modern classifications; and the psychopath stands accused of crime, of exploitation and of inability to profit from corrective procedures.

The background of "psychopathic personality" in nineteenth-century psychiatry, although relevant as past history, need not dictate the present and future development of the concept. Nor can we afford to perpetuate the implication that social deviation is morally bad. We cannot ignore the effects of parental emphasis, of others' reactions and of self-reactions in training a growing child to socially deviant behavior. (pp. 190–191)

This plea that we progress beyond the perspective of moral and social judgments as a basis for clinical concepts is as relevant today as it was when written.

Following the line of thinking first presented by Reich, Fenichel (1945), the renowned psychoanalytic scholar, sought to clarify the distinction between the antisocial's impulsiveness and the neurotic's compulsions. He, too, emphasized the failure of the superego to be effective in its efforts to control the impulses of the id. In that same year, Friedlander (1945), another psychoanalytic theorist, stressed that the character structure of psychopathic youngsters remained under the dominance of the pleasure-principle, unguided by an adequately developed superego. A thoughtful analysis of delinquency acting-out by Eissler (1949) portrayed their behaviors as designed to restore feelings of omnipotence that had been severely injured in childhood. Having suffered these injustices or deprivations, these youngsters felt deeply betrayed and, hence, became mistrustful, narcissistic, self-inflating, material-seeking, and addicted to risk and excitement.

A recent psychoanalytic theorist, B. Bursten (1972), has proposed that the essential features of classical sociopaths are their need to bolster their self-esteem by being contemptuous of others and "needing to put something over them." Referring to this pattern as "the manipulative personality," Bursten wrote:

This conceptualization begins to throw some light on why the sociopath seems not to learn from experience; we are looking at the wrong experience.

Frequently these people are quite bright and do learn. They are quite adept at assessing social situations. Indeed it is their very sharpness and their ability to size up a situation which inspires simultaneously our admiration and our anger.

They have well learned from experience what to expect in certain social situations. Nevertheless, the sociopath's behavior has baffled us because we have misunderstood the main purpose of his behavior. (p. 319)

Of particular note also is Bursten's (1972) effort to counter the moral and judgmental implications of the "antisocial" label by substituting what he viewed to be a value-free designation. He phrased his proposal as follows:

By describing such people as manipulative personalities, we get further away from the mixture of psychiatric concepts and concepts involving offenses against society. The manipulation is an interpersonal event resting in great measure on the internal dynamics of the manipulative personality; whether he comes into conflict with society is now immaterial as far as the diagnostic category is concerned.

What the shift from antisocial personality to manipulative personality can add is the further separation of the personality configuration from the social conflict. For indeed, there are many people who are internally driven to manipulate and who do not get into serious conflict with society. People with similar character structures may manifest their dynamic processes in a variety of ways [depending on] the options for expression which society offers them.

The category . . . includes some successful businessmen, politicians, administrators . . . as well as those who come into open conflict with society. (p. 320)

Bursten's specific proposals for the manipulative personality are highly debatable, but his desire to protect personality diagnoses from value judgments and his assertion that these personalities are to be found in all sectors of social life are both relevant and appropriate.

Developing his views in a manner consistent with his psychoanalytic perspective, Shapiro (1965) adds an important cognitive dimension that has enriched this perspective. Although not addressing the antisocial personality directly, Shapiro elaborates the major characteristics of what he terms "impulsive styles"; many of these styles reflect central characteristics of what we term the antisocial in our current nomenclature. Shapiro describes the cognitive elements of these individuals as follows:

In many respects, the psychopath is the very model of the impulsive style. He exhibits in a thorough and pervasive way what for others is only a direction or tendency. He acts on a whim, his aim is the quick, concrete gain, and his interests and talents are in ways and means. (p. 157)

Lack of planning is only one feature of a style of cognition and thinking in which active concentration, capacity for abstraction and generalization, and reflectiveness in general are all impaired. (p. 147)

If we say that the impulsive person's attention does not search actively and analytically, we may add that his attention is quite easily and completely captured, he sees what strikes him, and what strikes him is not only the starting point of a cognitive integrative process, but also, substantially, it is its conclusion. (pp. 150, 151)

Kernberg (1970, 1984, 1989), as he has with many other personality disorders, presents a thoroughgoing analysis and reconceptualization of the antisocial personality. Integrating the views of many of his psychoanalytic precedents, Kernberg recommends a hierarchical differentiation among those of an antisocial nature, aligning them from the most to the least severe. He sees all antisocial personalities as possessing the fundamental features of the narcissistic personality, plus possessing unusual pathology in their sense of morality, that is, their superego functions. Special attention is given to the syndrome he terms "malignant narcissism," a personality pattern characterized by a combination of (a) a narcissistic personality disorder; (b) antisocial behavior; (c) ego-syntonic aggression or sadism directed either toward others or toward oneself, the latter producing a perverse sense of triumph in self-mutilation or suicide; and (d) a strong paranoid orientation.

Kernberg (1989) describes the typical symptoms of the antisocial personality disorder as follows:

These patients typically present a narcissistic personality disorder. The typical symptoms of the narcissistic personalities are, in the area of pathological self-love: excessive self-reference and self-centeredness; grandiosity and the derived characteristics of exhibitionism, an attitude of superiority, recklessness, and overambitiousness; overdependency on admiration; emotional shallowness. . . . Regarding the area of pathological object relations, *these patients' predominant symptoms are inordinate envy (both conscious and unconscious); devaluation of others as a defense against envy; exploitativeness reflected in greediness, appropriation of others' ideas or property, and entitlement. . . . The* basic ego state *of these patients is characterized by a chronic sense of emptiness, evidence of an incapacity to learn, a sense of aloneness, stimulus hunger, and a diffuse sense of meaninglessness of life.*

In addition, all of these patients present some degree of superego pathology. *Ordinary superego pathology of narcissistic personalities includes the incapacity to experience mournful, self-reflective sadness; the presence of severe mood swings; [and] a predominance of "shame" as contrasted to "guilt" in their intrapsychic regulation of social behavior. (pp. 559–560)*

Approaching the subject of the antisocial from a particular cognitive orientation, Beck and Freeman (1990b) does not modify the conventional view of the characteristics of the disorder, but does address the dysfunctional beliefs that shape many aspects of the antisocial's behavior:

These personalities view themselves as loners, autonomous, and strong. Some of them see themselves as having been abused and mistreated by society, and therefore justify victimizing others because they believe that they have been victimized.

The core *beliefs are "I need to look out for myself," "I need to be the aggressor or I will be the victim." The antisocial personality also believes that "Other people are patsies or wimps," or "Others are exploitative, and therefore I'm entitled to exploit them back." This person believes that he or she is entitled to break rules—rules are arbitrary and designed to protect the "haves" against the "have nots." (pp. 48, 49)*

Antisocial patients' automatic thoughts and reactions are frequently distorted by self-serving beliefs that emphasize immediate, personal satisfactions and minimize future consequences. The underlying belief that they are always right makes it unlikely that they will question their actions. Patients may vary in the degree of trust or mistrust they have in others, but they are unlikely to seek guidance or advice on any particular course of action. . . . Their behavior tends to be objectionable and even infuriating to others.

Instead of evaluating the potential helpfulness of such input, ASPD patients tend to dismiss input from others as irrelevant to their purposes. In addition, antisocial distortions tend to show a loss of future time perspective. (p. 154)

The interpersonal model of the antisocial personality pattern was formulated most clearly in recent years by the work of Leary (1957). In what he refers to as "adjustment through rebellion," Leary outlines a common motivation for several of the personality disorders. The subgroup he refers to as "distrustful" comes closest to what we consider today to be the typical aims and behavior of the antisocial. In his insightful portrayal, Leary writes:

Pain and discomfort are traditionally associated with alienation from others, but for these subjects this discomfort is less than the anxiety involved in trustful, tender feelings. For the person who has experienced past rejections or humiliations there are certain comforts and rewards in developing a rebellious protection. The essence of this security operation is a malevolent rejection of conventionality. Trust in others, cooperation, agreeability, and affiliation seem to involve a certain loss of individuality. Giving or sharing or trusting requires a sacrifice of pure narcissism and some relinquishing of the critical function. The rebellious adjustment provides a feeling of difference and uniqueness which is most rewarding to some individuals. Inevitable . . . a rebellious freedom, a retaliatory pleasure in rejecting the conventional, a delight in challenging the taboos, commitments, and expectations which are generally connected with a durable affiliative relationship. (p. 270)

Continuing the interpersonal tradition, Benjamin (1974, 1993a) has furnished an extended series of analysis of numerous personality disorders. In her characterization of the interpersonal dimensions of the antisocial personality, she notes the following as core characteristics:

There is a pattern of inappropriate and unmodulated desire to control others, implemented in a detached manner. There is a strong need to be independent, to resist being controlled by others, who are usually held in contempt. There is a willingness to use untamed aggression to back up the need for control or independence. The ASP usually presents in a friendly, sociable manner, but that friendliness is always accompanied by a baseline position of detachment. He or she doesn't care what happens to self or others. (p. 203)

The interpersonal analysis of ASP suggests that the "criminality" depicted by the DSM can be characterized as inordinate autonomy taking, addiction to control, and lack of attachment to self or others. These dimensions also describe the "antisocial" lawyers, doctors, and politicians not diagnosable by the DSM. Like the criminals described by the diagnostic manual, individuals within these higher-socioeconomic-status groups misuse their positions in the service of control for control's sake. They have no regard for the impact of their actions on other people. (p. 209)

The discussion now turns to the often overlooked but important empirical work of research psychologists. For example, Eysenck (1957, 1967) offers evidence for the thesis that psychopaths possess an inherited temperamental disposition to extroversion that inclines them to acquire antisocial behaviors. According to the learning theory espoused by Eysenck, extroverts condition slowly and therefore, in contrast to normals, are able to acquire the values and inhibitions of their social group to only a minimal degree. Eysenck's thesis leaves many details of psychopathic development unclear, and laboratory evidence for its central assumptions is scanty at best.

Whereas Eysenck's theory rests on the assumption of innate constitutional dispositions, other learning theorists who have studied aggressive sociopathic behavior base their interpretations solely in terms such as vicarious learning and reinforcement. Thus, Bandura and Walters (1959), following a social learning model that is not dissimilar in content from the views of many analysts, gave primary attention to the role of parent-child interactions. For example, hostile parents are viewed as models that the child imitates and uses as a guide to establish antisocial relationships with others. In other cases, parents may mete out rewards and punishments in a manner that produces a style of superficial affability cloaking fundamentally devious attitudes. A series of extensive studies by Quay and his associates (Quay, 1964; Quay & Werry, 1979) focused on delinquent populations and used multivariate statistical techniques to identify distinct clusters or types. Four characteristic patterns have been obtained repeatedly across a variety of population samples: conduct disorder, anxiety-withdrawal, immaturity, and socialized-aggressive disorder.

An empirical approach of special note is the work of Robins (1966) and her colleagues, which has attempted to unravel the juvenile antecedents of adult psychopathy and antisocial behavior. What is noteworthy in her findings is the close correspondence they show to the behaviors specified as characteristic of psychopathic personalities some half-century earlier by Kraepelin. What made these data so important is that they comprised, in almost every detail, the diagnostic criteria promulgated in the DSM-III antisocial personality. Despite the history of alternative models and theories available for consideration, the DSM-III Task Force voted to base its diagnostic guidelines in accord with this single, albeit well-designed, follow-up study of delinquency cases referred to one child guidance clinic in a large midwestern city.

A rather dispassionate approach to the characterization of the antisocial personality may be achieved best by methods that seek to coordinate the traits of each syndrome as objectively as possible. Thus, the five-factor approach espoused by Costa and Widiger (1993) achieves this goal by virtue of a statistical rather than a clinical and hence subjective manner. In their summary of the traits found to underlie the antisocial disorder, they state:

The diagnostic criteria essentially provide a set of behavioral examples of excessively low conscientiousness and low agreeableness. . . . Persons who are low in conscientiousness tend to be aimless, unreliable, lax, negligent, and hedonistic; the most extreme variants of these tendencies describe the indulgent and irresponsible antisocial individual. The antisocial person, however, is also manipulative, exploitative, vengeful, criminal, and ruthless, which are aspects of antagonism (particularly the facets of excessively low straightforwardness, altruism, compliance, and tendermindedness). (p. 45)

The work of Hare and his associates (Hare, 1986, 1991) has drawn on Cleckley's formulation of the psychopathic personality, reconceptualizing his descriptive texts in the form of the Psychopathy Checklist (PCL). Two correlated factors have emerged from this work. The first factor appears to represent a narcissistic personality variant of the psychopathic pattern, evidencing tendencies toward selfishness, egocentricity, superficial charm, and a lack of remorse and empathy. The second factor appears more directly related to those with an overtly antisocial lifestyle, evidencing early periods of delinquency, low frustration tolerance, frequent substance abuse, a parasitic lifestyle, impulsivity, and frequent illegal or criminal behaviors.

Hare's work appears to support the ideas of both Kernberg and Millon concerning the two major features of the psychopathic lifestyle. It represents Millon's view that psychopathy has at its core a *deficiency* in concerns for "others," manifesting, on the one hand, a *passive* variant in the narcissistic's self-focus and, on the other, an *active* variant as seen in the self-focus of the antisocial. Similarly, these data reflect Kernberg's recognition that the antisocial and the narcissist share essential and major features, despite aspects of dissimilarity in their overt behaviors, notably the prominent lack of conscience or morality in the antisocial.

Reference to the biogenic origins of the antisocial has been made by many investigators seeking to uncover the underlying biophysical correlates of the disorder. However equivocal these results may be, biological theorists continue to explore its potential substrates. Thus, Siever and Davis (1991) have formulated the following thesis regarding the antisocial syndrome. With his associates (Siever, Klar, & Coccaro, 1985), Siever writes:

In antisocial personality disorder (APD), the impulsive characteristics take the form of repetitive behaviors that conflict with social constraints, for example, stealing, lying, and fighting behaviors that are normally suppressed or inhibited in the service of societal rules. Clinically, these behaviors are often conceptualized in terms of a failure of social learning or internalization of societal constraints in the course of development—that is, a faulty superego or capacity for experiencing guilt. A number of studies suggest that such individuals may demonstrate lowered cortical arousal and more disinhibited motoric responses to a variety of stimuli. Thus, patients with antisocial personality disorder may be considered to be more likely to act than to reflect prior to their taking action, so that internalization of societally sanctioned controls may be more problematic. (p. 43)

A similar notion has been formulated by Cloninger (1987a) in his efforts to deduce the underlying neurobiologic elements of this personality:

Antisocial personality is defined here as the personality variant characterized by the basic response characteristics of high novelty seeking, low harm avoidance, and low reward dependence. This combination is associated with second-order traits of impulsive-aggressive, oppositional, and opportunistic behavior. This description is essentially identical to the traditional concept of the "primary psychopath" described by Cleckley and others. (p. 584)

An earlier model of contemporary thought sought to anchor "psychopathic" behaviors to developmental learning and psychological dynamics. Proposed by Millon (1969) in his formulation of the active-independent personality, the following descriptions and criteria served as the initial working draft in 1975 for what was ultimately labeled by the DSM-III Task Force as the "antisocial personality." A synthesis of the more concretistic and research-oriented criteria in the final DSM-III draft and the more abstract and clinically oriented criteria that follow may prove useful to the reader. The 1975 draft proposal stated:

This pattern is typified by a self-assertive, temperamentally hostile and socially forceful and intimidating manner. There is pride in self-reliance, unsentimentality and hard-boiled competitive values. Malicious personal tendencies are projected outward, precipitating frequent outbursts of explosive anger. Vindictive gratification is obtained by humiliating and dominating others. A rash willingness to risk harm is notable as is a fearlessness in the face of threats and punitive action. Frank antisocial behaviors (e.g., truancy, non-traffic arrests, frequent fighting) are common among adolescent and post-adolescent aggressive personalities, as well as in certain socioeconomic sub-populations. However, the majority of these personalities do not exhibit flagrant antisocial behaviors, finding a sanctioned niche in conventional roles.

Since adolescence or early adulthood at least 3 of the following have been present to a notably greater degree than in most people and were not limited to discrete periods nor necessarily prompted by stressful life events.

1. *Hostile affectivity (e.g., pugnacious and irascible temper flares readily into argument and attack; exhibits frequent verbally abusive and physically cruel behaviors).*

2. *Assertive self-image (e.g., proudly characterizes self as self-reliant, vigorously energetic and hard-headed; values tough, competitive and power-oriented life style).*

3. *Interpersonal vindictiveness (e.g., reveals satisfaction in derogating and humiliating others; contemptuous of sentimentality, social compassion and humanistic values).*

4. *Hyperthymic fearlessness (e.g., high activation level evident in impulsive, accelerated and forceful responding; attracted to and undaunted by danger and punishment).*

5. *Malevolent projection (e.g., claims that most persons are devious, controlling and punitive; justifies own mistrustful, hostile and vengeful attitudes by ascribing them to others).*

Although the preceding characterizations were not utilized as a framework for the DSM-III antisocial personality description, owing to its heavy emphasis on Aggressive-Sadistic components, this model served subsequently as a basis for the DSM-III-R characterization of a Sadistic personality pattern. The DSM-III model for the antisocial personality was based essentially on the work of Lee Robins (1966) in which specific behavioral acts became the foundation of the criteria employed. The DSM-III-R criteria remained consistent with the initial criteria employed in Robin's work, although one additional criterion was added to represent the concept of these individuals' typical absence of guilt or remorse.

The issue of whether the antisocial form is but only one of several manifestations of a more complex personality substrate continues as controversial in the literature. The DSM-III committee voted to retain the decision promulgated for the first time in the DSM-II that the" antisocial" label serve to represent a distinct personality type rather than a form of behavior observed in several personality types. This decision signified a shift from the DSM-I, which considered "sociopathic reactions" to be a syndrome symptomatic of any of several underlying personality disorders. As contended earlier, undue prominence is given the delinquent or criminal expression of the personality by designating it as antisocial. This formulation fails to recognize that the same fundamental personality structure, with its characteristic pattern of ruthless and vindictive behavior, is often displayed in ways that are not socially disreputable, irresponsible, or illegal. Using personal repugnance and conventional morals as a basis for diagnostic syndromes runs contrary to contemporary efforts to expunge social judgments as clinical entities (e.g., the reevaluation of the concept of homosexuality as a syndrome). The label "antisocial" continues a struggle to resolve issues associated with earlier value-laden concepts.

The ICD-10 reverts to an earlier term as the label for the DSM's antisocial personality, entitling

it the "dissocial personality." The following features are summarized in their criteria listing: a callous unconcern for the feelings and needs of others; a persistent and gross attitude of irresponsibility, as evident in a disregard for prevailing social norms, rules, and obligations; though having no difficulty in establishing relationships, there is an incapacity to maintain them over extended periods; a very low tolerance for frustration and a low threshold for discharging aggression, including violence; an incapacity to experience guilt and to profit from troublesome experiences, particularly punishment; a marked proneness to blame others and to offer plausible rationalizations for behaviors that bring the person into conflict with society. Noted as associated features are the presence of persistent irritability, and childhood or adolescent conduct disorders. We should be mindful that this characterization includes features that are normally associated with aggressive/sadistic personality styles. These features have been fused into the dissocial personality disorder criteria owing to the failure to include the sadistic personality pattern in the ICD taxonomy.

Extensive reviews of the literature, several reanalyses of diagnostic efficiency statistics, and a major field trial study were carried out, all toward the end of trying to develop a more trait-oriented basis for the antisocial personality diagnosis. Specifically, efforts were made to compare the Robins' criteria of behavioral acts that served usefully in the DSM-III and DSM-III-R with trait characterizations based on the work of Cleckley (1964) and Hare (1970); the desire was to bring the DSM-IV criteria more in line with the personality trait format employed in all the other disorder categories of Axis II. Despite these extensive efforts, the DSM-IV resulted in only modest changes. Specifically some aspects of the earlier criteria sets were condensed and simplified. Two items (irresponsible parenting and failure to sustain monogamous relationships) were deleted; two items pertaining to irresponsibility (failure to sustain consistent work or honor financial obligations) were collapsed into one. The criterion relating to early evidence of a conduct disorder was clarified and simplified.

The final set of seven DSM-IV criteria places primary emphasis on Interpersonal conduct, although a number of criteria are listed for the Behavioral, Cognitive, and Mood domains. The following criteria are noted in the Interpersonal realm: a failure to conform to social norms and a disinclination to engage in lawful behaviors; signs of consistent irresponsibility in one's dealings with others; deceitfulness and the conning of others for personal profit or pleasure; indifference to the welfare of others, as evident in a lack of remorse or the rationalization of why one has hurt or mistreated others. There is a single criterion in the Behavioral area: a reckless disregard for one's own safety as well as those of others. Partially behavioral but also Cognitive is another single criterion: a failure to plan ahead, resulting in behavioral impulsivity. Finally, there is a Mood domain criterion that may be more suitable for the aggressive-sadistic personality pattern, namely: irritability and aggressiveness, as seen in repeated physical assaults.

Several major theorists have recognized the strong similarity between the antisocial and the narcissistic personality (e.g., Kernberg, 1992). As described in prior pages, many studies have been done investigating the attributes of these individuals, yet clarity regarding their central features seems to escape us. The evolutionary model, with its polarity schema, may provide us with insights that other approaches have only hinted at faintly, but have not established firmly. Reviewing Figure 12.1, we can see the prominence assigned to both the self (individuating) and active (modifying) polarities. What this suggests is that the antisocial is driven, first, to benefit himself and, second, to take vigorous action to see that these benefits do accrue to himself. This pattern is similar to, yet different, than seen in narcissists, where an unjustified self-confidence assumes that all that is desired will

come to them with minimal effort on their part. The antisocial assumes the contrary. Recognizing by virtue of past experience that little will be achieved without considerable effort, cunning, and deception, the antisocial knows that desired ends must be achieved through one's own actions. Moreover, these actions serve to fend off the malice that one anticipates from others, and undo the power possessed by those who wish to exploit the antisocial.

Figure 12.2 offers a useful summary of the major historical contributors.

CLINICAL FEATURES

The following sections should provide the reader with a systematic analysis of the prototypal domains and personality variants of the antisocial disorder.

PROTOTYPAL DIAGNOSTIC DOMAINS

The major features of this personality pattern are approached in line with the domain levels used in previous chapters. Here we will identify characteristics that are relatively specific to the prototypal antisocial disorder. Unless noted, the domains described should be generally applicable to most of the adult subtypes (see Table 12.1 and Figure 12.3).

Expressive Behavior: Impulsive

Many of these personalities evidence a low tolerance for frustration, seem to act impetuously, and cannot delay, let alone forgo, prospects for immediate pleasure. They are precipitous and irrepressible, acting hastily and spontaneously in a restless, spur-of-the-moment manner. Their impulsive behaviors are short-sighted, incautious, and inprudent. There is minimal planning, limited consideration of alternative actions, and consequences are rarely examined or heeded. Antisocial types appear easily bored and restless, unable to endure the tedium of routine or to persist at the day-to-day responsibilities of marriage or a job. Others of this variant are characteristically prone to taking chances and seeking thrills, acting as if they were immune from danger. There is a tendency to jump from one exciting and momentarily gratifying escapade to another, with little or no care for potentially detrimental consequences. When matters go their way, these antisocial variants often act in a gracious, cheerful, saucy, and

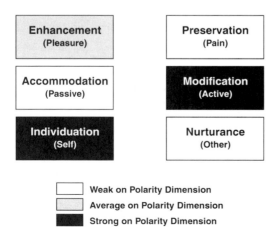

ANTISOCIAL PROTOTYPE

Enhancement (Pleasure)	Preservation (Pain)
Accommodation (Passive)	Modification (Active)
Individuation (Self)	Nurturance (Other)

☐ Weak on Polarity Dimension
▨ Average on Polarity Dimension
■ Strong on Polarity Dimension

Figure 12.1   Status of the antisocial personality prototype in accord with the Millon Polarity Model.

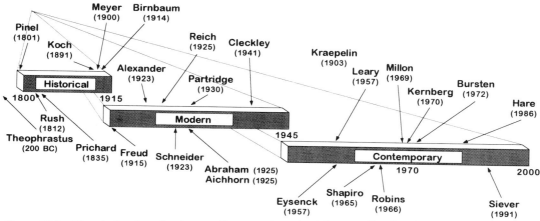

Figure 12.2   Historical review of major contributors to the antisocial personality disorder.

clever manner. More characteristically, their behavior is brash, arrogant, and resentful.

Although the preceding relates to the prototypal antisocial, it does suggest a typecast that is somewhat misleading. Many individuals who are intrinsically antisocial in the broad sense that we conceive them appear quite conventional in their appearance, manners, and styles of behavior. These nonstereotypical antisocials portray themselves in a manner consistent with their often rather conventional occupations. Hence, an aggrandizing and self-seeking physician will look and act like a physician, not like some riffraff gang member. The point to be made is that one should not be mislead into assuming that antisocials advertise their inclinations by superficial appearances.

Interpersonal Conduct: Irresponsible

It can be safely assumed that most antisocials are untrustworthy and unreliable in their personal relationships. They frequently fail to meet or intentionally negate obligations of a marital, parental, employment or financial nature. Not only do these personalities intrude upon and violate the rights of others, but they seem to experience a degree of pleasure in transgressing established social codes by engaging in deceitful or illegal behaviors. Not only do they covet both power and possessions, but they gain special joy in usurping and taking from others. For some, what can be plagiarized, swindled, and extorted are fruits far sweeter than those earned through honest labor. Once having drained all one can from one source, others are sought to exploit, bleed, and then cast aside. Pleasure in the

misfortunes of those in power or of means is particularly gratifying among most antisocial types.

Having learned to place their trust only in themselves, these personalities have few feelings of loyalty and may be treacherous and scheming beneath a veneer of politeness and civility. People are used as a means to an end, often subordinated and demeaned so that they can vindicate themselves for the grievances, misery, and humiliations they experienced in the past. By provoking fear and intimidating others, they seek to undo the lowly caste into which they feel they were thrust in childhood. Their search for power and material gains, therefore, is not benign; it springs from a deep well of resentment and the desire for retribution and vindication.

The most distinctive characteristic of antisocials is their tendency to flout conventional authority and rules. They act as if established social customs and guidelines for self-discipline and cooperative behavior do not apply to them. In some, this disdain is evidenced in petty adolescent disobedience or in the adoption of unconventional values, dress, and demeanor. Many express their arrogance and social rebelliousness in illegal acts and deceits, coming into frequent difficulty with educational and law-enforcement authorities.

Despite the disrespect they show for the rights of others, many antisocial types present a social mask, not only of civility but of sincerity and maturity. Untroubled by guilt and loyalty, they develop a talent for pathological lying. Unconstrained by honesty and truth, they weave impressive tales of competency and reliability. Many are disarmingly charming in initial encounters and become skillful

TABLE 12.1   Clinical Domains of the
Antisocial Prototype

Behavioral Level

(F) Expressively Impulsive. Is impetuous and irrepressible, acting hastily and spontaneously in a restless, spur-of-the-moment manner; is shortsighted, incautious, and imprudent, failing to plan ahead or consider alternatives, no less heed consequences.

(F) Interpersonally Irresponsible. Is untrustworthy and unreliable, failing to meet or intentionally negating personal obligations of a marital, parental, employment or financial nature; actively intrudes upon and violates the rights of others, as well as transgresses established social codes through deceitful or illegal behaviors.

Phenomenological Level

(F) Cognitively Deviant. Construes events and relationships in accord with socially unorthodox beliefs and morals; is disdainful of traditional ideals, fails to conform to social norms, and is contemptuous of conventional values.

(S) Autonomous Self-Image. Sees self as unfettered by the restrictions of social customs and the constraints of personal loyalties; values the image and enjoys the sense of being free, unencumbered, and unconfined by persons, places, obligations, or routines.

(S) Debased Objects. Internalized representations comprise degraded and corrupt relationships that spur revengeful attitudes and restive impulses which are driven to subvert established cultural ideals and mores, as well as to devalue personal sentiments and to sully, but intensely covet, the material attainments that society has denied them.

Intrapsychic Level

(F) Acting-Out Mechanism. Inner tensions that might accrue by postponing the expression of offensive thoughts and malevolent actions are rarely constrained; socially repugnant impulses are not refashioned in sublimated forms, but are discharged directly in precipitous ways, usually without guilt or remorse.

(S) Unruly Organization. Inner morphologic structures to contain drive and impulse are noted by their paucity, as are efforts to curb refractory energies and attitudes, leading to easily transgressed controls, low thresholds for hostile or erotic discharge, few subliminatory channels, unfettered self-expression, and a marked intolerance of delay or frustration.

Biophysical Level

(S) Callous Mood. Is insensitive, irritable and aggressive, as expressed in a wide-ranging deficit in social charitableness, human compassion or personal remorse; exhibits a coarse incivility, as well as an offensive, if not reckless disregard for the safety of self or others.

(F) = Functional domain.
(S) = Structural domain.

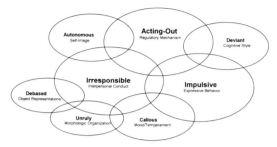

Figure 12.3   Salience of personologic domains in the antisocial prototype.

swindlers and impostors. Alert to weaknesses in others, they play their games of deception with considerable skill. However, the pleasure they gain from their ruse often flags once the rewards of deceit have been achieved. Before long, their true unreliability may be revealed as they stop "working at" their deception or as their need grows to let others know how clever and cunning they have been.

Cognitive Style: Deviant

Many antisocials construe events and interpret human relationships in accord with socially unorthodox beliefs and morals. In the main, they are disdainful of traditional ideals, fail to conform to acceptable social norms, and are often contemptuous of conventional ethics and values. It should be noted that these personalities exhibit both clarity and logic in their cognitive capacities, an observation traceable to Pinel's earliest writings. Yet they actively disavow social conventions, show a marked deficit in self-insight, and rarely exhibit the foresight that one would expect, given their capacity to understand (at least intellectually) the implications of their behavior. Thus, although they have a clear grasp of why they should alter their less attractive behaviors, they fail repeatedly to make such modifications. To them, right and wrong are irrelevant abstractions. It is not their judgment that is defective, but rather their ethics. Whereas most youngsters learn to put themselves in the shoes of others in a responsible and thoughtful way, antisocials use that awareness to their own purposes. To them, every opportunity pits their personal desires against those of others, resulting in the decision that they alone deserve every break and every advantage.

It should be evident that many of these personalities are unable to change because they possess deeply rooted habits that are largely resistant to conscious reasoning. To make their more repugnant behaviors more palatable to others, antisocial types are likely to concoct plausible explanations and excuses, often those of "poor upbringing" and past "misfortunes." By feigning innocent victimization, they seek to absolve themselves of blame—to remain guiltless and justified in continuing their irresponsible behaviors. Should their rationalizations fail to convince others, as when they are caught in obvious and repeated lies and dishonesties, many will affect an air of total innocence, claiming without a trace of shame that they have been unfairly accused.

Self-Image: Autonomous

There are two aspects to the image of self that are found among antisocials. The first, and more obvious, aspect is the sense of being unconventional and disdainful of the customs that most persons in society admire and seek to achieve for themselves. Inasmuch as antisocials reject societal values and goals, the more dissimilar they can be from "ordinary" people, the more gratified they will be with themselves. Hence, to be clever and cunning or disrespectful and deviant are both valued self-images.

Underlying these public presentations is a more fundamental desire, that of being unfettered by the constraints of personal attachments, that is, being free and unencumbered by connections and responsibilities to others. The sense of autonomy that drives this image of self is one in which the antisocial feels unconfined by persons, places, obligations, and routines. It is also important to the antisocial to arrogate to self a sense of magisterial self-sufficiency. This independence from others often makes the antisocial too proud to ask for anything, unwilling to be on the receiving end of the kindness and care others may express. It is not only humiliating to be the recipient of the goodwill of others, but antisocials can never trust others to act out of genuine concern and interest. They must remain inviolable so that they will never be humiliated or hurt again. It is the antisocial who must be the one to intimidate and reject others.

Antisocials do what they believe is right for them, disregarding that the behavior is patently dishonest or deceptively manipulative. Rarely would they designate the term "antisocial" as applicable to themselves; rather, in the view of antisocials, their behavior is suitable to those whose actions they disdain. Should they acknowledge being involved in behaviors that skirt the spirit of the law, perhaps even exaggerating the extent of these deviations, they will defend themselves by saying that "others not only do it, but get away with it," or that "everything in society is rotten to the core." White-collar antisocials have contempt for violent antisocials who possess the same basic personality; similarly, violent antisocials will scorn the white-collar type for being slyly devious and cowardly.

Object-Representations: Debased

If we look at the world through the eyes of antisocials—a place fraught with frustration and danger, where they must be on guard against the malevolence and cruelty of others—we can better understand why they behave as they do. They have no choice. You cannot trust what others will do. They will abuse, exploit, and dispossess you, strip you of all gratifications, and dominate and brutalize you, if they can. To avoid a fate such as this, one must arrogate all the power one can to oneself; one must block others from possessing the means to be belittling, exploitive, and harmful. Only by an alert vigilance and vigorous counteraction can one withstand and obstruct their malice. Displaying weakness or being willing to appease and compromise are fatal concessions to be avoided at all costs. Only by acquiring personal and material power can one be assured of gaining control of one's life. Further, only by usurping the powers that others command can one thwart them from misusing it. Given these fears and attitudes, we can readily see why these personalities have taken the course they have. It is only through self-sufficiency and decisive action that they can forestall the dangers in the environment and maximize the bounties of life.

Partly a result of their past experiences and partly a result of their current opportunities, the internalized objects of the antisocial consist of memories and images of a degraded and corrupt nature. These debased objects spur the antisocial's restive impulses and revengeful attitudes. Not only are these personalities driven to subvert established cultural ideals, but they seek to devalue personal sentiments and to sully, while intensely coveting, the material wealth that society has denied them.

Regulatory Mechanisms: Acting Out/Projection

The inner tensions that normally accrue by postponing the overt expression of manipulative thoughts and malicious feelings are *not* constrained by most antisocials. Rather, these exploitive and resentful dispositions are discharged directly and precipitously, enacted without guilt or remorse. In contrast to most other personalities, where socially repugnant impulses and feelings are either refashioned or repressed, the antisocial permits them open exposure, acts them out, so to speak, despite their disingenuous and socially offensive character.

Projection is another mechanism employed by antisocials. Accustomed throughout life to anticipate indifference or hostility from others and exquisitely attuned to the subtlest signs of contempt and derision, they are ever ready to interpret the incidental behaviors and remarks of others as fresh attacks on them. Given their perception of the environment, they need not rationalize their outbursts. These are fully justified as a response to the malevolence of others. The antisocial is the victim, an indignant bystander subjected to unjust persecution and hostility. Through this projection maneuver, then, they not only disown their malicious impulses but attribute the evil to others. As persecuted victims, they feel free to counterattack and gain restitution and vindication.

Morphologic Organization: Unruly

Constraints that help form a structure for one's personality organization are both few and undeveloped among antisocials. Their psychic system is poorly constructed to achieve the purposes for which the components of the intrapsychic mind are designed. As a consequence of this unruly organization, efforts to curb refractory energies and pernicious attitudes are weak or ineffectual. Controls are easily transgressed, and there is a consequential low threshold for both deviousness and irresponsible actions, as well as for hostile and erotic discharge. There is also an intolerance for delaying frustrations, unfettered self-expression, and few subliminatory channels developed to orient impulses of a problematic nature.

Acts that devalue their past leave a deep emptiness within antisocials. Having been jettisoned by one's own actions, there is now an inner scarcity of internalized objects. And it is this inner emptiness, at least in part, that drives the antisocial to aggrandizing behaviors. This is done with surface appearances, covering up or filling inner deficiencies by exploiting and usurping what others possess. Aggrandizing actions serve as much to make up for internal scarcities as for external deprivations.

The morphologic organization of antisocials is an open system possessing few valued components and few mechanisms for dynamic processing. It is the unruly and empty character of their intrapsychic world that necessitates aggrandizing self through superficial materialistic attainments—the big ring, the expensive and colorful car, fancy suits and shoes, and so on. Having ousted their past life from their inner world, antisocials are alienated from themselves, unable to feel any form of experiential depth. And because nothing and no one can be trusted, neither possesses value to the antisocial, other than momentarily. Hence, we see a hedonistic need to experience things that provide only immediate pleasure or achieve momentary recognition and significance. These, too, will be quickly jettisoned lest they "take over" and control their lives. Nothing is permitted permanence, be it a person, or a once-appealing material object.

Mood/Temperament: Callous

As noted, most of these personalities act out their impulses, rather than reworking them through intrapsychic mechanisms. Although showing restraint under certain conditions, there is a tendency to blurt out feelings and vent urges directly. Rather than inhibit or reshape thoughts, this personality is inclined to express them precipitously and forcibly. This directness may be viewed by some as commendable, an indication of a frankness and forthrightness. Such an appraisal may be valid at times, but this personality manifests these behaviors, not as an expression of "honesty and integrity," but from a desire to shock or put off others. Hence, among antisocials, we see an emotional disposition to be irritable and aggressive.

Among many antisocials, there is a wide-ranging deficit in social charitability, in human compassion, and in personal remorse and sensitivity. Beyond their lack of deeper sensitivity, many antisocials possess "a lust for life," a passion with which they are willing to pursue excitement and hedonistic pleasures. There appears also to be an impulse to explore the forbidden, an enjoyment in testing the limits of one's tolerance of pain and one's assertive powers. Thus, their passion appears to be for intensity and excitement, not just pleasure.

Related to antisocials' expansive and risky inclination is their seeming disdain for human compassion and sensitivity. Callousness thrives on adventures and risk, rather than on concern and empathy. From these deeper temperamental sources, if we can speak of them in this manner, we see the emergence of cynicism and skepticism, their distrust of the ostensive goodwill and kindness of others. Not uncommon among the less socially advantaged antisocial is a coarse incivility, as well as an offensive, if not reckless disregard for the safety or welfare of both oneself and others.

PROTOTYPAL PERSONALITY VARIANTS

Normal Styles

In the minds of many psychiatrists and psychologists, the antisocial personality is almost invariably seen as a severe character type and rarely conceived as potentially normal. A major reason for this perception is the pejorative implication of the antisocial label. If the syndrome were formulated in clinical rather than social terms, it might be recognized that the behaviors that characterize the disorder are not necessarily repugnant in their social consequences. Rather, the diverse manifestations of this personality should be viewed and interpreted as expressions of the individual's latent psychic makeup. From this broader, more clinical viewpoint, we know that the latent components of this personality often express themselves in behaviors that are minimally obtrusive, especially when manifested in sublimated forms, such as independence strivings, ambition, competition, risk-taking, and adventuresomeness.

The description of the "normal antisocial" style by Oldham and Morris (1990) is worth quoting here:

Throw caution to the winds—here comes the Adventurer. Who but Adventurers would have taken those long leaps for mankind—crossed the oceans, broken the sound barrier, walked on the moon? The men and women with this personality style venture where most mortals fear to tread. They are not bound by the same terrors and worries that limit most of us. They live on the edge, challenging boundaries and restrictions, pitting themselves for better or for worse in a thrilling game against their own mortality. No risk, no reward, they say. Indeed, for people with the Adventurous personality, the risk *is the reward. (p. 217)*

A slightly different slant on the normal antisocial may be seen in Millon et al.'s (1994) description of the "dissenting" individual:

These include unconventional persons who seek to do things their own way and are willing to take the consequence for doing so. They act as they see fit regardless of how others judge them. Inclined at times to elaborate on or shade the truth, as well as to ride close to the edge of the law, they are not conscientious—that is, they do not assume customary responsibilities. Rather, they frequently assert that too many rules stand in the way of people who wish to be free and inventive, and that they prefer to think and act in an independent and often creative way. Many believe that persons in authority are too hard on people who don't conform. Most dislike following the same routine day after day and, at times, act impulsively and irresponsibly. They will do what they want or believe to be the best without much concern for the effects of their actions on others. Being skeptical about the motives of most people, and refusing to be fettered or coerced, they exhibit a strong need for autonomy and self-determination. (p. 33)

The normal antisocial is action oriented, independent thinking, nonconforming, and innovative. These persons are enterprising and confrontational; they stretch the limits of the laws that prevail, do their best to keep within socially tolerable boundaries, but always focus on their own desires as primary. Seeking to make their own way, to find a place in which they alone can take charge, they assert themselves, push forward by sheer willpower, overcoming obstacles and cleverly maneuvering just within the boundaries of danger and legalities. Undeterred by difficulties, they possess a knack for turning setbacks into new opportunities. Many are extremely resourceful and self-motivated, taking the initiative to make things work toward their own ends. Some are effective leaders, masterful in their authority, ready to take charge, resolute and decisive. In sum, they are entrepreneurial adventurers and rugged individualists who use the free enterprise system to pursue their desires. The entrepreneurs have made their "aggrandizing talents" work successfully for them; in contrast, the aggrandizing aspirations of the antisocial have failed them. Successful aggrandizers are our industrialists, businesspeople, and lawyers who are no less driven than are antisocials to fill whatever void they feel within themselves. Enterprising and risk taking, most are wise enough, however, to stay clearly within societal boundaries.

Childhood Syndromes

The history of juvenile delinquency has been a long and detailed one, too far-ranging to be spelled out in the few paragraphs that we have to discuss this and associated childhood syndromes (ranging from infancy through adolescence). At the present time, these disorders are described in the DSM-IV as "conduct disorders," a rather broadly encompassing collection of repugnant behaviors as seen by society. Looking over the DSM, we see a long list—15 as of our last count—of characteristics that may be best differentiated into those that typify the antisocial construct and those that appear to be forerunners of what we term the sadistic construct. The features enumerated in this latest manual include initiating physical fights, intimidating others, and exhibiting physical cruelty at one end, and such behaviors as destroying the property of others, running away from home, truancy, staying out late at night, and breaking promises at the other end.

Those in the antisocial group are more akin to what Quay (1986) has described as the "socialized conduct disordered." The DSM-III spoke of this type as the nonaggressive variant of the conduct disorder; unfortunately, the distinction between aggressive and nonaggressive conduct disorders was eliminated in DSM-IV, a distinction in part attributable to the elimination of the sadistic personality disorder from the manual. As a consequence, both aggressive and nonaggressive types have been combined.

In our view, the distinctions between aggressive and nonaggressive is an important one conceptually. That youngsters exhibit mixtures of both in clinical settings is not to be dismissed; many children and adolescents evidencing conduct disorders display both features. Nevertheless, for conceptual and pedagogical purposes, these distinctions should be kept clearly in mind. In the following paragraphs, we will discuss the nonaggressive variants, for whom the disposition to violence and aggressive conduct is only a small element of their behavioral repertoire.

In what we might call the delinquent and partially socialized syndrome, we see chronic violations of social rules (e.g., truancy, substance abuse, persistent lying, nonconfrontive stealing) each of which tends, and is often, perhaps most frequently, executed in a peer group context. In what Millon (1969) has termed the "rebellious syndrome," there

is a more vigorous attack on established societal norms by intentional antisocial acts directed at representatives and symbols of the larger society. Thus, theirs is not a passive and semi-intellectual indifference to traditional customs, but a direct and challenging assault against the powers that be. Their energies are channeled into opposition toward the end of upsetting or destroying the customs or rules of a society they resent.

There are innumerable ways in which youngsters can react rebelliously to the strain of growing up. A common and relatively mild form is running away from home, of simply picking up one day and leaving for a—hopefully—better world. These youngsters typically are responding to the pressures and expectations of their parents and use the running-away mechanism not only as an escape, but as a means of causing their parents public embarrassment and forcing them to desist in their demands. Quite often, this behavior arises as a consequence of intolerable parental conflicts that spill over into childhood scapegoating.

More severe rebellious reactions take the form of persistent truancy, vandalism, and sexual misbehavior. These acts signify the youngsters' contempt for what they see as the oppressive rules and customs of a harsh or hypocritical society. Cases like these of so-called juvenile delinquency are found in all kinds of families and neighborhoods; they are not limited by any means to the slums and the underprivileged. Every court is acquainted with privileged adolescents who have reacted to parental indifference, deceptions, and hostility by stealing, drinking, and committing a wide variety of other antisocial acts. Every school, both in the "good" and "poor" communities, has its share of defiant, belligerent, and truant youngsters. Deprived of affection and interest, many adolescent girls, for example, rebel against the narrow values of unkind and strict parents by acting out sexually. The increase of teenage pregnancies in recent years attests to the number of unsatisfactory family relationships that precipitate this careless form of social defiance.

Adult Subtypes

The following combinations describe the great majority of so-called antisocial personality types. Although the focus in this section is on those features that distinguish the various antisocial amalgams, all combinations exhibit certain commonalities, most notably their marked self-centeredness and disdain for others. Security and gratification are achieved primarily by attending to oneself; the interests and needs of others are given incidental consideration, if attended to at all. Each of these personality mixtures views the world at large as comprising opportunities for exploitation and self-aggrandizement.

Psychopaths, sociopaths, sadists, and antisocial personalities have been lumped together in various ways in the past century. Each has been described by a parade of both common and contradictory characteristics. Some clinicians have described them as sharing a number of features, such as being impulsive, immature, naive, aimless, and flighty. No less frequently, it has been said that they are sly, cunning, and well-educated sorts who are capable of making clever long-range plans to deceive and exploit others. To complicate the clinical picture further, they have been noted for their cruel aggressiveness and for the keen pleasures they derive in disrupting and intimidating others. At still other times, they are pictured as lacking true hostility and are believed to feel considerable discomfort when their actions prove harmful to others. This confusion stems in part from a failure to recognize that these repugnant behaviors may spring from appreciably different personality combinations or mixtures. In this section, we will limit ourselves to variants that have at their core the aggrandizing elements that we believe are central to the antisocial personality pattern.

The Covetous Antisocial

In what we are terming the *covetous antisocial* we see, in its most distilled form, the essential feature we judge as characterizing the antisocial personality, the element of aggrandizement. Here we observe individuals who feel that life has not given them their due, that they have been deprived of their rightful level of emotional support and material rewards, that others have received more than their share, and that they personally never were given the bounties of the good life. What drives these personalities is envy and a desire for retribution. These goals can be achieved by the assumption of power, and it is best expressed through avaricious greed and voracity. To usurp that which others possess is the highest of rewards for covetous antisocials. Not only can they gain retribution, but they can fill the emptiness within. More pleasure comes from taking than in merely having.

Although similar in certain central characteristics to some narcissistic personalities, the covetous antisocial does not manifest a benign attitude of entitlement, but an active exploitiveness in which

greediness and the appropriation of what others possess are central motivating forces. Whereas the prototypal narcissist feels a sense of inner fullness and satisfaction, the covetous antisocial experiences a deep and pervasive sense of emptiness, a powerful hunger for the love and recognition they did not receive early in life. No matter how successful, no matter how many possessions they may have acquired, these antisocials still feel empty and forlorn. Owing to the belief that they will continue to be deprived, these antisocials show minimal empathy for those whom they exploit and deceive. They expend much effort in manipulating others to supply desired services and commodities—without offering any genuine reciprocation. Some may become successful entrepreneurs, exploiters of others as objects to satisfy their desires. Not expecting that people will comply willingly, covetous antisocials must be cleverly deceptive to overcome the reluctances of their victims.

Although the chief goal of these personalities is aggrandizement through the possession of goods usurped from others, it should not be forgotten that insecurity has been central to the construction of this personality's strategy and to the avaricious character of its pathology. Like a hungry animal after its prey, covetous antisocials have an enormous drive, a rapacious outlook in which they manipulate and treat others as possessions in their power games. Although they have little compassion for the effects of their behaviors, feeling little or no guilt for their actions, they remain at heart quite insecure about their power and their possessions, never feeling that they have acquired enough to make up for their earlier deprivations. They are pushy and greedy, anxious lest they lose the gains they have achieved. Their life is openly materialistic, characterized by both conspicuous consumptions and ostentatious displays. Regardless of their voracious desires and achievements, they remain ever jealous and envious. For the most part, they are completely self-centered and self-indulgent, often profligate and wasteful, unwilling to share with others for fear that they will take again what was so desperately desired in early life. Hence, these antisocials never achieve a deep sense of contentment, and feel unfulfilled no matter what successes they have had, remaining forever dissatisfied and insatiable.

The Reputation-Defending Antisocial

Not all antisocials desire to fill their sense of emptiness by pursuing material acquisitions. It is their reputation and status that they wish to defend or enlarge. For some, antisocial acts are self-enhancing, designed to ensure that others recognize them as persons of substance—people who should "not be trifled with." These antisocials need to be thought of as invincible and formidable persons, indomitable and inviolable; others should be aware that they possess qualities of strength and invulnerability. In these latter features, we see a strong amalgamation between the characteristics of the *reputation-defending* antisocial and those of the narcissistic personality.

Reputation-defending antisocials wish to convey to others that they are a tough and potent persons, who cannot be pushed around readily, and who will not allow anyone to slight their status. These antisocials react with great intensity when their status and capabilities are questioned. Most are perpetually on guard against the possibility that others will denigrate or belittle them. Some react instantaneously to a slight, whereas others brood and work themselves up until the proper moment arises to act defensively and assertively.

Reputation-defending, particularly among adolescents, reflects the youngster's social position and group status. The need of antisocials to overcome the past deficits in life makes them particularly sensitive to signs of indifference and disinterest, no less that of criticism. Both as an expression of internal needs and public reputation, these antisocials must do things that demonstrate to their peers that they are "contenders" of potential significance. This may require acts of aggressive leadership or risk-taking behaviors, often of a violent or criminal nature; the high prevalence of drug involvement and of turf wars among gangs illustrates these activities. The strengthening of the antisocial's reputation is often a by-product of these acts. What was initially intended as a defensive step to protect the person's standing, may become a major drive and aim in itself. But for most of these personalities, being tough and assertive, proving one's strength among one's peers, remains largely a reputation-defending act, and not a hostile one, as is often the case in antisocial/sadistic personality types.

The Risk-Taking Antisocial

Risk-taking is often carried out for itself, for the excitement it provides, for the sense of feeling alive and engaged in life, rather than for purposes such as material gain or reputation-defending. As noted elsewhere in this chapter, some people respond before thinking, act impulsively, behaving in an unreflective and uncontrolled manner. Beyond this inability to control their behaviors and feelings, the *risk-taking antisocial* appears to be substantially fearless, unblanched by events that most people experience as dangerous or frightening. They give evidence of a venturesomeness that appears blind to the potential of serious consequences. Their riskiness seems foolhardy, not courageous. Yet, they persist in an hyperactive search for hazardous challenges and for gambling with life's dangers. Descriptively, we may characterize these antisocials as being dauntless, intrepid, bold, and audacious. Perhaps more significantly, they are recklessly foolhardy, seem uninhibited by genuine hazards, and disposed to pursue truly perilous ventures. We see here an admixture or commingling of both antisocial and histrionic features.

In contrast to other antisocials, where the basic motivations are largely aggrandizement and revenge, these individuals are driven by the need for excitement and stimulation, for momentary and fleeting adventures that are intrinsically treacherous. They are, in effect, thrill seekers, easily infatuated by opportunities to test their mettle or open their possibilities. What makes them antisocial is the undependability and irresponsibility of their actions, their disdain for the effects of their behaviors on others as they pursue a restless chase to fulfill one capricious whim or another.

The actions of these risk-takers are driven by the feeling of being trapped and burdened by responsibilities, by feeling suffocated and constrained by routine and boredom. Unwilling to give up their need for autonomy, lacking the habits of self-discipline, unsure that they can ever achieve or fulfill the emptiness they feel within themselves in the real world, they are tempted to pursue the potentials of new and exciting ventures, traveling on a desultory and erratic course of chancy and hazardous activities.

The Nomadic Antisocial

It is commonly held that the central features that characterize antisocials are their overtly oppositional, hostile, and negativistic behaviors, intentionally enacted to undermine the values of the larger society. Although this characterization may apply to many who are labeled antisocial, it would be incorrect to overlook other individuals whose adjustments are equally problematic from a social viewpoint. In what we are terming the *nomadic antisocial,* we find individuals who seek to run away from a society in which they feel unwanted, cast aside, and abandoned. Instead of reacting antagonistically to this rejection by seeking retribution for having been denied the normal benefits of social life, these antisocials drift to the periphery of society, scavenging what little remains they can find of what they could not achieve through acceptable social means. These individuals are angry at the injustices to which they were exposed, but now feel sorry for themselves and have distanced from conventional social affairs because they feel they have little influence on others and are fearful of being further rejected. These peripheral drifters and vagrants feel jinxed, ill-fated, and doomed in life. They are gypsylike in their roaming, itinerant vagabonds and wanderers who have become misfits or dropouts from society. Their isolation, however, is not benign. Beneath their social withdrawal are intense feelings of resentment and anger. Under minor provocation, or as a consequence of alcohol or substance abuse, these antisocials may act out impulsively, precipitously discharging their pent-up frustrations in brutal assaults or sexual attacks upon those weaker than themselves.

In certain respects the nomadic antisocial represents a mixture of antisocial characteristics and those of either or both the schizoid or avoidant personalities. A lifelong pattern of wandering and gypsylike migrant roaming becomes more and more ingrained by the accumulation of repeated disappointments, the conviction of being worthless and useless, and the sense of being abandoned and not belonging anywhere. This pattern is not infrequently seen among adopted children who feel uneasy about their place in this world, experience being dissatisfied and lonely in their homes, and fear the possibility of total rejection. Their migrant and straying ways may be a symbolic search for what they hope may be their "true home" or their "natural parents." Many feel like misfits, dropouts from a world where they never felt fully accepted. With little regard for their personal safety or comfort, and with minimal planning, these nomadic antisocials drift from one setting to another as itinerant wanderers, homeless persons drifting often into prostitution and alcoholism as a way of life.

The urge to remain autonomous, to live as vagrants if necessary, to keep from establishing a continuous residency, is in many ways akin to the common adolescent pattern of running away from home. Insecure where they live, feeling like failures, perhaps unwilling to assume the responsibilities of family life, the vagabond style may be experienced as an optimal life strategy. Despite its problematic consequences and the necessity to live a life of petty crimes, many choose to drift aimlessly, to show little serious forethought, and to possess few if any inclinations toward serious endeavors. They exhibit what may be called a "passive asociality," a well-suited lifestyle in which one neither works nor assumes any responsibilities other than basic survival.

Most nomadics are comparatively harmless, owing to their general indifference and disengagement from life. However, in contrast to the *remote* and *affectless schizoid,* these personalities are deeply angry and resentful. Moreover, many have normal needs for life's pleasures, especially those of an erotic character. Stirred by alcohol, in the main, they may become brutal when "liberated," or engage in criminal-like sexual behaviors in lascivious assaults on the weak and inadequate, such as children. What justifies our calling them "antisocial," therefore, is that their impulses are not benign, despite their peripheral and nomadic existence. When stirred by inner needs or environmental circumstances, their pent-up hostility will be discharged against those who are not likely to react forcefully.

The motives of nomadic antisocials are short-term, to reduce tensions and the discomforts of everyday life. They have difficulty envisaging life beyond the moment. They can find no place to settle down; no place has ever given them the acceptance and support they have needed or wanted. This sense of "being no place" is both similar to and different from the experience of depersonalization; nomadics appear vaguely disconnected from reality, possess no clear sense of self, and seem to be transients both within themselves and their environments.

The Malevolent Antisocial

This subtype epitomizes the least attractive of the antisocial variants because it includes individuals who are especially vindictive and hostile. Their impulse toward retribution is discharged in a hateful and destructive defiance of conventional social life. Distrustful of others and anticipating betrayal and punishment, they have acquired a cold-blooded ruthlessness, an intense desire to gain revenge for the real or imagined mistreatment to which they were subjected in childhood. Here we see a sweeping rejection of tender emotions and a deep suspicion that the goodwill efforts expressed by others are merely ploys to deceive and undo them. They assume a chip-on-the-shoulder attitude, a readiness to lash out at those whom they distrust or those whom they can use as scapegoats for their seething impulse to destroy. Descriptively, we may summarize their traits with the following adjectives: belligerent, mordant, rancorous, vicious, malignant, brutal, callous, truculent, and vengeful. They are distinctively fearless and guiltless, inclined to anticipate and search out betrayal and punitiveness on the part of others. The primary antisocial characteristics of these individuals may be seen as features that blend with either or both the paranoid or sadistic personality, reflecting not only a deep sense of deprivation and a desire for compensatory retribution, but intermingling within them an intense suspiciousness and hostility.

Dreading that others may view them as weak, or may manipulate them into submission, they rigidly maintain an image of hard-boiled strength, carrying themselves truculently and acting tough, callous, and fearless. To prove their courage, they may even court danger and punishment. But punishment will only verify their anticipation of unjust treatment. Rather than being a deterrent, it may reinforce their rebelliousness and their desire for retribution. In positions of power, they often brutalize others to confirm their self-image of strength. If faced with persistent failure, beaten down in efforts to dominate and control others, or finding aspirations far outdistancing their luck, their feelings of frustration, resentment, and anger will only mount to a moderate level, rarely to a point where their controls give way to a raw brutality and vengeful hostility, as is seen in the *tyrannical sadist*. Spurred by repeated rejection and driven by an increasing need for power and retribution, their aggressive impulses will, however, surge into the open. At these times, their behaviors may become outrageously and flagrantly antisocial. Not only will they show minimal guilt or remorse for what they have done, but they are likely to display an arrogant contempt for the rights of the others.

What distinguishes the *malevolent antisocial* from the tyrannical sadist is the former's capacity to understand guilt and remorse, if not necessarily to experience it. They are capable of giving a perfectly rational explanation of ethical concepts, that is, they *know* what is right and what is wrong, but they seem incapable *of feeling it*. We cannot ascertain whether this experiential deficit is constitutionally built in or consequential to deficiencies in early learning. Nevertheless, there appears to be a defect in the capacity to empathize with the rightness or wrongness of their actions. As with the tyrannical sadist, these antisocials may come to relish menacing others, to make them cower and withdraw. They are combative and seek to bring more pressure on their opponents than

their opponents are willing to tolerate or to bring against them. Most make few concessions, are inclined to escalate as far as necessary, never letting go until others succumb. In contrast to the tyrannical sadist, however, antisocials recognize the limits of what can be done in their own self-interests. They do not lose self-conscious awareness of their actions and will press forward only if their goals of self-aggrandizement are likely to be achieved. Their adversarial stance is often contrived, a bluffing mechanism to ensure that others will back off. Infrequently are actions taken that may lead to a misjudgment and counterreaction in these matters.

COMORBID DISORDERS AND SYNDROMES

This section will aid the clinician in fulfilling the tasks of identifying overlapping or mixed syndromes, and in discriminating among similar, but fundamentally different, syndromes.

Axis II Comorbidities

As can be seen in Figure 12.4, the antisocial (ATS) personality disorder overlaps most frequently with the narcissistic (NAR) and sadistic (SAD) personality patterns. The correspondence with the narcissistic personality derives in part from their common self-orientation. In addition to the preceding two comorbid personalities, we find that the basic antisocial disorder covaries with the histrionic (HIS), borderline (BDL), negativistic (NEG), and paranoid (PAR) personalities. A number of other variants of the antisocial personality may be seen in the patterns described under the Adult Subtype section.

Axis I Comorbidities

Despite the misconception that most of these personalities are devoid of emotional sensitivity,

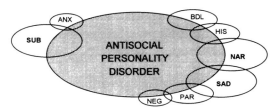

Figure 12.4 Comorbidity between antisocial personality disorder and other DSM Axis I and Axis II disorders.

there is ample clinical evidence that all variants often experience inner tensions and dysphoric moods. What appears to differentiate them from other personality types is their unwillingness to tolerate extended periods of psychic discomfort and frustration. It is the quick warding off of anxiety and the immediate discharge of tensions that is characteristic, not their failure or inability to experience either anxiety or tension. Their defense is geared toward rapid relief and impulsive acting out, rather than internal and intrapsychic resolutions.

Depressive Syndromes (DEP).   While inner tensions, frustrations, and dysphoria may occur, such discomforts are not tolerated for very long, being discharged through acting-out, rather than intrapsychic mechanisms.

When depression does occur in the antisocial personality, and if not "masked" through an exaggeration of acting-out behaviors, it is likely to be colored by bitterness, angry complaints, and accusations. Periods of self-loathing may occur at the perception of inner weakness and ineffectualness, and the sympathy of others would be actively shunned.

Anxiety Syndromes (ANX).   Despite their general infrequency, antisocial personalities do experience brief periods of anxiety prior to discharge and acting out. The major precipitant for these feelings is the dread of being controlled by others. Events that reactivate memories of similar and painful experiences in the past will evoke strong mixtures of anxiety and hostility. A severe panic attack may occur if the patient senses being particularly helpless or at the mercy of an obviously more powerful and hostile force. In contrast to the "free-floating" anxiety that persists in most other personality patterns, these patients quickly find an external source to which they ascribe their inner discomfort. Chronic anxiety, therefore, is rarely seen. For many, especially the nonantisocial variant, the surplus energy generated by anxiety is transformed and utilized to spur vigorous self-assertive action. Much of the aggressive drive that characterizes these persons reflects the exploitation of anxious energy in the service of manipulating and dominating others.

Substance Syndromes (SUB).   There is major degree of overlap between antisociality and substance use disorders. In great measure, this covariation can be attributed to economic influences and social dynamics, rather than to intrapsychic processes that are distinctive to any specific personality.

Among antisocials, the opportunities for material gain (at least for those who deal in drugs) and status enhancement are a powerful draw. For others, elements of dissolving feelings of guilt and self-destructiveness may contribute some share to their intrapsychic motivation.

DIFFERENTIAL DIAGNOSES

As noted in an earlier chapter, differential diagnostic considerations have diminished in importance because of the DSM-IV multiaxial format. Nevertheless, there are assessment pitfalls that clinicians should be alert to and avoid. For example, the persuasiveness and facile emotions of some antisocial aggressive personalities, particularly those with either histrionic or narcissistic features, may be so masterful as to con even experienced diagnosticians into believing that these patients are "depressed," "normal," "schizophrenic," or what have you. It is imperative when dealing with such glib and charming, but duplicitous, patients to inquire into their past history and to investigate inconsistencies. The discussion now turns from matters of deception to specific syndrome differentiations.

An important distinction to be drawn here is that between the antisocial personality and the condition labeled in the DSM-IV as *adult antisocial behavior*. This latter designation is essentially what previously was termed "dyssocial reaction"; it is now grouped among "conditions not attributable to a mental disorder that are a focus of attention of treatment." Both antisocial conditions are characterized by a disdain for social conventions. They differ in terms of the extent to which the behaviors they manifest reflect the operation of deeply ingrained and pervasive personality characteristics. As conceived in the DSM-IV, the behavior of antisocial personalities stems from internal psychological dynamics and broadly generalized environmental sensitivities. The actions of those evidencing the "adult antisocial behavior" condition are stimulus specific, usually provide material gain, and are acquired and sustained by the operation of vicarious or imitative group learning. Although the actions of the adult behavior group develop as a result of a less than ideal past, these experiences and associations did not destroy the acquisition of loyalty, trust, and the capacity for personal affection. Nor are these antisocial behaviors driven by unconscious and irrational needs; rather, they appear to be both discriminating and understandable in terms of material advantages and practical realities. Adult antisocial behaviors often grow as a consequence of group loyalties in which the individual joins others in shared criminal acts or plans collaborative illegal operations to achieve a tangible and profitable reward. By contrast, true antisocial personalities tend to be loners with little or no loyalty to anyone or anything. Driven primarily by the need to discharge unconscious tensions stirred up from the past, their goals often appear indiscriminate and impulsively pursued. For example, an antisocial personality, following a disagreement with an employer, may impulsively pilfer essentially worthless office items or decide to forge a series of small checks, for which there is no financial need. As a result, the person may end up losing a decent job and create a personal and family scandal. Compelled by the dictates of the unconscious, this behavior is objectively foolish and seemingly purposeless, enacted without apparent rhyme or reason.

Although they often coexist, a clear distinction between antisocial and *paranoid* personalities may be justified. In general, the paranoid patient exhibits fewer emotional controls and is more inclined to irrational behaviors. The prime distinction is the hypervigilance and suspiciousness of paranoids. They are extremely guarded and secretive, hypersensitive and readily slighted. Paranoids have difficulty relaxing and invariably expect to be tricked by others. This tense, edgy, and suspicious quality is usually lacking in antisocials, who typically act in a socially manipulative and emotionally constrained manner, despite their vigilance and mistrust. Paranoids may also be readily differentiated from the antisocial in that few paranoids ever engage in explicit illegal acts.

As noted in Chapter 11, problems arise in differentiating antisocials from *narcissistic* personality disorders. Although both are exploitive and unempathic, narcissists do not manifest the antisocial's characteristic impulsivity and active manipulativeness, nor do they usually possess a history of childhood conduct disorders, nor adult criminal or illegal behaviors.

Similarly, antisocials often covary with *histrionic* personality disorders. Histrionics, however, do not characteristically exhibit overt hostility and socially repugnant behaviors. Nevertheless, both of these disorders have a tendency to be seductive, stimulus-seeking, and emotionally impulsive.

The common element of interpersonal manipulativeness may at times cause difficulties in distinguishing *borderline* personalities and antisocials. However, the antisocial is primarily aggrandizing, manipulating others to gain power or other material gratifications; whereas the borderline's

manipulations reflect either emotional instabilities or the need to evoke supportive and nurturing attention from others.

Distinctions may be made as well between the *sadistic* personality and the antisocial. Although they often covary, the sadistic is essentially violent and explosive, primarily oriented to the destruction and derogation of others, solely for purposes of revenge and psychic discharge. By contrast, antisocials who are not sadistic, are motivated in a more restrained and cleverly manipulative fashion, often with no clear evidence of hostile intent, other than to exploit and to deceive others.

ASSESSING THE ANTISOCIAL: A CASE STUDY

The following are some of the features of the antisocial personality as they may be inferred from the Rorschach, TAT, and MMPI.

A disparity is often seen on the Rorschach between nontest behaviors and the responses to the test itself. Antisocials frequently display a rather casual and indifferent air as they approach the task, offering side comments of a rather obnoxious character. By contrast, their responses tend to be defensive and constrained. The protocol may contain rejected cards that have provoked the suspiciousness or irritability of the respondent. Similarly, perceptions may be voiced in a somewhat vague and nondetailed manner. Responses, especially to the color cards, may be delayed or reacted to in a particularly primitive and coarse manner, including blood and weapons as content. Beyond the generally reduced number of items, M, W, and shading responses may be especially limited. Also, $F+$ percents tend to be unusually low. Conversely, animal and popular responses may be proportionally high.

The TAT cards evoke either defensiveness or expansiveness, as also seen in narcissistic individuals. The underlying adolescent quality of the lives of many antisocials appears to show up in the juvenile character of many of their story themes. The world of many antisocials appears fixated at this age range, and acting-out fantasies of these personalities are readily portrayed. Although these themes are "oppositional" in character, that is, comprising irresponsible and childish activities in which illegal or antisocial acts predominate, there is little reference to perpetrators being punished or feeling guilty.

The MMPI will likely show the classical 4-9/9-4 profile, although variations containing these two scales are not uncommon and should be noted as a basis of differentiating various antisocial subtypes. Among those who are disposed to sadistic or violent behaviors, the most prevalent pattern shows high scores on Scales 4, 6, and 8; the addition of a high score on Scale 9 to this configuration suggests a particularly violent inclination. Where Scale 6 is prominently elevated, along with 4 and 9, we may infer a somewhat constrained and suppressed paranoid suspiciousness and hostility. Not infrequent among certain antisocials is a 2-4/4-2 profile, a pattern suggesting a measure of contrition and guilt for the person's sociopathic behaviors; this profile is often seen among individuals shortly after being apprehended or indicted. Similarly, where evidence of clear antisocial acts have been judicially proven, high scores may shift to Scales 2, 3, and 7.

The following sections summarize a case study of an antisocial personality, followed by a parallel MCMI-III profile and interpretive report segments.

CASE 12.1

Terrence W., Age 50, Unmarried

Terrence was picked up as a vagrant in a town 70 miles from his home. He had been drinking, caused considerable commotion outside a bar, made lewd comments to passersby and seemed unclear as to his whereabouts. In police headquarters, he seemed stuporous and apathetic, and was minimally communicative; he remained so for the following week, during which time he was remanded to a state hospital for observation.

Family history showed Terrence to be the third of seven children; his mother, a hardworking woman, died when he was 11, and his father, a drifter and periodic drunkard, died when Terrence was 16. Terrence was the "outsider" in his family, always by himself, teased by his siblings and shunned by his peers. He left school at 16, wandered for a year, took odd jobs to sustain himself, joined the Navy for a 4-year tour of duty, did not care for it, and has lived by himself since then in a rundown part of the city, working irregularly as a dishwasher, cook, and park attendant. He married a "pick-up" while in the Navy, and lived with her "miserably" for a few months. Upon his discharge, his wife disappeared; he has not seen her since, although he heard that she was remarried; she never legally divorced Terrence.

For several years thereafter, Terrence got himself into "lots of trouble." He became the getaway driver for a small gang of bank thieves. After drifting in this role for several years, he began to deal in drugs and numbers, serving as a front man in a cigar store, the back room being the setting for various illegal activities. Caught in a raid, he was convicted and sent to the state prison for 5 to 10 years. After a 4-year stint, Terrence returned to the community and has essentially gone straight, at least as far as overt criminal behavior is concerned.

When not in trouble, Terrence does not bother people; he simply prefers to be alone. Every couple of months he goes on a binge, a wild spree in which he spends all his money, gets into a drunken brawl, and usually lands in jail. Between these episodes, he does not drink and is quiet and unobtrusive.

Psychological tests and interviews with Terrence showed that he was of better than average intelligence, had great mistrust of others, and felt humiliated by his low status in life and the shame he brought to his more successful brothers in town. He admitted being suspicious of everyone's motives, having been made a fool of so much of the time. As he put it, "nobody gives a damn about you, especially if you're not worth a damn."

With regard to his wild sprees, he claimed that he "had to do something" every so often so as "not to go crazy doing things that don't mean nothing." When his isolation and monotony became unbearable he would "hit the bottle, and start feeling some life again."

Note should be made of the preceding case study in that it portrays a pattern that does not represent the stereotyped character of antisocials. A great majority of antisocials show mixed pictures, several of which do not portray the ostensibly hostile and mean-spirited qualities we tend to associate with these personalities. When we see an antisocial configuration that includes sadistic tendencies, the stereotyped picture would be applicable. However, when the configuration of personality traits combines antisocial elements with those of the schizoid, as in the preceding case, or with the narcissistic or borderline, for example, the overall pattern differs substantially from the stereotyped one.

The characteristics of the preceding antisocial/schizoid case are not very different than seen in the MCMI-III profile (Figure 12.5) and interpretive report that follows.

INTERPRETIVE SUMMARY

The MCMI-III personality profile of this man suggests a depressive apprehensiveness and the

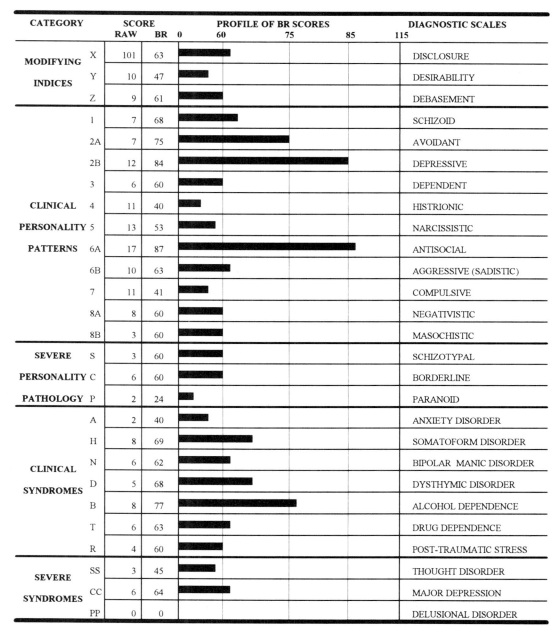

CATEGORY		SCORE RAW	BR	PROFILE OF BR SCORES 0 60 75 85 115	DIAGNOSTIC SCALES
MODIFYING INDICES	X	101	63		DISCLOSURE
	Y	10	47		DESIRABILITY
	Z	9	61		DEBASEMENT
CLINICAL PERSONALITY PATTERNS	1	7	68		SCHIZOID
	2A	7	75		AVOIDANT
	2B	12	84		DEPRESSIVE
	3	6	60		DEPENDENT
	4	11	40		HISTRIONIC
	5	13	53		NARCISSISTIC
	6A	17	87		ANTISOCIAL
	6B	10	63		AGGRESSIVE (SADISTIC)
	7	11	41		COMPULSIVE
	8A	8	60		NEGATIVISTIC
	8B	3	60		MASOCHISTIC
SEVERE PERSONALITY PATHOLOGY	S	3	60		SCHIZOTYPAL
	C	6	60		BORDERLINE
	P	2	24		PARANOID
CLINICAL SYNDROMES	A	2	40		ANXIETY DISORDER
	H	8	69		SOMATOFORM DISORDER
	N	6	62		BIPOLAR MANIC DISORDER
	D	5	68		DYSTHYMIC DISORDER
	B	8	77		ALCOHOL DEPENDENCE
	T	6	63		DRUG DEPENDENCE
	R	4	60		POST-TRAUMATIC STRESS
SEVERE SYNDROMES	SS	3	45		THOUGHT DISORDER
	CC	6	64		MAJOR DEPRESSION
	PP	0	0		DELUSIONAL DISORDER

Figure 12.5   Millon Clinical Multiaxial Inventory-III.

expectation that people will be rejecting and disparaging. Despite a long-suppressed desire to relate to others and to be accepted by them, he may feel that maintaining a safe distance is best. Recurrent anxieties and a pervasive depressive mood may typify his emotional life. A surface apathy may be exhibited in his effort to conceal his deeper sensitivity. Behind this front of restraint and sadness may lie intense contrary feelings that are likely to break through in the form of oppositional behaviors and an angry resentment toward those he views as being critical and disapproving. When this resentment is expressed, however, the security and acceptance that he needs are threatened. To restrain his anger and thereby protect himself against further rejection, he may attempt—unsuccessfully—to conceal his oppositional urges.

It is characteristic of this man to display an edgy irritability and broad-ranging negativism. Innumerable wrangles and disappointments with others may occur as he vacillates among depressive withdrawal, sullen passivity, and explosive anger. These moods may punctuate extended periods of loneliness. He is likely to feel misunderstood, unappreciated, and demeaned by others and may be characteristically pessimistic and disillusioned about life. His resulting low self-esteem may be further compounded by a tendency toward introspection and self-derogation. The alienation that he feels from others may parallel a feeling of alienation from himself. He may hesitate to express this self-contempt publicly, however, lest it invite a chorus of further derision from others.

This patient is both antisocial and depressively inclined; he also experiences a constant and confusing undercurrent of tension and anger. Moreover, he may frequently turn against himself, feeling remorseful and self-condemnatory, Vacillation may be exhibited among his oppositional urges, his loneliness, and his general numbness of feeling.

As a result, he has learned to guard against anticipated ridicule and contempt. Able to detect the most minute traces of annoyance expressed by others, he may interpret a minor slight as major derision and condemnation. Moreover, he appears to have learned that good things do not last and that support and friendship end with disappointment and rejection. Anticipating disillusionment, he may often react with impulsive hostility. A cyclical variation may be observed in his behavior as depressive constraint is followed by angry and antisocial outbursts, which are followed in turn by remorse and regret. These erratic emotions are intrinsically distressing and upset his capacity to cope effectively with everyday life.

This man's responses to the MCMI-III indicate that he is subject to episodes of alcohol abuse that unfold at times of frustration, disappointment, and resentment. Unable to restrain his intense and unstable emotions, he is likely to become stormy and destructive during times of drinking. Provocative complaints and discontent are likely to be mixed with subsequent feelings of guilt and contrition. Both tend to be short-lived, although the destructive and injurious consequences may persist for some time. During drinking bouts, his chronic level of anger and irritability is greatly aggravated and may lead to irrational accusations and intimidation, if not brutality, toward family members. In more quiescent periods, his drinking primarily serves to moderate the deep ambivalence he feels toward himself, his work, and his relationships with others.

PATHOGENIC DEVELOPMENTAL BACKGROUND

For pedagogical purposes, biogenic factors are again differentiated from experiential influences. The usual caveat concerning the conjectural nature of the hypotheses that follow is also applicable. There is a marked paucity of established empirical findings, even in this group of disorders where more research has been undertaken than in any other personality syndrome. Although some of the conjectures proposed in the following paragraphs derive from findings that are reasonably consistent, it would still be wise to view them with a skeptical eye.

HYPOTHESIZED BIOGENIC FACTORS

Perhaps more than for any other personality disorder, there exists an extensive number of biologically oriented studies that explore the genetic bases, neuropsychological factors, and arousal levels among this group of pathologies. Scholarly reviews may be found in several useful references (Meloy, 1988; Widiger, Corbitt, & Millon, 1991). In previous discussions concerning the role of biogenic influences, we noted both the marked paucity and equivocal nature of established empirical findings; as a consequence, etiologic propositions are highly speculative and the hypotheses presented here must be viewed in this light.

Heredity

The high frequency of correspondence in overt oppositional behavior commonly observed among family members suggests that constitutional dispositions traceable to genetic origins may play a role in the development of the antisocial pattern. Of course, observed similarities in family behaviors can be accounted for in large measure by shared experiences and common training methods. Nevertheless, it seems reasonable to posit that if there are biophysical substrates for antisocial tendencies, they may in part be transmitted by heredity.

Evidence in support of this thesis may be found in a number of large sample studies, such as those by Cadoret and Cain (1981); Cloninger, Reich, and Guze (1978); Eysenck and Eysenck (1969); Schulsinger (1977); Centerwall and Robinette (1989); and Grove, Eckert, and Heston (1990).

Parmic Infantile Reaction Patterns

Parents who bring their acting-out children to clinics often report that their youngsters "always were that way." Not uncommonly, parents remark that these children seemed undaunted by punishment, unimpressionable, unbending, and unmanageable. Furthermore, they evidenced a daring and boldness, an audacious and foolhardy willingness to chance punishment and physical harm; they seemed thick-skinned and unaffected by pain.

The possession of such temperamental attributes from early life are significant not only in themselves but for the experiences they produce, and the reactions they evoke from others. Being more venturesome, such children explore the challenges and competitions of their environment more assertively; moreover, they intrude themselves and upset the peaceful existence that others seek. Not only are they likely to encounter and precipitate more conflict and trouble than most children, but their seeming recalcitrance in the face of punishment results in their receiving more punishment than that required to control most children.

Neurological Characteristics

Proposals have been made to the effect that aspects of the antisocial personality style may be attributed to deficiencies in those frontal lobe processes associated with attentional regulation, emotional responsivity, and behavioral persistence. Others investigating the role of frontal lobe dysfunctions have produced equivocal or contradictory findings (Hare, 1970), leading some to note that although such neurological deficits were possible, the existing evidence does not prove to be conclusive and that dysfunctions in this area may result from impairments in other regions of the brain.

Early work by Lykken (1957), Eysenck (1964), and Quay (1965), resulted in the proposition that deficits in arousal might account for the antisocial disposition. Noting that antisocials were slow to condition to warning signals of fear and were inclined to be unresponsive to painful stimuli, they suggested that nonfrontal lobe disturbances of hypoarousal and rapid stimulus habituation might serve to undergird the antisocial's "fearless" behaviors. Other investigators (Blackburn, 1993) who have researched this area concluded that the data on arousal are essentially equivocal. Along a similar line, some investigators have suggested that antisocial tendencies may stem from a weak or deficient behavioral inhibition system. All these hypotheses have generated contradictory findings, although the likelihood that biogenic factors dispose some individuals to learn antisocial behaviors cannot be dismissed.

An unusual anatomic distribution in the limbic system also may contribute to the distinctive pattern of affectivity found in the antisocial. Conceivably, the "pain" center of the brain may be functionally sparse, accounting, in part at least, for the hardheadedness and insensitivity seen in many antisocial personalities, and for the bold and seemingly fearless quality of their outlook. Furthermore, we may speculate that the biophysical substrate for anger may be either copious or extensively branched, resulting in more intense and more frequently activated resentful reactions.

CHARACTERISTIC EXPERIENTIAL HISTORY

Although there are indications of a biogenic nature that disposes youngsters to acquire the antisocial personality pattern, psychogenic and sociogenic factors will play a significant role in shaping the timing, character, and form of expression with which these dispositions manifest themselves. It should also be recognized that psychosocial influences may be sufficient in and of themselves to give rise to these repugnant behaviors. To restate matters, both biogenic and psychosocial factors are likely to be involved in various complex interactions. Widiger, Corbitt, and Millon (1991) summarize a model outlined by Wilson and Hernstein (1985) that sought to demonstrate the highly interactive nature of antisocial development:

[It] includes a complex interaction of constitutional factors (level of impulsivity, intelligence, and arousal), failed socialization within the family (absence of a consistent enforcement of clear rules in the context of an atmosphere of warm support), and early experiences within the school (cold and permissive schools that do not provide sufficient alternatives and may even indirectly reinforce antisocial behavior patterns), as well as secondary sociological factors (peer influences, neighborhood

boundaries, unemployment, and opportunities for crime). (p. 69)

Early Parental Indifference

Infants who are exposed to parental neglect, indifference, even hostility during the *sensory-attachment* stage are likely to "feel" the world as a cold and ungiving place, hence creating a template for a lack of human sensibility and attachment behaviors. Moreover, established within them are enduring resentments, as well as the incorporation of the parental model of human indifference and deficient empathy. It is not that they have learned to deny human attachments, but rather they have never experienced it sufficiently to seek it or gain gratification from close relationships. Much of the antisocials' habits of social indifference and personal exploitation are driven not by a hateful revenge, as is typical among sadistic personalities, but by their having neither a basic awareness of others' feelings, nor a disposition to care for their welfare. This early neglectful background is most common in the antisocial personality, but by no means is it the only psychogenic source for the development of this pattern.

Deficient Parental Models

Conducive to the antisocial personality is a lack of a parental presence. This begins during the *sensorimotor-autonomy* stage when children quickly learn to assert their independence rather freely, and not to experience the normal restraints imposed by parental attention and action. In these cases, parents provide little or no guidance. The child is either left to fend for him- or herself or to observe and emulate whatever behavioral models are available (usually sibs who are as mischievous and autonomous as the observing child is likely to become). Broken families, especially those in which the father has abandoned his wife and children, characterize this state of affairs. With the model and authority of the breadwinner out of sight, and the mother harassed by overwork and financial insecurity, the youngster often is left to explore the world, unguided and unrestrained by the affection and controls of an attending parent.

The disappearance of the father and the preoccupations of a distracted mother are also felt, perhaps implicitly, as a sign of rejection, especially by young boys. As a result, there emerges a freewheeling, lusty, and predatory approach to life. The

antisocial has, by now, given up the expectation of being cared for, certainly to say nothing of love. The young boy learns quickly that he will get only what it is that he can take on his own. He will have nothing should he be concerned with the needs and feelings of others. Any feeling of empathy must be discarded if he wishes to create some place for himself in this world, minor though it may be in the larger scheme of things. Limited in feelings of human tenderness, he must now suppress all such tendencies and become a coolly indifferent, rapacious, and grasping person.

Maldeveloped Conscience

Doubting the values of the larger society, knowing that little of its material benefits will be forthcoming without extreme efforts on their own part, and increasingly convinced of the need to assert their own powers of self-sufficiency, these youngsters begin their *pubertal-gender identity* stage with a determination to reject the conventions of traditional societal values and acquire behaviors consistent with the values of their peer group. Why should these children accept the restrictions and demands that adults seek to impose on them when they have nothing to gain and, in addition, are convinced that they can manage better either by turning to themselves or by emulating the only society that they feel is relevant—that of the chosen peer group.

Having been subjected to parental neglect, indifference, or hostility throughout their growing years, future antisocials learn not only to reject their parents' questionable values, but to actively oppose the standards of most of the adult world. Thus, antisocials set out in the *intracortical-integrative* stage to shape their own identity—one that is contrary to those espoused by their "persecutors"—and in so doing, embark on a course of independence and mistrust characterized by self-assertion and autonomy. A major consequence of these actions is to undermine the development of an empathic conscience or superego. Not only has the capacity for these acquisitions been maldeveloped, but the opportunities for them to mature through identification with loving adult figures has failed to materialize. Moreover, parents who contributed to the future antisocial's early deprivations and neglect may have provided problematic and nonempathic models of identification. The same parent whose deficient care led to the child's sense of basic distrust may have exhibited a distorted sense of moral right or wrong that was incorporated by the child. Also possible as a consequence of parental neglect is what has been termed "a superego lacunae," a massive deficit in social conscience.

To find some model, some credo to mobilize and give meaning to their fate during the intracortical-integration stage, these children will most often turn to peers, to those other barren and lost souls who are similarly bereft of parental attention and who wander aimlessly in an indifferent if not hostile world. Together with these fellow outcasts, future antisocials quickly learn that they are viewed as misfits in society, that their misfortunes will be compounded by the deprecatory and closed-minded attitudes of the larger community. What they see around them is a world of predators, not a world of empathic and caring people. Having been a prey for others in early childhood, these youngsters learn that it is better to be predator than prey. Looking at the desperation and devastation of adult life in their underclass community, they see no future for themselves, no connection between conscientiousness and schooling, on the one hand, and postadolescent respect and employment, on the other. They learn that they will find a means of survival only by toughness and cunning. But this adaptive strategy sets into play a vicious circle; as these youngsters assert themselves, as they venture into the deviant remains left for them and their fellow scavengers by the larger society, that very same society castigates and condemns them further. Their resentments mount, and the circle of rejection and counterrejection gains momentum.

Another consequence of rejecting "authorities" is to lose the guidance and controls society provides for handling and directing impulses. By failing to accept traditional values and customs, youngsters are left largely to their own devices. They must devise, anew, ways and means to handle their emotions. Going it alone is no simple task, and in this sphere, where these children are strongly driven by unempathic, if not vengeful impulses, we find that few of them acquire self-developed controls adequate to their emotions. For this reason, among others, antisocial youngsters have difficulty in deferring gratifications, in resisting temptations, and in inhibiting angry reactions to even the slightest frustrations; in short, they pursue desires with little concern for the dangers or complications they invite.

With no hope of changing their fate, no promise of advancement, and struggling throughout to keep a foothold in the dog-eat-dog world into which they have been cast, they are driven further into a self-aggrandizing and exploitive lifestyle. Because no one will provide the material benefits of society, because they have been deprived of object-love and caring, they have no one but themselves to draw on to achieve these ends. Hence, they become almost totally self-oriented and will employ whatever means, legal or illegal, to fill the void they feel within. At its foundation, the antisocial demonstrates an aggrandizing personality pattern, a search to fill within the self that which the child did not receive from either parents or society-at-large.

Secondary Family Status

It is not only in socially underprivileged families or underclass communities that we see the emergence of antisocial individuals. The key problem for all has been their failure to experience the feeling of being treated fairly and having been viewed as a person/child of value in the family context. Such situations occur in many middle- and upper-middle-class families. Here, parents may have given special attention to another sibling who was admired and highly esteemed, at least in the eyes of the "deprived" youngster. Thus, even if the youngster is the recipient of considerable caring and material rewards, he or she *feels* neglected and deprived. This is a comparative rather than an absolute judgment, but a powerful and deeply felt one, nevertheless.

These materially privileged, but emotionally deprived youngsters become persistently acquisitive and driven by an aggrandizing need, such as power, status, and inexhaustible accumulations. Inasmuch as they are not part of the underclass of society, they may also progress educationally and professionally to positions of respect and stature. Nonetheless, they continue to be driven to overcome the emptiness of early indifference, to fill the void they experienced in childhood. Not seen as antisocials in the conventional sense, owing to their public propriety and success, these individuals remain, at heart, aggrandizers, invariably competitive, avaricious, and self-magnifying. These socially sublimated antisocials are among our most successful law and business professionals, comprising a major segment of our respected competitive society.

SELF-PERPETUATION PROCESSES

An essential element of personality disorders is that their efforts to cope with their world are themselves pathogenic; they create self-defeating actions.

Distrustful Anticipations

If we look at the world through the eyes of antisocial personalities—a place fraught with little love and much frustration, a place where they must be on guard against the indifference or cruelty of others—we can better understand why they behave as they do.

Their strategy is clear: "I cannot trust others; they will abuse and exploit their power, they will be indifferent to my needs, even dispossess me, strip me of all gratifications, perhaps dominate and brutalize me, if they can. To avoid this fate, I must arrogate all the power I can to myself, I must block others from possessing the means to be belittling, exploitive and harmful. Only by alert vigilance to disinterest, only by vigorous counteraction can I withstand and obstruct the insensitivity and hostility of others. Getting close, displaying weakness, and being willing to appease and compromise, are fatal concessions to be avoided at all costs. Only by acquiring power for myself can I be assured of gaining the rewards of life; only by usurping the powers that others command can I thwart them from misusing it." Given these fears and attitudes, we can readily see why antisocials have taken their course of action and independence. Only through self-sufficiency and decisiveness can they forestall the indifference or dangers of their environment, and thereby maximize achieving the bounties of life.

Unfortunately, these self-protective attitudes set into motion a vicious circle of suspiciousness and distrust, provoking others to react in a similarly cool and rejecting fashion. Potential sources of warmth and affection become wary, creating the indifference and rejection that prompted the antisocial's distrust in the first place. Hence, the antisocial has activated a repetition of the past, further intensifying resentments, the sense of isolation, and the need for autonomy.

Vindictive Interpersonal Behavior

The defensive actions of antisocials serve more than the function of counteracting exploitation and indifference. They are driven by a need to vindicate themselves, a desire to dominate and humiliate others, to wreak vengeance upon those who have mistreated them. Not only do they covet possessions and powers but they gain special pleasure in usurping and taking from others (a symbolic sib, for example); what they can plagiarize, swindle, and extort are fruits far sweeter than those they can earn through honest labor. And once having drained what they can from one source, they turn to others to exploit, bleed, and then cast aside; their pleasure in the misfortunes of others is unquenchable.

Having learned to trust only themselves, antisocials have no feelings of genuine loyalty and may be treacherous and scheming beneath a veneer of politeness and civility. People are used as a means to an end; they are to be subordinated and demeaned so that antisocials can vindicate themselves for the grievances, misery, and humiliations of the past. By provoking fear, by intimidating others, and by being ascendant and powerful, they will undo the lowly caste of childhood. Their search for power, then, is not benign; it springs from a desire for retribution and vindication.

Not only does the strategy of autonomy and domination gain a measure of release from past injustices but, as with most coping maneuvers, it proves partially successful in achieving rewards in the present. Most people find themselves intimidated by the antisocials' calculated pose of resentment and provocative look, no less than the overt threat of an emotional outburst, if not physical violence. In using these terrorizing behaviors, antisocial personalities possess a powerful instrumentality at their disposal for coercing others, for frightening them into fearful respect and passive submission.

Although many persons with the basic antisocial personality style find a niche for themselves in society where their exploitive and intimidating behaviors are sanctioned, even admired, they are ultimately self-defeating, no less so than occurs among more socially troublesome antisocials. The cleverly conniving businessperson, the physically brutal army sergeant, the stern and punitive school principal set into motion angry and resentful reactions from others, recreating once more what they had experienced in earlier life, a menacing and rejecting environment of persons who learn neither to trust them nor to care for them.

Weak Intrapsychic Controls

Threats and sarcasm are not endearing traits. How does one justify them to others, and by what means does the antisocial handle the fact that these behaviors may be unjust and irrational?

As noted in an earlier section, antisocial personalities have usually rebelled against the controls their parents and society have proposed to manage and guide impulses. Rarely do these youngsters substitute adequate controls in their stead; as a consequence, they fail to restrain or channel the emotions that well up within. As feelings surge forth, they are vented more or less directly; thus, we see the low tolerance, the impulsive rashness, the susceptibility to temptation, and the acting out of emotions so characteristic of this pattern.

Obvious and persistent acting out and rebelliousness cannot be overlooked. To make it acceptable, antisocials fabricate rather transparent rationalizations. They espouse such philosophical balderdash as "Might is right," "This is a dog-eat-dog world," "I'm being honest, not hypocritical like the rest of you," "It's better to get these kids used to tough handling now before it's too late," and "You've got to be a realist in this world, and most people are either foolish idealists, appeasers, commies, or atheists." Seen in this way, antisocials feel fully justified in their actions, and need not be restrained; if anything, they consider their own behavior more valid than ever.

Accustomed throughout life to indifference and hostility from others, and exquisitely attuned to the subtlest of signs of contempt and derision, well-entrenched antisocials begin to interpret the incidental behaviors and innocent remarks of others as signifying fresh attacks. Increasingly, they find evidence that now, as before, others are ready to persecute, to slander, and to vilify them. With this perception of the environment, the antisocial need not rationalize outbursts; they are "justified" reactions to the disinterest and malevolence of others. It is "they" who are contemptible, slanderous and belligerent and who hate and wish to destroy the antisocial. He or she is the victim, an innocent and indignant bystander subject to unjust persecution and hostility. Through this intrapsychic maneuver, then, the antisocial not only disowns and purges these exploitive and malicious impulses but attributes this evil to others. The person has absolved him- or herself of the irrationality of the resentful outbursts; moreover, as a persecuted victim, the individual is free to counterattack and to gain restitution and vindication. As expected, the antisocial has now created an imaginary world that continues to haunt and derogate the person—an inescapably malicious environment of rejection and deprecation that is, in effect however, of the antisocial's own making.

made between losing a job, being expelled from school, ending a marriage or relationship with children, or giving up a chance at probation and psychological treatment. Under other circumstances, treatment is usually forced on them; most prisons and other correctional facilities require inmates to attend psychotherapy sessions. In either case, a therapist working with an antisocial personality is likely to experience frustration and exasperation regarding the patient's clear lack of insight and/or motivation to change. Antisocials do not regard their behavior to be problematic for themselves, and its consequences for others, who are judged to be potentially unreliable and disloyal, is not a concern of theirs.

The patient's attitude toward the therapist will typically take one of two forms. Either the antisocial will try to enlist the therapist as an ally against those individuals who forced the antisocial to enter therapy or, alternatively, will try to con the therapist into being impressed with his or her insight and reform in an effort to secure advantage with some legal institution. The therapist's most effective recourse is to try to impress upon the antisocial the ways in which his or her behavior is in fact disadvantageous to him or her in the long run. The therapist can only hope that this insight will lead to behavior that is also advantageous to those who deal with antisocials; that is to say, behavior that is less abusive, exploitive, and criminal. The chances of the antisocial changing duplicitous patterns owing to the development of a real concern for others is slim.

Some clinicians believe that the chances for real gains increase with the patient's age. Although the incidence of antisocial personality does decline in middle age, it is likely that this statistic reflects two factors entirely incidental to the intrinsic character of the disorder. First, those whose antisocial behaviors persist are ultimately imprisoned for prolonged periods; they are, in effect, "out of commission" by 25 or 30 years of age. Second, those who survive in the mainstream of society are likely to have learned to channel their abusive and impulsive tendencies more skillfully or into more socially acceptable endeavors. It is not probable that their basic personality has been altered, only that it expresses itself in a less obviously flagrant and public way.

THERAPEUTIC INTERVENTIONS

Antisocials usually present for treatment as a result of an ultimatum. Therapy is often the choice

STRATEGIC GOALS

Ideally, therapeutic intervention would help reestablish a reasonable equivalence between the imbalanced polarities of the antisocial personality. The goal would be to help patients increase their other-orientation and decrease their use of active exploitation as a means of securing rewards. This would reflect an increased sensitivity to the needs and feelings of others. More realistically, the antisocials' problem-perpetuating tendencies are usually curbed only by convincing them that it is in their immediate best interests to do so.

Reestablishing Polarity Balances

The underlying motive for antisocial behavior is to "exploit before being exploited." As children, antisocials typically learn that the world will treat them unfairly, if not harshly; others are perceived, not as a source of rewards, but rather as potential exploiters or degraders. Antisocials defensively turn to themselves, not only to protect themselves against potential harm, but to secure gratification as well. When rewards involve other persons, it is not in the sense that the antisocial derives pleasure from sharing and intimacy. Others are essentially treated like objects; even highly personal interactions such as friendships and sexual relations are essentially instances of simple self-gratification. Retribution for past and present injustices is sought indiscriminately, whether or not the antisocial's victims are among the original offenders. Compensations for past deprivations are ruthlessly sought out and taken wherever they can be obtained. This active quest for self-gain, combined with a lack of other-orientedness leads to the manipulative, exploitive, and often criminal behavior so characteristic of the antisocial personality.

Ideally, therapeutic intervention would lead to increased balance on the self-other polarity, where others would be perceived as relatively benign and as having the potential to meet the antisocial personality's needs without exploitation. An appreciation and respect for the feelings and desires of others might result. The active stance toward securing rewards (at the expense of others) would ideally shift toward a more socially and personally adaptive one.

Countering Perpetuating Tendencies

Antisocials learn early that they do best by anticipating and reacting to an indifferent and unreliable environment with defensive autonomy, if not suspicion and hostility. The protective shell of anger and resentment that develops also acts as a perceptual and cognitive filter well past childhood. In their effort not to overlook any signs of threat, they persistently misinterpret incidental events as evidence of the devious and untrustworthy impulses of others. Often overlooked or suspiciously dismissed, on the other hand, are signs of objective goodwill. Expressions of affection and cooperative prosocial tendencies that do not escape the awareness of antisocials are demeaned so as to ensure that they do not put themselves in a dangerously vulnerable position. This also ensures that they do not experience their environment in a way that would encourage them to bring their defenses down. In fact, antisocials feel the need to demonstrate their invulnerability, both to themselves and to potentially threatening others by provoking them, both physically and verbally. Alternatively, antisocials may engage in illegal "beat the system" schemes that lead to run-ins with the law and aggressive, mean-spirited, and punitive officials. The defensive counterhostility on the part of others helps maintain the antisocial's conviction that the world is a denigrating place.

In working with antisocial patients, the therapist would probably do well to try to impress on them the possible advantages (for themselves) of altering socially repugnant behaviors. Despite self-interest being the primary motivator in increasing prosocial acts, the consequent decrease in abrasive social encounters may over time alter the antisocial's belief about the degree of intrinsic threat in the environment. Attempts at altering such beliefs directly would be likely to elicit disdain for the therapist that can lead to an increased desire to con, manipulate, or teach a lesson to the "sappy and naive wimp."

Modifying Domain Dysfunctions

The primary domain dysfunctions of the antisocial personality are seen in their socially evident irresponsible interpersonal conduct, impulsive expressive behavior, and acting-out regulatory mechanism. The antisocial is constantly calculating how to maximize personal benefits in any given situation; broken promises, failed obligations, and illegal behaviors are the inevitable consequences of always putting personal desires before marital, parental, employment, or financial responsibilities. Expressive behavior is impulsive, incautious, and shortsighted. Consequences do not play a role in the antisocial's behavioral decisions. Intrapsychic tensions are coped with by using acting out as a regulatory mechanism; offensive thoughts and malevolent actions are neither constrained for any length of time, nor are they sublimated into more adaptive forms. Instead, impulses are directly expressed with no concern for the damaging effects they will have on others. Once again, teaching antisocials to consider the consequences of their actions, and to see personal advantages in behaving in prosocial ways and in accordance with others' wishes is a first step in altering their dysfunctional personality style.

Changes in behavior that prove to be beneficial to the antisocial's lifestyle may have some positive effects on other dysfunctional domains. The antisocial has an autonomous self-image and enjoys seeing his or her personal freedom unrestrained by the loyalties or social customs that "bog down" most individuals. Once again, the personal advantages in adhering to the norms can help shift this image somewhat toward a more adaptive interdependent one. Interventions like wilderness therapy (discussed in the following section) can also be useful in this regard. Morphologic organization of the few weak inner defensive operations antisocials possess are unruly; impulses are rarely restrained or modulated. Learning cognitive and behavioral strategies for acting as a result of consequences can help provide guidelines for some personally and societally adaptive personality traits. The antisocial's debased inner object-representations are a juxtaposition of impulses to seek revenge and subvert established mores, as well as to demean personal sentiments and material attainments that were denied them in early life. Increased personal satisfaction and stability may lead to a decreased drive to actively rebel against "the system" and an increased motivation to work with it to the antisocial's advantage.

Other dysfunctional domains are more difficult to influence. The antisocial's deviant cognitive style consists of socially unorthodox beliefs and morals, disdain for traditional ideals, and contempt of conventional rules. The characteristic callous temperament is marked by an insensitive and unempathic, even ruthless, indifference to the welfare of others. These features are more likely to be masked than changed in a majority of cases.

TACTICAL MODALITIES

Developing rapport with the patient is a real challenge for the therapist working with an antisocial. Benjamin (1993a) suggests that it is virtually impossible to achieve collaboration with an antisocial patient in ordinary dyadic therapy without adjunct intervention geared toward that very aim (discussed in the following section). Power struggles

need to be avoided at all costs. Frances (1985) suggests that the therapist openly acknowledge the vulnerability of the therapy setting to the patient's manipulative talents. The goal is to decrease the chance that the patient feels challenged by the therapist and thus decide to become oppositional and counterreact. Toward this end, it is also crucial that the therapist does not assume the role of an evaluator. This is easiest to achieve in therapeutic settings that involve a team of therapists, usually inpatient settings, where a clinician other than the primary therapist provides access to privileges. The personality style of the therapist is even more important when working with antisocial personality disorder than with most other patients. Beck and Freeman (1990b) suggest that the following therapist characteristics are particularly helpful when working with an antisocial patient: self-assurance, a reliable but not infallible objectivity, a relaxed and nondefensive interpersonal style, clear sense of personal limits, and a strong sense of humor.

Domain-Oriented Techniques

Although the frequency of certain repugnant actions may be reduced using *behavioral* techniques such as aversive conditioning, gains rarely extend beyond the treatment setting and do not generalize to other equally offensive habits, no less attempt to correct the underlying causative dysfunctions. Because the vast majority of antisocial personalities have good social skills and are not impaired in their functioning by anxiety, most behavioral techniques prove of minimal value in a treatment program.

The *interpersonal* approach to therapy outlined by Benjamin (1993a) is based on the assumption that antisocials have not had a learning history with warm and caring figures that could lead to normal attachment and bonding experiences. Instead, the antisocial maintains an interpersonal position of cool detachment and autonomy that is masked by a friendly charm that gives the antisocial a good measure of interpersonal control. This superficial social ease may lead some therapists to believe that a therapeutic alliance can be achieved with this patient. Benjamin emphasizes, however, that the antisocial cannot be expected to genuinely collaborate with the therapist, and thus initial interventions cannot take the typical dyadic form of interpersonal therapy. Treatment interventions aim at providing these patients with consistent and well-modulated warmth needed to overcome their marked socialization deficits.

Benjamin suggests several methods that may facilitate this objective. One possibility is based on a milieu treatment program. This program does not try to bring antisocial patients from their suspicious and cynical baseline position with likely futile efforts of friendliness and helpfulness. Instead, the staff is advised to adopt the patient's baseline position and to ignore him or her. After the patient is familiarized with the milieu program, punishment would ensue from noncompliance. As the patient exhibits behaviors in accordance with the treatment plan, progressively greater autonomy and friendly interaction is granted by the staff.

Interventions that provide opportunities for interdependence are encouraged. The need for cooperation and deference to the group (to ensure one's ultimate welfare) can be taught in a *wilderness therapy* program. Here, difficult and often dangerous group tasks require individual and group commitment. Inappropriate behavior carries with it the risk of rapid unpleasant consequences from either hard-to-con nature or fellow antisocial participants. Exercises that require cooperation, such as getting everybody over a 14-foot sheer wall and "blind trust walks," also necessitate that participants gain trust and yield control. Benjamin reports that a group of male incest perpetrators manifested increases in self-perceived self-control after a one-day intervention of this type, while controls from the same population that had engaged in a daylong hike exhibited no such changes. Benjamin states that once the processes of bonding and interdependence have begun, the antisocial should now have the capacity to collaborate with the therapist. At this point, self-destructive features of their lifestyle can be recognized and understood, and skills such as self-care, delay of gratification, and empathy for others can be discussed and perhaps acquired.

Family approaches are often attempted in inpatient settings. Depending on the degree of antisocial tendencies of family members, intervention can range from supportive (of baffled and often despairing relatives) to active system-change (in cases where the family inadvertently or knowingly supports or encourages antisocial habits). Success depends largely on the situation; working with families of several antisocial personalities is likely to be doomed for failure. *Group* situations allow antisocials to help learn long-term problem-solving techniques by aiding others in similar situations, and successes in the lives of other group members can serve as positive models for antisocial patients.

Cognitive techniques are outlined in Beck and Freeman (1990b), and are based on the assumption that changes in affect and behavior can be brought about by the patient's reevaluation of basic assumptions regarding key problem areas in his or her life. Beck and Freeman note that this model does not try to improve moral and social behavior through the induction of shame or anxiety, but rather through enhancement of cognitive functioning. They suggest that the treatment plan be based on a cognitive-growth fostering strategy: helping the patient move from concrete operations and self-determination to abstract thinking and interpersonal thoughtfulness (formal operations).

A thoroughgoing review of the patient's life needs to be undertaken to identify special problem areas. The patient's significant others can be particularly helpful in this regard. Cognitive distortions related to each problem area need to be identified; these frequently include the following: Justifications—"Wanting something or wanting to avoid something justifies my actions"; Thinking is believing—"My thoughts and feelings are completely accurate, simply because they occur to me"; Personal infallibility—"I always make good choices"; Feelings make facts—"I know I am right because I feel right about what I do"; The impotence of others—"The views of others are irrelevant to my decisions, unless they directly control my immediate consequences." Such assumptions are self-serving and minimize future consequences. The goal of therapy is for the patient to recognize the implications of his or her behavior and how it affects others, and to consider the long-range consequences. This does not represent real moral development, but rather constitutes a change from not caring what others think or feel to caring what they think or feel, because their reactions can be for or against the antisocial's advantage. The chances of an antisocial patient truly caring about others' welfare is very slim.

Beck and Freeman offer suggestions about how to overcome antisocials' resistance to enter and stay with therapy. Antisocial behavior should be described as a "disorder"; the chances of the patient feeling accused thereby diminishes, thus increasing the probability of cooperation. The so-called disorder can further be framed as causing long-term negative consequences for the afflicted individual, such as incarceration, physical harm from others, and broken contact from friends and family. An initial experimental trial can be suggested, in which therapy can be explained as "a series of meetings that take place with an interested observer for the purpose of evaluating situations that might be interfering with the patient's independence and success in getting what he or she wants" (p. 156). Noncompliance with therapy guidelines such as missing sessions, not doing homework, or being hostile or noncommunicative despite the therapist's stance as a "helper" warrants discussion of the patient's feelings about therapy.

Therapeutic intervention includes helping the patient set clear priorities and examine a full range of possibilities and consequences before drawing a conclusion about appropriate behavior. The choice review exercise is very useful in this regard. A problem situation is rated on a scale of 1–100 to represent the patient's satisfaction. A series of behavioral responses to the problem are then listed, each with a rating of 1–100 in terms of their effectiveness in solving the problem. Advantages and disadvantages of all the alternatives are listed and a final decision can be made on the basis of the overall attractiveness of the consequences of each choice. Persistent choices of ineffective alternatives indicate a need to examine particular skill deficits or undetected dysfunctional beliefs.

Psychodynamic approaches tend to be difficult to undertake because antisocials are not apt to internalize therapeutic insights without external controls or interventions, even if they do stay in treatment more than a few sessions. If severe limits are put on the antisocial personality (such as in highly controlled incarceration settings), anxiety and depression may lead some patients to be more amenable to change. Almost any other treatment orientations would have a greater (if limited) chance at success given the antisocial's opposition to insight and low tolerance for boredom or slowly progressive changes.

It may be useful to review the major strategies and tactics as depicted in Figure 12.6.

Potentiated Pairings and Catalytic Sequences

If the resources are at all available, a therapist working with an antisocial would do well to involve the patient in an adjunct intervention that explores the diversity of human interdependence: wilderness therapy or supervised "nurturant" role exposure (working with children or animals) can activate cooperative schemas that may increase the chances of a real relationship developing between patient and therapist. In the case of aggressive

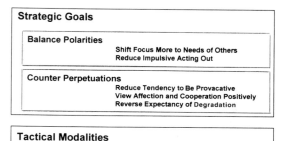

Figure 12.6 Therapeutic strategies and tactics for the prototypal antisocial personality.

antisocial patients, the therapist can consider evaluating the appropriateness of psychopharmacological intervention to help control physically abusive behavior. Group therapy with other antisocial patients can provide the patient with an opportunity to come in contact with credible role models. Potential benefits of changing the antisocial behavioral style can be observed in others' positive experiences. Helping people with similar life difficulties come up with solutions can also help provide insight about behavioral consequences in the patient's own life. Another adjunct that may in some cases prove to be a helpful addition to dyadic therapy is family intervention, particularly in cases where family dynamics inadvertently support antisocial behavior.

RISKS AND RESISTANCES

Despite the therapeutic focus on the disadvantages of the antisocial lifestyle, many emotional and material advantages mitigate against possible therapeutic headway. Feelings of control, power, and even rage can produce a "high" that the patient is understandably not willing to give up. Unlike other personality types who experience considerable discomfort in association with their symptoms, the antisocial's dysfunctional behaviors are rewarded more often than punished, and consequences are contingent on reactions of others and tend not to be immediate. Since neither antisocial "symptoms" nor their consequences generate immediate and internally generated discomfort, they do not serve to directly extinguish antisocial behavior. A cooperative and congenial attitude often is a mask for evasive behavior that is adopted to gain advantage with the therapist and legal authorities. Some antisocial patients who come to therapy as an alternative to jail may clearly not be participating in therapy. Therapists may feel compelled to continue with the intervention process in order to "rescue" patients from incarceration, but in fact unwittingly reward antisocial behavior and support the lifestyle by helping patients avoid the legal consequences of their choices. It can also undermine the very purpose of the legal system: to protect innocent society members from harm.

A different kind of countertransference reactions can lead to animosity that can interfere with potential therapeutic gains: therapist suspiciousness and anger about being lied to and manipulated, feelings of frustration and helplessness about apparent lack of intervention success, and disdain and disgust for the antisocial patient and his or her lifestyle are common. Therapy with this group can prove to be highly frustrating and nongratifying, and in the opinion of many therapists, generally unsuccessful. As antisocials are very sensitive to negative evaluation, power struggles and evaluation of

the patient by the therapist should be avoided if at all possible. In inpatient settings, this is easier to achieve because a clinician other than the therapist can be responsible for providing access to privileges; the primary therapist should not be viewed by the patient as an evaluator, but rather as a strategic helper. However, the therapist should resist intervening on the patient's behalf.

Many therapists are discouraged by the conviction that even when some behavioral changes are secured, it is highly unlikely that they reflect any change in moral character. Rather, they represent an accommodation to the constraints of society to yield a more profitable lifestyle for the antisocial individual. Whereas some therapists try to keep in mind that circumscribed goals that decrease problems for the patient and for those around the patient are valid, others worry that a veneer of socialization may lead to disastrous personal consequences for people who are more likely to be duped by the antisocial who has had therapy and has learned to present him- or herself well in the short term.

PART IV

INTRAPSYCHICALLY-CONFLICTED PERSONALITIES

CHAPTER 13

Sadistic Personality Disorders: The Abusive Pattern

The personalities to be discussed in the following four chapters—sadistic, compulsive, negativistic, and masochistic—are grouped together under the term "conflicted personality styles." They contrast with those we previously labeled "deficient," in that the latter group represents those who are incapable of experiencing the life-enhancing qualities inherent in the pleasure polarity; deficient personalities center their lives either on the pain polarity (avoidant, depressive), or neither polarity (schizoid). Similarly, in the group we have labeled "imbalanced personality styles," we find four personality disorders that are strongly inclined to orient their lives either toward themselves or toward others. By contrast, *conflicted* personalities experience the full measure of life's potentials, that is, both ends of the pain-pleasure and the self-other polarities. What is problematic in their case is that they reverse the components that make up these polarities.

Stated differently, the four personalities in this section are "double-minded," to use Kierkegaard's descriptive term. They are not, as are most personality disorders, "single-minded." At the most fundamental level, the primary motives that guide their lives conflict directly with one another. No matter what their other inclinations may be, their internal orientations move in opposing ways; to remain at war with oneself is intrinsic to their psychic makeup. To illustrate, obsessive-compulsives take great pride in controlling their lives, leaving little to chance, constantly evaluating both their own and others' actions. However, they play multiple roles: prosecutor, defendant, and judge. These multiple perspectives not only fail to resolve their internal conflicts but are likely to intensify them. Thus, if the defendant wins the case, the prosecutor must lose, and vice versa. For example, individuals with masochistic personalities consciously hold high expectations of others who, of course, almost invariably fail to meet them. As a consequence,

masochists unconsciously wish retribution by derogating others, but to do so would mean assaulting the very persons they hope will love and care for them. As the saying goes, these personalities can't win for losing, nor can they lose for winning.

More specifically, in both the sadistic/abusive and masochistic/self-defeating types, the conflict between the pain-pleasure polarities represents a transposition such that normally pleasurable experiences are viewed as painful, and normally painful experiences are felt as pleasurable. In the compulsive and negativistic personalities, it is the self and other polarities that are in conflict—the more they are disposed toward one component of the polarity pair, the more they are inclined to reverse themselves and turn toward the second. In sum, in the sadistic and masochistic types we find a psychic *dissonance* between the survival functions of pain and pleasure, and in the compulsive and negativistic types, we find an *ambivalence* between the survival functions of the self-other polarity. This chapter will focus on the sadistic/abusive personality, where we find a marked discordance between the most fundamental of the polarities, that representing the basic survival functions of enhancing and of preserving life.

As will be evident in the following historical survey, the notion of a abusive, explosive, and violent character type (individuals who are destructive to life) long preceded the decision of the DSM to introduce the sadistic personality disorder in 1987. The official proposals at that time coalesced viewpoints of numerous theorists and clinicians. As is well known, the introduction in the DSM-III-R was shortly followed by the deletion of the disorder in DSM-IV. Fiester and Gay (1991) reviewed its history in the DSM, as follows:

During the process of development of DSM-III-R, sadistic personality disorder (SPD) was suggested for inclusion by several psychiatrists who felt there was a clinical need for a category to describe persons, usually seen in forensic settings, who demonstrated a long-standing maladaptive pattern of cruel, demeaning, and aggressive behavior toward others but whose personality disturbance did not fit any other DSM-III-R diagnosis. They saw this disorder as distinct from the other personality disorders including antisocial personality disorder. As a result of discussions with the Advisory Committee on Personality Disorders, eight criteria were subsequently developed along with an exclusion criterion. These criteria were subsequently approved for inclusion in an appendix of the DSM-III-R entitled "Proposed Diagnostic Categories Needing Further Study." (p. 377)

There has been considerable controversy about this personality type throughout its brief official history. The elements that compose the reservation to include the disorder also vary. A number of these issues will be dealt with throughout this chapter.

For the present, it should be self-evident that our society has become increasingly preoccupied with matters of public violence and private abuse. Some commentators have characterized our times as a period when incivility and crudeness have not only come to the fore as inevitable products of a declining society, but also as sanctioned, encouraged, and even admired qualities of life. One need not look very far to see the pervasiveness of this plague of murder and mayhem in our daily news, our films and TV, as well as in the lyrics of our popular songs. And yet, at this point in time, the DSM-IV Task Force saw fit to delete the characterization of a violence-prone personality. Offering rationalizations galore, the Task Force sought to justify the decision to delete the Sadistic disorder from the nomenclature. Having been privy to these justifications, the senior author of this text cannot help but conclude that the true motive for this decision was essentially a political one, a decision to sweep under the rug what was difficult to sustain in the face of unrelenting criticisms by a small minority of mental health professionals. How ludicrous it will appear to clinicians in the next decade when they reflect on a course of action that essentially "ran away" from perhaps the most significant personality problem of the 1990s.

Sadistic behaviors are not limited to the actions of violent psychopaths who are seen only in the back wards of state prisons, those crudely vicious and brutalizing members in society's periphery. Through sublimation, if nothing else, many such individuals may be found at the center of everyday society. They are seen, for example, in the arrogant patriotism of nationalists whose truculence is "justified" by the "arrogant demands" of "alien" immigrant groups. Such behavior is evident also in the machinations of politicians whose facade of so-called good intentions cloaks a lust for power that leads to repressive and socially demeaning legislation. Less dramatically, and more frequently, these individuals participate in the ordinary affairs of life: the harshly punitive and abusive father; the puritanical fear-producing minister; the vengeful dean; and the irritable, shame-inducing mother.

HISTORICAL ANTECEDENTS

The entertainments of Rome, one of the cradles of western civilization, included spectacles of people slaughtering animals and animals slaughtering people. Eighty thousand citizens of the empire were packed close in the major amphitheaters, eating, drinking, and reveling in blood lust as the gladiators made battle. As the crowd cried out for the death of the soon-to-be vanquished, the victors plunged their weapons into the prone bodies of their helpless foes. Orgies of cruelty were not incidental to the civilization of ancient Rome; they were part of its mores and essence. To Rome, greatness and cruelty were interwoven. Insight into what characterological features would facilitate such a willingness to adhere to a cruel course of action can best be inferred from the popularity of early Roman legends where duty and patriotism prevailed over torture and death.

The point to be made by this brief excursion into ancient times is that there is a phenomenon revolving about cruelty, dominance, and suffering which is well known and perhaps intrinsic in the character of humans, this despite the DSM-IV's recent decision to eliminate the deeper character elements from which it springs. It is as if the elimination of such personality types would be sufficient to eliminate the character that it represents; denial, however, is not a feature that the psychiatric community should utilize as a principle of diagnostic classification. The themes of domination and evil can be seen throughout history. In its cultural and social form, it is intimately associated with totalitarian power structures. Note should be made of its enduring nature, as seen in the medieval church inquisitions, in the tyranny of slavery, and in the horrors of Nazi Germany and Soviet communism.

However, as a formal psychological construct representing an individual's features of domination and cruelty, the concept can be traced to the late 19th-century writings of Krafft-Ebing (1867, 1882/1937). Drawing on the letters and short stories of the 18th-century French nobleman and author, Marquis de Sade, whose novels extolled the administration of pain and sexual dominance, as well as cruelty and humiliation associated with sexual pleasure, Krafft-Ebing (1882/1937) introduced the term "sadism," as well as its counterpart, "masochism." He defined the term as:

the experience of sexual, pleasurable sensations (including orgasm) produced by acts of cruelty, bodily punishment, afflicted on one's own person or when witnessed in others, be they animals or human beings. (p. 80)

Krafft-Ebing wrote of an "innate desire to desire to humiliate and hurt" that was characteristic of all humans. He speculated that this sadistic force was stimulated by the natural shyness or innate coyness of women (p. 82) and was especially troublesome if the male was hypersexual. He notes:

Sexual emotion, if hyperaesthetic, might degenerate into a craving to inflict pain . . . under pathological conditions, man's active role of winning women may become an unlimited desire for subjugation. (p. 214)

Krafft-Ebing believed that the only adequate explanation for the lustful quality seen in these acts was the involvement of the sexual drives. He reasoned that the roots of sadism lie in an exaggeration of normal male sexual impulses, of which aggressive tendencies are a natural component. However, he noted, if such impulses were to be found in a psychopathic individual, the likelihood of acting out these urges more broadly was greatly increased. Phrased differently, psychopathy, though oblique to the sadistic tendency, could act as a catalyst in the actualization of broad-based destructive urges.

In 1895, Schrenck-Notzing introduced the term "Algolagnia" to describe the sadomasochistic phenomenon. The term comes from the Greek and roughly translates into "pain enjoyment." What was special about his proposal was the view that the pain experienced was in effect pleasurable, an acquired synthesis that fused normally contrasting emotional or affective experiences. The term Algolagnia did not become popular and was not revived until the work of Havelock Ellis (1933). To Ellis, and in contrast to his predecessors who focused on cruelty and hostility, Ellis considered sadism as an expression of love. To him:

Sadism and masochism may be regarded as complementary emotional states; they cannot be regarded as opposed states. The sadist desires to inflict pain, but in some cases, if not in most, he desires it to be felt as love. (pp. 159–160)

MODERN FORMULATIONS

Both K. Schneider (1923/1950) and E. Kahn (1931) presented detailed and thoughtful personality typologies to which they gave the label "psychopathic." Although some of their types correspond with current notions of a psychopathic personality, they are largely more detailed descriptions of what Kraepelin presented in the final edition of his text a decade or so earlier.

As noted in Chapter 12, Kraepelin (1909–1915) described a variety of different personality disorders, among which was the excitable, the unstable, and the impulsive, each possessing characteristics akin to our current notions of the sadistic/aggressive personality type.

Schneider (1923/1950) likewise concluded that the aggressive and impulsive characteristics described by Kraepelin were found in a variety of different psychopathic personalities. His description of the "explosive psychopath" comes closest to our current thinking regarding a sadistic personality. As with Kraepelin, however, he viewed the feature of hostile explosiveness to be an unspecific type of reaction, an important hallmark of a subgroup of otherwise diverse personalities. He commented that Kraepelin's notion of an "irritable personality" failed to reflect the "outgoing nature of the discharge." Schneider also referred to the work of Baer (1893), who spoke of the "impulsively violent type," but here also Schneider rejected Baer's notion that criminal conduct was necessarily associated with explosiveness. A quote from Schneider (1923/1950) describing his conception of these individuals may be informative:

They tend to make an unholy row for the slightest of reasons or they will hit out without warning, reactions which have been well labeled short-circuit reactions. . . .

There are many links with other psychopathic personalities-the blustering hyperthyme, the morose or paranoid depressive and the labile personality. . . . These and associated drunkenness often cause explosive personalities to be hospitalised. In addition, as is well known in states of violent affect, consciousness becomes blurred and at times these explosive excitements may develop into psychogenic twilight states.

These "hotheads" often present a social problem in their disturbed marriages, their incapacity to care for their children properly and their criminal outbreaks. In these, all sorts of impulsive delinquency may take place, assault, truculence, damage to property. (pp. 122–124)

To follow the line of *psychiatric* thinking concerning personality disorders, we should progress from Kraepelin to Schneider to Kahn (1931). In Kahn's view, the expressive and explosive qualities derive from a complex mixture of character and temperament:

Peculiar to them is a very pronounced tendency to respond to outer stimuli in the form of a sudden discharge . . . these explosive states of excitement can lead to particularly serious and dangerous acts of violence. Alcohol among other poisons is especially suited to intensify and magnify the explosiveness, and its destructive effect on the excitable in general should not remain unmentioned. (p. 184)

There are furthermore the ruthless natures who "walk over dead bodies" for the sake of their own advantage, that is, in pursuance of their entirely autistic goals; there are again unyielding, tyrannical personalities who live more frequently in smaller circles undeviatingly according to their own laws and subject their environment to themselves; less frequently as genuine dominating leaders (Cesare Borgia), unburdened by affective experience and undiverted by the affective needs of others. (p. 355)

As with many a notion concerning personality or character, the more subtle and intricate aspects are to be found in the unique perspectives that Sigmund Freud brought to bear on the subject. And as was typical of him, his conception of a particular idea (such as character type) evolved through his long career, changing in its portrayal and its developmental origins. Freud's notions concerning sadism and masochism clearly reflect this shift in perspective and in interpretation.

In his earliest writings, notably *Three Essays on the Theory of Sexuality* (1905/1926), Freud viewed sadism and masochism as bipolar dimensions (active versus passive forms) of the aggressive component of the sexual instinct. He wrote:

. . . Sadism would correspond to an aggressive component of the sexual instinct which has become independent and exaggerated and, by displacement, has usurped the leading position. . . . The connotation of sadism oscillates between, on the one hand, cases merely characterized by an active or violent attitude to the sexual object, and, on the other hand, cases in which satisfaction is entirely conditional on the humiliation and maltreatment of the object. (p. 158)

In these first formulations, Freud interpreted sadistic behavior as the upshot of libidinal psychosexual development. More specifically, he conceived sadism as a psychosexual regression from the oedipal period to that of the latter anal stage. Tension associated with excretory desires that are constrained in toilet training are seen as the foundation of an aggressive-expulsive tendency. Excretory tensions, once suppressed by external forces, build up within the organism. During the oedipal period, the child fears castration and domination, and may regress back to these internalized and pent-up anal tensions. According to Freud, the male child, originally identified with the mother, begins to view her as weak and humiliated, suffering under the strong and ravaging impulses of a dominant father. Refusing to identify with the submissive mother, and fearing genital castration should he remain passive and submissive, the boy increasingly identifies with the father and the aggressive impulses he represents. Drawing energy from his early suppressed anal impulses, he now discharges his hostility and cruel impulses in a form we term "sadistic behavior."

Freud shifted his interpretation of aggressive behaviors when he presented his "second drive theory" in his 1920 book, *Beyond the Pleasure Principle.* Here, for the first time, he proposed a new dichotomy of Eros and Thanatos, thereby replacing his original dichotomy between the ego and the sexual instincts. Henceforth, the sexual instincts were seen as components of Eros. Stating his new conception concerning the role of aggression, Freud (1920/1925) wrote:

. . . How can the sadistic instinct, whose aim it is to injure the object, be derived from Eros, the preserver of life? Is it not possible to suppose that this sadism is in fact a death instinct which, . . . has been forced away from the ego and has consequently only emerged in relation to the object?

If such an assumption as this is permissible, then we have met the demand that we should produce an example of a death instinct—though, it is true, a displaced one. (p. 48)

Freud himself was not convinced that his formulations concerning the death instinct were basically sound. As he wrote (1920/1925),

It may be asked whether and how far I am myself convinced of the truth of the hypotheses that have been set out in these pages. My answer would be that I am not convinced myself, that I do not seek to persuade other people to believe them. (p. 53)

In his final major work on the subject, Freud (1924/1925) notes the intertwined character of sadism and masochism, giving primacy to the role of masochism. Nevertheless, he states:

To the libido falls the task of making this destructive instinct harmless, and it manages to dispose of it by directing it to a great extent and early in life—with the help of . . . the musculature—towards the objects of the outer world. It is then called the instinct of destruction, of mastery, the will to power. (p. 260)

Following the views of Freud, his mentor, Abraham (1921/1927) held closely to the relationship of psychosexuality and character development. Focusing on a division he proposed in both the oral and anal stages, Abraham saw the origins of jealousy and hostility in what he termed the oral-biting stage, which became a regression point for later relationships. Both the negativistic/passive-aggressive, and aggressive/sadistic personality disorders can trace their origins to the frustrations consequent to experiences at both the oral-biting and anal-expulsive periods of libidinal development. To quote from Abraham:

The component instinct of sadism, as it exists in the infantile libido, also shows us two opposite pleasurable tendencies at work. One of these tendencies is to destroy *the object (or the external world); the other is to* control *it. I shall later try to show in detail that the tendency to spare the object and to preserve it has grown out of the more primitive, destructive tendency by a process of repression. For the present I shall speak of this process quite in general; but I should like to say at once that psychoanalysis has given us a perfectly sound knowledge of these stages and the succeeding ones in the development of object-love. For the moment, we will confine our interest to that sadistic instinct which threatens the existence of its object. And we see that the removal or loss of an object can be regarded by the unconscious either as a sadistic process of destruction or as an anal one of expulsion. (p. 428)*

Another close adherent to the Freudian model was Wilhem Stekel (1929/1939). Deviating slightly from early psychoanalytic traditions, Stekel proposed that a deeper instinctual ego undergirds the development of sadistic qualities owing to personal frustrations and culturally imposed behaviors. However, Stekel claims:

That which opposes the satisfaction of instinct is looked upon as hostile. The primitive attitude of man is hatred. Love is indeed a cultural production. Hate belongs to life. . . . There is no love without hatred. (p. 39)

As Stekel presents it, instinct frustration engenders retaliation of hate and hostility. This is universal. The sadist, however, has failed to develop a genuine love identification, and hence is unable to constrain his hate by the "voice of morality." Stekel goes on:

Many authors see in sadomasochism only a quantitative heightening of the normal sexual impulse, whereby sadism corresponds to the masculine, masochism to the feminine component of the sexual instinct. But it will not do simply to compare with each other the ideas, masculine-sadistic and feminine-masochistic.

Sadomasochism is a disorder of the environment, to be referred to therefore to definite influences in childhood.

Brutality of the pathological individual is to be understood as a persistence or breaking through of a primitive disposition common to all man. Sadists are relatively unrestrained by moral and love considerations in this expression of the will to power that is sexually accentuated.

All sadomasochists are affect-hungry individuals. They are in constant need of an affective spectacle. It is solely to be proved how and why they have come precisely to the specific affect. We shall see from many examples that it concerns a definite repressed affect, a specific attitude of hate toward a person of the environment. The hatred then turns itself against substitute objects or against one's own person. It is, however, withdrawn from its original object. (p. 60)

Although a small segment of his rich descriptive portrayals of several of the major character types, Wilhelm Reich (1933) extends several of Freud's early formulations concerning sadism. In his comments regarding these modifications, Reich notes:

Freud discovered that masochism and sadism are not absolute opposites, that the one instinctual aim is never present without the other.

Freud's theory of libidinal development further distinguishes the three stages of childhood sexuality (oral, anal, and genital) and, in the beginning, relegated sadism to the anal phase. Later it was found that every stage of sexual development is characterized by a corresponding form of sadistic aggression. Following up this problem, I was able to find in each of these three forms of sadistic aggression a reaction of the psychic apparatus to the specific frustration of the corresponding partial libidinal impulse. According to this concept, the sadism of each stage results from the mixture between the sexual demand itself and the destructive impulse against the person responsible for its frustration; oral sadism (frustration of sucking—destructive impulse, biting); anal sadism (frustration of anal pleasure—crushing, stomping, beating); phallic sadism (frustration of genital pleasure—piercing, puncturing). (pp. 227–228)

Another of Freud's early scholars was Otto Fenichel (1945) who commented along the following lines regarding the place of sadism in character development:

Sadism initially develops from the instinctive greediness with which the incorporation aims of the pregenital impulses are prosecuted, representing a way of striving for instinctive aims rather than an original instinctual aim in itself. Another root of sadism is the negative instinctual aim of getting rid ("splitting away") of painful stimuli. Both greediness and hate become condensed when the destruction or the damage of an object turns into an instinctual aim of its own, the completion of which produces a kind of erogenous pleasure.

All pregenital impulses, in their aims of incorporation, seem to possess a certain destructive component. Unknown constitutional factors, and above all, experiences and frustration, greatly increase this destructive element. In addition to oral and anal sadism other erogenous zones may serve as sources of sadism. It is often the specific repression of this sadistic component of infantile sexuality that later leads to conflicts and thus to neuroses. (p. 73)

Before turning to the writings of the psychoanalysts during the fourth and fifth decades of this century, the views of several other pre-World War II contributors should be noted briefly. G. E. Partridge (1927, 1928, 1930), a leading American clinician of the period, systematically studied several populations of diagnosed psychopathic personalities and concluded that the label was "meaningless" and should be dropped in favor of Birnbaum's concept of sociopathy. Efforts to divide these personalities into subtypes would be only a futile endeavor, according to Partridge; to him, the only justification for membership among the "essential sociopaths" was that the individual's behavior consistently deviated from the norms of his or her social group.

The leading British theorist of the 1930s, D. K. Henderson (1939), allied himself with Partridge's basic conclusions but felt that a useful distinction could be drawn between three subtypes: (a) the predominantly aggressive, (b) the predominantly passive or inadequate, and (c) the predominantly creative. Original at the time was Henderson's suggestion that these individuals feel themselves to be outcasts, rarely understood by others, and stigmatized and scapegoated unjustly. Because of his prominence in British circles, certain of Henderson's views gained quick attention and stirred much debate. Notable among the issues he raised was his inclusion of a passive-inadequate type, considered by most of his psychiatric colleagues to be more properly diagnosed as neurotic; even more controversial was his proposal of a "creative psychopath," a brilliant, aggressively active, though erratic and moody person, exemplified by individuals such as Lawrence of Arabia. As elsewhere, controversy raged, not over matters of empirical substance or theoretic logic but as a consequence of terminological confusion and issues of syndromal scope.

Although Horney's contributions were seen by her orthodox psychoanalytic colleagues as deviating from the mainstream, the distinctions she drew were deeply rooted in analytic theory. Attentive to conditions encountered in conventional clinical practice, as opposed to juvenile courts and prisons, Horney was fully aware that "sadistic trends" were prevalent in all walks of life. Describing such a personality pattern, Horney (1945) wrote:

The assumption that sadistic trends are the expression of sexual drive has no basis in fact. It is true that they can be expressed in sexual behavior . . . they are no exception to the general rule that all are our character attitudes are bound to manifest themselves in the sexual sphere. (p. 199)

What is typical of sadism is not a niggardliness in the sense of withholding but a much more active, though unconscious, impulse to thwart others—to kill their joy and to disappoint their expectations. Any satisfaction or buoyancy of the partner's almost irresistibly provokes the sadistic person to spoil it in some way. If the partner looks forward to seeing him, he tends to be sullen. If the partner wants sexual intercourse, he will be frigid or impotent.

As significant as any of these is the sadistic person's tendency to disparage *and* humiliate *others. He is remarkably keen at seeing shortcomings, at discovering the weak spots in others and pointing them out. He knows intuitively where others are sensitive and can be hurt. And he tends to use his intuition mercilessly for derogatory criticism. . . .*

In degrading others he not only allays his intolerable self-contempt but at the same time gives himself a feeling of superiority. . . . When he exploits others emotionally he provides a vicarious emotional life for himself that lessens his own sense of barrenness. When he defeats others he wins a triumphant elation which obscures his own hopeless defeat. This craving for vindictive triumph is perhaps his most intense motivating force.

Last but not least, his sadistic dealings with others provide him with a feeling of strength and pride which reinforce his unconscious feeling of omnipotence. (pp. 197–207)

CONTEMPORARY PROPOSALS

Drawing inspiration from the psychoanalytic framework, but more in keeping with the ideas formulated together with Horney, Erich Fromm (1973) contributed his own views concerning the role of sadism both from an individual and cultural perspective. Fromm places primary emphasis on the role of historical and societal influence on both the development and manifestation of sadism. As he notes:

Social groups tend to reinforce all those characteristic elements that correspond to (sadistic cruelties), while the opposite elements become dormant. (p. 333)

Fromm recognizes the specific conditions in which sadistic behaviors manifest themselves in stating the following:

There is no simple relation between environment and character. This is because the individual character is determined by such individual factors as constitutionally given dispositions, idiosyncrasies of family life, exceptional events in a person's life . . . environmental factors . . . also . . . religious or

philosophical—moral traditions, small town and big cities. (pp. 296, 297)

In what Fromm speaks of as "exploitative-sadistic" character, he finds a "passion" to exploit and control. In such people, the sadistic impulse is constantly active, waiting only for proper situations and a fitting rationalization in order to be acted out. As with Horney, Fromm takes exception to the association between sexuality and sadistic behaviors:

Sadism (and masochism) as sexual perversions constitute only a fraction of the vast amount of sadism in which no sexual behavior is involved. Nonsexual sadistic behavior, aiming at the infliction of physical *pain up to the extreme of death, has as its object a powerless being, whether man or animal.*

Mental cruelty, the wish to humiliate and to hurt another person's feelings, is probably even more widespread than physical sadism. This type of sadistic attack is much safer for the sadist; after all, no physical force but "only" words have been used. On the other hand, the psychic pain can be as intense or even more so than the physical.

I propose that the core of sadism, common to all its manifestations, is the passion to have absolute and unrestricted control over a living being. *To force someone to endure pain or humiliation without being able to defend himself is one of the manifestations of absolute control, but is by no means the only one. . . . Most sadism is malevolent. Complete control over another human being means crippling him, choking him, thwarting him. (pp. 283–289)*

Although adhering to the fundamentals of analytic thought, as well as being appreciative of Fromm's concepts of sadism and masochism, Shapiro (1981) takes exception to the view that sadism may have degrading ambition as its sole element:

The aims of sadism are, as I said, not only to make the victim suffer but especially to humiliate or degrade him, to make him feel helpless or powerless, to "put him in his place" or "show him who's boss." In the mildest case, the sadist wishes to make his victim feel ridiculous and small; in the most extreme case, to abuse him in such a way as to destroy his self-respect, break his will, and make him give in. These are aggressive aims of a special kind.

This view accounts for many aspects of sadism: for example, the important fact that the sadistic person regularly chooses his victims from those who are subordinate to him, the comparatively powerless, those he can control. . . . There are aspects of sadism, of cruelty, that, it seems to me, cannot plausibly be explained by any degree of interest in mere control of another individual. An aggressive satisfaction—a satisfaction in the other's suffering as such, perhaps even a hatred—is an essential and undeniable part of sadism. (p. 103)

In a different twist from those of his predecessors, Avery (1977) used the sadistic-masochistic pairing in a new light, albeit one that is still anchored to the analytic metapsychology. To Avery, these relationships are conducted under strict rules. There is a mutual trading of blows, the provocation of punishment, and the introduction of guilt in which both partners know precisely what the "bursting point" is of their object ties. Seeking to understand the logic that keeps the pairing bonded, Avery writes:

The thesis that now emerges is that dissolution is imminent and, should it occur, the weaker, needier partner will suffer the greater loss.

As in a poker game, it costs something to challenge the other. Submission to the threat means one has accepted the subordinate, more painful, position. However, the pain is borne within the boundaries of a relationship. To challenge or call the threatener is to possibly win—that is, to become dominant if the threat is not substantiated. Should the threat of a decision materialize, however, one has taken the ultimate risk—separation. (p. 102)

In his usual perceptive and integrative manner, Kernberg (1988a) outlines what he refers to as a "sadomasochistic personality disorder." This constellation of psychopathology is viewed as one variant of a broader category of masochistic pathology. As is typical for those who follow the analytic orientation, sadism and masochism are often seen as two sides of the same coin. However, Kernberg recognizes that there are subtypes within the larger framework of character pathologies; the sadomasochistic disorder is one of these. Kernberg (1988a) views this subtype as follows:

The patients I refer to alternate self-demeaning, self-debasing, self-humiliating behaviors with sadistic attacks on the same objects they feel they need and are deeply involved with. . . . These patients usually experience themselves as the victims of others' aggression, bitterly complain

about being mistreated, and adamantly justify their own aggressions toward those upon whom they are dependent. (p. 1009)

Another contemporary analyst of note is Michael Stone (1993) who has explored not merely the annals of crime as they relate to personality but the biographies of rather notorious and violent individuals that he has drawn on to examine his notions of psychopathy. In reviewing his examination of these individuals, Stone writes:

Forensic specialists mention several attributes, personality traits among them, noted with unusual frequency in persons who murder. Rebelliousness and aggressivity are common, as are mendacity, entitlement, and social isolation. Murderers are typically beset by surpluses of hatred and impulsivity. These attributes, especially when fueled by alcohol, conduce to ragefulness, *characterized by episodic outbursts of violent behavior directed against others. (p. 454)*

In describing the many forms in which "callousness" is expressed, Stone (1993) points out numerous character types who are especially amenable to therapeutic efforts. Among these highly destructive persons:

Despotic bosses whose abrasiveness and insensitivity make torture chambers of the workplace are known all too well. . . .

Certain explosive tempered, violent persons stop short of murder, but come to our attention (or to the attention of the authorities) because of pathological jealousy and wife-battering. . . .

Power-mad narcissistic leaders constitute a truly untreatable group. . . .

Mendacious psychopaths who cheat and betray, relying on their charm and acting skill to "con" and exploit others, may be said, as is true of power-mad leaders, to inhabit the realm of evil. . . .

The realm of evil is defined by the presence of malice; the active desire to harm others . . . enough to bring about, possibly, the psychological death of the victim. (pp. 451–452)

Tracking back a few decades is the work of Leary (1957). He presents a systematic model of personality styles that is largely indebted to the theoretical work of Sullivan and Horney. A major exponent of the interpersonal school of thought, Leary's sadistic conception includes not merely the obvious acts of verbal aggression and physical violence, but also those behaviors that inspire fear in others. Hence, according to Leary:

. . . the great majority of punitive sadistic characters are to be found in the ranks of the socially approved. Those persons who consistently maintain a punishing attitude towards others, or a disciplinary attitude, or a guilt-provoking attitude fall in this diagnostic category. Stern toughness is frequently admired and endorsed as a positive social adjustment. (p. 341)

We think here, for example, of the stern unforgiving father, the bad-tempered wife, the moralistic guilt-provoking mother, the sharp-tongued mocking husband, the grim-faced punitive official, the truculent fiery-natured colleague, the disciplinarian. We include all those law-abiding, often pious and self-righteous, individuals who maintain a role of potential insult, derogation, or punishment. (p. 342)

In recent years, several variants of the interpersonal school have been proposed, each of which provides a formal framework for explicating sadistic patterns for personality functioning (Benjamin, 1974, 1993a; Kiesler, 1982; Wiggins, 1982). Also of note are the social learning models formulated by Bandura (1977) stressing the role of imitative behavior and eschewing the construct of an sadistic personality. According to Bandura (1979):

At one extreme are persons who have adopted behavioral standards and codes that make aggressive feats a source of personal pride. Such individuals readily engage in aggressive activities and derive enhanced feelings of worth from physical conquests . . . Lacking self-reprimands for hurtful conduct, they are deterred from cruel acts mainly by reprisal threats. Idiosyncratic self-systems of aggressive cultures where prestige is closely tied to fighting prowess, members take considerable pride in aggressive exploits. (p. 5)

Statistical methods of analysis have often proved useful in identifying latent traits that manifest themselves in various forms of overt pathology. Despite the decision of the DSM-IV Task Force to eliminate the sadistic personality from its manual, various factor-analytic theorists have sought to give the disorder a measure of scientific credibility. Among them are Costa and Widiger (1993). In their various studies, they have come to the following brief description of the sadistic individual:

The proposed criteria in DSM . . . are all extreme variants of antagonism. The only other dimension of personality that is involved in the diagnostic criteria for this disorder is the extraversion facet of assertiveness (dominance and control). (p. 54)

Biologically oriented theorists have formulated conceptions based on their observations of aggressive behavioral tendencies which have clear implications for a sadistic personality type. Thus, Siever and Davis (1991) write as follows:

Impulsivity/aggression can be formulated as a low threshold for active responses to internal or external stimuli, i.e., motor disinhibition, manifest as a tendency toward action-oriented and aggressive behavioral strategies. Impulsive/aggressive individuals have difficulty anticipating the effects of their behavior, learning from undesirable consequences of their previous behaviors, and inhibiting or delaying action appropriately. They tend to externalize the source of their difficulties, are prone to the excessive expression of aggression and frustration, and may be less likely to experience guilt or anxiety. (p. 1650)

Along a similar line, Cloninger (1987a) refers to the explosive personality, whose features are akin to those of certain sadistic subtypes. He describes them as follows:

Explosive personality is defined here in terms of the basic response characteristics of high novelty seeking, high harm avoidance, and low reward dependence, which are associated with the second-order traits of being alienated, opportunistic, and hyperthymic. This corresponds to the ICD description of individuals who are characterized by their difficulty in inhibiting their outbursts of rage. These individuals are moody and experience frequent unfriendly feelings toward others. (p. 584)

In an early biosocial formulation, Millon (1969) proposed the following characterization as a subset of the antisocial personality disorder. In this early proposal, the aggressive/sadistic type was seen as a variant of the larger construct "antisocial," a formulation that preceded the separation of the sadistic type in DSM-III-R and was subsequently dropped in DSM-IV. Specifying the criteria for this disorder in the form of four criteria, Millon portrayed features in 1969 that remain more appropriate to his current conception of the sadistic than that of the antisocial. The following records this early formulation:

We might note the following characteristics as typical of the aggressive (sadistic) personality: hostile affectivity *(irritable and easily provoked to anger),* cognitive projection *(tending to ascribe one's own malicious motives to others),* assertive self-image *(proud of his energy, "realism," and hard-headedness), and* interpersonal vindictiveness *(socially blunt, intimidating and punitive). (p. 270)*

In his 1981 book, Millon formulated this personality pattern as follows:

The actions of these personalities appear to spring from their anticipation that others will be hostile. Their anger and vengeful behaviors are a preemptive counterattack, a fending off of the malice and humiliation they have learned to expect; in effect, they want to "beat the other fellow to the punch." To accomplish this, they seek to grab as much power as they can to prevent others from having and using it to exploit and harm them. Once seizing power, however, they become even more ruthless and vindictive than others may have been to them. They now use their strength for retribution striking back at those who they feel mistreated and betrayed them in the past. (p. 200)

The DSM-III-R added two personality disorders to the original list presented in DSM-III, the Sadistic and the Self-Defeating personality disorders. Both resided in the Appendix as "Diagnostic Categories Needing Further Study." In the listing of diagnostic criteria proposed for study of the sadistic personality, the attributes specified were primarily in the Interpersonal domain, although a few Cognitive and Mood indicators were noted as well. Of the eight criteria, five were clearly of an Interpersonal character: the use of physical cruelty or violence for the purpose of establishing dominance; the public humiliation and demeaning of others; harshly disciplining those under one's control; frightening or intimidating others to get them to do one's bidding; and restricting the autonomy of others with whom one has a close relationship. In the Cognitive realm: these individuals manifest a fascination with violence, weapons, torture, etc.; lying for the purpose of harming or inflicting pain on others. And in the Mood realm: amused by and enjoying the suffering of others.

As is known, the sadistic personality disorder was never introduced into either the ICD-9 or ICD-10. Moreover, it was dropped in DSM-IV, ostensibly owing to the minimal prevalence rates found in settings where these behaviors might normally be expected. Nevertheless, it is the judgment of the authors of this book that the decision to delete the sadistic/aggressive disorder was an error. It is our belief, as well as our observation, that persistent violence and abuse characterize a significant segment of the personality-disordered spectrum, hence the inclusion of the disorder in this chapter.

As the final paragraph of this contemporary section, we will turn our attention to the evolutionary model, specifically viewing the polarity schema as presented in Figure 13.1. As can be seen, the primary focus for the aggressive/sadistic centers in the pain (preservation) and active (modifying) polarities. At first glance, one might be inclined to note that the polarity focus is essentially the same as seen in the avoidant personality, where both pain and active polarities are preeminent as well. However, the avoidant actively anticipates and escapes from abuse, whereas the sadist actively assaults and degrades others. Both are active, but one imposes pain, whereas the second avoids pain. The reversal sign in the sadistic/aggressive figure

SADISTIC PROTOTYPE

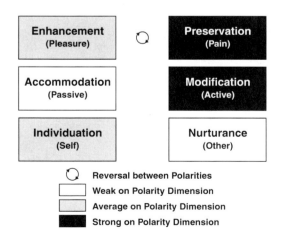

Figure 13.1   Status of the sadistic (aggressive) personality prototype in accord with the Millon Polarity Model.

signifies that sadists engage in discordant behaviors intrinsically at odds with the aims of the pleasure polarity, that is, seeking joy, optimism, and pleasure in relating to one's environment. In its stead, the sadist acts in a hostile and malevolent manner, actively working toward harmful and ruinous ends. Rather than uplifting and preserving life, the sadist is actively evil, violent, and deadly, assaulting and demeaning others instead of encouraging and enhancing them.

A visual chronology of the major historical contributors is presented in Figure 13.2.

CLINICAL FEATURES

As in prior chapters, we will furnish the reader with a variety of sources to assist in the appraisal of the sadistic personality, first noting how their features show up in eight clinical domains (Table 13.1) and then describing the several subtypes in which they express themselves.

PROTOTYPAL DIAGNOSTIC DOMAINS

The major features of this personality pattern are described in line with the domain paradigm used in previous chapters. Identifying characteristics often are similar to those noted in our discussion of the antisocial personality inasmuch as they frequently covary as personality mixtures (see Figure 13.3).

Expressive Behavior: Precipitate

Many people shy away from these personalities, feeling intimidated by their brusque and belligerent manner. They sense them to be cold and callous, insensitive to the feelings of others, gaining what pleasure they can competing with and humiliating everyone and anyone. These aggressively oriented personalities tend to be argumentative and contentious. Not infrequently, they are also abrasive, cruel, and malicious. They often insist on being seen as faultless, invariably are dogmatic in their opinions, and rarely concede on any issue despite clear evidence negating the validity of their argument. Most behave as if the softer emotions were tinged with poison. They avoid expressions of warmth and intimacy and are suspicious of gentility, compassion, and kindness, often seeming to doubt the genuineness of these feelings.

They have a low tolerance for frustration and are especially sensitive to reproachful or deprecating comments. When pushed on personal matters or faced with belittlement, they are likely to respond quickly and to become furious and vindictive; easily provoked to attack, their first inclination is to demean and to dominate. In sum, sadists are disposed to react suddenly and abruptly, evidencing outbursts of an unexpected and unwarranted nature. Although it is not true of all sadists, some tend to be recklessly reactive and daring, to be unflinching and undeterred by pain, as well as undaunted by danger and punishment.

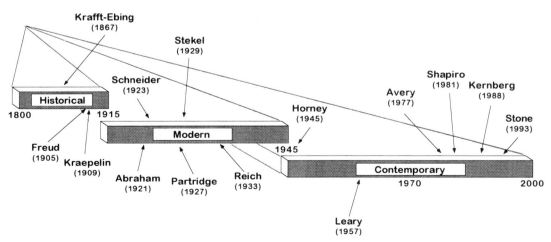

Figure 13.2   Historical review of major contributors to the sadistic personality disorder.

TABLE 13.1 Clinical Domains of the Sadistic/Aggressive Prototype

Behavioral Level

(F) Expressively Precipitate. Is disposed to react in sudden abrupt outbursts of an unexpected and unwarranted nature; recklessly reactive and daring, attracted to challenge, risk, and harm, as well as unflinching, undeterred by pain and undaunted by danger and punishment.

(F) Interpersonally Abrasive. Reveals satisfaction in intimidating, coercing, and humiliating others; regularly expresses verbally abusive and derisive social commentary, as well as exhibiting vicious, if not physically brutal behavior.

Phenomenological Level

(F) Cognitively Dogmatic. Is strongly opinionated and closed-minded, as well as unbending and obstinate in holding to one's preconceptions; exhibits a broad-ranging authoritarianism, social intolerance, and prejudice.

(S) Combative Self-Image. Is proud to characterize self as assertively competitive, as well as vigorously energetic and militantly hardheaded; values aspects of self that present pugnacious, domineering, and power-oriented image.

(S) Pernicious Objects. Internalized representations of the past are distinguished by early relationships that have generated strongly driven aggressive energies and malicious attitudes, as well as by a contrasting paucity of sentimental memories, tender affects, internal conflicts, shame or guilt feelings.

Intrapsychic Level

(F) Isolation Mechanism. Can be cold-blooded and remarkably detached from an awareness of the impact of own destructive acts; views objects of violation impersonally, as symbols of devalued groups devoid of human sensibilities.

(S) Eruptive Organization. A generally cohesive morphologic structure composed of routinely adequate modulating controls, defenses, and expressive channels; nevertheless surging powerful and explosive energies of an aggressive and sexual nature threaten to produce precipitous outbursts that periodically overwhelm and overrun otherwise competent restraints.

Biophysical Level

(S) Hostile Mood. Has an excitable and irritable temper that flares readily into contentious argument and physical belligerence; is cruel, mean-spirited, and fractious; willing to do harm, even persecute others to gets one's way.

(F) = Functional domain.
(S) = Structural domain.

AGGRESSIVE PROTOTYPE

Figure 13.3 Salience of personologic domains in the sadistic (aggressive) prototype.

Interpersonal Conduct: Abrasive

Sadistic personalities, by definition, reveal satisfaction in intimidating, coercing, and humiliating others. Some are experts in expressing verbally abusive and derisive social comments. Others exhibit physically vicious and brutal behaviors. Still others are sexually abusive, enjoying the process of demeaning members of their own or opposite gender.

Not only does the strategy of assertion and domination gain release from past injustices, but, as with most coping maneuvers, it often proves successful in achieving current psychological rewards. Because most persons are intimidated by hostility, sarcasm, criticism, and threats of physical violence, the aggressive demeanor of these personalities is a powerful instrumentality for coercing others and for frightening them into fearful respect and submission. Moreover, some sadistic/aggressive personalities frequently find a successful niche for themselves in roles where their hostile and belligerent behaviors are not only sanctioned but admired. The ruthless and cleverly conniving businessperson, the intimidating and brutalizing sergeant, the self-righteous and punitive headmistress, the demanding and dominating surgical chief, all illustrate roles that provide outlets for vengeful hostility cloaked in the guise of a socially responsible and admirable function.

Cognitive Style: Dogmatic

Despite their seemingly crude and callous actions, many sadists are finely attuned to the subtle elements of human interaction. A minor segment within this group may be constitutionally gross and insensitive, but the great majority, though appearing to be coarse and unperceptive, are in fact quite keenly aware of the moods and feelings of others. Their ostensive insensitivity stems from their tendency to use what weaknesses they see in others for purposes of upsetting the latter's equilibrium. In short, they take advantage of their perception of the foibles and sensitivities of others to manipulate and be intentionally callous.

It would not be inconsistent to find that most sadistic/aggressives are strongly opinionated and closed-minded with regard to their beliefs and values. Once they have a point of view, they will not change it. Hence, they tend to be unbending and obstinate in holding to their preconceptions. Of additional interest is the disposition of these personalities to a broad-ranging social intolerance and prejudice, especially toward envied or derogated social groups, ethnic, racial, or otherwise.

Of special note is the sadist's unusual sensitivity to signs of derision and derogation from others. Owing to their expectation of disparagement and belittlement, they are likely to see it in the most neutral and incidental of remarks or "looks." Should they be unable to vent the rage that such poor-mouthing and denigration evoke within them, they will probably discharge their fury toward the first person who is vulnerable to attack (most typically, after a few drinks, toward members of their immediate family).

Self-Image: Combative

The majority of sadistic personalities are likely to view themselves as assertive, energetic, self-reliant, and perhaps hard-boiled, but honest, strong, and realistic. If we accept their premise that ours is a dog-eat-dog world, we can understand why they would prefer a self-image of being tough, forthright, and unsentimental, rather than malicious and vindictive. Hence, these personalities seem proud to characterize themselves as competitive, vigorous and militantly hardheaded. Some value aspects of themselves that present a pugnacious, domineering, and power-oriented image, all of which enhance their sense of self and give a favorable interpretation to their malevolent behaviors.

Object-Representations: Pernicious

The inner templates that guide the perceptions and behaviors of the sadistic personality are composed of aggressive feelings and memories, and images comprising harsh relationships and malicious attitudes. Hence, whatever they experience in life is immediately recast to reflect the expectancy of hostility and the need to preempt it. Not to be overlooked, also, is that there is a marked paucity of tender and sentimental objects, and an underdevelopment of images that activate feelings of shame or guilt. In their deeply imbued jungle philosophy of life, where "might makes right," the only course to which they are disposed is to act in a bold, critical, assertive, and ruthless manner.

The harsh and antihumanistic dispositions of the sadistic personality are manifested in a number of ways. Some are adept at pointing out the hypocrisy and ineffectuality of so-called do-gooders. They rail against the devastating consequences of international appeasement. They justify their toughness and cunning by pointing to the hostile and exploitive behavior of others. Contemptuous of the weak and the underprivileged, they do not care one iota if they are looked on with disfavor. They claim that "good guys finish last," and so on. To them, the only way to survive in this world is to dominate and control it.

Regulatory Mechanisms: Isolation/Projection/Sublimation

Intrapsychically and dynamically, the most distinctive transformations of the sadists' inner world are those processed by the isolation mechanism. Many of these personalities are remarkably and cold-bloodedly detached from an awareness of the impact of their destructive acts. For example, their spouses and children are perceived as objects devoid of human feeling and sensibility. The painful consequences of their cruel behaviors are kept from mind. In the same manner, sadists who engage in group scapegoating view the objects of their violations impersonally, merely as despised symbols of a devalued people, empty of dignity and deserving degradation.

Despite the relative openness with which aggressives voice their thoughts and feelings, they have learned that there are times when it is best to restrain and transmute them. One cannot function effectively in society if one constantly bursts forth with hostility. To soften and redirect these urges, these individuals depend primarily on three mechanisms: rationalization, sublimation, and projection. The simplest means of justifying one's aggressive urges is to find a plausible and socially acceptable excuse for them. Thus, the blunt directness that characterizes the aggressive's social behavior is rationalized as signifying frankness and honesty, a lack of hypocrisy, and a willingness to face issues head-on—as being realistic and not mealy-mouthed and softheaded. More long-range and socially sanctioned resolutions of hostile urges are seen in the occupations to which these aggressive personalities gravitate. Many sublimate their impulses in highly competitive business enterprises, in military careers, the legal profession, and so on. Disposed to ward off threat by aggressive counteraction, this type accentuates the disapproval they anticipate from others by projecting their own hostility onto them. This act enables these personalities to justify their aggressive actions because they perceive themselves to be the object of unjust persecution.

Morphologic Organization: Eruptive

In the main, the morphologic structure of the sadist's inner world is composed of routinely adequate modulating controls, reasonable defensive operations, and numerous expressive channels. Nevertheless, powerful and explosive energies of an aggressive and sexual nature are so forceful that they periodically overwhelm and overrun these otherwise competent restraints. As a consequence, periodic eruptions are manifested, resulting in the harsh and cruel behaviors we see among these personalities.

Similarly, the psychic organization of the sadist possesses intense and explosive emotions derived from the nature of their early life experiences. Rather than backing off and restraining these internalized experiences and objects, they become quickly or persistently displayed in overt actions. Furthermore, these personalities dread the thought of being vulnerable, of being deceived, and of being humiliated. They assume they will receive no greater kindness from others than they have in the past. Others are seen as potentially threatening, and sadists claim they must be aggressive to defend themselves. Their principal task is to gain power over them before others can outfox and dominate them. People are seen as ruthless. It is this "fact" that makes them act as they do. They must outmaneuver others at their own game. Personal feelings are a sign of weakness and of maudlin and sloppy sentimentality. No one can make it in this life if he or she lets feelings get in the way.

Mood/Temperament: Hostile

Many sadists have an excitable and irritable temper that flares readily into contentious arguments and physical belligerence. Others are notably mean-spirited and fractious, willing to do harm, perhaps even to persecute others as a means of getting their own way. Beyond their callous disdain for the rights of others, these personalities may be deficient in the capacity to share tender feelings, to experience genuine affection and love for another or to empathize with their needs. Among the more vicious types, pleasure is gained in both the thought and process of hurting others and in seeing them downtrodden and suffering pain. Thus, many sadistic personalities are not only devoid of guilt or remorse for their malicious acts, but they may obtain a perverse and cruel satisfaction thereby. To achieve these malevolent ends, sadists may go out of their way to intimidate and harm others, enjoying not only the tangible fruits of their abuse and deceit but the distress and misery they leave in their wake.

PROTOTYPAL VARIANTS

There is no one sadistic personality but a variety of subtypes, some explosive, some calculating, some persistently tyrannical, and so on. This section will attempt to differentiate these variants.

Normal Styles

The sadistic personality is in some respects similar to the paranoid, schizotypal, and borderline, in that there are few forms of expression that can be considered potentially normal and socially adaptable. Limited though the range of normality may be for these individuals, when properly constrained, sublimated, and directed, it can serve as a pattern of behavior that proves to be effective socially and vocationally. The following two quotes attempt to characterize the characteristics of the sadistic/aggressive pattern as they manifest themselves in normal life. Listed first is the Oldham and Morris (1990) portrayal of this style:

While others may aspire to leadership, Aggressive men and women move instinctively to the helm. They are born to assume command as surely as is the top dog in the pack. Theirs is a strong, forceful personality style, more inherently powerful than any of the others. They can undertake huge responsibilities without fear of failure. They wield power with ease. They never back away from a fight. They compete with the supreme confidence of champions. . . . When put to the service of the greater good, the Sadistic personality style can inspire a man or women to great leadership, especially in the times of crisis. (p. 336)

Millon et al. (1994) depict these individuals as giving evidence of a controlling style:

These persons enjoy the power to direct and intimidate others, and to evoke obedience and respect from them. They tend to be tough and unsentimental, as well as gain satisfaction in actions that dictate and manipulate the lives of others. Although many sublimate their power-oriented tendencies in publicly approved roles and vocations, these inclinations become evident in occasional intransigence, stubbornness, and coercive behaviors. Despite these periodic negative expressions, controlling types typically make effective leaders, being talented in supervising and persuading others to work for the achievement of the common goal. (p. 34)

Childhood Syndromes

In Chapter 12, we discussed what the DSM has referred to as "conduct disorders." These characterizations subsume a variety of acting-out youth ranging from those early in childhood (ages 7–12), as well as those in adolescence (ages 13–19, or thereabouts). These troublesome youngsters may fall into two broad categories, the first noted primarily by a chronic disdain of societal norms, and the second by an aggressive acting out that takes the form of violence and interpersonal abuse. It is this latter group that mimics in many regards the characteristics of the sadistic personality disorder.

Hewitt and Jenkins (1946) were the first to separate this disorder from other behavioral and emotional problems of children attending a psychiatric clinic; they named these youngsters the "unsocialized aggressive" syndrome. Analyzing their data employing factor analytic techniques, they grouped the problematic behaviors into a pattern characterized by physical attacks, fighting, cruelty, noncompliance, and destructiveness. According to their

review, as well as the work of Rutter (1970) and Stewart (1985), boys with this disorder account for a third or more of the admissions to psychiatric clinics in the United States—with boys showing up approximately four times as frequently as girls. Stewart (1985) describes these youngsters as loud, obtrusive, given to teasing, physically aggressive, willfully resentful of directions, inclined to cheat rather than lose, insensitive to the feelings of others, prone to tantrums, and often associated with delinquent behaviors. Many are overactive and inattentive with consequent difficulties in school settings. The earlier the onset, the greater the likelihood of the problem persisting, often into adult life, although the aggressiveness may take different forms over time.

In the DSM-III, the principal characteristics of what are called undersocialized, aggressive types refer to their clinical features with terms such as violating the basic rights of others and physical violence against persons or property (e.g., vandalism, rape, mugging). Quay (1986), notes their principal characteristics as physical and verbal aggression, disruptiveness, lack of self-control, and a general pattern of aggressive conduct against others.

Although these youngsters may have a clear grasp of why they should alter their abusive behaviors, they fail repeatedly to make any modifications. Quite evidently, these youngsters are unable to change because they possess deeply rooted needs that are highly resistant to conscious reasoning and punitive consequences. In fact, punitive measures often reinforce those experiences and attitudes which initially served as models for their abusive behavior. Although they appear to gain pleasure in the thought and act of hurting others, in seeing them suffering pain and misery, in quieter and more reflective moments, they may show a measure of guilt and remorse for their malicious acts.

Millon (1969) has labeled a syndrome akin to the preceding characterization as "childhood pariosis." These youngsters show a mix of both sadistic and paranoid features. The paranoid elements are likely to be relatively minor aspects of the overall psychic picture, not having taken firm root in their suspicious, if not delusional features prior to late adolescence or adulthood.

The clinical picture of these youngsters is dominated by impulsive and aggressive behaviors. These children, ranging in age from 2 years through adolescence, are usually negativistic, belligerent, and defiant; they exhibit little concern regarding the consequences of their behaviors. Most of them seem unable to restrain their hostility or postpone receiving gratification; they reject dependency attachments, seem devoid of fear, are suspicious of others and cleverly manipulative, and tend to rationalize and project socially deviant motives onto others.

The dominant clinical features of these youngsters have often been noted in the literature, usually under the labels of "character" or "behavior disorders." The Child Psychiatry Committee of the Group for the Advancement of Psychiatry (1966) listed comparable syndromes under two titles, the "tension-discharge disorder: impulse ridden personality," and the "mistrustful personality"; others provide a somewhat similar picture in what is termed the "sociopathic-paranoid" type. The DSM-II provided a new classification that corresponded closely to the principal clinical features of child pariosis. Labeled unsocialized *aggressive reaction of childhood*, the description reads:

This disorder is characterized by overt or covert hostile disobedience, quarrelsomeness, physical and verbal aggressiveness, vengefulness, destructiveness. Temper tantrums, solitary stealing, lying, and hostile teasing of other children are common.

The role played by pathogenic constitutional dispositions or by adverse early experiences is likely to be more severe in the *pariotic* child than in adult counterparts. As noted in the etiology of sadistic patterns, which pariosis most resembles, many of these children exhibit both choleric and parmic temperaments in early life, traits which readily give rise to parental exasperation and anger. Whatever the initial source, these youngsters are subject to intense parental antagonism in the first 2 or 3 years of life. For various reasons, which were noted previously, these children do not yield to this harassment, but become contentious, arrogant, and belligerent. Not only do they refuse defiantly to "knuckle under," but they intentionally misbehave, engaging in a variety of conscious maneuvers to provoke and upset others. Their negativism, impulsiveness, and deep mistrust of their parents generalize to all interpersonal relations, creating a vicious circle of social tension and conflict. Many of these youngsters are labeled as "bad" early in life; this stereotype intensifies their resentment and anger, and often serves as an implicit sanction for continued arrogance and rebelliousness.

Adult Subtypes

It may seem strange in this text to discuss subtypes of the sadistic personality when the broader construct of a sadistic personality type has itself been deleted from the official DSM-IV classification system. One might ask, "Why bother describing multiple variants of a personality disorder that is no longer part of the DSM?" As noted elsewhere, we believe that the sadistic personality prototype should be retained as part of the official classification. Hence, the recognition that several varieties of the disorder are likely to exist seems to be a reasonable position. In the following sections, we have sought to describe some of the central features that may differentiate the major subtypes of this disorder.

The Explosive Sadist

The unpredictability and sudden emergence of hostility differentiates the *explosive sadist* from other variants of this personality type. The explosive sadist manifests adultlike tantrums, uncontrollable rage, and fearsome attacks on others, most frequently against members of his or her own family. Before its intensive nature can be identified and constrained, there is a rapid escalation of fury in which unforgivable things are said and unforgettable blows are struck.

Explosive behaviors erupt precipitously. Feeling thwarted or threatened, these sadists respond in a volatile and hurtful way, bewildering others with these abrupt changes. As with children, tantrums are instantaneous reactions to cope with frustration or fear. Often effective in intimidating others into silence or passivity, explosive behavior is not primarily an instrumentality, but rather an outburst that serves to discharge pent-up feelings of humiliation and degradation.

Disappointed and feeling frustrated in life, these persons lose control and seek revenge for the mistreatment and deprecation to which they feel subjected. In contrast to other sadists, the explosive type does not move about in a surly and truculent manner. Rather, their rages burst out uncontrollably, often unpredictably, and with no apparent provocation. In periods of explosive rage, they may unleash a torrent of abuse and storm about defiantly, cursing and voicing bitter contempt for all. This quality of sudden and irrational belligerence and the frenzied lashing out distinguish this form of sadistic disorder from the others. Many are hypersensitive to feelings of betrayal or may be deeply frustrated by the futility and hopelessness of their lives.

Faced with repeated failures, humiliations, and frustrations, this sadist's limited controls may be quickly overrun by deeply felt and undischarged resentments. Once released, the fury of the moment draws on the memories and emotions of the past that surge unrestrained to the surface and breaking out into a wild, irrational, and uncontrollable rage. From the preceding descriptions, it would not be unreasonable to hypothesize that explosive sadists possess beneath their surface controls an affective pattern akin to that seen in the instability of the borderline. Periodically under control, but lacking the cohesion of psychic structure to maintain these controls, these individuals at times erupt with the precipitous and vindictive behaviors that signify the sadistic personality style.

Whether justified or not, certain persons come to symbolize for sadists the sense of frustration and hopelessness they feel and that spark their explosive reactions. These symbolic figures must be obliterated: Unable to resolve the real sources of their resentment and frustration, these symbols of feelings of futility and hopelessness must be removed from the scene, lest they block all venues of escape. Feeling trapped and impotent, explosive sadists may be provoked into a panic and blind rage. Their violence is a desperate, lashing out against symbols rather than reality.

Physical assaults during these periods are often the product of verbally unskilled individuals seeking to terminate an altercation in which they feel incapable of responding effectively. Unable to verbalize what and why they feel the way they do, sensing that they are being outmaneuvered and humiliated, these personalities respond in the only way in which they can remove the irritation they feel. Impotence and personal failure provide the impetus for the aggressive act.

The violence of the attack serves to release accumulated tensions. In many ways, the identity of the victim is rather incidental and arbitrarily selected. The explosions are not so much a social response as an emotional release. However, social indifference accounts for but a small portion of explosive abuse. In the main, and as noted previously, the sadist has established "safe partners" for abuse, persons who have come to symbolize their failures and frustrations, and who know their inadequacies.

With minimal prompting, a full rush of hostile feelings is directed at the symbol of the sadist's discontent. Precipitous abuse is unleashed with minimal justification and minimal provocation. To explosive sadists, however, the mere presence of the symbol stirs their deep feelings of failure and reminds them of the violations that life has done to their hopes and their integrity. Although insidious in its development, once another person has come to symbolize their frustrations and life's impossibilities, little is required to prompt an explosive reaction.

The Tyrannical Sadist

Along with the malevolent antisocial, the *tyrannical sadist* stands among the most frightening and cruel of the personality disorder subtypes. Both relate to others in an attacking, intimidating, and overwhelming way, frequently accusatory and abusive, and almost invariably destructive. Some are crudely assaultive and distressingly "evil," whereas others are physically restrained, but overwhelm their victims by unrelenting criticism and bitter tirades. There is a verbally or physically overbearing character to their assaults, and minor resistances or weaknesses seem to stimulate tyrannical sadists, encouraging attack rather than deterring and slowing them down. It is the forcefulness, the unrestrained character, and the indiscriminate anger that is most notable. Descriptively, these sadists appear to relish the act of menacing and brutalizing others; forcing their victims to cower and submit seems to provide them with a special sense of satisfaction. Among those who are not physically brutal, we see verbally cutting and scathing commentaries that are both accusatory and demeaning. Many intentionally heighten and dramatize their surly, abusive, inhumane, and unmerciful behaviors. Although these individuals are in many respects the purest form of the "psychopathic" sadist, they do exhibit some features of other personality types, most notably the negativistic and/or the paranoid.

What is also especially distinctive is the desire and willingness of these sadists to go out of their way to be unmerciful and inhumane in their violence. More than any other personality, they derive deep satisfaction in creating suffering and in seeing its effect on others. Their mean-spirited disposition leads them to abandon universally held constraints that limit the viciousness of one's personal actions. In contrast to the explosive sadist, for whom hostility serves primarily as a discharge of pent-up feelings, tyrannical sadists employ violence as an intentionally utilized instrument to inspire terror and intimidation. Moreover, they can self-consciously observe and reflect on the consequences of his violence, and do so with a deep sense of satisfaction. Many other sadists, by contrast, experience second thoughts and feel a measure of contrition about the violence they have produced.

Often calculating and cool, *tyrannical sadists* are selective in their choice of victims, identifying scapegoats who are not likely to react with counterviolence. These sadists employ violence to secure cooperation and obeisance from their victims. Quite frequently, they display a disproportionate level of abusiveness and intimidation to impress not only the victim but those who observe the sadist's unconstrained power. Circumstances such as these are often seen in the behavior of street gangs and prisons.

Much of what drives the tyrannical subtype is their fear that others may recognize their inner insecurities and low sense of self-esteem. To overcome these deeply felt inner weaknesses, tyrannizing sadists have learned that they can feel superior by overwhelming others by the force of their physical power and brutal vindictiveness. "I am superior to you, I can defeat you in all things that matter, I will triumph over you despite your past achievements and superior talents. In the end, I will be the victor." Once unleashed, the power of vindication draws on deep fantasies of cruel and unmitigated revenge. There are no internal brakes to constrain them until their fury is spent. There is little remorse for the fury of their violence and the destructive consequences they create. The subjugation or elimination of others has become the primary goal.

The Enforcing Sadist

There are military sergeants, cops on the beat, deans in universities, and judges who sit on the bench, to name just a few whose hostile inclinations are employed ostensibly in the public interest. These individuals fall within the subtype we are naming the *enforcing sadist.* They represent persons who feel they have the right to control and punish others, who know when rules have been broken, and how these violators should be dealt with, even violently and destructively. Operating under the guise of sanctioned roles to meet the common interest, the deeper motives that spur these sadists' actions are of questionable legitimacy owing to the extraordinary force with which they mete out condemnation and punishment. As socially sanctioned referees, protectors of the weak, and arbiters of disputes, they search out rule-breakers and perpetrators of incidental infractions that fall within their societally endorsed roles, exercising whatever powers they possess to the most severe degree. Rather interestingly, these enforcing sadists have permeated within their configuration of characteristics some of the major features of the compulsive personality, those who are sticklers for rules, but now can openly discharge their otherwise deeply repressed angers against the weak and condemnable.

In all societies and cultures throughout history, from the most primitive to the most civilized, there are persons who are empowered to control and punish their fellow members, should they stray from the customs that have been set forth as proper. These powers often are executed with fairness and balance. However, for those so inclined, they also provide the opportunity to exercise that power in a vicious and unjustified manner. These become our sadistic enforcers, persons who impose their wills and malicious inclinations on others who have ostensibly "crossed the line." To meet an enforcing sadist is to do so at one's peril. Because their positions have been authorized by society, they can execute within their jurisdictions the means to prevail over and destroy others. Because they have permission "to be just," they are able to ventilate with a single-minded and steely determination the rights of society as they have been empowered to execute them. In carrying out their duties, they treat others in an inhumane and destructive manner. Despite their responsibility to be fair and balanced, these personalities are not able to put limits on the emotions that drive their sadistically vicious behaviors. Dominating everything and anyone becomes their goal.

What differentiates these sadists from others is their built-in and socially sanctioned power base, which allows them to exert any and all forms of control over others. Some of these personalities swagger about as prideful enforcers of the law; the more they dominate and discharge their venom, the more pridefully they swagger, and the more they feel righteously empowered. The more they discharge their hostility and exercise their wills, the more they display their dominance and feed their sadistic urges, the more they feel justified in venting their anger. Power has gone to their heads. Many begin to dehumanize their victims, further enlarging the sphere and intensity of their aggressive destructiveness. Increasingly opportunistic and manipulative, some may seek to usurp whatever they can from others. Beneath their ostensible good intentions, may lie a growingly deceptive viciousness, a malicious inclination that eventually produces the very destructiveness they have been authorized to control.

The Spineless Sadist

Not all sadists are intrinsically powerful and vicious executors of others. The explosive type acts so only periodically, and is often troubled and contrite about the consequences of his or her irrational actions. The tyrannical and enforcing varieties more closely fit the prototype of the sadist. However, there are types that are deeply insecure and irresolute, often fainthearted and cowardly, in fact. For them, their sadistic actions are responses to felt dangers and fears. Their aggression signifies an effort to show others that they are *not* anxious, nor ready to succumb to the inner weaknesses and external pressures they experience. It is these craven and cowardly types that we are calling the *spineless sadists*. These personalities commit violent acts as a means of overcoming their fearfulness and need to secure refuge. They are basically insecure, bogus, and cowardly personalities whose venom and cruelty is essentially a counterphobic act. Anticipating real danger, projecting their hostile fantasies, they strike first, hoping thereby to forestall their antagonist and ask questions later. An analysis of the psychic structure of these sadists indicates that their overt hostility and abuse maps onto a covert pattern of avoidant personality characteristics.

With fantasies that are peopled with powerful and aggressive enemies, and with a feeling of being precariously undefended, these personalities gain moments of peace by counteracting the dangers they see lurking about them. Experiencing panic, these sadists counteract their assaultors by engaging in the very acts they deeply fear. Among those who have been subjected repeatedly to physical brutality and intimidation, there is a subset that has learned to employ these instrumentalities of destruction and turn them against others who now seem threatening and abusive. In situations such as these, we see the fearful and spineless variant of the sadist, who copes with fears, not by withdrawing but with a preemptive attack.

For spineless sadists, aggressive hostility is a message to others that they are neither anxious nor intimidated. Hostility serves intrapsychically to diminish and control their real inner feelings, as well as to publicly display their opposite. Their behavior is counterphobic, as the analysts have pointed out so clearly. Not only does this mechanism enable them to master their personal fears, but it serves to divert and impress the public by a false sense of confidence and self-assurance. Here we may see the publicly swaggering spineless type, a belligerent and intimidating variant who wants the world to know, "I can't be pushed around." As with many other sadists, public aggressiveness is not a sign of genuine confidence and personal strength, but a desperate means to try to feel superior and self-assured. Neither naturally mean-spirited nor intrinsically violent, these spineless variants become caricatures of swaggering tough guys and petty tyrants.

Many spineless sadists join groups that search for a shared scapegoat, a people or ethnic population that has been "sanctioned to hate," so-called outsiders of all varieties. What makes them so special as an object of hate is that they invariably embody the very weaknesses that these sadists feel within themselves. In a perverse twist of psychic logic, by assaulting the scapegoat, these sadists assault the very elements within themselves that they wish and seek to deny.

COMORBID DISORDERS AND SYNDROMES

As in previous chapters, we will attempt to outline the most frequent comorbidities for the sadistic (SAD) personality disorder. These sections will be briefer than most owing to the recency with which this disorder was introduced in the official nomenclature (DSM-III-R), and then quickly withdrawn.

Axis II Comorbidities

Figure 13.4 outlines the major covariations seen among patients with a sadistic personality disorder. The conjunction with other personality

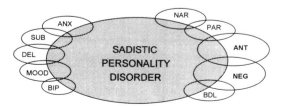

Figure 13.4 Comorbidity between sadistic personality disorder and other DSM Axis I and Axis II disorders.

disorders is most notable with the negativistic (NEG) and antisocial (ATS) types. In the negativistic, we see a strong common thread of resentment and anger. In the antisocial, the common theme appears to be a sense of having been reacted to with hostility and debasement by significant others, as well as society at large. Also associated with the sadistic pattern are features of the paranoid (PAR), borderline (BDL), and narcissistic (NAR) personalities. Several of these combinations are seen in the Adult Subtypes section of this chapter.

Axis I Comorbidities

A number of Axis I syndromes may be found at one or another time among sadistic personalities. *Anxiety* (ANX), *dysthymia* (DYS), and periods of *major depression* (MOOD) are not uncommon and should be expected among a small, but significant proportion of these individuals. Also typical among these individuals are periods that signify the presence of a bipolar (BIP) pattern of emotional expression. Another subset of these individuals are prone to substance use (SUB) disorders. In all these clinical syndromes, we see the emergence of qualities that are not hostile and vindictive in character. That is to say, a significant segment of those designated as sadistic personalities have feelings that are rather commonplace, signifying that there is more to them than destructive traits alone. Notable among their Axis I syndromes, however, are tendencies of a paranoidlike character.

Delusional Syndromes (DEL). Acute delusional episodes characterized by hostile excitement may be displayed by these personalities. Particularly prone to this disorder as a result of their hypersensitivity to betrayal, they have learned to cope with threat by acting out aggressively and, at times, explosively. Faced with repeated failures and frustrations, their fragile controls may be overwhelmed by undischarged and deeply felt angers and resentments. These hostile feelings, spurred by the memories and emotions of the past, may surge unrestrained to the surface, spilling into wild and delusional rages.

For the most part, the Axis I comorbidities tend to be episodic rather than enduring and characterological. Thus, a number of sadistic personalities may give evidence of *substance abuse* disorders, especially with those associated with alcohol. Periodically, the worst of the sadistic behavioral dispositions are elicited under the influence of these drugs. Similarly, *dysthymic* disorders may run concurrently for periods of time in the sadistic personality when they feel a strong measure of guilt for the destructive consequences of their behavior. Being kept from alcohol or observing the constraints of a religious belief system may enable sadists to inhibit their impulsive and destructive actions long enough to result in reflection and consequent contrition. *Bipolar* disorders may also covary with the sadistic characterological style, especially periods or episodes of a *manic* nature. During these latter phases, we may observe the irrational, if not explosive outbursts of hostility that typify the sadist. As noted, *delusional* disorders may occur owing to life's circumstances that force the sadist into patterns of social withdrawal, and these may lead, in turn, to fixed ideas of a delusional nature.

DIFFERENTIAL DIAGNOSES

As in previous chapters, the major issues of differentiation are found with those disorders with which the personality under discussion covaries or is comorbid.

Distinctions may be drawn between the sadistic personality and several personality types. Again, as has been noted previously, these difficult-to-discriminate personality styles may coexist as comorbid disorders.

Negativists and sadists share strong resentful and angry emotions that may exhibit themselves in overtly hostile behaviors. However, negativists are much more erratic in their emotional displays, and tend to discharge their resentments in a circuitous and indirect fashion rather than directly. Ambivalence feelings are found in both disorders, but are much more an intrinsic element of the negativist.

As noted in Chapter 12, sadists and *antisocials* commonly coexist as personality types. They differ in terms of the overtness and directness of their hostile discharge. The sadist is more openly violent and abusive, features that are not typical of antisocials, who tend to be cunningly manipulative and who also frequently engage in explicitly illegal or criminal activities.

Although *narcissists* are unempathic, insensitive, and exploitive of others, they rarely are openly hostile and destructive to personally significant others, as are sadists. Although *paranoids* and *borderlines* manifest periodically impulsive and explosive actions, these rarely are discharged in an overt fashion, as in the paranoid, or are merely one segment of an erratic sequence of vacillating actions, as in the borderline.

ASSESSING THE SADIST: A CASE STUDY

As described earlier, sadistic personalities encompass a wide range of individuals, from those who are explosive, and then express feelings of guilt and contrition, to those who gain uncontaminated pleasure by derogating and abusing others. More than most personality disorders, the subtype variations among the sadistic must be taken into account when assessing these individuals.

Let us briefly review a few of the features these individuals exhibit on major psychological assessment instruments.

In general, Rorschach profiles tend to be constrained and defensive. Human responses are relatively infrequent, whereas color responses, particularly *CF,* tend to be more common than average. Although considerable variation may be seen among different sadistic types, there is a tendency for evasiveness, as seen in a greater number than average of *Dd* responses, as well as an inclination toward proportionally more numerous *W* responses. Content on the Rorschach is likely to include explosions, dripping blood, as well as other themes of violence.

TAT responses reflect the sadist's degree of self-consciousness about the task. Those who are aware that they may be exposing themselves are inclined to provide rather constricted story themes, few of which provide any hint of their difficulties. Among those who are less sophisticated or who wish to be open, we see fairly explicit themes pertaining to violence and interpersonal conflict. A careful selection of cards will be called for on the part of the clinician to elicit useful information.

The MMPI configuration among sadistic personalities is not unlike that seen among antisocial types. High scores are usually obtained on Scales F, 4, and 9. Among the less controlled and more severe sadistic types, Scales 6 and 8 are also notable. There is evidence to suggest that 4-3 high point codes are prevalent among those likely to be explosive in expressing their abuse. Similar inferences may be made with the 3-9 high point code.

CASE 13.1

Michael R., Age 48, Supervising Foreman, Married, Two Children

The company for which Mr. R. worked recently contracted with a management consulting firm to have their middle and senior level executives "talk over their personal problems" on a regular basis with visiting psychologists. Mr. R. was advised to take advantage of the arrangement because of repetitive difficulties with his subordinates; he had been accused of being rough with his secretaries, and excessively demanding of engineers and technicians directly responsible to him. The validity of these accusations was attested to by a rapid turnover in his department, and the frequent requests for transfer on the part of his professional staff.

Mr. R. was seen as a tall, broad-shouldered, muscular, but slightly paunchy, man with a leathery, large-featured face, large hands, and brusque manner. He was the third child in a family of four; the oldest child was a girl, the others were boys. He recalled that his mother spoke of him as a strong-willed and energetic baby, who fought to have his way right from the start. Until he left for college at 18, he lived with his family on a small ranch in Montana. His father struggled to "make a go of things" through the depression, and died just as he was "starting to make ends meet." Mr. R. spoke of his father as a tough, God-fearing man; he dominated the household, was a "mean" disciplinarian, and showed no warmth or gentility. Toward the end of his life, while Mr. R. was in his teens, his father "got drunk three or four times a week," and often would come home and try to "beat up the kids and mom." He hated his father, but recognized that he served as a model for his own toughness and hardheaded outlook.

Mother was a background figure; she cooked, cleaned, and helped out on the ranch when father asked her to do so. She never interfered with her husband's wishes and demands, turning over all decisions and responsibilities to him. Mr. R.'s older sister was quiet like his mother; they both "sort of faded into the wall." The three brothers were quite different; they fought "tooth and nail" ever since they were young. Mr. R. proudly boasted, "I could beat up my older brother when I was 10 and he was 12"; he remained the dominant sibling from then on.

Mr. R. was given a "paid scholarship" to play college football but was drafted into the Army between his freshman and sophomore years. He served in the final European phase of the war and recalled his harrowing experiences with considerable pride; he currently is an active member of a veterans organization. Upon returning home, he continued his education on the G.I. Bill of Rights, played football for two seasons and majored in business economics. Upon graduation, he joined, as a field production assistant, the oil firm in which he is currently employed, married a girl he had "picked up" some months before and moved about from one field location to another as assigned by his company.

On the job, Mr. R. was known as a "hard boss." He was respected by the field hands, but got on rather poorly with the higher level technicians because of his "insistence that not a penny be wasted, and that nobody shirk their job." He was an indefatigable worker himself, and demanded that everyone within his purview be likewise. At times, he would be severely critical of other production chiefs who were, as he saw it, "lax with their men." Mr. R. "couldn't stand lazy, cheating people"; "softness and kindness were for social workers"; "there's a job that's to be done and easygoing people can't get it done the way it should be." Mr. R. feared "the socialists" who were "going to ruin the country." He had a similar distaste for "lazy and cheating" minority and racial groups.

Mr. R. was assigned to the central office of his company on the basis of his profitable production record; for the first time in his occupational life he had a "desk job." His immediate superior liked the way Mr. R. "tackled problems" but was concerned that he alienated others in the office by his gruffness and directness. It was only after considerable dissension within his department that Mr. R. was advised, as he put it, "to unload on someone other than my secretaries and my pussyfooting engineers."

The following sections include a parallel MCMI-III profile (Figure 13.5) and an interpretive report representing this sadistic pattern.

INTERPRETIVE SUMMARY

The MCMI-III profile of this man suggests that he is driven by his desire to display an image of daring and defiance, which may be characterized by outspokenness, brusqueness, imprudence, and cheekiness. Particularly notable may be inclinations to exploit and intimidate others and to expect, if not demand, recognition and consideration without assuming reciprocal responsibility. Actions that raise questions about his personal integrity, such as a ruthless indifference to the rights of others, may be present and may be indicative of a deficient social conscience. He is likely to be disdainful of traditional ideals and contemptuous of conventional values.

Personal displays of brashness and unsentimentality are viewed with pride. He may also

court danger and punishment, display a rash willingness to risk personal harm, and react fearlessly to threats and punitive action. Punishment appears only to reinforce his occasional rebellious and hostile feelings. Malicious tendencies seen in others may be used to justify his own aggressive inclinations and may lead not only to frequent personal and family difficulties but also to legal entanglements, antisocial behavior, alcoholism, or drug problems. The clinician may wish to corroborate these hypotheses.

When his life is under control, he may be adept at enticing the goodwill of others. More characteristically, he may be envious of others and wary of their motives. He may feel unfairly treated and is easily provoked to irritability and anger. His facade of sociability may give way to antagonistic and caustic comments, and gratification may often be obtained by humiliating others. A marked suspicion of those in authority may cause him to feel secure only when he has the upper hand. Socially repugnant impulses may not be refashioned in sublimated forms but may be directly discharged, usually with minimal guilt.

Deficient in deep feelings of loyalty and displaying an occasional indifference to truth, he may scheme beneath a veneer of charm. A guiding principle is that of outwitting others, exploiting them before they exploit him. Carrying a chip-on-the-shoulder attitude, he may exhibit an energy and readiness to attack those who are distrusting. If he is unsuccessful in channeling these aggressive impulses, resentments may mount into episodes of manic activity or into overt acts of hostility.

Testy and demanding, this man evinces an agitated, major depression that can be noted by his daily moodiness and vacillation. He is likely to display a rapidly shifting mix of disparaging comments about himself, anxiously expressed suicidal thoughts, and outbursts of bitter resentment interwoven with a demanding irritability toward others. Feeling trapped by constraints imposed by his circumstances and upset by emotions and thoughts he can neither understand nor control, he has turned his reservoir of anger inward, periodically voicing severe self-recrimination and self-loathing. These signs of contrition may serve to induce guilt in others, an effective manipulation in which he can give a measure of retribution without further jeopardizing what he sees as his currently precarious, if not hopeless, situation.

Failing to keep deep and powerful sources of inner conflict from overwhelming his controls, this characteristically difficult and conflicted man may be experiencing the clinical signs of an

CATEGORY		SCORE RAW	BR	PROFILE OF BR SCORES				DIAGNOSTIC SCALES
				0 60	75	85	115	

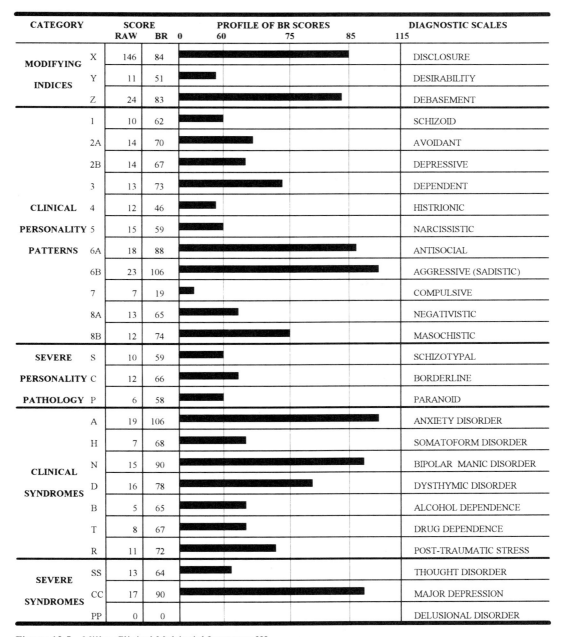

CATEGORY		RAW	BR		DIAGNOSTIC SCALES
MODIFYING INDICES	X	146	84		DISCLOSURE
	Y	11	51		DESIRABILITY
	Z	24	83		DEBASEMENT
CLINICAL PERSONALITY PATTERNS	1	10	62		SCHIZOID
	2A	14	70		AVOIDANT
	2B	14	67		DEPRESSIVE
	3	13	73		DEPENDENT
	4	12	46		HISTRIONIC
	5	15	59		NARCISSISTIC
	6A	18	88		ANTISOCIAL
	6B	23	106		AGGRESSIVE (SADISTIC)
	7	7	19		COMPULSIVE
	8A	13	65		NEGATIVISTIC
	8B	12	74		MASOCHISTIC
SEVERE PERSONALITY PATHOLOGY	S	10	59		SCHIZOTYPAL
	C	12	66		BORDERLINE
	P	6	58		PARANOID
CLINICAL SYNDROMES	A	19	106		ANXIETY DISORDER
	H	7	68		SOMATOFORM DISORDER
	N	15	90		BIPOLAR MANIC DISORDER
	D	16	78		DYSTHYMIC DISORDER
	B	5	65		ALCOHOL DEPENDENCE
	T	8	67		DRUG DEPENDENCE
	R	11	72		POST-TRAUMATIC STRESS
SEVERE SYNDROMES	SS	13	64		THOUGHT DISORDER
	CC	17	90		MAJOR DEPRESSION
	PP	0	0		DELUSIONAL DISORDER

Figure 13.5   Millon Clinical Multiaxial Inventory-III.

anxiety disorder. He is unable to rid himself of pre-occupations with his tension, fearful presentiments, recurring headaches, fatigue, and insomnia, and he is upset by their uncharacteristic presence in his life. Feeling at the mercy of unknown and upsetting forces that seem to well up within him, he is at a loss as to how to counteract them, but he

may exploit them to manipulate others or to complain at great length.

Periods of manic hyperactivity and excitement seem highly probable in the history of this man. During these periods, he is likely to exhibit a sequence of both euphoric and hostile periods that are marked by pressured speech, lessened need for sleep, hyperdistractibility, and a general restlessness. Periods of buoyant cheerfulness may be manifested for brief spans of time, only to be suddenly and unpredictably replaced by temper tantrums, belligerence, and explosive anger.

PATHOGENIC DEVELOPMENTAL BACKGROUND

As in prior chapters, an effort will be made to describe both biogenic and psychogenic influences underlying the sadistic personality disorder. Owing to the particular paucity of developmental evidence for this pathology, special care should be taken in evaluating the following propositions.

HYPOTHESIZED BIOGENIC FACTORS

In previous discussions concerning the role of biogenic influences, we noted both the marked paucity of established empirical findings and the highly speculative nature of etiologic propositions. This is especially true with the sadistic/aggressive personality. Although a number of studies of the antisocial personality are likely to contain many individuals with sadistic tendencies, the overlapping nature of the disorders makes it impossible to "deconfound" these results post hoc. As in a number of other personalities described in this text, we shall limit the number of hypotheses we will pose regarding the sadist's biogenic inclinations, referring the reader to a parallel section in Chapter 12.

Choleric Infantile Reaction Pattern

Parents often complain that their child displayed temper tantrums even as an infant, would get furious and turn "red" when frustrated, either when awaiting the bottle or feeling uncomfortable in a wet diaper. When older, these children are described as having had a "hot temper" and a bullying and demanding attitude toward other children. Thus, given a "nasty" disposition and an "incorrigible" temperament from the start, these youngsters provoke a superabundance of exasperation and counterhostility from others. Their constitutional tendencies may, therefore, initiate a vicious circle in which they not only prompt frequent aggression from others, but, as a consequence, learn to expect frequent hostility.

Mesomorphic-Endomorphic Body Build

Although aggressive personalities may be found to possess all varieties of body build, there appears to be an especially high proportion who are either mesomorphic, or a mesomorphic-endomorphic mixture. Whether the body builds are constitutionally linked to the previously hypothesized choleric temperament cannot be assessed with our present state of knowledge and technology. Even if a genetic linkage between them does exist, it is likely that the presence of a heavy, muscular morphology would increase the probability that the individual will find that assertive and aggressive behaviors "pay off." In other words, powerful and sturdy youngsters will more readily learn to utilize these behaviors because they are more likely than frail youngsters to experience success in achieving goals with them.

Neurological Disposition

Quite conceivably, a disposition to sadistic behavior may be based in part on low thresholds for activation. Should the reticular pathways for arousal be unusually dense, or should they be laid out so as to short-circuit the inhibitory and delaying effects of cortical intervention, the individual may exhibit both intense and impulsive behaviors, both of which are conducive to the learning of sadistic habits.

CHARACTERISTIC EXPERIENTIAL HISTORY

Although sadistic characteristics may be traced in part to biogenic dispositions, psychogenic factors will shape the content and direction of these dispositions; moreover, psychogenic influences often are sufficient in themselves to prompt these behaviors. The following hypotheses focus on the role of experience and learning, but keep in mind that as far as personality patterns are concerned, biogenic and psychogenic factors interrelate in a sequence of complex interactions.

Parental Hostility

Infants, who for constitutional reasons, are cold, sullen, testy, or otherwise difficult to manage, are likely to provoke negative and rejecting reactions from their parents. It does not take long before a child with this disposition will be stereotyped as a "miserable, ill-tempered, and disagreeable little beast." Once categorized in this fashion, momentum builds up and we may see a lifelong cycle of parent-child feuding.

Parental hostilities may stem from sources other than the child's initial disposition; for example, children often are convenient scapegoats for displacing angers that have been generated elsewhere. Thus, in many cases, a vicious circle of parent-child conflict may have its roots in a parent's occupational, marital, or social frustrations. Whatever its initial source, a major cause for the development of a sadistic personality pattern is exposure to parental cruelty and domination.

Before elaborating some of the features associated with parental hostility that lead to the sadistic personality, we might note some points that distinguish the patterns of the avoidant from those of the sadist. They are in many respects alike: Both are exposed to parental rejection and learn to be suspicious, viewing the world as hostile and dangerous.

Two factors may account for why the avoidant learns to withdraw from others whereas the sadist learns to rise up with counterhostility.

First, a close examination of the childhood of the *avoidant* personality indicates that parental rejection took the form primarily of belittlement, teasing, and humiliation. Although these children may have borne the brunt of occasional physical cruelty, the essential nature of the message conveyed by the persecutor was that the child was weak, worthless, and beneath contempt. As a result of this demeaning and deprecating attitude, the child learned to devalue him- or herself, and developed little or no sense of self-esteem. Being worthless, derided, and forlorn, the child felt powerless to counterattack, to overcome the humiliation and ridicule to which he or she was exposed.

Sadistic children were an object of similar parental aggression but received or experienced a different message. Rather than being devalued in the attack, they learned to feel that they were a power to contend with, that they could cause others to be upset, and that they had the wherewithal to influence the moods, attitudes, and behaviors of others. Thus, instead of feeling humiliated and belittled, each reaction—each hostile onslaught to which they were exposed—served to reinforce an image of influence and potency. Their perception of themselves as possessing the power of causing trouble spurred these children on to more vigorous action and counterhostility.

The second distinction between the avoidant and sadist may be traced to differences in temperamental attributes. It is not implausible that choleric/parmic (constitutionally fractious and fearless) and threctic (constitutionally fearful) youngsters would respond differently to parental hostility. This parental attitude would be likely to produce a withdrawn pattern in a threctic youngster, thus an avoidant personality, and an aggressive pattern in a choleric youngster, thus a sadistic personality.

Let us now return to the rationale for believing that parental hostility can lead to the acquisition of a sadistic personality style.

Hostility breeds hostility, not only in generating intense feelings of anger and resentment on the part of the recipient, but, perhaps more importantly, in establishing a model for vicarious learning and imitation. It appears to make little difference whether or not a child desires consciously to copy parental hostility; mere exposure to these behaviors, especially in childhood when alternatives have as yet not been observed, serves as an implicit guide as to how people feel and relate to one another. Thus, impulsive or physically brutal parents arouse and release strong counterfeelings of hostility in their children; moreover, they demonstrate in their roughshod and inconsiderate behavior both a model for imitation and an implicit sanction for similar behaviors to be exhibited whenever the child feels anger or frustration.

It may be useful next to trace the effects of parental hostility with reference to the major stages of neuropsychological development. This will provide us with additional insights into the complex pattern of habits and attitudes displayed by the sadistic personality.

The distinguishing feature of the *sensory-attachment* stage is likely to have been *not* the amount of stimulation to which the infant was exposed, but rather its quality. Rough, abrupt, or harsh treatment provides adequate, if not abundant, stimulation; but it also conveys a tone, a feeling, in the neonate that the world is an unkind, painful, and dangerous place, that discomfort and frustration are to be expected and to be prepared for. Early parental hostility is "felt"; it cues the infant to mistrust his or her environment and to view it with suspicion.

Having learned to expect harsh treatment in the world, such children enter the *sensorimotor-autonomy* stage with a feeling that they cannot depend on the goodwill of others, that to provide rewards and avoid discomforts they must turn inward to the self. By virtue of constitutional inclinations, or of parental reactions to their behaviors, which encourage a need to strengthen assertive powers, these youngsters rapidly acquire a disposition to stand on their own rather than expect support and interest from others. Thus, by the end of the second neuropsychological stage, these children are both deeply mistrustful and substantially independent of their parents.

Having been demeaned by their parents, and having learned to mistrust others, these youngsters enter their latter neuropsychological stages with a deep suspiciousness of others' motives, an indifference to parental guidance and control, and a strong aversion to close and intimate relationships. Although many such youngsters still seek to find a more loving and caring environment than they experienced with their parents, they cannot help but remain skeptical and untrusting. They have also learned to shape their own destiny and identity, predominantly one that runs contrary to those who assert that human sensitivity and caring are the highest of life's virtues. More particularly, they go out of their way to denigrate any values that represent what they themselves did not receive in childhood. In its stead, the future sadist asserts that the only "true" philosophy of life is guided by living for the moment, discharging hostile feelings, and distrusting the so-called goodwill of others.

With this background these youngsters enter the *pubertal-gender identity* stage harboring harsh and antagonistic attitudes toward the opposite sex. Although warmth and sensitivity are usual parts of most intimate encounters, nascent sadists view such encounters as likely preludes to later humiliations and the ultimate control by another. Hence, whatever its possibilities may have been, this phase usually reinforces the future sadist's suspiciousness and wish to maintain control over new relationships. These contradictory impulses, that of wishing to be intimate and dreading it at the same time, lead to sharp schisms in the mind of sadists during the *intracortical-integrative* stage. On the one hand, they very much seek the closeness and warmth they failed to receive in early life; on the other, each step in the direction of intimacy portends humiliation and derogation. The only course, as they see it, is one in which this dissonant schism is enacted both ways. For the greater part, they remain untrusting and harsh in their relationships with the world at large. In more personal settings, however, and for short periods of time, they may expose themselves by being close and affectionate. These latter circumstances often give way capriciously and precipitously to surges of hostility or outbursts of rage.

SELF-PERPETUATION PROCESSES

Although sadists may learn behavioral strategies to optimize positive experiences, these efforts produce, as do all pathological strategies, certain self-defeating actions. They are not only adaptively inflexible and thereby ineffective in dealing with novel challenges, but they rest on a rather tenuous and easily upset psychic balance. Perhaps their most destructive consequence is that they foster rather than resolve problems.

Perceptual and Cognitive Distortions

Most of what is communicated and experienced in life is fragmentary in nature—a few words, an intonation, a gesture. On the basis of these suggestive, but incomplete, messages, we come to some conclusion or inference as to what others seek to convey. We constantly read between the lines on the basis of past experiences, to give these incidental cues their coherence and meaning. Among the determinants of what we fill in are our moods and anticipations. If we expect someone to be cruel and abusive, we are likely to piece together the hazy elements of the communication in line with this expectancy. If we feel downhearted some days, it appears that the whole world is downcast and gloomy with us. The outlook and moods of most of us are episodic and temporary, and so these intrusions tend to be counterbalanced: We may be suspicious of certain persons but overly naive with others; we may feel blue some days but cheerful and optimistic on others.

This pattern of variability and balancing of mood and attitude is less typical of pathological than normal personalities. In the sadistic/aggressive individual, for example, there is an ever-present undertone of anger and resentment, a persistent expectation that others will be deviously denigrating, if not openly hostile. Because these moods and expectancies endure, these personalities are likely to repeatedly distort the incidental remarks and actions of others so that they appear to deprecate and vilify them. They persist in misinterpreting what they see and hear, and magnify minor slights into major insults and slanders.

Although this personality's aggressive reaction to external threat is understandable, given past experience, it promotes repetitive self-defeating consequences. For example, by perceiving derogation from others where none exists, these individuals prevent themselves from recognizing and appreciating the objective goodwill of others when it is there. Their reality is what they perceive, not what objectively exists. Thus, their vulnerability to deprecation blocks them from recognizing the presence of experiences that might prove gratifying and thereby change the course of their outlook and attitudes. Moreover, their distortion aggravates their misfortunes by creating, through anticipation, fictitious dangers and humiliations that duplicate those of the past. Rather than avoiding further pain and abuse, the hypersensitivity of sadists to derogation uncovers threats where they do not exist. In essence, their moods and defenses have fabricated dangers from which sadists cannot escape since they derive from within themselves.

Demeaning of Affection and Cooperative Behavior

This personality is not only suspicious of, but tends to depreciate sentimentality, intimate feelings, tenderness, and social cooperativeness. These individuals lack sympathy for the weak and oppressed, and are often contemptuous of those who express compassion and concern for the underdog. Given their past, there is little reason to expect that the sadistic personality would be empathic and sentimental. What affection and consideration did they enjoy in childhood? They learned too well that it is best to trust no one. Why be sympathetic and kindly? Should they chance again the rebuffs they believe they suffered at the hands of their parents and later, in the case of the several subtypes, from society as a whole? Will not others undo them and infringe on the fragile self-esteem that they so desperately seek to uplift, and that is so vital to them?

By denying tender feelings, they protect themselves against the memory of painful parental rejections. Furthermore, feelings of sympathy would be antithetical to the credo they have carved for themselves as a philosophy of life. To express softer emotions would only undermine the foundations of their coping strategy and reactivate feelings that they have rigidly denied for years. Why upset things and be abused and exploited again? Sympathy and tender feelings only get in the way, distracting and diverting them from their need to be hardheaded realists. Of course, this very attitude creates a vicious circle. By restraining positive feelings and repudiating intimacy and cooperative behaviors, these personalities provoke others to withdraw from them. Their cold and abusive manner intimidates others and blocks them from expressing warmth and affection. Once again, by

their own action, they create experiences that only perpetuate the frosty, condemning, and rejecting environment of their childhood.

Creating Realistic Antagonisms

Both the sadistic personality and the malevolent antisocial subtype evoke counterhostility, not only as an incidental consequence of their behaviors and attitudes but because they intentionally provoke others into conflict. They carry a chip on their shoulder, often seem to be spoiling for a fight, and appear to enjoy tangling with others to prove their strength and test their competencies and powers. Having been periodically successful in past aggressive ventures, they feel confident of their prowess. They may seek out dangers and challenges. Not only are they unconcerned and reckless, but they appear poised and bristling, ready to vent resentments, demonstrate their invulnerability, and restore their pride.

As with antisocials' perceptions and attitudes, these aggressive, conflict-seeking behaviors only perpetuate their fears and misery. More than merely fostering distance and rejection, they have now provoked others into justified counterhostility. By spoiling for a fight and by precipitous and irrational arrogance, they create not only a distant reserve on the part of others but intense and well-justified animosity. Now they must face real aggression, and now they have a real basis for anticipating retaliation. Objective threats and resentments do exist in the environment now, and the *vicious* circle is perpetuated anew. Their vigilant state cannot be relaxed; they must ready themselves, no longer for suspected threat and imagined hostility, but for the real thing.

THERAPEUTIC INTERVENTIONS

The prognostic picture for this personality cannot be viewed as promising unless the person has found a socially sanctioned sphere in which to channel his or her energies and hostilities. Even though a large majority of these individuals are able to disguise their pathological character by selecting vocations and hobbies that provide a socially acceptable outlet for their aggressive impulses, the persistent nature of their condition will eventually get them into trouble. At work, such individuals may have misused their status, and at home, domestic violence may have escalated. The strain on coworkers and family members has become so great that, as a last resort, these personalities are forced to seek help.

In other cases, the criminal justice system may have caught up with the transgressor. Violent and controlling behaviors that earlier were sanctioned are likely to have deteriorated into vengeful actions against arbitrary victims. These acts may no longer be tolerated, because the transgressions have become so blatant that the public can no longer claim ignorance, and societal pressures force law enforcers to take an active stance.

Not uncommonly, sadists lack insight into the nature of their interpersonal difficulties and the emotional distress they cause. More often, they simply do not care. Capacity for insight, however, is not a guarantee that treatment will succeed. Because it is impossible to force collaboration and coerce these patients to truly engage in treatment, it is unlikely that much of the underlying personality structure will be altered by the therapeutic process.

STRATEGIC GOALS

Cardinal aims of personologic therapy with the sadistic personality are to balance the polarities by reversing the discordance of pain-pleasure and reducing their active self-focus. Other important goals of treatment are to increase interpersonal sensitivity and reduce the sadist's hostile and, at times, volatile moods. Improvements in these and other domains are central to reversing the perpetuation of the maladaptive pattern.

Reestablishing Polarity Balances

The sadistic personality's primary mode of relating to others is by inflicting pain. The humiliation and victimization of others allows sadists to discharge pent-up anger and their own psychic pain. For some, this is experienced as pleasurable, even though it objectively runs counter to life enhancement. Sadists actively engage in behaviors that will allow them to control and display dominance over others. Ideally, therapeutic intervention would assist these personalities to recognize the rewards in interpersonal relationships devoid of destructive elements, and thereby remediate the reversal in the pain-pleasure polarity.

The active approach of these personalities involves manipulative schemes, venomous acts of cruelty and, at times, reckless outbursts of hostility, without self-control. The therapist must work with the sadistic personality to move him or her toward the passive end of the continuum and facilitate the acquisition of greater restraint and compassion. Sadists are generally unmoved by the hurtful consequences of their malicious intentions. Balancing the self-other polarity can be promoted by augmenting the sadists' ability not only to empathize with others, but to encourage them to engage in acts that lead to the preservation rather than the destruction of life.

Countering Perpetuating Tendencies

Given their early hurtful experiences, it is not surprising that sadists have come to expect abuse from others. However, this expectancy is often unrealistic in their current environment. These personalities have learned to attend selectively to stimuli from their surroundings that tend to support their distorted beliefs. Most of their current experiences are malevolently colored, and the benign motives of others are misconstrued. It is therefore important that therapeutic strategies focus on increasing accurate perceptual judgments and reducing cognitive distortions. Gradually, aiding the sadistic personality to interpret the environment in a more realistic manner will be an important step in exposing the person to potentially gratifying experiences and reversing the maladaptive pattern.

Sadists have further learned to be wary and distrustful of others. Displaying sentiments and responding sympathetically to others are interactional styles they carefully avoid to protect themselves from anticipated humiliation and abuse. Although this rigid coping style allows these individuals to practice great restraint in displaying emotions, others tend to be intimidated by this macho image, and are likely to withdraw as a result. To prevent the re-creation of earlier unloving and hostile experiences, sadistic personalities must learn to be more emotionally involved in their relationships with others. This will be facilitated if they allow their softer side to emerge. Intervention must stress further social cooperation rather then personal individuation.

A vital component of the vicious circle that sadists have created for themselves is their hostile and belligerent mode of interacting. One of the rewards of this interactional style is the feeling of self-importance. Not surprisingly, their aggressive and reckless ventures provoke counterhostility, and what once was an imagined foe, may now be an actual adversary. Sadists must learn to put down their weapons and let down their guard.

Assisting these individuals in finding alternative avenues for self-enhancement, without attacking others, may provide a link to a new chain of positive reactions. Their image will gradually improve once the acting-out behaviors are under control.

Modifying Domain Dysfunctions

The most salient dysfunctions in the sadistic personality are in the mood and interpersonal conduct domains. Hostile moods and an abrasive interpersonal style are central characteristics of this cruel and abusive personality. To these individuals, coercion and intimidation are instrumental in providing rewards and a sense of personal control. Teaching sadists alternative styles of interacting that will enhance their self-efficacy, as well as encouraging them to sublimate their aggression more appropriately, may have important therapeutic implications.

Other prominent dysfunctions are observed in the expressive behavior and morphologic organization domains. Uncontrolled outbursts of aggressive impulses will sporadically exceed otherwise adequate control mechanisms. Sadists, however, are undeterred by the consequences of their explosive reactions. This lack of regard for possible negative repercussions is one of the reasons these domains are so difficult to influence. One of the goals of personologic therapy with this disorder is to facilitate the acquisition of more prosocial behaviors. This includes teaching sadists to display greater restraint when impulses threaten to overwhelm them. Helping these individuals gain control over their eruptive behavior will facilitate work in other domains.

Sadists will be hard-pressed to give up those behaviors that have been instrumental for so long. Not only do their internalized representations of the past contain mainly destructive elements, but sadists also lack those sentiments that would allow them to show compassion for others and feel remorse for any harm done. Instead, they regard others merely as impersonal objects not worthy of respect. In contrast, most sadists view themselves as strong, hardheaded, and competitive. These personality features will be difficult to alter because their dogmatic and rigid cognitive style is likely to interfere with efforts to modify other domain dysfunctions. Cognitive restructuring can aid these individuals to broaden their perspective and enable them to make more accurate attributions.

Therapeutic efforts to improve cognitive as well as other areas of functioning should draw on the self-serving motives that underlie the sadist's behavior. Although it is unlikely that treatment will transform such individuals into compassionate self-sacrificing human beings, if they perceive that displaying such behaviors is in their best interest, progress can be made.

TACTICAL MODALITIES

The treatment of the sadistic personality presents quite a challenge for the therapist. Oftentimes, these individuals enter the therapeutic arena involuntarily and will comply only superficially to satisfy others' demands. The therapist will have to be careful not to be conned into believing that actual therapeutic gains have been achieved when they have not. Sadistic patients will be hard-pressed to recognize and admit their contribution to the presenting problem; instead, they will blame their victims.

Of therapeutic relevance are the resources available to the therapist and the patient's level of motivation. For example, a more controlled setting such as an institution allows the therapist to exercise greater control over the patient's immediate environment. Similarly, if family members or significant others can be targeted for intervention as well, the chances of maintaining progress are greater. It is unlikely that interventions targeting only specific symptoms will have long-range effects if the context or source of the sadist's problems remains as before.

Domain-Oriented Techniques

Behavioral intervention may be employed to target both aggressive and impulsive symptomatology. Appropriate methods should be selected depending on the function these behaviors serve. For some, explosive outbursts of violence signify a release of pent-up anger. Teaching these individuals impulse-management techniques may enhance their ability to keep their anger under control. Relaxation training can help reduce the frustration that tends to escalate and overwhelm them. Once the therapist has gained a greater understanding of the situations that tend to elicit anger, a hierarchy of anger-arousing stimuli can be set up as part of systematic desensitization. Anger-management efforts may also involve social skills training with an emphasis on improving less hostile forms of assertiveness, as well as making environmental modifications to help the patient avoid upsetting stimuli.

For other sadistic patients, aggression serves an instrumental purpose. The therapist may have to deal more directly with the calculated nature of their maliciousness by impressing on these patients the inevitability of adverse consequences. These individuals are, however, unlikely to benefit solely from aversive conditioning. Teaching them self-management techniques may be beneficial by presenting the rationale that they exert more control this way.

Sadistic personalities represent a rather heterogeneous group; interventions will have to be carefully selected to reflect the therapist's conceptualization of each patient's problems. A behavioral formulation based on a detailed functional analysis may aid the therapist in gaining a more accurate understanding of the contextual determinants that are instrumental to the maintenance and perpetuation of aggressive behaviors. For the most part, however, the effectiveness of behavioral methods is questionable. Some methods, such as contingency management programs are best utilized in institutional settings where more control can be exercised over the distribution of reinforcers. Treatment gains rarely extend far beyond the therapy setting. The problems with behavior generalization and maintenance may be due to the lack of environmental consistency. Working with the patient's surroundings whenever possible can enhance treatment efficacy.

Cognitive techniques, such as those proposed by Beck and Freeman (1990b) for the treatment of the antisocial personality, may also prove useful with sadistic patients. Cognitive therapy can help them shift their thinking from a rigid closed-mindedness to a broader range of cognitions that may generate greater tolerance for the beliefs and values of others. For example, the sadist's dysfunctional belief system includes the assumption that because he or she has been hurt in the past, similar treatment can be expected in the future. Therefore, it is best not to trust anyone. If others are out to get you, why not beat them first? Sadists' maladaptive schemas also include the belief that they should feel pleased with venting their powers, regardless of the damage done to others. When exploring these faulty assumptions, the therapist must take care not to attack the patient, yet must be sure to communicate that harmful actions are not acceptable. One of the goals of cognitive therapy is to assist the patient in reevaluating the consequences of aggressive behavior, how it adversely impacts everyone in the long run, and ultimately lowers quality of life.

The rationale for cognitive therapy is best explained by drawing on the self-serving nature of the sadistic personality. By engaging in prosocial behaviors, the patient will avoid the adverse consequences of hostility but, more importantly, may obtain additional rewards from more agreeable behaviors. The therapist can aid the patient in evaluating the advantages and disadvantages of various options that are available. Beck and Freeman (1990b) have suggested using a structured format when reviewing different problem areas in the patient's life, and evaluating the "risk-benefit ratio" of various choices. Ideally, cognitive interventions with the sadistic patient will result in a higher level of thinking and moral reasoning, characterized by tolerance for others, capacity for guilt, and open-mindedness.

Interpersonal techniques, such as those recommended by Benjamin (1993) for the treatment of the antisocial personality, can also be utilized with sadistic patients although collaboration, a vital component of the interpersonal approach, is hard to achieve. Benjamin suggests several alternative methods for eliciting collaboration and fostering bonding. One example is placing the patient in an institutional setting where more control can be exercised over the interpersonal messages from staff members. As a result, one of the links in the perpetuating chain (i.e., others reinforcing aggressive-sadistic acts) is broken. Another goal of these interventions is to set up alternative bonding experiences as well as situations that promote collaboration. Exposing the sadistic patient to a variety of life-enhancing experiences may fuel the desire to give up controlling and exploitive behaviors. Benjamin stresses, however, that unless the link between violent acts and the consequent highs that they may generate has been broken, sadists will see little reason to end their practices.

Psychodynamic approaches may prove useful if the patient is sincerely engaged in the therapeutic process. One of the goals of analytically-oriented intervention is to help patients recognize their own contribution to their difficulties and to minimize the use of defenses such as isolation, rationalization, and projection. Sadistic patients must relinquish claims that they deserve rewards for their behavior. There may be times that countertransference feelings such as impatience, annoyance, hatred, and riddance-wishes will be elicited (Stone, 1993). If perceived as such by the patient, this recreates the atmosphere of early home life. The therapist must contain his or her feelings instead of acting on them, thereby providing the patient with a new object relationship. Stone notes that, in time, patients may come to understand how the attack mode elicits defensiveness and counterattack from others. Eventually, they may be able to recognize that their preconceptions about others may be partially incorrect. These benevolent experiences may overpower the internal images of significant figures from the past as being malevolent.

Blackburn (1993) notes that therapy is unlikely to have favorable results unless the patient is able to express emotions. Strong affect will appear only after prolonged treatment. These new feelings are bound to be alien to the sadistic patient and may induce anxiety. The therapist must therefore continually provide encouragement.

Group therapy may be indicated for many sadists because this setting may present a less emotionally threatening environment than does individual therapy. The most effective groups are probably those in institutional settings where more control can be exerted over stable attendance, an important factor in the development of a cohesive group. Members in the group can exert pressure on the patient to express resentments and anger verbally, thereby reducing acting-out behavior. Gabbard (1994) notes that in some specialized settings treatment is enhanced by the homogenous compositions of the residents. This program uses group confrontation by peers, who may be more effective in engaging the sadistic patient owing to their considerable familiarity with the manipulative and cunning schemes he or she employs.

Family and *couples* therapy may be indicated when those individuals in the sadist's immediate surroundings are experiencing extreme discomfort. The family may inadvertently support the sadist's maladaptive patterns. Fostering growth of the family unit as a whole may depend on the cooperation of the other members. When working with families and couples, the therapist must take care to investigate both partners' history of abuse. A wife who has been abused in the past, may have come to expect re-victimization. As Stone (1993) notes, unhappy marriages often consist of a victimizer-victim pairing. He further points out that the therapist may have difficulty empathizing with the more openly abusive partner. If these countertransference feelings persist, it may be wise to use a cotherapist. The therapist can help family members communicate more clearly with each other without criticism and derisive commentary.

Pharmacotherapy plays a minor role in the treatment of the sadistic personality. To these personalities, the use of medications may be viewed as a threat to self-control and may further signify weakness. The utility of lithium may be evaluated when aggressive and impulsive behaviors predominate or when violent mood swings occur. To gain collaboration, the therapist must emphasize to the patient how the medication can increase self-control.

Figure 13.6 reviews the major strategies and tactics discussed in this section.

Potentiated Pairings and Catalytic Sequences

Although each of the approaches discussed previously has its own merits, programs that rely on a combination of techniques are more likely to influence the different domain dysfunctions. Interventions where the therapist has more control over the patient's environment should be considered if the resources are available. In these controlled settings, the patient will experience less difficulty in gaining control over hostile impulses. Anger-arousing stimuli can also be kept to a minimum. Growth in this area can then facilitate work in other domains.

Sadistic personalities who become involved in individual psychotherapy first must perceive possible gains from treatment or they are likely to drop out. Once again, the therapist will have to emphasize that the techniques employed are in the patients' best interest. For example, gaining control over their volatile nature will reduce others' tendency to withdraw or react with counterhostility. Adjuncts such as group and family methods should be considered from the onset because they promote system change rather than individual change. Family therapy may increase empathy and emotional involvement with the other members of the system,

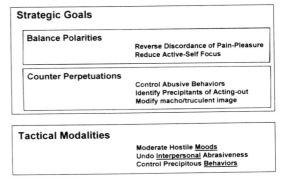

Figure 13.6 Therapeutic strategies and tactics for the prototypal sadistic (aggressive) personality.

thereby promoting the development of trust and tolerance for others. Over time, interpersonal and psychodynamic approaches may aid the patient in developing more secure object-relations.

RESISTANCES AND RISKS

The aggressive pattern will not be readily altered since mistrust is both chronic and deep. Moreover, these individuals will resist exploring their motives, and their defenses are resolute. One of the major challenges the therapist faces is to gain collaboration. It is an understatement to say that these personalities are not willing participants in therapy. The submissive and help-seeking role of patient is anathema to these power-oriented people. When they submit to therapy, it is usually under the press of severe marital discord or work conflicts. For example, they may be in a jam as a consequence of aggressive or abusive behavior on their job, or as a result of incessant quarrels and brutality toward their spouse or children. Rarely do they experience guilt or accept blame for the turmoil they cause. To them, the problem can always be traced to the other person's stupidity, laziness, or hostility. Even when they accept a measure of responsibility for their difficulties, one senses an underlying resentment of their "do-gooder" therapist, who tricked them into admitting it.

Not uncommonly, these personalities will challenge therapists and seek to outwit them. They will set up situations to test the therapist's skills, to catch inconsistencies, to arouse ire and, if possible, to belittle and humiliate the therapist. It is no easy task for the therapist to restrain the impulse to do battle or to express a condemning attitude; great effort must be expended at times to check these counterhostile feelings. The therapist must avoid getting in a power struggle with these patients. Beck and Freeman (1990) note that therapists may actually gain credibility if they acknowledge the patient's skill in manipulating others, including the therapist. Therapists may have to remind themselves that these patients' plight was not of their own doing, that they were the unfortunate recipients of a harsh upbringing, and that only by a respectful and sympathetic approach can they be helped to get on the right track.

To accomplish this goal, therapists must not only be ready to see things from the patient's point of view but must convey a sense of trust and create a feeling of sharing an alliance. It is important, however, that the building of rapport not be interpreted by the patient as a sign of the therapist's capitulation, of the latter having been intimidated by bluff and arrogance. Attempts to build rapport must not exceed personal boundaries and the therapist must set clear limits. A balance of professional firmness and authority, mixed with tolerance for the patient's less attractive traits, must be maintained. By building an image of being a fair-minded and strong authority figure, the therapist may encourage these patients to change their expectancies. Through quiet and thoughtful comments, the therapist may provide a model for learning the mix of power, reason, and fairness. By this process, patients may develop more wholesome attitudes toward others and be led to direct their energies more constructively than in the past.

CHAPTER 14

Compulsive Personality Disorders: The Conforming Pattern

This chapter continues the discussion of personality patterns judged to be of a *conflicted* personality style. As with the previously discussed sadistic personality disorder, and as with the negativistic and masochistic types, to be discussed in subsequent chapters, these personality styles are divided in their orientation, thereby possessing traits that are in conflict with one another and, hence, not having the potential of being intrinsically satisfying and consistently adaptive. This occurs because the interpersonal style and intrapsychic structures of these personalities can never be fully focused nor coherent. Both the *pleasure-deficient* (SZD, AVD, DPR) and *interpersonally imbalanced* personalities (DPD, HIS, NAR, ATS) are *either* dependent or independent in outlook, enabling them to think of themselves and deal with others in a nonconflictual manner. The deficient and imbalanced types contrast with the two *ambivalently conflicted* (OBC, NEG) styles and the two *discordantly conflicted* (SAD, MAS) personalities in that their feelings about themselves are not "split," nor are their attitudes toward others divided and divergent. Problematic though they may be, the imbalanced personality pathologies are able to relate to others in a manner that is often personally satisfying. This state of personal satisfaction is not as possible in the four conflicted types. Even if their environments were both benign and accepting, these individuals would either undo their chances for satisfaction or simply find themselves unable to experience contentment. The two *ambivalently conflicted* types—the compulsive and the negativist—are beset by severe internal schisms that they can neither escape (because they are an intrinsic part of themselves) nor resolve through external manipulation. This chapter elaborates the psychic entrapments of compulsive personalities who strive to find a niche in society that others will judge responsible and productive. However, they face an internal struggle in which the more they adapt, the more they feel anger and resentment.

Feeling ambivalent and experiencing conflict are inevitable parts of living. Each of us faces these no-win struggles periodically, but some individuals are constantly plagued in that ambivalence is an ongoing part of their makeup. Most of the conflicts we experience are fairly obvious and conscious to us, but some—usually the more troubling ones—tend to be kept from awareness (i.e., are unconscious). Certain conflicts may be considered as especially troublesome in the sense that they disrupt significant segments of life or lead to resolutions that have broad and enduring effects. One of these more troublesome conflicts is relevant to the two ambivalent personality patterns. It relates to whether individuals turn primarily to themselves *or* to others to find the security and rewards they desire. Stated in the form of the conflict it represents, it is a struggle between *obedience* and *defiance,* the terms suggested by Rado (1959). What distinguishes the ambivalent personalities from other pathological types is their failure to adequately resolve this conflict. This section elaborates the nature of ambivalence in these personalities.

Most individuals learn to feel comfortable with themselves *and* with others; they are able to seek rewards and satisfactions from both sources. The pathological personalities discussed in previous chapters may have faced a conflict between turning to others for comfort versus turning to themselves; each has opted, albeit unconsciously, to choose one course rather than the other, at least in great measure. Dependent and histrionic personalities have "decided" to obtain their rewards from the outer world; as a consequence, they will look only rarely for pleasure or comfort within themselves. The situation is reversed among narcissistic and antisocial personalities; experience has taught them that the bounties and securities of life are to be found within oneself. Although individuals from each of these personality types will occasionally reconsider their choice, the decision as to where to turn for reward and protection is essentially settled. With minor exceptions, they feel comfort with their choice and have little doubt that it is best for them.

This resoluteness does not characterize all pathological personalities; in fact, it is the failure to come to terms with the choice of self versus others that is the central difficulty among the ambivalent patterns. Two types have been identified: those whose ambivalence is seen clearly in their overt vacillation and inconsistencies (negativists), and those who, on surface impression, appear to have resolved their conflict through obedience but are struggling at a deeper level to restrain their defiance (compulsives). Both of these personalities have intense, conflictual feelings toward both themselves and others.

The active-ambivalent pattern, what we prefer to label the negativistic personality, referred to in the DSM-IV appendix as the passive-aggressive (negativistic) personality, experiences the turmoil of indecision daily. These persons get into endless wrangles and disappointments as they vacillate between showing submissive obedience and conformity at one time, and exhibiting stubborn defiance and resolute autonomy the next. The compulsive pattern, referred to in the DSM-IV as the obsessive-compulsive personality, appears entirely different. These individuals manifest extraordinary consistency, a rigid and unvarying uniformity in all significant settings. They accomplish this by repressing urges toward autonomy and independence. They comply with the strictures and conform to the rules set down by others. Their restraint, however, is merely a cloak with which they deceive both themselves and others; it serves also as a straitjacket to control intense resentment and anger.

The conflict within the compulsive personality may be understood best as comprising the diametrically opposite qualities of two milder pathological patterns, the dependent and the antisocial personalities. These personalities are like the antisocial in that they possess a strong, albeit unconscious, desire to assert themselves, act independent, and even defy the regulations imposed by others. At the same time, their conscious attitudes and overt behaviors are akin to the dependent; they are not only overly obedient but fully incorporate the strictures of others and submerge all vestiges of individuality. Inwardly, they churn with defiance like the antisocial personality; consciously and behaviorally, they submit and comply like the dependent. To bind

their rebellious and oppositional urges, and to ensure that these do not break through their controls, compulsives become overly conforming and overly submissive. Not only do they adhere to societal rules and customs, but they vigorously espouse and defend them. As a consequence, they are often seen as moralistic, legalistic, and self-righteous. Their insistence that events and relationships be systematized and regulated becomes a caricature of the virtues of order and propriety. Proceeding meticulously through their daily routines, they are likely to get lost in the minutiae, in the form and not the substance of everyday life. These rigid behaviors are necessary if compulsives are to succeed in controlling their seething, if repressed, antagonisms. Moreover, they cling grimly to the rules of society because these help restrain and protect them against their own impulses. They dare not risk deviating from an absolute adherence to these injunctions lest their anger burst out of control, and lest they expose to others and themselves the resentment they really feel.

The DSM-IV employs the label "obsessive-compulsive personality" to characterize this syndrome. We consider this designation to be inappropriate since the great majority of these patients exhibit neither compulsions nor obsessions. Moreover, there is an Axis I "obsessive-compulsive" clinical syndrome with which the personality diagnosis may readily be confused.

HISTORICAL ANTECEDENTS

The first portrayals of what we now refer to as compulsive states were rendered by German and French clinicians at the beginning of the 19th century. The German term for compulsion (Zwang) was first used by Krafft-Ebing in 1867; however, he did not utilize the label in the same sense as we do today, applying it to represent the constricted thinking of depressives. A posthumous paper of Griesinger's, published in 1868, employed the term Zwang in a manner more consistent with contemporary usage; in describing several of his cases, he identified the properties of compulsive questioning, compulsive curiosity, and compulsive doubting. In the last quarter of the 19th century a debate arose as to whether compulsions necessarily signified the operation of hidden emotions; Westphal (1877) was the prime naysayer, whereas Kraepelin (1887) was among those convinced that emotions were centrally involved. To represent this latter view, Donath (1897) proposed that the label Zwang, which by now had acquired differing meanings and translations (e.g., obsession in London, compulsion in New York), be replaced by the designation *anankast,* a term that has gained some favor on the Continent, but none in the United States.

MODERN FORMULATIONS

It was not until the second or third decades of this century that the literature turned from an exclusive interest in obsessive and compulsive symptoms to that of the personality or character type of the same name. This change evolved as a consequence of the writings of Freud and Abraham, particularly their formulations concerning the "anal character." Before detailing the contributions made by psychoanalytic thinkers, this discussion steps ahead in time to record briefly the views of K. Schneider and E. Kretschmer, two nonanalytic theorists of note who wrote important treatises on personality disorders in the first third of this century.

In his description of the "insecure" personality type, Schneider (1923/1950) brought together several earlier proposals made by clinical observers that he felt could be grouped under the designation *anankast.* Among the prime features were the following:

[This personality] is always trying to hide a nagging inner uncertainty under various forms of compensatory or overcompensatory activity, especially where the inferiority feelings are of a physical or social character. Outer correctness covers an imprisoning inner insecurity. . . .

To the onlooker anankasts appear as carefully dressed people, pedantic, correct, scrupulous and yet with it all somehow exceedingly insecure. The compensations they reach often seem unnatural and constrained. . . .

Severe anankasts with their compulsion to control . . . are extremely constricted people and indeed at times become reduced to almost complete immobility. (pp. 87, 92, 93)

Kretschmer described what we would consider to be the essential features of the compulsive personality under the designation of "sensitive types" (1918). By this term, Kretschmer meant persons who are burdened by affect-laden complexes that they must deal with intrapsychically because of their inability to externalize or discharge them. Highly impressionable but deficient in powers of active expression, they engage in a

"pent-up working over" of even minor and irrelevant daily experiences. Beset by their inability to take decisive action, they become uncertain over both large and small matters. In order to compensate for their indecisiveness and lack of self-confidence, they hold fast to standards set with conviction by others, often becoming "men of conscience." Ethical and moral issues are prominent matters in their thinking, as are conflicts over sexuality. Experienced as especially humiliating and shameful are their sexual fantasies, which appear to lodge in their thoughts and resist all efforts at suppression. The contrast between their internalized standards and these persistent and intrusive ideas contribute to the affect-laden complexes and tension so characteristic of this personality.

The descriptive approach to the study of personality types was carried forward by E. Kahn in 1931. Especially interesting is his conception of the "ambitendency" that characterizes what we now speak of as the obsessive-compulsive and the negativistic (passive-aggressive) personalities. Kahn describes the features of the former in this way:

Here are two *poles between which such persons may be constantly torn. Through the ambitendent attraction in extreme cases, even moderately definite goal-direction is made possible, so that every attempt to hold any goal in view must lead to conflict. . . . It appears however that in many cases there results even so a "satisfaction" to the personality in that it has succeeded in avoiding a decision of its own or in postponing a decision until its behavior is compelled by the total situation or by some definite event. In this way it has been possible to avoid personal responsibility.*

This dichrotic attitude may be called ambitendency, *if one has in mind the set-goals,* ambivalency *referring to the value system. From the angle of rationality it is at this point that* doubt *becomes effective—the doubt from which . . . hesitation and blocking arise. (pp. 274–275)*

The psychoanalytic approach to the compulsive personality was initiated in Freud's brief essay "Character and Anal Eroticism" (1908). It is notable not only for its clear description of the "anal character," the prime forerunner of contemporary conceptions of the compulsive personality, but for having stimulated all subsequent formulations of analytic character types. In this early paper, Freud specified three distinct and pronounced anal character traits:

The persons whom I am about to describe are remarkable for a regular combination of the 3 following peculiarities: they are exceptionally orderly, parsimonious, and obstinate. Each of these words really cover a small group or series of traits which are related to one another. "Orderly" comprises both bodily cleanliness and reliability and conscientiousness in the performance of petty duties; the Opposite of it would be "untidy" and "negligent." "Parsimony" may be exaggerated up to the point of avarice; and "obstinacy" may amount to defiance, with which irascibility and vindicativeness may easily be associated.

The latter two qualities—parsimony and obstinacy—hang together more closely than the third, orderliness; they are, too, the more constant element in the whole complex. It seems to me, however, incontestable that all 3 in some way belong together. (p. 83)

J. Sadger (1908, 1910) elaborated Freud's portrayal by noting that anal characters display a split or ambivalence in their behaviors; on the one hand they exhibit responsibility and perseverance in assuming assigned tasks and on the other, are strongly disposed to put off doing things until the very last moment.

Freud sought in 1913 to differentiate compulsive neurotic symptoms from the anal character type to which it corresponded. He concluded that the symptom reflects a breakdown in the individual's efforts to repress prohibited impulses and thoughts; in contrast, the character reflects successful repressions with supplementary reaction formations and sublimations. In a parallel essay, Jones (1918/1950) extended the distinctions Freud had made between "obsessional" neuroses and "obsessional" (anal) character traits.

The most detailed of the early anal character formulations were those of Abraham (1921/1927). Drawing on Freud's and Jones's papers, Abraham presented a range of clinical features that characterized the "obsessional" type. The following excerpts from this seminal paper illustrate the diverse traits Abraham saw within this personality:

[They] are inclined to be exaggerated in their criticism of others, and this easily degenerates into mere carping. . . . In some cases we meet with inaccessibility and stubbornness. . . . In others we find perseverence and thoroughness. . . .

There are [others] who avoid taking any kind of initiative . . . [and] we must not forget the

tendency, often a very obstinate one, of postponing every action. . . .

Almost all relationships in life are brought into the category of having (holding fast) and giving. . . . We have now come very close to one of the classical traits . . . namely, his special attitude to money, which is usually one of parsimony and avarice.

[This] over-emphasis of possession explains the difficulty . . . in separating . . . from objects of all kinds, when these have neither practical use nor monetary value.

Pleasure in indexing and classifying . . . in drawing up programmes and regulating work by timesheets . . . is so marked . . . that the forepleasure they get in working out a plan is stronger than their gratification in its execution, so that they often leave it undone. (pp. 378–388)

The next major analytic conception of the "compulsive" character was advanced by W. Reich (1933). Reich's own words convey the flavor of his views:

Even if the neurotic compulsive sense of order is not present, a pedantic sense of order is typical of the compulsive character. In both big and small things, he lives his life according to a preconceived, irrevocable pattern. . . .

This is related to another character trait, the ever-present penchant for circumstantial, ruminative thinking. There is a marked inability to focus attention on what is rationally important about an object and to disregard its superficial aspects.

Frugality, often pushed to the point of parsimony, is a character trait in all compulsive characters and is intimately related to the others we have named. Pedantry, circumstantiality, tendency to compulsive rumination, and frugality are all derived from a single instinctual source: anal eroticism.

We have indecision, doubt, and distrust. In external appearance, the compulsive character exhibits strong reserve and self-possession; he is just as ill disposed towards affects as he is acutely inaccessible to them. He is usually even-tempered, lukewarm in his displays of both love and hate. In some cases, this can develop into a complete affect-block. (pp. 209–211)

CONTEMPORARY PROPOSALS

As Abraham was the prime explicator of the "anal" character in the 1920s and Reich the major contributor to the "compulsive" character in the 1930s, E. Fromm (1947) was the prime analytic theorist of the 1940s to provide additional insights into what he labeled the "hoarding orientation." Again, a quotation lets the theorist speak for himself:

[These] people have little faith in anything new they might get from the outside world; their security is based upon hoarding and saving, while spending is felt to be a threat. They have surrounded themselves, as it were, by a protective wall, and their main aim is to bring as much as possible into this fortified position and to let as little as possible out of it.

To him the outside world threatens to break into his fortified position; orderliness signifies mastering the world outside by putting it, and keeping it, in its proper place in order to avoid the danger of intrusion. His compulsive cleanliness is another expression of his need to undo contact with the outside world. Things beyond his own frontiers are felt to be dangerous and "unclean." . . . A constant "no" is the almost automatic defense against intrusion. (1947, pp. 65–67)

A more classical analytic rendition of "obsessive character traits" was formulated by the major 1950s theorist of the disorder, S. Rado. In his fine clinical portrayal of these personalities, Rado (1959) wrote:

The patient is overconscientious in his particular way. What he is mostly concerned about are the minutiae, the inconsequential details, the meticulous observance of minor rules and petty formalities.

A rough sketch . . . would depict him as highly opinionated and proud of his . . . avowed rationality, keen sense of reality, and "unswerving integrity." He may indeed be an honest man, but he may also turn out to be a sanctimonious hypocrite. He is the ultimate perfectionist. While very sensitive to his own hurt, he may, at the same time, be destructively critical, spiteful, vindictive, and given to . . . bearing grudges in trivial matters. Or, on the contrary, he may be overcautious, bent on avoiding . . . conflict. His "common sense" militates against what he views as fancies of the imagination: he is a "man of facts," not of fancies. (pp. 325–326)

Rado's thesis concerning the origins of obsessive traits are well stated and also deserve selective quoting. Remaining true to Freud's assertion that

the impact of the anal period is crucial to the development of the pattern, Rado (1959) continued:

If the mother is overambitious, demanding and impatient . . . then the stage is set for the battle of the chamber pot.

Irritated by the mother's interference with his bowel clock, the child responds to her entreaties with enraged defiance, to her punishments and threats of punishment with fearful obedience. The battle is a seesaw, and the mother . . . makes the disobedient child feel guilty, undergo deserved punishment and ask forgiveness. . . . It is characteristic of the type of child under consideration that his guilty fear is always somewhat stronger; sooner or later, it represses his defiant rage. Henceforth, his relationship to the mother, and soon to the father will be determined by . . . guilty fear over defiant rage or obedience *versus* defiance.

A few words should be added about the obsessive patient's "ambivalence." . . . we trace these manifestations uniformly to the underlying obedience-defiance conflict. . . . He ponders unendingly: must he give in, or could he gain the upper hand without giving offense. (pp. 330, 336)

As noted in previous chapters, a number of contemporary theorists have sought to bridge traditional psychoanalytic conceptions by adding features that are focused on the role of cognitive styles and distortions. David Shapiro (1965) has contributed significantly to this effort, especially as regards "rigid styles," exemplified best in the obsessive-compulsive personality pattern. Shapiro details a facet of this cognitive dimension in the following:

The obsessive-compulsive's attention, although sharp, is in certain respects markedly limited in both mobility and range. These people not only concentrate; they seem always to be concentrating. And some aspects of the world are simply not to be apprehended by a sharply focused and concentrated attention. Specifically, this is a mode of attention that seems equipped for the casual or immediate impression. (p. 27)

Another analytic theorist of note, Salzman (1985) has described features associated with the obsessive-compulsive personality in a series of papers and books. To him:

The overriding purpose of the behavior is to attempt to achieve some security and certainty for the person who feels threatened and insecure in an uncertain world. The possibility of controlling oneself and the forces outside oneself by assuming omniscience and omnipotence can give one a false illusion of certainty. Therefore, the main ingredient is control. (p. 12)

As the defenses become overriding, a person may form patterns of behavior which are congealed and enduring. The obsessive personality, then, is manifested by meticulous, overly cautious, fearful and phobic behavior. Such obsessive individuals are afraid to risk new adventure or to go into new situations where the issues are unclear. They always take exaggerated precautions with regard to every move in their lives. (p. 19)

A recent analytic characterization that draws on elements of interpersonal conduct, self-esteem, and cognitive style has been presented by Gabbard (1994). In the following passage, he seeks to explicate the developmental background of the compulsive that goes beyond the early analytic focus on the vicissitudes of the anal phase of development:

Obsessive-compulsive persons are also characterized by a quest for perfection. They seem to harbor a secret belief that if they can only reach a transcendent stage of flawlessness, they will finally receive the parental approval and esteem they missed as children. These children often grow up with the conviction that they simply did not try hard enough, and as adults, they chronically feel that they are "not doing enough." The parent who seems never satisfied is internalized as a harsh superego that expects more and more from the patient. (p. 593)

In his intriguing work on character style and stress response syndromes, Horowitz (1974) explicates the obsessive-compulsive personality in terms of how information is processed in interpersonal communications. Of interest is Horowitz's effort to integrate traditional analytic conceptions with those that represent the patients' cognitive and perceptual styles.

Applying the synthesis of psychoanalytic and cognitive approaches to the study of personality, Beck and Freeman (1990b) formulate several of the major features of the obsessive-compulsive as follows:

There are certain cognitive distortions (i.e., systematic errors in information processing) that are characteristic of OCPD. Among these is a dichotomous thinking, the tendency to see things as all-or-nothing and in strictly black-and-white terms. It is this tendency that underlies the obsessive's rigidity, procrastination, and perfectionism. Without this primitive, global style of thinking, the obsessive would see the shades of gray that are obvious to others.

Another cognitive distortion in which the obsessive-compulsive frequently engages is magnification or catastrophizing. For the obsessive, the importance or consequences of an imperfection or error become greatly exaggerated.

A characteristic of many obsessives is thinking in terms of "shoulds" and "musts." This primitive, absolutistic, and moralistic style of thinking leads them to do what they should or must do according to their strict internalized standards, rather than what they desire to do or what is preferable to do. (pp. 316, 317)

They see themselves as responsible for themselves and others. They believe they have to depend on themselves to see that things get done. They are accountable to their own perfectionistic conscience. They are driven by the "shoulds." (p. 46)

Their instrumental beliefs are imperative: "I must be in control," "I must do virtually anything just right," "I know what's best," "You have to do it my way," "Details are crucial," "People should do better and try harder," "I have to push myself (and others) all the time," "People should be criticized in order to prevent future mistakes." (p. 47)

Picking up from the ideas of Horney and Sullivan, Leary (1957) made major contributions to the interpersonal school of thought. Hence we turn to Leary in this brief history of contemporary interpersonal proposals. His conception of what we call the obsessive-compulsive personality is as follows:

These individuals employ strong and conventional security operations. They present themselves as reasonable, successful, sympathetic, mature. They avoid the appearance of weakness or unconventionality. . . . These individuals often give the impression of maturity and parental strength.

Patients whose overt security operations strive towards normality do not present the typical neurotic symptoms when they appear in the psychiatric clinic. They are not anxious or depressed. They do not report interpersonal failures. They do not complain of timidity, isolation, distrust, etc. They tend to describe their emotional adjustment as adequate and normal.

Why then, do they come to the clinic? The overwhelming majority of these patients are not *self-referred, but have come at the request of a physician. Their symptoms are psychosomatic or physical. (pp. 315, 317–318)*

Continuing in the interpersonal tradition, Benjamin (1993a) outlines the following characteristics as central to the obsessive-compulsive style:

There is a fear of making a mistake or being accused of being imperfect. The quest for order yields a baseline interpersonal position of blaming and inconsiderate control of others. The OCD's control alternates with blind obedience to authority or principle. There is excessive self-discipline, as well as restraint of feelings, harsh self-criticism, and neglect of the self. (p. 251)

Forces himself or herself and others to follow very strict and harsh standards, and is mercilessly self-critical if he or she makes a mistake. Rigidly deferential to authority and rules. Compliance with authority, rule, or principle is quite literal. No rule bending or consideration of extenuating circumstances is likely. Rigidly follows his or her moral principles. For example, he or she won't lend a dollar to a needy friend because he or she believes: "Neither a borrower or a lender be." (p. 254)

As was characteristic of the 1960s, the theoretical and clinical features ascribed to the compulsive were subjected to critical and quantitative scrutiny. For example, Sandler and Hazari (1960) evaluated the responses of 100 patients to an "obsessional" questionnaire using the centroid method of factor analysis. Their results indicated that obsessional character traits cluster in a different group than do obsessional symptoms. More significantly, they found that the character pattern cluster did indeed correspond to classical analytic features (e.g., systematic, methodical, thorough, well ordered, consistent, punctual, and meticulous). In another factor analytic study, a similar pattern of findings was obtained and cross-validated with both preselected and random patients (Lazare, Klerman, & Armor, 1966, 1970). As they phrased their results: "The obsessive factor both in the original and in the current study contains defining traits which were all predicted from psychoanalytic theory" (p. 283). Among these traits were emotional constriction, orderliness, parsimony, rigidity, superego, perseverance, and obstinacy. Also reflecting the empirical bent of the period, Walton and Presley (1973a, 1973b) rated 140 patients in an effort to extract distinctive components using a factor analytic matrix. Although

blurred by certain intrusive "schizoid" elements, one of the components extracted was termed obsessional, having comprised features such as stubbornness, meticulousness, and officiousness.

Drawing on the work of earlier five-factor analysts, Costa and Widiger (1993) offer the following characterizations as essential to the obsessive-compulsive character type:

These features are clearly maladaptive, extreme variants of conscientiousness. Conscientiousness involves a person's degree of organization, persistence, and motivation in goal-directed behavior. Conscientious individuals tend to be organized, reliable, hard-working, self-disciplined, businesslike, and punctual. People who are overly conscientious are excessively devoted to work, perfectionistic to the point that tasks are not completed. (p. 51)

Also of interest in formulating basic variables which combine in different configurations to derive personality disorders is the theoretical work of Cloninger (1987a). In discussing the obsessive-compulsive derivation, Cloninger describes this pattern as follows:

Obsessional personality is narrowly defined here in terms of the basic response characteristics of low novelty seeking, high harm avoidance, and low reward dependence, which is associated with the second-order traits of being rigid, alienated, and self-effacing. The second-order cluster of "rigid-patient" traits caused by the combination of low novelty seeking and high harm avoidance includes patient or unassertive behavior and preoccupation with maintaining order and safety by attention to rules and organizational details. (p. 584)

More theoretical formulations were advanced by the end of the decade. Reinforced by both empirical data and conceptions concerning the role of ambivalence, such as posited by Rado, Millon (1969) put forth a theory-derived syndrome labeled "passive-ambivalence," a clinical pattern that paralleled in all major respects the character type variously called "anal," "compulsive," and "obsessional." To represent the deferential and self-constricting manner in which the obedience-defiance conflict is resolved, Millon proposed that the pattern be termed the "conforming" personality. The following descriptions and diagnostic criteria were developed in 1969 in accord with this pattern:

The four features we would abstract from the foregoing as characterizing the conforming (obsessive-compulsive) personality are; restrained affectivity *(emotionally controlled; grim and cheerless),* cognitive constriction *(narrow-minded; overly methodical and pedantic in thinking),* conscientious self-image *(practical, prudent and moralistic), and* interpersonal respectfulness *(ingratiating with superiors; formal and legalistic with subordinates). (p. 281)*

Drawing on the preceding obsessive-compulsive criterion listing presented in 1969, Millon wrote the initial 1975 working draft for the DSM-III Task Force as follows:

This pattern is typified by behavioral rigidity, emotional overcontrol and a conscientious compliance to rules and authority. Everyday relationships have a conventional, formal and serious quality to them and there is a conspicuous concern with matters of order, organization and efficiency. Perfectionism, small-mindedness and a lack of cognitive spontaneity are manifested in a cautious indecisiveness, procrastination and a tendency to be upset by deviations from routine. The characteristic air of austere and disciplined self-restraint precludes informality and easy relaxation.

Since adolescence or early adulthood at least 3 of the following have been present to a notably greater degree than in most people and were not limited to discrete periods nor necessarily prompted by stressful life events.

1. *Restrained affectivity (e.g., appears unrelaxed, tense, joyless and grim; emotional expression is kept under tight control).*

2. *Conscientious self-image (e.g., sees self as industrious, dependable and efficient; values self-discipline, prudence and loyalty).*

3. *Interpersonal respectfulness (e.g., exhibits unusual adherence to social conventions and properties; prefers polite, formal and correct personal relationships).*

4. *Cognitive constriction (e.g., constructs world in terms of rules, regulations, hierarchies; is unimaginative, indecisive and upset by unfamiliar or novel ideas and customs).*

5. *Behavioral rigidity (e.g., keeps to a well-structured, highly regulated and repetitive life pattern; reports preference for organized, methodical and meticulous work).*

In response to preliminary personality committee discussions, the following modifications in criteria were proposed for a later draft.

A. *Excessive emotional control (e.g., unable to relax, lack of spontaneous emotional response).*

B. *Excessive concern with matters of order, organization and efficiency (e.g., unduly meticulous, reliance on schedules).*

C. *Interpersonal reserve (e.g., relations with people are unduly conventional, serious and formal).*

D. *Excessive conformity to internalized standards (e.g., moralistic, or excessively judgmental of self or others).*

E. *Indecisiveness (e.g., procrastination, rumination).*

The characteristics included in the DSM-III were carried over in most details to the DSM-III-R. The only significant change was in the label assigned the disorder. Whereas DSM-III had eliminated the term "obsessive" to minimize confusion with the Axis I Obsessive-Compulsive disorder, the committee for the DSM-III-R believed that important features of the disorder were conveyed by the term "obsessive" and hence reintroduced the traditional terminology.

Terminology continues to plague this personality disorder. Thus, in its formulations the ICD-10 continues to employ the European term "anankastic," although it adds the label "obsessive-compulsive" within parentheses. The following characteristics are noted as descriptive of this disorder: feelings of excessive doubt, hesitation, and caution; preoccupation with rules, lists, organization, details, and schedules, perfectionism that interferes with the completion of tasks; excessive conscientiousness and scrupulousness, as well as an undue preoccupation with matters of productivity to the exclusion of pleasure and social relationships; inappropriate pedantry, conformity to social conventions; rigidity and stubbornness in interpersonal transactions; unreasonable insistence that others do exactly as he or she wishes, and an unreasonable reluctance to allow others to do things; the intrusion of unwelcome and persistent thoughts or impulses.

For the most part, the DSM-IV criteria remained consistent with those of preceding manuals. Grouping the criteria into the major clinical domains indicates that the Behavioral and Cognitive realms are most prominent. The following were listed within the Behavioral domain: a perfectionism that intrudes and interferes with the completion of tasks; a devotion to work and productivity that is excessive in that it excludes appropriate leisure activities and friendships; an inability to discard worthless or worn out objects even when they have no personal or sentimental value; a generalized rigidity and stubbornness. Three criteria fall primarily in the Cognitive domain: an excessive preoccupation with details, rules, organization, or schedules, such that the major reason for these activities are lost; an overconscientiousness, scrupulousness and inflexibility about many issues, especially those related to values, morality, or ethics; following a miserly style of spending both for self and others, implying that money is viewed as something to be hoarded for future catastrophes. A distinct Interpersonal criterion is noted as follows: a reluctance to delegate tasks or to work with others unless they accede to doing things exactly his or her way.

A brief summary of the obsessive-compulsive personality pattern as interpreted by the evolutionary model is portrayed in the polarity schema of Figure 14.1. Notable here is the dominance of the passive (accommodating) and other (nurturing) polar extremes. Worthy of note also is the arrow that is placed between the "self" and "other" boxes, which signifies the conflict experienced between these two orientations. As has

been described previously, and as will be elaborated in later pages, the compulsive is one of two "ambivalent" personality disorders; both compulsives and negativists struggle between doing the bidding of others versus doing their own bidding. The compulsive resolves this conflict by submerging all indications of self-interest, and devoting in its stead all efforts toward meeting the desires of others. The weak intensity seen in the self/individuating polarity and the contrasting strong intensity in the other/nurturing polarity represent this resolution. To ensure that one's unconscious self-desires do not become overtly manifest, the compulsive is extraordinarily accommodating, never taking the initiative about matters, always awaiting signals from others as to what they should do. Notable also in the polarity figure is the relative strength of the preservation focus over that of enhancement. This difference signifies the strong interest on the part of compulsives to protect themselves against potential harm and criticism, and a contrasting indifference to the experience of pleasure and joy; it is here where we can see the grim and cheerless demeanor that typifies these personalities.

A useful summary of the major historical contributors is represented in Figure 14.2.

CLINICAL FEATURES

Our analysis of the characteristics of the obsessive-compulsive personality may be usefully differentiated in accord with the several domains in which their pathology is manifested (see Table 14.1 and Figure 14.3), and in the several subtypes in which their prime features are displayed.

PROTOTYPAL DIAGNOSTIC DOMAINS

The major characteristics of the compulsive personality are organized in terms of the usual eight clinical domains.

Expressive Behavior: Disciplined

The grim and cheerless demeanor of compulsives is often quite striking. This is not to say that they are invariably glum or downcast but rather to convey their characteristic air of austerity and serious-mindedness. Posture and movement reflect their underlying tightness, a tense control of emotions

OBSESSIVE-COMPULSIVE PROTOTYPE

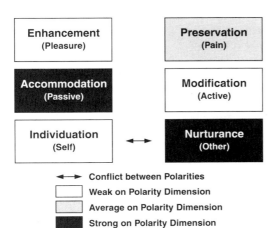

Figure 14.1   Status of the obsessive-compulsive personality prototype in accord with the Millon Polarity Model.

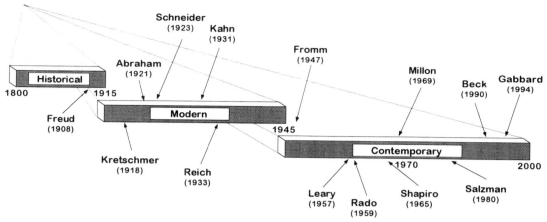

Figure 14.2   Historical review of major contributors to the obsessive-compulsive personality disorder.

that are kept well in check. Most significantly, their emotions are constrained by a regulated, highly structured, and carefully organized life. They appear emotionally tight, displaying features that signify an inner rigidity and control. There is a tendency for them to speak precisely, with clear diction, and well-phrased sentences. Clothing is formal and proper, consistent with current fashions, but restrained in color and style. Perfectionism limits the alternatives they consider in their everyday actions, often interfering with their ability to make choices and complete ordinary tasks.

Interpersonal Conduct: Respectful

Compulsives display an unusual adherence to social conventions and proprieties, preferring to maintain polite, formal, and "correct" personal relationships. Most are quite scrupulous about matters of morality and ethics. In a similar vein, they usually insist that subordinates adhere to their personally established rules and methods of conduct. The social behavior of compulsives may be characterized as formal. They relate to others in terms of rank or status and tend to be authoritarian rather than egalitarian in their outlook. This is reflected in their contrasting behaviors toward "superiors" and "inferiors." Compulsive personalities are deferential, ingratiating, and even obsequious with their superiors, going out of their way to impress them with their efficiency and serious-mindedness. Many seek the reassurance and approval of authority figures, experiencing considerable anxiety when they are unsure of their position. These behaviors

contrast markedly with their attitudes toward subordinates. Here the compulsive is quite autocratic and condemnatory, often appearing pompous and self-righteous. This haughty and deprecatory manner is usually cloaked behind regulations and legalities. Not untypically, compulsives will justify their aggressive intentions by recourse to rules or authorities higher than themselves.

The compulsive person is extraordinarily careful to pay proper respect to those in authority. These individuals are not only correct and polite but unctuous and flattering. Their conduct is beyond reproach; they are ever punctual and meticulous in fulfilling the duties and obligations expected of them. These behaviors serve a variety of functions beyond gaining approval and the avoidance of displeasure. For example, by allying themselves with a "greater power," compulsives gain considerable strength and authority for themselves. Not only do they enjoy the protection and the prestige of another, but by associating their actions with the views of an external authority, they relieve themselves of blame should these actions meet with disfavor. Of course, by submerging their individuality and becoming chattels of some other power or person, compulsives alienate themselves, preclude experiencing a sense of true personal satisfaction, and lose those few remnants of personal identity they may still possess.

As noted, compulsives are usually uncompromising and demanding in relationships with subordinates. This behavior bolsters their deep feelings of inadequacy. Disrespect and disloyalty on the part of subordinates remind them all too painfully

TABLE 14.1   Clinical Domains of the
Compulsive Prototype

Behavioral Level

(F) Expressively Disciplined. Maintains a regulated, highly structured and strictly organized life; perfectionism interferes with decision-making and task completion.

(F) Interpersonally Respectful. Exhibits unusual adherence to social conventions and proprieties, as well as being scrupulous and overconscientious about matters of morality and ethics; prefers polite, formal, and correct personal relationships, usually insisting that subordinates adhere to personally established rules and methods.

Phenomenological Level

(F) Cognitively Constricted. Constructs world in terms of rules, regulations, schedules and hierarchies; is rigid, stubborn, and indecisive and notably upset by unfamiliar or novel ideas and customs.

(S) Conscientious Self-Image. Sees self as devoted to work, industrious, reliable, meticulous and efficient, largely to the exclusion of leisure activities; fearful of error or misjudgment and, hence overvalues aspects of self that exhibit discipline, perfection, prudence and loyalty.

(S) Concealed Objects. Conscious awareness or behavioral expression is allowed only for those internalized representations, with their associated inner affects and attitudes, that can be socially approved; as a result, actions and memories are highly regulated, forbidden impulses sequestered and tightly bound, personal and social conflicts defensively denied, kept from awareness, maintained under stringent control.

Intrapsychic Level

(F) Reaction-Formation Mechanism. Repeatedly presents positive thoughts and socially commendable behaviors that are diametrically opposite one's deeper contrary and forbidden feelings; displays reasonableness and maturity when faced with circumstances that evoke anger or dismay in others.

(S) Compartmentalized Organization. Morphologic structures rigidly organized in a tightly consolidated system that is clearly partitioned into numerous, distinct, and segregated constellations of drive, memory, and cognition, with few open channels to permit interplay among these components.

Biophysical Level

(S) Solemn Mood. Is unrelaxed, tense, joyless, and grim; restrains warm feelings and keeps most emotions under tight control.

(F) = Functional domain.
(S) = Structural domain.

OBSESSIVE-COMPULSIVE PROTOTYPE

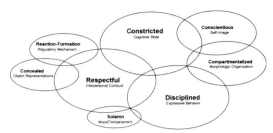

Figure 14.3   Salience of personologic domains in the obsessive-compulsive prototype.

of their own inner urges and weaknesses. Moreover, this power over others provides them with a sanctioned outlet to vent hostile impulses. Should the others fail to live up to their standards, compulsives feel just in reprimanding and condemning them.

Cognitive Style: Constricted

The thinking of compulsive personalities is organized in terms of conventional rules and regulations as well as personally formulated schedules and social hierarchies. They tend to be rigid and stubborn about adhering to formal schemas for constructing and shaping their lives. They also are easily upset by having to deal with unfamiliar customs and novel ideas. In these circumstances, compulsives feel unsure of the proper course of action, often ending up immobilized and indecisive. Especially concerned with matters of propriety and efficiency, compulsives tend to be rigid and unbending about regulations and procedures. These behaviors often lead others to see them as perfectionistic, officious, and legalistic.

Compulsives are contemptuous of those who behave "frivolously and impulsively"; emotional behavior is considered immature and irresponsible. To them, people must be judged by "objective" standards and by the time-proven rules of an organized society. Reactions to others must be based on established values and customs, not on personal judgments. What compulsives invariably fail to recognize is that they seek to judge others in accord with rules that they themselves unconsciously detest. They impose harsh regulations on others largely to convince themselves that these rules can, in fact, be adhered to. If they succeed in restraining the rebellious impulses of others, perhaps they can be confident of successfully restraining their own.

Compulsives are viewed by others as industrious and efficient, though lacking in flexibility and spontaneity. Many consider them to be stubborn, stingy, possessive, uncreative, and unimaginative. As noted previously, they tend to procrastinate, appear indecisive, and are easily upset by the unfamiliar or by deviations from routines to which they have become accustomed. Content with their "nose to the grindstone," many work diligently and patiently with activities that require being tidy and meticulous. Some judge these behaviors to be a sign of being orderly and methodical; others see it as reflecting a small-minded and picayune nature.

Self-Image: Conscientious

These personalities see themselves as devoted to work, as industrious, reliable, meticulous, and efficient individuals. They tend to minimize the importance of recreational and leisure activities in favor of those that signify productive efforts. Fearful of being viewed as irresponsible or slack in their efforts, as well as being seen as one who fails to meet the expectancies of others, or is error-prone, compulsives overvalue those aspects of their self-image that signify perfectionism, prudence, and discipline.

Compulsives are good "organization men," typifying what we have termed the bureaucratic personality type. The compulsive's self-image is that of a conscientious, selfless, loyal, dependable, prudent, and responsible individual. Not only do these individuals willingly accept the beliefs of institutional authorities, but they believe that these authorities' demands and expectations are "correct." Compulsives identify with these strictures, internalizing them as a means of controlling their own repressed impulses and employing them as a standard to regulate the behavior of others. Their vigorous defense of institutional authorities often brings them commendation and support, rewards that serve to reinforce their inclination toward public obedience and moral self-righteousness.

It is characteristic of compulsives to be as harsh in their self-judgments as they are with others. In addition, they voice a strong sense of duty to others, feeling that they must not let others down and, more significantly, not engage in behaviors that might provoke their displeasure. Although compulsives feel self-doubt or guilt for failing to live up to some ideal, they have no awareness that it is often their own ambivalence about achieving, their own unconscious desire to defy authority, that blocks them from attaining their public aspirations. They may rationalize their indecisiveness by the "wisdom" of "looking before one leaps," of delaying action until one is sure of its correctness, and of "aiming for high standards," which, of course demand the most careful and reflective appraisal. These philosophical clichés merely cloak an unconscious desire to undo the rigid mold into which compulsives have allowed their life to be cast.

Object-Representations: Concealed

It is of special importance to the compulsive that only those internalized representations of the past that are socially acceptable be permitted into conscious awareness or given expression behaviorally. Inner impulses and attitudes, as well as residual images and memories are all highly regulated and tightly bound. Forbidden impulses are sequestered in the unconscious. Similarly, current personal difficulties and social conflicts anchored to past experiences are defensively denied, kept from conscious awareness, and maintained under the most stringent of controls.

Compulsives take great pains to avoid recognizing the contradictions between their unconscious impulses and their overt behaviors. This they do by devaluing self-exploration. Thus, compulsives often exhibit little or no insight into their motives and feelings. To bolster this defensive maneuver, they demean the "personal equation," claiming that self-exploration is antithetical to efficient behavior and that introspection only intrudes on rational thinking and self-control. Protectively, then, they avoid looking into themselves and build a rationale in which they assert that analyses such as these are signs of immature self-indulgence, traits that they view as anathema to civilized life.

Regulatory Mechanisms: Reaction-Formation/Identification

Compulsives engage in numerous "mechanisms of defense" to keep a tight reign on their contrary feelings and dispositions. More than any other personality, they actively exhibit a wide range of regulatory actions. Most distinctive, perhaps, is their use of reaction-formation. This is seen in their repeated efforts to present a positive spin on their thoughts and behaviors, to engage in socially commendable actions that in fact, diametrically oppose their deeper forbidden and contrary feelings. Hence, they tend to display publicly a mature reasonableness when faced with circumstances that would evoke dismay or irritability in most persons. The ingratiating and obsequious manner of many compulsives, especially in circumstances that normally evoke frustration and anger in others, may be traced to a reversal of their hidden and oppositional urges. Not daring to expose their true feelings of defiance and rebelliousness, they bind these feelings so tightly that their opposite comes forth.

Two of the most effective techniques for transforming negative impulses, yet finding outlets for them at the same time, are identification and sublimation. If compulsives can find a punitive model of authority to emulate, they can justify venting their hostile impulses toward others and perhaps receive commendation as well. For example, in one case the author observed that a child identified with his parents' strict attitudes by tattling and reproaching his brother; this enabled the child to find a sanctioned outlet for his otherwise unacceptable hostility. Much of the compulsive's self-righteous morality reflects the same process. Mechanisms of sublimation serve similar functions. Unconscious feelings of hostility that cannot be tolerated consciously are often expressed in socially acceptable ways through occupations such as judge, dean, soldier, or surgeon. Fiercely moralistic fathers and "loving," but overcontrolling, mothers are more common ways of restraint that often camouflage hidden hostility.

Two other intrapsychic mechanisms—isolation and undoing—do not provide an outlet for submerged rebellious impulses but do serve to keep them in check. Compulsive individuals also compartmentalize or isolate their emotional response to a situation. They block or otherwise neutralize feelings that are normally aroused by a stressful event and thereby ensure against the possibility of reacting in ways that might cause embarrassment and disapproval. Should compulsives trespass the injunctions of authority figures or fail to live up to their expectations, they may engage in certain ritualistic acts to "undo" the evil or wrong they feel they have done. In this manner, they seek expiation for their sins, and they thereby regain the goodwill they fear may be lost.

Morphologic Organization: Compartmentalized

The structure of the compulsive's mind is rather distinctive among the personality patterns. To keep oppositional feelings and impulses from affecting one another, and to hold ambivalent images and contradictory attitudes from spilling forth into conscious awareness, the organization of their inner world must be rigidly compartmentalized. There is a tightly consolidated system that is clearly partitioned into numerous, distinct, and segregated constellations of dispositions, memories, and feelings. Crucial is that these compartments be tightly sealed, hence precluding any open channels through which these components can interrelate.

Appearing deliberate and well poised on the surface, the compulsives sit atop this tightly constrained but internal powder keg. Beset by deep ambivalences and conflicts, their inner turmoil threatens to upset the balance they have so carefully wrought throughout their lives. They must preserve that balance and protect themselves against the intrusion into both conscious awareness and overt behavior of their intensely contrary impulses and feelings. They must carefully avoid events that could dislodge and unleash these forces, causing them to lose favor with those in authority. Having opted for a strategy in which rewards and security are granted to those in power, they must, at all costs, prevent losing the powerful's respect and protection. To achieve this, they must take no risks and operate with complete certainty that no unanticipated event will upset their equilibrium. Avoiding external disruptions is difficult enough, but their greatest task is that of controlling their own emotions, that is, restraining the impulses that surge from within and from which they cannot escape. Their only recourse for dealing with these intrusive and frightening urges is either to transmute them or to seal them off. As noted previously, they do this by the extensive use of intrapsychic mechanisms. Because of the depth of their ambivalence and the imperative nature of its control, compulsive personalities employ more varied defensive mechanisms than any of the other pathological patterns.

A major force behind the tightly structured world of compulsives is their fear of disapproval and their concern that their actions will not only be frowned on, but severely punished. This fear can be understood given their likely history of exposure to demanding, perfectionistic, and condemnatory parents. One would assume that by toeing the line and behaving properly and correctly, compulsives could put this concern aside and be relaxed and untroubled. But this does not prove to be possible because their conformity and propriety are merely a public facade behind which lurks deeply repressed urges toward defiance and self-assertion. The ever-present threat that their rebellious and angry feelings will break into the open intensifies their fear of provoking condemnation. At some level, they sense the pretentiousness and insincerity of their public behavior. Thus, their fantasies may be a constant reminder of the disparity that exists between the front they present to others and the rebelliousness they feel beneath. No matter how perfect their behavior may be in fact, no matter how hard they may attempt to prove themselves, this inner ambivalence remains. They must be alert to the possibility of detection at all times. Condemnation is a constant threat since their true feelings may be readily uncovered. To cope with both their fears and their impulses, compulsives engage in the characteristic control mechanisms and formal interpersonal behaviors that have been addressed in previous sections.

Mood/Temperament: Solemn

It is typical to find compulsives to be unrelaxed, tense, joyless, and grim. Most restrain warm and affectionate feelings, keeping their emotions under a measure of firm control. Some compulsives exhibit a marked diminution in activity and energy, attributable in all probability to their lifelong habit of constraint and inhibition. Few evidence a lively or ebullient manner; most are rigidly controlled and emotionally tight, and their failure to release pent-up energies is likely to dispose them to psychophysiological disorders. Any speculation that the ambivalence of compulsives might reflect some intrinsic antagonism between opposing temperamental dispositions would seem presumptuous. Yet we do observe an opposition between intense fear and intense anger among these individuals. Both tendencies may be great and may account in part for their frequent indecisiveness and immobilization. Given their grim and joyless quality, we might also conjecture that many possess a constitutionally based anhedonic temperament. Translating these notions into tangible substrates, it might be hypothesized that regions of the limbic system associated with both fear and anger may be unusually dense or well branched; conflicting signals from these areas might underlie the hesitancy, doubting, and indecisive behaviors seen in these patients. Similarly, the substrate for experiencing pleasure may be poorly developed, leading to the compulsive's typical stern countenance. Speculations such as these are highly conjectural.

Prototypal Variants

Although certain key features typify the prototypal compulsive, we can observe a number of different ways in which these characteristics are configured and express themselves, ranging from so-called normal styles, to childhood syndromes, to clinical adult subtypes.

Normal Styles

Perhaps more than any other personality style, especially in advanced and successful societies, are those who evince a mild variant of the obsessive-compulsive personality disorder. Here we see not so much the driven, tense, and rigid adherence to external demands and to a perfectionism that typifies the disordered state; rather we see a well-disciplined and organized lifestyle that enables individuals to function efficiently and successfully in most of their endeavors. When things go wrong, there is a measure of discomfort that leads to a resolution, not indecisiveness and anxiety. Those reading this text are themselves likely to possess partial traits of the compulsive style; how else could one be sufficiently diligent to get through graduate or medical school?

In discussing this normal-compulsive personality, Oldham and Morris (1990) refer to them as demonstrating "the conscientious style":

Conscientious style people are the men and women of strong moral principle and absolute certainty, and they won't rest until the job is done and done right. They are loyal to their families, their causes, and their superiors. Hard work is a hallmark of this personality style; Conscientious types achieve. (p. 56)

Preferring to focus on their conventionality, their inclination to follow established rules and standards, Millon et al. (1994) label this normalized variant of the compulsive personality as exhibiting the "conforming style." The following paragraph depicts this view:

Their ideal is to be proper, conventional, orderly, and perfectionistic. . . . They are notably respectful of tradition and authority, and act in a responsible, proper, and conscientious way. They do their best to uphold conventional rules and standards, following given regulations closely, and tend to be judgmental of those who do not. Well-organized and reliable, prudent and restrained, they may appear to be overly self-controlled, formal and inflexible in their relationships, intolerant of deviance, and unbending in their adherence to social proprieties. Diligent about their responsibilities, they dislike having their work pile up, worry about finishing things, and come across to others as highly dependable and industrious. (p. 33)

Those evidencing characteristics of the normal compulsive style demonstrate an unusual degree of integrity, adhering as firmly as they can to society's ethics and morals. Extremely principled in their behavior, they tend to follow standards from which they hesitate to deviate, attempt to act in an objective and rational manner, and decide matters in terms of what they believe is right. Many are religious, following their church or temple's beliefs and principles to an extreme degree. Maintaining personal integrity ranks high among their goals; exhibiting virtuous behaviors and voicing moral values gives them a deep sense of satisfaction. On the other hand, problems arise as a consequence of their being superrational, of seeing complex matters in black or white, good or bad, or right or wrong terms. Their devaluation of the place of emotion tends to preclude relativistic judgments and subjective preferences.

Childhood Syndromes

Although the DSM-IV has subsumed the construct "over-anxious disorder in children," introduced in the DSM-III, into the overall category of "anxious disorders," there is reason to review this decision and specify some of the features included in the original DSM-III designation. We do this because the characteristics outlined appear to be precursors of the obsessive-compulsive personality disorder. For example, the essential feature noted was excessive worrying and fearful behavior that is not focused on a specific situation or object. Of particular interest in this section is the statement that these children may seem "hyper-mature with their precocious concerns." Also noted in this regard are perfectionistic tendencies, with obsessional self-doubt, excessive conformity, and a seeking of approval. The criteria enumerated include overconcern about competence; preoccupation with the appropriateness of one's behavior, excessive need for reassurance, somatic complaints, and marked feelings of tension or inability to relax.

As described in Chapter 3, several negative consequences may result from parental overcontrol and perfectionism. To reiterate, overly trained and overly disciplined youngsters are given little opportunity to shape their own destiny. Whether by coercion or enticement, children who learn early to control emergent feelings and to focus their thoughts and behaviors to meet the prescriptions of parental demands acquire a pattern that is the model of adult orderliness and propriety. Such overly socialized youngsters become rigid, tense, and anxious, lest they fail to hold to the true parental pathway. Not only are they overly anxious, should failures occur, but they now lack the spontaneity, flexibility, and creativeness normally seen in the young. They are fixed on a restrictive course and have been deprived of the rewards of exploring and experiencing life for themselves.

Although adults are comforted by the propriety and good manners of such youngsters, contrasting them with the omnipresent undisciplined and diffusely oriented behaviors of many of our current youth, the price to be paid by the children themselves is not always as slight as it may appear. Many are uptight, agitated in their inner life, and often inclined to act out in some later point in their life when the constraints of parental demands have been loosened.

Adult Subtypes

With perhaps three or four notable exceptions (antisocials, borderlines), compulsives have been found to blend with almost every other personality type. The variants described here reflect these combinations in part, but they are mostly accentuations of a number of the more prominent clinical domains of the prototypal obsessive-compulsive personality.

The Conscientious Compulsive

The behavior of the *conscientious compulsive* is typified, more than any other compulsive type, by a conforming dependency, a compliance to rules and authority, and a willing submission to the wishes and values of others. There is a tendency to be self-effacing and noncompetitive, a fear of independent self-assertion, and a surface compliance to the expectations and demands of others. They voice a strong sense of duty, feeling that others must not have their expectations unmet. Their self-image, on the surface, is that of being a considerate, thoughtful, and cooperative person, prone to act in an unambitious and modest way. There are deep feelings of personal inadequacy as conscientious compulsives tend to minimize attainments, underplay tangential attributes, and grade abilities by their relevance to fulfilling the expectations of others. We may characterize these compulsives by the following descriptive adjectives: earnest, duty-bound, hardworking, meticulous, painstaking, and rule-bound. Dreading the consequences of making errors or mistakes, they react to situations that are unclear or ambiguous by acting indecisively and inflexibly, evincing marked self-doubts and hesitations about taking any course of action. From the foregoing, we can see that the basic compulsive structure of these individuals combines in a variety of significant ways with features associated primarily with the dependent personality.

The conscientious patient is overly respectful, even ingratiating with those in authority. The fear of failure and of provoking condemnation creates considerable tension, as well as occasional expressions of guilt. Submissive behavior with those in authority may also be traced to a reversal of hidden rebellious feelings. Lurking behind the front of propriety and restraint may be intense contrary feelings that occasionally break through their controls. Rarely daring to expose these feelings, the conscientious compulsive binds them so tightly that life becomes overorganized in an anxiously tense and disciplined self-restraint. As a consequence the patient lacks spontaneity and flexibility, is often indecisive, tends to procrastinate, and is easily upset by deviations from routine. There is a marked denial of discordant emotions and a tendency to neutralize feelings normally aroused by distressful events.

The conscientious compulsive's marked self-doubts and deflated sense of self-esteem is given support by the person's attachment to institutional or religious organizations. In this way, the patient seeks to associate his or her actions by identifying them with those in authority. Efforts are made to maintain a behavioral pattern that is consistent and unvarying, to restrain independent actions, and to comply rigidly with the strictures of approved rules. The conscientious tendency to perfection and a preoccupation with minor irrelevancies distract the patient's attention from deeper sources of anxiety and inadequacy, as well as anticipated derogation.

Most central to the psychic makeup of these patients is the dread of making mistakes and the fear of taking risks. There is a persistent reworking over of things, a feeling of never being satisfied with the results of their efforts, and a concomitant anxiety of being unprepared for any new task. Their conscientiousness reflects a deep sense of inadequacy, of

potential failure, and ultimate exposure for inner deficiencies and untenable impulses.

These compulsives are meticulous and fastidious, not because the tasks facing them require such conscientious behavior, but because they anticipate criticism and derogation: "What can I do to prevent others from seeing how empty and shallow I am; what can I do to make sure that no one sees beneath my surface proprieties to the obnoxious and immoral impulses that keep welling up within me?" Fearing to commit themselves and make a mistake, conscientious compulsives keep within a narrow rut, unwilling to gamble with the possibility that they may choose wrong. Totally lacking in the gambling spirit, they are unwilling to chance placing their destiny in unpredictable events. To avoid misguided transgressions and to obviate the unknown and potentially dangerous, conscientious compulsives seek to convey a front of equanimity and social agreeableness. They display minimal introspection and a rigorous internal conscience, inner gauges that serve to counter any oppositional urges and unacceptable thoughts.

The Puritanical Compulsive

The *puritanical compulsive* is typified by an austere, self-righteous, highly controlled, but deeply conflictful conformity to the conventions of propriety and authority. The intense anger and resentment felt by these individuals is given sanction, at least as they see it, by virtue of their being on the side of righteousness and morality. Evident are periodic displays of suspiciousness, irritability, obsessional ideation, and severe judgmental attitudes. There is a tendency toward denial, with an extreme defensiveness about admitting emotional difficulties and psychosocial problems. However, despite the preceding efforts, there are clear signs that these personalities are unusually tense and high-strung. Anticipating public exposure and humiliation, periods of self-deprecation and self-punishment give way to outbursts of extrapunitive anger and persecutory accusations. This conflictual struggle against expressing emotions and directing anger endangers their efforts at maintaining control.

In addition to their harsh judgments of the behavior of others, puritanical compulsives make efforts to maintain a disciplined self-restraint; they rarely relax or let down a guarded defensiveness. They typically appear grim and cheerless, exhibiting an anxiously tense and serious-minded prudish morality. Beneath a cooperative and controlled facade are marked feelings of personal insecurity, and they are vigilantly alert to avoid social transgressions that may provoke humiliation and embarrassment. This puritanical variant of the compulsive shows distinct features of the paranoid personality, including bigoted, dogmatic, and zealous characteristics.

There is a pattern among these compulsives of avoiding situations that may result either in personal censure or derision, and there is a dread of making mistakes or taking risks, lest these provoke disapproval. As a defensive maneuver, they restrict activities, operate within narrow boundaries, and confine themselves to a rigid and, at times, self-righteous conformity to rules and regulations. By adhering vigorously to propriety and convention, by following the straight and narrow path, they seek to minimize criticism and punitive reactions, particularly from persons in authority.

The conforming style of these patients has been undermined repeatedly, and there is a consequent tendency to be argumentative, resentful, and critical of others. Lurking behind the facade of propriety is a growing bitterness and disillusionment. These animosities churn within the individual. They will either break through to the surface in angry upsurges or be countered in ritualistic precautions or obsessive ruminations. Guilt and self-condemnation may be periodically exhibited, as when the person turns feelings inward and self-imposes severe punitive judgments and actions. Despite the tension it generates, such self-reproval is likely to serve as a release for hostile and forbidden feelings. However, ambivalence is constantly present. On the one hand, there are strong desires to discharge hostility and, on the other, a constant fear that such expressions will prompt derision and rejection. As a residual of this ambivalence, the patient may have a history of persistent tensions, possibly evident in psychosomatic symptoms.

Beneath the surface, these puritanical compulsives feel the press of irrational impulses, including what they judge to be repugnant impulses and sexual desires. Their puritanical attitudes have developed as a protection against their own as well as the world's uncontrollable passions. Rather than allowing these impulses to wreak public havoc, should they ever be let loose and allowed expression, compulsives keep them tightly under control, resist their emergence, and ensure that such emotions be kept from desirable objects. Their ascetic and austere lifestyle—their constraint of themselves and others—serves as a method of prohibiting their own darker impulses and fantasies.

Indignant and judgmental about the lack of perfection in others, their puritanical attitudes are abrasive and irritating. These behaviors intimidate others at first, and then provoke them into acts of defiance and disobedience. Progressing over time from acts of an impersonal propriety and politeness, these puritanical compulsives deteriorate into an ascerbic dogmatism, a harsh and opinionated style that seeks constantly to fix the mistakes of others, and to endlessly criticize as inadequate or improper that which others have done. Uptight and straitlaced, these personalities quickly lose their temper over trivial matters. They become harsh and stern disciplinarians, faultfinding and moralistic prigs. Not only must they prove others to be wrong and immoral, but they judge them as deserving punishment. Because others are seen as sinners and perpetrators of immoral acts, they can justly be condemned without guilt. Justice requires a punitive attitude; morality sanctions it. Hence, puritanical compulsives, who have feared condemnation in the past, now become merciless condemnors. Once concerned with just treatment for themselves, they now become the perpetrator of injustices.

The Bureaucratic Compulsive

Not unlike other compulsive personalities, the variant we are labeling the *bureaucratic compulsive* finds that an alliance with time-tested traditional values, established authorities, or formal organizations, works extremely well. Instead of feeling angered and oppressed by authoritarian and organizational rules, these compulsives feel strengthened and comforted by these associations. Being part of a group or a bureaucracy makes them feel that they are not alone and that their ability to act firmly and decisively has thereby been empowered. They feel that their alliance with a company, a union, or a religious organization fortifies their self-esteem. The group not only provides a powerful identification, but an established set of rules and values that gives them a framework and a direction for action. Moreover, it is of great comfort to them to have the structure and goals of their group organize their lives and show them what "really" matters in life. Fearful that they cannot constrain their inner impulses, they seek firm boundaries that will guide them to make proper decisions. At the deepest level, therefore, they believe that by following the rules of their organization, no one can fault and punish them. They do "what they are told to do." Although obedience limits the range of their opportunities, it frees these compulsives from the anxiety of taking responsibility for making decisions on their own.

The hierarchy of who is an authority and who is a subordinate, enables bureaucratic compulsives to clearly define their place and responsibilities in the system. Once established, they will now become extremely loyal and dependable. Now that they know they are protected, compulsives can give of themselves freely within the boundaries the organization has established. Moreover, knowing what is expected of them and that others also have clearly defined roles and expectancies as well enables them to feel secure within the organization. Not only do they feel that they are no longer alone, but they are less fearful of being abandoned by the system. For these personalities, union with others provides secure and deep identifications; the bureaucracy becomes an important index of who they are, giving them both a sense of identity and a purpose for being. As long as they stay within the organization, they know that they will be highly valued. To reciprocate, they are loyal, trustworthy, and diligent group members, faithfully committed to the community's goals and values.

More than most members of a formal hierarchical organization—church, police, union, university, company—bureaucratic compulsives are rigid adherents to the structure of the organization. They are sticklers in following the details and aspirations of the system. Rules are set out precisely, lists and plans are formed to arrange their work, they know who is above and below them, they keep to precise time schedules. Punctual and meticulous, most adhere to the so-called Protestant work ethic, have a hierarchical or authoritarian schema for placing all personnel, for evaluating and ranking others on an explicit rating system. Personal inclinations are put aside; such inclinations are always suspect in that they may come to override the goals and values of the system. As in totalitarian societies, the bureaucratic person denies individuality and submits to the impersonal values of the system.

As a consequence of their narrow and rigid adherence to bureaucratic policies and rules, these compulsives are often seen as officious, high-handed, unimaginative, closed-minded, as well as intrusive, nosy, and meddlesome. It is these petty-minded and trifling bureaucrats that often make dealing with public agencies so trying and tiresome.

Owing to the status and security they gain by their alliance with institutional standing and perquisites, many of these otherwise rigid and constrained individuals exhibit a public sense of pride and self-importance. As a consequence, they may display overt features that appear similar to those seen among narcissistic personalities. However, in contrast to prototypal narcissists, their air of superiority and status is but skin-deep.

The Parsimonious Compulsive

Fromm's discussion of the hoarding orientation gets close to the characterization of the *parsimonious compulsive*. What is most notable in these individuals is their miserliness, the protective wall they place between themselves and the outer world, keeping tight to that which they possess, being ungiving and unsharing. These individuals are notably niggardly, tightfisted, and penny-pinching. Their parsimony, as we view it, reflects a wariness and a self-protective stance against the exposure that would permit the possibility of loss.

Another aspect of the parsimonious compulsive relates to property and possessions. The behavior of these compulsives conveys the attitude, "What is mine is mine and what is yours is yours; I will leave alone what you possess as long as you do likewise with mine." Just as these personalities learned in their struggle with parental restrictions to find a small sphere of behavior that was safe and above reproach, so too do they now gather and hold tight to their limited body of rights and possessions. As Fromm (1947) has put it, they will hoard and protect against all intrusions those few prized belongings they have struggled to acquire for themselves. Having been deprived of so many wishes and desires in childhood, they now nurture and protect what they have achieved. They fortify themselves and stave off those vultures who wish to deprive them of their resources. They are miserly and ungiving, and act as if their "fortune" could never be replenished. In this latter regard, we see the basis for clinical observations indicating that these compulsive personalities share a number of significant features more typically seen in the schizoid personality, a cool distancing and an apparent self-protectiveness from external intrusions.

There is a deeper and more devious basis for compulsives' demand that their possessions and privacy be secure. They dare not permit anyone to explore the emptiness of their inner self, the truly barren quality of their attainments and competencies. Of even greater import, they dread that others will uncover their rebellious urges, those angry and defiant feelings that lurk beneath their cloak of respectability and propriety. They must quickly stop others from exploring and possibly exposing the pretense of their very existence. Respect is a way of maintaining distance, then, a means of hiding what compulsives must keep from others and from themselves.

The Bedeviled Compulsive

As with some variants of both negativistic and compulsive ambivalent personality types, this subtype possesses an amalgamation of both prototypes. These individuals experience a deep struggle beneath the surface between the need to comply with the wishes of others one moment, and the desire to assert their own interests the next. Contending somewhat unsuccessfully with this ambivalence is what undermines the personality we are calling the *bedeviled compulsive.* For the most part, the compulsive strategy of self-denial works reasonably well for these individuals; they submerge their oppositional desires, and put forth a proper and correct front. For some compulsives, however, notably the bedeviled subtype, this strategy has not held. Although appearing on the surface to be in psychic control, underneath they are going around in circles, unable to decide which course to follow, increasingly unsure of who they are and what they want to do. When these persons are expected to act decisively, they oscillate and procrastinate, feel tormented and befuddled, become cautious and timid, delaying decisions and using complex rationales to keep their inner confusion under control. Unable to get a hold of who they are, feeling great pressure to meet their obligations, they begin to doubt what it is that they believe and what it is that they want. Caught in their upsurging ambivalence, with one part of themselves accelerating in one direction, and the other part resisting movement, they may become exhausted, grumpy, and discontent but, more than anything else, perplexed and confused, driven by thoughts and impulses that can no longer be contained and directed. There is a feeling of being overwhelmed against both one's will and one's better knowledge. Thoughts and impulses that are usually contained and that adhere to guiding principles, seem contradictory and uncontrolled. Inner uncertainties come to the fore, arising from unknown conflictual attitudes and feelings.

The persistence of these oscillating directions may result in the tendency of bedeviled compulsives to engage in "self-torture," to create a self-punitive resolution that seeks to undo the powerful emotions that bedevil them. The emergence of obsessions and compulsions may be seen as the futile attempt to control irrational thoughts and feelings.

Such attempts also signify, however, that the compulsive's habitual controls have been crumbling. At these times, *bedeviled compulsives* may come to feel possessed by demons. Unable to acknowledge that what upsets them is the ambivalence of their inner life, they seek an outlet for their contradictory emotions through obsessions and compulsions, hoping thereby that these irreconcilable feelings will not undermine or overwhelm them. The eruption of untoward thoughts and distressing impulses makes these persons feel as if they are caught in the grip of an unresolvable state. Most troublesome during these times is the recognition that they may be driven by temptations that may overwhelm their moral strength. They cannot have it both ways. They see themselves as succumbing to corruption, perhaps controlled by the devil himself. Constrained and deformed by these contradictory tendencies, they may come to feel that they are on the edge of psychic dissolution.

COMORBID DISORDERS AND SYNDROMES

This section attempts to identify the most frequent Axis I and Axis II syndromes that covary with the personality under discussion. In addition, brief descriptions are given of the vulnerabilities that activate Axis I symptoms and the typical aims the Axis II personality seeks to achieve in coping with these vulnerabilities.

Axis II Comorbidities

As can be seen from Figure 14.4, the obsessive-compulsive personality disorder (OBC) covaries to a modest degree with just a few other personality types. As noted, the core OBC may be found to be comorbid with the dependent personality

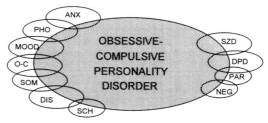

Figure 14.4 Comorbidity between obsessive-compulsive personality disorder and other DSM Axis I and Axis II disorders.

(DPD) and the schizoid personality (SZD). Each of the preceding two personalities share with the OBC a passive style of accommodating to the environment, evincing minimal intrusions or interventions on their part. This passive constellation, however, is not seen where the OBC covaries with the paranoid (PAR) and negativistic (NEG) personality disorders. In these latter comorbidities, we see much more of the irritabilities and obduracy that characterize certain of the subtypes of the OBC personality. It should be noted in general that the OBC personality pattern tends to be fairly circumscribed when compared with other personality disorders; the frequency of comorbidity is perhaps the lowest among the Axis II classifications.

Axis I Comorbidities

Before proceeding, note should be made again of some of the factors we have discussed in previous chapters to differentiate and to interrelate Axis I and Axis II disorders. Axis I clinical disorders usually take the form of dramatic signs that stand out in sharp relief against the more prosaic background of the patient's everyday style of functioning—what we have termed the *personality*. It has been our thesis that the patient's personality is the foundation for understanding his or her pathology. Axis I clinical syndromes are extensions or disruptions in patients' characteristic personality styles; anchored to their past experience, they take on significance and meaning largely in that context. Because personality disorders possess pervasive vulnerabilities, a wide array of feelings and memories are quickly reactivated and unleashed in response to duplicates of the past. These inner forces rapidly override current realities and take over as the primary stimuli to which the person responds. As a consequence, the Axis I clinical symptom is less a function of present precipitants than it is of the past associations they evoke. This primacy of the reactivated past gives clinical disorders much of their irrational and symbolic quality. However, the hidden meaning of the Axis I clinical symptom can be understood if seen in terms of the inner stimulus intrusions of Axis II personality vulnerabilities. In addition to reflecting the eruption of past memories and emotions, the Axis I disorder is shaped by the habitual coping style that characterizes the patient's Axis II personality. The behaviors exhibited, then, are rational and appropriate if seen in terms of the past that has been stirred up and the manner in which the patient has learned to cope

with his or her vulnerabilities. With this as a précis, the discussion turns to the most prevalent Axis I disorders found among compulsive personalities.

Obsessive-Compulsive Syndromes (O-C). It is probable that compulsive personalities do in fact exhibit obsessive-compulsive disorders to a slightly greater degree than do other personality patterns. Some theorists contend that obsessive-compulsive symptoms are not so much a matter of "disordered" coping as deeply ingrained strategies learned to contain socially forbidden impulses. Through widely generalized reaction-formations, compulsives not only control their contrary inclinations but present a socially attractive front of conformity and propriety. The symptom of obsessive doubting leads these patients to reexamine the most trivial of decisions and acts. This excessive preoccupation with minor irrelevancies distracts them, however, from the real source of their anxieties. Although self-doubting is a general characteristic of these personalities, it may become especially pronounced if a sudden eruption of feelings threatens to "expose them" or "give them away." Their pretense of equanimity may be readily disrupted by the intrusion of bizarre, hostile, or erotic thoughts. Stirring up intense fears of social condemnation, compulsives may "undo" these thoughts by a series of repetitive acts or rituals. For example, each morning, by washing his face and knotting his tie repeatedly, a compulsive man assured himself of his purity; the repetition of these easily mastered, if insignificant acts, strengthened his confidence in his ability to "clean up" and "tie down" his impulses.

Phobic Syndromes (PHO). Compulsives develop simple phobias primarily as a function of three anxiety precipitants: decision-making situations in which they anticipate being faulted or subjected to criticism; real failures that they wish to rationalize or avoid facing again; and surging impulses that they seek to counter, transform, or externalize lest these overwhelm controls and provoke social condemnation. In contrast to dependent and histrionic personalities, compulsives hide their phobias since their self-image would be weakened by such "foolish" and irrational symptoms. Thus, without public awareness, they displace their tensions into a variety of external phobic sources. This not only enables them to deny the internal roots of their discomforts, but, by making their anxiety into something tangible and identifiable, it becomes subject to control or avoidance.

Anxiety Syndromes (ANX). Compulsives are among the more frequent candidates for generalized anxiety disorders. Every act, thought, or impulse that may digress from the straight and narrow path is subject to the disapproval of an internal conscience or the punitive reactions of an external authority. Of equal importance, their anxiety is compounded by the presence within themselves of deeply repressed impulses that threaten to erupt and overwhelm their controls. Without rigid constraints, their tenuous social facade and psychic cohesion may be torn apart. Ever concerned that they will fail to live up to the demands of authority and constantly on edge lest their inner defiance break out of control, they often live in chronic states of anxiety. The constant presence of tension is so much a part of their everyday life that it is difficult to say where personality ends and where the anxiety symptom begins. On the positive side, many of these patients utilize the energy they derive from their tension to effective ends. Thus, the characteristic diligence and conscientiousness of compulsives reflect, in large measure, their control and exploitation of anxious energy. However, should these controls be shaken, there is a high probability that an acute attack of panic disorder will ensue.

Somatoform Syndromes (SOM). Compulsive personalities succumb to *conversion* disorders, albeit infrequently, as another means of containing the upsurge of forbidden impulses. Conversion disorders are not an easy "choice" for these patients, however, since to be ill runs counter to their image of self-sufficiency. Nevertheless—and in contrast to phobic symptoms, which are especially embarrassing in this regard—conversion symptoms enable these patients to advertise their illness as one of physical origin. It allows them not only to achieve the important secondary gains of attention and nurture but also to continue their belief that they are basically self-sufficient and merely unfortunate victims of "passing" sickness. Despite these gains, however, compulsives will feel most comfortable if they underplay their ailment, acting quite indifferent about it. Because they are likely to feel guilt over the surreptitious pleasure they gain in dependency, the conversion symptoms they acquire tend to be rather severe. Thus, they may exhibit the total immobilization of a bodily function (e.g., blindness, mutism, or complete paralysis of the legs). The severity of their symptoms not only reflects the sweeping character of their controls, as well as their need to "prove" the seriousness of their illness, but it frequently serves

as punishment for intense guilt feelings. By becoming blind or by disabling their limbs, they sacrifice a part of themselves as penance for their "sinful" thoughts and urges.

Somatization and *hypochondriacal* disorders are also employed by compulsives as a way of rationalizing failures and inadequacies. Fearful that they will be condemned for their shortcomings, compulsives may seek to maintain self-respect and the esteem of others by ascribing deficiencies to some ill-defined ailment or legitimate physical illness. This maneuver may not only shield them from rebuke but may evoke praise from others for the few accomplishments they do manage to achieve. How commendable others must think they are for their conscientious efforts, despite their illness and exhaustion. Compulsives do frequently suffer real fatigue and physiological symptoms as a consequence of their struggle to control undischarged inner angers and resentments. Bodily ailments may also represent a turning inward of repressed hostile impulses. Not infrequently, ailments such as these function as a displaced and symbolic self-punishment, a physical substitute for the guilt they feel after having expressed condemned emotions. Suffering not only discharges tension but serves as a form of expiation.

As noted previously, compulsives keep under close wraps most of the tensions generated by their dependence-independence conflict. Through repression and other mechanisms, their resentments and anxieties are tightly controlled and infrequently discharged. As a consequence, physiological tensions are not dissipated, tend to cumulate, and result in frequent and persistent psychosomatic ailments, especially of the gastrointestinal variety. Also notable is the close correspondence between the compulsive life pattern and what is now termed "Type A" behavior, a style ostensibly correlated with cardiovascular difficulties.

Dissociative Syndromes (DIS). Compulsive personalities succumb to dissociative disorders on occasion and for a variety of reasons. Experiences of depersonalization and estrangement stem from the overcontrol of feeling. By desensitizing their emotions or by withdrawing feelings as part of everyday life, they begin to experience the world as flat and colorless, a place in which events seem mechanical, automatic, and unreal. Episodes of *amnesia* may occur if compulsives are otherwise unable to isolate and control their intense ambivalence. The coexistence of conflicting emotions may become too great a strain. Not only will the eruption of hostile or erotic impulses shatter the compulsive's self-image of propriety, but they may provoke the severe condemnation from others that is dreaded. Failing to restrain their urges, compulsives may be driven to disown their identity or to obliterate all past memories. *Fugue* states may be another way to discharge unbearable tensions in that they allow these patients to vent their contrary impulses without any conscious awareness and, hence, without having to assume responsibility for them. Multiple personality disorders, although rare, will enable the patient to retain his or her true identity most of the time yet gain periodic release through "other" selves.

Mood Syndromes (MOOD).   More typical than the extreme psychotic episode noted shortly is the compulsive's proclivity to affective disorders, most frequently evident in periods of tense and anxious dejection. Faced with difficult decisions but unable to gain clear direction from others, these patients may experience intense anger toward themselves for their weakness and deep resentment toward others for what is seen as the latter's unyielding demands. Despite the intensity and direction of these feelings, compulsives dare not expose their own shortcomings nor their hostility toward others. Complicating matters further is that they have been well trained to express self-reproval and guilt. Thus, rather than voice their defiance and vent their resentment, and thereby be subject to severe social rebuke, they turn their feelings inward and discharge anger toward themselves. This act of self-reproval serves as a form of expiation for their hidden oppositional thoughts and feelings. Moreover, by acting contrite, they assume that no one will condemn and humiliate them. Unfortunately, compulsives have usually been subjected in the past to severe condemnation for any sign of weakness or incompetence. Thus, they find themselves trapped in a bind. Whether they are contrite or whether they are defiant, they cannot be free of the fear that their actions will provoke further rejection. The agitated and apprehensive quality of their *major depressions* reflects both a struggle to contain their resentments and their fear that contrition will only prompt derision and condemnation.

On occasion, compulsives display a relatively benign but chronic "melancholy," currently termed *dysthymic disorder.* This may occur if they realize how empty their lives have been, how often they have denied themselves, and how much they have given up by conforming to external standards. Extended depressions of a melancholic nature are often interrupted, however, by brief periods of self-assertion and self-expression. Quite typically, feelings of anxiety will be activated during these brief "flings," turning them into rather short-lived episodes. More commonly, compulsives will exhibit classic forms of agitated depression, noted primarily by diffuse apprehension, marked feelings of guilt, and a tendency to complain about personal sin and unworthiness. As noted earlier, compulsives are likely to turn the angry and resentful components of their ambivalence inward and against themselves, claiming that they truly deserve punishment and the misery they now suffer.

Schizophrenic Syndromes (SCH).   Brief reactive psychoses and schizophreniform disorders occur on occasion in compulsive personalities. This usually follows a shattering of controls employed to restrain the repressed obedience-defiance conflict. Unable to keep these divisive forces in check, these patients may feel torn apart or engulfed in a sea of surging and contrary feelings that spill forth in a flood of incoherent verbalizations and bizarre emotions. Stereotyped grimacing, posturing, and mannerisms often reflect the patients' feeble efforts to contain their impulses or to damp down the confusion and disharmony that they feel.

DIFFERENTIAL DIAGNOSIS

Few problems of differential diagnosis are likely to arise with the compulsive personality. Difficulties are most probable, as is generally the case, with syndromes that frequently overlap or covary with the syndrome in the first place; these should be recorded as concurrent diagnoses.

Separating the Axis I *obsessive-compulsive* disorder from the Axis II compulsive personality is at times problematic, mostly owing to their shared diagnostic labels. Where the broad-ranging and varied features of personality have been present for an extended period, the Axis II diagnosis is fully justified, whether or not distinctive symptoms of obsessions or compulsions are evident.

Turning to Axis II discriminations, obsessive-compulsive and *dependent* personalities exhibit clear tendencies to conform to the demands and expectations of others. Dependent personalities do so out of a habit of leaning on others owing to their lack of self-confidence and their limited repertoire of adult competence, deficits not notable among obsessive-compulsives. Whereas dependents exhibit their compliance to significant *persons,* compulsives are constrained by an adherence to authorities, institutions, and the formal rules and regulations of "required" behaviors. The former is personally attached, the latter is institutionally attached.

Similarities may be seen between compulsive and *schizoid* personalities. Both exhibit a passivity, a tendency not to take the initiative, nor to venture freely into the outer world. However, schizoids remain disengaged by virtue of their deep lack of social interest, an inability to be *stirred* to actions, rather than a *fear* of taking actions that may be disapproved.

ASSESSING THE COMPULSIVE: A CASE STUDY

A brief review of obsessive-compulsive personality features on the Rorschach, TAT, and MMPI will be presented initially in this section. Following this introduction, a case history of a compulsive will be described, and an MCMI-III profile and interpretive statements will be presented to conclude this assessment overview.

The Rorschach among these personalities will show a preponderance of *D* and *d* responses; relatively few *W* responses are likely. A high proportion of form responses are probable, most of which are likely to be of good quality (*F*+). Conversely, color-related responses, particularly *CF* and *C* are infrequent. Overall response level is often high, and a tendency toward preoccupation or elaboration of detail is also notable. If a sufficient number of location responses are given, they tend to be presented in an orderly sequence (e.g., moving from *W* to *D* to *d*). Similarly, the content of responses tends to be Popular and mundane.

The TAT story themes among compulsives are rather conventional in their character, often portraying what idealized persons "should do." Although infrequent, there is an occasional slippage of control, resulting in expressed resentments or overt hostility. The main characters tend to be "plastic" caricatures of proper and righteous persons. Elaborations of interest on the TAT are minimal, however; they are usually comprehensive in that they have a beginning, middle, and end.

For the most part, the profile of the MMPI with these personalities is rather flat, often with a higher than average K score; as on the MCMI-III, these personalities tend not to be self-disclosing and to present a favorable or socially desirable image. When scales are elevated, they tend to be on 3 and 1, especially if somatic difficulties are part of the clinical picture. Also characteristic is a high score on Scale 7, signifying a willingness to disclose underlying tensions and irritabilities.

CASE 14.1

Joseph L., 44, Married

Joseph was advised to seek assistance from a therapist following several months of relatively sleepless nights and a growing immobility and indecisiveness at his job. When first seen, he reported feelings of extreme self-doubt and guilt and prolonged periods of tension and diffuse anxiety. It was established early in therapy that he always had experienced these symptoms; they were now merely more pronounced than before.

The precipitant for this sudden increase in discomfort was a forthcoming change in his academic post. New administrative officers had assumed authority at the college, and he was asked to resign his deanship to return to regular departmental instruction.

In the early sessions, Joseph spoke largely of his fear of facing classroom students again, wondered if he could organize his material well, and doubted that he could keep classes disciplined and interested in his lectures. It was his preoccupation with these matters that he believed was preventing him from concentrating and completing his present responsibilities. At no time did Joseph express anger toward the new college officials for the demotion he was asked to accept; he repeatedly voiced his "complete confidence" in the "rationality of their decision." Yet, when face-to-face with them, he observed that he stuttered and was extremely tremulous.

Joseph was the second of two sons, younger than his brother by 3 years. His father was a successful engineer, and his mother a high school teacher. Both were "efficient, orderly, and strict" parents. Life at home was "extremely well planned," with "daily and weekly schedules of responsibility posted" and "vacations arranged a year or two in advance." Nothing apparently was left to chance. Both boys were provided with the basic comforts of life, enjoyed the rewards of a well-run household, but knew exactly what was expected of them, and knew that their parents would be punitive and unyielding if they failed to adhere to these expectations.

Joseph perceived his brother as the more preferred and dominant child in the family. He felt that his brother "got away with things," was a "show-off" and knew how to "get around his mother." Begrudgingly, Joseph admitted that his brother may have been a brighter and more attractive child. Nevertheless, he asserted that there was "not much of a difference" between them, and that he had been "cheated and overlooked by the fraud." This latter comment spilled forth from Joseph's lips much to his surprise. Obviously, he harbored intense resentments toward his brother that he had desperately tried to deny throughout his life. He feared expressing hostility in childhood because "mother and father would have nothing to do with emotions and feelings at home, especially angry feelings toward one another." The only way in which Joseph could express his resentment toward his brother was by tattling; he would experience great pleasure when able to inform his parents about things his brother had done with which they would disapprove. Not until therapy, however, did Joseph come to recognize that these self-righteous acts were less a matter of "sticking to the rules" than of trying to "get back at him."

Joseph adopted the "good boy" image. Unable to challenge his brother either physically, intellectually, or socially, he became a "paragon of virtue." By being punctilious, scrupulous, methodical, and orderly, he could avoid antagonizing his perfectionistic parents, and would, at times, obtain preferred treatment from them. He obeyed their advice, took their guidance as gospel, and hesitated making any decision before gaining their approval. Although he recalled "fighting" with his brother before he was 6 or 7, he "restrained my anger from that time on and never upset my parents again."

Peer experiences were satisfactory throughout schooling, although he was known as a rather serious and overconscientious student. With the exception of being thought of as "a sort of greasy grind," his relationships during adolescence were adequate, if not especially rewarding.

At 27, Joseph completed his doctorate in political economics, married a rather plain but "serious-minded" girl and obtained his first regular academic appointment at a small college. Two years later, he moved to his present institution. His "fine work" in advising freshmen students led to his appointment as Dean of Freshmen, and eventually to that of Dean of Students, a position he has held for seven years.

Although Joseph demonstrated a talent for "keeping the rules" and for assuming his responsibilities with utmost conscientiousness, he had been accused by both students and faculty as being a "stuffed shirt," a "moralist" with no real sympathy or understanding for the young. His lack of warmth and frequent, harshly punitive decisions with students were out of keeping with the new administration's policies and led to the request that he step down.

The MCMI-III profile of a compulsive personality configuration shown in Figure 14.5 is quite typical of these individuals in that few scales score high owing to their general denial tendencies. Nevertheless, we do see the primary features of the personality, as well as the clinical syndromes that are manifest under conditions of environmental stress. The interpretive report statements that follow the profile represent this personality's features, without reference to any knowledge of the patient's biographical history.

INTERPRETIVE SUMMARY

The MCMI-III profile of this man suggests anxious conformity to the expectations of others, rigidity and compulsiveness, and defensiveness about admitting psychological problems. He anticipates criticism and derogation and is inclined toward self-blame and self-punishment. A fear of expressing emotions and of losing control is evident. He is likely to appear grim, cheerless, and serious-minded. Beneath this controlled facade are probably strong feelings of insecurity that are evident in his tendency to downgrade himself, to distance himself from others, and to anticipate rejection.

This man's major defenses appear to be excessive conformity and the suppression of any social affect that might evoke ridicule, contempt, or punitive action. Limiting the extent to which this MCMI-III report may disclose his current difficulties is a tendency to deny discordant attitudes and to neutralize any distressful feelings. Because he fears making mistakes and taking risks, his activities have become restricted, confined largely to a repetition of the familiar.

It is possible that his self-doubts and low self-esteem may result in a chronic pattern of quiet conformity to a supportive institution such as his church or a bureaucratic organization such as his place of work. In this way, he may gain a measure of security and be able to identify himself with those whose actions cannot possibly—he believes—be met with disfavor. A consistent and rigid behavioral pattern may be maintained in which signs of autonomy and independence are

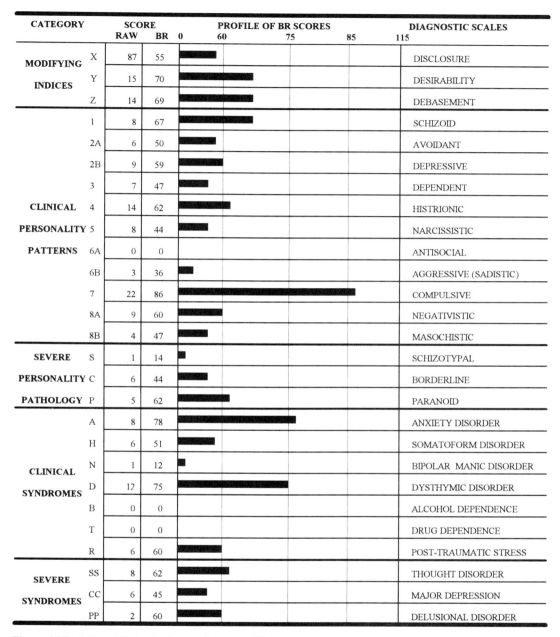

CATEGORY		SCORE RAW	BR	PROFILE OF BR SCORES 0 60 75 85 115	DIAGNOSTIC SCALES
MODIFYING INDICES	X	87	55		DISCLOSURE
	Y	15	70		DESIRABILITY
	Z	14	69		DEBASEMENT
CLINICAL PERSONALITY PATTERNS	1	8	67		SCHIZOID
	2A	6	50		AVOIDANT
	2B	9	59		DEPRESSIVE
	3	7	47		DEPENDENT
	4	14	62		HISTRIONIC
	5	8	44		NARCISSISTIC
	6A	0	0		ANTISOCIAL
	6B	3	36		AGGRESSIVE (SADISTIC)
	7	22	86		COMPULSIVE
	8A	9	60		NEGATIVISTIC
	8B	4	47		MASOCHISTIC
SEVERE PERSONALITY PATHOLOGY	S	1	14		SCHIZOTYPAL
	C	6	44		BORDERLINE
	P	5	62		PARANOID
CLINICAL SYNDROMES	A	8	78		ANXIETY DISORDER
	H	6	51		SOMATOFORM DISORDER
	N	1	12		BIPOLAR MANIC DISORDER
	D	12	75		DYSTHYMIC DISORDER
	B	0	0		ALCOHOL DEPENDENCE
	T	0	0		DRUG DEPENDENCE
	R	6	60		POST-TRAUMATIC STRESS
SEVERE SYNDROMES	SS	8	62		THOUGHT DISORDER
	CC	6	45		MAJOR DEPRESSION
	PP	2	60		DELUSIONAL DISORDER

Figure 14.5   Millon Clinical Multiaxial Inventory-III.

restrained and conformity to the rules of others is emphasized.

There is likely to be an overconcern with minor irrelevancies that serves to distract his attention from deep feelings of inadequacy and anticipated derogation. Although his facade of conformity may hide deeply repressed anger toward those who have humiliated him, periodic surges of resentment break through the surface.

It is probable that feelings of guilt and self-condemnation have become prominent features, and he may impose punitive judgments on himself as a form of symbolic expiation. His deep emotional ambivalence may constantly intrude, however, as strong desires to express long-felt resentment conflict with his fear that such expression will prompt derision and humiliation. As a result, he may experience a chronic state of tension, often evident in functional somatic disorders such as headaches and gastrointestinal difficulties.

This man appears to be suffering from an anxiety disorder. Sensitive to criticism and public reproval, he is experiencing the discomfort of having his normally controlled emotions exposed. Although conscientious in fulfilling his work and other responsibilities, he may have begun to feel intense self-doubts and concerns about his security and his ability to depend on others. Symptoms such as fatigue, insomnia, and abdominal pain may be evident, as well as a general apprehensiveness over matters such as social humiliation and disapproval.

A mild dysthymic disorder seems evident in this man's current symptomatology. Although he is usually disinclined to admit personal shortcomings or to acknowledge that psychological factors play a role in his growing emotional and physical discomfort, he appears sufficiently troubled at this time to concede to a modicum of general malaise and dejection about his life. Increasingly blue and pessimistic, he may recognize his decreased interest in matters with which he was formerly preoccupied, that he may be readily upset by the trivial problems of daily life, and his increasing disappointment in himself. His growing expressions of self-recrimination may serve to deflect the severe reproaches that he fears his behavior deserves. Moreover, acts of self-deprecation often succeed in prompting others to express supportive and encouraging words rather than condemnatory ones.

PATHOGENIC DEVELOPMENTAL BACKGROUND

This section explores factors that have been posited as contributing to the compulsive personality pattern. As before, the speculative nature of these determinants must be kept in mind.

HYPOTHETICAL BIOGENIC FACTORS

There is little evidence to suggest that biogenic influences contribute in any distinctive manner to the development of the compulsive personality. Stated differently, a wide variety of overt physical traits, infantile reaction patterns, and so on may be found among compulsives; no biogenic features are especially discriminable or highly correlated with this style of life.

Following the suppositions regarding mood/temperament presented in the preceding section, we might hypothesize that the neurological regions of the limbic system associated with the expression of fear and anger may be unusually dense or well branched among these patients; these conflicting dispositions might underlie the hesitancy, doubting, and indecisive behaviors seen in these patients. Speculations such as these, however, cannot be assigned much credibility, given the inchoate state of our knowledge.

CHARACTERISTIC EXPERIENTIAL HISTORY

The foundations of the compulsive pattern are rooted primarily in interpersonal experience and the coping behaviors with which the child learns to deal with these experiences. We will elaborate these strategies and the processes of self-perpetuation in a later section; for the present we will concern ourselves with influences that initiate the development of the compulsive style.

Parental Overcontrol by Contingent Punishment

The notion of overcontrol as a concept of child rearing may best be understood by comparing it to other rearing practices associated with several of the pathological patterns that were previously described.

First, it differs from overprotection in that it stems from an attitude of parental firmness and repressiveness. Overprotection, most common in the history of the dependent pattern, usually reflects a gentle and loving parental concern, a desire to cuddle and care for the child without harshness or hostility; overcontrolling parents may be caring, but display this concern with the attitude of "keeping the child in line," of preventing the youngster from causing trouble not only for him- or herself but for them. Thus, overcontrolling parents frequently are punitive in response to transgressions, whereas overprotective parents restrain the child more gently, with love, and not with anger and threat.

Overcontrol is similar in certain respects to the techniques of parental hostility, a training process more typical of the history of the antisocial and sadistic patterns. But there is an important distinction here, as well. The hostile parent is punitive *regardless of* the child's behavior, whereas the overcontrolling parent is punitive *only if* the child misbehaves. Thus, the parents of compulsives expect their children to live up to parental expectations, and condemn them only if they fail to achieve the standards the parents have imposed. We may speak of overcontrol as a method of contingent punishment; it is selective, occurring only under clearly defined conditions.

The contingency aspect of parental overcontrol makes it similar to the methods of child rearing that characterize the history of the histrionic personality. But, again, there are important differences. The histrionic child experiences irregular *positive* reinforcements contingent on the performance of good behaviors, tending not to receive negative reinforcements for bad behavior. In contrast, compulsive children receive reinforcements, *not* irregularly, but consistently, and they experience mostly *negative* reinforcements rather than positive reinforcements. They learn what they must *not do, so as to avoid negative* reinforcements, whereas histrionics learn what they can do, so as to achieve positive reinforcements. Compulsives learn to heed parental restrictions and rules; for them, the boundaries of disapproved behaviors are rigidly set. However, as a function of experiencing mostly negative injunctions, they have little idea of what *is* approved; they seem to know well what they must *not* do, but do not know so well what they *can* do. Thus, compulsive youngsters' achievements are usually "taken for granted" and are rarely acknowledged by parents; comments and judgments are limited almost exclusively to pointing out the occasional infraction of rules they set forth.

To summarize, then, parental overcontrol is a method of restrictive child rearing in which punitive procedures are used to set distinct limits on children's behavior. As long as they operate within the parentally approved boundaries, children are secure from parental criticism and condemnation. It is a highly efficient training procedure but is fraught with pathological possibilities.

Let us next examine some of these consequences in terms of the latter three neuropsychological stages of development (the first stage is likely to have been "highly scheduled," but this is neither pathogenic nor distinctive to the upbringing of the compulsive personality).

In the second stage of development, children begin the struggle to acquire autonomous skills and to achieve a sense of self-competence. During this period, most children become assertive and resistant to parental direction and admonition.

Overcontrolling parents will respond to these efforts with firm and harsh discipline; they will physically curtail the child, berate the child, withdraw love, and so on; in short, they will be relentless in their desire to squelch troublesome transgressions. Children who are unable to find an area of refuge from parental onslaught either will submit entirely, withdraw into a shell, or be adamant and rebel. However, children who uncover a sphere of operation that leaves them free of parental condemnation are likely to reach a compromise; they will restrict their activities just to those areas which meet parental approval. This, then, becomes the action available to the compulsive child; the youngster sticks within circumscribed boundaries and does not venture beyond them.

But there are several consequences of taking this course. Autonomy has been sharply curtailed; these children will not develop the full measure of self-competence that other, less restricted, children acquire. As a result, they will have marked doubts about their adequacy beyond the confines to which they have been bound, will fear deviating from the "straight and narrow path," will hesitate and withdraw from new situations, and will be limited in spontaneity, curiosity, and venturesomeness. Thus, having little self-confidence and fearing parental wrath for the most trivial of misdeeds, these children will submerge impulses toward autonomy and avoid exploring unknowns lest they transgress the approved boundaries. They are like the dependent child in this regard but, in contrast, have accepted dependency not from the comfort of love and acceptance, but from the discomfort of punishment and the fear of rejection.

To add insult to injury, overcontrolling parents continue to overtrain and overdirect their children in the third neuropsychological stage (pubertal: individuation versus nurturance). They provide constant advice and admonishments to guide the child's behavior. Not only is the child enriched excessively by parental directives, but these directives usually follow a narrow and well-defined course. As a consequence, the youngster not only fails to learn to think independently but is guided to think along conventional and adult lines. Rather than engaging in the usual imaginative gender-related explorations that are typical of adolescent thought, he or she is shaped to think and believe in an overly mature fashion. Both young boys and girls proceed at an accelerated pace toward adulthood, and are made to "toe the line" in acquiring proper and upright attitudes. For instance, boys such as these might have taken pride in being referred to as a "little gentleman"; as a further indication of their premature adherence to adult conventions, they might have worn jackets and ties to high school classes, a sartorial style that would help fashion a rather prudish image among peers.

The fourth neuropsychological stage is characterized by the assumption of initiative on the part of the young adolescent, and the growing image of a distinctive personal identity. But a prerequisite to the emergence of these signs of individuality is a well-established sense of self-competence, autonomy, and gender differentiation, three features already lacking in the compulsive child.

Parental overcontrol at this stage has divested these youngsters of the opportunity to learn initiative and to find their own identity; thus, they quickly become a caricature of adult propriety, but an automaton, as well. They are unable to face the novel and the unanticipated. They can act only if they are absolutely certain that their narrow band of established behaviors is applicable and correct. They do not venture on their own for fear that they may be ill equipped to the task, or that they will overstep approved boundaries. Their best course, then, is to simplify and organize their world, to be absolutely sure of what they can do and to eliminate complexities that require decisions and initiative. Their environment must be one of familiarity, guided by explicit rules and standards and one that stipulates the expected and approved course of action.

Let us recapitulate the major learning experiences of the compulsive. First, children learn instrumentally to avoid punishment by acquiescing to parental demands and strictures; they have been shaped by fear and intimidation to be obedient and to conform to the expectations and standards set down by their elders.

Second, children learn vicariously and by imitation; they model themselves after the parental image; they incorporate "whole hog" the rules and inhibitions that characterize their parents' behaviors. Moreover, they learn to make a virtue of necessity; boys and girls become proud and self-satisfied in being "good" and "proper" young people. This enables them not only to master their fear of parental rejection but to gain approval and commendation. Adoption of the parental model has its seamy side, however. Along with the air of adult propriety, children incorporate their parents' strictness and punitive attitudes. They learn to take on a role parallel to theirs, and become stern, intolerant, and self-righteous tyrants who condemn the "immaturity and irresponsibility" of others.

The third characteristic of the compulsive's learning is its insufficiency, its narrow range of competencies and its inadequacies for dealing with novel and unforeseen events. Thus, the compulsive personality not only is fearful of violating rules but lacks the wherewithal to chance the unknown. This behavioral rigidity is partly a matter of instrumental choice and partly a matter of having no alternatives.

Guilt and Responsibility Training

Another feature found commonly in the developmental history of the compulsive personality is the exposure to conditions that teach children a deep sense of responsibility to others, and a feeling of guilt when these responsibilities have not been met. These youngsters often are "moralized" to inhibit their natural inclinations toward frivolous play and impulse gratification. They are impressed by the shameful and irresponsible nature of such activities, and are warned against the "terrifying" consequences of mischief and sin.

Others are told how pained and troubled their parents will be if they are inconsiderate, cause them embarrassment, or deviate from the "path of righteousness." Long before children can grasp the significance of these injunctions, they learn that they must adopt them as their own. In due course, they internalize these strictures and develop a core of self-discipline and self-criticism, a "conscience" by which they prevent their behavior from transgressing the rights of others.

Guilt often is employed by overcontrolling parents as a means of diverting the early, rebellious behaviors of their offspring. Youngsters are made to feel disloyal and disrespectful of their "well-meaning" parents when they balk at their impositions and restraints. How inconsiderate a child must be "after all the things we have done." By promoting a sense of guilt, the child's anger is diverted from its original object, and turned inward toward the self. Now it can be used in the service of further curtailing the child's rebellious feelings. The child not only is made fearful of the consequences of aggressive impulses but learns in time to feel guilt for possessing them, an attitude that aids in their control. Moreover, by self-condemnation, such children demonstrate "good" intentions, and thereby ward off or diminish the intensity of reproach and criticism from others; thus, as their own persecutor, they may forestall a more devastating attack from parents.

SELF-PERPETUATION PROCESSES

This section addresses the features that perpetuate the personality style—that is, prove to be themselves pathogenic of the pattern—followed by a brief exploration of some of the remedial steps that may prove useful.

With all the conflicts and anxieties engendered by their strategy, why do compulsives resist exploring alternative coping methods? One answer is that they experience less pain by continuing, rather than changing, their style of behavior. Thus, discomforting as the strategy may be, it is less anguishing and more rewarding than any other they can envisage. Another answer is that much of what they do is merely the persistence of habit, the sheer continuation of what they have learned in the past. Thus, compulsives persevere, in part at least, not because their behavior is instrumentally so rewarding but because it is deeply ingrained, so much so that it persists automatically. None of this is unique to the compulsive personality: It is true of all personality patterns. Each style fosters a vicious circle such that the individual's adaptive strategy promotes conditions similar to those that gave rise initially to that strategy. Pathological personality traits are traps, self-made prisons that are perniciously self-defeating because they promote their own continuation. The following paragraphs look at three of these self-perpetuating processes.

Pervasive Rigidity

Compulsives dread making mistakes and fear taking risks lest they provoke disapproval. Defensively, they learn to restrict themselves to situations with which they are familiar and to actions they feel confident will be approved. They keep themselves within narrow boundaries and confine themselves to the repetition of the familiar. Rarely do they wander or view things from a different perspective than they have in the past. Moreover, compulsives are characteristically single-minded, have sharply defined interests, and can stick to "the facts" without deviation. To avoid the unknown—the potentially dangerous—they maintain a tight and well-organized approach to life. They hold onto the "tried and true" and keep their nose to old and familiar

grindstones. The price paid for this rigid and narrow outlook is high. Subtle emotions and creative imagination are simply incompatible with the deliberate and mechanical quality of the compulsive's style. Further, the repetition of the same dull routine prevents these persons from experiencing new perceptions and new ways of approaching their environment. By following the same narrow path, compulsives block their chances of breaking the bonds of the past. Their horizons are confined as they duplicate the same old grind.

Guilt and Self-Criticism

By the time compulsives attain adolescence, they are likely to have fully incorporated the strictures and regulations of their elders. Even if they could "get away with it" and be certain that no external power would judge them severely, they now carry within themselves a merciless internal "conscience," an inescapable inner gauge that ruthlessly evaluates and controls them, one that intrudes relentlessly to make them doubt and hesitate before they act. The proscriptions of "proper" behavior have been well learned and they dare not deviate irresponsibly. The onslaughts of guilt and self-recrimination are persistent and insidious; external sources of restraint have been supplanted by the inescapable controls of internal self-reproach. Compulsives are now their own persecutor and judge, ready to condemn themselves not only for overt acts but for thoughts of transgression as well. These inner controls stop them from exploring new avenues of behavior and thereby perpetuate the habits and constraints of the past.

Creation of Rules and Regulations

Most persons strive to minimize the constraints that society imposes. Laws are the price for a civilized existence, but we prefer as few as necessary. Compulsives are different. Not only do they live by rules and regulations, but they go out of their way to uncover legalities, moral prescriptions, and ethical standards to guide themselves and judge others. This attitude is understandable, deriving from their intense struggle to control raging impulses toward defiance that well up within them. The more restrictive the injunctions they find in legalities and external authority, the less effort they must expend on their own to control these contrary urges. Once more, they trap themselves in a self-defeating circle. By creating or discovering new percepts to heed, they draw the noose even tighter around themselves and shrink their world into an ever-narrowing shell. Opportunities for learning new behaviors, or to view the world afresh and more flexibly, are further curtailed. Their own characteristic habits have increasingly narrowed their boundaries for change and growth.

THERAPEUTIC INTERVENTIONS

Compulsive personalities often seek therapy as a result of psychophysiological discomforts. These symptoms are the psychosomatic manifestations of the difficulty compulsives have in discharging internal tensions caused by repressed emotions that churn within them. Symptoms often include attacks of anxiety, spells of immobilization, sexual impotence, and excessive fatigue. The therapist is enlisted to help the compulsive cope as the symptoms begin to be perceived as a threat to the efficient and responsible lifestyle that defines the compulsive's identity. This is not to say, however, that compulsives believe their symptoms are of a psychological nature. Compulsives are in fact so well defended against distressing emotions that they are typically oblivious to the possibility that internal ambivalence and repressed resentments exist, much less that they underlie the very symptoms they genuinely believe to be caused by an isolated (if unidentifiable) "disease."

STRATEGIC GOALS

Given the complex and ambivalent character of the compulsive's inclinations, what goals should the therapist keep in mind to guide his or her strategies?

Compulsives' subconscious conviction about the dire consequences of facing desires and discontent leads them to repress "inappropriate" feelings. Although this keeps the compulsive stable, it also makes it difficult for the therapist to elicit in the patient the emotional insight needed to reestablish balance in the self-other polarity and the active-passive dimension. Focused and steady work on countering the emotional and behavioral rigidities that lead to clinical domain dysfunctions can ultimately result in self-examination and risk-taking which may provide increased balance in the personality structure.

Reestablishing Polarity Balances

What polarity imbalances underlie the compulsive's difficulties? A typical early learning history of being punished for rule transgressions and praised for virtually nothing results in compulsives operating from the basic premise that their own wishes and desires are wrong and that expressing them leads to intimidation and punishment. Unlike the negativistic personality style, whose resentment at having to concede to the wishes of others is at times all too clear, the compulsive personality internalizes others' strictures as "true." Feelings of hostility about wishes and desires that may conflict with those of powerful others are unconsciously repressed in an attempt to avoid further social disapproval and punishment. The conflict between turning to others versus self for approval has been termed the ambivalent pattern. Normal personalities more or less balance their efforts at securing rewards between both alternatives. Compulsives, who deal with ambivalence by forcing it out of consciousness, exhibit their ambivalence passively. Although they are characterized by overt diligence and conscientious work patterns, most compulsives' efforts are a response to the demands and expectations of others, real or imagined. Compulsives are almost exclusively reactive (passive) in relation to their environment. They rarely exhibit initiative to change their circumstances due to their excessive fear of making a mistake. Because of this obsessive need to achieve perfection, they often turn tasks into paralyzing chores marked by indecision and delay. Even more fundamental to the passive style of compulsives is being out of touch, not only with their unconscious oppositional feelings, but with most of their emotions. Even if hesitation were not a behavioral obstacle to self-exploration, the inability to identify what they really feel and want certainly would be.

To reestablish balance within the self-other polarity, compulsives must work toward establishing an identity that differentiates their own feelings and desires from those perceived as expected of them. Before this can be accomplished, repressed anger and fear of disapproval must become conscious and worked through emotionally. Ultimately, both the expectations of others and the needs of self should be recognized and taken into consideration as valid. The resurrection of a personal self composed of genuine feelings and desires can set the groundwork for a shift in the active-passive polarity. Once wishes are acknowledged as acceptable, only perfectionism stands between the compulsive and a more active goal-seeking style. Therapeutic work to undermine impossibly high standards may help put an end to inertia.

Countering Perpetuating Tendencies

The compulsive decides early on in life that making mistakes leads to punishment. The only way to avoid disapproval is to be perfect. By the time a compulsive comes to the attention of a therapist, parental injunctions have been internalized and the simple yet foolproof mechanism of potential guilt prevents any deviation from the firmly entrenched rules. Self-criticism functions in much the same manner; by engaging in internal reprimands, compulsives proves their good intentions and obviate the need for disapproval from external sources. In familiar or straightforward situations, compulsives can ward off anxiety and self-reprisals by "doing the right thing." In new or ambiguous situations, however, they are paralyzed by indecision and anxiety because the consequences of different potential responses are unknown. At best, compulsives can decide how to react based on an educated guess, but this does not satisfy the need for complete control. To avoid anxiety-provoking ambiguity, compulsives becomes pervasively rigid. As they stick to a well-rehearsed routine, they encounter few confusing stimuli. Thought processes become limited to the realm of the tried and acceptable so as not to evoke guilty intrusions of conscience. To further ensure that they are not caught off guard in an unknown (threatening) situation, compulsives become extraordinarily sensitive to conventions, regulations, laws, and rules that can help them control unacceptable impulses, guide thinking, dictate behavior, and ensure that they are always beyond reproach.

These behavioral patterns, although allowing compulsives to control their guilt and anxiety over social disapproval, severely narrow their thinking and limit their experiences. Compulsives have no opportunity to explore new ways of approaching and integrating stimuli in their environment and thus adaptive learning cannot occur. More personally satisfying habits cannot be acquired and relationships remain restricted. Helping compulsives loosen their unattainable standards of perfection for themselves and others is a basic therapeutic goal that lays the foundation for experimentation with more spontaneous behavior and mental ventures into uncharted "dangerous" cognitive territory. As the

constant fear of making a mistake dissipates, restrictive behavior patterns can be varied and more profitable modes can be discovered. Overreliance on rules can be restricted, and creativity, given freer rein, allows for flexible behavior that can prove to be gratifying in and of itself. The possibility of enjoying non-task-oriented activities, including relationships, may then open up.

Modifying Domain Dysfunctions

The compulsive personality is characterized by primary dysfunctions in the domains of cognitive style, expressive behavior, and interpersonal conduct. The compulsive handles life's ambiguities and internal anxieties by adopting a constricted cognitive style that relies on rules, regulations, schedules, and hierarchies for their resolution. Unfamiliar situations and ideas are emotionally and cognitively disruptive because creative mental processes are not available to deal with and integrate novel stimuli. Exploratory therapies that examine the historical development of cognitive rigidities, as well as cognitive approaches that confront the validity of the compulsive's assumptions, can help the patient develop a more fluid and creative cognitive style that allows for more adaptive and rewarding interaction with the environment.

More fluid thinking can also help compulsives recognize that their disciplined expressive acts lead to limited experiences. Rather than make the most of each situation, compulsives adhere to structured and organized life patterns, regardless of whether they are optimally suited to the context. Insisting that all those around them behave in the same way ensures that exposure to alternate ways of doing or thinking about things is minimized. Once again, exploratory work that challenges internalized strictures and helps dissolve fears about the potential consequences of possibly making a mistake can help patients experiment with alternate behaviors.

Overly respectful interpersonal relations again reflect the compulsive's reliance on rules; propriety guarantees that the compulsive is always beyond reproach. Lack of interpersonal imagination, however, also leads others to find the compulsive boring and uptight, and the compulsive rarely enjoys rich and rewarding interpersonal feedback. As fears about being judged and punished decrease, the therapist may be able to convince the compulsive to try more spontaneous and potentially gratifying interaction styles, despite the patient's initial anxiety. Couples and sex therapy approaches can be particularly effective as an adjunct to individual therapy in helping the compulsive develop a healthier and more fruitful relationship.

Improvements in functioning in the primary clinical domains can be bolstered by therapeutic intervention in the realms of self-image and object-representations. The compulsive's self-image is conscientious; the self is seen as industrious, reliable, meticulous, and efficient. Fear of making an error and making a bad impression leads the patient to fixate on discipline, perfection, prudence, and loyalty. Exploratory work can help the patient get in touch with deep seated aspects of the self that have been repressed, and cognitive work can help the compulsive realize that while these traits are indeed attractive and valuable, other repressed tendencies can balance them and lead to a more functional, healthy, and appealing persona. Similarly, object-representations are concealed, and only socially approved affects, attitudes, and actions are acknowledged. As a wider range of internal experiences come to be tolerated, the therapist can encourage a wider range of expressive communication and sociability. Intrapsychic coping mechanisms can get stronger as compulsives acknowledge the existence of the deeper emotional experiences they have been unconsciously repressing. The compulsive deals with these (unacceptable) feelings by using the regulatory mechanism of reaction-formation and thus will display exactly the opposite emotion. For example, a compulsive who believes that anger is a weakness will suppress these feelings, even when they would be appropriate.

As work in the other domains helps the patient develop an individual identity, there will no longer be as much need as previously to present oneself in a socially proper light. The compartmentalized morphologic organization of the compulsive's personality may also become more fluid and integrated; distinct and segregated memories, cognitions, and drives can be drawn on in various contexts and be profitably applied. The typically solemn emotional affect should become sunnier as the need to control every aspect of behavior and environment diminishes. Decreased obsessive behavior and lessened concern with outcomes can increase the patient's enjoyment of the process of living.

TACTICAL MODALITIES

As they do in all of life's undertakings, compulsives wants to perform "perfectly" in therapy. To this end, they may desire highly structured therapeutic approaches that provide a yardstick against which to measure progress. Successful intervention with this personality style, however, entails the encouragement of open and spontaneous communication. Not only does this approach provide no specific procedural framework, spontaneity terrifies the compulsive, resulting itself in a host of possible resistances and transference reactions with which the therapist must cope. As the compulsive's deep-seated fear of losing control is inevitably kindled by the therapy process (which threatens to disequilibrate the much labored-for balance the patient has achieved), so is the ever-present rage that is activated by the pressure to maintain (unattainable) perfection. Some patients may express their resentments and anger by becoming openly critical of themselves, the therapy, or the therapist; justification for all interventions may be demanded of the therapist. Patients who view anger as an unacceptable form of expressing displeasure may become so "busy" at work that they are "forced" to miss sessions. In either case, as Benjamin points out (1993a), therapists can make use of the compulsive's intellectual curiosity to secure cooperation where emotional guardedness would cause the patient to flee. A therapist's initial kindly and logical discussion of some of the patient's behaviors and their causes, if they ring true to the patient, can foster the trust in the therapist that is an essential requirement for success. Without this trust, very few compulsives are likely to accept as viable such therapeutic goals as increasing interpersonal openness and warmth.

Domain-Oriented Techniques

What methods and procedures are likely to be most efficacious with these personalities?

Behavioral methods are useful in treating many of the undesirable manifestations of the compulsive personality disorder, particularly phobic avoidance and ritualistic or highly restrictive and rigid behavior. Treatment involves desensitizing the patient to the anxiety-provoking stimuli (whatever they may be for the particular compulsive) that promote the problematic behavior. The first step involves establishing a hierarchy of stimuli within a relevant context, followed by relaxation training. Covert desensitization can then be carried out. Other effective techniques used with these disorders include flooding, modeling, response prevention, satiation training, and thought stopping.

One of the techniques that approaches treatment by working on causative factors is the *interpersonal* approach. Benjamin (1993a) assumes that the majority of compulsive patterns are acquired as a response to a cold and demanding parent that the child must placate to avoid verbal or physical punishment. Constant frustration of the desire for parental love and approval is transformed into an identification with the critical parent, followed by the internalization of self-criticisms. The first step toward emotional healing is to enable the patient to openly recognize the character of these early learning experiences, and to develop a measure of empathy, if not compassion, for the child he or she once was. Lifelong striving for perfection and absolute control needs to be exposed and accepted as an unrealistic effort. More realizable and less frustration-producing standards can then be integrated. The inevitable anxiety produced by failing to live up to such lofty early goals can then begin to dissipate. Benjamin also suggests employing cognitive techniques (outlined a little later in this discussion) to help the compulsive recognize that black-and-white values and relationships are best seen as variegated and multidimensional phenomena.

Couples therapy is also recommended as useful. The sexual arena is one in which many of the compulsives' patterns can be easily identified. Power struggles manifest themselves in the female compulsive's inability to give up sexual control (and frequent consequent anorgasmia). The male compulsive patient will be likely to interpret any lack of submission to his sexual overtures as a seizure of control, if not rejection, on the part of his partner. The therapist can help mediate communication and clarify that sexual (as well as other) reluctance can in fact result from differences in desire, and not necessarily from a will to control or put down. Sexual therapy may help some compulsives interact in a less controlling and more open way through the practice of sexual "exercises." Prescribed by the therapist, these procedures require the patient to follow instruction (which the compulsive is good at) and thus paradoxically yield control to his or her partner (as the doctor ordered).

Benjamin (1993a) notes that a common aim of compulsive patients is to finally come to an understanding with their critical parent. *Family* therapy generally represents an attempt to bring members together, straighten out misunderstandings, and allow for the expression of long-stifled sentiments. Most often, satisfactory resolution of long-standing issues does not occur. Talking about relationship difficulties can be problematic here, as compulsives have a tendency to dominate other family members, and problems may even be aggravated. The compulsive needs to give up the wish for harmonious understanding before any structural changes in personality can occur. A different form of family therapy can occur in the compulsive's current family. Better success may be had where playful contact is encouraged between the patient, the spouse, and children, in an effort to emphasize the rewards inherent in even non-task-oriented activity, and in being warm and spontaneous. *Group* therapy can prove to be largely fruitless with compulsive patients; they will often ally themselves with the therapist, refusing to participate wholeheartedly as patients. They often develop contempt for the other patients, or suffer extreme anxiety if forced to relinquish their defenses and expose their feelings in front of others.

Cognitive reorientation methods are particularly well suited to the compulsive, who tends to overintellectualize in an effort to ward off emotional reactivity. The cognitive therapy approach offered by Beck and Freeman (1990b) suggests that helping patients alter basic cognitive assumptions about themselves and the world will lead to a therapeutic shift in emotions and behaviors. These assumptions include "There are right and wrong behaviors, decisions, and emotions"; "To make a mistake is to have failed, to be deserving of criticism"; "Failure is intolerable"; "I must be perfectly in control of my environment as well as of myself, loss of control is intolerable and dangerous"; "I am powerful enough to initiate or prevent the occurrence of catastrophes by magical rituals or obsessional ruminations"; and "Without my rules and rituals, I'll collapse into an inert pile." At the onset of therapy, the patient is taught the cognitive theory of emotion, and specific goals related to the compulsive's difficulties are established. Goals are ranked according to solvability and importance; some easily resolved difficulties should be put at the top of the list to motivate the patient with experiences of therapeutic success. The automatic thoughts that interfere with the attainment of goals should be identified. Thoughts, feelings, and behaviors related to specific goals are monitored during the week so that the compulsive can become aware of anxiety-provoking stimuli and the cognitive assumption they elicit. Finally, after the negative consequences of these assumptions have been grasped, the patient and therapist can work at refuting them in a way that makes sense to the patient.

One of the more useful behavioral approaches is teaching patients how to truly relax. A common problem in convincing compulsives to make use of helpful relaxation techniques is that they are perceived as a waste of productive time. Adopting a stance of short-term behavioral experimentation, where patients assess the helpfulness of relaxation exercises within their lifestyles, helps overcome resistance. If a patient is afraid of giving up worrying, due to an irrational conviction that it is somehow useful in preventing disaster, he or she may agree to try limiting worry behavior to a particular time of the day. Beck and Freeman also suggest that patients be warned about the likelihood of relapse, and the probable need for booster sessions; in this way, it may be possible to minimize patients' tendencies to want to be perfect, thereby avoiding feelings of shame over failure that may prevent them from requesting a needed session.

Psychodynamic approaches focus on interpreting displaced and repressed elements that result in overt symptoms. The transference relationship can be used as a starting point for exploring earlier relationships that may have been causative in the development of symptoms. Early traumas may be investigated. Dreams and free association can be helpful in getting past the patient's intellectual guard to deep-seated fears and feelings; often patients are surprised at the blatant and emotionally revealing content of their dreams. Fantasies about a relaxed and flexible approach to life can also be explored. As fears and feelings of shame become conscious, they can be productively worked through. While the valuable aspects of compulsivity need to be acknowledged by the therapist, its creativity-blocking and frequently inefficient aspects need to be pointed out.

Pharmacological intervention with compulsive patients, if indicated, usually involves the use of anxiolytic, antidepressant, or antiobsessive medications as an adjunct to psychotherapy. Relieving the anxiety and depression that help maintain compulsive symptoms often lead to more cooperative patients, enabling therapists to make inroads into the rigid structure of the compulsive personality.

Figure 14.6 reviews the strategies and tactics described in this section.

Potentiated Pairings and Catalytic Sequences

How can therapies best be combined and sequenced to optimize therapeutic progress?

After establishing treatment goals and a solid alliance with the patient, behavioral techniques such as relaxation training, desensitization, and thought-stopping can have good early results as an

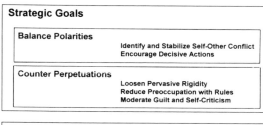

Figure 14.6   Therapeutic strategies and tactics for the prototypal obsessive-compulsive personality.

adjunct to the cognitive or interpersonal individual therapies. The possible benefits of anxiolytic or antidepressant medication can then be evaluated for the specific individual, since premature administration can lead, as with every personality disorder, to temporary alleviation of emotional symptoms and termination before longer term reconstructive work can be done. Once the patient has achieved some initial insight and behavior change in the course of individual treatment, the therapist may decide that couples, sex, or less commonly, family therapy may further increase self-understanding and help provide environmental conditions that bolster the process of reorganizing the functional structure of the compulsive personality.

Risks and Resistances

In the early phases of treatment, it is particularly important for the therapist to keep in mind that compulsives, even more than other personality-disordered patients, perceive change as a possible route to danger and increased vulnerability. Security and stability for them depend on a simple and well-ordered life. Should the unanticipated occur, or should stress supersede their defenses, equanimity may falter. They may vacillate between diffuse anxiety, explosive outbursts, expressions of doubt and contrition, and any number of bizarre compulsions. If pressure mounts or continues over prolonged periods, compulsives may decompensate into a florid disorder.

Compulsive personalities are likely to regard therapy as an encroachment on their defensive armor. They seek to relieve their symptoms, but at the same time want desperately to prevent self-exploration and self-awareness. The patient's defensiveness is deeply protective and must be honored by the therapist; probing should proceed no faster than the patient can tolerate. Only after building trust and self-confidence may the clinician chance exposing the patient's anger and resentment. It is important for therapists who are trying to establish rapport with compulsive patients in the initial phases of therapy not to push a close emotional relationship too quickly. Whereas this is a valid therapeutic for the later phases of treatment, anything but a respectful, problem-focused therapist manner may cause the compulsive enough discomfort to lead to premature termination.

Insight may be a first step, but not a guarantee, toward consenting to take risks, both in and out of therapy. For every piece of defensive armor removed, the therapist must be sure to bolster the patient's autonomy twofold. To remove more defenses than the patient can tolerate is to invite disaster. Fortunately, compulsives themselves are usually so well guarded that precipitous movement by the therapist is often ignored or intellectualized away. The therapist's best recourse against excessive hesitation is to reiterate often that life offers no guarantees, and that taking risks, while opening one up to the possibility of pain, disappointment, and failure, also offers the only hope of real reward and success. Discussion of how the patient would cope were things to turn out badly, may give the patient a modicum of security even in the face of threatening new situations.

Therapists often experience exasperation at a compulsive patient's focus on detail, particularly when the details come to obscure the larger picture. Sometimes the patient is perceived as boring and dry. Frustration often results from the tendency of compulsives to avoid significant emotional issues; rather than examine the anxiety that underlies their actions, they often justify their behavior as the best response to confusing goals, or, alternatively, to the psychological problems of others. Anger is a common reaction when the patient's need for control manifests itself through the passive refusal to do assignments. The astute therapist will manage to use his or her own reactions as a tool in understanding the patient's resistances, and will keep in mind that a power struggle will do little to help the patient. Polarity conflicts and perpetuating tendencies should always remain the focus of therapy.

CHAPTER 15

Negativistic Personality Disorders: The Vacillating Pattern

The negativistic personality (we will use this label rather than the outmoded passive-aggressive term to represent these personalities) usually evolves when a child internalizes the inconsistencies and vacillations in parental attitudes and behaviors to which he or she was exposed, a feature of experience that is not uncommon in our complex and ever-changing society. What distinguishes so-called negativists is that they were subjected to appreciably more than their share of contradictory parental messages. Their erraticism and capriciousness, their tendency to shift from agreeableness to negativism, simply mirror the inconsistent models and reinforcements to which they were exposed.

The overt picture of the DSM-IV's negativistic syndrome is strikingly *dissimilar* from that of the compulsive personality. According to Millon (1969, 1981, 1990), however, both share an intense and deeply rooted ambivalence about themselves and others. Compulsives deal with this ambivalence by vigorously suppressing the conflicts it engenders, and they appear as a consequence to be well controlled and single-minded in purpose; their behavior is perfectionistic, scrupulous, orderly, and quite predictable. In contrast, the negativist fails either to submerge or to otherwise resolve these very same conflicts; as a consequence, the ambivalence of negativists intrudes constantly into their everyday life, resulting in indecisiveness, fluctuating attitudes, oppositional behaviors and emotions, and a general erraticism and unpredictability. They cannot decide whether to adhere to the desires of others as a means of gaining comfort and security *or* to turn to themselves for these gains, whether to be obediently dependent on others *or* defiantly resistant and independent of them, whether to take the initiative in mastering their world *or* to sit idly by, passively awaiting the leadership of others. They vacillate, and then like the proverbial donkey,

they move first one way and then the other, never quite settling on which bale of hay is best.

The erratic pattern of behaviors observed among the negativistic is similar to that employed by young children who explore, through trial and error, various actions and strategies in the hope of discovering which ones succeed for them. In this exploratory phase, children display considerable spontaneity, shifting in an almost random fashion from assertion to submission, to avoidance, to exploitation, to obstinacy, and so on. Most children meet with fairly stable parental responses to their varied behaviors, and as a consequence, most learn to discern which actions and attitudes are acceptable and achieve their goals. This predictability in gauging the consequences of one's behaviors is not learned by future negativists, for these children experience little in the way of parental consistency. Because they cannot discern a clear pattern of consequences for their behaviors, they continue on an erratic, childish course. The persistence of these childlike and capriciously unpredictable behaviors accounts in part for the frequency with which these personalities are referred to in adulthood as "emotionally immature."

The DSM-III characterization and diagnostic criteria of the passive-aggressive were unlike the other personality descriptions in that manual. In each of the other portrayals, several relatively distinct traits were identified as composing the syndrome or personality pattern. In contrast, only one essential trait was specified in characterizing the passive-aggressive personality type, that of resistance to external demands. Several illustrations and consequences are spelled out in the manual, but they cannot substitute for the matrix of distinct, yet interrelated, traits that constitute a true *personality disorder*. In line with this objection, the senior author, as a member of the DSM-III personality subcommittee, submitted the following critique in response to the sketchy and deficient penultimate draft. Unfortunately, in the author's opinion, the recommendations suggested had no impact on the final version.

I think the descriptive material for this personality is narrowly focused. As evident in the diagnostic criteria, we seem to be dealing with a tendency to resist authority as the prime and almost singular trait. Should we not be dealing with a much broader complex when we describe a disorder as a personality disorder? I would like to see additional factors added so as to characterize this as a personality rather than a symptom disorder. The following are my suggestions. First, I would like to see the name changed; "passive-aggressive" has a long history of mixed meanings; I think terms such as oppositional personality disorder or negativistic personality disorder capture the flavor of these patients more clearly. As far as essential features and diagnostic criteria, I would suggest some of the following: frequently irritable and erratically moody; a tendency to report being easily frustrated and angry; discontented self-image, as evidenced in feeling misunderstood and unappreciated by others; characteristically pessimistic, disgruntled and disillusioned with life; interpersonal ambivalence, as evidenced in a struggle between being dependently acquiescent and assertively independent; the use of unpredictable and sulking behaviors to provoke discomfort in others. I think each of the above will enrich the descriptive material we have. It will broaden the personality pattern and provide a complex of traits.

Relevant to the issue of the syndrome's narrow and limited focus were data obtained during the DSM-III Task Force's field trials. Research seeking to gauge diagnostic agreement for each disorder resulted in a *Kappa* reliability figure of .21 for the passive-aggressive; the next poorest reliability among the personality disorders was .39, with the remainder of the group averaging close to .60. In effect, of all personality disorder descriptions, the passive-aggressive produced by far the poorest diagnostic agreement. Did the passive-aggressive portrayal suffer by comparison because it provided only one trait as a basis for identifying the clinical syndrome? The senior author believed the answer was yes! Before proceeding to elaborate the more comprehensive conception for the passive-aggressive/negativistic, the descriptive features of this personality, now placed in the 1994 DSM-IV Appendix, will

be outlined as originally formulated by Millon (1969).

Referring to this pattern as the "negativistic personality," these individuals were noted by their general contrariness and disinclination to doing things that others wish or expect of them. But beyond this passive-resistance there is a capricious impulsiveness, an irritable moodiness, a grumbling, discontented, sulky, unaccommodating, and faultfinding pessimism that characterizes their behaviors. They not only obstruct but dampen everyone's spirits as sullen malcontents and perennial complainers whose very presence demoralizes others. Although anguished and discontent with themselves, they never appear satisfied with others either. Even in the best of circumstances, they always seem to seek the "dark lining in the silver cloud." If they find themselves alone, they would prefer to be with others; if they are with others, they prefer to be alone. If someone gives them a gift, they dislike being obligated; if they fail to receive one, they feel slighted and rejected. If they are given a position of leadership, they complain bitterly about the lack of support they get from others; if they are not allowed to lead, they become critical and unsupporting of those who are.

HISTORICAL ANTECEDENTS

Although earlier writers such as Theophrastus characterized individuals displaying features akin to what we refer to today as passive-aggressive/negativistic personalities, little of a formal nature concerning these individuals has been described systematically in the literature. Perhaps, the portrayal of "neurotic personalities" in recent times comes closest to what we see in these individuals, an emotionally labile, inconsistent, and capricious pattern of behaviors, quite unpredictable and irrational, interspersed with moments of guilt and contrition as well as rational behavior and thought. Nevertheless, the formal history of these characterizations begin in modern times.

MODERN FORMULATIONS

The term "passive-aggressive personality" was first listed as part of the medical nomenclature in a War Department technical bulletin in 1945. Following a trial study of its utility in the Veterans Administration, it was formally introduced in the U.S. Joint Armed Services nosology in 1949. It was included next in the *Standard VA Classification* in 1951 as part of a new and broad category labeled "Character and Behavior Disorders," the first official recognition of the popular psychoanalytic designation *character disorder.* Character and behavior disorders subsumed two major syndromes: "Pathological Personalities" and "Immaturity Reactions." "Passive-aggressive" was listed among the latter group, along with "emotional instability," "passive-dependency," and "aggressive reaction." Guided by the VA nosology, the *Diagnostic and Statistical Manual of Mental Disorders* (DSM) developed by the American Psychiatric Association in 1952 included a passive-aggressive personality, differentiating it into three subtypes: a "pure" passive-aggressive, a passive-dependent, and an aggressive. Each of these types was considered a manifestation of the same underlying psychopathology and was ostensibly interchangeable in the same person. Although the 1968 edition (or second issue) of the DSM included a passive-aggressive type, it now took only one form; both passive-dependent and aggressive variants were dropped. The 1980 edition, or DSM-III, retained the earlier passive-aggressive personality, reactivated the passive-dependent type as a separate syndrome under the "dependent personality" label, and included some aspects of the aggressive type as part of the antisocial personality description.

Although the negativistic/passive-aggressive syndrome appears to be a prevalent disorder, its diagnostic reliability, as noted earlier, is extremely poor. Surprisingly, it has received rather scant theoretical and clinical attention despite having been listed in all three earlier editions of the DSM. Tracing its ancestry and clinical forerunners proves to be a job of major proportions, requiring the uncovering of descriptively similar characterizations formulated under widely diverse syndrome labels. This worthy but comprehensive task is not attempted in this text. Rather a few clinical ancestors and a number of descriptively similar current conceptions are identified.

Clinicians inclined to biogenic explanations of psychopathology turn to the writings of Kraepelin, Bleuler, and Schneider most often for their hypotheses. What do these theorists offer us that is suggestive of the constellation of traits currently designated as the negativistic/passive-aggressive personality?

Kraepelin, for one, wrote about individuals with constitutions that incline them to behave in the characteristically ambivalent and contradictory manner that typifies the negativistic. Employing the term "cyclothymia," first coined by Kahlbaum in the 1870s, Kraepelin (1913) referred to a depressively inclined variant as possessing "a special sensitiveness to the cares, troubles and disappointments of life. They take all things hard and feel the unpleasantness in every occurrence" (p. 219). Another variant of cyclothymia, those imbued with an irascible makeup, show "an extraordinary fluctuating emotional equilibrium and are strongly affected by all experiences, often in an unpleasant way" (p. 222).

Bleuler (1924) spoke of these personalities as being "irritable of mood" (*reizbare Verstimmung*), and Aschaffenburg (1922) described them as dissatisfied personalities who go through life as if they were perpetually wounded. Applying the label "amphithymia," Hellpach (1920) depicted a similar pattern of fussy people who tend to be of a sour disposition, constantly fret over whatever they do, and make invidious and painful comparisons between themselves and those of a more cheerful inclination whose simpler and brighter outlook is both envied and decried.

Of the constitutionalists, Schneider (1923/1950) did best in capturing the essence of this personality type, whom he designated as "ill-tempered depressives." He summarized their prime features as follows:

These tend to be cold, egotistical, morose and cantankerous. Sometimes also they are irritable and given to nagging and can be spiteful and malicious. They are doggedly pessimistic and rejoice when things go wrong. They are not given to wishing anyone well. (p. 81)

Theory-based explanations for these behaviors are to be found primarily in the writings of the early psychoanalysts. The clinical features of the negativist have been described in two different character types: the "oral sadistic melancholiac" and the "masochist." The first stems from ambivalences consequent to difficulties arising in the "oral biting" stage. The suppositions that these consequences give rise to the "oral-sadistic" character and that sadism and masochism are ostensibly two sides of the same coin suggest the inevitable similarity between the two characterizations. The notion of the oral-sadistic, or melancholiac, character is discussed first.

It was Abraham (1924/1927a) who first articulated a division of the oral stage into sucking and biting, with fixations arising at either substage and distinctive traits consequent to these fixations. In his initial descriptions, Abraham contrasted the clinical consequences of oral gratification with those who had been traumatized during the oral biting phase as follows: "The orally gratified person is identifying himself with the bounteous mother. Things are very different in the next, oral-sadistic stage, where envy, hostility, and jealousy make such behaviors impossible" (p. 398).

Since the theoretical framework that guides this chapter's clinical analysis is Millon's (1969) formulation of the "negativistic" personality pattern, it is worthy of note that Abraham was the first to recognize that ambivalence was at the core of the oral-sadistic problem. Speaking of "melancholiacs," he asserted that their moods and behaviors signified their effort to escape or otherwise deal with unresolved and deep rooted oral-sadistic ambivalence. Abraham (1924/1927b) wrote as follows:

In the biting stage of the oral phase the individual incorporates the object in himself and in so doing destroys it. . . . It is in this stage that the ambivalent attitude of the ego to its object begins to grow up. We may say, therefore, that in the child's libidinal development the second stage, the oral sadistic phase, marks the beginning of its ambivalence conflict; whereas the first (sucking) stage should be regarded as preambivalent.

The libidinal level, therefore, to which the melancholiac regresses after the loss of his object contains in itself a conflict of ambivalent feelings in its most primitive and therefore most unmodified form. . . . This ambivalent attitude remains inherent in the tendencies of the libido during subsequent phases of its development. . . . We meet this ambivalence everywhere in the patient's emotional life.

We are now in a position to understand why it is that the ambivalence of his instinctual life involves the melancholiac in quite especially grave conflicts which strike at the roots of his relation to his love-objects. The act of turning away from that original object round whom his whole emotional life revolved does not end there. It extends . . . finally to every human being. (pp. 451–453)

Although his orientation was more akin to the descriptive approach taken by Kraepelin and Schneider, Kahn (1931) also drew upon the concept of ambivalence as a basis for understanding a character type similar to what we refer to today as the negativistic (passive-aggressive) personality. He writes:

The types of ego-overvaluation and ego-undervaluation are "unipolar" and their conflicts are generally to be deduced and understood from this unipolarity; in the ambitendency it is different. These types oscillate between the ego and the environment, between overvaluation and undervaluation of the ego. . . . Every decision, every attitude, every act, in a way every experience, is reflected in the opposed concave mirrors of ego-overvaluation and ego-undervaluation and bandied back and forth between them. The oscillation leads inevitably to long-enduring inner tension, to persistent conflicts, or to persistent readiness to conflicts, and it takes effect in the daily bearing of the personality (pp. 273–274).

Menninger (1940) aptly portrayed the characteristic outlook and behavior of the oral-sadistic "melancholiac" in the following passage:

In the late oral stage the sadistic element of oral behavior develops. And this sadism in place of passive dependence makes the late oral-sadistic character in many ways the characterological opposite of the early oral character. The basic reaction is one of pessimistic distrust of the world. The world still owes the individual a living but instead of viewing it optimistically he is inclined to blame the world for everything unpleasant which happens to him. Instead of being easygoing, he is cantankerous, contemptuous, petulant. Instead of feeling that everything is right with the world, he is inclined to find everything wrong with it. Such individuals go through life making enemies instead of friends and constantly blame the other fellow for their shortcomings in accomplishment. Their social attitude is overdemanding and they are emotionally soured with the real world. . . . They become the perpetually discontented, moody people of unhappy temperament. (pp. 393–394)

CONTEMPORARY PROPOSALS

Little systematic research or clinical theorizing was published in the first few decades following World War II, other than the introduction of the term "passive-aggressive personality" into DSM-I in 1952.

Sandler (1985) clarified the themes originally proposed for the concept of "oral pessimists" that had been formulated some decades earlier by classical psychoanalysts. Bringing these earlier notions into contemporary thinking, he states:

The orally frustrated or ungratified character has a characteristically pessimistic outlook on life which may be associated with moods of depression, attitudes of withdrawal, passive-receptive attitudes, feelings of insecurity with a need for constant reassurance . . . a dislike of sharing, and a general feeling of demanding coupled with dissatisfaction. (p. 137)

Because of the rather skimpy and unfocused history of the negativistic personality, it is necessary to turn to very recent contributors in the literature for insights into this character type. Matters will become more problematic with the decision to shift this personality disorder into the Appendix of DSM-IV, a step that may further limit the extent to which both theorists, researchers, and clinicians are likely to employ this designation in their work. Despite this turn of events, the construct of a *negativistic* disorder has been expanded in the DSM-IV Appendix to represent the notion of a personality disorder more extensive in its clinical characteristics than its forerunner, the passive-aggressive disorder. It is hoped that this expanded range of clinical features may stimulate more work than has heretofore been carried out.

As noted, the syndrome designated "passive-aggressive" has generated few theoretical papers and research studies since its inclusion in the official 1952 nomenclature. However, a number of investigators have studied its features and utility; their findings are briefly summarized next.

Whitman, Trosman, and Koenig (1954) studied a group of 62 patients diagnosed as passive-aggressive and compared their features with those of 338 other psychiatric outpatients. Despite differences, most patients showed "an intense ambivalent" relation to their parents and "came in complaining of anxiety." In deciphering the psychodynamics of their behaviors, Whitman et al. wrote:

When the aggression is inhibited by internal guilt or fear of external retaliation, regression to a dependent position occurs. This is revealed by passive behavior. Passive behavior may also be stimulated by inability to deal with the ambiguity of a role re-

quirement. . . . The final step, dynamically, would be guilt over dependent needs . . . leading to pseudoaggression, the behavioral counterpart being hostility. On the behavioral level, shame over a culturally unacceptable passive role leads to hostility. (p. 346)

In a somewhat more recent study (Small, Small, Alig, & Moore, 1970), 100 patients diagnosed as passive-aggressive personalities were followed for periods of 7 to 15 years and compared with matched controls. The investigators concluded their thoroughly detailed study as follows:

All of the investigators were impressed with . . . the subjects' ability to manipulate and misconstrue interpersonal situations. . . .

Nevertheless, the majority of the subjects retained an active interest in interpersonal involvement. They were capable of giving and receiving affection, and most of their relatives and friends continued to hold them in esteem. In many instances this was despite frequent verbal battles and emotional outbursts, with the patients trying to influence and coerce others. The quality of the subjects' interactions with other people seemed to be intense, variable, and manipulative but with enduring relationships over long periods of time. . . .

The illness was as likely to occur in males as in females and was characterized by interpersonal strife, verbal (not physical) aggressiveness, emotional storms, impulsivity, and manipulative behavior. Suicidal gestures and lack of attention to everyday responsibilities commonly accompanied this intensive style of relating. In both sexes there were prominent disturbances of affect, generally consisting of frequent, short-lived outbursts of anger or rage and often accompanied by tearfulness. (pp. 979–980)

Formulations from a cognitive point of view have been proposed by Beck and Freeman (1990b) that are well worth summarizing in the following quotes that address the cognitive dysfunctions typical of these individuals:

Their conflicts are expressed in beliefs such as "I need authority to nurture and support me" versus "I need to protect my identity." (The same kind of conflicts are often expressed by borderline patients.) The conditional belief is expressed in terms such as "If I follow the rules, I lose my freedom of action." (p. 46)

The automatic thoughts of individuals with PAPD reflect their negativism, autonomy, and desire to follow the path of least resistance. For example, they see any requests from others as intrusive and demanding. Their response is to resist the request automatically rather than evaluate whether they want to do it. They vacillate between thinking that others have taken advantage of them and that they are unworthy. This negativism is pervasive in their thinking. Negativistic patients look for a negative interpretation of most events. Even during neutral or positive events, they seek out and focus on the negative aspects. . . . They believe that open conflict is terrible and will result in disapproval or even rejection. However, while negativistic persons fail to assert themselves, they nevertheless deeply resent submitting to other's demands. (pp. 336–337)

Another perspective has been introduced by Lorna Benjamin (1993a). In an insightful analysis of the interpersonal facets of the negativistic personality, Benjamin notes:

There is a tendency to see any form of power as inconsiderate and neglectful, together with a belief that authorities or caregivers are incompetent, unfair, and cruel. The NEG agrees to comply with perceived demands or suggestions, but fails to perform. He or she often complains of unfair treatment, and envies and resents others who fare better. His or her suffering indicts the allegedly negligent caregivers or authorities. The NEG fears control in any form and wishes for nurturant restitution. (p. 272)

Points out how others are treated with leniency and generosity while he or she is asked to do an unfair share of the work. Says that the others actually do less, but are acknowledged and rewarded more. Feels cheated and robbed of his or her due. (p. 276)

Those promulgating the five-factor statistical model of personality and its disorders have briefly described the major elements of this form of pathology as follows:

It is evident that PAG involves primarily low agreeableness (low compliance and low straightforwardness) and excessively low conscientiousness (low competence, low dutifulness, and low self-discipline). The negativistic person may also be high in the neuroticism facet of hostility (resents demands,

sulky, and irritable). (Costa & Widiger, 1993, p. 52)

Turning from the more psychological approaches of the past several decades, Klein and his associates (Klein & Davis, 1969; Klein, Honigfeld, & Feldman, 1973) have sought to identify syndromal personality groups in terms of their pharmacological response. They consider the negativistic type to be a dubious clinical entity, providing an alternative in what they term the "emotionally unstable character." The clinical features of the unstable character encompass characteristics that broaden the limited scope of the DSM negativistic portrayal. Their description stresses the likely biological instability and mood lability of these patients, which consists of:

. . . short periods of tense, empty unhappiness, accompanied by inactivity, withdrawal, depression, irritability, and sulking, alternating suddenly with impulsiveness, giddiness, low frustration tolerance, rejection of rules, and shortsighted hedonism. . . .

Patients with emotionally unstable personalities . . . are usually young, with a poorly developed conscience and generally immature attitudes, and are frequently irresponsible, hedonistic, extractive, and exploitive. Their marked affective lability is often not immediately noted as core pathology because of their complicated self-presentations. These range from a fragile, immature, dependent image, eliciting protectiveness from the observer, to a hard "wise guy" presentation expressing independence and lack of need for care. The patients are perplexed about their life goals, stating that they do not know who they are, what they are, or what they want to be. They are also confused about issues of dependency, intimacy and self-assertion, often reacting in a disorganized, flighty, and despairing fashion. (1973, p. 186)

Another biologically oriented thesis concerning the passive-aggressive style was derived from Cloninger's basic neurobiological-behavioral traits. He (1987a) writes:

Passive-aggressive subjects were described as being high in novelty-seeking ("impulsive," "sudden, unpremeditated action," "frequent outbursts of verbal anger," "neglects responsibilities"), as well as high in both harm avoidance and reward dependence or passive-avoidant (no physical aggression but "indirectly manipulative"). As expected of individuals high in all three dimensions, they were easily distressed ("nervous") and moody ("gloomy, cries often"), without meeting full criteria for major depression. (p. 584)

From a completely different vantage, that of a humanistic-existential perspective, we find a descriptive portrayal of the negativist in the following characterization by Mahrer (1983):

1. *The person behaves in ways which are helpless and needy . . . supplemented by temper tantrums, and these generally occur within the context of being helpless and needy.*

2. *The person behaves in passively infuriating ways ranging from thinly disguised anger to apparently helpful cooperativeness.*

3. *The person is negativistic, obstructionistic, uncooperative and stubborn in ways which are passive, indirect, and irresponsible.*

4. *The person behaves in ways which are superficially compliant and acquiescent, with undertones of whining, complaining, and grumbling. (p. 100)*

Although few analytically oriented theorists have addressed the construct of a negativistic (passive-aggressive) personality, there are a few who have sought to describe the pattern in a useful manner. For example, in his usual insightful fashion, Stone (1993) characterizes the origin and course of this disorder as follows:

The captiousness, verbal nitpicking, contrariness, and sulkiness that characterize PAgPD . . . would seem to have its origin in a pattern of unending power struggles with one's parents. The comparative helplessness of youth made it impossible to "win" these battles at the time, certainly not in any directly confrontive way. . . . The effects of parental nagging tend to grow more severe over the years: Constant nagging may interfere with a child's steps toward self-fulfillment; lowered achievement may then make the child (or adolescent) more vulnerable to criticism and more impaired in self-esteem; this renders the child more sensitive to, and resentful of, further parental criticism and nagging; allusions to his failures cut deeper with the advancing years, as the possibilities of living up to the parents' (often unrealistic) expectations grow even dimmer. (p. 361)

Descriptive material and diagnostic criteria for this personality syndrome were furnished by

Millon (1969) to the DSM-III Task Force to represent his theoretically derived "negativistic personality pattern," which stated the following:

We will list four major characteristics that distinguish the personality type under review. These characteristics have been labeled as follows: irritable affectivity *(is moody, high-strung and quick-tempered),* cognitive ambivalence *(holds incompatible ideas and shifts erratically among them),* discontented self-image *(feels misunderstood, disillusioned, a failure) and* interpersonal vacillation *(is impatient and unpredictable with others; switches from resentment to guilt). (p. 291)*

The features and criteria listed in the following quote encompassed a broad range of characteristics reported in both the theoretical and research literature and included features beyond those few which were ultimately included in the final DSM-III draft. Millon's formulation was derived primarily by conceptualizing the features of this personality, not only in terms of the passiveness of its aggression, but in the activeness of its ambivalence. The 1975 draft proposed by Millon included the following:

This pattern is typified by unpredictable moods, edgy irritability, social contrariness and a generally pessimistic outlook, notably the feeling of being cheated, misunderstood and unappreciated. An intense conflict between dependence and self-assertion contributes to an impulsive and quixotic emotionality. There is a pattern of sullen pouting, fault-finding, and stubbornness that is punctuated periodically by short-lived enthusiasms, angry outbursts and genuine expressions of guilt and contrition. Personal relationships are fraught with wrangles and disappointments, provoked often by the characteristic fretful, complaining and negativistic behaviors.

Since adolescence or early adulthood at least 3 of the following have been present to a notably greater degree than in most people and were not limited to discrete periods nor necessarily prompted by stressful life events.

1. *Irritable affectivity (e.g., is high-strung, quick-tempered and moody; reports being easily piqued and intolerant of frustration).*

2. *Behavioral contrariness (e.g., frequently exhibits passively-aggressive, obstinate, petulant, fault-finding and sulking behaviors;*

reveals a measure of gratification in demoralizing, obstructing and undermining the pleasures of others).

3. *Discontented self-image (e.g., reports feeling misunderstood, unappreciated and demeaned by others; is characteristically pessimistic, disgruntled and disillusioned about life).*

4. *Deficient regulatory controls (e.g., fleeting thoughts and emotions are impulsively expressed in unmodulated form; external stimuli evoke rapid, capricious and fluctuating reactions).*

5. *Interpersonal ambivalence (e.g., conflicting and changing roles are assumed in social relationships, particularly dependent acquiescence and assertive independence; unpredictable and vacillating behaviors provoke edgy discomfort and exasperation in others).*

Although serious doubts were raised with regard to the DSM-III passive-aggressive formulation, the DSM-III-R committee failed to undertake the necessary revision that was called for, namely the need to broaden the concept to represent a wide range of oppositional characteristics, of which negativism was merely one. Further, owing to its problematic character, the ICD-10 committee did not include any element of the passive-aggressive/negativistic personality within its taxonomy. Unclear as to what direction it should move, no changes in the conception or criteria were introduced into the DSM-III-R.

The need to examine again and to expand on the scope of the passive-aggressive/negativistic personality led the DSM-IV Axis-II Work Group to propose the alternative originally recommended in 1975, that is, that the conception and designation be formulated as a "negativistic" personality; it is this latter conceptualization that forms the basis and clinical details of the negativistic (passive-aggressive) disorder in this chapter.

Owing to the fundamental changes that were introduced, the DSM-IV Task Force made the decision to include the new formulation in its Appendix rather than in the main body of the text. Listed under the designation, Passive-Aggressive (Negativistic) Personality Disorder, owing to the concern that an entirely new nomenclature might prove "too radical," its diagnostic criteria fall into several clinical domains. Two criteria are presented within the Interpersonal domain: a passive resistance to fulfilling routine social expectancies

and occupational tasks; unreasonably critical and scornful of authorities. Two essentially Cognitive domain attributes are noted as well: feels cheated and unappreciated, complaining of being misunderstood and unappreciated by others; expresses resentment and envy of those ostensibly more fortunate. Two features reflect Mood/Temperament characteristics: tends to be sullen, irritable, argumentative, skeptical, and contrary; vacillates between expressing hostile defiance and being contrite (e.g., asking forgiveness as a means of mollifying those scorned and criticized).

A final commentary in this contemporary section on the negativistic personality turns our attention toward the evolutionary model and the polarity characterization represented in Figure 15.1. Little stands out in this portrayal, other than the element of conflict and ambivalence signified by the double pointed arrow between the self and other polarities. What this indicates is the inability of negativistic personalities to find a comfortable ground between acting on their own behalf versus doing so for others. They cannot find a consistent or single-minded purpose. As a consequence, they shift erratically back and forth, manifesting fluctuating attitudes and unpredictable behaviors. If they move toward the fulfillment of what others desire, they become irritated and annoyed with themselves for doing so, quickly shifting their thoughts and feelings in favor of doing their own thing. In so doing, however, they

NEGATIVISTIC PROTOTYPE

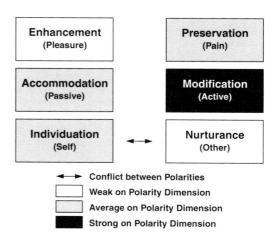

Figure 15.1   Status of the negativistic (passive-aggressive) personality prototype in accord with the Millon Polarity Model.

jeopardize the security and support they need from others, leading them quickly to become contrite and to reverse their position again. Negativists are active, not passive, shifting from one moment to the next in their behaviors, thoughts, and feelings. Little joy is experienced in this process; fear and self-preservation predominate. Whichever direction they take, there are discomforting consequences to pay. It is this unsettled character of the self-other orientation that keeps negativists in a perpetual state of discontent and dysphoria.

A useful chronology of the major contributors is presented in Figure 15.2.

CLINICAL FEATURES

The following sections provide the reader with several perspectives on the negativistic personality. We will first organize clinical data sources in line with the eight domains. Attention will next turn to the several normal, childhood, and adult varieties of the negativistic prototype, followed by considerations of comorbidity and differential diagnosis (see Table 15.1 and Figure 15.3).

PROTOTYPAL DIAGNOSTIC DOMAINS

This section discusses the central features of the so-called negativistic pattern, detailing these characteristics in accord with the eight domains of clinical analysis utilized in earlier chapters. As noted previously, the traits of the negativistic are more broadly conceived here than in the DSM-IV Appendix, and it is thereby conceptualized as a comprehensive personality disorder. This extended formulation is guided by the personality pattern described as the negativistic type by Millon in 1969.

Expressive Behavior: Resentful

One of the problems that arise when focusing on the distinctive characteristics of a pathological personality type is that the reader is led to believe, incorrectly, that these individuals always display the features that have been described. This is not the case. Most personalities behave normally much of the time; their behaviors are appropriate to the reality conditions of their environment. What a text such as this seeks to stress are those features that, by virtue of their frequency and intensity, *distinguish* certain personalities. Thus, "resentfulness" may be used as a descriptor to characterize the negativistic. But almost everyone behaves resentfully sometimes, and the negativistic is not resentful much of the time. What distinguishes negativists is the ease with which they can be made to act in a resentful manner and the regularity with which this behavior is manifested. With this qualification in mind, the discussion turns to a brief note of the resentful feature as typically found in the negativist.

As seen in these personalities, resentfulness is manifested in a variety of forms that signify their resistance to fulfilling the expectancies of others. Thus, they exhibit procrastination, inefficiency, obstinate, as well as contrary and socially irksome

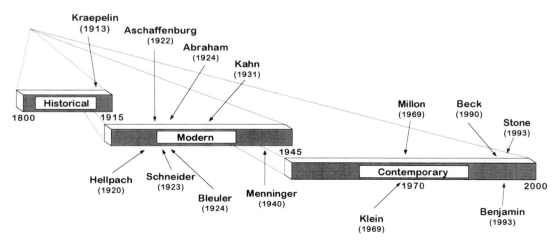

Figure 15.2   Historical review of major contributors to the negativistic (passive-aggressive) personality disorder.

TABLE 15.1   Clinical Domains of the Negativistic (Passive-Aggressive) Prototype

Behavioral Level

(F) Expressively Resentful. Resists fulfilling expectancies of others, frequently exhibiting procrastination, inefficiency, and obstinacy, as well as oppositional and irksome behaviors; reveals gratification in demoralizing and undermining the pleasures and aspirations of others.

(F) Interpersonally Contrary. Assumes conflicting and changing roles in social relationships, particularly dependent and contrite acquiescence and assertive and hostile independence; conveys envy and pique toward those more fortunate, as well as acting concurrently or sequentially obstructive and intolerant of others, expressing either negative or incompatible attitudes.

Phenomenological Level

(F) Cognitively Skeptical. Is cynical, doubting, and untrusting, approaching positive events with disbelief, and future possibilities with pessimism, anger, and trepidation; has a misanthropic view of life, whines and grumbles, voicing disdain and caustic comments toward those experiencing good fortune.

(S) Discontented Self-Image. Sees self as misunderstood, luckless, unappreciated, jinxed, and demeaned by others; recognizes being characteristically embittered, disgruntled and disillusioned with life.

(S) Vacillating Objects. Internalized representations of the past comprise a complex of countervailing relationships, setting in motion contradictory feelings, conflicting inclinations, and incompatible memories that are driven by the desire to degrade the achievements and pleasures of others, without necessarily appearing so.

Intrapsychic Level

(F) Displacement Mechanism. Discharges anger and other troublesome emotions either precipitously or by employing unconscious maneuvers to shift them from their instigator to settings or persons of lesser significance; vents disapproval by substitute or passive means, such as acting inept or perplexed, or behaving in a forgetful or indolent manner.

(S) Divergent Organization. A clear division in the pattern of morphologic structures such that coping and defensive maneuvers are often directed toward incompatible goals, leaving major conflicts unresolved and full psychic cohesion often impossible because fulfillment of one drive or need inevitably nullifies or reverses another.

Biophysical Level

(S) Irritable Mood. Frequently touchy, temperamental, and peevish, followed in turn by sullen and moody withdrawal; is often petulant and impatient, unreasonably scorns those in authority and reports being annoyed easily or frustrated by many.

(F) = Functional domain.
(S) = Structural domain.

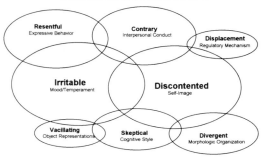

Figure 15.3   Salience of personologic domains in the negativistic prototype.

behaviors. These actions also reflect the gratification that negativists feel in demoralizing and undermining the pleasures and aspirations of others.

Interpersonal Conduct: Contrary

Most persons acquire styles of relating to others that enable them to achieve an optimal level of satisfaction and security, as well as to maintain a reasonable degree of self-harmony. So-called normals may be differentiated from pathological personalities by the variety and character of the strategies they employ to achieve these goals. Healthy personalities draw on their strategies flexibly as they face changing demands and pressures. Psychologically impaired individuals, however, tend to be inflexible. They approach different events as if they were the same and utilize the same strategies they acquired in childhood, even though these are presently inappropriate. Once having learned a particular style that has worked for them, it continues to be used as if it were a sacred rulebook for navigating the future.

The problem that faces negativists (and borderlines also) is quite different from that of most pathological personalities. Their difficulties stem *not* from the rigid character of their coping style but from its exaggerated fluidity. They are actively and overtly ambivalent, unable to find a satisfactory direction or course for their behavior. They vacillate and cannot decide whether to be dependent or independent of others and whether to respond to events actively or passively. Their dilemmas do not arise from an overcommitment to one strategy but from a lack of commitment. As a consequence, they vacillate indecisively in a tortuous and erratic manner from one mood and one course of action to another. They behave by fits and starts, shifting capriciously down a path that leads nowhere and precipitates them into endless wrangles with others and disappointments with themselves.

The contrary character seen in this domain of the negativistic personality takes the form of changing and conflicting social relationships. Most notable is the contrast between dependent and contrite acquiescence, on the one hand, and assertive and hostile independence, on the other. They exhibit envy and pique toward those who seem to be more fortunate than themselves and are actively obstructive toward those with whom they must relate regularly, expressing either critical or incompatible attitudes toward them.

It would appear from the foregoing that the ambivalence and erratic course of the negativistic would fail to provide the individual with any satisfactions or security. If this were the case, we would expect them to decompensate quickly. Few do. Hence, we are forced to inquire as to what gains and supports these individuals achieve by behaving in their vacillating and ambivalent manner.

Quite simply, being "difficult," quixotic, unpredictable, and discontent will produce certain rewards and avoid certain discomforts. The following are examples, drawn from the sphere of marital life, of the ingenious, though unconscious, mechanisms these personalities employ.

A negativistic man, who is unwilling or unable to decide whether to "grow up" or remain a "child," explodes emotionally whenever his wife expects "too much" of him. Afterward, he expresses guilt, becomes contrite, and pleads forbearance on her part. By turning toward self-condemnation, he evokes her sympathy, restrains her from making undue demands, and maneuvers her into placating rather than criticizing him.

A woman, feeling the ambivalence of both love and hate for her husband, complains bitterly about his loss of interest in her as a woman. To prove his affections, he suggests that they go on a "second honeymoon"—take a vacation without the children. To this proposal, she replies that his plan only proves that he is a foolish spendthrift; in the same breath, however, she insists that the children come along. No matter what he does, he is wrong. She has not only trapped him but confused him as well. Her ambivalence maneuvers him, first one way and then the other. It forces him to be on edge, always alert to avoid situations that might provoke her ire, yet he can never quite be sure that he has succeeded.

The negativists' inconsistent strategy, of being discontent and unpredictable, of being both seductive and rejecting, and of being demanding and then dissatisfied, is an effective weapon not only with an intimidated or pliant partner but with people in general. Switching among the roles of the martyr, the affronted, the aggrieved, the misunderstood, the contrite, the guilt-ridden, the sickly, and the overworked, is a tactic of interpersonal behavior that gains negativists the attention, reassurance, and dependency they crave while, at the same time, allowing them to subtly vent their angers and resentments. For all its seeming ineffectuality, vacillation recruits affection and support, on the one hand, and provides a means of discharging the tensions of frustration and hostility, on the other. Interspersed with self-deprecation and contrition, acts that relieve unconscious guilt and serve to solicit forgiveness and reassuring comments from others, this strategy proves *not* to be a total failure at all.

Cognitive Style: Skeptical

It is typical for negativists to be cynical, doubting, and untrusting, approaching most events in their life with a measure of disbelief and skepticism. Future possibilities are viewed with a degree of trepidation, if not pessimism and suspicion. Most negativists display a misanthropic view of life, tend to appraise matters in a whining and grumbling manner, and voice disdain and caustic comments toward circumstances and persons that appear to be experiencing good fortune.

It should also be noted that negativists are usually quite articulate in describing their subjective discomforts. Only rarely, however, are they willing to explore or to admit any insight into its roots. In talking about their sensitivities and difficulties, they will *not* recognize that these reflect, in largest measure, their own inner conflicts and ambivalences. Self-reports alternate between preoccupations with personal inadequacies, bodily ailments, and guilt feelings, on the one hand, and social resentments, frustrations, and disillusionments, on the other. They will voice dismay about the sorry state of their life, their worries, their sadness, their disappointments, their "nervousness," and so on. Although most will express a desire to be rid of distress and difficulty, they seem unable, or perhaps unwilling, to find any solution.

Ambivalence also characterizes the thinking of these persons. No sooner do they "see" the merits of approaching their problems one way than they find themselves saying, "but. . . ." Fearful of committing themselves and unsure of their own desires or competencies, they find their thoughts shifting erratically from one solution to another. Because of their intense ambivalences, they often act precipitously, on the spur of the moment. Any other course for them would lead only to hesitation or vacillation, if not total immobility.

Self-Image: Discontented

Negativists often assert that they have been trapped by fate, that nothing ever "works out" for them, and that whatever they desire runs aground. These negativistic persons express envy and resentment over the "easy life" of others. They are frequently critical and cynical about others' attainments, yet covet these achievements themselves. Life, negativists claim, has been unkind to them. They feel cheated and unappreciated. Whatever they have done has been for naught. Their motives and behaviors have always been misunderstood and they are now bitterly disillusioned. The obstructiveness and pessimism that others have attributed to them are only a reflection, they feel, of their sensitivity or the pain they have suffered from physical disabilities or the inconsideration that others have shown toward them. But here again, the negativists' ambivalence intrudes. Perhaps, they say, it has all been a consequence of their own unworthiness, their own failures, and their own "bad temper." Maybe it is their own behavior that is the cause of their misery and the pain they have brought to others. Among these personalities, the ambivalent struggle between feeling guilt and feeling resentment permeates every facet of thought and behavior.

Object-Representations: Vacillating

The inner templates of the past among negativistic personalities are composed of complexly conflicting images and memories. Few components of this template are composed of internally consistent qualities. Most internalized objects are associated with contradictory feelings, countervailing inclinations, and incompatible memories. Hence, the foundation of dispositions that serve to organize the negativist's ongoing perceptions and personal relationships are divergently oriented and in a constant state of flux. Adding to these internally vacillating objects is the fact that they are generally colored by negative emotions, resulting in a disposition to undermine the

pleasures and achievements of self and others, without necessarily appearing to do so.

The behaviors of these overtly ambivalent personalities are even more erratic and vacillating than we might expect from their reinforcement history. They appear to have labored under a double handicap. Not only were they deprived of external consistency and control in childhood but, as a consequence of these experiences, never acquired the motivation and competencies of internal control. Unsure of what their environment expects of them and unable themselves to impose self-discipline and order, these persons seem adrift in their environment, bobbing up and down erratically from one mood to another.

As will be noted in later paragraphs, these individuals failed to experience consistent parental discipline. What they did acquire was largely through implicit modeling. In essence, they imitated the contradictory or capricious style of their parents. Deprived of conditions for acquiring self-control and modeling themselves after their opposing or erratic and ambivalent parents, these personalities never learn to conceal their moods for long and cannot bind or transform their emotions. Whatever inner feelings well up within them—be it guilt, anger, or inferiority—they spill quickly to the surface in pure and direct form.

Regulatory Mechanisms: Displacement

A distinguishing clinical feature of negativists is their paucity of intrapsychic controls and mechanisms. Their moods, thoughts, and desires tend not to be worked out internally. Few unconscious processes are employed to handle the upsurge of feelings, and, as a consequence, these come readily to the surface, untransformed and unmoderated. These negativistic persons are like children in that they often react spontaneously and impulsively to passing emotions. As a result, there is little consistency and predictability to their reactions.

Perhaps the most consistent mechanism seen among negativists is their use of displacement, that is, their tendency to shift their anger both precipitously and unconsciously from their true targets (e.g., persons or settings) to those of lesser significance. Thus, through their passive-aggressive maneuvers, negativists will vent their resentments by substitute means, such as acting inept or perplexed or behaving in a forgetful or indolent manner.

Displacement, and the confusion of attitudes and feelings that this creates, is paralleled by a variety of other, often erratic and contradictory mechanisms. Sometimes patients will turn their externally directed, hostile feelings back toward themselves, a mechanism termed by some as introjection, the converse of projection. For example, hatred felt toward others may be directed toward self, taking the form of guilt or self-condemnation. True to form, however, negativists will alternate between introjection and projection. At one time, by projection, these persons will ascribe their destructive impulses to others, accusing the others, unjustly, of being malicious and unkind to them. At other times, by introjection, they will reverse the sequence, accusing themselves of faults that justifiably should be ascribed to others.

Thus, even in the use of unconscious mechanisms, the negativist behaves in an vacillating and contradictory manner. Those at the receiving end of these seemingly bizarre intrapsychic processes cannot help but conclude that the person is behaving in an irrational way and exhibiting uncalled for outbursts and emotional inconsistencies.

Morphologic Organization: Divergent

The pattern of morphologic structures in the negativistic personality exhibits a clear division among its components. Hence, controls and defensive maneuvers are often employed to achieve incompatible goals and purposes. Major conflicts may remain unresolved, therefore, and full psychic cohesion may become impossible to achieve because the fulfillment of one goal or purpose will nullify or undo and reverse another.

Weakness of intrapsychic control would not prove troublesome if the negativist's feelings were calm and consistent, but they are not. Rooted in deep personal ambivalences, negativists experience an undercurrent of perpetual inner turmoil and anxiety. Their equilibrium is unstable. Their inability to anticipate the future as consistent or predictable gives rise to a constant state of insecurity. The frustration and confusion they feel turn readily to anger and resentment. Guilt often emerges and frequently serves to curtail this anger. In short, the actively ambivalent suffers a range of intense and conflicting emotions that, because of weak controls and lack of self-discipline, surge quickly and capriciously to the surface.

Mood/Temperament: Irritable

The personality pattern is best characterized by the rapid succession of changing behaviors and moods. Much of the time, these patients seem restless, unstable, and erratic in their feelings. They are easily nettled, offended by trifles, and readily provoked into being sullen and contrary. There is often a low tolerance for frustration. Many are chronically impatient and irritable and fidgety unless things go their way. There are periods when they vacillate from being distraught and despondent at one moment, to being petty, spiteful, stubborn, and contentious, the next. At other times they may be enthusiastic and cheerful, but this mood is usually short-lived. In no time, they are again disgruntled, critical, and envious. They often begrudge the good fortunes of others and are jealous, quarrelsome, and easily piqued by signs of indifference or minor slights. Emotions are "worn on their sleeves." Many are excitable and impulsive. Others suddenly burst into tears and guilt at the slightest upset. Still others often discharge anger or abuse at the least of provocations. The impulsive, unpredictable, and often explosive reactions of these personalities make it difficult for others to feel comfortable in their presence or to establish rewarding and enduring relationships with them. Although there will be periods of pleasant sociability and warm affection, most acquaintances of these personalities often feel "on edge," waiting for them to display a sullen and hurt look or become obstinate or nasty.

Negativists do not exhibit a distinctive or characteristic level of biological activation. There is reason, however, to believe that they may possess an intrinsic irritability or hyperreactivity to stimulation. They seem easily aroused, testy, highstrung, thin-skinned, and quick-tempered. Minor events provoke and chafe them. They become inflamed and aggrieved by the most incidental and insignificant acts of others. Of course, these hypersensitivities could stem from adverse experiences as well as constitutional proclivities. We may speculate further that these personalities possess some unusual mixture of temperaments. Their behavioral ambivalences may reflect the back-and-forth workings of conflicting dispositions and result in the erratic and contradictory emotional reactions they characteristically display. The reader must note that there is no substantive evidence to warrant placing confidence in these biogenic conjectures.

The negativistic pattern may be more prevalent among women than among men. Although speculative as a thesis, women are subject to hormonal changes during their menstrual cycles that could regularly activate marked, short-lived, and variable moods. Rapid changes in affect such as these may set into motion erratic behaviors and interpersonal reactions that lead to both the acquisition and perpetuation of an ambivalently oriented pattern. Whereas obstreperous and uncontrolled characteristics among men are likely to be judged as a sign of being "tough-minded," these same characteristics among women may be viewed as being "bitchy" and "negativistic." Note again that conjectures such as these are no more than unconfirmed speculations.

PROTOTYPAL PERSONALITY VARIANTS

Despite its recency as a formal designation and its placement in the appendix of DSM-IV, there is good reason to recognize that the disorder has several variants, or different forms of expression, as described in the following sections.

Normal Styles

Popular literature in the 1940s and 1950s spoke frequently of the "neurotic personality." In laypeople's terms, these individuals exhibited features of emotional lability, erraticism, capriciousness, combined with sadness, contrition, guilt-ridden feelings, as well as a smattering of hostility and occasional irritability and negativism. Here was seen a mix of troublesome emotions that served to unsettle not only the individual but those around him or her as well. Although the roots of the concept of a negativistic personality may be partially traced, at least historically, to the syndrome labeled "passive-aggressive," a more complete portrayal can be found in the literature of neurotic personalities.

Oldham and Morris (1990) portray these individuals in several ways, but it is their "mercurial style" that most closely corresponds to the personality disorder of which we speak in this chapter. Ascribed by them to the normal range of the "borderline personality," a not inappropriate deduction, what is seen is in many ways a portrayal of the milder borderline, or what we are referring to here as the negativistic personality. Moving further to the normal range, Oldham and Morris characterize these individuals as follows:

Life is a roller coaster for those with the Mercurial personality style—and they'll insist that you come along for the ride. From the peaks to the valleys, intensity imbues their every breath. Mercurial women and men yearn for experience, and they jump into a new love or lifestyle with both feet, without even a glance backward. No other style . . . is so ardent in its desire to connect with life and

with other people. And no other style is quite so capable of enduring the changes in emotional weather that such a fervidly lived life will bring. (p. 282)

Viewing the normal negativistic pattern as a "discontented" individual, Millon et al. (1994) present a portrayal of this style in the following quote:

These individuals often assert that they have been treated unfairly, that little of what they have done has been appreciated, and that they have been blamed for things they did not do. Opportunities seem not to have worked out well for them, and they "know" that good things do not last. Often resentful of what they see as unfair demands placed on them, they may be disinclined to carry out responsibilities as well as they could. Ambivalent about their lives and relationships, they may get into problematic wrangles and disappointments as they vacillate between acceptance one time and resistance the next. When matters go well, they can be productive and constructively independent-minded, willing to speak out to remedy troublesome issues. (p. 34)

Childhood Syndromes

Several descriptions akin to a childhood negativistic personality disorder have been proposed in recent decades. For example, the Committee on Child Psychiatry of The Group for the Advancement of Psychiatry (1966) has labeled this pattern as "oppositional personality" and "tension-discharge disorder: neurotic personality." Others have employed the title "immature-labile" to characterize these youngsters. In the DSM-III, the term used was "oppositional disorder." Here described was a pattern of disobedience, negativism, and provocative opposition to authority figures. To contrast with the diagnosis of conduct disorder, the basic rights of others or major age-appropriate societal norms or rules are not violated. Important also is the persistence of oppositional behaviors and attitudes even when they are destructive to the interests and well-being of the child or adolescent. Typically, these youngsters do not see themselves as acting in an oppositional manner, but rather see the problem as arising from others who are making unreasonable demands.

The DSM-IV labels these youngsters as evincing an "oppositional defiant disorder." The designation assigns characteristics such as: losing one's temper frequently: arguing with adults: refusing to comply with requests or rules: deliberately annoying others; blaming others for one's own mistakes or misbehaviors; being touchy or irritated by others, often angry and resentful; and frequently spiteful or vindictive.

In 1969, Millon presented a childhood variant of the negativistic pattern under the title "childhood ambiosis." Most notable in these children are their behavioral unpredictability and erratic moods. There are prolonged periods of crankiness and testiness; at times they display a hypermobility and restlessness, a sense of inner trouble and conflict and a tendency to severe temper tantrums for no apparent reason. At other times, these same youngsters become extremely attached and cling to their parents in a manner not unlike that of the symbiotic child; this attachment seems to be born of fear, however, rather than of affection. Not uncommon are phobias and hypochondriacal traits. The impairment may be displayed as early as the end of the first year but is more frequently exhibited between the third and fifth years of life.

Many children display similar immature and negativistic behaviors in mild form; these less severe forms may evolve into a pattern of adolescent or adult active ambivalence, that is, they may develop into negativistic personalities. The label of ambiotic was reserved, however, for children whose impairment occurs in prepuberty and is so severe as to seriously upset the run of normal home life. Moderately severe cases may be categorized as "child-ambiosis: moderate severity" to signify a nonpsychotic yet extremely troublesome pattern.

Central to the impairment is likely to be a history of markedly contradictory parental feelings and attitudes. These may have resulted from conflicting behavioral styles between parents, as is often the case in schismatic families, or from the ambivalence and cyclical moods of a single parent. Rapid shifting between pampering and hostility, parental signals conducive to the "double-bind," and simultaneous exposure to easily manipulated and hostile caretakers, may have inflicted serious emotional damage and served as pathogenic models for these ambiotic children.

Adult Subtypes

In contrast to the DSM-III and DSM-III-R formulations, the passive-aggressive/negativistic personality has been introduced into the appendix of DSM-IV to represent a comprehensive pattern of traits. This wider ranging concept of the disorder will result in part in overlaps and combinations with other personality disorders. As such, we should anticipate finding amalgams and mixtures that display the features of several personalities, a number of which will be described in the following paragraphs.

The Circuitous Negativist

The *circuitous* subtype of the negativistic personality disorder closely corresponds to the classification previously labeled the passive-aggressive personality disorder. Here we see a prominent, if not singular feature, that characterized by a resistance to the expectations of others that is expressed indirectly rather than directly. Despite the passive nature of their resentments, these personalities are grumbling and oppositional, habitually angry at those who demand of them a level of performance that they are deeply unwilling to carry out. As noted, their oppositional behaviors are displayed indirectly, and as the descriptive label suggests, in a circuitous fashion through maneuvers such as procrastination, dawdling, stubbornness, forgetfulness, and a general, but intentional inefficiency.

If we can recall the early DSM history of the passive-aggressive designation, we will remember that this label had been grouped together with the passive-dependent type in the DSM-I. It is the *circuitous* variant of the negativistic (passive-aggressive) personality introduced in this text for the first time, which reflects the alliance that had been proposed in the early manual. The circuitous subtype is largely a psychic blend of both negativistic and dependent traits.

Unwilling or fearful of expressing resentments directly and overtly, circuitous negativists often fulfill the requirements set forth by others, but with a foot-dragging slowness and a bumbling inefficiency. Resistance is usually expressed in areas in which others cannot easily conclude that the negativist is acting in an intentionally oppositional manner and, hence, cannot readily be criticized for this behavior. Despite these frequently successful maneuvers at self-protection, negativists effectively, if unconsciously, sacrifice their own opportunities for achievement. They retaliate against the rejection and depreciation they have felt in the past in a way that ultimately undoes them in the future. They pay a severe personal penalty, therefore, for expressing their anger through a stubborn and oppositional style of behavior. In seeking to undo others, they efficiently undo themselves.

In the main, circuitous negativists are not consciously aware of the problems they have caused; a few do so, however, quite intentionally and consciously. Most resist facing the guilt feelings and interpersonal conflicts they would have to deal with were they not protecting themselves against conscious awareness. Moreover, by maintaining a high degree of repression, their neglectfulness and disagreeable behaviors can remain impervious to efforts to pressure them to change. They become highly defensive with others who wish to expose their maneuvers or seek to force them to do anything they resolutely deny resisting on a conscious or intentional basis.

Most cannot deal with the internal tension or external pressure created by their own indirectly retaliatory behaviors. It is an exhausting process to put on the brakes constantly. On the one hand, they must relate to others who either implore them to function better or are furious at them for their repeated incompetencies and deficiencies. On the other hand, they must control their own intensely conflictual and smoldering impulses that are surging in their unconscious. Some feel dismay over their obvious negligence and failures; most are spared from dealing with these feelings by their successful repressive efforts. Many, however, realize that their lack of success and failure of self-fulfillment result from their own *inactions*, a decision that cannot be undone, nor perhaps even remedied.

The Abrasive Negativist

In contrast to circuitous negativists, who exhibit the struggle between doing what others wish and doing what they wish in an oblique, if not passive, manner, *abrasive negativists* act in an overtly and directly contentious and quarrelsome way. An irascible and derogating personality, to the abrasive negativist everything and anyone serves as a sounding board for discharging inner irritabilities, readily available objects for nagging and assaulting, if not for litigious action. More than merely irritable in a general way, these persons are intentionally abrasive and antagonistic. Not surprisingly, many of these negativists exhibit features usually associated with the sadistic personality prototype.

Abrasive negativists have incessant discords with others that magnify every minor friction into repeated and bitter personal struggles. The following descriptive adjectives may be useful to characterize this abrasive type: contentious, intransigent, fractious, irritable, caustic, debasing, quarrelsome, acrimonious, and corrosive. They also appear to have few qualms and little conscience or remorse about contradicting or derogating even their most intimate associates.

Some abrasive negativists insist that their quarrelsomeness is dedicated to certain high principles; though a kernel of truth may be found in their beliefs, these higher principles invariably correspond to positions they themselves hold, never with those taken by others. Others are unquestionably wrong; they are unquestionably right. Faultfinding and dogmatic, these negativists achieve special delight in contradicting and derogating others. Their pleasure is greatest, not so much in the legitimacy and logic of their arguments, but in their use to demean others and retaliate against them.

Patterns akin to the abrasive personality are seen among adolescents who seek to establish their separateness and individuality by acting in ways that clearly oppose those of their parents. Thus, boys will let their hair grow long, and girls will wear their skirts short. The sons of deeply committed conservatives will favor highly liberal or socialistic values, whereas the teenagers of liberal parents will adopt intensely conservative points of view. But the rebellion of adolescents against the customs and standards of their parents is largely time-limited, a stage of development in which strategies of self-assertion are appropriate. Once a sense of independence is achieved, oppositional teenagers will likely drop this style of behavior, not infrequently reverting to the parental customs they previously sought to overturn. The hostile and opposing manners of abrasive negativists, however, are part of the core of their being. Their knack of belittling and denigrating anyone in the name of whatever principle they happen to espouse is well rehearsed and persistent. Derogation of others is "good for them." Believing that they possess no personal satisfaction in telling people off or in having ulterior motives for doing so, they feel unconstrained, free to say and do anything they please "to set people right."

It is evident to those with whom *abrasive negativists* relate that their pretentions of principled behavior is but a thin veneer. Faced with any opposition, especially from persons they consider of lesser stature than themselves, they will spew forth bitter complaints of how they have been ill treated by others and how unappreciated they have been. As a result of these direct attacks, the deeper origins of their personality style are reactivated. Recriminations and counteractions are refueled. They claim that anything personal they have done to others does not really reflect their character, but is merely a justified reaction to the uncaring treatment to which they have been exposed. They feel justified in what they say and do, with no qualms of conscience nor little remorse for having acted in a most obnoxious way.

The Discontented Negativist

Somewhere between the circuitous and abrasive negativist lies the pattern we have termed the *discontented negativist*. These individuals are embittered, complaining, and pessimistic, but they are neither indirect in their expression of disillusion and displeasure nor are they intentionally contentious and abrasive. These negativists are consummate gripers. They do not assault others in a harsh and brutal fashion; rather they attack under cover, from behind some pretense, one not readily transparent, from which they take piecemeal potshots, evincing niggling and annoying criticisms and complaints. There is a nonplayful teasing, a not-too-subtle dig, and various clever innuendoes. They leave their object of criticism somewhat unprotected, often with no clear response to make. Descriptively, we might note this discontented variant of the negativist is testy, cranky, petty, complaining, vexed, and fretful, one who avoids direct confrontation but is constantly griping with marginal and trivial complaints. Many exhibit features akin to depressive personalities, especially those of the ill-humored subtype, with its sour and grumbling qualities.

Owing to their clever camouflage, these negativists give the impression that they have something worthwhile to say, a recommendation or observation that justifies their comments and criticisms. These complaints, however, essentially reflect their hidden resentments and their deep discontents about life. They rarely provide real solutions to the problems they gripe about. Hence, their apparently worthwhile observations are merely sly ways to discharge their personal dissatisfactions and ultimately intensify problems rather than result in their resolution.

As with the circuitous negativist, the discontented are not so unwise as to risk open battles and confrontations. Rather, they seek to undercut their adversaries, to make them look inept or ridiculous, hence reaffirming the correctness of their own views, without directly endangering themselves or being overwhelmed by the counteractions of others. They have learned to choose a subtle and hidden rather than a frontal attack. They use small darts and stones rather than cannons and tanks. Having a distaste for and a fear of confrontational scenes, they use the cover of minor and tangential slights to avoid being exposed and punished. Whereas the circuitous negativist hides completely behind a veneer of seeming indifference and passivity, the discontented subtype is open, but not confrontational, using small cuts rather than coarse and abrasive actions.

These negativists are malcontents who gripe about everything, find fault with all matters of things, appearing to have legitimate complaints that they seek to bring to someone's attention. As noted, these complaints are merely safe ploys to discharge their deeper discontents, struggles, and conflicts. They act is if they were exasperated with the problems at hand, giving evidence thereby of being a person of goodwill and good intentions who has had to struggle with the inefficiencies and ineptitude of others. Hence, they cannot be criticized for their "occasionally" unpleasant behaviors and attitudes. There is a sense of puzzlement, if not bewilderment, among those who perceptively recognize the underlying anger of the discontented negativist. Should they try to examine the legitimate problems about which the discontented negativist has complained, or should they confront the negativist for being an annoyingly persistent crank and grumbler? The talent of the discontented is that they can quickly turn the tables on those to whom they complain, putting them on the defensive rather than on the offensive. Minor, trivial, and tangential though their charges may be, they are frequently real and justified.

Discontented negativists rarely dump personal accusations on significant others. Rather they complain to them about the awful and terrible characteristics of associates and relatives, accusing them of being incompetent and negativistic, precisely those attributes they possess themselves. Not able to fulfill their own wishes successfully, nor to discharge their resentments directly, they demean the power and stature of competing others and thereby appear to rise up in relative stature. They claim that it is others who have fallen short; they, personally, are blameless and innocent. Now that they have brought problems to the forefront, it is up to others to right the wrongs that have been pointed out. Unable to fulfill their own strivings, nor to settle within themselves the struggle between self and others, they must derogate competitors, often in an avaricious and greedy manner. Desiring the privileged status of self-fulfillment, they seek to be honored by those in power, yet are resentful of those who possess that power. Hence, they are caught again in a conflict between the need for self-expression and their resentment of those who have achieved it. This clash between envying others and being repulsed by them, further intensifies the inner conflict that gave rise to their fundamental problem between self and other.

The Vacillating Negativist

Although the primary characteristic of the *vacillating negativist* is seen among most negativists, the quality of rapid fluctuation from one emotional state or interpersonal attitude to another is particularly notable in this group. These individuals are experienced by others as upsetting and frustrating because of their sharp and frequent reversals of mood and behavior. At times they are affectionate and predictable, as well as interesting and charming. Before one can blink an eye, they may become irritable, oppositional, and disagreeable. The next moment they may act self-assured, decisive, and competent; before one can get accustomed to these behaviors, vacillating negativists may revert to being dependently clinging and childlike. Tantrums are quite common, frequently moving to the foreground, and evidencing their characteristic recalcitrant behaviors and emotional instabilities. They can become almost childlike in other ways, being disagreeably disobedient one moment, and submissively conforming the next. What is most characteristic, however, is their bewildering and enigmatic emotions, their inability to fathom their own capricious and mystifying moods, as well as their subjective wavering and intrapsychic fluctuations.

Vacillating negativists are considered to be difficult to understand by most. Few feel comfortable with them; not only are they enigmatic to themselves, but they are invariably baffling to those with whom they live and work. It is their contradictory qualities and the ease with which they oscillate in their behaviors and attitudes that distinguishes them from "run of the mill" negativists. As described elsewhere in this chapter, negativists are actively ambivalent. Their oscillation is rapid, with extremes of emotion. What makes them difficult to grasp is that their behaviors and emotional states are unpredictable, changing from one moment to the next for no obvious reason. Their ambivalence is not only a matter of public appearance, that is, seen in overt emotions and manifest interpersonal behaviors. Their conflict is also internal. For example, their self-image shifts rapidly, and they disparage themselves one time and act pleased and superior the next.

In many ways, the vacillating negativist is a dilute variant of the borderline personality. However, the ambivalence of the borderline is exhibited in all spheres of expression, between being passive or active, between seeking pleasure or pain, and between being self-focused and other-focused. By contrast, the negativist's struggle is centered largely on the polarity of self versus other. As a result, their intrapsychic ambivalence is more limited in its underlying scope and makeup, resulting in a less severe form of pathology than seen in the borderline.

COMORBID DISORDERS AND SYNDROMES

This section outlines the major Axis I and Axis II disorders that frequently covary with the personality type under discussion. Matters of differential diagnosis will be touched on in the next section.

Axis II Comorbidities

As can be seen from Figure 15.4, the negativistic (NEG) personality is notable by the large number of other personality disorders with which it covaries. Features of irritability and resentment often manifest themselves jointly with the characteristics of several of the major personalities we have previously discussed, and will be elaborating later in the text. More specifically, Figure 15.4 indicates that comorbidities are particularly pronounced with the paranoid (PAR), the borderline (BDL), and the sadistic (SAD) personality patterns. Each of these comorbid types demonstrate features that typify the negativistic, notably their anger and hypersensitivity to signs of displeasure and rejection. However, the traits of the negativist are themselves contradictory; hence, certain features may be found to covary with disorders that are substantially different from the three preceding types. For example, there are negativistic features that overlap with the depressive (DPS), the avoidant (AVD) and the masochistic (MAS) personality patterns. Here we see the covariance with the negativist's self-rejecting and guilt-ridden psychic characteristics.

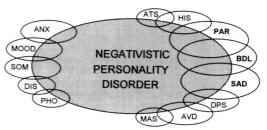

Figure 15.4 Comorbidity between negativistic personality disorder and other DSM Axis I and Axis II disorders.

And, once more, at the opposite end of the scale, we see strong negativistic combinations with the histrionic (HIS) and the antisocial (ATS) personalities.

Axis I Comorbidities

The negativistic (NEG) personality displays a wide range of associated Axis I syndromes. Only the more prominent of these will be discussed in the following paragraphs.

Anxiety Syndromes (ANX). Negativistic personalities experience prolonged and *generalized anxiety* disorders. In contrast to compulsive personalities, their passive-ambivalent counterparts, their discomfort and tension are exhibited openly and are utilized rather commonly as a means of either upsetting others or soliciting their attention and nurture. Which of these two instrumental aims takes precedence depends on whether the obedient-dependent or the defiant-independent facet of their ambivalence comes to the fore. Typically, negativists color their apprehensions with depressive complaints, usually to the effect that others misunderstand them and that life has been full of disappointments. These complaints not only crystallize and vent their tensions but are also subtle forms of expressing anger and resentment. Most commonly, negativists discharge their tensions in brief and frequent doses, thereby decreasing the likelihood of a significant, cumulative buildup and a consequent massive outburst. It is only when these negativistic persons are unable to discharge their inner anguish and hostile impulses that a full-blown *panic* attack may be precipitated. Having learned to utilize anxiety as a means of subtle aggression or as a way of gaining attention and nurture, some negativists claim to be experiencing anxiety when they may not be genuinely feeling it.

Phobic Syndromes (PHO). As indicated, these personalities are more open about discharging their feelings than most other personality types. This ready and diffuse discharge of emotion has its self-defeating side. By connecting anxieties freely to any and all aspects of their life, they increase the likelihood that many formerly innocuous experiences and events will be fused with phobic qualities. These phobic symptoms may then be utilized for secondary gains, being employed to attract attention and to control or manipulate the lives of others.

Somatoform Disorders (SOM). These negativistic personalities often display *hypochondriacal* and *somatization* symptoms in conjunction with frequent "psychosomatic disorders." Discontent, irritable, and fractious, they often use physical complaints as a weak disguise for hostile impulses, a veil to cloak their deeply felt anger and resentment. Feelings of retribution for past frustrations often underlie the excessive demands they make for special treatment. They seek not only to create guilt in others but to control the lives of family members and to cause them grief and financial cost. Although a significant proportion of these personalities were subjected in childhood to inconsistent parental treatment, most learned that they could evoke reliable parental attention and support when they were ill or complained of illness. As a consequence, when they need care and nurture, they may revert back to the ploy of physical complaints. Some may be sufficiently aware of the maneuvers they engage in so as to be justly diagnosed as exhibiting a *factitious disorder.* Others, less successful in evoking the care and sympathy they desire, have learned to nurture themselves, that is, to tend symbolically to their own bodily needs. Disillusioned by parental disinterest or inconsistency, these patients have learned to provide a hypochondriacal ministering to themselves, ensuring thereby a consistency in self-sympathy and self-gratification that can be obtained from no one else.

Because these personalities express their feelings rather openly and directly, tension builds up more slowly than in their passive ambivalent counterpart, the compulsive personality. Moreover, when emotional tension is discharged, it is less likely to be camouflaged. Thus, *conversion symptoms* among negativists are exhibited in fleeting or transitory forms such as intestinal spasms, facial tics, or laryngitis. Symptoms of this type often signify sporadic efforts to control anger and resentment. "Trained" to use physical ailments as instruments for manipulating others, their complaints of vague sensations and pains are designed in part to draw attention and nurturance, as well as to create concern and guilt in others.

Among the principal origins of psychosomatic disorders (termed "psychological factors affecting medical conditions" in the DSM) are repetitive upsets of the body's homeostatic balance and chronic failures to dissipate physiological tension. These problems arise most frequently in patients who repeatedly find themselves in unresolvable conflict situations, such as when the discharge of tensions associated with one side of a conflict only increases the tensions engendered by the other side. This state of affairs describes the typical experience of ambivalent personalities. Both compulsives and negativists are trapped between acquiescent dependency, on the one hand, and hostile or assertive independence, on the other. When they submit or acquiesce to the wishes of others, they experience resentment and anger for having allowed themselves to be "weak" and having given up their independence. Conversely, if they are defiant and assert their independence, they experience anxiety for having endangered their tenuous dependency security. Although negativists do periodically discharge both sources of tension, their repetitive and chronically irritable behaviors reactivate these troublesome conflicts time and again. As a consequence, they often generate and accumulate tension faster than they can dissipate it. Moreover, because of their constantly fretful behaviors, they subject their bodies repeatedly to vacillations in mood and emotion. As they swing from one intense feeling to another, their homeostatic equilibrium, so necessary for proper physiological functioning, is thrown off balance again and again. Not only do they experience an excess of chronic tension, then, but their systems rarely settle down into a smooth and regularized pattern. By keeping their bodies churning, they set themselves up for repeated bouts of psychosomatic discomfort.

Dissociative Syndromes (DIS). Accustomed to venting their contrary feelings quite directly, negativists exhibit dissociative symptoms only if they feel unduly restrained, shamed, or fearful of severe condemnation. Even under these circumstances, the frequency of dissociative disorders is low. Temper tantrums, which approach frenzied states in their overt appearance, are more common. In these episodes, however, the patient rarely loses conscious awareness and is usually able to recall the events that transpired.

Mood Syndromes (MOOD). These disorders are quite common among negativistic personalities, ranging from occasional severe depressive episodes to more chronic forms of *dysthymic disorder.* Similarly, *cyclothymic disorders* with brief manic periods are not uncommon. Most frequently, negativistic personalities display an agitated form of dysphoria. They characteristically vacillate between anxious futility, despair,

and self-deprecation, on the one hand; and a bitter discontent and demanding irritability with friends and relatives, on the other. Accustomed to the direct ventilation of feelings, these personalities restrain their anger and turn it inward only when they fear its expression will result in severe humiliation or rejection. There is a great struggle between acting out defiantly and curtailing resentments. They exhibit as grumbling and sour a disaffection with themselves as they do with others. Moody complaints and generalized pessimism pervade the air. These attitudes serve as a vehicle of tension discharge, relieving them periodically of mounting inner- and outer-directed anger. Not to be overlooked also is that sour moods and complaints often intimidate and make others feel guilty. These maneuvers enable the negativist to gain a measure of retribution for past disappointments by making life miserable for others.

DIFFERENTIAL DIAGNOSES

Conceived in the broad sense in which the negativistic personality is formulated here, the traits composing this pattern share innumerable features with other symptom and personality disorders. Thus, the moodiness of this personality is a central feature of most affective disorders; the quick-tempered irritability and the behavioral contrariness that characterize negativists are also found among antisocial types; the self-discontent and interpersonal ambivalence of this pattern are similar to the borderline, though in less intense form: their feelings of discouragement and disappointment are matched by the derogation that typify dependent personalities. In fact, it is the variegated, complex, inconstant, and erratic quality that is so unusual about the negativist. With exception of the borderline, it alone among the personality disorders possesses the entire mixture of traits seen more consistently and with less diversity among other types. This very heterogeneity and changeability are among its distinguishing hallmarks.

As far as Axis I disorders are concerned, the characteristic irregularity of mood and behavior of the negativist may require differentiation from the DSM-IV *cyclothymic disorder.* Both are "chronic," display either alternate or intermixed periods of intense affect that fail to approach psychotic proportions, and rarely, if ever, exhibit features such as delusions, hallucinations, or incoherence. There are two essential distinctions: first, the lifelong and consistent character of the personality pattern (negativistic), which differs from the episodic and discontinuous nature of the disorder (cyclothymic); and second, the persistently negative tone of the negativist, as contrasted to the periodic manic or euphoric phases of the cyclothymic.

A distinction may also be needed to differentiate the negativist's pessimistic and negative tone from that seen in the DSM-IV *dysthymic disorder*, previously termed the "depressive neurosis." Both share a measure of chronicity, but the personality pattern is both more consistent and of greater duration. More significantly, the negativist exhibits a persistent resentful quality in interpersonal relations, a bitter, complaining, and quarrelsome irritability that is not evident in the down-in-the-dumps, more melancholic, and sad quality seen in the dysthymic syndrome. As encouraged in the multiaxial DSM-IV format, concurrent diagnoses of Axis I and Axis II syndromes should be recorded if appropriate.

Distinctions between the negativistic personality and other Axis II disorders are also worthy of brief note. Most significant are difficulties in differentiating the negativist from the *borderline*. The borderline is functionally a more severe and a more structurally defective character type. Notable among these personality disorders is the extreme variability that can be observed in the affective, cognitive, and interpersonal spheres. In many ways, negativists may be seen as a dilute or less troubled variant of the borderline, in which the primary realm of ambivalence and inconsistency lies essentially in their problematic relationships with others. Owing to their more limited areas of difficulty, negativistic personalities do not evince cognitive extremes, rapid shifts in affectivity, nor dysfunctional conflicts in their behaviors.

As noted earlier, negativists and *sadists* exhibit a common disposition toward anger and resentment. However, sadists are more vicious and brutal, manifesting their hostility intensely and persistently. Negativists are more indirect and circuitous in their angry expressions.

There are notable similarities between *depressive* personalities and negativists. However, negativists usually direct their resentment against others, blaming them for their experience of discontent and disappointment. By contrast, depressives typically derogate themselves, identifying their own deficiencies and failures as the source of their unhappiness.

Some *paranoids* are more severe variants of the negativistic personality, hence accounting for their apparent comorbidity and problems of differential diagnosis. At the paranoid level, however, there is a more active manifestation of suspiciousness, with minidelusional beliefs regarding the malice and betrayal of others. Negativists are more forthright in their suspiciousness; they voice their beliefs openly, as opposed to paranoids, who ruminate about them, working over their fears and suspicions in an internal monologue.

ASSESSING THE NEGATIVIST: A CASE STUDY

Clinical signs associated with this personality disorder on the Rorschach, TAT, and MMPI are noted next. These will be followed by a presentation of a case study of a negativistic (passive-aggressive) personality, an associated MCMI-III profile, and an interpretive report.

The Rorschach is likely to reflect the irritability and ambivalence of this personality by a high number of harsh texture and flagrant color responses, a reasonable proportion of which will evidence only a modest degree of psychic control (e.g., CF and cF). Not untypically, the level of white-space responses may be greater than average. The ambivalence of these individuals regarding their opposing inclinations may show up in contrasting content responses, some characterized by passive child or animal responses, intermingled with aggressive and argumentative responses such as fire fighting, explosions, and the like. Location responses are likely to show prominent D proportions. Sequencing is likely to be unsystematic, if not illogical, vacillating within cards from passivity to activity and from sorrowfulness to anger.

TAT stories likewise reflect the discordance experienced by the negativist, especially between their doing what others want versus what they wish to do themselves. It may be difficult to follow themes that evoke this patient's deeper ambivalences. For example, on Card 1, the youngster in the story may voice his sense of responsibility in taking up the violin, owing to his parents' desire that he do so; after reflection and internal discomfort, the same youngster may decide rather precipitously to break the violin by smashing it against his parents' bedposts, but then feel very guilty for having done so. It is this back-and-forth element that should be looked for to identify the mixed and contradictory feelings that typify the negativist.

Several profile combinations may be seen with the negativistic personality on the MMPI. A common pattern is a high 3-4 code, in which both a hesitant and socially desirable quality suggested by the high Scale 3 conflicts with the aggressive inclinations associated with a high Scale 4. An additional high score on Scale 9 suggests that the energy of the individual is likely to take the form of overtly hostile and aggressive characteristics. Where Scales 6 and 8 are also present, we are likely to see a severely disturbed variant of the negativistic pattern. Similarly severe in its implications would be an elevated Scale 2. The particular configuration of high point codes on the MMPI may be useful in differentiating among the negativistic subtypes described previously.

CASE 15.1

Ann B., 31, Married, Four Children

For many years Ann had periodic spells of fatigue, backaches, and a variety of discomforting gastrointestinal ailments. These recurred recently and, as in the past, no physical basis for her complaints could be established. In his interviews with her, Ann's physician concluded that there was sufficient evidence in her background to justify recommending psychiatric evaluation, with the thought of hospitalization.

In his report, her physician commented that Ann had withdrawn from her husband sexually and implored him to seek a new job in another community although he was content and successful in his present position. She disliked the neighborhood in which they lived and had become increasingly alienated from their friends in past months. The physician noted that a similar sequence of events had occurred twice previously, resulting in her husband's decision to find new employment as a means of placating his wife. This time Ann's husband was "getting fed up" with her complaints, her crying, her sexual rebuffs, her anger, and her inability to remain on friendly terms with people. He simply did not want to "pick up and move again, just to have the whole damn thing start all over."

When Ann first was seen by her present therapist, she appeared depressed, contrite, and self-condemning; she knew that the physical problems she had been experiencing were psychosomatic, that she caused difficulties for her husband, that she precipitated complications with their friends, and that she periodically became very depressed, if not "crazy." This self-deprecation did not last

long; almost immediately after placing the burden of responsibility on her own shoulders, she reversed her course, and began to complain about her husband, her children, her parents, her friends, her neighborhood, and so on. Once she spilled out her hostility toward everyone and everything, she recanted, became conscience-smitten and self-accusing again.

The first item to which Ann referred when discussing her past was the fact that she was an unwanted child, that her parents had to marry to make her birth "legitimate." Her parents remained married, though it was a "living hell much of my life." A second girl was born two years after Ann, and a third child, this time a boy, five years thereafter. In the first two years of life, Ann was "clung to" by her mother, receiving a superabundance of mother's love and attention. "It seems as if my mother and I must have stuck together to protect ourselves from my father." Apparently, parental bickering characterized home life from the first day of their marriage; Ann's father remained antagonistic to her from the very beginning, since Ann represented for him the cause of his misery.

The protection and affection that Ann received from her mother in her first two years was substantially reduced with the advent of her sister's birth: Mother's attention turned to the new infant and Ann felt abandoned and vulnerable. She recalled the next several years as ones in which she tried desperately to please her mother, to distract her from her sister and recapture her affection and protection. This "worked at times." But as often as not, Ann's mother was annoyed with her for demanding more than she was able to provide.

By the time the third child appeared on the scene, parental conflicts were especially acute, and Ann was all the more demanding of support and attention as a means of assuaging her increased anxieties. It was not long thereafter that she began to hear the same comment from her mother that she had heard all too often from her father: "You're the cause of this miserable marriage." Mother would feel pangs of guilt following these outbursts, and would bend over backward for brief periods to be kind and affectionate. But these moments of affection and love were infrequent; more common were long periods of rejection or indifference.

Ann never was sure what her mother's attitude would be toward her, nor what she could do to elicit her love and attention. Thus, at times when she attempted to be helpful, she gained her mother's appreciation and affection; at other times when mother felt tired, distraught, or preoccupied with her own problems, the same behavior would evoke hostile criticism.

Ann hated her sister "with a vengeance" but feared to express this hostility most of the time. Every now and then, as she put it, she would "let go," tease her unmercifully, or physically attack her. Rather interestingly, following these assaults, Ann would "feel terrible" and be contrite, becoming nurturant and protective of her sister. She quickly recognized in therapy that her behavior with her sister paralleled that of her mother. And, in time, Ann observed that this vacillating and ambivalent pattern served as the prototype for her relationships with most people.

Until college, Ann's peer relationships were not unusual, although she reported never having been a member of the "in group"; she had her share of friends nevertheless. Ann attended an all-girls college where she frequently experienced problems in social relationships. She had a sequence of ill-fated friendships; for example, during her first two years, she had four different roommates. Typically, Ann would become "very close" to her roommate; after a short period, usually less than a semester, she would become disillusioned with her friend, noting faults and finding her disloyal; eventually, Ann would become "blue," then "nasty" and hostile.

When Ann met her future husband, during the first semester of her junior year, she decided to move into a single room in her dormitory; though not a total isolate, she rarely mingled socially with the other girls. The courtship period with her boyfriend had its trying moments, Ann was inordinately jealous of his friends, and feared that he would leave her. Quite often, she would threaten to break off the romance so as not to be hurt should it progress further—this threat served to "bring him back" to her.

Ann's marriage has mirrored many of the elements she experienced and observed in her childhood. She is submissive and affectionate, then sickly, demanding, and intimidating of her husband—a pattern not unlike she saw her mother use to control her father. Ann's husband spent much of his energies trying to placate her but "Ann is never content." During the 9 years of their marriage, she seemed satisfied only when they first moved to a new location. But these "bright periods" dimmed quickly, and the same old difficulties emerged again. This time, however, her husband would have "none of this," and refused to budge. Ann again began to experience her physical symptoms, to withdraw affection, to vent anger and vacillate in her moods.

For the first time, Ann has shown bipolar features, as evidenced in rapid shifts between manic excitement and depressive withdrawal; similarly, aspects of her thought processes appear to have become increasingly disorganized. She has also become suspicious of the motives of her husband, as well as evidencing a growing pattern of borderline behaviors. Owing to her apparent need to disclose her past as fully as possible, she may be overdramatizing her emotional difficulties, signifying a "cry for help."

The MCMI-III profile (Figure 15.5) and interpretive statements of this personality pattern follow.

INTERPRETIVE SUMMARY

The MCMI-III profile of this woman suggests her marked dependency needs, deep and variable moods, and impulsive, angry outbursts. She may anxiously seek reassurance from others and is especially vulnerable to fear of separation from those who provide support, despite her frequent attempts to undo their efforts to be helpful. Dependency fears may compel her to be alternately overly compliant, profoundly gloomy, and irrationally argumentative and negativistic. Almost seeking to court undeserved blame and criticism, she may appear to find circumstances to anchor her feeling that she deserves to suffer.

She strives at times to be submissive and cooperative, but her behavior has become increasingly unpredictable, irritable, and pessimistic. She often seeks to induce guilt in others for failing her, as she sees it. Repeatedly struggling to express attitudes contrary to her feelings, she may exhibit conflicting emotions simultaneously toward others and herself, most notably love, rage, and guilt. Also notable may be her confusion over her self-image, her highly variable energy levels, easy fatigability, and her irregular sleep-wake cycle.

She is particularly sensitive to external pressure and demands, and she may vacillate between being socially agreeable, sullen, self-pitying, irritably aggressive, and contrite. She may make irrational and bitter complaints about the lack of care expressed by others and about being treated unfairly. This behavior keeps others on edge, never knowing if she

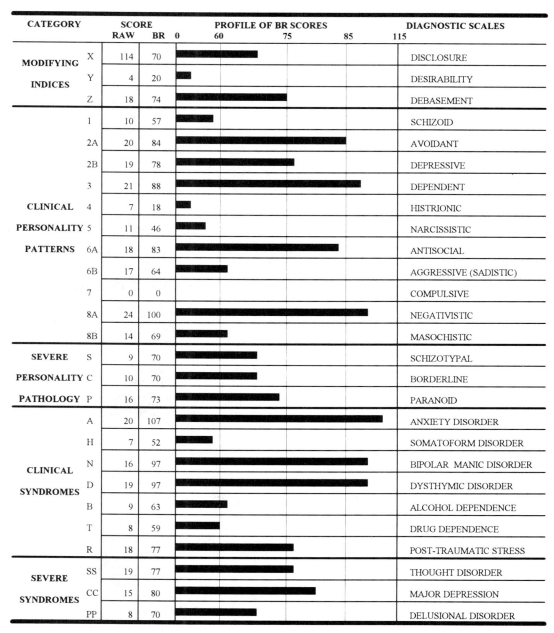

CATEGORY		SCORE		PROFILE OF BR SCORES				DIAGNOSTIC SCALES
		RAW	BR	0 60 75 85 115				
MODIFYING INDICES	X	114	70					DISCLOSURE
	Y	4	20					DESIRABILITY
	Z	18	74					DEBASEMENT
CLINICAL PERSONALITY PATTERNS	1	10	57					SCHIZOID
	2A	20	84					AVOIDANT
	2B	19	78					DEPRESSIVE
	3	21	88					DEPENDENT
	4	7	18					HISTRIONIC
	5	11	46					NARCISSISTIC
	6A	18	83					ANTISOCIAL
	6B	17	64					AGGRESSIVE (SADISTIC)
	7	0	0					COMPULSIVE
	8A	24	100					NEGATIVISTIC
	8B	14	69					MASOCHISTIC
SEVERE PERSONALITY PATHOLOGY	S	9	70					SCHIZOTYPAL
	C	10	70					BORDERLINE
	P	16	73					PARANOID
CLINICAL SYNDROMES	A	20	107					ANXIETY DISORDER
	H	7	52					SOMATOFORM DISORDER
	N	16	97					BIPOLAR MANIC DISORDER
	D	19	97					DYSTHYMIC DISORDER
	B	9	63					ALCOHOL DEPENDENCE
	T	8	59					DRUG DEPENDENCE
	R	18	77					POST-TRAUMATIC STRESS
SEVERE SYNDROMES	SS	19	77					THOUGHT DISORDER
	CC	15	80					MAJOR DEPRESSION
	PP	8	70					DELUSIONAL DISORDER

Figure 15.5   Millon Clinical Multiaxial Inventory-III.

will react to them in a cooperative or a sulky manner. Although she may make efforts to be obliging and submissive to others, she has learned to anticipate disillusioning relationships, and she often creates the expected disappointment by constantly questioning and doubting the genuine interest and support shown by others. Self-destructive acts and suicidal gestures may be employed to gain attention. These irritable testing maneuvers may exasperate and alienate those on whom she depends. When threatened by separation and disapproval, she may express guilt, remorse, and self-condemnation in the hope of regaining support, reassurance, and sympathy.

Beyond her helplessness and clinging behavior, she may exhibit an irritable argumentativeness. Recognizing that others may have grown weary of this behavior, she may alternate between voicing gloomy self-deprecation, being apologetic and repentant, and being petulant and bitter. A struggle between dependent acquiescence and assertive independence constantly intrudes into most relationships. Her inability to regulate her emotional controls, her feeling of being misunderstood, and her erratic moodiness contribute to innumerable wrangles and conflicts with others and to persistent tension, resentfulness, and depression.

Testy and demanding, this woman evinces an agitated, major depression that can be noted by her daily moodiness and vacillation. She is likely to display a rapidly shifting mix of disparaging comments about herself, anxiously expressed suicidal thoughts, and outbursts of bitter resentment interwoven with a demanding irritability toward others. Feeling trapped by constraints imposed by her circumstances and upset by emotions and thoughts she can neither understand nor control, she has turned her reservoir of anger inward, periodically voicing severe self-recrimination and self-loathing. These signs of contrition may serve to induce guilt in others, an effective manipulation in which she can give a measure of retribution without further jeopardizing what she sees as her currently precarious, if not hopeless, situation.

Failing to keep deep and powerful sources of inner conflict from overwhelming her controls, this characteristically difficult and conflicted woman may be experiencing the clinical signs of an anxiety disorder. She is unable to rid herself of preoccupations with her tension, fearful presentiments, recurring headaches, fatigue, and insomnia, and she is upset by their uncharacteristic presence in her life. Feeling at the mercy of unknown and upsetting forces that seem to well up within her, she is at a loss as to how to counteract them, but she may exploit them to manipulate others or to complain at great length.

Related to but beyond her characteristic level of emotional responsivity, this woman appears to have been confronted with an event or events in which she was exposed to a severe threat to her life, a traumatic experience that precipitated intense fear or horror on her part. Currently the residuals of this event appear to be persistently reexperienced with recurrent and distressing recollections, such as in cues that resemble or symbolize an aspect of the traumatic event. Where possible, she seeks to avoid such cues and recollections. Where they cannot be anticipated and actively avoided, as in dreams or nightmares, she may become terrified, exhibiting a number of symptoms of intense anxiety. Other signs of distress might include difficulty falling asleep, outbursts of anger, panic attacks, hypervigilance, exaggerated startle response, or a subjective sense of numbing and detachment.

PATHOGENIC DEVELOPMENTAL BACKGROUND

As noted in earlier chapters, under this topic a number of plausible etiologic hypotheses are proposed for the personality under study. The reader should be well conditioned by now to the highly conjectural nature of several of the speculations posited.

HYPOTHESIZED BIOGENIC FACTORS

As mentioned several times earlier, the role of biogenic influences in pathological personality development can only be speculated at this time. We know that these factors contribute a not insignificant share to the unfolding of behavioral traits, but we are far short of possessing the requisite data either for accepting this assertion with conviction, or specifying the character of the presumed biogenic effects. Nevertheless, as before, we will enumerate and describe briefly several plausible biogenic hypotheses.

Heredity

Many clinical features of the negativistic personality may be observed in common among family members. No doubt, this commonality can arise entirely from the effects of learning. But an equally reasonable thesis is that the biophysical substrate for affective irritability and for a sullen, peevish and testy temperament may be transmitted by genetic mechanisms.

Irregular Infantile Reaction Pattern

Infants whose behaviors and moods vary unpredictably may develop rather normal and stable patterns as they mature. The possibility arises, however, that a disproportionately high number of such "difficult to schedule" infants will continue to exhibit a "biologically erratic" pattern throughout their lives, thereby disposing them to develop the features of the negativistic.

Fretful and "nervous" youngsters are good candidates for the negativistic pattern also because they are likely to provoke bewilderment, confusion, and vacillation in parental training methods. Such "irregular" children may set into motion erratic and contradictory reactions from their parents which then serve, in circular fashion, to reinforce their initial tendency to be spasmodic and variable.

Uneven Maturation

Children who mature in an unbalanced progression, or at an uneven rate, are more likely to evoke inconsistent reactions from their parents than normally developing children. Thus, very bright but emotionally immature youngsters may precipitate anger in response to the childish dimensions of their behavior, but commendation in response to the cleverness displayed while behaving childishly. Such children will be confused whether to continue or to inhibit their behavior because it prompted contradictory reactions. Additionally, such children may possess mature desires and aspirations but lack the equipment to achieve these goals; this can lead only to feelings of discontent and disappointment, features associated with the negativistic pattern.

Neurological and Physiochemical Characteristics

Conceivably, the affective excitability of the negativistic personality may arise in part from a high level of reticular activity or a dominance of the sympathetic division of the autonomic nervous system.

Equally speculative, but plausible, are hypotheses that implicate segments of the limbic system. Anatomically dense or well-branched centers subserving several different, and irreconcilable, emotions such as anger, sadness, and fear could account for the ambivalent behavioral proclivities seen in this pattern. Of interest in this regard is the recently uncovered "ambivalence" center in the limbic region; hypotheses concerning this area may also be considered as plausible.

Negativistic personalities develop with somewhat greater frequency among women than men. Conceivably, many negativistic women may be subject to extreme hormonal changes during their menstrual cycles, thereby precipitating marked, short-lived, and variable moods. Such rapid mood changes may set into motion sequences of erratic behavior and associated interpersonal reactions conducive to the acquisition and perpetuation of this pattern. As noted in prior paragraphs, obstreperous traits among men are judged as "tough-mindedness," whereas these same characteristics among women may be spoken of as "bitchy" and "negativistic." Once again, keep in mind that these conjectures are merely unconfirmed speculations.

CHARACTERISTIC EXPERIENTIAL HISTORY

Biogenic influences may dispose the individual to certain forms of behavior, but the ultimate form and pattern we observe clinically is largely a product of the environmental influences to which the person was exposed. These influences will be differentiated for pedagogical purposes, but they often coexist in individual cases.

Parental Inconsistency

The central role of inconsistent parental attitudes and contradictory training methods in the development of the negativistic personality has been referred to repeatedly in our discussions. Although every child experiences some degree of parental inconstancy, negativistic youngsters are likely to have been exposed to appreciably more than their share. Their parents may have swayed from hostility and rejection at one time, to affection and love another; and this erratic pattern has probably been capricious, frequent, pronounced, and lifelong.

As a consequence, children may develop a variety of pervasive and deeply ingrained conflicts such as trust versus mistrust, competence versus doubt and initiative versus guilt and fear. Their self-concept will be composed of contradictory appraisals; every judgment they make of themselves will be matched by an opposing one; Am I good or am I bad? Am I competent or am I incompetent? Every course of behavior will have its positive and its negative side. Thus, no matter what these children do or think, they will experience a contrary inclination or value by which to judge it.

Internal ambivalence is paralleled by the inability to gauge what they can expect from their environment. How can they be sure that things are going well? Have they not experienced capricious hostility and criticism in the past when things appeared to be going well? Their plight is terribly bewildering. Unlike the avoidant and antisocial personalities, who can predict their fate, who "know" they will consistently experience humiliation or hostility, negativists are unable to predict what the future will bring. At any moment, and for no apparent reason, they may receive the kindness and support they crave; equally possible, and for equally unfathomable reasons, they may be the recipient of hostility and rejection. They are in a bind; they have no way of knowing which course of action on their part will bring relief; they have not learned how to predict whether hostility or compliance will prove instrumentally more effective. They vacillate, feeling hostility, guilt, compliance, assertion and so on, shifting erratically and impulsively from one futile action to another.

Unable to predict what kinds of reactions their behavior will elicit and having learned no way of reliably anticipating whether parents will be critical or affectionate, these children take nothing for granted; they must be ready for hostility when most people would expect commendation; they must assume they will experience humiliation when most would anticipate reward. They remain eternally "on edge," in a steady state of tension and alertness. Keyed up in this manner, their emotions build up and they become raw to the touch, overready to react explosively and erratically to the slightest provocation.

We may summarize the effects of parental inconsistency as follows. First, children learn vicariously to imitate the erratic and capricious behavior of their parents. Second, children fail to learn what "pays off" instrumentally; they never acquire a reliable strategy that achieves the desired reinforcements. Third, children internalize a series of conflicting attitudes toward self and others; for example, they do not know whether they are competent or incompetent; they are unsure whether they love or hate those upon whom he depends. Fourth, unable to predict the consequences of their behaviors, these children get "tied up in emotional knots," and behave irrationally and impulsively.

Contradictory Family Communications

Closely akin to parental inconsistency are patterns of intrafamilial communication that transmit simultaneous incompatible messages. Such families often present a facade of pseudomutuality that serves both to cloak and to control hidden resentments and antagonisms. This may be illustrated by parents who, although smiling and saying, "Yes, dear," convey through their facial expression and overly sweet tone of voice that they mean, "No, you

miserable child." Overt expressions of concern and affection may be disqualified or negated in various subtle and devious ways. A parent may verbally assert his love for the child, and thereby invite the child to demonstrate reciprocal affection, but the parent always may find some feeble excuse to forestall or rebuff the affectionate response.

These children constantly are forced into what are termed approach-avoidance conflicts. Furthermore, they never are sure what their parents really desire, and no matter what course they take, they find that they cannot do right. This latter form of entrapment has been referred to as a double-bind; thus, children are unable not only to find a clear direction for their behavior but to extricate themselves from the irreconcilable demands that have been made of him. The double-bind difficulty is often compounded because the contradictions in the parental message are subtle or concealed. Thus, children cannot readily accuse their parents of failing to mean what they overtly say since the evidence for such accusations is rather tenuous; moreover, the consequences of making an accusation of parental dishonesty or deception may be rather severe. Unable to discriminate, and fearful of misinterpreting, the intent of these communications, children become anxious, and may learn to become ambivalent in their thinking and erratic in their own behavior.

Family Schisms

Paradoxical and contradictory parental behaviors often are found in "schismatic" families, that is, in families where the parents are manifestly in conflict with each other. Here, there is constant bickering, and an undermining of one parent by the other through disqualifying and contradicting statements. Children raised in this setting not only suffer the constant threat of family dissolution, but, in addition, often are forced to serve as mediators to moderate tensions generated by the parents. These children constantly switch sides and divide their loyalties; they cannot simply be themselves for they must shift their attitudes and emotions to satisfy changing and antagonistic parental desires and expectations. The different roles they must assume to placate parents and to salvage a measure of family stability are markedly divergent; as long as the parents remain at odds, children must persist with behavior and thoughts that are intrinsically irreconcilable.

This state of affairs prevents children from identifying consistently with one parent; as a consequence, they end up modeling themselves after two intrinsically antagonistic figures. Such children form opposing sets of attitudes, emotions, and behaviors. As is evident, schismatic families are perfect training grounds for the development of an ambivalent pattern.

Guilt and Anxiety Training

Schismatic families generate considerable anxiety and guilt on the part of children. They are in constant dread that the affections and supports of family life will dissolve; they are made to feel guilty for their contribution to family difficulties and cannot help but feel dishonest and disloyal when they are forced to ally themselves first with one parent and then the other.

But guilt and anxiety, internal experiences that lead to hesitations in behavior and ambivalences in thought and feeling, can be produced in non-schismatic families. Children may learn these constraints through direct parental tuition. They may be taught to develop a "conscience" by which they must gauge the "correctness" of their behaviors and thoughts. The rationale and methods of inculcating such feelings were outlined in our discussion of the compulsive pattern; they are similar in most respects to that employed by the parents of the actively ambivalent child. But there is one significant difference. The compulsive child is likely to have been taught guilt in a consistent and unyielding manner, whereas the negativistic child experiences such training more irregularly. Thus, the guilt of the negativist is less firmly ingrained and it often fails to serve its control function; the child gives in to impulses more frequently than does the compulsive. As a consequence, he or she exhibits behavioral ambivalence, a vacillation between acting out one moment, and feeling guilty the next.

Sibling Rivalry

Many negativists felt that they had been "replaced" by a younger sibling and that their parents' affections were withdrawn and redirected to a newborn child. Of course, such sibling relationships are experienced by many children, and what distinguishes the negativist in this regard is not clear. It would be plausible to hypothesize that these youngsters experienced a sharp and marked change between their initial feeling of parental security and its sudden termination upon the birth of the newborn child. It is not uncommon for mothers to become unusually preoccupied and attached to their "babies," at the expense of their older children. A child who previously experienced a deep bond with his or her mother may become severely upset upon the advent of a new child. This event may prove so distressing that it leads to a lifelong expectation that affection and security are not durable and that one must anticipate losing tomorrow what seemed safe and solid today.

How do these events and attitudes evolve into a negativistic pattern? The shock and pain of being "replaced" is likely to generate intense anxieties and strong feelings of jealousy and resentment. However, children will hesitate venting these latter feelings for fear of provoking more of the parental rejection and withdrawal they have experienced; not infrequently, these children are made to feel guilty for their envious feelings and hostile outbursts. As a consequence, "replaced" youngsters may learn to restrain their emotions when parents are present, but be "sneaky" and physically aggressive when parents are absent. This erraticism in relating to the sibling may become a prototype for later relationships. We see this typical sequence of the negativist in many cases; a friendly, even overly enthusiastic, early relationship with others is followed by disappointment and hard feelings. Such youngsters may become attached to a series of friends, only to find each of them "unlikable and disloyal" in short order; and as they move from one community to the next over the course of their lives, their early enthusiasms and friendships quickly deteriorate into disillusionments and neighborhood animosities.

Adding further to their feelings of ambivalence is that these children often are told how rewarding it is to "be a big sister"; however, the youngster cannot help but observe that "baby" gets all of mother's attention and affection. Thus, the child faces another bind: Should she desire to grow up and get the dubious rewards and powers of an older child or should she try to recapture the idyllic state of infancy? This, too, may set the stage for future ambivalent behaviors: assertive independence at one period and clinging dependency at the next.

SELF-PERPETUATION PROCESSES

Most pathological personalities feel some measure of stability and self-content with the lifestyle they have acquired. This is not typical among negativistic personalities. Their feelings, attitudes, and behaviors allow for little internal equilibrium or consistent external gratification. They frequently live in a phenomenological state of discontent and self-dissatisfaction. Their irritability provokes them to behave unpredictably and to appear restless, sullen, and obstructive much of the time. Not only do they suffer an ever-present sense of inner turmoil, but they act out their discontent for all to see.

The following sections describe three aspects of the negativistic style that perpetuate and intensify the troublesome behaviors and attitudes acquired in childhood.

Negativistic and Unpredictable Behaviors

Acting erratically, vacillating from one course to another, is a sheer waste of energy. By attempting to achieve incompatible goals, these persons scatter their efforts and dilute their effectiveness. Caught in their own crosscurrents, they cannot commit themselves to one clear direction; they swing indecisively back and forth, performing ineffectually and experiencing a sense of paralyzing inertia or exhaustion.

In addition to the wasteful nature of ambivalence, negativists may actively impede their own progress toward conflict resolution and goal attainment. Thus, they frequently undo what good they previously had done. Driven by contrary feelings, they retract their kind words to others and replace them with harshness, or they undermine achievements they struggled so hard to attain. In short, their ambivalence often robs them of what few steps they secured toward progress. This inconstant "blowing hot and cold" behavior precipitates others into reacting in a parallel capricious and inconsistent manner. By prompting these reactions, negativists recreate the very conditions of their childhood that fostered the development of their unstable behaviors in the first place.

Most people weary of the sulking and stubborn unpredictability of these actively ambivalent personalities. Others are frequently goaded into exasperation and confusion when their persistent efforts to placate the negativist so frequently meet with failure. Eventually, everyone is likely to express both anger and disaffiliation, reactions that serve then only to intensify the negativist's dismay and anxiety.

Anticipating Disappointment

Not only do negativists precipitate real difficulties through their negativistic behaviors, but they often perceive and anticipate difficulties where none in fact exist. They have learned from past experience that "good things don't last," that positive feelings and attitudes from those whom they seek love will end abruptly and capriciously and be followed by disappointment, anger, and rejection.

Rather than be disillusioned and embittered, rather than allowing themselves to be led down the "primrose path" to suffer the humiliation and pain of having their hopes dashed again, it would be better to put a halt to illusory gratifications and to the futility and heartache of short-lived pleasures. Protectively, then, negativists may refuse to wait for others to make the turnabout. Instead, they "jump the gun," pull back when things are going well, and thereby cut off experiences that may have proved gratifying had they been completed. The anticipation of being set back and left in the lurch prompts negativists into a self-fulfilling prophecy. By their own hand, they defeat their chance to experience events that could have promoted change and growth.

By cutting off the goodwill of others and by upsetting their pleasurable anticipations, negativists gain the perverse and negative gratification of venting hostility and anger. These acts, however, prove to be pyrrhic victories; not only do they sabotage their own chances for rewarding experiences, but they inevitably provoke counterhostility from others and increased guilt and anxiety for themselves. Their defensive action has instigated responses that perpetuate the original difficulty, setting into motion a vicious circle in which they feel further discontent and disappointment.

Re-Creating Disillusioning Experiences

As noted earlier, interpersonal vacillation does gain partial gratifications for the negativist. And partial reinforcements, as we know from experimental research, strengthen habits and cause them to persist and recur. In the negativist, this appears to take the form of unconscious repetition-compulsions in which the individual re-creates disillusioning experiences that parallel those of the past.

Despite their ambivalence and pessimistic outlook, negativists operate on the premise that they can overcome past disappointments and capture, in full measure, the love and attention they only partially gained in childhood. Unfortunately, their search for complete fulfillment can no longer be achieved because they now possess needs that are in fundamental opposition to one another; for example, they both want and do not want the love of those on whom they depend. Despite this ambivalence, negativists enter new relationships as if a perfect and idyllic state could be achieved. They go through the act of seeking a consistent and true source of love that will not betray them as their parents and others have in the past. They venture into new relationships with enthusiasm and blind optimism; this time, all will go well. Despite this optimism, they remain unsure of the trust they really can place in others. Mindful of past betrayals and disappointments, they begin to test their new found "loves" to see if they are loyal and faithful. They may irritate others, frustrate them, and withdraw from them, all in an effort to check whether they will prove as fickle and insubstantial as those of the past. Soon these testing operations exhaust the partner's patience; annoyance, exasperation, and hostility follow. The negativist quickly become disenchanted; the "idol" has proved to be marred and imperfect; and the negativist is once more disillusioned and embittered. To vent their resentment at having been naive, these persons may turn against their "betrayers," disavow and recoil from the affections they had shown, and thereby complete the vicious circle. These experiences recur repeatedly, and with each recurrence, the negativists further reinforce their pessimistic anticipations. In their efforts to overcome past disillusionment, they have thrown themselves into new ventures that have led to further disillusion.

THERAPEUTIC INTERVENTIONS

The impression that negativists convey is that of childlike rebellion. They are likely to come to therapy at the request of others because their oppositional behavior has interfered with their marital, parental, or occupational responsibilities. Relationships with authority figures tend also to be problematic. This personality's characteristic negative outlook on life is likely to extend to therapy as well; therefore, it is improbable that they have entered the therapeutic arena voluntarily. Convinced that others are to blame for their misfortunes, they avoid taking responsibility for altering their provocative behaviors.

Progress in therapy is not promising. These personalities appear compliant on the surface, yet covertly they resist and manage to undermine the therapist's efforts. It may be difficult for these patients to see the therapist as a collaborator rather than an adversary.

STRATEGIC GOALS

The goals of therapy are to guide negativistic patients to recognize the source and character of their ambivalences toward self and others, and to reinforce a more consistent approach to life. Treatment must further attempt to mitigate the negativist's tendency to overreact in an obstructive and sullen manner. Recognition of the factors that foster the cyclical and recurrent nature of their interactions with others will assist in planning interventions, especially those oriented to the mood/temperament and self-image domains.

Reestablishing Polarity Balances

The conflictual coping style of the negativistic personality is manifested by extreme vacillations between submission to others and gratification of self needs. They may seek to obtain nurturance from others without examining their own adaptive capabilities. Not uncharacteristically, they may shift gears and quickly turn against those from whom they sought assistance. This self-other conflicted orientation provokes others to respond angrily in return. Assisting these patients in finding a comfortable balance within these bipolar orientations should be considered a major goal of therapy. Negativists need to learn to differentiate between the self and others and to adopt coping mechanisms that will allow them to move flexibly from fulfilling their own desires, without guilt, to being oriented toward others, without resentment.

Unlike the obsessive-compulsive who is overly controlled and represses urges to act out, the negativist employs an active mode of adaptation, displaying both erraticism and hyperreactivity. In these efforts to avoid distress, these personalities enact behaviors that not only upset others but also harm themselves. The observed imbalance in the active-passive polarity must be attenuated. It would be beneficial for negativists to take a more passive stance, especially in ambiguous situations where carefully exploring options and gathering more evidence when needed are more adaptive than reacting impulsively and erratically.

Countering Perpetuating Tendencies

The inconsistencies to which negativists were exposed in childhood reinforced the belief that disappointments are inevitable in life. In anticipation of this, they may withdraw prematurely from potentially gratifying experiences, upsetting their focus and changing their goals, only to repeat the same dysfunctional cycle. This behavior not only alienates others but also induces guilt in themselves. To interrupt this pattern, negativists must not only learn to commit to a specified plan of action, but to actively follow through as well. Acquiring control over their impulses is a paramount therapeutic goal.

Through their erratic and oppositional behaviors, negativistic personalities place themselves in double-bind situations, vacillating between incompatible goals and unable to commit and fulfill personal needs. Scornful, moody, and unpredictable emotional displays tend to exasperate others, causing them to react in a similar fashion. This, in turn, intensifies the negativist's beliefs that others cannot be relied on and will generate new conflictual behaviors. A major goal of personologic therapy with this disorder is to temper the volatile expression of behaviors and affect. When these patients learn to appropriately express their discontent, resentful encounters will give way to more mature interactions.

It is in the realm of interpersonal relations that the erratic cycle is played out in its full form. Not knowing whether they can rely on their partners, negativists proceed to test their fidelity and trustworthiness, eventually exasperating even the most compliant partner. Unable to find security and disillusioned once again, they will turn to their next victim. To prevent this recapitulation of past experiences, the dyadic relationship between the therapist and the patient may serve as a stable model to emulate, a starting block from which the patient can learn new ways of connecting.

Modifying Domain Dysfunctions

Central to this disorder are dysfunctions in the mood/temperament and self-image domains. Negativists feel that the world does not understand them, fearing there is little hope they will ever receive fair treatment. Their discontent is manifested through fickle and volatile emotional displays. Therapeutic efforts must be directed toward balancing the emotional seesaw, helping these patients gain control over the expression of negative affects. These personalities vacillate between blaming others and attributing the cause of their woes to themselves. Therapeutic goals include strengthening a consistent self image, as well as improving their perceptions of the real basis of their misfortunes.

Negativists have a very pessimistic outlook on life, believing that good things don't last. This skepticism often leads them to pull back and choose an opposite course of action when things seem to be going their way, thereby causing their predictions to come true. Therapy must assist these patients to challenge the faulty assumptions, and allow them to actively test reality. This negative outlook expresses itself particularly in interpersonal relationships. Believing that personal needs will never be met satisfactorily and that they will not be treated fairly, negativists develop a conflictual interpersonal style. They also resent others' good fortune, feeling personally deprived when observing what others may have received. Therapy must strive to help patients regulate contrary behaviors and develop tolerance for others so that their social behaviors will be more charitable and consistent.

Problems in relatedness began early in life and characterize their domain of inner object-representations. Experiences from the past have left a residue of internalized dispositions that are essentially ambivalent. Intervention must work toward replacing these conflictual and vacillating objects with more stable, dependable ones.

When expressing their discontent and troublesome feelings, negativists quite often fail to recognize its original and primary unconscious source. More direct and consciously assertive ways of voicing discontent should be explored in real life. As noted, the internal morphologic structures of negativists are divergent, consisting of coping mechanisms that are directed toward incompatible goals. The ultimate therapeutic objective in this area is a more consistent coping strategy, as well as a commitment to follow through in achieving its goal, that of psychic cohesion.

TACTICAL MODALITIES

The therapist must seek to demonstrate the effectiveness of therapy to these patients whose skeptical nature is likely to discount the possibility of progress ever being achieved. When everything seems to be moving along well and progress is made steadily, these patients may suddenly decide to discontinue therapy, stating that it was a waste of time. Major life issues that were brought up just prior to the end of the previous session may be discounted by the next meeting. The therapist will have to go with the flow, so to speak, keeping in mind their plan of action, not giving in to counter-transference feelings or reactions. Much therapy time will be devoted to exploring resistances and a slow pace of progression with many ups and downs can be expected.

Domain-Oriented Techniques

Formal *behavior modification* methods may be fruitfully explored to achieve greater consistency in social behaviors. Lacking appropriate role models in childhood, some negativists may have learned that goals may be achieved only through indirect means. The thought of dealing with matters in a straightforward way is anxiety arousing. During the course of therapy, negativists will be asked to engage in behaviors that are likely to raise anxiety levels. Teaching anxiety-management techniques can help them tolerate the expected discomforts and frustrations that normally would cause them to change their mode of action.

Controlling untimely expressions of anger may require impulse control and assertiveness skills training. These patients need to learn to "count to 10." By encouraging the direct expression of appropriate anger, the negativist will be less inclined to displace resentments to substitute objects. Within the therapeutic context, role playing and videotaped playback of interactions may facilitate an understanding of the negativist's dysfunctional interpersonal style. A functional analysis will reveal that there are contextual determinants to the negativist's behavior. Stimulus control procedures, such as removal of environmental pressures that aggravate the patient's anxieties, may be explored and appropriate modifications should be made.

Engaging the patient in behavioral contracting at the onset of treatment may foster compliance with therapy. Contracts should initially be short-term and concise to avoid giving the negativist an opportunity to use ambiguity as an excuse for not following through. Accomplishing the stated goals in the contract will help the patient develop a view of the self as competent. Self-management procedures are generally contraindicated as a first approach because these patients believe that others are to blame for their misfortunes.

Interpersonal techniques can be used to help these patients gain insight into the origin of their destructive behaviors and how these early learning experiences are played out in their current relationships. The transference reactions manifested in therapy will shed light on these patterns. Gradually, the therapist can start pointing out possible connections between the patient's early experiences and his or her current style of interacting. It is vital that the therapist point out the commonalities between the patient's behavior in the family of origin and his or her behavior in treatment, so that therapy will not recapitulate them or end in premature termination (Benjamin, 1993a).

Interpersonal work with negativists is a slow and arduous process. Benjamin notes that for negativists to recognize their maladaptive patterns, they must be partly adept at blocking these cycles and must have some desire to give up their mode of interaction. Successfully working through the obstructive behaviors in therapy will provide a corrective emotional experience. The therapist may be the first person who has not expressed criticism or counterreacted with hostility.

More directive *cognitive* techniques may be used to confront these patients with the obstructive and self-defeating character of their interpersonal relations. Cognitive approaches must be handled with caution, however, lest the patient become unduly guilt ridden, depressed, and suicidal. The greatest benefit derived through these approaches is to stabilize these patients, to "set them straight," and to put reins on their uncontrollable vacillations of mood and behavior, very much like must be done with borderline personalities.

Beck and Freeman (1990b) highlight a number of cognitive interventions with this disorder. From the onset, patients need to be engaged in a collaborative and practically oriented series of tasks. Because they are extremely resistant to external control, the therapist must take special care to actively involve negativists in treatment planning, reinforcing the autonomy they so desire. The therapist must avoid challenging the accuracy of their dysfunctional beliefs too directly or prematurely.

Typical automatic thoughts of the negativistic person include "Nothing ever works out for me in life"; "I never get what I deserve"; and "How dare others tell me how to lead my life?" These faulty assumptions can be explored and subsequently challenged. A dysfunctional thought record will be useful to help identify the automatic thoughts and accompanying emotions. The validity of the negativist's thinking can then be determined by setting up alternative hypotheses and trials to test them. Reality testing will provide patients with more precise information about the probability of anticipated misfortune, hence taking the edge off their skepticism.

Another important strategy Beck and Freeman discuss is maintaining consistency in treatment.

Negativists will inevitably try to blame lack of progress on the therapist, but by setting strict rules, structuring sessions, and giving clear rationales for each intervention, the ambiguity that provides an excuse for their lack of responsibility should be reduced. It is also important to examine which of the negativist's assumptions contribute to his or her success in obtaining satisfactions from others, exploring both pros and cons as well as short-term versus long-term gains.

Because *family* and *marital* treatment methods focus on the complex network of relationships that often sustain this personality style, these may prove to be the most useful techniques available. When negativists come in for marital therapy, it is not unusual for the identified patient in the dyad to be the victim of the misplaced hostility. Quite commonly, however, both partners have their own conflicts and dysfunctional style and in turn perpetuate each other's pathology. The negativist often projects undesirable traits onto the marital partner and subsequently expresses dismay, yet proceeds to behave in such a manner that actually generates this behavior in the partner. In couples therapy, it is not uncommon that improvement in one member of the dyad may result in increased symptomatology in the other. The therapist must be attuned to this possibility.

Group methods may be fruitfully employed to assist the patient to acquire more self-control and consistency in social situations. When group members share their reaction to the obstructiveness of the negativistic person, recognition of his or her pathological patterns may be facilitated. Unfortunately, premature dropout may ensue, especially in the early phases. Because their interactions are consistently negative, these patients do not usually obtain positive responses from others. Group members may inadvertently hold them responsible for their own misfortunes, or may contribute in other ways to sustaining the pattern. The therapist may need to be especially alert when group members combine forces against the negativist.

Because of the deeply rooted character of these problems and the high probability that unconscious resistances will impede the effectiveness of other therapeutic procedures, it may be necessary to explore the more extensive and prolonged techniques of *psychodynamic* therapy. A thorough reconstruction of personality may be the only means of altering the pattern. An awareness of the origins of the paradoxical behavior should enhance the negativist's understanding of how the same behaviors are played out in negative transference responses to the therapist. The neutrality of responses with which the therapist engages the patient can be a major corrective force. Once these personalities see that they can express their anger overtly, without disapproval and rejection from this authority figure, a more consistent model and self-image may then be internalized. Replacement of the vacillating objects with stable ones will allow negativists to view their interactions with others as consistent and as safe ground.

Unless there is a greater harmony in the negativist's internal structural elements, coping and defensive maneuvers will continue to be used to fulfill contradictory goals. The therapist must help the patient understand that his or her behavior actually serves to exacerbate conflicts. Encouraging patients to make sense of the confused mix of emotions they carry inside will help them be in touch with internal stimuli. Once they understand these feelings, the internal confusion may no longer be overwhelming. The patient can then sort through internal reserves to select appropriate coping mechanisms.

Stone (1993) notes that dream analysis can be helpful to get at the heart of the central conflicts. If the therapist can work through the patient's resistance, underlying feelings of impotence and unworthiness may be exposed and examined. Stone further points out that the patient has received primarily conditional love in the past, and enters treatment with the belief that the therapist will not be much different. When the therapist communicates an understanding of the issues important to the patient, and provides support rather than telling the person what to do, the negativistic personality can start to develop a more secure self-image.

Intense anxieties may preoccupy the patient in the early phases of treatment. *Pharmacological* tranquilizing agents may prove helpful in their relief. If depressive features predominate, antidepressant drugs may be prescribed. However, the therapist must be aware of the potential for misuse of medication.

A useful review of the major strategies and tactics is depicted in Figure 15.6.

Potentiated Pairings and Catalytic Sequences

What combinations and sequences should be taken to optimize the effectiveness of the various domain-oriented techniques described previously?

Therapy must initially help the negativistic personality to settle down and calm erratic

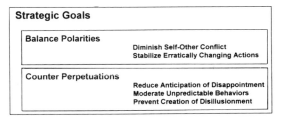

Figure 15.6   Therapeutic strategies and tactics for the prototypal negativistic (passive-aggressive) personality.

emotions. Supportive techniques may be used as a first approach, especially if combined with pharmacological intervention. Without curtailing the patient's emotional lability, other interventions are not likely to prove beneficial. Behavioral techniques can be of use to desensitize the patient to established anxiety-arousing stimuli. These methods should promote increasingly autonomous behavior, allowing the patient to feel more in control. This will subsequently decrease the resentfulness and contrariness displayed in interpersonal situations. Concurrent modifications in the patient's cognitive style will help the individual attend in more detail to attitudes and assumptions about self and others.

Throughout the therapy process, the use of interpersonal techniques will facilitate the negativist's recognition of interactive patterns. Understanding his or her own contributions to interpersonal difficulties may pave the way for a transition in object-relatedness. Only when therapy has progressed for some period of time, will dynamic techniques be able to help the patient get in touch with innermost fears and contradictions. Understanding and acknowledgment of these feelings will significantly reduce the need for displacement and other externalizing defenses. Gradually, the careful application of the preceding techniques can result in psychic cohesion.

RESISTANCES AND RISKS

Negativistic patients frequently decompensate into anxiety and depressive disorders. Therapists must be on guard to anticipate suicidal attempts since ambivalent personalities can act quite impulsively when they feel guilt, need attention, or seek a dramatic form of retribution. Because these patients often enter treatment in an agitated state, an early treatment task is to calm their anxieties and fears. Relieved of tension, many will lose the incentive to continue treatment. Motivating them to pursue a more substantial course of therapy may call for considerable effort on the part of the therapist because these personalities are deeply ambivalent about dependency relationships. They desire to be nurtured and loved by a powerful parental figure, but such submission poses the threat of loss and undermines the desire to maintain independence.

A seesaw struggle is often enacted between patient and therapist; the negativist is likely to exhibit an ingratiating submissiveness on one occasion, and a taunting and demanding attitude on another. Similarly, these patients may solicit the therapist's affections, but when these are expressed, the patient rejects them, voicing doubt about the genuineness of the therapist's feelings. When the therapist points out these contradictory attitudes, the patients may verbally appreciate the therapist's perceptiveness, but not alter their attitudes at all. The roundabout tactics negativists employ to air their grievances can take many different forms in the therapeutic setting. Delaying payments, late arrivals, forgetting appointments, not remembering to do homework, poor boundaries, and anger projection are just a few examples of the many resistances encountered. These patients are likely to use the ambiguity inherent in the therapeutic setting as an excuse for withdrawing or enacting passive-aggressive maneuvers.

If therapy has moderated the negativist's pathology to the point where he or she can satisfactorily fulfill social and occupational obligations without causing friction, treatment should be considered successful. Only in select cases can therapy become a major corrective force for more fundamental personality change.

CHAPTER 16

Masochistic Personality Disorders: The Aggrieved Pattern

Although the existence of a self-abasing character has been observed for centuries, it failed to gain official recognition as a personality disorder until 1987. An effort to include the psychoanalytic construct, "masochistic personality disorder," was made in early discussions of the DSM-III (1980). Given the antitheoretical orientation of that manual's Task Force, the concept of masochistic behaviors, originally conceived as a potential Axis II disorder, was formulated instead as a feature of the Axis I "affective" group of syndromes. Soon after the appearance of DSM-III, several clinical theorists continued to press for an Axis II category that would encompass the self-abasive and self-undoing qualities of a "depressive/masochistic" personality. This proposal was taken seriously by the Work Group assigned the task of revising the DSM-III. The proposal quickly generated both professional and public controversy. To minimize substantive objections and harassing debates, the label was changed from masochistic to *self-defeating*. The initially proposed criteria were then modified to rule out depressive symptomatology, as well as to minimize gender biases (e.g., to exclude from the list abusive relationships in which female victims were in effect blamed for ostensibly precipitating the abuse). The committee then decided to place the diagnosis of a self-defeating personality in the DSM-III-R Appendix, along with the sadistic personality diagnosis, because they were "new" disorders and hence required further clinical and empirical study.

Although the original label masochism acquired a somewhat confusing array of meanings (e.g., a sexual perversion, a moral character type), the selection of self-defeating as an alternative did not achieve either clarity or precision in its potential usage. Moreover, all personality disorders are essentially self-defeating in that they all set into motion self-perpetuating behaviors and reactions that further intensify the very problems that

gave rise to them in the first place. Any number of terms would have proved more apt, we believe; for example, self-abasing, deferential, obsequious, abject, servile, and self-denigrating.

The need to clarify the meaning of the construct, which we prefer to label again "masochistic personality disorder," is a central task for those who wish to extend the boundaries of the DSM-IV, and from which the disorder has been deleted. Two quotes may be useful in this regard, the first by a contemporary analytic theorist, S. Asch (1988):

The disorder can perhaps be best defined as a lifelong pattern of unconsciously arranged difficulties or failures in multiple areas of functioning. This is the "loser" in our society, the person who needs to be unnecessarily encumbered or even to fail. He tends to fail at work and love despite what are sometimes the best credentials. He either cannot form a gratifying relationship or, if he does, he inevitably, although unconsciously, arranges for it to flounder. He may achieve great preliminary success but somehow snatches defeat from the jaws of victory and fails at the penultimate moment. (p. 2)

Another useful perspective that recognizes masochism as a complex and diverse phenomenon is presented by another distinguished analytic thinker, N. Shainess (1987):

She—and it is usually she—does not incite rejecting responses, she elicits them; there is a big difference between these two words and their meanings. She does not turn down opportunities for pleasure, but rather, pleasurable occurrences turn sour.... In fact, the masochist does not enjoy suffering. If one paraphrases the credo of Descartes "Cogito ergo sum" (I think therefore I am), a statement of what distinguishes humans, the masochist's credo can be expressed as "I suffer, therefore I am." This is a constant reenactment of early experience, which has had virtually nothing pleasurable in it. (p. 174)

The reason for describing the masochistic/self-defeating prototype in this text is to broaden the readers' perspective by including in the scope of their clinical work a constellation of cohering self-abasive and self-undoing personality characteristics. With such knowledge in hand, clinicians should be able to better understand and treat their patients. While it is true that all labeling and diagnoses possess the potential for misuse, we cannot bypass valid syndromes simply because interpretations given these disorders may at times be fallacious and misguided. Personality disorders of all stripe result from interacting biogenic, psychogenic, and sociogenic factors. While it is especially regrettable that such complexly formed pathologies are interpreted by some solely in terms of their potential social and political implications, we must reject all such interpretations lest mental disorders be recast, as they have been in Germany and Russia this past century, as social defects, rather than as *intrinsic clinical phenomena,* in this case as one of the several persistently chronic and widely pervasive pathologies of persons.

HISTORICAL ANTECEDENTS

The label "masochism" was initially proposed by Krafft-Ebing (1882) when he sought to catalog the sexual perversions. In a manner similar to the term "sadism," the label masochism was created by employing the name of a well-known writer of the time, Leopold Von Sacher-Masoch. In Masoch's novel, *Venus In Furs* (1870), the hero was a man who suffered torture, subjugation, and deprecation from a female tormentor. Krafft-Ebing asserted that flagellation and physical punishment were necessary elements in the perversion, but they were less significant than the interpersonal relationship that included enslavement, passivity, and psychological serfdom. Hence, from its first formulations, the concept of masochism, although centrally sexual in nature, included the need for the experience of suffering itself and was not limited to cases in which physical pain was a necessary ingredient for sexual arousal. To quote Krafft-Ebing(1882/1937):

The wish to suffer pain and be subjected to force, the idea of being completely and unconditionally subject to the will of the person of the opposite sex [defines masochism]; [essential is] being treated by this person, as by a master, humiliated and abused. (p. 131)

To Krafft-Ebing, masochism was a sexual anomaly where the male was functionally impotent except when experiencing suffering, subjugation, and abuse. Few cases of masochistic perversions were reported in women.

In what might be called characterological masochism, typically expressed in love relationships, Krafft-Ebing wrote:

When the idea of being tyrannized is for a long time closely associated with a lustful thought of the beloved person, the lustful emotion is finally transferred to the tyranny itself and the transformation to the perversion is completed. (p. 207)

Hence, from the start, masochism is more typically seen as a masculine form of pathology, rather than as a feminine form.

MODERN FORMULATIONS

Although the concepts of sadism and masochism were first formulated by Krafft-Ebing in his studies of psychopathological sexual behavior in 1882, it was Freud and his disciples who developed a more contemporaneous explication of both phenomena. Freud's primary writings on masochism began with his "Three Essays on Sexuality," a paper in 1905, and were then brought to their fullest development in 1924 with his paper entitled "The Economic Problem of Masochism." In his early papers, Freud spoke of sadism and masochism as paired opposites. Sadism was an elaboration of a biologically driven aggressive instinct to survive and was equated with activity and masculinity. Masochism was seen initially when the aggressive instinct was turned from the external world to the person's inner self. In his 1919 paper "A Child Is Being Beaten," Freud shifted his focus and considered masochism to be a result of unconscious guilt. Summing up his views at that time, Freud (1919/1959) states:

Masochism is not the manifestation of the primary instinct, but originates from sadism which has been turned around upon the self, that is to say, by means of regression from an object into the ego. Instincts with a passive aim must be taken for granted as existing, especially among women. The passivity is not the whole of masochism. The characteristic of unpleasure belongs to it as well—a bewildering accompaniment to the satisfaction of an instinct. The transformation of sadism into masochism appears to be due to the influence of the sense of guilt which takes part in the act of repression. (p. 193)

Prior to formulating his hypothesis that destructive behaviors are conceived best as derivatives of a death instinct, Freud (1918/1925) described the role of guilt in masochism as follows:

A child who behaves [with inexplicable naughtiness] is making a confession and trying to provoke punishment as a simultaneous means of setting his sense of guilt at rest and of satisfying his masochistic sexual trend. (p. 28)

In 1924, Freud formulated his concept of masochism in an entirely different fashion. Written after "Beyond the Pleasure Principle" (1923), pleasure and tension reduction were no longer associated with the concept of "tension reduction" but rather its deeper biological basis in what he referred to as the "death instinct." This new formulation drew much criticism. Assumption of a death instinct serving as the basis for human aggression and masochistic behaviors continues to be either ignored or attacked by later writers, both analytic and nonanalytic.

The concept of individuals who seek to sacrifice themselves at the alter of some stronger other was also elaborated by nonanalytic theorists, such as Kahn (1931). In his study of "psychopathic character types," he describes the following:

Much sacrificial courage all too loudly stresses and much compassion only too evidently courting the attention of the environment belong here . . . The personality seems to say: I am worth nothing and so I sacrifice myself for the others! I exist only for others! Behold how I sacrifice myself!

In the passion and longing for subjection and suffering *the self-deprecation is lived out most impassively. This reaches even a so-called bondage, that is a bearing in which the personality seems to find its highest pleasure in slavish obedience to a master or mistress, the associated humiliations of every sort being almost eagerly sought and enjoyed. (pp. 269–270)*

Although embracing most features of Freud's theories, Wilhelm Reich (1933) grew increasingly distant from crucial elements of the master's formulations. Deeply imbued, however, with the

significance of libidinal development, Reich was convinced that early experiences, their complexes and conflicts, led to the emergence of what he termed "a character armoring." Specifically, masochistic characters, as Reich conceived them, were victims of abuse and aggression. Masochists developed a complex compromise formation of defensive maneuvers that served to become their distinctive character armor. To Reich, the future masochist had suffered deep disappointments and became extraordinarily demanding of love that could be gained or rebuilt by suffering at the hand of the desired love-object: Moreover, they willingly submitted to minor and repetitive punishments as a means of forestalling and perhaps avoiding more severe ones.

Hence, it was Reich (1933/1949) who first conceptualized a comprehensive syndrome termed the "masochistic character," describing its essence as reflecting a submissive form of love-manipulation and aggression. The major traits he identified were:

. . . a chronic, subjective feeling of suffering which is manifested objectively and especially stands out as a tendency to complain. *Additional traits of the masochistic character are chronic tendencies to inflict pain upon and to debase oneself ("moral masochism") and an intense passion for tormenting others, from which the masochist suffers no less than his object. (pp. 237–238)*

A major feature of Reich's formulation of the masochist is the disposition to obstruct others through passively provocative behaviors. Reflecting on the "infantile spite reaction" of one of his patients, Reich observed:

These provocations were attempts to make me strict and drive me into a frenzy. It is not at all a question of punishment but of putting *the analyst or his prototype, the parent, in the wrong, of causing him to act in a way which would give a rational foundation to the reproach "See how badly you are treating me."*

There must be a meaning in the fact that the masochist provokes the analyst to put him in the wrong. The meaning is: "You are a bad person; you don't like me; on the contrary, you treat me horribly; I am right in hating you."

A deep disappointment in love lies behind the provocation. The masochist is especially fond of provoking those objects through whom he suffered a disappointment. Originally, these objects were intensely loved, and either an actual disappointment was experienced or the love demanded by the child was not sufficiently satisfied. (1949, pp. 242–243)

Reich's thesis of disappointment and disillusion is similar to formulations concerning other character types. What appears to distinguish the genesis of the masochistic pattern is the strategy that children acquire to spitefully "get back" at and torture their rejecting parents. Reich described this process by positing a series of hypothetical questions and patient responses. He illustrated the patient's complaint as follows:

"You see how miserable I am—love me!" "You don't love me enough—you are mean to me!" "You have to love me; I will force you to love me. If you don't love me, I'll make you angry!" The masochistic passion for torment, the complaints, the provocation, and the suffering can, in terms of their meaning—we shall discuss their dynamics later— be explained on the basis of the fantasized or actual non-fulfillment of a quantitatively inordinate demand for love.

The masochistic character seeks to bind the inner tension and threat of anxiety by an inadequate method, namely by courting love through provocation and defiance.

The defiance and the provocation are directed at the person who is loved and from whom love is demanded. In this way, the fear of losing love and attention is increased, just as the guilt feeling which one wants to be rid of is not diminished but intensified, for the beloved person is in fact tormented. This explains the extremely peculiar behavior of the masochist, who becomes more and more enmeshed in the situation of suffering, the more intensely he tries to extricate himself from it. (1949, pp. 245–246)

As will be evident in presentations of the DSM-III-R's self-defeating pattern, Reich's conception of the masochistic character comes close to the mark of contemporary views.

Horney's formulation of "masochistic phenomena" bridges the theme of ambivalence first posited as central to these personalities by Abraham and the notion of spiteful suffering proposed by Reich. As she views it, the masochist establishes "a value in suffering" as a means of defending against fears associated with a sense of intrinsic weakness and insignificance, both of which leave the person with an inordinate need for affection and an extraordinary fear of disapproval. In her early writings on the subject, Horney (1939) noted:

Certain wishes of the masochistic person may be expressed directly. . . . The specific masochistic way of expressing wishes, however, consists in the person impressing on others how great his need is because of his bad condition.

The conflict on the score of dependency is one between weakness and strength, between merging and self-assertion, between self-contempt and pride. . . .

The specific form of expressing wishes appears as a desperate cry . . . implying something like . . . "You have done me so much harm you are responsible for all my misery—you must do something for me."

The specifically masochistic way of expressing hostility is by suffering, helplessness, by the person representing himself as victimized and harmed.

The hostility . . . is not altogether merely defensive. It often has a sadistic character. . . . [It] springs from the vindictiveness of a weak and suppressed individual . . . who craves to feel that he too can subject others to his wishes and make them cringe. (pp. 261–263)

Elaborating her thoughts, Horney recognized that the suffering of the masochist often serves the defensive purpose of avoiding recriminations and responsibilities; it is a way of expressing accusations in a disguised form. For some, it is a way of demanding affection and reparations. For others it is a virtue that justifies claims for love and acceptance. Important to Horney's way of thinking is a clarification of what the masochistic experience entails. She goes on to write:

The conflicts and painful experiences are neither secretly wanted nor enjoyed, but are unavoidable and are as painful to the masochistic person as they would be to anyone else. . . . The masochistic type despises himself for being dependent; because of his excessive expectations of his partner he is bound to become disappointed and resentful; he is bound to feel frequently unfairly treated.

Therefore only by eliminating conflicts and narcotizing the pains involved can satisfaction be derived from such a relationship. Conflicts can be eliminated and psychic pain lulled in several ways . . . Unbearable pain can be alleviated and turned into something pleasurable by submerging the self in a feeling of misery. (pp. 271–272)

Reik (1941) took a different turn from his neo-analytic predecessors, conceiving the masochistic character as a more manipulative and cunning individual. Far from feeling as Reich and Horney did that the masochist was a victim, Reik conceived them as revengeful, aggressive, and defiant individuals, driven by sadistic fantasies. Disagreeing with the view that the primary motive of the masochist is an unconscious need for punishment, Reik focuses instead on the masochist's compensatory drive to regain the sense of personal significance, if not glory. To the masochists, then, suffering can become a sign as well as an expression of one's own value. He writes:

This new interpretation endeavors to draw masochistic pleasure from the defeat, a pleasure which first of all is concerned with the rehabilitation of the injured ego. The claim to be better than the environment may be hidden, may be below the consciousness of the claiming person. Yet it must be acknowledged as one of the most intensive pleasure gains in social masochism. As far as I can see the feature of superiority, even of vainglory, in masochistic characters has not been discovered hitherto. The humility and emphasized dependence, the weakness and submissiveness, have disguised those tendencies. The claim to be superior in psychic and moral qualities, however, is not refuted but only masked by the servile, self-deprecating behavior of the masochist. (p. 259)

In the ensuing two or three decades, several analytically oriented theorists contributed further insights concerning the unconscious processes that motivated masochistic individuals. Menaker (1942, 1953) stressed the role of children in protecting the mother's need for control by a willing sacrifice of the child's own autonomy, hence sustaining the illusion that love from the mother will be forthcoming forever. She expresses this theme as follows:

The hatred of the self, originating at the earliest level of ego differentiation, and the accompanying feeling of powerlessness become the prototype for later feelings of worthlessness, which characterize the moral masochist. These very feelings are used in the service of ego to protect it from the fear of being abandoned, and to gain for it a fantasy gratification of love. This is the essence of moral masochism, in the defense of the ego. (1953, p. 209)

Paralleling the views of Menaker, Berliner (1940, 1942, 1947, 1958) takes a strong stand on the theme that masochistic phenomena derive from early parent-child relationships. Disagreeing with his forerunners, Berliner does not see masochism as an instinctual force, nor as a quality of sadism turned upon the self, but rather as a "disturbance of object-relations" and a "pathological way of loving":

Masochism is neither a pure instinctual phenomena (death instinct), nor the expression of component sexual drive, nor is it the subject's own sadism turned upon himself. It is in the sexual as well as moral form a disturbance of object-relations, a pathological way of loving. Masochism means loving a person who gives hate and ill treatment. (1958, p. 40)

Both Berliner and Menaker suggest that masochists have developed an unusual blind spot for judging others' abuses because of their experiences with an abusive mother. These children have learned to misidentify cruelty as love. As Berliner (1947) phrases it:

The dependent child, in order not to lose the vitally needed love object, submits and accepts the suffering which the object imposes as if it were love, and is not conscious of the difference. (p. 461)

In this way, the masochistic person has learned to gravitate toward punitive others because this is the only kind of intimacy that he or she knows.

Reverting back to earlier themes in analytic thought, Loewenstein (1957) restates the notion that masochism serves as a "seduction of the aggressor":

Masochism seems to be the weapon of the weak—i.e., of every child—faced with the danger of human aggression. The masochistic perversion does not deal with the survival of the individual, but one can say that it permits a limited and precarious survival. . . . The mechanism . . . appears at that early age to ensure the existence of parental love, at a time when parental love is as necessary for the development of sexuality as it is for survival. It continues to be operative in both, even when they have parted ways and at times even oppose one another. (p. 230)

We close this section on modern formulations with two neoanalytic theorists, Beiber (1966), and Sullivan (1947), the former opening a cognitive perspective on the masochistic character, the latter an interpersonally oriented one. Agreeing with Reich that masochistic acts are defenses against the possibility of greater injury, Beiber views this individual to be unrealistically, if not irrationally disposed to expect injury. He recognizes that this pattern of expectancy must have been adaptive at some point in the individual's personal history, even though it may now have been perpetuated into a maladaptive general attitude. He describes the pathology as consisting "of irrationally held beliefs . . . associated with erroneous expectations of injury" (1966, p. 269).

Along similar lines, Sullivan (1947) describes these people as demonstrating "an astigmatic slant on life," such that unpleasant experiences and anticipations are what concern them. Sullivan states:

A large number of people go to extraordinary lengths to get themselves imposed on, abused, humiliated . . . but as you go on, you discover this quite often pays, i.e., they get the things they want. And the things they want are satisfaction and security from anxiety. (p. 120)

CONTEMPORARY PROPOSALS

A major adherent of Sullivan's interpersonal approach, Leary (1957) characterizes a variety of different personality types, including the masochist. As he sees it, the masochistic style induces others into feeling strong, superior, and supportive, at least initially. Because suffering evokes within others these natural responses, masochists will likely exaggerate or dramatize them so that the needs for rescue will be especially compelling. In his descriptive portrayal of what he terms "the self-effacing-masochistic" personality, Leary writes:

The message which they communicate to others in their face-to-face relations is "I am a weak, inferior person." Through their autonomous reflex operations they train others to look down upon them with varying intensities of derogation and superiority. . . . In either case the person employing this general mechanism avoids anxiety by means of retiring, embarrassed diffidence. He is automatically mobilized to shun the appearance of outward strength and pride.

The individuals who employ this security operation do so because they feel that this social role is the safest and least dangerous position to be assumed in this particular situation. (p. 282)

Whenever we observe or measure this security operation, we may assume that an individual has learned to employ self-deprecation as a protective device in certain situations. (p. 283)

In the early 1970s, a number of analytically oriented thinkers began to offer ideas concerning the disorder that opened up new vistas on its development and unfolding. For example, MacKinnon and Michels (1971) described masochism in the depressive character as follows:

Pain has become a means of assuaging the superego and explaining guilt. The patient atones for his real or fantasied wrong-doing by his masochistic behavior. He avoids, or at least lessens, the pangs of conscience by arranging punishment in the real world . . . The child whose life is marked by frequent punishment may feel loved only if abused, and may feel insecure if he goes for any length of time without punishment. He learns to seek out situations that recreate his early experiences, and is uncomfortable if he cannot re-establish the role of the victim. (pp. 190–191)

Whereas MacKinnon and Michels focused on the relationship between masochism and depression, Stolorow (1975) drew attention to the interweaving of narcissistic elements and masochistic behavior. He describes this connection as follows:

I shall attempt to show that masochistic activities may, in certain instances, represent abortive (and sometimes primitively sexualized) efforts to restore and maintain the structural cohesiveness, temporal stability and positive affective colouring of a precarious or crumbling self-representation . . . Masochistic activities, as one of their multiple functions, may serve as abortive efforts to restore, repair, buttress and sustain a self-representation that had been damaged and rendered precarious by injurious experiences. (pp. 441–442)

Although Sack and Miller (1975) find a diversity of mechanisms underlying masochistic behavior, suggesting that there is no single preeminent dynamic process, more recent theorists suggest that there may be a common thread in all these disorders and a special one at that. For example, some suggest that masochists derive their sense of identity and self-esteem from the pain and suffering they experience. For them to give up their inner conflicts and external discomforts would mean to give up a major element of their sense of self. As just noted, a parallel position has been suggested by Stolorow (1975). In his view, achieving a cohesive self-representation is one of the major functions of the masochistic pattern.

An articulate writer on character disorders, Shapiro (1965, 1981) has written thoughtfully on various personality disorders. His descriptive portrayal of masochistic patterns is captured well in the following quote:

I am referring particularly to those individuals who are chronically aggrieved, constantly preoccupied with their suffering. These people complain a great deal about having been victimized or unfairly treated, and they seem to exaggerate their troubles— for example, by constant and melodramatic reference to their "hurt" or "pain." . . . They dwell upon and exaggerate their misfortunes not merely, nor even primarily, for an external audience. They exaggerate their sufferings to themselves. To put it simply, they seem to work themselves up, to try to experience more suffering than they actually feel at the time. . . . When an old misfortune comes to mind in an incidental or peripheral way, or when an old grievance threatens to grow faint, he tries to retrieve it and to revive the experience of it. He cannot allow the grievance to dissipate or himself to forget it. In short, he is obsessed with his misfortunes. (1981, p. 113)

Perhaps the most gifted theorist in contemporary psychoanalytic literature is Kernberg (1988a). Arguing for the universality of masochistic behaviors, Kernberg outlines an overall classification of masochistic psychopathology based on the severity of the disorder. We will make reference to the various subtypes of the masochistic personality disorder in other sections. For the moment, it will suffice to record the major categories that Kernberg enumerates. First, Kernberg outlines the logic for "normal" masochism. Here he refers to realistic self-criticism and guilt feelings when repressed impulses of an oppositional nature are experienced. Also referred to is a depressive-masochistic disorder as one of the three "higher-level" or "neurotic" forms of character pathology. Condensing his characterizations of the depressive-masochistic

type, Kernberg (1988a) describes three trait constellations, the first reflecting severe superego functioning, the second reflecting overdependency on support, love, and acceptance from others, and the third, reflecting difficulty in the expression of aggression:

A tendency to be excessively serious, responsible, and concerned about work performance and responsibilities.

A tendency to excessive guilt feelings toward others because of unconscious ambivalence toward loved and needed objects, and an excessive reaction of frustration when their expectations are not met.

These patients [tend] to become depressed under conditions that would normally produce anger or rage . . . Unconscious guilt over anger expressed to others. . . . Followed by depression and overly apologetic, submissive, or compliant behavior, only to be followed by a second wave of anger over the way they are treated and their own submissiveness. (pp. 1008–1009)

In other papers, Kernberg (1984) outlines what he sees as the "scenario" that is responsible for the pathology of object-relations and superego development in the masochistic pattern of the sadomasochistic personality disorder:

(1) The experience of external objects as omnipotent and cruel; (2) a sense that any good, loving, mutually gratifying relationship with an object is frail, easily destroyed, and, even worse, contains the seeds for attack by the overpowering and cruel object; (3) a sense that total submission to that object is the only condition for survival and that, therefore, all ties to a good and weak object have to be severed. (p. 1025)

Recent theorists of the analytic school have offered variations on the themes described by Kernberg and earlier psychodynamically oriented thinkers. Especially significant are the contributions of Cooper (1993) and Stone (1993). In extending earlier formulations by Stolorow, Cooper proposes the following synthesis of masochistic and narcissistic features, a theme elaborated previously in Chapter 11:

My conviction [is] that masochism is a variant of narcissistic personality disorder and that in every masochistic patient one finds prominent narcissistic traits. . . . Masochistic patients are those who as children were especially intolerant of the hurts to their self-esteem . . . These children resort to a special defense. In effect, they deny their childhood helplessness by claiming control over their frustrators . . . asserting that the frustrations were delivered because the child forced the parent to do so. What's more, the child claims to be so powerful that the parent cannot really hurt him because he enjoys the injury that has been suffered. (p. 4)

Showing his breadth of perspective and open-mindedness, Stone (1993) refers to masochistic phenomena in a contemporary and sophisticated manner:

Currently, we no longer understand masochistic personality as an exaggerated form of femininity, recognizing that the typical personality traits occur about as frequently in men as in women. . . .

I used the term pain-dependent in the chapter heading to avoid both the narrowness of "masochistic" and the excessive breadth of "self-defeating." As Cooper rightly underlines, all neurotic persons suffer, and they also undermine their own ambitions. Not many people seek the help of a psychotherapist who are not in some sense "self-defeating." To be sure, DSM attempts to give the label meaning by defining it as, in effect, very self-defeating, i.e., chooses people and situations that lead to hurt or disappointment, rejects help, elicits angry responses, is unattracted to persons who would be genuinely caring, engages in unnecessary self-sacrifice, etc. But the new definition conflates items from concepts which, for clinical reasons, have generally been distinguished within the psychoanalytic community—namely, masochistic, and sadomasochistic. (p. 374)

Approaching the subject from a cognitive perspective, Beck (1967, 1976), views the masochistic pattern as a paradox among his depressive subtypes, noting that these individuals do not consider themselves worthy of experiencing pleasure, and paradoxically experience actual success as depressing rather than joyful. Considering masochistic behavior as related, but distinct from the symptoms of depression, Beck writes (1967):

Some typical repetitive behavior patterns observed in individuals considered masochistic but not necessarily depressed are: the tendency to interpret the lack of complete success as failure: to have self doubts even when successful: to magnify the importance of personal defects: to react to criticism with self-debasement; and to expect rejection. (p. 163)

An analysis of the self-defeating pattern in accord with the statistical methods utilized by Costa and Widiger (1993) spells out a number of the latent traits associated with this pattern. In their brief description, they note:

The self-defeating person is characterized by low conscientiousness (e.g., fails to accomplish tasks despite an ability to do so and chooses situations that lead to failure) and low agreeableness (incites angry responses from others, rejects people who treat them well, and rejects or renders ineffective the help of others). (p. 53)

Being informed by psychoanalytic, cognitive, and interpersonal worldviews, several new investigators and theorists have approached the subject of self-defeating behaviors from a social-psychological and experimental orientation, a markedly different perspective than the preceding authors. Developing their ideas on the basis of interpersonal processes that have been tested out in the laboratory, these contributors provide a scientific credibility to the subject that heretofore depended entirely on clinical observations, as well as frequent, ingenious inferences from them. Most theorists of this new persuasion follow recent analytic notions to the effect that masochism results from efforts to maintain extant self-representations and inner notions of self-esteem. Significant among these are Curtis (1989) and Berglas (1989). The following quote from Berglas typifies the views of these psychologically oriented thinkers:

Instead of manipulating self-disclosures, the self-handicapper controls impressions by getting into situations or circumstances that may look painful or problematic but, paradoxically, sustain a lofty image of competence.

Self-handicapping is accomplished in one of two ways: (1) by finding or creating impediments that make successful performances less likely, or (2) by withdrawing effort in order to invite probable failure. . . . The self-handicapper's true abilities cannot be assessed because extraneous factors (impediments, lack of effort) have prevented their manifestation. If and when this state of judgmental ambiguity is created, the self-handicapper has achieved his or her tactical goal: the preservation of the favorable competence image attained prior to the evaluative interaction.

In response to the fear of damaging an inflated self-conception, the self-handicapper reaches out for impediments or exposes himself or herself to incapacitating circumstances that inhibit his or her capacity to succeed again. (p. 269)

Despite considerable discussion and favorable recommendations from the wider advisory group, a "masochistic personality disorder" was not included in the DSM-III. Support for the concept, although heavily criticized by many politically sensitive groups, led finally to its introduction in the DSM-III-R Appendix under the title "self-defeating personality." Many clinicians suggested that there was no personality disorder in the official taxonomy that described a pattern of personality disturbance in which individuals are drawn into situations or relationships that will cause them to suffer; similarly, these individuals ostensibly undermine the experience of pleasurable activities and prevent others from helping them. The name of the category was changed to avoid the historical association of the "masochistic" term with psychoanalytic notions about female characteristics and, in particular, the implication that these individuals unconsciously derive pleasure from the experience of suffering.

The characteristics noted as official DSM-III-R diagnostic criteria included the following clinical features, which we have grouped into four clinical domains. In the Interpersonal realm we find that four criteria had been noted: choosing people and situations that led to disappointment or mistreatment, even when better options are clearly available; rejecting or rendering ineffective the attempts of others to be helpful; inciting rejecting or angry responses from others and then feeling hurt or humiliated; being uninterested in or rejecting people who are consistently supportive and helpful. Two Mood criteria were included: responds with depression or guilt following some positive personal event or achievement: rejects opportunities for pleasure or hesitant about acknowledging enjoyable experiences. The following criterion is noted in the Behavioral sphere: despite clear ability to do so, fails to complete tasks central to his or her objectives. And finally one criterion relates to Self-Image: engages in self-sacrifice that is not solicited or even expected by recipients of these behaviors.

The ICD-10 does not include a Self-Defeating or Masochistic personality designation. Similarly,

as noted previously, self-defeating personality disorder is no longer part of the DSM diagnostic taxonomy. It may be of interest to the reader, nevertheless, to review some of the features that were proposed in discussions of the DSM-IV Work Group. The following paragraphs summarize the Work Group's initial descriptive portrayals:

It was clearly felt that the characteristics of self-defeating behaviors would be pervasive, occurring in several areas of functioning such as school, work, social relationships, etc. Notable is the assumption that self-defeating persons would avoid or undermine achieving pleasurable experiences or were drawn to situations or relationships in which they would suffer and/or prevent others from helping them. Also noteworthy is the tendency to repeatedly become involved with people or situations that result in troublesome and problematic consequences. When the self-defeating personality experiences rewarding or gratifying personal events, instead of experiencing pleasure or pride, the person might become dysphoric, feel guilty, claim to be undeserving, even undertake things which result in psychic or physical pain. These persons repeatedly reject offers of assistance, prefer to remain in discomforting situations, and undermine what efforts others may make to assist them. Not infrequently, these personalities act in ways that prompt distressing, angry, or rejecting responses from others. Opportunities for pleasure may repeatedly be avoided. Similarly, these personalities may participate in an objectively enjoyable activity, but deny having experienced any pleasure. A tendency to undermine one's own achievements may also be notable, demonstrating a willingness to contribute to the tasks of others, but failing to complete tasks for which one alone is responsible. Relationships have a perverse quality to them in that caring and nurturing people are spoken of as boring, and opportunities to relate further to such persons are avoided or fail to be pursued. Similarly, exploitive or insensitive persons are seen as attractive. A willingness to engage in excessive self-sacrifice is often made to please such exploitive and insensitive individuals. Such self-sacrifice does not, however, usually make the self-defeating person feel content, more valued, or desirable. (Axis-II Work Group Memos, 1991)

Although the construct of a self-defeating personality has not attracted a substantial degree of research attention, the time between the DSM-III-R and DSM-IV may have been much too brief a period to test its empirical base and justify its deletion from the diagnostic manual. In this regard, it should be noted that a majority of the personality disorders are deficient in the number of research studies they have engendered in recent decades. That the masochistic disorder has generated considerable controversy in its short official life (e.g., hurtful to women, sex-biases, confused as an affective disorder) is all the more reason to explore and refine more precisely its characteristics in ongoing research; excluding it from the manual will only leave its problems unresolved. To say that the description of the disorder is unusually problematic, owing to the diverse mix of its unconscious motivations is, once more, all the reason to keep it as an active category in the manual. If clinicians have difficulty in sorting out components, should we not continue to disentangle and elaborate these intricacies in our research, or should we simply sweep it under the rug and leave mental health professionals in the dark. In our judgment, and as noted in earlier paragraphs, all the preceding reasons for deleting the disorder are rationalizations to obviate the deeply troubling political implications of keeping it in the manual. So be it—at least for DSM-IV.

As in prior chapters, brief notes will be made of the evolutionary theory as a framework for explicating the key elements of the masochistic/self-defeating pattern that were included in the DSM-III-R Appendix. Figure 16.1 provides a visual picture of the strength of the three major polarities of the theory. As can be seen, the major pathologic component is the reversal between the pain and pleasure segments of the first polarity. This signifies that the individual has learned to experience pain in a manner that makes it preferable to experiences of pleasure. Of course, this preference may be a relative one, that is, the individual may be willing to tolerate significant discomfort and abuse as long as it is the lesser of greater degrees of anguish and humiliation. To be moderately distressed and disheartened may be better than to be severely pained and demoralized.

The masochistic, self-defeating disorder is passive and accommodating in a manner similar to the depressive personality. The distinction is a fine one, but is significant nevertheless. For depressives, passivity indicates an acceptance of their fate, a sense that loss and hopelessness are justified and that depression is inevitable; further, that these experiences can never be overcome and, hence, the depressive should accept his or her state and the irretrievability of happiness. In the self-defeating, there is a measure of both control and desirability in giving in to their suffering and discomfort. For them, a measure of moderate anguish may be a preferable state, that is, it may be the best of all possible alternatives available to the person. Passivity, therefore, indicates an acceptance of pain as a realistic choice, given the individual's inescapable options, not a final and irretrievable state of hopelessness.

A pictorial review of the major historical contributors is represented in Figure 16.2.

CLINICAL FEATURES

The following sections encompass several perspectives in our attempt to illuminate the major characteristics of the prototypal masochistic/self-defeating personality pattern (see Table 16.1 and Figure 16.3).

PROTOTYPAL DIAGNOSTIC DOMAINS

This section discusses the central features of the so-called masochistic (self-defeating) pattern, detailing these characteristics in accord with the eight domains of clinical analysis utilized in earlier chapters.

Expressive Behavior: Abstinent

Overtly, masochistic personalities are inclined to act in a self-effacing and unpresuming manner. For

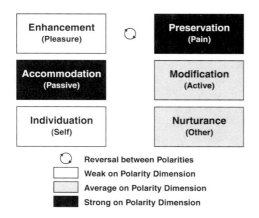

MASOCHISTIC PROTOTYPE

Figure 16.1 Status of the masochistic (self-defeating) personality prototype in accord with the Millon Polarity Model.

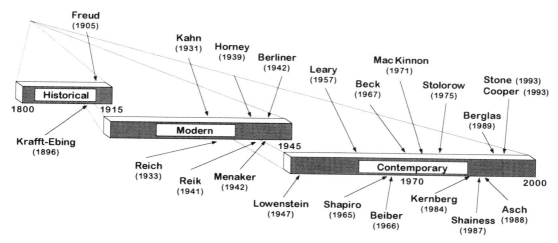

Figure 16.2 Historical review of major contributors to the masochistic personality disorder.

public consumption, they place themselves in an inferior light or abject position, are reluctant to seek pleasurable experiences, and refrain from exhibiting signs of enjoying life. For the most part, they present themselves as being nonindulgent, frugal, and chaste. Some appear shabby in public. Their clothes are designed to signify poverty or a disinterest in common forms of attractiveness. Others may actually abuse their bodies in ways that lead to self-starvation and anorexia. Most merely fail to dress up and appear appropriate given their socioeconomic status.

What we see in these abstinent behaviors is an active expression of self-denigration, an act of frustrating personal choices and self-respect. There is a taboo on most forms of enjoyment and self-enhancement. They are saying, in effect, that they do not wish to gain pleasure or gratification, that good things are not good for them, that any form of self-indulgence is best forbidden and denied. Some of these self-taboos are cast in the form of social concern and altruism. To them, self-denial is a sign of social conscience and responsibility; material gains would be ill-gotten were they not shared equally by others. In its most extreme form, the determination to self-denial can generate feelings of panic if the person realizes that he or she has failed to jettison an attractive trait or material possession.

Interpersonal Conduct: Deferential

These personalities prefer relationships in which they can be self-sacrificing, even servile and obsequious in manner. The tendency to place themselves in a general deferential position is notable. It is not untypical for them to allow, if not encourage, others to be exploitive and mistreating, even to take advantage of them. Equally problematic is a tendency to distance from those who are supportive and helpful. At times, they may render ineffectual the attempts of others to be kindly and of assistance. Most pathological is their inclination to solicit condemnation from others and to accept undeserved blame, as well as to court unjust criticism for their actions and performance.

By self-sacrifice, the masochist aims to arouse guilt in others, and such self-denigration helps explain relationships that would otherwise seem perplexing. Rather puzzling is that this pattern of repetitive self-flagellation persists even when a hurtful partner shows no sign of guilt or remorse. Instead, masochists continue to humiliate themselves before their denigrating partner. By intensifying their self-disparagement, they hope ultimately to provoke their unprincipled partner not only to admit their acts of dishonor and exploitation, but to feel contrite and loving. This signifies, in effect, the masochists' belief that they must submit and denigrate themselves to be loved and cared for by another.

The self-contempt that masochists feel necessitates that they assume an inferior and contemptible role with others. Hence, even when making an appropriate request, masochists feel that they may be taking undue advantages of another. Either they refrain from the request or do so apologetically and deferentially. Along this line, they will fail to

TABLE 16.1   Clinical Domains of the Masochistic (Self-Defeating) Prototype

Behavioral Level

(F) Expressively Abstinent. Presents self as nonindulgent, frugal, and chaste; is reluctant to seek pleasurable experiences, refraining from exhibiting signs of enjoying life; acts in an unpresuming and self-effacing manner, preferring to place self in an inferior light or abject position.

(F) Interpersonally Deferential. Distances from those who are consistently supportive, relating to others where one can be sacrificing, servile, and obsequious; allowing, if not encouraging them to exploit, mistreat, or take advantage; renders ineffectual the attempts of others to be helpful and solicits condemnation by accepting undeserved blame and courting unjust criticism.

Phenomenological Level

(F) Cognitively Diffident. Hesitant to interpret observations positively for fear that, in doing so, they may not take problematic forms, or achieve troublesome and self-denigrating outcomes; as a result, there is a habit of repeatedly expressing attitudes and anticipations contrary to favorable beliefs and feelings.

(S) Undeserving Self-Image. Is self-abasing, focusing on the very worst personal features, asserting thereby that one is worthy of being shamed, humbled, and debased; feels that one has failed to live up to the expectations of others and hence, deserves to suffer painful consequences.

(S) Discredited Objects. Object-representations composed of failed past relationships and disparaged personal achievements, of positive feelings and erotic drives transposed into their least attractive opposites, of internal conflicts intentionally aggravated, of mechanisms for reducing dysphoria being subverted by processes that intensify discomfort.

Intrapsychic Level

(F) Exaggeration Mechanism. Repetitively recalls past injustices and anticipates future disappointments as a means of raising distress to homeostatic levels; undermines personal objectives and sabotages good fortunes so as to enhance or maintain accustomed level of suffering and pain.

(S) Inverted Organization. Owing to a significant reversal of the pain-pleasure polarity, morphologic structures have contrasting and dual qualities—one more or less conventional, the other its obverse—resulting in a repetitive undoing of affect and intention, of a transposing of channels of need gratification with those leading to frustration, and of engaging in actions that produce antithetical, if not self-sabotaging consequences.

Biophysical Level

(S) Dysphoric Mood. Experiences a complex mix of emotions, at times anxiously apprehensive, at others forlorn and mournful, to feeling anguished and tormented; intentionally displays a plaintive and wistful appearance, frequently to induce guilt and discomfort in others.

(F) = Functional domain.
(S) = Structural domain.

Figure 16.3   Salience of personologic domains in the masochistic (self-defeating) prototype.

defend themselves when treated in an insulting and derogatory fashion. They behave as if they were defenseless, easily exploitable, a ready prey for those who seek to take advantage.

There is an inverse ratio, as Horney has put it, between success and inner security. Achievements in relationships or in occupation do not make masochists more secure, but more anxious. Fearing retribution, even total annihilation for their presumption of possessing worthy gains, they will neither stand up for their rightful awards, nor will they counter any expression of anger and resentment directed at them. Their dismay can only be expressed in disguised or denied forms. Only in the most extraordinary circumstances will masochists reprimand, reproach, or accuse others, even in a joking or sarcastic way. Of course, to be self-effacing, to suffer and refrain from success and self-assertion provide an alibi for not achieving much in life. They can thereby save face, both in their own eyes and in the eyes of others, for self-induced deficiencies and failings.

Cognitive Style: Diffident

Masochists are unsure of themselves, reluctant to assert their views, and tend to be self-effacing and restrained in their interpretation of life events. Disposed to construe events as troublesome and problematic, they are hesitant to see life in a positive light for fear that optimism will ultimately result in troublesome and self-denigrating aftermaths. As a result, masochists bring to their interpretive inclinations a habit of expressing views and anticipations that are pessimistic in orientation and contrary to favorable consequences. Not only do they express pessimistic and negative feelings, but whatever positive attitudes may be engendered are likely to be voiced without any genuine enthusiasm.

One might wonder how masochists can maintain this singularly heavy outlook without being devastated or collapsing under its weight. What is surprising is that masochists appear never to be undone by their persistent apologetic and self-deprecating attitudes. Observation over a period of time is likely to find that these self-reproachful attitudes are largely overdone, artificial, and forced, presenting an exaggerated facade of simulated communications. In great measure, their public posture of inadequacy, their voiced deficiencies and sense of demoralization, are designed (unconsciously so) to deflect or defeat those who they believe may assault and demean them. They are like the forest wolf, an animal that avoids continuing a fight-to-the-finish which would result in its annihilation. Instead, the wolf effectively thwarts its enemy by admitting its inadequacy, exposing its weakest link, the jugular vein, and thereby exhibiting that it is no longer a threat to the enemy. Similarly, by overtly exaggerating their weaknesses and ineffectuality, masochists turn away the aggression of others.

Self-Image: Undeserving

Masochists are overtly self-abasing, inclined in public to focus on their very worst personal features. As they see it, they have failed to live up to the expectations of others, despite their repeated efforts at self-sacrifice. Hence, they deserve to suffer painful consequences and, thereby, should feel shamed, humbled, and debased. In some masochists, this self-effacing, nondeserving image is so extreme as to lead them to conclude that anything that exemplifies personal achievement or competence could only have been the result of good luck or the contributions of others. To have a strong personal conviction or opinion is potentially endangering, a position that the masochist will quickly yield when facing an opposing viewpoint or interpretation. A public commendation of their work is usually judged to have been mistaken, an erroneous observation that fails to recognize their core deficiencies and inadequacies. Masochists do not seek to strive, to reach out for more than they have, because to do so challenges the fates, and exposes them to potential humiliation and denigration. Nothing should ever be done just for oneself. Requiring little keeps them in a small and protective shell, where they can maintain to a minimum any ridicule and deprecation.

As in the previously described Cognitive Style section, closer examination reveals that many self-sacrificing and unassertive masochists are preoccupied, not with the welfare of others, but with their own suffering and resentments. What appears on the surface to be a sympathetic and self-sacrificial attitude often cloaks a lack of genuine empathy and a distrust of others.

Object-Representations: Discredited

Reflecting on aspects of their past experience, but even more so by transforming their memories, the inner template of their objects and events come to have a distinctly negative tone. As masochists retrospectively view it, their past relationships are recast to signify problematic failures, and their own personal achievements are disparaged. Affectionate and erotic feelings of the past are transposed to their least attractive opposites. Adding further insult to these transmutations of past realities, unmodified internal conflicts are intentionally aggravated. In a similar fashion, mechanisms for reducing dysphoric feelings are subverted by processes that intensify the discomfort level of the masochist's recollections.

Owing to their early life experiences, masochists are likely to assume that all close relationships contain at their roots the potential of new frustrations and deprecations. In the main, they transmute their current everyday experiences to reproduce the frustrations and cruelty that remain from the past in their intrapsychic world. Some recognize that there are genuinely caring persons in their environment, but they judge it to be the invariable misfortune with which they are cursed in life that such persons are not the people to whom they relate.

As part of their intrapsychic dissonance, masochists struggle between internal images of being a tormentor themselves, on the one hand, and an innocent and abused victim, on the other. Thus, the self and other objects of their inner world are split into opposing elements, one convinced that others will continue to seek to destroy them, the other that they themselves wish to destroy others. Incapable of resolving this schism and thereby provide a genuinely positive attitude, the masochist bends over backward, as in a reaction-formation, attempting with every resolve to be an unambivalently reliant and ever-sacrificing partner.

Regulatory Mechanisms: Exaggeration

Whereas regulatory mechanisms are internal dynamic processes designed to resolve or soften the psychic pain of objective realities, these processes are inverted in the masochist, at least for public consumption. Rather than lessen their public discomforts, these personalities recall and exaggerate past injustices to raise their overt experience of distress. Similarly, they go out of their way to anticipate and magnify likely future disappointments as a means of raising their expectation of distress to levels consonant with their negative orientation. Furthermore, masochists often undermine their personal plans and sabotage their good fortunes so as to maintain or enhance the level of suffering and pain to which they have become accustomed.

As noted by Shapiro (1981), these patients dwell on their misfortunes, not only for public purposes, but to manage their personal discomfort and private suffering. Despite the melodramatic public fashion in which they exaggerate the incidental grievances of the past, exaggeration reflects the operation of a useful defensive maneuver in that it enables masochists to control and recast their sources of bitterness. By repetitively recreating in their mind early humiliations and injustices, masochists are able to diminish the actual pain and deprecation they indeed suffered. As in the implosive therapeutic technique, excessive exposure to painful and threatening stimuli ultimately diminishes their impact and power. So too is exaggeration an inverted form of self-protection and pain diminution. By exaggeration, they have diminished their suffering. They can now control it, compartmentalize it, bring it up at will, transform and moderate it; in effect, they can now be in charge of past discomforts, play them out, manipulate them, and make them less painful than they may have been, should that be the masochist's intrapsychic desire.

Morphologic Organization: Inverted

As is typical of personalities who are intrapsychically ambivalent or discordant, such as the masochist, their morphological structures possess contrasting and dual qualities. One segment of their inner world is structured in a more or less conventional fashion; the other reflects opposing or contradictory components. Thus, masochists exhibit a reversal of the pain-pleasure polarity, experiencing pleasure when pain would be more appropriate, and vice versa. As a consequence, they exhibit a repetitive undoing of intention and affect. There is a frequent transposition of channels of need-gratification so that frustration results. Most problematic, their inverted structural organization and dynamic processes result in actions that produce perplexing—and often antithetical, if not self-undoing—consequences.

As with most complex phenomena, the structure of personality undergirds many functions in the economy of the mind. Conventionally structured, the components of the mind serve to gratify

instinctual drives, impose social constraints by means of psychic expiation and punishment, and provide methods of adapting to life's realities. As in the case of the sadist, the compulsive, and the negativist, the masochist possesses intrapsychic structures that are in intrinsic opposition. For example, structural inversion of the basic polarities results in masochists assuming that they are loved most when they suffer most, generating the conviction that when they desire love, they must first seek to suffer. Rather than pursue affection in a straightforward fashion, masochists may need to engage in a form of "naughtiness," hoping thereby to elicit a rejecting or scolding response from the significant other; the assumption that carries them forward is the belief that forbidden behaviors will ultimately evoke love in return.

It is often quite puzzling and perplexing to track these reversals of what are usually straightforward and natural orientations. By defeating themselves, masochists seek not only to avoid being beaten and humiliated, but to elicit nurture and affection. The direct pursuit of pleasure threatens them by evoking experiences of anxiety and guilt. Whether these processes stem from "internalized bad objects" is one analytic way to formulate the problem. What this means simply is that the person has internalized a punitive system that must be enacted when normal affectional desires are sought. One must suffer, therefore, to be loved.

Mood/Temperament: Dysphoric

Masochists experience a complex of countervailing emotions. At times, they are anxiously apprehensive; at other times, they are forlorn and mournful. Many are disposed to feel anguished and tormented; these same individuals may exhibit a socially pleasant and engaging manner at other points in time. Some intentionally display a plaintive and wistful appearance, seemingly designed to induce discomfort and guilt in others.

Suffering among masochists is not invariably designed to impress others; it serves as much to ennoble the self. Once established, masochists effectively accuse others and excuse themselves. They seek in every way possible to dampen their own spirits, as well as those of others. At times of deepening distress, however, there is a powerful appeal for masochists to simply "let things go," just giving up what is felt to be a hopeless struggle for consistent and reliable love, for meeting the self-sacrificial demands imposed on self, to be free of the terror of everyday life. All of these feelings can create a sense of ultimate triumph, a way to escape forever, to be "done with it all." The broad dysphoric mix of emotions we often see in masochists serves to glorify their ultimate state of misery, providing proof of the fundamental nobility of their suffering.

PROTOTYPAL VARIANTS

The following sections detail a number of subtypes of the prototypal masochistic personality, subdividing them, as previously, into Normal, Child, and Adult variants.

Normal Styles

As with the dependent personality styles, the masochistic or self-defeating pattern is often a consequence of cultural values and customs rather than unique personal experiences. Again, there are societies, today, that still foist on certain individuals, particularly women, roles that are self-demeaning and servile, creating the impression for them and others that this is a deserving role and one that the individual should be proud to assume. Such are the values of some societies.

Oldham and Morris (1990) portray this normalized variant as seen in Western society as the "self-sacrificing" style characterizing them as follows:

To live life is to serve; to love life is to give. These are axioms for individuals who have the Self-Sacrificing personality style. The way they see it, their needs can wait until others' are well served. Knowing that they have given of themselves, they feel comfortable and at peace, secure with their place in the scheme of things. At its best and most noble, this is the selfless, magnanimous style of which saints and good citizens are made. (p. 308)

Some Self-Sacrificers feel unworthy and undeserving of love, attention, and pleasure. Therefore, they are always trying to earn it. Others may, deep down, have a very good sense of who they are and what they want for themselves—but they may feel that they should not indulge their "selfish" desires but instead tend to the needs of others. (p. 316)

A similar characterization may be found in the "yielding" interpersonal trait dimension that Millon et al. (1994) have formulated:

These persons show a disposition to act in a subservient and self-abasing manner. Placing themselves in an inferior light or abject position, they may even encourage others to take advantage of them. They are unassertive and deferential, if not servile. Often viewing themselves as their own worst enemies, they behave in an unpresuming, self-effacing, even self-derogating manner, and tend to avoid displaying their talents and aptitudes. Obsequious and self-sacrificing in their interactions with others; they can be depended on to adhere to the expectations of those they follow. Most people in this category possess abilities far in excess of those they lay claim to. (p. 33)

Childhood Syndromes

There is modest evidence to indicate the presence of a self-defeating pattern in children. The literature here is sparse and what can be gleaned from the odds and ends of clinical writings suggests a pattern that is perhaps more likely to be thought of as depressive in character.

Nevertheless, one does see in children a proclivity to suffer unduly as a means of soliciting attention and nurturance from their caregivers, a way of forestalling criticism and parental indifference, a style that signifies that the youngster judges at some level that his or her life is improved on balance when he or she is not faring well. Hence, there are children who learn in a rather simple and straightforward way that their parents are kindly and nonpunitive *only* when the child is feeling down, is ill, or is remorseful. At these times, the child experiences a respite from an otherwise hostile or neglectful family environment.

As yet, no formal designation or characterization has been applied to these youngsters. Rather, as noted, they are more likely to come to the attention of clinicians as depressive children, or children who have made suicidal attempts.

Adult Subtypes

As noted previously, there has been considerable controversy concerning the concept of a masochistic or self-defeating personality disorder. The decision to delete this personality pattern from the DSM-IV nosology is an unfortunate one, as we, the authors, perceive it. That the original formulation was interpreted in a specific and narrow manner by psychoanalytic thinkers early in this century was also unfortunate. The intense reaction by feminists to the original psychoanalytic formulation was justified. The solution favoring dropping the disorder from the official classification, however, was unwise, in our estimation. A better solution would have been to illustrate the many routes that individuals travel to become manifestly "self-defeating," only one of which reflects the developmental theme proposed by analytic thinkers.

Almost all the personality disorders are self-defeating in the sense that they engage in self-perpetuating patterns that foster the continuation of their already established pathologies. Hence, we have also argued that the original term assigned this personality type—masochistic—would be the better choice of the two designations. As we have stressed, the original analytic conception describes only one of several types of masochistic behavior. Its developmental dynamics are manifold, and it is the purpose of the following sections to illustrate a number of the subtypes of the personality that differ not only in the descriptive picture they manifest, but in the developmental course that leads to the clinical state.

The Self-Undoing Masochist

The classical psychoanalytic conception of the masochist represents individuals who have actively and repetitively, although unconsciously, sought out circumstances that lead to their own suffering, if not destruction. These behaviors do not necessarily bring pleasure, but may be the less distressing choice of two painful states. What is most notable is that these persons ostensibly create or provoke circumstances in which they will experience misfortune or abuse. They achieve what Reik (1941) called "victory through defeat" or what Freud (1916/1925) described as patients "wrecked by success." They appear, at least from an outsider's perspective, to be gratified by experiencing their own personal misfortunes, failures, humiliations, or ordeals. They eschew their own best interests, choosing in their stead, to be disgraced, victimized, even ruined.

A major manifestation of these behaviors is found in what has been termed the "success neurosis"; here, the deeper layers of psychic experience react to being successful by provoking intense anxieties and guilt, rather than pleasure and happiness. Success is responded to as if it were a horrible disaster. Rather than suffering these consequences, the individual undoes the success, behaving in ways that provoke failure, humiliation, or punishment. This process of undoing one's good fortunes is what characterizes the *self-undoing masochists*. In effect, these personalities repetitively do the opposite of what objectively is in their best interests. Although striving to achieve and perform their

best, they either stop short of its attainment, or quickly prove themselves insufficient to the task or undeserving of its rewards. In describing the "depressive psychopath," Schneider (1923/1950) wrote that these individuals "overtly express distress, but are covertly gratified at the prospect of the satisfaction they could bring from their misfortune."

For undoing masochists, there may be more relief in sharing one's troubles and failures than in experiencing the pressure of trying to live up to being successful and happy. In many regards, these self-undoing masochists are akin to avoidant personalities in that avoidants anticipate that they will ultimately fail or be disillusioned, even when matters appear to be going well for the moment. Rather than be disappointed when things inevitably turn sour, these personalities quickly undo themselves before they are undone by others. They would rather be seen as a victim of unfortunate circumstance, largely self-created of course, than as someone who has sought rewards and gains, and is expected thereby to maintain them and to behave in a valued and prideful way.

Moreover, in the developmental background of masochists, there are those whose lives have been better for them when they are suffering than when things are going well. Thus, a young child who learns that an otherwise mean-spirited and critical parent stops these abusive behaviors when the child is ill will also learn that being ill is the more comfortable state. Such persons may acquire a general belief that suffering is greatest when things are apparently going well than when they are manifestly in pain and discomfort. Hence, when faced in later life with opportunities for achievement and happiness, the undoing masochist steps back from these possibilities, fearing that more suffering will happen in "good" circumstances than when things are apparently problematic.

The Possessive Masochist

As with other masochists, these subtypes are constantly giving of themselves. Insinuating themselves may be perhaps a more descriptive and pertinent way of describing their actions. They are unable to let go of those to whom they are attached. Their need to be indispensable is so intensely self-sacrificial that others are unable to withdraw from the masochist without feeling irresponsible, unkind, or guilty. The *possessive masochist* entraps others, draws them into a reciprocal dependency, disarmed by the depth of concern and interest the masochist feels for them. Sacrificial to a fault, these possessive types find ways to make others feel simultaneously needy and fulfilled, less capable of functioning without the kindnesses and labors the masochist engages in to meet their narcissistic desires. In effect, they control others by an obligatory dependence. Moreover, they are jealously overprotective and indispensable collaborators, dominating those they possess by sacrificing themselves in every way others desire. This pattern of behaviors is seen in personality admixtures composed of core masochistic components permeated by characteristics most common to the negativistic style.

They make ostentatious sacrifices, intruding themselves repeatedly into the daily affairs of their children, their spouses, friends, and peers. They make it their business to always be there, to be vital and necessary contributors and advice-givers. They meddle into all areas of the possessed person's activities—love life, health, job situation—any and all problems in which masochists feel they can help and insinuate themselves. In this way, they seek to induce so profound a sense of obligation on the part of others that they are unable either to repay the masochist fully or to function effectively without that aid. This stratagem is effective; it creates an emotional and obligatory dependence that forces others to be both submissive and yielding by virtue of psychic need and personal guilt.

As a result of their maneuvers, masochists believe they have proprietary rights and are justified in enveloping and possessing others. They have suffered and have been kind and giving, all for the benefit of others. Whatever the possessive masochist has done ostensibly has been done for others, kindnesses intended to advance and better, rather than to control and dominate their lives. On the surface, what they do appears to be the opposite of what their ulterior motives may be. Masochists, in essence, bribe others to love them, give to others to control them, and become indispensable, and hence possessive of them.

The Oppressed Masochist

The *oppressed masochists* make use of all kinds of psychic symptoms and physical diseases to dominate and make their families and friends feel guilt. Anyone who is not responsive to the maneuver of psychological or medical illness may be quickly prompted to fall in line by their guilt-inducing moans and groans, saying, in effect, "Don't let my suffering make you think twice about me; overlook my suffering if you will and do only what you think is best for you." Ultimately, the apparent victim, the oppressed masochist, effectively triumphs over his or her true victims by making them feel guilty and obligated. Let us not be misled into

thinking that oppressed masochists are merely feigning their anguish; they experience genuine misery and despair, feel tormented and are often physically ill. However, these grievances are used secondarily, but quite effectively, to create guilt in others, enabling masochists to vent the resentments they feel, and exempting them from responsibilities they may normally be asked to carry out. As can be inferred from the preceding, these masochists frequently form an amalgam with features seen most prominently in the depressive personality disorder, accounting in part for their frequently judged coalescence by knowledgeable clinicians (Kernberg, 1988a).

Hypochondriacal manipulations may come to the fore when no other method of gaining love and dependence has been constructively achieved. Symptoms of illness are an effective and reliable way of assuring the receipt of attention and appreciation. Becoming a sorrowful invalid is a rather pathetic solution, a genuine, but self-created suffering that forces others to be caring and nurturing. The oppressed masochist does not actually enjoy his or her state of suffering; it is merely a necessary, if discomforting instrumentality to produce small benefits. By exaggerating real but minor discomforts, they are not merely making them public but, in effect, intensifying and making their suffering greater. It is the small secondary gains that make the process somewhat worthwhile.

Not to be overlooked is that the state of being oppressed enables the masochist to be exempt from fulfilling responsibilities, and also to discharge resentments toward others for not having been sufficiently caring or supportive in the past. Feeling victimized by the ingratitude of others, the oppressed masochist seeks to make them feel guilty and to act responsibly and caring, attitudes and feelings they have failed to demonstrate previously. As noted elsewhere in this chapter, oppressed masochists exaggerate their plight by moping about helplessly, placing added burdens on others, as well as causing them not only to be attentive and nurturing, but to suffer and feel guilty while doing so.

The Virtuous Masochist

These masochists are *proudly* unselfish and self-sacrificial. Their self-denial and asceticism are judged, at least by themselves, to be noble and righteous acts that signify that they are, in essence, meritorious, if not saintly. Rather than negate their altruism, depreciate their esteem in the eyes of others, and accept the inferior status that typifies most other masochists, prideful or *virtuous masochists* assert a sense of specialness and the high status and veneration in which they should be seen. Have they not consistently demonstrated their concern for the welfare of others, have they not deprived themselves of the good life, have they not sacrificed themselves at the altar of others?

Turning their life pattern on its heels, they cry out that others have been ungrateful and thoughtless and should be mindful of how faithful and loyal and giving the masochist has been to them. In effect, they, as the self-sacrificing servant, should be seen as the master; they should receive a constant stream of gratitude and attention, deserving to be repaid for their lifelong sacrifices, real or imagined. The overt demonstration of self-sacrifice is turned periodically into a display of pride and egocentrism. Having submerged themselves and been indispensable to others, they now praise themselves and become self-congratulatory: "I am good and virtuous. I am special and deserve special considerations," say these masochists. However, these narcissistic displays have but a shallow depth. Beneath the surface remains a low sense of self-esteem, and unsureness about their self-assertions, that whatever recognition they now get was manipulated and solicited rather than genuinely felt by others. For reasons consistent with the foregoing, these masochists will, at times, exhibit overt narcissistic features and, at other times, appear more like dependent styles. Hence, despite their self-approval and self-congratulatory tone, these virtuous masochists continue to be self-sacrificing, persistently doing for others what they wish others would do for them . . . but more genuinely so.

COMORBID DISORDERS AND SYNDROMES

This section outlines the major Axis I and Axis II disorders that frequently covary with the personality type under discussion. Matters of differential diagnosis are touched on briefly in the next section. It should be noted that this section is briefer than those for other personality disorders owing to the short period of time in which the masochistic (self-defeating) disorder was part of the official classification system (DSM-III-R). As a consequence, relatively little comorbidity research has been carried out to provide us with a basis for identifying the Axis I and Axis II covariants of the disorder.

Axis II Comorbidities

Figure 16.4 identifies those disorders that preliminary research suggests as combining with the

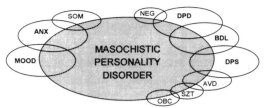

Figure 16.4   Comorbidity between self-defeating personality disorder and other DSM Axis I and Axis II disorders.

masochistic personality type. The overlap portrayal of Figure 16.4, shows that masochists (MAS) are associated primarily with the dependent (DPD), borderline (BDL), and depressive (DEP) personalities; all give evidence of reduced self-esteem, depressive symptomatology, and a tendency to devalue themselves with others (the traits just described are prominent only in a subset of borderline covariants). Also notable is a conjunction with the avoidant (AVD) pattern and, to a lesser extent, with the obsessive-compulsive (OBC), the negativistic (NEG), and the schizotypal (SZT) personality disorders.

Axis I Comorbidities

As noted previously, little data are available to justify making clear statements about the comorbidities between the masochistic personality and the Axis I clinical syndromes. A brief notation will be in order in the following paragraphs.

Mood Syndromes (MOOD).   It is almost redundant, as in the case of the depressive personality, to state that the masochistic individual is subject to mood disorders. *Dysthymia,* in particular, is in great measure an intrinsic feature of the masochistic pathology, a chronic and long-standing disposition to express, as well as to feel, extended periods of melancholy and sadness. Of course, and more than is typical of the depressive, these unhappy mood states are part of the self-sacrificial instrumental strategy employed by the masochist, a tendency to publicly display dejection and sadness as a vehicle to deflect serious condemnation, to evoke guilt in its stead, to elicit sympathy, and to avoid assuming onerous responsibilities.

Anxiety Syndromes (ANX).   As part of the general dysphoric state that typifies the masochist, we often see a diffuse, though usually moderate level of anxiety. As with similar personalities, such as the dependent (DPD) and depressive (DPS), the masochistic is highly susceptible to fears of loss and abandonment. The anticipation of such eventualities remains a persistent and underlying source of concern, leaving these persons vulnerable to the fear of finding that their desperate self-sacrificial efforts will not suffice to protect them against personal loss. States of *panic* may also emerge under these conditions, especially when the attachments needed to maintain their equilibrium are in serious jeopardy.

Somatic Syndromes (SOM). As described in other sections of this chapter, various forms of illness, most notably *hypochondriacal* disorders, are experienced and utilized by masochists as a decoy to deflect hostile actions on the part of others. Instrumentally, such ailments may also serve the unconscious purpose of self-depredation, a means of inducing suffering in oneself to accommodate feelings of guilt and to reflect acts of self-flagellation. Also notable is that many masochists have learned that illness is associated with genuine parental care and attention, an attitude on their part that would not otherwise be forthcoming.

DIFFERENTIAL DIAGNOSES

Overlap with Axis I syndromes is not usually problematic insofar as differential diagnosis is concerned. As noted in the prior section, masochists exhibit a wide range of concurrent clinical syndromes and, for the most part, these are comorbid in that they intrinsically penetrate the broader trait pathology seen in the personality type.

Distinctions may be made with a number of personality disorders, notably the depressive, the dependent, the borderline, and the obsessive-compulsive.

As noted in an earlier chapter describing the *depressive* personality, there are numerous theorists who describe these two pathologies as different facets of the same disorder (Kernberg, 1988). Despite their frequent comorbidity, it may be useful to distinguish them along certain lines. Both personalities operate with a heavy burden of guilt, suffering from a self-critical and overly severe conscience. However, they seek to appease these self-derogating inclinations in distinctively different ways, especially insofar as to how punishment should be meted out. Masochists seek to create situations in which others will be punitive; depressives engage in self-punishment. Masochist take an active stance, permitting or encouraging others to inflict and destroy what is of value to the masochist, experiencing thereby a perverse and momentary sense of expiation. By contrast, depressive personalities need no other agent to demonstrate their unworthiness. They persistently undermine themselves and hold fast to the belief that nothing and no one can remedy their unhappy state.

A similar pattern of comorbid pathology makes the distinction between masochism and the *dependent* personality a problematic one. Both seek to placate the object of their security and nurturance needs. Both behave in a submissive, noncompetitive, and self-demeaning manner. However, their psychodynamics are quite dissimilar. Whereas dependents merely manifest an intrinsic lack of self-esteem and neediness, masochists permit or intentionally create circumstances in which someone else will minimize their self-worth. The masochist, therefore, is active in arranging or provoking derogation from others; the dependent accepts his or her own diminished reality without taking any action.

Distinctions between the masochist and the *borderline* personality should not prove complicated in that the borderline is a much more severely defective structural pathology, exhibiting a much wider range of clinical symptoms. However, they do share a common tendency toward chronic self-mutilation and suicidal behaviors. Although not typical, masochists who blend into a borderline level of pathology will begin to exhibit hostile recriminations and angry rebukes, along with their more characteristic self-denial and self-derogation. The borderline, however, does not seek to undo or make up for repugnant and hostile behaviors to the extent that is frequently seen in the masochist. The primitive nature of the borderline's antagonistic behaviors signifies their greater pathology.

Brief note should be made of a feature that connects masochism and *obsessive-compulsive* pathology. Both personalities give evidence of extreme guilt feelings and the anticipation of punishment. Both seek forgiveness but do so in different ways. Both adhere to the demands and expectancies of others, but also do it in a different way. Whereas the masochist elicits punishment and is submissive, the compulsive eschews punishment and adheres to others in a perfectly proper manner. Distinctions are not especially problematic, because other characteristics and traits of the two disorders differ appreciably.

ASSESSING THE MASOCHIST: A CASE STUDY

Despite the paucity of research and assessment studies of the masochistic (self-defeating) personality pattern in the clinical literature, some preliminary data do provide us with guidelines for what may be found on the Rorschach, TAT, and MMPI. These will be commented on briefly in this section. Additionally, a case history and an associated MCMI-III profile and interpretation will be presented.

The pattern of responses on the Rorschach is likely to reflect the current state of the patient and the expectations that the examining clinician communicates. Although contaminated by the momentary status of the patient's emotions, masochists are prone to produce what they think would please the examiner. In general, masochists will generate fewer than an average number of responses. They tend to generate *D* and *d* responses rather than *Ws* and *dds*. There is a tendency also to give more than an average number of shading and color responses, usually with a reasonable measure of control and form quality. Animal movement may be more frequent than human movement responses; both are likely to be passive in character; response popularity is likely to be high. As far as content is concerned, depending on the comfort level of the respondent, there may be fractious interactions portrayed between the two sides of each card, particularly where one side seems to be overwhelming its parallel on the other.

The TAT often provides clearer evidence regarding the masochist's inclinations and current discomforts than does the Rorschach. Story themes frequently reflect events that are close to the respondent's life; for example, dominance and submission relationships are portrayed more frequently than the so-called "objective" content of the cards suggest. Themes of suffering, being beaten, and generally despised are fairly common. Gender identifications are evident, as is the oppressed character.

The MMPI is likely to reflect the current emotional state of these patients rather than their deeper character patterns. Perhaps most common is the 2-7/7-2 profile, inasmuch as most masochists come for treatment when their depressive feelings and anxieties are especially high. Scales 9 and 4 are likely to fall at the low end of the distribution of scores. These scores reflect the masochist's usual nonaggressive and nonenergetic styles of behavior. Should hostility and anger become increasingly manifest, Scale 9 may be much more elevated than is typical.

CASE 16.1

Jacqueline C., Age 44, Married

This masochistic woman has decompensated over several years into a borderline level of pathology following persistent quarrels with her exasperated husband, a man she married in her teens who began to spend weeks away from home in recent years, presumably with another woman. For brief periods, Jacqueline sought to regain her husband's affections, but these efforts were for naught.

Despite her willingness to submit to all his wishes, despite her efforts to deny herself any of her goals and ambitions, he was essentially immovable and increasingly nasty and critical. Despite his hostility and rejection, she would become a "doormat for him," permitting herself to do his bidding in spite of the humiliation she felt owing to his increasingly public and flagrant behaviors. She would make excuses to her neighbors and friends for public scenes he had with other women, attempting to cover up these embarrassing behaviors. At home, she would prepare food she knew he liked, arrange for vacations to places he enjoyed, all to no avail. In fact, there were periods when "he stood her up," failing to come home for a special dinner she prepared, and simply disappearing during periods they were to travel together with friends. Throughout these years, Jacqueline would quietly suffer, brood, and worry about her life, fearing "What would happen to me should he ever leave for good?" She was willing to do anything to forestall abandonment. The only upside was that he was never physically abusive and gave her sufficient funds to permit her to maintain an adequate home. As the years continued, Jacqueline became more depressed than masochistic. Over time, her resentfulness and bitterness were intensified, but nevertheless, she continued in her self-abnegating ways.

As she became increasingly disenchanted with life with her husband, she also became more guilt-ridden and self-deprecating. Her erratic mood swings not only intensified her feelings of psychic disharmony, but further upset her efforts to gain her husband's attention and support. As she persisted in vacillating between gloomy despondency, accusatory attacks, and clinging behaviors, more of her primary source of affection was withdrawn, thereby accentuating both her separation anxieties and the maladaptive character of her behaviors. The next step, that of a regression to a borderline level of functioning, was especially easy for her because it was consistent with her lifelong pattern of self-deprecation and inadequacy feelings.

Figure 16.5 presents a masochistic profile on the MCMI-III, and includes the following parallel interpretive commentary.

INTERPRETIVE SUMMARY

The MCMI-III profile of this woman suggests that she is often melancholy and blue, fearful, socially shy, and self-pitying. Expressing feelings of self-reproach and inappropriate guilt, she has learned to turn to others for security, and she assumes the role of a submissive, cheerless, and self-sacrificing partner in close relationships. Exceedingly insecure and vulnerable if separated from those who provide support, she willingly places herself in inferior or demeaning positions, permitting others to be inconsiderate, if not exploitive. She probably feels considerable resentment toward those who fail to appreciate her intense needs for affection and nurturance. Although emotionally irritable and overtly angry at times, she hesitates to discharge any negative feelings because her security is threatened when she expresses her resentment; most typically, she does so in a cranky and grumbling manner. Ever fearful of rebuff, she would rather withdraw from painful social relationships or try to convince herself that being isolated and sad is a worthy state.

It is likely that her masochistic depression, loneliness, and isolation are getting worse. Her underlying tension and emotional dysphoria appear to be present in disturbing mixtures of anxiety, sadness, and guilt. Insecurity and fear of abandonment may account for her mournful, self-denigrating, and dispirited attitudes. Aside from her periodic outbursts and expressions of resentment, she is likely to be conciliatory, placating, and even ingratiating. By acting dejected and weak, by expressing self-derogation, by being self-depriving, communicating a need for assurance and direction, and displaying a willingness to submit and comply, she hopes to evoke nurturance and protection. By submerging her individuality, voicing thoughts of death or suicide, focusing on her worst features and lowly status,

subordinating her personal desires, and submitting at times to abuse and intimidation, she hopes to avoid total abandonment. These hypotheses are worth reflecting on by her clinician.

Her preoccupation with and complaints of inadequacy, fatigability, and illness probably reflect her underlying mood of depression. Simple responsibilities may demand more energy than she can muster. Life may be referred to by her as empty with constant feelings of weariness and apathy. By withdrawing, being dependent and self-abnegating, or restricting her social involvement to those few situations in which she is not exploited or rejected, she precludes the possibility of new, potentially favorable experiences redirecting her life.

A pattern of anxiety and dysthymia is likely to have emerged over time in this edgy and ambivalently dependent woman. Unsure of the fealty of those on whom she has learned to depend and ambivalent about her neediness in this regard, she feels strong emotions of a resentful and hostile nature. Because of her dread of rebuke and rejection, she tries to restrain these emotions, albeit only partially successfully. Rather than chance total abandonment, she turns much of her anger inward, leading to self-generated feelings of unworthiness and guilt. Her increasingly hopeless feeling springs from a wide and pervasive range of events that have caused her to see her life as being filled with inadequacies, resentments, fears, diminished pleasures, and self-doubts.

PATHOGENIC DEVELOPMENTAL BACKGROUND

We will attempt to outline some of the biogenic and psychogenic factors conducive to the development of the masochistic personality pattern. Similarly, we will discuss a variety of self-perpetuating features of masochists that they themselves contribute to the intensification of their established pathology.

HYPOTHESIZED BIOGENIC FACTORS

There is little in the literature at this time to support the view that the vicissitudes of the masochist can be traced to genetic or constitutional dispositions. Hypotheses regarding the biological substrates of this disorder would seem to be both highly convoluted and speculative. Not that it is inconceivable that the anatomic wiring and biochemical

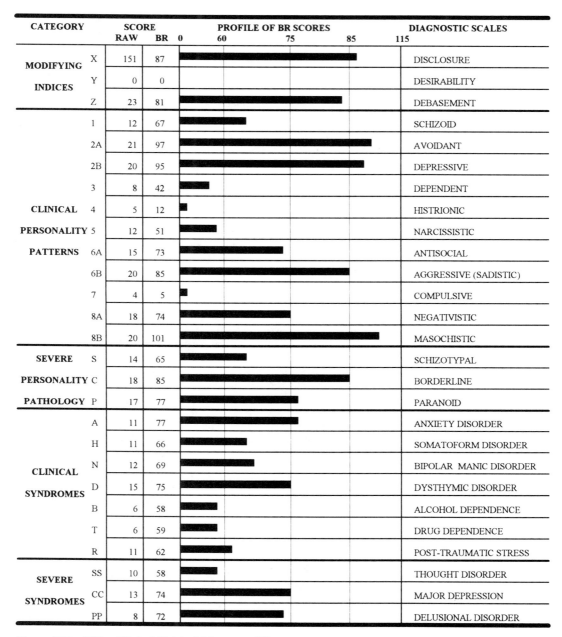

CATEGORY			SCORE		PROFILE OF BR SCORES				DIAGNOSTIC SCALES
			RAW	BR	0 60	75	85	115	
MODIFYING INDICES		X	151	87					DISCLOSURE
		Y	0	0					DESIRABILITY
		Z	23	81					DEBASEMENT
CLINICAL PERSONALITY PATTERNS		1	12	67					SCHIZOID
		2A	21	97					AVOIDANT
		2B	20	95					DEPRESSIVE
		3	8	42					DEPENDENT
		4	5	12					HISTRIONIC
		5	12	51					NARCISSISTIC
		6A	15	73					ANTISOCIAL
		6B	20	85					AGGRESSIVE (SADISTIC)
		7	4	5					COMPULSIVE
		8A	18	74					NEGATIVISTIC
		8B	20	101					MASOCHISTIC
SEVERE PERSONALITY PATHOLOGY		S	14	65					SCHIZOTYPAL
		C	18	85					BORDERLINE
		P	17	77					PARANOID
CLINICAL SYNDROMES		A	11	77					ANXIETY DISORDER
		H	11	66					SOMATOFORM DISORDER
		N	12	69					BIPOLAR MANIC DISORDER
		D	15	75					DYSTHYMIC DISORDER
		B	6	58					ALCOHOL DEPENDENCE
		T	6	59					DRUG DEPENDENCE
		R	11	62					POST-TRAUMATIC STRESS
SEVERE SYNDROMES		SS	10	58					THOUGHT DISORDER
		CC	13	74					MAJOR DEPRESSION
		PP	8	72					DELUSIONAL DISORDER

Figure 16.5   Millon Clinical Multiaxial Inventory-III.

susceptibility of the nervous system could not incline some individuals to learn masochistic forms of behavior, but proposals of this nature would be so deficient in their substantive grounding as to suggest it is best to leave this section blank.

Characteristic Experiential History

Our previous recognition that there are few grounds to implicate biogenic factors in the masochistic development does not mean that such factors play no role in the acquisition of masochisticlike behaviors. Aspects of their role will be noted in the following descriptive sections relating to the neuropsychological stages of development.

Pairing Pain and Pleasure

Events in the first stage of development, that termed *sensory-attachment,* may set the ground for an association between sensory pain experiences and psychic attachment behaviors. For most of life, a pain stimulus will decrease the likelihood that the organism will continue to make an approach response (i.e., organisms will distance from pain stimuli). However, there is a sensitive "imprinting" period that produces just the opposite response, that is, painful stimuli will increase the organisms approach/attachment response instead of decreasing it. In effect, what we see is a masochistic form of attachment behavior in the sense that punishment increases rather than decreases attachment to the punishing figure.

Experimental studies during these early imprinting periods (e.g., Melzack & Scott, 1957) showed that animals became significantly more attached to punishing objects, and would absorb repeated punitive experiences to a much greater degree than animals not subjected to these noxious stimuli. These organisms demonstrated the physiological reactivity that pain typically activates, but the usual aversive behavioral reaction was not only lacking, but was reversed.

If one wishes to translate such experiences to the human level, such individuals appear to be willing to endure suffering and discomfort, rather than mere indifference or deprivation. Unable at this early stage in life to connect the pain with the perpetrator, it feels greater security and warmth by attaching itself to the "accepting" perpetrator. In effect, it comes to believe that this "accepting love object" provides a significant level of security and protection. One might conclude, to extrapolate

further, that such experiences set the groundwork for masochistic behaviors, that is, subjecting oneself to degradation and suffering under the mistaken assumption that such behaviors ultimately provide protection, fear reduction and, perhaps, the diminishment of further pain.

As a result of the preceding, we see an insistent form of clinging behavior on the part of the child to his or her parent during the early imprinting sensory-attachment period, even though the care given may have been punitive or otherwise noxious. Moreover, the danger of being totally abandoned in a punitive world generates greater anxiety than to be attached to another when such negative consequences are being experienced. Unable to understand the source of the noxious experience, the infant has learned to feel more secure when it is close to or clings onto an attachment object, albeit a frequently rejecting and hostile one. Such patterns are likely to be intensified when the punitive parent is an inconsistent caretaker. At times, parents such as these are likely to be frustrating, depriving, or rejecting and, at other times, guiltily oversolicitous and possessively nurturing. The grounds for developing these masochistic inclinations are only further strengthened by this form of vacillatory behavior.

Acquiring a Self-Handicapping Attitude

The *sensorimotor-autonomous* stage is a crucial period in that children begin to acquire capacities to function on their own. Difficulties can arise to disrupt this natural progression toward increasing independence and self-confidence. Several such problematic events help establish aspects of the masochist's servile and self-denigrating attitudes.

Parental support and encouragement may not be forthcoming for achievements and autonomy during this crucial stage. For example, children who receive nonambivalent parental affection and support *only* when they are ill, injured, or deficient are likely to conclude not only that they are defective and incompetent, but that they are loved and encouraged only when things are problematic or go wrong. Further, they learn that they can deflect otherwise hostile and critical parents by enacting deficiencies or illnesses on their own. Hence, if parents exhibit affection and attention only when the child is suffering or handicapped, that child will learn willingly to appear disadvantaged or ill as an instrumentally effective style of behavior, an attitudinal orientation that sets the seeds for what ultimately takes the shape of masochistic behaviors.

Elaborating on the preceding, parents of future masochists may seek to undermine their child's increasing independence and autonomy. Whatever the reasons may be for this subversive behavior—fear of losing their child's affection, a broad-based negativism, a specific hostility to the child—by being alternately intrusively critical or emotionally remote, they create within the youngster a sense of confusion that is strongly weighted in the direction of self-doubt, self-derogation, and self-injury. Only at times of weakness and despair does the child evince genuine attention and concern from the significant parent. This sense of inadequacy and disadvantage is strongly reinforced during periods when parental concern for the child is especially oversolicitous and overprotective. Its impact is great because at this time the child not only learns that it is better to be handicapped than to be competent, but to believe that he or she is particularly needful of others for support and nurturance. Overprotective actions restrain the development of autonomous behaviors and deepen the image within the child of inadequacy and dependency. Such children will fear confronting the world on their own; moreover, they must submit to the will of others to function effectively. In effect, in the *sensorimotor-attachment* phase, where self-confidence and competence are generated, the child's development is stunted and interfered with by a restrictive parental attitude; such children become further convinced that they are most loved when they are most handicapped.

In its extreme form, these children may actually harm themselves—banging their body against hard objects, burning themselves, intentionally falling down stairs or off porches—enacting anything that intensifies public pain and suffering. Such acts ward off further physical punishment, but they also give children what little power they can gain for themselves, even if it is only to take charge over their own hurtful experiences. In this perverse way, these children find some small sphere with which they can undo their parents' domination. Finding this niche of self-control may provide the basis of the future masochist's pleasurable self-abusive behaviors.

Learning Discordant Gender Roles

The groundwork for acquiring a clear sense of male or female identity is given a major push during the *pubertal-gender identity* stage. The model for each of these two gender roles emerges progressively, but it does not take on a firm character until this phase of life. Parents are the model, and difficulties observed in the parental relationship serve as a basis for what youngsters are likely to incorporate unconsciously as perhaps inevitable for themselves. Although a parental myth of harmony is often presented for public consumption, the realities of the true relationship—argumentation, disillusionment, mutual distrust—are implicitly observed and incorporated by children, setting a framework for what it means to be intimately connected to another. Distant and cold fathers, uninvolved in the everyday give-and-take of family life, mothers lacking in personal achievement and emotional fulfillment, going through the motions of motherhood and womanhood, each creates an image for the child to adopt, usually unintentionally, but nevertheless deeply and firmly. Rarely do youngsters experience in early life a conscious awareness of their parents' relationship as being unusual or deviant. For the most part, what they observe is taken for granted as the way in which heterosexual relationships are enacted. Owing to the pseudo-harmony that is portrayed for many, most youngsters are willing to accept what they see as inevitable; alternative styles are observed only peripherally, but what remains as the core is the model they experience in everyday family interactions.

For the young female future-masochist, the family setting is often one in which the mother's marital role is an unhappy one, filled with disillusionment, irritability, and anger. The presence of an involved father is often lacking, an absence which serves as a model for what she may expect from her future male suitors. Observing her distant and ineffectual father, she will feel "most at home" with equally ineffectual and distant suitors. For other young women who have observed the devaluation of a father's role in the family, there may develop a perverse conclusion that any man who in fact desires her could not possibly be a good enough suitor. In this inversion of logic, the teenager assumes that it is only those who reject her who could possibly love her. This perverse logic may also stem from self-rejection and an unwillingness to value her true self-worth. Thus, anyone who genuinely cares must not be a "real" man, perhaps even be a "fool"; if he knew what was good for him he could not possibly desire her.

Another variant of this distorted female role is an attraction for men who are untrustworthy and unreliable, who can make life momentarily exciting, but ultimately miserable and unhappy. These problematic attachments often arise in families where the father has been characterized by the mother as a cleverly disreputable and deceitful human being. Should the father have been distant in the youngster's early life, the adolescent girl may be driven, albeit unconsciously, to seek out an equally charming ne'er-do-well, that is, to regain that which she desired but lost in early life. What we see in these cases is a repetitive sequence of searching for and initiating relationships that often begin as intensely passionate, but ultimately result in a sequence of unrequited love, temporary reconciliations, and lifelong patterns of misery and discontent. Seeking the unattainable or treacherous love-object re-creates for this youngster what might be judged to be a form of masochistic behavior.

In the young man with a similar dysfunctional background that inclines him toward problematic gender relationships, we often find an early sequence in which the mother was dominating, seductive, and hypercritical of the father. Ambivalent about their feminine role, these mothers often turn to their sons as an alternate to their distant and cold husbands. Although initially compliant and overidealizing of their mothers, these boys acquire a mixed attraction to the opposite sex. On the one hand, they can be easily seduced by the openness with which girls express their thoughts and affections. Mirroring their early role with their mothers, these boys find themselves attracted and drawn into an intimate relationship. In short order, however, contrary feelings come to the fore, reflecting their confused and distrustful feelings toward women that were engendered in their relationship with their mother. Hence, the young man may be initially seduced, but then withdraws and becomes rejecting. The young woman is drawn to men who show an initial interest in her, but then becomes equally untrusting and derogating, that is, until he withdraws, at which time she is attracted and drawn to him once more. The vicissitudes of this "sadomasochistic" pattern typify the gender roles played out by such youngsters.

Both male and female premasochistic personalities may be irresistibly attracted to those who are unable to respond in a healthy and reliable manner. Whether in the courtship phase or after marriage, there is a search on the part of both genders for the unobtainable, setting in motion a vicious circle in which each will be drawn to the other initially, but will, unconsciously, undo that relationship, leading to discontent and disillusionment on both parties.

Failing to Integrate Good Fortune

It is in the last of the major neuropsychological stages, termed *intracortical-integration,* that the final synthesis of development takes firm hold. Whereas the major task for females is given primary focus during the pubertal-gender identity stage, that is, where *self-in-relationship-to-another* plays itself out prominently, the major task for the male, the cohesion of a *sense-of-self,* begins to come together in the intracortical-integrative stage.

For the premasochistic young man, this last phase of development is partially undone by an image of mother (female) as the more powerful and omnipotent parent. The male adolescent, raised in a discordant family system, finds his masculine image to be one of powerlessness and dependency, in which the identity he may prefer is confused, but nevertheless diminished in its self-worth. Perceiving himself as weak and helpless in comparison to his mother, he cannot integrate the image of what he believes a man should be, and what it is that he has experienced that image to be. Not only is mother (women) a troubled and troublesome victim, but she is the indomitable force that has created the system of his life.

Given this background, the integration of the male role becomes a formidable task. Not only is the youngster likely to have learned to be overly submissive and humble, but his behaviors may have become parasitic in nature. Although he does not wish to internalize his personal limitations, he finds himself not only clinging to another, but never sure that the object of his attachment will fulfill his needs. He feels inadequate and dependent as a male, but "knows" that females cannot be trusted or depended on. At a time when he should be developing a sense of initiative, personal opinions, and self-confidence, he possesses a set of self-denigrating attitudes and perceptions. No less a consequence of the warped relationships of his past, he feels that the world around him will also be derogating and demeaning. He thereby dreads asserting himself, believing that such initiatives will likely engender further proofs of his inadequacies and imperfections.

What the young premasochistic male has come to see as his means of security is to publicly belittle himself and withdraw into unobtrusiveness. Not only does he seek to make himself insignificant and inconspicuous, but he will attempt to undo any venture that may lead others to expect more of him. He therefore fears success, becomes alarmed should he attain even a small measure of achievement or good fortune. He would rather "not matter," not be conspicuous in any way, diminish his value, and thereby deprive himself of even a modest level of conventional satisfaction.

For both male and female premasochists, there is an openly expressed belief that one does not deserve success, despite clear evidence to the contrary. There are claims that advancements and rewards carry increased responsibility and continuing expectations. Beneath these public disavowals, however, are deeply held fears of being exposed as inadequate, and the dread of assuming genuinely adult responsibilities. No less significant is the fear of retaliation for having asserted oneself and become independent of others. They have learned that good fortune often elicits emotional withdrawal and derogating commentary from a rejecting parent, an aggression that subsides, even inverts into care and affection, when they are in a one-down or disabled position.

It is this inability to cohere a sense of self-worth during the *intracortical-integrative* stage that prevents the individual from completing the full circle of mature development. In its stead, these personalities recreate undesirable experiences for themselves, possess a "repetition compulsion" to undo themselves. Rather than moving forward, they retreat repeatedly to the only life they know, that of weakness, disability, and suffering. Unable to feel secure in a world of successful, no less caring and considerate people, they intentionally preclude their own advancement. Familiar with a world of indifference and hurt, they distance from relationships that are kindly and supportive. Not only do they search out that which will make them suffer, but they look for new difficulties, and are prone wherever they can to see the worst in life. To be uncared for, to be derogated, and to live in a world of failure and misery is a familiarity that breeds a perverse form of security in their lives.

SELF-PERPETUATION PROCESSES

As the interim label for masochistic personality clearly indicates, these individuals are "self-defeating"; what they do further intensifies their difficulties and undoes what promising advances may have happened in their lives. Although the very notion of self-perpetuation is therefore intrinsic to the masochistic construct, it may be useful to specify some of the more explicit ways in which these personalities undermine their own healthful progress.

Demeaning of Self

Masochists are specialists in beating themselves down, disparaging themselves, belittling themselves, ridiculing themselves, being contemptuous of themselves. Although there are considerable differences among masochists in the degree to which they are aware of these denigrating processes, they all add up to diminishing their capacity to take anything that they do seriously; they are surprised, if not astonished, when others judge their opinions and attitudes to be of consequence. Not only are they unable to appreciate their own talents and achievements but, as has been stated previously, they seek to undo whatever good fortune may accidentally have come their way.

As a consequence of demeaning their own self-worth, these individuals greatly impair themselves, preclude any form of spontaneous self-assertive behavior, exaggerate their difficulties and, in effect, submerge themselves in a pervasive feeling of helplessness and ineffectuality. Not only do these behaviors undermine their competence and self-esteem, but they throw themselves into an abyss of lifelong misery that is quite disproportionate to the circumstances that their life's experiences would justify. Hence, through their own actions and exaggerations, they place themselves repeatedly in positions of almost irrevocable disgrace and contempt.

Dependence on Others

In a manner similar to the dependent personality, masochists have devalued themselves to such an extent that their self-worth depends wholly on the judgment of others. Their psychic state rises or falls with others' opinions of them. Devaluing the self has made the masochist entirely dependent on others for judging the adequacy with which self-sacrificial behaviors have met their desires. Self-minimization forces the masochist to turn to others to provide not only feelings of security, but a sense of salvation. Should the self-denigrating and self-abasing behaviors fail to be recognized, the individual's search for appreciation may begin to take on a frantic character, further reducing the sense of self-esteem.

The fear of being abandoned and isolated becomes prominent at times when masochists are unsure of their value in the eyes of significant others. They are unable to be alone for any length of time, and feel lost and rejected, cut off from the stream of life that they need. Fearful as these insecurities may be, they can be overcome by any form of connection to others; abuse can be tolerated as long as it is kept within extreme limits. As long as masochists can remain connected and needed, regardless of how much abuse they receive, they will not feel the nameless terror of being totally abandoned. Hence, they must keep attached at all costs, regardless of the humiliation and derogation they experience. To be alone is the ultimate proof that they are not only unwanted and rejected, but disgraced and forsaken.

Intensifying Self and Other Abuse

Although the masochist has undoubtedly experienced troublesome early relationships, we know that they also transform new life events to conform with those of the past. This distorting process creates a series of unrealities. Not only do they suffer anguish, shame, and guilt for every shortcoming or failure in their lives, but they are hyperscrupulous about their own behaviors and circumstances, such that everything they do or observe deserves to be ridiculed and disparaged. They are "injustice collectors," seeing unfairness, if not derogation in those who do not appreciate their self-sacrificial behaviors.

A problem that may arise here is a growing indignation felt toward those whom they see as having humiliated them. This reversal from self-denial into a more openly critical and negative attitude toward others reflects a desire to quiet their idealized self-image and conscience. Although they judge themselves to be unworthy, they do not judge themselves so unworthy as to continue to have abuse heaped upon them *in spite of* their willingness to carry undue burdens and to persist in their self-sacrifice. As this reversal of characteristic behaviors becomes intensified, the masochist begins to discharge this misery and to assert a feeling of entitlement, a confused and disillusioned state that leads the masochist to want others to make up for the perceived injuries that have been perpetrated on him or her throughout life.

No longer are such masochists merely self-pitying persons who feel unfairly treated; they now rise up in a rather pathetic form of righteous indignation. The more they distort the actions of others as being accusatory and abusive, the more frantically are they likely to exaggerate the wrongs that have been done to them and the more deeply they feel that recompense is their due. Should their vindictive anger break into consciousness, it will mar their idealized image of being virtuous and magnanimous, violating the inner image of being self-sacrificing and all-forgiving. Hence, the expression of previously repressed resentments becomes a disruptive element of considerable magnitude. In addition to creating inner turmoil, it may provoke others into rejecting the masochist even further, leading the person thereby to be doubly ignoble, both victim and perpetrator.

THERAPEUTIC INTERVENTIONS

Although the masochistic patient's self-defeating behavior pervades all aspects (personal, social, and occupational) of functioning, the self-sabotaging tendencies are seen primarily in the area of interpersonal relationships. Despite relatively adaptive adjustment in some spheres of life, there often exists a long history of abusive relationships that combines with an apparent lack of understanding of his or her role in inviting maltreatment. Patients may lament years of undeserved victimization and suffering while continuing to behave in excessively deferential and self-demeaning ways and making no attempt to constructively alter the dynamics of exploitive relationships. The therapist may marvel as a patient sabotages potentially positive interactions and rejects opportunities for involvement with caring and considerate individuals, dismissing them as boring or otherwise inappropriate companions.

Lacking the experience of deriving rewards from behaving in an interpersonally competent and self-respecting manner, and having no coherent personal identity other than victim, the masochist is threatened with a loss of self in giving up his or her usual ways of relating. Suffering provides the masochist with an identity, a sense of value, and predictable interactions. The therapist working with a masochist has to keep in mind that much work will have to be done to provide the patient with the foundations of a healthier self-concept. Resistance to adopting new modes of interaction will be reduced as self-respecting behavior can be meaningfully incorporated, rather than posing a threat to the only identity they have known. The therapist must point out behaviors that provoke hostile reactions from others, while empathizing with the patient's tendency to perpetuate victimization.

Eventually the patient may internalize the therapist's empathy and positive regard, thus becoming more amenable to change.

STRATEGIC GOALS

Much of the masochist's difficulty is based on a pain-pleasure discordance that draws them to situations and individuals that cause them pain. Reestablishing a balance on this polarity can help patients acquire more adaptive behaviors. Also, a shift on the active-passive dimension can lead to constructive rather than self-defeating attitudes and actions.

Interventions within the masochist's dysfunctional domains are intertwined with the former objectives. Cognitive interventions that produce change within the patient's cognitive style, exploring the developmental history of the patient's difficulties, and behavioral interventions that teach assertiveness and social skills may allow masochists to replace customary interpersonal deference with respect-fostering relationships. Strategic plans of action, as well as increased insight, can help patients reduce their tendencies to allow others to abuse them.

Reestablishing Polarity Balances

To restructure the masochist's disordered personality, a balance needs to be established on the pain-pleasure and active-passive polarities. A major problem of masochists is their distorted and inverted focus on life-preserving experiences. The tendency to perpetuate unpleasant situations stems from the masochist's identity being intertwined with suffering and the role of victim. As described throughout the chapter, many masochists learned in childhood to misidentify abuse as love. To modify their self-sabotaging and abuse-perpetuating behavior, they first need to clarify and internalize the difference between loving and abusive behavior, that is, between pleasure and pain. Work must also be done to help the masochist develop a more adaptive and positive self-image. Interventions aimed at cognitive reorientation can be effective in this regard.

Once patients become cognizant of, and begin to overcome, their victimized self-image and self-inflicted pain, they may be ready to start overcoming their self-defeating passivity. Behavioral intervention, including assertiveness and social skills training, can prepare the patient to relate to others in a more equity-fostering way. Patients can be taught to set time aside daily to engage in pleasurable activities, and can reward themselves in prespecified ways for appropriate interactions.

Modifying Domain Dysfunctions

Central to masochistic personalities' characteristic difficulties are their undeserving self-image and their dysphoric mood. Convinced that they have failed to achieve others' expectations, masochists genuinely believe they deserve to be shamed and punished. Suffering is actively sought to ease their sense of guilt about perceived failings. Consistent with this self-image, the masochists' mood is dysphoric, and ranges from anxiety to anguish. After years of believing themselves to be both inadequate and victimized, masochists display extreme self-denial and deferential interpersonal conduct. These modes of expressing themselves and relating interpersonally serve a preconscious purpose. They help maintain consistent and predictable internal and external representations of the self as a suffering, inferior individual. By behaving in a self-effacing and unpresuming manner, and by declining to participate in pleasant activities and denying any experiences of joy, masochists can also "atone" for inadequacies and render themselves beyond reproach.

Convinced that pleasure and fun are undeserved and, in fact, beyond their very capacity, masochists find that suffering not only eases their guilt but is the only feeling they can allow that is better than the prospect of an inner nothingness. Not only do these patients feel unjustified in attempting to feel better, but their suffering and helplessness serve to provide a tangible identity and social role. The role of depression in the patient's dysphoric mood should be carefully evaluated. Psychopharmacological intervention in the form of antidepressants may be indicated for some patients. Improved affect and self-esteem can help provide motivation to continue working toward more permanent structural personality changes.

For some masochists, the tendency to be self-sacrificing, even to invite exploitation and accept undeserved blame, have other self-serving functions. Experiences with punitive adults in childhood may lead to equating maltreatment with love; thus, some masochists may search out powerful and oppressive others and play the complementary part to satisfy their need for affection. Others have learned that a punitive parent was in fact most loving, or at least less cruel, when the masochist's suffering was most evident. Overt expressions of suffering in adulthood may thus serve to appease significant others or, as the only weapon in the masochist's arsenal, to punish them and make them feel guilty for not meeting the person's needs.

A therapist working with a masochistic personality is going to encounter much resistance in trying to modify the patient's poor self-concept. Methods of cognitive reorientation can help patients realize that their diffident cognitive style maintains their difficulties. Self-effacing and unsure of themselves, masochists construe events as troublesome and problematic for fear that optimism will ultimately result in anguishing and discouraging consequences. More adaptive ways of thinking can help to alter the basis on which these masochistic behaviors are built. In time, patients may stop repetitively recalling past injustices, anticipating future humiliations, and undermining personal objectives and good fortune in order to maintain their accustomed level of suffering and pain.

Insight-oriented therapy can help identify the developmental causes of the masochist's discredited object-relations. The patient can learn that while his or her parents confused love and abuse, not all people do. Behavioral interventions can teach assertive social skills that provide the patient with new modes of interacting. Successful therapeutic intervention should help reorganize the patient's personality structure so that its organization is no longer inverted. Once the pain-pleasure polarity has been rebalanced, the channels of need gratification and frustration should no longer be transposed. This adjustment can help the patient strive for reward rather than pain, resulting in more adaptive behaviors.

Countering Perpetuating Tendencies

A therapist working with a masochistic personality would be well-advised to focus efforts on helping the patient become aware of and change problem-perpetuating behaviors. Goals here are to counter the patient's willingness to be abused, to be involved in self-demeaning experiences, and to engage in self-sabotage through the undoing of positive events.

Cognitive interventions and exploratory therapies can help the patient expand understanding of a fuller range of human interactions, allowing the patient to conceive relational experiences that can work without victimization. Some masochists have learned to feel important or validated when others are hostile toward them. Masochists learn

that a significant other's cruelty relents when the masochist is suffering, and from that conclude that their value increases with increments in their unhappiness. A growing understanding of this process may encourage patients to adopt new attitudes and interaction styles. Bolstering the patient's self-esteem will further increase the likelihood that self-demeaning experiences will be avoided as they become less consistent with a changed and more positive self-image.

Some patients may benefit from pharmacological intervention as an adjunct to dyadic treatment. Antidepressants may bolster improvements in self-esteem and reduce guilt. In conjunction with new ways of thinking about themselves and their environments, decreased guilt can help patients prevent the undoing of positive events that in the past had served as self-punishment for failings, as well as preserving their sense of identity.

TACTICAL MODALITIES

Masochistic patients are likely to elicit a number of antitherapeutic countertransference reactions from their therapists. However, a consistently warm and empathic alliance can provide a prototype for self-evaluation that the masochist can internalize over time and draw on in working to overcome self-defeating tendencies.

Domain-Oriented Techniques

A useful initial approach with the masochist, as it is with all personality disorders, is the adoption of a supportive orientation. Most masochistic patients will anticipate rejection and/or humiliation by the therapist and will provoke him or her to fulfill expectations. Establishing a therapeutic alliance in which the therapist expresses sympathy for the patient's tendency to elicit negative reactions from others, as a form of self-punishment, can help the patient adopt a less harsh self-concept. This should help the patient understand that he or she does not deserve to suffer and, hence, contribute to building a more positive identity.

Much like depressive patients, masochists often suffer from excessive guilt. The therapist's sympathetic reassurance that the patient has suffered enough can mobilize the patient to work toward a more adaptive and satisfying way of life. Also like depressives, masochists may deny or repress their resentment of others failing to recognize that hostility and a desire to punish others, induce guilt, and reactivate the vicious circle that leads to personal suffering. Helping patients to acknowledge their feelings of resentment and to express them more directly can make it easier for them to develop a self-concept that is inconsistent with the victim role. Once the patient comes to trust that the therapist's supportive empathy toward these self-destructive tendencies will not be transformed into abusive derision, the probability of the patient benefiting from other interventions is greatly increased.

Behavioral interventions can help masochists change their tendency to be victimized in relationships. Social skills training can expand their interactional repertoire beyond their typical abuse-inviting and self-denigrating subservience. Assertiveness training can help patients learn how to enforce personal limits that prevent abuse. Learning to express their desires allows masochists to have their needs fulfilled directly and obviates the need for passive-aggressive behaviors, as well as manipulative displays of martyrdom and suffering. Helping the patient overcome individual self-defeating behaviors begins with a careful analysis of the patient's interactions. Masochistic behaviors need to be identified, as do the circumstances that trigger them. Enjoyable and esteem-building events and activities should also be noted. By keeping a record of daily events, behaviors, and moods, interventions to help change self-sabotaging tendencies can be devised. The patient's dysphoric mood also needs to be targeted. Esteem-building activities, as well as material reinforcers, can be used as rewards for behaving more adaptively and for carrying out assignments successfully.

Some behavioral intervention programs include the patient's significant others who are drawn upon to facilitate communication and to guide and support interactions in the patient's natural environment. Toward this end, *interpersonal* approaches can highlight the role of the patient's own actions in initiating and maintaining self-defeating patterns. In interpreting the patient's behavior, the therapist needs to keep in mind that many masochists are not fully aware that they have contributed to their own abuse, nor that their own behavior leads them to fall repeatedly into the victim role. The process by which they seek abusive partners and by which they provoke benign others to denigrate them is largely unconscious. Although it is important for the therapist to point out to patients that parents' punitive attitudes have been internalized in the form of self-criticism, outright blaming by the therapist of parents may create patient resistance that can

interfere with therapeutic progress. Guilt over anger at idealized parents can be too much for some patients to bear. The therapist can point out the victim role that the patient is playing in present relationships. The value of asserting one's rights and of learning skills to avoid or stop maltreatment need to emphasized. More adaptive modes of interaction should be explored.

Including masochistic patients in treatment *groups* can be helpful in providing the patient both with support and with assertive role models. However, the group therapist should watch out for the possibility that such patients will sacrifice their own needs for the benefit of other members, and inadvertently be reinforced for the "martyr" role. Alternatively, group members may become frustrated when after hours of attempting to find solutions for the masochist's difficulties and providing overt support, the masochist continues to protest that the situation is hopeless and that he or she is also hopeless. The unpleasant feedback may be destructive to a newly burgeoning sense of self.

Couples intervention can be helpful if the partner is willing to cooperate, but we know that masochists often pair up with a range of abusive types. If the partner is willing, role-playing and role-reversals can help both understand the dynamics of their interaction and how it perpetuates self-defeating tendencies.

Cognitive approaches in the treatment of the masochistic personality are similar to the ones employed for reducing depressive symptomatology, and emphasize directly challenging the patient's self-sabotaging assumptions through logical reasoning. By keeping track of events, thoughts, and moods, masochistic patients can learn how much of their suffering is directly related to their appraisal of their environment and of themselves, and how much to their self-demeaning attitudes and behaviors.

Once negative automatic thoughts have been identified, they can be evaluated and modified by teaching patients to ask themselves such questions as "What's the evidence?" "Is there any other way to look at it?" "How could alternative (less pessimistic) explanations be tested?" and "What can I do about it (to make it better)?" The tacit beliefs upon which automatic thoughts rest also need to be identified and altered in order for lasting change to occur and for negative thoughts not to resurface in a new form. Past experiences that have led to the patient's poor self-image can be discussed, and the role of dysfunctional cognitive habits such as overgeneralization, arbitrary inference, emotional reasoning, and dichotomous thinking in maintaining it can be confronted directly. A basic strategy is to help patients realize that their thoughts are inferences and not facts about themselves and the world. Predictions can then be made and experiments devised to test their validity.

Psychodynamic approaches to treating the masochistic personality tend to conceptualize the patient's behavior to be a result of his or her childhood relationship to a withholding or cruel parent. The child defended against his or her greatest fear—abandonment by the parent—by assuming a self-deprecating and defeated position that served to complement the parent's behavior. As in most other approaches, the importance of the patient-therapist relationship is emphasized. Whereas the classic psychodynamic therapist stance is neutral and reserved, with the masochistic patient this approach may create an atmosphere of inequality that is too conducive to masochistic transference reactions reminiscent of the parent-child relationship. It has been suggested that a conscious self-presentation as a fallible human being by the therapist may help prevent the patient from trying to act out the unconscious wish for submission to avoid abandonment.

Regardless of the therapist's sensitivity, masochistic patients will likely seek to frustrate the therapist's efforts with negative therapeutic reactions, as well as to challenge the therapist by claiming that nothing can help them (sometimes even blaming the therapist for making them worse). Brenner (1959) sees masochistic tendencies as serving four separate functions: repetition of the patient's reactions to childhood conflict; defense against feelings of loss or helplessness; expiation; and unconscious gratification. Persistent yet sympathetic interpretations of the patient's self-defeating attitudes are recommended; objective statements are likely to leave the patient feeling criticized and worthless. The realistic need to point out the patient's less attractive tendencies should be balanced by a warm and relatively self-revealing therapeutic stance so as to avoid having the patient internalize the therapist's interpretations as insults. Berliner (1947) suggests that the therapist begin to bring the patient's self-defeating behaviors to awareness through examination of relationships outside the therapy. By pointing out that the patient's accusations and complaints all relate to individuals the masochist loves or cares about, the therapist can avoid an intense transference reaction that might lead to excessive acting

out. Once the patient achieves some insight into his or her own masochistic patterns, any acting out that does occur in the context of the therapy becomes easier to interpret.

Berliner suggests that the patient and therapist can then proceed to working through the patient's identification with the aggressor. The patient can thus come to appreciate how much of his or her self-criticism is due to external reinforcement, and can thus learn to differentiate between love and cruelty. Eisenbud (1967) suggests that another avenue that leads to therapeutic success is to target the masochist's feelings of inadequacy and need for efficacy.

Masochistic personalities often develop depression after years of abuse and self-sabotaging, which then serves to maintain the masochistic tendencies. Evaluating the appropriateness of *psychopharmacological* intervention for the patient may serve as a useful first road to regulate mood. It is also important for the therapist to emphasize that there is a lag between the onset of antidepressant medication and its psychoactive effects so as to guard against the patient giving up in the interim.

The major strategies and tactics discussed in this section are reviewed in Figure 16.6.

Catalytic Sequences and Potentiated Pairings

What arrangements should be planned to maximize the efficacy of the individual domain-oriented techniques one might employ with these difficult patients?

Masochistic patients tend to have negative reactions to therapy and to resist change, making a supportive stance a useful way for the therapist to establish initial rapport. Patience and consistency,

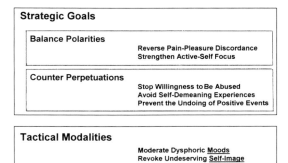

Figure 16.6 Therapeutic strategies and tactics for the prototypal masochistic personality.

despite the patient's provocations, can aid in solidifying the masochist's trust that the therapist will not abuse his or her "superior" position in the relationship. If after careful evaluation the patient is judged to be suffering from a concomitant depression, appropriate antidepressant medication can help provide the motivation to persevere through more anxiety-provoking exploratory and cognitive work.

If the patient's partner is amenable to entering couples therapy, it can help provide the patient with a supportive home environment and insight into interaction patterns. Behavioral couples intervention can teach the couple more adaptive ways of relating. Group treatment is another potential adjunct that can help increase the patient's social appropriateness and assertiveness skills. If it is deemed more preferable, behavioral interventions can also be integrated into the primary dyadic therapy.

RISKS AND RESISTANCES

Most therapists may initially be able to empathize with the patient's low self-esteem and complaints of years of abuse. However, as the patient's tendency to arrange situations to ensure the continuation of pain becomes increasingly evident, the therapist may come to harbor the suspicion that the patient enjoys suffering. The patient's pathetic self-presentation and ineffectual implementation of the therapist's suggestions begin to call forth an almost sadistic therapeutic style. Many provoke defensiveness by devaluing both the therapeutic process and the therapist. Many a well-meaning therapist can be seduced in this manner to complement the masochistic patient's role with subtly punishing comments.

Although a defensive reaction on the part of the therapist is understandable, challenging the masochist's negative distortions too early in the therapeutic process may be counterproductive. Such confrontation may prove too threatening to the patient's undeserving self-image, which requires that anything the patient is involved in must not be very good, including therapy. If the

therapist can resist the temptation to insist that the therapy may be very helpful or valuable, the patient will not be as threatened by the possibility of being judged a failure by the "superior" therapist. Countertransferential anger is often also provoked as the patient meets constructive suggestions with replies that his or her suffering cannot be overcome; the patient acts passively helpless and succumbs to a defensive sullenness. Even worse, the patient's negative therapeutic reactions and regressions may be interpreted as being staged to serve as proof that the therapist can be of more harm than help.

To prevent this antitherapeutic interaction from developing, it is important for therapists to understand that masochists' apparent need to suffer is based not in their perverse enjoyment of pain, but rather in their belief that they will experience less of it by doing what they do. Defensiveness only confirms and perpetuates the patient's expectation that all significant others are cruel and insensitive. Conversely, being overly encouraging rarely serves to snap the patient out of masochistic behavior or into taking a more assertive and confident stand. Therapist's working with these patients should also remember that pushing the patient too fast can precipitate too much distress, possibly resulting in a psychotic decompensation.

Before the masochist can give up self-defeating patterns, a slow process of building up a new identity and new attitudes must take place. Negating patients' problematic sense of identity, without offering integratable alternatives, can leave a psychic void that may foster even more difficulties than they already have. Pitying patients and harboring "rescue" fantasies toward them can also lead to disappointment when these patients fail to live up to the therapist's expectations. Countertransference reactions toward patients' resistance or slow progress often include defensiveness and hostility. Harm to the patient can be avoided by sympathizing with the tendency of masochists to sabotage their own potential, and by keeping in mind that success threatens the masochist's identity and instigates strong feelings of guilt. Patients should not be blamed for their failures.

PART V

STRUCTURALLY-DEFECTIVE PERSONALITIES

CHAPTER 17

Schizotypal Personality Disorders: The Eccentric Pattern

All patterns of pathological personality—be they of mild, moderate, or marked severity—comprise deeply etched and pervasive characteristics of functioning that unfold as a product of the interplay of constitutional and experiential influences. The behaviors, self-descriptions, intrapsychic mechanisms, and interpersonal coping styles that evolve out of these transactions are embedded so firmly within the individual that they become the very fabric of his or her makeup, operating automatically and insidiously as the individual's way of life. Present realities are often mere catalysts that stir up these long-standing habits, memories, and feelings. Past learnings frequently persist inflexibly, irrespective of how maladaptive or irrational they now may be. Sooner or later they may prove to be the person's undoing. Self-defeating *vicious* circles are set up that precipitate new difficulties and often reactivate and aggravate earlier unfavorable conditions of life.

ON THE CONCEPT OF PERSONALITY STRUCTURE

Central to this and the following three chapters is the concept of *structural cohesion* in personality organization, an element of clinical significance that has been brought to the foreground in the creative work of Otto Kernberg (1967, 1970, 1975, 1984). In this and the following chapters, we stress the significance of the structural makeup of personality, contrasting this element with the *stylistic features* that have played a prominent part in our discussion of the less severe personality patterns outlined in previous chapters. Structure and style coexist. Style relates largely to the functional manner in which the individual relates to the internal and external world. It represents dynamic processes that transpire within the mind and between the self and the person's psychosocial environment. As

has been described in earlier chapters, functional styles represent expressive modes of regulatory action. By contrast, structural elements represent deeply embedded and relatively enduring templates of imprinted memories, attitudes, needs, fears, conflicts, and so on, which undergird and transform the character of ongoing life events. Psychic structures, in addition to serving as the underlying architecture of the mind, have a fundamental preemptive effect in that they alter the character and impact of subsequent experiences so as to make them fit preformed inclinations and expectancies. They serve selectively to lower experiential thresholds or transactions so that these events become consonant with constitutional proclivities and early learnings. As a consequence, ongoing events are often experienced as minor variations of the past. As described in an earlier book by the senior author (Millon, 1969):

Significant experiences of early life may never recur again, but their effects remain and leave their mark. Physiologically, we may say they have etched a neurochemical change; psychologically, they are registered as memories, a permanent trace and an embedded internal stimulus. In contrast to the fleeting stimuli of the external world, these memory traces become part and parcel of every stimulus complex which activates behavior. Once registered, the effects of the past are indelible, incessant, and inescapable. They now are intrinsic elements of the individual's makeup; they latch on and intrude into the current events of life, coloring, transforming and distorting the passing scene. Although the residuals of subsequent experiences may override them, becoming more dominant internal stimuli, the presence of earlier memory traces remains in one form or another. In every thought and action, the individual cannot help but carry these remnants into the present. Every current behavior is a perpetuation, then, of the past, a continuation and intrusion of these inner stimulus traces.

The residuals of the past do more than passively contribute their share to the present. By temporal precedence, if nothing else, they guide, shape, or distort the character of current events. Not only are they ever present, then, but they operate insidiously to transform new stimulus experiences in line with the past. (p. 200)

For purposes of definition, structures may be considered to be a quasi-permanent framework. They comprise a network of interconnecting substrates, the internalized residues of the past that serve as the undergirding foundation for action, thought, and feeling.

For our purposes, it is necessary to recognize that the overall architecture that serves as the structure of one's psychic interior may display weaknesses in its cohesion, or exhibit deficient coordination among its components, or possess few mechanisms to maintain balance and harmony, or regulate internal conflicts, or mediate external pressures. The concept of structural organization refers to the strength, interior congruity, and ultimate functional and stylistic efficacy of the personality. As a complex system of internal dispositions and traits, the structure and organization of the mind is almost exclusively derived from inferences of intrapsychic phenomena; hence the difficulty in articulating its strength and character.

The concept of psychic structure is similar to current psychoanalytic notions of normal, neurotic, borderline, and psychotic "organizational levels." We recognize the utility of these analytic notions in the following chapters where distinctions have been made between *defective structures* and *decompensated structures*. This usage is somewhat limited inasmuch as it relates essentially to quantitative degrees of structural pathology, not to their variations in character or configuration. In this regard, we are following the innovative model, but not the content, of Kernberg's proposals. Thus, we have introduced stylistic variants of structure in our description of "morphologic organization" domains, proposing a distinctive style for each personality prototype. In this and following chapters, we have limited our focus to degrees rather than styles of structural cohesion. The schizotypal, borderline, and paranoid styles are represented as exhibiting *defects* in their personality organization in Chapters 17, 18, and 19; in Chapter 20 they are described in a more severe form of pathology in which they exhibit a major *decompensation* in their organizational structure.

ON SEVERITY OF PERSONALITY PATHOLOGY

Chapters 17 through 20 describe the most severe variants of personality pathology, the so-called borderline, paranoid, schizotypal, and decompensated syndromes. As discussed previously, the senior author's prior theoretical and clinical work has led to a differentiation of the major personalities in terms of their level of structural coherence and interpersonal flexibility. As a précis of this final group of chapters, it may be useful to outline some of the criteria employed to assist in concluding that certain pathological patterns are more severe or grave than others.

Although all these personalities display an adaptive inflexibility, tend to promote self-perpetuating vicious circles, and hang on a tenuous emotional balance, there are substantive grounds for differentiating them in terms of levels of severity. Before doing so, it should be restated that personality structure is composed of complex traits that lie on a continuum of adaptiveness. Adaptiveness is a gradient, a matter of degree, and not a dichotomy. Notions such as health versus disease, abnormal versus normal, or psychotic versus nonpsychotic are polar extremes of a continuum that has intervening shades or gradations. An infinite number of discriminations may be made along these lines, but for certain purposes, refined distinctions may be neither feasible nor necessary. As long as we keep in mind that the pathological dimension of personality lies on a continuum, it will suffice to differentiate patients into a few broad classes such as mild, moderate, advanced, or severe.

In general, the patients discussed in the following chapters differ from those in preceding chapters by the frequency with which certain unusual symptoms arise, such as emotional outbursts, peculiar thinking, and bizarre behaviors. Inner (ego) controls have significantly weakened and these patients are driven to rather extreme measures in maintaining their psychological balance and cohesion. As a consequence of their failed background, those with defective structures will have had rather checkered histories in their personal relationships and in school and work performance. Most will have exhibited an extreme unevenness in fulfilling normal social functions and responsibilities. Rarely do they persevere to attain mature goals. Their histories show repeated setbacks, a lack of judgment and foresight, tendencies to digress from earlier aspirations, and failures to utilize their natural aptitudes and talents. It is often easy to trace the consequences of their adaptive inflexibility and their involvement in self-defeating vicious circles. Many may have shown flashes of promise, stability, and achievement, but these periods usually are either short-lived or are dependent on the presence of a highly tolerant and supportive social system. Most fail to learn from their experiences and involve themselves repeatedly in the same imbroglios, quandaries, and disappointments. Life is like a merry-go-round of getting into predicaments and discord, and then spending time extricating oneself from them. Few things are ever accomplished and much in life is undone. The defectively structured patient goes round in circles, covering the same ground as before, getting nowhere, and then starting all over again. This pattern contrasts with personalities at milder levels of pathological functioning whose strategies and behaviors, though self-perpetuating, are often instrumentally successful. The defectively structured style of functioning falters frequently and leads these individuals to endless impasses and serious setbacks. Rather than finding and holding a secure niche for themselves in society, as many of the less severe personalities do, they upset their progress repeatedly, achieve a low level of social attainment, and find that they must start again from scratch. Despite these ups and downs, personalities at this structural level do manage to recoup, to gain the wherewithal to pull themselves together, to find an out, and to get enough of a foothold in normal life to prevent themselves from slipping into more pernicious and serious states. In contrast to the structurally decompensated personality patterns, where realistic efforts to mobilize and defend oneself have been abandoned, defectively structured patients gain enough reinforcement to motivate themselves to make a "go of it" again.

Despite this capacity to "regain one's wits" and take hold of life, these patients experience transient periods in which bizarre behaviors, irrational impulses, and delusional thoughts are exhibited. These confusing episodes signify the tenuous character of their stability and controls. During these disturbed states, they may drift out of contact with their environment as if caught up in a momentary dream in which reality is blurred and fears and urges that derive from an obscure inner source take over and engulf them in an ocean of primitive anxieties and behaviors. Unable to grasp the illusory character of these inner stimuli, they may be driven to engage in erratic and hostile actions or embark on wild and chaotic sprees they may only vaguely recall. These episodes of emotional discharge serve a useful homeostatic function because they afford temporary relief from mounting internal pressures. When pressures cumulate beyond tolerable limits, they erupt through the patient's tenuous controls and are manifested in bizarre acts and thoughts. On release, these patients may sense a feeling of easement and quiescence. They may now regain a measure of psychic equilibrium until such time as these tensions again cumulate beyond manageable proportions. These transitory breaks from reality, traditionally termed "psychotic disorders," occur infrequently in the milder pathological personalities. Although less severely disturbed personalities do lose control occasionally, they usually retain a full awareness of reality. This contrasts not only with the defective-borderline patient but with the defective-paranoid and defective-schizotypal as well. Each of these more severe structurally defective personalities exhibits marked breaks with reality at relatively frequent intervals. Every so often, their intrapsychic world erupts and overwhelms them, blurring their awareness and releasing bizarre impulses, thoughts, and actions.

Patients who exhibit the structurally defective pattern can develop a healthier mode of adjustment or, conversely, decompensate into a more severe pattern of disorder. However, barring the presence of change-inducing events, they are likely to preserve their characteristic structure and style of functioning. Through all their ups and downs, and despite the fluctuating mix of both mild and marked pathological features, these patients remain sufficiently different from both the less and more severe personality syndromes to justify considering them a distinct clinical group.

As described earlier, these patients are ineffective in mobilizing their coping strategies, are less able to realistically appraise the stresses they face, and are unable to draw on their prior competencies and resources. Some become overly rigid and constrictive in their thinking and behavior, such as the paranoid; or, conversely, they experience being cognitively confused and emotionally scattered, as borderlines and schizotypals often are. Should difficulties mount or their restitutive efforts continue to fail, these structurally more disturbed personalities may abandon their attempts to mobilize their resources or to maintain their psychic cohesion, and thereby deteriorate into a florid psychotic disorder. In these more severe Axis I states, patients fail to discriminate between inner subjective experience and external reality; they are unable to carry out normal responsibilities or otherwise behave in accord with conventional social standards and expectations. As reality recedes further into the background, rational thinking disappears, previously controlled emotions erupt, and a disintegration and demoralization of self often takes hold. The upsurge of formerly repressed feelings and memories combines with new adverse experiences to undermine the individual's remaining coping capacities. Fearful of losing a tenuous hold on reality and threatened by surging emotions and uncontrollable and bizarre thoughts, these individuals succumb further. Deteriorating to more primitive levels of functioning and retreating into an inner and unreal world, they may ultimately fall into a persistent and more pernicious pattern of life. Despite the insidious and destructive sequence of decompensation, they will retain essentially the same basic perceptions, attitudes, and emotions they evidenced earlier in life. Defective levels of structural pathology, no matter how bizarre and maladaptive they may become, remain consonant with the individual's lifelong history and style of functioning.

The levels to which structural deterioration proceeds may be usefully separated into two broad categories. As noted previously, the first level is termed the *structurally defective* personalities, and includes the defective-schizotypal, defective-borderline, and defective-paranoid personalities. The second is termed the *structurally decompensated* personality patterns; the characteristics of this structurally more severe group will be elaborated in Chapter 20.

In what we describe here as disorders evidencing *defective personality structures,* patients can no longer depend on their prior mechanisms and strategies to work for them. No longer secure on a foundation of structural cohesion, their strategies have lost their prior effectiveness and their styles are no longer as coordinated and focused as previously; these individuals are likely to become overly concerned about receiving the attention and support they previously assumed they could readily obtain. They may seek to mobilize their resources, shore up their strategies, and take a more active role than before. For example, a previously dependent personality may begin to feel severely threatened by separation anxieties. As former strategies waver and stumble, a less functional pattern of behaviors may evolve. The patient may engage in a series of frantic actions to regain security or display frustration at having failed. Individuals who stabilize at these more extreme or advanced levels of structural defect often remain ambulatory, despite transient psychotic episodes. The borderline, paranoid, and schizotypal syndromes are the major variants of these defective personality structures. Although deterioration may proceed to lower levels of decompensation, these syndromes do not signify diagnostic indecision, nor are they a way station between normality and total psychotic disintegration. Rather, they should be seen as crystallized, habitual, and enduring pathological patterns.

Two features distinguish these defective personality structures from those at less severe levels. The first has been termed *deficit social competence* (Millon, 1969) and refers to the erratic personal history of these patients and their failure to attain a level of social achievement commensurate with their natural aptitudes and talents. Faulty starts and repeated disruptions characterize their educational, vocational, and marital life. In contrast to the less severe types, who progress and achieve a modicum of social and vocational effectiveness, structurally defective personalities create endless complications for themselves and experience the same setbacks time and again. Despite these failures, many are fortunate in having strongly supportive or beneficent environments. Hence, they are able to pull themselves together periodically and make a go of it again. This rapid recovery process contrasts with the fate of those at more severe levels of personality decompensation, who exhibit a more persistent downhill regression that eventuates in prolonged and often total social invalidism.

As evident from the foregoing, the second distinguishing feature of the structurally defective group is their *periodic, but reversible, psychotic episodes.* These severe transient disorders are characterized by the loss of reality contact and by both cognitive and emotional dyscontrol. Although psychotic eruptions occur with some frequency, their reversibility differentiates them from those at the decompensated level. Thus, in the structurally defective patient, the reality break is brief and transitory; whereas in severely decompensated personalities, it is prolonged and often permanent. Caught in their own adaptive inflexibilities and tendencies to foster new difficulties and self-defeating vicious circles, defective personalities experience constant upsets in their equilibrium and are subject to emotional eruptions and uncontrollable behaviors and thoughts. Once these intense feelings are discharged, however, these patients regain a modicum of psychic balance—until such time as their tensions again mount beyond manageable portions.

As noted, these three structurally defective personalities parallel, in somewhat less discriminable (but more severe) form, the 11 personality patterns described in previous chapters. Thus, the *schizotypal* is a more structurally defective and dysfunctional variant of two pleasure-deficient patterns: the schizoid and avoidant types. The *borderline* is usually a structurally defective depressive, dependent, histrionic, narcissistic, antisocial, or negativistic pattern; and the *paranoid* is a structurally defective personality type that is akin to the narcissistic, antisocial, sadistic, compulsive, and negativistic patterns. A detailed review of the schizotypal is presented in this chapter; the borderline and paranoid personalities are detailed in Chapters 18 and 19. The structurally decompensated personality types will be discussed in Chapter 20.

PRELIMINARY COMMENTS ON THE SCHIZOTYPAL PERSONALITY CONSTRUCT

Manifest in the schizotypal personality are a variety of persistent and prominent eccentricities of behavior, thought, and perception. These characteristics mirror—but fall short of, in either severity or peculiarity—features that would justify the diagnosis of clinical schizophrenia. It is the author's contention (Millon, 1969) that these "odd" schizotypal symptoms contribute to and are derivatives of a more fundamental and profound social isolation and self-alienation. Although the schizotypal syndrome should be seen as an advanced form of structural pathology, akin in severity to both the borderline and paranoid types, it may also be understood as a more grave form of the pathologically less severe schizoid and avoidant patterns.

In general, these three syndromes—schizoid, avoidant, and schizotypal—are characterized by an impoverished social life, a distancing from close interpersonal relationships, and an autistic, but nondelusional, pattern of thinking. Because of their more advanced state of pathology, schizotypals frequently lead a meaningless, idle, and ineffectual existence, drifting from one aimless activity to another, remaining on the periphery of societal life, and rarely developing intimate attachments or accepting enduring responsibilities. Their characteristic oddities in behavior and thought—such as magical thinking, illusions, circumstantial speech, suspiciousness, and ideas of reference—stem in part from their withdrawn and isolated existence. This separateness from conventional relationships and modes of communication precludes their being exposed to corrective perspectives that might mitigate their autistic preoccupations. To paraphrase

what was stated in an earlier chapter, the more individuals turn inward, the more they lose contact with the styles of behavior and thought of those around them. As they become progressively estranged from their social environment, they lose touch with the conventions of reality and with the checks against irrational thought and behavior that are provided by reciprocal relationships. Increasingly detached from the controls and stabilizing influences of repetitive, though ordinary, human affairs, they may lose their sense of behavioral propriety and suitability, and gradually begin the process of acting, thinking, and perceiving in peculiar, unreal, and somewhat "crazy" ways—hence, their manifest and prominent eccentricities.

In consequence, and because they lack either the means or the desire to experience the joy and vibrancy of a personal life, schizotypals become devitalized and numb, wander in a dim and hazy fog, and engage in bizarre activities and curious thoughts that have minimal social purpose or meaning. As the reader proceeds through this chapter, it will become easier to understand why schizotypals avoid participating in social reality. Briefly, they have no reason to aspire to be part of normal social life when they believe that nothing can spark their flat existence or provide them with feelings of joy. As a consequence, they move through life, not only like automatons possessing impenetrable barriers to shared meanings and affections, but also estranged from the aspirations, spontaneity, delight, and triumph of selfhood.

Before proceeding to the more detailed presentation of the schizotypal, a few words should be said about controversies concerning its selection as a diagnostic label. Perhaps second only to the disputation that surrounded the choice of the borderline term, the introduction of this new designation raised serious objections on the part of several members of the DSM-III Task Force. The issue of the substantive validity of the syndrome as a distinct personality entity remained active in the deliberations of the committee to the very end, resolved in part only by a study undertaken by Spitzer, Endicott, and Gibbon (1979). The reader's appraisal of the internal coherence and differential diagnostic properties of the schizotypal constellation may be aided by a review of its historical and theoretical antecedents, furnished in the next section. For the present, attention is focused on problems associated with the use of "schizoid" and "schizotypal" as two, ostensibly distinct, personality designations. Numerous objections concerning potential confusions these terms might engender were raised by Task Force members. Thus, in a memo to his Task Force colleagues in December 1978, the senior author of this text wrote:

I took upon myself the opportunity to explore empirically views . . . concerning possible confusions that might exist with the terms schizoid and schizotypal as separate personality disorders . . . my own data, limited though they are in terms of the size and diversity of the sample, show that many would be inclined to think that schizoid and schizotypal are synonymous, particularly in suggesting dispositions to schizophrenia. . . . [I] think the introduction of the term schizotypal and the reapplication of the label schizoid to mean something different than it meant in DSM-II, is only going to lead to confusion and to a diminishment in utility of the Personality Disorders axis.

Two, among several, concurring views expressed at this late date by Task Force members are excerpted here:

Using both schizoid and schizotypal is asking for trouble. I have a nagging feeling that if we cut out schizoid and leave schizotypal then what will happen is that people will equate schizotypal with schizoid and not understand the other term.

Introducing the term Schizotypal, which will be new to most clinicians, met with dismay and annoyance when I described it to a sophisticated clinical group here. Both Schizoid and Schizotypal Personality Disorders are described with a central criterion of severe social isolation.

As noted earlier, the reader should be able to assess distinctions between these two syndromes following opportunities to review their associated histories and data, and opportunities to test DSM-IV differential criteria with real, rather than theoretically abstract, patients. It was the senior author's view that substantive clinical grounds existed for separating them, if for no other reason than their levels of severity and their consequences. Nonetheless, the selection of such similar diagnostic labels seems to have been most unwise when appropriate alternative designations were available.

HISTORICAL ANTECEDENTS

In contrast with the comparatively extensive early literature on the paranoid syndrome, and more similar to the borderline label in their shared recency, the diagnostic term schizotypal provides few leads to the diligent investigator who seeks to trace its historical roots. Coined as a syndromal designation as late as the 1950s, the constellation of traits it encompasses may be found under descriptive labels that are quite far afield. This review is not limited, therefore, to a literature bound by adherence to the schizotypal designation. On the other hand, the purview is not enlarged so broadly as to include historical entities more properly conceived as forerunners of the new borderline syndrome, a diagnostic class identified by its characteristic affective and interpersonal instability. Rather, attention is focused on earlier syndromes that closely approximate the principal characteristics of the schizotypal pattern—social isolation and eccentricities in behavior, thought, and perception. First, a few paragraphs are devoted to reviewing the historical evolution of schizophrenia, the syndromal prototype of which schizotypal is ostensibly a dilute and nonpsychotic personality variant.

An English neurologist, Willis (1668; 1684/1912), reported having observed a pathological sequence in which "young persons who, lively and spirited, and at times even brilliant in their childhood, passed into obtuseness and hebetude during adolescence." Better known historically are the texts written by the Belgian psychiatrist Morel (1852–1853), who described the case of a 14-year-old boy who had been a cheerful and good student, but who progressively lost his intellectual capacities and increasingly became melancholy and withdrawn. Morel considered cases such as these to be irremediable and ascribed the deterioration to an arrest in brain development that stemmed from hereditary causes. He named the illness "dementia praecox" *(demence precoce)* to signify his observation that the degenerative processes began at an early age and progressed rapidly.

K. L. Kahlbaum (1863) and E. Hecker (1871) described two other forms of mental deterioration. They applied the term "hebephrenia" to conditions that began in adolescence, usually started with a quick succession of erratic moods followed by a rapid enfeeblement of all functions, and finally progressed to an unalterable psychic decline. The label "catatonic" was introduced to represent "tension insanity" in cases where the patient displayed no reactivity to sensory impressions, lacked "self-will," and sat mute and physically immobile. These symptoms ostensibly reflected brain structure deterioration.

Kraepelin (1896) considered hebephrenia and dementia praecox to be synonymous prior to the fifth edition of his psychiatric text. In that highly original treatise, he concluded that the diverse symptom complexes of catatonia and hebephrenia, as well as certain paranoid disturbances, displayed a common theme of early deterioration and ultimate incurability. As he conceived them, each of these illnesses was a variation of Morel's original concept of dementia praecox. By subsuming the disparate symptoms of these formerly separate syndromes under the common theme of their ostensive early and inexorable mental decline, Kraepelin appeared to bring order and simplicity to what had previously been diagnostic confusion. In line with the traditions of German psychiatry, Kraepelin assumed that a biophysical defect lay at the heart of this new coordinating syndrome. In contrast to his forebears, however, he speculated that sexual and metabolic dysfunctions were the probable causal agents, rather than the usual hypothesis of an anatomic lesion. Among the major signs that Kraepelin considered central, in addition to the progressive and inevitable decline, were discrepancies between thought and emotion, negativism, and stereotyped behaviors, wandering or unconnected ideas, hallucinations, delusions, and a general mental deterioration.

Kraepelin's observations and syntheses were challenged and modified in significant proposals offered by Eugen Bleuler in Switzerland and Adolf Meyer in the United States.

Observing hundreds of dementia praecox patients in the early 1900s led Bleuler (1911) to conclude that it was misleading to compare the type of deterioration they evidenced with that found among patients suffering from metabolic deficiencies or brain degeneration. Moreover, the reactions and thoughts of his patients were qualitatively complex and often highly creative, contrasting markedly with the simple or meandering thinking that Kraepelin observed. Furthermore, not only did many of his patients display their illness for the first time in adulthood, rather than in adolescence, but a significant proportion evidenced no progressive deterioration, which Kraepelin considered the sine qua non of the syndrome. Thus, to Bleuler, the label dementia praecox was a misleading designation in that it characterized an age of onset and a course of development that were not supported by the evidence.

The primary symptoms, as Bleuler saw them, were disturbances in the associative link among thoughts, a breach between affect and intellect, ambivalence toward the same objects, and an autistic detachment from reality. The variety of cases that displayed these fragmented thoughts, feelings, and actions led Bleuler, in 1911, to term them "the group of schizophrenias," a label selected to signify what he saw to be a split (schism) within the mind (phrenos) of these patients. Although he considered schizophrenia to be a diverse set of disorders, he retained the Kraepelinian view that the impairment stemmed from a unitary disease process that was attributable to physiological pathology. Schizophrenics shared a neurological ailment that produced their common primary symptoms. Schizophrenics also exhibited several secondary symptoms, such as hallucinations and delusions, the content of which Bleuler ascribed to the patients' distinctive life experiences and to their efforts to adapt to their basic disease. Psychogenic factors shaped the particular character of the schizophrenic impairment, but Bleuler was convinced that experience could not in itself cause the ailment.

Along similar lines, Meyer suggested in 1906 that dementia praecox was not an organic disease but a maladaptive way of reacting to stress, fully understandable in terms of the patient's constitutional potentials and life experiences. To him, these maladaptive reactions led to what he termed "progressive habit deteriorations," that reflected "inefficient and faulty attempts to avoid difficulties" (Meyer, 1912, p. 98). Symptoms of psychopathology were seen as the end product of abortive and self-defeating efforts to establish psychic equilibrium. His well-reasoned "psychobiological" approach to schizophrenia, which he preferred to call "paregasia" to signify its distorted or twisted character, was the most systematic recognition to date of the interactive and progressive nature of pathogenesis. Of special note also was Meyer's view that paregasia could be present in dilute and nonpsychotic form, that is, without delusions, hallucinations, or deterioration. He considered the classic psychotic symptoms to be advanced signs of a potentially, but not inevitably, evolving habit system that might stabilize at a prepsychotic level. In its nonclinical state, paregasia could be detected by a variety of attenuated and soft signs that merely suggested the manifest psychotic disorder. Meyer's proposal of a self-defeating and maladaptive reaction system (personality) that parallels schizophrenia in inchoate form was a highly innovative, but unheeded, notion. In many respects, Bleuler and Meyer's ideas on this matter were the primary forerunners of the schizotypal syndrome; they shared the view that a constitutional defect or disposition can evolve into a moderately dysfunctional and enduring personality system under a regimen of life experiences that prevent these potentials from being exacerbated into a manifest clinical state.

MODERN FORMULATIONS

Both Bleuler and Meyer expanded Kraepelin's more limited conception of the inevitable and fixed course of dementia praecox by recognizing both nondeteriorating and intermediary cases, a position that Kraepelin (1919) accepted in his later years when writing of "autistic personalities" and those whose dementia is "brought to a standstill short of its full clinical course" (p. 237). Nevertheless, there were those who retained Kraepelin's earlier insistence on the inevitable deterioration in dementia praecox. For example, Langfeldt (1937) stressed the notion that some schizophrenic patients follow an inevitable course of decompensation, whereas others do not. This distinction led him to reserve the schizophrenic label for those he termed "process" types, who eventually did deteriorate; he coined the word "schizophreniform" for those he referred to as "reactive" types, whose symptoms were more affectively tinged and followed intense and acute precipitants. Process schizophrenics presumably possessed premorbid schizoid personalities that would progress insidiously to the clinical state with minimal external promptings. As this deterioration progresses, previously inchoate signs of "ego-boundary disturbances," associative thought defects, and feelings of depersonalization gain increasing prominence.

The theme of a nonpsychotic form of schizophrenia was brought into sharp focus in a seminal paper by G. Zilboorg (1941). Referring to these patients as "ambulatory schizophrenics," Zilboorg took strong exception to the practice of creating "euphemistic labels" (such as "borderline cases," "incipient schizophrenia," and the like) when what was observed were merely less advanced forms of the basic schizophrenic disease process. Devising new terms was seen as both misleading and unjustified. To quote Zilboorg (1941), it is as if we would:

. . . refuse to make a diagnosis of appendicitis merely because the appendix has not ruptured and no peritonitis has as yet set in. . . . Schizophrenia is not dementia praecox . . . [it] is a generic name covering a certain type of psychopathological processes. That these . . . should present themselves in various degrees of intensity, various stages of development—from the earliest to most advanced forms—and in various degrees of overtness of clinical manifestations, should be self-understood. (p. 151)

Considering the flagrant symptoms of delusions, hallucinations, and flatness of affect to be "terminal phenomena" that belong to advanced cases only, Zilboorg (1941) wrote of the ambulatory schizophrenic as follows:

These patients seldom reach the point at which hospitalization appears necessary either to the relatives or to the psychiatrist, and . . . they appear "to walk about life" like any other "normal" person—although they remain inefficient, peregrinatory, casual in their ties to things and to people. . . . Such individuals remain more or less on the loose in the actual or figurative sense, outwardly and inwardly. . . .

Suffice it here to say that the shallowness of affect so conspicuous in the external aspects of the clinical picture should not be mistaken either for the absence of affect or for some special mysterious disturbance of what is called the "emotional sphere." . . . The emotion appears lacking in the schizophrenic only because that part of his personality which deals with external realities of life . . . play a minor role in his life. (pp. 154–155)

Another early, yet formal, recognition of a stable, prepsychotic form of schizophrenia evolved in psychodiagnostic studies undertaken by Rapaport et al. (1945–1946, 1968). Searching for subgroups within the broad spectrum of clearly diagnosed schizophrenics, they identified an important patient population that they termed "preschizophrenics," described as follows:

These were cases . . . whose adjustment was so precarious that schizophrenialike withdrawal tendencies in the guise of anxiety and inhibition, or schizophrenialike ideational productions in the guise of obsessive-phobic thought, had already penetrated into their everyday life; thus any strain or stress could precipitate a schizophrenic psychosis, but under favorable conditions they might continue with such preschizophrenic behavior or ideation without an acute break. (1968, p. 57)

Of particular note was the subdivision of the preschizophrenic group into two categories, the "inhibited" (coarctated) type and the "over-ideational" type. They described these types as follows:

[The preschizophrenic] group was subdivided into two categories. One of these, [the inhibited] was characterized by blocking, withdrawal, marked anxiety, feelings of strangeness, incompetence, extreme inhibition of affect and some kind of sexual preoccupation. The other group [the overideational], was

characterized by an enormous wealth of fantasy, obsessive ideation, obsessions and a preoccupation with themselves and their bodies; these subjects were immensely introspective and preoccupied with their own ideas. (1968, p. 58)

Although following similar lines of diagnostic assessment, Schafer (1948) concluded that clearer distinctions should be made among the preschizophrenic group; thus, he replaced the labels "coarctated" (inhibited) and "over-ideational," substituting in their stead the terms "schizoid character," "incipient schizophrenia," and "schizophrenic character." The schizoid was described briefly and possessed essentially the same features that are included under that designation in this text. The incipient form reflected what the term implies—behaviors, thoughts, and perceptions that suggest a psychotic break is imminent. Last, Schafer's notion of a schizophrenic character approached in certain details many of the symptoms incorporated in the DSM-III schizotypal personality syndrome. Taking as his guide Zilboorg's (1948) formulation of ambulatory schizophrenia, Schafer (1948) wrote:

This diagnostic term is applied to those patients in whom a lifelong, insidious, and extensive development of schizophrenic disorganization has taken place, and in whom this development appears to have reached an essentially stable state, the schizophrenic mechanisms seeming to be integrated into the character make-up. There has been no acute break and there is no reason to anticipate a rapid process of deterioration. The classical secondary symptoms (hallucinations, delusions) are absent, but the primary disorders of thinking and affect are evident upon clinical examination. Usually the major diagnostic features are bizarre, impulsive and which are fantastically and blandly rationalized, and wild flights of fancy, the products of which often remain indistinguishable from fact in the patient's mind. Phobic, obsessive-compulsive, psychopathic, and histrionic features may all merge in these cases. As a rule, the orderly front they put up is adequate for most routines or simple social situations. (p. 86)

CONTEMPORARY PROPOSALS

The concept of "latent schizophrenia," signifying the presence of "concealed" catatonic and paranoid symptoms, was first posited by Bleuler, but it was not brought to the fore as a potential diagnostic entity until so formulated in a paper by P. Federn (1947) and, later, in the concept of "latent psychosis" described by G. Bychowski (1953). Referred to as persons who cloak their deeper pathology under the guise of neurotic manifestations, latent schizophrenia "reveals itself by the patient's behavior and mannerisms, earlier than by his verbal productions" (Federn, 1947, p. 141). To Bychowski, the cardinal feature was the ease with which "primary processes" spilled into their thoughts and speech. Social communication was thereby often scattered, evidencing excesses in condensation and personal allusions. The depressive inclinations that Bychowski observed in these patients suggest that many may have been more typical of what we currently label borderline personalities. The superimposition of neurotic symptoms as a cloak for deeper schizophrenic processes was brought to its clearest and most articulate form by P. Hoch and P. Polatin (1949) in their formulation of "pseudoneurotic schizophrenia." Elaborating the concept in detail in later papers (Hoch & Cattell, 1959; Hoch, Cattell, Stahl, & Pennes, 1962), these investigators took pains to stress that the entity they described was a stable variant of schizophrenia, which, though occasionally precipitated into a clinical psychosis, more characteristically retained its distinctive features and ambulatory status over extended periods of time. Displaying a conglomeration of traits and clinical features that formed a unique constellation, the pseudoneurotic schizophrenic exhibited a variety of signs that both mimicked and dramatized classical neurotic symptomatology, as well as suggesting in a more subtle or less striking form the thought disorders and dysregulated emotions that typify clinical schizophrenia. In the first paper on the syndrome, Hoch and Polatin (1949) offered the following descriptive features as a basis for the diagnosis:

Some inappropriate emotional connections . . . are not rarely present, and a lack of modulation, of flexibility in emotional display is demonstrated. . . . Many of these patients show the cold, controlled, and at the same time, hypersensitive reactions to emotional situations, usually over-emphasizing trivial frustrations and not responding to, or bypassing, major ones. At times lack of inhibition in displaying certain emotions is especially striking in otherwise markedly inhibited persons. . . .

From the diagnostic point of view the most important presenting symptom is what the writers call pan-anxiety and pan-neurosis. Many of these patients show, in contrast to the usual neurotic, an all-pervading anxiety structure which does not leave any life-approach of the person free from tension. . . . In connection with this diffuse anxiety, a pan-neurosis is also present. The patients usually do not have one or two different neurotic manifestations, but all symptoms known in neurotic illness are often present at the same time. . . .

In all the writers' cases they observed that the patient usually told of a great many sexual preoccupations showing autoerotic, oral, anal homosexual and heterosexual tendencies. . . .

Quite a number of the patients with this pseudoneurotic symptomatology develop psychotic episodes which are, however, often of short duration. . . . In these short-lived psychotic attacks (micropsychosis) usually three elements appear simultaneously which are very significant. The patient expresses hypochondriacal ideas, ideas of reference, and feelings of depersonalization. They are often interlocked. (pp. 250–253)

The specific term "schizotypal" was coined by S. Rado in a paper delivered in 1950 to the New York Academy of Medicine; this concept was briefly expanded in an address in 1953 to the American Psychiatric Association and further developed in several publications in 1956 and later. Conceiving the label as an abbreviation of "schizophrenic phenotype" (indicating its ostensive representation in overt form of an underlying hereditary predisposition or genotype), Rado specified the existence of two inherited defects, that of an "integrative pleasure deficiency" and a "proprioceptive diathesis." The following excerpt from one of Rado's early papers (1956) details these defects and articulates their consequences with clinical clarity and astuteness:

In general, absence of sufficient pleasure slows down and hinders psychodynamic integration. . . . In particular, (1) it weakens the motivating power of the welfare emotions, such as pleasurable desire, joy, affection, love and pride; (2) it weakens the counter balancing effect ordinarily exerted by the welfare emotions on the emergency emotions, thus allowing fears and rages to rise to excessive strength; (3) it reduces the coherence of the action-self, which is viewed as the highest integrative system of the organism, and the very basis of its self-awareness; (4) it undermines the schizotype's self-confidence and sense of security in relation to both himself and his social environment; (5) it makes the development of a well-integrated sexual function impossible; (6) it limits the

schizotype's capacity for the appropriate enjoyment of his life activities, as well as for love and affectionate give and take in human relationships.

The proprioceptive diathesis further damages the composition of the action-self. This two-fold impairment of the action-self appears to be the deepest root of the patient's tormenting lack of self-confidence and also, of his feeling that he is hopelessly different from other people. Furthermore, brittleness of the impaired action-self predisposes the patient to disintegrative breakdown marked by thought disorder. (p. 226)

Referring to the efforts individuals make to compensate for their innate defects as "schizoadaptation," Rado stated that its success depends on the interplay of three reparative processes: the careful husbanding of the scare pleasure capacity; the ability to shift the burden of adaptive tasks to others despite ambivalent overdependency; and the adequacy with which nonemotional thoughts can replace limited pleasurable feelings. He did not see the schizotypal pattern as inevitably fixed but as an adaptive developmental process that can move forward and back between four stages: compensated, decompensated, disintegrated, and deteriorated. Rado (1969) described the stages and sequence as follows:

Compensated schizotypal behavior means that in favorable circumstances the schizotype may go through life without a breakdown. . . . In decompensated schizotypal behavior, "emergency dyscontrol" is marked by the production of inappropriate or excessive fears and rages. An attack of emergency dyscontrol is bound to break the compensatory system of adaptation and thus precipitate decompensation, characterized by what appears to be a scramble of phobic, obsessive, depressive, and still other overreactive mechanisms. . . .

The stage of disintegrated schizotypal behavior is known as overt schizophrenic psychosis. Disorganization of his action-self has reduced the patient to adaptive incompetence, the disintegrative process resulting in thought disorder, activity disorder, and the like. . . . The process of schizotypal disintegration may go on for an indefinite period of time. There is, however, a chance of spontaneous remission, as well as a threat of progressive deterioration. Deteriorated schizotypal behavior is marked by a progressive cessation of function, a nearly complete withdrawal from the adaptive task. (pp. 254–255)

Attracted by Rado's schizotypal formulation, P. Meehl (1962, 1973, 1991) constructed a brilliant, speculative theoretical model. Essentially, Meehl sought to articulate how an inherited "neural integrative defect," which he labeled "schizotaxia," evolved through "all known forms of social history" into the phenotypic personality organization that Rado termed the "schizotype." The reader is referred to Meehl's paper for his masterly neurological-social-learning thesis. A brief quote summarizing his general theme will suffice here:

I hypothesize that the statistical relation between schizotaxia, schizotypy, and schizophrenia is class inclusion: All schizotaxics become, on all actually existing social learning regimens, schizotypic in personality organization; but most of these remain compensated. A minority, disadvantaged by other (largely polygenically determined) constitutional weaknesses, and put on a bad regimen by schizophrenogenic mothers (most of whom are themselves schizotypes) are thereby potentiated into clinical schizophrenia. What makes schizotaxia etiologically specific is its role as a necessary *condition. I postulate that a nonschizotaxic individual, whatever his other genetic makeup and whatever his learning history, would at most develop a character disorder or a psychoneurosis; but he would not become a schizotype and therefore could never manifest its decompensated form, schizophrenia. (1962/1973, p. 832)*

In line with the growing conviction that schizophrenia is genetically based yet possesses a variety of phenotypic forms depending on polygenic mixtures and environmental potentiators, S. Kety, D. Rosenthal, P. Wender, and F. Schulsinger (1968; Wender, 1977) set out to develop a strategy to disentangle genetic and environmental variables. Unsure of what clinical conditions the concept of schizophrenia actually subsumed, they reviewed its history and concluded that there were basically four variants that had been designated as either schizophrenia itself or as closely related to schizophrenia. They grouped these variants into what they spoke of as the "schizophrenic spectrum" since it was possible to align and differentiate them reasonably well on grounds such as clinical severity and chronicity. The first subcategory, termed "chronic schizophrenia," was seen to correspond to Kraepelin's initial formulation of dementia praecox, with its poor prepsychotic adjustment, progressive deterioration, and prominence of

Bleuler's primary symptoms; this group is variously referred to as "true" and "process" schizophrenia in contemporary literature. The second group, labeled the "acute schizophrenic reaction," exhibited a good premorbid history, appeared to have been precipitated by external events into a rapid decompensation, was noted by Bleuler's more dramatic secondary symptoms, and had a good long-term prognosis. The third, or "borderline" schizophrenic, group is summarized in greater detail shortly because it best parallels the DSM-III schizotypal syndrome. The fourth, final, and most distal variant, whose location on the schizophrenic spectrum is questioned by some, received the label "inadequate personality"; more akin to the DSM-III schizoid than schizotypal personality, its historical ancestry and diagnostic features can be reviewed best by reference to Chapter 10. Returning to the borderline schizophrenic subgroup, Wender (1977) has summarized its essential characteristics as follows:

[There is] a chronic history of psychological maladaptation with abnormalities in the following areas: (1) Thinking—strange, vague, illogical mentation which tends to ignore reality, logic and experience, and results in poor adaptation to life experiences; (2) Affective life—characterized by "anhedonia," the inability to experience intense pleasure, so that the individuals report a history of never having been happy (although they may never have been seriously depressed); (3) Interpersonal relations—characterized by a tendency to polar opposites which may include either the absence of deep, intense involvement with other people or excessively "deep" and dependent involvement with others. There also exist possible difficulties in sexual adjustment which may be characterized by either a very low sexual drive or a promiscuous and chaotic pattern of sexual interaction; (4) Psychopathology—characterized not only by its intensity but by its lack of constancy with multiple neurotic manifestations that may shift frequently (obsessive concerns, phobias, conversion symptoms, psychosomatic symptoms, etc.); severe, widespread anxiety and occasionally short-lived episodes, designated as "micropsychotic," during which the individual experiences transient delusions, hallucinations, feelings of depersonalization or de-realization. The course of these disturbances tends to be lifelong, generally without deterioration, and the illnesses seem refractory to neuroleptic drugs. (p. 112)

Picking up the themes suggested by Kety et al., Siever (Siever & Davis, 1991) draws on a variety of sources in his proposal that argues strongly for a psychobiological foundation among schizotypal personalities. He writes (1991):

Subtle disturbances in cognitive controls may be expressed not only as persistent symptoms reflecting cognitive/perceptual distortions but also as traits of eccentricity, peculiar speech, and social detachment, as observed in schizotypal personality disorder. . . .

The dimension of cognitive/perceptual organization reflects an individual's capacity to perceive and attend to important incoming stimuli, process this information in relation to previous experience, and select appropriate response strategies. Disturbances in this dimension will be apparent in defects in the attention/selection processes that organize an individual's cognitive/perceptual evaluation of and relatedness to his or her environment. The result may be impairment and discomfort in social interactions and a misunderstanding or suspiciousness of others' motivations. Social isolation may represent the major strategy to cope with defective information processing of social cues. In more severe cases, such individuals may be prone to cognitive/perceptual distortions, amplified by social detachment, which forestalls the possibility of potentially corrective input for reality testing. (pp. 1648–1649)

Approaching the schizotypal from a nonbiological cognitive vantage point, Beck and Freeman (1993b) throw a different light on this disorder. Beck does not reject the genetic-constitutional thesis presented by others, but rather focuses on the content of the cognitive dysfunctions so central to this disorder. They describe these core features as follows:

Some schizotypal individuals may focus on details and lose sight of the overall situation, while others may exclude attention to detail. Many schizotypals will engage in the cognitive distortions of emotional reasoning and personalization. In emotional reasoning, a person believes that because he or she feels a negative emotion, there must be a corresponding negative external situation. With personalization, the individual believes that he or she is responsible for external situations when this is not the case. These patients are often very concrete, and are unable to assess accurately the probability of an imagined outcome. (p. 138)

Although she does not reject the biological perspectives that have been presented concerning the schizotypal personality, Benjamin (1993a) prefers to focus her attention on the interpersonal consequences of these cognitive dysfunctions. In line with her major approach to the problems of personality disorders, Benjamin states the following regarding the schizotypal:

There is a fear of attacking, humiliating control; the wish is that others will leave the SZT alone. His or her baseline position is one of hostile withdrawal and self-neglect. The SZT believes that he or she has a capacity for magical influence that can be implemented directly (telepathy) or indirectly (control through ritual). Usually the SZT imposes these "powers" from a distance. He or she is aware of aggressive feelings, but usually restrains them. (p. 356)

The SZT elects to live separately, rejecting the rest of the world. In childhood this often assumed the form of watching TV excessively, listening to music alone, and so on. If the withdrawal is relatively complete over a long period of time, he or she will lose touch with social norms, and develop his or her own rules for personal hygiene, dressing, and social stereotypes. (p. 360)

As with other personality disorders, an effort has been made by five-factor theorists Costa and Widiger (1993) to identify the underlying traits that may best represent the schizotypal personality. In their descriptive summary, Costa and Widiger write:

Both are largely characterized by excessive introversion but they are differentiated by the relative emphasis on social and physical anhedonia in SZD and by the relative emphasis on cognitive-perceptual aberrations in SZT . . . Prototypal schizoid and schizotypal patients are largely differentiated by their respective degree of neurotocism: The prototypal schizoid person displays low hostility and low self-consciousness, whereas the prototypical schizotypal displays excessively high self-consciousness (social anxiety and pervasive discomfort with others). (p. 44)

In an early, pre-DSM-III formulation, Millon (1969) drew on his theoretically based biosocial model of psychopathology to construct a syndrome at the mid-level of personality severity. Based on an advanced or severe detached coping style, he labeled this disorder the "schizoid personality"; its features, however, corresponded to the new DSM-III schizotypal syndrome. The following quote summarizes the major criteria for the disorder as presented in 1969:

Detachment from others and alienation from self are principal features of this personality. Notable are: deficient social behaviors *(a lack of social competence and intelligence derivable from and contributing to deficits in interpersonal interest and feelings of social unworthiness);* cognitive disjunctiveness *(unable to orient thoughts logically; they lack "touch" with others and are unable to order ideas in terms relevant to reciprocal social communications);* depersonalization anxiety *(feel themselves to be insubstantial, foreign and disembodied, detached and uninvolved observers of the passing scene, looking from the outside in);* impoverished affect *(blandness of mood, listlessness and lack of spontaneity, a lack of ambition and interest in life activities). (pp. 308–309)*

As previously noted, this disorder was conceived in the theory as a more severe variant of the passively detached DSM-III schizoid and the actively detached DSM-III avoidant personalities. Although these two subtypes share many clinical features, important characteristics differentiate them, especially those associated with the experience and expression of affect and anxiety. As in the case of the DSM-III borderlines and paranoids, several subtypes of the schizotypal may be found because the more advanced and dysfunctional personality patterns are superimposed on the less severe character types. The following descriptive text and criteria were conceived with these considerations in mind. They were written by the author in 1975 for the DSM-III personality subcommittee as the first working draft of what was ultimately labeled the "schizotypal" syndrome:

This pattern is typified by a marked deficit in social interest, a shunning of close interpersonal relationships, frequent behavioral eccentricities, nondelusional autistic thinking and depersonalization anxieties. There is a tendency to follow meaningless, idle and ineffectual lives, drifting aimlessly and remaining on the periphery of societal living. Some possess significant activation, affective and cognitive deficiencies, appearing listless, bland, unmotivated and obscure, only minimally connected to the external world. Others are anxiously tense and withdrawn, fearful and intentionally seclusive,

inclined to damp down hypersensitivities and to disconnect from anticipated external threats.

An appraisal of personal background and history reveals both of the following:

1. *Social attainment deficits (e.g., experienced serious, self-precipitated setbacks in scholastic, marital or vocational pursuits; repeated failure to maintain durable, satisfactory and secure roles consonant with age and aptitudes).*

2. *Periodic mini-psychotic episodes (e.g., experienced several brief and reversible periods in which either bizarre behaviors, extreme moods, irrational impulses or delusional thoughts were exhibited; short-lived breaks from "reality," however, are often recognized as peculiar or deviant).*

Since adolescence or early adulthood at least 3 of the following have been present to a notably greater degree than in most people and were not limited to discrete periods nor necessarily prompted by stressful life events.

1. *Social detachment (e.g., prefers life of isolation with minimal personal attachments and obligations; has drifted over time into increasingly peripheral social and vocational roles).*

2. *Behavioral eccentricity (e.g., exhibits frequent odd or peculiar habits; is perceived by others as unobtrusively strange or different).*

3. *Non-delusional autistic thinking (e.g., social communication interspersed with personal irrelevancies, obscurities and tangential asides; appears self-absorbed and lost in daydreams with occasional blurring of fantasy and reality).*

4. *Either (a) Anxious wariness (e.g., reports being hypersensitive, apprehensively ill-at-ease, particularly in social encounters; is guarded, suspicious of others and secretive in behavior) or (b) Emotional flatness (e.g., manifests a drab, sluggish, joyless, and spiritless appearance; reveals marked deficiencies in activation and affect).*

5. *Disquieting estrangement (e.g., reports periods of depersonalization, derealization and dissociation; experiences anxious feelings of emptiness and meaninglessness).*

The final text and criteria for the syndrome were based on a study carried out and reported by

Spitzer, Endicott, and Gibbon (1979) to clarify distinctions that might be drawn between what were then tentatively termed in the deliberations of the DSM-III Task Force as the "Unstable (Borderline)" and "Schizotypal" personalities. Following guidelines established earlier by relevant Task Force members, Spitzer et al. consulted other theorists and researchers at work in the field for further advice toward the goal of constructing two subsets of potentially discriminating criteria. Although procedures for data gathering, analyzing, and cross-validating these criterion sets were carried out with exceptional diligence, the final item lists were found to highly correlate when utilized with a heterogeneous patient population. However, within a select group of more disturbed or dysfunctional patients, borderline and schizotypal item subsets did show a high degree of independence. The data of these studies—though far from fully convincing either clinically, methodologically, or statistically—provided sufficient hard evidence to justify separating the two syndromes and to utilize their respective item lists as inclusion criteria for the DSM-III.

The diagnostic criterion set for the schizotypal personality was modified in the DSM-III-R by alterations in two criteria. The first was the deletion of depersonalization and derealization as a criterion, owing to the observation that these features were not clinically evident in most patients who otherwise exhibit the disorder. A new item representing, odd, eccentric, or peculiar behaviors or appearance was added in the DSM-III-R because such characteristics were frequently recorded in persons with the disorder.

The ICD does not include the schizotypal as part of personality disorder conditions: rather, it records them as a component of a broad schizophrenic disorders spectrum.

The DSM-IV continues the line of thinking described in earlier manuals and characterizes the schizotypal disorder as evincing a pervasive pattern of social and interpersonal deficits, particularly a reduced capacity for and discomfort with close relationships, and by cognitive distortions and behavioral eccentricities. The criterion list is heavily weighted in the Cognitive domain, although aspects of other domains are noted as well. Specifically, five criteria relate to Cognitive dysfunctions: the presence of ideas of reference; odd beliefs or magical thinking that are inconsistent with subcultural norms (e.g., superstitions, bizarre fantasies); unusual perceptual illusions; odd, circumstantial, and metaphorical

thinking and speech; paranoid ideation and persistent suspicions. Two criteria are noted in the area of Mood/Temperament: constricted or inappropriate affect; excessive social anxieties of a paranoid character that do not diminish with familiarity. One criterion may be found in the Behavioral domain: odd, eccentric, or peculiar appearance or behaviors. Likewise, one criterion is essentially Interpersonal in character: a lack of close friends other than first-degree relatives.

As a final illustration of contemporary proposals, we will turn briefly to the evolutionary polarity model as presented in Figure 17.1. The primary theme illustrated is the vacancy or weakness that exists in each of the six polarity boxes. Notable, however, are the reversal signs between each of the three pairs. In essence, this signifies that none of the survival motives and aims of the schizotypal have a firm grounding. Rather, they are feeble in their intensity and focus, and can be easily reversed or distorted in their usual objectives and goals. The figure portrays their rather ineffectual existence, as well as the meaningless and eccentric character of their activities. Possessing little spark or drive, these individuals become increasingly estranged from social conventions, resulting in the purposeless nature of their behaviors, the curious character of their thoughts, and the frequent inappropriateness of the emotions they express.

In line with the view that the severe personality disorders are largely structural pathologies, rather than stylistic ones, an understanding of

SCHIZOTYPAL PROTOTYPE

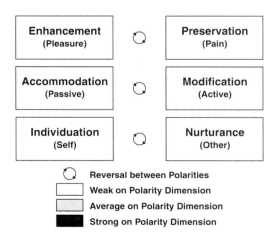

Figure 17.1 Status of the schizotypal personality prototype in accord with the Millon Polarity Model.

these patients requires that we combine the particular structural pathology of the patient with the less severe personality style with which it is fused. Schizotypals usually demonstrate either a schizoid or an avoidant stylistic pattern. The features of these less severe pathological styles then conflate with the pathology of structure that typifies the schizotypal, thereby producing the particular configuration of characteristics of the patient under study.

A chronological review of the major contributors is shown in Figure 17.2.

CLINICAL FEATURES

Several clusters of symptoms are found in common among patients classed in the schizotypal category; these will be noted before arranging them into clinical domains and specifying characteristics that differentiate the two major subvarieties. The three aspects of the schizotypal picture described here are the source of anxiety that tends to prompt psychotic episodes; characteristic cognitive processes and preoccupations; and general mood and behavior:

• *Depersonalization Anxiety.* The deficient or disharmonious affect of these patients deprives them of the capacity to relate to things or to experience events as something different from flat and lifeless phenomena. This persistent detachment or disavowal of self distinguishes the unreal and meaningless quality of his life, and may give rise to a frightening

sense of emptiness and nothingness. Every so often, the schizotypal may be overwhelmed by the dread of total disintegration, implosion, and nonexistence. These severe attacks of depersonalization may precipitate wild psychotic outbursts in which the patient frantically searches to reaffirm reality.

• *Cognitive Autism and Disjunctiveness.* The slippage and interference in thought processes that characterize the milder detached patterns are even more pronounced in the schizotypal. When motivated or prompted to relate to others, they are frequently unable to orient their thoughts logically and they become lost in personal irrelevancies and in tangential asides that have no pertinence to the topic at hand. They lack "touch" with others and are unable to order their ideas in terms relevant to reciprocal, social communication. This pervasive disjunctiveness, this scattered and autistic feature of thinking, only further alienates them from others.

• *Deficient Social Behaviors and Impoverished Affect.* Examination of the developmental achievements of the typical schizotypal will indicate an erratic course in which the person has continually failed to progress toward normal social attainments. School and employment history of these patients shows marked deficits and irregularities, given their intellectual capacities as a base. Not only are they frequent drop outs, but they drift from one source of employment to another, and, if married, often are separated or

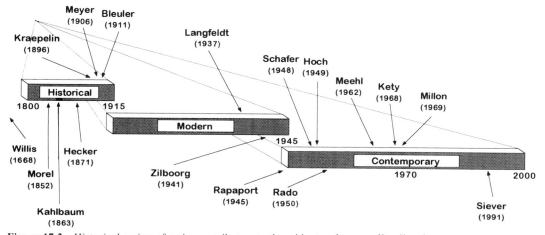

Figure 17.2   Historical review of major contributors to the schizotypal personality disorder.

divorced. This deficit in social competence and attainment derives from, and in part contributes to, their lack of drive and their feelings of unworthiness.

PROTOTYPAL DIAGNOSTIC DOMAINS

Although important distinctions exist among subvariants of the schizotypal syndrome, they share a number of features, and it is these to which attention is directed in the following sections (see Table 17.1 and Figure 17.3).

Expressive Behavior: Eccentric

What is most distinctive about schizotypal personalities is their socially gauche and peculiar mannerisms, and their tendency to evince unusual actions and appearances. Many dress in strange and unusual ways, often appearing to prefer a "personal uniform" from day to day (e.g., wearing a baseball cap with the visor in the back and invariably dressed in a horizontally striped t-shirt, always draped over a khaki pants belt). The tendency to keep to peculiar clothing styles sets them distinctively apart from their peers. As a consequence of their strange behaviors and appearances, schizotypals are readily perceived by others as aberrant, unobtrusively odd, curious, or bizarre.

Some schizotypals are aloof and isolated and behave in a bland and apathetic manner because they experience few pleasures and have need to avoid few discomforts. It would appear, then, that they should have little reason to acquire instrumental behaviors.

Other schizotypals more actively control expressions of intense affect because they fear being humiliated and rejected. They are inexpressive and socially isolated for protective reasons. Their constricted affect and interpersonal reserve do not arise because of intrinsic emotional or social deficits but because they have bound their feelings and relationships to protect against the possibility of rebuff.

Interpersonal Conduct: Secretive

Perhaps as a consequence of their unusual cognitive dysfunctions, schizotypals may have learned to prefer privacy and isolation. Unable to achieve a reasonable level of interpersonal comfort and satisfaction, they may have learned to withdraw from social relationships, to draw increasingly into themselves, with just a few tentative attachments

TABLE 17.1   Clinical Domains of the Schizotypal Prototype

Behavioral Level

(F) Expressively Eccentric. Exhibits socially gauche and peculiar mannerisms; is perceived by others as aberrant, disposed to behave in an unobtrusively odd, aloof, curious, or bizarre manner.

(F) Interpersonally Secretive. Prefers privacy and isolation, with few highly tentative attachments and personal obligations; has drifted over time into increasingly peripheral vocational roles and clandestine social activities.

Phenomenological Level

(F) Cognitively Disorganized. Capacity to read thoughts and feelings of others is markedly dysfunctional, mixes social communications with personal irrelevancies, circumstantial speech, ideas of reference, and metaphorical asides; often ruminative, appearing self-absorbed and lost in daydreams with occasional magical thinking, bodily illusions, obscure suspicions, odd beliefs, and a blurring of reality and fantasy.

(S) Estranged Self-Image. Exhibits recurrent social perplexities and illusions as well as experiences of depersonalization, derealization and dissociation; sees self as forlorn, with repetitive thoughts of life's emptiness and meaninglessness.

(S) Chaotic Objects. Internalized representations consisting of a piecemeal jumble of early relationships and affects, random drives and impulses, and uncoordinated channels of regulation that are only fitfully competent for binding tensions, accommodating needs, and mediating conflicts.

Intrapsychic Level

(F) Undoing Mechanism. Bizarre mannerisms and idiosyncratic thoughts appearing to reflect a retraction or reversal of previous acts or ideas that have stirred feelings of anxiety, conflict, or guilt; ritualistic or magical behaviors that serve to repent for or nullify assumed misdeeds or "evil" thoughts.

(S) Fragmented Organization. Possesses permeable ego-boundaries; coping and defensive operations are haphazardly ordered in a loose assemblage of morphologic structures, leading to desultory actions in which primitive thoughts and affects are discharged directly, with few reality-based sublimations, and significant further disintegrations into a psychotic structural level, likely under even modest stress.

Biophysical Level

(S) Distraught or Insentient Mood. Excessively apprehensive and ill at ease, particularly in social encounters; agitated and anxiously watchful, evincing distrust of others and suspicion of their motives that persists despite growing familiarity; *or* manifests drab, apathetic, sluggish, joyless, and spiritless appearance; reveals marked deficiencies in face-to-face rapport and emotional expression.

(F) = Functional domain.
(S) = Structural domain.

SCHIZOTYPAL PROTOTYPE

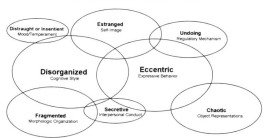

Figure 17.3 Salience of personologic domains in the schizotypal prototype.

and personal obligations. Depending on the difficulty they have experienced in these limited social relationships, they may have drifted over time into increasingly peripheral vocational roles, finding a degree of satisfaction in unusual and clandestine social activities.

As noted previously, the social achievements of the typical schizotypal usually indicate an erratic course, with a failure to make normal progress. Academic and work histories show marked deficits and irregularities, given their intellectual capacities as a base. Not only are they frequent drop outs, but they tend to drift from one job to another and are often separated or divorced, if they ever married. Their deficits in achievement competence derive from and, in part, contribute to their social anxieties and feelings of unworthiness. Moreover, there is a listlessness and a lack of spontaneity, ambition, and interest in life.

Schizotypals are able to talk about only a few relatively tangible matters, usually those things that demand their immediate attention. If they do sustain a conversation. they may press it beyond the appropriate or suitable, digressing into highly personal, odd, or metaphorical topics. More commonly, they lack the spark to initiate action or to participate socially, seemingly enclosed and trapped by some force that blocks them from responding to and empathizing with others. This inability to take hold of life to become a member of a real society, and to invest their energies and interests in a world of others, lies at the heart of their pathology.

Cognitive Style: Disorganized

Crucial to the pathology of schizotypals is their inability to organize their thoughts, particularly in the realm of interpersonal understanding and empathy. They interpret things "differently" than

most of us. The capacity to differentiate what is salient from what is tangential seems lacking in these personalities. They attribute unusual and special significance to peripheral and incidental events, construing what transpires between persons in a manner that signifies a fundamental lack of social comprehension and logic. They do not evince a general deficit in cognitive capacity that is pervasively awry or is broadly deficient. Rather, their distortions and deficiencies appear limited to the interpersonal facets of the cognitive domain. As a consequence of their misrenderings of the meaning of human interactions, they construct idiosyncratic conceptions regarding the thoughts, feelings, and actions of others. They are unable to grasp or resonate to the everyday elements of human behavior and thought. Daily transactions are transformed in bizarre ways, rendering them as odd and peculiar to most observers. In sum, the capacity to "read" the thoughts and feelings of others is markedly distorted. They interpose personal irrelevancies, circumstantial speech, ideas of reference, and metaphorical asides in ordinary social communications. Lacking in the ability to implicitly understand the give-and-take that coheres interpersonal transactions, they may gradually withdraw from such transactions, becoming highly ruminative, self-absorbed, lost in daydreams. Owing to their problematic information gathering and disorganized processing, their ideas may result in the formation of magical thinking, bodily illusions, odd beliefs, peculiar suspicions, and cognitive blurring that interpenetrates reality with fantasy.

Why else do they develop superstitions, referential ideas, and illusions, and engage at times in frenetic activity and vigorous coping? In essence, schizotypals have enough awareness of the fruits of life to realize that other people do experience joy, sorrow, and excitement, whereas they, by contrast, are empty and barren. They desire *some* relatedness, *some* sensation, and *some* feeling that they are part of the world about them. Although avoiding more than they can handle comfortably, they also feel considerable discomfort with less than they need, especially since less brings them close to nothing. Their recurrent illusions, their magical and telepathic thinking, and their ideas of reference may be viewed as a coping effort to fill the spaces of their emptiness, the feeling that they are "going under" and are bereft of all life and meaning.

Alienated from others and themselves, they too may sense the terror of impending nothingness and of a barren, depersonalized, and nonexistent self. Such feelings prompt them also to engage in bizarre behaviors, beliefs, and perceptions that enable them to reaffirm reality. It is for this reason among others that we observe the ideas of reference, the clairvoyance, the illusions, and the strange ideation that typify the schizotypal.

Self-Image: Estranged

Owing to their unsatisfactory social and cognitive dysfunctions, most schizotypals evidence recurrent social perplexities as well as self-illusions, depersonalization, and association. Many see themselves as alienated from the world around them, as forlorn and estranged beings, with repetitive ruminations about life's emptiness and meaninglessness. The deficient cognitions and disharmonious affects of schizotypals deprive them of the capacity to experience events as something other than lifeless and unfathomable phenomena. They suffer a sense of vapidness in a world of puzzling and washed-out objects. As noted in prior paragraphs, many schizotypals see themselves to be more dead than alive, insubstantial, foreign, and disembodied. As existential phenomenologists might put it, they are threatened by nonbeing. Detached observers of the passing scene, these patients remain uninvolved, looking from the outside not only with regard to others but with regard to themselves as well. Many pathological personalities experience periods of inner void and social detachment, but the feeling of estrangement and depersonalization is an ever-present and insistent feature of the schizotypal's everyday existence.

Object-Representations: Chaotic

The inner world of the schizotypal is grounded in a piecemeal jumble of early memories, perceptions, and feelings. The inner template that comprises this chaotic melange of objects, impulses, and thoughts is almost random, resulting in an ineffective and uncoordinated framework for regulating the patient's tensions, needs, and goals. Perhaps for the greater part of their lives, these internalized representations have been only fitfully competent for accommodating to their world, binding their impulses, and mediating their interpersonal difficulties.

When motivated or prompted to relate to others, schizotypals are frequently unable to orient their inner dispositions in a logical manner; as noted previously, they become lost in personal irrelevancies and in tangential asides that seem vague, digressive, and with no pertinence to the topic at hand. They are out of touch with others and are unable to

order their ideas in terms relevant to reciprocal, social communication. The pervasive disjunctiveness of their inner templates—the scattered, circumstantial, and autistic elements of their thinking—only further alienates these patients from others.

Regulatory Mechanisms: Undoing

It appears that many of the bizarre mannerisms and idiosyncratic thoughts of the schizotypal reflect a retraction or reversal of previous acts or ideas. Intrapsychically, this regulatory mechanism may serve to counteract feelings of anxiety, conflict, or guilt. By utilizing this dynamic process, the patient "repents for" or nullifies the ostensive misdeed or "evil thought." The outcropping of this undoing process may be seen in their magical beliefs and ritualistic behaviors.

This persistent undoing mechanism, combined with the schizotypal's periodic disavowal of self, may come to characterize the unreal and meaningless quality of their lives and may give rise to their frequent and frightening sense of emptiness and nothingness. As already noted, schizotypals are often overwhelmed by the dread of total disintegration, implosion, and nonexistence—feelings that may be countered by imposing or constructing new worlds of self-made reality, an idiosyncratic reality composed of superstitions, suspicions, illusions, and so on. The more severe attacks of depersonalization may precipitate psychotic episodes, irrational outbursts in which these patients frantically search to build a sense of reality to fill their vacant existence.

Morphologic Organization: Fragmented

If one looks into the intrapsychic organization of the schizotypal's mind, one is likely to find highly permeable boundaries among psychic components that are commonly well segregated. There is a haphazardly ordered and loose assemblage of morphologic structures. As a consequence of these less than adequate and poorly constructed defensive operations, primitive thoughts and impulses are usually discharged in a helter-skelter way, more or less directly and in a sequence of desultory actions. The intrinsically defective nature of the schizotypal's internal structures results in few reality-based sublimations and few successful achievements in life. These defects make the patient vulnerable to further decompensation—even under modest degrees of stress.

The inner structures of the schizotypal may be overwhelmed by excess stimulation. This is likely to occur when social demands and expectations press hard against their preferred uninvolved or withdrawn state. Unable to avoid such external impositions, some schizotypals may react either by "blanking out," drifting off into another world, or by paranoid or aggressive outbursts. Undue encroachments on their complacent world may lead them to disconnect socially for prolonged periods, during which they may be confused and aimless, display inappropriate affect and paranoid thinking, and communicate in odd, circumstantial, and metaphorical ways. At other times, when external pressures may be especially acute, they may react with a massive and psychotic outpouring of primitive impulses, delusional thoughts, hallucinations, and bizarre behaviors. Many schizotypals have stored up intense repressed anxieties and hostilities throughout their lives. Once released, these feelings burst out in a rampaging flood. The backlog of suspicions, fears, and animosities has been ignited and now explodes in a frenzied cathartic discharge.

Mood/Temperament: Distraught/Insentient

Although variable in nature, schizotypals tend to display one of two predominant affective states. The *insipid* schizotypal, to be discussed shortly, manifests a drab, apathetic, sluggish, and joyless demeanor, a pattern of behaviors that appears to overlie an intrinsically spiritless and affectless temperament. Rarely do they display an ease in emotional expression; as a consequence, they exhibit marked deficiencies in their face-to-face rapport with others. Whether this deficit derives from some inborn constitutional disposition, or a lack of affective attachment experiences in early life, cannot be ascertained readily; more will be said regarding this matter in a later section.

A contrasting predominant mood may be seen among patients labeled *timorous* schizotypals; these actively detached persons exhibit many features of the avoidant personality as well. These schizotypals are excessively apprehensive and ill at ease, particularly in social encounters, and evidence a generally agitated and anxious watchfulness. Many exhibit a distrust of other persons and are suspicious of their motives, a disposition that rarely recedes despite growing familiarity.

PROTOTYPAL VARIANTS

It will be useful in this section to outline and describe a number of personality variations that

have at their core the prototypal schizotypal pattern; however, they display features that give the individual's personality structure a somewhat different coloration.

Normal Styles

Among the notable characteristics of the three structurally defective personalities—schizotypal, paranoid, borderline—is the low probability that they can function in a normal fashion. Each possesses characteristics that make it difficult to relate in an effective and socially acceptable way in everyday life. These personalities are either too withdrawn and eccentric (SZT), too impulsive and unpredictable (BDL), or too suspicious and antagonistic (PAR). Consequently, we will leave this section on normal styles blank, as we will in describing the other structurally defective personalities.

Childhood Syndromes

Chapters 6 and 7 outlined features of schizoid and avoidant personality trends in children and discussed such disorders as autism, Asperger's syndrome, and threctism, the latter two perhaps being the same pathology listed under different labels. The features of the schizotypal personality have often been found in what has historically been called "childhood schizophrenia." In the DSM-IV, the label "childhood disintegrative disorder" has been introduced to portray features formerly signifying a degeneration of an otherwise and previously normal child into a disorganized state in which a significant loss of language, competence, social skills, and adaptive behavior have become notable. Whether this recent characterization or this deteriorating course signifies a pattern akin to the schizotypal personality pattern can only be speculated at this time.

In what we prefer to term an "interpersonal-cognitive disorder of childhood," we may find the forerunner of the schizotypal pattern. In contrast to the autistic child, where we see a deficit in the capacity for affective and attachment behaviors, or the threctic child (Asperger's syndrome), where we see an extreme hypersensitivity to environmental stimuli, especially those having emotional significance, the child with an interpersonal-cognitive dysfunction is likely to possess an intrinsic defect (constitutional or experiential) in the capacity to accurately read the psychic state of other humans, or to interpret their communications accurately. Such children may be normal with regard to most cognitive and intellectual functions, but evidence a marked defect in the interpersonal sphere. Their social intelligence is what is retarded, not their other aptitudes and capacities.

Rarely is this deficiency evident in the first year or two of life where the sensibility for interpreting the thoughts and communications of others has not yet come into play as an expected capability. However, by the age of 4 or 5, and certainly in later years, these children may become the butt of others' jokes and derogations. Interpreting events in the family and in the schoolyard in a peculiar and distorted manner, misinterpreting the intentions of others, and responding in a somewhat irrelevant and tangential manner, these children are quickly judged as peculiar and eccentric. The more they experience the critical and derogating commentary that their own behaviors and communications elicit, the more likely a vicious circle of new difficulties arise. Hence, many may begin to acquire a pattern of protective withdrawal behaviors, becoming increasingly isolated and fearful of social relationships. Although the origins of their difficulties are in the cognitive sphere, life experiences frequently become entangled with emotional and behavioral consequences that intensify over time.

Adult Subtypes

There are two major variants of the defective schizotypal personality. The first derives from the *passive-detached style,* noted as the schizoid personality; the second reflects an *active-detached style* and has been termed the avoidant personality. Although there are several adult subtypes of each of these broad personality styles (e.g., "languid" and "remote" to represent two of the schizoid subtypes) we will limit our discussion to the two broad variations of the defective-schizotypal disorder.

The Insipid Schizotype

Notably insensitive to feelings, these individuals often experience a separation between their mind and their physical body. There is a strange sense of nonbeing or nonexistence as if their floating conscious awareness carried with it a depersonalized or identityless human form. Behaviorally, these personalities tend to be drab, sluggish, and inexpressive. They possess a marked deficit in affectivity and appear bland, indifferent, unmotivated, and insensitive to the external world. Cognitive processes seem obscure, vague, and tangential.

They are either impervious to, or miss the shades of, interpersonal and emotional experience. Social communications are responded to minimally or with inappropriate affect or peculiar ideas, or in a circumstantial and confused manner. Speech is often monotonous, listless, or inaudible. Most people consider them to be unobtrusive and strange persons who drift on the periphery of life or who fade into the background, self-absorbed, woolgathering, and lost to the outside world. Most typically the *insipid schizotype* derives from and coalesces with the schizoid pattern. In a very modest number of cases, we see a fusion with depressive and dependent personality features.

The insipid schizotype will occasionally experience the awesome terror of feeling "dead," nonexistent, petrified. Detached from the world and insensitive to their own feelings, these patients may become terrified by a frightening sense of "nothingness," of passing through a barren, cold, lifeless existence. The disaster of losing "self," of becoming a walking automaton, a petrified object without meaning or purpose, may overwhelm these patients driving them into a bizarre psychotic state in which they create tangible illusions to which they can relate, self-referential ideas that give them a significance they otherwise lack, bizarre telepathic powers that enable them to communicate with mythical or distant others—all in a desperate effort to reaffirm their existence in reality. Sinking into a lifeless void, they find themselves struck by a sense of becoming a thing and not a being. This dread, this catastrophic sense of nothingness causes them to grasp at anything, real or fantasized, by which they can convince themselves that they do in fact exist. On the brink of feeling totally annihilated, they struggle desperately to confirm their being, clinging tenaciously to whatever meaning and feeling they can find in or impute to their surroundings. As in their pure schizotypal counterpart, these eccentricities are attempts to forestall the void of oblivion and nothingness.

These schizotypals occasionally succumb to psychotic disorders when faced with too much, rather than too little, stimulation. Painfully uncomfortable with social obligations or personal closeness, they will feel encroached if pressed into responsibilities beyond their limited tolerance. During these periods, schizotypal-schizoids may either explode, bursting into frenetic activity to block the intrusions forced on them, or simply "fade out," become blank, lose conscious awareness, and "turn off" the pressures of the outer world.

The Timorous Schizotype

As with their less severe avoidant counterparts, these *timorous schizotypals* are restrained, isolated, apprehensive, guarded, and shrinking. Protectively, they seek to "kill" their feelings and desires, bind their impulses, and withdraw from social encounters, thereby defending themselves from the pain and anguish of interpersonal relationships. The surface apathy and seeming indifference of these patients is not, as it is in the insipid schizotypal, owing to an intrinsic lack of sensitivity but to their attempt to restrain, damp down, or deaden excessive sensitivity. In addition to their social isolation, timorous schizotypals depreciate their self-worth. There is an abandonment of self and a disowning and remoteness from feeling and desire. The "real" selves of these personalities have been devalued and demeaned, split off, cast asunder, and rejected as humiliating or valueless. Not only are these schizotypals alienated from others, then, but they find no refuge and comfort in turning to themselves. Their isolation is twofold. So little is gained from others, and only a despairing sense of shame is found within themselves. Without the rewards of self or others to spur them, they drift into personal apathy and social isolation. As described previously, this timorous schizotypal pattern either emerges from or is interwoven with the more basic avoidant personality style.

Having little hope of gaining affection and security, timorous schizotypals learn that it is best to deny real feelings and aspirations. Cognitive processes are intentionally confused in an effort to disqualify and discredit rational thinking. In their stead are substituted fantasy worlds that might provide some respite from the anguish of realistic thought. But these, too, hold brief interest because the outer world keeps intruding and "shames" these patients back to reality.

Disharmonious affects, irrelevant and tangential thoughts, and an increasingly severe social bankruptcy develop as timorous schizotypals are forced to build an ever-tighter armor around themselves. Their characteristic eccentricities derive from this wall of isolation and insularity that they have constructed. Like the insipid schizotypal, they are subject to the devastating terror of nothingness, the feeling of imminent nonexistence. By insulating themselves, shrinking their world, and deadening their sensitivities, they have laid the groundwork for feeling emptiness and unreality. To counter the anxieties of depersonalization and derealization, they may be driven into excited and bizarre behaviors, contrive peculiar and hallucinating images, and shout utterly unintelligible but beseeching sounds, all in an effort to draw attention and affirm their existence as living beings. They may maneuver irrationally just to evoke a response from others, simply create a stir to prove that they are real and not a mirage of empty, floating automatons such as they sense themselves to be. Failing in this effort to quiet their anxieties, as is likely, they may turn to a "make-believe" world of superstitions, magic, and telepathy—anything that they can fashion from their imagination that will provide them with a "pseudocommunity" of fantasized persons and objects to which they can safely relate.

COMORBID DISORDERS AND SYNDROMES

As in the prior two chapters, the focus here is concentrated on personalities that most frequently covary with the syndrome under review. Brief attention is given both to the schizotypal's concomitant Axis I clinical syndromes and Axis II personality disorders. Points of differential diagnosis will be discussed in a later section.

Axis II Comorbidities

A review of Figure 17.4 suggests that the schizotypal (SZT) syndrome covaries most frequently with the schizoid (SZD), avoidant (AVD), and paranoid (PAR) personalities. As has been discussed in prior sections of the text, the schizotypal pattern often develops insidiously, becoming an increasingly integral, but more dysfunctional and structurally defective pattern that supersedes a less severe AVD and SZD personality disorder. Hence, what we observe clinically in a number of schizotypals is a mixture of its own constellation of traits

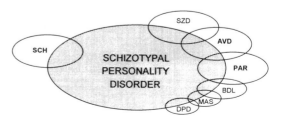

Figure 17.4 Comorbidity between schizotypal personality disorder and other DSM Axis I and Axis II disorders.

superimposed on either a passively detached SZD style or an actively detached AVD style. The comorbidity derives from a different source in the SZD and PAR disorders. Their personality features covary by virtue of a shared severity of pathology and a tendency in common to be fearful and suspicious of the motives of others. Lesser SZT comorbidities are found with the borderline (BDL), masochistic (MAS), and dependent (DPD) personalities. The conjunction with the BDL derives primarily from the fact that they share a more severe, structurally defective personality pattern.

Axis I Comorbidities

Although schizotypals occasionally exhibit a wide range of DSM-IV anxiety, somatoform, and dissociative disorders, these are touched on only in passing as the chapter progresses. Primary interest is directed to the more severe, psychotic-level schizophrenic disturbances to which the schizotypal is especially prone.

Schizophrenic Syndromes (SCH). Particularly subject to *disorganized* (hebephrenic) *schizophrenic* disorders, schizotypals are identifiable by their incongruous and fragmented behaviors. At these times, they seem totally disoriented and confused, unclear as to time, place, and identity. Many will exhibit posturing, grimacing, inappropriate giggling, and peculiar mannerisms. Speech tends to ramble into "word salads" composed of incoherent neologisms and a chaotic mishmash of irrelevancies. Ideas are colored with fantasy, illusion, and hallucination, and scattered with bizarre and fragmentary delusions that have no apparent logic or function. Regressive acts such as soiling and wetting are not uncommon, and these patients often consume food in an infantile or ravenous manner.

Catatonic states tend to occur after a period when the tide of unconscious anxieties and impulses have surged forward, overwhelming these patients, and sinking them into a hazy world of fleeting and dreamlike impressions. Subjective moods and images become fused with, and ultimately dominate, objective realities. Overt behaviors are distorted and guided by primary process thinking and thereby appear purposeless, disjointed, irrational, stereotyped, and bizarre. There is a disunity and disorganization to speech and communication. Ideas are conveyed in an inchoate or jumbled fashion, reflecting delusions that are projected onto the world in hallucinatory perceptions. Controls are abandoned and random emotions break loose. No seeming purpose exists

to their behaviors, other than the ventilation of momentary impulses. Unable to grasp reality or coordinate feelings and thoughts, these schizotypals may regress into a motorically rigid and immobile state, a totally helpless form of catatonic invalidism.

In the *residual schizophrenic* state, where a prior experience of overt schizophrenia has been evident, bizarre thoughts and emotions continue to churn close to the surface, but are managed and held in check by the schizotypal. Although the positive signs of schizophrenia are now under control, such that delusions and hallucinations are no longer absent, there is continuing evidence of the disorder by virtue of the presence of a number of so-called negative symptoms. Should the underlying feelings constrained by the few schizotypal controls overpower the patient's tenuous state, certain disorders are likely to occur, such as *hebephrenic* states or brief *schizophreniform* episodes. These latter episodes tend to be characterized by a mixture of terror and fury. In less severe reactions, we observe more terror than fury; violence usually is controlled or neutralized. In more extreme cases, a full-fledged catatonic excitement may emerge, with unconscious impulses rising to the foreground and producing the turbulent picture that typifies these disorders. These eruptions often are useful safety valves. By discharging hidden and pent-up feelings, the schizotypal's cumulative tensions subside temporarily. For a brief period, these patients can vent emotions that they would not dare express in the course of their everyday life. Chaotic and aberrant as they appear, and as they are, these outbursts serve an adaptive function.

Differential Diagnoses

Only a few points are noted in this differential diagnostic section. The major considerations relevant to distinguishing among similar syndromes have been recorded several times in earlier chapters. Thus, given the multiaxial system of the DSM-IV, the schizotypal designation may be diagnosed concurrently with any number of Axis I and Axis II disorders.

Differential concerns regarding Axis I syndromes should be few. The schizotypal syndrome is a chronic and pervasive lifestyle that exhibits and subsumes a wide constellation of Axis I features that may be diagnosed as separate symptoms when they are found singly or for brief time periods. Thus, *depersonalization disorder,* so intrinsic a part of the schizotypal syndrome, would be independently diagnosed if there were no co-variant patient symptoms such as social isolation, suspiciousness, or a host of eccentricities of thought, perception, and behavior.

Various other *schizophrenic disorders* may be seen concomitantly with the schizotypal syndrome, an expected covariance given the theoretical and empirical basis for constructing the personality syndrome in the first place. A major issue, more of nosologic consistency than substantive discrimination, is the separation of *schizophrenia: residual type* from schizotypal personality. The diagnostic criteria are highly similar. However, "residual" is to be employed only if a prior psychotic episode has occurred. Since schizotypals ostensibly experience transient psychotic episodes, usually of a schizophrenic nature, then it would appear that they always must coexist multiaxially—except before the schizotypal's first schizophrenic episode. So be it.

As noted in previous chapters, the schizotypal may require more precise discriminations from certain other Axis II disorders, particularly schizoid, avoidant, and paranoid.

Differentiation from the *schizoid* is particularly important in that the two are often discussed and presented as if they were interchangeable (Beck & Freeman, 1990b; Benjamin, 1993a). The commingling of schizoid and schizotypal characteristics is certainly a valid observation. Despite the similarity in the *consequences* of their fundamental defects, they can and should be separated both conceptually and pedagogically, owing to differences in their *basic impairment.* Schizoids are intrinsically deficient in the capacity to experience emotion or *affect*; this results ultimately in interpersonal difficulties. Schizotypals are intrinsically dysfunctional in their *cognitive* capacity to understand human motivations and communications; this, too, results ultimately in interpersonal difficulties. Apart from the interpersonal consequences of their deeper impairments, both schizoids and schizotypals have to be treated therapeutically in different ways, the former by activating their capacity to feel and become attached to others, the latter by "straightening out" their cognitive capacity to read correctly what others think and feel.

As in the previously described schizoid, the *avoidant* is often a precursor of the schizotypal personality structure. That is, both schizoid and avoidants often decompensate in the direction of acquiring many of the structurally defective features that are present in schizotypals from the start. As a consequence of this developmental pathogenic course, the task of separating avoidants and schizotypals can be a difficult one indeed, if necessary at all. Nevertheless, where there are long-term signs of behavioral eccentricity and cognitive dysfunctions, the diagnostician can safely assume that he or she is dealing with schizotypal pathology. By contrast, avoidant personalities have actively distanced from close relationships owing to their deep fear of being rejected, despite a persistent longing for such attachments. Schizotypal disengagement stems from their social peculiarities and their inability to connect to others.

Separation from the *paranoid* personality can also be problematic in that many features are shared (e.g., ideas of reference, suspiciousness, social isolation), as is their general structurally defective level of pathology. It is the peculiarities of the schizotypal, the tangential thinking and eccentric behaviors, not found in the paranoid, that helps the differentiation process. The paranoid, by contrast to the schizotypal, displays cold and restricted affect, and evinces a clarity of thought that is focused in its intentions.

ASSESSING THE SCHIZOTYPAL: A CASE STUDY

There are few indications on the Rorschach, TAT, and MMPI for identifying the schizotypal personality pattern that differ appreciably from what is seen on these instruments with moderately severe and chronic schizophrenia. Little data have accumulated to aid us in the task of differentiating the personality variant of the schizophrenic spectrum from those evidencing the clinical syndrome; this reflects the fact that the designation schizotypal has been in active clinical use only a decade or two. What follows, therefore, is a distillation of schizophreniclike characteristics. Following a discussion of the response patterns seen on these three well-established assessment tools, we will turn to a case history and to the profile and interpretation on the MCMI-III, an instrument that has now become the second most frequently used of the major clinical inventories.

The major feature seen on the Rorschach is the generally poor or confused quality of the patient's responses. There is considerable scatter within the content employed; much of this content is of an odd and unusual nature. There are peculiar verbalizations, contaminations, incongruous sequences, and fabulized responses. Pure color responses are not infrequent; at the other end, there are responses that are based on form alone. There is a low number of human movement responses, but a significant proportion of animal responses, both of which are usually of poor quality. In contrast to manifestly schizophrenic patients, however, schizotypals tend not to perseverate, that is use the same perceptions repeatedly from card to card. Similarly, clinical schizophrenics will perceive many more unusual or odd objects, or exhibit a so-called massing of repetitive pure color responses. Although the F-percent is likely to be the highest among all personality disorders, it will tend to be appreciably less than clinical schizophrenics.

The inclination to tell rambling and disorganized stories on the TAT is likewise higher among schizotypals than among other personalities, but less frequent and more coherent than found in schizophrenics. Story themes directly reflect the character of the schizotypal's current life history. Whereas schizophrenics are inclined to be symbolic in their responses, evidencing the primary process nature of their thinking, schizotypals are more reality-oriented. Nevertheless, the schizotypal's themes seem to be confused and sequentially illogical, with frequent comments of a self-referential nature.

The schizotypal MMPI is likely to show a higher than average score on Scale 8, although this is not an inevitable finding. It is their tendency to be drawn into a fantasy world, and their preoccupation with feelings of isolation and alienation that results in this high scale score. Whether they are of the flat and barren variety, where the response pattern is likely to be close to a 2-7-8 code type, or of an anguished and timorous variety, where a 7-8/8-7 code type is most likely present, it is wise for the clinician to examine the implications of various code combinations, as long as Scale 8 is prominent. For example, high 8-4 profiles suggest that schizotypallike features may be associated with intense resentments toward those who have been rejecting and humiliating. Similarly, high pairings between Scales 6 and 8 may suggest particularly severe decompensation among these schizotypal individuals.

The following sections include a typical schizotypal personality, following which the MCMI-III profile and interpretive report will be presented.

CASE 17.1

Thelma C., Age 37, Unmarried

Thelma was the youngest of four sisters. Since early life, she was known to be quiet and shy, the "weakest" member of the family. Thelma's father was a chronic alcoholic who, during frequent drinking sprees, humiliated and regularly beat various members of his family. Her mother seemed detached from Thelma, but she often would be critical of her for being "stupid and slow."

Thelma completed the 10th grade with better than average grades; however, she had to leave school shortly thereafter because of her mother's death. Thelma was given a job as a seamstress as a means of contributing to the family income since her father had abandoned his family two years prior to his wife's death, never to be heard from again.

Unfortunately, Thelma was unable to hold her position because the factory in which she worked had closed down; she failed to keep the next three jobs her sisters got for her over a 2-year period; as Thelma put it, "I was not interested and slow." Periodically, Thelma began to drink, becoming somewhat of an alcoholic as was her father. This pattern of drinking has continued on and off since her early 20s.

Following dismissal from her last position, Thelma simply withdrew from work, becoming entirely dependent on her older sister. Thelma claimed that work was too difficult for her and, more significantly, that she thought that everyone felt "I was stupid and would mess up the job." In a similar vein, several young men sought to court her, but she persistently refused their overtures since she knew "they wouldn't like me after they took me out." Alone much of the time, Thelma began to ruminate about the overtures that others had made toward her, gradually developing a broad-based suspiciousness that people were out to undo her, to humiliate her and embarrass her. These paranoid-like suspicions have remained relatively entrenched in Thelma's thinking, periodically becoming clinical in their severity, occasionally reaching levels of clear-cut delusions.

For the most part, however, Thelma has remained quietly unobtrusive, drawn into herself, and voicing slightly disorganized thoughts and impressions of what "really makes the world go around." Not especially eccentric in her appearance, except when she has gone on an alcoholic binge, Thelma has numerous peculiar beliefs about "influences that get to me," as well as mythological notions of a somewhat disorganized character.

For several years, Thelma took care of the house for her unmarried sister; however, Thelma felt that she had never done a "good job" since, "I spent most of my time sleeping or watching TV."

She reported further, "I don't like to read or to watch TV, but it's better than thinking about people or myself."

Upon her older sister's marriage, it was decided that Thelma, who was both afraid and incapable of being on her own, should be institutionalized. The decision, made by her sisters, was not responded to by Thelma as a painful rejection; she accepted it, at least overtly, without protest.

Upon entrance to the hospital, Thelma seemed hazy and disconnected, although she evidenced no hallucinations or prominent delusions. She spoke minimally, answered questions with a yes or no, seemed controlled, took care of herself reasonably well, and fit quietly into the admissions ward. She voiced relief to an attendant at being away from the expectations and demands of the outer world; however, she established no personal relationships with other patients or with the hospital personnel.

Were it not that no one made the effort to assist her in initiating a transition back to society, Thelma would have been recommended for discharge. Lacking such environmental support and recognizing her inability to relate easily with others or to assume independence, there seemed no option but to keep her hospitalized.

The MCMI-III profile is shown in Figure 17.5 on the next page; its interpretation follows below.

INTERPRETIVE SUMMARY

The MCMI-III profile of this man appears to reflect an intense conflict between his desire to withdraw from personal relationships, his fear of independence, and a growing sense of unworthiness and despondency. He would very much like to depend on friends and family, but he has learned to anticipate disillusionment and discouragement in these relationships. His deflated sense of self-worth and his expectation of personal failure and social humiliation limit any efforts he might make to become autonomous or to overcome his dispirited feelings. Moreover, he believes that others have either deprecated or disapproved of his occasional attempts at confidence building or self-assertion. He sees no alternative but to give up hopelessly or to give in to his gloomy and sorrowful state. This restriction of choice stirs deep resentments within him. As a consequence, he may experience anxiety and dejection, interspersed occasionally with odd, peculiar, erratic, passive-

aggressive acts, and periodic criticism of others for their lack of support. The dependency security that he seeks, however, may be seriously jeopardized when he voices his discontent too strongly. To bind his resentments and thereby protect against further loss, he will characteristically withdraw, becoming even more anxious and confused. The referring clinician may want to determine whether this man's moods change almost from day to day and whether he feels empty and hollow at times.

The erratic moodiness of this man may only add to the humiliating reactions he gets from others, which may serve to further reinforce his self-protective and erratic withdrawal. Every avenue of potential gratification seems full of conflict. He fears standing on his own because of his shaky sense of self-esteem. On the other hand, he cannot depend on others because of his fearful mistrust of them. Anticipating disillusionment, he may behave in an eccentric and irrational manner, thereby incurring the very rejection and disappointment he expects but seeks to avoid.

Unable to overcome the feeling that life is meaningless and empty, and unable to muster the skills to overcome the deficits he sees within himself, he is likely at times to become cranky, if not explosive, but then to turn against himself, expressing self-pity and a deep sense of personal unworthiness and uselessness. Often feeling misunderstood, unappreciated, and demeaned by others, he may add to his dismay by turning ridicule and contempt on himself. He sees few of the attributes he admires in others within himself, and this awareness intrudes upon his thoughts and interferes with his behavior, ultimately upsetting his sense of identity and his capacity to cope effectively with ordinary life tasks. Extended periods of irrational and suspicious thinking may be typical. Simple tasks may demand more energy than he can muster. What few efforts he can make may give way to emotional outbursts under the slightest of family or social pressures.

A reasonable conclusion from his MCMI-III responses is that this man also experiences repeated episodes of alcohol abuse. Anxiously troubled, lonely, and socially apprehensive much of the time, he appears to turn to alcohol to fulfill a number of otherwise difficult-to-achieve psychological functions. Alcohol not only may serve to medicate his social anxiety and thereby enhance his confidence but also may help him relate more comfortably to others by bolstering his feelings of self-esteem and well-being. For him, alcohol provides a quick dissolution of psychic pain, a method

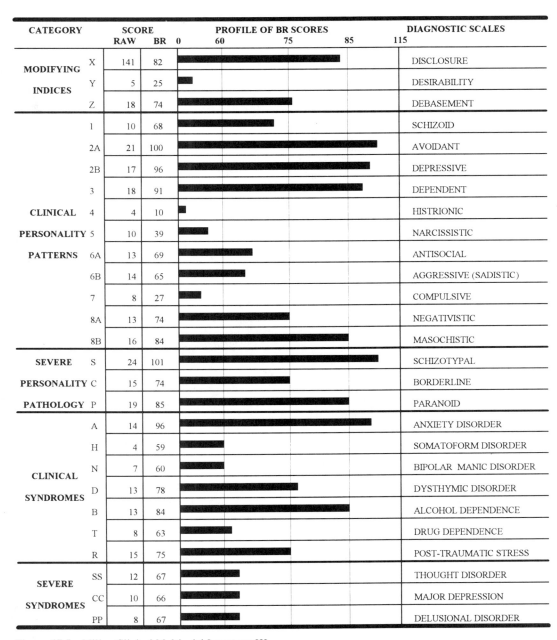

CATEGORY		SCORE		PROFILE OF BR SCORES				DIAGNOSTIC SCALES
		RAW	BR	0 60	75	85	115	
MODIFYING INDICES	X	141	82					DISCLOSURE
	Y	5	25					DESIRABILITY
	Z	18	74					DEBASEMENT
CLINICAL PERSONALITY PATTERNS	1	10	68					SCHIZOID
	2A	21	100					AVOIDANT
	2B	17	96					DEPRESSIVE
	3	18	91					DEPENDENT
	4	4	10					HISTRIONIC
	5	10	39					NARCISSISTIC
	6A	13	69					ANTISOCIAL
	6B	14	65					AGGRESSIVE (SADISTIC)
	7	8	27					COMPULSIVE
	8A	13	74					NEGATIVISTIC
	8B	16	84					MASOCHISTIC
SEVERE PERSONALITY PATHOLOGY	S	24	101					SCHIZOTYPAL
	C	15	74					BORDERLINE
	P	19	85					PARANOID
CLINICAL SYNDROMES	A	14	96					ANXIETY DISORDER
	H	4	59					SOMATOFORM DISORDER
	N	7	60					BIPOLAR MANIC DISORDER
	D	13	78					DYSTHYMIC DISORDER
	B	13	84					ALCOHOL DEPENDENCE
	T	8	63					DRUG DEPENDENCE
	R	15	75					POST-TRAUMATIC STRESS
SEVERE SYNDROMES	SS	12	67					THOUGHT DISORDER
	CC	10	66					MAJOR DEPRESSION
	PP	8	67					DELUSIONAL DISORDER

Figure 17.5   Millon Clinical Multiaxial Inventory-III.

for blotting out awareness of his loneliness and troubled existence, but one that also intensifies his cognitive confusions.

PATHOGENIC DEVELOPMENTAL BACKGROUND

As noted in earlier chapters, it is the author's contention that personality patterns evolve from a complex interaction of biogenic and psychogenic factors. Prior descriptions of personality syndromes have sought, albeit too briefly, to identify the most probable combinations of influence that contribute to these psychopathologies. Among the more significant factors were heredity, constitutional dispositions; stimulation at sensitive periods of neurological maturation; parental feelings, communications, and methods of behavioral control; and the individual's own self-defeating attitudes, behaviors, and coping strategies. In the following sections, we will focus on background features that characterize the two major variants of the detached-schizotypal personality, the schizoid style (insipid) and the avoidant style (timorous). In Chapter 20, attention is given to the deterioration process that takes form in a decompensated schizotypal pattern.

HYPOTHESIZED BIOGENIC FACTORS

We will divide our discussion of the background of the defective-schizotypal pattern into their two major subtypes.

Passive-Detached Schizotypal. The passively detached schizotypals (*schizoid/insipid*) may be unfortunate carriers of a defective family inheritance. There are some data supporting the contention that genetic factors conducive to affective and cognitive deficits underlie the eccentricities of many of these personalities. Although families do "breed" the characteristics of the *insipid-schizotypal,* it is difficult to conceptualize the nature of the genetic mechanisms involved or even to state unequivocally that such mechanisms do in fact operate. Families may very well "breed" this pattern through interpersonal experience and not through biological inheritance at all. Among other biogenic factors that may be conducive to the development of this schizotypal is a passive infantile pattern, which may initiate a sequence of impoverished stimulation and parental

indifference. Also possible, though speculative, are anatomic deficits or neurochemical dysfunctions in either reticular, limbic, sympathetic, or synaptic control systems, resulting in diminished activation, minimal pleasure-pain sensibilities, and cognitive dysfunctions.

Active-Detached Schizotypal. The other, more actively detached schizotypal personality (*avoidant/ timorous*) often has a family history of apprehensive or cognitively "muddled" relatives, suggesting the possibility that genetic dispositions may be operative. A history of a fearful infantile pattern is not uncommon in this personality, often precipitating parental exasperation and rejection. Some have evidenced an irregular sequence of maturation, resulting in the development of an imbalance among competencies, an inability to handle excess emotionality, and the emergence of social peculiarities. The possibility of an underlying excess in limbic and sympathetic system reactivity, or a neurochemical acceleration of synaptic transmission, likewise may be posited. Dysfunctions such as these could give rise to the hypersensitivity and cognitive flooding that characterize these patients.

CHARACTERISTIC EXPERIENTIAL HISTORY

As in the preceding section, we will divide the typical developmental background of the two major variants of the defective-schizotypal in the following subsections.

Passive-Detached Schizotypal. *Insipid schizotypals* are likely to have been hindered in early life with constitutional insensitivities, resulting in a marked stimulus impoverishment during their oral, or sensory-attachment stage. This may set in motion an underdeveloped biophysical substrate for affectivity and deficient learning of social attachment behaviors. Other experiential factors of note are family atmospheres of indifference, impassivity, or formality, which may provide models for imitative learning and thereby establish the roots for lifelong patterns of social reticence interpersonal insensitivity, and discomfort with personal affection and closeness. Family styles of fragmented and amorphous communication may also contribute. Thus, exposure to disjointed, vague, and pointless interactions may give rise to the development, not only of inner cognitive confusions, but to unfocused, irrelevant, and tangential interpersonal relations. Experiences paralleling those of early childhood are often repeated and cumulative. In addition, stereotypes of the child's early "character" often take firm root, shape subsequent social attitudes, and preclude any changes in interpersonal style. Problematic relationships of this nature often get caught in a web of reciprocally destructive reactions, which then only aggravate earlier maladaptive tendencies.

Often overlooked among processes that perpetuate the individual's initial experiences are his or her own behaviors and coping styles. In the developmental background of these *insipid* schizotypals, the following appear to be especially self-defeating: affective deficits that flatten emotional experiences and perceptual insensitivities and cognitive obscurities that blur distinctions among events that might otherwise enhance and enrich their lives. As a consequence, opportunities for realizing stimulating and varied experiences, so necessary to alter the characteristically apathetic state, are precluded or diluted. To add further insult to these injuries, the early passive and cognitively insensitive behaviors of these insipid schizotypals make them unattractive and unrewarding social companions. Unable to communicate with either affect or clarity, they likely were shunned, overlooked, and invited to share few of the more interesting experiences to which others were drawn. Failing to interchange ideas and feelings with others, they remained fixed and undeveloped, continuing therefore in their disjointed, amorphous, and affectless state. Restricted in their social experiences, they acquired few social skills, found it increasingly difficult to relate socially, and perpetuated a vicious circle that not only fostered their isolated life but accentuated their social inadequacies and cognitive deficiencies.

Alienated from others and marginal members of society, these insipid schizotypals turned increasingly to solitary thoughts. Over time, shared social behaviors became fully subordinate to private fantasy. In solitude, their thoughts were left to wander unchecked by the logic and control of reciprocal social communication and activity. What they found within themselves was hardly rewarding, a barren, colorless void that offered no basis for joyful fantasy. Their inner personal world proved to be as dead and ungratifying as objective reality. They had no choice, so it seemed, but to turn to unreal fantasies. These, at least, might fill in the void and give their existence some substance. Interest moved toward the mystical and magical, to "needed" illusions and ideation that

enabled the person to become a central, rather than a peripheral and insignificant figure.

Active-Detached Schizotypal. Many *timorous schizotypals* were exposed to an early history of deprecation, rejection, and humiliation, resulting in feelings of low self-esteem and a marked distrust of interpersonal relations. Others may have been subjected to belittlement, censure, and ridicule, not only from parents but also from sibs and peers. During the sensory-attachment phase of development, they may have been treated in a harsh and unwelcoming fashion, thereby learning protectively to keep distance from their environment and to insulate their feelings. Ridicule from others in response to their efforts during the sensorimotor-autonomy stage may have led to feelings of personal incompetence and low self-worth. A further consequence of these experiences is that the children learned not only to avoid the appraisals of others but to demean themselves as persons as well. Continuation into the *gender-identity* and the *intracortical-integrative* stages is likely to have intensified feelings of low self-esteem and increased self-critical attitudes. Future timorous-schizotypals now devalue, censure, and belittle themselves as others had in the past. Some are subjected to deprecation and humiliation at the hands of their adolescent peers. Social alienation, heterosexual failure, and minimal vocational and competitive success during this period add further insults to the earlier injuries.

Unfortunately, the coping strategies acquired by these *timorous* schizotypals to fend off the pain of life have fostered rather than resolved their difficulties. In an effort to minimize their awareness of external discomfort, they turned inward to fantasy and rumination, but this also proved to be self-defeating. Not only were their inner conflicts intense, but they spent much of their reflective time reliving and duplicating the painful events of the past. Their protective efforts only reinforced their distress. Moreover, given their low self-esteem, their inner reflections often took the form of self-reproval. Not only did they fail to gain solace from themselves, but they found that they could not readily escape from their own thoughts of self-derogation, from feelings of personal worthlessness and the futility of being themselves. In an effort to counter these oppressive inner thoughts, they may have sought to block and destroy their cognitive clarity, that is, to interfere with the anguish of their discordant inner emotions and ideas.

This maneuver not only proved self-defeating, in that it diminished their ability to deal with events rationally, but it further estranged them from communicating effectively with others. Even more destructive self-reproval and cognitive interference alienated them from their own existence. Having no place to go, they began to create a new, inner world, populated by magical fantasies, illusions, telepathic relationships, and other odd thoughts that would provide them not only with an existence but one that was more significant and potentially rewarding than that found in reality.

SELF-PERPETUATION PROCESSES

The future of the schizotypal syndrome is perhaps the least promising of all personality types. This section briefly summarizes factors that contribute toward the downward progression.

In the preceding discussion, we have referred to several of the strategies employed by the schizotypal personality. This reflects the assertion that the adaptive efforts utilized by pathological personalities are themselves pathogenic, because many of their coping strategies are self-defeating and foster new difficulties; all pathological patterns are alike in this regard. The central distinction between the more and less severe patterns is that the strategies of the former group are instrumentally less successful and more self-defeating than those of the latter, either because they were never learned adequately, or because they have faltered under persistent and cumulative stress. Since their adaptive facilities are instrumentally so deficient, it seems best to focus on the restitutive and defensive efforts these patients employ. Thus, these patients are distinguished from their milder counterparts, not in their strategies but in what they do to shore up these strategies when they begin to crumble, albeit to minimal avail.

As formerly effective strategies begin to falter, the schizotypal may be driven to engage in a variety of extreme and frequently dramatic restitutive maneuvers; these are often displayed in the form of brief psychotic episodes in which previously dormant or controlled thoughts and impulses break into consciousness, producing primary process symptoms of bizarre ideation and behavior. If sufficient tension is discharged during these upsurges, and if environmental pressures are adequately relieved, the individual may regain composure and equilibrium; the temporary "disordered state" has

ended, and the person returns to the previous level of pathological personality functioning. For the present, we will focus our attention on what schizotypals seek to achieve in their attempts to cope with stress now that their former strategies have failed them.

Earlier, we noted two sets of conditions that precipitate schizotypals into temporary psychotic disorders. One occurs when they feel a frightening sense of petrifaction, "deadness," depersonalization, and emptiness—a degree of outer and inner stimulation that is much *less* than that to which they are accustomed. The second occurs when they feel an oppressive sense of being encroached on, pressured and obligated to others—a degree of external stimulation that is much more than that to which they are accustomed. We will next discuss the restitutive measures they employ to deal with these conditions.

Countering Depersonalization

To cope with depersonalization, the schizotypal frequently bursts into frenetic activity; becomes hyperactive, excited, and overtalkative; spews forth a flight of chaotic ideas and is unrestrained, grabbing objects and running hurriedly from one thing to another, all in an effort to reaffirm existence, to validate life, to avoid the catastrophic fear of emptiness and nothingness.

Insipid schizotypals generally behave in a bland and apathetic manner because they experience few positive reinforcements and seek to avoid few negative reinforcements. As a result, they have little reason to acquire instrumental behaviors. Why then do they become active, frenetic, and feverish and engage in vigorous coping efforts?

Insipid schizotypals have enough awareness of the fruits of life to realize that other people experience joy, sorrow, and excitement whereas they, by contrast, are empty and barren. They seek to maintain the modest level of sensation and feeling to which they have become accustomed; although they avoid more than they can handle comfortably, they also feel considerable discomfort with less than they need, especially since less brings them close to nothing. Their frantic, erratic, and bizarre outbursts may be viewed, then, as a coping effort to counter the feeling that they are "going under," bereft of all life and meaning.

Timorous schizotypals control expressions of affect because they fear humiliation and rejection; they are bland and socially withdrawn, then, for protective reasons. Their overt appearance is similar to the insipid schizotypal, not because of an intrinsic affectivity deficit, but because they have bound their emotions against possible rebuff. However, the consequences of their coping strategy are the same as those experienced by the insipid schizotypal. Alienated from others and themselves, they may sense the terror of impending nothingness and of a barren, depersonalized and nonexistent self. Such feelings prompt them to engage in a frenetic round of behaviors to reaffirm reality.

Deflecting Overstimulation

At the other extreme, both insipid and timorous schizotypals may be faced with excess stimulation.

Unable to avoid external impositions, insipid schizotypals may react either by blanking out, drifting off into another world, or by wild and aggressive outbursts. Undue encroachments on their complacent world may lead them to disappear for prolonged periods of time, during which they seem confused and aimless, and which they only vaguely recall. At other times, where pressure may be especially acute, they may instrumentally turn away these pressures by reacting with a massive outpouring of primitive impulses, delusional thoughts, hallucinations, and bizarre behaviors.

As with insipid schizotypals, external pressures may be too great for timorous schizotypals, going beyond their tolerance limits and leading them also either to drift out or to become wild and uncontrollable. During these outbursts, the probability of delusions, hallucinations, and bizarre and aggressive behaviors is even greater than that found in the insipid schizotypal. The timorous schizotypal has stored up intense repressed anxieties and hostilities throughout life. Once released, they burst as in a rampaging flood; the backlog of fears and animosities has been ignited and now explodes in a frenzied, cathartic discharge.

THERAPEUTIC INTERVENTIONS

Schizotypal individuals are one of the easier personality disorders for clinicians to diagnose. Odd speech, cognitive slippage, peculiar mannerisms, and even unusual dressing patterns give hints about the correct personality diagnosis. Confusion can sometimes arise, however, in attempting to differentiate between a schizotypal experiencing a temporary psychotic break and a diagnosis of

schizophrenia. In general, however, schizotypals do not exhibit the delusions, hallucinations, and loose associations of either the schizophreniform or schizophrenic disorder.

Therapists working with schizotypals are likely to find themselves giving a lot more "advice" to schizotypals than to other patients. Although the general aim of therapy may be to help patients help themselves, many schizotypals have trouble generalizing from one situation to another, and hence need repeated "lessons" about similar life circumstances. Despite the probability that personality reconstruction is not a likely outcome, except with mild cases of the disorder, many schizotypal patients benefit from the therapeutic relationship owing to the limits it provides on reality-distorting social isolation, and for the lessons it teaches about more adaptive functioning.

A primary focus of therapy should be to enhance these patients' self-worth and to encourage them to recognize their positive attributes. Their pride in self and in the self's constructive capacities are necessary for rebuilding motivation. No longer alienated from themselves, they will have a basis for overcoming their alienation from others. By building on this a sense of self-worth, the therapist may guide these patients to explore positively rewarding social activities. Initiating such experiences may be crucial in preventing what otherwise might be a downward progression.

Strategic Goals

When formulating the therapeutic goals for a particular patient, the therapist would do well to keep in mind that schizotypals can be either active or passive regarding their characteristic social isolation and detachment; the cognitive dysfunctions and behavioral eccentricities that are the hallmark of the disorder usually map onto less pathological avoidant or schizoid personality disorders. Although the avoidant variant is more likely to be seen clinically, the therapist needs to distinguish between the two types in order to maximize treatment goals and strategies.

Reestablishing Polarity Balances

As one of the three more severe and structurally defective personality disorders, schizotypals are burdened with disturbances in several polarity realms. As discussed previously, the constellation of these disturbances falls into one of two general patterns, the active-detached (avoidant/timorous) or the passive-detached (schizoid/insipid) variants. Those who fall into the passive category are unlikely to be motivated by either pain or pleasure: the capacity for feelings appear to be markedly reduced. Those of the actively detached type, on the other hand, are highly sensitive to environmentally produced and intrapsychically generated painful experiences, leading them to feel self-alienated and to withdraw from social interactions. Internally, however, anxiety and shame unremittingly continue to intrude. Neither active nor passive variants balance their social disengagement with an adaptive self-strategy. Daydreaming, magical thinking, and ideas of reference serve either to replace the turmoil and anxiety of the timorous schizotypal or to fill the frightening inner void of the insipid variant.

An increase in an adaptive other-oriented focus can be achieved with behavioral interventions such as social-skills training and modeling. A first potential benefit is to limit cognitive distortions through socially provided reality controls. Quality of life may be improved by increasing sensitivity to pleasure. Should these goals be realized, the passive subtype will probably also shift toward the active end of the active-passive dimension, and the active subtype will likely channel energy into more gratifying goals and may become more passive in relation to avoiding potential (mostly illusory) threats. In the case of timorous schizotypals, decreasing their fear of rejection or insult may be achieved by making them aware of the common and mutually rewarding rules of social exchange.

Modifying Domain Dysfunctions

The schizotypal's most salient personologic domain dysfunctions are evidenced in their cognitive style and expressive behavior. Their disorganized cognitive functioning underlies disturbances in almost all the other domains. Schizotypals mix social communication with personal irrelevancies, perceive the environment as imbued with material that feeds their ideas of reference and their metaphorical mental tangents. Nonproductive daydreaming often supports magical thinking and irrational suspicions, and obscures the line between reality and fantasy. Such thinking is the foundation for aberrant expressive behavior. Paired with a lack of human interaction that could provide normalizing feedback about thinking and behavior leads schizotypals to exhibit socially gauche habits and peculiar mannerisms. The estranged self-image contributes to permeable ego-boundaries and increases the tendency to be

perplexed by social interactions and to experience depersonalization, derealization, and dissociation. A preference for privacy and isolation tends to drive schizotypals toward clandestine activities and peripheral roles. A result of this secretive interpersonal conduct is that others usually find the schizotypal odd, although unobtrusive.

As a result of consistent misperception of the world (and of possible early abusive experiences), the schizotypal's object-representations tend to be chaotic. The schizotypal's main stress-reducing regulatory mechanisms are bizarre mannerisms and idiosyncratic thoughts that reflect a retraction or reversal of previous acts or ideas that have stirred conflict or anxiety. Their ritualistic or magical thinking are meant to counteract evil thoughts and deeds, both of the schizotypal and of others. All of these dysfunctions contribute to the fragmented morphologic organization of the schizotypal's personality. Few reality-based sublimations bind primitive thoughts and affect. Mood is typically distraught in active schizotypals and insentient in the passive ones. Complaints of being ill at ease, agitated, and watchful of others' motives are typical of active variants. Drab, apathetic, or otherwise markedly deficient face-to-face rapport and emotional expression are typical of passive variants.

In the case of the insipid schizotypal, a primary goal would be to help the patient identify those spheres of life toward which some positive inclination exists. Even if enthusiasm is not likely, increased participation in such activities can decrease the need for bizarre internal gratifications. It may also provide a window of reality-based experiences through which to objectively examine cognitive dysfunctions and distorted object-relations. Psychopharmacological intervention can be helpful in increasing affectivity and laying the groundwork for increased motivation and active adaptation. Group and/or behavioral interventions can help the patient develop social and other skills, leading to more satisfying social interactions that may strengthen other-oriented and active behaviors. Vocational and other areas of functioning can be enhanced, even if real intimacy with others is not likely to be achieved.

Interventions that foster feelings of self-worth and that encourage active schizotypals to realistically appraise their positive attributes and capacities can help provide patients with an improved self-image and motivation. Energy previously channeled into avoidance strategies can now be more productively directed into securing pleasure through much craved for social contact and/or vocational accomplishments. Improved social skills and increased self-esteem can help prevent extreme isolation and the cognitive distortions that result from the subsequent lack of socially provided reality checks, difficulties that so readily lead to decompensation.

Countering Perpetuating Tendencies

Both social isolation and dependency training not only perpetuate the schizotypal personality style, but in fact intensify deficits in cognitive organization and social skills. Environmental conditions that foster dependency can develop easily in the schizotypal's home, where well-intentioned family members may, with the best intentions for the patient's welfare, inadvertently coddle and patronize him or her. Schizotypals who relinquish their activities and learn to depend on others too much are likely to regress further into an amotivated and isolated state. Patients who remain in understaffed hospitals for extended periods of time are likely to end up in a similar condition. In the latter case, this is likely to result from staff neglect and a failure to encourage involvement with friends, relatives, fellow patients, and staff, even while basic needs are provided for. Finally, many schizotypals contribute to their own deterioration by consistently avoiding social interactions that could provide the stimulation and feedback that can keep them functional.

One main objective when working with a schizotypal patient is to encourage the development and maintenance of relatively normal social relationships, through social skills training, cognitive reorientation, and environmental management. Patients should be taught basic skills and encouraged to do as much for themselves as possible. The contact with a therapist is in itself helpful in preventing deterioration. Compensating for isolation through fantasy can sustain the schizotypal for but brief periods before preoccupations turn to past misfortunes and injustices. Unable to escape misery by turning inward, they may disavow their own existence, scramble what organization there is between thoughts and feelings, and sink into nothingness.

TACTICAL MODALITIES

Most schizotypals seen by therapists are of the active-detached or timorous variant. Their extreme social anxiety and frequent paranoia can make it difficult for the therapist to establish a solid relationship because these patients will try to defensively distance themselves. Many schizotypals interpret the therapist's behavior in unusual ways that may not be conducive to a positive therapeutic alliance. Schizotypal patients often believe that they can read minds or influence others through telepathic means; thus, the therapist would do well to enquire about the patient's therapy experience to make sure that the patient's perception mirrors reality. Benjamin (1993a) suggests that the process of forging a good relationship can be greatly aided by the therapist's respect for the schizotypal patient's particular sensitivities. Not pushing the patient too hard or too fast can prevent the patient from experiencing severe anxiety and paranoid reactions. Schizotypals' peculiar and rambling cognitive style can make it difficult for them to maintain focus in therapy sessions. Providing well-structured interventions and sessions can be very helpful with this group of individuals.

Domain-Oriented Techniques

A *supportive* approach is often the only kind of therapy that a schizotypal patient can handle during the early stages of treatment. Although other approaches can be used concomitantly, a realistic positive outcome may involve increasing the patient's pleasure in living rather than changing fundamental aspects of personality style or structure. The therapist's acceptance, empathic understanding, and benevolent advice can serve to realize this aim. The therapist may need to serve as the patient's "reality-testing auxiliary-ego" for a very long time.

Many of schizotypal's behaviors are amenable to *behavioral* interventions. Marked peculiarities of speech, dress, and mannerism can be reduced through modeling, social-skills training, and simple advice.

Benjamin's outline for *interpersonal* intervention with schizotypal patients focuses largely on the role of undoing aspects of the schizotypals' histories. Magical thinking is seen as being provoked by placement in situations in which the young child was led to believe that he or she had control when in fact he or she had none. In other circumstances, the child may have been given undue or inappropriate responsibility, for example, being led to believe that abuse could be prevented by certain behaviors that did not achieve this end. It is suggested that patients need to see how the content of such ideas mirrors past interpersonal dynamics before they will be willing to attempt to interpret and cope with life differently.

Problematic early experiences are often discussed without expression of any affect. It is recommended that sympathizing and empathizing with others who experienced similar treatment can help lead the patient to understand his or her own position, as well as to generate appropriate affect. Also possible with these patients is the tendency to do the opposite of what was intended therapeutically, for example, identifying with the perpetrator of aggression, and experiencing guilt or feeling the need for punishment as a result of having traitorous thoughts, or what they interpret as their part in instigating an abusive situation. Alternatively, the feelings can be projected on the therapist, who may be seen as an enemy.

Teaching the schizotypal to recognize when he or she is distorting reality can be done within the context of the therapeutic relationship, as these patients usually harbor unrealistic ideas about the therapist's communication and intent. Many schizotypals may even fear that harm will befall the therapist because of the therapeutic association. As ideas and predictions are countered, more realistic thinking can be learned. The learning of new cognitive skills can alter maladaptive patterns as the patient gives up the pathogenic wish, which Benjamin sums up as "the wish to magically protect the self and others while maintaining loyalty to early abusers." Interpreting symptomatic behavior, such as suicidal fantasies that reflect this underlying wish, can help the patient realize the function of these behaviors. Benjamin's example of such an interpretation is "Well, he (abusive father) would sure be happy to see what a good job you are doing of punishing yourself this time. This will prove that you love him and want to stay with him forever." As long as the therapist consistently displays sympathy for the patient's "terror of defying the internalized wishes and fears implanted by abusers," as well as convincing the schizotypal that he or she can think about self and others differently than previously, more adaptive patterns may come to replace the old.

Leszcz (1989) recommends that *group* therapy is appropriate for schizotypals who do not display prominently eccentric behavior, thereby causing other group members too much discomfort. Similarly, if the patient has paranoid features, these attributes may cause more turmoil than desirable. If the patient is appropriate for group therapy, the experience can help the schizotypal overcome social anxiety and awkwardness by providing a supportive environment and an opportunity to realize that others have similar insecurities.

Cognitive approaches are more directly focused on altering the content of schizotypals' thoughts. Beck and Freeman's (1990b) outline of their cognitive intervention procedures for treating schizotypal personality disorders suggests that a first therapeutic step is to identify the patient's dysfunctional automatic thoughts. Examples of such thoughts include: "Is that person watching me?" "I can feel the devil in her," and "I am a nonbeing." Dysfunctional thoughts generally fall into one of four categories: ideas of reference in which the patient believes that unrelated events are related to him or her, paranoid ideation, magical thinking such as a conviction that a dead relative is present, or the experiencing of illusions such as seeing people in shadows. Another common cognitive distortion seen among schizotypals is emotional reasoning, which cause them to believe that emotions are "evidence" about circumstances; if they feel bad, they believe that there is necessarily a problem, and vice versa. Schizotypals also engage in personalization, in which they believe that they are responsible for external circumstances, when in fact they are not.

An important first step would be to establish a good therapeutic alliance. In the context of a solid relationship, the patient is less likely to be handicapped by the deleterious effect of social isolation on reality testing and is more likely to be receptive to cues and interventions to improve social appropriateness. Social-skills training, including modeling of appropriate behavior and speech, can be very helpful in reducing the patient's social anxiety and awkwardness. Beck and Freeman suggest that a group setting can be ideal for identifying and challenging automatic thoughts about social functioning, as well as for learning and practicing new skills. They also point out that keeping the session structured is helpful with these patients, as their rambling cognitive style can result in little getting accomplished.

Teaching patients to evaluate their thoughts against environmental evidence, rather than against their feelings, can help reduce emotional reasoning and the drawing of incorrect conclusions about life circumstances. Although dysfunctional thoughts are not likely to disappear, it may be possible for the patient to learn to disregard them, rather than to respond either emotionally or behaviorally. Instead, a cognitive coping statement can be employed to counter the dysfunctional one. An example of such a statement is "There I go again. Even though I'm thinking this thought, it doesn't mean that it's true." A particularly useful suggestion is to keep track of the patient's predictions, and systematically to test them. The patient can then see that emotion does not predict or necessarily reflect circumstance. Communication style problems, whether they include circumstantiality, tangentiality, or fixation on or exclusion of detail, can usually be reduced when the patient can identify the reason the particular style is used. It is also recommended that the patient be taught practical ways to improve his or her life, whether this means learning about personal hygiene, finding employment, or initiating relationships.

Psychodynamic approaches focus on the need for the schizotypal patient to internalize a healthy "related" bond with another person, often the therapist. Gabbard (1994) suggests that the therapist should expect the patient to react to increased closeness with silence and emotional distance. This silence should be accepted as a legitimate part of the patient's personality. It is also suggested that the patient may then begin to reveal hidden aspects of the self and integrate them in adaptive ways. Offering classic psychodynamic interpretations to the patient about his or her behavior is not likely to be very successful or helpful. Moreover, psychoanalytic methods should not be considered until the patient's tendency toward detachment is well under control. Analytic procedures such as free association, the neutral attitude of the therapist, or the focus on dreams may actually foster an increase in autistic reveries and social withdrawal.

Psychopharmacological intervention can prove very helpful in controlling many of the symptoms of the schizotypal personality disorder. Illusions, ideas of reference, phobic anxiety, obsessive-compulsive symptoms, and "psychoticism" have been shown at times to respond favorably to low doses of neuroleptics. Some patients, however, appear to tolerate such medications poorly due to excessive sedation. Stone (1993) recommends that patients who show relatively better functioning, and the milder signs of the disorder (cognitive slippage, odd speech) probably do not need medications at any point in their treatment.

Institutionalization, when necessary, should be brief. Hospital settings too often breed isolation, reward quiet behaviors, and provide models of eccentric belief and perception, each of which can lead to increased detachment and bizarre preoccupations.

The major strategies and tactics are reviewed in Figure 17.6.

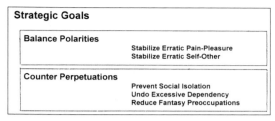

Figure 17.6 Therapeutic strategies and tactics for the prototypal schizotypal personality.

Potentiated Pairing and Catalytic Sequences

Establishing a good relationship with a schizotypal patient is a necessary first objective. In fact, providing a healthy, steady relationship is therapeutic in and of itself. A good alliance is most likely to result from an initial, almost exclusively supportive therapist stance. Silence may need to be tolerated, empathy expressed, and encouragement of participation in pleasurable activities emphasized. The therapist's practical advice can often provide structure and foster improvements in the patient's life. When the patient comes to trust the therapist, cognitive and behavioral interventions can help the patient learn to identify distortions in interpretation of the environment, and provide the skills necessary for more enhancing relationships. As noted earlier, patients who evidence psychotic thinking above and beyond the oddities of speech and mannerism may benefit from low doses of neuroleptics. This is likely to be more true of timorous schizotypals than of insipid ones. If behavioral eccentricities are not too great, the patient may also benefit from group therapy, particularly if a major presenting problem is social anxiety and a lack of social skills. Unfortunately, most schizotypals are not likely to undergo substantial changes in the structure of their personality, or in the level of intimacy involved in their relations with others. Gains are more likely to be made, however, in nonintimate interactions, in reality testing, and in participation in activities that the schizotypal can enjoy.

RISKS AND RESISTANCES

Both insipid and timorous schizotypals have poor prognostic prospects. Although great therapeutic gains can be made with some mildly affected individuals, many more do not alter their core personality. The pattern is deeply ingrained, if not strongly genetically predisposed. These patients rarely live in an encouraging or supportive environment. Probing into personal matters is experienced as painful or even terrifying. Schizotypals distrust close personal relationships such as occur in most forms of psychotherapy. Therapy sets up what they see as false hopes and necessitates painful self-exposure. Most would rather leave matters be, keep to themselves, and remain insulated from the potential of further humiliation and anguish. Should they enter treatment, timorous schizotypals tend to be guarded, constantly testing the therapist's sincerity. Excessive probing into the patient's sensitivities or another "false move" is likely to be interpreted as an attack or as verification of the disinterest and deprecation the patient has learned to anticipate from others.

Trust is therefore essential. Without a feeling of confidence in the genuineness of the therapist's motives, these patients will block the therapist's efforts and, ultimately, terminate treatment. Equally important is that the patient find a supportive social environment. Treatment will be more than usually difficult, a long and an uphill battle, unless external conditions are favorable.

CHAPTER 18

Borderline Personality Disorders: The Unstable Pattern

The label "borderline" has had a varied, if brief history. Despite its recent status as an official diagnostic entity in the DSM-III nomenclature, gained after considerable dispute, its use as a formal syndromal designation is most lamentable in our view. In its pure linguistic sense, the term *borderline* conveys with clarity and utility a midlevel severity, or intermediary degree, of either personality functioning (Millon, 1969) or structural organization (Kernberg, 1967, 1970). However—and in contrast with other labels that were new to the DSM-III, such as narcissistic and avoidant—the borderline term neither connotes nor communicates a behavioral pattern that portrays distinctive stylistic features (Perry & Klerman, 1978). In concert with other colleagues on the DSM-III Task Force, the senior author strongly argued for the selection of alternative and more clearly descriptive designations. For example, his original working draft for this syndrome, prepared for the DSM-III personality subcommittee in 1975, termed it the "cycloid" personality. Since the descriptive features and diagnostic criteria for the final draft of the borderline personality disorder remained highly consistent with this early formulation, the author joined other outspoken committee members who vigorously dissented from the decision to choose so general and vague a label as borderline to represent what was a distinctive syndromal trait constellation. In his final memo on the issue, written in June 1978, the senior author commented as follows:

I very much like the description of the borderline personality disorder; it portrays a very important population that has not been adequately described in previous DSM publications. However, I would like to register my strong agreement with the point raised . . . to the effect that the label, borderline, is perhaps the most poorly chosen of all the terms selected for the DSM-III. I know a small segment of the profession feels that this is the most apt descriptive term for this population, but frankly, I find the word, borderline, to mean, at best, a level of severity and not a descriptive type. . . . Unless the word is used to signify a class that borders on something, then it has no clinical or descriptive meaning at all.

If we look at the clinical description that we have created for this disorder I am sure we can find a label that is more suitable and communicative than borderline. . . .

I would like the Personality Committee to reassess the term borderline . . . [in addition to the original suggestions of borderline and unstable] other alternative labels that might be considered are the following: ambivalent *personality disorder,* erratic *personality disorder,* impulsive *personality disorder,* quixotic *personality disorder, etc. Any one of these (*labile *captures the flavor most clearly for me) would be far preferable than the meaningless borderline label. Please let's try not to fall prey to absurdities in the literature; let's not get hooked into a poor label which, when closely examined, has absolutely no relationship to the syndrome's clinical descriptions. One of the major advances of DSM-III is that it has sought to create labels and descriptions that are clearer, more explicit and more relevant than in the past. Let's not regress by introducing a bad and misleading label.*

Although the term borderline was retained, its evolution in the deliberations of the DSM-III committee reinforced the notion that it is a specific diagnostic entity that stabilized at an advanced level of dysfunction. More importantly, its clinical characteristics are not only those of a personality syndrome but one that falls within the broad spectrum of *affective disorders*. In this sense, it parallels the schizotypal syndrome, which was also conceived as an advanced level of personality dysfunction but within the schizophrenic disorder spectrum.

With the foregoing as an introduction, the major characteristics of the DSM borderline personality syndrome are briefly reviewed.

The most salient feature of this person is the depth and variability of moods. Borderlines tend to experience extended periods of dejection and disillusionment, interspersed occasionally with brief excursions of euphoria and significantly more frequent episodes of irritability, self-destructive acts, and impulsive anger. These moods are often unpredictable and appear prompted less by external events than by internal factors.

This text stresses the divergent background histories found among borderlines. In effect, they are conceived as advanced dysfunctional variants of the less structurally defective dependent, histrionic, narcissistic, antisocial and, in particular, negativistic (passive-aggressive) personalities. The variety of borderline personalities reported in the literature are thereby more clearly differentiated and their frequently mixed symptom pictures are clarified. The model presented states that when these less dysfunctional personalities prove deficient or falter under the strain of persistent environmental stress, they will frequently deteriorate into what we have labeled the "defective-borderline personality structure." For example, a *dependent* personality, faced with intense problems in areas of special vulnerability, will experience a sense of helplessness and hopelessness; these persons will exhibit brief, frantic, but futile efforts either to assert themselves and stand on their own, or to recapture by behaving in a forced, cheerful, and outgoing manner the attachment and support they desperately need. Similarly, the characteristic gregarious strategy of a *histrionic* personality may reach a feverish pitch of euphoric excitement, only to fall into the depths of futility, despondency, and self-destructiveness, should the persons restitutive efforts fail. The collapsing security of the troubled *narcissistic* personality may lead the person to vacillate among marked self-condemnation, protestations of piety and good intentions, and impulsive outbursts of anger, followed by feelings of intense shame and feelings of emptiness. The preborderline pattern of behavior vacillation in a *negativistic* personality will continue under increased stress but reach a more intense, unpredictable, and erratic pace, swinging into profound gloom at one time, and irrational negativism and chaotic excitement, the next. It is the instability of both behavior and

affect, combined with their shared search for acceptance and approval, that justifies bringing these patients together into a single "structurally defective borderline" disorder, despite their divergent histories and coping styles.

Prior to its current fashionable status, the label borderline was typically assigned when a clinician was uncertain about the diagnosis of a patient. Every clinician faces dilemmas as to whether certain observed ominous symptoms signify the presence of more severe pathology than first meets the eye. Such patients appear to display both normal and psychotic features. At these times, clinicians handle this seeming incongruence by hedging, "sitting on the fence." They wait until they can obtain a clearer picture of their patient's status or until some change occurs in behaviors before making the decision as to whether the patient is suffering a neurosis or a psychosis. This common use of the borderline designation rests on the false premise that patients must fall in one of two categories of a dichotomy, that of "slightly sick" (neurosis) or "very sick" (psychosis). We now recognize that personality pathology lies on a continuum; it is not an all-or-none phenomenon but one that may fall at any point along a continuous gradient. Borderline need not be used as a wastebasket for clinical indecision. It is currently conceived as a meaningful designation that reflects a real rather than a spurious or incongruous state of affairs: an advanced and potentially serious level of maladaptive personality functioning. Moreover, borderline syndromes need not represent transitory states between normality and frank pathology—a way station leading inevitably to more severe illness. The label signifies a habitual level of behavior, a durable pattern of disturbed functioning that stabilizes for substantial periods of time.

Although several clinical theorists have formulated the concept of borderline as representing a level of personality organization (Kernberg, 1967, 1970) or a degree of personality severity (Millon, 1969; Stone, 1980), rather than a specific character type possessing distinctive features, the DSM-III Task Force chose the latter course and applied the label to a discrete syndromal entity. Hence, this review of the literature is more narrowly focused than it would have been—if it had encompassed notions such as "borderline schizophrenia," "pseudoneurotic schizophrenia," and "latent psychoses," each of which is considered by some as part of a broad borderline spectrum. These latter clinical entities are bypassed in the present rendering of the historical forerunners of the DSM borderline because they more properly prefigure the schizotypal personality syndrome presented in Chapter 17.

Complicating this review further, the particular constellation of traits making up the DSM borderline syndrome has historical and theoretical precursors that antedate the latter, and the discussion therefore cannot be restricted to propositions that employ the recent designation of borderline. There is a substantial body of literature on syndromes, *not* termed borderline, that possess clinical features clearly representing the pattern of affective and interpersonal instability that characterizes the DSM personality type. This review, therefore, does not begin with the borderline concept but with formulations that differ in designation but are clinically akin to it.

A further source of difficulty in furnishing a comprehensive yet relevant survey of borderline antecedents is the plethora of terms and the not inconsiderable disagreement that exists among theorists concerning the prime attributes of the syndrome (Perry & Klerman, 1978). Popular among psychoanalytic thinkers is the position that it is best conceived as a structural configuration or character organization that exists at a level of personality cohesion midway between neurotic and psychotic levels (Frosch, 1960; Kernberg, 1970; Knight, 1953). Certain biologically oriented researchers hold the view that it is best considered as a set of personality variants within an affective disorders spectrum (Akiskal, Djenderedjian, Rosenthal, & Khani, 1977; Klein, 1977). As noted earlier, those who consider it as essentially an incipient precursor or inchoate substrate for schizophrenia are discussed in Chapter 17, dealing with the schizotypal personality. Still others have formulated it as a stable and moderately severe level of functioning that encompasses a variety of different personality subtypes (Grinker et al., 1968, Millon, 1969).

The presentation must be formally divided to represent these diverse viewpoints. The ensuing paragraphs provide a prime example of how theoretically dissimilar perspectives can conceptualize the same diagnostic syndrome in divergent fashions.

HISTORICAL ANTECEDENTS

From the earliest literary and medical history, writers have recognized the coexistence within single persons of intense and divergent moods such as euphoria, irritability, and depression. Homer,

Hippocrates, and Aretaeus described with great vividness the related character of impulsive anger, mania, and melancholia, noting both the erratic vacillation among these "spells" and the personalities likely to be subject to them. However, as with most medical and scientific knowledge, these early writings were suppressed in medieval times. With the advent of the Renaissance, many of the observations of early Greek and Roman physicians were brought again to light, and studies of these patients were begun anew.

The first theorist to revive the notion of the covariation between impulsive and erratic moods in a single syndrome was Bonet, who applied the term *folie maniaco-mélancolique* in 1684. Schacht and Herschel in the 18th century reinforced the view suggested in Bonet's terminology that these erratic and unstable moods followed a rhythmic or periodic regularity of highs and lows. Fixed in the minds of all subsequent clinicians was the belief in an inevitable periodicity of the manic-depressive covariation. In fact, the case histories described by Bonet, Schacht, and Herschel rarely followed so regular a pattern. Rather, they were episodic, erratic, and desultory in sequence, shifting almost randomly from depression, to anger, to guilt, to elation, to boredom, to normality, and so on in an unpredictable and inconsistent course. In 1854, Baillarger and Falret summarized the results of 30 years' work with depressed and suicidal persons. They reported that a large portion of these patients showed a course of extended depression, broken intermittently by periods of irritability, anger, elation, and normality. The terms *la folie circulaire* (Falret, 1854) and *folie a double forme* (Baillarger, 1854) were applied to signify the syndrome's contrasting and variable character. It was Kahlbaum who, in 1882, clearly imprinted the current belief in the fixed covariation of mania and melancholia. Although he saw them as facets of a single disease that manifested itself in different ways at different times—occasionally euphoric, occasionally melancholic, and occasionally excitable or angry—it was the primacy of the former two which rigidified future conceptions of the syndrome and redirected thinking away from its more typical and fundamental affective instability and unpredictability. He termed the milder variant of the illness, notable for its frequent periods of normality, *cyclothymia*. A more severe and chronic form of the same pattern was designated *vesania typica circularis*.

From a vantage quite different from Kahlbaum's, an American psychiatrist, C. Hughes, wrote in 1884, "The borderland of insanity is occupied by many persons who pass their whole life near that line, sometimes on one side, sometimes on the other" (p. 297). Also writing of "borderline insanity," J. C. Rosse (1890) spoke of patients who drifted in a twilight between "reason and despair."

As noted earlier, Kraepelin (1921) identified four temperament variants disposed to clinical manic-depressive disease. The irritable temperament, elsewhere described by Kraepelin as the "excitable personality," was conceived as a "mixture of the fundamental states." It parallels the borderline features closely, as illustrated in the following excerpts:

The patients display from youth up extraordinarily great fluctuations in emotional equilibrium and are greatly moved by all experiences, frequently in an unpleasant way. . . .

They flare up, and on the most trivial occasions fall into outbursts of boundless fury.

The coloring of mood is subject to frequent change . . . periods are interpolated in which they are irritable and ill-humored, also perhaps sad, spiritless, anxious; they shed tears without cause, give expression to thoughts of suicide, bring forward hypochondriacal complaints, go to bed. . . .

They are mostly very distractible and unsteady in their endeavors.

In consequence of their irritability and their changing moods their conduct of life is subject to the most multifarious incidents, they make sudden resolves, and carry them out on the spot, run off abruptly, go traveling, enter a cloister. (pp. 130–131)

Of special note is the extent to which Kraepelin's description encompasses the central diagnostic criteria of the DSM-IV borderline, especially the impulsivity, unstable relationships, inappropriate and intense anger, affective instability, and physically self-damaging acts.

MODERN FORMULATIONS

Kretschmer (1925) provided a more modern precursor of the borderline in portraying patients who exhibited what he considered to be a mixed cycloid-schizoid temperament. Not quite as apt or congruent as is Kraepelin's text, it nevertheless captures a number of important elements of the borderline syndrome. Kretschmer depicted these patients as follows:

Cases of agitated melancholia with violent motility symptoms, alien influences in the constitution . . . may be distinguished [by] . . . an admixture of humourless dryness, of a hypochondriacal, hostile attitude towards the world . . . of sharpness, nervousness, and jerky restless moodiness (not rhythmic cyclic modifications), of insufficient affective response, of a grumbling dissatisfaction, and of a display of sulky pessimism. . . . This kind . . . is not at all the prototype . . . of the borderline character. . . . Out of our material one could form a continuous series leading . . . from the typical cycloid over to the typical schizoid. (1925, p. 140)

Schneider (1923/1950), Kretschmer's prime European contemporary, came even closer to the mark of the borderline in his portrait of the "labile" personality. In his characterization of this type, Schneider (1923/1950) wrote:

The labile . . . has no chronic moodiness but is specifically characterized by the abrupt and rapid changes of mood which he undergoes.

Sometimes the smallest stimulus is sufficient to arouse a violent reaction. . . . It appears that there is some constitutional tendency toward sporadic reactions of a morose and irritable character. . . .

We are only interested here in behavior which clearly arises from periodic lability of mood. Such behavior has sometimes been called impulsive but the impulse . . . is only secondary and takes place against the periodic crisis of mood.

Labile [persons] present a picture of shiftless, social instability. They develop sudden dislikes and distastes. They experience sudden restlessness. . . . Many . . . are socially shiftless and inconstant.

As a social group . . . the more irritable ones are apt to get into trouble through impulsive violence, and the more inconstant ones have all sorts of chance lapses.

We may wonder whether the mood shift of our labile personalities is a matter of cyclothymic . . . mood. Clinically everything speaks against cyclothymia. The transience of the mood and the general volatility are the chief contraindications. (pp. 116–120)

Although his focus centered on what he referred to as "impulsive characters," Reich (1925) described these individuals as demonstrating a predominance of infantile aggression, a primitive narcissism, and severe superego impairments. The intense ambivalence and rapidly changing character presentations of these individuals were seen by

Reich as a "borderline" group of disorders falling between mild and severe levels of pathology

A brief note should also be made of the contribution of J. Kasanin (1933), who first coined the label "schizoaffective." Reviewing the atypical premorbid characteristics of several cases of young psychotics who were initially hospitalized with the diagnoses of acute schizophrenic episodes, Kasanin concluded that they appeared to possess the social dispositions and affective inclinations that are more typical of manic-depressives. The acute nature of the disorder and the blend of features portrayed in Kasanin's syndrome are somewhat tangential to the borderline formulation, yet the following quote suggests elements of comparability:

A subjective review of their . . . personalities reveals that they are very sensitive, critical of themselves, introspective, very unhappy and preoccupied with their own conflicts, problems, and sometimes with life in general. These conflicts and problems may go on for years before the patient breaks down. . . . The fact that there is comparatively little of the extremely bizarre, unusual and mysterious, is what perhaps gives these cases a fairly good chance of recovery. They do not exhibit any profound regression socially. . . . Their reaction is one of protest, or a fear, without the ready acceptance of the solution offered by the psychosis. (p. 101)

The first major psychoanalytic publication to employ the designation of borderline was written by Adolf Stern in 1938. His paper was prompted by the increasing number of patients seen who could not be fit readily into standard neurotic or psychotic categories, and who were, in addition, refractory to psychotherapeutic interventions. Stern labeled these patients as comprising a "border line group of neuroses." Close examination led him to identify 10 symptoms, character traits, and "reaction formations" that, though not unique to the borderline group, were judged by him to be both more pronounced than in other neurotics and especially resistant to psychoanalytic efforts at resolution. Since a number of these 10 characteristics have remained as criteria for contemporary borderline conceptions, it may be useful to record them briefly: "narcissism," a character trait consequent to deficient maternal affection; "psychic bleeding," a self-protective lethargy or immobility in response to stress; "inordinate hypersensitivity," an undue caution or exquisite awareness of minor slights; "psychic rigidity," a persistent, protectively reflexive body stiffness in anticipation of danger; "negative therapeutic reactions," a quickness to display anger, depression, or anxiety in response to interpretive probes involving self-esteem; "feelings of inferiority," despite demonstrable evidence of self-competence, claiming a personal inadequacy so as to avoid adult responsibilities; "masochism," a depressively toned, self-pity, "wound-licking," and self-commiseration; "somatic anxiety," a presumption of one's constitutional inadequacy to function without external assistance; "projection mechanism," a tendency to attribute internal difficulties to ostensive hostile sources in the environment; and "difficulties in reality testing," nonpsychotic deficits in judgment and empathic accuracy.

Although close to a decade would pass before the borderline label reemerged in the formal literature, it was a popular, if colloquial, term that conveyed little more than the patient's intermediary or inchoate status, a loosely conceived designation bandied about informally at case conferences or in passing diagnostic dialogues. Two informal and occasionally overlapping trends emerged. Psychoanalysts such as Stern focused on the problem of identifying the "borderline" between neurotic characters or symptom disorders and similarly appearing, but more ominous and severe, forms of pathology. Although the roots and characteristic features of the syndrome are more broadly conceived by others, it was the analysts' concern and their related line of thinking that gradually evolved into the DSM-III formulation that has been labeled the "borderline personality." The other, overlapping yet distinct, concern that arose was found among hospital-based clinicians, often biologically oriented, who sought to differentiate the manifest forms of schizophrenia from their "borderline" variants, characterized by designations such as "latent," "ambulatory," or "incipient." It was this latter desire and its related line of thought and research that ultimately shaped the syndrome and criteria for the DSM-III schizotypal personality. As indicated earlier, this chapter proceeds with antecedents more directly relevant to the contemporary borderline formulation.

CONTEMPORARY PROPOSALS

Melitta Schmideberg (1947, 1959) was among a small group of clinicians to employ the borderline term in early post-World War II publications. In her first papers, she characterized borderlines as unable to tolerate routine, incapable of developing insight, inclined to lead chaotic lives, and deficient in empathic capacity. To Schmideberg, the borderline concept represented a stable level of functioning that blends features of normality, neuroses, psychoses, and psychopathy. Also notable was her contention that there was no single and distinct entity that could be labeled borderline; rather, the term encompassed several trait mixtures and symptom constellations. She wrote of the syndrome as follows:

It is not just quantitatively halfway between the neuroses and psychoses; the blending and combination of these modes of reaction produce something qualitatively different. . . .

One reason why the borderline should be regarded as a clinical entity is that the patient, as a rule, remains substantially the same throughout his life. He is stable in his instability, whatever ups and downs he has, and often keeps constant his pattern of peculiarity.

Borderlines should be broken down into major subgroups, such as depressives, schizoids, paranoids. . . .

Borderlines suffer from disturbances affecting almost every area of their personality and life, in particular, personal relations and depth of feeling. (1959, p. 399)

Another early theorist of the borderline syndrome, A. Wolberg (1952), posited a number of clinical features that also resemble those found in the DSM-III formulation. Of particular interest was her notion of the vicious circle within which the borderline-prone child becomes trapped. Notable in this sequence are ambivalence between wishing to be seen as "good" by one's parents, accompanied by a resistance to obeying them; a mixed feeling of anxiety and depression leading to the need for constant reassurance of love that fails to be forthcoming; a consequent hypersensitivity to anticipated rejection from others; a growing feeling of personal failure, loneliness, and emptiness; a projected hostile acting out against others, followed by contrition and guilt; self-punitive and self-damaging behaviors such as drug or alcohol addiction; and increased anxiety and depression—and the vicious circle begins anew.

Although Knight (1953) focused his attention on young adults undergoing schizophreniclike states or transient psychotic episodes, his paper was a seminal contribution in that he brought to the foreground the importance of "ego weakness" as a crucial element in characterizing the borderline personality structure. In essence, he concluded that psychotic episodes were likely to occur in borderline character structures. Superficial neurotic symptoms provide a "holding position," but, ultimately, the weak ego defenses display themselves in both microscopic (interview behavior) and macroscopic (life history and behavior) forms. Conceptualizing his incisive and fruitful studies from an ego-analytic perspective, Knight wrote:

The superficial clinical picture—hysteria, phobia, obsessions, compulsive rituals—may represent a holding operation in a forward position, while the major portion of the ego has regressed far behind this in varying degrees of disorder.

We conceptualize the borderline case as one in which normal ego functions of secondary process thinking, integration, realistic planning, adaptation to the environment, maintenance of object relationships, and defenses against punitive unconscious impulses are severely weakened.

Other ego functions, such as conventional (but superficial) adaptation to the environment and superficial maintenance of object relationships may exhibit varying degrees of intactness. And still others, such as memory, calculation, and certain habitual performances, may seem unimpaired.

In addition to these . . . evidences of ego weakness [there is a] . . . lack of concern about the realities of his life predicament; . . . the illness developed in the absence of observable precipitating stress, or under . . . relatively minor stress; . . . the presence of multiple symptoms and disabilities, especially if these are regarded with an acceptance that seems ego-syntonic; . . . lack of achievement over a relatively long period, indicating a chronic and severe failure of the ego to channelize energies constructively; . . . vagueness or unrealism in planning for the future with respect to education, vocation, marriage, parenthood, and the like. (1953, pp. 5–8)

Frosch initiated a series of explorations in the 1950s into what he termed the "disorders of impulse control," many of which typify the DSM-III borderline (e.g., quick-tempered irritability). It was not until his papers on the "psychotic character" (1960, 1964, 1970), however, that Frosch made his contributions more directly relevant to contemporary borderline conceptions. Adhering to a more orthodox psychoanalytic perspective than Knight's ego-orientation, Frosch summarized his position as follows:

We are not dealing with a transitional phase on the way to or back from psychosis, or a latent, or larval psychosis which may become overt. We are dealing with characterological phenomena peculiar to persons who may never show psychosis and who establish a reality-syntonic adaptation. . . .

The psychotic character is dominated by psychotic processes and modes of adaptation. . . . There is a propensity for regressive dedifferentiation and an underlying fear of disintegration and dissolution of the self. The psychotic reactions of fragmentation, projective identification, ego splitting, etc., can also be observed in the psychotic character, especially during periods of decompensation. . . .

He retains a relative capacity to test reality, albeit with techniques frequently consistent with earlier ego states. Object relations, although at times prone to primitivization, as in psychosis, are nonetheless at a higher infantile level. There appears to be a push toward establishing contact with objects, though the simultaneously existing fear of engulfment by the object frequently leads to complications.

The ego is constantly threatened by breakthroughs of id-derived impulses. (1970, pp. 47–48)

Although referring only tangentially to Kraepelin's views, which address the same thesis directly and cogently, Jacobson (1953), an important analytic theorist, recorded her experiences with a group of "cyclothymic depressives" who gave evidence of "simple depression . . . without psychotic symptoms, yet belong to the manic-depressive group" (p. 52). As would be anticipated, Jacobson sought to interpret the behavior of these "borderline" cyclothymics in psychoanalytic terms. To her, their behaviors reflected an effort to find solutions to psychosexual conflicts through regressive maneuvers. An "inherited constitution" might be operative, but, according to Jacobson, these affective borderlines more than likely experienced emotional deprivation, had poor self versus object differentiations, and displayed a "remarkable vulnerability, and intolerance of frustration, hurt and disappointment" (p. 55). Jacobson played a seminal role in describing the structural consequences of problematic early introjections. To her, these primitive object-relations led to marked disturbances in both identity and intimate relationships, as well as "an

adolescent fluidity of moods." As Jacobson (1964) conceived the problem, these patients:

at times experience their mental functions or their bodily organs as belonging to their own self and, at other times, as objects, i.e., foreign bodies which they want to expel. Or they may at one time attach part of their own mental or body self to external objects, and at another time attribute realistic object qualities to the latter. (p. 48)

The work of Grinker et al. (1968) is especially noteworthy in being the first systematic empirical investigation employing explicit criteria both for including a borderline population sample and excluding potentially confounding schizophreniclike patients. Selection criteria resulted in young adults with short-term hospitalizations, good interim functioning, and florid, attention-gaining behaviors; these criteria were employed to minimize the schizophrenic confound and oriented the study population along affective lines. Data from 51 patients were subjected to a cluster analysis and resulted in both common features and differentiation into four major subtypes. Among the elements that appear to be shared by all variants are "*anger* as the main or only affect, defect in *affectional* relationships, absence of indications of *self-identity* and *depressive* loneliness" (p. 176).

The four subgroups were described as follows. The first, which Grinker et al. termed the "psychotic border," was:

characterized clinically by inappropriate and negative behaviors. . . . These patients were careless in their personal grooming and slept and ate erratically. . . . [Their] perception of self and others . . . revealed deficiencies. . . . These patients manifested essentially negative effects . . . with occasional angry eruptions in an impulsive manner. In addition, depression of recognizable duration was present. (p. 83)

The second cluster, or "core" borderline group, was characterized by the following:

1. Vacillating involvement with others

2. Overt or acting-out expressions of anger

3. Depression

4. Absence of indications of consistent self identity. (p. 87)

The third group, the affectless, defended "as if" persons, represents a syndrome similar to the DSM schizoid personality. As discussed in Chapter 6, Deutsch's as if type appears to be the forerunner, not of the borderline disorder as we currently conceive it to be, but of the affectless, unempathic, interpersonally detached schizoid.

The fourth borderline category, labeled "the border with the neurosis," revealed defects in self-esteem and confidence, and a depressive quality not associated with anger or guilt feelings. The prime qualities were summarized by Grinker et al. as follows:

1. *Childlike clinging depression (anaclitic)*
2. *Anxiety*
3. *Generally close resemblance to neurotic narcissistic characters. (p. 90)*

A review of the findings reported by Grinker et al. suggests that this fourth group, rather than exhibiting parallels with the DSM narcissistic pattern, is appreciably more similar to the manual's newly formulated dependent personality. The first of their subtypes, referred to as the "psychotic border" is akin to Klein's hysteroid dysphorics, to Millon's borderline personalities, and to the initial DSM-III borderline characterization. Their so-called core borderline group overlaps also with the DSM borderline description and has affinities with Klein's emotionally unstable character and Millon's negativistic personality.

More directly relevant to current conceptions of the borderline are the affective symptoms that B. R. Easser and S. R. Lesser (1965) described in their psychoanalytic formulation of the "hysteroid" borderline type. This group of patients exhibits the outward behaviors of the classical hysterical (histrionic) personality but are unquestionably a more deeply disturbed variant. Worthy of mention is that the features of Easser and Lesser's hysteroid are akin to the symptoms outlined in Kernberg's portrayal of the infantile personality (1967, 1970), a character type he judged structurally at the "lower level" (borderline) of organization. The affinity of the hysteroid to both an affective style and a borderline severity is well portrayed in the following (Easser & Lesser, 1965):

In many instances the hysteroid would appear to be a caricature of the hysteric, much as the hysteric has been said to be a caricature of femininity. Each characteristic is demonstrated in even sharper dramatic relief. The bounds of social custom and propriety are breached. The latent aggressivity of the

exhibitionism, the competitiveness and the self-absorption becomes blatant, insistent, and bizarre. The chic becomes the mannequin; the casual, sloppy; the bohemian, beat.

The adaptational functioning of the hysteroid is erratic. Inconstancy and irresponsibility cause the patient to suffer realistic rebuffs, injuries, and failure.

The hysteroid starts friendships with great hopes and enthusiasm. The friendship commences with idolatry and ends in bitterness when the expectation of rescue, nurture and care is not fulfilled. These relational ruptures are often succeeded by detachment, isolation, depression, and paranoid-like trends.

The hysteroid's family life is often . . . disturbed, disorganized, and inconsistent.

Grosser fluctuations of the hysteroid personality are to be anticipated from the more infantile fixation and the consequent weaker integration and synthesis of the ego. Thus we encounter less emotional control, a lessened ability to hold and tolerate tension, and more proneness to action and depression. (pp. 399–400)

Drawing more from the British object-relations school of thought than from classical analytic conceptions, Modell (1963) spoke of various borderline cases as persons characterized by a tendency toward "transitional relatedness," an inclination to attribute to those they idealize as possessing "magical omnipotence," a reality-based dependency combined with an illusion of self-sufficiency, and a divided self-image composed of contrasting elements, such as being either "omnipotently giving" or "omnipotently destructive."

Important contributions to the understanding of borderline pathogenesis were contributed by Mahler and her associates (1958, 1967; Mahler, Pine, & Bergman, 1975). As the child asserts autonomy, he or she challenges the "good" mother, who seeks to maintain the closeness of an earlier stage. At this "separation-individuation" phase, the child develops an intense ambivalence toward the mother, alternating between the mother's coercive clinging and the child's negativistic withdrawal. Wishing to retain the mother's nurturance, yet desiring increasing independence, leads to a schism, a splitting process that protects the child's image of the good mother from the contrasting image as being a constraining and limiting force. By seeking to separate these two incompatible images, the child fails to achieve "object constancy," nor does a parallel coherence develop in the child's own identity. According to Mahler, this deep schism creates the fundamental structural defect of the borderline personality.

Influenced by the theses of Stern and Knight, as well as the British object-relations theorists Klein, Fairbairn, and Winnicott in particular, Kernberg's writings (1967, 1975, 1980, 1984) on the "border-line personality organization" have become a prime force in establishing the status and attention given the syndrome in contemporary literature. Combining the central role assigned by Knight to impaired ego functions and the diverse symptom criteria spelled out by Stern, Kernberg has constructed a complex, multilevel, and multidimensional nosology based on psychoanalytic metapsychology. This schema encompasses not only the borderline ego structure, or organization, but a wide range of syndromes that are hierarchically ordered in terms of both specific type and pathological severity. Paralleling a similar nosological matrix by Millon (1969), which was based on a social-learning rather than a psychoanalytic metapsychology, it conceives the borderline concept as a particular form of significantly weakened personality organization. Neither Kernberg nor Millon, nor for that matter Knight, Schmideberg, or Grinker, suggest that the borderline label be employed as a specific or distinct diagnostic type; rather, they contend that it is best treated as a supplementary diagnosis that conveys the dimension of severity in ego functioning and object relations.

Despite the diversity of forms this personality may take, borderlines do possess certain stable and enduring psychostructural features in common, according to Kernberg (1979). In reviewing the clinical manifestations of the borderline personality, which Kernberg (1975) considers intermediary between neurotic and psychotic organizations, he wrote:

Clinically, when we speak of patients with border-line personality organizations, we refer to patients who present serious difficulties in their interpersonal relationships and some alteration in their experience of reality but with essential preservation of reality testing. Such patients also present contradictory characteristics, chaotic co-existence of defenses against and direct expression of primitive "id contents" in consciousness, a kind of pseudo-insight into their personality without real concern for nor awareness of the conflictual nature of the material, and a lack of clear identity and lack of understanding in depth of other people. These patients present primitive defensive operations rather than repression and related defenses, and above all, mutual dissociation of contradictory ego states reflecting what might be called a "nonmetabolized" persistence of early, pathological internalized object relationships. They also show "nonspecific" manifestations of ego weakness. The term "nonspecific" refers to a lack of impulse control, lack of anxiety tolerance, lack of sublimatory capacity, and presence of primary process thinking, and indicates that these manifestations of ego weakness represent a general inadequacy of normal ego functioning. In contrast, the primitive defensive constellation of these patients and their contradictory, pathological character traits are "specific" manifestations of ego weakness. (pp. 161–162)

It was mentioned earlier that a drift has occurred in the theoretical and research literature, as well as in the formulations of the DSM, toward conceiving the borderline syndrome as a personality variant that falls within the spectrum of affective disorders; in this respect, it parallels the schizotypal personality syndrome, which has been increasingly conceived as fitting the schizophrenic spectrum. The major exponents of this view are found most prominently among researchers of a biological persuasion, but a number of psychoanalytically oriented theorists have also offered suggestions of a similar cast.

The recent work of Gunderson and his colleagues (Gunderson, 1977, 1979; Gunderson, Carpenter, & Strauss, 1975; Gunderson & Singer, 1975) has led them to strongly advocate the borderline as a discrete personality disorder that can be clearly described and differentially diagnosed from both schizophrenic syndromes and neurotic states. Benefiting from a thorough review of prior work and opportunities to carry out a series of empirical studies, Gunderson et al. characterized the borderline as showing intense affect, either hostile or depressed; an absence of flatness or pleasure, but frequent depersonalization; a background of episodic and impulsive behavior that may include self-damaging acts such as drug overdoses, alcoholism, or promiscuity; identity disturbances that are often cloaked by superficial identifications; brief psychotic episodes; and interpersonal relationships that vacillate between superficiality, dependency, and manipulativeness.

Gunderson has modified his views over the past two decades, increasingly refining his conceptions to highlight the distinctive features that differentiate the borderline from other similar personality disorders or clinical syndromes. In his most recent formulations, carried out with his associates at McLean Hospital (Zanarini, Gunderson, & Frankenburg, 1989), he has proposed the following distinguishing features: self-mutilation; manipulative suicide efforts; abandonment-engulfment annihilation concerns; demandingness-entitlement; quasi-psychotic thought; treatment regressions; and countertransference difficulties. A significant extension of this work is the thesis advanced by Zanarini (1993) to the effect that borderlines might best be seen as an "impulse spectrum disorder" rather than a variant of the affective disorder spectrum. Zanarini has been able to marshal a broad-ranging body of research in support of her formulation.

The ideas proposed by Masterson (1972, 1976) draw heavily on the developmental theses of Bowlby and of Mahler. Stressing the belief that the mother may have been borderline herself, Masterson sees the child as being encouraged to continue symbiotic clinging, while the mother threatens to withdraw love should the child persist in striving toward autonomy. Relating to mothers who are intensely conflicted about their child's growing independence, these youngsters are faced with a dilemma; becoming autonomous will mean a loss of maternal love. This ambivalence creates an intrapsychic schism; any form of assertiveness threatens abandonment. This deep template within the future borderline's psyche sets the groundwork for unstable relationships, repeated intrapsychic ruptures, fruitless searches for idealized unions, and periodic states of emptiness and depression.

Working originally with Masterson, Rinsley (Masterson & Rinsley, 1975; Rinsley, 1977) shifted his earlier emphasis on the central role of separation-individuation to that of an "insufficiency" conception. As he viewed it, a seriously deficient maternal presence lay at the core of the borderline's pathogenesis, a viewpoint developed further in the work of Adler (1985).

Further developing the analytic approach to the borderline, Gabbard (1994) provides a series of descriptive insights into this disorder's intrapsychic processes, especially as seen in this personality's therapeutic encounters:

Near-delusional perceptions of abandonment by loved ones are common, and psychotic transference regressions may appear when patients become attached to their therapists. Clinicians who witness this kaleidoscope display of shifting ego states are prone to a variety of intense countertransference reactions, including rescue fantasies, guilt feelings,

transgressions of professional boundaries, rage and hatred, anxiety and terror, and profound feelings of helplessness. (p. 452)

Also within the analytic framework are a series of important contributions by Michael Stone (1980, 1985, 1993). The following brief quote only touches lightly on his many writings on this subject. In it, he addresses the emergence of the borderline pattern in the teen and 20s period:

The usual debut of BPD is in the later part of the second decade of life to the early part of the third. In my experience, there are two main sets of underlying factors. One has to do with an innate predisposition to affective illness, especially of the depressive/irritable sort, surfacing in late adolescence as rebelliousness, extreme moodiness, demandingness, and self-damaging acts. The other has to do with parental abusiveness.

There is a general tendency for BPD patients to do rather poorly during their 20s, struggling with the difficulties of leaving home and of achieving emotional and occupational security. . . . They crave closeness but fear being hurt or disappointed. This paradox can come about either because of innate nervous system irritability in those from relatively nurturing homes or because of deep (and quite understandable) distrust of others engendered by abusive caretakers during the formative years. (pp. 224–225)

We move next to contemporary thinkers of a nonanalytic persuasion, although the roots of many can be traced to an earlier psychodynamic orientation.

Although Aaron Beck and Freeman (1990b) are best known for their analysis of the depressive syndrome, they approach the borderline disorder from a cognitive rather than an affective point of view. Distinctive to Beck's analysis of the personality disorders has been his ability to highlight the dysfunctional beliefs that undergird so much of the disorder's pathological behaviors and emotional responses. The following quotes represent his view of the problematic qualities of cognitive style in the borderline disorder:

The most striking features of BPD are the intensity of client's emotional reactions, the changeability of their moods, and the great variety of symptoms they present. These individuals may abruptly shift from a pervasive depressed mood to anxious agitation or intense anger, or they may impulsively engage in actions that they later recognize as irrational and counterproductive (p. 178).

Three key basic assumptions are often uncovered in cognitive therapy with borderline individuals and appear to play a central role in the disorder. These are "The world is dangerous and malevolent," "I am powerless and vulnerable," and "I am inherently unacceptable" (p. 186).

Dichotomous thinking is the tendency to evaluate experiences in terms of mutually exclusive categories (e.g., good or bad, success or failure, trustworthy or deceitful) rather than seeing experiences as falling along continua. The effect of this "black-or-white" thinking is to force extreme interpretations on events that would normally fall in the intermediate range of a continuum, since there are no intermediate categories. According to the cognitive view, extreme evaluations of situations lead to extreme emotional responses and extreme actions.

In addition, a dichotomous view of experience can easily result in abrupt shifts from one extreme view to the opposite. (p. 187)

The role of interpersonal difficulties, especially those of erratic and inconsistent response styles, are taken to be central to understanding the borderline according to Benjamin (1993a). In her descriptive portrayals of this disorder, Benjamin notes the following as crucial to the personality's difficulties:

There is a morbid fear of abandonment and a wish for protective nurturance, preferably received by constant physical proximity to the rescuer (lover or caregiver). The baseline position is friendly dependency on a nurturer, which becomes hostile control if the caregiver or lover fails to deliver enough (and there is never enough). There is a belief that the provider secretly if not overtly likes dependency and neediness, and a vicious introject attacks the self if there are signs of happiness or success. (p. 122)

A love of intensity in relationship is shown by a desire to share very private information in great detail early in the history of the relationship. There are demands to spend large amounts of time together, and potential caregivers or lovers are idealized at the first or second meeting. However, the BPD switches easily and without reason from idealization of caregivers or lovers to devaluation. The caregiver's fall from grace is allegedly because he or she does not care enough, does not give enough,

is not "there" enough. There is an ability to empathize with and nurture the caregiver, but this is accompanied by the expectation that in return, the caregiver will "be there" to fulfill a compelling dependency upon demand. (p. 124)

An unusually perceptive analysis of the role of childhood trauma and abuse, including a careful review of empirical studies, has been argued persuasively by Perry and Herman (1993). They write:

Many of the most troubling and difficult features of BPD become more comprehensible in the light of a history of early, prolonged, severe childhood trauma. The psychopathology becomes an understandable adaptation to an environment of fear, secrecy, and betrayal rather than an innate defect in the self. Chronic childhood abuse takes place in a familial climate of pervasive terror. The abused child cannot turn to a parent for protection, either because the parent is himself the abuser, or because the abuser has succeeded in alienating the child from his or her primary caretaker. . . .

When ordinary caregiving relationships are disrupted, the abused child faces formidable developmental tasks in isolation. He or she must find a way to form primary attachments to caretakers who are either dangerous or incapable of protecting him or her. The capacity to trust must develop in an environment where trust is not warranted. . . . The capacity to experience and modulate affect must develop in an environment that provokes extreme feelings of terror and rage and that does not provide reliable soothing.

The characteristic borderline defense of splitting may be understood as an adaptive attempt to maintain some positive image of an idealized, nurturing parent as a figure for attachment while segregating the image of the abusive or neglectful parent. (pp. 135–136)

An interesting series of formulations concerning the nature of borderline pathology and pathogenesis have been articulated by Linehan (1993). In her proposals, which characterize borderlines as suffering from "emotional dysregulation," Linehan suggests that the core pathology is a combination of emotional vulnerability and the inability to regulate affect. The key element in the development of the borderline's emotional dysregulation derives from what she terms an "invalidating environment." Linehan describes the latter as follows:

A defining characteristic of the invalidating environment is the tendency of the family to respond

*erratically and inappropriately to private experi-
ence and, in particular, to be insensitive (i.e., non-
responsive) to private experience. . . . Invalidating
environments contribute to emotion dysregulation
by: (1) failing to teach the child to label and modulate arousal, (2) failing to teach the child to tolerate stress, (3) failing to teach the child to trust his
or her own emotional responses as valid interpretations of events, and (4) actively teaching the
child to invalidate his or her own experiences by
making it necessary for the child to scan the environment for cues about how to act and feel.
(pp. 111–112)*

In an unusually sensitive portrayal of the psychic processes undergirding the borderline pathology, Kroll (1993) suggests a close affinity between
the borderline's difficulties and that of the posttraumatic stress disorders. In the following quote,
he aptly describes disturbances in the "stream of
consciousness":

*The PTSD/borderline person suffers first and fore-
most from a disorder of the stream of consciousness. More specifically, the PTSD/borderline
person suffers from the inability to turn off a
stream of consciousness that has become its own
enemy, comprised of actual memories of traumatic
events, distorted and fragmented memories, unwelcome somatic sensations, negative self-commen-
taries running like a tickertape through the mind,
fantasied and feared elaborations from childhood
of the abuse experiences, and concomitant strongly
dysphoric moods of anxiety and anger. Much that
the adult PTSD/borderline does . . . is a response
to, or an attempt to terminate or modify, the intolerable presence of this stream of consciousness.
(p. xv)*

Turning to another psychologically grounded
thesis concerning the borderline personality,
Costa and Widiger (1993) have sought to reformulate the various DSM-IV personalities in terms of
the five-factor model they espouse as an optimal
schema of dimensions. In effect, they identify the
borderline personality as essentially equivalent to
the "facets" of what they term the Neurotic factor,
describing their view as follows:

*These features correspond closely to the five neuro-
tocism facets of hostility, impulsivity, vulnerability,
depression, and anxiety. A person who is elevated
on neurotocism tends to be hot-tempered, angry,
and easily frustrated (hostility); unable to resist*
*impulses and transient urges (impulsivity); easily
rattled, panicked, and unable to deal with stress
(vulnerable); tense, fearful, worried, and apprehensive (anxiety); hopeless, guilty, and blue (depressed); and is stricken by feelings of shame,
inferiority, and embarrassment (self-consciousness). (p. 45)*

Entering from the perspective of differential responsiveness to pharmacological agents, D. Klein
(1975, 1977) has raised serious questions concerning the validity of the borderline syndrome as a
unified diagnostic entity. This challenge notwithstanding, he has proposed a series of ostensibly distinct personality disorders that exhibit clinical
features frequently associated with recent descriptions of the borderline syndrome. In addition to asserting that the borderline designation subsumes, in
effect, several heterogeneous subtypes, he contends further that their characterological and severity dimensions are secondary to their shared
affective symptomatology. In essence—and in accord with Kraepelin's contention some 70 years
earlier to the effect that an endogenous metabolic
defect was at the core of the disturbance—Klein argued that an affective dysfunction lies at the heart
of the vulnerability of these syndromes. Three personality types—the phobic-anxious, the emotionally unstable, and the hysteroid dysphorics—are
identified as subject to this vulnerability; each
displays a long-term and somewhat atypical affective disorder. Several brief excerpts characterizing
these patterns are provided in earlier chapters,
and these are not repeated here. Worthy of note,
however, is the symptomatologic affinity between
Klein's pharmacologically deduced hysteroid dysphoric type and Easser and Lesser's analytically
derived hysteroid portrayal. Also notable are the
close parallels between Klein's three "atypical
affective" syndromes and three of the four borderline syndromal clusters obtained empirically by
Grinker, Werbel, and Drye (1968).

Brief mention must be made, however, of
another group of contemporary biological researchers, H. S. Akiskal et al. (1977), who have
studied and marshaled data from a variety of
pharmacological and family sources that support
the position that what they term "cyclothymia"
is, in essence, a subclinical or borderline personality condition found in biological relatives of
manic-depressives, which predisposes those afflicted to the clinical form of the illness, a view
quite reminiscent once more of Kraepelin's early
thesis.

The theoretical model of Siever (Siever & Davis, 1991) has attempted to link neurotransmitter properties to the various personality disorders. Extrapolating his four-system framework, he associates the borderline primarily to abnormalities in impulse action. He hypothesizes that these disorders may stem from a combined dysfunction in which serotonin is diminished and norepiniphrine is overactive. As he sees it, activation without behavioral inhibition might underlie the risk of borderline pathology. Intriguing as these and parallel neurotransmitter speculations may be, the mix of multiple neurochemical sites and sequences suggests that these hypotheses require further research before neurobiological markers specific to any complex disorder such as the borderline can be pinpointed.

Most of the conceptual models discussed thus far in this chapter derive their inspiration from psychoanalytic and biological schools of thought. Increasingly, however, contributors to the Borderline personality literature are recognizing that the disorder may reflect the operation of social forces, as well. In a particularly illuminating and comprehensive review of this literature, Paris (1994) has proposed what he terms a "multidimensional approach." In his analysis, Paris recommends that we include "social risks" as central to the genesis of this protean syndrome:

Social integration is a protective factor against BPD and . . . social disintegration is a risk factor for BPD. . . . Impulsive personality traits could be associated with sociocultural conditions in which high levels of autonomy are expected from the young at the same time that the level of social supports is decreased. Impulsivity also increases when social containment for deviant behavior decreases. Societies can either specifically proscribe characteristically "borderline" behaviors such as self-mutilation, recurrent parasuicide, and substance abuse, or create an unstructured and permissive environment in which these behaviors are more likely to occur. (p. 82)

An innovative, if somewhat controversial proposal of this nature has been promulgated by this book's senior author (Millon, 1987b, 1990); its essential argument will be described further in the section termed "Characteristic Experiential History." Recognizing that other pathogenic influences are operative, this culturally based thesis was written not to supplant either psychogenic or biogenic models, but to provide an addendum that supplements them with a sociogenic perspective. A brief summary of the role of sociocultural factors as indirectly influencing the pathogenesis of the borderline is noted in the following quote (Millon, 1987b):

Recent cultural changes have led to a loss of key cohering experiences that once protected against problematic parent-child relationships. Traditional societies provided ameliorative and reparative relationships (grandparents, aunts, older siblings, neighbors) and institutions (church, school) that offered remedies for parental disaffiliation; such societies provided a backup, so to speak, that insured that those who had been deprived or abused would be given a second chance to gain love and to observe models for developmental coherence. [The BPD patient's] aimless floundering and disaffiliated stagnation . . . might be substantially lessened if concurrent or subsequent personal encounters and social customs were compensatory or restitutive; that is, if they repaired the intrapsychically destabilizing and destructive effects of problematic experiences. Unfortunately, the converse appears to be the case. Whereas the cultural institutions of most societies have retained practices that furnish reparative stabilizing and cohering experiences, thereby remedying disturbed parent-child relationships . . . the changes of the past two to three decades (in Western societies) have not only fostered an increase in intrapsychic diffusion and splintering, but have also resulted in the discontinuation of psychically restorative institutions and customs, contributing thereby to both the incidence and exacerbation of features that typify borderline pathology. Without the corrective effects of undergirding and focusing social mentors and practices, the diffusing or divisive consequences of unfavorable earlier experience take firm root and unyielding form. (p. 367)

Finally, the classification model formulated initially by Millon in 1969 provided a schema for conceptualizing the borderline as a level of personality decompensation with several subvariants. As described previously, the notion that personality disorders should be differentiated in terms of degrees of severity or disorganization parallels the innovative schema articulated by Kernberg (1967). To Millon, the so-called borderline, schizotypal, and paranoid personalities that were initially presented in the DSM-III were likely to exhibit a series of characteristics in common, notably a chronic and periodically severe pathology in their overall structure and a checkered history of disruptions, predicaments, and disappointments in personal relationships and in school and work performance. Deficits in social attainments may also be prominent, as evidenced in an apparent inability to learn from prior difficulties, a tendency to precipitate self-defeating vicious circles, digressions and setbacks from earlier aspirations, and a failure to achieve a consistent niche in life that is consonant with natural aptitudes and potentials. Although all these personalities are able to function on an ambulatory basis, there is likely to have been repetitive but transient episodes in which extreme or bizarre behaviors were exhibited. More specifically, the descriptions and criteria that follow were written by Millon in 1969:

In contrast to his less severe counterparts, the "borderline" must try harder, employing his characteristic strategies with greater fervor or to abandon them, seeking to institute new but equally ineffectual techniques. The central features or criteria may be differentiated as follows: erratic behaviors *(for short periods, acquiescent and ingratiating, soon to be followed by a rageful outburst or, seeking to buoy flagging spirits, running frenetically here and there, changing excitedly from one behavior to another);* cognitive conflict *(finds himself repeatedly in a terrible bind; should he "go it" alone, no longer depending on others who are perceived as being unkind, or should he submit to them for fear of losing what little security he has gained);* separation anxiety *(inordinately vulnerable to separation from external sources of support, constantly on edge, and ripe for feelings of inevitable desertion);* mood vacillation *(typically exhibits a dominant mood, usually that of a depressive tone, which, gives way on occasion to displays of anxious agitation, euphoric activity, or hostile outbursts). (pp. 317–318)*

Elaborating on the preceding descriptors, Millon presented the following text as the initial working draft of what he termed the "cycloid borderline" to the DSM-III Task Force personality subcommittee in 1975:

This pattern is typified by intense, variable moods and by irregular energy levels, both of which appear frequently to be unrelated to external events. Those with predominant euphoric moods often experience brief spells of dejection, anxiety or impulsive anger; *where the characteristic mood is depressed, transient periods of anxiety, elation and anger may be interspersed. There is a notable fear of separation and loss with considerable dependency reassurance required to maintain psychic equilibrium. Strong ambivalent feelings, such as love, anger and guilt, are often felt toward those upon whom there is dependence.*

An appraisal of personal background and history reveals both of the following:

1. *Social attainment deficits (e.g., experienced serious, self-precipitated setbacks in scholastic, marital or vocational pursuits; repeated failure to maintain durable, satisfactory and secure roles consonant with age and aptitudes).*

2. *Periodic mini-psychotic episodes (e.g., experienced several brief and reversible periods in which either bizarre behaviors, extreme moods, irrational impulses or delusional thoughts were exhibited; short lived breaks from "reality," however, are often recognized subsequently as peculiar or deviant).*

Since adolescence or early adulthood at least 3 of the following have been present to a notably greater degree than in most people and were not limited to discrete periods nor necessarily prompted by stressful life events:

1. *Intense endogeneous moods (e.g., repetitive failure to be in normal mood not readily attributable to external sources; affective state either characteristically depressed or excited, or noted by recurring periods of dejection and apathy interspersed with spells of anger, anxiety or euphoria).*

2. *Dysregulated activation (e.g., experiences desultory energy level and irregular sleep-wake cycle; describes time periods suggesting that affective activation equilibrium was constantly in jeopardy).*

3. *Self-condemnatory conscience (e.g., reveals recurring self-mutilating and suicidal thoughts; periodically redeems moody behavior through contrition and self-derogation).*

4. *Dependency anxiety (e.g., preoccupied with securing affection and maintaining emotional support; reacts intensely to separation and reports haunting fear of isolation and loss).*

5. *Cognitive-affective ambivalence (e.g., portrays repeated struggle to express attitudes contrary to inner feelings; conflicting emotions and thoughts simultaneously experienced toward others, notably love, rage and guilt).*

The preceding text was subsequently revised in line with Klein's characterizations of the "emotionally unstable character disorder" and was labeled the "unstable personality disorder." Still later work reported by Spitzer, Endicott, and Gibbon (1979) was undertaken with the view of including criteria proposed by several clinical theorists specializing in this disorder. Following extended discussions and compromises of a political rather than substantive nature, the syndrome was designated the "borderline personality" in the DSM-III.

The DSM-III-R criteria essentially duplicated those of DSM-III. Minor changes were introduced in DSM-IV by adding a single criterion to represent the tendency of those with this disorder to exhibit transient, stress-related ideation of a paranoid character, or display brief but severe dissociative symptoms.

The diagnostic criteria outlined in DSM-IV make up perhaps the most broad-based listing among the personality disorders, a not surprising finding considering the vast literature that has developed regarding this disorder in the past two or three decades. In the Behavioral sphere are recorded two criteria: impulsivity that is potentially self-damaging in two or more spheres (e.g., substance abuse, reckless driving); self-mutilating behaviors, or recurrent suicidal gestures, threats, or actions. In the Interpersonal realm, one criterion of note is recorded: unstable and intense relationships that alternate between extremes of idealization and devaluation. A single Cognitive domain criterion is listed: the presence of transient, stress-related paranoid ideation or severe dissociative symptoms. Two criteria relate to Self-Image difficulties: unstable sense of self as in persistent identity disturbances or distortions; the presence of chronic feelings of emptiness. One Object-Relations criterion is noted: frantic efforts to avoid imagined abandonment from significant supportive figures. Finally, there are two significant criteria relating to Mood/Temperament: affective instability owing to a marked reactivity of mood (e.g., episodic dysphoria and irritability lasting usually a few days at most); intense and inappropriate anger signifying a loss of emotional control,

as evident in displays of bitterness, verbal outbursts, irritability, and sarcasm.

ICD-10 includes for the first time a disorder akin to the borderline construct as conceived in the DSMs. However, this characterization is designated "Emotionally Unstable" personality disorder, a reversion to the DSM-III formulation during the 1970s prior to a last-minute vote to designate this pattern of symptoms under the label "borderline." The ICD divides the emotionally unstable category into two subvarieties. Both share a general pattern of impulsivity and lack of control. There is affective instability, a less than average ability to plan ahead, outbursts of intense anger, often with periodic behavioral "explosions." The so called Impulsive type displays predominant characteristics of emotional instability and lack of impulse control. Threatening behavior or outbursts of violence are not uncommon, especially when being criticized. The Borderline type of the emotionally unstable gives evidence of an unclear or disturbed self-image and exhibits chronic feelings of emptiness, as well as a tendency to become involved in intense and unstable relationships that precipitate repeated emotional crises and that may be associated with efforts to avoid abandonment and to engage in suicidal threats or acts of self-harm.

The evolutionary model for the borderline personality construct, as seen in the polarity schema of Figure 18.1, shows that all the usual motives and aims reflected in the model are present, albeit to a

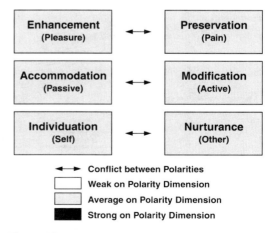

Figure 18.1 Status of the borderline personality prototype in accord with the Millon Polarity Model.

moderate degree. What is most significant is that all three pairs of polarities are in conflict, as indicated by the double-pointed arrows between them. This signifies the intense ambivalence and inconstancy that characterizes the borderline, their emotional vacillation, their behavioral unpredictability, as well as the inconsistency they manifest in their feelings and thoughts about others.

This conflictual pattern contrasts with the other two severe or structural pathologies, the schizotypal and paranoid. The borderline possesses distinct inclinations, but they clash and are disharmonious; hence, the borderline switches back and forth, going from one direction and then to its opposite. By contrast, the intensity of the polarity inclinations in the schizotypal is diffuse and undirected, hence producing the randomness and eccentricity that characterizes their thoughts, feelings, and behaviors. In the paranoid, the structural problem is one of rigidity and compartmentalization. There is an unbending and unvarying character to their polarity inclinations, an unwillingness to change their attitudes, behaviors, and emotions despite good reasons to do so. No such difficulty is evident in the borderline. In their case, each polarity position is but a temporary one, quickly jettisoned for its opposite.

As has been noted, the severe or structural pathologies, which includes the schizotypal, paranoid, and borderline disorders, almost invariably coexist with one or another of the stylistic personality disorders (e.g., avoidant, histrionic, negativistic). Hence, in evaluating a patient with distinct but conflictual structural defects that characterize the borderline, it is necessary to consider which stylistic personality pattern is also present. The polarity model requires the integration of both stylistic polarity features and structural borderline defects. A fusion of the two, style and structure, is necessary for a thorough and accurate assessment.

A review of the major contributors to borderline personality disorder is summarized in Figure 18.2.

CLINICAL FEATURES

Patients categorized as borderline personalities display an unusually wide variety of clinical symptoms. However, certain elements stand out and are common to most; these will be noted shortly. As with the preceding structurally-defective personality, the schizotypal, we will introduce these features first by dividing them into three broad categories: primary source of anxiety; cognitive processes and preoccupations; and general mood and behavior. Further differentiations will be made in terms of the eight basic clinical domains. The categories are as follows:

- *Separation Anxiety.* Borderline personalities are exceedingly dependent; not only do they require a great deal of protection, reassurance, and encouragement from others to maintain their equanimity, but they are inordinately vulnerable to separation from these external sources of support.

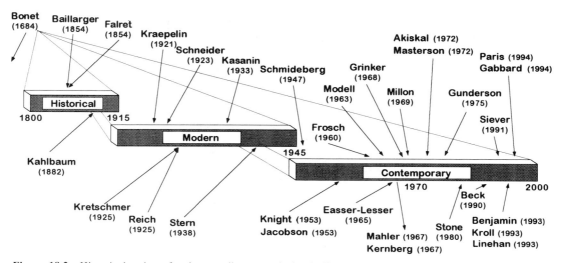

Figure 18.2 Historical review of major contributors to the borderline personality disorder.

Separation and isolation can be terrifying not only because borderlines do not value themselves or use themselves as a source of positive reinforcement, but because they lack the wherewithal, the know-how and equipment for independence and self-determination. Unable to fend for themselves, they not only dread signs of potential loss, but they anticipate it, and distort their perceptions so that they "see it" happening when, in fact, it is not. Moreover, because borderlines devalue their own self-worth, they have difficulty believing that others can value them; as a consequence, they are exceedingly fearful that others will depreciate and cast them off.

With so shaky a foundation of self-esteem, and lacking the means for an autonomous existence, these patients remain constantly on edge, prone to the anxiety of separation and ripe for feelings of inevitable desertion. Any event that stirs up these feelings may precipitate a psychotic episode, most notably those of depression or excitement.

- *Cognitive Conflict and Guilt.* Matters are bad enough for borderlines, given their separation anxiety, but these patients are also in conflict regarding their dependency needs, and often feel guilt for having tried to be self-assertive. In contrast to their mildly pathological counterparts who have found a measure of success utilizing their strategies, borderline patients have been less fortunate, and have struggled hard to achieve the few rewards they have sought. Moreover, in their quest for security and approval, most of them have been subjected to periods of isolation and separation; as a result, many have acquired feelings of distrust and hostility toward others.

  Borderlines cannot help but be anxious. To assert themselves would endanger the rewards they so desperately seek from others and perhaps even provoke total rejection and abandonment; yet because of past experiences, borderlines know they can never fully trust others nor hope to gain all the affection and support they need. Should they be excessively anxious about separation and therefore submit to protect themselves against desertion, borderlines will still feel insecure; moreover, they will experience anger toward those upon whom they depend because of their power to "force" the borderline to yield and acquiesce. To complicate matters, this very resentment

becomes a threat; if borderlines are going to appease others as a means of preventing abandonment, they must take great pains to assure that their anger does not get out of hand. Should these resentments be discharged, even in so innocuous a form as displays of self-assertion, their security may be undermined and severely threatened. Thus, borderlines are in a terrible bind; should they "go it" alone, no longer depending on others who have been so unkind, or submit for fear of losing what little security they can eke out?

To secure anger and constrain resentment, borderlines often turn against themselves and are self-critical and self-condemnatory. They begin to despise themselves and to feel guilty for their offenses, unworthiness, and contemptibility. They impose upon themselves the same harsh and deprecatory judgments they anticipate from others. Thus, we see in these patients not only anxiety and conflict but overt expressions of guilt, remorse, and self-belittlement.

- *Mood and Behavior Vacillation.* The most striking feature of borderlines is the intensity of their moods and the frequent changeability of their behaviors. These *rapid* swings from one mood and behavior to another are *not* invariably present in the borderline; they do, however, characterize periods in which there is a break in control or what we have referred to as a psychotic episode. More commonly, these patients exhibit a single dominant mood, usually a self-ingratiating and depressive tone that, on occasion, gives way to brief displays of anxious agitation, euphoric activity, or outbursts of hostility.

PROTOTYPAL DIAGNOSTIC DOMAINS

Although patients categorized as borderline personalities display a wide variety of clinical features, certain elements stand out as relatively distinct, and these are the prime focus in this section. As in prior chapters, these characteristics are separated into eight domains of clinical significance (see Table 18.1 and Figure 18.3).

Expressive Behavior: Spasmodic

Although the erratic qualities of the borderline are conceived as primarily of an emotional character, we see high levels of inconsistency and irregularity

TABLE 18.1   Clinical Domains of the
Borderline Prototype

Behavioral Level

(F) Expressively Spasmodic. Displays a desultory
energy level with sudden, unexpected, and impulsive
outbursts; abrupt, endogenous shifts in drive state and
inhibitory controls; not only places activation and emotional equilibrium in constant jeopardy, but engages in
recurrent suicidal or self-mutilating behaviors.

(F) Interpersonally Paradoxical. Although needing
attention and affection, is unpredictably contrary,
manipulative, and volatile, frequently eliciting rejection rather than support; frantically reacts to fears of
abandonment and isolation, but often in angry, mercurial, and self-damaging ways.

Phenomenological Level

(F) Cognitively Capricious. Experiences rapidly
changing, fluctuating, and antithetical perceptions or
thoughts concerning passing events, as well as contrasting emotions and conflicting thoughts toward self and
others, notably love, rage, and guilt; vacillating and
contradictory reactions are evoked in others by virtue
of one's behaviors, creating, in turn, conflicting and
confusing social feedback.

(S) Uncertain Self-Image. Experiences the confusions of an immature, nebulous, or wavering sense of
identity, often with underlying feelings of emptiness;
seeks to redeem precipitate actions and changing self-
presentations with expressions of contrition and self-
punitive behaviors.

(S) Incompatible Objects. Internalized representations comprise rudimentary and extemporaneously
devised, but repetitively aborted learnings, resulting in
conflicting memories, discordant attitudes, contradictory needs, antithetical emotions, erratic impulses, and
clashing strategies for conflict reduction.

Intrapsychic Level

(F) Regression Mechanism. Retreats under stress to
developmentally earlier levels of anxiety tolerance,
impulse control, and social adaptation; among adolescents, is unable to cope with adult demands and conflicts, as evident in immature, if not increasingly
infantile behaviors.

(S) Split Organization. Inner structures that exist in
a sharply segmented and conflictful configuration in
which a marked lack of consistency and congruency is
seen among elements; levels of consciousness often
shift and result in rapid movements across boundaries
that usually separate contrasting percepts, memories,
and affects; this leads to periodic schisms in what limited psychic order and cohesion may otherwise be
present, often resulting in transient, stress-related
psychotic episodes.

Biophysical Level

(S) Labile Mood. Fails to accord unstable mood
level with external reality; has either marked shifts
from normality to depression to excitement, or has
periods of dejection and apathy, interspersed with
episodes of inappropriate and intense anger, as well
as brief spells of anxiety or euphoria.

(F) = Functional domain.
(S) = Structural domain.

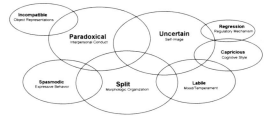

Figure 18.3   Salience of personologic domains in the
borderline prototype.

in all aspects of their behavior. Their dress and
their voice show this pattern of vacillation and
changeability. One day, they are dressed quite appropriately and attractively; the next, they are
sloppy and disheveled. One day, their voice has a
spirited and energetic quality to it; the next they are
hesitant, slow, and monosyllabic. Borderlines display a desultory energy level, occasioned at times
with sudden, unexpected, and impulsive outbursts.
Their activation and emotional equilibrium seem to
be in constant jeopardy, with endogenous shifts in
mood, drive, and inhibitory controls. Given this
lack of control and the intensity of their emotional
states, it should not be surprising that they are
vulnerable to recurrent suicidal or self-mutilating
impulses.

It is the unpredictability and the impetuous, erratic, and unreflected impulsivity that characterize the borderline's tempers and actions, rather
than the presence of a pattern of smoothly and
repetitively swinging emotions that go from one
end of the affective continuum to the other. This
brittle, labile, and unsustainable quality contrasts
to the cyclical regularity of contrasting moods that
is often believed to typify these patients.

Interpersonal Conduct: Paradoxical

Although borderlines need attention and affection, they act in an unpredictably contrary, manipulative, and volatile manner in their interpersonal
relationships. These paradoxical behaviors frequently elicit rejection rather than the support
they desperately seek. In an unpredictable and
frantic reaction to their fears of abandonment and
isolation, borderlines become mercurially angry
and explosive, hence damaging their security
rather than eliciting the care they seek.

As a secondary consequence of their unsure or
unstable self-identities, borderlines have become

exceedingly dependent on others, if they were not so already. Not only do they need protection and reassurance to maintain their equanimity, but they become inordinately vulnerable to separation from these external sources of support. Isolation or aloneness may be terrifying not only because borderlines lack an inherent sense of self but because they lack the wherewithal, the know-how, and equipment for taking mature, self-determined, and independent action. Unable to fend adequately for themselves, they not only dread potential loss but often anticipate it, "seeing it" happening when, in fact, it is not.

The borderline is more ambivalent about relationships with others than are most personality syndromes. Moreover, these individuals have been less successful in fulfilling their dependency needs, suffering thereby considerably greater separation anxieties. Their concerns are not simply those of gaining approval and affection but of not submitting to others, yet preventing further loss. Because they already are on shaky grounds, borderlines' actions are directed less toward accumulating additional reserves of support and esteem than toward preserving the little security they still possess.

At first, borderlines will employ their characteristic coping styles with increased fervor in the hope that they will regain their footing. Some may become martyrs, dedicated and self-effacing persons who are "so good" that they are willing to devote or sacrifice their lives for some greater purpose. The usual goal of these borderlines is to insinuate themselves into the lives of others who will not merely "use" them but need them and, therefore not desert them. Self-sacrificing though they may appear to be, these borderlines effectively manipulate others to protect against the separation they dread. Moreover, by sacrificing themselves, they not only assure continued contact with others but serve as implicit models for others to be gentle and considerate in return. Virtuous martyrdom, rather than a sacrifice, is a ploy of submissive devotion that strengthens the attachments borderlines need.

The intolerance of being abandoned and the feeling of emptiness and aloneness consequent to the borderline's failure to maintain a secure and rewarding dependency relationship, cumulate into a reservoir of anxiety, conflict, and anger. Like a safety valve, these tensions must be released either slowly or through periodic and often impulsive outbursts against others. Because borderlines seek the goodwill of those on whom they depend, they will

try at first to express their inner tensions subtly and indirectly. Depression is among the most common of these covert expressions. Thus, the pleading anguish, despair, and resignation voiced by borderlines serve to release tensions and to externalize the torment they feel within themselves. For some, however, depressive lethargy and sulking behavior are a means primarily of expressing anger. Depression serves as an instrument for them to frustrate and retaliate against those who have "failed" them or "demanded too much." Angered by the "inconsiderateness" of others, these borderlines employ their somber and melancholy sadness as a vehicle to get back at them or teach them a lesson. Moreover, by exaggerating their plight and by moping about helplessly, they effectively avoid responsibilities, place added burdens on others, and thereby cause their families not only to take care of them but to suffer and feel guilt while doing so. In addition, the dour moods and excessive complaints of these borderlines infect the atmosphere with tension and irritability, thereby upsetting what equanimity remains among those who have "disappointed" them. Similarly, suicidal threats, gambling, and other impulsively self-damaging acts may function as instruments of punitive blackmail, a way of threatening others that further trouble is in the offing, and that they had best make up for their prior neglect and thoughtlessness.

Cognitive Style: Capricious

It is characteristic of borderlines to experience rapidly changing, fluctuating, and antithetical perceptions and thoughts concerning persons and passing events. Not only do they experience contrasting emotions, but they have ambivalent attitudes toward themselves and others; for example, they may perceive a spouse with love one moment, feel rage the next, and then experience guilt thereafter. Most problematic is that their vacillating and contradictory perceptions evoke in others similarly conflicting and confusing feedback. This perpetuates the vicious circle of experiencing again and again that which prompted their actions in the first place.

A major problem for the borderline is the lack of a consistent purpose or direction for shaping attitudes, behaviors, or emotions. Unable to give coherence to their existence, they have few anchors or guideposts to either coordinate their actions, control their impulses, or construct a goal-oriented means for achieving their desires. Feeling scattered and unintegrated, they vacillate, responding as a child would to every passing interest or whim and shifting from one momentary course to another. In effect, borderlines appear to have deteriorated increasingly toward primary-process thinking. Under the press of upsurging affects and their inability to maintain a clear focus, there is a regression to a psychoticlike thought process, occasionally reflected in quasi-paranoid ideation and severe dissociated symptoms.

Self-Image: Uncertain

It is typical of the borderline to experience the confusions of an immature, nebulous, or wavering sense of identity, often with underlying feelings of emptiness. They have considerable difficulty in maintaining a stable sense of who they are, conveying rapidly shifting presentations of self, or in formulating any clear sense of their personal image. They remain aimless, unable to channel their energies or abilities, incapable of settling down on some path or role that might provide a basis for fashioning a unified and enduring sense of self. Seeking to redeem their precipitate actions and changing self-presentations accounts in part for their expressions of contrition, and for their self-punitive behaviors. Likewise, borderlines demonstrate highly contradictory self-representations. These reflect their lack of inner cohesion and the so-called splitting maneuvers that they employ. Portions of their schismatic psyche may be split off and projected onto others as a means of bewildering or controlling them, a defensive maneuver designed in part to create confusion in others that mirrors their own inner ambivalences.

Object-Representations: Incompatible

Inferring the internalized representations of the borderline on the basis of their thoughts and behaviors suggests that their inner objects comprise rudimentary and extemporaneously derived dispositions and images. Early learnings regarding significant others are likely to have been repetitively aborted, resulting in conflicting memories, discordant attitudes, contradictory needs, erratic impulses, and clashing strategies for conflict resolution. In effect, their inner templates for perceiving and thinking about current events are composed of complex antithetical dispositions.

Because borderlines are now very likely to devalue their self-worth, it is difficult for them to believe that those on whom they have depended in the past could ever have thought well of them. Consequently, at a deep intrapsychic level, they are exceedingly fearful that others will inevitably depreciate them and perhaps cast them off. With so unstable an inner template of self-esteem, and lacking the means for assuring their autonomous existence, borderlines remain constantly on edge, prone to the anxiety of separation and ripe for anticipating inevitable desertion. Anchored to these internalized objects stirs up deep fears that efforts at restitution such as idealization, self-abnegation, and attention-gaining acts of self-destruction or, conversely, self-assertion and impulsive anger, will inevitably fail. As a result of the schisms that characterize both their overt and covert psychic processes, borderlines fail to recognize that other persons possess a mix of both positive and negative feelings and attitudes. Instead, the inner templates of borderlines are sharply divided, split, so-to-speak, into polar extremes, that is, others are seen either as totally good or totally bad. Consequentially, as life experiences progress with significant others, borderlines may alternate on a regular basis between idealizing these persons, and then abruptly devaluing them, a process that both reflects their inner schisms and creates erratic shifts in the reactions of others.

Matters are bad enough for borderlines, given their identity diffusion and separation anxieties, but their internalized images and impulses are in intense conflict regarding dependency needs. Not only do they feel guilt for past attempts at self-assertion and independence, but these quests for self-determination and self-identity may have been subjected to ridicule and isolation, resulting in increased feelings of distrust and resentment toward others. Moreover, should they seek to become close to another, two contrasting, but distressful consequences come to mind. First, they fear that they will be engulfed by the person, thereby losing what little sense of autonomy and identity they possess. On the other hand, there is the fear that they will, without forewarning, be precipitously abandoned.

Regulatory Mechanisms: Regression

What is most significant among the regulatory mechanisms employed by the borderline is the tendency to retreat under stress to developmentally earlier levels of anxiety tolerance, impulse control, and social adaptation. Among adolescents who exhibit borderline tendency, we find an inability to cope with adult demands and life's conflicts, as evident in immature, if not increasingly infantile behaviors.

The hostility expressed by borderlines poses a serious threat to their security. To experience resentment toward others, let alone to vent it, endangers them since it may provoke the counterhostility, rejection, and abandonment they fear. Angry feelings and outbursts must not only be curtailed or redirected toward impotent scapegoats but may be intrapsychically reversed and condemned. To appease their conscience and to assure expiation, they may reproach themselves for their faults, and purify themselves to prove their virtue. To accomplish this regulatory goal, their hostile impulses may be dynamically inverted. Thus, aggressive urges toward others may be turned on themselves. Rather than vent their anger, they will openly castigate and derogate themselves, and voice exaggerated feelings of guilt and worthlessness. These borderlines become notably self-recriminating. They belittle themselves, demean their abilities, and derogate their virtues, not only to dilute their aggressive urges but to assure others that they themselves are neither worthy nor able adversaries. The self-effacement of these borderlines is an attempt, then, both to control their own hostility and to stave off hostility from others.

Among other borderlines, where hostile impulses are more deeply ingrained as a form of self-expression, these feelings must be counteracted more forcefully. Because these patients are likely to have displayed their anger more frequently and destructively, they must work all the harder to redeem themselves. Instead of being merely self-effacing and contrite, they will often turn on themselves viciously, claiming that they are despicable and hateful persons. These condemnatory self-accusations may at times reach delusional proportions, and such patients may reject every rational effort to dissuade them of their culpability. In these cases, the struggle to redeem oneself often leads to self-mutilation and physical destruction.

Morphologic Organization: Split

The structural concept termed "split" is especially apt in characterizing the intrapsychic organization of the borderline. Their mind comprises inner structures that exist in sharply segmented and conflictful configurations. There is a marked lack of systematic order and congruency among the elements of the mind. Levels of consciousness often shift to and fro. Similarly, rapid movements take place across boundaries that should separate contrasting perceptions, memories, and affects. This lack of control and cohesion produces periodic but serious schisms in psychic order and cohesion, resulting in a susceptibility to transient, stress-related psychotic episodes.

Borderlines cannot help but be intrapsychically ambivalent. To assert themselves endangers the security and protection they desperately seek from others by provoking the latter to reject and abandon them. Yet, given their past, they know they can never entirely trust others nor fully hope to gain the security and affection they need. Should their anxiety about separation lead them to submit as a way of warding off or forestalling desertion, they expose themselves to even further dependency and, thereby, an even greater threat of loss. Moreover, they know they experience intense anger toward those on whom they depend, not only because it shames them and exposes their weakness but also because of others' power in having "forced" them to yield and acquiesce. This very resentment becomes then a threat in itself. If they are going to appease others to prevent abandonment, they must take pains to assure that their anger remains under control. Should this resentment be discharged, even in innocuous forms of self-assertion, their security will be severely threatened. They are in a terrible bind. Should they strike out alone, no longer dependent on others who have expected too much or have demeaned them, or should they submit for fear of losing what little security they can gain thereby?

To secure their anger and to constrain their resentment, borderlines often turn against themselves in a self-critical and self-condemnatory manner. Despising themselves, they voice the same harsh judgments they have learned to anticipate from others. They display not only anxiety and conflict but overt expressions of guilt, remorse, and self-belittlement. It is these feelings that occasionally take hold, overwhelm them, and lead to the characteristic self-damaging and periodic self-destructive acts.

Mood/Temperament: Labile

The most striking characteristic of borderlines is the intensity of their affect and the changeability of their actions. Most fail to accord their unstable mood levels with external reality. They tend to show marked shifts from normality to depression to excitement. There are periods of dejection and apathy, interspersed with episodes of inappropriate and intense anger, followed by brief spells of anxiety or euphoria.

As noted previously, rapid shifts from one mood and attitude to another are not inevitable aspects of the everyday behavior of the borderline, but they do characterize extended periods when there has been a break in control. Most borderlines exhibit a single, dominant outlook or frame of mind, such as a self-ingratiating depressive tone, which gives way periodically, however, to anxious agitation or impulsive outbursts of temper or resentment. The self-destructive and self-damaging behaviors that often occur, are usually recognized subsequently as having been irrational and foolish.

PROTOTYPAL VARIANTS

As in prior chapters, the following sections will attempt to alert the reader to the many variations seen clinically that reflect a basic borderline pattern of adaptation. Owing to the observation that the borderline level of pathology is intrinsically severe or structurally defective, no variant of a normal type will be presented.

Childhood Syndromes

The reader is referred back to Chapter 15 for a discussion on childhood ambiosis. Here, we see childhood characteristics in milder form than may be present in the prepubertal borderline personality disorder. What we will describe in the following paragraphs characterizes these youngsters in more severe form. Thus, the features noted for what may be termed the moderately severe ambiotic child include a high degree of behavioral unpredictability, and capricious and erratic moods. Many are noted for their crankiness and testiness, their restlessness and hypermobility, and their tendency to manifest severe temper tantrums for no apparent reason. Some may be extremely clingy, unwilling to leave their parent's side, others seem unusually fearful in general, exhibiting unusual phobias and hypochondriacal behaviors.

Some suggest the roots of this disorder, particularly as a prelude to adolescent or adult borderline conditions, as traceable to attention deficit/hyperactivity disorders, evidencing themselves in neural developmental delays and unusual central nervous system sensitivities of a nonspecific origin. The influence of psychological mechanism in these disorders has also been widely promulgated; these are discussed in greater detail both in our historical review as well as in later sections of this chapter. Along these lines, some family studies appear to shed light on the developmental origins of childhood variance. Thus, proposals include faulty family boundaries, capricious relationships among family members, as well as the possibilities of childhood sexual abuse. How experiences of this nature are mediated developmentally, how they may lead from trauma and altered biological processes to the clinical state remain as issues yet to be resolved. A few words should be said of an adolescent pattern not unlike the borderline personality. In what Millon (1969) has referred to as "adolescent diffusion-reactions," a constellation of clinical features are seen that parallel and extend some the earlier notions of Erik Erikson (1950) in his concept of "identity crisis."

These youngsters are characterized by vague feelings of apathy and boredom, an inability to see any meaning or purpose to life other than momentary gratifications and an aimless and drifting existence without commitment of direction. These youngsters feel estranged from society's traditions and believe them to be false or deceiving, but are unable or unwilling to find an alternative to replace them. They appear to suffering from what Erikson (1950) speaks of as an "identity crisis," a sense of uncertainty as to who they are and where they are going.

As they ponder the grim realities of a society plagued with civil strife and engaged in hopeless and immoral wars, striving to maintain what these children see as adult hypocrisy and sham, as they sense the futility of long-range plans, they convince themselves that nothing really matters, that nothing is worth laboring for or aspiring to. Unable to find a purpose in life, a goal for the future, their behavior becomes aimless, geared only to the pleasures of the moment, with little heed paid to their consequences. Lacking guidelines and goals, they have no reason to act and become paralyzed, unable to plan or to commit themselves to anything.

Adolescent diffusion often remains latent until the age of 17 or 18, when youngsters go off to college and are free of parental control and surveillance. Here, they often learn scientific facts and the skills of critical thinking, which enable them to question naive social dogma and archaic childhood beliefs. They become conditioned to think that the world of his parents is phony, stupid, self-defeating, and meaningless. Moreover, among their peers, they find many who share their dismay over the failures and deceptions of the society.

Unable to discipline themselves and buckle down to the demands of academic life, lacking a coherent set of values by which they can channel their energies, and resistant to the "absurdity" of conventional education, these individuals fail to fulfill even the simplest assignments, and their grades sink precipitously. This event only verifies for them the stupidity and narrow conventions of the adult world. With their former self-image of intelligence shattered by poor academic performance, they seek to reaffirm status through promiscuous sexual activity, usually with minimal gratification or by the use of marijuana or cocaine, which serves as an emblem of "copping out" of society. Both of these "prove" the independence of their mortified parents.

Adult Subtypes

Both theory (Millon, 1969, 1981, 1990) and research (Millon, 1977, 1987, 1994) show that the borderline pattern overlaps almost invariably with every other personality disorder; the schizoid and compulsive types are about the only significant exceptions; narcissists and avoidants are also infrequent covariants of the borderline structure. Among the other stylistic personality disorders, it often develops insidiously as a structurally advanced or structurally more defective pattern.

However, what we observe in a number of personality styles are brief episodes of impulsivity and affective instability that mimic the more intrinsic and persistent traits of the borderline. A key notion in the previous sentence is brevity, that is, the evanescent nature with which these covariant symptoms exhibit themselves. Impulsive anger, affective instability, and self-destructive acts are not, nor do they appear to become, integral character traits of these non-borderline personalities. Some succumb to these behaviors fleetingly following severe psychic deflation, that is, a loss of a significant source of status or fantasized self-esteem; during these transitory episodes they will appear "borderline" but only until they can regain their more benign composure. Others may also succumb to the borderline's more overtly exhibitionistic symptoms following a painful psychic blow. However, these personalities are much more apt to decompensate, if at all, along schizotypal or paranoid lines. They intensify at these times their established pattern of social anxiety and isolation, their self-created cognitive interference, and their flat and constricted affect. The discussion returns now to those subtypes of the borderline that share

its prime features in a more enduring and integrated fashion.

It is the authors' contention that we will find the same complex of determinants in the borderline syndrome as we do in several of its less structurally-defective variants: the avoidant, depressive, dependent, histrionic, antisocial, sadistic, and negativistic personalities. The primary differences between them are the intensity, frequency, timing, and persistence of a host of potentially pathogenic factors. Those who function at the borderline level may begin with less adequate constitutional equipment or be subjected to a series of more adverse early experiences. As a consequence of their more troublesome histories, they either fail to develop an adequate coping style in the first place or decompensate slowly under the weight of repeated and unrelieved difficulties. It is the authors' view that most borderline cases progress sequentially through a more adaptive or higher level of functioning before deteriorating to the structurally defective state. Some patients, however, notably childhood variants, never appear to get off the ground and give evidence of a borderline pattern from their earliest years.

The borderlines' typical, everyday mood and behavior reflect their basic personality pattern. In the following paragraphs, we will note some of the clinical features that differentiate the several subtypes of the disorder.

The Discouraged Borderline

Discouraged borderlines typically have been pliant and submissive individuals who shun competition, are lacking in initiative, and are frequently, chronically sad or depressed. They may have attached themselves to one or two other persons on whom they depend, with whom they have been able to display affection and thoughtfulness and to whom they have been loyal and humble.

However, the borderline's strategy of quiet cooperation and compliance, in contrast to the less pathological dependent or depressive personalities, has not been notably successful. These patients may have put all their eggs in one basket, a specific loved one to whom they are excessively attached. But this attachment has not proved secure; their lifeline is connected to an unreliable anchor and their psychic equilibrium hangs on a thin thread and is in constant jeopardy. As a consequence, these patients exhibit a perennial preoccupation and concern with security; their pathetic lack of inner resources and their marked self-doubts lead them to cling tenaciously to whomever they can find, and to submerge every remnant of autonomy and individuality they possess. As can be expected from the preceding, the features just outlined demonstrate traits likely to be seen in mixed clinical pictures composed of deteriorated dependent and avoidant and structurally defective borderline personalities.

The insecurity experienced by these persons precipitates conflict and distress. *Discouraged borderlines* easily become dejected and depressed and feel hopeless, helpless, and powerless to overcome their fate. Everything becomes a burden; simple responsibilities demand more energy than they can muster; life seems empty but heavy; they cannot go on alone; and they begin to turn on themselves, feeling unworthy, useless, and despised. Should their sense of futility grow, they may regress to a state of marked depression or infantile dependency, requiring others to tend to them as if they were babies.

Sometimes, these borderlines reverse their habitual strategy and seek actively to solicit attention and security. For short periods, they may become exceedingly cheerful and buoyant, trying to cover up and counter their sense of underlying despondency. Others may disown their submissive and acquiescent past and display explosive though brief outbursts of angry resentment, a wild attack on others for having exploited and abused them and for failing to see how needful they have been of encouragement and nurturance. At these times, a frightening sense of isolation and aloneness may overwhelm and panic these patients, driving them to cry out for someone to comfort and hold them, lest they sink into the oblivion and nothingness of self.

Some discouraged borderlines appear to be extreme variants of the less pathological conforming and depressive personalities. Both have been conscientious and proper persons; they overcomply with the strictures of society, display an air of propriety, are overly respectful and deferential to authority and tend to be grim and humorless. They have learned to look to others for support and affection, but such rewards are contingent on compliance and submission. However, these personalities are less certain than their less disturbed counterparts that they will receive support for compliant behaviors. Try as they may, they no longer have confidence that diligence and acquiescence will forestall desertion, and that they will not be left adrift, alone and abandoned even when they submit and conform.

For such individuals, insecurity may stem from several sources; for example, they may have been reproached unfairly by perfectionistic parents or may not have been told with sufficient clarity "exactly" what was expected of them. Whatever the source, compliant and conscientious strategies have not always paid off, and the person is justly distressed and resentful; the pact the borderline has made with parents and other authorities has been abrogated too often, and they have failed to fulfill their share of the bargain.

The resentment and anger these borderlines feel for having been coerced into submission and then betrayed churns within them and presses hard against their usually adequate controls. Periodically, these feelings break through to the surface, erupting in an angry upsurge of fury and unbridled vituperation. This anger draws its strength not only from immediate precipitants but from a deep reservoir of animosity, filled through years of what was experienced as constraint. These outbursts of venom usually are directed toward weaker persons, innocent subordinates or children who, by virtue of their powerlessness, cannot retaliate.

Whether resentments are discharged overtly, or kept seething near the surface, these borderlines experience them as a threat to their equanimity; feelings such as these signify weakness and emotionality, traits which are anathema to their self-image of propriety and control. Moreover, contrary impulses create anxiety because they jeopardize their security, that is, their basic dependency on others. Hostility is doubly dangerous; not only may it lead to an attack on the very persons upon whom they depend, thereby undermining the strength of those to whom they look for support, but it may provoke their wrath, which may result in outright rejection and desertion by these important persons.

To counter these hostile impulses, the discouraged borderline may become excessively constrained. Guilt and self-condemnation frequently become dominant features. Struggling feverishly to control their aggressive impulses, these patients will likely turn their feelings inward, and impose on themselves severe punitive judgments and actions. Accusations of their own unworthiness are but mild rebukes for the guilt they feel. Self-mutilation and suicide, symbolic acts of self-desertion, may be a means to control their own expressions of resentment or to punish themselves for their anger.

The Impulsive Borderline

Impulsive borderlines typically are structurally-defective variants of certain of their less pathological counterparts, primarily the histrionic and antisocial personalities. Each is capricious, evasive, superficial, and seductive. However, at the border-line level, strategies are instrumentally less successful than heretofore. As a consequence, we observe more extreme efforts to cope with events, many of which serve only to perpetuate and deepen their difficulties. For example, former histrionics may not have mastered the techniques of soliciting approval and ensuring a stream of support and encouragement; because of an excessively flighty and capricious style of personal relationships, they may experience long periods in which they lack a secure base and a consistent source of attention.

Deprived of the attentions and rewards they seek, impulsive borderlines may intensify their strategy of seductiveness and irresponsibility. Those with a histrionic background may give evidence of extreme hyperactivity, flightiness, and distractibility. At moments, they may exhibit a frenetic gaiety, an exaggerated boastfulness and an insistent and insatiable need for social contact and excitement. Frightened lest they lose attention and approval, they may display a frantic conviviality, an irrational and superficial euphoria in which they lose all sense of propriety and judgment, and race hypomanically from one activity to another. Those with a stronger antisocial history may engage in a series of restless, spur-of-the-moment acts, failing to plan ahead or to consider more pragmatic alternatives, no less to heed the consequences of their actions. For some, the struggle to free themselves from the restrictions of social custom results in impetuous and irresponsible behaviors.

At times, these borderlines experience repeated rebuffs; at others, their efforts to solicit attention simply prove futile. Fearing a permanent loss of attention and esteem, they may succumb for brief periods to hopelessness and self-depreciation. Having lost confidence in their seductive or exploitive powers, dreading a decline in vigor, charm and youth, they may begin to fret and worry, to have doubts about their worth and attractiveness. Anticipating desertion and disillusioned with self, they begin to ponder their fate. Since worry begets further worry and doubts raise more doubts, their agitation turns to gloom, to increased self-derogation, and to feelings of emptiness and abandonment; ultimately, they begin to distort reality so that everything, no matter how encouraging or exciting it formerly was, now seems bleak and barren.

The Petulant Borderline

Petulant borderlines are often difficult to distinguish from certain of their less structurally-defective counterparts, most notably the negativistic personality. Simply stated, we can say that the petulant borderline's overt symptoms are more intense and that psychotic episodes occur with somewhat greater frequency than in the negativist. Petulant borderlines may be best characterized by their extreme unpredictability and by their restless, irritable, impatient, and complaining behaviors. Typically, they are defiant, disgruntled, and discontent, as well as stubborn, sullen, pessimistic, and resentful. Enthusiasms are short lived; they are easily disillusioned and slighted, tend to be envious of others and feel unappreciated and cheated in life.

Despite their anger and resentment, petulant borderlines fear separation, and are desirous of achieving affection and love; in short, they are ambivalent, trapped by conflicting inclinations to "move toward, away or against others," as Horney (1950) might put it. They oscillate perpetually, first finding one course of action unappealing, then another, then a third, and back again. To give in to others is to be drained of all hope of independence, but to withdraw is to be isolated.

Petulant borderlines have always resented their dependence on others, and hate those to whom they have turned to plead for love and esteem. In contrast to other borderline subtypes, petulants are not likely to have had even a small measure of consistency in the support they received from others; most have never had their needs satisfied on a regular basis and have never felt secure in their relationships. Petulant borderlines openly register their disappointments, are stubborn and recalcitrant, and vent anger only to recant and feel guilty and contrite. They are erratic and continue to vacillate between apologetic submission, on the one hand, and stubborn resistance and contrariness, on the other.

Unable to get hold of themselves and unable to find a comfortable niche with others, petulant borderlines may become increasingly testy, bitter, and discontent. Resigned to their fate and despairing of hope, they oscillate between two pathological extremes of behavior. For long periods, they may express feelings of worthlessness and futility, become highly agitated or deeply depressed, develop delusions of guilt, and be severely self-condemnatory and perhaps self-destructive. At other times, their habitual negativism may cross the line of reason, break out of control and drive them into maniacal rages in which they distort reality, make excessive demands of others and viciously attack those who have trapped them and forced them into intolerable conflicts. However, following these wild outbursts, these borderlines usually turn their hostility inward, are remorseful, plead forgiveness and promise "to behave" and "make up" for their unpleasant and miserable past. One need not be too astute to recognize that these "resolutions" will be short lived.

The Self-Destructive Borderline

As with other borderline subtypes, the *self-destructive borderline* vacillates perpetually, first finding one course of action unappealing, then another, then a third, and back again. To give in to others is to lose hope of independence, but to withdraw is to be isolated. They have always resented their dependence on others and often hate those to whom they have turned to seek security, love, and esteem. As with other borderline subtypes, they are indecisive and oscillate between apologetic submission, on the one hand, and stubborn resistance and contrariness on the other. In a manner similar to the *petulant borderline,* self-destructive subtypes are unable to "get hold of themselves" and unable to find a comfortable niche with others. However, in contrast to the petulant type, self-destructive borderlines *do not* become increasingly testy and bitter over time. Although expressing their discontent in an erratic and changeable manner, they become more inward turning and most typically vent their anger in an intropunitive way. Many have a long history of depressive or masochistic traits, and these features may now interpenetrate the borderline's defective psychic structure.

In the past, the self-destructive borderline's surface appearance may have presented a veneer of sociability and conformity. Beneath this superficial front, however, was a fear of genuine autonomy and a deeply conflictual submission to the expectations of others. This social propriety cloaked deep and increasingly intense, but suppressed antagonisms. To control these oppositional tendencies, there was a struggle to maintain a self-restraint and a self-sacrificial affability. Many evinced a longstanding pattern of being deferential and ingratiating with superiors, going out of the way to impress them with their adherence to their expectations and their serious-mindedness.

Failures to evoke needed emotional support and approval are likely to have led to periods of depression and chronic anxiety. They may have become high-strung and moody, straining to express attitudes contrary to their inner feelings of tension, anger, and dejection. To avoid these discomforts, they may have become overly sensitive to the moods and expectations of others. Although viewing themselves as self-sacrificial and submissive, the extreme other-directedness utilized in the service of achieving approval has resulted in an increasingly unstable lifestyle. Whereas in earlier years, these future borderlines successfully learned to be alert to signs of potential hostility and rejection, their success rate has diminished appreciably. In the past, they paid attention to the signals that others transmit and, thereby, usually avoided disapproval. The pattern of adapting their behaviors to comply with the desires of others had been central to their lifestyles. Not only has this preoccupation become less and less successful over time, but it has resulted in a growing sense of personal impotence and social dependency.

Self-destructive borderlines have sought to deny an awareness of their inner deficiencies because to do so would point up the fraudulence that exists between the overt impressions they sought to create and their internally felt sterility and emotional poverty. This tendency to seal off and deny the elements of their inner life further intensifies their dependence on others, a dependency that has become increasingly insecure. As noted, deep resentments toward those to whom they have sacrificed themselves begin to emerge. These antagonisms periodically break through their surface constraints, erupting in outbursts of anger and resentment, followed by sorrowful expressions of guilt and contrition. These vacillations between periods of submissive compliance and depressive negativism further compound their discomforts.

Moreover, public displays of inconsistency and impulse expression contrast markedly with these borderline's self-images. There are bitter complaints about being treated unfairly, of expecting to be disillusioned and disapproved by others, and of no longer being appreciated for their diligence, submissiveness, and self-sacrifice. With the persistence of these ambivalent feelings, self-destructive borderlines often begin to suffer somatic discomforts, voicing growing distress about a wide range of physical symptoms. Increasingly upset, labile in mood and impulse, these self-destructive borderline types turn their anger inward, seeking to maintain their earlier image of propriety and responsibility. Anger becomes intropunitive rather than extrapunitive. They rarely express their deep antagonisms and resentments. More and more, we begin to see a depressive, self-abnegating tone to their verbal and emotional expressions. Although abrupt outbreaks of contrary feelings occasionally emerge, for the most part we observe an increasingly self-destructive and self-depreciating pattern of behaviors and attitudes. The possibilities of suicide are now almost always present.

COMORBID DISORDERS AND SYNDROMES

This section outlines several of the major Axis I clinical syndromes and Axis II disorders that are associated with the personality under review. Special attention was given in a previous section to the several subtypes of the borderline pattern. In this section, we will briefly discuss the many covariations that are found with this personality disorder. Points useful in the differential diagnosis of the borderline pattern will be briefly discussed shortly thereafter.

Axis II Comorbidities

Because the borderline (BDL) personality pattern is so varied in its symptomatology, there is a high probability that its features will be comorbid with a wide range of other personality disorders. Furthermore, the borderline has been conceived as a more advanced or structurally-defective level of pathology that interpenetrates several of the less severe personality styles. On both accounts, therefore, its protean pattern of symptomatology and its dysfunctional level of pathology, we find that the borderline disorder overlaps considerably with numerous other personality disorders. These comorbidities are illustrated clearly in Figure 18.4.

As can be seen in the figure, the borderline overlaps to a considerable extent with the negativistic (NEG) and masochistic (MAS) types. To a lesser degree, and reflecting the more impulsive

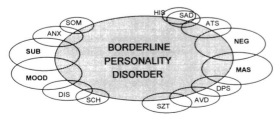

Figure 18.4 Comorbidity between borderline personality disorder and other DSM Axis I and Axis II disorders.

and hostile features of certain borderlines, we see conjunctions with the antisocial (ATS), sadistic (SAD), and histrionic (HIS) disorders. Signifying the more introversive and intropunitive characteristics of certain borderline disorders is their tendency to be associated with the depressive (DPS), the avoidant (AVD), and the schizotypal (SZT) personality disorders, the latter overlap also reflecting their common level of structural defect.

Axis I Comorbidities

As has been described throughout the chapter, one of the distinguishing features of borderline personalities is the wide variety of covariant symptoms they exhibit over time. The affective instability and diminished controls that characterize the pattern result in the periodic emergence of a number of different Axis I disorders. Only the more common of these are noted here.

Anxiety Syndromes (ANX). Brief eruptions of uncontrollable emotion occur in borderline patients, who often experience states of *generalized anxiety.* For varied reasons, traceable to particular vulnerabilities or coping inadequacies, these patients fear the imminence of an impending disaster or feel that they are being overwhelmed or will disintegrate from the press of forces that surge within them. These anxieties may follow a period of mounting stress in which a series of objectively trivial events cumulate to the point of being experienced as devastating and crushing. At other times, it is when the patients' unconscious impulses have been activated and break through their controls that we see this dramatic upsurge and emotional discharge. As the more acute phases of these attacks approach their culmination, the patient's breathing quickens, the heart races, and the patient perspires profusely and feels faint, numb, nauseous, chilly, and weak. After a few minutes (or at most one or two hours), the diffuse sense of fear, with its concomitant physical symptoms, begins to subside, and the patient returns to a more typical level of composure. There are other, more intense periods when a sweeping disorganization and overwhelming *panic disorder* take hold. This borderline's controls have completely disintegrated and the patient is carried by a rush of irrational impulses and bizarre thoughts that often culminate in a wild spree of chaotic behavior, violent outbursts, terrifying hallucinations, suicidal acts, and so on. These extreme behaviors may be justly diagnosed as *brief psychotic disorder,* a category listed under the schizophrenia classification. In either case, we see transitory states of both intense anxiety and ego decompensation that terminate after a few hours, or at most no more than one or two days, following which the patient regains his or her normal equilibrium. Should these eruptions linger for weeks or recur frequently, with bizarre behaviors and terrifying anxieties persisting, it would be more correct to categorize the impairment as a specific psychotic disorder.

Somafotorm Syndromes (SOM). These have as their primary goal the blocking from awareness of the true source of the borderline's anxiety. Despite the price these patients must pay in diminished bodily functioning, they remain relatively free of tension by accepting their disability. The "choice" of the symptom and the symbolic meaning it expresses reflect the particular character of an individual's underlying difficulties and the secondary gains he or she wishes to achieve. Both the problems and the gains that borderlines seek stem from their basic vulnerabilities and habitual coping style. This interplay can be illustrated with three brief examples: One borderline patient, whose pattern of life has been guided by the fear of social rebuke, may develop an arm paralysis to control the impulse to strike someone whom he hates; another borderline may suddenly become mute for fear of voicing intense anger and resentment; a third patient may lose her hearing as a way of tuning out ridiculing voices, both real and imagined. Somatoform symptoms rarely are the end product of a single cause or coping function. Overdetermined, they reflect a compromise solution that blends several emotions and coping aims. Thus, a paralyzed arm may not only control an angry impulse but also may attract social sympathy, as well as discharge the patient's self-punitive and guilt feelings.

Dissociative Syndromes (DIS). Borderline personalities are likely to vent brief, but highly charged, angry outbursts during *psychogenic fugue* states. Repressed resentments occasionally take this form and erupt into the open when these patients have felt trapped and confused or betrayed. Moreover, it is not unusual for borderlines to brutalize themselves, as well as others, during these fugues. They may tear their clothes, smash their fists, and lacerate their bodies, thereby suffering more themselves than do their presumed assailants. Most frequently, these violent discharges

are followed by a return to their former state. In some cases, however, borderlines may disintegrate into one or another of the more prolonged psychotic disorders. Though strange and fearsome, fugues do not come as totally unexpected to friends and family members of borderlines because the symptoms of this disorder are but extremes of their long-term pattern of impulsiveness, behavioral unpredictability, and self-damaging acts.

Mood Syndromes (MOOD). Overt and direct expressions of hostility tend to be exhibited only impulsively by borderlines because they fear these actions will lead others to reject them. A major form of anger control is to turn feelings of resentment inward into hypochondriacal disorders and mild depressive episodes. Not only may they overplay their helplessness and futile state, but the borderline's "sorrowful plight" may create guilt in others and cause them no end of discomfort as they try to meet the borderline's "justified" need for attention and care. Of course, devious coping maneuvers such as these often prove fruitless and may evoke exasperation and rebuke from others. Should such a course prevail, borderlines may turn their anger on themselves even more intensely. Protestations of guilt and self-reproval come to the fore as they voice a flood of self-deprecatory comments about their own personal shortcomings, the inordinate and despicable demands they have made of others, their history of irresponsibility, unworthiness, evil actions, and so on. Self-derision and thinly veiled suicidal threats not only discharge borderlines' anger but manage to get others to forgive them and offer assurances of their devotion and compassion.

As evident from the preceding, borderlines succumb frequently to *major depressions.* In the more retarded form of depression, borderlines gain some measure of control over their inner conflicts and hostile impulses. Referred to earlier, they do this by turning their angry feelings inward and taking out their hatred on themselves. Guilt and self-disparagement are voiced for their failures, impulsive acts, contemptuous feelings, and evil thoughts. Feelings of emptiness, boredom, and "deadness" also are frequently reported. In the more self-punitive depressions, borderlines manage to cloak their contrary impulses by seeking redemption and asking absolution for their past behaviors and forbidden inclinations. Not infrequently, this sadness and melancholy solicit support and nurture from others. As in other symptom disorders, this is a subtle and indirect means of venting hidden resentment and anger. Helplessness and self-destructive acts make others feel guilty and burden them with extra responsibilities and woes.

The *mood* disorder features of the borderline are rather mixed and erratic, varying in quality and focus according to the patient's special vulnerabilities. It is essentially a composite of depression and hostility, although not as extreme as either, when one of these is the predominant affect. Quite often, we see an incessant despair and suffering, an agitated pacing, a wringing of hands, and an apprehensiveness and tension that are unrelieved by comforting reassurances. The primary components at these times are hostile depressive complaints and a demanding and querulous irritability. These patients may bemoan their sorry state and their desperate need for others to attend to their manifold physical ailments, pains, and incapacities. In other borderlines, the depressive picture is colored less by critical and demanding attitudes, and more by self-blame and guilt. In others still, we see anxious self-doubting, expressions of self-hate, a preoccupation with impending disasters, suicidal thoughts, feelings of unworthiness, and delusions of shame and sin. Borderlines are especially prone, however, to agitated depressions. These disorders are an extension of their personality style—unstable relationships and feelings, self-destructiveness, identity confusion, complaints, irritability, and grumbling discontent, usually interwoven with expressions of guilt and self-condemnation. Their habitual style of acting out their conflicts and ambivalent feelings becomes more pronounced at these times and results in vacillations between bitterness and resentment, on the one hand, and intropunitive self-deprecation, on the other.

Some borderlines display periods of *bipolar disorder* similar to *schizoaffective* states, displaying a scattering of ideas and emotions, and a jumble of disconnected thoughts and aimless behaviors. In some cases, there may be an exuberance—a zestful energy and jovial mood—that is lacking among true schizophrenic types. Although the ideas and hyperactivity of these borderlines tend to be connected only loosely to reality, they have an intelligible logic to them and appear consonant with the predominant mood. In other cases, behaviors and ideas are fragmented, vague, disjointed, and bizarre. Here, the borderlines' moods are varied and changeable, inconsistent with their thoughts and actions, and difficult to grasp and relate to, let alone empathize with. Albeit briefly,

some borderlines successfully infect others for short periods with their conviviality and buoyant optimism. They may become extremely clever and witty, rattling off puns and rhymes, and playing cute and devilish. This humor and mischievousness rapidly drains others, who quickly tire of the incessant and increasingly irrational quality of the borderlines' forced sociability. In addition to their frenetic excitement and reckless race from one topic to another, they may display an annoying pomposity and self-expansiveness as well. Boastfulness becomes extremely trying and exasperating, often destroying what patience and goodwill these patients previously evoked from others.

Schizophrenic Syndromes (SCH). Without external support and lacking a core of inner competence, borderlines may disintegrate into a *schizoaffective* disorder. However, and in line with most patients exhibiting this disorder, we often see beneath their confusion and bizarre acts a need for affection and emotional support. Their regressive eating and soiling, for example, may reflect a search for nurturant care and attention. Even their stereotyped grimacing may signify their pathetic effort to attract the goodwill and approval of those on whom they now wish to depend.

Substance Use Syndromes (SUB). There is a strong association in contemporary society between borderline personality characteristics and heavy involvements in substance abuse. The association does not appear to be an intrinsic element of these two disorders, but appears to signify the borderline's desire to experience varied forms of reality and an effort to search for an identity that may give structure to divergent impulses and confusions. Hence, borderlines are inclined to be abusers of many different substances, including alcohol, cocaine, speed, and crack.

DIFFERENTIAL DIAGNOSES

Borderlines typically manifest so many and so wide-ranging a group of associated disorders that differential diagnosis becomes an academic matter of minor clinical significance. This is true of both covariant Axis I symptoms and Axis II personality disorders. The major issue that deserves a modicum of attention relates to the distinction between the psychotic Axis I *mood disorders* and various borderline personality patterns, a distinction often difficult to make on the basis of overt clinical features alone. The principal difference between them lies in the developmental history of the impairment; psychotic mood disorders usually have a rapid onset. Although those disposed to severe affective disorders have evidenced prior social difficulties and competency deficits, most have managed to maintain their psychic equilibrium for extended periods. In contrast, borderline personalities show a consistently lower level of functioning. Another distinction between the Axis I mood disorders and the borderline patterns is the role of external precipitants. The borderline patient's disturbance appears to reflect the operation of internal and ingrained defects in personality, whereas in the psychotic symptom disorders there is evidence that the current maladaptive behavior is, in part at least, a product of external or environmental stress. Further, as these stresses are reduced, disordered patients quickly regain their coping power and former level of functioning. This rapid return to equilibrium is not evident among borderline personalities. Disorders, therefore, are transitory, of relative short duration, in contrast to the more permanent and disturbed lifestyle of the borderline personality.

This brings us to another distinction between these severe psychic states. Axis I patients feel their symptoms to be discordant and therefore exert some, albeit futile, efforts to fight them off. The emotions they experience may be spoken of as *ego-dystonic,* that is, they are alien, strange, and unwanted. In contrast, borderlines tend to become indifferent or accepting of their pathological behaviors. Their actions and moods are taken for granted, are *ego-syntonic,* that is, they seem to be an inevitable or natural part of their lives.

The relative comfort with which bizarre traits are experienced in borderline patients reflects in large measure the insidious manner in which these traits developed. They are integrated bit by bit into the very fabric of the patient's personality makeup. In contrast, Axis I *psychotic disorders* often appear relatively abruptly, disrupting the patient's accustomed mode of functioning. In this respect, Axis I symptoms often stand out as isolated and dramatic deviations from a more typical style of behavior: They erupt, so to speak, as bizarre accentuations or caricatures of the person's more prosaic style.

Despite the points of distinction noted, the line between Axis I mood disorders and the Axis II borderline personality is often blurred. Diagnostic complications are compounded further in these cases because episodes of symptom disorder may gradually blend into a more permanent borderline pattern. For a variety of reasons—persistent stress, the comforts of hospitalization, and so on—patients often get caught in the web surrounding their disorder and fail to pull out of what may otherwise have been a transitory episode.

Turning to discriminations among Axis II disorders, difficulties in separating borderline from *schizotypal* personalities will occur because these patterns occasionally blend, especially when the borderline decompensates further. Nevertheless, the key distinction lies in the features that differentiate schizophreniclike and mood-type symptoms. The diagnostic criteria spelled out in the DSM-IV represent the key differentiations well. Thought and perceptual pathologies are primary in the socially isolated schizotypal, whereas mood instability and ambivalence typify the interpersonally connected borderline. Where psychotic like symptoms occur among borderlines, they are considerably more transient and reactive to external events than is found in the schizotypal personality.

Distinctions with the *histrionic* personality disorder are problematic as well. Both borderlines and histrionics give evidence of labile emotions associated with interpersonal manipulations and attention-seeking. However, borderlines are also noted by their angry disruptions in relationships with others and by their repetitive feelings of emptiness and loneliness.

Similarly, borderlines show some features in common with the *paranoid* personality in that both reflect severe structural defects. Although the paranoid shares the same level of severity as the borderline, there is a tendency toward rigidity and consistency in behavior that is lacking in the borderline, who also demonstrates a self-destructiveness and sense of aloneness not seen among paranoids.

The similarity between the *antisocial* personality and the borderline, both of whom are manipulative in their actions, can be differentiated by the fact that antisocials seek to gain profit and power, whereas the borderline manifests similar actions to discharge emotion and self-expression, as well as to evoke the attention and care of others.

Similar diagnostic difficulties may be seen between the borderline and the *dependent* in that both are driven in part by fears of abandonment. However, dependents are led to engage in submissive and appeasing behaviors, seeking desperately to gain attention and care, whereas the borderline reacts to abandonment fears with demands, impulsive actions, and interpersonal rage, further alienating his or her relationship with the desired supportive figure.

ASSESSING THE BORDERLINE: A CASE STUDY

This section will include a brief review of response patterns on the Rorschach, TAT, and MMPI. Following this survey, a case history of a borderline personality will be presented, along with an MCMI-III profile and interpretive comments.

The Rorschach picture will reflect the current emotional state of the patient. Some borderlines provide a picture that suggests the predominance of depressive features; under these circumstances, there may be a high proportion of monochromatic responses (e.g., gray and dark colors). Similarly, the content will have a quality of sadness and forlornness on the part of the figures perceived. Most location scores during this period will be of the *D* and *d* character. On the other hand, the Rorschach may portray a more resentful and hostile quality if the patient is going through a phase of acting-out behaviors. Under these circumstances, color responses may predominate, most notably *CF* and *C,* as well as a high number of shading responses, especially those signifying rough surfaces (e.g., stormy seas). The content at these periods will likely signify irritability and aggressive behavior. Of particular interest are sequences between cards that shift back and forth from depressive to aggressive features, as noted in the preceding.

The TAT should be quite illuminating given the propensity of these personalities to be quite open about their emotions and moods. The content of their stories is likely to directly represent their current interpersonal and intrapsychic difficulties. For example, fractious relationships between the patient and spouse or parents may be described relatively explicitly. Personal identifications may be readily observed, with the current emotional state and attitudes presented in a straightforward manner. Given a careful selection of appropriate cards, the TAT should provide useful assessment data.

The MMPI will likewise reflect the current state of the borderline under study. Some of these patients give evidence of elevations on Scales 2, 7, and 8; these are likely to occur with those in whom the depressive and anxious components are currently prominent. Other borderlines may show high scores on Scales 3 and 4, perhaps with a secondary elevation in Scale 6; patterns high on these scales

usually reflect a current state in which resentment and anger are prominent. Should a manic state be present, we would expect an elevation on Scale 9 and a corresponding lowering on Scale 2. The inclusion of a high score on Scale 8 in the picture suggests a diminished level of psychic structure; the higher Scale 8 is located in the configuration, the more severe the likely degree of pathology.

CASE 18.1

Timothy D., Age 47, Married

Tim has shown a lifelong development typical of a masochistic borderline. He claimed that he was never fully appreciated by anyone, especially his mother, wife, and employers.

Tim was the middle child of a family of modest means. His father was a traveling salesman who brought in a barely sufficient income to support the family; his mother was primarily a housewife who occasionally worked to supplement the family income. The second son of three children, Tim was repetitively compared unfavorably to his older brother, an excellent student who became a lawyer and has remained in the community as one of its most successful and respected citizens. By contrast, Tim was an average student, although his teachers felt that he could do much better than he did. Tim was referred to within the family as a "no-gooder," meaning that he never met his mother's expectations of him. She would constantly berate him, tell him he wasn't worth a "plugged-nickel" and should have been abandoned when the family saw how "lousy a kid" he was.

Tim's employment history has been rather erratic, with few jobs lasting more than two or three years, usually ending when Tim became angry or annoyed with his supervisor. The pattern he established with his mother has been extended into his relationship with his wife, a woman whose feelings toward Tim appear to have changed over the years. At present, she views Tim as a troubled man who "can't seem to get his life put together." At times, Tim becomes "very despondent," and then he gets "angry or foolish," "ranting and raving at everybody and everything." Presently, Tim has been hospitalized for treatment of his depression.

Desirous of seeking affection and approval from others, yet unsure of their feelings toward him, smothered by deep resentments, yet fearful of the consequences of assertion and anger, Tim would often be in a state of turmoil, in an unresolvable conflict that precluded finding a single and stable course of action. For short periods, he would be acquiescent and ingratiating; but as soon as he felt unsuccessful, unloved, and deserted, he would burst into a rage. When he momentarily felt confident and successful again, he would become euphoric and was "up in the clouds," making grandiose plans for the future; with his high hopes dashed shortly thereafter, he again became overtly hostile; then, protectively, he would turn his resentments inward and feel abject, worthless, and guilty; to counter the oppressiveness of these feelings, he would divert his thoughts from himself, seek to buoy his spirits, run frenetically here and there, and speak hurriedly and without pause, changing excitedly from one topic to another. The denouement would follow shortly again.

The material that follows includes an illustrative MCMI-III profile (Figure 18.5), with interpretive suggestions of the preceding borderline personality disorder.

INTERPRETIVE SUMMARY

There is reason to believe that at least a moderate level of pathology characterizes the overall personality organization of this man. Defective psychic structures suggest a failure to develop adequate internal cohesion and a less than satisfactory hierarchy of coping strategies. This man's foundation for effective intrapsychic regulation and socially acceptable interpersonal conduct appears deficient or incompetent. He is subjected to the flux of his own enigmatic attitudes and contradictory behavior, and his sense of psychic coherence is often precarious. He has probably had a checkered history of disappointments in his personal and family relationships. Deficits in his social attainments may also be notable as well as a tendency to precipitate self-defeating vicious circles. Earlier aspirations may have resulted in frustrating setbacks and efforts to achieve a consistent niche in life may have failed. Although he is usually able to function on a satisfactory basis, he may experience periods of marked emotional, cognitive, or behavioral dysfunction.

The MCMI-III profile of this man is suggestive of marked dependency needs, anxious seeking of reassurance from others, and his melancholic fear of separation from those who provide support. Dependency strivings push him to be overly compliant, to be self-sacrificing, to downplay his personal strengths and attributes, and to place himself in inferior or demeaning positions. Significant relationships appear to have become increasingly insecure and unreliable. This has resulted in increased moodiness, prolonged periods of futility and dejection, episodes of obstructive anger, and a seeking of situations in which he may act out as a martyr.

He is mostly seen as submissive and cooperative. At other times, he is thought of as alternately petulant, self-debasing, and pessimistic. He may vacillate between being socially agreeable, sullen, aggrieved, despondent, obstructive, and contrite. He may often complain of being treated unfairly, yet he also may undermine himself and appear to court blame and criticism, behavior that keeps others on edge, never knowing if he will react in an apologetic, agreeable, or sulky manner. He may often undo the efforts of others to be helpful, frequently provoking rejection and then feeling hurt. Although struggling to be obliging and submissive, he may anticipate disillusioning relationships and often creates the expected disappointment by testing the behavior of others and questioning the genuineness of their interest and support. Self-defeating habits and an attitude that he deserves to suffer may exasperate and eventually alienate those on whom he depends. When threatened by separation and disapproval, he may express guilt and self-condemnation in the hope of regaining support, reassurance, and sympathy.

This man may exhibit helplessness as well as experience anxious periods and prolonged depressive moods. Fearing that others may grow weary of his plaintive and aggrieved behavior, he may have begun to alternate between voicing self-deprecation and remorse and being petulant and bitter. A struggle between being dependently acquiescent and inducing guilt in others over what he sees as their abuse and lack of interest may now intrude into most relationships. His seeming inability to control his sorrowful state and his feelings of being treated unjustly and being misunderstood may contribute to a persistent attitude of discontent and affective dysthymia.

The self-demeaning comments and feelings of inferiority that mark this man's major depression are part of his overall and enduring characterological structure, a set of chronic self-defeating attitudes and depressive emotions that are intrinsic to his psychological makeup. Feelings of emptiness and loneliness and recurrent thoughts of death and suicide are accompanied by expressions of low self-esteem, preoccupations with failures and physical unattractiveness, and assertions of guilt and unworthiness. Although he complains about

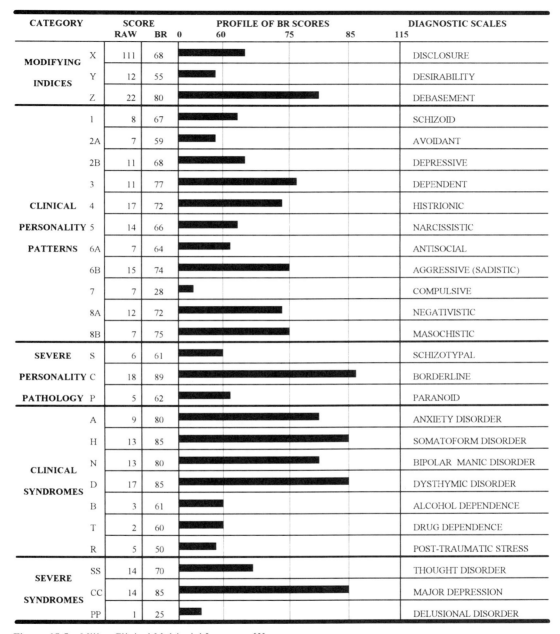

CATEGORY		SCORE		PROFILE OF BR SCORES					DIAGNOSTIC SCALES
		RAW	BR	0	60	75	85	115	
MODIFYING INDICES	X	111	68						DISCLOSURE
	Y	12	55						DESIRABILITY
	Z	22	80						DEBASEMENT
CLINICAL PERSONALITY PATTERNS	1	8	67						SCHIZOID
	2A	7	59						AVOIDANT
	2B	11	68						DEPRESSIVE
	3	11	77						DEPENDENT
	4	17	72						HISTRIONIC
	5	14	66						NARCISSISTIC
	6A	7	64						ANTISOCIAL
	6B	15	74						AGGRESSIVE (SADISTIC)
	7	7	28						COMPULSIVE
	8A	12	72						NEGATIVISTIC
	8B	7	75						MASOCHISTIC
SEVERE PERSONALITY PATHOLOGY	S	6	61						SCHIZOTYPAL
	C	18	89						BORDERLINE
	P	5	62						PARANOID
CLINICAL SYNDROMES	A	9	80						ANXIETY DISORDER
	H	13	85						SOMATOFORM DISORDER
	N	13	80						BIPOLAR MANIC DISORDER
	D	17	85						DYSTHYMIC DISORDER
	B	3	61						ALCOHOL DEPENDENCE
	T	2	60						DRUG DEPENDENCE
	R	5	50						POST-TRAUMATIC STRESS
SEVERE SYNDROMES	SS	14	70						THOUGHT DISORDER
	CC	14	85						MAJOR DEPRESSION
	PP	1	25						DELUSIONAL DISORDER

Figure 18.5   Millon Clinical Multiaxial Inventory-III.

being aggrieved and mistreated, he is likely to assert that he deserves anguish and abuse. Such self-debasement is consonant with his self-image, as is his tolerance and perpetuation of relationships that foster and aggravate his misery.

Feeling anxious and aggrieved, this moody and ambivalent man also appears to be preoccupied with physical fears and complaints that are indicative of a somatoform disorder (e.g., gastrointestinal discomfort, pain). His low self-esteem and dread of reproval and rejection prevent him from directly or consistently venting his discontent and resentment. As a consequence, his emotions remain largely bottled up, precluding his ability to relax or to give his bodily functions a chance to improve. Beyond the detrimental effects of unrelieved physical tension, his symptoms may represent an assault against his body. Psychodynamically, he may be treating his body as an object of repudiation, a symbol of his psychic self, which he views as defective and undesirable.

This man may be expressing the symptom cluster of a mild manic episode. Although brief spells of euphoric excitement may be understandable in this man, such behavior is not characteristic of his personality pattern, In fact, he may appear composed, perhaps even uptight, at the motoric level; at the same time, his speech may be rushed and his thinking accelerated. Physical hyperactivity also may be exhibited at times (e.g., restless pursuit of multiple activities). Inconsistent with his typically restrained and hesitant behavioral style, hypomanic periods signify a marked reversal, a posture that he may adopt briefly as a means of nullifying, if not countermanding, the upsurge of painful thoughts and feelings that he cannot otherwise deny or neutralize.

PATHOGENIC DEVELOPMENTAL BACKGROUND

The developmental history of the borderline personality is reviewed here by subdividing the presentation into several of the styles the authors believe are disposed to deteriorate into the disorder. This review should help clarify the varied pictures that are seen among patients diagnosed as borderline. With exceptions relevant to the more defective-borderline stage, these hypotheses frequently summarize material presented in earlier chapters.

As frequently noted, a continuum exists between what we have termed the mild and moderately severe pathological personality patterns. This gradient refers not only to severity of symptoms but also to similarities in developmental history where the major distinction is one of emphasis and configuration.

HYPOTHESIZED BIOGENIC FACTORS

Constitutional dispositions to the borderline pattern differ somewhat depending on the variant of the disorder under review.

1. Among those inclined to be of the *discouraged* and *self-destructive* borderline variety, we are likely to find families with disproportionately numerous bland, sweet, and unenergetic relatives. As infants many display both melancholic and threctic reaction patterns; the reticence and gentle sadness of these temperamental dispositions frequently evoke parental warmth and overprotection. Many of the patients possess either ectomorphic or endomorphic builds, resulting in deficits in competitive abilities, and few positive reinforcements for assertiveness. Dysfunctions and imbalances in the reticular, limbic and adrenal systems may be hypothesized; specifically, the combination of low activation and high fear reactions may elicit dependency and bring forth protective and nurturant responses from others.

2. *Impulsive* and *petulant* borderlines may frequently be found in families in which many members display high autonomic reactivity. A hyperresponsive infantile pattern is not uncommon among these patients; their alertness and activity in childhood not only exposes them to considerable stimulation but evokes it from others. To account for their high sensory reactivity, one may point the presence of neurally dense and responsive limbic, reticular, and adrenal systems.

Also notable among these latter two borderline subtypes is an irregular infantile reaction pattern and an uneven course in the development of various capacities, both of which would increase the probability of inconsistent reactions from others. Low thresholds in neurological and physiochemical systems may be hypothesized to account, in part, for their hyperactivity and irritable affectivity.

CHARACTERISTIC EXPERIENTIAL HISTORY

The following brief summary of the developmental experiences of the subvariants of the defectively-structured borderline personality may be supplemented by reference to prior chapter discussions of their more basic personality styles.

Self-Destructive and Discouraged Subtypes

Those *self-destructive* and *discouraged* borderlines that are likely to be exacerbations of the more basic dependent and depressive personality styles may have been subjected to parental overprotection during the first stage of neuropsychological maturation. Many became unduly attached to a single caretaking figure with whom they developed a symbiotic dependence. This early attachment typically persisted through the second, or sensori-motor autonomy, stage, during which time the child's parents discouraged autonomy and venture-someness. By the third stage, dependent youngsters may have failed to develop a clear sense of gender-identity, other than to view themselves as hetero-sexually confused, weak, inadequate, or inept. In this history of the depressive subvariant, we may have experiences of severe personal loss, upsetting prior securities and creating a sense of hopeless-ness and futility.

The general psychogenic history of these two defectively structured borderlines differ from their mildly pathological counterparts in matters of de-gree, rather than kind (e.g., the borderline may have been more attached or been given less oppor-tunity for initiative). Borderline children are also likely to have experienced less competence in the competitive give-and-take with siblings and peers; furthermore, their efforts to attach themselves in later life to new "caretakers" may have been less rewarding, resulting in greater insecurities and, in turn, to increasingly pathological coping behaviors. These *self-destructive* and *discouraged* borderline types perpetuated their plight by abdicating self-responsibility and clinging tenaciously to others. This placed them in a most vulnerable position be-cause they were increasingly devoid of capacities for autonomy, and they found themselves viewed with exasperation by those on whom they de-pended. Failure to achieve support from others may have led either to marked self-disparagement or to frenetic efforts to solicit attention and approval. These erratic behaviors and mood swings fostered increased inner disharmony and maladaptation, re-sulting in the loss of intrapsychic control and con-sequent brief psychotic episodes.

The Impulsive Subtype

The *impulsive* subtype of the borderline is likely to have a foundation in the active-dependent or histrionic basic personality style. Many of these individuals had enriching and diverse experiences during their first years of life, leading to a pen-chant for stimulus variety and excitement and an inability to tolerate boredom and routine. Parental control by contingent and irregular reward was typical, that is, the child received periodic posi-tive reinforcements for fulfilling parentally ap-proved expectations. This resulted in feelings of competence and security *only* when others ac-knowledged and encouraged the child's perfor-mance. Furthermore, many of these youngsters were exposed to histrionic and exhibitionistic parental models; others were unusually attractive, and thereby learned to depend on favorable external comments as a basis for their feelings of adequacy. Another contributing factor may have been expo-sure to rapid changes in parental standards and so-cietal values; this often results in the development of an exteroceptive orientation, a learning to be adept in "reading" what, where, and when certain behaviors are approved. The acquisition of this radar system, geared to changing external stimuli, leads to an excessive flexibility and other-directed-ness. The skillful seductiveness of this impulsive borderline not only may foster new difficulties, but may falter as an instrumental strategy. These per-sonalities are not only shallow and capricious, but give little in return for their subtle though exces-sive demands on others; as a result, they are unable to establish enduring close relationships. Further-more, because of their exteroceptive orientation and their intrapsychic repressions, they fail to ac-quire inner resources from which they can draw sustenance. As a consequence, they are always on unsure footing, constantly on edge and never quite sure that they will secure the attention and esteem they require from others. Anxious lest they be cut adrift and left on their own, they proceed through cyclical swings of simulated euphoria in which they seek to solicit the attention they need, and periods of brooding dejection, hopelessness, and self-depreciation. When their dread of desertion reaches monumental proportions, they lose all con-trol, and are swept either into a chaotic and manic cry for help or into a deep and intransigent gloom.

The Petulant Subtype

The *petulant* variant of the defectively structured borderline comprises exacerbations primarily of the active-ambivalent or negativistic basic person-ality style. Their discontented and erratic behav-iors result from parental inconsistency; they failed to be treated in even a moderately predictable fashion, being doted on one moment and castigated the next, ignored, abused, nurtured, exploited, promised, denied and so on, with little rhyme or reason as they saw it. As a consequence, they learned to anticipate irrationality, to expect contra-dictions and to know, however painfully, that their actions will bring them rewards one time, but con-demnation the next. Their parents may also have served as models for vacillation, capriciousness, and unpredictability; moreover, schisms often ex-isted between their parents, tearing their loyalties first one way and then the other. They learned that nothing is free of conflict and that they are trapped in a bind. Yet, despite the feeling that they were mishandled and cheated, they received enough attention and affection to keep them hoping for ultimate harmony and secure dependency. These hopes rarely are fulfilled in those who deteriorate to the borderline level; external circumstances continue to be inconsistent. Furthermore, borderlines themselves create inconsistency by their own vacillations, unpredictability, unreasonableness, sullenness and revengeful nature. Because they have learned to anticipate disappointment, they often "jump the gun," alienating others before being subjected to alienation. Moreover, tensions keep churning close to the surface, leading these borderlines to act petulantly, impulsively, and precipitously. Their lack of controls results in endless wrangles with others and precludes achieving the affections borderlines so desperately seek. Dejected, angry, and pessimistic, they may periodically become violent, exploding with bitter complaints and recriminations against the world or, conversely, turn against themselves, become self-sacrificing, plead forgiveness and contrition, and reproach and derogate their self-worth.

Special Role of Childhood Abuse

In the past two decades, there have been persuasive reports suggesting a high incidence of abuse during childhood in the history of borderline patients (Herman, Perry, van der Kolk, 1989; Paris, 1994; Perry & Herman, 1993). Although sexual abuse appears the most prominent of the abusive triad, both verbal and physical abuse may play a role as well. Some investigators (Kroll, 1993) have seen an overlap between posttraumatic stress disorder and borderline personalities, noting it is not only abuse that generates the psychic discordance which can give rise to borderline processes. Other investigators suggest that borderline patients experience their parents as emotionally neglectful rather than overtly abusive (Paris, 1994).

The results of empirical studies seeking to verify the preceding hypotheses indicate that there is a mixed and complex picture in the pathogenic background of the borderline personality. For example, although childhood sexual abuse appears to be relatively common in borderline patients, not all borderlines have a history of such abuse, and many nonborderlines, as well as nonpatients, also have such histories. It is evident that a number of pathways lead to the development of borderline pathology, some of which include abuse, neglect, parental loss, and so on. The possible mechanisms

of abuse or trauma require an explication of several interacting forces, including such secondary elements as feelings of betrayal, shame, and guilt, as well as stigmatization and powerlessness.

Special Role of Societal Inconsistency

Broad and pervasive sociocultural forces may also play a significant role in the development of all of the borderline personality patterns. This is likely to be found where a society's values and practices are fluid and inconsistent, such as appears increasingly prominent in current Western societies, notably the United States. Under these circumstances, individuals are likely to evolve deficits in psychic solidity and stability, especially as it affects the processes that develop during the *intracortical-integrative* stage; it is here where the coordination and synthesis of thought and feeling must take place, the failure of which results in the psychic schisms and vacillations that typify the borderline personality structure.

An amorphous cultural state, so characteristic of our modern times, is mirrored in the interpersonal vacillations and affective instabilities that characterize the borderline personality. As noted earlier, central to our recent culture have been the increased pace of social change and the growing pervasiveness of ambiguous customs to which children are expected to subscribe. Under the cumulative impact of rapid industrialization, immigration, mobility, technology, and mass communication, there has been a steady erosion of traditional values and standards. Instead of a simple and coherent body of practices and beliefs, children find themselves confronted with constantly shifting styles and increasingly questioned norms whose durability is uncertain and precarious (Millon, 1987b).

No longer do youngsters find the certainties and absolutes that guided earlier generations. The complexity and diversity of everyday experience play havoc with simple archaic beliefs, and render them useless as instruments to deal with contemporary realities. Lacking a coherent view of life, maturing youngsters find themselves groping and bewildered, swinging from one set of principles and models to another, unable to find stability either in their relationships or in the flux of events; each of these elements is a core characteristic of the borderline disorder.

Few times in history have so many children faced the tasks of life without the aid of accepted and durable traditions. Not only does the strain of making choices among discordant standards and goals beset them at every turn, but these competing beliefs and divergent demands also prevent them from developing either internal stability or external consistency. And no less problematic in generating such disjoined psychic structures is the escalation of emotionally capricious and interpersonally discordant role models.

The fabric of traditional and organized societies not only comprises standards designed to indoctrinate and inculcate the young, but also provides "insurance," if you will, backups to compensate and repair system defects and failures. Extended families, church leaders, schoolteachers, and neighbors provide nurturance and role models by which children experiencing troubling parental relationships can find a means of support and affection, enabling them thereby to be receptive to society's established body of norms and values. Youngsters subject to any of the diffusing and divisive forces so typical in the developmental background of borderlines (Millon, 1987b), must find one or another of these culturally sanctioned sources of surrogate modeling and sustenance to give structure and direction to their emerging capacities and impulses. Without such bolstering, maturing potentials are likely to become diffuse and scattered. Without admired and stable roles to emulate, such youngsters are left to their own devices to master the complexities of their varied and changing worlds, to control the intense aggressive and sexual urges that well up within them, to channel their fantasies, and to pursue the goals to which they may aspire. Many borderlines become victims of their own growth, unable to discipline their impulses or find acceptable means for expressing their desires. Scattered and unguided, intracortically discordant, they are unable to fashion a clear or integrated sense of personal identity, a consistent direction for feelings and attitudes, a coherent purpose to their existence.

SELF-PERPETUATION PROCESSES

As in prior chapters, this section describes how aspects of the behavioral style of the personality pattern under discussion perpetuate and intensify the difficulties that characterize that personality.

It is difficult to see the utility of any of the borderline's characteristic behaviors, let alone to grasp what gains the patient may derive by vacillating among them. Clinging helplessness, resentful stubbornness, hostile outbursts, pitiable depression, and self-denigrating guilt seem notably wasteful and self-destructive. Although these genuinely felt emotions are instrumentally useful in eliciting attention and approval, releasing tensions, wreaking revenge, and avoiding permanent rejection by redeeming oneself through contrition and self-derogation, they ultimately intensify and subvert the borderline's efforts for a better life.

Despite short-term gains, these behaviors are self-defeating in the end. By their affective instability and self-deprecation, these patients avoid confronting and resolving their real interpersonal difficulties. Their coping maneuvers are a double-edged sword, relieving passing discomforts and strains, but in the long run fostering the perpetuation of faulty attitudes and strategies. It will be instructive to outline several of the dysfunctional efforts the borderline exhibits in seeking to overcome difficulties.

Countering Separation

In contrast to milder counterparts, borderlines have been less successful in fulfilling dependency needs, suffering, thereby, considerably greater separation anxieties. As a consequence, their concerns are not simply those of gaining approval and affection, but of preventing further loss; because they already are on shaky ground, their actions are directed less toward accumulating a reserve of support and esteem, than of preserving the little security they still possess.

At first, borderlines will employ characteristic strategies with even greater vigor than usual. Whichever style typifies their established personality pattern, will be applied with increased fervor in the hope of regaining footing with others. Thus, borderlines with *self-destructive* and *discouraged* styles may begin to view themselves as martyrs, dedicated and self-effacing persons who are "so good" that they are willing to sacrifice their lives for a higher or better cause. This they do, but not for the reasons they rationalize. Their goal is to insinuate themselves into the lives of others, to attach themselves to someone who will not only "use" them, but need them, and therefore not desert them. Self-sacrificing though they may appear to be, these borderlines have effectively manipulated the situation so as to assure against the separation they dread. Furthermore, by demeaning themselves, they not only assure contact with others, but often stimulate them to be gentle and considerate in return. Virtuous martyrdom, rather than being a sacrifice, is a means of exploiting the generosity and responsibility of others, a ploy of submissive devotion that strengthens attachments.

But what if the borderlines' efforts fail to counter the anxiety of separation? What occurs when exaggerations of the characteristic strategy fail to produce or strengthen the attachments they need?

Under these conditions, we often observe a brief period in which the patient renunciates the lifelong coping style. For example, discouraged borderlines, rather than being weak and submissive, may reverse their more typical behaviors, and assert themselves, becoming frivolous, demanding, or aggressive. They may employ a new and rather unusual mode of coping as a substitute method for mastering the anxiety of separation. Unable to quiet their fears, faced with situations that refuse to be solved by the habitual adaptive styles, and discouraged and annoyed at the futility of using them, they disown them, divest themselves of these deficient coping devices and supplant them with dramatically new instrumentalities. Their goal remains the same, that of denying or controlling anxiety, but they have "found" a new strategy by which to achieve it that is diametrically opposed to that used before. It is this shifting from one strategy to another that accounts in part for the variable or borderline pattern observed in these patients.

These novel efforts are not only often bizarre but typically even less effective in the long run than the patient's more established strategies. The borderline has sought to adopt attributes and behaviors that are foreign to the person's more "natural" self; unaccustomed to the feelings he or she tries to simulate and the behaviors he or she strives to portray, the individual acts in an "unreal," awkward and strained manner with others. The upshot of this reversal in strategy is a failure to achieve goals, leading to increased anxiety, frustrations, dismay, or hostility. Not only have the simulations alienated the person from his or her real feelings, but the pretensions displayed before others have left the patient vulnerable to exposure and humiliation.

Releasing Tensions

The ever-present fear of separation and the periodic failure of the borderline to achieve secure and rewarding dependency relationships cumulate an inner reservoir of anxiety, conflict, and hostility. Like a safety valve, these tensions are released either slowly and subtly or through periodic and dramatic outbursts.

Because borderlines seek to retain the good will of those on whom they depend, they try, at first, to express indirectly the inner tensions they experience. Dejection and depression are among the most common forms of such covert expression. The pleading, the anguish, and the expressed despair and resignation of borderlines serve to release their inner anxieties and to externalize and vent the fright and torment they sense within themselves.

But of even greater importance, depressive lethargy and sulking behaviors are means of expressing anger. In the self-destructive and discouraged styles, for example, depression may serve as an instrument to frustrate and retaliate against those who now seek to buoy the borderline's spirits. Angered by others' previous failures to be thoughtful and nurturant, these borderlines employ their somber depression as a vehicle to "get back" at others or to "teach them a lesson." By exaggerating their plight and by moping about helpless and exhausted, borderlines effectively avoid responsibilities, place added burdens on others, and thereby cause their families not only to care for them, but to suffer and feel guilt while doing so.

Impulsive (histrionic) borderlines vent anger in similar ways. Because their manner is generally gregarious and affable, their glum moroseness and sluggish and gloomy manner become doubly frustrating to others. By withdrawing into this dismal and sullen attitude, borderlines construct a barrier between themselves and others in which they can no longer experience the pleasures of the impulsive's dramatic and cheerful behaviors. Thus, in the form of recalcitrant depression, they gain revenge, punish, sabotage, and defeat others who have failed to appreciate them.

Petulant borderlines are equally adroit in venting their tensions and expressing their angers. Their frequent fatigue and minor somatic ailments force others not only to be attentive and kind but, by making them carry excess burdens, to suffer as well. Moreover, the dour moods and excessive complaints of these borderlines infect the atmosphere with tension and irritability, thereby upsetting the equanimity of those who have disappointed them. In the same way, this borderline's cold and stubborn silence may function as an instrument of punitive blackmail, a way of threatening others that further trouble is in the offing or a way of forcing them to make up for the inconsiderations they previously had shown.

Despite the temporary gains achieved by these indirect forms of tension and hostility discharge, they tend to be self-defeating in the long run. The gloomy, irritable, and stubborn behavior of this borderline wears people down and provokes them to exasperation and anger that, in turn, will only intensify the anxieties, conflicts and hostilities that the patient feels.

As these more subtle means of discharging negative feelings prove self-defeating, the patient's tensions and depressions mount beyond tolerable limits and the person may begin to lose control. Bizarre thoughts and psychotic behaviors may burst forth and discharge a torrential stream of irrational emotion. Discouraged and self-destructive borderlines, for example, may shriek that others despise them, are seeking to depreciate their worth and are plotting to abandon them. Inordinate demands for attention and reassurance may be made; patients may threaten to commit suicide and thereby save others the energy of destroying them slowly. Under similar circumstances, usually restrained preborderlines may burst into vitriolic attacks upon "loved ones," as deep and previously hidden bitterness and resentment surge into the open. Not unjustifiably, they accuse others of being aggressors, protesting that others are contemptuous and unjustly view the borderline as a deception, a fraud, and a failure. Utilizing the distorting process of intrapsychic projection, these patients ascribe to others the weakness and ineptness they feel within themselves; it is "they" who have fallen short and who should be punished and humiliated. With righteous indignation, the borderline rails outward, castigating, condemning, and denouncing others for their frailty and imperfections.

Redemption through Self-Derogation

The hostility of borderlines poses a serious threat to their security. To experience resentment toward others, let alone to vent it, is dangerous because it may provoke the dreaded counterhostility, rejection, and abandonment. Angry feelings and outbursts must not only be curtailed but condemned. To appease their conscience and to assure expiation, borderlines must reproach themselves for faults, purify themselves, and prove their virtue. To accomplish this goal, hostile impulses are inverted; thus, aggressive urges toward others are turned on oneself. Rather than express anger, the borderline castigates and derogates self, and suffers exaggerated feelings of guilt and worthlessness.

Discouraged and self-destructive borderlines, for example, are notably self-recriminating; they belittle themselves, demean their competence and

derogate their virtues, not only in an effort to dilute their aggressive urges, but also to assure others that they are neither worthy nor able adversaries. The self-effacement of these borderlines is an attempt, then, to control their hostile outbursts, and to stave off aggression from others. Among petulant and impulsive borderlines, where hostile urges are more profound and enduring than in discouraged and self-destructive borderlines, patients must counteract these feelings more forcefully. Furthermore, because they have displayed anger more frequently and destructively, they must work all the harder to redeem themselves. Instead of being merely self-effacing and contrite, they may turn on themselves viciously, as being despicable and hateful. Condemnatory self-accusations may reach delusional proportions in these patients; moreover, they often reject rational efforts to dissuade them of their culpability and dishonor. In some cases, the struggle to redeem oneself may lead to self-mutilation and destruction.

THERAPEUTIC INTERVENTIONS

Borderlines are notoriously difficult patients for therapists. They run through the whole gamut of emotions in therapy, and their erratic and frequently threatening behaviors stir many therapists to react negatively. Because the risk of burnout is so high, therapists should limit the number of borderline patients in their caseload, if possible. This having been said, however, it should be noted that therapy work with a borderline can prove to be a gratifying experience. Unlike working with some personalities, such as antisocials or schizotypals, with whom the therapist can hope at best only for modestly increased levels of adaptive behavior, borderline disturbances are much more amenable to personality change and reorganization. Many borderlines have a range of highly developed social skills, along with the intrinsic motivation to restrain contrary and troublesome impulses. Therapeutic gains can lead to extended periods of productive functioning and interpersonal harmony in the patient's life, and can provide the therapist with an unusual, if not satisfying, relationship as well as the opportunity to realize therapeutic goals.

Before gauging the patient's prognostic picture and recommending a remedial course of therapy, it is well to remember that borderlines, despite their common defining characteristics, are frequently more severe variants of other personality disorders, notably the negativistic, depressive, histrionic, avoidant, and compulsive. As a result, they are even less homogeneous a classification than are other personality disorder categories. Some are well-compensated; most are not. Some are bolstered by supportive families, whereas others face destructive environmental conditions. Despite symptom commonalities, these differences in the clinical picture must be attended to closely for effective remedial intervention.

STRATEGIC GOALS

Reorganizing the structure of the borderline personality is no trivial undertaking. The clinical picture represents a state of imbalance on all four of the pain-pleasure, passive-active, other-self, and thinking-feeling polarities. Not only are the personality's coping mechanisms ineffective and problem-perpetuating, but their lack of consistency lead to identity confusions as well. Personologic domain dysfunctions include the morphologic structure of the personality itself, handicapping the borderline above and beyond the difficulties presented by disturbances in the other domains. These many deviations from optimal functioning make the borderline, along with the schizotypal and paranoid personalities, one of the three more severe disorders of personality. The borderline's characteristic desire for gratifying relationships (unlike the schizotypal) and flexibility in the personality structure (unlike the paranoid), however, work to the borderline's advantage, giving these patients an edge over the other two severe variants.

Reestablishing Polarity Balances

Borderlines vacillate between being motivated by pain and pleasure, turning to others and to self for gratification, and taking an active and passive stance in regard to manipulating their environments. Although most borderline patients have fundamental tendencies toward particular orientations within the polarities, they often adopt diametrically opposed strategies when they find that their usual behavior patterns are not resulting in the desired consequences. For example, a borderline that tends toward dependency can become suddenly aggressive and independent in an effort to "bully" the partner into caretaking behavior. Fluctuation between extremes of dependency and aggression are not likely to produce desired results, however, as they tend to leave significant others confused, frightened, or worse. Additionally, such behavior on the part of borderlines leads to

repeatedly undoing and even reversing previous actions. This leaves patients with distress from failing to secure nurturing responses from others and increases feelings of emptiness and confusion from being without a clear sense of who they are.

Therapeutic interventions help patients to moderate their vacillations between extreme polarity behaviors until they are stabilized in a more adaptive balance between the active-passive, self-other, and pain-pleasure polarities. An important first step is to gently illustrate the inevitably unfavorable consequences of extreme behaviors, and to help the borderline patient learn more moderate and adaptive coping strategies. Consideration of the particular environmental context, whether deciding between relying on themselves or others or between passive and active strategies, can prove to be an invaluable skill. Ultimately, a decrease in vacillation between extremes can serve to stabilize not only the borderline's life, but his or her uncertain self-image, providing thereby a more solid grounding to prevent painful and disruptive breaks with reality.

Countering Perpetuating Tendencies

Teaching the borderline patient to overcome the tendency to engage in deeply ingrained problem-perpetuating behavioral strategies is only a first step; the therapist faces the additional challenge of overcoming the largely unnatural behaviors that borderlines desperately adopt when their more-or-less typical behaviors fail to produce desired results. The tactic of reversing their habitual attitudes and roles, whether these be clinging helplessness, resentful stubbornness, hostile outbursts, pitiable depression, or self-denigrating guilt, serves to alienate borderlines even further from their fragile sense of self and their relationships with others. In addition, most people can sense the unreal quality of these dramatic behavioral changes, and often fail to respect or respond to the borderline's needs. Even when these momentary reversals provide the patient with attention and support, the long-term effect of these forced strategies will likely wear down and exasperate others. Borderlines sense the growth of these unpleasant sentiments in others, becoming thereby more conflicted about what they should do, and leading them to be increasingly anxious about potential abandonment.

Once patients grasp the counterproductive nature of their strategies, a major therapeutic goal is to help the borderline tolerate the anxiety that causes the switching from one extreme behavior to another. These extremes represent a frantic desire to discharge anxiety. Learning to contain these feelings long enough to delay responses will provide the time to evaluate whether the perceived threat is real, and to choose a healthier response. This serves to eliminate the negative effects of failing to cope adequately with the consequent diminished self-esteem and interpersonal dislocations. A painful and disruptive break with reality thereby becomes less likely, extreme reactions more moderate, and opportunities for healthier emotional experiences more probable.

Modifying Domain Dysfunctions

The three most salient domain dysfunctions of the borderline personality are their paradoxical interpersonal conduct, split morphologic organization, and uncertain self-image. The paradoxical interpersonal conduct of borderlines is the hallmark of the disorder, the immediate source of the chaos and uncertainty that typifies their life. While their overwhelming motivation is to secure attention and nurturance, a fundamental split in the morphologic organization of this personality leads to nonintegrated emotional functioning and cognitive black-and-white thinking. The result is often inconsistent and paradoxical behaviors, such as seen in displays of anger when the prospect of separation is threatened. Although such hostile acts sometimes elicit the desired nurturance in the short term, they greatly increase the probability of abandonment over time.

Such erratic tendencies are further aggravated by the borderline personality's uncertain self-image. This tentative sense of identity creates confusion regarding what behavior is appropriate. When behavioral strategies do not yield desired results, borderlines intensify them: They will try harder, not necessarily more wisely. Ultimately, failure compels them to redeem themselves with expressions of contrition and self-punitive behaviors that seek to forestall further rejection. Unfortunately, they also negate important aspects of the self, intensify the uncertainty about their identity, and reinforce the vicious circle of personality decline.

Therapeutic interventions that aim to solidify the patient's identity can indirectly lead to decreases in the anxiety produced by the threat of abandonment, and thus can serve to undermine maladaptive behaviors at their source. A stable and solid self-image can also provide grounding and security needed for borderlines to risk exploring the validity of long-held and ingrained assumptions, to face the futility of their behavioral patterns, and to motivate patients to tolerate useful interventions that may produce temporary increases in anxiety. One consequence of helping the patient tolerate anxiety long enough to explore inner conflicts and to experiment with moderate behaviors can be to initiate the integration of the many splits within the morphologic structure of the personality. Tolerance for unpleasant reactions can also diminish the tendency to regress to earlier modes of coping and anxiety-reduction.

Improvements in the primary domain dysfunctions can be bolstered by intervention into the secondary dysfunctional domains. Focusing on altering the borderline's capricious style will help patients assess whether the anxiety-provoking environment is actually a product of their own misperceptions and misinterpretations. Life events have been perceived in contradictory ways, leading to inconsistent responses. In turn, individuals associated with the patient have also responded in conflicting ways, leaving the patient with the distressing reality of an unpredictable and seemingly irrational world. Coming to realize that the world is not structured in black-and-white categories is a large part of overcoming the tendency to overreact. If people are seen as either all good or all bad, the appropriate reaction is to either love or to hate them; if they do one imperfect thing to negate their goodness, they must by default be bad, and need to be treated as such. Extreme and categorical behavior is thus built on the foundation of extreme categorical thinking. The borderline's incompatible object representations are an example of such thinking. Examining early memories can lead to insight into antithetical emotions, contradictory needs, and readily aborted schemas about others. Spasmodic expressive acts that reflect impulsive outbursts and abrupt endogenous shifts in drive state can be stabilized also by the former interventions. Whereas the borderline's labile temperament can often be somewhat stabilized with medication, therapeutic gains in other domains help bring about stability in the structure of the personality that will be reflected in less fluctuating mood states.

TACTICAL MODALITIES

Despite changes in the borderline diagnostic conceptions and definitions over time, one aspect has remained stable: therapists have many difficulties dealing with borderline patients. Despite the near inevitability of therapist frustrations, the importance of a solid alliance between therapist and patient cannot be overestimated. More than other personality disorders, borderlines have erratic interpersonal relationships that take a great toll on their lives and that will be mirrored in their relationship with a therapist. These patients' strong positive and negative reactions, and their rapidly fluctuating attitudes toward the therapist can evoke powerful countertransference responses. The patient may have bouts with therapist idealization and devaluation, threats of legal repercussions, suicidality, self-harm, and other uncontrollable behaviors, each of which may evoke empathy, anger, frustration, fear, as well as inadequacy feelings.

Benjamin (1993a) sees this interactional pattern as deriving from the patient's long history and expectation of abandonment, and as a recent consequence of therapist burnout after prolonged but failed attempts to effect significant therapeutic changes. It is when the patient realizes that the therapist will never be able to provide enough nurturance, that desperate and extreme behaviors, such as suicidal gestures, cause the therapist to begin to withdraw. The borderline in turn accuses the therapist of not caring, and often "ends" therapy in a dangerous and dramatic way. At times, the therapist is held responsible or even threatened with lawsuits. If the patient decides to return to treatment, the therapist may have lost enthusiasm but may fear legal repercussions or charges of professional irresponsibility. The vicious circle for continued failure is now set. Another possible pattern is one in which the patient starts to get better but fears that improvements will lead to being "kicked out" of therapy. The patient will therefore preemptively regress.

In either of these troublesome sequences, the therapist may experience a blurring of personal boundaries, an invasion of privacy that leaves the clinician at a loss. Borderlines may not hesitate to intrude into the therapist's space, ask the therapist for lunch, call at home at off hours, or use abusive tactics to manipulate and "set the therapist up." The patient may plead for inappropriate intimacies and then turn the tables around and accuse the therapist of taking advantage of his or her more powerful position. These difficulties should be avoided as much as possible by making it clear at the beginning of therapy that the goal of treatment is to foster independence, and that limits must be set to aid its achievement. This does not imply that the therapist should refuse to help or provide support in a crisis, but rather that help should also support the goal of strength-building;

long hand-holding phone calls and special arrangements are replaced with a supportive but brief reminder of treatment goals, contracts, and gains in therapeutic work. In short, clear limits should be set in the first few sessions. Then the therapist should be as responsive and supportive as possible within those clear limits. A failure to be responsive will lead to accusations of abandonment and hypocrisy; overstepping agreed-on boundaries will lead to further testing of the therapist by the patient. Some potential clients may decide from the beginning that they need a therapist to provide a more nurturant position.

If the patient accepts the therapist's terms, the two can begin working on building an alliance. A good therapeutic relationship can take quite some time to develop. Much can be gained therapeutically as the borderline realizes that not all individuals are dangerous and that not all self-disclosure necessarily leads to being judged unacceptable and worthy of abandonment. Beck and Freeman (1990b) note that the patient's difficulty trusting the therapist cannot be resolved quickly and easily. Explicit acknowledgment of the patient's difficulty with trust; special care to communicate clearly, assertively, and honestly; and especially the maintenance of congruity between verbal and nonverbal cues by the therapist, can all help. The importance of a basic attempt to behave in a trustworthy manner cannot be overestimated. Although it may not be appropriate for the therapist to flood the client with information regarding his or her reactions, any strong emotions that the therapist fails to contain should be partially acknowledged, lest the patient find reason to mistrust the therapist.

Many borderlines are uncomfortable with intimacy (due to their basic mistrust of others) and can become quite anxious in therapy if their boundaries are overstepped. It is suggested by Beck and Freeman (1990b) that the therapist solicit the client's feedback regarding how to make therapy more comfortable for him or her. Many borderlines experience greater comfort with the intimacy involved in the therapeutic process if they feel that they have some control over the pace and the topics discussed in therapy.

It is very important to make it clear from the beginning of therapy that getting better will not mean that the patient will be thrown out of treatment, and that termination will be a mutual decision. Otherwise, the therapist will be faced with the threat that the patient will feel the need to regress or resist progress to get attention from the therapist. Benjamin suggests that in the event of such manipulation by the client, whether in the form of lethal attacks or seductive gestures, the appropriate response would be to be firm, yet nonattacking. The terms of the therapy and its goals should be stated clearly and in a supportive tone, giving the patient safe grounding despite habitual emotional turmoil.

Domain-Oriented Techniques

A *supportive* approach is often the best intervention strategy in the beginning phases of therapy. Therapist sympathy, reassurance, education about interpersonal dynamics, advice, limit-setting, and safeguarding of the patient's self-disclosure and secrets (Stone, 1993) make up the larger body of patient-therapist interactions within this initial approach.

Dialectic behavior therapy (Linehan, 1987, 1992) is conceptually related to several cognitive approaches in that it emphasizes a dialogue between patient and therapist that seeks through persuasion to bring the patient's worldview in line with that of the therapist. To this end, therapist self-disclosure is considered a valid and useful technique. The ultimate goal of therapy is to create a "responsible autonomy" in the patient's attitudes and behaviors; this aim is arrived at gradually by moving through a series of hierarchical steps designed to prevent suicidal and self-injurious behavior, secure a therapeutic alliance, deal with symptoms that disrupt functioning (e.g., substance abuse), counter less disruptive problems in living, and finally, contend with the patient's cognitive schemas (hopes, ambitions, beliefs) and explore healthy psychic reorganization. Linehan's outline for individual therapy includes adjunct group therapy in which behavioral interventions such as skill-training, rehearsal, and didactic analysis aim to decrease dependency and improve tolerance for negative feedback and affect.

The *interpersonal* approach outlined by Benjamin (1993a) places great emphasis on the development of a solid alliance. The next therapy objective is for the patient to recognize his or her maladaptive patterns. Dream analysis, free association, role-plays, and discussion can all help achieve this goal. Helping the borderline understand the connection between his or her present symptomatic behavior and early history can bring relief and generate motivation. Validating the patient's sense of reality about having been victimized (often refuted by family members) can also help set the patient on the path toward healing. Any guilt the borderline feels needs to be acknowledged as normal, although

his or her role in supposedly "asking for" early abuse needs to be clarified as being patently false. Once the maladaptive patterns are recognized, the therapist and patient need to work on blocking them. The therapist can point out to the borderline that a "nosedive" often follows periods when things "go well" in therapy. Plans can be created for averting or at least minimizing damaging actions. The reasons for self-destructive behavior can be uncovered by examining internal fantasies; parents are appeased, and abusers realize that they are still loved and will be good to the patient. Benjamin suggests strengthening the will to resolve old attachments by asking penetrating questions such as "Do you still love your brother (or any significant other) enough to give him this (self-destructive result)?"

Benjamin believes that borderlines will give up self-destructive behavior if they can "divorce" the "internalized abusive attachment figure." A dislike of the internalization can be fostered, or an attachment to someone else can serve to replace it. The therapist can become an "emotional cheerleader" who encourages healthy life choices and behaviors; direct attachment to the therapist as a significant other, however, should be avoided. On the other hand, if patients can permit themselves to trust the therapist enough, they can internalize the therapist's compassion for the patient as a young abused child, and help build self-protective and self-nurturing inclinations. If direct blaming of the abuser is avoided, borderlines can for the first time dare to be disloyal to the abuser by emotionally detaching from his or her internalized figure. Pushing borderlines in this direction too quickly, however, can precipitate great anxiety, self-sabotaging behavior, and withdrawal from therapy. The therapist should make it clear that the goal of therapy is for patients to make their own decisions, and know that they can stay on good terms with the abusive person(s) if needed, as long as their welfare is not jeopardized.

Family intervention is often useful when the borderline has frequent interaction with parents or other family members who are overinvolved but not supportive of the patient's individual therapy. In these cases, borderlines often feel guilty about being disloyal to the family and terminate therapy prematurely. Involving the family in helping the patient with his or her "problem" by not reinforcing dependent behavior can help tremendously in meeting treatment objectives. In families where abuse and/or incest have led to symptomatology (more common), there is often strong resistance to participation. Independent meetings with the parents may be required to emphasize that family intervention will be focused on increasing the patient's independence, and not on blaming parents or other family members.

Group approaches have some benefits that are not provided by dyadic therapy, and therefore often serve as a useful adjunct to individual intervention. A peer group is less likely than an individual therapist to be accused of being controlling or of having bad intentions when confronting maladaptive patterns. This rich interpersonal setting also provides a wealth of opportunities for these patterns to be acted out and identified. New behaviors are often actively encouraged by the group and can be practiced in this highly supportive setting.

In their book outlining *cognitive* interventions with personality disorders, Beck and Freeman (1990b) note that one of the initial setbacks in working with borderlines is that their lack of clear identity makes it difficult for them to set goals and maintain priorities from week to week. Beck and Freeman suggest that a focus on concrete behavioral goals is a useful initial therapeutic intervention for several reasons. The patient does not need to reveal deeply personal thoughts and feelings before trust can be established, and initial success can provide motivation to continue in therapy. As therapy shifts to more extensive goals, the therapist may find that the patient's concerns and goals change from week to week; discussion about the advantages of keeping focused, or about setting aside time in each session for immediate as well as long-term problems can be very helpful. The therapist should make a special effort to point to underlying commonalities among problems as they come up, attempting thereby to illustrate the presence of persistent behavioral and cognitive patterns to the patient.

It is sometimes difficult to convince borderline patients to complete homework assignments. Discussing the advantages and the disadvantages of trying out new behaviors often helps patients feel as though the therapist is not trying to control or manipulate them. Asking patients to pay attention to their thoughts at those times when they decide *not* to do their homework can help identify what may be disturbing or obstructing progress. Sometimes therapists find that they are ascribing incorrect intentions to patients, thinking that they do not want to get better. Careful consideration of the meaning of noncompliance for the patient may need to be evaluated before it can be overcome.

A main therapeutic focus of cognitive therapy with borderline clients is decreasing their dichotomous thinking. Borderlines tend to think in terms of discrete categories such as "good," "bad," "reliable," and "unreliable," rather than more realistic continuous dimensions. Beck and Freeman recommend pointing out to patients examples of their black-and-white thinking, and then asking them to consider whether it is reality-based in their experience. One example provided involves asking a client to provide a description of the salient polarities "trustworthy" and "not trustworthy." After the client defines these extremes operationally, the therapist and client examine whether people actually exhibit constant trustworthy or untrustworthy behavior, and the client realizes that while some may be more trustworthy than others, very few are always or never reliable. Examination of the patient's own behavior and motivation can help clarify that not all instances of so-called unreliable behavior are motivated by bad intentions or lack of concern for others.

Effecting a decrease in dichotomous thinking leads to a decrease in the intensity and vacillation of moods, as problem situations are not evaluated in such extreme terms. Additional methods to control nonadaptive emotional symptoms can also be taught. Many borderlines believe that if they express anger or other unpleasant emotions they will be jeopardizing their relationships. They suppress those feelings until they erupt in ways that bear negative consequences and reinforce the conviction that expressing emotions causes problems. The therapist can encourage the client to express negative feelings in moderate ways and provide feedback and consequences that help speed the accomplishment of therapeutic goals.

In helping patients learn to control impulses, it is important to first address the borderline's need not to be controlled by the therapist. Once clients understand the ways in which controlling their impulses can improve their life, they are less likely to be resistant to intervention. The therapist and client need to work on identifying the first hints of impulsive inclinations; through self-instructional training (Meichenbaum, 1977) useful steps can be taken to help patients implement new appropriate behaviors. Self-destructive impulses, particularly, need to be addressed. Once the intent and tendencies toward acting-out are understood, other means to the same ends can be developed. Hospitalization may have to be considered if the impulse to self-mutilate or suicide are strong.

All the preceding interventions should help strengthen the borderline's sense of identity, and pointing out strengths and accomplishments will serve to further this goal. Discussions about what constitutes self can also be helpful. Basic beliefs about life's inherent dangers and the borderline's helplessness can also be addressed through behavioral experiments and the development of new coping skills. Certain ideas can be confronted using contrary evidence from the patient's own life. Most borderline patients strongly believe that self-disclosure will lead to inevitable rejection. The therapeutic relationship can serve as a good example that this assumption is not universally true. Discussion of fear of rejection, and helping patients understand that a certain amount of rejection is a normal part of living, can help patients feel less singled out, and that rejection or personal slight need not be testimony to their inherent flaws.

Approaches of a *psychodynamic* character emphasize the need to monitor and control countertransference reactions. Borderline patients tend to have intense negative as well as positive reactions toward the therapist that can easily disrupt the therapeutic process. These must be properly handled. Controversy abounds regarding how strict the therapist's personal limits should be, how to handle crises appropriately, and how soon and how much confrontation is effective. Classic approaches such as free association and minimal therapist action are tolerated quite poorly by most borderline patients, owing to their poorly structured psychic boundaries. Their natural proclivity toward psychoticlike episodes may be prompted by such methods. The usual length of treatment by psychodynamic techniques appears to be needlessly time-consuming given the availability of equally effective alternatives.

Psychopharmacological medications are often prescribed to borderline personalities in light of their multiple symptom disorders. Depression is a common presenting complication, suggesting the potential value of serotonin uptake inhibitors. A study by Soloff et al. (1986) suggests that different presenting depressions warrant different classes of antidepressant medication: Irritable and hostile patients may do better when treated with monoamine oxidase inhibitors (MAOIs), whereas others may do just as well on tricyclic medication or low doses of neuroleptics. The latter appear to be most useful when depression, hostility, and anxiety are accompanied by psychoticlike symptoms such as illusions, ideas of reference, derealization, and depersonalization. Anxiety and panic may be controlled with benzodiazepines, though some borderlines become more irritable when taking these anxiolytics. As noted, the effectiveness of serotonin uptake inhibitors is promising, but unclear, with these patients as of this time.

Discretion must be exercised when prescribing any medications. For example, when evaluating the possible benefits of MAOIs for suicidal patients, it is particularly important to consider that they are lethal in overdose. Another factor therapists should keep in mind when prescribing medications for borderlines is that many report feeling worse when medications seem objectively to be fostering improvements. One possible explanation is that borderlines may feel that they will be "abandoned" by the therapist if they truly get better; another reason suggests that decreases in anxiety and/or depression may lead to disinhibited behavioral controls.

The major strategies and tactics are reviewed in Figure 18.6.

Potentiated Pairing and Catalytic Sequences

The most important first step in helping a borderline begin progress toward adaptive personality change is to establish a solid working alliance that can help alter the patient's schema about the inherent dangers of relationships. Supportive interventions are a useful way to accomplish this first goal. To bolster motivation without delving into anxiety-provoking self-exploration, the therapist can help patients to realize behavioral goals that provide them with an initial success in treatment. Severe anxiety and depression can then be

Figure 18.6   Therapeutic strategies and tactics for the prototypal borderline personality.

evaluated as candidates for psychopharmacological intervention. Behavioral interventions, in conjunction with psychopharmacological agents, may then help bring about a measure of predictability in the borderline's social relationships. At this point, the therapist may decide that a group approach would be a useful adjunct. Here, objective feedback and a supportive environment can help keep the patient from feeling attacked as more searching cognitive and emotional work begins. When the therapist feels that the patient has grasped some of the main issues, family therapy can help speed the healing process and solidify control over the patient's maladaptive and erratic patterns.

RISKS AND RESISTANCES

If borderlines find an emotionally nurturant environment and are reinforced in their need for acceptance and attachment, they can live in relative comfort and tranquillity, maintaining a reasonably secure hold on reality. However, should the attention and support that borderlines require be withdrawn, and should their strategies prove wearisome and exasperating to others, precipitating their anger and unforgiveness, then their tenuous hold on reality often disintegrates and their capacity to function withers.

Many therapists worry that somber depression and explosive hostility, which often signify acute breaks with reality, can lead to a more permanent decompensation process. Among the early signs of a growing breakdown are marked periods of discouragement and a persistent dejection. At this phase, it is especially useful to employ supportive therapy and cognitive reorientation. Efforts should be made to boost these patients' sagging morale, to encourage them to continue in their usual sphere of activities, to build their self-confidence, and to deter them from being preoccupied with their melancholy feelings. They should not be pressed

beyond their capabilities, nor told to "snap out of it," because their failure to achieve these goals will only strengthen the patients' growing conviction of their own incompetence and unworthiness. Should depression be the major symptom picture, it is advisable to prescribe any of the suitable antidepressant agents as a means of buoying the patient's flagging spirits. Should suicide become a threat, or should the patient lose control or engage in hostile outbursts, it may be advisable to arrange for brief institutionalization in the hope of obviating future needs for more serious institutional intervention.

Some therapists may overreact to a borderline patient's tendency toward psychoticlike experiences or actual breaks with reality. In order not to bias therapeutic work against the patient, it is important for the therapist to remember that brief hospitalizations should not be interpreted by the patient as a sign of being "crazy" or of outpatient therapeutic work being futile. When a therapist does feel that his or her efforts are futile or feels threatened by a patient's behavior, countertransference reactions can include a variety of problematic reactions. Therapists who realize they are experiencing such feelings need to examine them to ensure that they do not bias their interaction with the patient against the patient's best interest. It may be best for the therapist to seek consultation with a colleague if this becomes a pattern in the therapy with a particular client.

On the other hand, some patients become excessively dependent owing to the lack of responsibilities during a period of hospitalization. Therapists working with such borderline behaviors can help break this dependency by suggesting to the patient that hospitalization is not a cure, but just a "life preserver" that will keep the patient from sinking. Not conducting therapy while the patient is hospitalized can help the person view hospitalization as a temporary solution to problems, and thereby strengthen the will to return to a more functional lifestyle.

CHAPTER 19

Paranoid Personality Disorders: The Suspicious Pattern

Among the more prominent features of paranoid personalities are their mistrust of others and their desire to stay free of relationships in which they might lose the power of self-determination. They are characteristically suspicious, guarded, and hostile; tend to misread the actions of others; and respond with anger to what they frequently interpret as deception, deprecation, and betrayal. Their readiness to perceive hidden motives and deceit precipitates innumerable social difficulties, which then confirm and reinforce their expectations. Their need to distance from others, combined with their tendency to magnify minor slights, results in distortions that occasionally cross the bounds of reality.

A feature that justifies considering paranoids among the more structurally defective personalities is the inelasticity and constriction of their coping skills. The obdurate and unyielding structure of their personality contrasts markedly with the lack of cohesion and instability of the borderline's personality. Whereas borderlines are subject to a dissolution of controls and to a fluidity in their responsiveness, paranoids display such inflexible controls that they are subject to having their rigid facade shattered.

Entirely insignificant and irrelevant events are often transformed by paranoids so as to have personal reference to themselves. They may begin to impose their inner world of meanings on the outer world of reality. As Cameron once put it (1963), they create a "pseudo-community" composed of distorted people and processes. Situations and events lose their objective attributes and are interpreted in terms of subjective expectations and feelings. Unable and unwilling to follow the lead of others and accustomed to drawing power within themselves, paranoids reconstruct reality so that it suits their dictates. Faced by a world in which others shape what occurs, they construct a world in which they determine events and have power to do

as they desire. In contrast to their less structurally defective counterparts, the paranoid's need for autonomy and independence has been undermined often and seriously. These personalities counter the anxiety their experiences create by distorting objective reality and constructing in its stead a new reality in which they can affirm their personal stature and significance.

HISTORICAL ANTECEDENTS

The term *paranoia* can be traced back over 2000 years in the medical literature, preceding the writings of even Hippocrates. Translated from the Greek it means "to think beside oneself," and it was used rather freely in ancient times as a general designation for all forms of serious mental disturbance. The word disappeared from the medical lexicon in the second century and was not revived again until the 18th century. Heinroth, following the structure of Kantian psychology, utilized the term in 1818 to represent a variety of disorders. Those of the intellect were termed paranoia; disturbances of feeling were called *paranoia ecstasia*. Also proposed were the parallel concepts of *Wahnsinn* and *Verrucktheit* (the latter term is still in use as a label for paranoia in modern-day Germany). Griesinger picked up the term *Wahnsinn* in 1845 to signify pathological thought processes and applied it to cases that exhibited expansive and grandiose delusions. In 1863, Kahlbaum suggested that paranoia be the exclusive label for delusional states.

The French psychiatrist V. Magnan (1886) described a subgroup of patients, which he termed *bouffées délirantes des dégenéres,* who gave evidence of preexisting traits that disposed them to psychotic disorders. Among the paranoic group displaying these preconditions, he isolated a subset that he labeled *délire chronique*. This syndrome followed a course similar to dementia praecox, but it usually began later in life and was characterized by delusions that showed a "striking degree of systematization." Magnan considered the development of *délire chronique* to progress slowly through four stages. At first, patients exhibited a general irritability, pessimism, and hypochondriacal preoccupation; subsequently, they deteriorate to the point of making delusional interpretations of events, visualizing florid hallucinations, and, finally, succumbing to the inevitable dementia. Magnan's developmental thesis appears to have been the first formulation of the paranoid concept to have explicitly conceived from its premorbid personality history.

Following the German usage, particularly the proposals of Kahlbaum, in 1895 Kraepelin narrowed the meaning of the term *paranoia,* restricting it to highly systematized and well-contained delusions in patients who otherwise lacked signs of personality deterioration. Recognizing that paranoia, as he described it, applied to a small portion of cases, Kraepelin adopted a label first used by Guslain in the early 19th century, *paraphrenia,* to signify impairments displaying a mixture of the delusional elements of paranoia and the deterioration features of dementia praecox. Kraepelin believed that as many as 40% of patients who exhibited paranoid delusions ultimately deteriorated to dementia praecox, that the bulk of the remainder decompensated to the paraphrenic level, and that a very small proportion retained the characteristic nondeterioration of pure paranoia. In his early writings on the subject, Kraepelin appears to have conceived the systematized delusions of paranoia to be a first stage of what could turn out to be a general deterioration process. In the second stage, if it occurs at all, the patient decompensates to paraphrenia, identified by bizarre thoughts and perceptual hallucinations; in this form, Kraepelin specified that many functions of personality that are not directly associated with thought and intellect remain moderately well preserved. For example, the patient's mood is not unstable or fragmented but is consistent with his or her disordered ideas. For many patients, however, paraphrenia is a transitional second stage that eventuates in dementia praecox. At this final level, all personality functions have disintegrated. Thus, the patient's moods are both incongruous and random, and no longer consonant with the delusional content. In his early publications, Kraepelin (1896) referred to the totally deteriorated cases of paranoia by the term *dementia paranoides.* Subsequently,

he claimed "When the delusions and . . . emotions . . . may be observed with complete indifference to the natural relations of life . . . [these disorders] are more correctly to be brought under the head of dementia praecox" (p. 512).

In an earlier chapter, we took the master synthesist to task for rejecting Kahlbaum's observation that moderately well-preserved manic-depressive patterns do, on occasion, decompensate; Kraepelin did not make this error, as we see it, with the paranoid patterns. Unfortunately, however, Kraepelin was consistent in one respect; he conceived the end point in this continuum to be that of dementia praecox (schizophrenia). Thus, once again, he categorized together, in a final group, deteriorated personalities with widely divergent developmental histories. As we have said before, a classification that includes all deteriorated personalities would be valid and useful; this grouping is what we have termed the "decompensated personality patterns." But we have contended further that this larger category be subdivided in accord with the premorbid histories and coping strategies that differentiate these patients. Thus, in Chapter 20, we have proposed several categories within a *decompensated* group—decompensated schizotypals, decompensated borderlines, and also decompensated paranoids.

It is important to stress that in contrast with his view of the "circular insanities," Kraepelin asserted that delusional states not only vary along a continuum of severity—from paranoia to paraphrenia to dementia praecox—but also often progress from one stage to another. Kraepelin's use of the term paraphrenia is especially significant to our thesis because it represents his recognition that premorbid paranoid tendencies do decompensate to more structurally severe levels; however, in his aspiration to simplify matters, Kraepelin once again assumed that if a final stage of deterioration was reached, the impairment *must* be that of dementia praecox. We are inclined to return to Kraepelin's earlier thinking on this score, suggested by his use of the term dementia paranoides; here Kraepelin recognized that the paranoid trend has its own developmental end point, independent of dementia praecox.

It was not until the monumental eighth edition of his Lehrbuch (1909–1915) that Kraepelin formally addressed the premorbid character of individuals disposed to paranoid conditions. Writing about those he explicitly termed paranoid personalities, Kraepelin (1921) portrayed their characteristics as follows:

The most conspicuously common feature was the feeling of uncertainty and of distrust towards the surroundings. . . . The patient feels himself on every occasion unjustly treated, the object of hostility, interfered with, oppressed. His own people treat him badly. . . . In indefinite hints he speaks of secret connections, of the agitation of certain people. Things are not as they ought to be; everywhere he scents interested motives, embezzlement, intrigues. . . .

Such delusional ideas, which emerge sometimes on one occasion, sometimes on another, are closely accompanied by a great emotional irritability *and a* discontented, dejected *mood. The patient is difficult to get on with, is faultfinding, makes difficulties everywhere, perpetually lives at variance with his fellow-workers, on trivial occasions falls into measureless excitement, scolds, blusters and swears.*

As a rule, heightened self-consciousness can be easily demonstrated. The patients boast of their performances, consider themselves superior to their surroundings, make special claims, lay the blame for their failure solely on external hindrances.

[The paranoid] seems to me to be essentially a combination of uncertainty with excessive valuation of self, *which leads to the patient being forced into hostile opposition to the influences of the struggle for life and his seeking to withdraw himself from them by inward exaltation. Further a strong personal coloring of thought by vivid feeling-tones, activity of the power of imagination and self-confidence might be of significance. (pp. 268–271)*

As in his depiction of so many of the disorders for which he is better known, Kraepelin beautifully portrayed the essential features of the paranoid personality, a description as apt today as it was when written.

Other theorists of repute in the first decade of the century also wrote of traits they associated with the paranoid condition. Albeit briefly and tangentially, each formulated concepts similar to contemporary notions of the paranoid character. For example, K. Birnbaum (1909), best known for his progressive views of the sociopath, preceded Kraepelin in speaking of paranoids as possessing overvalued ideas that were heavily charged with emotion and dominated the individual's psychic life. Even earlier, E. Bleuler (1906) ascribed the development of paranoia to the patient's premorbid "excessive stability" of affect. He asserted

that paranoids made no more errors or misinterpretations of life events than did normal persons. The essential pathological feature is the "fixity" of their errors. They possess a resistance to change that leads to the rigidification of beliefs and ultimately, by being compounded over time, the implacable delusional system we term paranoia. However, Bleuler spoke of those with "paranoid constitution" whose false assumptions and inordinate sensitivities do not necessarily attain the form of obvious delusions. A. Meyer (1908, 1913) conceived the paranoid developmental process in a fashion similar to Bleuler. In addition to the inability of paranoids to adjust their beliefs to the facts, he noted their inclination to isolate themselves and to counter the efforts of others to correct or otherwise influence their misinterpretation of events.

MODERN FORMULATIONS

A modern nonanalytic theorist of note was Schneider (1923/1950). He characterized these traits as a specific personality type, speaking of such individuals as "fanatic psychopaths." Although disavowing the appropriateness of the label paranoid personality, his portrayal of the fanatic is very much in line with our contemporary conception of the paranoid. Schneider spoke of two variants of the fanatic psychopaths. The "combative" types were actively quarrelsome about their fallacious beliefs, complaining bitterly about injustices done to them, often seeking retribution and frequently litigious. The second variant, the "eccentrics," were quietly suspicious, carried hidden assumptions about others' motives, and were drawn to the beliefs of secretive sects. The following excerpts taken from the final edition of his personality text illustrate a number of these features:

Ideas of fanatic personalities differ from those of depressive or insecure personalities in that the ideas are held much more assertively and combatively. Where sthenic [drive energies] are less in evidence there is a tendency for the fanatic ideas to issue in schemes and programmes. If the overvalued idea relates to a personal difference or a civil dispute, every effort is concentrated on laying low the offender utterly. . . .

There are fanatics who are expansive . . . tenacious personalities who elaborate their experience in a most vigorous way and are uninhibitedly aggressive. (pp. 97–98)

A tangential note is Schneider's (1923/1950) strong stance on the separation he believed should be made between personality and pathology, nowhere stated more directly than in his discussion of how delusions are independent of the personality structure of the "fanatic" patient. His position on this controversial issue was stated as follows:

In our view delusion-formation has nothing to do with traits of personality and there are serious objections to attempts which endeavor to associate the two. Delusion cannot be explained away in terms of a particular personality, its development and inner conflicts. (1950, p. 99)

Schneider's assertions on this issue were set in clear opposition to the well-known psychoanalytic contention that clinical symptoms have distinct ontogenetic origins and character substrates. It is appropriate, therefore, that the discussion turns next to the analyst's prime exponent.

Freud first conceived paranoia in 1896 as a "neuropsychosis of defense," a formulation that laid the foundation for considering all mental disorders to result from a psychodynamic process with specific developmental roots. Not only did this early paper establish the important concept of projection, but his success in elucidating the delusional symptom as a faulty attempt at self-remediation contributed significantly toward establishing the utility of an intrapsychic approach to psychopathology.

Specifically, Freud considered the paranoid symptom to signify a series of intrapsychic transformations. First, there is a breakdown in the effectiveness of repression as a defense against unacceptable impulses. This results in the alternative use of denial, reaction formation, and projection mechanisms. The product of these more circuitous intrapsychic maneuvers gains conscious form in a delusion. Freud utilized this particular intrapsychic sequence to elucidate how paranoia derives from unsuccessfully repressed homosexual urges. In the famous case of Schreber, Freud (1911/1925) was provided with an excellent opportunity to illustrate this previously formulated model. In simple terms, Freud's logic was that Schreber's homosexual impulse for another man, in the form "I love him," was *denied*; because the urge was viewed consciously as repugnant, it was altered through *reaction-formation* to its opposite, "I do not love him, I hate him." The next step, that of *projection*, altered the attitude further: "It is not that I hate him, but

that he hates me." Finally, because his newly emergent hatred required an acceptable justification, he reverted to the more conventional mechanism of *rationalization* and concluded, "I hate him because of his hatred for me."

Freud conceived a wide range of persecutory, erotic, and jealousy delusions as essentially progressing through similar psychodynamic sequences and transformations. Thus, he hinted at the possibility that a fundamental connection might exist between sadomasochism and paranoid behaviors. In describing persons who harbor unconscious fantasies of being beaten, Freud (1919/1959) wrote that such individuals:

. . . often develop a special sensitiveness and irritability toward anyone whom they can include in the class of fathers. They are easily offended by a person of this kind, and in that way (to their own sorrow and cost) bring about the realization of the imagined situation of being beaten by the father. I should not be surprised if it were one day possible to prove that the phantasy is the basis of the delusional litigiousness of paranoia. (p. 195)

Despite the seminal role he played in formulating his model of paranoia, Freud did not construct a fully explicit basis for either the origins or the structure of a paranoid character type. It was S. Ferenczi (1919, 1952) and K. Abraham (1921/1927) who suggested that the foundation for this personality might be first established during the anal period. Picking up a theme just lightly touched on by Freud in the preceding quote, Abraham (1921/1927) wrote:

If we bear in mind the great significance of anal eroticism in the psychogenesis of paranoia . . . we can understand this . . . behavior as an anal-character formation, and therefore as a precursor of paranoia. (p. 391)

Explicating this connection more fully, Menninger (1940) wrote:

The character traits of the anal expulsive period are chiefly those of megalomania and suspiciousness. . . . The individual who constantly is extremely conceited, very ambitious, and makes unwarranted claims upon his own abilities but is inclined to attribute his failures to the jealousy of rivals is a personality determined chiefly by fixations in the anal expulsive period. Such individuals are closely related to the paranoid character, on the one hand, and to homosexual characters, on the other. . . . These character traits [derive] from the megalomania connected with early consciousness of sphincter control and from the reaction formation against the homosexuality of this period. (p. 394)

A few words concerning the contributions of E. Kretschmer and W. Sheldon should be recorded to identify yet another explanatory schema for the paranoid character. In 1918, Kretschmer wrote of a syndrome that he labeled *paranoia sensitiva;* these personalities were noted as being extraordinarily sensitive to the negative judgments of others, hence leading them to restrict their social contacts. Although formulated in this early book as a subset of paranoid disorders, the primary traits that Kretschmer ascribed to them depict the characteristics of the recently formulated avoidant personality. For example, Kretschmer noted that they were anxiety-prone, liable to feelings of inferiority and melancholy, socially shy or hesitant, and morbidly disposed to introspection. In his later writings (1925), these same features were ascribed also to patients considered close to the hyperaesthetic pole of the schizoid temperament, as discussed in Chapter 7. More consistent with present-day conceptions of the paranoid personality was Kretschmer's "expansive reaction type." This temperament inclined those who were so endowed to become sensitive, suspicious, irritable, tenacious, uninhibitedly aggressive, and, ultimately, combatively paranoid.

Sheldon (1940; Sheldon & Stevens, 1942), Kretschmer's prime disciple, proposed a temperament variant that he labeled *somatatonia*. It served as the substrate for what he termed the "paranoid component," an inclination to "fight against something" and to be antagonistic and resentful of others. Those possessing this component will be openly aggressive if they can successfully present themselves in this manner. Those who fail in these overt actions will use indirect methods of attack or, if need be, limit themselves to internal ruminations of hostility or persecution.

CONTEMPORARY PROPOSALS

Brief mention should be made of the perceptive analyses of paranoid phenomena by N. Cameron (1943, 1963). A short excerpt will illustrate the aptness and clarity of his formulation of the paranoid personality:

The paranoid personality is one that has its origin in a lack of basic trust. There is evidence that in many cases the paranoid person has received sadistic treatment during early infancy and that he has, in consequence, internalized sadistic attitudes toward himself and others. Because of his basic lack of trust in others the paranoid personality must be vigilant in order to safeguard himself against sudden deception and attack. He is exquisitely sensitive to traces of hostility, contempt, criticism or accusation. (1963, p. 645)

Shapiro (1965, 1981) has provided several significant analyses of the underlying features of the paranoid personality, stressing both their rigidity and their need for autonomy. A psychoanalyst strongly influenced by the views of early cognitive psychologists (e.g., G. Klein, P. Holzman) Shapiro has sought to bridge these two perspectives in his analysis of character disorders. Writing on features of the paranoid personality, Shapiro (1965) differentiates two types, and then outlines the cognitive distortions that they share:

Aside from the dimension of severity, there are, descriptively and quite roughly speaking, two sorts of people who fall within the category of this style: furtive, constricted, apprehensively suspicious individuals and rigidly arrogant, more aggressively suspicious, megalomanic ones. Of course . . . these are only two differentiations of a more general style. . . .

When we describe a person as "suspicious," we usually refer to certain ideas, preoccupations, or unwarranted apprehensions of his, such as a continual expectation of trickery. In other words, we usually refer primarily to what he thinks, to the contents of his mind, which are, technically speaking, projective contents. But "suspiciousness," especially when it is not merely occasional, but chronic and habitual, also describes a mode of thinking and cognition.

A suspicious person is a person who has something on his mind. He looks at the world with fixed and preoccupying expectation, and he searches repetitively, and only, for confirmation of it.

The fact is, furthermore, that their dismissal and disregard of anything that does not confirm their prior supposition is an active and intentional process. (pp. 54–57)

Kernberg (1975) includes the characteristics of the paranoid personality in describing variations of the borderline personality organization. At this lower level of functioning, Kernberg sees a notable decrease in both ego and superego activity. The dynamic processing of repression is diminished, and the central defensive operations that take hold are prominently those of splitting, denial, and projective identification. Primary process thinking becomes increasingly prominent as the conflict-free areas of the ego are restricted. In an unpublished paper (1982), Kernberg also notes the frequent comorbidity of narcissistic and paranoid personality features. Which of the two character types is seen as preeminent depends on whether the cold and suspicious features of the paranoid are more central, or the exploitiveness and enviousness of the narcissistic.

As noted earlier, Freud related paranoid tendencies to the repudiation of latent homosexual impulses that are turned around, so-to-speak, through projection, a position that has been debated and remains controversial in the psychoanalytic literature. Among others, Blum (1980, 1981), considers hostility, rather than a defense against homosexual impulses, to be the primary difficulty in paranoid personality types. As he judges it, the central driving force is the actual threats children experience to their survival during early development. Following Mahler's (1975) theory of separation-individuation, Blum notes that children prone to future paranoid inclinations experience an inability to internalize a comforting, constant mother. As a result of the "inconstant object," these children remain deeply ambivalent regarding future loved objects, feeling that they are both desperately needed and, at the same time, persecutory. There is a consequent lack of ego-integration, intense feelings of infantile omnipotence, a tendency toward separation-anxiety, and a constant fear of betrayal and loss.

An astute attempt at synthesis regarding the paranoid personality has been formulated by Akhtar (1992), who differentiates the overt from the covert features of these individuals as follows:

The individual with a paranoid personality disorder is overtly arrogant, mistrustful, and suspicious of others; is driven, industrious, and even successful in solitary professions; and is unromantic, idiosyncratically moralistic, and sharply vigilant toward the external environment. However, covertly he is frightened, timid, gullible, chronically experiencing interpersonal difficulties in the work situation, corruptible, vulnerable to erotomania and sadomasochistic perversions, and cognitively unable to grasp the totality of actual events in their proper context. (p. 167)

Stone (1993) brings together a number of features of several varieties of the paranoid disorder. In his usual insightful and descriptively articulate manner, he writes:

The grandiosity . . . may be either secret or blatant, [and reflects] the paranoid person's intense fear of dissolution of self (loss of identity) as a central dynamic . . .

The characteristic hypervigilance of paranoid persons has relevance both to their hostility and to their fear of boundary-loss. The need for a wide psychological and even geographical space between paranoid persons and those with whom they interact is a reflection of both (a) fear of hostile invasion by others (for which real distance has survival value) and (b) fear of being "unduly" influenced by others, to the point of losing a sense of separate self (for which extra psychological "space"—not getting intimate with others—is a solution). (p. 200)

Beck and Freeman (1990b) have carried the role of cognitive elements in the paranoid to its fullest and richest extent. Paranoid personalities have cognitive dysfunctions central to their disorder and Beck helps explicate the content of these distorting components and beliefs. He writes:

The paranoid personalities see themselves as righteous and mistreated by others.

They see other people essentially as devious, deceptive, treacherous, and covertly manipulative. They believe that other people want to interfere with them, put them down, discriminate against them—but all in a hidden or secret way under the guise of innocence. Paranoids may think that others form secret coalitions against them.

The paranoid personalities are driven to be hypervigilant and always on guard. They are wary, suspicious, and looking all the time for cues that will betray the "hidden motives" of their "adversaries."

The main affect is anger over the presumed abuse. Some paranoid personalities, however, may additionally experience constant anxiety over the perceived threats. (pp. 47–48)

As in her descriptive analysis of all of the preceding personality disorders, Benjamin (1993a) focuses her attention on the interpersonal facets of the pathology. This is also true of her characterization of the paranoid, where she writes:

There is fear that others will attack to hurt or blame. The wish is that others will affirm and understand. If affirmation fails, the hope is that others will either leave the PAR alone or submit. The baseline position is to wall off, stay separate, and tightly control the self. If threatened, the PAR will recoil in a hostile way or attack to countercontrol or gain distance.

Is quick to see degradation, attack, and negation; responds with long-lasting revenge. Expects to be misunderstood and misused, so if someone shows the slightest annoyance, he or she responds with a perceptive, fierce, well-focused rage. Can attack harshly with virtually no justification because of the belief that he or she was about to be attacked by the target. (pp. 322–326)

Although the five-factor approach fails to provide an adequate understanding of the development and dynamics of the paranoid personality, Costa and Widiger (1993) furnish us with a clear description of the primary traits of this disorder. They note:

PAR is . . . characterized primarily by excessively low agreeableness (antagonism), particularly on the facet of suspiciousness (low trust), which provides an explicit representation of the core feature of this personality disorder. However, PAR also includes the low agreeableness facets of excessively low straightforwardness, which represents the paranoid tendencies to be secretive, devious, and scheming, and excessively low compliance, which represents the paranoid tendency of antagonistic oppositionalism. (p. 41)

In 1969, Millon formulated the characteristics of the paranoid personality by noting the following diagnostic criteria:

The paranoid personality may be viewed as a moderately severe form of psychopathology founded on the strategy of turning to oneself, rather than others, as the primary source of protection and gratification. The central traits are: cognitive suspicions *(oversensitivity, readily disposed to detect signs of hostility and deception, a tendency to pick up, magnify, and distort the behaviors of others so as to confirm their expectations);*

attachment anxieties *(a need to be the maker of one's own fate, free of entanglements and obligations, even more, not to be subject to the control of others or to have one's power curtailed or infringed upon);* defensive vigilance *(constantly on guard, mobilized and ready for any threat; maintaining a fixed level of preparedness, an alertness to the possibility of attack and derogation);* veiled hostility *(a current of deep resentment, a bitterness for having been overlooked, treated unfairly, and slighted by others who seek to dupe them; only a thin veil hides these bristling animosities). (pp. 327–328)*

The following text and criteria were written for the DSM-III Task Force personality subcommittee by Millon in 1975 as the initial draft for the paranoid personality syndrome. Derived from his theoretical model to be an extreme variant of the "independent" coping style, it places the paranoid personality at an advanced level of structural defect and dysfunction, equal in that respect to the DSM borderline and schizotypal syndromes:

This pattern is typified by a suspicious and vigilant mistrust of others, resistance to external sources of influence and a fear of losing the power of self-determination. There is an undercurrent of veiled hostility, tendencies toward self-importance, the presence of fixed, but essentially irrational, belief systems, and an inclination to misinterpret the incidental actions of others as signs of deception and malevolence. The hypersensitive readiness to perceive threat, to experience envy or jealousy and to assign malice to others precipitates frequent social difficulties.

An appraisal of personal background and history reveals both of the following:

1. *Social attainment deficits (e.g., experienced serious, self-precipitated setbacks in scholastic, marital or vocational pursuits; repeated failure to maintain durable, satisfactory and secure roles consonant with age and aptitudes).*

2. *Periodic mini-psychotic episodes (e.g., experienced several brief and reversible periods in which either bizarre behaviors, extreme moods, irrational impulses or delusional thoughts were exhibited; short-lived breaks from "reality," however, are often recognized subsequently as peculiar or deviant).*

Since adolescence or early adulthood at least 3 of the following have been present to a notably greater degree than in most people and were not limited to discrete periods nor necessarily prompted by problematic life events.

1. *Vigilant mistrust (e.g., exhibits edgy defensiveness against anticipated criticism and deception; conveys extreme suspiciousness, envy and jealousy of others).*

2. *Provocative interpersonal behavior (e.g., displays a disputatious, fractious and abrasive irritability; precipitates exasperation and anger by hostile, deprecatory demeanor).*

3. *Tenacious autonomy (e.g., expresses fear of losing independence and power of self-determination; is grimly resistant to sources of external influence and control).*

4. *Mini-delusional cognitions (e.g., grossly distorts events into personally logical, but essentially irrational, belief systems; embellishes trivial achievements in line with semi-grandiose self-image).*

5. *Persecutory self-references (e.g., entirely incidental events are construed as critical of self; reveals tendency to magnify minor and personally unrelated tensions into proofs of purposeful deception and malice).*

The DSM-III-R modified the DSM-III paranoid personality criteria only modestly, dropping the criterion of "restricted affectivity" and introducing this feature into the schizoid personality criterion list.

The ICD has long carried a descriptive portrayal for the paranoid personality. The following features are noted in its ICD-10 form: an excessive sensitivity to setbacks and rebuffs; a tendency to bear grudges, being unforgiving of insults and injuries; suspiciousness, as seen in a pervasive tendency to distort and misconstrue friendly or neutral actions of others as being hostile or contemptuous; a combative sense of personal rights; recurrent suspicions, without justification, regarding sexual fidelity of spouse or partner; a persistent self-referential attitude as in beliefs of superior self-importance; preoccupation with "conspiratorial" explanations of events without substantiation.

Only modest changes were introduced in the DSM-IV characterization. Included in the criteria for the DSM-IV were seven descriptive features, most of which, as might be expected, in the Cognitive domain. Thus, in this sphere is recorded the

following diagnostic criteria: without sufficient basis suspects that others are deceiving or exploiting him/her; is reluctant to confide in others because of an unwarranted assumption that such information will be maliciously used; reads hidden threats and demeaning implications into benign remarks or events; perceives attacks on one's character or reputation that are not apparent to others; experiences recurrent suspicions regarding fidelity of spouse or partner with no justification. One behavioral criterion is represented: when perceiving an attack on one's character is quick to react angrily or to counterattack. Two criteria appear to reflect representations of objects internalized from the past: is preoccupied with unjustified doubts of the loyalty or trustworthiness of significant others; persistently bears grudges as in being unforgiving of past insults or slights.

In terms of the evolutionary model of the paranoid personality, as seen in Figure 19.1, what is most notable is the presence of a double box and a block between each pair of the polarity groups. This signifies the rigid enclosure and compartmentalization of the paranoids' thoughts and feelings about themselves and others, as well as the unyielding and constricted nature with which they perceive and relate to the world. Whatever motives and aims they have developed in life remain concealed, firmly fixed, unchangeable, and uninfluenced by life circumstances.

The obduracy and inelasticity of their polarity inclinations characterizes paranoids and distin-

PARANOID PROTOTYPE

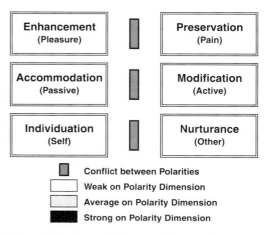

Figure 19.1 Status of the paranoid personality prototype in accord with the Millon Polarity Model.

guishes them from the two other severe/structural pathological types, the schizotypal and borderline. Despite commonalities in the eccentricity of their beliefs and attitudes, the schizotypal comes to this characterization by virtue of excessive structural fluidity, whereas in the paranoid it reflects an unwillingness to adapt to external realities, and a fixity in one's psychic structure that is unbending and inelastic. Similarly, the paranoids' inflexibility and rigidity differs from the borderlines' extraordinary inconstancy and changeability.

As with the two other severe/structural pathologies, the paranoid disorder almost invariably covaries with one or more of the usually less severe personality "styles." In reviewing cases of most paranoids, we are likely to see a conflation of paranoid structural pathologies combined with a stylistic disorder (e.g., paranoid-avoidant, paranoid-antisocial, paranoid-obsessive/compulsive). The task of the clinician is not to disentangle these components, but to recognize that they almost invariably coexist as a stylistic/structural fusion. These mixtures result in what we have described as prototypal variants or subtypes in prior chapters; they will be illustrated in later paragraphs of this chapter.

Figure 19.2 offers a summary of the major historical contributors to the study of paranoid personality.

CLINICAL FEATURES

Certain symptom characteristics are shared among paranoids. As in the two previous struc-

turally defective patterns, we shall divide these characteristics initially into three broad areas of clinical significance: primary sources of anxiety; cognitive processes and preoccupations; and typical moods and behaviors. Five of the major subtypes that develop into variants of the paranoid personality will be discussed in detail later in this chapter. Characteristics which will further aid in distinguishing the prototypal paranoid in accord with our schema of eight clinical domains will immediately follow this elaboration of the three major areas of significance:

• *Attachment Anxiety.* Paranoids detest being dependent not only because it signifies weakness and inferiority, but because they are unable to trust anyone. To lean on another is to expose oneself to intimate betrayal and to rest on ground that will only give way when support is needed most. Rather than chance deceit, paranoids aspire to be the maker of their own fate, free of entanglements and obligations. Bad as it is to place trust in others, it is even worse to be subject to their control and to lose autonomy.

To be coerced by external authority and to be attached to a stronger power than self provokes extreme anxiety. Paranoids are acutely sensitive to threats to autonomy, resist all obligations, and are cautious lest any form of cooperation be a subtle ploy to seduce them and force their submission to the will of others. It is this attachment anxiety, with its consequent dread of losing personal control and independence, that underlies the

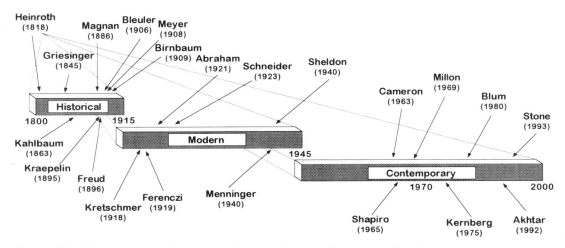

Figure 19.2   Historical review of major contributors to the paranoid personality disorder.

paranoids' characteristic resistance to influence. Ever fearful of domination, they watch carefully to ensure that no one robs them of their will.

Any circumstance that prompts feelings of helplessness and incompetence, decreases their independence and freedom of movement, or places them in a vulnerable position subject to the powers of others, may precipitate a psychotic episode. Trapped by the danger of dependency, struggling to regain their integrity and status and dreading deceit and betrayal, they may strike out aggressively, accuse others of seeking to persecute him, and ennoble themselves with grandiose virtues and superiority. Should paranoids find themselves thinking, feeling, and behaving in ways that are alien to a preferred self-image, they will claim that powerful sources have manipulated them and coerced them to submit to malicious intent. That these accusations are pathological is evident by their vagueness and irrationality; for example, paranoids safely locate these powers in unidentifiable sources such as "they," "a voice," "communists," or "the devil."

The paranoid's dread of attachment and fear of insignificance are similar to the anxieties of the schizotypal. Both shy from close personal relationships and are vulnerable to the threat of nothingness. These commonalities account, in part, for the difficulties that clinicians have faced in differentiating between these syndromes. There is, however, a crucial difference between these patients. Schizotypals find little reinforcement in themselves; their fantasies generate feelings of low self-worth. Moreover, they turn away from others *and* from themselves; thus, they are neither attached nor possess a sense of self. Though paranoids turn away from others, as do schizotypals, they find reinforcements within themselves. Accustomed to self-determination, they use their active fantasy world to create a self-enhanced image and rewarding existence apart from others. Faced with the loss of external recognition and power, they revert to internal sources of supply. Thus, in contrast to the schizotypal, their inner world compensates fully for the rebuffs and anguish of experience; through delusional ideation, they reconstruct an image of self that is more attractive than reality.

- *Cognitive Suspicions and Delusions.* The paranoids' lack of trust colors their perceptions, thoughts, and memories. No doubt, all

people selectively perceive events and draw inferences based on their needs and past experiences. But the feelings and attitudes generated in the life history of paranoids have produced an intense mistrust of others, creating within them a chronic and pervasive suspiciousness; they are oversensitive and readily detect signs of hostility and deception. They tend to be preoccupied with these perceived suspicions and actively pick up, magnify, and distort the actions and words of others so as to confirm their expectations.

The unwillingness of paranoids to attach themselves to others or to share their ideas and points of view, leaves them isolated and bereft of the reality checks that might restrain their suspicions and fantasies. Driven to maintain their independence, they are unable to see things as others see them. Apart from others and with no one to counter the proliferations of their imagination, paranoids concoct events to support their fears or wishes. They ponder incessantly along a single deviant track, put together the flimsiest of evidence, reshape the past to conform to their beliefs and build an intricate logic to justify anxieties and desires. Thus, left to their own devices, they cannot validate speculations and ruminations; no difference exists in the mind between what they have seen and what they have thought; fleeting impressions and hazy memories become fact; a chain of unconnected facts is fitted together; conclusions are drawn. The inexorable course from suspicion to supposition to imagination has given birth to a delusion; a system of invalid and unshakable beliefs has been created.

Delusions are a natural outgrowth of the paranoid personality pattern. Two conditions, dependence on self for both stimulation *and* reinforcement, are conducive to the emergence of minidelusions. Insistent on retaining independence, paranoids isolate themselves and are unwilling to share the perspective and attitudes of others. They have ample time to cogitate and form idiosyncratic suppositions and hypotheses; these then are "confirmed" as valid because it is the paranoid *alone* who is qualified to judge them.

The delusions of the paranoid differ from those seen in other pathological patterns. Accustomed to self-reinforcement and independent thought and "convinced" of their competence and superiority, these patients are both skillful in formulating beliefs and confident in their correctness; their delusions tend, therefore, to be systematic, rational, and convincing. In contrast, the occasional delusions of the schizotypal and borderline appear illogical and unconvincing, tending to arise under conditions of unusual emotional duress; moreover, in further distinction, they are usually bizarre, grossly irrational, scattered, and unsystematic.

- *Defensive Vigilance and Veiled Hostility.* Paranoids are constantly on guard, mobilized and ready for any emergency or threat. Whether faced with real dangers or not, they maintain a fixed level of preparedness, an alert vigilance against the possibility of attack and derogation. There is an edgy tension, an abrasive irritability and an ever-present defensive stance from which they can spring to action at the slightest hint of threat. This state of rigid control never seems to abate; rarely do they relax, ease up, or let down their guard.

Beneath the surface mistrust and defensive vigilance in the paranoid lies a current of deep resentment toward others who "have made it." To the paranoid, most people have attained their status unjustly; thus, he or she is bitter for having been overlooked, treated unfairly, and slighted by the "high and mighty," "the cheats and the crooks" who dupe the world. Only a thin veil hides these bristling animosities.

Unable to accept their own faults and weaknesses, paranoids maintain their self-esteem by attributing their shortcomings to others. They repudiate their own failures and project or ascribe them to someone else. They possess a remarkable talent for spotting even the most trifling of deficiencies in others; both subtly and directly they point out and exaggerate, with great pleasure, the minor defects they uncover among those they despise. Rarely does their undercurrent of envy and hostility subside; they remain touchy and irascible, ready to humiliate and deprecate anyone whose merits they question, and whose attitudes and demeanor evoke their ire and contempt.

No universal attributes may be spoken of as the "essence" of the paranoid personality. The great majority of these patients evidence the constellation of anxieties, cognitions, and behaviors we have described, but we must be careful not to let our focus on these common symptoms obscure the variety of forms into which this impairment unfolds or

the different coping patterns that underlie them. In the section Prototypal Variants, we shall describe some of the features that differentiate five basic subtypes of the paranoid personality. We must be mindful, however, that these distinctions are not well defined in reality; there are overlappings, with traces of the more distinctive features of each subvariety found often in the others. Few pure textbook cases ever are met. Experienced clinicians will have to search back to their history of paranoid patients to find such a pure type.

PROTOTYPAL DIAGNOSTIC DOMAINS

As in prior chapters, the presentation of the characteristics of the personality under review is divided into the domains that are this text's standard format, supported by Table 19.1 and Figure 19.3.

Expressive Behavior: Defensive

Paranoids appear tense and guarded. Eyes tend to be fixed, sharply focused on whatever facet of their worldview draws their attention. It is not uncommon for them to make quick movements, should they hear or see something they view as untoward; otherwise they are likely to remain fixed and unmovable. These characteristics represent the vigilant quality of the paranoids' attention to their environment. They are notably alert to anticipate and to ward off any potential malice, deception, or derogation of themselves. It also signifies that they are tenaciously and firmly resistant to external influence and control. As just noted, paranoids are ready for any real or imagined threat. Whether faced with danger or not, they are at a fixed level of preparedness, an alert vigilance against the possibility of deception and derogation. They exhibit an edgy tension, an abrasive irritability, and an ever-present protective stance from which they can spring into action at the slightest offense. Their state of rigid control never seems to abate, and they rarely relax or let down their guard.

Interpersonal Conduct: Provocative

Paranoids not only bear grudges and are unforgiving of those with whom they have related in the past, but are also likely to display a quarrelsome, fractious, and disputatious attitude toward recent social acquaintances. Interpersonally, they tend to be provocative in their transactions with others, precipitating exasperation and anger by testing their loyalty and by intrusive and searching

TABLE 19.1 Clinical Domains of the
Paranoid Prototype

Behavioral Level

(F) *Expressively Defensive.* Is vigilantly guarded,
alert to anticipate and ward off expected derogation,
malice, and deception; is tenacious and firmly resistant to sources of external influence and control.

(F) *Interpersonally Provocative.* Not only bears
grudges and is unforgiving of those of the past, but
displays a quarrelsome, fractious, and abrasive attitude
with recent acquaintances; precipitates exasperation
and anger by a testing of loyalties and an intrusive and
searching preoccupation with hidden motives.

Phenomenological Level

(F) *Cognitively Suspicious.* Is unwarrantedly skeptical, cynical, and mistrustful of the motives of others,
including relatives, friends, and associates, construing
innocuous events as signifying hidden or conspiratorial
intent; reveals tendency to read hidden meanings into
benign matters and to magnify tangential or minor difficulties into proofs of duplicity and treachery, especially regarding the fidelity and trustworthiness of a
spouse or intimate friend.

(S) *Inviolable Self-Image.* Has persistent ideas of
self-importance and self-reference, perceiving attacks
on character not apparent to others, asserting as personally derogatory and scurrilous, if not libelous,
entirely innocuous actions and events; is pridefully
independent, reluctant to confide in others, highly
insular, experiencing intense fears, however, of losing
identity, status, and powers of self-determination.

(S) *Unalterable Objects.* Internalized representations of significant early relationships that are a fixed
and implacable configuration of deeply held beliefs and
attitudes; these also are driven by unyielding convictions that, in turn, are aligned idiosyncratically with a
fixed hierarchy of tenaciously held, but unwarranted
assumptions, fears, and conjectures.

Intrapsychic Level

(F) *Projection Mechanism.* Actively disowns undesirable personal traits and motives, and attributes them
to others; remains blind to his or her own unattractive
behaviors and characteristics, yet is overalert to, and
hypercritical of, similar features in others.

(S) *Inelastic Organization.* Systemic constriction
and inflexibility of undergirding morphologic structures, as well as rigidly fixed channels of defensive coping, conflict mediation, and need gratification, create
an overstrung and taut frame that is so uncompromising
in its accommodation to changing circumstances that
unanticipated stressors are likely to precipitate either
explosive outbursts or inner shatterings.

Biophysical Level

(S) *Irascible Mood.* Displays a cold, sullen, churlish, and humorless demeanor; attempts to appear
unemotional and objective, but is edgy, envious, jealous, quick to take personal offense and react angrily.

(F) = Functional domain.
(S) = Structural domain.

PARANOID PROTOTYPE

Figure 19.3 Salience of personologic domains in the
paranoid prototype.

preoccupations with possible hidden motives. As
noted in prior pages, beneath the obvious mistrust
and defensive vigilance of the paranoid stirs a
current of deep resentment toward those who
"have made it." To paranoids, most people have
attained their status and esteem unjustly. To make
matters worse, they feel that they have been personally overlooked and are bitter for having been
treated unfairly and slighted by those who dupe
the world. Only a thin veil hides their bristling
animosities.

Every trivial rebuff is a painful reminder to
paranoids of their past, part of the plot whose history can be traced back to early mistreatments.
Trapped in what they see as a timeless web of deceit and malice, the fears and angers of paranoids
may mount to monumental proportions. Should
their defenses fall into shambles, their controls dissolved, and their fantasies of doom run rampant,
their underlying dread and fury may surge into the
open. A flood of hostile energies may erupt, letting
loose a violent and uncontrollable torrent of vituperation and aggression. These psychotic outbursts
are usually brief. As the surge of fear and hostility
is discharged, these patients typically regain their
composure and seek to rationalize their actions, reconstruct their defenses, and bind their aggression.
This subsiding of bizarre emotions does not lead to
a normal state but merely a return to their former
personality pattern.

Cognitive Style: Suspicious

Perhaps the most distinctive feature of paranoids is
their pervasive suspiciousness. Moreover, they
are unwarrantedly skeptical, cynical, and mistrustful of the motives of others, including relatives,
friends, and associates. Innocuous events are construed as signifying hidden or conspiratorial intent.

Most reveal tendencies to search for hidden meanings in completely benign matters, and to magnify tangential or minor difficulties into proofs of duplicity or treachery, especially regarding the fidelity of a spouse or intimate friend.

To restate a prior comment, what we perceive and infer is based on our pattern of needs and past experiences. Unfortunately, the learned feelings and attitudes of paranoids produce a deep mistrust and pervasive suspiciousness of others. They are notoriously oversensitive and disposed to detect signs everywhere of trickery and deception; they are preoccupied with these thoughts, actively picking up minute cues, then magnifying and distorting them so as to confirm their worst expectations. To complicate matters further, events that fail to confirm their preformed suspicions "only prove how deceitful and clever others can be." As noted in a prior section, in an effort to uncover the assumed pretense, paranoid personalities will test others and explore every nook and cranny to find some justification for their beliefs. These preconceptions rarely are upset by facts. Paranoids dismiss contradictions and confirm their expectations by seizing on real, although trivial or irrelevant, data. Even more problematic is that they create an atmosphere that provokes others to act as they anticipated. After testing the honesty of their friends and constantly cajoling and intimidating others, the paranoid will provoke almost everyone into exasperation and anger.

Self-Image: Inviolable

The majority of paranoids have persistent ideas of self-reference and self-importance. They perceive attacks on their character not apparent to others, asserting as personally derogatory and scurrilous, if not libelous, entirely innocuous actions or events. As a consequence, they seek to be inviolable, are pridefully independent-minded, reluctant to confide in and be dependent on others. This highly insular attitude derives from their intense fear of losing their identity and, more importantly, their powers of self-determination.

As a further means of assuring self-determination, paranoids assume an attitude of invincibility and pride. Convincing themselves that they have extraordinary capacities, they can now master their fate alone, as well as overcome every obstacle, resistance, and conflict. All traces of self-doubt are dismissed, and they repudiate all nurturant overtures from others. Thus assured, they will never dread having to need or to depend on anyone.

As discussed in prior paragraphs, circumstances that prompt feelings of helplessness and incompetence, or decrease their freedom of movement, or place them in a vulnerable position subject to the powers of others, may precipitate a sudden and ferocious counterattack. Feeling trapped by the dangers of dependency, struggling to regain their status, and dreading deceit and betrayal, they may strike out aggressively and accuse others of seeking to persecute them. Should others accuse them accurately of thinking, feeling, or behaving in ways that are alien to their self-image, they are likely to claim that powerful and malevolent sources have coerced them with malicious intent.

Object-Representations: Unalterable

The internalized representation of significant early relationships among most paranoids are limited and rigidly fixed. There is an implacable configuration of objects representing firmly held images, beliefs, and attitudes. These intrapsychic components are driven to yield unwarranted convictions regarding the attitudes and dispositions of others with whom they interact in their current world. What is most notable about this inner template of objects is its idiosyncratic character, which comprises fixed and tenaciously held assumptions.

The experiential history of paranoids often gives them reason to be mistrustful and to fear betrayal or sadistic treatment. To counter these sources of threat, they have learned to distance themselves from others and to remain strong and vigilant, not only as a protective stance but as a means of vindication and triumph over potential attackers. To assure their security, they go to great pains to avoid any weakening of their resolve and to develop new and superior powers to control others.

As must be evident from the foregoing, the confidence and pride of paranoids cloak but a hollow shell. Their arrogant pose of autonomy rests on insecure internal footings. Extremely vulnerable to challenge, their defensive facade is constantly weakened by real and fantasied threats. In their efforts to reassert their power and invincibility, they will resort to any course of action that will shore up their defenses or thwart their detractors.

Regulatory Mechanisms: Projection/Fantasy

Perhaps second only to suspiciousness as a sign of the paranoid disorder, is the use of the projection regulatory mechanism. These personalities actively disown their undesirable personal traits and motives, attributing them freely to others. Not only are they blind, therefore, to their own unattractive behaviors and characteristics, but they are hyperalert to similar features that may be present to a limited degree in others. Thus, troubled by mounting and inescapable evidence of inadequacy and hostility, paranoids are driven to go beyond mere denial. They not only disown these personally humiliating traits but throw them back at their real or imagined accusers. Through the mechanism of projection, they are able to claim that it is "they" who are stupid, malicious, and vindictive. Moreover, it is the patient himself who is an innocent and unfortunate victim of the incompetence and malevolence of others.

Unable to accept faults and weaknesses within themselves, paranoids maintain their self-esteem by attributing their shortcomings to others. Repudiating their own failures, they project or ascribe them to someone else. They possess a remarkable talent for spotting the most trifling deficiencies in others. Both indirectly and directly they point to and exaggerate the minor defects they uncover among those they learn to despise. Rarely does their envy and hostility subside. They are touchy and irritable, ready to humiliate and deprecate anyone whose merits they question, and whose attitudes and demeanor evoke their ire or contempt. By a simple reversal, paranoids not only absolve themselves of fault but find a "justified" outlet for their resentment and anger. If paranoids are found to have been in error, others should be blamed for their ineptness. If they have been driven to become aggressive, it is only because the evil of others has provoked them. They are innocent, and justifiably indignant, unfortunate, and maligned scapegoats for the blundering and the slanderous.

Faced with persistent derogation and threat, paranoids will seek vigorously to redeem themselves and reestablish their sense of autonomy and power. However, they may have no recourse to achieve these ends except through fantasy. Unable to face their feelings of inadequacy and insignificance, they may begin to fabricate an image of superior self-worth. Left to ruminate alone, they may construct proofs of their eminence through intricate self-deceptions. Renouncing objective reality, they supplant it with a glorified self-image. They endow themselves with limitless powers and talents and hence need no longer be ashamed of themselves or fear others. They can now rise above petty jealousies, "understanding all too clearly" why others seek to undermine their stature and virtue. The meaning of the malicious and persecutory attacks of others is obvious; it is the paranoid's eminence and superiority that they envy and seek to destroy.

Morphologic Organization: Inelastic

The structural organization of the intrapsychic world of the paranoid is composed of highly controlled and systematically arranged images and impulses. Particularly notable is its constriction and inflexibility such that channels for defensive coping are few and persistently employed; similarly, processes for conflict mediation and need gratification are fixed and immutable. This inelastic structure creates an overstrung and taut frame that is so uncompromising in its accommodation to changing circumstances that unanticipated stressors are likely to precipitate either explosive outbursts or inner shatterings. In contrast to other severe personality disorders, the defective nature of the paranoid's structural organization is *not* its lack of cohesion, but rather its overly constrained and rigid character.

To preclude the possibility of external outbursts or internal shatterings, paranoids seek to transform the ongoing events of their everyday life to make them fit their interior structures and objects. As noted previously, they utilize the projection mechanism and its variants (e.g., projective identification) to achieve these ends. Moreover, even those patients who are noted for their rigidity and their hyperalertness to the environment may begin to lower their controls and loosen their usually firm boundaries between reality and fantasy. This latter process of blurring formerly segregated features of their psychic world will inevitably create new and troublesome consequences.

Mood/Temperament: Irascible

Underlying many of the paranoid's more general characteristics appears to be a cold, sullen, churlish, and humorless temperament. Whether learned or constitutionally based, paranoids tend to be unemotional and objective in outlook. On the other hand, they are typically edgy, envious, jealous, and quick to take personal offense, reacting angrily with minimal provocation. One of their major goals is to desensitize their tender and affectionate feelings. They become hard, unyielding, immune, and insensitive to the suffering of others. By so doing, they protect themselves against entrapment and against being drawn into a web of anticipated deceit and subjugation. To assume a callous and unsympathetic stance is not difficult for paranoids. Not only is it a successful defensive maneuver against entrapment, but it also allows them to discharge their resentments and angers.

Hostility for the paranoid serves both defensive and restitutive measures. Not only is it a means of countering threats to their equilibrium, but it helps restore their image of self-determination and autonomy. Once released, this hostility draws on a reserve of earlier resentments. Present angers are fueled by animosities from the past. Desire for reprisal and vindication spurred by prior humiliations are brought to the surface and discharged into the stream of current hostility.

PROTOTYPAL VARIANTS

There are both theoretical rationales (Millon, 1969, 1981, 1990) and supportive empirical data (Millon, 1977, 1987, 1994) to indicate that the paranoid covaries in profile combination with specific other personality types. In these mixed cases, the paranoid dimension is often an insidious and secondary development, fusing slowly into the fabric of an earlier and less defective structural pattern. Although paranoidlike features may be exhibited in almost every other personality disorder, they tend to become integral components of only a few of the patterns previously described (e.g., narcissistic, avoidant, compulsive, sadistic, negativistic).

Before proceeding to mention a few of these personality configurations, it should be noted that no single attribute may be found universally in all paranoid personalities. The great majority of patients evidence the constellation of behaviors described in the Clinical Features section, but the focus on these common symptoms should not obscure the many variations of the impairment. What follows expresses but a small fraction of the diversity seen among paranoids. As a further caveat, let us note again that the distinctions drawn here are not so sharply defined in reality. There are numerous prototypal variants in which traces of features associated with each subtype may be found in the others. Single-dimension textbook cases are rarely met.

Normal Styles

Along with the other structurally defective personality styles, it is hard to conceive normal paranoids.

Although a number of these individuals restrain their markedly distorted beliefs and assumptions from public view, at no point does their fundamental paranoid inclination manifest itself in an acceptable, no less successful personality style. Hence, we leave this section blank and turn to basic paranoid characteristics seen in children and adults.

Childhood Syndromes

As with other childhood syndromes, there is no direct correlation between the patterns seen in childhood and roughly comparable adult types. First of all, it is difficult to place any of the previously described childhood patterns at a specified level of severity. Children evidencing paranoidlike qualities appear to be extensions of the avoidant (i.e., threctic syndrome), on the one hand, and the sadistic (i.e., pariotic child), on the other. Both give evidence of fearful suspicion and a hypervigilance in scanning a potentially threatening environment. Threctic children are largely fearful and self-isolating youngsters, whose suspicions are kept largely to themselves, who maintain vigilance at a distance, so to speak, and whose anxious withdrawal and hesitation relate to all potential degraders in their world. Conversely, pariotic children are characterized by what might be called a parmic temperament, in which they act in a fearless and largely abrasive and truculent manner. Their paranoidlike qualities also are of a suspicious, if not slightly delusional character. However, unlike the avoidant type, they do not withdraw, slink away, and hide from potential threateners; rather they are truculent, hostile, willing to attack those who they feel have "done them in."

As is seen in the paranoid, there are several subvarieties and combinations. The same set of distinctions can be seen in childhood and adolescence; on the one hand, the fearfully withdrawn and hypersuspicious type, on the other, the hostile and cynical sadistic type with a readiness to attack.

It should be noted in this penultimate chapter that patterns of behavior seen in children vary more than those seen in adults. For example, different pariotic children will manifest different degrees of impulse control and reality adaptability; similarly, different symbiotic children may exhibit different degrees of overattachment and initiative. It may be useful in this regard to append the level of psychopathological severity to each of these youngsters; for example, "child pariosis: moderate severity." We would suggest limiting these notations to "moderate" and "marked" severity, since mild forms of these impairments may be only temporary affairs, given the relative fluidity of childhood personality.

For the most part, and as is well known, the personality of the child is less firmly fixed than that of adults; thus, not only will children fluctuate more than their older counterparts, but as time progresses, they may "grow out of" their earlier coping pattern. It seems wise, nevertheless, to view as moderately and markedly severe those children whose difficulties are so deviant as to warrant clinical treatment or hospitalization. This view is based on the belief that severe early patterns of pathology tend to be perpetuated and intensified over time; this consequence reflects the likely repetition of injurious parental influences and the child's own self-defeating and provocative behaviors. Unless remedial procedures are instituted early, "the twig" will likely grow in the direction it was originally "bent."

As noted earlier, not all basic pathological personality patterns have counterparts in childhood disturbances. Thus, the child who is exposed to parental overvaluation and indulgence, that is, the passive-independent (narcissistic) child, rarely exhibits severe pathological traits in early life. Although this type of parental management builds a false sense of self-worth in the child, the consequences of having been "spoiled" do not usually reach structurally defective proportions until adolescence or later.

Adult Subtypes

Several attributes may be spoken of, somewhat loosely, as the "core features" of the paranoid personality. The great majority of these patients evidence the constellation of anxieties, cognitions and behaviors described in prior sections, but we must be careful not to let our focus on these common symptoms obscure the variety of forms into which this disorder unfolds. In what follows, we shall describe some of the features that differentiate five adult subtypes of the paranoid personality.

The Fanatic Paranoid

The *fanatic paranoid* is similar to a less structurally defective parallel, the narcissistic personality, with whom the fanatic is often interwoven. Both seek to retain their admirable self-image, act in a haughty and pretentious manner, are naively self-confident, ungenerous, exploitive, expansive, and presumptuous, as well as display an air of supercilious contempt and benign arrogance toward others.

In contrast to narcissists, who achieve a modicum of success with their optimistic veneer and exploitive behaviors, *fanatic paranoids* run hard against reality. Their illusion of omnipotence has periodically been shattered, toppling them from a vaulted image of eminence. Accustomed to being viewed as the center of things and to being a valued and admired figure, at least in their own eyes, they cannot tolerate the lessened significance circumstances have now assigned to them. Their narcissism has been profoundly wounded.

Not only must fanatic paranoids counter the indifference, the humiliation, and the fright of insignificance generated by reality, they must reestablish their lost pride through extravagant claims and fantasies. Upset by assaults on self-esteem, they reconstruct their self-image and ascend once more to their former status. To do this, they endow themselves by illusory self-reinforcement with superior powers and exalted competencies. They dismiss events that conflict with their newly acquired and self-designated importance; flimsy talents and accomplishments are embellished, creating a new self-image that supplants objective reality.

Because these patients lack internal discipline and self-control, they allow their reparative fantasies free rein to embroider a fabric of high sheen and appeal, caring little that their claims are unwarranted. These grandiose assertions become fixed and adamant; they are too important to the patient's need to regain importance and to become an identity of significance and esteem. Fanatic paranoids go to great lengths to convince themselves and others of the validity of their claims, insisting against obvious contradictions and the ridicule of others that they deserve to be catered to and that they are entitled to special acknowledgment and privileges.

But the evidence in support of the fanatic paranoids' assertions is as flimsy as a house of cards, easily collapsed by the slightest incursion. Unable to sustain this image before others and rebuffed and unable to gain the recognition they crave, they turn more and more toward themselves for salvation. Taking liberties with objective facts and wandering further from social reality and shared meanings, paranoids concoct an ever more elaborate fantasy world of grandiose delusions. Not uncommonly, they may begin to assume the role and attributes of some idolized person, whose repute cannot be questioned by others. As this identification takes root, the fanatic paranoid asserts a new identity, a noble and inspired leader, a saint or a god, a powerful and rich political figure, or an awesome and talented genius. Grandiose missions are proposed for "saving the world"; plans are made for solving insurmountable geographic, social, and scientific problems, for creating new societies, interplanetary arrangements and so on. These schemes may be worked out in minute detail, often correspond to objective needs, and are formulated with sufficient logic to draw at least momentary attention and recognition from others.

The Malignant Paranoid

Malignant paranoids tend be structurally defective variants of the sadistic personality, whose features frequently commingle and blend with those of the paranoid. They are characterized best by their power orientation; by their mistrust, resentment, and envy of others; and by their autocratic, belligerent, and intimidating manner. Underlying these features is a ruthless desire to triumph over others, to vindicate themselves for past wrongs by cunning revenge or callous force, if necessary.

In contrast to their less structurally defective counterpart, malignant paranoids have found that in their efforts to abuse and tyrannize others, they have only prompted them to inflict more of the hostility and harsh punishment to which they were subjected in childhood. Their strategy of arrogance and brutalization has backfired too often, and they now seek retribution, not as much through action as through fantasy.

Repeated setbacks have confirmed the malignant paranoids' expectancy of aggression from others; by their own hand, they stir up further hostility and disfavor. Because of their argumentative and chip-on-the-shoulder attitudes, they provoke ample antagonism from others. Isolated and resentful, they increasingly turn to themselves, to cogitate and mull over their fate. Left to their own ruminations, they begin to imagine a plot in which every facet of the environment plays a threatening and treacherous role. Moreover, through the intrapsychic mechanism of projection, they attribute their own venom to others, ascribing to them the malice and ill-will they feel within themselves. As the line draws thin between objective antagonism and imagined hostility, the belief takes hold that others are intentional persecutors; alone, threatened, and with decreasing self-esteem, the suspicions of the malignant paranoid now have been transformed into delusions. Not infrequently, persecutory delusions

combine with delusions of grandeur; however, these latter beliefs play a secondary role among malignant patients, in contrast to their primacy among fanatic paranoids.

Preeminent among malignant paranoids is their need to retain their independence; despite all adversity they cling tenaciously to the belief in their self-worth. This need to protect their autonomy and strength may be seen in the content of their persecution delusions. Malevolence on the part of others is viewed neither as casual nor random; rather, it is designed to intimidate, offend, and undermine the patient's self-esteem. "They" are seeking to weaken the patient's "will," destroy his or her power, spread lies, thwart talents, conspire to control thoughts, and immobilize and subjugate him or her. These paranoids dread losing their independence; their persecutory themes are filled with fears of being forced to submit to authority, of being made soft and pliant, and of being tricked to surrender their self-determination.

The Obdurate Paranoid

Obdurate paranoids are more pathological variants of the less structurally defective obsessive-compulsive personality disorder, whose rule-bound and rigid characteristics typically mesh and unite with those of the paranoid. However, in contrast to their compulsive counterparts, who retain the hope of achieving gratification and protection through the good offices of others, obdurate paranoids break their self-other conflict, renouncing their dependency submission and taking on a stance of self-assertion. Despite their growing hostility and repudiation of conformity as a way of life, obdurate paranoids retain their basic rigidity and perfectionism; they remain grim and humorless, tense, controlled and inflexible, small-minded, unyielding and implacable, dyspeptic, peevish and cranky, legalistic and self-righteous. These features of their basic psychic makeup are deeply embedded, internalized as a fixed system of habits, feelings, and thoughts. Though obdurate paranoids now may find it necessary to discard others as their primary source of security, the remnants of lifelong habits of overcontrol and faultlessness are not so readily abandoned; the basic personality style remains immutable.

Obdurate paranoids continue to seek the clarity of rules and regulations; they cannot tolerate suspense and must create an order and system in life. Deprived of the customary guidelines they now spurn, they learn to lean increasingly on themselves and to be their own ruthless slave driver in search of order, power, and independence. This leads to an obsessive concern with trivial details and an excessive intellectualization of minor events, all to the end of obtaining internal perfection and faultlessness.

In their newfound independence, obdurate paranoids free themselves from the constraints of submission and propriety. They begin to discharge the reservoir of hostility they previously had repressed and impose their self-created standards on others, using the same demands and punitive attitudes to which these paranoids were earlier subjected. Setting impossible regulations for others allows paranoids to vent hostilities and condemn failures; to know they can give to others what they themselves have received. They can despise and hate others for their weaknesses, their deceits, and their hypocrisy—precisely those feelings that the paranoids previously had experienced within themselves, had once sought to repress, and still try to conceal by condemning them in others.

Despite their overt repudiation of conformity and submission, obdurate paranoids cannot free themselves entirely of conflict and guilt: despite efforts to justify their newly found hostility, they are unable to square these actions with past beliefs. Furthermore, their present arrogance reactivates past anxieties; they cannot escape the memories of retaliation which their own hostile actions provoked in the past.

Deep within these paranoids, then, live the remnants of guilt and the fear of retribution; these two elements rise to persecutory delusions. First, obdurate paranoids have learned from past experience to anticipate disfavor and criticism in response to contrary and nonconforming behaviors; thus, as they look about them, they "see," in the movements and remarks of others, the hostility they anticipate. Second, in order to deny or justify their behaviors, obdurate paranoids project their anger on others—this mechanism, however, causes them to "find" hostile intent where none, in fact, exists. Last, inner feelings of guilt reactivate self-condemnatory attitudes; thus, part of the person feels that he or she deserves to be punished for resentments and behaviors. Thus, as a result of anticipation, projection, and guilt, the patient begins to believe that others are "after him [her]," seeking to condemn, punish, belittle and undo him or her.

Certain encapsulated and well-defined delusions often exist apart from the main body of a patient's normal beliefs. These rare delusional systems have been referred to as cases of classical *paranoia* in the past. When they are seen, they tend to be found among these obdurate paranoid types. The overly rigid and tightly controlled thought processes of these paranoids often enable them to segment their beliefs and to keep them as separate and compartmentalized units. Thus, the patient may appear to function much of the time in a normal manner; however, once a topic associated with the delusion is broached, the irrational, but normally hidden and encapsulated, belief becomes manifest.

The Querulous Paranoid

These personalities may be differentiated from several of their less structurally defective counterparts by the presence of both overt hostility and frank delusions. Along with their milder variants, such as the negativistic style with whom shared characteristics continue to coexist, *querulous paranoids* are noted by their discontent, pessimism, stubbornness, and vacillation. However, at this defective-structural level, the pathology is more aggressively negativistic and faultfinding, sullen, resentful, obstructive, and peevish at all times, and openly expressive of feelings of jealousy, of being misunderstood, and of being cheated. As a consequence, querulous paranoids rarely can sustain good relationships, creating endless wrangles wherever they go. Demoralized by these events, they forgo all hopes of gaining affection and approval from others, and decide to renounce these aspirations in preference for self-determination. Notable as characteristics distinguishing the querulous paranoid are the following adjectives: contentious, fractious, resentful, choleric, jealous, waspish, and whiny.

Despite the strength with which they assert their newfound independence, querulous paranoids remain irritable, dissatisfied, and troubled by discontent and ambivalence. They rarely forget their resentments—the feelings of having been mistreated and exploited. Not uncommonly, they begin to perceive the achievements of others as unfair advantages, preferential treatments that are undeserved and that have been denied to the paranoid. Disgruntlement and complaints mount; fantasies expand and weave into irrational envy; grumbling turns to anger and spite; each of these feed into the central theme of unjust misfortune, and are whipped, bit by bit, into delusions of resentful jealousy.

Erotic delusions are not uncommon among these patients. Although consciously repudiating their need for others, querulous paranoids still seek affection from them. Rather than admit to these desires, however, these patients defensively project them, interpreting the casual remarks and actions of others as subtle signs of their amorous intent. However, they cannot tolerate these "attentions" because they dread further betrayal and exploitation. Thus, in conjunction with erotic delusions, these paranoids demand "protection" and may accuse innocent victims of committing indignities, of making lewd suggestions, or of molesting them.

The Insular Paranoid

Notably hypervigilant, the *insular paranoid type* is extremely moody and apprehensive, overly reactive to criticism, particularly in response to judgments made of the person's status, beliefs, and achievements. In earlier stages of their pathology, these patients often are avoidant personalities, frequently withdrawn from the world, increasingly reclusive and isolated. Extremely vulnerable, many *insular paranoids* seek solace in a variety of self-focused ways; for example, some engage in abstruse intellectual activities to enhance their fantasied self-esteem, others indulge in alcohol or drugs as a way of calming the frightening nature of troublesome fantasies, still others pursue sexual escapades with prostitutes, not only to provide a measure of physical relief from their insular state, but also to purchase a willing ear to listen to their fears and grandiosities.

More than other paranoid types, insular variants seek to protect themselves from a world judged to be both threatening and destructive. As are other paranoids, they are hypervigilant, exceptionally observant of their environment, especially the judgments others make regarding themselves. In this way, they apparently spot problems in their earliest stages, quickly anticipating what could be troubling, and defending themselves against both real and imagined dangers. As evident in the preceding, these self-protective insular types share certain core features with the avoidant personality. Typically, these subtypes come to premature conclusions about rather incidental and trivial events that are given meaning largely by projecting their own anxieties and hostility. The natural complexities of their social world are narrowed to signify one or two persistent and all-embracing ideas; in this way, paranoids can effectively deal with the problems they face by "knowing" that everything represents basically one or two variants of the same thing.

Part of the reason for insulating themselves stems from their need to prevent anything or anyone from influencing them. Insular paranoids have an unusual fear of being controlled. Not only do they seek to divert or preclude external sources of influence, but they have a strong desire to remain autonomous, to keep to themselves and to rely solely on their own ideas and beliefs. Ultimately, this isolation, this unwillingness to check their thoughts against reality results in the insular paranoid becoming more and more out of touch with reality. As a consequence of believing that the only reality is the one they have created, insular paranoids have no defense against external forces because their world is a product of their own imagination. Hence, they not only have difficulty in accurately observing external reality, but have no escape from the false reality that inheres within themselves.

As with their precursor, the avoidant personality, their inner thoughts may become so painful and terrifying that they must undo or destroy them. Their intense feelings of insecurity and threat have escalated as a consequence of their own defensive actions. Everything is now seen as parts of a general assault intended to destroy them. But the conspiracies and the persecution they perceive are self-created. To defend against these frightening feelings, insular paranoids intentionally disrupt their own thoughts, seeking to distance themselves from their own mind. Their inner world becomes a void, a chaotic melange of distorted and incidental thoughts. It is at this point that they regress into the decompensated paranoid state. They have become detached from themselves, empty vessels devoid of the cohesion and focus that dominated their life until their own imagination made existence so painful as to require that it be ultimately purged.

COMORBID DISORDERS AND SYNDROMES

The paranoid personality is a well-established and clinically familiar syndrome. This section touches only briefly on the concomitant Axis I clinical syndromes and Axis II disorders associated with the paranoid pattern. Issues of differential diagnosis will be briefly presented in a later section.

Axis II Comorbidities

The multidiagnosis format of the DSM-IV encourages concurrent personality diagnosis. For this reason, and in contrast to discussions of the syndrome by most other authors, attention in this section is allotted to comorbid personalities with the paranoid.

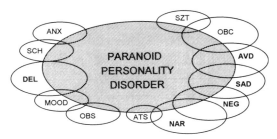

Figure 19.4 Comorbidity between paranoid personality disorder and other DSM Axis I and Axis II disorders.

Figure 19.4 summarizes the pattern of overlap seen between the paranoid and several other personality disorders. Aspects of these covariant features are described in our earlier description of the Adult Subtypes of the paranoid personality. As can be visualized, notable levels of conjunction are found with the narcissistic (NAR), the negativistic (NEG), the sadistic (SAD), the avoidant (AVD), and the obsessive-compulsive (OBC). Less frequent covariances are seen with the schizotypal (SZT) and the antisocial (ATS), both of which are also of more than modest frequency.

Axis I Comorbidities

Paranoids are usually overly sensitive about appearing "strange or bizarre" and, hence, display few of the milder and more controllable Axis I symptoms. When their defenses disintegrate or shatter, however, we see several of both the milder and psychotic level symptoms.

Delusional Syndromes (DEL). Paranoid personalities develop *delusional* paranoid disorders and paranoia insidiously, usually as a consequence of anticipating or experiencing repeated mistreatment or humiliation. Acute paranoid episodes may be precipitated by the shock of an unanticipated betrayal. In these acute phases, previously repressed resentments may surge to the surface and overwhelm the patient's former controls, quickly taking the form of a delusional belief, usually persecutory in nature. During these episodes, typically brief and rather chaotic, patients both discharge their anger and project it on others. Note that the resentments and suspicions of the paranoid usually do not cumulate and burst out of control. Rather, these patients continue to be persistently touchy, secretive, and irritable, thereby allowing them to vent their

spleen in regular, small doses. Only if their suspicions are aggravated suddenly do they take explosive or irrational form.

Anxiety Syndromes (ANX). Severe *generalized* anxiety disorders may take the form of diffuse apprehensions or fears of the unknown, often distracting the patient from dealing effectively with matters of daily routine. Paranoids may complain of their inability to concentrate and of being unable to enjoy previously pleasurable activities and pursuits. No matter what they do, they feel unable to avoid pervasive and interminable apprehension. They sense themselves incapable of distinguishing the safe from the unsafe. Some become notably irritable and view minor responsibilities as momentous and insurmountable tasks. Distress mounts when they become aware and self-conscious of their growing incompetence and tension. Soon this self-awareness becomes a preoccupation. Observing themselves, paranoids sense tremors, palpitations, muscular tightness, "butterflies in the stomach," cold sweats, a feeling of foreboding, and, ultimately, the dread of imminent collapse. Their awareness of their own frailty has not only perpetuated their fright but feeds on itself until it builds to monumental proportions. Unless they can distract or divert their attention elsewhere, the paranoids' controls may give way. The upsurge of unconscious fears and images that flood to the surface may inundate and overwhelm them, resulting in an acute anxiety attack or *panic disorder.*

Obsessive-Compulsive Syndromes (OBC). Paranoid patients will occasionally exhibit *compulsive disorders,* as seen in an irresistible preoccupation with some absurd but "safe" activity that serves to distract them from confronting more painful sources of discomfort. Also, through reaction-formation, they may pursue these activities as a subterfuge for socially unacceptable impulses. Thus, symbolic acts of compulsive "undoing" serve not only to void past sins but to ward off anticipated future punishment and social rebuke. Moreover, the self-punitive and redemptive aspects of the undoing ritual often diminish the oppressive buildup of guilt. For example, insistence on order and cleanliness, not usually typical of the paranoid's characteristic behavior, and the self-righteous air with which they perform these acts, distract others from the paranoid's previous irrationalities, and this often also evokes a number of secondary gains.

Mood Syndromes (MOOD).   Paranoids, especially those with a strong blend of narcissistic features, may evidence a self-exalted and pompous variant of *bipolar manic disorder.* Faced with realities that shatter their illusion of significance and omnipotence, they may lose perspective and frantically seek to regain their status. No longer secure in their image of superiority, they attempt through cheerful and buoyant behaviors to instill or revive the blissful state of former times when they believed their mere existence was of value. They are driven to their excited state in the hope of reestablishing their lost exalted status.

Schizophrenic Syndromes (SCH).   In contrast to the buoyant and manic hyperactivity that may be seen in *fanatic* paranoids, *malignant* paranoid personalities are subject more to the *schizophrenic: catatonic excited* disorders. These paranoids move about in a surly and truculent manner and explode into uncontrollable rages during which they threaten and occasionally physically assault others with little or no provocation. At these times, they unleash a torrent of abuse and storm about defiantly, cursing and voicing bitterness and contempt for all. They may lunge at and assail passersby quite unpredictably, shouting obscenities at unseen but hallucinated attackers and persecutors. The quality of irrational belligerence and fury, the frenzied lashing out, distinguishes these paranoids from others.

Obdurate and *querulous* paranoids are also subject to schizophrenic disorders, but of the *catatonic stupor and negativism* varieties. Their physical uncooperativeness is but a passive expression of deeply felt resentments and angers. The body tightness we observe reflects an intense struggle to control seething hostility, and their physical withdrawal and obduracy helps avoid contacts with events that could provoke and unleash their hostile impulses. Their catatonic postures both communicate and control their anger. They may be seen as bizarre extensions of their habitual coping style, a means of controlling contrary urges by protective restraint and rigid behavior. The gestures and grimaces of these patients convey symbolically an abbreviated and immediately restrained expression of their aggressive urges.

DIFFERENTIAL DIAGNOSES

Several listings in the DSM-IV resemble the paranoid personality. Most relevant are "delusional disorder," and "schizophrenic disorder, paranoid type." Both syndromes are distinguished by persistent psychotic symptoms such as delusions and hallucinations, which are not intrinsic to the paranoid personality syndrome unless a psychotic episode is superimposed. The description of the former (DSM-III) "paranoia" category stated that this syndrome develops insidiously and possesses "a permanent and unshakable delusional system accompanied by preservation of clear and orderly thinking." "Paranoid disorder," termed *delusional* disorder in DSM-IV, is the broader syndrome within which paranoia was subsumed; it does not require that the delusional system be "permanent and unshakable." Finally, the long-established syndrome, noted as "schizophrenia paranoid type," present in all recent manuals, has been described as evidencing incoherence, loose associations, hallucinations, and fragmented delusions. In surveying these descriptions, it appears that the progression from "paranoia" to "paranoid disorder" to "schizophrenia, paranoid type" reflects, primarily, differences in degree of personality deterioration. Thus, in "paranoia," the delusions are highly systematized and the personality largely intact; in the "paranoid (delusional) disorder," the delusions lack the systematization seen in paranoia but fall short of the fragmentation and deterioration of the "schizophrenic paranoid."

As described previously, the paranoid's fear of close attachments is similar to the concerns of the *schizotypal.* Both distance from intimate personal relationships and are vulnerable to the threat of external control. These commonalities are associated with their shared level of structural defect in their personality organization. Several clear distinctions, however, may be made to differentiate them. For example, schizotypals experience little satisfaction in being themselves; thus, their fantasies generate feelings of low, rather than high, self-worth. They turn from others *and* from themselves, being neither socially attached nor possessing a valued sense of self. Paranoids also turn from others, but their active fantasy life creates an enhanced self-image. Faced with the loss of external recognition or power, paranoids draw on their internal sources of supply to compensate for rebuff and anguish. On other dimensions—and in contrast with schizotypals, who tend toward the apathetic and indifferent—paranoids are often energetic, driven, argumentative, and hostile. As noted earlier, in the more decompensated states, the pictures of schizotypals, paranoids, and borderlines begin to merge, making discrimination extremely difficult at the symptomatological level. Differentiation in these cases may be more accurately made with reference to developmental histories; a review of distinctions noted in Chapter 17 may also be useful.

Discrimination between the paranoid personality and the avoidant, antisocial, sadistic, and narcissistic personalities is worthy of brief note; reference should be made to earlier chapters that touch on these differentiations, as well.

Problematic distinctions with *avoidants* are likely to occur owing to their shared hyperalertness and suspiciousness regarding the motives and intentions of others. As touched on previously, avoidants may very well decompensate in the direction of the paranoid's structurally defective level of pathology; as such, the problem of differentiation becomes moot. The key difference is that the avoidant has a broad sense of personal unattractiveness and a low sense of self-worth; by contrast, most paranoids have a sense of high self-esteem, at least publicly, and are willing when faced with a conflictual situation to directly vent their resentments and anger.

As previously noted, the avoidant may gravitate over time in the direction of acquiring paranoid characteristics; so, too, may the *narcissistic* personality drift or, in response to unrelieved pressures of a self-deflating character, begin to evidence the grandiosity that typifies the paranoid disorder. Under these conditions, narcissists not only compensate and defend themselves by self-inflation, but come to display the social withdrawal and suspiciousness seen from the start among paranoids. Until this paranoid decompensation progresses, narcissists evince a cool sense of superiority, a capacity to deal with their life in a manner that is quite successful and competent, often eliciting admiring responses and tribute from others. These signs of social ease and comfort are not seen with paranoids, who typically evoke resentment and countersuspiciousness on the part of those to whom they relate.

Mention should be made concerning the pathogenic progression toward paranoid pathology found also among *antisocial* and *sadistic* personalities. Prior to acquiring fears of exploitation and deception that almost reach psychotic proportions, the structural cohesion of these two personality disorders are relatively well maintained. However, when the circumstances of reality become intensely threatening, when their imperfections and misbehaviors are revealed for what they are, when their capacity to freely discharge their hostility is curtailed, or when their efforts to manipulate and exploit repetitively fail, there is a progressive breakdown in psychic cohesion. It is at this time that we see the paranoid pattern of distrust, of holding misguided grudges, of perceiving persistent personal attacks, of perverse accusations of disloyalty and infidelity, coming to the fore.

ASSESSING THE PARANOID: A CASE STUDY

As in the preceding chapters, we will describe a number of the response characteristics of paranoid personalities as seen on the Rorschach, TAT, and MMPI. In a later segment of this section, we will describe a paranoid personality case study and illustrate the clinical features of this disorder on the MCMI-III.

Owing to the highly ambiguous Rorschach stimuli, paranoids are likely to react in an extremely suspicious manner to the clinician's "devious ways." One may learn more about these patients from their extratest behaviors than from their actual response styles and content. Not uncommonly, for example, paranoids will examine the cards carefully, turning them over, checking little marks here and there, and then rejecting them as "defective." Critical commentary signifying their resentment and displeasure at the task are worthy pieces of information. As far as the formal responses are concerned, there is likely to be a high level of W combined with small and unusual location responses (e.g., dd). Owing to their suspiciousness and its consequent constriction, there probably will be relatively few M responses, except for one or two grandiose characterizations. The F percents are typically high and often of a very good quality. Popular and animal responses may also be frequent.

The problems that arise with the Rorschach also show up on the TAT. Paranoids are quite suspicious owing to the relative ambiguity of the cards. Story themes are limited for fear of exposing characteristics about oneself that one cannot suppress on a knowledgeable basis. Stories are orderly but brief. Should a particular theme strike a responsive chord within the patient, he or she may loosen constraints and develop an extensive storyline, possibly connected explicitly to present life circumstances. A careful selection of cards may prompt such self-disclosures.

As with the MCMI, high scores on the MMPI do not invariably correspond to what might be expected. Thus, although paranoids may score high on Scale 6, this result does not invariably occur. Knowing what has been said about them, paranoids seek to prevent or misabuse people of such attributions; as a consequence, the very paranoid quality of the items on the MMPI (and MCMI) alerts the patient to the self-disclosures the clinician may be seeking, hence leading the patient to refuse to respond in the expected manner. As a result, Scale 6 may not evidence as much success as a gauge of paranoid tendencies as might be desired. Moreover, and as with the Rorschach and TAT, paranoids often do what is *not* expected of them. Hence, one might find them responding in strange, if not random ways to the inventory. Similarly, forced to make simple binary choices, they may produce highly deviant responses that show up as inconsistent or high K scores. When more straightforward in their responses, that is, not disposed to deny or misguide, moderately elevated Scales 6 and 4 are usually helpful in identifying this personality disorder. Should Scale 8 also be elevated, we may safely infer for the presence of a more defective or decompensated level of psychic structure.

CASE 19.1

Peter M., Age 41, Married

Peter, an only child of informally educated parents, had been considered to be a "child genius" in his early school years. He received a PhD degree at 24, and subsequently held several middle-level positions as a research physicist in a number of industrial firms, going from one to another.

Peter's father also had considerable difficulty in his vocational career. Although uneducated in a formal sense, he acquired and thoroughly understood a great deal of technical information. He became of considerable value to several smaller companies who sought someone with his detailed knowledge and inventive mind. These positions were not held for very long. In usually less than a year or two, Peter's father alienated almost all his colleagues, accusing them of trying to steal his ideas and of not paying him what he was worth. Peter recalled quite vividly conversations that took place at the family table. Here, his father would be furious at the fact that he was "fired again" because he was "too smart for everyone around him."

In a pattern not dissimilar from his father's, Peter's haughty arrogance and egocentricity often resulted in conflicts with his superiors. They felt that Peter spent too much time working on his own "harebrained" schemes and not enough on company projects. Over time, Peter was assigned to jobs of lesser importance than that to which he was accustomed. He began to feel, not unjustly, that both his superiors and his subordinates were "making fun of him" and not taking him seriously. To remedy this attack on his status, Peter began to work on a scheme that would "revolutionize the industry," a new thermodynamic principle which, when applied to his company's major product, would prove extremely efficient and economical. After several months of what was conceded by others as "brilliant thinking," he presented his plans to the company president. Brilliant though it was, the plan overlooked certain obvious, simple facts of logic and economy.

Upon learning of its rejection, Peter withdrew to his home and began a well-established habit of drinking to excess. Moreover, he became obsessed with "new ideas," proposing them in intricate schematics and formulas to a number of government officials and industrialists. These resulted in new rebuffs that led to further efforts at self-inflation. It was not long thereafter that he lost all semblance of reality and control; for a brief period, he convinced himself of the grandiose delusion that he was Albert Einstein. Whether these delusions could be attributed fully to his alcoholic problems or were a direct outgrowth of his paranoid personality pattern was a major question for clinical assessment.

The following page portrays a paranoid personality MCMI-III profile (Figure 19.5) and below is its associated interpretive report.

INTERPRETIVE SUMMARY

There is reason to believe that at least a moderate level of pathology characterizes the overall personality organization of this man. Defective psychic structures suggest a rigidity in his intrapsychic morphology and a less than satisfactory flexibility of coping strategies. This man's foundation for effective intrapsychic regulation and socially acceptable interpersonal conduct appears deficient or overly constrained. He is subjected to the flux of his own suspicious attitudes and contradictory behavior, and his sense of psychic stability is often precarious. He has probably had a checkered history of disappointments in his personal and family relationships. Deficits in his social attainments may also be notable as well as a tendency to precipitate self-defeating vicious circles. Earlier aspirations may have resulted in frustrating setbacks,

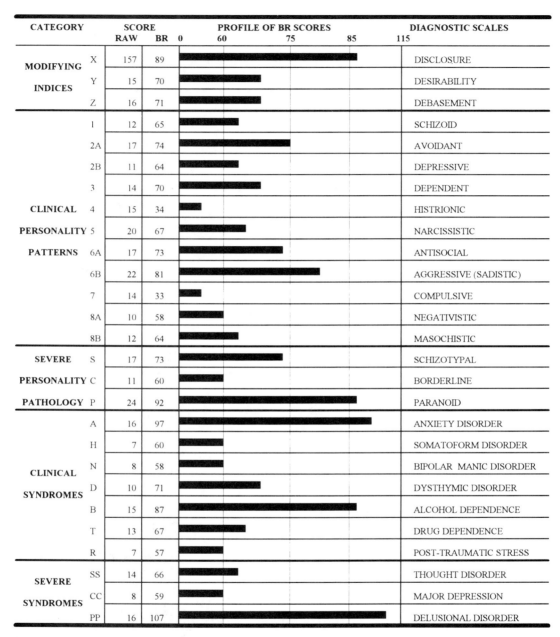

CATEGORY		SCORE RAW	BR	PROFILE OF BR SCORES 0 60 75 85 115	DIAGNOSTIC SCALES
MODIFYING INDICES	X	157	89		DISCLOSURE
	Y	15	70		DESIRABILITY
	Z	16	71		DEBASEMENT
CLINICAL PERSONALITY PATTERNS	1	12	65		SCHIZOID
	2A	17	74		AVOIDANT
	2B	11	64		DEPRESSIVE
	3	14	70		DEPENDENT
	4	15	34		HISTRIONIC
	5	20	67		NARCISSISTIC
	6A	17	73		ANTISOCIAL
	6B	22	81		AGGRESSIVE (SADISTIC)
	7	14	33		COMPULSIVE
	8A	10	58		NEGATIVISTIC
	8B	12	64		MASOCHISTIC
SEVERE PERSONALITY PATHOLOGY	S	17	73		SCHIZOTYPAL
	C	11	60		BORDERLINE
	P	24	92		PARANOID
CLINICAL SYNDROMES	A	16	97		ANXIETY DISORDER
	H	7	60		SOMATOFORM DISORDER
	N	8	58		BIPOLAR MANIC DISORDER
	D	10	71		DYSTHYMIC DISORDER
	B	15	87		ALCOHOL DEPENDENCE
	T	13	67		DRUG DEPENDENCE
	R	7	57		POST-TRAUMATIC STRESS
SEVERE SYNDROMES	SS	14	66		THOUGHT DISORDER
	CC	8	59		MAJOR DEPRESSION
	PP	16	107		DELUSIONAL DISORDER

Figure 19.5 Millon Clinical Multiaxial Inventory-III.

and efforts to achieve a consistent niche in life may have failed. Although he is usually able to function on a satisfactory basis, he may experience periods of marked emotional, cognitive, or behavioral dysfunction.

The MCMI-III profile of this man posits arrogance, an inflated yet insecure sense of self-worth, an edgy defensiveness against anticipated criticism, provocative interpersonal behavior, indifference to the welfare of others, and a seductive or baiting social manner. His disputatious and abrasive tendencies are ultimately likely to exasperate and anger others. He may be exploitive and may expect special consideration from friends and relatives, often without assuming much reciprocal responsibility. Actions that raise questions of personal integrity, such as disregarding social conventions and the rights of others, may indicate a deficient social conscience.

This man fears domination and dependence, resists external influence, and carefully protects his right to self-determination and autonomy. Failures and social irresponsibility may often be justified with expansive fantasies and prevarications. It may be important to him to maintain an image of cool strength, arrogance, and fearlessness. Self-reliance, unsentimentality, and hardboiled competitiveness may be viewed with pride. More significantly, he may exhibit a rash willingness to risk harm and may be notably fearless in the face of threats and punitive action. In fact, punishment may only reinforce his rebellious and hostile feelings. Malicious tendencies seen in others may be used to justify his own aggressive inclinations and may lead to personal and family difficulties as well as occasional legal entanglements. Antisocial behavior or drug problems may be prominent.

In all likelihood, this man is envious of others and wary of their motives. He feels unfairly treated and is easily provoked to irritability and anger. His thin facade of sociability can quickly give way to antagonistic and caustic comments, and he may obtain vindictive gratification by humiliating and dominating others. A marked suspicion of those in authority may cause him to feel secure only when he has power.

Probably skilled in the ways of social influence, he may be adept at deceiving others. Possibly lacking deep feelings of loyalty, he may successfully scheme beneath a veneer of civility. A guiding principle for him may be to outwit others, controlling and exploiting them before they control and exploit him. With a chip-on-the-shoulder attitude, he may exhibit readiness to attack those he distrusts. Incidental events may be misconstrued as critical and then offered as evidence of purposeful deception and malice on the part of others. If he is unsuccessful in channeling his omnipresent suspicions and impulses, his resentment may mount into acts of abuse.

The features and dynamics of the following Axis I clinical syndromes appear worthy of description and analysis. They may arise in response to external precipitants but are likely to reflect and accentuate several of the more enduring and pervasive aspects of this man's basic personality makeup.

There is reason to believe that this man is experiencing the clinical symptoms of a delusional (paranoid) disorder (e.g., irrational jealousy, ideas of reference) and that this disorder is probably set within a broad context of other problematic characteristics and personality pathologies. Given his dispositional background, he may exhibit periods of aggressive behavior and uncontrollable rages. Even when these are moderated successfully by medication, an undertone of surliness and bitterness remains, inclining him to be easily inflamed and unpredictable in his responses to what he perceives as the provocations of others.

Unable to control deep or powerful sources of threat, this characteristically angry, conflicted, and irritable man is now experiencing the clinical signs of an anxiety disorder. Various symptoms may be evident, notably, muscular tightness, headache, fatigue, perspiration, and chest palpitations, as well as such behavioral indexes as edginess and distractibility. These experiences probably derive from his feeling of being trapped by the upwelling of uncontrollable inner conflicts or by the feeling of being exposed to events or forces that he cannot counteract. His restlessness and jumpiness derive energy from the press of these unchecked sources of danger.

That this man experiences repeated episodes of alcohol abuse may be reliably assumed. These bouts may be prompted in part by the frustration and disappointment in his life. He is characteristically unpredictable, moody, and impulsive, and these behaviors may be intensified when he is drinking heavily. At these times, his brooding resentment breaks out of control, often resulting in stormy and destructive consequences. He may subsequently express genuine feelings of guilt and contrition, but the destructive and injurious effects of his behavior are likely to persist. Deep resentment that is restrained in his sober state may be unleashed in full force when he is drinking and manifests itself in irrational accusations and physical intimidation, if not brutality, toward family members. He may evince a self-destructive facet to his extropunitive hostility, and this serves to undermine both himself and others.

PATHOGENIC DEVELOPMENTAL BACKGROUND

There is no unique set nor sequence of determinants in the dispositional background of paranoid personalities. Different combinations and orders of events may give rise to the syndrome. The preceding discussion has formally recognized some of these divergent lines by differentiating the paranoid syndrome into several variants; the discussion of backgrounds is arranged according to these differences. Note again that the propositions presented are provisional hypotheses, not facts. There is little in the way of dependable evidence from systematic and well-designed research to justify making definitive statements.

HYPOTHESIZED BIOGENIC FACTORS

The roots that lead to the paranoid personality stemming from genetic or constitutional factors appear unclear at this time. Nevertheless, a few speculations that go beyond current empirical findings may be useful for future investigators to explore.

1. *Malignant* paranoids appear to come from families with a disproportionately high number of members who display vigorous energy, an irascible choleric temperament, or a fearless parmic temperament. As children, these patients tend to be active and intrusive, have frequent temper outbursts, are difficult to manage, and precipitate difficulties with others by their thick-skinned, aggressive manner. Many possess a constitutional mesomorphic-endomorphic build, a physique that tends to reinforce the learning of assertive behaviors. It may be speculated that aspects of their temperament can be traced to low thresholds of reactivity in portions of the limbic and reticular systems.

2. *Querulous* paranoids often evidence irregular infantile reaction patterns and an uneven course of maturation, traits that tend to promote inconsistent and contradictory styles of parental behavior management. Their characteristic hyperactivity and irritable affectivity may be attributed to low neurophysiological thresholds for responsivity.

3. *Insular* paranoids, similar in background to many timorous schizotypals, often have a family history of apprehensive relatives, suggesting the possibility that genetic dispositions may be operative. An anxiously threctic infantile reaction pattern is not uncommon in these personalities, and may precipitate parental exasperation and rejection. Many may have shown an irregular sequence of maturation, resulting in imbalances among competencies, an inability to handle intense emotions, and the emergence of rigidly aversive behaviors. The possibility that there may exist an underlying

excess in limbic and sympathetic system reactivity, or a neurochemical acceleration of synaptic transmission, likewise may be posed; such dysfunctions can give rise to the hypersensitivity, cognitive autism, and social isolation that characterize these patients.

CHARACTERISTIC EXPERIENTIAL HISTORY

A number of the roots by which certain milder personality styles eventuate in a paranoid pattern will be described briefly in the following paragraphs.

The Fanatic Subtype

A major group of defective-paranoids, the *fanatic* subtype is likely to have been overvalued and indulged by their parents, given the impression that their mere existence was of sufficient worth in itself. Few developed a sense of interpersonal responsibility, failing to learn how to cooperate, to share, or to think of the interests of others. Unrestrained by their parents and unjustly confident in their self-worth, their fantasies had few boundaries, allowing them to create fanciful images of their power and achievements. The social insensitivity and exploitiveness of these future paranoids led inevitably to interpersonal difficulties. Once beyond the protective home setting, they ran hard against objective reality. Their illusion of omnipotence was challenged and their self-centeredness and ungiving attitudes were attacked. In time, their image of eminence and perfection was shattered. Rather than face or adapt to reality, or build up their competencies to match their high self-esteem, they turned increasingly to the refuge of fantasy. Rationalizing their defects and lost in their imaginary gratifications, they retreated and became further alienated from others. As new rejections and humiliations cumulated, the narcissistic defective-paranoids moved more into themselves, soon beginning to confuse their fantasy compensations for objective reality. In their imaginative world, they redeemed themselves and reasserted their pride and status. Their lifelong habit of self-reinforcement enabled them to weave alibis and proofs of their own perfection and grandiosity with supreme facility. Protected by these fantasies, they remained indifferent to others, successfully compensating for the others' "jealous criticism" and their malevolent lies and "distortions."

These individuals are similar to their less structurally defective counterparts. They seek to retain their admirable self-image, tend to act in a haughty and pretentious manner, and are naively self-confident, ungenerous, exploitive, expansive, and presumptuous, displaying a supercilious contempt and arrogance toward others. In contrast to the more mildly dysfunctional narcissists, who are likely to have achieved a modicum of success with their optimistic veneer and exploitive behaviors, defective-paranoid fanatics have run hard against reality. Their illusions of omnipotence may periodically have been shattered, toppling them from their vaulted self-image of eminence. Accustomed to seeing themselves as the center of things, they cannot bear the lessened significance now assigned them. Their narcissism has been severely wounded. To restate our prior descriptions, not only must they counter the humiliation found in reality, but they must reestablish their pride through extravagant claims. Upset by assaults against their self-esteem, defective-paranoid fanatics reconstruct their image of themselves even further and ascend beyond the status from which they fell. By self-reinforcement, they endow themselves with exalted competencies and powers. They dismiss any evidence that conflicts with their newly acquired and self-designated importance. Whatever flimsy talents and accomplishments they possess are embellished, creating thereby a new self-image that brushes aside objective reality.

As noted before, lacking internal discipline and cognitive control, *fanatic* paranoids allow their reparative fantasies free rein to create a fabric of high appeal, caring little that their claims are unwarranted. Their grand assertions become fixed and adamant, for they are necessary elements in regaining an identity of significance and esteem. Restating earlier phrasings, these defective-paranoids go to great lengths to convince themselves and others of the validity of their claims, insisting against obvious contradictions that they deserve to be catered to, and that they are entitled to special acknowledgment and privileges. But the evidence in support of their assertions is as flimsy as a house of cards, easily collapsed by the slightest incursion. Unable to sustain this image before others and rebuffed and powerless to gain the recognition they crave, these fanatic paranoids turn more and more inward for salvation. Taking liberties with objective facts and wandering further from social reality and shared meanings, they concoct an ever more elaborate world of fantasy. They may don the role and attributes of some idolized person, whose repute cannot be questioned by others. As this identification takes root, these paranoids begin to

assert a new identity: a noble and inspired leader, a saint or powerful political figure, or an awesome and talented genius. Crossing the line into psychotic delusions, they may propose grandiose schemes for "saving the world," for solving insurmountable scientific problems, for creating new societies, and so on. These schemes may be worked out in minute detail and are formulated often with sufficient logic to draw at least momentary attention and recognition from others.

The Malignant Subtype

The characteristic experiential history of the *malignant* paranoids suggests that they were subjected to parental antagonism and harassment. Many served as scapegoats for displaced parental aggression. Instead of responding with anxiety as a consequence of this mistreatment, they acquired the feeling that they had "to be contended with" and that they could cause trouble and "get a rise" out of others through their unyielding and provocative behaviors. In addition, many learned vicariously to model themselves after their aggressive parents. The *malignant* paranoid learned to perceive the world as harsh and unkind, a place calling for protective vigilance and mistrust. Many also acquired the self-confidence to fend for themselves.

Through their own aggressive actions, these future paranoids found they could disturb others and manipulate events to their suiting. Mistrustful of others and confident of their powers, they rejected parental controls and values, and supplanted them with their own. Rebellious of parental authority, they developed few inner controls, often failing to learn to restrain impulses or to avoid temptations.

Similar learning is acquired by children reared in broken families and disorganized subcultures. Impulse controls are not learned, and children gain their outlook on life wandering "on the street" in concert with equally destitute and disillusioned peers. There are few congenial and socially successful models for them to emulate, and the traditional values and standards of society are viewed as alien, if not downright hypocritical and hostile. Aggressive toughness seems mandatory for survival, and these youngsters learn quickly to adopt a "dog-eat-dog" attitude and to counter hostility with the same. Anticipating resentment and betrayal from others, future *malignant* paranoids moved through life with a chip-on-the-shoulder attitude, bristling with anger and reacting before hostility and duplicity actually occurred. Resentment and antagonism were projected. Dreading being attacked, humiliated, or powerless, they learned to attack first.

In contrast to their less structurally defective prototype, *malignant* paranoids experienced repeated rebuffs. Their confidence weakened, they could not successfully sustain their assertive and vindictive strategy. Faced with repeated setbacks, they redoubled their isolation from others, preferring fantasy as a means of nursing their wounds. Their growing apartness from social life, their gnawing mistrust of relationships, and the devastating feeling that they may have lost their powers of self-determination, led these paranoids into increasingly irrational suspicions and, ultimately, their delusions of persecution.

These paranoids are characterized best by their power orientation, their mistrust and resentment of others, and their belligerent and intimidating manner. There is a ruthless desire to triumph over others, to vindicate themselves for past wrongs by cunning revenge or callous force, if necessary. In contrast to their nonparanoid counterpart, these personalities have found that their efforts to outwit and frustrate others have only prompted the others to inflict more of the harsh punishment and rejection to which they were previously subjected. Their strategy of arrogance and brutalization has backfired and they seek retribution, no longer as much through direct action as through fantasy.

Persistent and humiliating setbacks have confirmed these paranoids' expectancy of aggression from others. Of course, they have by their own hand stirred up much hostility and disfavor. Their argumentative and "chip-on-the-shoulder" attitude has provoked ample antagonism from others. Isolated and resentful, they now turn increasingly to themselves to cogitate and to mull over their fate. Left to their own ruminations, they begin to concoct plots in which every facet of their environment plays a threatening and treacherous role. Moreover, through projection, they attribute their own venom to others, ascribing to them the malice and ill will these patients feel within themselves. The line draws thin between objective antagonism and imagined hostility. Slowly, the belief takes hold that others are intentionally persecuting them. Alone, feeling all the more threatened, and with decreasing self-esteem, their suspicions now cross the line into psychotic delusions.

The Obdurate Subtype

In the *obdurate* subtype of the defective-paranoid pattern, children learned to conceive their worth in

proportion to the degree of their success in meeting parental demands, feeling that they would be punished and abandoned if they failed to heed their parent's strictures. Future paranoids may have felt especially vulnerable to error, knowing that they had to keep within approved boundaries, yet being unsure of exactly what these boundaries were. Fearing transgression, they modeled themselves closely after authority figures, repressing all inclinations toward autonomy and independence lest these behaviors provoke wrath and desertion. They learned to follow rules, failed to develop initiative, and lacked spontaneity and imagination. Overtrained to be conventional and to feel guilt and self-reproach for failing to subscribe to the rigid prescriptions of their elders, these children sacrificed their own identity to gain favor and esteem from others. This lifestyle perpetuated their difficulties. Their rigidity and conformity precluded growth and change, kept them from genuinely warm human relationships, and alienated them from their own inner feelings. Constantly tense for fear that they would overstep approved lines, they found themselves unable to make decisions or act assertively. Their indecisiveness may have turned to guilt for having let others down. Thinking of themselves as frauds and failures led to increased self-derogation. In time, these paranoids learn to anticipate that others cannot be trusted to be considerate of their efforts to adhere to their expectations, perceiving them as insensitive and potentially dangerous, enhancing a fear of betrayal and treachery on the part of those on whom they may have previously depended and looked to for guidance. The obdurate subtype stems from a conflation of paranoid and compulsive personality features. These persons have a background of parental overcontrol through contingent punishment. Most have striven to meet parental demands and to avoid errors and transgressions, thereby minimizing punitive treatment and the threat of abandonment. In early life, they sought to model themselves after authority figures, forgoing their independence and following the rules with utmost precision. As a consequence of their rigid conformity, they lack spontaneity and initiative, are unable to form deep and genuine relationships, and are indecisive and fearful of the unknown. For various reasons, differing from case to case, the security these paranoids sought to achieve through submission and propriety was not attained. Lacking guidance and support from others, intolerant of suspense, and dreading punishment lest repressed anger erupt, they drew into themselves, turned away from their dependent conformity, and sought solace, if they could, within their own thoughts. Although renouncing their dependency, obdurate paranoids cannot relinquish their lifelong habits. Thus, feelings of guilt and fear become acute as they begin to assert themselves. Anticipating punishment for their nonconforming behaviors and feeling that such actions deserve condemnation, they project these self-judgments on others and now view them to be hostile and persecutory.

These individuals are similar to the moderately severe compulsive personality. However, in contrast to their milder counterparts, who retain the hope of achieving protection through the good offices of others, obdurate paranoids renounce their dependency aspirations and assume a firm and absolute stance of independence. Despite their growing hostility and the repudiation of conformity and submissive respect as a way of life, they retain their basic rigidity and perfectionism. They are now all the more grim and humorless, tense, controlled and inflexible, small-minded, legalistic, and self-righteous. These features of their makeup are even more deeply embedded and internalized as a fixed habit system. They may have found it necessary to discard their dependence on others as their primary source of reward, but the remnants of their lifelong habit of overcontrol and faultlessness are not as readily abandoned. As described in previous pages, they continue to seek the clarity of rules and regulations, cannot tolerate suspense, and impose order and system on their life. Deprived now of the guidelines of those others they have spurned, these paranoids lean increasingly on themselves. With little hesitation, they will impose their self-created standards on others, demand that others submit to their way of doing things, and attack them with the same punitive attitudes to which they themselves were earlier subjected. The impossible regulations they set for others allow them to vent hostilities and to condemn others for their failures.

Despite their public repudiation of being conforming and submissive persons, obdurate paranoids cannot free themselves entirely of feeling conflict and guilt. Although they try to justify their aggressive manner, they cannot fully square these actions with their past beliefs. Moreover, their present overt arrogance reactivates past anxieties, for they cannot escape remembering the retaliation their own hostile actions provoked in the past. They have learned from past experience to anticipate disfavor and criticism in response to contrary and nonconforming behaviors. Consequently, as they scan their environment they "see" in the movements and remarks of others the hostility they anticipate. Further, to deny or justify their behaviors, they project their anger on others. This mechanism proves self-defeating because it leads them to "find" hostile intent where none, in fact, exists. Last, inner feelings of guilt reactivate self-condemnatory attitudes. Part of their self feels that they should be punished for their resentments and behaviors. Thus, in combination, their anticipations, projections, and guilt lead them inexorably to believe that others are "after them," seeking to condemn, punish, belittle, and undo them.

The Querulous Subtype

The *querulous* paranoid is a variant related in part to a basic negativistic personality. These paranoids often evidence irregular infantile patterns and an uneven course of maturation, traits that often promote inconsistent and contradictory styles of parental management. Their characteristic irritable affectivity may be attributed to low neurophysiological thresholds of responsivity.

Most of these patients are likely to have acquired their irritability and discontent in response to inconsistent parental treatment. Many were subjected to capricious vacillations in parental emotion and interest. Thus, their parents may have been affectionate one moment and irrationally hostile the next. These erratic behaviors often serve as a model for vicarious learning and imitation. Similar learnings are often acquired in schismatic families where parents vie for their children's loyalties, creating not only confusion and contradictory behaviors but feelings of guilt and anxiety. Early learnings are perpetuated by the future paranoids' own actions. Intransigence, disgruntlement, and behavioral inconsistency result in difficult personal relationships and the persistence of chaotic and erratic experiences. Should these events lead to painful setbacks and severe disappointments, these paranoids will have learned to forgo their dependency needs, gradually relinquishing all hope of affection and approval from others. They begin to see others as having been given preferential and undeserved treatment. Their complaints and discontent begin to take on an irrational quality. Jealousy delusions may come to the fore, and accusations of infidelity, deceit, and betrayal are made against innocent relatives and friends.

These patients may be differentiated from their less structurally defective counterparts and the equally ill *petulant* borderline by the presence of periodic delusions. In common with their affiliated syndromal patterns, these paranoids are noted by their discontent, pessimism, stubbornness, and vacillation. However, this paranoid is more aggressively negativistic and faultfinding, and is almost invariably sullen, resentful, obstructive, and peevish, openly registering feelings of jealousy, of being misunderstood, and of being cheated. Rarely can these patients sustain good relationships, and they re-create endless wrangles wherever they go. Demoralized by these failures, they forgo all hopes of gaining affection and approval from others and decide to renounce these aspirations in preference for self-determination.

As described previously, the paranoids' fantasies expand and weave into irrational envy. Their grumbling comments turn to overt anger and hostility. Each of these may feed into a theme of unjust misfortune. If unchecked, they take the form of a psychotic delusion of resentful jealousy. In similar fashion, erotic delusions may evolve among these patients. Although they consciously repudiate their need for others, these paranoids still seek affection from them. Rather than admit these desires, however, they will defensively interpret the casual remarks of others as signs of amorous intent. However, they are unable to tolerate these "attentions" because they dread further betrayal and exploitation. As a consequence, querulous paranoids will insist that they must be "protected" against erotic seduction by others. Innocent victims may be accused of committing indignities.

The Insular Subtype

The *insular* paranoids are the most likely of the paranoid personalities to be precipitated into a frank psychotic disorder when confronted with painful humiliation and derogation from others. Although they have sought by active withdrawal and isolation to minimize their social contacts, this coping defense is not impenetrable. Should their armor be pierced and their protective detachment assaulted and encroached on, they will not only experience the anguish of the present but will have reactivated within them the painful memories of past assaults.

Deep resentments from the past may remain seething near the surface, but are experienced as a threat to equanimity. These angry impulses create anxiety because they jeopardize the insular paranoid's security. Such hostility is doubly dangerous.

Not only may it be directed at the very persons whom the paranoid fears trusting, thereby undermining what faith they may still have in these relationships but, in addition, it will likely provoke their wrath, leading to outright condemnation and desertion. To counter their angry impulses, these defectively structured *insular* paranoids may find themselves unable to muzzle and bind their deep reservoir of resentment. Struggling feverishly to control their surging anger, they may turn their feelings inward and impose on themselves harsh judgments and punitive actions. These efforts may not succeed, however. Accusations of their own unworthiness are but mild rebukes for the suspicion and fury they feel. Self-mutilation and suicide, symbolic acts of self-desertion, or brutal attacks against others—a direct expression of their rage—may become the only punishments that "fit the crime."

Under these pressures, the insular paranoid may, instead, burst into a flood of erratic, hostile, and bizarre reactions. Fearful lest they be further humiliated and injured, and unable to govern the onrush of previously repressed anxieties and resentments, these patients may lose all controls and be drowned in a wave of chaotic and primitive impulses. Thus, at the moment their external world inundates them, their inner world erupts. What we see is a frantic struggle to escape being smothered and submerged.

SELF-PERPETUATION PROCESSES

The instrumental behaviors of the structurally defective patterns are less adaptive and more self-defeating than those of the less severely ill. Moreover, they are more vulnerable to the strains of life, and are easily precipitated into psychotic disorders. Situations that promote the anxieties of attachment, expectations of sadistic treatment, or the loss of self-determination result in defensive vigilance, withdrawal, and ultimately in the delusions that are so characteristic of the paranoid personality. Not infrequently, the isolation and fantasy ruminations of the patient become deeply entrenched, leading to more permanent psychotic habits and attitudes. We will postpone to the next chapter a discussion of the more structurally decompensated paranoid patterns. For the present, we will discuss the coping efforts of paranoids, by which they seek to prevent further decompensation but that only intensify their difficulties.

Countering Attachment

Paranoids have reason to be mistrustful and to fear betrayal and sadistic treatment. To counter these sources of anxiety, they have learned to keep their distance from others and to remain strong and vigilant, not only as a protective stance but as a means of vindication and triumph over potential attackers. To assure their security, they engage in a variety of measures both to prevent the weakening of their resolve and to generate new powers for controlling others.

One of the major steps in this quest is a desensitization of tender and affectionate feelings. They become hard and unyielding and immune and insensitive to the suffering and pleading of others. By so doing, they secure themselves against entrapment and against being drawn into the web of deceit and subjugation. Assuming a callous and unsympathetic posture is not difficult for the paranoid; not only does it serve as a defensive maneuver against attachment, but it also allows for the discharge of resentments and anger.

As a further means of affirming self-determination, paranoids assume an air of invincibility and pride. They convince themselves that they have extraordinary capacities, that they can master their fate alone and overcome every obstacle, resistance, and conflict. They dismiss all traces of self-doubt and repudiate the nurturant overtures of others; in this way they need never dread having to lean on anyone.

But the paranoids' autonomy is spurious. They maintain an illusion of superiority by rigid self-conviction and exaggerated bluff. Time and again, their competencies are proved defective and they are made to look foolish; thus, their precarious equilibrium, self-appointed certainty, and pride are upset too easily and too often. To redeem their belief in their invincibility, these patients begin to employ extreme and grossly pathological measures. Rather than accepting their obvious weaknesses and faults, they assert that some alien influence is undermining their efforts and causing them to fail and be humbled before others. Frailty, ineffectuality, shame, or whatever predicament paranoids find themselves in, must be attributed to an irresistible destructive power. As the suspicion of a "foreign force" grows and as vigilance against belittlement and humiliation crumbles, they begin increasingly to distort reality. Not only can paranoids not accept that their failures are self-caused, they are unwilling to ascribe these failures to pedestrian

powers and events; rather, their loss must reflect the malicious workings of devils, X rays, magnetism, poisons, and so on. Their delusions of influence and persecution signify, then, both the dread of submission and the need to bolster pride by attributing shortcomings to the action of insidious deceits or supernatural forces.

Discharging Hostility

As we have just noted, the confidence and pride of the paranoid are but hollow shells; their pose of independence stands on insecure footings. They are extremely vulnerable to challenge, and their defensive facade is constantly weakened by real and delusional threats. To reassert power and invincibility, these patients must resort to some course of action that will shore up their defenses and thwart attackers. Hostility in the paranoid is just such a defensive and restitutive measure, a means of countering threats to the equilibrium and a means of reestablishing an image of self-determination and autonomy.

Once released, the paranoids' hostility draws on a deep reserve of earlier resentments. The fires of present angers are fed by animosities reactivated from the past; intense impulses for reprisal and vindication are brought to the surface and discharged into the stream of current hostility. To restate a previous paragraph, every trivial rebuff by others is a painful reminder of the past, part of a plot traceable to early humiliations and mistreatments. Trapped in a timeless web of deceit and malice, their fears and angers may mount to monumental proportions. With defenses down, controls dissolved, and fantasies of doom running rampant, their dread and fury increase. A flood of frantic and hostile energies may erupt, letting loose a violent discharge, an uncontrollable torrent of vituperation and aggression.

These psychotic outbursts are usually of brief duration. As the swell of fear and hostility is discharged, these patients regain their composure and seek to rationalize their actions, reconstruct defenses, and bind their aggression. But this subsiding of bizarre emotions does not lead to normality; rather, the patient merely returns to the former paranoid personality pattern.

Reconstructing Reality

The paranoid transforms events to suit his self-image and aspirations; delusions may be seen as an extreme form of this more general process of reality reconstruction. Even the passive-ambivalent, noted for excessive rigidity, exhibits this lowering of controls, this loosening of boundaries between what is real and what is fantasied. These reconstructions take many forms, but it will suffice for us to describe the two that are most commonly found among paranoids: denial of weakness and malevolence, and their projection on others; and aggrandizement of self through grandiose fantasies.

As previously noted, troubled by the mounting evidence of their inadequacy and hostility, paranoids must go further than mere denial; they not only disown these objectionable traits, but throw them back at their accusers, real or imagined. It is "they" who are stupid, malicious and vindictive; the paranoid, in contrast, is an innocent and unfortunate victim of the ineffectuality and malevolence of others. With this simple reversal, the paranoids not only absolve themselves of fault, but find an outlet and a justification for resentment and anger. If they are in error, others should be blamed for their ineptness; if they have been aggressive, it is only because the evil in others has provoked them. They have been an innocent, and justifiably indignant, scapegoat for the blundering and the slanderous.

But the gains of the projection maneuver are short lived; moreover, it ultimately intensifies the paranoids' plight. By ascribing slanderous and malevolent urges to others, they now face threat where none in fact existed; thus, by subjective distortion, they have created an ever-present hostile environment that surrounds them and from which there is no physical escape. Furthermore, their unjust accusations are bound to provoke in others feelings of exasperation and anger; thus, the strategy of projection has transformed what may have been overtures of good will from others into the feared hostility.

Restating an earlier comment, faced with genuine derogation and threat, paranoids must reestablish their sense of autonomy. Once more, they may have no recourse but to turn to fantasy. Unable to confront feelings of inadequacy and insignificance, they fabricate an image of superior self-worth and importance. Left alone to ruminate, they unfold proofs of their eminence through intricate self-deceptions. These patients renounce or distort objective reality and supplant it with a glorified image of self. Having endowed themselves with limitless virtues, powers, and talents, they need not now be ashamed of themselves or

fear anyone; they can "rise above" petty jealousies and can "understand all too clearly" why others seek to undermine and persecute them. The meaning of others' malicious attacks is obvious; it is the paranoids' eminence—their infinite superiority—which others envy and seek to destroy.

Step by step, self-glorifications and persecutory delusions form into a systematic pattern; the "whole picture" comes into sharp relief. One delusion feeds on another, unchecked by the controls of social reality. Fabrications, employed initially to cope with the despair of reality, become more "real" than reality itself; it is at this point that we see the clear emergence of a psychotic phase.

THERAPEUTIC INTERVENTIONS

Like other structurally defective personality patterns, the prospects for the paranoid are not promising. Their habits and attitudes are deeply ingrained and pervade the entire fabric of their functioning. Modest improvements are possible, but these are likely merely to diminish the frequency of troublesome episodes rather then revamp the basic personality style. Impairment in the paranoid is more likely to be as much an interpersonal as an intrapsychic nature and tends to be less disturbing to the patient than to others. Most paranoid personalities do not succumb to serious and persistent delusions and tend to come in contact with psychological services only at the request of others, or when their defenses crumble, triggering the onset of a more severe condition. They are regarded by most associates as suspicious and testy people. A very small number attain considerable success, especially if they are unusually talented or happen by good fortune to attract a coterie of disciples.

Despite difficult social relationships, the long-range prognosis for the paranoid is not as poor as that of the schizotypal, one of its structurally defective counterparts. Paranoids can obtain satisfactions from themselves; schizotypals do not. Faced with external derogation, paranoids can nurture themselves until their wounds are sufficiently healed. Schizotypals, lacking faith both in themselves and others, remain empty-handed. Compared with borderlines, their other structurally defective counterpart, paranoids have both a disadvantage and an advantage insofar as prognosis is concerned. Borderlines characteristically maintain reasonably good interpersonal relations. Paranoids do not. As a consequence, borderline personalities may gain some of the support and encouragement they need. Furthermore, unlike the paranoid, they turn to others during difficult periods, often soliciting enough affection and security to forestall a further decline. In contrast, paranoids tend to remain socially difficult and keep to themselves when relationships turn sour. Behaviors such as these increase their isolation, not only resulting in an intensification of their suspicions and secretiveness but giving rise to further social estrangement. To the borderlines' disadvantage is their lack of internal reserve, which leads them to slip into a state of helplessness should they fail to evoke external support. This is not the case with paranoids. Not only will they refuse to submit to weakness and indolence, but they will struggle to "pull themselves up by their own bootstraps."

Strategic Goals

Despite each patient's unique combination of presenting complaints, reasons for entering therapy, and personality presentation, a cardinal aim of personologic therapy with paranoid personalities is to loosen up the extreme constriction and inflexibility that pervades all clinical domains. Concurrently, an attempt must be made to balance the confused mix of polarity reversals that may have contributed to perpetuating the paranoid pattern. If paranoids can learn to let down their guard and obtain satisfaction and reinforcement from interpersonal relationships, instead of being constantly on the defensive, they may open themselves up to many life-enhancing experiences.

Reestablishing Polarity Balances

The paranoid personality displays an extreme sensitivity to psychic pain, anticipating rejection and humiliation at every turn. For this reason, they try to avoid situations that are aversive or negatively reinforcing. Always wary of what others can do to hurt them and fearful of external control, paranoids have learned to withdraw from others and turn to themselves. Therapy then should begin to focus on reducing the predominant self-orientation as well as attenuating the extreme insensitivity to the needs of others. Countering vigilant paranoid mistrust of others is fundamental to balancing the pain-pleasure polarity. Gradually aiding the patient in identifying possible rewards from interactions with others will fuel their desire to seek positive experiences within the realm of interpersonal contact.

Countering Perpetuating Tendencies

The suspicious nature and extreme distrust of others are at the core of this personality's problems. They remain ever so vigilant to signs of rejection that they inevitably uncover them. Accusations and provocations, combined with projection of personal insecurities onto others, cannot help but antagonize people. Interrupting the cycle that perpetuates the paranoid may best be accomplished in an indirect manner. Beck and Freeman (1990) suggest increasing the paranoid's sense of self-efficacy. This in turn will reduce the likelihood that projection will be employed as a defense. Empowering the self may take the edge off the extreme hypervigilance that paranoids use to scan the environment for the expected signs of hostilities.

As a result of these delusional thought patterns, paranoids tend to turn from others to avoid rejection and rebuff. Withdrawal thus serves a self-protective function, yet it also makes them more susceptible to reality distortions, leaving them to ruminate and construct elaborate fabrications without the necessary reality checks. Inadequate reality testing combined with a suspicious attitude toward others fosters the development of delusional thought processes. A major goal of personologic therapy with this disorder is to minimize the tendency of paranoids to engage in self-protective withdrawal by encouraging them to gather additional information from the environment before reevaluating assumptions about others. When paranoids establish that their perceptions about the dangers in their surroundings are largely inaccurate, the use of self-protective withdrawals may decrease, thereby further attenuating their pathology.

Modifying Domain Dysfunctions

The paranoid personality displays prominent dysfunctions in the cognitive style and expressive behavior domains. Their suspicious nature extends rigidly, inflexibly, and virtually indiscriminately to all situations encountered. Helping the paranoid see that most fears are imaginary and invalid will assist in alleviating the guardedness. It will furthermore diminish the need to engage in self-protective withdrawal.

The projective thinking displayed by paranoids not only protects their self-image, it often elicits attack and rejection. As personal faults are disavowed and attributed to others, the belief that the source of all misery lies in the malevolent nature of their adversaries becomes stronger. Therapeutic efforts must aim to strengthen the paranoid's self-sufficiency, gradually encouraging these patients to accept minor faults in themselves. Affectively, paranoids display a touchiness and irritability that, combined with their interpersonally provocative style, will be experienced as abrasive even by otherwise affable individuals. Interventions must teach paranoids to express anger and criticism in a more subtle, socially accepted manner, as well as encourage the expression of positive emotions.

Early relational experiences have been internalized and have left the paranoid with a set of fixed, unyielding, and unwarranted beliefs about others. The systemic constriction and inflexibility of their morphologic organization, and their tenacious and unalterable coping styles present a major dilemma. Work in this area must emphasize the acquisition of more diverse coping mechanisms. It is also essential for paranoids to encounter new relational experiences.

Tactical Modalities

What then is a good approach to take with paranoid patients? Essentially, the therapist must build trust through a series of slow, progressive steps and must show a quiet, formal, genuine respect for these patients. The therapist must accept, but not confirm, patients' unusual beliefs and allow them to explore their thoughts and feelings at a pace that can be tolerated. The major initial goal of therapy is to free paranoids of mistrust by showing them that they can share their anxieties with another person without the humiliation and maltreatment to which they are accustomed. If this can be accomplished, paranoids may learn to look at the world not only from their own perspective but through the eyes of others. If they can trust the therapist, they can begin to relax, relinquish their defenses, and open themselves to new attitudes. Once they have accepted the therapist as trustworthy, they may be able to lean on him or her and accept the therapist's thoughts and suggestions. This may become a basis for a more generalized lessening of suspicions and for a wider scope of trusting and sharing.

Domain-Oriented Techniques

Regarding specific modes of therapy, it is simplest to say that technique is secondary to building trust. There are, however, a variety of procedures that can be employed along the way. Regardless of the particular approach used at any given time, the therapist can avoid arousing further suspicion by carefully explaining each move to the patient (Gabbard, 1994). The treatment rationale should be straightforward and clear, and treatment planning must acknowledge the paranoid's need for control. At no time should the patient be directly confronted with the delusions.

Behavioral interventions can target the paranoid's need to be constantly on guard, actively resisting sources of external control. Because they are so fearful of being externally influenced, behavioral techniques will need to emphasize personal control. Contingency management programs that rely on others to provide reinforcement are likely to fail and should be avoided. In situations where others represent a threat to their autonomy, paranoids may lash out aggressively in an attempt to regain control and relieve anxiety. The immediate gains, however, are temporary and ultimately serve only to perpetuate the paranoid style. A reduction in defensiveness, as well as enhanced feelings of competence and self-control, can be achieved through assertiveness training. The therapist may have to educate the patient about the differences between aggression and assertiveness. Teaching paranoids that they can express thoughts in a constructive manner, without the intensity of the negative affect will take the edge off their explosive nature. Relaxation training can help them feel more at ease and may also lessen the need for alternative modes of relaxation such as substance abuse.

A functional analysis often will reveal particular people or environments that promote paranoid reactions. Impulse control can be strengthened by assisting patients to recognize these contextual determinants and subsequently avoid them if the situation cannot be handled. If possible, environmental irritants should be removed. To gain patients' cooperation, the therapist can use verbal reinforcers, emphasizing that acquiring the skills will enhance their self control.

Turkat (1990) demonstrates the use of behavioral techniques in his case description of Mr. E. His approach focused on diminishing the patient's anxiety about criticism. Components of the anxiety-reduction approach include construction of a fear hierarchy, teaching progressive muscle relaxation, and developing a repertoire of adaptive cognitions in response to fear-eliciting stimuli. Criticism and negative feedback may be the result of deficits in interpersonal skills; therefore, anxiety management training procedures should be followed by social-skills training. Paranoids are often extremely self-absorbed, unable to tune in other's thoughts and feelings. Assisting them in overcoming this inattentiveness can be accomplished by communication-skills training. The therapist can engage the client in role-playing, providing immediate feedback. In summary, treatment with this patient was aimed at diminishing hypersensitivity to social evaluation and eliminating those behaviors that invited criticism.

Interpersonal approaches may help establish a collaborative relationship between the paranoid and the therapist. An important goal of interpersonal therapy with this disorder is to facilitate what Benjamin (1993a) calls pattern recognition. She notes, however, that paranoids often are hesitant to discuss family history. This reluctance is thought to stem from fear that talking about family issues will elicit punishment. Nevertheless, paranoid patients need to learn that, although the expectations of attack are understandable considering their early learning experiences, they are no longer appropriate or adaptive in their current environment.

The abuse and harassment paranoids suffered at the hands of parents can have a profound impact on child-rearing practices, and if intervention does not target this area, future generations may repeat the pattern of abuse. Benjamin suggests helping paranoids recall how it felt to be abused. This in turn can foster a more empathic attitude toward their own children. Substituting maladaptive patterns will require the paranoid to change from identification to differentiation from the aggressors, while rechanneling the anger that often has been misdirected.

The therapist may at times have to draw back to allow for interpersonal breathing space. Intensive therapy, as Stone (1993) notes, encourages self-revelation and transference reactions that are extremely anxiety provoking. Allowing more space between appointments may prevent premature dropout.

Cognitive techniques can additionally help paranoids gain insight into their dysfunctional behaviors. This personality style is maintained by the core beliefs and schemas that others cannot be trusted and will intentionally try to hurt you. Interventions should aim to modify the individual's basic assumptions, because these are the root cause of this disorder, yet schema-driven cognitive distortion must not be directly challenged because confrontation will be seen as a personal attack. Beck and Freeman (1990b) note that modifications of the client's basic assumptions would require the patient to relax enough to reduce hypervigilance

and defensiveness. Instead, it is suggested that increasing the paranoid's sense of self-efficacy must precede attempts to modify other aspects of automatic thoughts, interpersonal behavior, and basic assumptions. These authors propose two ways of accomplishing this goal. If paranoids overestimate the threat posed by the situation, or underestimate their capacity to solve the problem, interventions that promote a more realistic appraisal of coping ability will increase their sense of self-efficacy. Second, if it is determined that the appropriate skills to contend with the situation are lacking, interventions that cultivate coping skills will serve to increase self-efficacy.

The paranoid's suspicious cognitive style manifests itself in cognitive errors frequently characterized by dichotomous thinking and over-generalizations. For example, others are likely to be viewed as either to be trusted or totally untrustworthy, or fully competent or entirely incompetent. Paranoids tend to reason backward from preconceived ideas to the evidence, which reinforces such beliefs. Several techniques can be employed to help establish a new perspective on people. Initially, the patient can be instructed to monitor interpersonal experiences along with the cognitions and emotions that accompany these interactions. Gathering more information can help fill in the inevitable gaps that exist in the paranoid's fund of knowledge about others' motives. Alternative explanations can then be explored. The therapist must take care not to interpret the assumptions as being faulty, but must seek instead to shift the weight of probability the paranoid attributes to the alternative hypotheses. The therapist should strive to introduce an element of doubt in the paranoid's mind regarding the validity of his or her beliefs (Stone, 1993).

Assisting the patient in reviewing past experiences to establish that past beliefs of danger have not always proven true will additionally facilitate the development of a more flexible cognitive style. Reluctance to engage in interpersonal relationships can be addressed by encouraging the patient to explore the benefits of being alone versus having intimate relationships. When paranoids can accept that interactions with others may actually have something positive to offer, an important step in reducing isolation has been achieved.

Beneath the flimsy exterior that conveys a sense of grandiosity and self-importance, paranoids carefully shelter a fragile self-image. Unable to admit to personal faults, they project them onto others. Cognitive interventions can address the patient's need to blame others and utilize projection as a defense. Toward the end of therapy, Beck and Freeman suggest that the therapist can help the patient refine interpersonal skills by improving the ability to empathize with others and see things from their perspective. This can be done by asking the patient to anticipate the impact of his or her actions on others and to imagine what it would feel like to be in their shoes. The validity of the patient's beliefs about the feelings and thoughts of others can be examined by investigating how closely the conclusions match the available evidence.

With most personality disorders, *group therapy* can provide an ideal forum for reality testing. Yet, because of the paranoid's intrinsic mistrust, rigidity, and refusal to examine interpersonal distortions, group methods are generally contraindicated. The tendency to misinterpret feedback or contributions from other group members may provoke hostility, putting a strain on the group's cohesion and placing the paranoid at risk for premature dropout.

Paranoids may, however, benefit from examining group processes while maintaining a secure distance. Possibly allowing the paranoids to be passive observers can encourage these patients to examine different hypothesis for people's behavior without actually having to defend their own actions.

Similarly, *marital* and *family* techniques run the risk of running aground if careful attention is not paid to paranoid processes. Paranoids may question the fidelity and trustworthiness of their partners and may see the therapist as combining forces with the other family members; therefore, it would be wise to use cotherapists. The predominance of negative affect in family dynamics, as well as in interactions with others, must be counterbalanced by encouraging the patient to express more positive statements and emotions.

Gabbard (1994) highlights the goals of *psychodynamic* interventions with this disorder. The purpose of therapy is to help patients shift their beliefs about the origin of their problems from an external cause to an internal one. Letting go of the rigid defensive structure can free up energy to help acquire more satisfying interpersonal relationships. Paranoids also spend a great deal of energy ruminating about the past and feeling that they should receive retribution for past wrongdoings. Goals in this area center on having patients accept reality. Frustrations are an inevitable part of everyone's life and paranoids must relinquish these claims at compensation. As the paranoid's defenses gradually ease up, the innermost feelings of vulnerability, inferiority, and worthlessness come to the

foreground. Depression may result, calling for a shift in the focus of therapy to resolve these depressive components.

At times, the therapeutic balance may be challenged by the patient's attempts to elicit a counter reaction from the therapist. Gabbard (1994) emphasizes that the therapist must contain feelings instead of acting on them, thereby providing the patient with a new object-relationship unlike those previously encountered. Gradually, these new experiences will be internalized.

Despite the relative paucity of research reporting therapeutic benefit from *pharmacological* intervention, trials with medication may be indicated when the paranoid's characterological defenses fail and specific symptoms such as anxiety or depression occur. Only when contact with reality worsens and a psychotic breakdown is imminent are antipsychotics called for. Medication may represent a threat to the paranoid's need for internal control, and as a result, resistance can be expected. With medications, as with other therapeutic efforts, the therapist must involve the patient in treatment planning, outlining in detail the potential benefits as well as the possible side effects. To gain collaboration, the therapist must emphasize to the patient how the medication can increase self-control.

A review of the major strategies and tactics is presented in Figure 19.6.

Potentiated Pairings and Catalytic Sequences

Early on in therapy, focus should be placed on developing the therapeutic relationship. Other techniques can have the desired effect only when the patient has developed enough trust in the

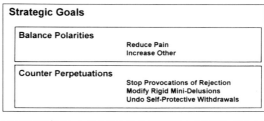

Figure 19.6 Therapeutic strategies and tactics for the prototypal paranoid personality.

therapist and when the alliance has stabilized. Nondirective cognitive approaches that focus on increasing self-efficacy, may be indicated as a first course of action, to be followed, where appropriate, by other measures. The choice of second-stage therapeutic methods depends on both practical and ultimate goals. At best, therapy is likely to control or moderate rather than reverse the basic personality pattern.

Developing a trusting relationship and increasing the patient's feelings of self-esteem will lay the groundwork for other therapeutic modalities and have profound effects across clinical domains. Feeling more secure with their own strengths, for example, will lessen the need for patients to engage in projective defense. Other cognitive techniques can subsequently be employed to target the paranoids' unrealistic perception of their environment. Creating an element of doubt in patients' minds about the accuracy of their beliefs will encourage them to explore potentially positive characteristics of others in interpersonal relationships. At the same time, behavioral methods can teach patients to be less defensive and to inhibit expressions of hostility. Equipped with a better outlook on life and the potential for obtaining reinforcement from others, these patients may be able to handle the more searching psychodynamic procedures. Rebuilding the paranoid's basic personality structure necessitates the careful utilization and sequencing of these techniques, and must proceed slowly and carefully to uncover unconscious elements.

If it is determined that the family contributes to the paranoid pattern or that the marital partner bears the brunt of the malicious accusations, marital or family therapy should be pursued concurrently. In the course of therapy, medication should be considered when anxiety crops up or when the paranoid becomes extremely hostile or starts acting out. Institutionalization may be required if reality controls break down. At this point, the carefully orchestrated therapeutic efforts that have led to some progress previously will have to be put on hold. If the patient decides to continue therapy, the therapist will, quite likely, have to start from scratch with rebuilding the fragile trusting bond that may have been severed by the therapist's decision to institutionalize the patient.

RESISTANCES AND RISKS

Therapeutic work with paranoids is a touchy proposition at best. Few come willingly for treatment. Therapy to them signifies weakness and dependency, both of which are anathema. When they do come in, the therapeutic work may be complicated because paranoids' suspicious and distrustful nature guards them against revealing emotional and interpersonal difficulties, making it extremely difficult to examine internal processes.

Many therapists fall into the trap of disliking these patients because their suspicions and hostility readily provoke discomfort and resentment. Therapists must resist being intimidated by the arrogance and demeaning comments of these patients. Weakness is not a trait paranoids could accept in someone in whom they have placed their trust. Other problems can complicate the therapeutic effort. Excessive friendliness and overt sympathies often connote deceit to these patients, a seductive prelude to humiliation and deprecation. As paranoids tend to view it, they have suffered pain at the hands of deceptively kind people. A comfortable distance must be maintained. Nor can therapists question these patients directly about their distorted attitudes and beliefs. This may drive them to concoct new rationalizations. It may intensify their distrust and destroy whatever rapport has been built. Conceivably, it may unleash a barrage of defensive hostility or precipitate an open psychotic break. The beliefs, self-confidence, and image of autonomy and strength of paranoids should not be directly challenged. These illusions are too vital a part of their style; to question them is to attack the patient's fragile equilibrium.

Despite the risks involved and therapeutic modifications required in working with these personalities, it is possible to put them on the road to recovery, providing them with a glimpse of a positive, healthy way of relating that might ultimately draw them further into the process of therapy.

CHAPTER 20

Decompensated Personality Disorders: The Terminal Pattern

Structurally decompensated is the term the authors suggest for the most profoundly deteriorated of the personality types. As with their less severe counterparts, decompensated features are deeply rooted, pervasive, and relatively enduring. They usually require institutional care and treatment, and are distinguished from Axis I psychotic disorders by the breadth and persistence of their deterioration. Although psychotic disorders represent equal severity, they are of relatively briefer duration, are usually confined to a particular sphere of functioning (e.g., mood, thought, or behavior), and do not eventuate in a broad and enduring deterioration of the personality pattern.

Little difficulty should be encountered in diagnosing the decompensated personality. In contrast to structurally defective patterns, in which patients exhibit mixed signs and fluctuate between relatively normal and distinctly pathological behaviors, decompensated patterns display a consistent and pervasive impairment that rarely is broken by lucid thoughts and conventional behaviors. Almost invariably, decompensated patients require institutionalization because they are unable to fend alone in everyday life, make few efforts to "get hold" of themselves, and fail to fulfill any acceptable societal role.

The two central features of all structurally decompensated personalities, be they schizotypal, borderline, or paranoid in character, are a *diminished reality awareness* and a *cognitive and emotional dyscontrol*. Psychotic-level *clinical syndromes* and decompensated *personality disorders* patterns fail to discriminate between subjective fantasy and objective reality; events take on a dreamlike quality, a hazy and phantasmagoric world of fleeting and distorted impressions colored by internal moods and images. These patients cannot appraise correctly the threats they face or the rewards they may gain; the difference between positive and negative reinforcements blur, causing them to behave in a

purposeless, irrational, and bizarre manner. Control functions are markedly deficient; patients are unable to direct or coordinate an effective coping strategy. There is a sense of disunity and disorganization to their communications; ideas are inchoate and jumbled, or take the form of peculiar beliefs and delusions. Absurd and stereotyped behaviors are exhibited. Subjective images become reality and are projected on the world as hallucinatory perceptions.

Before we proceed to systematize these general clinical features, let us note that the line we have drawn between the defective and decompensated patterns is an arbitrary one, established for the purpose of alerting the reader to clinical features that characterize particular points along the continuum of pathological severity. Let us not forget that imperceptible gradations differentiate the points on this continuum and that patients can fall anywhere along the way. In this section, we will be focusing on states that lie close to the extreme pole of severity, where the decompensated state is clear-cut.

GENERAL CLINICAL PICTURE

Psychotic disorders and decompensated personality patterns share a common level of pathological severity; both lack reality awareness and emotional and cognitive control. The principal distinction between them is the pervasiveness and relative permanence of these impairments among the decompensated personalities.

We will describe three major clinical features that further characterize the decompensated pattern in this section. These features present themselves regardless of other differences in personality makeup. They consist of: developmental immaturity and social invalidism; cognitive disorganization; and feelings of estrangement.

DEVELOPMENTAL IMMATURITY AND SOCIAL INVALIDISM

In Chapters 17, 18, and 19, we noted that structurally defective patients display a deficit in social competence; they evidence an uneven attainment of conventional goals, experience repeated setbacks in their vocational and marital plans, get involved in foolish predicaments, and spend much of their life extricating themselves from unnecessary difficulties, seeking to recoup the gains they once had achieved and then lost. Although defective patients do not make appreciable progress, they have managed, at least, to attain some social success, and they do exert some effort to continue moving forward.

Such is not the case among decompensated patterns. A number of investigators have indicated that these severely impaired individuals can best be described in terms of their social incompetence, inefficiency, and immaturity. In both their history and current functioning, these patients evidence a profound deficit in social skills. These deficiencies develop usually in one of two ways: by a general *developmental immaturity,* or by a progressive decompensation to *social invalidism.* Let us briefly discuss these two processes:

1. The concept of *fixation* was formulated originally as an intrapsychic mechanism employed by children that resulted in an arrested development and in a persistence into adulthood of childlike behaviors. We need not agree with the specific rationale of this psychoanalytic formulation to recognize that early behaviors are perpetuated throughout life; several alternative explanations for this persistence of early learning were provided in Chapter 3.

Whatever the reason, or combination of reasons, the upshot of fixation or behavior perseveration is a consequent failure of children to acquire a fully mature repertoire of social skills. As new and greater tasks come to challenge their immature skills and as they fail more and more to fulfill expected roles, their incompetence and ineffectuality become increasingly apparent. Over time, the disparity between competence and responsibility grows; these children get further and further behind others, become less able to "catch up" or to compensate for their already established lag. In individuals who have never achieved social maturity, the process of decompensation to a markedly severe level of functioning may progress both rapidly and early in life.

2. Many decompensated personalities have achieved a measure of social competence and maturity during their lives. Unfortunate circumstances, however, bore down heavily, and they deteriorated gradually into a more severe pathological state. The concept of *regression* has been used in the psychoanalytic literature to signify a process of decompensation in which the individual returns under pressure to behaviors that characterized an early developmental stage; more specifically, the individual ostensibly reverts back to fixated childhood characteristics.

There is no need for us to accept the psychoanalytic formulation that decompensation is a backward retracing and revival of childhood fixations. Although elements of the past will emerge under extreme duress, there is no reason to assume that decompensation is a return to the past. Rather, it seems more reasonable to say that the individual's established repertoire of mature strategies disintegrates under pressure and gives rise to a wide range of deviant and generally *immature* behaviors. Among these behaviors is a childlike dependency and invalidism, colored no doubt by the particulars of the individual's own history.

Invalidism, a term coined by Cameron and Magaret (1951) in the mental health realm, underlies the regressive or childlike character of the decompensated patient. In the face of progressively hopeless adverse conditions, these patients withdraw into a totally dependent state, entirely devoid of social concerns and responsibilities. Unable to cope with the pressures of normal social life and unable to overlook their deficits, failures, and humiliations, patients retreat into homelessness, accepting both the discomforts of total disability and the few gains it provides. No longer will they be burdened with life's struggles or face unfavorable comparisons. Ultimately, they may allow themselves to slide into the security and the obscurity of a hospital environment. Cared for by others and excused from social expectancies and self-responsibilities, they begin to learn the "art" of the invalid. Within this controlled setting and its undemanding routines, they relinquish progressively whatever competence and social maturity they previously achieved. Two broad clinical characteristics typify this level of pathological functioning, cognitive disorganization and feelings of estrangement; we will describe each briefly before we proceed to more specific features.

Cognitive Disorganization

In most persons, ideas are associated in a logical and orderly progression so as to convey meaningful communications. This coherence and intent often are lost among the severely ill. Of course, disturbances in thought frequently are evident among certain patients long before they succumb to the decompensated level; this is somewhat the case among the less severely detached (e.g., schizoid, avoidant) personalities, but especially so among the defective-schizotypal (e.g., insipid, timorous) patterns. However, no matter what the basic pattern may originally have been, cognitive controls loosen as these patients decompensate. They display an increasing number of irrelevant and bizarre notions; connections among thoughts become vague or involved; communications directed to others lose their focus and wander into generalities and abstractions, the significance of which is difficult to grasp. Sequences of ideas are disjointed and fragmented. Metaphorical and stereotyped phrases may be endlessly repeated; unrelated thoughts may be fused, creating neologisms which in turn may be thrown together in a "word salad" of disconnected nouns and verbs. The following illustrates the mumbo-jumbo character of these disorganized flights of verbigeration:

Improper wave length-wave length changes, later visible death. That is a moving trollysis similar to circulation of life action. Born high focusing action may die through wave length charge and still live until visible death takes place.

Education comes from radiation of action. Anyone can study all science in a compositive way. It takes a compositive mind to be able to understand. Can tell compositive minds by stromonized conception. The mind at birth takes on a birthification, becomes environmental by the radiation to it. Metabolism to dimension differ in every person is of actions of metabolism and dimension balancing.

Quite commonly, delusions and hallucinations accompany cognitive disorganization. These tend to be loosely structured and transitory, in contrast to the more logical, ingrained, and systematized delusional beliefs of the defectively structured paranoid. Decompensated patients piece together entirely unrelated observations and ideas from which they draw peculiar and bizarre inferences about the nature of the world. Typically, these unsystematized delusions and perceptions are dissolved and forgotten almost as readily as they were formed; some, however, seem to "stick" although they never attain the logic and coherence shown in the beliefs of the defective paranoid patient.

The bizarre and chaotic thought processes of these patients are not wholly meaningless; their irrational quality stems from mixing internal images in a rather chancelike manner with unrelated environmental events. Because of their lack of cognitive control, these patients allow stimuli from divergent origins to flow together into a common stream, resulting in odd perceptions, disjointed behaviors, and incoherent verbalizations. In essence, by abandoning their cognitive controls, these patients have lost choice and selectivity. The hierarchy of potency that differentiated among stimuli and responses has been leveled; all stimuli have equal impact, and all responses have an equal probability of expression. Unable to scan their environment selectively and unable to distinguish the relevant from the irrelevant, their thoughts and actions become scattered and disorganized, a potpourri of fragmented delusions, transitory hallucinations, and obscure tangential talk.

It will be instructive next to explore why cognitive disorganization occurs. Certainly, these patients have little reason to face reality or to perceive with clarity a life full of anguish and humiliation. Failing repeatedly to cope with adversity, they have no option but to withdraw, tune out reality, and reduce contact with events that evoke nothing but shame and agony. The potency of inner thought and memory increases as they withdraw from external events, and the balance of the stimulus world shifts inward.

At first, patients invite this respite from painful reality; memories and thoughts dominate thinking, thereby shutting out the conflict and humiliation of external intrusions. Unchecked by logic or social consensus, fantasies have free rein to salve wounds unencumbered by realities. In time, these reveries blur into a dreamlike state, lose their organization, and become fragmented, discontinuous, and ephemeral.

Despite the usefulness of fantasy in healing wounds and blocking reality, patients find, ultimately, that the dream world is not a haven but a nightmare. Whatever order and meaning they extract from these disorganized reveries, remind them, in one way or another, of their misery, of past misfortunes and of being nothing but a failure, a humiliated invalid bereft of status and hope. Their private world, then, proves no less painful than that of reality. Faced with the pain of self, they turn away, not only from others but also from the self. But this is no simple task; thoughts remain within, fixed and adamant, cropping up no matter how hard the patient tries to deny them.

How can they be dismembered? Among the person's few alternatives is the capacity to destroy his or her own cognitive processes, befuddle memories, block logic and meaning, and create internal confusion where clarity, consensus, and order existed; everything, then, is intentionally mixed up, disconnected, reversed, and jumbled.

But this effort, like so many that preceded it, proves a further undoing of self. Patients become trapped in this web of self-made confusion; try as they may, they cannot gain clear focus and cannot organize the self to find some meaning and purpose to existence. In the end they sink further into an abyss of nothingness, an estrangement from both objective reality and subjective self.

FEELINGS OF ESTRANGEMENT

The invalidism of the patient may be traced initially to a combination of causes including social disaffection, protective isolation, and a final collapse of habitual coping strategies. Once invalidism is established, however, hopeless dependency and social incompetence become a basis for further alienation, and thus perpetuate the breach between these homeless or hospitalized patients and the community.

As they succumb to their new social role, patients jettison most traces of pride and self-control, abandoning whatever social amenities and facades they may have acquired; more importantly, they begin to lose touch with the meaning and structure of social behavior and with the form and syntax of language and communication. Their actions and verbalizations take on a peculiar and idiosyncratic quality. The patterns and rules of interpersonal relations increasingly mystify them, and they seem incapable of comprehending the sequence or purpose of social discourse, the reciprocal flow of person-to-person interaction. Unable to participate in or make sense out of their environment, patients begin to experience life as something unreal, a game whose moves are made by unseen hands in accord with strange and unfathomable regulations. They sense a "nonbeing in the world," as the existentialists might phrase it. They are perplexed and bewildered, are unable to grasp the logic and significance of what surrounds them, and feel doomed to wander in a vague, alien, and frightening environment; they are homeless, estranged nonparticipants at the mercy of enigmatic, capricious, and hazardous powers; moreover, they stand alone, confused and devoid of any means of mitigating despair and dread of the unknown or of the strange and ominous forces that surround them; at any moment, these unpredictable forces may destroy them or leave them totally isolated and helpless.

The decompensated patient's social estrangement is paralleled by an equally terrifying estrangement from self. As noted earlier, cognitive disorganization often reflects a process in which patients seek to destroy, disarrange, or clutter painful thoughts and memories. They purposely make their behavior incongruous, jumble their ideas, and swing fitfully from one mood to another without rhyme or reason. Cognitive disorganization as a strategy serves its function well; patients successfully interfere with "real" thinking and feeling, and thereby protect themselves from the anguish such thoughts produce.

But several disturbing consequences arise as a result of purposeful self-disjunction. As these patients observe their own behavior, they see something foreign, a strange, unknown, and peculiar being, a frightening and unpredictable creature they cannot recognize. Being both participant and spectator, they observe the self with terror and cannot match what now emanates from that self with what they know to have been the self. They look on aghast, unable to control their impulses, bizarre grimaces, and strange outbursts. Perhaps, they conclude, some alien force resides within, some power that causes them to act in this way; clearly, this body and these behaviors belong to someone else.

Try as they may, patients cannot escape the pain and fright of self-awareness. Their divorce from self must be total; they must disembody the self and not only dismember feelings and thoughts, but disown behavior and body. It is at this point of self-abandonment, of rejecting self as a viable being, that the unfortunate patient disintegrates into the final and profoundly severe state we have termed the "terminal personality pattern." We shall elaborate differences between the terminal and decompensated patterns later in this chapter.

Before we proceed, we must note several similarities between the decompensated and the schizotypal patterns. As all personality patterns decompensate, they begin to exhibit qualities of social detachment and self-estrangement, traits found more commonly and permanently among schizotypals. The defective schizotypals, however, maintain a measure of reality contact and often manage, albeit poorly and irregularly, to function as a peripheral member of society.

The clinical similarity between psychotic clinical syndromes and decompensated personality disorders accounts in part for the common practice of labeling all severely deteriorated patients as "schizophrenic"; this latter diagnostic label should be limited, however, to Axis I clinical syndromes of marked severity, and should *not* be used for other, similar appearing patients who have followed a different developmental course before exhibiting these symptoms. As we will point out later, sufficient differences exist to make useful diagnostic distinctions.

GENERAL PATHOGENIC BACKGROUND

It will be useful, as a précis, to outline briefly the principal determinants that contribute to the development of decompensated personalities; distinctions will later be made among the three subvarieties of this pattern. Several etiologic factors have been discussed in detail in earlier chapters and these should be referred to by the reader.

HYPOTHESIZED BIOGENIC FACTORS

A small but not insignificant portion of these patients are hampered by constitutional impairments or tendencies that strongly dispose them to psychopathology. Marked sensitivities, congenital injuries, or any of a wide range of constitutional anomalies will increase both the probability and the likely severity of abnormal development.

It should be noted that constitutional dispositions associated with decompensated personality patterns differ from serious organic impairments. First, dispositions connected to pathological personalities are not readily identifiable by current diagnostic techniques, that is, their presence is unclear and inferred, not known or observable in fact. Second, where they are observable, they tend to be of the "soft" variety, that is, not so severe as to preclude the possibility of a normal course of development.

CHARACTERISTIC EXPERIENTIAL HISTORY

Not all decompensated patients are constitutionally disposed to pathology. Some, born with entirely normal biophysical equipment, have been subjected to unusually destructive experiences during the years of early maturation and learning. Excessively impoverished or enriched stimulation and any number of pathogenic family attitudes and methods of behavior control may prepare the soil for the progressive unfolding of markedly pathological perceptions and strategies. The more intense, pervasive, and enduring these experiences are, the more likely that they will result in a decompensated personality pattern.

SELF-PERPETUATION PROCESSES

Tendencies toward decompensation may be aggravated by the cumulation of repetitive pathogenic experiences. Not only are early behaviors and attitudes difficult to extinguish but, in addition, the individual may be exposed to a continuous stream of destructive events that accelerate the pathological decline. Not the least of decompensated patterns to justify our making these accelerating factors are the patient's coping behaviors that foster new problems and perpetuate vicious circles.

PROLONGATION OF PSYCHOTIC EPISODES

Defectively structured patients experience serious incursions on their psychic equilibrium, giving rise usually to short-lived and reversible psychotic episodes. These bizarre periods normally subside following the ventilation of feelings and the reduction of stress.

In some cases, however, the psychotic episode persists until it becomes an ingrained and enduring pattern. Perhaps the conditions of stress did not diminish, or the patient may have become "caught" in the web of his or her own coping maneuvers. Perhaps the reinforcements acquired during the episode were greater than those obtained preceding it; for example, even though the conditions which precipitated the episode disappeared, the patient may have achieved unusually gratifying exemptions and privileges as a function of the illness, which then reinforced its continuance.

Whatever the cause or combination of causes, some patients fail to pull themselves together or to override what is usually a transient psychotic period. In these cases, we may see a progressive deterioration into a more permanent decompensated personality pattern.

PROGRESSIVE DECOMPENSATION

It is evident from the preceding statements that the emergence of the decompensated personality pattern is a progressive and insidious process. Typically, the kernel of the pattern was set in place at childhood and developed into its manifest state through imperceptible steps. We need not elaborate each step in the developmental sequence preceding the formation of the final pattern; that can best be done by reviewing the clinical features and strategies of the milder and more moderate personality patterns discussed in previous chapters. It will be useful, however, to describe the final step in the decompensation sequence.

Patients begin to slip into a deteriorated state when they feel that their normal relations with others have become bogged down and hopeless; they experience at the same time an intolerable decline in their self-worth. As they protectively isolate themselves from social contact, their feelings of hopelessness and self-derogation increase; yet they also sense a measure of relief as they assume the pattern of invalidism. Minor gains have been eked out through collapse and withdrawal; others will care for them, and they need meet no responsibilities or struggle to achieve goals in a world with which they cannot cope. They have given up not only their aspirations but their struggle for a meaningful social existence; they allow themselves to sink increasingly into a persistent homelessness, a disorganization of control and thought, an emotional flatness and an invalidism in which they care little and do little to care for themselves.

At this stage, external events are seen as a distant screen on which phantoms move in a strange and purposeless automaticity; voices emanate from alien sources, creating a muted cacophony of obscure and bewildering sounds; a fog descends, enshrouding eyes and ears, dampening senses, and giving events a shadowy, pantomimic quality. Inner thoughts prove no more articulate or meaningful; within themselves they find a boundless region of fantasy, delusion, inchoate images, and sensations. Like an unanchored and rudderless ship in a whirling sea, they drift without compass, hither and yon, buffeted by waves of past memories and future illusions. Dreams, reality, and the past and present—a potpourri of random pieces—merge and are then dismembered. For such patients, their own physical presence seems foreign, a detached corpse; they sense the self as floating, a disembodied mind with its rummage of fleeting, disconnected, jumbled, and affectless impressions. This frightening collapse of meaning and existence is shared by most decompensated patterns as their zest for life is drained.

Considerable space has been allotted thus far to a discussion of characteristics shared by the different decompensated patterns. This has been done in recognition of the notable similarity they exhibit in their clinical picture and in the final steps of their deterioration; despite appreciably different constitutional tendencies and developmental experiences, most patients become increasingly alike as they face repeated coping failures and social humiliation. These similarities have already been described, enabling us, therefore, to present a less extensive description of each of the separate decompensated patterns than was previously given to other personality patterns. As we have stated before, sufficient differences exist among these patterns to justify our making useful diagnostic distinctions. Thus, despite their overt commonalities, patients differ markedly in the content of their thinking, the strategies they previously employed, the type of reinforcements to which they may respond in a therapeutic regime, and so on. In the following sections, we will differentiate the three major decompensated patterns, as well as the terminal personality pattern, noting briefly their distinguishing clinical features and developmental histories.

To point up the continuum that we believe exists between the defective and decompensated personalities, we shall label the three structurally decompensated patterns with terms that parallel the structurally defective personalities, referring to them as *decompensated schizotypals, decompensated borderlines, and decompensated paranoids.*

DECOMPENSATED-SCHIZOTYPAL PERSONALITIES

It will be instructive to briefly review the history and clinical conditions associated with the syndrome label "schizophrenia." This term has been applied to almost 50% of all hospitalized mental patients; such a striking statistic may signify either the impressive prevalence of this particular impairment or the indiscriminate lumping into one gross category of equally disturbed but basically different patients.

It is our contention that the traditional category of schizophrenia should be seen as a *spectrum* with several subclassifications, including one for patients who have displayed a *lifelong and deeply ingrained pattern of social detachment;* this group should be labeled as decompensated schizotypals.

Many patients who fall within this schizophrenic spectrum should be assigned an Axis I clinical syndrome, such as schizophrenia proper, because their impairments are of relatively brief duration. Other severely disturbed patients also possess deeply ingrained personality patterns, but the pattern they exhibit is *not* characterized by a lifelong schizotypal structure and style. Rather, they may have possessed a variety of other styles of life; if so, they should be labeled, at this severe stage of pathology, either as decompensated borderlines or decompensated paranoids.

Comments on the Schizophrenia Diagnostic Label

The system of classification currently used in psychiatry retains the basic typology of dementia praecox as formulated by Kraepelin in the fifth edition (1896) of his text. However, for the greater part of this century, the label dementia praecox was replaced by the term "schizophrenic reaction types," representing modifications in accord with the thinking of Bleuler and Meyer. In recently revised DSMs, the nomenclature was simplified to that of "schizophrenia."

Although Kraepelin's categories rested on dubious assumptions regarding etiology and prognostic course, they have been retained with minimal change, albeit clothed in more fashionable language. For many and divergent reasons, few diagnosticians are satisfied with the Kraepelinian typology; it remains in popular usage today largely as a result of habit and inertia. Like patients who are unable to extricate themselves from their past, perpetuating and fostering new difficulties as a consequence, so too does the profession of psychiatry find itself unable to break its old though admittedly poor classificatory habits. The Kraepelinian typology remains with us because no new formulation possessing sufficient distinction to overcome the inertia of the past has been proposed.

The term schizophrenia is applied in current practice to almost all patients who evidence chronic decompensation, without regard to the character of their premorbid personality pattern; in addition, it is used as a designation for almost all acute impairments that are noted by the primacy of disorganized thinking. We consider the application of the schizophrenic term to a wide spectrum of severe ailments to be a reasonable extension of the Kraepelinian system. On the one hand, there are the relatively brief and acutely severe syndromes that may be still referred to as schizophrenia. On the other hand, there are a group of similar symptom pictures that are more enduring and pervasive: it is these that we will term "decompensated-schizotypal personalities."

In the formulation presented in this text, all severely deteriorated personalities will be classified as *decompensated patterns* to signify nothing more than the pervasiveness, durability, and severity of their pathology. Further distinctions, reflecting premorbid personality differences among these patients (e.g., schizoid, avoidant) will be made by reference to the labels schizotypal, borderline, and paranoid. Markedly severe though brief episodes, usually with acute onsets, should be noted as clinical syndromes and labeled in accord with the particular constellation of symptoms characterizing the disorder (e.g., schizophrenia, mood disorder).

The label decompensated schizotype shall apply exclusively to severely deteriorated personality patterns characterized by a lifelong and pervasive strategy of detachment, as seen in the schizoid and avoidant personality styles. It is most akin in its clinical features to the official schizophrenic syndrome labeled "disorganized," with its social withdrawal, emotional blunting or disharmony, bizarre thinking, and general disintegration of personality functions. The correspondence proposed between the present usage of the decompensated-schizotype label and the DSM-IV clinical features termed disorganized may be viewed as a return to Kraepelin's conceptions prior to the fifth edition of his classic work. We believe that Kraepelin was carried away by his attempt to subsume nearly all severe forms of decompensation under one label; this effort rested on the erroneous assumption that these divergent pathologies stem from a single constitutional defect or experiential origin, an oversimplification of the problem if there ever was one.

We next can turn to a description of the *decompensated-schizotypal personality pattern,* as conceived in this text.

CLINICAL FEATURES

This disorder is a markedly decompensated variant of certain of the mild and moderately severe detached patterns, the schizoid, avoidant, and the defective-schizotypal (insipid and timorous) personalities. Reference should be made to prior discussions of these less severe disorders; briefer descriptions will be presented in the following pages.

Though the decompensated schizotypes' clinical appearance is clearly more deteriorated than that of *defective*-schizotypal counterparts, they still retain many of their attributes, in addition to those they share with the other decompensated patterns. Their lack of social relatedness and competence is most striking. Cognitive processes are markedly disorganized, evidencing both autistic and fragmented qualities. Speech, when proffered, frequently is tangential if not incoherent, and may be scattered with neologisms mixed into rambling word salads. Behavior is extremely bizarre and spotted with peculiar mannerisms and automatisms. Emotional affect either is totally lacking, creating a drab and flat appearance (insipid type), or is characterized by its inappropriateness and incongruity (timorous type). Hallucinations and delusions are quite common, tending to be fleeting, unconnected, and totally illogical.

The severity of the three cardinal signs noted in common among decompensated patterns is particularly pronounced in the decompensated schizotype since these traits have always existed as part of these patients' makeup, although in less prominent form. In the *schizoid-insipid* variant of the decompensated-schizotype, for example, there is a premorbid affectivity deficit, cognitive slippage, and interpersonal insensitivity; these patients always appeared perplexed, vacant, and drab and were drawn within themselves, unable to communicate clearly and with feeling toward others. As conditions led them to retreat to what we have termed the defective-schizotypal pattern, they began to experience feelings of depersonalization and became even more unresponsive, socially inadequate, detached, and inarticulate. Thus, prior to their decompensation, they evidenced clear signs of cognitive disjunctiveness, depersonalization anxieties, and deficient social behaviors, each of which parallels the cardinal traits of the markedly severe personality level. For these reasons, as we shall later discuss more fully, disintegration into the decompensated pattern occurs with greater frequency and at an earlier age among detached personalities than among other premorbid personality types. Thus, we would expect to find that a major proportion of institutionalized psychotic patterns would be classified as decompensated schizotypes; similarly, the age at which the psychosis first becomes evident in these patients should be appreciably earlier than in that of other decompensated personality patterns.

Although the premorbid clinical picture of the *avoidant-timorous* decompensated-schizotypal pattern differs in certain fundamental respects from that of the more *schizoid-insipid* types, these pat-

terns progressively become more alike as they decompensate. As in the schizoid-insipid patterns, the avoidant-timorous types are disposed to a rapid and early development of schizotypal features. Their affective disharmony, alienated self-image, cognitive interference and interpersonal aversiveness are early forerunners of the estrangement feelings, cognitive disorganization, and social incompetence of the decompensated level. The road toward disintegration may well have been laid in childhood and may require little external prompting to be traveled fully and rapidly in early life.

Although many more mildly detached personalities (e.g., schizoid, avoidant) remain well compensated, a substantial proportion falter along the way, either deteriorating to the defective-schizotypal level, with its periodic psychotic eruptions, or decomposing further to the more chronically maladaptive decompensated-schizotypal pattern. At this stage of abject surrender and coping collapse, we see behavioral regressions, a frightening depersonalization and estrangement, bizarre and fragmented thinking, and a marked social invalidism. These characteristics may be seen in the following case.

CASE 20.1

Gerald T., Age 31, Unmarried

Gerald was the fourth of seven children. His father, a hard-drinking coal miner, had been on relief throughout most of Gerald's early life; his mother died giving birth to her seventh child when Gerald was 8. The family was raised by two older sisters, ages 15 and 11 at the time of their mother's death; partial household assistance was provided by a widowed maternal aunt with eight children of her own.

"Duckie," as Gerald was known, had always been a withdrawn, frightened, and "stupid" youngster. The nickname Duckie represented a peculiar waddle in his walk; it was used by others as a term of derogation and ridicule. Gerald rarely played with his sibs or neighborhood children; he was teased unmercifully because of his walk and his fear of pranksters. Gerald was a favorite neighborhood scapegoat; he was intimidated even by the most innocuous glance in his direction.

His father's brutality toward the other children of the family terrified Gerald. Although Gerald received less than his share of this brutality because his father thought him to be a "good and not troublesome boy," this escape from paternal hostility was more than made up for by resentment and teasing on the part of his older siblings. By the time Gerald was 10 or 11, his younger brothers joined in taunting and humiliating him.

Gerald's family was surprised when he performed well in the first few years of schooling. He began to falter, however, on entrance to junior high school. At about the age of 14, his schoolwork became extremely poor, he refused to go to classes and he complained of a variety of vague, physical pains. By age 15, he had totally withdrawn from school, remaining home in the basement room that he shared with two younger brothers. Everyone in his family began to speak of him as "being tetched." He thought about "funny religious things that didn't make sense"; he also began to draw "strange things" and talk to himself. When he was 16, he once ran out of the house screaming "I'm gone, I'm gone, I'm gone, . . ." saying that his "body went to heaven" and that he had to run outside to recover it; rather interestingly, this event occurred shortly after his father had been committed by the courts to a state mental hospital. By age 17, Gerald was ruminating all day, often talking aloud in a meaningless jargon; he refused to come to the family table for meals.

The scheduled marriage of his second oldest sister, who had been running the household for five years, brought matters to a head. Gerald, then 18, was taken to the same mental hospital to which his father had been committed two years previously.

When last seen, Gerald had been institutionalized periodically for the past 14 years; no appreciable change was evident in his behavior or prognosis since admission. Most notable clinically is his drab appearance, apathy, and lack of verbal communication; on rare occasions he laughs to himself in an incongruous and peculiar manner. He stopped soiling, which he had begun to do when first admitted, and will now eat by himself. When left alone with pencil and paper, he draws strange religiouslike pictures but is unable to verbalize their meaning in a coherent fashion. Drug therapy has had no effect on his condition; neither has he responded to group therapeutic efforts.

PATHOGENIC DEVELOPMENTAL BACKGROUND

We shall not review in detail the background of the decompensated schizotype because their histories essentially duplicate conditions already discussed in our presentations of the schizoid, avoidant, and schizotypal personalities.

Hypothesized Biogenic Factors

As has been stressed repeatedly throughout the text, markedly severe decompensated patterns lie at one polar extreme of a continuum of pathology, with the other extreme occupied by the mild personality types. The same complex of etiologic factors found in mild pathologies is seen in the background of more severe variants; the principal differences are the greater intensity and frequency of pathogenic elements in the latter. Thus, where constitutional factors are operative, the presence of a severe biophysical impairment is more likely to result in a marked rather than a mild pathological pattern. Similarly, in the severely disabled patterns we are likely to discover a history of persistent and unrelieved environmental adversity. We will briefly summarize some of the pathogenic elements associated with the insipid (schizoid) and timorous (avoidant) patterns of decompensated-schizotypal development.

There is a reasonable likelihood that genetic anomalies conducive to affective and cognitive deficits are present in the biogenic background of the *schizoid-insipid* decompensated schizotypes. Many have shown a passive reaction pattern in infancy, which in turn may have initiated a sequence of impoverished stimulation and parental indifference. Fragile ectomorphic builds may have resulted in physical incompetencies and vulnerabilities to stress; speculations may be offered to the effect that deficits in reticular, limbic, sympathetic, or synaptic control centers underlie their low activation, minimal capacity for reinforcement experiences, and cognitive disorders.

The biogenic background of *avoidant-timorous* decompensated schizotypes will often give evidence of apprehensive or cognitively obscure relatives, indicating the possible contribution of genetic factors to pathology. Threctic infantile patterns are common, often precipitating parental tension and derogation, which then aggravate the established temperament. Irregularities in maturation may frequently be noted, producing uneven competencies, difficult-to-handle emotions, and notable social "peculiarities." Low thresholds for sympathetic, reticular, and synaptic functioning may be hypothesized to account for the hypersensitivity and cognitive flooding found among these patients.

Characteristic Experiential History

We will now differentiate the experiential histories of the two decompensated schizotypes.

Schizoid-Insipid Type

In the psychogenic background of the *schizoid-insipid* variant of the decompensated schizotype, there is a reasonable probability of marked stimulus impoverishment during the sensory-attachment stage, reflecting either parental neglect or indifference; these experiences may lay the groundwork for a biophysical underdevelopment of affectivity substrates and a deficit learning of interpersonal attachment behaviors. A family atmosphere of cold formality may have served as a model for imitative learning, resulting in a lifelong style of social reticence and insensitivity and a discomfort with personal closeness. Fragmented and amorphous styles of parental communication may have prompted the development of disjointed and unfocused patterns of thinking.

Repeated exposure to these conditions and to peer experiences that aggravate them may accumulate to produce an inextricable web of pathogenicity. Once established, early styles of behavior and coping may perpetuate and intensify past difficulties. Social detachment, emotional impassivity, and cognitively obscure thinking will progressively alienate these youngsters from others and lead them to subordinate overt activity to autistic fantasy; unchecked by social consensus, these inner thoughts begin to lose their logic and coherence, causing a new spiral of self-defeating processes that further the decompensation trend.

Ruminations of inner emptiness in these persons will prompt depersonalization anxieties. At the same time, they experience anxieties in response to social encroachments and responsibilities. Both depersonalization and encroachment result in periodic psychotic breaks. Ultimately, the slow and insidious process of personality deterioration will produce the social invalidism, cognitive disorganization, and feelings of estrangement that characterize the decompensated level.

Avoidant-Timorous Type

The psychogenic histories of *avoidant-timorous* decompensated-schizotypes typically show a background of parental deprecation and peer group humiliation, resulting in lowered self-esteem and social distrust. These experiences often begin as early as the first or sensory-attachment stage of development, leading these youngsters to protectively insulate their feelings. Ridicule in response to second-stage autonomy efforts contributes markedly to a sense of personal inadequacy and incompetence; the persistence of belittling and derogating attitudes through later childhood and adolescence leads eventually to self-criticism and self-deprecation.

The coping strategies these persons employ to protect against further social ridicule only perpetuate and intensify their plight. Thus, many youngsters deny themselves opportunities for remedial experiences, perceive censure and threat where none existed, and preoccupy themselves with autistic fantasies that focus on past misfortunes. To counter these oppressive thoughts, they begin to block or destroy their cognitive clarity, thereby fostering further self-estrangement and social incompetence. As feelings of depersonalization and unreality grow, periodic psychotic episodes blend into one another, and they deteriorate gradually into a more permanent decompensated state.

The prognostic picture for the milder detached patterns (schizoid and avoidant personalities) is generally unfavorable; this contrasts with other mild personality patterns (e.g., dependent, histrionic, narcissistic). Each of these latter patterns has elicited a modicum of positive experience through their coping strategies, and has sought and maintained some measure of social relatedness. Schizoids and avoidants, both mild and defective (insipid, timorous) variants, however, have lost the ability to evoke these positive experiences and have disengaged themselves from reality and the controls of social interaction. Without positive experiences to motivate them and without the support and controls of social life, the prospects are high that they will undergo rapid personality decompensation. For these reasons, we find defective-schizotypal patterns emerging typically early in life, usually, but not invariably, between the ages of 15 and 25. This same paucity of developed social skills and sense of deep unworthiness and incompetence are the reasons these patients often remain in a permanent decompensated state. Decompensated schizotypes represent the greater bulk of the chronic or hard-core patients in most mental institutions.

Let us again be mindful that schizotypal levels of pathology evolve gradually. Few cases have their origin in such markedly adverse biological or psychological handicaps as those found in infantile autism and threctism. Adolescent or adult forms of schizotypal pathology may have their roots in conditions that are qualitatively comparable to those that produce childhood impairments, but these adverse conditions were likely to have been quantitatively less severe. However, these less severe early difficulties may have been compounded and intensified throughout development, leading to a slow and inexorable decompensation that eventuates in an adult schizotypal personality pattern that is no less severe than that found in childhood types.

DECOMPENSATED-BORDERLINE PERSONALITIES

The label "decompensated borderlines" is a new term, coined in this text to represent a syndrome whose structural decompensation is deeply ingrained and pervasive; its distinguishing feature as a personality pattern is that it overlies a more basic or evolved ambivalent personality style. The estrangement, invalidism, and cognitive disorganization of these decompensated patients emerge following the disintegration of a defective-borderline pattern of coping; thus, the syndrome reflects one further step in pathological severity that began with one of several milder personality patterns (e.g., dependent, negativistic).

There is no term in the psychiatric nomenclature for severely deteriorated patients whose earlier life style is noted by ambivalent struggles. It has been customary in psychiatric circles to label as schizophrenic all markedly decompensated patients, regardless of their premorbid or underlying personality structures and styles; for reasons noted earlier in the chapter, the failure to draw distinctions at the markedly severe level has been most unfortunate.

We have taken several steps to establish clarity along these lines. First, we have applied the general label "structurally decompensated personalities" for all chronic, severe, and pervasively deteriorated personality patterns. And second, even though we recognize that severe pathology does not fall into sharply defined subtypes, we have differentiated several structurally deteriorated patterns in accordance with their dominant predecompensated personality styles.

The choice of the designation decompensated borderline has been made to match the label decompensated schizotypal; both are structurally deteriorated personality patterns, as are decompensated paranoids, to be discussed in a later section. Furthermore, the label borderline, in addition to maintaining consistency with both its schizotypal and paranoid counterparts, seeks to focus on the essential feature found among these patients—their psychic ambivalence, and their vacillation in mood, thought, and behavior.

Comparison of the Decompensated Borderline and Similar Syndromes in the Official Classification

As previously noted, we reject the historic practice of classifying as schizophrenic most patients evidencing a progressive and marked decompensation. It is our contention that distinctions should be made in accord with premorbid personality styles.

There is one diagnostic label in the official DSM-IV nosology that corresponds to the clinical picture of decompensated borderlines; this designation is listed as *schizoaffective disorder*. Portions of the descriptive text state:

The essential feature of Schizoaffective disorder is an uninterrupted period of illness during which, at some time, there is a Major Depressive, Manic, or Mixed Episode concurrent with symptoms [of] Schizophrenia. In addition, during the same period of illness, there have been delusions or hallucinations for at least two weeks in the absence of prominent mood symptoms. Finally, the Mood symptoms are present for a substantial portion of the total duration of the illness.

There may be poor occupational functioning, a restricted range of social contact, difficulties with self-care, and increased risk of suicide. (pp. 292, 293)

This brief description represents in crude form some of the overt clinical features of what we have termed the decompensated borderline; in essence, these patients exhibit cognitive disorganization, estrangement, and invalidism (which are features of all decompensated patterns); in addition, they display both a strong affective tone and a social relatedness that are not found in decompensated-schizotypal personalities. The affectivity and sociability of decompensated borderlines reflect their lifelong basic strategy of seeking interpersonal support, approval, and nurture. Thus, decompensated borderlines possess both the features of decompensated personalities and those of most nondetached personality styles. This combination distinguishes them from the official classifications of manic-depression (episodic but severe mood syndromes) and schizophrenia (episodic cognitive disorganization).

CLINICAL FEATURES

The previously described defective-borderline personality variants tend to exhibit mixed clinical signs, and they fluctuate between relatively normal and distinctly pathological behaviors. This contrasts with the decompensated-borderline, who displays a consistently severe and pervasive impairment that rarely is broken by lucid thoughts and conventional behaviors. Decompensated borderlines often require institutionalization because they are unable to manage alone, appear to make few efforts to get hold of themselves, and are incapable of filling any acceptable societal role. They possess two features in common with all severely decompensated states: diminished reality awareness and cognitive and emotional dyscontrol. These patients fail to discriminate between subjective fantasy and objective reality. External events take on a dreamlike quality and become a hazy and phantasmagoric world of fleeting and distorted impressions colored by internal moods and images. They no longer grasp the threats they face or the rewards they may gain. Pain and pleasure become blurred, causing them to behave in a purposeless, irrational, or bizarre manner. Controls in thought and emotion are deficient, and there is a sense of internal disunity and disorganization in their social communications. Ideas are jumbled and take the form of peculiar beliefs or delusions. Stereotyped behaviors may be exhibited. Subjective imaginings become reality and are projected on the outer world as hallucinatory perceptions.

Notable at this stage is the emergence of a persistent social invalidism, most clearly evident in these patients' inability to assume responsibility for their own care, welfare, and health. Acceptance of social invalidism as a way of life is not difficult for borderline patients, given their lifelong orientation to dependency. As their efforts to maintain a normal social life are abandoned, they succumb readily into a helpless and disoriented state. There is a withdrawal into self, without external purpose or the controls of social reality, which increases the likelihood of cognitive disorganization. Whatever coherent thoughts these borderlines do possess are colored by an oppressive and melancholy tone. To avoid painful preoccupations such as these, they may try to focus on offbeat or cheerful thoughts, a process that accounts in part for their erratic ramblings. These cognitive digressions rarely are sustained. Sensing the futility of their efforts to alter their mood and preoccupation, decompensated borderlines block or retard their thought processes, resulting thereby in the slow and laborious responses that often characterize them. Should these efforts fail also, they may disassemble or disorganize their ruminations to protect themselves against the anguish their thoughts evoke. As a consequence, their cognitive processes are disjunctive and autistic, manifesting themselves either in sudden changes of focus or as incoherent ramblings.

Behaviors and emotions also tend toward the bizarre, with capricious bursts of energy and irrational hostility scattered unpredictably in an otherwise more sluggish and lugubrious style. Some may exhibit no motor activity, a physical inertia, a weighty and stooped posture, and downcast and forlorn expression. Fragmented delusions and hallucinations are not uncommon. These symptoms usually express themselves as obsessive fears of impending disaster or in strange and undiagnosable bodily ailments. Self-deprecation, remorse, and guilt are prominent aspects of their disorganized delusions. Feelings of estrangement in these borderlines are rooted in their growing sense of aloneness and apartness from the attachments they previously had established. Socially rebuffed and often institutionalized, they not only experience separation from loved ones but are immersed in new and strange environments. Geared to turn to others for guidance and support, these borderlines are now keenly aware of their aloneness and the frightening unfamiliarity of their surroundings. Most feel desperately removed and lost, perplexed and bewildered in a strange and unreal world.

As indicated earlier, the decompensated borderline is a markedly deteriorated variant of various milder personality patterns (e.g., negativistic, histrionic, antisocial); reference should be made to earlier portions in the text for a fuller description of the characteristics of these pre-decompensated clinical pictures. Despite greater deterioration, decompensated borderlines retain many traces of the behaviors and moods that typified their earlier adjustment.

Although defective and decompensated borderlines lie on a continuum of severity, with only imperceptible shades of difference separating them, it will be useful to note certain features that distinguish at least the prototypes of these two impairments.

Decompensated borderlines exist in a structurally deteriorated state, unable to survive without a total caretaking environment. Reality contact is minimal in these patients, preventing them from maintaining meaningful communications with others or gaining the benefits of their reassurance and support. Lifelong controls and coping strategies have collapsed, resulting in the total disintegration of personality functioning. In contrast, defective borderlines experience only transient and reversible psychotic episodes; at other times, reality contact is maintained, their controls and coping strategies are adequately preserved, and they are able to evoke a modicum of positive experiences in their interpersonal relationships.

Some distinctions may be made between the decompensated schizotypals and decompensated borderlines. Here the essential difference lies in their developmental histories, that is, the lifelong pattern of relationships, attitudes, and coping strategies they have acquired. Briefly, decompensated borderlines have shown a capacity to relate to others, although in an ambivalent fashion; their thoughts focus on their own inadequacies, conflicts, guilt, and self-deprecation; frequent periods of angry resentment and mood swings are notable. In contrast, decompensated schizotypals have characteristically been detached, self-contained, and socially deficient; their cognitive processes have always been disjointed and somewhat autistic; affect has been either lacking or markedly apprehensive; periods of panic and bizarre impulses and feelings of alienation and depersonalization are notable.

Because of their social motivation and skills, the long-range prognosis for ambivalent personalities (e.g., borderlines) is considerably better than that for detached patterns (e.g., schizotypals); thus, the proportion of ambivalent patterns that decompensate to moderate and markedly severe levels of structural pathology is relatively small, appreciably less than that found among detached personalities. Borderline personalities have a built-in protection against further decompensation stemming from their strong proclivity for maintaining social relationships; for this reason, the incidence of decompensated borderlines is appreciably less than that of decompensated schizotypes, but by no means zero.

A number of the symptomatological features distinguish among the several personality subtypes that deteriorate to decompensated borderlines:

1. One subgroup of decompensated borderlines (e.g., dependent-immature) tends to be consistent in its pattern of helpless invalidism and depression; earlier efforts to forgo and reverse their stylistic pattern, as evidenced in bursts of self-assertion or gregarious cheerfulness, have failed miserably. Convinced of their unworthiness and the inevitability of abandonment and desertion, they crumble and sink into a state of utter hopelessness. Though frightened by their separation from past sources of security, they quickly learn that they can gain a more consistent level of support in the "womb" of a totally nurtural hospital. Here they can comfortably regress to a childlike dependency, to a limpet-like attachment to whoever supplies their needs for protection and nurture. However, their infantile simpering and clinging behaviors often prove a drain on their caretakers and fellow patients.

2. Another group of decompensated borderlines (e.g., histrionic-theatrical), despite their social invalidism and the bizarre character of their thinking and behavior, frequently make an effort to be charming, gay, and attractive. Their lifelong pattern of soliciting attention and approval reemerges periodically in displays of irrational conviviality, often accompanied by garish clothes and ludicrous makeup. During these brief but wild flights into euphoria, there is a gushing forth of frenetic conversation and a latching on to any and all passersby in a frantic effort to rekindle the human warmth they so desperately need. But these bizarre and hyperactive episodes usually are short lived, and the patient succumbs once more to a less agitated and more dolorous and downcast state. Even during these more prolonged and somber periods, we may observe that the patient retains some former seductive and exhibitionistic features; thus, although thoughts may be disorganized and irrational, the clinician can see the histrionic quality of complaints and self-deprecations, and can sense that they are expressed in such ways as to solicit the listener's attention and compassion. Despite the genuineness of the patient's misery and the obviously delusional thinking, habit systems acquired in earlier life still come through in discernible form.

3. In another group of decompensated borderlines (e.g., negativist-abrasive), we observe a much tighter and restrained picture than that found in either of the types discussed previously. The woebegone look has an air of tension; behaviors are more rigid and stereotyped and all sorts of mannerisms and grimaces may be displayed. On rare occasions, they may exhibit explosive outbursts of rage directed at unseen persecutors; at other times, they may assault themselves viciously. Many remain mute and unresponsive for long periods. Cognitive processes generally are labored, emitted in a slow and deliberate manner and tending, where coherent, to be self-deprecatory and tinged with delusions of persecution and guilt; their cognitive distortions usually are more organized or systematic than those of other decompensated borderlines. Tension and inner agitation are more manifest; conflicts and impulses are frequently acted out, and a stream of complaints is often voiced in irritable and disorganized commentaries. Behavior varies from listless pacing to hostile immobility. Delusions of guilt and self-condemnation may precipitate periodic flare-ups of violence and bickering. Most times, however, these patients are subdued and downcast, complaining in a quiet, almost unfeeling and automatic manner, as if by sheer habit alone. Their sour pessimism, although now dissipated, still colors their attitudes and behaviors, making relationships with fellow patients and hospital workers difficult to sustain.

There are many variants of the decompensated borderline owing to the numerous developmental origins among these patients. The following case depicts a typical decompensated type giving evidence of aspects of a poorly integrated histrionic pattern of coping and relating.

CASE 20.2

Edith S., Age 49, Separated

Edith has been institutionalized three times, the first of which, at the age of 24, was for 8 months; the second, at 31, lasted about 3 years; this third period has continued since she was 37.

Edith was the fifth child, the only girl, of a family of six children. Her early history is unclear, although she "always was known to be a tease" with the boys. Both parents worked at semiskilled jobs throughout Edith's childhood; her older brothers took care of the house. By the time she entered puberty, Edith had had sexual relations with several of her brothers and many of their friends. As she reported it in one of her more lucid periods, she "got lots of gifts," that would not otherwise have been received for "simply having a lot of fun." Apparently, her parents had no knowledge of her exploits, attributing the gifts she received to her vivaciousness and attractiveness.

A crucial turning point occurred when Edith was 15; she became pregnant. Although the pregnancy was aborted, parental attitudes changed, and severe restrictions were placed on her. Nevertheless, Edith persisted in her seductive activities, and by the time she was 17 she again had become pregnant. At her insistence, she was married to the father of her unborn child. This proved to be a brief and stormy relationship, ending 2 months after the child's birth. Abandoned by her husband and rejected by her parents, Edith turned immediately to active prostitution as a means of support.

In the ensuing 6 years, she acquired another child and another husband. Edith claims to have "genuinely loved" this man; they had "great times" together, but also many "murderous fights." It was his decision to leave her that resulted in her first, clear, psychotic break.

Following her 8-month stay in the hospital, Edith picked up where she left off—prostitute, dance-hall girl, and so on. Periods of drunkenness and despondency came more and more frequently, interspersed with shorter periods of gay frivolity and euphoria. For a brief time, one that produced another child, Edith served as a "plaything" for a wealthy ne'er-do-well, traveling about the country having "the time of her life." She fell into a frantic and depressive state, however, when he simply "dumped her" on hearing that she was pregnant.

Hospitalized again, this time for 3 years, Edith's personality was beginning to take on more permanent psychotic features. Nevertheless, she was remitted to the home of her father and older brother; here she served as a housemaid and cook. Her children had been placed in foster homes; her mother had died several years earlier.

The death of her father, followed quickly by the marriage of her brother, left Edith alone again. Once more, she returned to her old ways, becoming a bar girl and prostitute. Repeated beatings by her "admirers," her mental deterioration, and her growing physical unattractiveness, all contributed to a pervasive despondency that resulted in her last hospitalization.

For the past several years she has been doing the work of a seamstress in the institution's sewing room; here, in addition to her mending chores, she makes rather garish clothes for herself and others. Every now and then, she spruces herself up, goes to the beauty parlor, puts on an excess of makeup, and becomes transformed into a "lovely lady." More characteristically, however, her mood is somber; though responsive and friendly to those who show interest in her, her ideas almost invariably are bizarre and irrational.

PATHOGENIC DEVELOPMENTAL BACKGROUND

We find the same complex of determinants in the decompensated-borderline syndrome as we do in its less severe counterparts; the primary differences between them are the intensity, frequency, timing, and persistence of pathogenic factors. Decompensated borderlines may begin with less adequate constitutional equipment or be subjected to a series of more adverse early experiences; as a consequence, they may fail to develop an adequate coping style in the first place or decompensate slowly under the weight of repeated and unrelieved difficulties. Most decompensated-borderline cases progress sequentially through the stylistic and defective-borderline patterns before deteriorating to the decompensated level. However, some patients, notably the childhood syndromes, never appear to "get off the ground," and give evidence of the decompensated-borderline pattern from their earliest years.

We shall review next the developmental history of several of the less severe personality patterns that serve as the forerunners of the decompensated borderlines; with the exception of minor elaborations relevant to the final stages of decompensation, this review summarizes material already presented in prior pages of the text.

Hypothesized Biogenic Factors

The biogenic background of certain decompensated borderlines (e.g., dependents) includes a disproportionately high number of bland and unenergetic relatives. A melancholic and threctic infantile reaction pattern is not infrequent, and often gives rise to parental overprotection. Ectomorphic or endomorphic body builds are more common than mesomorphic builds, predisposing deficits both in autonomy and competitive skills. Hypotheses may be proposed regarding various limbic, reticular, or adrenal imbalances to account for their apparent lowered activation levels and their vulnerability to fear—both of which may elicit protective and nurtural responses in beneficent environments.

In another group of decompensated borderlines (e.g., histrionic) we find numerous close relatives who exhibit high autonomic reactivity. Other evidence suggesting a biogenic predisposition is hyperresponsivity in early childhood; this temperamental factor not only exposed them to a high degree of sensory stimulation, but tended to elicit more frequent and intense reactions from others. It may be speculated further that neurally dense or low threshold limbic, reticular, or adrenal systems underlie their sensory reactivity.

Other decompensated borderlines (e.g., negativistic) appear to have displayed both an irregular infantile reaction pattern and an uneven course of development, thereby increasing the likelihood of inconsistent treatment at the hands of others. Their hyperactivity and irritable affectivity may

be hypothesized to be a consequence of various neurological and physiochemical imbalances or dysfunctions.

Characteristic Experiential History

Several developmental backgrounds appear in the history of decompensated borderlines. A brief summary of a number of these will be presented in the following paragraphs; reference to earlier sections of the text may be helpful in elaborating the points discussed.

1. The central psychogenic influence for one group of decompensated borderlines (e.g., dependent) appears to have been parental overprotection, leading to an unusually strong attachment to, and dependency on, a single caretaking figure. The perpetuation of overprotection throughout childhood fostered a lack in the development of autonomous behaviors and a self-image of incompetence and inadequacy. The coping style of these children accentuated these weaknesses; by abdicating self-responsibility and by clinging to others, they restricted their opportunities to learn skills for social independence.

In contrast to personalities who stabilize at the milder levels of pathology, these future decompensated borderlines may have found themselves increasingly rebuffed by those on whom they depended. The intense separation anxieties that these experiences engendered precipitated behaviors referred to as the defective-borderline pattern, characterized by mood vacillations, marked self-disparagements and guilt, as well as frequent psychotic episodes.

2. Among the more important psychogenic influences in another group of decompensated borderlines (e.g., histrionic) is an unusually varied and enriched sequence of sensory experiences in the first neuropsychological stage that built in a "need" for stimulus diversity and excitement. Parental control by contingent and irregular reward may also have occurred, establishing in these children the habit of feeling personally competent and accepted only if their behaviors were explicitly approved by others. Many of these youngsters were exposed to exhibitionistic and theatrical parental models. Another background contributor may have been exposure to variable and rapidly changing parental and societal values, resulting in an extreme of exteroceptivity, that is, an excessive dependence on external cues for guiding behavior. The emergent pattern of capriciousness and seductiveness in interpersonal relations fostered rather than resolved difficulties. Their emotional shallowness and excessive demands for attention and approval often resulted in a paucity of enduring relationships.

Unable to sustain a consistent external source of nurture and fearful that their capacity to elicit attention and support was waning, these patients began to evidence the cyclical mood swings that are characteristic of the borderline level of functioning. Persistent shifts between brooding dejection, simulated euphoria and impulsive outbursts of resentment and hostility only resulted in further interpersonal complications and a mounting of separation anxieties. As these self-defeating behaviors and coping efforts failed repeatedly, there may have been a pervasive structural deterioration, and a gradual slipping into the more permanent decompensated-borderline pattern.

3. A primary psychogenic influence among other decompensated borderlines (e.g., negativistic) was the presence of parental inconsistency in upbringing; as youngsters, these patients are likely to have been exposed to extreme oscillations between smothering or guilt-laden affection on the one hand, and indifference, abuse, or castigation on the other. Many were products of schismatic families. In addition to the emotional consequences of these experiences, parents served as models for learning erratic and contradictory behaviors. Such youngsters often were trapped in a "double-bind." Despite their discontent at having been mishandled and deceived, they obtained sufficient affection so as not to forgo the hope that matters ultimately would improve.

Patients who decompensated beyond the milder stylistic patterns continued to be subjected to marked conflicts and disappointments. These difficulties were fostered by their own sullen and vacillating behaviors. Rarely could they sustain a prolonged harmonious relationship. As a consequence of their negativism and moodiness, they turned away the very affections and support they so desperately needed; this only intensified their erratic and troublesome behaviors. At this point, the defective-borderline pattern may have emerged in the form of violent and irrational outbursts of recrimination and revenge; interspersed with these bizarre episodes were periods characterized by severe selfreproaches and redemptive pleas for forgiveness.

Unable to get hold of themselves, control their churning resentments and conflicts, or elicit even the slightest degree of approval and support from others, guilt-ridden and self-condemnatory, these patients slide from the cyclical episodes of the defective-borderline pattern into the more permanent structural abyss of becoming a decompensated borderline. Here they linger as invalids, away from the turmoil of reality; disorganized cognitively and estranged from themselves, they sink into the sheltered obscurity of institutional life.

DECOMPENSATED-PARANOID PERSONALITIES

The label "paraphrenia" was first used by Kraepelin in 1893 to describe an insidiously developing pathology that he viewed as lying halfway between the paranoid conditions and dementia praecox (schizophrenia); we have discussed aspects of the history and logic of this syndrome in earlier chapters. The concept behind Kraepelin's term shall be revived in this text because it seems especially appropriate for those cases of markedly severe personality decompensation that have been preceded by a premorbid history of strivings for independence, power, and recognition. In our view, the label "decompensated paranoid" parallels both decompensated schizotypal and decompensated borderlines in its insidious course of decompensation, and in the pervasiveness and severity of deterioration; it differs from these two parallel structural pathologies in that it applies to cases of paranoid deterioration rather than to cases of schizotypal or borderline deterioration.

As noted earlier, it is customary in current psychiatric practice to apply the label of schizophrenia to all cases of personality decompensation, regardless of differences in premorbid styles of functioning. This practice unwisely groups widely divergent personalities into a single syndrome, causing endless diagnostic complications. To help resolve these difficulties, we have designated all severely and chronically deteriorated cases decompensated-personality patterns, reserving more specific labels to represent particular types of premorbid coping styles.

Comparison of the Decompensated-Paranoid and Similar Syndromes in the Official Classification

A number of listings in the DSM-IV resemble the decompensated-paranoid syndrome as described in this section. Most relevant are *delusional disorder* and *schizophrenia, paranoid type*. Both syndromes are distinguished by the presence of persecutory and grandiose delusions. More specifically, the DSM-IV description of the delusional disorder category states, "The essential feature . . . is the presence of one or more nonbizarre delusions that persist for at least one month . . . auditory or visual hallucinations, if present, are not prominent." In prior manuals, a category termed *paranoid state* was differentiated from other paranoid disorders by the fact that "it lacks the logical nature of (delusional) systematization . . . yet it does not manifest the bizarre fragmentation and deterioration of the schizophrenic reactions." Finally, the syndrome posited as *schizophrenia, paranoid type* is described in the 1994 manual by its "prominent delusions or auditory hallucinations in the context of a relative preservation of cognitive functioning and affect . . . none of the following is prominent: disorganized speech, disorganized or catatonic behavior, or flat or inappropriate affect."

In surveying these descriptions, one cannot help but be struck by the observation that the differences among the preceding categories reflect differences in degree of personality deterioration; all they have in common is the presence of delusions. Thus, in one category, the delusions are highly systematized and the personality is essentially intact; in another, the delusions lack the systematization seen in the former category, but fall short of fragmentation and deterioration; in the third, thinking is autistic and unrealistic, and the personality tends to be deteriorated. In effect, the distinctions relate almost exclusively to degree of structural personality decompensation.

What appears especially peculiar in this regard, and is viewed as such by many clinicians, is the separation of these subcategories into a number of different syndromes. This bifurcation reflects the persistence of Kraepelin's original notions reviewed earlier. It was inconsistencies such as these that prompted the revisions formulated for this text. We do not consider the decompensated-paranoid syndrome to be a variant of schizophrenia; rather, it is a parallel level of pathology structurally equivalent to the other severely deteriorated personality patterns—the decompensated-schizotypal and the decompensated-borderline syndromes. It differs in that its roots derive from a developmental history of independence strivings, and it follows the defective-paranoid pattern as the last of a series of personality decompensations of that coping strategy.

CLINICAL FEATURES

The contrast in the clinical picture between the defective- and decompensated-paranoid patterns is more striking than that found between other defective patterns and their decompensated counterparts. Although the transition is a gradual one, spotted along the way with several "syndromal episodes," the final decompensated state appears to reflect a major transformation. Actually, this is not the case; certain fundamental changes have taken place, of course, but superficial appearances tend to accentuate them. It is this overt and dramatic clinical difference that may, in part, have accounted for Kraepelin's decision to subsume these cases, which he originally termed "dementia paranoides," under the dementia praecox label.

The air of independence and self-assertion that characterizes so many paranoid personalities is sharply deflated when they succumb to the decompensated paranoid pattern. In contrast to schizotypals and borderlines, who have always appeared more or less either weak or vacillating, paranoids have fostered the image of being cocky, self-assured, willful, and dominant; they fall a far distance when they finally topple, and the contrast is quite marked.

Despite these dramatic overt changes, decompensated paranoids retain many elements of the basic personality style that characterized their earlier functioning; reference should be made to previous chapters for an extensive discussion of these premorbid features.

Though cognitively disorganized, estranged, and invalided, decompensated paranoids remain defensively on guard against influence, coercion, or attachments of any kind. They still are mistrustful and suspicious, ever fearful that those on whom they now must depend for survival will be deceitful or injurious. Through the haze of disorganized thought processes, they still distort objective reality to fit their delusional "pseudo-community." Not only are paranoids estranged from others and therefore unable to share a common social perspective, but they continue the habit of actively resisting the other person's viewpoint. And despite the general collapse of their coping strategy, they persist, however feebly, in the struggle to retain independence and to keep intact the remnants of a shattered self-image.

These traces of the decompensated paranoid's past assertiveness and self-assurance are submerged, however, in the ineffectualities and confusions of severe decompensation. Where self-determination and independence had characterized earlier behavior, we now observe a pervasive invalidism and dependence on others, an inability to assume responsibility for even the most mundane tasks of self-care and survival. Although cognitive processes were always distorted, delusional and narrow in focus, they possessed intrinsic order and logic to them; now they are fragmented, disjunctive, and irrational. Previously, ideas were conveyed in a self-confident and often articulate manner; they now tend to be stated with hesitation and doubt; remarks frequently are tangential, expressed in incoherent phrases or scattered in disjointed flights of fancy. Emotions still retain their quality of veiled hostility but the "fight" is lacking; words of anger seem devoid of feeling and the spark of intense resentment has burned out. Behavior, once dominant, intimidating, or contemptuous, has become aversive, secretive, and bizarre. The whole complex of paranoid self-assurance and social belligerence has disintegrated, leaving an inner vacancy, a fearful hesitation, and a fragmented shadow of the former being.

The role of invalidism in these patients has been hard for them to accept. Their mistrust of others and their lifelong orientation of hardboiled self-determination make it difficult to accept the weakness and dependence that the role of hospital patient imposes on them. But they have had no choice; their behavior has been grossly disturbing, impossible to tolerate in normal social life. For a few, institutional life is a sanctuary; illness may be a convenient rationalization to account for their repeated failures. Others assert that their "forced" hospitalization only proves the correctness of their persecutory delusions; it verifies the inevitable deceit of others, the inescapable resentment the world has always felt toward them. Distorted in this manner, many accept their fate of hospital invalidism and become less contentious and resistive; though still suspicious and easily affronted, they may no longer be as difficult to manage as when they were first committed.

The collapse of their formerly organized cognitive world has several roots. First, as their difficulties mounted, they became increasingly detached from social contact; lost in their own reveries, they had little need to maintain the logic of consensual thinking. They slipped, then, into an inchoate world of dreamlike fantasy, with all its disjointed and phantasmagoric elements. In addition, as their formerly prideful self-image collapsed as a consequence of repeated social failures and the painful realities of their increasing dependence, they begin to engage in the destruction of their own cognitive processes; these patients would rather not think about their humiliations and the "shameful" state in which they find themselves. When these painful thoughts intrude into consciousness, they disassemble and twist them into digressive and irrelevant paths, ultimately creating disorganization where cognitive order and clarity previously existed.

Decompensated paranoids become estranged from self for similar reasons. Always apart from others by choice, they now disengage their thoughts and feelings from themselves. Unable to tolerate their present state of helpless dependency, they reject their own being and often adopt in its stead the identity of others.

There are many similarities in the clinical pictures of decompensated paranoids and timorous schizotypals, a fact that may result in diagnostic difficulties, especially if reference is not made to their different developmental histories. Decompensated paranoids exhibit many characteristics at this stage of decompensation that have existed throughout the life history of certain schizotypal personalities. They now experience a deep sense of personal humiliation and low self-esteem where pride and high self-esteem existed before; cognitive interference and disjunctiveness have come to the foreground to replace their former clarity and logic; behaviors now are noted by aversiveness in contrast to dominance and directness; there is a growing impoverishment of affect, where once there was intense anger and resentment; and a sense of alienation and depersonalization has taken over from that of social involvement and self-assurance.

Both decompensated paranoids and timorous schizotypals (e.g., avoidants) learned in early life to be mistrustful and suspicious of others. The major difference between them is that the paranoids acquired a sense of self-confidence and learned to fight back, whereas avoidant/timorous youngsters did not. But now that confidence and spirit have been shattered in paranoids, they experience in adulthood the same derogation and humiliation of self that was the lot of young, avoidant/timorous schizotypals. Thus, both types have not only been mistrustful of others, but both now lack a feeling of self-worth and self-confidence. Their clinical pictures begin to blend, making discriminations extremely difficult at the observational level.

Because of these difficulties, it is important to differentiate decompensated paranoids and decompensated schizotypals in terms of their developmental histories. Furthermore, from a prognostic point of view, the prospects for decompensated paranoids, though far from good, are more favorable than those for schizotypals; they have had moderate success in their past social life and retain some residue of their former feelings of self-worth.

The following are clinical features of several of the less pathological personality patterns that often deteriorate to decompensated paranoids:

1. Before their final stage of decompensation, several of the defective paranoids (e.g., narcissistic types) usually construct delusional self-pictures of illustriousness and omnipotence as a means of countering the painful reality of their failures and embarrassments. But these efforts at narcissistic restitution have not been supported or encouraged; these patients have repeatedly been rebuffed and humiliated. As they progressively disengage themselves from reality, sinking further into a state characterized by autistic fantasy and feelings of futility, their overt behavior begins to lose its former color and their grandiose statements seem vapid, lacking the flavor of self-confidence; delusional beliefs no longer seem inspired, suggesting that the patients themselves may sense their emptiness and invalidity.

Quite typically, these decompensated paranoids spend endless hours ruminating over memories of a better yesteryear, such as when they experienced realistic adulation and encouragement in childhood. Many revert to childlike behaviors and attitudes, as if hoping that these reversions will revive the good will and commendation of the past. Most no longer act haughty and arrogant; on the contrary, they seem to accept their helpless invalidism and to bask in the care that others provide them; this transformation to a passive receptive role often is baffling to those who previously knew them. Strange as these behaviors may seem, they are not inconsistent with the defectively structured narcissist's former exploitive strategy; moreover, the return to a role in which they benignly accept the goodwill of others may be an unconscious attempt to resurrect the rewards they experienced in childhood.

2. Despite their common invalidism, disorganization, and estrangement, other decompensated paranoids (e.g., antisocials, sadists) exhibit a strained and hostile demeanor; though repeatedly humiliated and deflated, an undercurrent of suspicion and resentment remains in these patients and pervades their every mood and behavior.

Each setback to their aspirations for power and revenge has only reinforced their persecutory delusions, and there is no diminishment in their tendency to project their anger on others. However, because of possible hospital confinement and their growing doubts of omnipotence, these decompensated paranoids become relatively subdued, usually working out their hostility and desire for retribution through fantasy and hallucination. Unconscious impulses may periodically erupt into bizarre and violent behavior; more often, however, these feelings are directed toward hallucinated images.

3. The clinical picture of a third group of decompensated paranoids (e.g., negativistic) is difficult to distinguish from its decompensated-borderline counterpart. Although the underlying ambivalent style that characterizes these personalities often splits in separate directions at the defective-structural level, this divergence terminates as patients deteriorate to the markedly severe or decompensated structural level. Basically alike in their personalities from early life, these ambivalent patients took different directions when faced with the threat of separation and abandonment; some asserted their independence, thereby turning in the defective-paranoid direction; others clung to the hope of reestablishing their security through connections with others, thus turning toward the defective-borderline pattern. Now, sharing a common fate of failure and personal devastation, they revert to similar decompensated characteristics.

It should be noted that despite differences in their basic personalities, distinctions are difficult to make between the clinical pictures of the various decompensated patterns because their behaviors and moods, under the impact of external and internal pressures, have become appreciably similar. Moreover, the task of sorting patients on the basis of clinical symptomatology alone is complicated by the inevitable intrapatient variability in overt symptomatology. For example, delusions may be dominant in a patient at one time, but are hardly noticed at other times. Thus, the only sound basis for differential classification, given overt clinical similarities among groups and intrapatient symptomatological variabilities, rests on the patient's developmental history. These background data should provide the diagnostician with a clearer picture of a patient's basic personality pattern; with knowledge of the experiential background and the instrumental strategies the patient has undergone and habitually employed in the past, the clinician should have a sound foundation for recommending a plan of remedial treatment.

The following case history relates to a sadistic/malignant subtype of the decompensated paranoid, illustrating numerous developmental experiences and characteristics that typify this structurally defective personality.

Case 20.3

Jack R., Age 59, Separated

Jack lived in foster homes from the age of 3 months; at 8 years of age he settled with one family, remaining there until he was 15, when he left to go on his own. Eventually enlisting in the Navy, he was given a medical discharge on psychiatric grounds, after three years of service.

As a child, Jack was known to be a "bully"; he was heavy, muscular, burly in build, had an inexhaustible supply of energy, and prided himself on his physical strength and endurance. Though quite intelligent, Jack was constantly in trouble at school, teasing other children, resisting the directives of teachers, and walking out of class whenever he pleased.

Jack was the foster son of a manager of a coal mine, and spoke with great pride of his capacity, at the age of 12, to outproduce most of the experienced miners. When he was 14, his foster mother died, leaving Jack alone to take care of himself; his foster father, who lived periodically with a mistress, rarely came home. Jack worked at the mine and quarreled bitterly with his father for a "fair" wage; when he was 15, he got into one of his "regular fights" with his father and beat him so severely that the man was hospitalized for a month. After this event, Jack left his hometown, wandered aimlessly for 2 years, and enlisted in the Navy. In the service, Jack drank to excess, "flew off the handle at the drop of a hat," and spent an inordinate amount of time in the brig. The persistence of this behavior and the apparent bizarre features that characterized some of these episodes resulted in his discharge.

For several years thereafter, Jack appeared to make a reasonable life adjustment. He married, had four sons, and started a small trash-collecting business. Drinking was entirely eliminated, though Jack remained a "hot-headed" fellow who happily "took on all comers" to prove his strength.

Greater success—and difficulty—followed when Jack "took up" with a teenage girl; this younger woman was quite attractive and built up Jack's self-image. More importantly, she bore him, illegitimately, what his own wife failed to—a little girl. With mistress and child in hand, he left his legal family, moving some 600 miles to a new city where he "started life again." Within three years, Jack founded a successful contracting company and became moderately wealthy; at 36, he ran for a local political office, which he won.

Trouble began brewing immediately thereafter. Jack was unable to compromise in the give-and-take of politics; he insisted at public meetings, to the point of near violence, that his obviously impractical and grandiose plans be adopted. After many outbursts, one of which culminated in the assault of a fellow official, Jack was asked to resign from office, which he refused to do. To assure his resignation, as he put it, "They dredged up all the dirt they could get to get rid of me"; this included his Navy psychiatric discharge, his abandonment of his legal family, his illicit "marriage," illegitimate child, and so on. The final collapse of his world came when his present "wife," in whose name alone his business was registered, rejected him, sold the company and kept all of the proceeds.

Jack became physically violent following these events, and was taken to a state institution. Here, his well-justified feelings of persecution were elaborated until they lost all semblance of reality. Jack remained hospitalized for 2 years, during which he managed gradually to reorient himself, although still retaining his basic, aggressive paranoid pattern. On remission, he returned to his legal family, working periodically as a driver of heavy contracting equipment. He began drinking again and got involved in repeated fist fights in local bars. When Jack came home after a night's drinking, he frequently attempted to assault his wife. To his dismay, his teenage sons would come to their mother's defense; Jack invariably was the loser in these battles.

After living with his family for 4 years, Jack disappeared, unheard from for about 18 months. Apparently, he had lived alone in a city some 90 miles from his home; the family learned of his whereabouts when he was picked up for vagrancy. After he was bailed out, it was clear that Jack was a beaten and destitute man. He returned to the state hospital where he has since remained for some 10 years. Although subdued and periodically cooperative, Jack is still suspicious, has delusions of persecution that he keeps largely to himself, tends to be easily affronted, and occasionally flares up in a hostile outburst. He ruminates to himself all day, occasionally speaking in an angry voice to hallucinated images.

The deterioration to the decompensated-paranoid level is now deeply entrenched.

Pathogenic Developmental Background

As should be evident from the general thesis presented in the text, the pathogenic determinants that shape the development of the decompensated-paranoid pattern are similar to those found in its less severe counterparts, differing essentially only in intensity, frequency, timing, and persistence. The roots of these difficulties may be traced to a variety of sources: constitutional defects, adverse early experiences, periodically severe or unrelieved stress, and so on. Thus, the patient's capacity to cope with his or her environment may never have been adequately developed, or it may have crumbled under the weight of persistent misfortune.

We shall next summarize the developmental background of several variants of the decompensated-paranoid personality; this review abbreviates more extensive discussions provided in earlier chapters.

Hypothesized Biogenic Factors

The background of certain decompensated paranoids (e.g., sadists) may include a number of biogenic factors. This is suggested by the frequent presence among family members of high levels of activation and energy, irascible choleric temperaments, and fearless parmic temperaments. Along these lines, many of these patients as young children exhibited a vigorous aggressive and thick-skinned obtrusiveness. Mesomorphic-endomorphic physical builds are disproportionately frequent, increasing the likelihood that assertive and competitive behaviors will be positively reinforcing. Speculations may be made as to the neurological substrate of these tendencies in the limbic and reticular systems.

Characteristic Experiential History

As in prior discussions, decompensated-paranoid personality disorders originate in a number of diverse developmental histories; a few of these will be noted in the following paragraphs.

1. Many future decompensated paranoids (e.g., antisocial, sadistic) have been exposed to parental indifference or harsh treatment. These children apparently learn to counterattack in response to this experience rather than to withdraw into docility; this coping response may reflect the operation of a constitutional parmic temperament or a rapid learning that they possess the power to disrupt others by provocative behaviors or a simple process of imitating parental models. As a consequence of their experiences, these children acquire a deep mistrust of others, a desire for self-determination, and a confident sense of competence and autonomy. With this as a base, they frequently reject parental controls and social values, developing in their stead an impulsive, aggressive, and often hedonistic style of life.

Experiences such as these frequently arise in broken families and in disorganized subcultural groups. Here, children lack nurtural and consistent parental models, and acquire their outlook on life through contact with equally disillusioned and angry peers; as a consequence, they learn to emulate the wrong models; the customs and values of the larger society are viewed as alien, hypocritical, and hostile; aggressive toughness becomes a necessary style of coping.

The expectations of attack and the chip-on-the-shoulder attitudes of these youngsters provoke new tensions and conflicts, and thereby reactivate old fears and intensify new mistrusts. In decompensated cases, we see either deficiencies in the skill with which aggressive and vindictive strategies were learned or a gradual weakening of them as a result of repeated setbacks. Under these conditions, inchoate suspicions of malignment and deceit gradually are transformed into irrational delusions of persecution. Unable to cope directly with the threats that surround them, their tensions either erupt into overt hostile attacks or are resolved in increasingly delusional fantasies. This paranoid stage with its periodic psychotic episodes may disintegrate further.

Unrelieved or severe stress may prompt a marked withdrawal from social contact; the shock and humiliation of hospitalization, the loss of self-determination and the terrifying dependence on others may shatter their fragile underpinnings and the last remnants of their delusional self-image. As they protectively withdraw further, they sink into a primitive and diffuse world of fantasy, unchecked by reality and social controls. The former logic of their delusional system loses its coherence and order; disorganized fantasies blur into objective reality. Hallucinations are projected and cognitive associations are dismembered; bizarre feelings and a sense of barrenness, disorientation, and estrangement come to the fore as these paranoids now pass the line into decompensation.

2. An early pattern of parental overvaluation and indulgence is common among another group of decompensated paranoids (e.g., narcissistic). Many fail to learn interpersonal responsibility, rarely think of the desires and welfare of others, and seem markedly deficient in group sharing and social cooperation. Undisciplined by parental controls and given an illusory sense of high self-worth, these youngsters place no reins on their imagination; they tend through excessive self-reinforcement to weave glorious fantasies of their own power and achievements; most of them, however, lack true substance to support their illusions and aspirations. Once beyond the confines of home, their haughty, exploitive, presumptuous, and selfish orientation provokes repeated ridicule, humiliation, and ostracism by peers. Unwilling to adjust to reality and accept a lowered self-esteem, they begin to withdraw from direct social competition and find consistent gratification in the refuge of fantasy. A vicious circle of rebuff, increased isolation, and fantasy develops.

As these patients revert to the coping style characterizing the defective-paranoid level, they harshly reject all forms of dependence, refuse to ally themselves with those whom they view as "inferior," and begin to suspect that others will undo them the first moment they can. Their resentment toward others for failing to appreciate them or to be willing subjects for their narcissistic exploitation comes to the surface in the form of overt anger and vituperation. Unable to gain recognition and humiliated time and again, they reconstruct reality to suit their desires and illusions. As fantasy supplants reality and as their delusions lead them further astray from others, the decompensation process speeds up. The more involved they become within their boundless and undisciplined inner world, the more their thoughts become fluid and disorganized. Repeated experiences of belittlement and censure take their toll; now their reveries are interrupted more and more with thoughts of persecution, dismay, and anguish.

The final shameful collapse to the role of hospital invalid is a further blow to their once vaunted self-image. As they become conceptually more disorganized and as they try to deny and destroy the intrusions of their own painful thoughts and memories, they become increasingly estranged from themselves. All that remains is a thin thread connecting the present to memories of a happier yesteryear; these few mementos they hold fast to,

turning them over and over again in their thoughts, embellishing and nurturing them, lost in the distant past that now becomes their only reality.

3. With the exception of a divergency in coping aims during the defective-structural level of paranoid functioning, the developmental histories of most other deteriorated paranoid personalities are essentially alike; reference should be made in this regard to earlier chapters, rather than repeat them in this discussion. The major distinction between these decompensated personalities, as just noted, is that the more ambivalent paranoids progressed through a defective-paranoid stage prior to final decompensation, whereas the more ambivalent borderlines followed a defective-borderline course. During this earlier phase of decompensation, the decompensated paranoids abandoned their basic ambivalence and shifted in the direction of independence and self-assertion; at this point in deterioration, they will have exhibited overt hostility, and psychotic episodes were marked by delusions of influence and persecution; all traces of dependency needs were denied, and inner conflicts and guilt feelings were projected onto others. As coping efforts crumbled under repeated adversity, these patients usually disintegrate to the structurally decompensated personality level; because their efforts to assert autonomy failed, they may revert back again to the basic ambivalent personality style.

In general, the prognostic picture for decompensated paranoids is extremely grave; this is true of all variants. The chronic and pervasive nature of their decompensation augurs a poor future adjustment. Because of their earlier self-confidence and capacity to draw self-reinforcements, their prognosis is somewhat better than that of schizotypals, but circumstance has devastated the paranoids' self-image, leaving but a few remnants of self-esteem in its wake. Moreover, the undercurrent of mistrust and hostility in these patients makes it extremely difficult to establish therapeutic relationships that might alter the course of their illness.

TERMINAL PERSONALITY PATTERN

It may be inappropriate to speak of this last and most decompensated state of psychopathology as a personality pattern because the syndrome represents the total disintegration of functions that normally compose what we speak of as personality. These long-term and profoundly deteriorated patients are seen in every mental institution; some sit mutely on benches, vegetating and transfixed, attired in drab or peculiar garb; others wander aimlessly, seem unaware of the presence of other people, and stare vacantly into space, absorbed in nothingness; occasionally they grimace or stop in a corner, rocking to and fro.

There is little in the recent literature or in the DSM-IV to separate these more advanced states from those we have termed decompensated patterns. Kraepelin noted several end stages of dementia praecox, differentiating the last two of the series, "silly dementia" and "apathetic dementia," as terminal points. More recently, Menninger (1963) spoke of a "fifth order of dyscontrol" in the decompensation process; here the patient regresses to an irreversible impairment, exhibiting not even the feeblest and most ineffectual survival efforts.

CLINICAL FEATURES

Distinctions cannot readily be made between the decompensated and *terminal* patterns since these lie on a gradient of severity; not only do they shade imperceptibly into one another, but there is enough intrapatient variability in the clinical picture to make clear-cut discriminations practically impossible. The essential distinction we seek to draw may be largely academic, yet it may have practical implications.

Basically, we would categorize as decompensated those who exhibit signs giving promise, albeit small, that they can be rehabilitated. In contrast, in those we shall call the terminal pattern, the prognosis appears totally hopeless. These patients have been immersed in their disintegrated state for so long that their previous social habits and attitudes have largely been extinguished; they have deteriorated into a state of permanent invalidism. All efforts at self-care and self-determination have long since been relinquished, and the patient now seems devoid of any but the most rudimentary competencies necessary for survival. At this stage of decompensation, the fabric of former personality structure has completely decayed.

It is important to note that not all decompensated patterns deteriorate further over time, neither is there a simple one-to-one relationship between duration of illness and severity of deterioration. Many patients of long-standing chronicity not only adjust to the hospital routine, but assume a variety of simple tasks that help to deter further disintegration. Though they are social invalids according to any standard of normal behavior and responsibility, they perform these hospital chores with a reasonable measure of adequacy

(e.g., changing their beds, eating without supervision or assistance, lining up to await medication).

Among other features that may distinguish decompensated from terminal patterns is the persistence among the former of their distinctive premorbid attributes and coping styles. For example, decompensated patients tend to hallucinate actively and retain their "pet" delusional beliefs, characteristics that terminal patients rarely possess. Although decompensated patients' distorted cognitive ideas and idiosyncratic behaviors indicate the severity of their illness, the continued presence of these personal processes signifies the preservation of some remnants of their former personality style. In contrast, carryovers from the past, in the form of personal delusions and behaviors, are burned out in terminal patients; there is now a vegetablelike colorlessness, a loss of all those subtle features of thought and action that distinguished their former style of functioning. Some deteriorated cases continue to exhibit minor and peculiar habits and occasional bizarre acts, but these seem random and aimless, unrelated to their preterminal personality patterns. All terminal patients display, in common, a flat and insipid uniformity; those who were once identifiable and distinguishable now converge into a single, undifferentiated class.

PATHOGENIC DEVELOPMENTAL BACKGROUND

The downward spiral to total structural deterioration usually occurs only after a prolonged period of institutionalization; prior to ultimate disintegration, each patient passes through one of the three decompensated patterns. There is no need, therefore, to review the long history of events that preceded this terminal stage; it simply picks up where the decompensated stage leaves off.

It will be instructive to separate the influences that contribute to the terminal stage of decay into those arising from external as contrasted with internal sources (i.e., those deriving from the conditions of hospitalization as opposed to those stemming from the patient's own thoughts and behaviors).

Conditions of Hospitalization

Among the experiences of hospitalization that foster further deterioration are those of *social isolation* and *dependency training;* both of these are usually consequences of poor therapeutic planning or understaffed hospital management.

Social Isolation. Patients who are cut off from social contact, who are segregated or neglected and who are allowed to drift into the bleak back wards of institutions, without opportunities to communicate with fellow patients, staff, and relatives, are bound to deteriorate with the passage of time. Others, homeless and withdrawn not only perpetuate, but intensify deficits in cognitive organization and social skills; ultimately, under these stimulus deprivations, patients lose whatever competencies they may have had as participants of social life.

Dependency Training. At the other extreme, and perhaps no less damaging, is an excess in custodial care, a tendency to overprotect and coddle the patient. Though decompensated patients are "mental" invalids, they will not be helped to regain normal skills and responsibilities if they are exposed to a regime of inadvertent dependency training. Extreme devotion to the welfare of patients may be of great value in many respects, but it may do them an ultimate disservice. Patients who are guided unwisely to relinquish their former interests and activities or to restrict themselves to the directives and suggestions provided by hospital personnel may learn to lean too much on others and not enough on themselves. Under prolonged guidance and care of this kind, they may undergo a progressive impoverishment of competencies and self-motivations, resulting ultimately in a total lack of interest and an utter helplessness. In short, many decompensated patients are reinforced to learn dependency and apathy as a consequence of the "good care" to which they were exposed.

Patient Behavior

Two factors that stem directly from the patient's own behavior foster further personality deterioration: *protective insulation* and *self-abandonment.*

Protective Insulation. It is not only through neglect and mismanagement that patients experience a decrease in social contact. To protect themselves from painful humiliation and rejection, decompensated patients learn to withdraw from reality and to disengage themselves from social give-and-take. Thus, even though they may be exposed to active and inviting hospital programs, many patients are reluctant to participate, preferring to keep to themselves. The consequences are not different for them than for those who are isolated by neglectful management. Without the controls and

support of interpersonal relations, these patients recede further into a social stagnancy and become increasingly impoverished and deteriorated.

Self-Abandonment. Progressively decompensating patients cut off relationships not only with others but with themselves as well. Fantasy may have been an early refuge, but few decompensated types gain consistent gratification from this source. As noted previously, the content of these fantasies turns too often into preoccupations with past misfortune and injustice. More importantly, patients may find that they cannot escape the futility and anguish of being who they are. To protect themselves from self-inflicted misery, they must destroy their thoughts, cluttering, blocking, and disarranging memories and feelings, and thus contributing to the cognitive disorganization that characterizes the terminal level. Confused and disoriented as they may be, however, these patients still sense the irrational and bizarre elements of their behavior. Try as they may to divert awareness or disorient themselves, they cannot escape "being" what they are. Nothing less than a total divorce and abandonment of self will do. Humiliated and terror stricken, they jettison the self and disavow their own existence. In contrast to less severe personality patterns, terminal patients accept the calm and deathlike emptiness that takes hold; depersonalization becomes a welcome relief, a permanent escape from the self. They have "chosen" nothingness; they have disgorged their very being, with all of its turmoil and anguish.

THERAPEUTIC INTERVENTIONS

Most patients are institutionalized when they reach the markedly severe levels of personality decompensation; thus, treatment occurs within a hospital setting. In general, the initial focus of treatment is to relieve patients of unbearable environmental tensions, rebuild social skills, and prepare them for approaches that may modify the distortions of personality makeup; only after a modest degree of social rapport and cognitive clarity have occurred can the therapist begin to turn attention to the attributes of specific personality patterns. Therapy for decompensated patients may be viewed, then, as a two-stage process. We shall concern ourselves in this section only with the first, that of preparing the groundwork for treatment methods geared to specific personality types.

As noted earlier, three central features characterize all decompensated personality patterns: social invalidism, cognitive disorganization, and estrangement. These characteristics are the focus of the first stage of this therapeutic sequence. Let us deal with them in order.

Social Invalidism. The hospital environment serves as an excellent protection against the incursions and stresses of reality; in this setting the patient is safe from further onslaught and anguish. But the supportive character of the hospital milieu may itself become a pathogenic influence. Specifically, patients may be encouraged to slip into obscurity and relinquish whatever social skills they previously may have possessed; in other words, institutional life may foster *social invalidism.* Thus, although the important role that the hospital serves as a refuge must be granted, it should not blind us to the deleterious consequences of custodial overprotectiveness, social inactivity, personal idleness, and physical vegetation.

Toward the end of countering these consequences, and for the purpose of rebuilding social competencies and motivations, it is advisable to encourage patients to participate in a variety of normal-life activities, such as vocational therapy and social recreation. Involvement in even the simplest and most menial productive tasks will help forestall further regression to total invalidism and perhaps stimulate some growth toward feelings of adequacy and self-worth. Similarly, structured ward programs, group projects, attendance at social affairs, visits with congenial relatives and repeated contact with volunteers from outside the hospital will help to prevent the deterioration of social skills and possibly aid in learning new ones. Keeping in touch with the realities of normal productive and social life is a prerequisite to further therapy and an essential phase in the early handling of decompensated personalities.

Cognitive Disorganization. The cognitive disorganization of these patients is extremely difficult to break through, and it may require months of laborious therapy to rebuild clearer and more orderly thinking. The therapist must pick up the patients' "symbolism" and trend of thought and grasp the elusive and jumbled threads of their communications. By listening carefully and responding in a "connected" yet logical manner, the therapist may help patients to a more socially meaningful and disciplined way of thinking. Until some measure of cognitive control is established, and until a degree of consensual meaning replaces these patients' inchoate and confused communications, it will be almost impossible to utilize more focused therapeutic approaches.

Estrangement. The reestablishment of reality contact and the rebuilding of a sense of personal identity and self-worth are the two principal goals to counter the patients' estrangement. Attainment of these goals rests, first, on the development of trust between patient and therapist. Many hours of untiring perseverance, usually at a low key, are required before these patients will gain enough faith in their therapist to dare face the world of reality again. Having been humiliated, anguished, and abandoned so often, such patients have learned to insulate themselves; they have every reason to move cautiously before relating to others. The therapist must feel genuine respect for the patient; a sincere desire to be of assistance is needed to help carry the therapist through the long, slow, and not too promising process of treatment. Should trust and a cognitively clear line of communication be developed, the therapist will have established the foundation for further progress.

Now feeling less estranged from others, the patient has taken the first step in learning to feel less estranged from the self. As the patient's cognitive processes take on greater clarity, and as feelings of trust develop further, the therapist can begin to rebuild the patient's sense of self-worth. At this point, sufficient inroads have been made into the decompensation process itself so that the therapist may direct attention to the specific features of the patient's personality and background. The therapist is no longer primarily concerned with the general state of the patient's decompensation and can shift now to those features that distinguish the patient's lifelong attitudes and styles of coping (i.e., the specific personality pattern).

A few words should be said concerning a number of the specific modalities that may prove helpful with decompensated personalities; the details and focus of this work have been discussed partially in previous Therapeutic Interventions sections presented in conjunction with the less severe personality patterns.

Certain personality patterns possess attitudes and coping styles that undermine chances for recovery; some resist therapeutic rapport whereas others are difficult to motivate. For example, decompensated-schizotypal personalities frequently deteriorate rapidly despite all treatment efforts. These personalities often succumb to catatonic disorders with their flat and difficult-to-activate qualities or to disorganized disorders that, given their characteristic cognitive disruptions, are highly resistant to meaningful therapeutic communication. Other patterns are conducive to better prognoses because they provide a handle, so to speak, that the therapist can use to relate to and motivate the patient. For example, dependent and histrionic borderline patterns are desirous of social approval and can be motivated by therapeutic attitudes of gentility and nurture during their typical disorders. For different reasons, notably the drive to assert themselves and to reestablish their autonomy, antisocial and sadistic patterns—despite episodes such as delusional disorders and "manic excitement"—have modestly promising prognostic pictures.

Therapists have employed practically every therapeutic modality and technique in rehabilitating decompensated patients. In the following paragraphs, we will note some of the measures that have been used and comment briefly on their respective merits.

Environmental management is a necessary step in the handling of decompensated disorders. This should consist of more than the mere removal of adverse conditions in life. Proper institutional placement should provide the patient not only with a refuge from environmental stress, but also with opportunities to resolve tensions and to employ programs which will orient the person toward social recovery. In what is termed "milieu therapy," the patient's daily routine is scheduled to maximize both emotional support and the acquisition of attitudes and skills conducive to a better social adjustment than existed previously.

Psychopharmacological treatment methods can be of notable value in several disorders. Antipsy-chotics and antidepressants may fruitfully be utilized to reactivate patients suffering schizotypal or borderline decompensated patterns. Each of these biophysical methods is of value not only in its immediate and direct effects, but in bringing the patient to a state in which other therapeutic measures may be employed (e.g., a lethargic and unresponsive depressed borderline patient who benefitted by drugs may now readily communicate in verbal psychotherapy).

Psychological therapeutic measures have not been especially successful in the early phases of a decompensating disorder. *Phenomenological* and *intrapsychic* methods cannot be used effectively until the patient possesses a modicum of cognitive clarity and emotional quietude. Nevertheless, the sympathetic attitude, patience, and gentle manner that these procedures employ may establish rapport and build a basis for further therapy.

Behavior modification techniques appear especially promising as instruments both for extinguishing or controlling specific symptoms and shaping more adaptive alternative responses. Although the durability of and the ability to generalize from these beneficial effects have not been adequately researched, these techniques are among the most encouraging of the initial treatment approaches to the decompensating disorders.

Group therapeutic methods may be especially efficient and adaptable to hospital settings, given the shortage of professional institutional personnel and the feasibility with which sessions can be arranged. They are particularly valuable as vehicles for resocializing patients and enabling them to express their confused attitudes and feelings in a highly controlled yet sympathetic environment.

References

Abraham, K. (1911). Notes on the psychoanalytic investigation and treatment of manic-depressive insanity and allied conditions. In *Selected papers of Karl Abraham*. London: Hogarth.

Abraham, K. (1927). Contributions to the theory of the anal character. In *Selected papers on psychoanalysis*. London: Hogarth. (Original work published 1921)

Abraham, K. (1927a). The influence of oral eroticism on character formation. In *Selected papers on psychoanalysis*. London: Hogarth. (Original work published 1924)

Abraham, K. (1927b). A short study of the development of the libido, viewed in the light of mental disorders. In *Selected papers on psychoanalysis*. London: Hogarth. (Original work published 1924)

Abraham, K. (1927). Character-formation on the genital level of the libido. In *Selected papers on psychoanalysis*. London: Hogarth. (Original work published 1925)

Ackerman, N. W. (1958). *The psychodynamics of family life*. New York: Basic Books.

Adler, A. (1964). *Problems of neurosis*. New York: Harper.

Adler, G. (1981). The borderline-narcissistic personality disorders continuum. *American Journal of Psychiatry, 138,* 16–50.

Adler, G. (1985). *Borderline psychopathology and its treatment*. Northvale, NJ: Aronson.

Aichorn, A. (1935). *Wayward youth*. New York: Viking. (Original work published 1925)

Ainsworth, M. D. S. (1967). *Infancy in Uganda*. Baltimore: John Hopkins University Press.

Ainsworth, M. D. S., Blehar, M., Waters, E., & Wall, S. (1978). *Patterns of attachment: A psychological study of the strange situation*. Hillsdale, NJ: Erlbaum.

Akhtar, S. (1987). Schizoid personality disorder: A synthesis of developmental, dynamic, and descriptive features. *American Journal of Psychotherapy, 41,* 499–518.

Akhtar, S., & Thomson, A. J. (1982). Overview: Narcissistic personality disorder. *American Journal of Psychiatry, 139,* 12–20.

Akiskal, H. S. (1981). Subaffective disorders: Dysthymic, cyclothymic and bipolar II disorders in the "borderline" realm. *Psychiatric Clinics of North America, 4,* 25–46.

Akiskal, H. S. (1983). Dysthymic disorder: Psychopathology of proposed chronic depressive subtypes. *American Journal of Psychiatry, 140,* 11–20.

Akiskal, H. S. (1984). Characterologic manifestations of affective disorders: Toward a new conceptualization. *Integrative Psychiatry, 2,* 83–88.

Akiskal, H. S., & Akiskal, K. (1992). Cyclothymic, hyperthymic and depressive temperaments as subaffective variants of mood disorders. In A. Tasman & M. B. Riba (Eds.), *Annual review of psychiatry, 11,* 43–62. Washington, DC: American Psychiatric Press.

Akiskal, H. S., Djenderedjian, A. H., Rosenthal, T. L., & Khani, M. K. (1977). Cyclothymic disorder: Validating criteria for inclusion in the bipolar affective group. *American Journal of Psychiatry, 134,* 1227–1233.

Alexander, F. (1930). The neurotic character. *International Journal of Psychoanalysis, 11,* 292–313.

Alexander, F. (1930). *Psychoanalysis of the total personality*. New York: Nervous and Mental Disease Publications. (Original work published 1923)

Alexander, F. (1935). *Roots of crime*. New York: Knopf.

Allen, F. (1942). *Psychotherapy with children*. New York: Norton.

Allen, F. (1950). The psychopathic delinquent child. *American Journal of Orthopsychiatry, 20,* 223–265.

Allport, G. (1937). *Personality: A psychological interpretation*. New York: Holt.

American Psychiatric Association. (1952). *Diagnostic and statistical manual of mental disorders* (DSM-I). Washington, DC: Mental Hospitals Service.

American Psychiatric Association. (1968). *Diagnostic and statistical manual of mental disorders* (DSM-II). Washington, DC: American Psychiatric Association.

American Psychiatric Association. (1980). *Diagnostic and statistical manual of mental disorders* (DSM-III). Washington, DC: American Psychiatric Association.

American Psychiatric Association. (1994). *Diagnostic and statistical manual of mental disorders* (DSM-IV). Washington, DC: American Psychiatric Association.

Anchin, J. C., & Kiesler, D. J. (Eds.). (1982). *Handbook of interpersonal psychotherapy.* New York: Pergamon.

Andreas-Salome, L. (1921). The dual orientation of narcissism. *Psychoanalytic Quarterly, 31,* 1–30.

Andrews, J. D. W. (1991). *The active self in psychotherapy.* Boston: Allyn & Bacon.

Ansbacher, H. L., & Ansbacher, R. (1956). *The individual psychology of Alfred Adler.* New York: Basic Books.

Arieti, S. (1955). *Interpretation of schizophrenia.* New York: Brunner/Mazel.

Arieti, S., & Bemporad, J. (1978). *Severe and mild depression.* New York: Basic Books.

Arkowitz, H. (1992). Integrative theories of therapy. In D. Freedham (Ed.), *The history of psychotherapy: A century of change.* Washington, DC: American Psychological Association.

Armstrong, J. S., & Solberg, P. (1968). On the interpretation of factor analysis. *Psychological Bulletin, 70,* 361–364.

Asch, S. (1988). The masochistic personality. In R. Michels (Ed.), *Psychiatry.* New York: Basic Books.

Aschaffenburg, G. (1922). Constitutional psychopathies. In *Handbook of medical practice, 4.* Leipzig: Barth.

Asperger, H. (1944). Die autistichen psychopathen im kindesalter. *Archieve fur Psychiatrie und Nerven Krankheiten, 177,* 76–137.

Avery, N. (1977). Sadomasochism: A defense against object loss. *Psychoanalytic Review, 64,* 101–109.

Baer, A. (1893). *Anthropological study of the delinquent.* Leipzig: Barth.

Bagby, R. M., Parker, J. D., & Joffe, R. T. (1992). Confirmatory factor analysis of the Tridimensional Personality Questionnaire. *Personality and Individual Differences, 13,* 1245–1246.

Baillarger, M. (1854). De la folie a double forme. *Annee medicales psychologie, 27,* 369–384.

Baldessarini, R. J., Finklestein, S., & Arieti, G. W. (1983). The predictive power of diagnostic tests and the effects of prevalence of illness. *Archives of General Psychiatry, 40,* 569–573.

Bandura, A. (1969). *Principles of behavior modification.* New York: Holt, Rinehart & Winston.

Bandura, A. (1977). *Social learning theory.* Englewood Cliffs, NJ: Prentice Hall.

Bandura, A., & Walters, R. H. (1959). *Adolescent aggression.* New York: Ronald.

Bartemeier, L. H. (1930). The neurotic character as a new psychoanalytic concept. *American Journal of Orthopsychiatry, 1,* 512–519.

Bartholomew, K., & Horowitz, L. M. (1991). Attachment styles among young adults: A test of a four-category model. *Journal of Personality and Social Psychology, 61,* 226–244.

Bartko, J. J., Strauss, J. S., & Carpenter, W. T. (1971). An evaluation of taxometric techniques for psychiatric data. *Classification Society Bulletin, 2,* 1–28.

Bates, J. E. (1980). The concept of difficult temperament. *Merrill-Palmer Quarterly, 26,* 299–319.

Bates, J. E. (1987). Temperament in infancy. In J. D. Osofsky (Ed.), *Handbook of infancy* (2nd ed., pp. 1101–1149). New York: Wiley.

Bateson, G., Jackson, D., Haley, J., & Weakland, J. (1956). Toward a theory of schizophrenia. *Behavioral Science, 1,* 251–256.

Bateson, G., & Ruesch, J. (1951). *Communication, the social matrix of psychiatry.* New York: Norton.

Baumrind, D. (1967). Child care practices anteceding three patterns of preschool behavior. *Genetic Psychology Monographs, 75,* 43–83.

Beach, F., & Jaynes, J. (1954). Effects of early experience upon the behavior of animals. *Psychological Bulletin, 51,* 239–262.

Beck, A. T. (1963). Thinking and depression: Idiosyncratic content and cognitive distortions. *Archives of General Psychiatry, 9,* 324–344.

Beck, A. T. (1967). *Depression: Clinical, experimental, and theoretical aspects.* New York: Harper & Row.

Beck, A. T. (1976). *Cognitive therapy and the emotional disorders.* New York: International Universities Press.

Beck, A. T. (1983). Cognitive therapy of depression: New perspectives. In P. Clayton & J. Barrett (Eds.), *Treatment of depression.* New York: Raven.

Beck, A. T., & Freeman, A. (1990a). Belief questionnaire. In A. T. Beck & A. Freeman (Eds.), *Cognitive therapy of personality disorders.* New York: Guilford.

Beck, A. T., & Freeman, A. (1990b). *Cognitive therapy of personality disorders.* New York: Guilford.

Beiber, I. (1966). Sadism and masochism. In S. Arieti (Ed.), *American handbook of psychiatry, 3,* 256–270. New York: Basic Books.

Beiber, I. (1974). Sadism and masochism. In S. Arieti (Ed.), *American handbook of psychiatry* (Vol. 3). New York: Basic Books.

Belsky, J., & Rovine, M. (1987). Temperament and attachment security in the strange situation: An empirical rapprochement. *Child Development, 58,* 787–795.

Bem, D. J., & Allen, A. (1974). On predicting some of the people some of the time: The search for cross-situational consistencies in behavior. *Psychological Review, 81,* 506–520.

Benjamin, L. S. (1974). Structural analysis of social behavior. *Psychological Review, 81,* 392–425.

Benjamin, L. S. (1984). Principles of prediction using structural analysis of social behavior (SASB). In R. A. Zucker, J. Aranoff, & A. J. Rubin (Eds.), *Personality and prediction of behavior* (pp. 121–174). New York: Academic Press.

Benjamin, L. S. (1993a). *Interpersonal and treatment of personality disorders.* New York: Guilford.

Benjamin, L. S. (1993b). Commentary. In M. H. Klein, D. J. Kupfer, & M. T. Shea (Eds.), *Personality and depression: A current view.* New York: Guilford.

Benjamin, L. S. (1993c). Every psychopathology is a gift of love. *Psychotherapy Research, 3,* 1–24.

Berglas (1989). Self-handicapping behavior and the self-defeating personality disorder: Toward a refined clinical perspective. In R. C. Curtis (Ed.), *Self-defeating behaviors: Experimental research, clinical impressions, and practical implications* (pp. 261–288). The Plenum series in social/clinical psychology. New York: Plenum.

Berliner, B. (1940). Libido and reality in masochism. *Psychoanalytic Quarterly, 9,* 322–333.

Berliner, B. (1942). The concept of masochism. *Psychoanalytic Review, 29,* 386–400.

Berliner, B. (1947). On some psychodynamics of masochism. *Psychoanalytic Quarterly, 16,* 459–471.

Berliner, B. (1958). The role of object relations in moral masochism. *Psychoanalytic Quarterly, 27,* 38–56.

Berne, E. (1961). *Transactional analysis in psychotherapy.* New York: Grove.

Beutler, L. E., & Clarkin, J. F. (1990). *Systematic treatment selection.* New York: Brunner/Mazel.

Bibring, E. (1953). The mechanism of depression. In P. Greenacre (Ed.), *Affective Disorders.* New York: International Universities Press.

Billings, A. G., & Moos, R. H. (1982). Psychosocial theory and research on depression: An integrative framework and review. *Clinical Psychology Review, 2,* 213–237.

Binswanger, L. (1942). *Grundformen und erkenntnis menschlichen daseins.* Zurich: Niehaus.

Binswanger, L. (1947). *Ausgewählte vorträge und aufsätze.* Berne: Francke.

Binswanger, L. (1956). Existential analysis and psychotherapy. In F. Fromm-Reichmann & J. L. Moreno (Eds.), *Progress in psychotherapy* (Vol. 1). New York: Grune & Stratton.

Birnbaum, K. (1909). *Die psychopathischen Verbrecker.* Leipzig: Thieme.

Birnbaum, K. (1914). *Die psychopathischen Verbrecker* (2nd ed.). Leipzig: Thieme.

Binet, A. (1890). Double consciousness in health. *Mind, 15,* 46–57.

Blackburn, R. (1993). *The psychology of criminal conduct.* Chichester: Wiley.

Blashfield, R. K. (1984). *The classification of psychopathology.* New York: Plenum.

Blashfield, R. K. (1986). Structural approaches to classification. In T. Millon & G. Klerman (Eds.), *Contemporary directions in psychopathology.* New York: Guilford.

Blashfield, R. K., & McElroy, R. (1995). Confusions in terminology about classificatory models. In W. J. Livesley (Ed.), *The DSM-IV personality disorders.* New York: Guilford.

Blatt, S. J. (1974). Levels of object representation in anaclitic and introjective depression. *Psychoanalytic Study of the Child, 29,* 107–157.

Blatt, S. J., & Schichman, S. (1983). Two primary configurations of psychopathology. *Psychoanalysis and Contemporary Thought, 6,* 187–254.

Bleuler, E. (1906). *Affectivitat, suggestibilitat, paranoia.* Halle: Marhold.

Bleuler, E. (1911). *Dementia praecox oder gruppe der schizophrenien.* Leipzig: Deuticke.

Bleuler, E. (1922). Die probleme der schizoidie und der syntonie. *Zeitschrift fuer die gesamte Nurologie und Psychiatrie, 78,* 373–388.

Bleuler, E. (1924). *Textbook of psychiatry.* New York: Macmillan.

Bleuler, E. (1929). Syntonie-schizoidie-schizophrenie. *Neurologie und Psychopathologie, 38,* 47–64.

Bleuler, E. (1950). *Dementia praecox.* New York: International Universities Press.

Block, J. (1961). *The Q-sort method in personality assessment and psychiatric research.* (Reprint ed. 1978). Palo Alto, CA: Consulting Psychologists Press.

Block, J. (1971). *Lives through time.* Berkeley: Bancroft.

Block, J. (1977). Advancing the psychology of personality: Paradigmatic shift or improving the quality of research. In D. Magnusson & N. S. Endler (Eds.), *Personality at the crossroads: Current issues in interactional psychology.* Hillsdale, NJ: Erlbaum.

Blum, H. (1980). Paranoia and beating fantasy: Psychoanalytic theory of paranoia. *Journal of the American Psychoanalytic Association, 28,* 331–361.

Blum, H. (1981). Object inconstancy and paranoid conspiracy. *Journal of American Psychoanalytic Association, 29,* 789–813.

Boss, M. (1957). *Psychoanalyse und daseinsanalytik.* Berne: Hans Huber.

Boss, M. (1963). *Psychoanalysis and daseinanalysis.* New York: Basic Books.

Boszormenyi-Nagy, I., & Framo, J. L. (1965). *Intensive family therapy.* New York: Harper & Row.

Bowlby, J. (1952). *Maternal care and mental health.* Geneva: World Health Organization.

Bowlby, J. (1958). The nature of the child's tie to his mother. *International Journal of Psychopathology, 39,* 350–373.

Bowlby, J. (1960). Grief and mourning in infancy and early childhood. *Psychoanalytic Study of the Child, 15,* 9–52.

Bowlby, J. (1969). *Attachment and loss. Vol. I. Attachment* (pp. 228–232). New York: Basic Books.

Bowlby, J. (1973). *Attachment and loss. Vol. 2. Separation: Anxiety and anger.* New York: Basic Books.

Bowlby, J. (1980). *Loss: Sadness and depression.* New York: Basic Books.

Bowlby, J. (1982). *Attachment and loss. Vol 1. Attachment.* New York: Basic Books. (Original work published 1969)

Breger, L., & McGaugh, J. L. (1965). Critique and reformulation of "learning-theory" approaches to psychotherapy and neurosis. *Psychological Bulletin, 63,* 338–358.

Brenner, C. (1959). The masochistic character: Genesis and treatment. *Journal of the American Psychoanalytic Association, 7,* 197–266.

Bretherton, I. (1985). Attachment theory: Retrospect and prospect. *Monograph of Social Research in Child Development, 50* (Serial No. 209), 3–35.

Bridgman, P. W. (1927). *The logic of modern physics.* New York: Macmillan.

Briquet, P. (1859). *Traite clinique et therapeutique a l'hysterie.* Paris: J. B Balliere & Fils.

Burnham, D. L., Gladstone, A. I., & Gibson, R. W. (1969). *Schizophrenia and the need-fear dilemma.* New York: International Universities Press.

Bursten, B. (1972). The manipulative personality. *Archives of General Psychiatry, 26,* 318–321.

Bursten, B. (1973a). *The manipulator: A psychoanalytic view.* New Haven, CT: Yale.

Bursten, B. (1973b). Some narcissistic personality types. *International Journal of Psychoanalysis, 54,* 287–300.

Bursten, B. (1989). The relationship between narcissistic and antisocial personalities.

Buss, A. H. (1966). *Psychopathology.* New York: Wiley.

Buss, A. J., & Plomin, R. (1975). *A temperament theory of personality development.* New York: Wiley.

Buss, A. J., & Plomin, R. (1984). *Temperament: Early developing personality traits.* Hillsdale, NJ: Erlbaum.

Buss, D. M., & Chiodo, L. M. (1991). Narcissistic acts in everyday life. *Journal of Personality, 59,* 179–215.

Buss, D. M., & Craik, K. H. (1983). The act frequency approach to personality. *Psychological Review, 90,* 105–126.

Buss, D. M., & Craik, K. H. (1987). Act criteria for the diagnosis of personality disorders. *Journal of Personality Disorders, 1,* 73–81.

Butcher, J. N., Graham, J. R., Williams, C. L., & Ben-Porath, Y. (1990). *Development and use of the MMPI-2 content scales.* Minneapolis: University of Minnesota Press.

Butler, J. M., & Rice, L. N. (1963). Audience, self-actualization, and drive theory. In J. I. Wepman & R. Heine (Eds.), *Concepts of personality.* Chicago: Aldine.

Bychowski, G. (1953). The problem of latent psychosis. *Journal of the American Psychoanalytic Association, 4,* 484–503.

Cadoret, R., & Cain, C. (1981). Environmental and genetic facors in predicting adolescent antisocial behavior in adoptees. *Psychiatric Journal of the University of Ottawa, 6,* 220–225.

Cameron, N. (1943). The paranoid pseudo-community. *American Journal of Sociology, 49,* 32–38.

Cameron, N. (1947). *The psychology of the behavior disorders.* Boston: Houghton Mifflin.

Cameron, N. (1963). *Personality development and psychopathology.* Boston: Houghton Mifflin.

Cameron, N., & Margaret, A. (1951). *Behavior pathology.* Boston: Houghton Mifflin.

Campbell, D. T., & Fiske, D. W. (1959). Convergent and discriminant validation by the multitrait-multimethod matrix. *Psychological Bulletin, 56,* 81–105.

Campbell, S. B. (1973). Mother-infant interaction in reflective, impulsive, and hyperactive children. *Developmental Psychology, 8,* 341–349.

Cantor, N., & Genero, N. (1986). Psychiatric diagnosis and natural categorization: A close analogy. In T. Millon & G. L. Klerman (Eds.), *Contemporary directions in psychopathology. Towards the DSM-IV* (pp. 233–256). New York: Guilford.

Cary, G. L. (1972). The borderline condition: A structural-dynamic viewpoint. *Psychoanalytic Review, 59,* 33–54.

Cattell, R. B. (1947). Confirmation and clarification of primary personality facots. *Psychometrika, 12,* 197–220.

Cattell, R. B. (1957). *Personality and motivation structure and measurement.* New York: World.

Cattell, R. B. (1965). *The scientific analysis of personality.* Chicago: Aldine.

Cattell, R. B. (1970). The integration of functional and psychometric requirements in a quantitative and computerized diagnostic system. In A. R. Mahrer (Ed.), *New approaches to personality classification* (pp. 9–52). New York: Columbia University Press.

Centerwall, B. S., & Robinette, D. C. (1989). Twin concordance for dishonorable discharge from the military: With a review of the genetics of antisocial behavior. *Comprehensive Psychiatry, 30,* 442–446.

Child, C. M. (1941). *Patterns and problems of development.* Chicago: University of Chicago Press.

Charcot, J. (1875). *Léons sur les maladies du systéme nerveux* (2nd ed.). Paris: Delahaye.

Chess, S., & Thomas, A. (1984). *Origins and evolution of behavior disorders.* New York: Brunner/Mazel.

Choca, J., Shanley, L., Van-Denburg, E., Agresti, Albert, et al. (1992). Personality disorder or personality style: That is the question. *Journal of Counseling and Development, 70,* 429–431.

Chodoff, P. (1974). The diagnosis of hysteria: An overview. *American Journal of Psychiatry, 131,* 1073–1078.

Chodoff, P., & Lyons, H. (1958). Hysteria, the hysterical personality and "hysterical" conversion. *American Journal of Psychiatry, 114,* 734–740.

Cicchetti, D., & Beeghly, M. (1987). Symbolic development in maltreated youngsters: An organizational perspective. In D. Cicchetti & M. Beeghly (Eds.), *Atypical symbolic development.* San Francisco: Jossey-Bass.

Cicchetti, D., & Carlson, V. (Eds.). (1989). *Child maltreatment: Theory and research on the causes and consequences of child abuse and neglect.* New York: Cambridge University Press.

Circirelli, V. G. (1982). Sibling influence throughout the lifespan. In M. E. Lamb & B. Sutton-Smith (Eds.). *Sibling relationships* (pp. 267–284). Hillsdale, NJ: Erlbaum.

Clark, L. A. (1990). Toward a consensual set of symptom clusters for assessment of personality disorder. In J. N. Butcher & C. D. Spielberger (Eds.), *Advances in personality assessment.* Hillsdale, NJ: Erlbaum.

Clark, L. A. (1993). Personality disorder diagnosis: Limitations of the five-factor model. *Psychological Inquiry, 4,* 100–104.

Clark, L. A., Vorhies, L., & McEwen, J. L. (1994a). Personality disorder symptomatology from the five-factor perspective. In P. T. Costa, Jr., & T. A. Widiger (Eds.), *Personality disorders and the five factor model of personality.* Washington, DC: American Psychological Association.

Clark, L. A., Vorhies, L., & McEwen, J. L. (1994b). Personality structure and the structure of personality disorders. In P. T. Costa & T. Widiger (Eds.), *Personality disorders and the five factor model of personality* (pp. 73–95). Washington, DC: American Psychological Association.

Cleckley, H. (1941). *The mask of sanity.* St. Louis: Mosby.

Cleckley, H. (1964). *The mask of sanity.* (2nd ed.). St. Louis: Mosby.

Cloninger, C. R. (1986). A unified biosocial theory of personality and its role in the development of anxiety states. *Psychiatric Developments, 3,* 167–226.

Cloninger, C. R. (1987a). A systematic method for clinical description and classification of personality variants. *Archives of General Psychiatry, 44,* 573–588.

Cloninger, C. R. (1987b). *The Tridimensional Personality Questionnaire (TPQ),* Version IV. St. Louis, MO: Department of Psychiatry and Geriatrics, Washington University School of Medicine.

Cloninger, C. R. (1993). *A general biosocial model of personality and psychopathology.* Presidential address presented at the 83rd annual meeting of the American Psychological Association, New York.

Cloninger, C. R., Przybeck, T. R., & Svrakic, D. M. (1991). The tridimensional personality questionnaire: U. S. normative data. *Psychological Reports, 69,* 1047–1057.

Cloninger, C. R., Reich, T., & Guze, S. B. (1978). Genetic-environmental interactions and antisocial behavior. In R. D. Hare & D. Schalling (Eds.), *Psychopathic behavior: Approaches to research.* Chichester: Wiley.

Cloninger, C. R., Svrakic, D. M., & Przybeck, T. R. (1993). A psychobiological model of temperament and character. *Archives of General Psychiatry, 50,* 975–990.

Coolidge, J. C., & Brodie, R. D. (1974). Observations of mothers of 49 school phobic children. *Journal of the American Academy of Child Psychiatry, 13,* 275–285.

Coolidge, F. L., & Merwin, M. M. (1992). Reliability and validity of the Coolidge Axis II Inventory: A new inventory for the assessment of personality disorders. *Journal of Personality Assessment, 59,* 223–238.

Cooper, A. M. (1984). Narcissism in normal development. In M. R. Zales (Ed.), *Character pathology: Theory and treatment* (pp. 39–56). New York: Brunner/Mazel.

Cooper, A. M. (1988). The narcissistic-masochistic character. In R. A. Glick & D. Meyers (Eds.), *Masochism: Current psychoanalytic perspectives* (pp. 117–138). Hillsdale, NJ: Analytic Press.

Cooper, A. M. (1993). Psychotherapeutic approaches to masochism. *Journal of Psychotherapy Practice and Research, 2,* 51–63.

Cooper, A. M., & Sacks, M. (1991). Sadism and masochism in character disorders and resistance: Panel report. *Journal of the American Psychoanalytic Association, 39,* 215–226.

Cooper, S. H., Perry, J. C., & Arnow, D. (1988). An empirical approach to the study of defense mechanisms: I. Reliability and preliminary validity of the Rorschach Defense Scales. *Journal of Personality Assessment, 52,* 187–203.

Cooper, S. H., Perry, J. C., & O'Connell, M. (1991). The Rorschach Defense Scales: II. Longitudinal perspectives. *Journal of Personality Assessment, 56,* 191–201.

Coriat, R. C. (1927). Discussion of "the constitutional psychopathic inferior." *American Journal of Psychiatry, 6,* 686–689.

Costa, P. T., & McCrae, R. R. (1985). *The NEO Personality Inventory manual.* Odessa, FL: Psychological Assessment Resources.

Costa, P. T., & McCrae, R. R. (1990). Personality disorders and the five-factor model of personality. *Journal of Personality Disorders, 4,* 362–371.

Costa, P. T., & McCrae, R. R. (1992). The five-factor model of personality and its relevance to personality disorders. *Journal of Personality Disorders, 6,* 343–359.

Costa, P. T., & Widiger, T. (Eds.). (1993). *Personality disorders and the five-factor model of personality.* Washington, DC: American Psychological Association.

Coyne, J. C. (1986). *Essential papers on depression.* New York: New York University Press.

Crockenberg, S. (1985). Toddler's reaction to maternal anger. *Merrill-Palmer Quarterly, 31,* 361–373.

Cronbach, L. J., & Meehl, P. E. (1955). Construct validity in psychological tests. *Psychological Bulletin, 52,* 281–302.

Cronbach, L. J., & Gleser, G. C. (1965). *Psychological tests and personnel decisions* (2nd ed.). Urbana: University of Illinois Press.

Cummings, J. S., Pellegrini, D. S., Notarius, C. I., & Cummings, E. M. (1989). Children's responses to angry adults as a function of marital distress and history of interparent hostility. *Child Development, 60,* 1035–1043.

Curtis, R. C. (Ed.). (1989). *Self-defeating behaviors: Experimental research, clinical impressions, and practical implications.* New York: Plenum.

Davidson, E. H. (1986). *Gene activity in early development.* Orlando, FL: Academic Press.

Davison, G. C. (1968). Systematic desensitization as a counterconditioning process. *Journal of Abnormal Psychology, 73,* 91–99.

Degerman, R. L. (1972). The geometric representation of some simple structures. In R. N. Shepard, A. K. Romney, & S. B. Nerlove (Eds.), *Multidimensional scaling* (Vol. 1). New York: Seminar Press.

Dejerine, J., & Gaukler, E. (1913). Psychoneurosis and psychotherapy. Philadelphia: Lippincott.

Deutsch, H. (1942). Some forms of emotional disturbance and their relationship to schizophrenia. *Psychoanalytic Quarterly, 11,* 301–321.

Dodge, K., Murphy, R., & Buchsbaum, K. C. (1984). The assessment of intention-cue detection skills in children: Implications for developmental psychopathology. *Child Development, 55,* 163–173.

Donath, J. (1897). The anankast (psychic compulsive states). *Archiv fuer Psychiatrie und Neurologie, 29,* 211–230.

Dornbusch, S. M., Ritter, P. L., Leiderman, P. H., et al. (1987). The relation of parenting style to adolescent school performance. *Child Development, 58,* 1244–1257.

Dorr, A. (1985). Contexts for experience with emotion, with special attention to television. In M. Lewis & C. Saarni (Eds.), *The socialization of emotions* (pp. 55–85). New York: Plenum.

DuBois, P. (1909). *The psychic treatment of mental disorders.* New York: Funk & Wagnell.

Dunn, J., & Kendrick, C. (1981). Interaction between young siblings: Associations with the interactions between mothers and first-born. *Developmental Psychology, 17,* 336–343.

Easser, R., & Lesser, S. (1965). Hysterical personality: A re-evaluation. *Psychoanalytic Quarterly, 34,* 390–402.

Eisenbud, J. (1967). Why psy? *Psychoanalytic Review, 53,* 47–163.

Eissler, K. R., (Ed.). (1949). *Searchlights on delinquency: Essays in honor of August Aichhorn.* New York: International Universities Press.

Ekehammer, E. (1974). Interactionism in personality from a historical perspective. *Psychological Bulletin, 81,* 1026–1048.

Ellis, A. (1962). *Reason and emotion in psychotherapy.* New York: Lyle Stuart.

Ellis, A. (1967). Goals of psychotherapy. In A. R. Mahrer (Ed.), *The goals of psychotherapy.* New York: Appleton-Century-Crofts.

Ellis, A. (1970). *The essence of rational psychotherapy: A comprehensive approach to treatment.* New York: Institute for Rational Living.

Ellis, H. (1933). Auto-erotism: A psychological study. *Alienist and Neurologist, 19,* 260–299. (Original work published 1898)

El Sheikh, M., Cummings, E. M., & Goetsch, V. (1989). Coping with adult's angry behavior: Behavioral, physiological, and verbal responses in preschoolers. *Developmental Psychology, 25,* 490–498.

Emde, R. N. (1989). The infant's relationship experience: Developmental and affective aspects. In A. Sameroff & R. N. Emde (Eds.), *Relationship disturbances in early childhood: A developmental approach* (pp. 33–51). New York: Basic Books.

Emery, R. E. (1982). Interparental conflict and the children of discord and divorce. *Psychological Bulletin, 92,* 310–330.

Endler, N. S., & Magnusson, D. (1976). Toward an interactional psychology of personality. *Psychological Bulletin, 83,* 956–974.

Epstein, S. (1977). Traits are alive and well. In D. Magnusson & N. S. Endler (Eds.), *Personality at the crossroads: Current issues in interactional psychology.* Hillsdale, NJ: Erlbaum.

Epstein, S. (1979). The stability of behavior: 1. On predicting most of the people much of the time. *Journal of Personality and Social Psychology, 37,* 1097–1126.

Erikson, E. (1950). *Childhood and society.* New York: Norton.

Erikson, E. (1959). Growth and crises of the healthy personality. In G. S. Klein (Ed.), *Psychological Issues.* New York: International University Press.

Escalona, S. (1968). *Roots of individuality.* Chicago: Aldine.

Escalona, S., & Heider, G. (1959). *Prediction and outcome.* New York: Basic Books.

Escalona, S., & Leitch, M. (1953). *Early phases of personality development.* Evanston: Child Development Publications.

Esquirol, E. (1838). *Maladies mentales* (2 Vols.). Paris: Bailliere.

Ey, H. (1964). History and analysis of the concept. *La Revue du Practicien, 14,* 1417–1434.

Eysenck, H. J. (1952). *The scientific study of personality.* London: Routledge and Kegan Paul.

Eysenck, H. J. (1957). *The dynamics of anxiety and hysteria.* New York: Praeger.

Eysenck, H. J. (1960). *The structure of human personality.* London: Routledge and Kegan Paul.

Eysenck, H. J. (1964). *Crime and personality.* Boston: Houghton Mifflin.

Eysenck, H. J. (1967). *The biological basis of personality.* Springfield, IL: Thomas.

Eysenck, H. J., & Eysenck, S. B. G. (1969). *Personality structure and measurement.* London: Routledge and Kegan Paul.

Fairbairn, W. R. D. (1952). Schizoid factors in the personality. In W. R. D. Fairbairn (Ed.), *Psychoanalytic studies of the personality.* London: Tavistock. (Original work published 1940)

Falret, J. (1854). De la folie circulaire. *Bulletin del l'Academie Medicale, 19,* 382–394.

Farrar, C. F. (1927). Quoted in D. Henderson & R. D. Gillespie, *A textbook of psychiatry.* London: Oxford.

Faust, D., & Miner, R. A. (1986). The empiricist and his new clothes: DSM-III in perspective. *American Journal of Psychiatry, 143,* 962–967.

Federn, P. (1947). Principles of psychotherapy in latent schizophrenia. *American Journal of Psychotherapy, 1,* 129–139.

Feinstein, A. R. (1977). A critical overview of diagnosis in psychiatry. In V. M. Rakoff, H. C. Stancer, & H. B. Kedward (Eds.), *Psychiatric diagnosis* (pp. 189–206). New York: Brunner/Mazel.

Fenichel, O. (1945). *The psychoanalytic theory of the neurosis.* New York: Norton.

Fenigstein, A., Scheier, M. F., & Buss, A. H. (1975). Public and private self consciousness: Assessment and theory. *Journal of Consulting and Clinical Psychology, 43,* 522–527.

Ferenczi, S. (1919). Sonntagsneurosen. *International Journal for Psychoanalysis, 5,* 46–48.

Ferenczi, S. (1952). *Further contributions to theory and technique of psychoanalysis.* New York: Basic Books.

Ferri, E. (1976). *Growing up in a one-parent family.* Slough, England: NFER.

Ferster, C. B. (1973). A functional analysis of depression. *American Psychologist, 28,* 857–871.

Feuchtersleben, E. (1847). *Lehrbuch der arztlichen Seelenkunde.* Vienna: Gerold.

Field, T. M. (1985). Affective responses to separation. In T. B. Brazelton & M. W. Yogman (Eds.), *Affective Development in Infancy.* Norwood, NJ: Ablex.

Fiester, S. J., & Gay, M. (1991). Sadistic personality disorder: A review of data and recommendations for DSM-IV. *Journal of Personality Disorders, 5,* 376–385.

Fisher, S., & Greenberg, R. P. (1977). The scientific credibility of Freud's theoretical therapies. New York: Basic Books.

Fiske, D. W. (1949). Consistency of the factorial structures of personality ratings from different sources. *Journal of Abnormal & Social Psychology, 44,* 329–344.

Fiske, D. W., & Maddi, S. R. (Eds.). (1961). *Functions of varied experience.* Homewood, IL: Dorsey.

Fleiss, J. L., & Zubin, J. (1969). On the methods and theory of clustering. *Multivariate Behavior Research, 4,* 235–250.

Forgus, R., & Schulman, B. (1979). *Personality: A cognitive view.* Englewood Cliffs, NJ: Prentice Hall.

Forman, M. (1975). Narcissistic personality disorders and the oedipal fixations. *Annual of Psychoanalysis, 3,* 65–92. New York: International Universities Press.

Forth, A. E., Hart, S. D., & Hare, R. D. (1990). Assessment of psychopathy in male young offenders. *Psychological Assessment, 2,* 342–344.

Fox, N. A., Kimmerly, N. L., & Schafer, W. D. (1991). Attachment to mother/attachment to father: A meta-analysis. *Child Development, 62,* 210–225.

Frances, A. (1985). Validating schizotypal personality disorder: Problems with the schizophrenia connection. *Schizophrenia Bulletin, 11,* 595–597.

Frances, A., Clarkin, J. F., Gilmore, M., Hurt, S. W., & Brown, R. (1984). Reliability of criteria for borderline personality disorder: A comparison of DSM-III and the diagnostic interview for borderline patients. *American Journal of Psychiatry, 141,* 1080–1084.

Frances, A., Clarkin, J. F., & Perry, S. (1984). Differential therapeutics in psychiatry. New York: Brunner/Mazel.

Frank, L. K. (1936). *Projective methods.* Springfield, IL: Thomas.

Frankl, V. E. (1955). The doctor and the soul: An introduction to logotherapy. New York: Knopf.

Frankl, V. E. (1966). Logotherapy and existential analysis: A review. *American Journal of Psychotherapy, 20,* 252–260.

Freud, S. (1900). *The interpretation of dreams.* New York: Norton.

Freud, S. (1923). The ego and the id. In *The standard edition of the works of Sigmund Freud* (Vol. 21, pp. 3–66). New York: Norton.

Freud, S. (1924). The economic problem of masochism. In *The standard edition of the works of Sigmund Freud* (Vol. 19, pp. 159–170). New York: Norton.

Freud, S. (1925). Further remarks on the defence-neuropsychoses. In *Collected papers* (Vol. 2). London: Hogarth. (Original work published 1896)

Freud, S. (1925). *Three essays on the theory of sexuality.* In J. Strachey (Ed. and Trans.), *The standard edition of the works of Sigmund Freud* (Vol. 7). London: Hogarth. (Original work published 1905)

Freud, S. (1925). Character and anal eroticism. In *Collected papers* (Vol. 2). London: Hogarth. (Original work published 1908)

Freud, S. (1925). Psychoanalytic notes upon an autobiographical account of a case of paranoia (Dementia paranoides). In *Collected papers* (Vol. 3). London: Hogarth. (Original work published 1911)

Freud, S. (1925). On narcissism: An introduction. In *Collected papers* (Vol. 4). London: Hogarth. (Original work published 1914)

Freud, S. (1925a). Some character types met with in psycho-analytic work. In *Collected papers* (Vol. 4). London: Hogarth. (Original work published 1915)

Freud, S. (1925b). The instincts and their vicissitudes. In *Collected papers* (Vol. 4). London: Hogarth. (Original work published 1915)

Freud, S. (1925). Some character-types met with in psychoanalytic work. In J. Strachey (Ed. and Trans.), *The standard edition of the works of Sigmund Freud* (Vol. 14, pp. 310–333). London: Hogarth. (Original work published 1916)

Freud, S. (1925). Mourning and melancholia. In J. Strachey (Ed. and Trans.), *The standard edition of the works of Sigmund Freud* (Vol. 14, pp. 237–260). London: Hogarth. (Original work published 1917)

Freud, S. (1925). From the history of an infantile neurosis. In *Collected papers* (Vol. 3). London: Hogarth. (Original work published 1918)

Freud, S. (1925). *Beyond the pleasure principle.* In *The standard edition of the works of Sigmund Freud* (Vol. 18, pp. 7–64). New York: Norton. (Original work published 1920)

Freud, S. (1950). Libidinal types. In *Collected papers* (Vol. 5). London: Hogarth. (Original work published 1931)

Freud, S. (1957). Leonardo da Vinci and a memory of his childhood. In J. Strachey (Ed. and Trans.), *The standard edition of the works of Sigmund Freud* (Vol. 2). London: Hogarth. (Original work published 1910)

Freud, S. (1959). *Turnings in the ways of psychoanalytic therapy.* In J. Rivier (Ed.), *Collected papers,* (Vol. 2, pp. 392–402). New York: Basic Books. (Original work published 1919)

Freyhan, F. A. (1959). Clinical and integrative aspects. In N. S. Kline (Ed.). Psychopharmacology frontiers. Boston: Little, Brown.

Friedlander, K. (1945). Formation of the antisocial character. *Psychoanalytic Study of the Child, 1,* 189–203.

Fromm, E. (1947). *Man for himself.* New York: Holt, Rinehart & Winston.

Fromm, E. (1973). *The anatomy of human destructiveness.* New York: Holt, Rinehart & Winston.

Frosch, J. (1960). Psychotic character. *Journal of the American Psychoanalytic Association, 8,* 544–555.

Frosch, J. (1964). The psychotic character. *Psychiatric Quarterly, 38,* 81–96.

Frosch, J. (1970). Psychoanalytic considerations of the psychotic character. *Journal of the American Psychoanalytic Association, 18,* 24–50.

Gabbard, O. G. (1994). *Psychodynamic psychiatry in clinical practice.* Washington, DC: American Psychiatric Press.

Garmezy, N. (1986). Developmental aspects of children's responses to the stress of separation and loss. In M. Rutter, C. E. Izard, & P. B. Read (Eds.), *Depression in young people: Developmental and clinical perspectives* (pp. 297–323). New York: Guilford.

Gedo, J. D., & Goldberg, A. (1973). *Models of the mind.* Chicago: University of Chicago Press.

Gewirtz, J. L. (1963). A learning analysis of the effects of normal stimulation upon social and exploratory behavior in the human infant. In B. M. Foss (Ed.), *Determinants of infant behavior II.* New York: Wiley.

Gill, M. M. (1963). *Topography and systems in psychoanalytic theory.* New York: International Universities Press.

Gilligan, C. (1981). *In a different voice.* Cambridge, MA: Harvard University Press.

Glasser, W. (1961). Mental health or mental illness. New York: Harper & Row.

Glasser, W. (1965). Reality therapy. New York: Harper & Row.

Godel, K. (1931). *On formally undecidable propositions of principia mathematica and elated systems.* Unpublished doctoral dissertation, University of Vienna.

Gold, J. R., & Stricker, G. (1993). Psychotherapy integration with character disorders. In G. Stricker & J. R. Gold (Eds.), *Comprehensive handbook of psychotherapy integration* (pp. 323–336). New York: Plenum.

Goldberg, L. R. (1990). An alternative "description of personality": The big-five factor structure. *Journal of Personality and Social Psychology, 59,* 1216–1229.

Goldberg, L. R. (1992). The development of markers for the big-five factor structure. *Psychological Assessment, 4,* 26–42.

Golden, R., & Meehl, P. E. (1979). Detection of the schizoid taxon with MMPI indicators. *Journal of Abnormal Psychology, 88,* 217–233.

Goldfarb, W. (1955). Emotional and intellectual consequences of psychologic deprivation in infancy: A reevaluation. In P. Hoch & J. Zubin (Eds.), *Psychopathology of childhood*. New York: Grune & Stratton.

Goldsmith, H. H., & Gottesman, I. I. (1981). Origins of variation in behavioral style: A longitudinal study of temperament in young twins. *Child Development, 52*, 91–103.

Gottman, J. M., & Katz, L. F. (1989). Effects of marital discord on young children's peer interaction and health. *Developmental Psychology, 25*, 373–381.

Gouster, M. (1878). Moral insanity. *Review of Scientific Medicine, 38*, 115–131.

Green, C. J. (1987). The Structured Interview for DSM-III Personality Disorders (SIDP): A review. *Journal of Personality Disorders, 1*, 288–290.

Greenacre, P. (1945). Conscience in the psychopath. *American Journal of Orthopsychiatry, 15*, 495–509.

Greenacre, P. (Ed.). (1953). *Affective disorders*. New York: International Universities Press.

Greenberg, J. R., & Mitchell, S. A. (1983). *Object relations in psychoanalytic theory*. Cambridge, MA: Harvard University Press.

Greenberg, L. S., & Safran, J. D. (1987). Emotion in psychotherapy. New York: Guilford.

Griesinger, W. (1867). *Mental pathology and therapeutics*. London: New Syndenham Society. (Original work published 1845)

Griesinger, W. (1868). A little recognized psychopathic state. *Archiv fuer Psychiatrie und Neurologie, 1*, 626–631.

Grinker, R. R., Werble, B., & Drye, R. C. (1968). *The borderline syndrome*. New York: Basic Books.

Group for the Advancement of Psychiatry. (1966). *Psychopathological disorders in childhood*. New York: GAP Publications.

Grove, W. M., Eckert, E. D., & Heston, L. (1990). Heritability of substance abuse and antisocial behavior: A study of monozygotic twins reared apart. *Biological Psychiatry, 27*(12), 1293–1304.

Grunbaum, A. (1984). The foundations of psychoanalysis: A philosophical critique. Berkeley: University of California Press.

Grunberger, B. (1979). *Narcissism: Psychoanalytic essays*. New York: International Universities Press.

Gunderson, J. G. (1977). Characteristics of borderlines. In P. Hartcollis (Ed.), *Borderline personality disorders* (pp. 173–192). New York: International Universities Press.

Gunderson, J. G. (1979). The relatedness of borderline to schizophrenic disorders. *Schizophrenia Bulletin, 5*, 17–23.

Gunderson, J. G. (1988). Narcissistic traits in psychiatric patients. *Comprehensive Psychiatry, 29*(6), 545–549.

Gunderson, J. G., Carpenter, W., & Stauss, J. (1975). Borderline and schizophrenic patients: A compara-

tive study. *American Journal of Psychiatry, 132,* 1257–1264.

Gunderson, J. G., Kolb, J. E., & Austin, V. (1981). The diagnostic interview for borderline patients. *American Journal of Psychiatry, 138*, 896–903.

Gunderson, J. G., Links, P. S., & Reich, J. H. (1991). Competing models of personality disorders. *Journal of Personality Disorders, 5*, 60–68.

Gunderson, J. G., & Ronningstam, E. (1990a, May). Differentiating narcissistic and antisocial personality disorders. Paper presented at the American Psychiatric Association annual convention, Los Angeles.

Gunderson, J. G., & Ronningstam, E. (1990b). Identifying critieria for narcissistic personality disorder. *American Journal of Psychiatry, 147*, 918–922.

Gunderson, J. G., & Ronningstam, E. (1991). Is narcissistic personality disorder a valid diagnosis? In J. M. Oldham (Ed.), *Personality disorders: New perspectives on diagnostic validity* (Vol. 20, pp. 107–119). Washington, DC: American Psychiatric Press.

Gunderson, J. G., Ronningstam, E., & Bodkin, A. (1990). The diagnostic interview for narcissistic patients. *Archives of General Psychiatry, 47*, 676–680.

Gunderson, J. G., Ronningstam, E., & Smith, L. E. (1991). Narcissistic personality disorder: A review of data on DSM-III-R descriptions. *Journal of Personality Disorders, 5*, 167–177.

Gunderson, J. G., & Singer, M. T. (1975). Defining borderline patients: An overview. *American Journal of Psychiatry, 132*, 1–10.

Guntrip, H. (1952). A study of Fairbairn's theory of schizoid reactions. *British Journal of Medical Psychology, 25*, 86–104.

Gurman, A., & Kniskern, D. (Eds.). (1981). *The handbook of family therapy*. New York: Brunner/Mazel.

Guslain, J. (1826). *Traitesur l'alienation mentale*. Amsterdam.

Hall, G. S. (1916). *Adolescence*. New York: Appleton.

Hare, R. D. (1970). *Psychopathy: Theory and research*. New York: Wiley.

Hare, R. D. (1984). Performance of psychopaths on cognitive tasks related to frontal lobe function. *Journal of Abnormal Psychology, 93*, 133–140.

Hare, R. D. (1985). *The Psychopathy Checklist*. Unpublished manuscript, University of British Columbia, Vancouver, Columbia.

Hare, R. D. (1991). *The Hare Psychopathy Checklist—Revised*. Toronto: Multihealth Systems.

Harkness, A. R. (1993). Fundamental topics in the personality disorders: Candidate trait dimensions from lower regions of the hierarchy. *Psychological Assessment, 4*, 251–259.

Harpur, T. J., & Hare, R. D. (1989). Two-factor conceptualization of psychopathy: Construct validity and assessment implications. *Psychological Assessment, 1,* 6–17.

Hartmann, H. (1939). *Ego psychology and the problem of adaption.* New York: International Universities Press.

Hartmann, H. (1958). *Ego psychology and the problem of adaptation.* New York: International Universities Press.

Healy, W., & Bronner, A. (1926). *Delinquents and criminals: Their making and unmaking.* New York: Macmillan.

Heathers, G. (1955). Emotional dependence and independence in a physical threat situation. *Child Development, 24,* 169–179.

Hecker, E. (1871). Die hebephrenie. *Archive fuer Pathologie, Anatomie und Physiologie, 52,* 394–429.

Heinrichs, R. W. (1993). Scizophrenia and the brain: Conditions for a neuropsychology of madness. *American Psychologist, 48,* 221–233.

Heinroth, J. C. (1818). *Lehrbuch der storungen des seelenlebens.* Leipzig: Thieme.

Hellpach, W. (1920). Amphithymia. *Zeitschrift fuer d ie gesamte Neurologie und Psychiatrie, 19,* 136–152.

Hempel, C. G. (1961). Introduction to problems of taxonomy. In J. Zubin (Ed.), *Field studies in the mental disorders.* New York: Grune & Stratton.

Hempel, C. G. (1965). *Aspects of scientific explanation.* New York: Free Press.

Henderson, D. K. (1939). *Psychopathic states.* London: Chapman and Hall.

Henderson, D. K., & Gillespie, R. D. (1927). *A textbook of psychiatry.* London: Oxford.

Henderson, D. K., & Gillespie, R. D. (1940). *A text-book of psychiatry* (5th ed.). London: Oxford.

Herman, J. L., Perry, J. C., & van der Kolk, B. A. (1989). *Childhood trauma in borderline personality disorder.* New York: Guilford.

Hetherington, E. M. (1972). Effects of paternal absence on personality development in adolescent daughters. *Developmental Psychology, 7,* 313–326.

Hetherington, E. M., Cox, M., & Cox, C. R. (1982). Effects of divorce on parents and children. In M. Lamb (Ed.), *Nontraditional families* (pp. 223–288). Hillsdale, NJ: Erlbaum.

Hewitt, L. E., & Jenkins, R. L. (1946). *Fundamental patterns of maladjustment: The dynamics of their origin; a statistical analysis based upon five hundred case records of children examined at the Michigan Child Guidance Institute.* Springfield, IL: State of Illinois.

Heymans, G., & Wiersma, E. (1906–1909). Beitrage zur speziellen psychologie auf grundeiner massenuntersuchung. *Zeitsehrift fuer Psychologie, 42, 46, 49, 51.*

Hinde, R. A. (1982). Attachment: Some conceptual and biological issues. In J. Stevenson-Hinde & C. P. Parkes (Eds.), *The place of attachment in human behavior* (pp. 60–76). New York: Basic Books.

Hirt, E. (1902). *Die temperamente.* Leipzig: Barth.

Hoch, A. (1910). Constitutional factors in the dementia praecox group. *Review of Neurology and Psychiatry, 8,* 463–475.

Hoch, P. H., & Cattell, J. P. (1959). The diagnosis of pseudoneurotic schizophrenia. *Psychiatric Quarterly, 33,* 17–43.

Hoch, P. H., Cattell, J. P., Stahl, M. O., & Pennes, H. H. (1962). The course and outcome of pseudoneurotic schizophrenia. *American Journal of Psychiatry, 118,* 106–115.

Hoch, P. H., & Polatin, P. (1949). Pseudoneurotic form of schizophrenia. *Psychiatric Quarterly, 23,* 248–276.

Hogan, R. (1986). *Hogan Personality Inventory manual.* Minneapolis: National Computer Systems.

Horney, K. (1937). *The neurotic personality of our time.* New York: Norton.

Horney, K. (1939). *New ways in psychoanalysis.* New York: Norton.

Horney, K. (1942). *Self-analysis.* New York: Norton.

Horney, K. (1945). *Our inner conflicts.* New York: Norton.

Horney, K. (1950). *Neurosis and human growth.* New York: Norton.

Horowitz, L. M., Post, D. L., French, R. de S., Wallis, K. D., & Siegelman, E. Y. (1981). The prototype as a construct in abnormal psychology: 2. Clarifying disagreement in psychiatric judgments. *Journal of Abnormal Psychology, 90,* 575–585.

Horowitz, M. (1974). *Stress response syndromes.* New York: Jason Aronson.

Hughes, C. H. (1884). Moral (affective) insanity: Psycho-sensory insanity. *Alienist and Neurologist, 5,* 296–315.

Hyler, S. E., & Rieder, R. O. (1987). PDQ-R: Personality Diagnostic Questionnaire—Revised. New York: New York State Psychiatric Institute.

Hyler, S. E., Skodol, A. E., Andrew, E., Kellman, H. D., & Oldham, J. M. (1990). Validity of the Personality Diagnostic Questionnaire—Revised: Comparison with two structured interviews. *American Journal of Psychiatry, 147,* 1043–1048.

Hyler, S. E., Skodol, A. E., Kellman, D., Oldham, J. M., & Rosnick, L. (1990). Validity of the Personality Disorder Questionnaire—Revised: Comparison with two structured interviews. *American Journal of Psychiatry, 147,* 1043–1048.

Ihilevich, D., & Gleser, G. C. (1986). Defense mechanisms: The classification, correlates, and measurement with the Defense Mechanisms Inventory. Owosso, MI: DMI Associates.

Ihilevich, D., & Gleser, G. C. (1991). Defenses in psychotherapy: The clinical application of the Defense Mechanisms Inventory. Owosso, MI: DMI Associates.

Jackson, D. N. (1971). The dynamics of structured tests. *Psychological Review, 78,* 229–248.

Jackson, D. N., & Livesley, W. J. (1995). Contributions from personality assessment to the classification of personality disorders. In W. J. Livesley (Ed.), *The DSM-IV personality disorders.* New York: Guilford.

Jacobson, E. (1953). Contribution to the metapsychology of cyclothymic depression. In P. Greenacre (Ed.), *Affective disorders* (pp. 49–83). New York: International Universities Press.

Jacobson, E. (1964). *The self and the object world.* New York: International Universities Press.

Jahoda, M. (Ed.). (1958). *Current concepts of positive mental health.* New York: Basic Books.

Janet, P. (1901). *The mental state of hystericals: A study of mental stigmata and mental accidents* (English translation). New York: Putnam.

Jaspers, K. (1913). *Allegemaine psychopathologie.* Berlin: Springer.

Jaspers, K. (1925). *Allegemaine psychopathologie* (2nd ed.). Berlin: Springer.

Jaspers, K. (1948). *General psychopathology* (English translation). London: Oxford.

John, O. P. (1990). The "big five" factor taxonomy: Dimensions of personality in the natural language and in questionnaires. In L. A. Pervin (Ed.), *Handbook personality theory and research* (pp. 66–100). New York: Guilford.

John, O. P. (1990). The search for basic dimensions of personality: A review and critique. In P. McReynolds, J. C. Rosen, & G. L. Chelune (Eds.), *Advances in psychological assessment* (Vol. 7, pp. 1–37). New York: Plenum.

Jones (1950). Anal erotic character traits. In Tindall & Cox (Eds.) *Papers on psychoanalysis* (pp. 413–437). London: Bailliere. (Original work published 1918)

Jones, S. S., & Raag, T. (1989). Smile production in older infants: The importance of a social recipient for the facial signal. *Child Development, 13,* 147–165.

Jung, C. G. (1916). *Psychology of the unconscious.* New York: Moffat, Yard.

Jung, C. G. (1921). *Psychological types.* Zurich: Rasher Verlag.

Jung, C. G. (1923). *Psychological types.* Zurich: Rasher Verlag.

Jung, C. G. (1961). *Memories, dreams, reflections.* New York: Vintage Books.

Kagan, J. (1989). Temperamental contribution to social behavior. *American Psychologist, 44,* 668–674.

Kagan, J., Reznick, J. S., & Snidman, N. (1989). Issues in the study of temperament. In G. A. Kohnstamm,

J. E. Bates, & M. K. Rothbart (Eds.), *Temperament in childhood.* New York: Wiley.

Kahlbaum, K. L. (1863). *Die gruppierung der psychischen kranke? Zheiteri.* Danzig: A. W. Kafemann.

Kahlbaum, K. L. (1882). *Uber zyklisches irresein, irrenfreund.* Berlin: Springer.

Kahlbaum, K. L. (1890). Heboidophrenia. *Allgemaine Zeitschrift fuer Psychiatrie, 46,* 461–482.

Kahn, E. (1931). *Psychopathic personalities.* New Haven: Yale University Press.

Kahn, M. M. (1960a). Clinical aspects of the schizoid personality: Affects and technique. *International Journal of Psychoanalysis, 41,* 430–437.

Kahn, M. M. (1960b). *A polygraph study of the catharsis of aggression.* Unpublished doctoral dissertation, Harvard University.

Kallman, F. J. (1938). *The genetics of schizophrenia.* New York: Augustin.

Kanfer, F. H., & Saslow, G. (1965). Behavioral analysis: An alternative to diagnostic classification. *Archives of General Psychiatry, 15,* 114–127.

Kanner, L. (1943). Autistic disturbances of affective contact. *Nervous Child, 2,* 217–250.

Karpman, B. (1941). On the need for separating psychopathy into two distinct clinical types: Symptomatic and idiopathic. *Journal of Clinical Psychopathology, 3,* 112–137.

Kasanin, J. (1933). Acute schizoaffective psychoses. *American Journal of Psychiatry, 97,* 97–120.

Kasanin, J., & Rosen, Z. A. (1933). Clinical variables in schizoid personalities. *Archives of Neurology Psychiatry, 30,* 538–566.

Kelly, G. A. (1955). *The psychology of personal constructs.* New York: Norton.

Kendall, R. E. (1975). The role of diagnosis in psychiatry. Oxford: Blackwell.

Kenrick, D. T., & Stringfield, D. O. (1980). Personality traits and the eye of the beholder: Crossing some traditional philosophical boundaries in the search for consistency in all of the people. *Psychological Review, 87,* 88–104.

Kernberg, O. F. (1967). Borderline personality organization. *Journal of the American Psychoanalytic Association, 15,* 641–685.

Kernberg, O. F. (1970). Factors in the psychoanalytic therapy of narcissistic patients. *Journal of the American Psychoanalytic Association, 18,* 51–85.

Kernberg, O. F. (1975). *Borderline conditions and pathological narcissism.* New York: Jason Aronson.

Kernberg, O. F. (1979). Two reviews of the literature on borderlines: An assessment. *Schizophrenia Bulletin, 5,* 53–58.

Kernberg, O. F. (1980). *Internal world and external reality.* New York: Jason Aronson.

Kernberg, O. F. (1982). *Paranoid regression, sadistic control and dishonesty in the transference.* Unpublished manuscript.

Kernberg, O. F. (1984). *Severe personality disorders.* New Haven: Yale University Press.

Kernberg, O. F. (1988a). Clinical dimensions of masochism. *Journal of the American Psychoanalytic Association, 36,* 1005–1029.

Kernberg, O. F. (1988b). Object relations theory in clinical practice. *Psychoanalysis Quarterly, 57,* 481–504.

Kernberg, O. F. (1989a). Narcissistic personality disorder in childhood. *The Psychiatric Clinics of North America, 12*(3), 671–294.

Kernberg, O. F. (1989b). The narcissistic personality disorder and the differential diagnosis of antisocial behavior. In O. F. Kernberg (Ed.), *Narcissistic personality disorder. Psychiatric Clinics of North America,* Vol. 12.

Kernberg, O. F. (1992). *Aggression in personality disorders and perversions.* New Haven, CT: Yale University Press.

Kety, S. S., Rosenthal, D., Wender, P. H., & Schulsinger, F. (1968). Mental illness in the biological and adoptive families of adopted schizophrenics. In D. Rosenthal & S. S. Kety (Eds.), *Transmission of schizophrenia* (pp. 345–362). Oxford: Pergamon.

Khan, M. M. R. (1963). The concept of cumulative trauma. *Psychoanalytic Study of the Child, 18,* 286–306. New York: International Universities Press.

Khan, M. M. R. (1974). *The privacy of the sea.* New York: International Universities Press.

Kiesler, D. J. (1966). Some myths of psychotherapy research and the search for a paradigm. *Psychological Bulletin, 65,* 110–136.

Kiesler, D. J. (1983). The 1982 interpersonal circle: A taxonomy for complementarity in human transactions. *Psychological Review, 90,* 185–214.

Kiesler, D. J. (1986). The 1982 interpersonal circle: An analysis of DSM-III personality disorders. In T. Millon & G. L. Klerman (Eds.), *Contemporary directions in psychopathology.* New York: Guilford.

Killackey, H. P. (1990). Neocortical expansion: An attempt toward relating phylogeny and ontogeny. *Journal of Cognitive Neuroscience, 2,* 1–17.

Klar, H., & Siever, L. (Eds.). (1985). *Biologic response styles: Clinical implications.* Washington, DC: American Psychiatric Press.

Klein, D. F. (1967). The importance of psychiatric diagnosis in prediction of critical drug effects. *Archives of General Psychiatry, 16,* 118–126.

Klein, D. F. (1970). Psychotropic drugs and the regulation of behavior at activation in psychiatric illness. In W. L. Smith (Ed.), *Drugs and cerebral function.* Springfield, IL: Thomas.

Klein, D. F. (1971). Approaches to measuring the efficacy of drug treatment of personality disorders: An analysis and program. In *Principles and problems in establishing the efficacy of psychotropic agents.* U.S. Department of Health, Education and Welfare, Public Health Service, Publication Number 2138 (pp. 187–204).

Klein, D. F. (1972). *Psychiatric case studies: Treatment, drugs and outcome.* Baltimore: Williams & Wilkins.

Klein, D. F. (1975). Psychopharmacology and the borderline patient. In J. E. Mack (Ed.), *Borderline states in psychiatry* (pp. 75–92). New York: Grune & Stratton.

Klein, D. F. (1977). Psychopharmacological treatment and delineation of borderline disorders. In P. Hartcollis (Ed.), *Borderline personality disorders* (pp. 365–383). New York: International Universities Press.

Klein, D. F., & Davis, J. (1969). *Diagnosis and drug treatment of psychiatric disorders.*

Klein, D. F., Gittleman, R., Quitkin, F., & Rifkin, A. (1980). *Diagnosis and drug treatment of psychiatric disorders* (2nd ed.). Baltimore: Williams & Wilkins.

Klein, D. F., Honigfeld, G., & Feldman, S. (1973). Prediction of drug effect in personality disorders. *Journal of Nervous and Mental Diseases, 156,* 183–198.

Klein, M. H. (1946). Notes on some schizoid mechanisms. In J. Riviere (Ed.), *Development in psychoanalysis.* London: Hogarth.

Klein, M. H. (1948). *Contributions to psychoanalysis, 1921–1945.* London: Hogarth.

Klein, M. H., Benjamin, L. S., Rosenfeld, R., Treece, C., Husted, J., & Greist, J. H. (1993). The Wisconsin Personality Disorders Inventory: Development, reliability, and validity. *Journal of Personality Disorders, 7,* 285–303.

Klerman, G. L., Weissman, M., Rounsaville, B., & Chevron, E. (1984). *Interpersonal psychotherapy of depression.* New York: Basic Books.

Knight, R. P. (1953). Borderline states. *Bulletin of the Menninger Clinic, 17,* 1–12.

Koch, J. L. (1891). *Die psychopathischen minderwertigkeiten.* Ravensburg: Maier.

Kohut, H. (1966). Forms and transformations of narcissism. *Journal of the American Psychoanalytic Association, 14,* 243–272.

Kohut, H. (1968). The psychoanalytic treatment of narcissistic personality disorders. *Psychoanalytic Study of the Child, 23,* 86–113.

Kohut, H. (1971). *The analysis of self.* New York: International Universities Press.

Kohut. H. (1977). *The restoration of the self.* New York: International Universities Press.

Kolb, J., & Gunderson, J. G. (1980). Diagnosing borderline patients with a semistructured interview. *Archives of General Psychiatry, 37,* 37–41.

Kollarits, J. (1912). *Charakter und nervositat.* Budapest: Knoedler.

Kraepelin, E. (1887). *Psychiatrie: Ein lehrbuch* (2nd ed.). Leipzig: Abel.

Kraepelin, E. (1889). *Psychiatrie: Ein lehrbuch* (3rd ed.). Leipzig: Barth.

Kraepelin, E. (1896). *Psychiatrie: Ein lehrbuch* (5th ed.). Leipzig: Barth.

Kraepelin, E. (1903–1904). *Psychiatrie: Ein lehrbuch* (7th ed.). Leipzig: Barth.

Kraepelin, E. (1904). *Lectures on clinical psychiatry.* New York: Wood.

Kraepelin, E. (1909–1915). *Psychiatrie* (8th ed., Vol. 4). Leipzig: Barth.

Kraepelin, E. (1913). *Psychiatrie: Ein lehrbuch* (8th ed., Vol. 3). Leipzig: Barth.

Kraepelin, E. (1919). *Dementia praecox and paraphrenia.* Edinburgh: Livingstone.

Kraepelin, E. (1921). *Manic-depressive insanity and paranoia.* Edinburgh: Livingstone.

Krafft-Ebing, R. (1867). *Moral insanity—Its recognition and forensic assessment.* Berlin: Erlangn.

Krafft-Ebing, R. (1937). *Psychopathia sexualis.* New York: Physicians and Surgeons Books. (Original work published 1882)

Kretschmer, E. (1918). *Der sensitive beziehungswahn.* Berlin: Springer.

Kretschmer, E. (1925). *Korperbau und charakter.* Berlin: Springer Verlag.

Kretschmer, E. (1926). *Hysteria.* New York: Nervous and Mental Disease Publishers.

Kroll, J. (1993). *PTSD/borderlines in therapy.* New York: Norton.

Kuhn, T. S. (1962). *The structure of scientific revolutions.* Chicago: University of Chicago Press.

Kuhn, T. S. (1969). *The structure of scientific revolutions.* (rev. ed.). Chicago: University of Chicago Press.

Laing, R. D. (1960). *The divided self.* Chicago: Quadrangle.

Lamb, M. E., Thompson, R. A., Gardner, W., & Estes, D. (1985). *Infant-mother attachment.* Hillsdale, NJ: Erlbaum.

Langfeldt, G. (1937). The prognosis in schizophrenia and the factors influencing the curse of the disease. *Acta Psychiatrica Scandinavica,* Supplementurn 13.

Lasch, C. (1978). *The culture of narcissism.* New York: Norton.

Lazare, A., Klerman, G. L., & Armor, D. (1966). Oral, obsessive, and hysterical personality patterns. *Archives of General Psychiatry, 14,* 624–630.

Lazare, A., Klerman, G. L., & Armor, D. (1970). Oral, obsessive and hysterical personality patterns: Replication of factor analysis in an independent sample. *Journal of Psychiatric Research, 7,* 275–290.

Lazarus, A. A. (1968). Learning theory and the treatment of depression. *Behavior Research and Therapy, 6,* 83–89.

Lazarus, A. A. (1981). *The practice of multimodal therapy.* New York: McGraw-Hill.

Lazursky, A. (1906). *An outline of a science of characters.* St. Petersburg: Lossky.

Leary, T. (1957). *Interpersonal diagnosis of personality.* New York: Ronald.

Leonhard, K. (1968). *The classification of endogenous psychoses.* New York: Irvington.

Leszcz, M. (1989). Group therapy. In T. Karasu (Ed.), *Treatments of psychiatric disorders* (pp. 2667–2678). Washington, DC: American Psychiatric Press.

Levine, J. B., Green, C. G., & Millon, T. (1986). The Separation-Individuation Test of adolescence. *Journal of Personality Assessment, 50,* 123–137.

Levy, D. M. (1951). Psychopathic behavior in infants and children. *American Journal of Orthopsychiatry, 21,* 223–272.

Lewinsohn, P. M. (1974). A behavioral approach to depression. In R. J. Friedman & M. M. Katz (Eds.), *The psychology of depression: Contemporary theory and research.* Washington, DC: V. H. Winston.

Lewis, A. (1934). The story of unreason. In A. Lewis, *The state of psychiatry.* London: Routledge & Kegan Paul.

Lewis, A. (1974). Psychopathic personality: A most elusive category. *Psychological Medicine, 4,* 133–140.

Linehan, M. M. (1987). Dialectical behavior therapy for borderline patients. *Menninger Clinic, 51,* 261–276.

Linehan, M. M. (1992). Behavior therapy, dialectics, and the treatment of borderline personality disorder. In D. Silver & M. Rosenbluth (Eds.), *Hand of borderline disorders* (pp. 415–434). Madison, CT: International Universities Press.

Linehan, M. M. (1993). *Cognitive-behavioral therapy of borderline personality disorder.* New York: Guilford.

Lipton, S. A., & Kater, S. B. (1989). Neurotransmitter regulation of neuronal outgrowth, plasticity, and survival. *Trends in Neuroscience, 12,* 265–269.

Livesley, W. J. (1986). Trait and behavioral prototypes of personality disorder. Paper presented at the 138th annual meeting of the American Psychiatric Association (1985, Dallas, Texas). *American Journal of Psychiatry, 143,* 728–732.

Livesley, W. J. (1987). Theoretical and empirical issues in the selection of criteria to diagnose personality disorders. *Journal of Personality Disorders, 1,* 88–94.

Livesley, W. J., Jackson, D. N., & Schroeder, M. L. (1989). A study of the factorial structure of personality pathology. *Journal of Personality Disorders, 3,* 292–306.

Livesley, W. J., Jackson, D. N., & Schroeder, M. L. (1992). Factorial structure of traits delineating personality disorders in clinical and general population samples. *Journal of Abnormal Psychology, 101,* 432–440.

Livesley, W. J., Reiffer, L. I., Sheldon, A. E. R., & West, M. (1987). Prototypic ratings of DSM-III criteria for a personality disorder. *Journal of Nervous & Mental Disorders, 178,* 395–401.

Livesley, W. J., & Schroeder, M. L. (1990). Dimensions of personality disorder: The DSM-III Cluster-A diagnoses. *Journal of Nervous & Mental Disorders, 178,* 627–635.

Livesley, W. J., Schroeder, M. L., & Jackson, D. N. (1990). Dependent person disorder and attachments. *Journal of Personality Disorders, 4,* 131–140.

Livesley, W. J., Schroeder, M. L., Jackson, D. N., & Lang, K. L. (1994). Categorical distinctions in the study of personality disorder: Implications for classification. *Journal of Abnormal Psychology, 103,* 6–17.

Loeber, R., & Stouthamer-Loeber, M. (1986). Family factors as correlates and predictors of juvenile conduct problems and delinquency. In M. Toury & N. Morris (Eds.), *Crime and justice* (Vol. 7). Chicago: University of Chicago Press.

Loevinger, J. (1957). Objective tests as instruments of psychological theory. *Psychological Reports, 3,* 635–694.

Loevinger, J. (1994). Has psychology lost its conscience? *Journal of Personality Assessment, 62,* 2–8.

Loewenstein, R. (1957). Denial and repression. *Journal of the American Psychoanalytic Association, 5,* 61–92.

Lombroso, C. (1872–1887). *L'Uomo delinquente.* Bocca: Torina.

Loranger, A. W., Susman, V. L., Oldham, J. M., & Russakoff, L. M. (1987). The Personality Disorder Examination: A preliminary report. *Journal of Personality Disorders, 1,* 1–13.

Lorenz, K. (1965). *Evolution and modification of behavior.* Chicago: University of Chicago Press.

Lorr, M. (1975). Convergences in personality constructs measured by four inventories. *Journal of Clinical Psychology, 31,* 182–188.

Lorr, M., & Manning, T. T. (1978). Higher-order personality factors of the ISI. *Multivariate Behavioral Research, 13,* 3–7.

Lykken, D. T. (1957). A study of anxiety in the sociopathic personality. *Journal of Abnormal and Social Psychology, 55,* 6–10.

Maccoby, E., & Martin, J. (1983). Socialization in the context of the family: Parent-child interaction. In E. M. Hetherington (Ed.), *Handbook of child psychology, Vol 4: Socialization, personality, and social development.* New York: Wiley.

MacKinnon, R. A., & Michels, R. (1971). *The psychiatric interview in clinical practice.* Philadelphia: Saunders.

Maddi, S. R. (1968). *Personality theories: A comparative analysis.* Homewood, IL: Dorsey.

Maddi, S. R., & Propst, B. (1971). Activation theory and personality. In S. R. Maddi (Ed.), *Perspectives on personality.* Boston: Little, Brown.

Magnan, V. (1886). *Lecons cliniques sur les madadies mentales.* Paris: Battaille.

Magnusson, D., & Endler, N. S. (Eds.). (1977). *Personality at the crossroads: Current issues in interactional psychology.* Hillsdale, NJ: Erlbaum.

Mahler, M. S. (1958). Autism and symbiosis: Two extreme disturbances of identity. *International Journal of Psychoanalysis, 39,* 77–83.

Mahler, M. S. (1967). On human symbiosis and the vicissitudes of individuation. In *The selected papers of Margaret S. Mahler* (Vol. 1, pp. 77–98). New York: International Universities Press.

Mahler, M. S. (1975). On the current status of the infantile neurosis. In *The selected papers of Margaret S. Mahler* (Vol. 2, pp. 189–194). New York: Jason Aronson.

Mahler, M. S., Pine, F., & Bergman, A. (1975). *The psychological birth of the human infant.* New York: Basic Books.

Mahrer, A. R. (1983). An existential-experiential view and operational perspective on passive-aggressiveness. In R. D. Parsons & R. J. Wickes (Eds.), *Passive-aggressiveness.* New York: Brunner/Mazel.

Marmor, J. (1953). Orality in the hysterical personality. *Journal of the American Psychoanalytic Association, 1,* 656–671.

Marmor, J. (1962). Psychoanalytic therapy as an educational process. In J. Masserman (Ed.), *Science and Psychoanalysis.* New York: Grune & Stratton.

Marmor, J. (1986). The question of causality. *Behavioral and Brain Sciences, 9,* 249–250.

Mash, E. J., & Johnston, C. (1982). A comparison of the mother-child interactions of younger and older hyperactive and normal children. *Child Development, 53,* 1371–1381.

Masterson, J. F. (1972). *Treatment of the borderline adolescent: A developmental approach.* New York: Wiley.

Masterson, J. F. (1976). *Psychotherapy of the borderline adult: A developmental approach.* New York: Brunner/Mazel.

Masterson, J. F., & Rinsley, D. (1975). The borderline syndrome: The role of the mother in the genesis and psychic structure of the borderline personality. *International Journal of Psycho-Analysis, 56,* 163–177.

Mattson, A., Sesse, L., & Hawkins, J. (1969). Suicidal behavior as a child psychiatric emergency. *Archives of General Psychiatry, 20,* 100–109.

Maudsley, H. (1874). *Responsibility in mental disease.* London: King.

Maxwell, A. E. (1971). Multivariate statistical methods and classification problems. *British Journal of Psychiatry, 119,* 121–127.

May, R., et al. (1958). *Existence.* New York: Basic Books.

May, R., & Van Kaam, A. (1963). Existential theory and therapy. In J. H. Masserman (Ed.), *Current psychiatric therapies* (Vol. 3). New York: Grune & Stratton.

McClelland, D. C. (1951). *Personality.* New York: Dryden.

McClelland, D. C., Koestner, R., & Weinberger, J. (1989). How do self-attributed and implicit motives differ? *Psychological Review, 96,* 690–702.

McDougall, W. (1932). *Introduction to social psychology.* New York: Scribners. (Original work published 1908)

McGraw, M. B. (1943). *The neuromuscular maturation of the human infant.* New York: Columbia University Press.

McLemore, C. W., & Brokaw, D. W. (1987). Personality disorders as dysfunctional interpersonal behavior. *Journal of Personality Disorders, 1*(3) 270–285.

Mead, G. H. (1934). Mind, self, and society. Chicago: University of Chicago Press.

Meehl, P. E. (1972). Specific genetic etiology, psychodynamics, and therapeutic nihilism. *International Journal of Mental Health, 1,* 10–27.

Meehl, P. E. (1973). Schizotaxia, schizotypy, schizophrenia. In T. Millon (Ed.), *Theories of psychopathology and personality* (2nd ed.). Philadelphia: Saunders. (Reprinted from *American Psychologist, 1962, 17,* 827–838).

Meehl, P. E. (1977). Specific etiology and other forms of strong influence: Some quantitative meanings. *Journal of Medicine and Philosophy, 2,* 33–53.

Meehl, P. E. (1978). Theoretical risks and tabular asterisks: Sir Karl, Sir Ronald, and the slow progress of soft psychology. *Journal of Consulting and Clinical Psychology, 46,* 806–834.

Meehl, P. E. (1986). Diagnostic taxa as open concepts: Metatheoretical and statistical questions about reliability and construct validity in the grand strategy of nosological revision. In T. Millon & G. Klerman (Eds.), *Contemporary directions in psychopathology: Toward the DSM-IV* (pp. 215–231). New York: Guilford.

Meehl, P. E. (1990). Schizotaxia as an open concept. In A. I. Rabin, R. Zucker, R. Emmons, & S. Frank (Eds.), *Studying persons and lives* (pp. 248–303). New York: Springer.

Meehl, P. E. (1991). Why summaries of research on psychological theories are often uninterpretable. In R. E. Snow & D. Wiley (Eds.), *Improving inquiry in social science: A volume in honor of Lee J. Cronbach* (pp. 13–59). Hillsdale, NJ: Erlbaum. (Reprinted from *Psychological Reports, 1990, 66,* 195–244.

Meehl, P. E. (1992). Factors and taxa, traits and types: Differences of degree and differences in kind. *Journal of Personality, 60,* 117–174.

Meichenbaum, D. (1977). *Cognitive-behavioral modification.* New York: Plenum.

Meissner, W. W. (1979). *The paranoid process.* New York: Jason Aronson.

Meloy, J. R. (1988). *The psychopathic mind.* Northvale, NJ: Jason Aronson.

Melzack, R. (1965). Effects of early experience upon behavior: Experimental and conceptual considerations. In P. Hoch & J. Zubin (Eds.), *Psychopathology of perception.* New York: Grune & Stratton.

Menaker, E. (1942). The masochistic factor in the psychoanalytic situation. *Psychoanalytic Quarterly, 11,* 171–186.

Menaker, E. (1953). Masochism, a defense reaction. *Psychoanalytic Quarterly, 22,* 205–220.

Mendelson, M. (1974). *Psychoanalytic concepts of depression* (2nd ed.). New York: Spectrum.

Menninger, K. (1930). *The human mind.* New York: Alfred Knopf.

Menninger, K. (1940). Character disorders. In J. F. Brown (Ed.), *The psychodynamics of abnormal behavior* (pp. 384–403). New York: McGraw-Hill.

Menninger, K. (1963). *The vital balance.* New York: Viking.

Meumann, E. (1910). *Intelligenz und wille.* Leipzig: Barth.

Meyer, A. (1906). Fundamental conceptions of dementia praecox. *British Medical Journal, 2,* 757–760.

Meyer, A. (1908). The problem of mental reaction-types, mental causes and diseases. *Psychological Bulletin, 5,* 245–261.

Meyer, A. (1912). Remarks on habit disorganizations in the essential deteriorations. *Nervous and Mental Disease Monographs, 9,* 95–109.

Meyer, A. (1913). The treatment of paranoic and paranoid states. In W. White & S. Jelliffe (Eds.), *Modern treatment of nervous and mental diseases* (pp. 274–285). Philadelphia: Lea and Febiger.

Meyer, A. (1951). *The collected papers of Adolf Meyer.* Baltimore: The Johns Hopkins Press.

Michelsson, K., Rinne, A., & Paajanen, S. (1990). Crying, feeding and sleeping patterns in 1- to 12-month-old infants. *Child Care, Health, and Development, 16,* 99–111.

Miller, A. (1981). *Prisoners of childhood.* New York: Basic Books.

Miller, G. A., Galanter, E., & Pribam, K. H. (1960). Plans and structure of behavior. New York: Holt, Rinehart & Winston.

Miller, H. R., Streiner, D. L., & Parkinson, A. (1992). Maximum likelihood estimates of the ability of the MMPI and MCMI personality disorder scales and the SIDP to identify personality disorders. *Journal of Personality Assessment, 59,* 1–13.

Millon, T. (Ed.). (1967). *Theories of psychopathology.* Philadelphia: Saunders.

Millon, T. (1969). *Modern psychopathology: A biosocial approach to maladaptive learning and functioning.* Philadelphia: Saunders.

Millon, T. (Ed.). (1973). *Theories of psychopathology and personality* (2nd ed.). Philadelphia: Saunders.

Millon, T. (1977). *Millon Clinical Multiaxial Inventory manual.* Minneapolis: National Computer Systems.

Millon, T. (1981). Disorders of personality: DSM-III, Axis II. New York: Wiley.

Millon, T. (1986a). Personality prototypes and their diagnostic criteria. In T. Millon & G. L. Klerman (Eds.), *Contemporary directions in psychopathology: Toward the DSM-IV.* New York: Guilford.

Millon, T. (1986b). A theoretical derivation of pathological personalities. In T. Millon & G. L. Klerman (Eds.), *Contemporary directions in psychopathology: Toward the DSM-IV.* New York: Guilford.

Millon, T. (1987a). On the nature of taxonomy in psychopathology. In C. G. Last & M. Hersen (Eds.), *Issues in diagnostic research* (pp. 3–85). New York: Plenum.

Millon, T. (1987b). On the genesis and prevalence of the borderline personality disorder: A social learning thesis. *Journal of Personality Disorders, 1,* 354–372.

Millon, T. (1987c). *Millon Clinical Multiaxial Inventory manual II.* Minneapolis: National Computer Systems.

Millon, T. (1988). Personologic psychotherapy: Ten commandments for a posteclectic approach to integrative treatment. *Psychotherapy, 25,* 209–219.

Millon, T. (1990). *Toward a new personology: An evolutionary model.* New York: Wiley.

Millon, T., & Disenhaus, H. (1972). Research Methods in psychopathology. New York: Wiley.

Millon, T., Millon, C., & Davis, R. D. (1994). *Millon Clinical Multiaxial Inventory—III.* Minneapolis: National Computer Systems.

Millon, T., & Millon, R. (1974). *Abnormal behavior and personality.* Philadelphia: Saunders.

Millon, T., Weiss, L., Millon, C., & Davis, R. (1994). *MIPS: Millon index of personality styles manual.* San Antonio: The Psychological Corporation.

Mischel, W. (1968). *Personality assessment.* New York: Wiley.

Mischel, W. (1969). Continuity and change in personality. *American Psychologist, 24,* 1012–1018.

Mischel, W. (1973a). On the empirical dilemmas of psychodynamic approaches: Issues and alternative. *Journal of Abnormal Psychology, 82,* 335–344.

Mischel, W. (1973b). Toward a cognitive social learning reconceptualization of personality. *Psychological Review, 80,* 252–283.

Mischel, W. (1979). On the interface of cognition and personality: Beyond the person-situation debate. *American Psychologist, 34,* 740–754.

Modell, A. (1963). Primitive object relationships and the predisposition to schizophrenia. *International Journal of Psycho-Analysis 44,* 282–292.

Morel, B. A. (1852–1853). *Traite theoriquee pratique des maladies mentales (Vols. 1 and 2).* Paris: Bailliere.

Morey, L. (1992). *The Personality Assessment Inventory.* Odessa, FL: Psychological Assessment Resources.

Morey, L. C., Blashfield, R. K., Webb, W. W., & Jewell, J. (1988). MMPI scales for DSM-III personality disorders: A preliminary validation study. *Journal of Clinical Psychology, 44,* 47–50.

Morey, L. C., Waugh, M. H., & Blashfield, R. B. (1985). MMPI scales for DSM-III personality disorders: Their derivation and correlates. *Journal of Personality Assessment, 49,* 245–251.

Morrison, J. R. (1980). Adult psychiatric disorders in parents of hyperactive children. *American Journal of Psychiatry, 137,* 825–827.

Mowrer, O. H. (1961). *The crisis in psychiatry and religion.* Princeton: Van Nostrand.

Mowrer, O. H. (1965). Integrity therapy: A self-help approach. *Psychotherapy, 3,* 14–19.

Mowrer, O. H. (1966). Learning theory and behavior therapy. In B. Wolman (Ed.), *Handbook of clinical psychology.* New York: McGraw-Hill.

Mueller, E., & Silverman, N. (1989). Peer relations in maltreated children. In D. Cicchetti & V. Carlson (Eds.), *Child maltreatment: Theory and research on the causes and consequences of child abuse and neglect* (pp. 529–578). New York: Cambridge University Press.

Murphy, G. (1947). *Personality: A biosocial approach to origins and structures.* New York: Harper.

Murphy, L. B. (1962). *The widening world of childhood.* New York: Basic Books.

Murphy, L. B., & Moriarty, A. E. (1976). *Vulnerability, coping and growth.* New Haven: Yale University Press.

Murray, E. J. (1988). Personality disorders: A cognitive view. *Journal of Personality Disorders, 2,* 37–43.

Murray, H. A. (Ed.). (1938). *Explorations in personality.* New York: Oxford University Press.

Nacke, P. (1899). Die sexuellen perversitaten in der irrenansalt. *Psychiatrie en Neurologie Bladen, 3,* 14–21.

Nagera, H. (1964). Autoeroticism, autoerotic activities, and ego development. *Psychoanalytic Study of the Child, 19,* 240–255.

Nanarello, J. (1953). Schizoid. *Journal of Nervous and Mental Diseases, 118,* 237–249.

Newton, G., & Levine, S. (Eds.). (1968). *Early experience and behavior.* Springfield, IL: Thomas.

Norcross, J. C., & Goldfried, M. R. (Eds.). (1992). *Handbook of psychotherapy integration.* New York: Basic Books.

Norman, W. (1963). Toward an adequate taxonomy of personality attributes: Replicated factor structure in peer nomination personality ratings. *Journal of Abnormal and Social Psychology, 66,* 574–583.

Offer, D., & Sabshin, M. (Eds.). (1974). *Normality: Theoretical and clinical concepts of mental health* (rev. ed.). New York: Basic Books.

Offer, D., & Sabshin, M. (Eds.). (1991). *The diversity of normal behavior.* New York: Basic Books.

Oldham, J. M., & Morris, L. B. (1990). *The personality self-portrait.* New York: Bantam.

Olweus, D. (1977). A critical analysis of the "modern" interactionist position. In D. Magnusson & N. S. Endler (Eds.), *Personality at the crossroads: Current issues in interactional psychology.* Hillsdale, NJ: Erlbaum.

Osofsky, J. D., & Danzger, B. (1974). Relationships between neonatal characteristics and mother-infant interaction. *Developmental Psychology, 10,* 124–130.

Palombo, J. (1976). Theories of narcissism and the practice of clinical social work. *Clinical Social Work Journal, 4,* 147–161.

Pap, A. (1953). Reduction-sentences and open concepts. *Methodos, 5,* 3–30.

Papousek, H., & Papousek, M. (1975). Cognitive aspects of preverbal social interaction between human infants and adults. In R. Porter & M. O'Conner (Eds.), *Parent-infant interaction* (pp. 241–260). Amsterdam: Elsevier.

Paris, J. (1994). *Borderline personality disorder: A multidimensional approach.* Washington, DC: American Psychiatric Press.

Parker, G. (1983). *Parental overprotection: A risk factor in psychosocial development.* New York: Grune & Stratton.

Partridge, G. E. (1927). A study of 50 cases of psychopathic personality. *American Journal of Psychiatry, 7,* 953–974.

Partridge, G. E. (1928). Psychopathic personality and personality investigation. *American Journal of Psychiatry, 8,* 1053–1064.

Partridge, G. E. (1930). Current conceptions of psychopathic personality. *American Journal of Psychiatry, 10,* 53–99.

Pepper, S. C. (1942). *World hypotheses: A study in evidence.* Berkeley: University of California Press.

Perry, J. C., & Cooper, S. H. (1989). An empirical study of defense mechanisms. *Archives of General Psychiatry, 46,* 444–452.

Perry, J. C., & Herman, J. (1993). Trauma and defense in the ideology of borderline personality disorder. In J. Paris (Ed.), *Borderline personality disorder: Ideology and treatment.* Washington, DC: American Psychiatric Press.

Perry, J. C., & Klerman, G. L. (1978). The borderline patient. *Archives of General Psychiatry, 35,* 141–150.

Person, E. S. (1986). Manipulativeness in entrepreneurs and psychopaths. In W. H. Reid, D. Dorr, J. I. Walker, & J. W. Bonner, III (Eds.), *Unmasking the psychopath: Antisocial personality and related syndromes* (pp. 256–273). New York: Norton.

Pfohl, B., Blum, N., Zimmerman, M., & Stangl, D. (1989). *Structured interview for DSM-III-R personality (SIDP-R).* Iowa City: University of Iowa, Department of Psychiatry.

Philips, E. L. (1956). *Psychotherapy: A modern theory and practice.* Englewood Cliffs, NJ: Prentice-Hall.

Phillips, K. A., Gunderson, J. G., Hirschfeld, R. M., & Smith, L. E. (1990). A review of the depressive personality. *American Journal of Psychiatry, 147,* 830–837.

Phillips, L. (1968). *Human adaptation and its failures.* New York: Academic Press.

Piaget, J. (1952). *The origins of intelligence in children.* New York: International Universities Press.

Piaget, J. (1956). The general problems of the psychobiological development of the child. In J. M. Tanner & B. Inhelder (Eds.), *Discussions on child development* (Vol. 4). New York: International Universities Press.

Pincus, A. L., & Wiggins, J. S. (1990). Interpersonal problems and conceptions of personality disorders. *Journal of Personality Disorders, 4,* 342–352.

Pinel, P. (1801). *Traite medico-philosophique sur l'alienation mentale.* Paris: Richard, Cailleet Ravier.

Pinel, P. (1806). *A treatise on insanity* (D. Davis, Trans.). New York: Hafner.

Plomin, R. (1990). The role of inheritance in behavior. *Science, 248,* 183–188.

Plomin, R., DeFries, J. C., & McClearn, G. E. (1990). *Behavioral genetics: A primer* (2nd ed.). New York: Freeman.

Plomin, R., & Dunn, J. (Eds.). (1986). *The study of temperament: Changes, continuities, and challenge.* Hillsdale, NJ: Erlbaum.

Popper, K. R. (1973). Debates with Schroedinger. In P. A. Schilpp (Ed.), *The philosophy of Karl Popper* (Vol. 1, sec. 30). Lasalle, IL: Open Court.

Prichard, J. C. (1835). *A treatise on insanity.* London: Sherwood, Gilbert and Piper.

Purves, D., & Lichtman, J. W. (1985). *Principles of neural development.* Sunderland, MA: Sinauer.

Quay, H. C. (1964). Personality dimensions in delinquent males as inferred from the factor analysis of behavior ratings. *Journal of Research in Crime and Delinquency, 1,* 33–37.

Quay, H. C. (1965). Psychopathic personality as pathological stimulus seeking. *American Journal of Psychiatry, 122,* 180–183.

Quay, H. C. (1986). A critical analysis of DSM-III as a taxonomy of psychopathology in childhood and adolescence. In T. Millon & G. L. Klerman (Eds.), *Contemporary directions in psychopathology: Toward the DSM-IV.* New York: Guilford.

Quay, H. C., & Werry, J. S. (Eds.). (1979). *Psychopathological disorders of childhood* (2nd ed.). New York: Wiley.

Queyrat, F. (1896). *Les caracteres et l'education morale.* Paris: Alcan.

Quine, W. V. O. (1961). *From a logical point of view* (2nd ed.). New York: Harper & Row.

Rado, S. (1928). The problem of melancholia. *International Journal of Psychoanalysis, 9,* 297–313.

Rado, S. (1956). Schizotypal organization: Preliminary report on a clinical study of schizophrenia. In S. Rado & G. E. Daniels (Eds.), *Changing concepts of psychoanalytic medicine* (pp. 225–236). New York: Grune & Stratton.

Rado, S. (1959). Obsessive behavior. In S. Arieti (Ed.), *American handbook of psychiatry* (Vol. 1). New York: Basic Books.

Rado, S. (1969). *Adaptational psychodynamics.* New York: Science House.

Rakic, P. (1985). Limits of neurogenesis in primates. *Science, 227,* 154–156.

Rakic, P. (1988). Specification of cerebral cortical areas. *Science, 241,* 170–176.

Rank, O. (1929). *The trauma of birth.* New York: Harcourt, Brace.

Rank. O. (1936). *Will therapy: An analysis of the therapeutic process in terms of relationship.* New York: Knopf.

Rapaport, D. (1958). The theory of ego autonomy: A generalization. *Bulletin of the Menninger Clinic, 22,* 13–35.

Rapaport, D. (1959). The structure of psychoanalytic theory: A systematizing attempt. In S. Koch (Ed.), *Psychology: A Study of a science.* New York: McGraw-Hill.

Rapaport, D., Gill, M. M., & Schafer, R. (1945–1946). *Diagnostic psychological testing* (2 Vols.). Chicago: Year Book Publishers.

Rapaport, D., Gill, M. M., Schafer, R., & Holt, R. R. (1968). *Diagnostic Psychological Testing* (rev. ed.). New York: International Universities Press.

Reich, A. (1960). Pathologic forms of self-esteem regulation. *Psychoanalytic Study of the Child, 15,* 215–232.

Reich, J., Noyes, R., Coryell, W., & Gorman, T. W. (1986). The effect of state anxiety on personality measurement. *American Journal of Psychiatry, 143,* 760–763.

Reich, W. (1925). *Der triebhafie charakter.* Leipzig: Internationaler Psychoanalytischer Verlag.

Reich, W. (1933). *Charakteranalyse.* Leipzig: Sexpol Verlag.

Reich, W. (1949). *Character analysis* (3rd ed.). New York: Farrar, Straus and Giroux.

Reid, J. B., Patterson, G. R., & Loeber, R. (1982). The abused child: Victim, instigator, or innocent bystander. In D. Bernstein (Ed.), *Response, structure and organization.* Lincoln: University of Nebraska Press.

Reik, T. (1941). *Masichism and modern man.* New York: Farvar and Rinehart.

Reiss, D. (1981). *The families' construction of reality.* Cambridge, MA: Harvard University Press.

Ribble, M. A. (1943). *The rights of infants.* New York: Columbia University Press.

Ribot, T. (1890). *Psychologie des sentiments.* Paris: Delahaye and Lecrosnier.

Riesen, A. H. (1961). Stimulation as a requirement for growth and function in behavioral development. In D. Fiske & S. Maddi (Eds.), *Functions of varied experience* (pp. 57–80). Homewood, IL: Dorsey.

Rinsley, D. B. (1977). An object relations view of borderline personality. In P. Hartocollis (Ed.), *Borderline personality disorders: The concept, the syndrome, the patient* (pp. 47–70). New York: International Universities Press.

Roback, A. A. (1927). *The psychology of character.* New York: Harcourt, Brace.

Robins, L. (1966). *Deviant children grown up.* Baltimore: Williams & Wilkins.

Robins, L., & Rutter, M. (Eds.). (1990). *Straight and devious pathways from childhood to adulthood.* New York: Cambridge University Press.

Rogers, C. R. (1942). *Counseling and psychotherapy.* Boston: Houghton Mifflin.

Rogers, C. R. (1951). *Client-centered therapy.* Boston: Houghton Mifflin.

Rogers, C. R. (1961). *On becoming a person.* Boston: Houghton Mifflin.

Rogers, C. R., et al. (1967). *The therapeutic relationship and its impact.* Madison: University of Wisconsin Press.

Romney, D. M., & Bynner, J. M. (1989). Evaluation of a circumplex model of DSM-III personality disorders. *Journal of Research in Personality, 23,* 525–538.

Rorer, L. G. (1990). Personality assessment: A conceptual survey. In L. A. Perwin (Ed.), *Handbook of Personality: Theory and Research* (pp. 693–724). New York: Guilford.

Rosch, E. (1978). Principles of categorization. In E. Rosch & B. B. Loyd (Eds.), *Cognition and categorization.* Hillsdale, NJ: Erlbaum.

Rosch, E., & Mervis, C. B. (1975). Family resemblances: Studies in the internal structure of categories. *Cognitive Psychology, 8,* 382–439.

Rosenfeld, H. (1964). On the psychopathology of narcissism. *International Journal of Psychoanalysis, 45,* 332–337.

Rosenthal, D., & Kety, S. S. (Eds.). (1968). *The transmission of schizophrenia.* Oxford: Pergamon.

Rosenzweig, M. R., et al. (1962). Effect of environmental complexity and training on brain chemistry and anatomy: A replication and extension. *Journal of Comparative Physiological Psychology, 55,* 429–437.

Rosse, J. C. (1890). Clinical cases of insanity and imbecility. *American Journal of Insanity, 47,* 263–267.

Rotter, J. B. (1954). *Social learning and clinical psychology.* Englewood Cliffs, NJ: Prentice-Hall.

Rush, B. (1812). *Medical inquiries and observations upon the diseases of the mind.* Philadelphia: Kimber and Richardson.

Rushton, J. P. (1985). Differential K theory: The sociobiology of individual and group differences. *Personality and Individual Differences, 6,* 441–452.

Rutter, M. (1970). *Maternal deprivation reassessed.* London: Penguin.

Rutter, M., & Giller, H. (1983). *Juvenile Delinquency: Trends and Perspectives.* Harmondsworth: Penguin.

Sacher-Masoch, L. (1870). *Venus in furs.* Dresden: Dohrn.

Sack, R. L., & Miller, W. (1975). Masochism: A clinical and theoretical overview. *Psychiatry, 38,* 244–257.

Sadger, J. (1908). Psychiatrish-neurologisches in psychoanalytischer beleuchtung. *Zeitschrift fuer gesamte Medizin, 7,* 92–104.

Sadger, J. (1910). Analerotik und analcharakter. *Die Heilkunde, 4,* 11–20.

Salzman, L. (1985). *Treatment of the obsessive personality.* New York: Aranson.

Sandler, J. (1985). *The analysis of defense.* New York: International Universities Press.

Sandler, J., & Hazari, A. (1960). The obsessional: On the psychological classification of obsessional character traits and symptoms. *British Journal of Medical Psychology, 33,* 13–122.

Sandler, J., & Joffe, W. G. (1965). Notes on childhood depression. *International Journal of Psychoanalysis, 46,* 88–96.

Sarwer-Foner, G. J. (1959). Theoretical aspects of the modes of action. In N. S. Kline (Ed.), *Psychopharmacology frontiers.* Boston: Little, Brown.

Schaefer, E. S. (1965). Configurational analysis of children's reports of parent behavior. *Journal of Consulting Psychology, 29,* 552–557.

Schafer, R. (1948). *The clinical application of psychological tests.* New York: International Universities Press.

Schmideberg, M. (1947). The treatment of psychopaths and borderline patients. *American Journal of Psychotherapy, 1,* 45–55.

Schmideberg, M. (1959). The borderline patient. In S. Arieti (Ed.), *American handbook of psychiatry* (Vol. 1, pp. 398–416). New York: Basic Books.

Schneider, K. (1950). *Psychopathic personalities* (9th ed.). London: Cassell. (Original work published 1923)

Schroeder, M. L., Wormworth, J. A., & Livesley W. J. (1993). Dimensions of personality disorder and the five-factor model of personality. In P. T. Costa, Jr. & T. A. Widiger (Eds.), *Personality disorders and the five-factor model of personality* (pp. 117–127). Washington, DC: American Psychological Association.

Schulsinger, F. (1977). Psychopathy: Heredity and environment. In S. A. Mednick & K. O. Christiansen (Eds.), *Biosocial basis of criminal behavior* (pp. 109–141). New York: Gardener.

Schwartz, R. A., & Schwartz, I. K. (1976). Are personality disorders diseases? *Diseases of the Nervous System, 86,* 613–617.

Schwartz, M. A., Wiggins, O. P., & Norko, M. A. (1989). Prototypes, ideal types, and personality disorders: The return of classical psychiatry. *Journal of Personality Disorders, 3,* 1–9.

Scott, J. P. (1968). *Early experience and the organization of behavior.* Belmont, CA: Brooks-Cole.

Scott, W. A. (1958). Social psychological correlates of mental illness and mental health. *Psychological Bulletin, 55,* 65–87.

Sechrest, L., & Smith, B. (1994). Psychotherapy is the practice of psychology. *Journal of Psychotherapy Integration, 4,* 1–29.

Serban, G., & Siegel, S. (1984). Response of borderline and schizotypal patients small doses of thiothixene and haloperidol. *American Journal of Psychiatry, 141,* 145S–148S.

Shainess, N. (1987). Masochism or self-defeating personality? *Journal of Personality Disorders, 1,* 174–177.

Shapiro, D. (1965). *Neurotic styles.* New York: Basic Books.

Shapiro, D. (1981). *Autonomy and rigid character.* New York: Basic Books.

Shea, P. (1994). Mental disorders and dangerousness. *International Journal of Mental Health, 22,* 71–79.

Sheldon, W. H. (1940). *The varieties of human physique: An introduction to constitutional psychology.* New York: Harper.

Sheldon, W. H. (1954). *Atlas of men: A guide for somatotyping the male of all ages.* New York: Harper.

Sheldon, W. H., & Stevens, S. S. (1942). *The varieties of temperament: A psychology of constitutional differences.* New York: Harper.

Shoben, E. J. (1957). Toward a concept of the normal personality. *American Psychologist, 12,* 183–189.

Siever, L. J., & Davis, K. L. (1991). A psychobiological perspective on the personality disorders. *American Journal of Psychiatry, 148,* 1647–1658.

Siever, L. J., Klar, H., & Coccaro, E. (1985). Biological response styles: Clinic implications. In L. J. Siever & H. Klar (Eds.), *Psychobiological substrates personality* (pp. 38–66). Washington, DC: American Psychiatric Press.

Singer, M. (1975). The borderline delinquent: the interlocking of intrapsychic and interactional determinants. *International Review of Psychoanalysis, 2,* 429–440.

Singer, M. T., & Wynne, L. C. (1965). Thought disorder and family relations of schizophrenics, III: Methodology using projective techniques. *A.M.A. Archives of General Psychiatry, 12,* 187–212.

Sjobring, H. (1914). *Den individual psykologiska fragestallningen inom psykiatrien.* Unpublished doctoral dissertation, Upsala University.

Sjobring. H. (1973). Personality structure and development: A model and its application. *Acta Psychiatrica Scandinavica, 244,* 1–204.

Skinner, B. F. (1953). *Science and behavior.* New York: Macmillan.

Skinner, H. (1986). Construct validation approach to psychiatric classification. In T. Millon & G. L. Klerman (Eds.), *Contemporary directions in psychopathology: Towards the DSM-IV* (pp. 307–329). New York: Guilford.

Skodal, A. E., Oldham, J. M., Rosnick, L., Kellman, H. D., & Hyler, S. E. (1991) *International Journal of Methods in Psychiatric Research, 1,* 13–26.

Slavsen, S. R. (1943). *An introduction to group therapy.* New York: Commonwealth Fund.

Small, I. F., Small, J. G., Alig, V. B., & Moore, D. F. (1970). Passive-aggressive personality disorder: A search for a syndrome. *American Journal of Psychiatry, 126,* 973–983.

Smith, P. B., & Pederson, D. R. (1988). Maternal sensitivity and patterns of infant-mother attachment. *Child Development, 59,* 1097–1101.

Sneath, P. H. A., & Sokal, R. R. (1973). *Numerical taxonomy.* San Francisco: Freeman.

Soloff, P. H., George, A., Nathan, S., Schulz, P. M., Ulrich, R. F., & Perel, J. (1986). Progress in pharmacotherapy of borderline disorders. *Archives of General Psychiatry, 43,* 691–697.

Soloff, P. H., & Ulrich, R. F. (1981). Diagnostic interview for borderline patients: A replication study. *Archives of General Psychiatry, 38,* 686–692.

Spitz, R. (1965). *The first year of life.* New York: International Universities Press.

Spitzer, R. L., Endicott, J., & Gibbon, M. (1979). Crossing the border into borderline personality and borderline schizophrenia. *Archives of General Psychiatry, 36,* 17–24.

Spitzer, R. L., Williams, J. B. W., & Gibbon, M. (1987). Structured Clinical Interview for the DSM-III-R Personality Disorders (SCID-II). New York: New York State Psychiatric Institute, Biometrics Research.

Sroufe, L. A., & Fleeson, J. (1986). Attachment and the construction of relationships. In W. Hartup & Z. Rubin (Eds.), *Relationships and development* (pp. 51–71). Hillsdale, NJ: Erlbaum.

Sroufe, L. A., & Waters, E. (1976). The ontogenesis of smiling and laughter: A perspective on the organization of development in infancy. *Psychological Review, 83,* 173–189.

Steinberg, L., Elmen, J. D., & Mounts, N. S. (1989). Authoritative parenting, psychosocial maturity, and academic success among adolescents. *Child Development, 60,* 1424–1436.

Stekel, W. (1929). *Sadism and masochism.* New York: Liverwright.

Stern, A. (1938). Psychoanalytic investigation of and therapy in the border line group of neuroses. *Psychoanalytic Quarterly, 7,* 467–489.

Stewart, M. A. (1985). Aggressive conduct disorder: A brief review. Sixth Biennial Meeting of the International Society for Research on Aggression. *Aggressive Behavior, 11,* 323–331.

Stolorow, R. D. (1975). The narcissistic function of masochism (and sadism). *International Journal of Psychoanalysis, 56,* 441–448.

Stone, M. H. (1980). *The borderline syndromes.* New York: McGraw-Hill.

Stone, M. H. (1985). Disturbances in sex and love in borderline patients. In R. C. DeFries, B. Friedman, & R. Corn (Eds.), *Sexuality: New perspectives* (pp. 159–186). Westport, CT: Greenwood Press.

Stone, M. H. (1986). *Essential papers on borderline disorders.* New York: New York University Press.

Stone, M. H. (1990a). *The fate of borderline patients.* New York: Guilford.

Stone, M. H. (1990b). Abuse and abusiveness in borderline personality disorder. In P. S. Links (Ed.), *Family environment and borderline personality disorder* (pp. 133–148). Washington, DC: American Psychiatric Press.

Stone, M. H. (1993). Etiology of borderline personality disorder: Psychobiological factors contributing to an underlying irritability. In J. Paris (Ed.), *Borderline personality disorder: Etiology and treatment* (pp. 87–101). Washington, DC: American Psychiatric Press.

Strack, S. (1987). Development and validation of an adjective check list to assess the Millon personality types in a normal population. *Journal of Personality Assessment, 51,* 572–587.

Strack, S. (1991). *Manual for the Personality Adjective Check List (PACL)* (rev.). South Pasadena, CA: 21st Century Assessment.

Strack, S. (1993a). *Manual for the Personality Adjective Checklist (PACL)* (rev.). South Pasadena, CA: 21st Century Assessment.

Strack, S. (1993b). Measuring Millon's personality styles in normal adults. In R. J. Craig (Ed.), The Millon Clinical Multiaxial Inventory: A clinical research information synthesis (pp. 253–278). Hillsdale, NJ: Erlbaum.

Strack, S., & Lorr, M. (Eds.). (1994). *Differentiating normal and abnormal personalities.* New York: Springer.

Strauss, J. S. (1973). Diagnostic models and the nature of psychiatric disorder. *Archives of General Psychiatry, 29,* 445–449.

Strauss, J. S. (1975). A comprehensive approach to psychiatric diagnoses. *American Journal of Psychiatry, 132,* 1193–1197.

Stricker, G., & Gold, J. (Eds.). (1993). *Comprehensive handbook of psychotherapy integration.* New York: Guilford.

Sullivan, H. S. (1947). *Conceptions of modern psychiatry.* New York: Norton.

Sullivan, H. S. (1953). *The interpersonal theory of psychiatry.* New York: Norton.

Sullivan, H. S. (1954). *The psychiatric interview.* New York: Norton.

Taft, J. (1933). *The dynamic of therapy in a controlled relationship.* New York: Macmillan.

Tartakoff, H. (1966). The normal personality in our culture and the Nobel Prize complex. In R. M. Loewenstein, L. M. Newman, & M. Schur (Eds.), *Psychoanalysis: A general psychology* (pp. 222–252). New York: International Universities Press.

Task Force on Nomenclature and Statistics, American Psychiatric Association. (1976). *DSM-III in midstream.* Conference Publication, Missouri Institute of Psychiatry.

Tellegen, A. (1982). *Brief manual for the Multidimensional Personality Questionnaire.* Unpublished manuscript, University of Minnesota, Department of Psychology, Minneapolis.

Tellegen, A. (1985). Structures of mood and personality and their relevance to assessing anxiety, with an emphasis on self-reoprt. In A. H. Tuma & J. Maser (Eds.), *Anxiety and the anxiety disorders* (pp. 681–706). Hillsdale, NJ: Erlbaum.

Tellegen, A. (1993). Folk concepts and psychological concepts of personality and personality disorder. *Psychological Inquiry, 4*(2), 122–130.

Thomas, A., & Chess, S. (1977). *Temperament and development.* New York: Brunner/Mazel.

Thomas, A., Chess, S., & Birch, H. G. (1963). *Behavioral individuality in early childhood.* New York: New York University Press.

Thomas, A., Chess, S., & Birch, H. G. (1968). *Temperament and behavior disorders in children.* New York: New York University Press.

Thomas, A., Chess, S., & Korn, S. J. (1982). The reality of difficult temperament. *Merrill-Palmer Quarterly, 28,* 1–20.

Thompson, W. R., & Schaefer, T. (1961). Early environmental stimulation. In D. Fiske & S. Maddi (Eds.), *Functions of varied experience.* Homewood, IL: Dorsey.

Thorne, F. C. (1944). A critique of nondirective methods of psychotherapy. *Journal of Abnormal and Social Psychology, 39,* 459–470.

Thorne, F. C. (1948). Principles of directive counseling and psychotherapy. *American Psychologist, 3,* 160–165.

Tizard, B., & Hodges, J. (1978). The effect of early institutional rearing on the development of 8 year old children. *Journal of Child Psychology and Psychiatry, 19,* 99–118.

Thurstone, L. L. (1934). The vectors of mind. *Psychological Review, 41,* 1–32.

Tramer, M. (1931). Psychopathic personalities. *Schweizer medizinische Wochenschrift, 217,* 271–322.

Trull, T. J., Goodwin, A. J., Schopp, L. H., Hillenbrand, T. L., & Schuster, B. (1993). Psychometric properties of a cognitive measure of personality disorders. *Journal of Personality Assessment, 61,* 536–546.

Trull, T. J., Widiger, T. A., & Guthrie, P. (1990). Categorical versus dimensional status of borderline personality disorder. *Journal of Abnormal Psychology, 99*(1), 40–48.

Tuke, D. H. (1892). *Dictionary of psychological medicine.* Philadelphia: Blakiston.

Tupes, E. R., & Christal, R. (1961). Recurrent personality factors based on trait ratings. *USAFD Technical Report, No. 67-97.* Lackland Airforce Base, Texas.

Turkat, I. D. (1990). *The personality disorders.* New York: Pergamon.

Tyrer, P. (1988). What's wrong with DSM-III personality disorders? *Journal of Personality Disorders, 2,* 281–291.

U.S. Joint Armed Services. (1949). *Nomenclature and method of recording psychiatric conditions.* Washington, DC: Department of Defense.

Vaillant, G. E. (1971). Theoretical hierarchy of adaptive ego mechanisms. *Archives of General Psychiatry, 24,* 107–118.

Veterans Administration. (1951). *Standard classification of diseases.* Washington, DC: Veterans Administration.

Volkmar, F., & Provence, S. (1990). *Disorders of affect* (Yale Child Study Center working paper). New Haven, CT: Yale Child Study Center.

von Neumann, J., & Morgenstern, O. (1944). *The theory of games and economic behavior.* Princeton, NJ: Princeton University Press.

Wachtel, P. L. (1973). Psychodynamics, behavior therapy and the implacable experimenter: An inquiry into the consistency of personality. *Journal of Abnormal Psychology, 82,* 324–334.

Wachtel, E., & Wachtel, P. (1988). *Family dynamics in individual psychotherapy.* New York: Guilford Press.

Waelder, R. (1925). The psychoses, their mechanisms and accessibility to influence. *International Journal of Psychoanalysis, 6,* 259–281.

Wagner, M. E., Schubert, H. J. P., & Schubert, D. S. P. (1979). Sibship-constellation effects on psychosocial development, creativity, and health. In H. W. Reese & L. P. Lipsitt (Eds.), *Advances in child development and behavior* (Vol. 14, pp. 58–148). New York: Academic Press.

Waldron, S., Shrier, D. K., Stone, B., & Tobin, F. (1975). School phobia and other childhood neuroses: A systematic study of the children and their families. *American Journal of Psychiatry, 132,* 802–808.

Waelder, R. (1925). The psychoses, their mechanisms and accessibility to influence. *International Journal of Psychoanalysis, 6,* 259–281.

Waller, N. G., Lilienfeld, S. O., Tellegen, A., & Lykken, D. T. (1991). The Tridimensional Personality Questionnaire: Structural validity and comparison with the Multidimensional Personality Questionnaire. *Multivariate Behavioral Research, 26,* 1–23.

Walsh, F. (1977). The family of the borderline patient. In R. Grinker & B. Werble (Eds.), *The borderline patient* (pp. 149–177). New York: Jason Aronson.

Walton, H. J., Foulds, G. A., Littman, S. K., & Presley, A. S. (1970). Abnormal personality. *British Journal of Psychiatry, 116,* 497–510.

Walton, H. J., & Presley, A. S. (1973a). Dimensions of abnormal personality. *British Journal of Psychiatry, 122,* 269–276.

Walton, H. J., & Presley, A. S. (1973b). Use of a category system in the diagnosis of abnormal personality. *British Journal of Psychiatry, 122,* 259–263.

War Department Technical Bulletin. (1945). *Nomenclature and recording diagnoses* (No. 203). Washington, DC: War Department.

Weissman, M. M., & Paykel, E. S. (1974). *The depressed woman: A study of social relationships.* Chicago: University of Chicago Press.

Wender, P. H. (1977). The scope and the validity of the schizophrenic spectrum concept. In V. M. Rakoff, H. C. Stancer, & H. B. Kedward (Eds.), *Psychiatric diagnosis.* New York: Brunner/Mazel.

Werner, H. (1940). *Comparative psychology of mental development.* New York: Follett.

Westphal, C. (1877). Iber zwangsvorstellungen. *Berliner klinische Wochenschrift, 2,* 239–262.

Wetzler, S. (1990). The Millon Clinical Multiaxial Inventory (MCMI): A review. *Journal of Personality Assessment, 55,* 445–464.

White, R. W. (1960). Competence and the psychosexual stages of development. In M. R. Jones (Ed.), *Nebraska symposium on motivation.* Lincoln: University of Nebraska Press.

Whitman, R. M., Trosman, H., & Koenig, R. (1954). Clinical assessment of passive-aggressive personality. *Archives of Neurology and Psychiatry, 72,* 540–549.

Widiger, T. A. (1982). Prototype typology and borderline diagnosis. *Clinical Psychology Review, 2,* 115–135.

Widiger, T. A., Corbitt, E. M., & Millon, T. (1991). Antisocial personality disorders. In A. Tasman & M. Riba (Eds.), *Review of psychiatry* (Vol. II). Washington, DC: American Psychiatric Press.

Widiger, T. A., & Frances, A. (1987) Interviews and inventories for the measurement of personality disorders. *Clinical Psychology Review, 7,* 49–75.

Widiger, T. A., & Sanderson, C. (1995). Toward a dimensional model of personality disorder in DSM-IV and DSM-V. In W. J. Livesley (Ed.), *The DSM-IV personality disorders.* New York: Guilford.

Widiger, T. A., Trull, T. J., Clarkin, J. F., Sanderson, C., & Costa, P. T. (1994). In P. T. Costa, Jr. & T. A. Widiger (Eds.), *Personality disorders and the five-factor model of personality* (pp. 41–56). Washington, DC: American Psychological Association.

Wiggins, J. S. (1966). Substantive dimensions of self-report in the MMPI item pool. *Psychological Monographs, 80,* (22 whole, No. 630).

Wiggins, J. S. (1973). *Personality and prediction: Principles of personality assessment.* Reading, MA: Addison-Wesley.

Wiggins, J. S. (1982). Circumplex models of interpersonal behavior in clinical psychology. In P. Kendall & J. Butcher (Eds.), *Handbook of research methods in clinical psychology.* New York: Wiley.

Wiggins, J. S., & Pincus, A. L. (1989). Conceptions of personality disorders and dimensions of personality. *Psychological Assessment, 1,* 305–316.

Will, H. (1994). Zur phanomenologie der depression aus psychoanalytischer sicht: The phenomenology of depression: A psychoanalytic view. *Psyche Zeitschrift fur Psychoanalyse und ihre Anwendungen, 48,* 361–385.

Williams, R. J. (1973). The biological approach to the study of personality. In T. Millon (Ed.), *Theories of psychopathology and personality* (2nd ed.). Philadelphia: Saunders.

Willis, T. (1668). *Pathologiae cerebri et nervosi generis.* Amsterdam: D. Elzevir.

Willis, T. (1684). Quoted in R. Semelaigne, *Alienistes et philanthropes* (1912). Paris: Battaille.

Wilson, E. O. (1978). *On human nature.* Cambridge, MA: Harvard University Press.

Wilson, J. Q., & Hernstein, R. J. (1985). *Crime and human nature.* New York: Simon & Schuster.

Winnicott, D. W. (1956). On transference. *International Journal of Psychoanalysis, 37,* 382–395.

Winnicott, D. W. (1958). Primitive emotional development. In D. W. Winnicott (Ed.), *Collected papers.* London: Tavistock. (Original work published 1945)

Wittels, F. (1930). The hysterical character. *Medical Review of Reviews, 36,* 186–190.

Wittels, F. (1937). The criminal psychopath in the psychoanalytic system. *Psychoanalytic Review, 24,* 276–283.

Wolberg, A. (1952). The "borderline patient." *American Journal of Psychotherapy, 6,* 694–701.

Wolberg, L. R. (1954). *The technique of psychotherapy.* New York: Grune & Stratton.

Wolberg, L. R. (1967). *The technique of psychotherapy* (2nd ed.). New York: Grune & Stratton.

Wolf, E. (1976). Recent advances in the psychology of the self: An outline of basic concepts. *Comprehensive Psychiatry, 17,* 37–46.

Wolff, S., & Barlow, A. (1970). Schizoid personality in childhood: A comparative study of schizoid, autistic and normal children. *Journal of Child Psychology and Psychiatry, 20,* 29–46.

Yalom, I. D. (1985). *The theory and practice of group psychotherapy.* New York: Basic Books.

Yarrow, L. J. (1961). Maternal deprivation: Toward and empirical and conceptual reevaluation. *Psychological Bulletin, 58,* 459–490.

Young, J. E., & Lindeman, M. D. (1992). An integrative schema-focused model for personality disorders. Special Issue: Personality disorders. *Journal of Cognitive Psychotherapy, 6,* 11–23.

Zanarini, M. C. (1993). Borderline personality as an impulse spectrum disorder. In J. Paris (Ed.), *Borderline personality disorder: Etiology and treatment.* Washington, DC: American Psychiatric Association Press.

Zanarini, M. C., Gunderson, J. G., Frankenburg, F. R., & Chauncey, D. L. (1989). The revised Diagnostic Interview for Borderlines: Discriminating BPD from other Axis II disorders. *Journal of Personality Disorders, 3,* 10–18.

Zanolli, K., Saudargas, R., & Twardosz, S. (1990). Two-year-olds' responses to affectionate and caregiving teacher behavior. *Child Study Journal, 20,* 35–54.

Zetzel, E. R. (1968). The so-called good hysteric. *International Journal of Psychoanalysis, 49,* 256–260.

Zilboorg, G. (1941). Ambulatory schizophrenia. *Psychiatry, 4,* 149–155.

Zimmerman, M., & Coryell, W. H. (1991). Diagnosing personality disorders in the community: A comparison of self-report and interview measures. *Archives of General Psychiatry, 47,* 527–531.

Zimmerman, M., Pfohl, B., Stangl, D., & Corenthal, C. (1986). Assessment of DSM-III personality disorders: The importance of interviewing an informant. *Journal of Clinical Psychiatry, 47,* 261–263.

Author Index

Subject Index

histrionic personality disorders, 363
narcissistic personality disorders, 401–402
negativistic personality disorders, 546, 572
paranoid personality disorders, 696–697
sadistic personality disorders, 502
schizotypal personality disorders, 620,
    640–641
theories, generally, 57–58
Benzodiazepines, 689
Beta-blockers, 284
Bias, as classification issue, 23–24
Bimodality thesis, 31
Biochemical dysfunctions, 89, 193–194
Biogenic dysfunction, personality development and,
    87–88
Biography, individualism and, 5, 7
Biophysical individuality, 88–89
Biophysical theorists, pathogenic analysis, 85
Biophysical treatment, 192–195
Biopsychosocial systems, 9
Biosocial-learning theory, 66–69
Bipolar disorder, 378, 673
Bipolar manic disorder, 711
Bipolar Syndromes (BIP), 492
Birnbaum, K.:
    antisocial personality disorder, 434
    paranoid personality disorders, 693
Birth order:
    first male, 420
    significance of, 118–119
Bizarre ideation, 637–638, 683
Bizarre thoughts, 692, 731
Blame:
    masochistic personality disorders, 606
    negativistic personality, 571
    paranoid personality, 722, 726
Bleuler, Eugen:
    dependent personality disorder, 218–219
    depressive personality disorder, 254
    histrionic personality, 358
    negativistic personality disorders, 543
    paranoid personality disorders, 693
    schizotypal personality disorders, 615–616,
        619
Blind trust walks, 467
Borderline personality disorders:
    adult subtypes, 667–671
    affective instability, 64
    antisocial personalities and, 454, 456
    biosocial-learning model, 69
    case study, 675–678
    characteristics of, 645–646
    clinical features:
        comorbidity, 671–673
        differential diagnoses, 673–675
        overview, 660–661
        prototypal diagnostic domains, 661–666
        prototypal variants, 666–671
    defined, 52

dependent personalities and, 343
depressive personalities and, 308
development of, generally, 25
early experience and, 84
gender diffusion, 105
hierarchy and, 7
historical perspective, 53
histrionic personalities and, 376, 379
impulse regulation and, 78
integration and, 106
in interpersonal theory, 57
maladaptive patterns, 13
masochistic personalities, 592–593
Millon Polarity Model, 659
narcissistic personality vs., 399, 415
negativistic personalities and, 558, 561
neuroticism and, 62
pathogenic developmental background:
    biogenic factors, hypothesized, 678
    experiential history, characteristic, 678–681
    self-perpetuation processes, 681–683
personologic prototype, 662
prognosis, 722–723
sadistic personality, 492
schizotypal personality and, 630
theoretical perspectives:
    contemporary proposals, 649–660
    historical antecedents, 647–648
    modern formulations, 648–649
therapeutic interventions:
    overview, 683–684
    resistances/risks, 690
    strategic goals, 684–685
    tactical modalities, 685–690
Bouffees delirantes des degeneres, 691
Boundaries, in domain-bound psychotherapy, 210
Brain physiology, 36
Brain structure:
    biochemical disturbance and, 193–194
    personality development and, 89
    stimulus nutriment, 94
Brain weight, 95
Brief psychotic disorder, 672
Brief reactive psychoses, 526
British Mental Deficiency Act (1913), 434
British object-relations theorists, 52
Bureaucratic compulsive, 521–522
Buss, Arnold, 63

Cabala, 97
Calculative character, 37
Calm depressive, 39
Calm euphoric, 39
Cameron, S.:
    paranoid personality disorders, 695
    invalidism, 730
Capacity, temperament and, 43
Case history, causal analysis and, 83
Castration anxiety, 83